❧ CELEBRATION ❧

❧ CELEBRATION ❧
INTRODUCTION TO LITERATURE

Paul A. Parrish
Texas A&M University

Winthrop Publishers, Inc.
Cambridge, Massachusetts

Library of Congress Cataloging in Publication Data

Main entry under title:

Celebration.

Includes indexes.
1. Literature — Collections. I. Parrish,
Paul A.
PN6014.C34   808.8   76-26134
ISBN O-87626-113-6

Acknowledgments begin on page xv.

© 1977 by Winthrop Publishers, Inc.
17 Dunster Street, Cambridge, Massachusetts 02138

10 9 8 7 6 5 4 3 2

For my mother and father

contents

POETRY / 271

Persona, Tone, Irony / 318

Imagery: Figurative Language / 331

preface

The fundamental aim of this book is simply stated: to bring together good works of literature and to encourage their reading for insight and pleasure. In fulfilling this aim I have not limited the selections along any particular lines. Many of the titles are familiar ones from the fields of English and American literature, but many others lie outside those traditions. The selections from contemporary authors include some which have achieved national and international recognition and some which are not well-known and which have never before been anthologized. Throughout I have pursued a balance between familiar and unfamiliar, old and new, standard and nonstandard selections.

The editorial sections of the book are written to guide and suggest without overwhelming the reader. Some comments about terms, concepts, and selections are undoubtedly helpful, but too many, I think, can be intimidating and can discourage independent thinking. The questions which follow most selections also suggest and guide without giving certain answers. Throughout the book I have interspersed comments and questions "for comparison"; these encourage the study of a given selection, not just in isolation, but in the context of other selections which are related to it thematically or formally. Finally, I have, as much as possible, arranged selections and categories to reveal increasingly more difficult or more complex examples. To cite only the fiction, for example, each story listed first under each of the elements discussed is a simpler or more limited illustration of that particular feature. Similarly, the first elements discussed, plot and character, generally present fewer difficulties for the student than do tone, irony, and symbolism.

I am grateful to Texas A&M University and to Dean W. David Maxwell for released time which enabled me to work on this project. I am also indebted to a number of colleagues who provided wise counsel during the time I worked on the book: Lawrence Clipper, Robert Cochran, and Tom Vander Ven of Indiana University at South Bend; Dennis Berthold, Forrest Burt, Carl Childress, Paul Christensen, Harrison Hierth, J. S. Jernigan, Harry Kroitor, Jerome Loving, Linda Schubert-Mohr, and Cleve Want of Texas A&M University. My colleague and friend, Larry Reynolds, has been an unyielding supporter throughout; his contributions are more numerous than I could name. Paul O'Connell and Catherine Searle of Winthrop have been generous in praise and kind in criticism and have contributed to a thoroughly enjoyable and stimulating situation for me. Primary recognition must go to my wife, Linda, who provided the kind of personal support and encouragement that can only be acknowledged, not repaid.

acknowledgments

Auden, W. H., "In Memory of W. B. Yeats," and "The Unknown Citizen." Copyright 1940 and renewed 1968 by W. H. Auden. Reprinted from *Collected Shorter Poems 1927—1957*, by W. H. Auden, by permission of Random House, Inc. Baldwin, James, "Sonny's Blues." Copyright© 1957 by James Baldwin. Originally published in *Partisan Review*. Reprinted from the book *Going to Meet the Man* by James Baldwin, with the permission of The Dial Press. Bambara, Toni Cade, "My Man Bovanne." Copyright © 1971 by Toni Cade Bambara. Reprinted from *Gorilla, My Love*, by Toni Cade Bambara, by permission of Random House, Inc. Barthelme, Donald, "The Sandman." Reprinted with the permission of Farrar, Straus & Giroux, Inc. from *Sadness* by Donald Barthelme, Copyright © 1970, 1971, 1972 by Donald Barthelme. Bergman, Ingmar, *Wild Strawberries*. From *Four Screen Plays of Ingmar Bergman*. Copyright © 1960, by Ingmar Bergman. Reprinted by permission of Simon and Schuster. Berryman, John, "A Strut for Roethke." Reprinted with the permission of Farrar, Straus & Giroux, Inc. from *77 Dream Songs* by John Berryman, Copyright © 1959, 1962, 1963, 1964 by John Berryman. Bishop, Elizabeth, "The Fish." Reprinted with the permission of Farrar, Straus & Giroux, Inc., from *The Complete Poems* by Elizabeth Bishop, Copyright © 1938, 1940, 1969 by Elizabeth Bishop. Black, Byron, "I, the Fake Mad Bomber and Walking It Home Again." Copyright 1961 by the University of Nebraska Press. Reprinted by permission from *Prairie Schooner*. Black, David, "Laud." Reprinted by permission of Harold Ober Associates Incorporated. Copyright © 1972 by David Black. Blackburn, Paul, "Good Morning Love!" From *The Nation*. Reprinted by the permission of the publisher. Bly, Robert, "The Great Society." From *The Light Around the Body* by Robert Bly. Copyright © 1962 by Robert Bly. Reprinted by permission of Harper & Row, Publishers, Inc. Bridges, Robert, "London Snow." From *The Poetical Works of Robert Bridges*, 2nd ed. by permission of the Clarendon Press, Oxford. Brooks, Gwendolyn, "The Chicago Picasso." From *The World of Gwendolyn Brooks* by Gwendolyn Brooks. Copyright © 1968 by Gwendolyn Brooks Blakely. Reprinted by permission of Harper & Row, Publishers, Inc. Camus, Albert, "The Guest." From *Exile and the Kingdom*, by Albert Camus, translated by Justin O'Brien. Copyright © 1957, 1958 by Alfred A. Knopf, Inc. Reprinted by permission of Alfred A. Knopf, Inc. Chekhov, Anton, "An Anna Round His Neck." From *Chekhov: Selected Short Stories*, translated by Jessie Coulson and published by Oxford University Press. © Oxford University Press 1963. Clifton, Lucille, "Good Times." From *Good Times*, by Lucille Clifton. Copyright © 1969 by Lucille Clifton. Reprinted by permission of Random House, Inc. Corso, Gregory, "Marriage," from *The Happy Birthday of Death*. Copyright © 1960 by New Directions Publishing Corporation. Reprinted by permission of New Directions Publishing Corporation. Creeley, Robert, "A Wicker Basket," (Copyright © 1959 by Robert Creeley) is reprinted by permission of Charles Scribner's Sons from *For Love* by Robert Creeley. cummings, e. e., "i thank You God." Copyright, 1950, by e. e. cummings. Reprinted from his volume, *Complete Poems 1913—1962*, by permission of Harcourt Brace Jovanovich, Inc. "if i have made, my lady." Copyright, 1926, by Horace Liveright; Copyright, 1954, by e. e. cummings. Reprinted from *Complete Poems 1913—1962* by e. e. cummings by permission of Harcourt Brace Jovanovich, Inc. "O sweet spontaneous." Copyright, 1923, 1951, by e. e. cummings. Reprinted from his volume, *Complete Poems 1913—1962*, by permission of Harcourt Brace Jovanovich, Inc. Dickinson, Emily, "To Make A Prairie," and "Because I Could Not Stop for Death." Reprinted by permission of the publishers and the Trustees of Amherst College from Thomas H. Johnson, Editor, *The Poems of*

and Schuster. Levertov, Denise, "The Wife," from *With Eyes at the Back of Our Heads.* Copyright © 1959 by Denise Levertov Goodman. Reprinted by permission of New Directions Publishing Corporation. MacLeish, Archibald, "Ars Poetica." From *Collected Poems 1917–1952.* Reprinted with the permission of Houghton Mifflin Company. Malamud, Bernard, "The Magic Barrel." Reprinted with the permission of Farrar, Straus & Giroux, Inc. from *The Magic Barrel* by Bernard Malamud, Copyright © 1954, 1958 by Bernard Malamud. Marín, Luís Muñoz, "Pamphlet," translated by Muna Lee de Muñoz Marín. *An Anthology of Contemporary Latin American Poetry,* edited by Dudley Fitts. Copyright 1942 by New Directions Publishing Corporation. Reprinted by permission of New Directions Publishing Corporation. McPherson, James Alan, "A Matter of Vocabulary." Copyright © 1968, 1969 by James Alan McPherson. From *Hue and Cry* by James Alan McPherson, by permission of Little, Brown and Co. in association with The Atlantic Monthly Press. Merwin, W. S., "Leviathan." From *The First Four Books of Poems* by W. S. Merwin. Copyright © 1955, 1956, 1975 by W. S. Merwin. Reprinted by permission of Atheneum Publishers. Momaday, N. Scott, "The Bear," from *New Mexico Quarterly,* XXXI, No. 1, (Spring 1961). Copyright © 1961 University of New Mexico. Reprinted with the permission of the author. Moore, Marianne, "Poetry." Reprinted with permission of Macmillan Publishing Co., Inc. from *Collected Poems* by Marianne Moore. Copyright 1935 by Marianne Moore, renewed 1963 by Marianne Moore and T. S. Eliot. Oates, Joyce Carol, "How I Contemplated the Detroit House of Correction and Began My Life Over Again." Reprinted from *The Wheel of Love and Other Stories* by Joyce Carol Oates, by permission of the publisher, Vanguard Press, Inc. Copyright © 1970, 1969, 1968, 1967 by Joyce Carol Oates. O'Connor, Flannery. "Revelation." Reprinted with the permission of Farrar, Straus & Giroux, Inc. from *The Complete Stories* by Flannery O'Connor, Copyright © 1964 by the Estate of Mary Flannery O'Connor. Piercy, Marge, "Community." Copyright © 1969 by Marge Piercy. Reprinted from *Hard Loving,* by Marge Piercy, by permission of Wesleyan University Press. Pirandello, Luigi, "The Captive." Copyright © By permission of the Pirandello Estate and Toby Cole. Randall, Dudley, "Roses and Revolutions." From *Cities Burning* by Dudley Randall. Reprinted with the permission of Broadside Press. Ransom, John Crowe, "Bells for John Whiteside's Daughter." Copyright 1924 by Alfred A. Knopf, Inc. and renewed 1952 by John Crowe Ransom. Reprinted from *Selected Poems,* Third Edition, Revised and Enlarged, by John Crowe Ransom, by permission of the publisher. Roethke, Theodore, "Elegy for Jane," Copyright 1950 by Theodore Roethke, and "The Dream," Copyright 1953 by Theodore Roethke from *The Collected Poems of Theodore Roethke.* Reprinted by permission of Doubleday & Company, Inc. "The Reply." From *The Collected Poems of Theodore Roethke.* Copyright © 1961 by Beatrice Roethke, Administratrix of the Estate of Theodore Roethke. Reprinted by permission of Doubleday & Company, Inc. Rukeyser, Muriel, "This Place in the Ways." Reprinted by permission of Monica McCall, International Creative Management. Copyright 1951 by Muriel Rukeyser. Sexton, Anne, "A Starry Night." From *All My Pretty Ones,* copyright © 1961, 1962 by Anne Sexton. Reprinted by permission of Houghton Mifflin Company. Shakespeare, William, *King Lear.* Edited by Russell Fraser. Copyright © Russell Frasher, 1961, Copyright © 1963 Sylvan Barnet. Reprinted by arrangement with The New American Library, Inc. New York, N. Y. Stevens, Wallace, "The Idea of Order at Key West," Copyright 1936 by Wallace Stevens and renewed 1964 by Holly Stevens, "Not Ideas About the Thing, but the Thing Itself," Copyright 1954 by Wallace Stevens. "Of Modern Poetry," Copyright 1942 by Wallace Stevens and renewed 1970 by Holly Stevens. Reprinted from *Collected Poems of Wallace Stevens,* by permission of Alfred A. Knopf, Inc. Synge, John Millington, *Riders to the Sea.* Reprinted from *The Complete Works of John M. Synge,* Random House, Inc. Thomas, Dylan, "Do Not Go Gentle Into That Good Night." *The Poems of Dylan Thomas.* Copyright 1952 by Dylan Thomas. Reprinted by permission of New Directions Publishing Corporation. Thurber, James, "Mr. Preble Gets Rid of His Wife." Copyright © 1935 James Thurber. Copyright © 1963 Helen W. Thurber and Rosemary Thurber Sauers. From *The Middle-Aged Man on the Flying Trapeze,* published by Harper & Row. Originally appeared in *The New Yorker.* Unamuno, Miguel de, "Saint Emmanuel the Good, Martyr," from *Abel Sanchez and Other Stories.* Reprinted with the permission of Henry Regnery Company. Updike, John, "A & P." Copyright © 1962 by John Updike. Reprinted from *Pigeon Feathers and Other Stories,* by John Updike, by permission of Alfred A. Knopf, Inc. Originally appeared in *The New Yorker.* Wain, John, "Reason for Not Writing Orthodox Nature Poetry." Reprinted by permission of Curtis Brown, Ltd. on behalf of the author from *Word Carved on a Sill* by John Wain. Welty, Eudora, "A Still Moment." Copyright, 1942, 1970, by Eudora Welty. Reprinted from her volume, *The Wide Net and Other Stories,* by permission of Harcourt Brace Jovanovich, Inc. Wilbur, Richard, "Love Calls Us to the Things of This World." From *Things of This World,* copyright, 1956, by Richard Wilbur. Reprinted by permission of Harcourt Brace Jovanovich, Inc. Williams, William Carlos, "The Gift," Copyright © 1962 by William Carlos

❧ CELEBRATION ❧

introduction

The Roman poet Horace once said that the aim of literature is to delight and instruct. He meant that literature provides pleasure during the reading experience and teaches the reader something at the same time. Since Horace, many readers have suggested more specific theories about the way literature affects us; it is doubtful, though, that anyone has offered a sounder basis for the continuing vitality and attraction of the literary art. Reading good literature continues to yield these two complementary results: pleasure and understanding. This belief lies behind the selections in this text and the introductory comments to fiction, drama, and poetry.

Precisely what kind of pleasure and what kind of understanding are large and complex questions. Each of the separate introductions suggests some answers appropriate to the genre with which it is concerned. Nonetheless, some initial comments are perhaps in order here.

The focus on pleasure does not mean, of course, that literature emphasizes amusement or comedy or only the fortunate side of life. Horace was well aware of tragedies, both in life and in literature, as are we all. Literature deals with the tragic experience — in fact, it deals with all kinds of experiences which evoke many different reactions from us. We may be amused, angered, enlightened, or disturbed, yet, in each instance, we respond to the lives and emotions of the human characters and the human situations revealed to us in literature. This, surely, is the key to the fundamental pleasure which literature as a whole — whatever its form, themes, or techniques — can be said to provide. It remains human throughout.

In defining the pleasurable quality of literature, we cannot afford to neglect, at the same time, its importance as art. Other kinds of writing focus on human beings; literature is not at all unique in that regard. What is unique is the sense of wholeness, of purpose, of order, in a creative framework which literature — and only literature — offers. Most of us are governed by a search for order rather than chaos, integration rather than fragmentation. Literature is an expression of what Wallace Stevens called the "rage for order" which human beings experience. That, too, brings satisfaction and enjoyment.

The second part of our focus, that literature is instructive, may be initially unexpected, since we have been taught that literature is far removed from those disciplines which emphasize more formal instruction and which focus on procedures, information, and facts. In reading literature, we do not expect to be informed in the way that we are when we read a history book or a newspaper. One is fictional, a representation of an imaginative life; the others are factual, dealing with historical or contemporary people or actions in "real life." Information as such may occasionally be provided. If we read a novel set in Spain or a poem about the Civil War, we may, incidentally, learn more about Spanish culture or about certain Civil War battles. A contemporary novelist, Ralph Ellison, even asserted once that he learned to shoot birds by reading Hemingway. But that kind of information is surely rare and, at best, tangential to a larger purpose. If we specifically set out to learn more about Spain or the Civil War or about bird-hunting, we will more likely go to books on culture, history, or hunting. What literature does teach is surely tied to what makes it enjoyable. That is, literature is enjoyable because it is about human beings, and it teaches us more about humanity and thus, in an important sense, more about ourselves. Horace's original phrase indicates that literature is "applicable to life"; the caution inherent in the wording is important. Literature does not tell us *how* to live in any explicit form. It seldom proposes solutions to sociological or political problems, nor is it like a moral treatise which dictates the best way to live. However, it remains applicable to life. We read it, and if we understand it, we understand more about our experiences and those of others.

Just as the artistic form of literature offers pleasure, so the artistic techniques of the author promote our understanding. In the several introductions which follow, there are discussions of the various elements of each form of literature to help us understand how and why an author writes as he or she does and thus how and why a story, poem, or play means what it does. If we read a newspaper account of an airplane crash we seldom have to ask why the author chose a particular point of view, or why a certain tone was developed, or why a particular setting was chosen, or why various people were described. All of that is essentially dictated by the factual event itself. The literary artist, though, has more freedom to effect a particular aim. It is appropriate, indeed, often necessary, that we single out the components of a story in order to understand better, not only the literary techniques, but also the human experiences described.

The foregoing discussion is deceptively analytical. We do not react to a story by dividing it into those parts which provide pleasure and those which provide understanding, or by dividing our satisfaction into that produced by the human subjects and that produced by the artistic form. Furthermore, our enjoyment often leads to increased understanding, and understanding may in itself be an enjoyable experience. These several responses exist, but not in isolation. They are, finally, complementary parts of the whole, which is the total experience of reading and appreciating literature.

Implicit in these comments is the belief that literature engages us in the concerns of imagined human beings — their joys, doubts, fears, and hopes. The title of this volume also aims at literature's capacity for involvement. "Celebration" implies, above all, a communal affirmation of life and values. In an era more frequently characterized by anxiety and alienation, such a focus would seem to be constructive and, perhaps, instructive. Although "celebration" is sometimes associated with almost any kind of affirmative occasion, whether frivolous or serious, it retains, nonetheless, the more profound meaning which allows us to say that literature is, collectively, a celebration of life. In his Nobel Prize acceptance speech, William Faulkner emphasized some of the truths and values which literature aims to celebrate. In the writer's workshop, he said, there are only "the old verities and truths of the heart, the old universal truths lacking which any story is ephemeral and doomed — love and honor and pity and pride and compassion and sacrifice." Affirmation is in some cases immediate and spontaneous, in others difficult or unattainable; in all, it must be honest to elicit our involvement. Ralph Ellison had in mind the "tough" form of affirmation when he asserted that "true novels, even when most pessimistic and bitter, arise out of an impulse to celebrate human life and therefore are ritualistic and ceremonial at their core." Explicit in Ellison's comment is the recognition that literature may be at once pessimistic and bitter and yet spurred by an affirmative impulse. The tension which results between these two poles is part of the vitality and integrity of literature; few works reveal total alienation, few reveal unequivocal celebration. Like the experiences of life itself, the experiences recorded in literature are seldom neatly classified. They engage us, evoke our response, encourage our analysis, and invite our understanding. When we work to let this happen we are not so much outsiders as participants in the creative experience of literature, and we become part of its celebration of life.

❧ FICTION ❧

introduction

Most of us enjoy a good story and, consequently, we find the narrative form a natural and familiar one. We have all, at one time or another, narrated a personal experience or listened to someone else's account of certain events. Furthermore, if book sales and personal testimonies are an accurate gauge, many of us enjoy reading fictional narratives. Whatever the effects of television or movies, we still spend a great deal of time and money reading fiction. In this respect, fiction is different from drama or poetry, for we do not characteristically sit down to read a good play or a good poem — we more often read a good story. But the very availability and popularity of fiction necessitates that we make some distinctions. Fiction is written for a variety of reasons. It appeals to a diverse audience which reads it for equally diverse reasons, and it varies greatly in quality and impact. Simply stated, not all narratives are alike, and not all narratives, even fictional ones, are literature. Since our concern here is not just telling or listening to stories but reading and understanding literary fiction, some important criteria need to be established.

Reading fiction ought to be a pleasurable activity; if it's not, few of us, except under constraint, will read at all. But the sources of pleasure derived from reading fiction vary considerably. We may be enthralled by the adventures of a super-hero, or titillated by the vivid description of a romantic affair, or held in suspense by the uncertainties of a murder mystery. We may, in a different sense, find it pleasurable when a story makes us think about people, about life in its infinite variety, or about ourselves. The first kind of pleasure, we notice, is essentially an emotional response to the action of a story — adventure, romance, mystery; the second undoubtedly includes the emotions but engages the mind as well. The first kind of pleasure is more transitory because the action which is stressed and the emotions which are evoked are transitory; the second kind of pleasure is more lasting since it leads to thoughtful reaction, in other words, to analysis and interpretation.

A reader's overall response to a given story will not likely fall completely into either of these forms, for few stories appeal only to the emotions or only to the intellect. The differing emphasis is nonetheless important and is related to an appropriate discrimination between what is termed "popular" fiction and what might be termed "serious" or literary fiction. The first is characterized by a surface presentation of action, characters, and situation; the second, exemplified by the selections in this text, may deal with similar action, characters, and situations, but does so with greater depth and meaning — in a word, with more significance. This aim can be achieved in a context that is light-hearted or humorous, as is the case with Barthelme's "The Sandman" or Bambara's "My Man Bovanne" and many of the stories of writers such as Mark Twain or James Thurber. In any case, though, the writer intends to make a point, to give the story some significance.

Perhaps this approach to fiction can be further clarified if we correlate it to the state of another popular art form, the contemporary film. Like fiction, film is a medium readily available to the public; it has wide appeal and for that reason the audience it appeals to is very heterogeneous. Increasingly, some films are regarded as important forms of art, yet because of its diversity, film as a category includes all types, ranging from the superficial to the profound, from the popular to the artistic. Audience reaction (and critical reaction) to films indicates that there are, broadly speaking, two classes — those films that primarily provide entertainment or escape and those that are more thoughtful and engaging, those that allow us to live in a world of fantasy or near-impossibility and those that force us to deal with life and human characters with a greater degree of honesty and seriousness. Most of us are able, depending on our mood or the occasion, to enjoy both types, but we generally recognize differences in purpose and effect. Many universities make evident these differences by sponsoring both a "popular" film series and a "classical" or art film series. Inevitably, there is overlapping and some necessary blurring of distinctions, but "classical" or serious films, like serious fiction, are usually judged to be more analytical, more thoughtful, and, from a human standpoint, more significant.

All of this points to an important conclusion: literary fiction is entertaining, but it is more than that, and as a result it encourages, indeed, in some instances requires, discussion and interpretation.

Interpretation need not be a forbidding term; it is, in brief, the activity through which we seek to understand what a literary work means, and how and why it affects us as it does. Understanding the meaning of literature is not the same thing as culling from it a one- or two-statement **theme**. There are themes in literature, of course, but we should avoid the temptation to equate an extracted theme with the meaning which, as Flannery O'Connor has said, is embodied in a story.

Interpretation is a matter of being open to all the elements which go toward the making of this embodied meaning. It implies, therefore, that literature is meaningful, that authors do write purposefully and artistically about human beings and human situations, and that we, as readers, may have to work as well to come to a satisfactory understanding of the literature. Initially, this may be hard to accept in its entirety, but if an honest effort of discovery is made, the results can be very rewarding. What we often find, if we've worked effectively, is that our effort has not only increased our understanding but enhanced our pleasure as well.

plot

ANONYMOUS FOLKTALE
How Buck Won His Freedom

Buck was the shrewdest slave on the big Washington plantation. He could steal things almost in front of his master's eyes without being detected. Finally, after having had his chickens and pigs stolen until he was sick, Master Henry Washington called Buck to him one day and said, "Buck, how do you manage to steal without getting caught?"

"Dat's easy, Massa," replied Buck, "dat's easy. Ah kin steal yo' clo'es right tonight, wid you a-guardin' 'em."

"No, no," said the master, "you may be a slick thief, but you can't do that. I will make a proposition with you: If you steal my suit of clothes tonight, I will give you your freedom, and if you fail to steal them, then you will stop stealing my chickens."

"Aw right, Massa, aw right," Buck agreed. "Dat's uh go."

That night about nine o'clock the master called his wife into the bedroom, got his Sunday suit of clothes, laid it out on the table, and told his wife about the prop-osition he had made with Buck. He got on one side of the table and had his wife get on the other side, and they waited. Pretty soon, through a window that was open, the master heard the mules and the horses in the stable lot running as if someone were after them.

"Here wife," said he, "you take this gun and keep an eye on this suit. I am going to see what's the matter with those animals."

Buck, who had been out to the horse lot and started the stampede to attract the master's attention, now approached the open window. He was a good mimic, and in tones that sounded like his master's he called out, "Ol'lady, ol'lady, ol'lady, you better hand me that suit. That damn thief might steal it while I'm gone."

The master's wife, thinking that it was her husband asking for his suit, took it from the table and handed it out the window to Buck. This is how Buck won his freedom.

Although brief, this tale from Black American folklore includes most of the elements of fiction to be discussed more fully in later sections. We are interested in the people, the **characters**, especially Buck. We do not have much direct characterization, but we are told that Buck "was the shrewdest slave on the big Washington plantation" and we understand, through the interaction between Buck and Washington, something of the personalities of each. Although unobtrusive, the **point of view** is clearly omniscient ("all-knowing") as the narrator describes what is happening at several different locations and tells us about the thoughts and motives of different characters. Near the end of the tale, for example, we are told what Buck has done and why he did it ("[he] had been out to the horse lot and started the stampede to attract the master's attention") and later, why the master's wife hands the suit out the window ("thinking that it was her husband asking for his suit"). We further sense a **tone**, an authorial attitude, of admiration and approval in the narrative about Buck and recognize a decisive **irony** which adds to the humor and attraction of the tale. The poor, uneducated slave is indeed shrewd and wins the contest; the wealthy owner of the "big" plantation is outwitted in spite of the apparently easy task he has.

Fundamentally, though, we are interested in what happens and why. The last sentence of the tale gives force to this level of the action by telling us that "this is how Buck won his freedom." We are interested, as the narrator implies, in the **plot** of the story, the selection and presentation of events which reveal how the freedom is won.

Plot is a basic feature of this and most stories. Without a clear perception of an action and its cause we are not likely to be able to go further in our understanding. At the same time, if we never move beyond the level of plot, we will be neglecting many of the more complex elements of fiction. The plot of a story is a little like the rudiments of education; you have to begin there but if you stay there you will miss out on more stimulating and compelling experiences.

Traditionally, the plot of a story is divided into four essential parts: the **introduction** or **exposition**, which contains background information or points to incidents which took place before the action of the story; the **complication**, which presents the tension, the essential conflict of the story which usually involves key characters; the **crisis** or **climax**, the point at which the tension builds to a peak and leads to a turning point in the story; and the **resolution** or **conclusion**, in which action and conflicts are settled or at least, for the moment, ended. The tale of Buck fits comfortably into this format. We are first introduced to Buck and to what he does. Immediately, then, we are introduced to Master Henry Washington and to the conflict he represents. The agreement Buck and Washington make leads to a building of the tension which climaxes with the fulfillment of Buck's scheme to get the suit of clothes. The conclusion confirms that preceding events led to Buck's freedom. Good stories are not constructed by a mechanical formula, of course, and some stories do not fit into the conventional mold. The divisions, nonetheless, provide a convenient way to discuss most developments in plot and action. The stories of Hawthorne, Chekhov, Melville, and Lessing are among many which develop a plot in a traditional manner.

While the plot includes the basic action of the narrative, it is more important than a mere retelling or paraphrase of what happens. One significant characteristic, pointed out by the late English novelist and critic E. M. Forster, is that of causality. Writing in *Aspects of the Novel*, Forster distinguishes between what he calls a story and a plot: " 'The king died and then the queen died' is a story. 'The king died, and then the queen died of grief' is a plot. The time-sequence is preserved, but the sense of causality overshadows it." In other words, the first example tells us what happens, the second tells us why. The plot of fiction is not merely a series of haphazard or unrelated incidents; the action fits together into a meaningful whole.

The traditional plot of fiction not only includes the four-part division mentioned above but also follows a chronological progression of events. Modern fiction writers have occasionally moved away from the chronological pattern, writing instead stories which consist of individual segments which must be fitted together to give the story its meaning. There is still a plot of sorts — that is, a design or conscious arrangement of episodes and action — but it does not fit the traditional, chronological pattern we find typical of most stories.

Faulkner's and Oates' stories reveal two different narrative patterns, and neither is tied to a strict chronological organization. Faulkner's "A Rose for Emily" begins near the end of the time sequence with the death of Emily Grierson. Within the first section the narrator moves back a few years before Emily's death and then, beginning in section II, goes back to her life as a young girl. From there the narrative moves in a compressed but chronological fashion to its conclusion. Because he already knows the outcome of his story, Faulkner's narrator makes significant use of **foreshadowing**, hinting at and implying what will later be revealed.

Joyce Carol Oates' "How I Contemplated the World from the Detroit House of Correction and Began My Life Over Again" is a more radical variation on the traditional plot structure, as it forces us to jump back and forth in order to pick up the time sequence of the events depicted. A chronology of events underlies the narrative but it is not the basis on which the events are related to the reader.

WILLIAM FAULKNER   (1897–1962)
A Rose for Emily

I

When Miss Emily Grierson died, our whole town went to her funeral: the men through a sort of respectful affection for a fallen monument, the women mostly out of curiosity to see the inside of her house, which no one save an old manservant — a combined gardener and cook — had seen in at least ten years.

It was a big, squarish frame house that had once been white, decorated with cupolas and spires and scrolled balconies in the heavily lightsome style of the seventies, set on what had once been our most select street. But garages and cotton gins had encroached and obliterated even the august names of that neighborhood; only Miss Emily's house was left, lifting its stubborn and coquettish decay above the cotton wagons and the gasoline pumps — an eyesore among eyesores. And now Miss Emily had gone to join the representatives of those august names where they lay in the cedarbemused cemetery among the ranked and anonymous graves of Union and Confederate soldiers who fell at the battle of Jefferson.

Alive, Miss Emily had been a tradition, a duty, and a care; a sort of hereditary obligation upon the town, dating from that day in 1894 when Colonel Sartoris, the mayor — he who fathered the edict that no Negro woman should appear on the streets without an apron — remitted her taxes, the dispensation dating from the death of her father on into perpetuity. Not that Miss Emily would have accepted charity. Colonel Sartoris invented an involved tale to the effect that Miss Emily's father had loaned money to the town, which the town, as a matter of business, preferred this way of repaying. Only a man of Colonel Sartoris' generation and thought could have invented it, and only a woman could have believed it.

When the next generation, with its more modern ideas, became mayors and aldermen, this arrangement created some little dissatisfaction. On the first of the year they mailed her a tax notice. February came, and there was no reply. They wrote her a formal letter, asking her to call at the sheriff's office at her convenience. A week later the mayor wrote her himself, offering to call or to send his car for her, and received in reply a note on paper of an archaic shape, in a thin, flowing calligraphy in faded ink, to the effect that she no longer went out at all. The tax notice was also enclosed, without comment.

They called a special meeting of the Board of Aldermen. A deputation waited upon her, knocked at the door through which no visitor had passed since she ceased giving chinapainting lessons eight or ten years earlier. They were admitted by the old Negro into a dim hall from which a stairway mounted into still more shadow. It smelled of dust and disuse — a close, dank smell. The Negro led them into the parlor. It was furnished in heavy, leather-covered furniture. When the Negro opened the blinds of one window, they could see that the leather was cracked; and when they sat down, a faint dust rose sluggishly about their thighs, spinning with slow motes in the single sun-ray. On a tarnished gilt easel before the fireplace stood a crayon portrait of Miss Emily's father.

They rose when she entered — a small,

fat woman in black, with a thin gold chain descending to her waist and vanishing into her belt, leaning on an ebony cane with a tarnished gold head. Her skeleton was small and spare; perhaps that was why what would have been merely plumpness in another was obesity in her. She looked bloated, like a body long submerged in motionless water, and of that pallid hue. Her eyes, lost in the fatty ridges of her face, looked like two small pieces of coal pressed into a lump of dough as they moved from one face to another while the visitors stated their errand.

She did not ask them to sit. She just stood in the door and listened quietly until the spokesman came to a stumbling halt. Then they could hear the invisible watch ticking at the end of the gold chain.

Her voice was dry and cold. "I have no taxes in Jefferson. Colonel Sartoris explained it to me. Perhaps one of you can gain access to the city records and satisfy yourselves."

"But we have. We are the city authorities, Miss Emily. Didn't you get a notice from the sheriff, signed by him?"

"I received a paper, yes," Miss Emily said. "Perhaps he considers himself the sheriff . . . I have no taxes in Jefferson."

"But there is nothing on the books to show that, you see. We must go by the—"

"See Colonel Sartoris. I have no taxes in Jefferson."

"But, Miss Emily —"

"See Colonel Sartoris." (Colonel Sartoris had been dead almost ten years.) "I have no taxes in Jefferson. Tobe!" The Negro appeared. "Show these gentlemen out."

II

So she vanquished them, horse and foot, just as she had vanquished their fathers thirty years before about the smell. That was two years after her father's death and a short time after her sweetheart — the one we believed would marry her — had deserted her. After her father's death she went out very little; after her sweetheart went away, people hardly saw her at all. A few of the ladies had the temerity to call, but were not received, and the only sign of life about the place was the Negro man — a young man then — going in and out with a market basket.

"Just as if a man — any man — could keep a kitchen properly," the ladies said; so they were not surprised when the smell developed. It was another link between the gross, teeming world and the high and mighty Griersons.

A neighbor, a woman, complained to the mayor, Judge Stevens, eighty years old.

"But what will you have me do about it, madam?" he said.

"Why, send her word to stop it," the woman said. "Isn't there a law?"

"I'm sure that won't be necessary," Judge Stevens said. "It's probably just a snake or a rat that nigger of hers killed in the yard. I'll speak to him about it."

The next day he received two more complaints, one from a man who came in diffident deprecation. "We really must do something about it, Judge. I'd be the last one in the world to bother Miss Emily, but we've got to do something." That night the Board of Aldermen met — three graybeards and one younger man, a member of the rising generation.

"It's simple enough," he said. "Send her word to have her place cleaned up. Give her a certain time to do it in, and if she don't . . ."

"Dammit, sir," Judge Stevens said, "will you accuse a lady to her face of smelling bad?"

So the next night, after midnight, four men crossed Miss Emily's lawn and slunk about the house like burglars, sniffing along the base of the brickwork and at the cellar openings while one of them performed a regular sowing motion with his hand out of a sack slung from his shoulder. They broke open the cellar door and sprinkled lime there, and in all the out-buildings. As they recrossed the lawn, a window that had been dark was lighted and Miss Emily sat in it, the light behind her, and her upright torso motionless as that of an idol. They crept quietly across the lawn and into the shadow of the locusts that lined the street. After a week or two the smell went away.

That was when people had begun to feel really sorry for her. People in our town, remembering how old lady Wyatt, her great-aunt, had gone completely crazy at last, believed that the Griersons held themselves a little too high for what they really were. None of the young men were quite good enough for Miss Emily and such. We had long thought of them as a tableau, Miss Emily a slender figure in white in the background, her father a spraddled silhouette in the foreground, his back to her and clutching a horsewhip, the two of them framed by the back-flung front door. So when she got to be thirty and was still single, we were not pleased exactly, but vindicated; even with insanity in the family she wouldn't have turned down all of her chances if they had really materialized.

When her father died, it got about that the house was all that was left to her; and in a way, people were glad. At last they could pity Miss Emily. Being left alone, and a pauper, she had become humanized. Now she too would know the old thrill and the old despair of a penny more or less.

The day after his death all the ladies prepared to call at the house and offer con-dolence and aid, as is our custom. Miss Emily met them at the door, dressed as usual and with no trace of grief on her face. She told them that her father was not dead. She did that for three days, with the ministers calling on her, and the doctors, trying to persuade her to let them dispose of the body. Just as they were about to resort to law and force, she broke down, and they buried her father quickly.

We did not say she was crazy then. We believed she had to do that. We remem-bered all the young men her father had driven away, and we knew that with nothing left, she would have to cling to that which had robbed her, as people will.

III

She was sick for a long time. When we saw her again, her hair was cut short, mak-ing her look like a girl, with a vague resemblance to those angels in colored church windows — sort of tragic and serene.

The town had just let the contracts for paving the sidewalks, and in the summer after her father's death they began the work. The construction company came with niggers and mules and machinery, and a foreman named Homer Barron, a Yankee — a big, dark, ready man, with a big voice and eyes lighter than his face. The little boys would follow in groups to hear him cuss the niggers, and the niggers singing in time to the rise and fall of picks. Pretty soon he knew everybody in town. Whenever you heard a lot of laughing anywhere about the square, Homer Barron would be in the center of the group. Presently we began to see him and Miss Emily on Sunday afternoons driving in the yellow-wheeled buggy and the matched team of bays from the livery stable.

At first we were glad that Miss Emily would have an interest, because the ladies all said, "Of course a Grierson would not think seriously of a Northerner, a day laborer." But there were still others, older people, who said that even grief could not cause a real lady to forget *noblesse oblige* — without calling it *noblesse oblige*. They just said, "Poor Emily. Her kinsfolk should come to her." She had some kin in

Alabama; but years ago her father had fallen out with them over the estate of old lady Wyatt, the crazy woman, and there was no communication between the two families. They had not even been represented at the funeral.

And as soon as the old people said, "Poor Emily," the whispering began. "Do you suppose it's really so?" they said to one another. "Of course it is. What else could . . ." This behind their hands; rustling of craned silk and satin behind jalousies closed upon the sun of Sunday afternoon as the thin, swift clop-clop-clop of the matched team passed: "Poor Emily."

She carried her head high enough — even when we believed that she was fallen. It was as if she demanded more than ever the recognition of her dignity as the last Grierson; as if it had wanted that touch of earthiness to reaffirm her imperviousness. Like when she bought the rat poison, the arsenic. That was over a year after they had begun to say "Poor Emily," and while the two female cousins were visiting her.

"I want some poison," she said to the druggist. She was over thirty then, still a slight woman, though thinner than usual, with cold, haughty black eyes in a face the flesh of which was strained across the temples and about the eyesockets as you imagine a lighthouse-keeper's face ought to look. "I want some poison," she said.

"Yes, Miss Emily. What kind? For rats and such? I'd recom—"

"I want the best you have. I don't care what kind."

The druggist named several. "They'll kill anything up to an elephant. But what you want is—"

"Arsenic," Miss Emily said. "Is that a good one?"

"Is . . . arsenic? Yes, ma'am. But what you want—"

"I want arsenic."

The druggist looked down at her. She looked back at him, erect, her face like a strained flag. "Why, of course," the druggist said. "If that's what you want. But the law requires you to tell what you are going to use it for."

Miss Emily just stared at him, her head tilted back in order to look him eye for eye, until he looked away and went and got the arsenic and wrapped it up. The Negro delivery boy brought her the package; the druggist didn't come back. When she opened the package at home there was written on the box, under the skull and bones: "For rats."

IV

So the next day we all said, "She will kill herself"; and we said it would be the best thing. When she had first begun to be seen with Homer Barron, we had said, "She will marry him." Then we said, "She will persuade him yet," because Homer himself had remarked — he liked men, and it was known that he drank with the younger men in the Elks' Club — that he was not a marrying man. Later we said, "Poor Emily" behind the jalousies as they passed on Sunday afternoon in the glittering buggy, Miss Emily with her head high and Homer Barron with his hat cocked and a cigar in his teeth, reins and whip in a yellow glove.

Then some of the ladies began to say that it was a disgrace to the town and a bad example to the young people. The men did not want to interfere, but at last the ladies forced the Baptist minister — Miss Emily's people were Episcopal — to call upon her. He would never divulge what happened during that interview, but he refused to go back again. The next Sunday they again drove about the streets, and the following day the minister's wife wrote to Miss Emily's relations in Alabama.

So she had blood-kin under her roof

again and we sat back to watch developments. At first nothing happened. Then we were sure that they were to be married. We learned that Miss Emily had been to the jeweler's and ordered a man's toilet set in silver, with the letters H. B. on each piece. Two days later we learned that she had bought a complete outfit of men's clothing, including a nightshirt, and we said, "They are married." We were really glad. We were glad because the two female cousins were even more Grierson than Miss Emily had ever been.

So we were not surprised when Homer Barron — the streets had been finished some time since — was gone. We were a little disappointed that there was not a public blowing-off, but we believed that he had gone on to prepare for Miss Emily's coming, or to give her a chance to get rid of the cousins. (By that time it was a cabal, and we were all Miss Emily's allies to help circumvent the cousins.) Sure enough, after another week they departed. And, as we had expected all along, within three days Homer Barron was back in town. A neighbor saw the Negro man admit him at the kitchen door at dusk one evening.

And that was the last we saw of Homer Barron. And of Miss Emily for some time. The Negro man went in and out with the market basket, but the front door remained closed. Now and then we would see her at a window for a moment, as the men did that night when they sprinkled the lime, but for almost six months she did not appear on the streets. Then we knew that this was to be expected too; as if that quality of her father which had thwarted her woman's life so many times had been too virulent and too furious to die.

When we next saw Miss Emily, she had grown fat and her hair was turning gray. During the next few years it grew grayer and grayer until it attained an even pepper-and-salt iron-gray, when it ceased turning. Up to the day of her death at seventy-four it was still that vigorous iron-gray like the hair of an active man.

From that time on her front door remained closed, save for a period of six or seven years, when she was about forty, during which she gave lessons in china-painting. She fitted up a studio in one of the downstairs rooms, where the daughters and granddaughters of Colonel Sartoris' contemporaries were sent to her with the same regularity and in the same spirit that they were sent to church on Sundays with a twenty-five-cent piece for the collection plate. Meanwhile her taxes had been remitted.

Then the newer generation became the backbone and the spirit of the town, and the painting pupils grew up and fell away and did not send their children to her with boxes of color and tedious brushes and pictures cut from the ladies' magazines. The front door closed upon the last one and remained closed for good. When the town got free postal delivery, Miss Emily alone refused to let them fasten the metal numbers above her door and attach a mailbox to it. She would not listen to them.

Daily, monthly, yearly we watched the Negro grow grayer and more stooped, going in and out with the market basket. Each December we sent her a tax notice, which would be returned by the post office a week later, unclaimed. Now and then we would see her in one of the downstairs windows — she had evidently shut up the top floor of the house — like the carven torso of an idol in a niche, looking or not looking at us, we could never tell which. Thus she passed from generation to generation — dear, inescapable, impervious, tranquil, and perverse.

And so she died. Fell ill in the house filled with dust and shadows, with only a doddering Negro man to wait on her. We did not even know she was sick; we had long since given up trying to get any information from the Negro. He talked to no one, probably not even to her, for his voice had grown harsh and rusty, as if from disuse.

She died in one of the downstairs rooms, in a heavy walnut bed with a curtain, her gray head propped on a pillow yellow and moldy with age and lack of sunlight.

V

The Negro met the first of the ladies at the front door and let them in, with their hushed, sibilant voices and their quick, curious glances, and then he disappeared. He walked right through the house and out the back and was not seen again.

The two female cousins came at once. They held the funeral on the second day, with the town coming to look at Miss Emily beneath a mass of bought flowers, with the crayon face of her father musing profoundly above the bier and the ladies sibilant and macabre; and the very old men — some in their brushed Confederate uniforms — on the porch and the lawn, talking of Miss Emily as if she had been a contemporary of theirs, believing that they had danced with her and courted her perhaps, confusing time with its mathematical progression, as the old do, to whom all the past is not a diminishing road but, instead, a huge meadow which no winter ever quite touches, divided from them now by the narrow bottle-neck of the most recent decade of years.

Already we knew that there was one room in that region above stairs which no one had seen in forty years, and which would have to be forced. They waited until Miss Emily was decently in the ground before they opened it.

The violence of breaking down the door seemed to fill this room with pervading dust. A thin, acrid pall as of the tomb seemed to lie everywhere upon this room decked and furnished as for a bridal: upon the valance curtains of faded rose color, upon the rose-shaded lights, upon the dressing table, upon the delicate array of crystal and the man's toilet things backed with tarnished silver, silver so tarnished that the monogram was obscured. Among them lay a collar and tie, as if they had just been removed, which, lifted, left upon the surface a pale crescent in the dust. Upon a chair hung the suit, carefully folded; beneath it the two mute shoes and the discarded socks.

The man himself lay in the bed.

For a long while we just stood there, looking down at the profound and fleshless grin. The body had apparently once lain in the attitude of an embrace, but now the long sleep that outlasts love, that conquers even the grimace of love, had cuckolded him. What was left of him, rotted beneath what was left of the nightshirt, had become inextricable from the bed in which he lay; and upon him and upon the pillow beside him lay that even coating of the patient and biding dust.

Then we noticed that in the second pillow was the indentation of a head. One of us lifted something from it, and leaning forward, that faint and invisible dust dry and acrid in the nostrils, we saw a long strand of iron-gray hair.

For Consideration

1. The story begins at the end, or near it, with the death of Miss Emily Grierson. Why does the narrator take away from the force of that event by presenting it first?

2. What is Miss Emily's position in the town? What are the various attitudes of the townspeople toward her?

3. Through what means does the narrator keep us interested in his story, especially in view of the fact that we already know one important outcome (Miss Emily's death)? How does he build the suspense of his account?

4. How much attention does the narrator give to characterization? How fully is Miss Emily portrayed?

5. What is the narrator's relationship to the story he tells? How involved does he appear to be in the events?

6. The story is suspenseful and, at the end perhaps, shocking. Are shock and suspense the only effects created by the narrative?

JOYCE CAROL OATES   (1938–   )

How I Contemplated the World from the Detroit House of Correction and Began My Life Over Again

Notes for an essay for an English class at Baldwin Country Day School; poking around in debris; disgust and curiosity; a revelation of the meaning of life; a happy ending . . .

I   Events

I. The girl (myself) is walking through Branden's, that excellent store. Suburb of a large famous city that is a symbol for large famous American cities. The event sneaks up on the girl, who believes she is herding it along with a small fixed smile, a girl of fifteen, innocently experienced. She dawdles in a certain style by a counter of costume jewelry. Rings, earrings, neck-laces. Prices from $5 to $50, all within reach. All ugly. She eases over to the glove counter, where everything is ugly too. In her close-fitted coat with its black fur collar she contemplates the luxury of Branden's, which she has known for many years: its many mild pale lights, easy on the eye and the soul, its elaborate tinkly decorations, its women shoppers with their excellent shoes and coats and hairdos, all dawdling gracefully, in no hurry.

Who was ever in a hurry here?

2. The girl seated at home. A small library, paneled walls of oak. Someone is talking to me. An earnest, husky, female voice drives itself against my ears, nervous, frightened, groping around my heart, saying, "If you wanted gloves, why didn't you say so? Why didn't you ask for them?" That store, Branden's, is owned by Raymond Forrest who lives on DuMaurier Drive. We live on Sioux Drive. Raymond Forrest. A handsome man? An ugly man? A man of fifty or sixty, with gray hair, or a man of forty with earnest, courteous eyes, a good golf game; who is Raymond Forrest, this man who is my salvation? Father has been talking to him. Father is not his physician; Dr. Berg is his physician. Father and Dr. Berg refer patients to each other. There is a connection. Mother plays bridge with . . . On Mondays and Wednesdays our maid Billie works at . . . The strings draw together in a cat's cradle, making a net to save you when you fall. . . .

3. *Harriet Arnold's.* A small shop, better than Branden's. Mother in her black coat, I in my close-fitted blue coat. Shopping. Now look at this, isn't this cute, do you want this, why don't you want this, try this on, take this with you to the fitting room, take this also, what's wrong with you, what can I do for you, why are you so strange . . . ? "I wanted to steal but not to buy," I don't tell her. The girl droops along in her coat and gloves and leather boots, her eyes scan the horizon, which is pastel pink and decorated like Branden's, tasteful walls and modern ceilings with graceful glimmering lights.

4. Weeks later, the girl at a bus stop.

Two o'clock in the afternoon, a Tuesday; obviously she has walked out of school.

5. The girl stepping down from a bus. Afternoon, weather changing to colder. Detroit. Pavement and closed-up stores; grillwork over the windows of a pawnshop. What is a pawnshop, exactly?

II Characters

1. The girl stands five feet five inches tall. An ordinary height. Baldwin Country Day School draws them up to that height. She dreams along the corridors and presses her face against the Thermoplex glass. No frost or steam can ever form on that glass. A smudge of grease from her forehead . . . could she be boiled down to grease? She wears her hair loose and long and straight in suburban teen-age style, 1968. Eyes smudged with pencil, dark brown. Brown hair. Vague green eyes. A pretty girl? An ugly girl? She sings to herself under her breath, idling in the corridor, thinking of her many secrets (the thirty dollars she once took from the purse of a friend's mother, just for fun, the basement window she smashed in her own house just for fun) and thinking of her brother who is at Susquehanna Boys' Academy, an excellent preparatory school in Maine, remembering him unclearly . . . he has long manic hair and a squeaking voice and he looks like one of the popular teen-age singers of 1968, one of those in a group, *The Certain Forces, The Way Out, The Maniacs Responsible.* The girl in her turn looks like one of those fieldsful of girls who listen to the boys' singing, dreaming and mooning restlessly, breaking into high sullen laughter, innocently experienced.

2. The mother. A Midwestern woman of Detroit and suburbs. Belongs to the

Detroit Athletic Club. Also the Detroit Golf Club. Also the Bloomfield Hills Country Club. The Village Women's Club at which lectures are given each winter on Genet and Sartre and James Baldwin, by the Director of the Adult Education Program at Wayne State University. . . . The Bloomfield Art Association. Also the Founders Society of the Detroit Institute of Arts. Also . . . Oh, she is in perpetual motion, this lady, hair like blown-up gold and finer than gold, hair and fingers and body of inestimable grace. Heavy weighs the gold on the back of her hairbrush and hand mirror. Heavy heavy the candlesticks in the dining room. Very heavy is the big car, a Lincoln, long and black, that on one cool autumn day split a squirrel's body in two unequal parts.

3. The father. Dr.   He belongs to the same clubs as #2. A player of squash and golf; he has a golfer's umbrella of stripes. Candy stripes. In his mouth nothing turns to sugar, however; saliva works no miracles here. His doctoring is of the slightly sick. The sick are sent elsewhere (to Dr. Berg?), the deathly sick are sent back for more tests and their bills are sent to their homes, the unsick are sent to Dr. Coronet (Isabel, a lady), an excellent psychiatrist for unsick people who angrily believe they are sick and want to do something about it. If they demand a male psychiatrist, the unsick are sent by Dr.   (my father) to Dr. Lowenstein, a male psychiatrist, excellent and expensive, with a limited practice.

4. Clarita. She is twenty, twenty-five, she is thirty or more? Pretty, ugly, what? She is a woman lounging by the side of a road, in jeans and a sweater, hitchhiking, or she is slouched on a stool at a counter in some roadside diner. A hard line of jaw. Curious eyes. Amused eyes. Behind her eyes processions move, funeral pageants, cartoons. She says, "I never can figure out why girls like you bum around down here. What are you looking for anyway?" An odor of tobacco about her. Unwashed underclothes, or no underclothes, unwashed skin, gritty toes, hair long and falling into strands, not recently washed.

5. Simon. In this city the weather changes abruptly, so Simon's weather changes abruptly. He sleeps through the afternoon. He sleeps through the morning. Rising, he gropes around for something to get him going, for a cigarette or a pill to drive him out to the street, where the temperature is hovering around 35°. Why doesn't it drop? Why, why doesn't the cold clean air come down from Canada; will he have to go up into Canada to get it? will he have to leave the Country of his Birth and sink into Canada's frosty fields . . . ? Will the F.B.I. (which he dreams about constantly) chase him over the Canadian border on foot, hounded out in a blizzard of broken glass and horns . . . ?

"Once I was Huckleberry Finn," Simon says, "but now I am Roderick Usher." Beset by frenzies and fears, this man who makes my spine go cold, he takes green pills, yellow pills, pills of white and capsules of dark blue and green . . . he takes other things I may not mention, for what if Simon seeks me out and climbs into my girl's bedroom here in Bloomfield Hills and strangles me, what then . . . ? (As I write this I begin to shiver. Why do I shiver? I am now sixteen and sixteen is not an age for shivering.) It comes from Simon, who is always cold.

III World Events

Nothing.

IV People & Circumstances Contributing to This Delinquency

Nothing.

V Sioux Drive

George, Clyde G. 240 Sioux. A manufacturer's representative; children, a dog, a wife. Georgian with the usual columns. You think of the White House, then of Thomas Jefferson, then your mind goes blank on the white pillars and you think of nothing. Norris, Ralph W. 246 Sioux. Public relations. Colonial. Bay window, brick, stone, concrete, wood, green shutters, sidewalk, lantern, grass, trees, blacktop drive, two children, one of them my classmate Esther (Esther Norris) at Baldwin. Wife, cars. Ramsey, Michael D. 250 Sioux. Colonial. Big living room, thirty by twenty-five, fireplaces in living room, library, recreation room, paneled walls wet bar five bathrooms five bedrooms two lavatories central air conditioning automatic sprinkler automatic garage door three children one wife two cars a breakfast room a patio a large fenced lot fourteen trees a front door with a brass knocker never knocked. Next is our house. Classic contemporary. Traditional modern. Attached garage, attached Florida room, attached patio, attached pool and cabana, attached roof. A front door mail slot through which pour *Time Magazine, Fortune, Life, Business Week*, the *Wall Street Journal*, the *New York Times*, the *New Yorker*, the *Saturday Review, M.D., Modern Medicine, Disease of the Month* . . . and also. . . . And in addition to all this, a quiet sealed letter from Baldwin saying: *Your daughter is not doing work compatible with her performance on the Stanford Binet. . . .* And your son is not doing well, not well at all, very sad.

Where is your son anyway? Once he stole trick-and-treat candy from some six-year-old kids, he himself being a robust ten. The beginning. Now your daughter steals. In the Village Pharmacy she made off with, yes she did, don't deny it, she made off with a copy of *Pageant Magazine* for no reason, she swiped a roll of Life Savers in a green wrapper and was in no need of saving her life or even in need of sucking candy; when she was no more than eight years old she stole, don't blush, she stole a package of Tums only because it was out on the counter and available, and the nice lady behind the counter (now dead) said nothing. . . . Sioux Drive. Maples, oaks, elms. Diseased elms cut down. Sioux Drive runs into Roosevelt Drive. Slow, turning lanes, not streets, all drives and lanes and ways and passes. A private police force. Quiet private police, in unmarked cars. Cruising on Saturday evenings with paternal smiles for the residents who are streaming in and out of houses, going to and from parties, a thousand parties, slightly staggering, the women in their furs alighting from automobiles bought of Ford and General Motors and Chrysler, very heavy automobiles. No foreign cars. Detroit. In 275 Sioux, down the block in that magnificent French-Normandy mansion, lives   himself, who has the C   account itself, imagine that! Look at where he lives and look at the enormous trees and chimneys, imagine his many fireplaces, imagine his wife and children, imagine his wife's hair, imagine her fingernails, imagine her bathtub of smooth clean glowing pink, imagine their embraces, his trouser pockets filled with odd coins and keys and dust and peanuts, imagine their ecstasy on Sioux Drive, imagine their income tax returns, imagine their little boy's pride in his experimental car, a scaled-down C   , as he roars around the neighborhood on the sidewalks frightening dogs and Negro maids, oh imagine all these things, imagine everything, let your mind roar out all over Sioux Drive and Du Maurier Drive and Roosevelt Drive and Ticonderoga Pass and Burning Bush Way and Lincolnshire Pass and Lois Lane.

When spring comes, its winds blow nothing to Sioux Drive, no odors of hollyhocks or forsythia, nothing Sioux Drive doesn't already possess, everything is planted and performing. The weather vanes, had they weather vanes, don't have to turn with the wind, don't have to contend with the weather. There is no weather.

VI Detroit

There is always weather in Detroit. Detroit's temperature is always 32°. Fast-falling temperatures. Slow-rising temperatures. Wind from the north-northeast four to forty miles an hour, small-craft warnings, partly cloudy today and Wednesday changing to partly sunny through Thursday . . . small warnings of frost, soot warnings, traffic warnings, hazardous lake conditions for small craft and swimmers, restless Negro gangs, restless cloud formations, restless temperatures aching to fall out the very bottom of the thermometer or shoot up over the top and boil everything over in red mercury.

Detroit's temperature is 32°. Fast-falling temperatures. Slow-rising temperatures. Wind from the north-northeast four to forty miles an hour. . . .

VII Events

1. The girl's heart is pounding. In her pocket is a pair of gloves! In a plastic bag! Airproof breathproof plastic bag, gloves selling for twenty-five dollars on Branden's counter! In her pocket! Shoplifted! . . . In her purse is a blue comb, not very clean. In her purse is a leather billfold (a birthday present from her grandmother in Philadelphia) with snapshots of the family in clean plastic windows, in the billfold are bills, she doesn't know how many bills. . . . In her purse is an ominous note from her friend Tykie *What's this about Joe H. and the kids hanging around at Louise's Sat. night? You heard anything?* . . . passed in French class. In her purse is a lot of dirty yellow Kleenex, her mother's heart would break to see such very dirty Kleenex, and at the bottom of her purse are brown hairpins and safety pins and a broken pencil and a ballpoint pen (blue) stolen from somewhere forgotten and a purse-size compact of Cover Girl Make-Up, Ivory Rose. . . . Her lipstick is Broken Heart, a corrupt pink; her fingers are trembling like crazy; her teeth are beginning to chatter; her insides are alive; her eyes glow in her head; she is saying to her mother's astonished face *I want to steal but not to buy.*

2. At Clarita's. Day or night? What room is this? A bed, a regular bed, and a mattress on the floor nearby. Wallpaper hanging in strips. Clarita says she tore it like that with her teeth. She was fighting a barbaric tribe that night, high from some pills; she was battling for her life with men wearing helmets of heavy iron and their faces no more than Christian crosses to breathe through, every one of those bastards looking like her lover Simon, who seems to breathe with great difficulty through the slits of mouth and nostrils in his face. Clarita has never heard of Sioux Drive. Raymond Forrest cuts no ice with her, nor does the C   account and its millions; Harvard Business School could be at the corner of Vernor and 12th Street for all she cares, and Vietnam might have sunk by now into the Dead Sea under its

tons of debris, for all the amazement she could show . . . her face is overworked, overwrought, at the age of twenty (thirty?) it is already exhausted but fanciful and ready for a laugh. Clarita says mournfully to me *Honey somebody is going to turn you out let me give you warning.* In a movie shown on late television Clarita is not a mess like this but a nurse, with short neat hair and a dedicated look, in love with her doctor and her doctor's patients and their diseases, enamored of needles and sponges and rubbing alcohol. . . . Or no: she is a private secretary. Robert Cummings is her boss. She helps him with fantastic plots, the canned audience laughs, no, the audience doesn't laugh because nothing is funny, instead her boss is Robert Taylor and they are not boss and secretary but husband and wife, she is threatened by a young starlet, she is grim, handsome, wifely, a good companion for a good man. . . . She is Claudette Colbert. Her sister too is Claudette Colbert. They are twins, identical. Her husband Charles Boyer is a very rich handsome man and her sister, Claudette Colbert, is plotting her death in order to take her place as the rich man's wife, no one will know because they are *twins*. . . . All these marvelous lives Clarita might have lived, but she fell out the bottom at the age of thirteen. At the age when I was packing my overnight case for a slumber party at Toni Deshield's she was tearing filthy sheets off a bed and scratching up a rash on her arms. . . . Thirteen is uncommonly young for a white girl in Detroit, Miss Brock of the Detroit House of Correction said in a sad newspaper interview for the *Detroit News*; fifteen and sixteen are more likely. Eleven, twelve, thirteen are not surprising in colored . . . they are more precocious. What can we do? Taxes are rising and the tax base is falling. The temperature rises slowly but falls rapidly. Everything is falling out the bottom, Woodward Avenue is

filthy, Livernois Avenue is filthy! Scraps of paper flutter in the air like pigeons, dirt flies up and hits you right in the eye, oh Detroit is breaking up into dangerous bits of newspaper and dirt, watch out. . . .

Clarita's apartment is over a restaurant. Simon her lover emerges from the cracks at dark. Mrs. Olesko, a neighbor of Clarita's, an aged white wisp of a woman, doesn't complain but sniffs with contentment at Clarita's noisy life and doesn't tell the cops, hating cops, when the cops arrive. I should give more fake names, more blanks, instead of telling all these secrets. I myself am a secret; I am a minor.

3. My father reads a paper at a medical convention in Los Angeles. There he is, on the edge of the North American continent, when the unmarked detective put his hand so gently on my arm in the aisle of Branden's and said, "Miss, would you like to step over here for a minute?"

And where was he when Clarita put her hand on my arm, that wintry dark sulphurous aching day in Detroit, in the company of closed-down barber shops, closed-down diners, closed-down movie houses, homes, windows, basements, faces . . . she put her hand on my arm and said, "Honey, are you looking for somebody down here?"

And was he home worrying about me, gone for two weeks solid, when they carried me off . . . ? It took three of them to get me in the police cruiser, so they said, and they put more than their hands on my arm.

4. I work on this lesson. My English teacher is Mr. Forest, who is from Michigan State. Not handsome, Mr. Forest, and his name is plain, unlike Raymond Forrest's, but he is sweet and rodentlike, he has conferred with the principal and my parents, and everything is fixed . . . treat her as if nothing has happened, a new

start, begin again, only sixteen years old, what a shame, how did it happen? — nothing happened, nothing could have happened, a slight physiological modification known only to a gynecologist or to Dr. Coronet. I work on my lesson. I sit in my pink room. I look around the room with my sad pink eyes. I sigh, I dawdle, I pause, I eat up time, I am limp and happy to be home, I am sixteen years old suddenly, my head hangs heavy as a pumpkin on my shoulders, and my hair had just been cut by Mr. Faye at the Crystal Salon and is said to be very becoming.

(Simon too put his hand on my arm and said, "Honey, you have got to come with me," and in his six-by-six room we got to know each other. Would I go back to Simon again? Would I lie down with him in all that filth and craziness? Over and over again.

                      a Clarita is being betrayed as in front of a Cunningham Drug Store she is nervously eying a colored man who may or may not have money, or a nervous white boy of twenty with sideburns and an Appalachian look, who may or may not have a knife hidden in his jacket pocket, or a husky red-faced man of friendly countenance who may or may not be a member of the Vice Squad out for an early twilight walk.)

I work on my lesson for Mr. Forest. I have filled up eleven pages. Words pour out of me and won't stop. I want to tell everything . . . what was the song Simon was always humming, and who was Simon's friend in a very new trench coat with an old high school graduation ring on his finger . . . ? Simon's bearded friend? When I was down too low for him, Simon kicked me out and gave me to him for three days, I think, on Fourteenth Street in Detroit, an airy room of cold cruel drafts

with newspapers on the floor. . . . Do I really remember that or am I piecing it together from what they told me? Did they tell the truth? Did they know much of the truth?

VIII   Characters

1. Wednesdays after school, at four; Saturday mornings at ten. Mother drives me to Dr. Coronet. Ferns in the office, plastic or real, they look the same. Dr. Coronet is queenly, an elegant nicotine-stained lady who would have studied with Freud had circumstances not prevented it, a bit of a Catholic, ready to offer you some mystery if your teeth will ache too much without it. Highly recommended by Father! Forty dollars an hour, Father's forty dollars! Progress! Looking up! Looking better! That new haircut is so becoming, says Dr. Coronet herself, showing how normal she is for a woman with an I.Q. of 180 and many advanced degrees.

2. Mother. A lady in a brown suede coat. Boots of shiny black material, black gloves, a black fur hat. She would be humiliated could she know that of all the people in the world it is my ex-lover Simon who walks most like her . . . self-conscious and unreal, listening to distant music, a little bowlegged with craftiness. . . .

3. Father. Tying a necktie. In a hurry. On my first evening home he put his hand on my arm and said, "Honey, we're going to forget all about this."

4. Simon. Outside, a plane is crossing the sky, in here we're in a hurry. Morning. It must be morning. The girl is half out of her mind, whimpering and vague; Simon her dear friend is wretched this morning . . . he is wretched with morning itself . . . he forces her to give him an in-

jection with that needle she knows is filthy, she has a dread of needles and surgical instruments and the odor of things that are to be sent into the blood, thinking somehow of her father. . . . This is a bad morning, Simon says that his mind is being twisted out of shape, and so he submits to the needle that he usually scorns and bites his lip with his yellowish teeth, his face going very pale. *Ah baby!* he says in his soft mocking voice, which with all women is a mockery of love, *do it like this — Slowly —* And the girl, terrified, almost drops the precious needle but manages to turn it up to the light from the window . . . is it an extension of herself then? She can give him this gift then? *I wish you wouldn't do this to me,* she says, wise in her terror, because it seems to her that Simon's danger — in a few minutes he may be dead — is a way of pressing her against him that is more powerful than any other embrace. She has to work over his arm, the knotted corded veins of his arm, her forehead wet with perspiration as she pushes and releases the needle, staring at that mixture of liquid now stained with Simon's bright blood. . . . When the drug hits him she can feel it herself, she feels that magic that is more than any woman can give him, striking the back of his head and making his face stretch as if with the impact of a terrible sun. . . . She tries to embrace him but he pushes her aside and stumbles to his feet. *Jesus Christ,* he says. . . .

5. Princess, a Negro girl of eighteen. What is her charge? She is closed-mouthed about it, shrewd and silent, you know that no one had to wrestle her to the sidewalk to get her in here; she came with dignity. In the recreation room she sits reading *Nancy Drew and the Jewel Box Mystery,* which inspires in her face tiny wrinkles of alarm and interest: what a face! Light brown skin, heavy shaded eyes, heavy eyelashes, a serious sinister dark brow, graceful fingers, graceful wristbones, graceful legs, lips, tongue, a sugar-sweet voice, a leggy stride more masculine than Simon's and my mother's, decked out in a dirty white blouse and dirty white slacks; vaguely nautical is Princess' style. . . . At breakfast she is in charge of clearing the table and leans over me, saying, *Honey you sure you ate enough?*

6. The girl lies sleepless, wondering. Why here, why not there? Why Bloomfield Hills and not jail? Why jail and not her pink room? Why downtown Detroit and not Sioux Drive. What is the difference? Is Simon all the difference? The girl's head is a parade of wonders. She is nearly sixteen, her breath is marvelous with wonders, not long ago she was coloring with crayons and now she is smearing the landscape with paints that won't come off and won't come off her fingers either. She says to the matron *I am not talking about anything,* not because everyone has warned her not to talk but because, because she will not talk; because she won't say anything about Simon, who is her secret. And she says to the matron, *I won't go home,* up until that night in the lavatory when everything was changed. . . . "No, I won't go home I want to stay here," she says, listening to her own words with amazement, thinking that weeds might climb everywhere over that marvelous $180,000 house and dinosaurs might return to muddy the beige carpeting, but never never will she reconcile four o'clock in the morning in Detroit with eight o'clock breakfasts in Bloomfield Hills. . . . oh, she aches still for Simon's hands and his caressing breath, though he gave her little pleasure, he took everything from her (five-dollar bills, ten-dollar bills, passed into her numb hands by men and taken out of her hands by Simon) until she herself was passed into the hands of other

men, police, when Simon evidently got tired of her and her hysteria. . . . *No, I won't go home, I don't want to be bailed out.* The girl thinks as a *Stubborn and Wayward Child* (one of several charges lodged against her), and the matron understands her crazy white-rimmed eyes that are seeking out some new violence that will keep her in jail, should someone threaten to let her out. Such children try to strangle the matrons, the attendants, or one another . . . they want the locks locked forever, the doors nailed shut . . . and this girl is no different up until that night her mind is changed for her. . . .

IX   That Night

Princess and Dolly, a little white girl of maybe fifteen, hardy however as a sergeant and in the House of Correction for armed robbery, corner her in that lavatory at the farthest sink and the other girls look away and file out to bed, leaving her. God, how she is beaten up! Why is she beaten up? Why do they pound her, why such hatred? Princess vents all the hatred of a thousand silent Detroit winters on her body, this girl whose body belongs to me, fiercely she rides across the Midwestern plains on this girl's tender bruised body . . . revenge on the oppressed minorities of America! revenge on the slaughtered Indians! revenge on the female sex, on the male sex, revenge on Bloomfield Hills, revenge revenge. . . .

X   Detroit

In Detroit, weather weighs heavily upon everyone. The sky looms large. The horizon shimmers in smoke. Downtown the buildings are imprecise in the haze. Perpetual haze. Perpetual motion inside the haze. Across the choppy river is the city of Windsor, in Canada. Part of the continent has bunched up here and is bulging outward, at the tip of Detroit; a cold hard rain is forever falling on the expressways. . . . Shoppers shop grimly, their cars are not parked in safe places, their windshields may be smashed and graceful ebony hands may drag them out through their shatterproof smashed windshields, crying *Revenge for the Indians!* Ah, they all fear leaving Hudson's and being dragged to the very tip of the city and thrown off the parking roof of Cobo Hall, that expensive tomb, into the river. . . .

XI   Characters We Are Forever Entwined With

I. Simon drew me into his tender rotting arms and breathed gravity into me. Then I came to earth, weighed down. He said, *You are such a little girl*, and he weighed me down with his delight. In the palms of his hands were teeth marks from his previous life experiences. He was thirty-five, they said. Imagine Simon in this room, in my pink room: he is about six feet tall and stoops slightly, in a feline cautious way, always thinking, always on guard, with his scuffed light suede shoes and his clothes that are anyone's clothes, slightly rumpled ordinary clothes that ordinary men might wear to not-bad jobs. Simon has fair long hair, curly hair, spent lanquid curls that are like . . . exactly like the curls of wood shavings to the touch, I am trying to be exact . . . and he smells of unheated mornings and coffee and too many pills coating his tongue with a faint green-white scum. . . . Dear Simon, who would be panicked in this room and in this house (right now Billie is vacuuming next door in my parents' room; a vacuum cleaner's roar is a sign of all good things), Simon who is said to have come from a home not much different from this, years ago, fleeing all

the carpeting and the polished banisters
... Simon has a deathly face, only desperate people fall in love with it. His face
is bony and cautious, the bones of his
cheeks prominent as if with the rigidity of
his ceaseless thinking, plotting, for he has
to make money out of girls to whom
money means nothing, they're so far gone
they can hardly count it, and in a sense
money means nothing to him either except
as a way of keeping on with his life. *Each
Day's Proud Struggle*, the title of a novel
we could read at jail. . . . Each day he
needs a certain amount of money. He
devours it. It wasn't love he uncoiled in me
with his hollowed-out eyes and his courteous smile, that remnant of a prosperous
past, but a dark terror that needed to press
itself flat against him, or against another
man . . . but he was the first, he came over
to me and took my arm, a claim. We
struggled on the stairs and I said, *Let me
loose, you're hurting my neck, my face*, it
was such a surprise that my skin hurt
where he rubbed it, and afterward we lay
face to face and he breathed everything
into me. In the end I think he turned me
in.

2. Raymond Forrest. I just read this
morning that Raymond Forrest's father,
the chairman of the board at   ,
died of a heart attack on a plane bound for
London. I would like to write Raymond
Forrest a note of sympathy. I would like to
thank him for not pressing charges against
me one hundred years ago, saving me, being so generous . . . well, men like Raymond Forrest are generous men, not like
Simon. I would like to write him a letter
telling of my love, or of some other emotion that is positive and healthy. Not like
Simon and his poetry, which he scrawled
down when he was high and never
changed a word . . . but when I try to
think of something to say, it is Simon's
language that comes back to me, caught in

my head like a bad song, it is always
Simon's language:

> There is no reality only dreams
> Your neck may get snapped when you
>   wake
> My love is drawn to some violent end
> She keeps wanting to get away
> My love is heading downward
> And I am heading upward
> She is going to crash on the sidewalk
> And I am going to dissolve into the
>   clouds

XII   Events

1. Out of the hospital, bruised and
saddened and converted, with Princess'
grunts still tangled in my hair . . . and
Father in his overcoat looking like a prince
himself, come to carry me off. Up the expressway and out north to home. Jesus
Christ, but the air is thinner and cleaner
here. Monumental houses. Heartbreaking
sidewalks, so clean.

2. Weeping in the living room. The ceiling is two stories high and two chandeliers
hang from it. Weeping, weeping, though
Billie the maid is *probably listening*. I will
never leave home again. Never. Never
leave home. Never leave this home again,
never.

3. Sugar doughnuts for breakfast. The
toaster is very shiny and my face is distorted in it. Is that my face?

4. The car is turning in the driveway.
Father brings me home. Mother embraces
me. Sunlight breaks in movieland patches
on the roof of our traditional-contempo-
rary home, which was designed for the
famous automotive stylist whose identity,
if I told you the name of the famous car he
designed, you would all know, so I can't
tell you because my teeth chatter at the

thought of being sued . . . or having someone climb into my bedroom window with a rope to strangle me. . . . The car turns up the blacktop drive. The house opens to me like a doll's house, so lovely in the sunlight, the big living room beckons to me with its walls falling away in a delirium of joy at my return, Billie the maid is *no doubt* listening from the kitchen as I burst into tears and the hysteria Simon got so sick of. Convulsed in Father's arms, I say I will never leave again, never, why did I leave, where did I go, what happened, my mind is gone wrong, my body is one big bruise, my backbone was sucked dry, it wasn't the men who hurt me and Simon never hurt me but only those girls . . . my God, how they hurt me . . . I will never leave home again. . . . The car is perpetually turning up the drive and I am perpetually break-ing down in the living room and we are perpetually taking the right exit from the expressway (Lahser Road) and the wall of the rest room is perpetually banging against my head and perpetually are Simon's hands moving across my body and adding everything up and so too are Father's hands on my shaking bruised back, far from the surface of my skin on the surface of my good blue cashmere coat (dry-cleaned for my release). . . . I weep for all the money here, for God in gold and beige carpeting, for the beauty of chande-liers and the miracle of a clean polished gleaming toaster and faucets that run both hot and cold water, and I tell them, *I will never leave home, this is my home, I love everything here, I am in love with everything here.* . . .

I am home.

For Consideration

1. This story is introduced as "notes for an essay for an English class at Baldwin Country Day School." Is that form important for the story? In what ways?

2. Isolate the several characters in the story. How complete is the descrip-tion of each? What is the young girl's relationship with her family? With Clarita? With Simon?

3. Chronology is not consistently maintained in the story. What effects are created by the shifts in the time sequence?

4. Of what importance is the specific action of stealing the gloves? Why don't we see it in greater detail?

5. What is so important about **That Night (IX)** that changes the girl? Is it more than fear of the physical beating?

6. At the beginning the narrator leads us to expect "a happy ending." Is the ending happy? Is it hopeful? Do we believe the girl when she says of her home that "I am in love with everything here"?

character

Most discussions of fiction focus on **character**, for it is the human dimension which gives literature its greatest appeal. We should not, of course, be so limited as to insist on reading only that literature which presents human types or personalities we already know. Such a demand forces our reading to confirm the rather limited world that most of us live in. Literature ought, rather, to expand our worlds, to introduce us to human beings and human emotions that may initially be foreign or unfamiliar to us. Discrimination among characters is essential, of course, if understanding is to follow. We need to distinguish between a character whose motives are corrupt and dishonest and one who acts unwisely but innocently. The point is that, ideally, we should keep strictly personal biases and preferences under control in order to let the story work in an honest way.

Characters in fiction can usually be placed along a continuum ranging from flat to round (the terms are E. M. Forster's). The flat character is the human type, often the stereotype, who is not really a complete person at all. The character is instead a representative of a certain class, an occupation, or perhaps of an emotion, a belief, or a bias. Flat characters are seldom very interesting in themselves because they are, by definition, simple and limited. They can be significant in a story, of course, but usually in the way they serve as a contrast to a character who is more complex and interesting: more round. Round characters include within themselves the ambiguities and ambivalences we assume to be a part of any human being. For that reason their motives may be less definite and more complex; they may be changeable and unpredictable. They may be at one moment selfless and kind, at another proud and unyielding.

Flat characters, as Forster suggests, are usually static; they undergo no appreciable change as the story progresses. They remain at the end essentially what they were at the beginning. Round characters, by contrast, are dynamic; events and other people influence and change them. Indeed, the principal focus of many stories is precisely on these alterations in a character's life. Malamud's "The Magic Barrel,"

Lawrence's "The Horse Dealer's Daughter," and Black's "Laud" are among the several stories in this book which portray changing and changeable characters as an important dimension of the narrative.

Conflict, as suggested in the discussion of plot, is a central element of most fiction. The conflict may be an internal one within a single individual or it may pit an individual against society or against some larger force such as Nature, God, or Fate. Often, though, conflicts in fiction are between individuals. One traditional pattern is the conflict between a prominent figure (the **protagonist**) and an opponent (the **antagonist**). We should remember, of course, that the pattern has many variations; the conflict is seldom seen in terms of a battle between good and evil. Whatever its particular qualities, however, the conflict itself adds much to our understanding of the individuals involved.

Both of the stories which follow present prominent characters, and, in each, conflict is important. Chekhov's "An Anna Round His Neck" develops the growing tension between a "flat" character, Modest Alexeich, and a "round" character, his wife Anya. Modest Alexeich is associated always with a staid, unchanging, and uninteresting middle-class existence. He serves as a significant counterpoint to Anya, who changes and develops significantly in the course of the story. The Modest Alexeich we see at the end of the story is little different from the person described at the beginning; Anya, though, has experienced a kind of rebirth into a new existence.

Melville's "Bartleby the Scrivener" also focuses on characters in conflict, but the terms of the conflict, and the qualities of the characters, are more difficult to define. Bartleby seems in many ways a "flat" character; we know little about him, he speaks and acts predictably, and he remains unmovable (literally and emotionally) throughout the story. Yet he is of great interest to the reader and seems always more complex than his surface action and speech indicate. The lawyer appears, by contrast, more fully human and more varied, yet in his own way he is superficial and predictable, driven always by his "profound conviction that the easiest way of life is the best." You may find that, by the end of the story, easy characterizations are no longer possible.

ANTON CHEKHOV (1860–1904)
An Anna Round His Neck

Translated by Jessie Coulson

I

After the wedding there was not even a light meal; the bride and groom drank a glass of champagne, changed their clothes, and went off to the station. Instead of a cheerful wedding-ball and supper, instead of music and dancing, a pilgrimage to a monastery a hundred and fifty miles away. Many people approved of this, saying that Modest Alexeich was not young and had already attained a high position in the civil service, and that a noisy wedding might perhaps have seemed a little unsuitable; and besides, it is boring to listen to music when a fifty-two-year-old official marries a girl who is barely eighteen. They said also that Modest Alexeich, as a man of principle, had planned this pilgrimage on purpose to give his young wife to understand that even in marriage he gave first place to religion and morality.

The couple were seen off at the station. A crowd of colleagues and relatives stood with glasses in their hands, waiting to cheer as the train left, and Peter Leontyich, the bride's father, wearing a top hat and the tailcoat of his teacher's uniform, already drunk and very pale, kept stretching up his glass towards the window and saying in an imploring tone,

"Anyuta! Anya! Anya, just a word!"

Anna leaned out of the window towards him, and he whispered something to her, enveloping her in stale wine-fumes, blowing into her ear — it was impossible to understand what he was saying — and making the sign of the cross over her face and breast and hands, while his breath came

unsteadily and tears glistened in his eyes. Anya's brothers, Petya and Andryusha, schoolboys, tugged at his coat from behind and whispered in embarrassment,

"Papa, stop it . . . Don't, papa . . ."

When the train moved Anna saw her father running a little way after it, staggering and splashing wine out of his glass, and saw how pathetic, kind, and guilty he looked.

"Hurrah!" he shouted.

The newly married pair remained alone. Modest Alexeich looked round the compartment, distributed their things on the racks, and sat down smiling opposite his young wife. He was an official of medium height, rather round and plump and very well nourished, with long whiskers but no moustache, and his round, shaven, sharply defined chin looked like a heel. The most characteristic thing about his face was the absence of a moustache, the freshly shaven bare place which gradually merged into fat cheeks quivering like a jelly. His demeanour was staid, his movements deliberate, his manners suave.

"I cannot help recalling just now a certain circumstance," he said smiling. "Five years ago, when Kosorotov was given the Order of St. Anne, second class, and called to thank the Governor, his Excellency expressed himself in these terms, 'Well, now you have three Annas, one in your buttonhole and two hanging round your neck.' I must tell you that at the time Kosorotov's wife, a shrewish and trivial creature, whose name is Anna, had just returned to him. I hope that when I receive my Anna of the second class, his Excellency will not have occasion to say the same thing to me."

He smiled with his little eyes. And she smiled too, agitated by the thought that at any moment this man might kiss her with his moist, full lips and that she no longer had the right to refuse him. The soft movements of his plump body frightened her; she felt both alarmed and revolted. He stood up and hurriedly removed the order he wore round his neck, took off his coat and waist-coat and put on his dressing-gown.

"There!" he said, sitting down beside Anya.

She was remembering how painful the wedding ceremony had been, when it had seemed to her that the priest, and the guests, and everybody in the church, had looked at her sadly: why, why was she, such a nice pretty girl, marrying that dull, elderly gentleman? This morning she had been delighted that everything was going so well for her, but during the ceremony and now in the railway carriage she felt guilty, cheated, and ridiculous. She had married a rich man, but all the same she had no money, her wedding clothes had not been paid for, and today, when her father and brothers were seeing her off, she could tell from their faces that they hadn't a single copeck. Would they have any supper tonight? And what about tomorrow? And for some reason she saw her father and the boys sitting at that moment without her, hungry and experiencing the same distress as on the first evening after her mother's funeral.

"Oh, how unhappy I am!" she thought. "Why am I so unhappy?"

With the awkwardness of a solid citizen unaccustomed to dealing with women, Modest Alexeich touched her waist and patted her shoulder, while she thought of money, of her mother, and of her mother's death. When her mother died, her father,

Peter Leontyich, a teacher of calligraphy and drawing in the high school, began to drink, and they felt the pinch; the boys had no boots or galoshes, their father was taken before the magistrate, the court bailiff came and made an inventory of the furniture . . . What shame! Anya had had to look after her drunken father, mend her brothers' stockings, go to market, and when she was complimented on her beauty, youth and elegant manners, she thought the whole world could see her cheap hat and the holes in her shoes smeared over with ink. And at night tears and the importunate, worrying thought that at any moment her father's weakness would get him dismissed from the school and that he would not be able to endure it, but would die like her mother. But now some of the ladies among their acquaintances bestirred themselves and began to look for a good husband for Anna. Before long they had found this same Modest Alexeich, not young or handsome, but well off. He had about a hundred thousand in the bank and a family estate which he let to tenants. He was a man of principle and stood well with his Excellency; it would cost him nothing, they told Anna, to get a note from his Excellency to the headmaster of the school, or even to the Director of Education, to prevent Peter Leontyich's dismissal . . .

As she recalled these details the sudden sound of music and voices was borne in through the window. The train had stopped at a halt. Among the crowd beyond the platform somebody was playing lively tunes on an accordion and a cheap, squeaky fiddle, and from behind the tall birches and poplars, and the summer villas flooded with moonlight, came the strains of a military band: evidently a dance was in progress. On the platform strolled summer visitors and people whom the fine weather had brought out from the town for a breath of fresh air.

Artynov, who owned the whole summer colony, was there too, a rich, tall, heavily built, dark-haired man with protruding eyes, like an Armenian in the face, and oddly dressed. He was wearing a shirt open down the front, high boots with spurs, and a long black cloak hanging from his shoulders and trailing on the ground like a train. Two borzois were at his heels, their sharp muzzles lowered.

Anya's eyes still glistened with tears, but she had already forgotten all about her mother, and money, and her marriage, and was shaking hands with officers she knew and boys from the high school, smiling cheerfully and hurriedly saying,

"Good evening! How are you?"

She went out on to the platform at the end of the coach, in the moonlight, and stood so that everybody could see her in her magnificent new dress and hat.

"Why have we stopped?" she asked.

"This is a loop-line," she was told, "and they are waiting for the mail train."

She saw that Artynov was watching her, and she coquettishly narrowed her eyes and began to speak French in a loud voice, and because her own voice sounded so splendid, because of the music, and the moon reflected in the pond, because Artynov, who was well known as a rake and Don Juan, was watching her with eager curiosity, and because everybody was cheerful, she felt suddenly gay, and when the train moved and her officer acquaintances saluted her by way of good-bye, she was humming the polka whose sound the military band, pounding away there behind the trees, sent in pursuit of her; and she returned to their compartment feeling as though something at the halt had convinced her that she could not fail to be happy, in spite of everything.

The couple spent two days in the monastery and then returned to the town. They lived in an official flat. When Modest Alexeich went to his office, Anya played the piano, or wept with boredom, or lay on the couch reading novels or looking through a fashion paper. At dinner Modest Alexeich ate a great deal and talked about politics, appointments, transfers, and awards, about the necessity for hard work, about how family life is not a pleasure but a duty, about how one must take care of the copecks and the roubles will take care of themselves, and about how he held religion and morals in higher esteem than anything else on earth. And holding his knife in his fist like a sword, he said:

"Every man ought to have his obligations."

And Anya listened to him and was afraid, could not eat, and usually rose from the table hungry. After dinner her husband rested for a time, snoring loudly, and she went to see her family. Her father and the boys looked at her rather peculiarly, as though just before she came in they had been criticizing her for marrying for his money a dreary bore whom she did not love; her rustling dresses, bracelets, and general appearance of a lady embarrassed and offended them; in her presence they were a little confused and did not know what to talk to her about; but all the same they still loved her as much as before, and they had not yet got used to dining without her. She would sit down with them and eat cabbage soup, buckwheat porridge, and potatoes fried in mutton fat and smelling like tallow candles. Peter Leontyich poured out a glass of vodka with shaking hands and drank it off quickly, greedily and with aversion, then he drank a second, and a third . . . Petya and Andryusha, pale-faced thin little boys with big eyes, would take hold of the decanter and say worriedly,

"Don't papa . . . That's enough, papa . . ."

Anya would be anxious also and beg him not to drink any more, and he would fly into a sudden rage and thump his fist on the table.

"I won't allow anybody to dictate to me!" he would shout. "Brats! I'll turn the lot of you out!"

But his voice revealed his weakness and goodness and nobody was afraid of him. After dinner he usually dressed himself up; pale-faced, with cuts on his chin from shaving, he would stand a full half-hour craning his thin neck and smartening himself up in front of the mirror, combing his hair, twisting his black moustache, spraying himself with scent, knotting his tie; then he put on his gloves and top hat and went off to his private pupils. If it was a holiday he stayed at home and painted or played the wheezy, growling harmonium, trying to draw melodious sounds from it and humming an accompaniment, or growing angry with the boys:

"Wretches! Scoundrels! You've ruined the instrument!"

In the evenings Anya's husband played cards with the colleagues who lived in official quarters under the same roof with him. At such times the officials' wives, unattractive, tastelessly dressed, as coarse as kitchen maids, would call, and the flat was filled with gossip as ugly and tasteless as the women themselves. It sometimes happened that Modest Alexeich went to the theatre with Anya. In the intervals he did not allow her to stir a step away from him, but walked with her on his arm through the corridors and about the foyer.

After exchanging bows with anybody he would immediately whisper to Anya, "He's high in the service, a State Councillor — on visiting terms with his Excellency," or "Well-to-do . . . owns his house." When they passed the buffet Anya would very much have liked something sweet; she loved chocolate and apple tarts, but she had no money and was too shy to ask her husband. He would take up a pear, squeeze it in his fingers and ask undecidedly,

"How much?"

"Twenty-five copecks,"

"Well, really!" he would say, putting the pear back; and because it was awkward to leave the buffet without buying anything, he would order seltzer-water and drink the whole bottle himself, making his eyes water; at such times Anya hated him.

Or, suddenly going red all over, he would say hurriedly,

"Bow to that old lady!"

"But I don't know her."

"That doesn't matter. She is the wife of the Director of the Treasury Office. Bow, I tell you," he would mutter insistently. "Your head won't fall off."

Anya bowed, and her head never did fall off, but she suffered torments. She did everything her husband wished, while she raged at herself for having been taken in by him like the silliest little ninny. She had married him only for money, and yet she had less now than before her marriage. At least then she had a few coins from her father, but now not a copeck. She could neither take any by stealth nor ask for it; she was afraid of her husband and trembled before him. It seemed to her that she had nursed her fear of this man in her heart for a very long time. At one time, when she was a child, the high-school headmaster had represented the most dread and awe-inspiring powers, looming like a thunder-cloud or advancing with crushing weight like a railway engine; another such power, always spoken of with fear in the house, was his Excellency; there were a dozen lesser powers, including the stern, implacable masters in the school, with their clean-shaven upper lips, and now, finally, there was Modest Alexeich, the man of principle, who resembled the headmaster even in looks. In Anya's imagination all these powers fused into one and advanced on the weak and erring, like her father, in the shape of a terrible, enormous white bear; and she was afraid to protest but met with a forced smile and an expression of feigned pleasure the coarse caresses and defiling embraces that filled her with horror.

Only once did Peter Leontyich dare to ask his son-in-law for a loan of fifty roubles to settle an unpleasant debt, but what an ordeal it was!

"Very well, I will give it you," said Modest Alexeich, "but I warn you that in future I shall not help you until you stop drinking. For a man who is in the service of the government, it is a disgraceful failing. I cannot refrain from reminding you of the well-known fact that many capable individuals have been ruined by this passion, whereas had they been abstinent, they might well, with time, have attained very high rank."

The long periods went rolling on; "inasmuch as . . . ," "arising out of that assumption . . . ," "in view of what has just been stated . . . ," while poor Peter Leontyich suffered agonies of humiliation and experienced a strong desire for a drink.

The boys, when they came to visit Anya, usually in shabby trousers and with holes in their boots, also had to listen to long sermons.

"Every man ought to have his obligations!" Modest Alexeich told them.

He never parted with money. On the other hand, he gave Anya rings, bracelets, and brooches, remarking that these were good things to possess against a rainy day. He often opened her drawers and carried out an inspection to see that all the things were safe.

II

Meanwhile winter set in. Long before Christmas there was an announcement in the local paper that the usual winter ball was to take place in the Assembly Rooms on 29 December. Every evening, after his game of cards, Modest Alexeich talked in excited whispers with the wives of his colleagues, throwing anxious glances at Anya, and then spent a long time thoughtfully pacing the room. At last, late one evening, he stopped in front of Anya and said,

"You must get a ball-dress. Do you understand? Only please ask the advice of Maria Grigoryevna and Natalya Kuzminishna."

And he gave her a hundred roubles. She took them; but when she ordered her ball-dress she did not consult anybody, only talked to her father and tried to imagine how her mother would have dressed for the ball. Her dead mother had always dressed in the latest fashion and always taken pains with Anya and dressed her exquisitely, like a doll; and she had taught her to speak French and to dance the mazurka superlatively well (before her marriage she had been a governess for five years). Like her mother, Anya knew how to make a new dress out of an old one, clean gloves with benzine, and hire *bijoux*; and, like her mother again, she could half close her eyes, lisp, adopt elegant poses, go into raptures when necessary, or look sad and enigmatic. From her father she had inherited dark eyes and hair, highly strung nerves, and his way of always making the best of his appearance.

When, half an hour before they left for the ball, Modest Alexeich came into her room without his frock-coat, in order to put his order round his neck in front of her long mirror, he was enchanted by her

beauty and the brilliant freshness and air-
iness of her dress, stroked his whiskers in a
self-satisfied manner and said,

"How nice you look . . . how very nice!
Anyuta!" he went on, with sudden solemnity, "I have made you happy, and today
you can make me happy. I beg you to introduce yourself to his Excellency's good
lady. In God's name! Through her I might
receive the senior secretaryship!"

They went to the ball. Here were the
Assembly Rooms, the porter at the entrance, the ante-room with its coat pegs,
fur coats, scurrying lackeys, ladies in low-
necked gowns shielding themselves from
the draught with their fans, and smell of
gas and soldiers. As Anya mounted the
stairs on her husband's arm, the sight of
her own reflection, full length and brightly
illuminated by a multitude of lights, in an
enormous mirror, awakened in her heart a
feeling of gladness and the same anticipation of happiness as she had experienced at the railway halt that moonlit
night. She walked proudly and confi-
dently, conscious for the first time that she
was a lady and not a little girl, and involuntarily imitating her dead mother in her
gait and carriage. For the first time in her
life she felt rich and free. Even the
presence of her husband did not embarrass
her, since from the moment she crossed
the threshold she had instinctively sensed
that the proximity of her elderly husband
in no way detracted from her but on the
contrary invested her with the piquant
mystery men like so much. In the great
ballroom the orchestra was already in full
swing and dancing had begun. Plunged,
after their official flat, into all the impressions of bright lights, colour, music
and noise, Anya threw a glance round the
room, and thought, 'Oh, how splendid!'
and at once picked out in the crowd all her
acquaintances, everybody she had met at
evening parties or out walking, all the officers, schoolmasters, lawyers, officials,
landowners, his Excellency, Artynov, the
great ladies, beautiful or plain, elaborately
dressed and extremely *decolletées*, who
had already taken up their positions
among the stalls of the charity bazaar,
ready to begin trading for the benefit of
the poor. An enormous officer, wearing
epaulettes — she had met him in Old Kiev
Street when she was a schoolgirl and now
could not remember his name — sprang
up as if out of the ground in front of her
and asked her for a waltz, and she whirled
away from her husband, feeling as though
she were in a sailing-boat in a violent
storm and he was left behind on the distant shore . . . With passionate enthusiasm
she danced the waltz, and a polka, and a
quadrille, passing from partner to partner,
dizzy with the music and the noise, mixing
French and Russian words, lisping,
laughing, and thinking neither of her husband nor of anybody or anything else. She
was a success with the men, that was clear,
and indeed it was inevitable; she was
breathless with excitement, feverishly
clutched her fan, and felt very thirsty. Her
father, Peter Leontyich, in crumpled tails
that smelt of benzine, came up to her,
holding out a saucer of pink ice-cream.

"You are charming tonight," he said,
gazing at her with immense pleasure, "and
I have never been so sorry that you were in
such a hurry to get married . . . Why? I
know you did it for our sakes, but . . ."
With shaking hands he pulled out a packet
of notes and said, "I was paid for some
lessons today, and I can settle my debt to
your husband."

She thrust the saucer into his hands and
was pounced on and swept away by
somebody else, catching a glimpse over
her cavalier's shoulder of her father
gliding over the polished floor, putting his

arm round a lady, and dashing off round the room with her.

"How nice he is when he's sober!" she thought.

She danced the mazurka with the enormous officer; solemnly and heavily, like a carcase in uniform, he walked along, twisted his shoulders and chest, stamped almost imperceptibly — he was terribly unwilling to dance, but she fluttered by his side, teasing him with her beauty and her bare neck; her eyes blazed with enthusiasm, her movements were full of passion, while he grew steadily more indifferent, and proffered his arm with the gracious condescension of a king.

"Bravo, bravo!" said the spectators.

Little by little even the enormous officer was carried away; he grew animated and excited, yielded to the spell, let himself go and began to move lightly and youthfully, while she only twisted her shoulders and looked arch, as if she was a queen and he a slave, and then it seemed to her that the whole room was watching them, and all these people were spell-bound and full of envy. The enormous officer had hardly had time to thank her before the spectators moved aside and the men drew themselves up rather oddly, with their arms by their sides. It was his Excellency, wearing two stars on his coat, who was coming towards her. Yes, his Excellency was indeed coming to her, since he was staring straight at her and smiling sweetly, and at the same time mumbling his lips, as he always did when he saw a pretty woman.

"Delighted, delighted . . .," he began. "I shall have your husband placed under arrest for concealing such a treasure from us until now. I am the bearer of a message from my wife," he continued, offering her his arm. "You must come and help us . . . Mm, yes . . . We shall have to give you a beauty-prize . . . as they do in America . . . Mm . . . yes. The Americans . . . My wife is waiting impatiently for you."

He led her into a stall in the shape of a little peasant hut and up to an elderly lady, the lower part of whose face was disproportionately big, so that she looked as if she was holding a large stone in her mouth.

"Come and help," she said in a drawling nasal voice. "All the pretty ladies are working in the charity bazaar, and you are the only one who is idle, for some reason. Why won't you help us?"

She went away and Anya took her place beside a silver samovar and some cups. She began to do a brisk trade at once. She would not accept less than a rouble for a cup of tea, and she made the enormous officer drink three cups. Artynov, the rich man with the protruding eyes, approached, wheezing asthmatically and wearing not the strange costume in which Anya had seen him in the summer, but tails like everybody else. Without taking his eyes off her, he drank a glass of champagne, for which he paid a hundred roubles, and then had a cup of tea and gave another hundred — and all without a word, wheezing with asthma . . . Anya invited customers in and took money from them, and was already profoundly certain that her smiles and glances afforded them nothing but the greatest pleasure. She now understood that she was created exclusively for this noisy, brilliant, laughing life with its music, dances, and admirers, and her long-standing terror of some power advancing upon and threatening to crush her seemed ridiculous; she no longer feared anybody, and her only regret was that her mother was not there to rejoice with her in her success.

Peter Leontyich, pale by now but still firm on his feet, came up to the stall and asked for a glass of cognac. Anya blushed, expecting him to say something unsuitable (she was already ashamed that her father was so poor and so ordinary), but he drank his cognac, threw down ten roubles out of his packet, and walked sedately away without saying a word. A little later she saw him dancing the *grand rond* with his partner, and this time he was staggering and shouting, to the great confusion of his lady, and Anya remembered that three years ago at the ball he had staggered and shouted in the same way — and ended by being taken home to bed by a police officer; and the following day the headmaster had threatened him with dismissal. How untimely these memories seemed!

When the samovars on the stalls were extinguished and the weary charitable ladies handed their takings to the elderly lady with a stone in her mouth, Artynov took Anya on his arm to the room where supper was served for all those who had taken part in the bazaar. There were about twenty people, not more, having supper, but it was very lively. His Excellency proposed a toast: "In this luxurious dining-room it is fitting that we should drink to the success of the cheap dining-rooms which were the object of our bazaar today." A brigadier-general proposed a toast "to the power before which even the artillery quails," and everybody clinked glasses with the ladies. It was all very gay.

When somebody took Anya home, it was already growing light and cooks were on their way to market. Gay, intoxicated, full of new impressions, and extremely weary, she undressed, fell into bed and was instantly asleep.

At one o'clock in the afternoon the maid wakened her and announced that Mr. Artynov had called. She dressed quickly and went into the drawing-room. Soon after Artynov left, his Excellency arrived to thank her for helping with the bazaar. Casting saccharine looks at her and mumbling his lips, he kissed her hand, asked permission to call again, and departed, and she stood in the middle of the room, amazed and enchanted, unable to believe that this change in her life, an astonishing change, could have happened so quickly; and at that moment her husband, Modest Alexeich, walked in . . . He stood before her with exactly the same ingratiating, sugary, slavishly deferential expression that she was accustomed to seeing on his face in the presence of the powerful and distinguished; and triumphantly, indignantly, contemptuously, sure that nothing would happen to her for it, she said, pronouncing every word with great distinctness,

"Go away, stupid!"

After this, Anya never had a free day, since she was always going out to picnics, or walking, or to the play. She returned home every day towards morning, and went to bed on the floor of the drawing-room, afterwards movingly telling everybody how she slept under the flowers. She needed a great deal of money, but she was no longer afraid of Modest Alexeich and spent his money as if it were her own; she did not ask him for any, or demand it, merely sent him her bills, or notes saying "Give the bearer of this 200 roubles," or "100 roubles; settle immediately."

At Easter Modest Alexeich received the Order of St. Anne, second class. When he went to express his thanks, his Excellency laid aside his newspaper and settled back in his armchair.

"Well, now you have three Annas," he said, studying his white hands with their pink nails, "one in your buttonhole and two round your neck."

Modest Alexeich laid two fingers to his lips, for fear of laughing too loud, and said,

"Now we must expect the appearance in the world of a little Vladimir. May I venture to ask your Excellency to be godfather?"

He was referring to the Order of St. Vladimir, fourth class, and he had already begun to imagine himself repeating his witty remark, so successful in its resourcefulness and audacity, everywhere he went; he intended to make another, equally successful, but his Excellency was once more buried in his newspaper and only nodded his head . . .

And Anya went on driving behind troikas, hunting with Artynov, taking part in one-act plays, and going out to supper, and was less and less frequently with her family. Now they always dined alone. Peter Leontyich drank more heavily than before, there was no money, and the har-monium had long ago been sold for debt. The boys no longer allowed him out alone, and always followed him to see that he did not fall; and when, among the carriages parading on Old Kiev Street, they met Anya in a showy turn-out with Artynov on the box instead of the coachman, Peter Leontyich took off his top-hat and seemed about to call out something, but Petya and Andryusha took his arms and said imploringly,

"Papa, don't . . . Stop, papa . . ."

For Consideration

1.   What kind of wedding do Modest Alexeich and Anya have? How is it characteristic of Modest Alexeich's way of life? How does his physical appearance reinforce his values in life?

2.   What is Anya's reaction to her marriage? Why, exactly, is she unhappy?

3.   When the train stops briefly Anya feels "suddenly gay." Why? Is that gaiety lasting?

4.   What is Anya's relationship to her family? How did that affect her decision to marry?

5.   When Anya and her husband go to the ball, what is the first thing that awakens her joy and confidence in herself? What else contributes to that feeling? How does she react to Modest Alexeich at the ball?

6.   At the ball Anya understands "that she was created exclusively for this noisy, brilliant, laughing life with its music, dances, and admirers, and her long-standing terror of some power advancing upon and threatening to crush her seemed ridiculous." Why has she reached this conclusion? Is the life she anticipates frivolous? How does it compare to life as Modest Alexeich desires it?

7.   In what ways has Anya changed by the end of the story? How has her relationship to Modest Alexeich changed? In what sense has she become "an Anna round his neck"?

8.   The ending seems curiously open-ended, with the final focus on Anya's father and her brothers pleading to him, "Papa, don't . . . Stop, papa. . . ." Where else in the story have they said this? Why do you think Chekhov concludes his story this way?

HERMAN MELVILLE   (1819–1891)
Bartleby the Scrivener

A Story of Wall Street

I am a rather elderly man. The nature of my avocations, for the last thirty years, has brought me into more than ordinary contact with what would seem an interesting and somewhat singular set of men, of whom, as yet, nothing, that I know of, has ever been written — I mean, the law-copyists, or scriveners. I have known very many of them, professionally and privately, and, if I pleased, could relate divers histories, at which good-natured gentlemen might smile, and sentimental souls might weep. But I waive the biographies of all other scriveners, for a few passages in the life of Bartleby, who was a scrivener, the strangest I ever saw, or heard of. While, of other law-copyists, I might write the complete life, of Bartleby nothing of that sort can be done. I believe that no materials exist for a full and satisfactory biography of this man. It is an irreparable loss to literature. Bartleby was one of those beings of whom nothing is ascertainable, except from the original sources, and, in his case, those are very small. What my own astonished eyes saw of Bartleby, *that* is all I know of him, except, indeed, one vague report, which will appear in the sequel.

Ere introducing the scrivener, as he first appeared to me, it is fit I make some mention of myself, my *employés*, my business, my chambers, and general surroundings; because some such description is indispensable to an adequate understanding of the chief character about to be presented. Imprimis: I am a man who, from his youth upwards, has been filled with a profound conviction that the easiest way of life is the best. Hence, though I belong to a profession proverbially energetic and nervous, even to turbulence, at times, yet nothing of that sort have I ever suffered to invade my peace. I am one of those unambitious lawyers who never addresses a jury, or in any way draws down public applause; but, in the cool tranquillity of a snug retreat, do a snug business among rich men's bonds, and mortgages, and title-deeds. All who know me, consider me an eminently *safe* man. The late John Jacob Astor, a personage little given to poetic enthusiasm, had no hesitation in pronouncing my first grand point to be prudence; my next, method. I do not speak it in vanity, but simply record the fact, that I was not unemployed in my profession by the late John Jacob Astor; a name which, I admit, I love to repeat; for it hath a rounded and orbicular sound to it, and rings like unto bullion. I will freely add, that I was not insensible to the late John Jacob Astor's good opinion.

Some time prior to the period at which this little history begins, my avocations had been largely increased. The good old office, now extinct in the State of New York, of a Master in Chancery, had been conferred upon me. It was not a very arduous office, but very pleasantly remunerative. I seldom lose my temper; much more seldom indulge in dangerous indignations at wrongs and outrages; but, I must be permitted to be rash here, and declare, that I consider the sudden and violent abrogation of the office of Master in Chancery, by the new Constitution, as a —— premature act; inasmuch as I had counted upon a life-lease of the profits, whereas I only received those of a few short years. But this is by the way.

My chambers were up stairs, at No. —— Wall Street. At one end, they looked upon the white wall of the interior of a spacious sky-light shaft, penetrating the building from top to bottom.

This view might have been considered rather tame than otherwise, deficient in what landscape painters call "life." But, if so, the view from the other end of my chambers offered, at least, a contrast, if nothing more. In that direction, my windows commanded an unobstructed view of a lofty brick wall, black by age and everlasting shade; which wall required no spyglass to bring out its lurking beauties, but, for the benefit of all near-sighted spectators, was pushed up to within ten feet of my window panes. Owing to the great height of the surrounding buildings, and my chambers being on the second floor, the interval between this wall and mine not a little resembled a huge square cistern.

At the period just preceding the advent of Bartleby, I had two persons as copyists in my employment, and a promising lad as an office-boy. First, Turkey; second, Nippers; third, Ginger Nut. These may seem names, the like of which are not usually found in the Directory. In truth, they were nicknames, mutually conferred upon each other by my three clerks, and were deemed expressive of their respective persons or characters. Turkey was a short, pursy Englishman, of about my own age — that is, somewhere not far from sixty. In the morning, one might say, his face was of a fine florid hue, but after twelve o'clock, meridian — his dinner hour — it blazed like a grate full of Christmas coals; and

continued blazing — but, as it were, with a gradual wane — till six o'clock P.M., or thereabouts; after which, I saw no more of the proprietor of the face, which, gaining its meridian with the sun, seemed to set with it, to rise, culminate, and decline the following day, with the like regularity and undiminished glory. There are many singular coincidences I have known in the course of my life, not the least among which was the fact, that, exactly when Turkey displayed his fullest beams from his red and radiant countenance, just then, too, at that critical moment, began the daily period when I considered his business capacities as seriously disturbed for the remainder of the twenty-four hours. Not that he was absolutely idle, or averse to business, then; far from it. The difficulty was, he was apt to be altogether too energetic. There was a strange, inflamed, flurried, flighty recklessness of activity about him. He would be incautious in dipping his pen into his inkstand. All his blots upon my documents were dropped there after twelve o'clock meridian. Indeed, not only would he be reckless, and sadly given to making blots in the afternoon, but, some days, he went further, and was rather noisy. At such times, too, his face flamed with augmented blazonry, as if cannel coal had been heaped on anthracite. He made an unpleasant racket with his chair; spilled his sand-box; in mending his pens, impatiently split them all to pieces, and threw them on the floor in a sudden passion; stood up, and leaned over his table, boxing his papers about in a most indecorous manner, very sad to behold in an elderly man like him. Nevertheless, as he was in many ways a most valuable person to me, and all the time before twelve o'clock meridian, was the quickest, steadiest creature, too, accomplishing a great deal of work in a style not easily to be matched — for these reasons, I was willing to overlook his eccentricities, though, indeed, occasionally, I remonstrated with him. I did this very gently, however, because, though the civilest, nay, the blandest and most reverential of men in the morning, yet, in the afternoon, he was disposed, upon provocation, to be slightly rash with his tongue — in fact, insolent. Now, valuing his morning services as I did, and resolved not to lose them — yet, at the same time, made uncomfortable by his inflamed ways after twelve o'clock — and being a man of peace, unwilling by my admonitions to call forth unseemly retorts from him, I took upon me, one Saturday noon (he was always worse on Saturdays) to hint to him, very kindly, that, perhaps, now that he was growing old, it might be well to abridge his labors; in short, he need not come to my chambers after twelve o'clock, but, dinner over, had best go home to his lodgings, and rest himself till tea-time. But no; he insisted upon his afternoon devotions. His countenance became intolerably fervid, as he oratorically assured me — gesticulating with a long ruler at the other end of the room — that if his services in the morning were useful, how indispensable, then, in the afternoon?

"With submission, sir," said Turkey, on this occasion, "I consider myself your right-hand man. In the morning I but marshal and deploy my columns; but in the afternoon I put myself at their head, and gallantly charge the foe, thus" — and he made a violent thrust with the ruler.

"But the blots, Turkey," intimated I.

"True; but, with submission, sir, behold these hairs! I am getting old. Surely, a blot or two of a warm afternoon is not to be severely urged against gray hairs. Old age — even if it blot the page — is honorable. With submission, sir, we *both* are getting old."

This appeal to my fellow-feeling was hardly to be resisted. At all events, I saw that go he would not. So, I made up my mind to let him stay, resolving, nevertheless, to see to it that, during the afternoon, he had to do with my less important papers.

Nippers, the second on my list, was a whiskered, sallow, and, upon the whole, rather piratical-looking young man, of about five and twenty. I always deemed him the victim of two evil powers — ambition and indigestion. The ambition was evinced by a certain impatience of the duties of a mere copyist, an unwarrantable usurpation of strictly professional affairs, such as the original drawing up of legal documents. The indigestion seemed betokened in an occasional nervous testiness and grinning irritability, causing the teeth to audibly grind together over mistakes committed in copying; unnecessary maledictions, hissed, rather than spoken, in the heat of business; and especially by a continual discontent with the height of the table where he worked. Though of a very ingenious, mechanical turn, Nippers could never get this table to suit him. He put chips under it, blocks of various sorts, bits of pasteboard, and at last went so far as to attempt an exquisite adjustment, by final pieces of folded blotting-paper. But no invention would answer. If, for the sake of easing his back, he brought the table lid at a sharp angle well up towards his chin, and wrote there like a man using the steep roof of a Dutch house for his desk, then he declared that it stopped the circulation in his arms. If now he lowered the table to his waistbands, and stooped over it in writing, then there was a sore aching in his back. In short, the truth of the matter was, Nippers knew not what he wanted. Or, if he wanted anything, it was to be rid of a scrivener's table altogether. Among the manifestations of his diseased ambition was a fondness he had for receiving visits from certain ambiguous-looking fellows in seedy coats, whom he called his clients. Indeed, I was aware that not only was he, at times, considerable of a ward-politician, but he occasionally did a little business at the Justices' courts, and was not unknown on the steps of the Tombs. I have good reason to believe, however, that one individual who called upon him at my chambers, and who, with a grand air, he insisted was his client, was no other than a dun, and the alleged title-deed, a bill. But, with all his failings, and the annoyances he caused me, Nippers, like his compatriot Turkey, was a very useful man to me; wrote a neat, swift hand; and, when he chose, was not deficient in a gentlemanly sort of deportment. Added to this, he always dressed in a gentlemanly sort of way; and so, incidentally, reflected credit upon my chambers. Whereas, with respect of Turkey, I had much ado to keep him from being a reproach to me. His clothes were apt to look oily, and smell of eating-houses. He wore his pantaloons very loose and baggy in summer. His coats were execrable; his hat not to be handled. But while the hat was a thing of indifference to me, inasmuch as his natural civility and deference, as a dependent Englishman, always led him to doff it the moment he entered the room, yet his coat was another matter. Concerning his coats, I reasoned with him; but with no effect. The truth was, I suppose, that a man with so small an income could not afford to sport such a lustrous face and a lustrous coat at one and the same time. As Nippers once observed, Turkey's money went chiefly for red ink. One winter day, I presented Turkey with a highly respectable-looking coat of my own — a padded gray coat, of a most comfortable warmth, and which buttoned straight up from the knee to the neck. I thought Turkey would appreciate the favor, and abate his rashness and obstreperousness of afternoons. But no; I verily believe that buttoning himself up in so downy and blanket-like a coat had a pernicious effect upon him — upon the same principle that too much oats are bad for horses. In fact, precisely as a rash, restive horse is said to feel his oats, so Turkey felt his coat. It made him insolent. He was a man whom prosperity harmed.

Though, concerning the self-indulgent habits of Turkey, I had my own private surmises, yet, touching Nippers, I was well persuaded that, whatever might be his faults in other respects, he was, at least, a temperate young man. But, indeed, nature herself seemed to have been his vintner, and, at his birth, charged him so thoroughly with an irritable, brandy-like disposition, that all subsequent potations were needless. When I consider how, amid the stillness of my chambers, Nippers would sometimes impatiently rise from his seat, and stooping over his table, spread his arms wide apart, seize the whole desk, and move it, and jerk it, with a grim, grinding motion on the floor, as if the table were a perverse voluntary agent and vexing him, I plainly perceive that, for Nippers, brandy-and-water were altogether superfluous.

It was fortunate for me that, owing to its peculiar cause — indigestion — the irritability and consequent nervousness of Nippers were mainly observable in the morning, while in the afternoon he was comparatively mild. So that, Turkey's paroxysms only coming on about twelve o'clock, I never had to do with their eccentricities at one time. Their fits relieved each other, like guards. When Nippers's was on, Turkey's was off; and *vice versa*. This was a good natural arrangement, under the circumstances.

Ginger Nut, the third on my list, was a lad, some twelve years old. His father was a car-man, ambitious of seeing his son on the bench instead of a cart, before he died. So he sent him to my office, as student at law, errand-boy, cleaner and sweeper, at the rate of one dollar a week. He had a little desk to himself; but he did not use it much. Upon inspection, the drawer exhibited a great array of the shells of various sorts of nuts. Indeed, to this quick-witted youth, the whole noble science of the law was contained in a nutshell. Not the least among the employments of Ginger Nut, as well as one which he discharged with the most alacrity, was his duty as cake and apple purveyor for Turkey and Nippers. Copying law-papers being proverbially a dry, husky sort of business, my two scriveners were fain to moisten their mouths very often with Spitzenbergs, to be had at the numerous stalls nigh the Custom House and Post Office. Also, they sent Ginger Nut very frequently for that peculiar cake — small, flat, round, and very spicy — after which he had been named by them. Of a cold morning, when business was but dull, Turkey would gobble up scores of these cakes, as if they were mere wafers — indeed, they sell them at the rate of six or eight for a penny — the scrape of his pen blending with the crunching of the crisp particles in his mouth. Rashest of all the fiery afternoon blunders and flurried rashnesses of Turkey, was his once moistening a ginger-cake between his lips, and clapping it on to a mortgage, for a seal. I came within an ace of dismissing him then. But he mollified me by making an oriental bow, and saying —

"With submission, sir, it was generous of me to find you in stationery on my own account."

Now my original business — that of a conveyancer and title hunter, and drawer up of recondite documents of all sorts — was considerably increased by receiving the master's office. There was now great work for scriveners. Not only must I push the clerks already with me, but I must have additional help.

In answer to my advertisement, a motionless young man one morning stood upon my office threshold, the door being open, for it was summer. I can see that figure now — pallidly neat, pitiably respectable, incurably forlorn! It was Bartleby.

After a few words touching his qualifications, I engaged him, glad to have among my corps of copyists a man of so singularly sedate an aspect, which I thought might operate beneficially upon the flighty temper of Turkey, and the fiery one of Nippers.

I should have stated before that ground glass folding-doors divided my premises into two parts, one of which was occupied by my scriveners, the other by myself. According to my humor, I threw open these doors, or closed them. I resolved to assign Bartleby a corner by the folding-doors, but on my side of them, so as to have this quiet man within easy call, in case any trifling thing was to be done. I placed his desk close up to a small side-window in that part of the room, a window which originally had afforded a lateral view of certain grimy back-yards and bricks, but which, owing to subsequent erections, commanded at present no view at all, though it gave some light. Within three feet of the panes was a wall, and the light came down from far above, between two lofty buildings, as from a very small opening in a dome. Still further to a satisfactory arrangement, I procured a high green folding screen, which might entirely isolate Bartleby from my sight, though not remove him from my voice. And thus, in a manner, privacy and society were conjoined.

At first, Bartleby did an extraordinary quantity of writing. As if long famishing for something to copy, he seemed to gorge himself on my documents. There was no pause for digestion. He ran a day and night line, copying by sun-light and by candle-light. I should have been quite delighted with his application, had he been cheerfully industrious. But he wrote on silently, palely, mechanically.

It is, of course, an indispensable part of a scrivener's business to verify the accuracy of his copy, word by word. Where there are two or more scriveners in an office, they assist each other in this examination, one reading from the copy, the other holding the original. It is a very dull, wearisome, and lethargic affair. I can readily imagine that, to some sanguine temperaments, it would be altogether intolerable. For example, I cannot credit that the mettlesome poet, Byron, would have contentedly sat down with Bartleby to examine a law document of, say five hundred pages, closely written in a crimpy hand.

Now and then, in the haste of business, it had been my habit to assist in comparing some brief document myself, calling Turkey or Nippers for this purpose. One object I had, in placing Bartleby so handy to me behind the screen, was to avail myself of his services on such trivial occasions. It was on the third day, I think, of his being with me, and before any necessity had arisen for having his own writing examined, that, being much hurried to complete a small affair I had in hand, I abruptly called to Bartleby. In my haste and natural expectancy of instant compliance, I sat with my head bent over the original on my desk, and my right hand sideways, and somewhat nervously extended with the copy, so that, immediately upon emerging from his retreat, Bartleby might snatch it and proceed to business without the least delay.

In this very attitude did I sit when I called to him, rapidly stating what it was I wanted him to do — namely, to examine a small paper with me. Imagine my surprise, nay, my consternation, when, without moving from his privacy, Bartleby, in a singularly mild, firm voice, replied, "I would prefer not to."

I sat awhile in perfect silence, rallying my stunned faculties. Immediately it occurred to me that my ears had deceived me, or Bartleby had entirely misunderstood my meaning. I repeated my request in the clearest tone I could assume; but in quite as clear a one came the previous reply, "I would prefer not to."

"Prefer not to," echoed I, rising in high excitement, and crossing the room with a stride. "What do you mean? Are you moon-struck? I want you to help me compare this sheet here — take it," and I thrust it towards him.

"I would prefer not to," said he.

I looked at him steadfastly. His face was leanly composed; his gray eye dimly calm. Not a wrinkle of agitation rippled him. Had there been the least uneasiness, anger, impatience, or impertinence in his manner; in other words, had there been any thing ordinarily human about him, doubtless I should have violently dismissed him from the premises. But as it was, I should have as soon thought of turning my pale plaster-of-paris bust of Cicero out of doors. I stood gazing at him awhile, as he went on with his own writing, and then reseated myself at my desk. This is very strange, thought I. What had one best do? But my business hurried me. I concluded to forget the matter for the present, reserving it for my future leisure. So calling Nippers from the other room, the paper was speedily examined.

A few days after this, Bartleby concluded four lengthy documents, being quadruplicates of a week's testimony taken before me in my High Court of Chancery. It became necessary to examine them. It was an important suit, and great accuracy was imperative. Having all things arranged, I called Turkey, Nippers, and Ginger Nut from the next room, meaning to place the four copies in the hands of my four clerks, while I should read from the original. Accordingly, Turkey, Nippers, and Ginger Nut had taken their seats in a row, each with his document in his hand, when I called to Bartleby to join this interesting group.

"Bartleby! quick, I am waiting."

I heard a slow scrape of his chair legs on the uncarpeted floor, and soon he appeared standing at the entrance of his hermitage.

"What is wanted?" said he, mildly.

"The copies, the copies," said I, hurriedly. "We are going to examine them. There —" and I held towards him the fourth quadruplicate.

"I would prefer not to," he said, and gently disappeared behind the screen.

For a few moments I was turned into a pillar of salt, standing at the head of my seated column of clerks. Recovering myself, I advanced towards the screen, and demanded the reason for such extraordinary conduct.

"*Why* do you refuse?"

"I would prefer not to."

With any other man I should have flown outright into a dreadful passion, scorned all further words, and thrust him ignominiously from my presence. But there was something about Bartleby that not only strangely disarmed me, but in a wonderful manner, touched and disconcerted me. I began to reason with him.

"These are your own copies we are about to examine. It is labor saving to you, because one examination will answer for your four papers. It is common usage. Every copyist is bound to help examine his copy. Is it not so? Will you not speak? Answer!"

"I prefer not to," he replied in a flutelike tone. It seemed to me that, while I had been addressing him, he carefully revolved every statement that I made; fully comprehended the meaning; could not gainsay the irresistible conclusion; but, at the same time, some paramount consideration prevailed with him to reply as he did.

"You are decided, then, not to comply with my request — a request made according to common usage and common sense?"

He briefly gave me to understand, that on that point my judgment was sound. Yes: his decision was irreversible.

It is not seldom the case that, when a man is browbeaten in some unprecedented and violently unreasonable way, he begins to stagger in his own plainest faith. He begins, as it were, vaguely to surmise that, wonderful as it may be, all the justice and all the reason is on the other side. Accordingly, if any disinterested persons are present, he turns to them for some reinforcement of his own faltering mind.

"Turkey," said I, "what do you think of this? Am I not right?"

"With submission, sir," said Turkey, in his blandest tone, "I think that you are."

"Nippers," said I, "what do *you* think of it?"

"I think I should kick him out of the office."

(The reader, of nice perceptions, will here perceive that, it being morning, Turkey's answer is couched in polite and tranquil terms, but Nippers replies in ill-tempered ones. Or, to repeat a previous sentence, Nippers's ugly mood was on duty, and Turkey's off.)

"Ginger Nut," said I, willing to enlist the smallest suffrage in my behalf, "what do *you* think of it?"

"I think, sir, he's a little *luny*," replied Ginger Nut, with a grin.

"You hear what they say," said I, turning towards the screen, "come forth and do your duty."

But he vouchsafed no reply. I pondered a moment in sore perplexity. But once more business hurried me. I determined again to postpone the consideration of this dilemma to my future leisure. With a little trouble we made out to examine the papers without Bartleby, though at every page or two Turkey deferentially dropped his opinion, that this proceeding was quite out of the common; while Nippers, twitching in his chair with a dyspeptic nervousness, ground out, between his set teeth, occasional hissing maledictions against the stubborn oaf behind the screen. And for his (Nippers's) part, this was the first and the last time he would do another man's business without pay.

Meanwhile Bartleby sat in his hermitage, oblivious to everything but his own peculiar business there.

Some days passed, the scrivener being employed upon another lengthy work. His late remarkable conduct led me to regard his ways narrowly. I observed that he never went to dinner; indeed, that he never went anywhere. As yet I had never, of my personal knowledge, known him to be outside of my office. He was a perpetual sentry in the corner. At about eleven o'clock though, in the morning, I noticed that Ginger Nut would advance toward the opening in Bartleby's screen, as if silently beckoned thither by a gesture invisible to me where I sat. The boy would then leave the office, jingling a few pence, and reappear with a handful of ginger-nuts, which he delivered in the hermitage, receiving two of the cakes for his trouble.

He lives, then, on ginger-nuts, thought I; never eats a dinner, properly speaking; he must be a vegetarian, then; but no; he never eats even vegetables; he eats nothing but ginger-nuts. My mind then ran on in reveries concerning the probable effects upon the human constitution of living entirely on ginger-nuts. Ginger-nuts are so called, because they contain ginger as one of their peculiar constituents, and the final flavoring one. Now, what was ginger? A hot, spicy thing. Was Bartleby hot and spicy? Not at all. Ginger, then, had no effect upon Bartleby. Probably he preferred it should have none.

Nothing so aggravates an earnest person as a passive resistance. If the individual so resisted be of a not inhumane temper, and the resisting one perfectly harmless in his passivity, then, in the better moods of the former, he will endeavor charitably to construe to his imagination what proves impossible to be solved by his judgment. Even so, for the most part, I regarded Bartleby and his ways. Poor fellow! thought I, he means no mischief; it is plain he intends no insolence; his aspect sufficiently evinces that his eccentricities are involuntary. He is useful to me. I can get along with him. If I turn him away, the chances are he will fall in with some less-indulgent employer, and then he will be rudely treated, and perhaps driven forth miserably to starve. Yes. Here I can cheaply purchase a delicious self-approval. To befriend Bartleby; to humor him in his strange willfullness, will cost me little or nothing, while I lay up in my soul what will eventually prove a sweet morsel for my conscience. But this mood was not invariable with me. The passiveness of Bartleby sometimes irritated me. I felt strangely goaded on to encounter him in new opposition — to elicit some angry spark from him answerable to my own. But, indeed, I might as well have essayed to strike fire with my knuckles against a bit of Windsor soap. But one afternoon the evil impulse in me mastered me, and the following little scene ensued:

"Bartleby," said I, "when those papers are copied, I will compare them with you."

"I would prefer not to."

"How? Surely you do not mean to persist in that mulish vagary?"

No answer.

I threw open the folding-doors near by, and, turning upon Turkey and Nippers, exclaimed:

"Bartleby a second time says, he won't examine his papers. What do you think of it, Turkey?"

It was afternoon, be it remembered. Turkey sat glowing like a brass boiler; his bald head steaming; his hands reeling among his blotted papers.

"Think of it?" roared Turkey; "I think I'll just step behind his screen, and black his eyes for him!"

So saying, Turkey rose to his feet and threw his arms into a pugilistic position. He was hurrying away to make good his promise, when I detained him, alarmed at the effect of incautiously rousing Turkey's combativeness after dinner.

"Sit down, Turkey," said I, "and hear what Nippers has to say. What do you think of it, Nippers? Would I not be justified in immediately dismissing Bartleby?"

"Excuse me, that is for you to decide, sir. I think his conduct quite unusual, and, indeed, unjust, as regards Turkey and myself. But it may only be a passing whim."

"Ah," exclaimed I, "you have strangely changed your mind, then — you speak very gently of him now."

"All beer," cried Turkey; "gentleness is effects of beer — Nippers and I dined together to-day. You see how gentle *I* am, sir. Shall I go and black his eyes?"

"You refer to Bartleby, I suppose. No, not to-day, Turkey," I replied; "pray, put up your fists."

I closed the doors, and again advanced towards Bartleby. I felt additional incentives tempting me to my fate. I burned to be rebelled against again. I remembered that Bartleby never left the office.

"Bartleby," said I, "Ginger Nut is away; just step around to the Post Office, won't you? (it was but a three minutes' walk), and see if there is anything for me."

"I would prefer not to."

"You *will* not?"

"I *prefer* not."

I staggered to my desk, and sat there in a deep study. My blind inveteracy returned. Was there any other thing in which I could procure myself to be ignominiously repulsed by this lean, penniless wight? — my hired clerk? What added thing is there, perfectly reasonable, that he will be sure to refuse to do?

"Bartleby!"

No answer.

"Bartleby," in a louder tone.

No answer.

"Bartleby," I roared.

Like a very ghost, aggreeably to the laws of magical invocation, at the third summons, he appeared at the entrance of his hermitage.

"Go to the next room, and tell Nippers to come to me."

"I prefer not to," he respectfully and slowly said, and mildly disappeared.

"Very good, Bartleby," said I, in a quiet sort of serenely-severe, self-possessed tone, intimating the unalterable purpose of some terrible retribution very close at hand. At the moment I half intended something of the kind. But upon the whole, as it was drawing towards my dinner-hour, I thought it best to put on my hat and walk home for the day, suffering much from perplexity and distress of mind.

Shall I acknowledge it? The conclusion of this whole business was, that it soon became a fixed fact of my chambers, that a pale young scrivener, by the name of Bartleby, had a desk there; that he copied for me at the usual rate of four cents a folio (one hundred words); but he was permanently exempt from examining the work done by him, that duty being transferred to Turkey and Nippers, out of compliment, doubtless, to their superior acuteness; moreover, said Bartleby was never, on any account, to be dispatched on the most trivial errand of any sort, and that even if entreated to take upon him such a matter, it was generally understood he would "prefer not to" — in other words, that he would refuse point-blank.

As days passed on, I became considerably reconciled to Bartleby. His steadiness, his freedom from all dissipation, his incessant industry (except when he chose to throw himself into a standing revery behind his screen), his great stillness, his unalterableness of demeanor under all circumstances, made him a valuable acquisition. One prime thing was this — *he was always there* — first in the morning, continually through the day, and the last at night. I had a singular confidence in his honesty. I felt my most precious papers perfectly safe in his hands. Sometimes, to be sure, I could not, for the very soul of me, avoid falling into sudden spasmodic passions with him. For it was exceedingly difficult to bear in mind all the time those strange peculiarities, privileges, and unheard of exemptions, forming the tacit stipulations on Bartleby's part under which he remained in my office. Now and then, in the eagerness of dispatching pressing business, I would inadvertently summon Bartleby, in a short, rapid tone, to put his finger, say, on the incipient tie of a bit of red tape with which I was about compressing some papers. Of course, from behind the screen the usual answer, "I prefer not to," was sure to come; and then, how could a human creature, with the common infirmities of our nature, refrain from bitterly exclaiming upon such perverseness — such unreasonableness. However, every added repulse of this sort which I received only tended to lessen the probability of my repeating the inadvertence.

Here it must be said, that according to the custom of most legal gentlemen occupying chambers in densely-populated law buildings, there were several keys to my door. One was kept by a woman residing in the attic, which person weekly scrubbed and daily swept and dusted my apartments. Another was kept by Turkey for convenience sake. The third I sometimes carried in my own pocket. The fourth I knew not who had.

Now, one Sunday morning I happened to go to Trinity Church, to hear a celebrated preacher, and finding myself rather early on the ground I thought I would walk around to my chambers for a while. Luckily I had my key with me; but upon applying it to the lock, I found it resisted by something inserted from the inside. Quite surprised, I called out; when to my consternation a key was turned from within; and thrusting his lean visage at me, and holding the door ajar, the apparition of Bartleby appeared, in his shirt sleeves, and otherwise in a strangely tattered *déshabillé*, saying quietly that he was sorry, but he was deeply engaged just then, and — preferred not admitting me at present. In a brief word or two, he moreover added, that perhaps I had better walk around the block two or three times, and by that time he would probably have concluded his affairs.

Now, the utterly unsurmised appearance of Bartleby, tenanting my lawchambers of a Sunday morning, with his cadaverously gentlemanly *nonchalance*, yet withal firm and self-possessed, had such a strange effect upon me, that incontinently I slunk away from my own door, and did as desired. But not without sundry twinges of impotent rebellion against the mild effrontery of this unaccountable scrivener. Indeed, it was his wonderful mildness chiefly, which not only disarmed me, but unmanned me as it were. For I consider that one, for the time, is somehow unmanned when he tranquilly permits his hired clerk to dictate to him, and order him away from his own premises. Furthermore, I was full of uneasiness as to what

Bartleby could possibly be doing in my office in his shirt sleeves, and in an otherwise dismantled condition of a Sunday morning. Was anything amiss going on? Nay, that was out of the question. It was not to be thought of for a moment that Bartleby was an immoral person. But what could he be doing there? — copying? Nay again, whatever might be his eccentricities, Bartleby was an eminently decorous person. He would be the last man to sit down to his desk in any state approaching to nudity. Besides, it was Sunday; and there was something about Bartleby that forbade the supposition that he would by any secular occupation violate the proprieties of the day.

Nevertheless, my mind was not pacified; and full of a restless curiosity, at last I returned to the door. Without hindrance I inserted my key, opened it, and entered. Bartleby was not to be seen. I looked round anxiously, peeped behind his screen; but it was very plain that he was gone. Upon more closely examining the place, I surmised that for an indefinite period Bartleby must have eaten, dressed, and slept in my office, and that, too, without plate, mirror, or bed. The cushioned seat of a rickety old sofa in one corner bore the faint impress of a lean, reclining form. Rolled away under his desk, I found a blanket; under the empty grate, a blacking box and brush; on a chair, a tin basin, with soap and a ragged towel; in a newspaper a few crumbs of ginger-nuts and a morsel of cheese. Yes, thought I, it is evident enough that Bartleby has been making his home here, keeping bachelor's hall all by himself. Immediately then the thought came sweeping across me, what miserable friendlessness and loneliness are here revealed! His poverty is great; but his solitude, how horrible! Think of it. Of a Sunday, Wall Street is deserted as Petra; and every night of every day it is an emptiness. This building, too, which of weekdays hums with industry and life, at nightfall echoes with sheer vacancy, and all through Sunday is forlorn. And here Bartleby makes his home; sole spectator of a solitude which he has seen all populous — a sort of innocent and transformed Marius brooding among the ruins of Carthage!

For the first time in my life a feeling of over-powering stinging melancholy seized me. Before, I had never experienced aught but a not unpleasing sadness. The bond of a common humanity now drew me irresistibly to gloom. A fraternal melancholy! For both I and Bartleby were sons of Adam. I remembered the bright silks and sparkling faces I had seen that day, in gala trim, swan-like sailing down the Mississippi of Broadway; and I contrasted them with the pallid copyist, and thought to myself, Ah, happiness courts the light, so we deem the world is gay; but misery hides aloof, so we deem that misery there is none. These sad fancyings — chimeras, doubtless, of a sick and silly brain — led on to other and more special thoughts, concerning the eccentricities of Bartleby. Presentiments of strange discoveries hovered round me. The scrivener's pale form appeared to me laid out, among uncaring strangers, in its shivering winding sheet.

Suddenly I was attracted by Bartleby's closed desk, the key in open sight left in the lock.

I mean no mischief, seek the gratification of no heartless curiosity, thought I; besides, the desk is mine, and its contents, too, so I will make bold to look within. Everything was methodically arranged, the papers smoothly placed. The pigeon holes were deep, and removing the files of documents, I groped into their recesses. Presently I felt something there, and dragged it out. It was an old bandanna handkerchief, heavy and knotted. I opened it, and saw it was a savings's bank.

I now recalled all the quiet mysteries which I had noted in the man. I remembered that he never spoke but to answer; that, though at intervals he had considerable time to himself, yet I had never seen him reading — no, not even a newspaper; that for long periods he would stand looking out, at his pale window behind the screen, upon the dead brick wall; I was quite sure he never visited any refectory or eating house; while his pale face clearly indicated that he never drank beer like Turkey, or tea and coffee even, like other men; that he never went anywhere in particular that I could learn; never went out for a walk, unless, indeed, that was the case at present; that he had declined telling who he was, or whence he came, or whether he had any relatives in the world; that though so thin and pale, he never complained of ill health. And more than all, I remembered a certain unconscious air of pallid — how shall I call it? — of pallid haughtiness, say, or rather an austere reserve about him, which had positively awed me into my tame compliance with his eccentricities, when I had feared to ask him to do the slightest incidental thing for me, even though I might know, from his long-continued motionlessness, that behind his screen he must be standing in one of those dead-wall reveries of his.

Revolving all these things, and coupling them with the recently discovered fact, that he made my office his constant abiding place and home, and not forgetful of his morbid moodiness; revolving all these things, a prudential feeling began to steal over me. My first emotions had been those of pure melancholy and sincerest pity; but just in proportion as the forlornness of Bartleby grew and grew to my imagination, did that same melancholy merge into fear, that pity into repulsion. So true it is, and so terrible, too, that up to a certain point the thought or sight of misery enlists our best affections; but, in certain special cases, beyond that point it does not. They err who would assert that invariably this is owing to the inherent selfishness of the human heart. It rather proceeds from a certain hopelessness of remedying excessive and organic ill. To a sensitive being, pity is not seldom pain. And when at last it is perceived that such pity cannot lead to effectual succor, common sense bids the soul be rid of it. What I saw that morning persuaded me that the scrivener was the victim of innate and incurable disorder. I might give alms to his body; but his body did not pain him; it was his soul that suffered, and his soul I could not reach.

I did not accomplish the purpose of going to Trinity Church that morning. Somehow, the things I had seen disqualified me for the time from churchgoing. I walked homeward, thinking what I would do with Bartleby. Finally, I resolved upon this — I would put certain calm questions to him the next morning, touching his history, etc., and if he declined to answer them openly and unreservedly (and I supposed he would prefer not), then to give him a twenty dollar bill over and above whatever I might owe him, and tell him his services were no longer required; but that if in any other way I could assist him, I would be happy to do so, especially if he desired to return to his native place, wherever that might be, I would willingly help to defray the expenses. Moreover, if, after reaching home, he found himself at any time in want of aid, a letter from him would be sure of a reply.

The next morning came.

"Bartleby," said I, gently calling to him behind his screen.

No reply.

"Bartleby," said I, in a still gentler tone, "come here; I am not going to ask you to do anything you would prefer not to do — I simply wish to speak to you."

Upon this he noiselessly slid into view.

"Will you tell me, Bartleby, where you were born?"

"I would prefer not to."

"Will you tell me *anything* about yourself?"

"I would prefer not to."

"But what reasonable objection can you have to speak to me? I feel friendly towards you."

He did not look at me while I spoke, but kept his glance fixed upon my bust of Cicero, which, as I then sat, was directly behind me, some six inches above my head.

"What is your answer, Bartleby," said I, after waiting a considerable time for a reply, during which his countenance remained immovable, only there was the faintest conceivable tremor of the white attenuated mouth.

"At present I prefer to give no answer," he said, and retired into his hermitage.

It was rather weak in me I confess, but his manner, on this occasion, nettled me. Not only did there seem to lurk in it a certain calm disdain, but his perverseness seemed ungrateful, considering the undeniable good usage and indulgence he had received from me.

Again I sat ruminating what I should do. Mortified as I was at his behavior, and resolved as I had been to dismiss him when I entered my office, nevertheless I strangely felt something superstitious knocking at my heart, and forbidding me to carry out my purpose, and denouncing me for a villain if I dared to breathe one bitter word against this forlornest of mankind. At last, familiarly drawing my chair behind his screen, I sat down and said: "Bartleby, never mind, then, about revealing your history; but let me entreat you, as a friend, to comply as far as may be with the usages of this office. Say now, you will help to examine papers to-morrow or next day: in short, say now, that in a day or two you will begin to be a little reasonable: — say so, Bartleby."

"At present I would prefer not to be a little reasonable," was his mildly cadaverous reply.

Just then the folding-doors opened, and Nippers approached. He seemed suffering from an unusually bad night's rest, induced by severer indigestion than common. He overheard those final words of Bartleby.

"*Prefer not*, eh?" gritted Nippers — "I'd *prefer* him, if I were you, sir," addressing me — "I'd *prefer* him; I'd give him preferences, the stubborn mule! What is it, sir, pray, that he *prefers* not to do now?"

Bartleby moved not a limb.

"Mr. Nippers," said I, "I'd prefer that you would withdraw for the present."

Somehow, of late, I had got into the way of involuntarily using this word "prefer" upon all sorts of not exactly suitable occasions. And I trembled to think that my contact with the scrivener had already and seriously affected me in a mental way. And what further and deeper aberration might it not yet produce? This apprehension had not been without efficacy in determining me to summary measures.

As Nippers, looking very sour and sulky, was departing, Turkey blandly and deferentially approached.

"With submission, sir," said he, "yesterday I was thinking about Bartleby here, and I think that if he would but prefer to take a quart of good ale every day, it would do much towards mending him, and enabling him to assist in examining his papers."

"So you have got the word, too," said I, slightly excited.

"With submission, what word, sir," asked Turkey, respectfully crowding himself into the contracted space behind the screen, and by so doing, making me jostle the scrivener. "What word, sir?"

"I would prefer to be left alone here," said Bartleby, as if offended at being mobbed in his privacy.

"*That's* the word, Turkey," said I — "*that's* it."

"Oh, *prefer*? oh yes — queer word. I never use it myself. But, sir, as I was saying, if he would but prefer —"

"Turkey," interrupted I, "you will please withdraw."

"Oh certainly, sir, if you prefer that I should."

As he opened the folding-door to retire, Nippers at his desk caught a glimpse of me, and asked whether I would prefer to have a certain paper copied on blue paper or white. He did not in the least roguishly accent the word prefer. It was plain that it involuntarily rolled from his tongue. I thought to myself, surely I must get rid of a demented man, who already has in some degree turned the tongues, if not the heads of myself and clerks. But I thought it prudent not to break the dismission at once.

The next day I noticed that Bartleby did nothing but stand at his window in his dead-wall revery. Upon asking him why he did not write, he said that he had decided upon doing no more writing.

"Why, how now? what next?" exclaimed I, "do no more writing?"

"No more."

"And what is the reason?"

"Do you not see the reason for yourself," he indifferently replied.

I looked steadfastly at him, and perceived that his eyes looked dull and glazed. Instantly it occurred to me, that his unexampled diligence in copying by his dim window for the first few weeks of his stay with me might have temporarily impaired his vision.

I was touched. I said something in condolence with him. I hinted that of course he did wisely in abstaining from writing for a while; and urged him to embrace that opportunity of taking wholesome exercise in the open air. This, however, he did not do. A few days after this, my other clerks being absent, and being in a great hurry to dispatch certain letters by the mail, I thought that, having nothing else earthly to do, Bartleby would surely be less inflexible than usual, and carry these letters to the post-office. But he blankly declined. So, much to my inconvenience, I went myself.

Still added days went by. Whether Bartleby's eyes improved or not, I could not say. To all appearance I thought they did. But when I asked him if they did, he vouchsafed no answer. At all events, he would do no copying. At last, in reply to my urgings, he informed me that he had permanently given up copying.

"What!" exclaimed I; "suppose your eyes should get entirely well — better than ever before — would you not copy then?"

"I have given up copying," he answered, and slid aside.

He remained as ever, a fixture in my chamber. Nay — if that were possible — he became still more of a fixture than before. What was to be done? He would do nothing in the office; why should he stay there? In plain fact, he had now become a millstone to me, not only useless as a necklace, but afflictive to bear. Yet I was sorry for him. I speak less than truth when I say that, on his own account, he occasioned me uneasiness. If he would but have named a single relative or friend, I would instantly have written, and urged their taking the poor fellow away to some convenient retreat. But he seemed alone, absolutely alone in the universe. A bit of wreck in the mid Atlantic. At length, necessities connected with my business tyrannized over all other considerations. Decently as I could, I told Bartleby that in six days time he must unconditionally leave the office. I warned him to take measures, in the interval, for procuring some other abode. I offered to assist him in his endeavor, if he himself would but take the first step towards a removal. "And when you finally quit me, Bartleby," added I, "I shall see that you go not away entirely unprovided. Six days from this hour, remember."

At the expiration of that period, I peeped behind the screen, and lo! Bartleby was there.

I buttoned up my coat, balanced myself; advanced slowly towards him, touched his shoulder, and said, "The time has come; you must quit this place; I am sorry for you; here is money; but you must go."

"I would prefer not," he replied, with his back still towards me.

"You *must*."

He remained silent.

Now I had an unbounded confidence in this man's common honesty. He had frequently restored to me sixpences and shillings carelessly dropped upon the floor, for I am apt to be very reckless in such shirt-button affairs. The proceeding, then, which followed will not be deemed extraordinary.

"Bartleby," said I, "I owe you twelve dollars on account; here are thirty-two; the odd twenty are yours — Will you take it?" and I handed the bills towards him.

But he made no motion.

"I will leave them here, then," putting them under a weight on the table. Then taking my hat and cane and going to the door, I tranquilly turned and added — "After you have removed your things from these offices, Bartleby, you will of course lock the door — since every one is now gone for the day but you — and if you please, slip your key underneath the mat, so that I may have it in the morning. I shall not see you again; so good-by to you. If, hereafter, in your new place of abode, I can be of any service to you, do not fail to advise me by letter. Good-by, Bartleby, and fare you well."

But he answered not a word; like the last column of some ruined temple, he remained standing mute and solitary in the middle of the otherwise deserted room.

As I walked home in a pensive mood, my vanity got the better of my pity. I could not but highly plume myself on my masterly management in getting rid of Bartleby. Masterly I call it, and such it must appear to any dispassionate thinker. The beauty of my procedure seemed to consist in its perfect quietness. There was no vulgar bullying, no bravado of any sort, no choleric hectoring, and striding to and fro across the apartment, jerking out vehement commands for Bartleby to bundle himself off with his beggarly traps. Nothing of the kind. Without loudly bidding Bartleby depart — as an inferior genius might have done — I *assumed* the ground that depart he must; and upon that assumption built all I had to say. The more I thought over my procedure, the more I was charmed with it. Nevertheless, next morning, upon awakening, I had my doubts — I had somehow slept off the fumes of vanity. One of the coolest and wisest hours a man has, is just after he awakes in the morning. My procedure seemed as sagacious as ever — but only in theory. How it would prove in practice — there was the rub. It was truly a beautiful thought to have assumed Bartleby's departure; but, after all, that assumption was simply my own, and none of Bartleby's. The great point was, not whether I had assumed that he would quit me, but whether he would prefer so to do. He was more a man of preferences than assumptions.

After breakfast, I walked down town, arguing the probabilities *pro* and *con*. One moment I thought it would prove a miserable failure, and Bartleby would be found all alive at my office as usual; the next moment it seemed certain that I should find his chair empty. And so I kept veering about. At the corner of Broadway and Canal Street, I saw quite an excited group of people standing in earnest conversation.

"I'll take odds he doesn't," said a voice as I passed.

"Doesn't go? — done!" said I; "put up your money."

I was instinctively putting my hand in my pocket to produce my own, when I remembered that this was an election day. The words I had overheard bore no reference to Bartleby, but to the success or non-success of some candidate for the mayoralty. In my intent frame of mind, I had, as it were, imagined that all Broadway shared in my excitement, and were debating the same question with me. I passed on, very thankful that the uproar of the street screened my momentary absent-mindedness.

As I had intended, I was earlier than usual at my office door. I stood listening for a moment. All was still. He must be gone. I tried the knob. The door was locked. Yes, my procedure had worked to a charm; he indeed must be vanished. Yet a certain melancholy mixed with this: I was almost sorry for my brilliant success. I was fumbling under the door mat for the key, which Bartleby was to have left there for me, when accidentally my knee knocked against a panel, producing a summoning sound, and in response a voice came to me from within — "Not yet; I am occupied."

It was Bartleby.

I was thunderstruck. For an instant I stood like the man who, pipe in mouth, was killed one cloudless afternoon long ago in Virginia, by summer lightning; at his own warm open window he was killed, and remained leaning out there upon the dreamy afternoon, till some one touched him, when he fell.

"Not gone!" I murmured at last. But again obeying that wondrous ascendancy which the inscrutable scrivener had over me, and from which ascendancy, for all my chafing, I could not completely escape, I slowly went down stairs and out into the street, and while walking round the block, considered what I should next do in this unheard-of perplexity. Turn the man out by an actual thrusting I could not; to drive him away by calling him hard names would not do; calling in the police was an unpleasant idea; and yet, permit him to enjoy his cadaverous triumph over me — this, too, I could not think of. What was to be done? or, if nothing could be done, was there anything further that I could *assume* in the matter? Yes, as before I had prospectively assumed that Bartleby would depart, so now I might retrospectively assume that departed he was. In the legitimate carrying out of this assumption, I might enter my office in a great hurry, and pretending not to see Bartleby at all, walk straight against him as if he were air. Such a proceeding would in a singular degree have the appearance of a home-thrust. It was hardly possible that Bartleby could withstand such an application of the doctrine of assumptions. But upon second thoughts the success of the plan seemed rather dubious. I resolved to argue the matter over with him again.

"Bartleby," said I, entering the office, with a quietly severe expression, "I am seriously displeased. I am pained, Bartleby. I had thought better of you. I had imagined you of such a gentlemanly organization, that in any delicate dilemma a slight hint would suffice — in short, an assumption. But it appears I am deceived. Why," I added, unaffectedly starting, "you have not even touched that money yet," pointing to it, just where I had left it the evening previous.

He answered nothing.

"Will you, or will you not, quit me?" I now demanded in a sudden passion, advancing close to him.

"I would prefer *not* to quit you," he replied, gently emphasizing the *not*.

"What earthly right have you to stay here? Do you pay any rent? Do you pay my taxes? Or is this property yours?"

He answered nothing.

"Are you ready to go on and write now?

Are your eyes recovered? Could you copy a small paper for me this morning? or help examine a few lines? or step round to the post-office? In a word, will you do anything at all, to give a coloring to your refusal to depart the premises?"

He silently retired into his hermitage.

I was now in such a state of nervous resentment that I thought it but prudent to check myself at present from further demonstrations. Bartleby and I were alone. I remembered the tragedy of the unfortunate Adams and the still more unfortunate Colt in the solitary office of the latter; and how poor Colt, being dreadfully incensed by Adams, and imprudently permitted himself to get wildly excited, was at unawares hurried into his fatal act — an act which certainly no man could possibly deplore more than the actor himself. Often it had occurred to me in my ponderings upon the subject, that had that altercation taken place in the public street, or at a private residence, it would not have terminated as it did. It was the circumstance of being alone in a solitary office, up stairs, of a building entirely unhallowed by humanizing domestic associations — an uncarpeted office, doubtless, of a dusty, haggard sort of appearance — this it must have been, which greatly helped to enhance the irritable desperation of the hapless Colt.

But when this old Adam of resentment rose in me and tempted me concerning Bartleby, I grappled him and threw him. How? Why, simply by recalling the divine injunction: "A new commandment give I unto you, that ye love one another." Yes, this it was that saved me. Aside from higher considerations, charity often operates as a vastly wise and prudent principle — a great safeguard to its possessor. Men have committed murder for jealousy's sake, and anger's sake, and hatred's sake, and selfishness' sake, and spiritual pride's sake; but no man, that ever I heard of, ever committed a diabolical murder for sweet charity's sake. Mere self-interest, then, if no better motive can be enlisted, should, especially with high-tempered men, prompt all beings to charity and philanthropy. At any rate, upon the occasion in question, I strove to drown my exasperated feelings towards the scrivener by benevolently construing his conduct. Poor fellow, poor fellow! thought I, he don't mean anything; and besides, he has seen hard times, and ought to be indulged.

I endeavored, also, immediately to occupy myself, and at the same time to comfort my despondency. I tried to fancy, that in the course of the morning, at such time as might prove agreeable to him, Bartleby, of his own free accord, would emerge from his hermitage and take up some decided line of march in the direction of the door. But no. Half-past twelve o'clock came; Turkey began to glow in the face, overturn his inkstand, and become generally obstreperous; Nippers abated down into quietude and courtesy; Ginger Nut munched his noon apple; and Bartleby remained standing at his window in one of his profoundest dead-wall reveries. Will it be credited? Ought I to acknowledge it? That afternoon I left the office without saying one further word to him.

Some days now passed, during which, at leisure intervals I looked a little into "Edwards on the Will," and "Priestley on Necessity." Under the circumstances, those books induced a salutary feeling. Gradually I slid into the persuasion that these troubles of mine, touching the scrivener, had been all predestinated from eternity, and Bartleby was billeted upon me for some mysterious purpose of an all-wise Providence, which it was not for a mere mortal like me to fathom. Yes, Bartleby, stay there behind your screen, thought I; I shall persecute you no more; you are harmless and noiseless as any of these old chairs; in short, I never feel so private as when I know you are here. At last I see it, I feel it; I penetrate to the predestinated purpose of my life. I am content. Others may have loftier parts to enact; but my mission in this world, Bartleby, is to furnish you with office-room for such period as you may see fit to remain.

I believe that this wise and blessed frame of mind would have continued with me, had it not been for the unsolicited and uncharitable remarks obtruded upon me by my professional friends who visited the rooms. But thus it often is, that the constant friction of illiberal minds wears out at last the best resolves of the more generous. Though to be sure, when I reflected upon it, it was not strange that people entering my office should by struck by the peculiar aspect of the unaccountable Bartleby, and so be tempted to throw out some sinister observations concerning him. Sometimes an attorney, having business with me, and calling at my office, and finding no one but the scrivener there, would undertake to obtain some sort of precise information from him touching my whereabouts; but without heeding his idle talk, Bartleby would remain standing immovable in the middle of the room. So after contemplating him in that position for a time, the attorney would depart, no wiser than he came.

Also, when a reference was going on, and the room full of lawyers and witnesses, and business driving fast, some deeply-occupied legal gentleman present, seeing Bartleby wholly unemployed, would request him to run round to his (the legal gentleman's) office and fetch some papers for him. Thereupon, Bartleby would tranquilly decline, and yet remain idle as before. Then the lawyer would give a great stare, and turn to me. And what could I say? At last I was made aware that all through the circle of my professional acquaintance, a whisper of wonder was running round, having reference to the strange creature I kept at my office. This worried me very much. And as the idea came upon me of his possibly turning out a long-lived man, and keep occupying my chambers, and denying my authority; and perplexing my visitors; and scandalizing my professional reputation; and casting a general gloom over the premises; keeping soul and body together to the last upon his savings (for doubtless he spent but half a dime a day), and in the end perhaps outlive me, and claim possession of my office by right of his perpetual occupancy: as all these dark anticipations crowded upon me more and more, and my friends continually intruded their relentless remarks upon the apparition in my room; a great change was wrought in me. I resolved to gather all my faculties together, and forever rid me of this intolerable incubus.

Ere revolving any complicated project, however, adapted to this end, I first simply suggested to Bartleby the propriety of his permanent departure. In a calm and serious tone, I commended the idea to his careful and mature consideration. But, having taken three days to meditate upon it, he apprised me, that his original determination remained the same; in short, that he still preferred to abide with me.

What shall I do? I now said to myself, buttoning up my coat to the last button. What shall I do? what ought I to do? what does conscience say I *should* do with this man, or, rather, ghost. Rid myself of him, I must; go, he shall. But how? You will not thrust him, the poor, pale, passive mortal — you will not thrust such a helpless creature out of your door? you will not dishonor yourself by such cruelty? No, I will not, I cannot do that. Rather would I let him live and die here, and then mason up his remains in the wall. What, then, will you do? For all your coaxing, he will not budge. Bribes he leaves under your own paper-weight on your table; in short, it is quite plain that he prefers to cling to you.

Then something severe, something unusual must be done. What! surely you will not have him collared by a constable, and commit his innocent pallor to the common jail? And upon what ground could you procure such a thing to be done? — a vagrant, is he? What! he a vagrant, a wanderer, who refuses to budge? It is because he will *not* be a vagrant, then, that you seek to count him *as* a vagrant. That is too absurd. No visible means of support: there I have him. Wrong again: for indubitably he *does* support himself, and that is the only unanswerable proof that any man can show of his possessing the means so to do. No more, then. Since he will not quit me, I must quit him. I will change my offices; I will move elsewhere, and give him fair notice, that if I find him on my new premises I will then proceed against him as a common trespasser.

Acting accordingly, next day I thus addressed him: "I find these chambers too far from the City Hall; the air is unwholesome. In a word, I propose to remove my offices next week, and shall no longer require your services. I tell you this now, in order that you may seek another place."

He made no reply; and nothing more was said.

On the appointed day I engaged carts and men, proceeded to my chambers, and, having but little furniture, everything was removed in a few hours. Throughout, the scrivener remained standing behind the screen, which I directed to be removed the last thing. It was withdrawn; and, being folded up like a huge folio, left him the motionless occupant of a naked room. I stood in the entry watching him a moment, while something from within me upbraided me.

I re-entered, with my hand in my pocket — and — and my heart in my mouth.

"Good-by, Bartleby; I am going — good-by, and God some way bless you; and take that," slipping something in his hand. But it dropped upon the floor, and then — strange to say — I tore myself from him whom I had so longed to be rid of.

Established in my new quarters, for a day or two I kept the door locked, and started at every footfall in the passages. When I returned to my rooms, after any little absence, I would pause at the threshold for an instant, and attentively listen, ere applying my key. But these fears were needless. Bartleby never came nigh me.

I thought all was going well, when a perturbed-looking stranger visited me, inquiring whether I was the person who had recently occupied rooms at No. — Wall Street.

Full of forebodings, I replied that I was.

"Then, sir," said the stranger, who proved a lawyer, "you are responsible for the man you left there. He refuses to do any copying; he refuses to do anything; he says he prefers not to; and he refuses to quit the premises."

"I am very sorry, sir," said I, with assumed tranquillity, but an inward tremor, "but, really, the man you allude to is nothing to me — he is no relation or apprentice of mine, that you should hold me responsible for him."

"In mercy's name, who is he?"

"I certainly cannot inform you. I know nothing about him. Formerly I employed him as a copyist; but he has done nothing for me now for some time past."

"I shall settle him, then — good morning, sir."

Several days passed, and I heard nothing more; and, though I often felt a charitable prompting to call at the place and see poor Bartleby, yet a certain squeamishness, of I know not what, withheld me.

All is over with him, by this time, thought I, at last, when, through another week, no further intelligence reached me. But, coming to my room the day after, I found several persons waiting at my door in a high state of nervous excitement.

"That's the man — here he comes," cried the foremost one, whom I recognized as the lawyer who had previously called upon me alone.

"You must take him away, sir, at once," cried a portly person among them, advancing upon me, and whom I knew to be the landlord of No. — Wall Street. "These gentlemen, my tenants, cannot stand it any longer; Mr. B——," pointing to the lawyer, "has turned him out of his room, and he now persists in haunting the building generally, sitting upon the banisters of the stairs by day, and sleeping in the entry by night. Everybody is concerned; clients are leaving the offices; some fears are entertained of a mob; something you must do, and that without delay."

Aghast at this torrent, I fell back before it, and would fain have locked myself in my new quarters. In vain I persisted that Bartleby was nothing to me — no more than to any one else. In vain — I was the last person known to have anything to do with him, and they held me to the terrible account. Fearful, then, of being exposed in the papers (as one person present obscurely threatened), I considered the matter, and, at length, said, that if the lawyer would give me a confidential interview with the scrivener, in his (the lawyer's) own room, I would, that afternoon, strive my best to rid them of the nuisance they complained of.

Going up stairs to my old haunt, there was Bartleby silently sitting upon the banister at the landing.

"What are you doing here, Bartleby?" said I.

"Sitting upon the banister," he mildly replied.

I motioned him into the lawyer's room, who then left us.

"Bartleby," said I, "are you aware that you are the cause of great tribulation to me, by persisting in occupying the entry after being dismissed from the office?"

No answer.

"Now one of two things must take place. Either you must do something, or something must be done to you. Now what sort of business would you like to engage in? Would you like to re-engage in copying for some one?"

"No; I would prefer not to make any change."

"Would you like a clerkship in a dry-goods store?"

"There is too much confinement about that. No, I would not like a clerkship; but I am not particular."

"Too much confinement," I cried, "why you keep yourself confined all the time!"

"I would prefer not to take a clerkship," he rejoined, as if to settle that little item at once.

"How would a bar-tender's business suit you? There is no trying of the eye-sight in that."

"I would not like it at all; though, as I said before, I am not particular."

His unwonted wordiness inspirited me. I returned to the charge.

"Well, then, would you like to travel through the country collecting bills for the merchants? That would improve your health."

"No, I would prefer to be doing something else."

"How, then, would going as a companion to Europe, to entertain some young gentleman with your conversation — how would that suit you?"

"Not at all. It does not strike me that there is anything definite about that. I like to be stationary. But I am not particular."

"Stationary you shall be, then," I cried, now losing all patience, and, for the first time in all my exasperating connection with him, fairly flying into a passion. "If you do not go away from these premises before night, I shall feel bound — indeed, I *am* bound — to — to — to quit the premises myself!" I rather absurdly concluded, knowing not with what possible threat to try to frighten his immobility into compliance. Despairing of all further efforts, I was precipitately leaving him, when a final thought occurred to me — one which had not been wholly unindulged before.

"Bartleby," said I, in the kindest tone I could assume under such exciting circumstances, "will you go home with me now — not to my office, but my dwelling — and remain there till we can conclude upon some convenient arrangement for you at our leisure? Come, let us start now, right away."

"No: at present I would prefer not to make any change at all."

I answered nothing; but, effectually dodging every one by the suddenness and rapidity of my flight, rushed from the building, ran up Wall Street towards Broadway, and, jumping into the first omnibus, was soon removed from pursuit. As soon as tranquillity returned, I distinctly perceived that I had now done all that I possibly could, both in respect to the demands of the landlord and his tenants, and with regard to my own desire and sense of duty, to benefit Bartleby, and shield him from rude persecution. I now strove to be entirely care-free and quiescent; and my conscience justified me in the attempt; though, indeed, it was not so successful as I could have wished. So fearful was I of being again hunted out by the incensed landlord and his exasperated tenants, that, surrendering my business to Nippers, for a few days, I drove about the upper part of the town and through the suburbs, in my rockaway; crossed over to Jersey City and Hoboken, and paid fugitive visits to Manhattanville and Astoria. In fact, I almost lived in my rockaway for the time.

When again I entered my office, lo, a note from the landlord lay upon the desk. I opened it with trembling hands. It informed me that the writer had sent to the police, and had Bartleby removed to the Tombs as a vagrant. Moreover, since I knew more about him than any one else, he wished me to appear at that place, and make a suitable statement of the facts. These tidings had a conflicting effect upon me. At first I was indignant; but, at last, almost approved. The landlord's energetic, summary disposition, had led him to adopt a procedure which I do not think I would have decided upon myself; and yet, as a last resort, under such peculiar circumstances, it seemed the only plan.

As I afterwards learned, the poor scrivener, when told that he must be conducted to the Tombs, offered not the slightest obstacle, but, in his pale, unmoving way, silently acquiesced.

Some of the compassionate and curious bystanders joined the party; and headed by one of the constables arm in arm with Bartleby, the silent procession filed its way through all the noise, and heat, and joy of the roaring thoroughfares at noon.

The same day I received the note, I went to the Tombs, or, to speak more properly, the Halls of Justice. Seeking the right officer, I stated the purpose of my call, and was informed that the individual I described was, indeed, within. I then assured the functionary that Bartleby was a perfectly honest man, and greatly to be compassionated, however unaccountably eccentric. I narrated all I knew, and closed by suggesting the idea of letting him remain in as indulgent confinement as possible, till something less harsh might be done — though, indeed, I hardly knew what. At all events, if nothing else could be decided upon, the alms-house must receive him. I then begged to have an interview.

Being under no disgraceful charge, and

quite serene and harmless in all his ways, they had permitted him freely to wander about the prison, and, especially, in the inclosed grassplatted yards thereof. And so I found him there, standing all alone in the quietest of the yards, his face towards a high wall, while all around, from the narrow slits of the jail windows, I thought I saw peering out upon him the eyes of murderers and thieves.

"Bartleby!"

"I know you," he said, without looking round — "and I want nothing to say to you."

"It was not I that brought you here, Bartleby," said I, keenly pained at his implied suspicion. "And to you, this should not be so vile a place. Nothing reproachful attaches to you by being here. And see, it is not so sad a place as one might think. Look, there is the sky, and here is the grass."

"I know where I am," he replied, but would say nothing more, and so I left him.

As I entered the corridor again, a broad meat-like man, in an apron, accosted me, and, jerking his thumb over his shoulder, said — "Is that your friend?"

"Yes."

"Does he want to starve? If he does, let him live on the prison fare, that's all."

"Who are you?" asked I, not knowing what to make of such an unofficially speaking person in such a place.

"I am the grub-man. Such gentlemen as have friends here, hire me to provide them with something good to eat."

"Is this so?" said I, turning to the turnkey.

He said it was.

"Well, then," said I, slipping some silver into the grub-man's hands (for so they called him), "I want you to give particular attention to my friend there; let him have the best dinner you can get. And you must be as polite to him as possible."

"Introduce me, will you?" said the grub-man, looking at me with an expression which seemed to say he was all impatience for an opportunity to give a specimen of his breeding.

Thinking it would prove of benefit to the scrivener, I acquiesced; and, asking the grub-man his name, went up with him to Bartleby.

"Bartleby, this is a friend; you will find him very useful to you."

"Your sarvant, sir, your sarvant," said the grub-man, making a low salutation behind his apron. "Hope you find it pleasant here, sir; nice grounds — cool apartments — hope you'll stay with us sometime — try to make it agreeable. What will you have for dinner to-day?"

"I prefer not to dine to-day," said Bartleby, turning away. "It would disagree with me; I am unused to dinners." So saying, he slowly moved to the other side of the inclosure, and took up a position fronting the dead-wall.

"How's this?" said the grub-man, addressing me with a stare of astonishment. "He's odd, ain't he?"

"I think he is a little deranged," said I, sadly.

"Deranged? deranged is it? Well, now, upon my word, I thought that friend of yourn was a gentleman forger; they are always pale and genteel-like, them forgers. I can't help pity 'em — can't help it, sir. Did you know Monroe Edwards?" he added, touchingly, and paused. Then, laying his hand piteously on my shoulder, sighed, "he died of consumption at Sing-Sing. So you weren't acquainted with Monroe?"

"No, I was never socially acquainted with any forgers. But I cannot stop longer. Look to my friend yonder. You will not lose by it. I will see you again."

Some few days after this, I again obtained admission to the Tombs, and went through the corridors in quest of Bartleby; but without finding him.

"I saw him coming from his cell not long ago," said a turnkey, "may be he's gone to loiter in the yards."

So I went in that direction.

"Are you looking for the silent man?" said another turnkey, passing me. "Yonder he lies — sleeping in the yard there. 'Tis not twenty minutes since I saw him lie down."

The yard was entirely quiet. It was not accessible to the common prisoners. The surrounding walls, of amazing thickness, kept off all sounds behind them. The Egyptian character of the masonry weighed upon me with its gloom. But a soft imprisoned turf grew under foot. The heart of the eternal pyramids, it seemed, wherein, by some strange magic, through the clefts, grass-seed, dropped by birds, had sprung.

Strangely huddled at the base of the wall, his knees drawn up, and lying on his side, his head touching the cold stones, I saw the wasted Bartleby. But nothing stirred. I paused; then went close up to him; stooped over, and saw that his dim eyes were open; otherwise he seemed profoundly sleeping. Something prompted me to touch him. I felt his hand, when a tingling shiver ran up my arm and down my spine to my feet.

The round face of the grub-man peered upon me now. "His dinner is ready. Won't he dine to-day, either? Or does he live without dining?"

"Lives without dining," said I, and closed the eyes.

"Eh — He's asleep, ain't he?"

"With kings and counselors," murmured I.

There would seem little need for proceeding further in this history. Imagina-tion will readily supply the meagre recital of poor Bartleby's interment. But, ere parting with the reader, let me say, that if this little narrative has sufficiently interested him, to awaken curiosity as to who Bartleby was, and what manner of life he led prior to the present narrator's making his acquaintance, I can only reply, that in such curiosity I fully share, but am wholly unable to gratify it. Yet here I hardly know whether I should divulge one little item of rumor, which came to my ear a few months after the scrivener's decease. Upon what basis it rested, I could never ascertain; and hence, how true it is I cannot now tell. But, inasmuch as this vague report has not been without a certain suggestive interest to me, however said, it may prove the same with some others; and so I will briefly mention it. The report was this: that Bartleby had been a subordinate clerk in the Dead Letter Office at Washington, from which he had been suddenly removed by a change in the administration. When I think over this rumor, hardly can I express the emotions which seize me. Dead letters! does it not sound like dead men? Conceive a man by nature and misfortune prone to a pallid hopelessness, can any business seem more fitted to heighten it than that of continually handling these dead letters, and assorting them for the flames? For by the cart-load they are annually burned. Sometimes from out the folded paper the pale clerk takes a ring — the finger it was meant for, perhaps, moulders in the grave; a bank-note sent in swiftest charity — he whom it would relieve, nor eats nor hungers any more; pardon for those who died despairing; hope for those who died unhoping; good tidings for those who died stifled by unrelieved calamities. On errands of life, these letters speed to death.

Ah, Bartleby! Ah, humanity!

For Consideration

1. How does the lawyer-narrator characterize himself at the opening of the story? What qualities are suggested by his preferring the "easiest way of life" and by his being "an eminently safe man"?

2. What are the lawyer's relations with his workers? How does he wish for Bartleby to fit into his office routine? Where does he place Bartleby's desk? Why?

3. What is the lawyer's initial response to Bartleby's refusal to do certain kinds of work? Why doesn't he become angry with Bartleby? For what reasons does he decide to keep Bartleby in his employ? What does the lawyer mean by intending to "cheaply purchase a delicious self-approval" by his action?

4. After the lawyer discovers Bartleby in his office on a Sunday morning, how does his reaction to the scrivener change? For what reasons does he begin to decide that Bartleby must be dismissed?

5. What do we know of Bartleby's motives throughout his encounters with the lawyer? Are his decisions involving the frequent "prefer not to" based on reason and logic? If not, on what?

6. At one point the lawyer decides that Bartleby's presence serves a mysterious and providential purpose and that he must continue to furnish Bartleby with a room in his office. Yet he decides later to follow through on Bartleby's dismissal. Why?

7. The lawyer's relationship with Bartleby is both close and distant. Not only is the lawyer unable to get rid of Bartleby but he also admits to strong feelings of responsibility to him. Furthermore, even after the lawyer moves his offices, others think of Bartleby as his obligation. On the other side, the lawyer never understands Bartleby and is frequently driven by a desire to eliminate Bartleby from his presence and memory. How are these ambivalent responses explained? What might be the psychological explanation for the concurrent feelings of "brotherhood" and repulsion?

8. What is the meaning of the epilogue? Is the lawyer's explanation of the significance of the Dead Letter Office credible? What is implied in the final exclamation, "Ah, Bartleby! Ah, humanity!"?

9. The sub-title of this story is "A Story of Wall Street." What is the function of walls here? Are they important in more than a physical sense?

10. Who is finally more dominant in the story, Bartleby or the lawyer?

point of view

One element of fiction that is often neglected by the beginning student is **point of view**. When we read a story we need to know through whose eyes and mind the events are being relayed, just as when we hear a person describe an event we are interested in his or her integrity and credibility as a witness. In other words, not everything we read in a story is to be accepted at face value; we need to know who is relating it and why. There are three basic, important narrative points of view: **third-person**, **third-person limited** (sometimes called limited or selective omniscience), and **first-person**.

The most prominent form of third-person narration is the **omniscient** ("all-knowing") point of view where the author assumes the god-like ability to see into the minds and hearts of all of the characters. In "The Horse Dealer's Daughter" (p. 140), for example, Lawrence allows a reader to see what the Pervin brothers are thinking, what the various moods and emotions of Mabel Pervin are, and how Jack Fergusson reacts to his life in the small town. In the following passage Lawrence describes the ambivalent response of Fergusson to the people he, as village doctor, must serve:

> It was a stimulant to him to be in the homes of the working people, moving as it were through the innermost body of their life. His nerves were excited and gratified. He could come so near, into the very lives of the rough, inarticulate, powerfully emotional men and women. He grumbled, he said he hated the hellish hole. But as a matter of fact it excited him, the contact with the rough, strongly-feeling people was a stimulant applied direct to his nerves.

As seen above, one obvious value in omniscient narration is that a reader is able to see characters revealed fully, not only through external actions and speech, but also through inner ideas and motives. If there is little or no revelation of the inner side of the characters but the third-person perspective is maintained, the form of narration is said to be **objective** or camera-eye. It is as if the author stands apart from the scene, records it, but does not comment on it. This type of narrative often includes a great deal of dialogue, as would be the case if the author were in fact a mere recorder.

A further variation on third-person narrative is third-person limited, where the author still commands a theoretical omniscience but focuses on one or two characters through whom we see most of the action. In "The Captive" (p. 174), we are almost completely absorbed in the mind and character of Vicé Guarnotta, though technically the point of view remains omniscient.

Of the three basic points of view mentioned earlier, the omniscient usually requires a less discriminating analysis by the reader. In it we assume the author-narrator's total control over the material and accuracy in presenting it. Limited omniscience requires sharper discrimination, since the author has chosen to limit the focus to one or two characters rather than move among many. The most complex possibilities for point of view are evident in a story told by someone actually present during the events recorded, either an observer or a participant. In those instances we have first-person narration, for some "I" tells the story. This form of narrative, especially, demands a reader's close attention. There is no guarantee of objectivity or truth since there is no semblance of omniscience. The narrator is a part of the subject of the story and is limited by personal knowledge; while the narrator may be a reliable witness he or she may just as easily be biased, inaccurate, or misleading. If the narrator is also the principal character, the story has the appearance of autobiography (of the narrator, not the author). Thus, Oates' story is primarily about the young narrator herself; "My Man Bovanne" (p. 254) focuses on an older woman who describes her own life. But the narrator is not always the focus of the story. "Bartleby the Scrivener" is as much about Bartleby as it is about the lawyer-narrator; "Laud" (p. 259) is more about the father than it is about the son who narrates the account. At the opposite extreme from the narrator who is the principal participant is the (apparently objective) observer who is a part of the events recounted though they seem only to be recorded in a more or less objective way.

The four stories which follow illustrate four variations in point of view. Hawthorne's "The Maypole of Merry Mount" is told from the perspective of traditional omniscience. Hawthorne's narrator describes the past as well as the present and freely informs us of what is going on both outside and within the characters.

"Hills Like White Elephants" is a classic example of objective or camera-eye narration. There are a few descriptive passages but most of the story is made up of dialogue between the two principal characters. The dialogue also contributes much to other elements in the story, including characterization and atmosphere.

The narrative perspective of Malamud's "The Magic Barrel," though technically omniscient, is usually limited to the thoughts and motives of Leo Finkle. When Leo sees the photograph of Salzman's daughter, for example, we are told exactly how it affects him:

> Her face deeply moved him. Why, he could at first not say. It gave him the impression of youth — spring flowers, yet age — a sense of having been used to the bones, wasted; this came from the eyes which were hauntingly familiar, yet absolutely strange. He had a vivid impression that he had met her before, but try as he might he could not place her although he could almost recall her name, as if he had read it in her own handwriting.

The point of view of "Saint Emmanuel the Good, Martyr" is the most complex of the four. It is a first-person account told by Angelita, who is greatly affected by the life of St. Emmanuel. The opening paragraph reveals that the narrator is intimately involved in the story she will tell, for she describes St. Emmanuel as "that matriarchal man who pervaded the most secret life of my soul, who was my true spiritual father, the father of my spirit, the spirit of myself, Angela Carballino." Angelita is, therefore, both storyteller and participant, acting within the experiences she recounts. By contrast, at the end of the narrative, the author, Unamuno, steps in and reveals that he has found Angelita's story and has presented it to us. The final perspective is therefore that of a detached outsider, though the narrative proper is highly personal.

NATHANIEL HAWTHORNE   (1804—1864)
The Maypole of Merry Mount

There is an admirable foundation for a philosophic romance in the curious history of the early settlement of Mount Wollaston, or Merry Mount. In the slight sketch here attempted, the facts, recorded on the grave pages of our New England annalists, have wrought themselves, almost spontaneously, into a sort of allegory. The masques, mummeries, and festive customs, described in the text, are in accordance with the manners of the age. Authority on these points may be found in Strutt's Book of English Sports and Pastimes.

Bright were the days at Merry Mount, when the Maypole was the banner staff of that gay colony! They who reared it, should their banner be triumphant, were to pour sunshine over New England's rugged hills, and scatter flower seeds throughout the soil. Jollity and gloom were contending for an empire. Midsummer eve had come, bringing deep verdure to the forest, and roses in her lap, of a more vivid hue than the tender buds of Spring. But May, or her mirthful spirit, dwelt all the year round at Merry Mount, sporting with the Summer months, and revelling with Autumn, and basking in the flow of Winter's fireside. Through a world of toil and care she flitted with a dreamlike smile, and came hither to find a home among the lightsome hearts of Merry Mount.

Never had the Maypole been so gayly decked as at sunset on midsummer eve. This venerated emblem was a pine-tree, which had preserved the slender grace of youth, while it equalled the loftiest height of the old wood monarchs. From its top streamed a silken banner, colored like the rainbow. Down nearly to the ground the pole was dressed with birchen boughs, and others of the liveliest green, and some with silvery leaves, fastened by ribbons that fluttered in fantastic knots of twenty different colors, but no sad ones. Garden flowers, and blossoms of the wilderness, laughed gladly forth amid the verdure, so fresh and dewy that they must have grown by magic on that happy pine-tree. Where this green and flowery splendor terminated, the shaft of the Maypole was stained with the seven brilliant hues of the banner at its top. On the lowest green bough hung an abundant wreath of roses, some that had been gathered in the sunniest spots of the forest, and others, of still richer blush, which the colonists had reared from English seed. O, people of the Golden Age, the chief of your husbandry was to raise flowers!

But what was the wild throng that stood hand in hand about the Maypole? It could not be that the fauns and nymphs, when driven from their classic groves and homes of ancient fable, had sought refuge, as all the persecuted did, in the fresh woods of the West. These were Gothic monsters, though perhaps of Grecian ancestry. On the shoulders of a comely youth uprose the head and branching antlers of a stag; a sec-

ond, human in all other points, had the grim visage of a wolf; a third, still with the trunk and limbs of a mortal man, showed the beard and horns of a venerable he-goat. There was the likeness of a bear erect, brute in all but his hind legs, which were adorned with pink silk stockings. And here again, almost as wondrous, stood a real bear of the dark forest, lending each of his fore paws to the grasp of a human hand, and as ready for the dance as any in that circle. His inferior nature rose half way, to meet his companions as they stooped. Other faces wore the similitude of man or woman, but distorted or extravagant, with red noses pendulous before their mouths, which seemed of awful depth, and stretched from ear to ear in an eternal fit of laughter. Here might be seen the Savage Man, well known in heraldry, hairy as a baboon, and girdled with green leaves. By his side, a noble figure, but still a counterfeit, appeared an Indian hunter, with feathery crest and wampum belt. Many of this strange company wore foolscaps, and had little bells appended to their garments, tinkling with a silvery sound, responsive to the inaudible music of their gleesome spirits. Some youths and maidens were of soberer garb, yet well maintained their places in the irregular throng by the expression of wild revelry upon their features. Such were the colonists of Merry Mount, as they stood in the broad smile of sunset round their venerated Maypole.

Had a wanderer, bewildered in the melancholy forest, heard their mirth, and stolen a half-affrighted glance, he might have fancied them the crew of Comus, some already transformed to brutes, some midway between man and beast, and the others rioting in the flow of tipsy jollity that foreran the change. But a band of Puritans, who watched the scene, invisible themselves, compared the masques to those devils and ruined souls with whom their superstition peopled the black wilderness.

Within the ring of monsters appeared the two airiest forms that had ever trodden on any more solid footing than a purple and golden cloud. One was a youth in glistening apparel, with a scarf of the rainbow pattern crosswise on his breast. His right hand held a gilded staff, the ensign of high dignity among the revellers, and his left grasped the slender fingers of a fair maiden, not less gayly decorated than himself. Bright roses glowed in contrast with the dark and glossy curls of each, and were scattered round their feet, or had sprung up spontaneously there. Behind this lightsome couple, so close to the Maypole that its boughs shaded his jovial face, stood the figure of an English priest, canonically dressed, yet decked with flowers, in heathen fashion, and wearing a chaplet of the native vine leaves. By the riot of his rolling eye, and the pagan decorations of his holy garb, he seemed the wildest monster there, and the very Comus of the crew.

"Votaries of the Maypole," cried the flower-decked priest, "merrily, all day long, have the woods echoed to your mirth. But be this your merriest hour, my hearts! Lo, here stand the Lord and Lady of the May, whom I, a clerk of Oxford, and high priest of Merry Mount, am presently to join in holy matrimony. Up with your nimble spirits, ye morris-dancers, green men, and glee maidens, bears and wolves, and horned gentlemen! Come; a chorus now, rich with the old mirth of Merry England, and the wilder glee of this fresh forest; and then a dance, to show the youthful pair what life is made of, and how airily they should go through it! All ye that love the Maypole, lend your voices to the nuptial song of the Lord and Lady of the May!"

This wedlock was more serious than most affairs of Merry Mount, where jest and delusion, trick and fantasy, kept up a continual carnival. The Lord and Lady of the May, though their titles must be laid down at sunset, were really and truly to be partners for the dance of life, beginning the measure that same bright eve. The wreath of roses, that hung from the lowest green bough of the Maypole, had been twined for them, and would be thrown over both their heads, in symbol of their flowery union. When the priest had spoken, therefore, a riotous uproar burst from the rout of monstrous figures.

"Begin you the stave, reverend Sir," cried they all; "and never did the woods ring to such a merry peal as we of the Maypole shall send up!"

Immediately a prelude of pipe, cithern, and viol, touched with practised minstrelsy, began to play from a neighboring thicket, in such a mirthful cadence that the boughs of the Maypole quivered to the sound. But the May Lord, he of the gilded staff, chancing to look into his Lady's eyes, was wonder struck at the almost pensive glance that met his own.

"Edith, sweet Lady of the May," whispered he reproachfully, "is yon wreath of roses a garland to hang above our graves, that you look so sad? O, Edith, this is our golden time! Tarnish it not by any pensive shadow of the mind; for it may be that nothing of futurity will be brighter than the mere remembrance of what is now passing."

"That was the very thought that saddened me! How came it in your mind too?" said Edith, in a still lower tone than he, for it was high treason to be sad at Merry Mount. "Therefore do I sigh amid this festive music. And besides, dear Edgar, I struggle as with a dream, and fancy that these shapes of our jovial friends are visionary, and their mirth unreal, and that we are no true Lord and Lady of the May. What is the mystery in my heart?"

Just then, as if a spell had loosened

them, down came a little shower of withering rose leaves from the Maypole. Alas, for the young lovers! No sooner had their hearts glowed with real passion than they were sensible of something vague and unsubstantial in their former pleasures, and felt a dreary presentiment of inevitable change. From the moment that they truly loved, they had subjected themselves to earth's doom of care and sorrow, and troubled joy, and had no more a home at Merry Mount. That was Edith's mystery. Now leave we the priest to marry them, and the masquers to sport round the Maypole, till the last sunbeam be withdrawn from its summit, and the shadows of the forest mingle gloomily in the dance. Meanwhile, we may discover who these gay people were.

Two hundred years ago, and more, the old world and its inhabitants became mutually weary of each other. Men voyaged by thousands to the West: some to barter glass beads, and such like jewels, for the furs of the Indian hunter; some to conquer virgin empires; and one stern band to pray. But none of these motives had much weight with the colonists of Merry Mount. Their leaders were men who had sported so long with life, that when Thought and Wisdom came, even these unwelcome guests were led astray by the crowd of vanities which they should have put to flight. Erring Thought and perverted Wisdom were made to put on masques, and play the fool. The men of whom we speak, after losing the heart's fresh gayety, imagined a wild philosophy of pleasure, and came hither to act out their latest day-dream. They gathered followers from all that giddy tribe whose whole life is like the festal days of soberer men. In their train were minstrels, not unknown in London streets: wandering players, whose theatres had been the halls of noblemen; mummers, rope-dancers,

and mounte-banks, who would long be missed at wakes, church ales, and fairs; in a word, mirth makers of every sort, such as abounded in that age, but now began to be discountenanced by the rapid growth of Puritanism. Light had their footsteps been on land, and as lightly they came across the sea. Many had been maddened by their previous troubles into a gay despair; others were as madly gay in the flush of youth, like the May Lord and his Lady; but whatever might be the quality of their mirth, old and young were gay at Merry Mount. The young deemed themselves happy. The elder spirits, if they knew that mirth was but the counterfeit of happiness, yet followed the false shadow wilfully, because at least her garments glittered brightest. Sworn triflers of a lifetime, they would not venture among the sober truths of life not even to be truly blest.

All the hereditary pastimes of Old England were transplanted hither. The King of Christmas was duly crowned, and the Lord of Misrule bore potent sway. On the Eve of St. John, they felled whole acres of the forest to make bonfires, and danced by the blaze all night, crowned with garlands, and throwing flowers into the flame. At harvest time, though their crop was of the smallest, they made an image with the sheaves of Indian corn, and wreathed it with autumnal garlands, and bore it home triumphantly. But what chiefly characterized the colonists of Merry Mount was their veneration for the Maypole. It has made their true history a poet's tale. Spring decked the hallowed emblem with young blossoms and fresh green boughs; Summer brought roses of the deepest blush, and the perfected foliage of the forest; Autumn enriched it with that red and yellow gorgeousness which converts each wildwood leaf into a painted flower; and Winter silvered it with sleet, and hung it round with icicles, till it flashed in the cold sunshine, itself a frozen sunbeam. Thus each alternate season did homage to the Maypole, and paid it a tribute of its own richest splendor. Its votaries danced round it, once, at least, in every month; sometimes they called it their religion, or their altar; but always, it was the banner staff of Merry Mount.

Unfortunately, there were men in the new world of a sterner faith than these Maypole worshippers. Not far from Merry Mount was a settlement of Puritans, most dismal wretches, who said their prayers before daylight, and then wrought in the forest or the cornfield till evening made it prayer time again. Their weapons were always at hand to shoot down the straggling savage. When they met in conclave, it was never to keep up the old English mirth, but to hear sermons three hours long, or to proclaim bounties on the heads of wolves and the scalps of Indians. Their festivals were fast days, and their chief pastime the singing of psalms. Woe to the youth or maiden who did but dream of a dance! The selectman nodded to the constable; and there sat the light-heeled reprobate in the stocks; or if he danced, it was round the whipping-post, which might be termed the Puritan Maypole.

A party of these grim Puritans, toiling through the difficult woods, each with a horseload of iron armor to burden his footsteps, would sometimes draw near the sunny precincts of Merry Mount. There were the silken colonists, sporting round their Maypole; perhaps teaching a bear to dance, or striving to communicate their mirth to the grave Indian; or masquerading in the skins of deer and wolves, which they had hunted for that especial purpose. Often, the whole colony were playing at blindman's bluff, magistrates and all, with their eyes bandaged, except a single scapegoat, whom the blinded sinners pursued by the tinkling of the bells at his garments. Once, it is said, they were seen following a flower-decked corpse, with merriment and festive music, to his grave. But did the dead man laugh? In the quietest times, they sang ballads and told tales, for the edification of their pious visitors; or perplexed them with juggling tricks; or grinned at them through horse collars; and when sport itself grew wearisome, they made game of their own stupidity, and began a yawning match. At the very least of these enormities, the men of iron shook their heads and frowned so darkly that the revellers looked up, imagining that a momentary cloud had overcast the sunshine, which was to be perpetual there. On the other hand, the Puritans affirmed that, when a psalm was pealing from their place of worship, the echo which the forest sent them back seemed often like the chorus of a jolly catch, closing with a roar of laughter. Who but the fiend, and his bond slaves, the crew of Merry Mount, had thus disturbed them? In due time, a feud arose, stern and bitter on one side, and as serious on the other as anything could be among such light spirits as had sworn allegiance to the Maypole. The future complexion of New England was involved in this important quarrel. Should the grizzly saints establish their jurisdiction over the gay sinners, then would their spirits darken all the clime, and make it a land of clouded visages, of hard toil, of sermon and psalm forever. But should the banner staff of Merry Mount be fortunate, sunshine would break upon the hills, and flowers would beautify the forest, and late posterity do homage to the Maypole.

After these authentic passages from history, we return to the nuptials of the Lord and Lady of the May. Alas! we have delayed too long, and must darken our tale too suddenly. As we glance again at the Maypole, a solitary sunbeam is fading from the summit, and leaves only a faint, golden tinge blended with the hues of the rainbow banner. Even that dim light is now withdrawn, relinquishing the whole domain of Merry Mount to the evening gloom, which has rushed so instantaneously from the black surrounding woods. But some of the black shadows have rushed forth in human shape.

Yes, with the setting sun, the last day of mirth had passed from Merry Mount. The ring of gay masquers was disordered and broken; the stag lowered his antlers in dismay; the wolf grew weaker than a lamb; the bells of the morris-dancers tinkled with tremulous affright. The Puritans had played a characteristic part in the Maypole mummeries. Their darksome figures were intermixed with the wild shapes of their foes, and made the scene a picture of the moment, when waking thoughts start up amid the scattered fantasies of a dream. The leader of the hostile party stood in the centre of the circle, while the route of monsters cowered around him, like evil spirits in the presence of a dread magician. No fantastic foolery could look him in the face. So stern was the energy of his aspect, that the whole man, visage, frame, and soul, seemed wrought of iron, gifted with life and thought, yet all of one substance with his headpiece and breastplate. It was the Puritan of Puritans; it was Endicott himself!

"Stand off, priest of Baal!" said he, with a grim frown, and laying no reverent hand upon the surplice. "I know thee, Blackstone![1] Thou art the man who couldst not abide the rule even of thine own corrupted church, and hast come hither to preach iniquity, and to give example of it

1. Did Governor Endicott speak less positively, we should suspect a mistake here. The Rev. Mr. Blackstone, though an eccentric, is not known to have been an immoral man. We rather doubt his identity with the priest of Merry Mount.

in thy life. But now shall it be seen that the Lord hath sanctified this wilderness for his peculiar people. Woe unto them that would defile it! And first, for this flower-decked abomination, the altar of thy worship!"

And with his keen sword Endicott assaulted the hallowed Maypole. Nor long did it resist his arm. It groaned with a dismal sound; it showered leaves and rosebuds upon the remorseless enthusiast; and finally, with all its green boughs and ribbons and flowers, symbolic of departed pleasures, down fell the banner staff of Merry Mount. As it sank, tradition says, the evening sky grew darker, and the woods threw forth a more sombre shadow.

"There," cried Endicott, looking triumphantly on his work, "there lies the only Maypole in New England! The thought is strong within me that, by its fall, is shadowed forth the fate of light and idle mirth makers, amongst us and our posterity. Amen, saith John Endicott."

"Amen!" echoed his followers.

But the votaries of the Maypole gave one groan for their idol. At the sound, the Puritan leader glanced at the crew of Comus, each a figure of broad mirth, yet, at this moment, strangely expressive of sorrow and dismay.

"Valiant captain," quoth Peter Palfrey, the Ancient of the band, "what order shall be taken with the prisoners?"

"I thought not to repent me of cutting down a Maypole," replied Endicott, "yet now I could find in my heart to plant it again, and give each of these bestial pagans one other dance round their idol. It would have served rarely for a whipping-post!"

"But there are pine-trees enow," suggested the lieutenant.

"True, good Ancient," said the leader. "Wherefore, bind the heathen crew, and bestow on them a small matter of stripes apiece, as earnest of our future justice. Set some of the rogues in the stocks to rest themselves, so soon as Providence shall bring us to one of our own well-ordered settlements, where such accommodations may be found. Further penalties, such as branding and cropping of ears, shall be thought of hereafter."

"How many stripes for the priest?" inquired Ancient Palfrey.

"None as yet," answered Endicott, bending his iron frown upon the culprit. "It must be for the Great and General Court to determine, whether stripes and long imprisonment, and other grievous penalty, may atone for his transgressions. Let him look to himself! For such as violate our civil order, it may be permitted us to show mercy. But woe to the wretch that troubleth our religion!"

"And this dancing bear," resumed the officer. "Must he share the stripes of his fellows?"

"Shoot him through the head!" said the energetic Puritan. "I suspect witchcraft in the beast."

"Here be a couple of shining ones," continued Peter Palfrey, pointing his weapon at the Lord and Lady of the May. "They seem to be of high station among these misdoers. Methinks their dignity will not be fitted with less than a double share of stripes."

Endicott rested on his sword, and closely surveyed the dress and aspect of the hapless pair. There they stood, pale, downcast, and apprehensive. Yet there was an air of mutual support, and of pure affection, seeking aid and giving it, that showed them to be man and wife, with the sanction of a priest upon their love. The youth, in the peril of the moment, had dropped his gilded staff, and thrown his arm about the Lady of the May, who leaned against his breast, too lightly to burden him, but with weight enough to express that their destinies were linked together, for good or evil. They looked first at each other, and then into the grim captain's face. There they stood, in the first hour of wedlock, while the idle pleasures, of which their companions were the emblems, had given place to the sternest cares of life, personified by the dark Puritans. But never had their youthful beauty seemed so pure and high as when its glow was chastened by adversity.

"Youth," said Endicott, "ye stand in an evil case thou and thy maiden wife. Make ready presently, for I am minded that ye shall both have a token to remember your wedding day!"

"Stern man," cried the May Lord, "how can I move thee? Were the means at hand, I would resist to the death. Being powerless, I entreat! Do with me as thou wilt, but let Edith go untouched!"

"Not so," replied the immitigable zealot. "We are not wont to show an idle courtesy to that sex, which requireth the stricter discipline. What sayest thou, maid? Shall thy silken bridegroom suffer thy share of the penalty, besides his own?"

"Be it death," said Edith, "and lay it all on me!"

Truly, as Endicott had said, the poor lovers stood in a woeful case. Their foes were triumphant, their friends captive and abased, their home desolate, the benighted wilderness around them, and a rigorous destiny, in the shape of the Puritan leader, their only guide. Yet the deepening twilight could not altogether conceal that the iron man was softened; he smiled at the fair spectacle of early love; he almost sighed for the inevitable blight of early hopes.

"The troubles of life have come hastily on this young couple," observed Endicott. "We will see how they comport themselves under their present trials ere we burden them with greater. If, among the spoil, there be any garments of a more decent fashion, let them be put upon this May Lord and his Lady, instead of their glistening vanities. Look to it, some of you."

"And shall not the youth's hair be cut?" asked Peter Palfrey, looking with abhorrence at the lovelock and long glossy curls of the young man.

"Crop it forthwith, and that in the true pumpkin-shell fashion," answered the captain. "Then bring them along with us, but more gently than their fellows. There be qualities in the youth, which may make him valiant to fight, and sober to toil, and pious to pray; and in the maiden, that may fit her to become a mother in our Israel, bringing up babes in better nurture than her own hath been. Nor think ye, young ones, that they are the happiest, even in our lifetime of a moment, who misspend it in dancing around a Maypole!"

And Endicott, the severest Puritan of all who laid the rock foundation of New England, lifted the wreath of roses from the ruin of the Maypole, and threw it, with his own gauntleted hand, over the heads of the Lord and Lady of the May. It was a deed of prophecy. As the moral gloom of the world overpowers all systematic gayety, even so was their home of wild mirth made desolate amid the sad forest. They returned to it no more. But as their flowery garland was wreathed of the brightest roses that had grown there, so, in the tie that united them, were intertwined all the purest and best of their early joys. They went heavenward, supporting each other along the difficult path which it was their lot to tread, and never wasted one regretful thought on the vanities of Merry Mount.

For Consideration

1. Why does Hawthorne, through the brief introduction to the story and the naming of historical personages, give his account the appearance of historical authenticity? What is the purpose of the festival which opens the story? Why are there costumes?

2. What is the source of mystery in Edith's heart? How is her recognition contrasted to the joys of Merry Mount?

3. Why is the Maypole at the center of Merry Mount's activities? What does it represent?

4. Isolate the characteristics which contrast the Puritans and Merry Mount. What is implied in Hawthorne's description of them as, respectively, "grizzly saints" and "gay sinners"? Is one group presented more favorably than the other?

5. Where do the lovers stand with respect to the opposite lifestyles of the Puritans and Merry Mount? What is the effect of the final portrait of them?

ERNEST HEMINGWAY   (1899–1961)
Hills Like White Elephants

The hills across the valley of the Ebro were long and white. On this side there was no shade and no trees and the station was between two lines of rails in the sun. Close against the side of the station there was the warm shadow of the building and a curtain, made of strings of bamboo beads, hung across the open door into the bar, to keep out flies. The American and the girl with him sat at a table in the shade, outside the building. It was very hot and the express from Barcelona would come in forty minutes. It stopped at this junction for two minutes and went on to Madrid.

"What should we drink?" the girl asked. She had taken off her hat and put it on the table.

"It's pretty hot," the man said.

"Let's drink beer."

"Dos cervezas," the man said into the curtain.

"Big ones?" a woman asked from the doorway.

"Yes. Two big ones."

The woman brought two glasses of beer and two felt pads. She put the felt pads and the beer glasses on the table and looked at the man and the girl. The girl was looking off at the line of hills. They were white in the sun and the country was brown and dry.

"They look like white elephants," she said.

"I've never seen one," the man drank his beer.

"No, you wouldn't have."

"I might have," the man said. "Just because you say I wouldn't have doesn't prove anything."

The girl looked at the bead curtain.

"They've painted something on it," she said. "What does it say?"

"Anis del Toro. It's a drink."

"Could we try it?"

The man called "Listen" through the curtain. The woman came out from the bar.

"Four reales."

"We want two Anis del Toro."

"With water?"

"Do you want it with water?"

"I don't know," the girl said. "Is it good with water?"

"It's all right."

"You want them with water?" asked the woman.

"Yes, with water."

"It tastes like licorice," the girl said and put the glass down.

"That's the way with everything."

"Yes," said the girl. "Everything tastes of licorice. Especially all the things you've waited so long for, like absinthe."

"Oh, cut it out."

"You started it," the girl said. "I was being amused. I was having a fine time."

"Well, let's try and have a fine time."

"All right. I was trying. I said the mountains looked like white elephants. Wasn't that bright?"

"That was bright."

"I wanted to try this new drink. That's all we do, isn't it — look at things and try new drinks?"

"I guess so."

The girl looked across at the hills.

"They're lovely hills," she said. "They don't really look like white elephants. I just meant the coloring of their skin through the trees."

"Should we have another drink?"

"All right."

The warm wind blew the bead curtain against the table.

"The beer's nice and cool," the man said.

"It's lovely," the girl said.

"It's really an awfully simple operation, Jig," the man said. "It's not really an operation at all."

The girl looked at the ground the table legs rested on.

"I know you wouldn't mind it, Jig. It's really not anything. It's just to let the air in."

The girl did not say anything.

"I'll go with you and I'll stay with you all the time. They just let the air in and then it's all perfectly natural."

"Then what will we do afterward?"

"We'll be fine afterward. Just like we were before."

"What makes you think so?"

"That's the only thing that bothers us. It's the only thing that's made us unhappy."

The girl looked at the bead curtain, put her hand out and took hold of two of the strings of beads.

"And you think then we'll be all right and be happy."

"I know we will. You don't have to be afraid. I've known lots of people that have done it."

"So have I," said the girl. "And afterward they were all so happy."

"Well," the man said, "if you don't want to you don't have to. I wouldn't have you do it if you didn't want to. But I know it's perfectly simple."

"And you really want to?"

"I think it's the best thing to do. But I don't want you to do it if you don't really want to."

"And if I do it you'll be happy and things will be like they were and you'll love me?"

"I love you now. You know I love you."

"I know. But if I do it, then it will be nice again if I say things are like white elephants, and you'll like it?"

"I'll love it. I love it now but I just can't think about it. You know how I get when I worry."

"If I do it you won't ever worry?"

"I won't worry about that because it's perfectly simple."

"Then I'll do it. Because I don't care about me."

"What do you mean?"

"I don't care about me."

"Well, I care about you."

"Oh, yes. But I don't care about me. And I'll do it and then everything will be fine."

"I don't want you to do it if you feel that way."

The girl stood up and walked to the end of the station. Across, on the other side, were fields of grain and trees along the banks of the Ebro. Far away, beyond the river, were mountains. The shadow of a cloud moved across the field of grain and she saw the river through the trees.

"And we could have all this," she said. "And we could have everything and every day we make it more impossible."

"What did you say?"

"I said we could have everything."

"We can have everything."

"No, we can't."

"We can have the whole world."

"No, we can't."

"We can go everywhere."

"No, we can't. It isn't ours any more."

"It's ours."

"No, it isn't. And once they take it away, you never get it back."

"But they haven't taken it away."

"We'll wait and see."

"Come on back in the shade," he said. "You mustn't feel that way."

"I don't feel any way," the girl said. "I just know things."

"I don't want you to do anything that you don't want to do ——"

"Nor that isn't good for me," she said. "I know. Could we have another beer?"

"All right. But you've got to realize ——"

"I realize," the girl said. "Can't we maybe stop talking?"

They sat down at the table and the girl looked across at the hills on the dry side of the valley and the man looked at her and at the table.

"You've got to realize," he said, "that I don't want you to do it if you don't want to. I'm perfectly willing to go through with it if it means anything to you."

"Doesn't it mean anything to you? We could get along."

"Of course it does. But I don't want anybody but you. I don't want any one else. And I know it's perfectly simple."

"Yes, you know it's perfectly simple."

"It's all right for you to say that, but I do know it."

"Would you do something for me now?"

"I'd do anything for you."

"Would you please please please please please please please stop talking?"

He did not say anything but looked at the bags against the wall of the station. There were labels on them from all the hotels where they had spent nights.

"But I don't want you to," he said, "I don't care anything about it."

"I'll scream," the girl said.

The woman came out through the curtains with two glasses of beer and put them down on the damp felt pads. "The train comes in five minutes," she said.

"What did she say?" asked the girl.

"That the train is coming in five minutes."

The girl smiled brightly at the woman, to thank her.

"I'd better take the bags over to the other side of the station," the man said. She smiled at him.

"All right. Then come back and we'll finish the beer."

He picked up the two heavy bags and carried them around the station to the other tracks. He looked up the tracks but could not see the train. Coming back, he walked through the barroom, where people waiting for the train were drinking. He drank an Anis at the bar and looked at the people. They were all waiting reasonably for the train. He went out through the bead curtain. She was sitting at the table and smiled at him.

"Do you feel better?" he asked.

"I feel fine," she said. "There's nothing wrong with me. I feel fine."

For Consideration

1. What is the setting of the story? How does it contribute an appropriate atmosphere for the conversation?

2. What appears to be the attitude of each speaker toward the other? Which of the two is more dominant?

3. In utilizing an objective point of view, Hemingway does not describe the motives or intentions of his characters. Through what means does he allow us to see them better? Does either of the two appear to be treated more sympathetically by the author?

4. What is the "awfully simple operation" which Jig and the American discuss? Why isn't it specified for us? What are the attitudes of the two people toward the operation?

5. Although the operation is apparently the important topic, much of the conversation is about other things, for example, drinks, and hills like white elephants. Are those other topics merely circumstantial or do they convey some meaning?

6. Does Jig mean it when she says, at the end, "There's nothing wrong with me. I feel fine."? On what do you base your judgment?

BERNARD MALAMUD (1914–   )
The Magic Barrel

Not long ago there lived in uptown New York, in a small, almost meager room, though crowded with books, Leo Finkle, a rabbinical student in the Yeshivah University. Finkle, after six years of study, was to be ordained in June and had been advised by an acquaintance that he might find it easier to win himself a congregation if he were married. Since he had no present prospects of marriage, after two tormented days of turning it over in his mind, he called in Pinye Salzman, a marriage broker whose two-line advertisement he had read in the *Forward*.

The matchmaker appeared one night out of the dark fourth-floor hallway of the graystone rooming house where Finkle lived, grasping a black, strapped portfolio that had been worn thin with use. Salzman, who had been long in the business, was of slight but dignified build, wearing an old hat, and an overcoat too short and tight for him. He smelled frankly of fish, which he loved to eat, and although he was missing a few teeth, his presence was not displeasing, because of an amiable manner curiously contrasted with mournful eyes. His voice, his lips, his wisp of beard, his bony fingers were animated, but give him a moment of repose and his mild blue eyes revealed a depth of sadness, a characteristic that put Leo a little at ease although the situation, for him, was inherently tense.

He at once informed Salzman why he had asked him to come, explaining that his home was in Cleveland, and that but for his parents, who had married comparatively late in life, he was alone in the world. He had for six years devoted himself almost entirely to his studies, as a result of which, understandably, he had found himself without time for a social life and the company of young women. Therefore he thought it the better part of trial and error — of embarrassing fumbling — to call in an experienced person to advise him on these matters. He remarked in passing that the function of the marriage broker was ancient and honorable, highly approved in the Jewish community, because it made practical the necessary without hindering joy. Moreover, his own parents had been brought together by a matchmaker. They had made, if not a financially profitable marriage — since neither had possessed any worldly goods to speak of — at least a successful one in the sense of their everlasting devotion to each other. Salzman listened in embarrassed surprise, sensing a sort of apology. Later, however, he experienced a glow of pride in his work, an emotion that had left him years ago, and he heartily approved of Finkle.

The two went to their business. Leo had led Salzman to the only clear place in the room, a table near a window that overlooked the lamp-lit city. He seated himself at the matchmaker's side but facing him, attempting by an act of will to suppress the unpleasant tickle in his throat. Salzman eagerly unstrapped his portfolio and removed a loose rubber band from a thin packet of much-handled cards. As he flipped through them, a gesture and sound that physically hurt Leo, the student pretended not to see and gazed steadfastly out the window. Although it was still February, winter was on its last legs, signs of which he had for the first time in years begun to notice. He now observed the round white moon, moving high in the sky through a cloud menagerie, and watched with half-open mouth as it penetrated a huge hen, and dropped out of her like an egg laying itself. Salzman, though pretending through eyeglasses he had just slipped on, to be engaged in scanning the writing on the cards, stole occasional glances at the young man's distinguished face, noting with pleasure the long, severe scholar's nose, brown eyes heavy with learning, sensitive yet ascetic lips, and a certain, almost hollow quality of the dark cheeks. He gazed around at shelves upon shelves of books and let out a soft, contented sigh.

When Leo's eyes fell upon the cards, he counted six spread out in Salzman's hand.

"So few?" he asked in disappointment.

"You wouldn't believe me how much cards I got in my office," Salzman replied. "The drawers are already filled to the top, so I keep them now in a barrel, but is every girl good for a new rabbi?"

Leo blushed at this, regretting all he had revealed of himself in a curriculum vitae he had sent to Salzman. He had thought it best to acquaint him with his strict standards and specifications, but in having done so, felt he had told the marriage broker more than was absolutely necessary.

He hesitantly inquired, "Do you keep photographs of your clients on file?"

"First comes family, amount of dowry, also what kind promises," Salzman replied, unbuttoning his tight coat and settling himself in the chair. "After comes pictures, rabbi."

"Call me Mr. Finkle. I'm not yet a rabbi."

Salzman said he would, but instead called him doctor, which he changed to rabbi when Leo was not listening too attentively.

Salzman adjusted his horn-rimmed spectacles, gently cleared his throat and read in an eager voice the contents of the top card:

"Sophie P. Twenty-four years. Widow one year. No children. Educated high school and two years college. Father promises eight thousand dollars. Has wonderful wholesale business. Also real estate. On the mother's side comes teachers, also one actor. Well known on Second Avenue."

Leo gazed up in surprise. "Did you say a widow?"

"A widow don't mean spoiled, rabbi.

She lived with her husband maybe four months. He was a sick boy she made a mistake to marry him."

"Marrying a widow has never entered my mind."

"This is because you have no experience. A widow, especially if she is young and healthy like this girl, is a wonderful person to marry. She will be thankful to you the rest of her life. Believe me, if I was looking now for a bride, I would marry a widow."

Leo reflected, then shook his head.

Salzman hunched his shoulders in an almost imperceptible gesture of disappointment. He placed the card down on the wooden table and began to read another:

"Lily H. High school teacher. Regular. Not a substitute. Has savings and new Dodge car. Lived in Paris one year. Father is successful dentist thirty-five years. Interested in professional man. Well Americanized family. Wonderful opportunity."

"I knew her personally," said Salzman. "I wish you could see this girl. She is a doll. Also very intelligent. All day you could talk to her about books and theyater and what not. She also knows current events."

"I don't believe you mentioned her age?"

"Her age?" Salzman said, raising his brows. "Her age is thirty-two years."

Leo said after a while, "I'm afraid that seems a little too old."

Salzman let out a laugh. "So how old are you, rabbi?"

"Twenty-seven."

"So what is the difference, tell me, between twenty-seven and thirty-two? My own wife is seven years older than me. So what did I suffer? — Nothing. If Rothschild's daughter wants to marry you, would you say on account her age, no?"

"Yes," Leo said dryly.

Salzman shook off the no in the yes.

"Five years don't mean a thing. I give you my word that when you will live with her for one week you will forget her age. What does it mean five years — that she lived more and knows more than somebody who is younger? On this girl, God bless her, years are not wasted. Each one that it comes makes better the bargain."

"What subject does she teach in high school?"

"Languages. If you heard the way she speaks French, you will think it is music. I am in the business twenty-five years, and I recommend her with my whole heart. Believe me, I know what I'm talking, rabbi."

"What's on the next card?" Leo said abruptly.

Salzman reluctantly turned up the third card:

"Ruth K. Nineteen years. Honor student. Father offers thirteen thousand cash to the right bridegroom. He is a medical doctor. Stomach specialist with marvelous practice. Brother in law owns own garment business. Particular people."

Salzman looked as if he had read his trump card.

"Did you say nineteen?" Leo asked with interest.

"On the dot."

"Is she attractive?" He blushed. "Pretty?"

Salzman kissed his finger tips. "A little doll. On this I give you my word. Let me call the father tonight and you will see what means pretty."

But Leo was troubled. "You're sure she's that young?"

"This I am positive. The father will show you the birth certificate."

"Are you positive there isn't something wrong with her?" Leo insisted.

"Who says there is wrong?"

"I don't understand why an American girl her age should go to a marriage broker."

A smile spread over Salzman's face.

"So for the same reason you went, she comes."

Leo flushed. "I am pressed for time."

Salzman, realizing he had been tactless, quickly explained. "The father came, not her. He wants she should have the best, so he looks around himself. When we will locate the right boy he will introduce him and encourage. This makes a better marriage than if a young girl without experience takes for herself. I don't have to tell you this."

"But don't you think this young girl believes in love?" Leo spoke uneasily.

Salzman was about to guffaw but caught himself and said soberly, "Love comes with the right person, not before."

Leo parted dry lips but did not speak. Noticing that Salzman had snatched a glance at the next card, he cleverly asked, "How is her health?"

"Perfect," Salzman said, breathing with difficulty. "Of course, she is a little lame on her right foot from an auto accident that it happened to her when she was twelve years, but nobody notices on account she is so brilliant and also beautiful."

Leo got up heavily and went to the window. He felt curiously bitter and upbraided himself for having called in the marriage broker. Finally, he shook his head.

"Why not?" Salzman persisted, the pitch of his voice rising.

"Because I detest stomach specialists."

"So what do you care what is his business? After you marry her do you need him? Who says he must come every Friday night in your house?"

Ashamed of the way the talk was going, Leo dismissed Salzman, who went home with heavy, melancholy eyes.

Though he had felt only relief at the marriage broker's departure, Leo was in low spirits the next day. He explained it as arising from Salzman's failure to produce a suitable bride for him. He did not care for

his type of clientele. But when Leo found himself hesitating whether to seek out another matchmaker, one more polished than Pinye, he wondered if it could be — his protestations to the contrary, and although he honored his father and mother — that he did not, in essence, care for the matchmaking institution? This thought he quickly put out of mind yet found himself still upset. All day he ran around in the woods — missed an important appointment, forgot to give out his laundry, walked out of a Broadway cafeteria without paying and had to run back with the ticket in his hand; had even not recognized his landlady in the street when she passed with a friend and courteously called out, "A good evening to you, Doctor Finkle." By nightfall, however, he had regained sufficient calm to sink his nose into a book and there found peace from his thoughts.

Almost at once there came a knock on the door. Before Leo could say enter, Salzman, commercial cupid, was standing in the room. His face was gray and meager, his expression hungry, and he looked as if he would expire on his feet. Yet the marriage broker managed, by some trick of the muscles, to display a broad smile.

"So good evening. I am invited?"

Leo nodded, disturbed to see him again, yet unwilling to ask the man to leave.

Beaming still, Salzman laid his portfolio on the table. "Rabbi, I got for you tonight good news."

"I've asked you not to call me rabbi. I'm still a student."

"Your worries are finished. I have for you a first-class bride."

"Leave me in peace concerning this subject." Leo pretended lack of interest.

"The world will dance at your wedding."

"Please, Mr. Salzman, no more."

"But first must come back my strength," Salzman said weakly. He fumbled with the portfolio straps and took out of the leather case an oily paper bag, from which he extracted a hard, seeded roll and a small, smoked white fish. With a quick motion of his hand he stripped the fish out of its skin and began ravenously to chew. "All day in a rush," he muttered.

Leo watched him eat.

"A sliced tomato you have maybe?" Salzman hesitantly inquired.

"No."

The marriage broker shut his eyes and ate. When he had finished he carefully cleaned up the crumbs and rolled up the remains of the fish, in the paper bag. His spectacled eyes roamed the room until he discovered, amid some piles of books, a one-burner gas stove. Lifting his hat he humbly asked, "A glass tea you got, rabbi?"

Conscience-stricken, Leo rose and brewed the tea. He served it with a chunk of lemon and two cubes of lump sugar, delighting Salzman.

After he had drunk his tea, Salzman's strength and good spirits were restored.

"So tell me, rabbi," he said amiably, "you considered some more the three clients I mentioned yesterday?"

"There was no need to consider."

"Why not?"

"None of them suits me."

"What then suits you?"

Leo let it pass because he could give only a confused answer.

Without waiting for a reply, Salzman asked, "You remember this girl I talked to you — the high school teacher?"

"Age thirty-two?"

But surprisingly, Salzman's face lit in a smile. "Age twenty-nine."

Leo shot him a look. "Reduced from thirty-two?"

"A mistake," Salzman avowed. "I talked today with the dentist. He took me to his safety deposit box and showed me the birth certificate. She was twenty-nine years last August. They made her a party in the mountains where she went for her vacation. When her father spoke to me the first time I forgot to write the age and I told you thirty-two, but now I remember this was a different client, a widow."

"The same one you told me about? I thought she was twenty-four?"

"A different. Am I responsible that the world is filled with widows?"

"No, but I'm not interested in them, nor for that matter, in school teachers."

Salzman pulled his clasped hands to his breast. Looking at the ceiling he devoutly exclaimed, "Yiddishe kinder, what can I say to somebody that he is not interested in high school teachers? So what then you are interested?"

Leo flushed but controlled himself.

"In what else will you be interested," Salzman went on, "if you not interested in this fine girl that she speaks four languages and has personally in the bank ten thousand dollars? Also her father guarantees further twelve thousand. Also she has a new car, wonderful clothes, talks on all subjects, and she will give you a first-class home and children. How near do we come in our life to paradise?"

"If she's so wonderful, why wasn't she married ten years ago?"

"Why?" said Salzman with a heavy laugh. "— Why? Because she is *partikiler*. This is why. She wants the *best*."

Leo was silent, amused at how he had entangled himself. But Salzman had aroused his interest in Lily H., and he began seriously to consider calling on her. When the marriage broker observed how intently Leo's mind was at work on the facts he had supplied, he felt certain they would soon come to an agreement.

Late Saturday afternoon, conscious of Salzman, Leo Finkle walked with Lily Hirschorn along Riverside Drive. He walked briskly and erectly, wearing with distinction the black fedora he had that morning taken with trepidation out of the dusty hat box on his closet shelf, and the heavy black Saturday coat he had thoroughly whisked clean. Leo also owned a walking stick, a present from a distant relative, but quickly put temptation aside and did not use it. Lily, petite and not unpretty, had on something signifying the approach of spring. She was au courant, animatedly, with all sorts of subjects, and he weighed her words and found her surprisingly sound — score another for Salzman, whom he uneasily sensed to be somewhere around, hiding perhaps high in a tree along the street, flashing the lady signals with a pocket mirror; or perhaps a cloven-hoofed Pan, piping nuptial ditties as he danced his invisible way before them, strewing wild buds on the walk and purple grapes in their path, symbolizing fruit of a union, though there was of course still none.

Lily startled Leo by remarking, "I was thinking of Mr. Salzman, a curious figure, wouldn't you say?"

Not certain what to answer, he nodded.

She bravely went on, blushing, "I for one am grateful for his introducing us. Aren't you?"

He courteously replied, "I am."

"I mean," she said with a little laugh — and it was all in good taste, or at least gave the effect of being not in bad — "do you mind that we came together so?"

He was not displeased with her honesty, recognizing that she meant to set the relationship aright, and understanding that it took a certain amount of experience in life, and courage, to want to do it quite that way. One had to have some sort of past to make that kind of beginning.

He said that he did not mind. Salzman's function was traditional and honorable — valuable for what it might achieve, which, he pointed out, was frequently nothing.

Lily agreed with a sigh. They walked on for a while and she said after a long silence, again with a nervous laugh,

"Would you mind if I asked you something a little bit personal? Frankly, I find the subject fascinating." Although Leo shrugged, she went on half embarrassedly, "How was it that you came to your calling? I mean was it a sudden passionate inspiration?"

Leo, after a time, slowly replied, "I was always interested in the Law."

"You saw revealed in it the presence of the Highest?"

He nodded and changed the subject. "I understand that you spent a little time in Paris, Miss Hirschorn?"

"Oh, did Mr. Salzman tell you, Rabbi Finkle?" Leo winced but she went on, "It was ages ago and almost forgotten. I remember I had to return for my sister's wedding."

And Lily would not be put off. "When," she asked in a trembly voice, "did you become enamored of God?"

He stared at her. Then it came to him that she was talking not about Leo Finkle, but of a total stranger, some mystical figure, perhaps even passionate prophet that Salzman had dreamed up for her — no relation to the living or dead. Leo trembled with rage and weakness. The trickster had obviously sold her a bill of goods, just as he had him, who'd expected to become acquainted with a young lady of twenty-nine, only to behold, the moment he laid eyes upon her strained and anxious face, a woman past thirty-five and aging rapidly. Only his self control had kept him this long in her presence.

"I am not," he said gravely, "a talented religious person," and in seeking words to go on, found himself possessed by shame and fear. "I think," he said in a strained manner, "that I came to God not because I loved Him, but because I did not."

This confession he spoke harshly because its unexpectedness shook him.

Lily wilted. Leo saw a profusion of loaves of bread go flying like ducks high over his head, not unlike the winged loaves by which he had counted himself to sleep last night. Mercifully, then, it snowed, which he would not put past Salzman's machinations.

He was infuriated with the marriage broker and swore he would throw him out of the room the minute he reappeared. But Salzman did not come that night, and when Leo's anger had subsided, an unaccountable despair grew in its place. At first he thought this was caused by his disappointment in Lily, but before long it became evident that he had involved himself with Salzman without a true knowledge of his own intent. He gradually realized — with an emptiness that seized him with six hands — that he had called in the broker to find him a bride because he was incapable of doing it himself. This terrifying insight he had derived as a result of his meeting and conversation with Lily Hirschorn. Her probing questions had somehow irritated him into revealing — to himself more than her — the true nature of his relationship to God, and from that it had come upon him, with shocking force, that apart from his parents, he had never loved anyone. Or perhaps it went the other way, that he did not love God so well as he might, because he had not loved man. It seemed to Leo that his whole life stood starkly revealed and he saw himself for the first time as he truly was — unloved and loveless. This bitter but somehow not fully unexpected revelation brought him to a point of panic, controlled only by extraordinary effort. He covered his face with his hands and cried.

The week that followed was the worst of his life. He did not eat and lost weight. His beard darkened and grew ragged. He stopped attending seminars and almost never opened a book. He seriously considered leaving the Yeshivah, although he was deeply troubled at the thought of the loss of all his years of study — saw them like pages torn from a book, strewn over the city — and at the devastating effect of this decision upon his parents. But he had lived without knowledge of himself, and never in the Five Books and all the Commentaries — mea culpa — had the truth been revealed to him. He did not know where to turn, and in all this desolating loneliness there was no *to whom*, although he often thought of Lily but not once could bring himself to go downstairs and make the call. He became touchy and irritable, especially with his landlady, who asked him all manner of personal questions; on the other hand, sensing his own disagreeableness, he waylaid her on the stairs and apologized abjectly, until mortified, she ran from him. Out of this, however, he drew the consolation that he was a Jew and that a Jew suffered. But gradually, as the long and terrible week drew to a close, he regained his composure and some idea of purpose in life: to go on as planned. Although he was imperfect, the ideal was not. As for his quest of a bride, the thought of continuing afflicted him with anxiety and heartburn, yet perhaps with this new knowledge of himself he would be more successful than in the past. Perhaps love would now come to him and a bride to that love. And for this sanctified seeking who needed a Salzman?

The marriage broker, a skeleton with haunted eyes, returned that very night. He looked, withal, the picture of frustrated expectancy — as if he had steadfastly waited the week at Miss Lily Hirschorn's side for a telephone call that never came.

Casually coughing, Salzman came immediately to the point: "So how did you like her?"

Leo's anger rose and he could not refrain from chiding the matchmaker: "Why did you lie to me, Salzman?"

Salzman's pale face went dead white, the world had snowed on him.

"Did you not state that she was twenty-nine?" Leo insisted.

"I give you my word—"

"She was thirty-five, if a day. *At least* thirty-five."

"Of this don't be too sure. Her father told me—"

"Never mind. The worst of it was that you lied to her."

"How did I lie to her, tell me?"

"You told her things about me that weren't true. You made me out to be more, consequently less than I am. She had in mind a totally different person, a sort of semi-mystical Wonder Rabbi."

"All I said, you was a religious man."

"I can imagine."

Salzman sighed. "This is my weakness that I have," he confessed. "My wife says to me I shouldn't be a salesman, but when I have two fine people that they would be wonderful to be married, I am so happy that I talk too much." He smiled wanly. "This is why Salzman is a poor man."

Leo's anger left him. "Well, Salzman, I'm afraid that's all."

The marriage broker fastened hungry eyes on him.

"You don't want any more a bride?"

"I do," said Leo, "but I have decided to seek her in a different way. I am no longer interested in an arranged marriage. To be frank, I now admit the necessity of premarital love. That is, I want to be in love with the one I marry."

"Love?" said Salzman, astounded. After a moment he remarked, "For us, our love is our life, not for the ladies. In the ghetto they—"

"I know, I know," said Leo. "I've thought of it often. Love, I have said to myself, should be a by-product of living and worship rather than its own end. Yet for myself I find it necessary to establish the level of my need and fulfill it."

Salzman shrugged but answered, "Listen, rabbi, if you want love, this I can find for you also. I have such beautiful clients that you will love them the minute your eyes will see them."

Leo smiled unhappily, "I'm afraid you don't understand."

But Salzman hastily unstrapped his portfolio and withdrew a manila packet from it.

"Pictures," he said, quickly laying the envelope on the table.

Leo called after him to take the pictures away, but as if on the wings of the wind, Salzman had disappeared.

March came. Leo had returned to his regular routine. Although he felt not quite himself yet — lacked energy — he was making plans for a more active social life. Of course it would cost something, but he was an expert in cutting corners; and when there were no corners left he would make circles rounder. All the while Salzman's pictures had lain on the table, gathering dust. Occasionally as Leo sat studying, or enjoying a cup of tea, his eyes fell on the manila envelope, but he never opened it.

The days went by and no social life to speak of developed with a member of the opposite sex — it was difficult, given the circumstances of his situation. One morning Leo toiled up the stairs to his room and stared out the window at the city. Although the day was bright his view of it was dark. For some time he watched the people in the street below hurrying along and then turned with a heavy heart to his little room. On the table was the packet. With a sudden relentless gesture he tore it open. For a half-hour he stood by the table in a state of excitement, examining the photographs of the ladies Salzman had included. Finally, with a deep sigh he put them down. There were six, of varying degrees of attractiveness, but look at them long enough and they all became Lily Hirschorn: all past their prime, all starved behind bright smiles, not a true personality in the lot. Life, despite their frantic yoo-hooings, had passed them by; they were pictures in a brief case that stank of fish. After a while, however, as Leo attempted to return the photographs into the envelope, he found in it another, a snapshot of the type taken by a machine for a quarter. He gazed at it a moment and let out a cry.

Her face deeply moved him. Why, he could at first not say. It gave him the impression of youth — spring flowers, yet age — a sense of having been used to the bone, wasted; this came from the eyes, which were hauntingly familiar, yet absolutely strange. He had a vivid impression that he had met her before, but try as he might he could not place her although he could almost recall her name, as if he had read it in her own handwriting. No, this couldn't be; he would have remembered her. It was not, he affirmed, that she had an extraordinary beauty — no, though her face was attractive enough; it was that *something* about her moved him. Feature for feature, even some of the ladies of the photographs could do better; but she leaped forth to his heart — had *lived*, or wanted to — more than just wanted, perhaps regretted how she had lived — had somehow deeply suffered: it could be seen in the depths of those reluctant eyes, and from the way the light enclosed and shone from her, and within her, opening realms of possibility: this was her own. Her he desired. His head ached and eyes narrowed with the intensity of his gazing, then as if an obscure fog had blown up in the mind, he experienced fear of her and was aware that he had received an impression, somehow, of evil. He shuddered, saying softly, it is thus with us all. Leo brewed some tea in a small pot and sat sipping it without sugar, to calm himself. But before he had finished drinking, again with excitement he examined the face and found it good: good for Leo Finkle. Only such a one could understand him and help him seek whatever he was seeking. She might, perhaps, love him. How she had happened to be among the discards in Salzman's barrel he could never guess, but he knew he must urgently go find her.

Leo rushed downstairs, grabbed up the Bronx telephone book, and searched for Salzman's home address. He was not listed, nor was his office. Neither was he in the Manhattan book. But Leo remembered having written down the address on a slip of paper after he had read Salzman's advertisement in the "personals" column of the *Forward*. He ran up to his room and tore through his papers, without luck. It was exasperating. Just when he needed the matchmaker he was nowhere to be found. Fortunately Leo remembered to look in his wallet. There on a card he found his name written and a Bronx address. No phone number was listed, the reason — Leo now recalled — he had originally communicated with Salzman by letter. He got on his coat, put a hat on over his skull cap and hurried to the subway station. All the way to the far end of the Bronx he sat on the edge of his seat. He was more than once tempted to take out the picture and see if the girl's face was as he remembered it, but he refrained, allowing the snapshot to remain in his inside coat pocket, content to have her so close. When the train pulled into the station he was waiting at the door and bolted out. He quickly located the street Salzman had advertised.

The building he sought was less than a block from the subway, but it was not an office building, nor even a loft, nor a store in which one could rent office space. It was a very old tenement house. Leo found Salzman's name in pencil on a soiled tag under the bell and climbed three dark flights to his apartment. When he knocked, the door was opened by a thin, asthmatic, gray-haired woman, in felt slippers.

"Yes?" she said, expecting nothing. She listened without listening. He could have sworn he had seen her, too, before but knew it was an illusion.

"Salzman — does he live here? Pinye Salzman," he said, "the matchmaker?"

She stared at him a long minute. "Of course."

He felt embarrassed. "Is he in?"

"No." Her mouth, though left open, offered nothing more.

"The matter is urgent. Can you tell me where his office is?"

"In the air." She pointed upward.

"You mean he has no office?" Leo asked.

"In his socks."

He peered into the apartment. It was sunless and dingy, one large room divided by a half-open curtain, beyond which he could see a sagging metal bed. The near side of a room was crowded with rickety chairs, old bureaus, a three-legged table, racks of cooking utensils, and all the apparatus of a kitchen. But there was no sign of Salzman or his magic barrel, probably also a figment of the imagination. An odor of frying fish made Leo weak to the knees.

"Where is he?" he insisted. "I've got to see your husband."

At length she answered, "So who knows where he is? Every time he thinks a new thought he runs to a different place. Go home, he will find you."

"Tell him Leo Finkle."

She gave no sign she had heard.

He walked downstairs, depressed.

But Salzman, breathless, stood waiting at his door.

Leo was astounded and overjoyed. "How did you get here before me?"

"I rushed."

"Come inside."

They entered. Leo fixed tea, and a sardine sandwich for Salzman. As they were drinking he reached behind him for the packet of pictures and handed them to the marriage broker.

Salzman put down his glass and said expectantly, "You found somebody you like?"

"Not among these."

The marriage broker turned away.

"Here is the one I want." Leo held forth the snapshot.

Salzman slipped on his glasses and took the picture into his trembling hand. He turned ghastly and let out a groan.

"What's the matter?" cried Leo.

"Excuse me. Was an accident this picture. She isn't for you."

Salzman frantically shoved the manila packet into his portfolio. He thrust the snapshot into his pocket and fled down the stairs.

Leo, after momentary paralysis, gave chase and cornered the marriage broker in the vestibule. The landlady made hysterical outcries but neither of them listened.

"Give me back the picture, Salzman."

"No." The pain in his eyes was terrible.

"Tell me who she is then."

"This I can't tell you. Excuse me."

He made to depart, but Leo, forgetting himself, seized the matchmaker by his tight coat and shook him frenziedly.

"Please," sighed Salzman. "*Please*."

Leo ashamedly let him go. "Tell me who she is," he begged. "It's very important for me to know,"

"She is not for you. She is a wild one — wild, without shame. This is not a bride for a rabbi."

"What do you mean wild?"

"Like an animal. Like a dog. For her to

be poor was a sin. This is why to me she is dead now."

"In God's name, what do you mean?"

"Her I can't introduce to you," Salzman cried.

"Why are you so excited?"

"Why, he asks," Salzman said, bursting into tears. "This is my baby, my Stella, she should burn in hell."

Leo hurried up to bed and hid under the covers. Under the covers he thought his life through. Although he soon fell asleep he could not sleep her out of his mind. He woke, beating his breast. Though he prayed to be rid of her, his prayers went unanswered. Through days of torment he endlessly struggled not to love her; fearing success, he escaped it. He then concluded to convert her to goodness, himself to God. The idea alternately nauseated and exalted him.

He perhaps did not know that he had come to a final decision until he encountered Salzman in a Broadway cafeteria. He was sitting alone at a rear table, sucking the bony remains of a fish. The marriage broker appeared haggard, and transparent to the point of vanishing.

Salzman looked up at first without recognizing him. Leo had grown a pointed beard and his eyes were weighted with wisdom.

"Salzman," he said, "love has at last come to my heart."

"Who can love from a picture?" mocked the marriage broker.

"It is not impossible."

"If you can love her, then you can love anybody. Let me show you some new clients that they just sent me their photographs. One is a little doll."

"Just her I want," Leo murmured.

"Don't be a fool, doctor. Don't bother with her."

"Put me in touch with her, Salzman," Leo said humbly. "Perhaps I can be of service."

Salzman had stopped eating and Leo understood with emotion that it was now arranged.

Leaving the cafeteria, he was, however, afflicted by a tormenting suspicion that Salzman had planned it all to happen this way.

Leo was informed by letter that she would meet him on a certain corner, and she was there one spring night, waiting under a street lamp. He appeared, carrying a small bouquet of violets and rosebuds. Stella stood by the lamp post, smoking. She wore white with red shoes, which fitted his expectations, although in a troubled moment he had imagined the dress red, and only the shoes white. She waited uneasily and shyly. From afar he saw that her eyes — clearly her father's — were filled with desperate innocence. He pictured, in her, his own redemption. Violins and lit candles revolved in the sky. Leo ran forward with flowers outthrust.

Around the corner, Salzman, leaning against a wall, chanted prayers for the dead.

For Consideration

1. Why is Leo Finkle looking for a wife? What kind of woman does he want to find? Why is he concerned about confirming the matchmaker's function as a traditional and honorable one?

2. How complete are the "machinations" of Salzman? How does his action determine the success — or lack of it — of the meeting between Leo Finkle and Lily Hirschorn?

3. Based on what evidence does Leo conclude that he is "unloved and loveless"? Is it possible that he is over-reacting to his disappointing meeting with Lily Hirschorn? What connection does he make between his relationship to God and his association with humankind?

4. What causes Leo's new thinking that love should precede marriage?

5. Why does Leo become so excited when viewing the face on the cheap snapshot? What is it about the face that attracts him?

6. From Salzman's description of his daughter it appears that she needs to be "redeemed," yet Leo, on seeing her, pictures "in her, his own redemption." What kind of redemption is he thinking of? Can the two be redeeming influences on each other? (Leo has previously said to Salzman of his daughter: "Perhaps I can be of service.") What is the significance of Salzman, in the final words of the story, chanting "prayers for the dead"?

MIGUEL DE UNAMUNO   (1864–1936)
Saint Emmanuel the Good, Martyr

Translated by Anthony Kerrigan

If with this life only in view we have had hope in Christ, we are of all men the most to be pitied.

Saint Paul: 1 Cor. 15:19.

Now that the bishop of the diocese of Renada, to which this my beloved village of Valverde de Lucerna belongs, is seeking (according to rumor), to initiate the process of beatification of our Don Manuel, or more correctly, Saint Emmanuel the Good, who was parish priest here, I want to state in writing, by way of confession (although to what end only God, and not I can say), all that I can vouch for and remember of that matriarchal man who pervaded the most secret life of my soul, who was my true spiritual father, the father of my spirit, the spirit of myself, Angela Carballino.

The other, my flesh-and-blood temporal father, I scarcely knew, for he died when I was still a very young girl. I know that he came to Valverde de Lucerna from the outside world — that he was a stranger — and that he settled here when he married my mother. He had brought a number of books with him: *Don Quixote*, some plays from the classic theatre, some novels, a few histories, the *Bertoldo*, everything all mixed together. From these books (practically the only ones in the entire village), I nurtured dreams as a young girl, dreams which in turn devoured me. My good mother gave me very little account either of the words or the deeds of my father. For the words and deeds of Don Manuel, whom she worshipped, of whom she was enamored, in common with all the rest of the village — in an exquisitely chaste manner, of course — had obliterated the memory of the words and deeds of her husband; him she commended to God, with full fervor, as she said her daily rosary.

Don Emmanuel I remember as if it were yesterday, from the time when I was a girl of ten, just before I was taken to the convent school in the cathedral city of Renada. At that time Don Emmanuel, our saint, must have been about thirty-seven years old. He was tall, slender, erect; he carried himself the way our Buitre Peak carries its crest, and his eyes had all the blue depth of our lake. As he walked he commanded all eyes, and not only the eyes but the hearts of all; gazing round at us he seemed to look through our flesh as through glass and penetrate our hearts. We all of us loved him, especially the children. And the things he said to us! Not words, things! The villagers could scent the odor of sanctity, they were intoxicated with it.

It was at this time that my brother Lazarus, who was in America, from where he regularly sent us money with which we lived in decent leisure, had my mother send me to the convent school, so that my education might be completed outside the village; he suggested this move despite the fact that he had no special fondness for the nuns. "But since, as far as I know," he wrote us, "there are no lay schools there yet, — especially not for young ladies — we will have to make use of the ones that do exist. The important thing is for Angelita to receive some polish and not be forced to continue among village girls." And so I entered the convent school. At

one point I even thought I would become a teacher; but pedagogy soon palled upon me.

At school I met girls from the city and I made friends with some of them. But I still kept in touch with people in our village, and I received frequent reports and sometimes a visit.

And the fame of the parish priest reached as far as the school, for he was beginning to be talked of in the cathedral city. The nuns never tired of asking me about him.

Ever since early youth I had been endowed, I don't very well know from where, with a large degree of curiosity and restlessness, due at least in part to that jumble of books which my father had collected, and these qualities were stimulated at school, especially in the course of a relationship which I developed with a girl friend, who grew excessively attached to me. At times she proposed that we enter the same convent together, swearing to an everlasting "sisterhood" — and even that we seal the oath in blood. At other times she talked to me, with eyes half closed, of sweethearts and marriage adventures. Strangely enough, I have never heard of her since, or of what became of her, despite the fact that whenever our Don Manuel was spoken of, or when my mother wrote me something about him in her letters — which happened in almost every letter — and I read it to her, this girl would exclaim, as if in rapture: "What luck, my dear, to be able to live near a saint like that, a live saint, of flesh and blood, and to be able to kiss his hand; when you go back to your village write me everything, everything, and tell me about him."

Five years passed at school, five years which now have evanesced in memory like a dream at dawn, and when I became fifteen I returned to my own Valverde de Lucerna. By now everything revolved around Don Emmanuel: Don Emmanuel, the lake and the mountain. I arrived home anxious to know him, to place myself under his protection, and hopeful he would set me on my path in life.

It was rumored that he had entered the seminary to become a priest so that he might thus look after the sons of a sister recently widowed and provide for them in place of their father; that in the seminary his keen mind and his talents had distinguished him and that he had subsequently turned down opportunities for a brilliant career in the church because he wanted to remain exclusively a part of his Valverde de Lucerna, of his remote village which lay like a brooch between the lake and the mountain reflected in it.

How he did love his people! His life consisted in salvaging wrecked marriages, in forcing unruly sons to submit to their parents, or reconciling parents to their sons, and, above all, of consoling the embittered and the weary in spirit; meanwhile he helped everyone to die well.

I recall, among other incidents, the occasion when the unfortunate daughter of old aunt Rabona returned to our town. She had been in the city and lost her virtue there; now she returned unmarried and castoff, and she brought back a little son. Don Emmanuel did not rest until he had persuaded an old sweetheart, Perote by name, to marry the poor girl and, moreover, to legitimize the little creature with his own name. Don Emmanuel told Perote:

"Come now, give this poor waif a father, for he hasn't got one except in heaven."

"But, Don Emmanuel, it's not my fault . . . !"

"Who knows, my son, who knows . . . ! And besides, it's not a question of guilt."

And today, poor Perote, inspired on that occasion to saintliness by Don Emmanuel, and now a paralytic and invalid, has for staff and consolation of his life the son he accepted as his own when the boy was not his at all.

On Midsummer's Night, the shortest night of the year, it was a local custom here (and still is) for all the old crones, and a few old men, who thought they were possessed or bewitched (hysterics they were, for the most part, or in some cases epileptics) to flock to the lake. Don Emmanuel undertook to fulfill the same function as the lake, to serve as a pool of healing, to treat his charges and even, if possible, to cure them. And such was the effect of his presence, of his gaze, and above all of his voice — the miracle of his voice! — and the infinitely sweet authority of his words, that he actually did achieve some remarkable cures. Whereupon his fame increased, drawing all the sick of the environs to our lake and our priest. And yet once when a mother came to ask for a miracle in behalf of her son, he answered her with a sad smile:

"Ah, but I don't have my bishop's permission to perform miracles."

He was particularly interested in seeing that all the villagers kept themselves clean. If he chanced upon someone with a torn garment he would send him to the church: "Go and see the sacristan, and let him mend that tear." The sacristan was a tailor, and when, on the first day of the year, everyone went to congratulate him on his saint's day — his holy patron was Our Lord Jesus Himself — it was by Don Emmanuel's wish that everyone appeared in a new shirt, and those that had none received the present of a new one from Don Emmanuel himself.

He treated everyone with the greatest kindness; if he favored anyone, it was the most unfortunate, and especially those who rebelled. There was a congenital idiot in the village, the fool Blasillo, and it was toward him that Don Emmanuel chose to show the greatest love and concern; as a consequence he succeeded in miraculously teaching him things which had appeared beyond the idiot's comprehension. The fact was that the embers of understanding feebly glowing in the idiot were kindled whenever, like a pitiable monkey, he imitated his Don Emmanuel.

The marvel of the man was his voice; a divine voice which brought one close to weeping. Whenever he officiated at Solemn High Mass and intoned the prelude, a tremor ran through the congregation and all within sound of his voice were moved to the depths of their being. The sound of his chanting, overflowing the church, went on to float over the lake and settle at the foot of the mountain. And when on Good Friday he intoned "My God, my God, my God, why hast Thou forsaken me?" a profound shudder swept through the multitude, like the lash of a northeaster across the waters of the lake. It was as if these people heard the Lord Jesus Christ himself, as if the voice sprang from the ancient crucifix, at the foot of which generations of mothers had offered up their sorrows. And it happened that on one occasion his mother heard him and was unable to contain herself, and cried out to him right in the church, "My son!," calling her child. And the entire congregation was visibly affected. It was as if the mother's cry had issued from the half-open lips of the Mater Dolorosa — her heart transfixed by seven swords — which stood in one of the chapels of the nave. Afterwards, the fool Blasillo went about piteously repeating, as if he were an echo, "My God, my God, my God, why hast Thou forsaken me?" with such effect that everyone who heard him was moved to tears, to the great satisfaction of the fool, who prided himself on this triumph of imitation.

The priest's effect on people was such that no one ever dared to tell him a lie, and everyone confessed themselves to him without need of a confessional. So true was this that on one occasion, when a revolting crime had been committed in a neighboring village, the judge — a dull fellow who badly misunderstood Don Emmanuel — called on the priest and said:

"Let us see, Don Manuel, if you can get this bandit to admit the truth."

"So that afterwards you may punish him?" asked the saintly man. "No, Judge, no; I will not extract from any man a truth which could be the death of him. That is a matter between him and his God . . . Human justice is none of my affair. 'Judge not that ye be not judged,' said our Lord."

"But the fact is, Father, that I, a judge . . ."

"I understand. You, Judge, must render unto Caesar that which is Caesar's, while I shall render unto God that which is God's."

And, as Don Emmanuel departed, he gazed at the suspected criminal and said:

"Make sure, only, that God forgives you, for that is all that matters."

Everyone went to Mass in the village, even if it were only to hear him and see him at the altar, where he appeared to be transfigured, his countenance lit from within. He introduced one holy practice to the popular cult; it consisted in assembling the whole town inside the church, men and women, ancients and youths, some thousand persons; there we recited the Creed, in unison, so that it sounded like a single voice: "I believe in God, the Almighty Father, Creator of heaven and earth . . ." and all the rest. It was not a chorus, but a single voice, a simple united voice, all the voices based on one on which they formed a kind of mountain, whose peak, lost at times in the clouds, was Don Emmanuel. As we reached the section, "I believe in the resurrection of the flesh and life everlasting," the voice of Don Emmanuel was submerged, drowned in the voice of the populace as in a lake. In truth, he was silent. And I could hear the bells of that city which is said hereabouts to be at the bottom of the lake — bells which are also said to be audible on Midsummer's

Night — the bells of the city which is submerged in the spiritual lake of our populace; I was hearing the voice of our dead, resurrected in us by the communion of saints. Later, when I had learned the secret of our saint, I understood that it was as if a caravan crossing the desert lost its leader as they approached the goal of their trek, whereupon his people lifted him on their shoulders to bring his lifeless body into the promised land.

When it came to dying themselves, most of the villagers refused to die unless they were holding on to Don Emmanuel's hand, as if to an anchor chain.

In his sermons he never inveighed against unbelievers, Masons, liberals or heretics. What for, when there were none in the village? Nor did it occur to him to speak against the wickedness of the press. On the other hand, one of his most frequent themes was gossip, against which he lashed out.

"Envy," he liked to repeat, "envy is nurtured by those who prefer to think they are envied, and most persecutions are the result of a persecution complex rather than of an impulse to persecute."

"But Don Emmanuel, just listen to what that fellow was trying to tell me . . ."

"We should concern ourselves less with what people are trying to tell us than with what they tell us without trying . . ."

His life was active rather than contemplative, and he constantly fled from idleness, even from leisure. Whenever he heard it said that idleness was the mother of all the vices, he added: "And also of the greatest vice of them all, which is to think idly." Once I asked him what he meant and he answered: "Thinking idly is thinking as a substitute for doing, or thinking too much about what is already done instead of about what must be done. What's done is done and over with, and one must go on to something else, for there is nothing worse than remorse without possible relief." Action! Action! Even in those early days I had already begun to realize that Don Emmanuel fled from being left to think in solitude, and I guessed that some obsession haunted him.

And so it was that he was always occupied, sometimes even occupied in searching for occupations. He wrote very little on his own, so that he scarcely left us anything in writing, even notes; on the other hand, he acted as scrivener for everyone else, especially mothers, for whom he composed letters to their absent sons.

He also worked with his hands, pitching in to help with some of the village tasks. At threshing time he reported to the threshing floor to flair and winnow, meanwhile teaching and entertaining the workers by turn. Sometimes he took the place of a worker who had fallen sick. One day in the dead of winter he came upon a child, shivering with the bitter cold. The child's father had sent him into the woods to bring back a strayed calf.

"Listen," he said to the child, "you go home and get warm, and tell your father that I am bringing back the calf." On the way back with the animal, he ran into the father, who had come out to meet him, thoroughly ashamed of himself.

In winter he chopped wood for the poor. When a certain magnificent walnut tree died — "that matriarchal walnut," he called it, a tree under whose shade he had played as a boy and whose fruit he had eaten for so many years — he asked for the trunk, carried it to his house and, after he had cut six planks from it, which he put away at the foot of his bed, he made firewood of the rest to warm the poor. He also was in the habit of making handballs for the boys and a goodly number of toys for the younger children.

Often he used to accompany the doctor on his rounds, adding his presence and prestige to the doctor's prescriptions. Most of all he was interested in maternity cases and the care of children; it was his opinion that the old wives' sayings "from the cradle to heaven" and the other one about "little angels belong in heaven" were nothing short of blasphemy.[1] The death of a child moved him deeply.

"A child stillborn," I once heard him say, "or one who dies soon after birth, is the most terrible of mysteries to me. It's as if it were a suicide. Or as if the child were crucified."

And once, when a man had taken his own life and the father of the suicide, an outsider, asked Don Emmanuel if his son could be buried in consecrated ground, the priest answered:

"Most certainly, for at the last moment, in the very last throes, he must certainly have repented. There is no doubt of it whatsoever in my mind."

From time to time he would visit the local school to help the teacher, to teach alongside him — and not only the catechism. The simple truth was that he fled relentlessly from idleness and from solitude. He went so far in this desire of his to mingle with the villagers, especially the youth and the children, that he even attended the village dances. And more than once he played the drum to keep time for the young men and women dancing; this kind of activity, which in another priest would have seemed like a grotesque mockery of his calling, in him somehow took on the appearance of a holy and religious exercise. When the Angelus would ring out, he would put down the drum and sticks, take off his hat (all the others doing the same) and pray: "The angel of the Lord declared unto Mary: Hail Mary . . ." And afterwards: "Now, let us rest until tomorrow."

"First of all," he would say, "the village must be happy; everyone must be happy

1. "Teta y gloria" and "angelitos al cielo."

to be alive. To be satisfied with life is of first importance. No one should want to die until it is God's will."

"I want to die now," a recently widowed woman once told him, "I want to be with my husband . . ."

"And why now?" he asked. "Stay here and pray God for his soul."

One of his well-loved remarks was made at a wedding: "Ah, if I could only change all the water in our lake into wine, into a dear little wine which, no matter how much of it one drank, would always make one joyful without intoxicating . . . or, if intoxicating, would make one joyfully drunk."

Once upon a time a band of poor acrobats came through the village. The leader — who arrived on the scene with a gravely ill and pregnant wife and three sons to help him — played the clown. While he was in the village square making all the children, and even some of the adults, laugh with glee, his wife suddenly fell desperately ill and had to leave; she went off accompanied by a look of anguish from the clown and a howl of laughter from the children. Don Emmanuel hurried after, and, a little later, in a corner of the inn's stable, he helped her give up her soul in a state of grace. When the performance was over and the villagers and the clown learned of the tragedy, they came to the inn, and there the poor bereaved clown, in a voice choked with tears, told Don Emmanuel, as he took his hand and kissed it: "They are quite right, Father, when they say you are a saint." Don Emmanuel took the clown's hand in his and replied before everyone:

"It is you who are the saint, good clown. I watched you at your work and understood that you do it not only to provide bread for your children, but also to give joy to the children of others. And I tell you now that your wife, the mother of your children, whom I sent to God while you worked to give joy, is at rest in the Lord, and that you will join her there, and that the angels, whom you will make laugh with happiness in heaven, will reward you with their laughter."

And everyone present wept, children and elders alike, as much from sorrow as from a mysterious joy in which all sorrow was drowned. Later, recalling that solemn hour, I have come to realize that the imperturbable joyousness of Don Emmanuel was merely the temporal, earthly form of an infinite, eternal sadness which the priest concealed from the eyes and ears of the world with heroic saintliness.

His constant activity, his ceaseless intervention in the tasks and diversions of everyone, had the appearance, in short, of a flight from himself, of a flight from solitude. He confirmed this suspicion: "I have a fear of solitude," he would say. And still, from time to time he would go off by himself, along the shores of the lake, to the ruins of the abbey where the souls of pious Cistercians seem still to repose, although history has long since buried them in oblivion. There, the cell of the so-called Father-Captain can still be found, and it is said that the drops of blood spattered on the walls as he flagellated himself can still be seen. What thoughts occupied our Don Emmanuel as he walked there? I remember a conversation we held once in which I asked him, as he was speaking of the abbey, why it had never occurred to him to enter a monastery, and he answered me:

"It is not at all because of the fact that my sister is a widow and I have her children and herself to support — for God looks after the poor — but rather because I simply was not born to be a hermit, an anchorite; the solitude would crush my soul; and, as far as a monastery is concerned, my monastery is Valverde de Lucerna. I was not meant to live alone, or die alone. I was meant to live for my village, and die for it too. How should I save my soul if I were not to save the soul of my village as well?"

"But there have been saints who were hermits, solitaries . . . ." I said.

"Yes, the Lord gave them the grace of solitude which He has denied me, and I must resign myself. I must not throw away my village to win my soul. God made me that way. I would not be able to resist the temptations of the desert. I would not be able, alone, to carry the cross of birth . . ."

I have summoned up all these recollections, from which my faith was fed, in order to portray our Don Emmanuel as he was when I, a young girl of sixteen, returned from the convent of Renada to our "monastery of Valverde de Lucerna," once more to kneel at the feet of our "abbot."

"Well, here is the daughter of Simona," he said as soon as he saw me, "made into a young woman, and knowing French, and how to play the piano, and embroider, and heaven knows what else besides! Now you must get ready to give us a family. And your brother Lazarus; when does he return? Is he still in the New World?"

"Yes, Father, he is still in the New World."

"The New World! And we in the Old. Well then, when you write him, tell him for me, on behalf of the parish priest, that I should like to know when he is returning from the New World to the Old, to bring us the latest from over there. And tell him that he will find the lake and the mountain as he left them."

When I first went to him for confession, I became so confused that I could not enunciate a word. "I recited the "Forgive me, Father, for I have sinned," in a stammer, almost a sob. And he, observing this, said:

"Good heavens, my dear, what are you afraid of, or of whom are you afraid? Certainly you're not trembling now under the weight of your sins, nor in fear of God. No, you're trembling because of me, isn't that so?"

At this point I burst into tears.

"What have they been telling you about me? What fairy tales? Was it your mother, perhaps? Come, come, please be calm; you must imagine you are talking to your brother . . ."

At this I plucked up courage and began to tell him of my anxieties, doubts and sorrows.

"Bah! Where did you read all this, Miss Intellectual. All this is literary nonsense. Don't succumb to everything you read just yet, not even to Saint Theresa. If you need to amuse yourself, read the *Bertoldo*, as your father before you did."

I came away from my first confession to that holy man deeply consoled. The initial fear — simple fright more than respect — with which I had approached him, turned into a profound pity. I was at that time a very young woman, almost a girl still; and yet, I was beginning to be a woman, in my innermost being I felt the juice and stirrings of maternity, and when I found myself in the confessional at the side of the saintly priest, I sensed a kind of unspoken confession on his part in the soft murmur of his voice. And I remembered how when he had intoned in the church the words of Jesus Christ: "My God, my God, why hast Thou forsaken me?" his own mother had cried out in the congregation: "My son!"; and I could hear the cry that had rent the silence of the temple. And I went to him again for confession — and to comfort him.

Another time in the confessional I told him of a doubt which assailed me, and he responded:

"As to that, you know what the catechism says. Don't question me about it, for I am ignorant; in Holy Mother Church there are learned doctors of theology who will know how to answer you."

"But you are the learned doctor here."

"Me? A learned doctor? Not even in thought! I, my little doctress, am only a poor country priest. And those questions, . . . do you know who whispers them into your ear? Well . . . the Devil does!"

Then, making bold, I asked him point-blank:

"And suppose he were to whisper these questions to you?"

"Who? To me? The Devil? No, we don't even know each other, my daughter, we haven't met at all."

"But if he did whisper them? . . ."

"I wouldn't pay any attention. And that's enough of that; let's get on, for there are some people, really sick people, waiting for me."

I went away thinking, I don't know why, that our Don Emmanuel, so famous for curing the bedeviled, didn't really even believe in the Devil. As I started home, I ran into the fool Blasillo, who had probably been hovering around outside; as soon as he saw me, and by way of treating me to a display of his virtuosity, he began the business of repeating — and in what a manner! — "My God, my God, why hast Thou forsaken me?" I arrived home utterly saddened and locked myself in my room to cry, until finally my mother arrived.

"With all these confessions, Angelita, you will end by going off to a nunnery."

"Don't worry, Mother," I answered her. "I have plenty to do here, in the village, and it will be my only convent."

"Until you marry."

"I don't intend to," I rejoined.

The next time I saw Don Emmanuel I asked him, looking straight into his eyes:

"Is there really a Hell, Don Emmanuel?"

And he, without altering his expression, answered:

"For you, my daughter, no."

"For others, then?"

"Does it matter to you, if you are not to go there?"

"It matters for the others, in any case. Is there a Hell?"

"Believe in Heaven, the Heaven we can see. Look at it there" — and he pointed to the heavens above the mountain, and then down into the lake, to the reflection.

"But we are supposed to believe in Hell as well as in Heaven," I said.

"That's true. We must believe everything believed and taught by our Holy Mother Church, Catholic, Apostolic, and Roman. And now, that will do!"

I thought I read a deep unknown sadness in his eyes, eyes which were as blue as the waters of the lake.

Those years passed as if in a dream. Within me, a reflected image of Don Emmanuel was unconsciously taking form. He was an ordinary enough man in many ways, of such daily use as the daily bread we asked for in our Paternoster. I helped him whenever I could with his tasks, visiting the sick, his sick, the girls at school, and helping, too, with the church linen and the vestments; I served in the role, as he said, of his deaconess. Once I was invited to the city for a few days by a school friend, but I had to hurry home, for the city stifled me — something was missing, I was thirsty for a sight of the waters of the lake, hungry for a sight of the peaks of the mountain; and even more, I missed my Don Emmanuel, as if his absence called to me, as if he were endangered by my being so far away, as if he were in need of me. I began to feel a kind of maternal affection for my spiritual father; I longed to help him bear the cross of birth.

My twenty-fourth birthday was approaching when my brother Lazarus came back from America with the small fortune he had saved up. He came back to Valverde de Lucerna with the intention of taking me and my mother to live in a city, perhaps even Madrid.

"In the country," he said, "in these villages, a person becomes stupefied, brutalized and spiritually impoverished." And he added: "Civilization is the very opposite of everything countryfied. The idiocy of village life! No, that's not for us; I didn't have you sent away to school so that later you might spoil here, among these ignorant peasants."

I said nothing, though I was disposed to resist emigration. But our mother, already past sixty, took a firm stand from the start: "Change pastures at my age?" she demanded at once. A little later she made it quite clear that she could not live out of sight of her lake, her mountain, and, above all, of her Don Emmanuel.

"The two of you are like those cats that get attached to houses." my brother muttered.

When he realized the complete sway exercised over the entire village — especially over my mother and myself — by the saintly priest, my brother began to resent him. He saw in this situation an example of the obscurantist theocracy which, according to him, smothered Spain. And he commenced to spout the old anti-clerical commonplaces, to which he added anti-religious and "progressive" propaganda brought back from the New World.

"In the Spain of sloth and flabby useless men, the priests manipulate the women, and the women manipulate the men. Not to mention the idiocy of the country, and this feudal backwater!"

"Feudal," to him, meant something frightful. "Feudal" and "medieval" were the epithets he employed to condemn something completely.

The failure of his diatribes to move us and their total lack of effect upon the village — where they were listened to with respectful indifference — disconcerted him no end. "The man does not exist who could move these clods." But, he soon began to understand — for he was an intelligent man, and therefore a good one — the kind of influence exercised over the village by Don Emmanuel, and he came to appreciate the effect of the priest's work in the village.

"This priest is not like the others," he announced. "He is, in fact, a saint."

"How do you know what the others are like," I asked. To which he answered:

"I can imagine."

In any case, he did not set foot inside the church nor did he miss an opportunity to parade his incredulity — though he always exempted Don Emmanuel from his scorning accusations. In the village, an unconscious expectancy began to build up, the anticipation of a kind of duel between my brother Lazarus and Don Emmanuel — in short, it was expected that Don Emmanuel would convert my brother. No one doubted but that in the end the priest would bring him into the fold. On his side, Lazarus was eager (he told me so himself, later) to go and hear Don Emmanuel, to see him and hear him in the church, to get to know him and to talk with him, so that he might learn the secret of his spiritual hold over our souls. And he let himself be coaxed to this end, so that finally — "out of curiosity," as he said — he went to hear the preacher.

"Now, this is something else again," he told me as soon as he came from hearing Don Emmanuel for the first time. "He's not like the others; still, he doesn't fool me, he's too intelligent to believe everything he must teach."

"You mean you think he's a hypocrite?"

"A hypocrite . . . no! But he has a job by which he must live."

As for me, my brother undertook to see that I read the books he brought me, and others which he urged me to buy.

"So your brother Lazarus wants you to read," Don Emmanuel queried. "Well, read, my daughter, read and make him happy by doing so. I know you will read only worthy books. Read even if only novels; they are as good as the books which deal with so-called 'reality.' You are better off reading than concerning yourself with village gossip and old wives' tales. Above all, though, you will do well to read devotional books which will bring contentment in life, a quiet, gentle contentment, and peace."

And he, did he enjoy such contentment?

It was about this time that our mother fell mortally sick and died. In her last days her one wish was that Don Emmanuel should convert Lazarus, whom she expected to see again in heaven, in some little corner among the stars from where they could see the lake and the mountain of Valverde de Lucerna. She felt she was going there now, to see God.

"You are not going anywhere," Don Emmanuel would tell her; "you are staying right here. Your body will remain here, in this land, and your soul also, in this house, watching and listening to your children though they do not see or hear you."

"But, Father," she said, "I am going to see God."

"God, my daughter, is all around us, and you will see Him from here, right from here. And all of us in Him, and He in all of us."

"God bless you," I whispered to him.

"The peace in which your mother dies will be her eternal life," he told me.

And, turning to my brother Lazarus: "Her heaven is to go on seeing you, and it is at this moment that she must be saved. Tell her you will pray for her."

"But —"

"But what? . . . Tell her you will pray for her, to whom you owe your life. And I know that once you promise her, you *will* pray, and I know that once you pray . . ."

My brother, his eyes filled with tears, drew near our dying mother and gave her his solemn promise to pray for her.

"And I, in heaven, will pray for you, for all of you," my mother responded. And then, kissing the crucifix and fixing her eyes on Don Emmanuel, she gave up her soul to God.

"Into Thy hands I commend my spirit," prayed the priest.

My brother and I stayed on in the house alone. What had happened at the time of my mother's death had established a bond between Lazarus and Don Emmanuel. The latter seemed even to neglect some of his charges, his patients and his other needy to look after my brother. In the afternoons, they would go for a stroll together, walking along the lake or toward the ruins, overgrown with ivy, of the old Cistercian abbey.

"He's an extraordinary man," Lazarus told me. "You know the story they tell of how there is a city at the bottom of the lake, submerged beneath the water, and that on Midsummer's Night at midnight the sound of its church bells can be heard . . ."

"Yes, a city 'feudal and medieval' . . ."

"And I believe," he went on, "that at the bottom of Don Emmanuel's soul there is a city, submerged and inundated, and that sometimes the sound of its bells can be heard . . ."

"Yes . . . And this city submerged in Don Emmanuel's soul, and perhaps — why not? — in yours as well, is certainly the cemetery of the souls of our ancestors, the ancestors of our Valverde de Lucerna . . . 'feudal and medieval!' "

In the end, my brother began going to Mass. He went regularly to hear Don Emmanuel. When it became known that he was prepared to comply with his annual duty of receiving Communion, that he would receive when the others received,

an intimate joy ran through the town, which felt that by this act he was restored to his people. The rejoicing was of such nature, moreover, so openhanded and honest, that Lazarus never did feel that he had been "vanquished" or "overcome."

The day of his Communion arrived; of Communion before the entire village, with the entire village. When it came time for my brother's turn, I saw Don Emmanuel — white as January snow on the mountain, and moving like the surface of the lake when it is stirred by the northeast wind — come up to him with the holy wafer in his hand, which trembled violently as it reached out to Lazarus's mouth; at that moment the priest had an instant of faintness and the wafer dropped to the ground. My brother himself recovered it and placed it in his mouth. The people saw the tears on Don Emmanuel's face, and everyone wept, saying: "What great love he bears!" And then, because it was dawn, a cock crowed.

On returning home I locked myself in with my brother; alone with him I put my arms around his neck and kissed him.

"Lazarus, Lazarus, what joy you have given us all today; the entire village, the living and the dead, and especially our mother. Did you see how Don Emmanuel wept for joy? What joy you have given us all!"

"It was for that reason that I did what I did," he answered me.

"For what? To give us pleasure? Surely you did it for your own sake, first of all; because of your conversion."

And then Lazarus, my brother, grown as pale and tremulous as Don Emmanuel when he was giving Communion, bade me sit down, in the very chair where our mother used to sit. He took a deep breath, and, in the intimate tone of a familiar and domestic confession, he told me:

"Angelita, the time has come when I must tell you the truth, the absolute truth, and I shall tell you because I must, because I cannot, I ought not, conceal it from you, and because, sooner or later, you are bound to intuit it anyway, if only halfway — which would be worse."

Thereupon, serenely and tranquilly, in a subdued voice, he recounted a tale that drowned me in a lake of sorrow. He told how Don Emmanuel had appealed to him, particularly during the walks to the ruins of the old Cistercian abbey, to set a good example, to avoid scandalizing the towns-people, to take part in the religious life of the community, to feign belief even if he did not feel any, to conceal his own ideas — all this without attempting in any way to catechize him, to instruct him in religion, or to effect a true conversion.

"But is it possible?" I asked in consternation.

"Possible and true. When I said to him: 'Is this you, the priest, who suggests I dissimulate?' he replied, hesitatingly: 'Dissimulate? Not at all! That is not dissimulation. "Dip your fingers in holy water, and you will end by believing," as someone said.' And I, gazing into his eyes, asked him: 'And you, celebrating the Mass, have you ended by believing?' He looked away and stared out at the lake, until his eyes filled with tears. And it was in this way that I came to understand his secret."

"Lazarus!" I cried out, incapable of another word.

At that moment the fool Blasillo came along our street, crying out his: "My God, my God, why hast Thou forsaken me?" And Lazarus shuddered, as if he had heard the voice of Don Emmanuel, or of Christ.

"It was then," my brother at length continued, "that I really understood his motives and his saintliness; for a saint he is, Sister, a true saint. In trying to convert me to his holy cause — for it is a holy cause, a most holy cause — he was not attempting to score a triumph, but rather was doing it to protect the peace, the happiness, the illusions, perhaps, of his charges. I understood that if he thus deceives them — if it *is* deceit — it is not for his own advantage. I submitted to his logic, — and that was my conversion.

"I shall never forget the day on which I said to him: 'But, Don Emmanuel, the truth, the truth, above all!'; and he, all atremble, whispered in my ear — though we were all alone in the middle of the countryside — 'The truth? The truth, Lazarus, is perhaps something so unbearable, so terrible, something so deadly, that simple people could not live with it!' "

" 'And why do you show me a glimpse of it now, here, as if we were in the confessional?' I asked. And he said: 'Because if I did not, I would be so tormented by it, so tormented, that I would finally shout it in the middle of the plaza, which I must never, never, never do . . . I am put here to give life to the souls of my charges, to make them happy, to make them dream they are immortal — and not to destroy them. The important thing is that they live sanely, in concord with each other, — and with the truth, with my truth, they could not live at all. Let them live. That is what the Church does, it lets them live. As for true religion, all religions are true as long as they give spiritual life to the people who profess them, as long as they console them for having been born only to die. And for each people the truest religion is their own, the religion that made them . . . And mine? Mine consists in consoling myself by consoling others, even though the consolation I give them is not ever mine.' I shall never forget his words."

"But then this Communion of yours has been a sacrilege," I dared interrupt, regretting my words as soon as I said them.

"Sacrilege? What about the priest who gave it to me? And his Masses?"

"What martyrdom!" I exclaimed.

"And now," said my brother, "there is one more person to console the people."

"To deceive them, you mean?" I said.

"Not at all," he replied, "but rather to confirm them in their faith."

"And they, the people, do they really believe, do you think?"

"About that, I know nothing! . . . They probably believe without trying, from force of habit, tradition. The important thing is not to stir them up. To let them live from their thin sentiments, without acquiring the torments of luxury. Blessed are the poor in spirit!"

"That then is the sentiment you have learned from Don Emmanuel. . . . And tell me, do you feel you have carried out your promise to our mother on her deathbed, when you promised to pray for her?"

"Do you think I *could* fail her? What do you take me for, sister? Do you think I would go back on my word, my solemn promise made at the hour of death to a mother?"

"I don't know. . . . You might have wanted to deceive her so she could die in peace."

"The fact is, though, that if I had not lived up to my promise, I would be totally miserable."

"And . . ."

"I carried out my promise and I have not neglected for a single day to pray for her."

"Only for her?"

"Well, now, for whom else?"

"For yourself! And now, for Don Emmanuel."

We parted and went to our separate rooms. I to weep through the night, praying for the conversion of my brother and of Don Emmanuel. And Lazarus, to what purpose, I know not.

From that day on I was fearful of finding myself alone with Don Emmanuel, whom I continued to aid in his pious works. And he seemed to sense my inner state and to guess at its cause. When at last I came to him in the confessional's penitential tribunal (who was the judge, and who the offender?) the two of us, he and I, bowed our heads in silence and began to cry. It was he, finally, Don Emmanuel, who broke the terrible silence, with a voice which seemed to issue from the tomb:

"Angelita, you have the same faith you had when you were ten, don't you? You believe, don't you?"

"I believe, Father."

"Then go on believing. And if doubts come to torment you, suppress them utterly, even to yourself. The main thing is to live . . ."

I summoned up courage, and dared to ask, trembling:

"But, Father, do you believe?"

For a brief moment he hesitated, and then, mastering himself, he said:

"I believe!"

"In what, Father, in what? Do you believe in the after life? Do you believe that in dying we do not die in every way, completely? Do you believe that we will see each other again, that we will love each other in a world to come? Do you believe in another life?"

The poor saint was sobbing.

"My child, leave off, leave off!"

Now, when I come to write this memoir, I ask myself: Why did he not deceive me? Why did he not deceive me as he deceived the others? Why did he afflict himself? Why could he not deceive himself, or why could he not deceive me? And I want to believe that he was afflicted because he could not deceive himself into deceiving me.

"And now," he said, "pray for me, for your brother, and for yourself — for all of us. We must go on living. And giving life."

And, after a pause:

"Angelita, why don't you marry?"

"You know why I do not."

"No, no; you must marry. Lazarus and I

will find you a suitor. For it would be good for you to marry, and rid yourself of these obsessions."

"Obsessions, Don Emmanuel?"

"I know well enough what I am saying. You should not torment yourself for the sake of others, for each of us has more than enough to do answering for himself."

"That it should be you, Don Emmanuel, who says this! That you should advise me to marry and answer for myself alone and not suffer over others! That it should be you!"

"Yes, you are right, Angelita. I am no longer sure of what I say. I am no longer sure of what I say since I began to confess to you. Only, one must go on living. Yes! One must live!"

And when I rose to leave the church, he asked me:

"Now, Angelita, in the name of the people, do you absolve me?"

I felt pierced by a mysterious and priestly prompting and said:

"In the name of the Father, the Son and the Holy Ghost, I absolve you, Father."

We quitted the church, and as I went out I felt the quickening of maternity within me.

My brother, now totally devoted to the work of Don Emmanuel, had become his closest and most zealous collaborator and companion. They were bound together, moreover, by their common secret. Lazarus accompanied the priest on his visits to the sick, and to schools, and he placed his resources at the disposition of the saintly man. A little more zeal, and he would have learned to help celebrate Mass. All the while he was sounding deeper in the unfathomable soul of of the priest.

"What manliness!" he exclaimed to me once. "Yesterday, as we walked along the lake he said: 'There lies my direst temp-tation.' When I interrogated him with my eyes, he went on: 'My poor father, who was close to ninety when he died, was tormented all his life, as he confessed to me himself, by a temptation to suicide, by an instinct to self-destruction which had come to him from a time before memory — from birth, from his *nation*, as he said — and was forced to fight against it always. And this fight grew to be his life. So as not to succumb to this temptation he was forced to take precautions, to guard his life. He told me of terrible episodes. His urge was a form of madness, — and I have inherited it. How that water beckons me in its deep quiet! ... an apparent quietude reflecting the sky like a mirror — and beneath it the hidden current! My life, Lazarus, is a kind of continual suicide, or a struggle against suicide, which is the same thing. ... Just so long as our people go on living!" And then he added: 'Here the river eddies to form a lake, so that later, flowing down the plateau, it may form into cascades, waterfalls, and torrents, hurling itself through gorges and chasms. Thus does life eddy in the village; and the temp-tation to suicide is the greater beside the still waters which at night reflect the stars, than it is beside the crashing falls which drive one back in fear. Listen, Lazarus, I have helped poor villagers to die well, ig-norant, illiterate villagers, who had scarce-ly ever been out of their village, and I have learned from their own lips, or divined it when they were silent, the real cause of their sickness unto death, and there at the head of their deathbed I have been able to see into the black abyss of their life-weariness. A weariness a thousand times worse than hunger! For our part, Lazarus, let us go on with our kind of suicide of working for the people, and let them dream their life as the lake dreams the heavens.'

"Another time," said my brother, "as we were coming back, we spied a country girl, a goatherd, standing erect on a height of the mountain slope overlooking the lake and she was singing in a voice fresher than its waters. Don Emmanuel took hold of me, and pointing to her said: 'Look, it's as though time had stopped, as though this country girl had always been there just as she is, singing in the way she is, and as though she would always be there, as she was before my consciousness began, as she will be when it is past. That girl is a part of nature — not of history — along with the rocks, the clouds, the trees, and the waters.' He has such a subtle feeling for nature, he infuses it with spirit!

"I shall not forget the day when snow was falling and he asked me: 'Have you ever seen a greater mystery, Lazarus, than the snow falling, and dying, in the lake, while a hood is laid upon the mountain?' "

Don Emmanuel had to moderate and temper my brother's zeal and his neophyte's rawness. As soon as he heard that Lazarus was going about inveighing against some of the popular superstitions he told him forcefully:

"Leave them alone! It's difficult enough making them understand where orthodox belief leaves off and where superstition begins. It's hard enough, especially for us. Leave them alone, then, as long as they get some comfort. . . . It's better for them to believe everything, even things that contradict one another, than to believe nothing. The idea that someone who believes too much ends by not believing in anything is a Protestant notion. Let us not protest! Protestation destroys contentment and peace."

My brother told me, too, about one moonlit night when they were returning to town along the lake (whose surface a mountain breeze was stirring, so that the moonbeams topped the whitecaps), Don Emmanuel turned to him and said:

"Look, the water is reciting the litany and saying: *ianua caeli, ora pro nobis;* gate of heaven, pray for us."

Two evanescent tears fell from his lashes to the grass, where the light of the full moon shone upon them like dew.

And time went hurrying by, and my brother and I began to notice that Don Emmanuel's spirits were failing, that he could no longer control completely the deep rooted sadness which consumed him; perhaps some treacherous illness was undermining his body and soul. In an effort to rouse his interest, Lazarus spoke to him of the good effect the organization of a type of Catholic agrarian syndicate would have.

"A syndicate?" Don Emmanuel repeated sadly. "A syndicate? And what is that? The Church is the only syndicate I know. And you have certainly heard 'My kingdom is not of this world.' Our kingdom, Lazarus, is not of this world . . ."

"And of the other?"

Don Emmanuel bowed his head:

"The other is here. Two kingdoms exist in this world. Or rather, the other world. . . . Ah, I don't really know what I'm saying. But as for the syndicate, that's a vestige from your days of 'progressivism.' No, Lazarus, no; religion does not exist to resolve the economic or political conflicts of this world, which God handed over to men for their disputes. Let men think and act as they will, let them console themselves for having been born, let them live as happily as possible in the illusion that all this has a purpose. I don't propose to advise the poor to submit to the rich, nor to suggest to the rich that they subordinate themselves to the poor; but rather to preach resignation in everyone, and charity toward everyone. For even the rich man must resign himself — to his riches, and to life; and the poor man must show charity — even to the rich. The Social Question? Ignore it, for it is none of our business. So, a new society is on the way, in which there will be neither rich nor poor, in which wealth will be justly divided, in which everything will belong to everyone — and so, what then? Won't this general well-being and comfort lead to even greater tedium and weariness of life? I know well enough that one of those chiefs of what they call the Social Revolution has already said that religion is the opium of the people. Opium . . . Opium . . . Yes, opium it is. We should give them opium, and help them sleep, and dream. I, myself, with my mad activity, give myself opium. And still I don't manage to sleep well, let alone dream well. . . . What a fearful nightmare! . . . I, too, can say, with the Divine Master: 'My soul is weary unto death.' No, Lazarus, no; no syndicates for us. If *they* organize them, well and good — they would be distracting themselves in that way. Let them play at syndicates, if that makes them happy."

The entire village began to realize that Don Emmanuel's spirit was weakening, that his strength was waning. His very voice — that miracle of a voice — acquired a kind of quaking. Tears came into his eyes for any reason whatever — or for no reason. Whenever he spoke to people about the other world, about the other life, he was compelled to pause at frequent intervals, and he would close his eyes. "It is a vision," people would say, "he has a vision of what lies ahead." At such moments, the fool Blasillo was the first to break into tears. He wept copiously these days, crying now more than he laughed, and even his laughter had the sound of tears.

The last Easter Week which Don Emmanuel was to celebrate among us, in this world, in this village of ours, arrived, and all the village sensed the impending end of tragedy. And how the words did strike home when for the last time Don Emmanuel cried out before us: "My God, my God, why hast Thou forsaken me?"! And when he repeated the words of the Lord to the Good Thief ("All thieves are good," Don Emmanuel used to tell us): "Tomorrow shalt thou be with me in Paradise." . . . ! And then, the last general Communion which our saint was to give! When he came to my brother to give him the Host — his hand steady this time —, just after the liturgical ". . . *in vitam aeternam*," he bent down and whispered to him: "There is no other life but this, no life more eternal . . . let them dream it eternal . . . let it be eternal for a few years . . ."

And when he came to me he said: "Pray, my child, pray for us all." And then, something so extraordinary happened that I carry it now in my heart as the greatest of mysteries: he bent over and said, in a voice which seemed to belong to the other world: ". . . and pray, too, for our Lord Jesus Christ."

I stood up, going weak as I did so, like a somnambulist. Everything around me seemed dream-like. And I thought: "Am I to pray, too, for the lake and the mountain?" And next: "Am I bewitched, then?" Home at last, I took up the crucifix my mother had held in her hands when she had given up her soul to God, and, gazing at it through my tears and recalling the "My God, my God, why hast Thou forsaken me?" of our two Christs, the one of this earth and the other of this village, I prayed: "Thy will be done on earth as it is in heaven," and then, "And lead us not into temptation. Amen." After this I turned to the statue of the Mater Dolorosa — her heart transfixed by seven swords — which had been my poor mother's most sorrowful comfort, and I prayed again: "Holy Mary, Mother of God, pray for us sinners, now and in the hour of our death. Amen." I had scarcely finished the prayer, when I asked myself: "Sinners? Sinners are we? And what is our sin, what is it?" And all day I brooded over the question.

The next day I presented myself before Don Emmanuel — Don Emmanuel now in the full sunset of his magnificent religiosity — and I said to him:

"Do you remember, my Father, years ago when I asked you a certain question you answered: 'That question you must not ask me; for I am ignorant; there are learned doctors of the Holy Mother Church who will know how to answer you?'"

"Do I remember? . . . Of course. And I remember I told you those were questions put to you by the Devil."

"Well, then, Father, I have come again, bedeviled, to ask you another question put to me by my Guardian Devil."

"Ask it."

"Yesterday, when you gave me Communion, you asked me to pray for all of us, and even for . . ."

"That's enough! . . . Go on."

"I arrived home and began to pray; when I came to the part 'Pray for us sinners, now and at the hour of our death,' a voice in me asked: 'Sinners? Sinners are we? And what is our sin?' What is our sin, Father?"

"Our sin?" he replied. "A great doctor of the Spanish Catholic Apostolic Church has already explained it; the great doctor of *Life is a Dream* has written 'The greatest sin of man is to have been born.' That, my child, is our sin; to have been born."

"Can it be atoned, Father?"

"Go and pray again. Pray once more for us sinners, now and at the hour of our death. . . . Yes, at length the dream is atoned . . . at length life is atoned . . . at length the cross of birth is expiated and atoned, and the drama comes to an end. . . . And as Calderón said, to have done good, to have feigned good, even in dreams, is something which is not lost."

The hour of his death arrived at last. The entire village saw it come. And he made it his finest lesson. For he would not die alone or at rest. He died preaching to his people in the church. But first, before being carried to the church (his paralysis made it impossible for him to move), he summoned Lazarus and me to his bedside. Alone there, the three of us together, he said:

"Listen to me: watch over these poor sheep; find some comfort for them in living, and let them believe what I could not. And Lazarus, when your hour comes, die as I die, as Angela will die, in the arms of the Holy Mother Church, Catholic, Apostolic, and Roman; that is to say, of the Holy Mother Church of Valverde de Lucerna. And now, farewell; until we never meet again, for this dream of life is coming to an end . . ."

"Father, Father," I cried out.

"Do not grieve, Angela, only go on praying for all sinners, for all who have been born. Let them dream, let them dream . . . O, what a longing I have to sleep, to sleep, sleep without end, sleep for all eternity, and never dream! Forgetting this dream! . . . When they go to bury me, let it be in a box made from the six planks I cut from the old walnut tree — poor old tree! — in whose shade I played as a child, when I began the dream. . . . In those days, I did really believe in life everlasting. That is to say, it seems to me now that I believed. For a child, to believe is the same as to dream. And for a people, too. . . . You'll find those six planks I cut at the foot of the bed."

He was seized by a sudden fit of choking, and then, composing himself once more, he went on:

"You will recall that when we prayed together, animated by a common sentiment, a community of spirit, and we came to the final verse of the Creed, you will remember that I would fall silent . . . When the Israelites were coming to the end of their wandering in the desert, the Lord told Aaron and Moses that because they had not believed in Him they would not set foot in the Promised Land with their people; and he bade them climb the heights of Mount Hor, where Moses ordered Aaron stripped of his garments, so that Aaron died there, and then Moses went up from the plains of Moab to Mount Nebo, to the top of Pisgah, looking into Jericho, and the Lord showed him all of the land promised to His people, but said to him: 'You will not go there.' And there Moses died, and no one knew his grave. And he left Joshua to be chief in his place. You, Lazarus, must be my Joshua, and if you can make the sun stand still, make it stop, and never mind progress. Like Moses, I have seen the face of God — our supreme dream — face to face, and as you already know, and as the Scripture says, he who sees God's face, he who sees the eyes of the dream, the eyes with which He looks at us, will die inexorably and forever. And therefore, do not let our people, so long as they live, look into the face of God. Once dead, it will no longer matter, for then they will see nothing . . ."

"Father, Father, Father," I cried again.

And he said:

"Angela, you must pray always, so that all sinners may go on dreaming, until they die, of the resurrection of the flesh and the life everlasting . . ."

I was expecting "and who knows it might be . . ." But instead, Don Emmanuel had another attack of coughing.

"And now," he finally went on, "and now, in the hour of my death, it is high time to have me brought, in this very chair, to the church, so that I may take leave there of my people, who await me."

He was carried to the church and brought, in his armchair, into the chancel, to the foot of the altar. In his hands he held a crucifix. My brother and I stood close to him, but the fool Blasillo wanted to stand even closer. He wanted to grasp Don Emmanuel by the hand, so that he could kiss it. When some of the people nearby tried

to stop him, Don Emmanuel rebuked them and said:

"Let him come closer. . . . Come, Blasillo, give me your hand."

The fool cried for joy. And then Don Emmanuel spoke:

"I have very few words left, my children; I scarcely feel I have strength enough left to die. And then, I have nothing new to tell you, either. I have already said everything I have to say. Live with each other in peace and contentment, in the hope that we will all see each other again some day, in that other Valverde de Lucerna up there among the nighttime stars, the stars which the lake reflects over the image of the reflected mountain. And pray, pray to the Most Blessed Mary, and to our Lord. Be good . . . that is enough. Forgive me whatever wrong I may have done you inadvertently or unknowingly. After I give you my blessing, let us pray together, let us say the Paternoster, the Ave Maria, the Salve, and the Creed."

Then he gave his blessing to the whole village, with the crucifix held in his hand, while the women and children cried and even some of the men wept softly. Almost at once the prayers were begun. Don Emmanuel listened to them in silence, his hand in the hand of Blasillo the fool, who began to fall asleep to the sound of the praying. First the Paternoster, with its "Thy will be done on earth as it is in heaven;" then the Ave Maria, with its "Pray for us sinners, now and in the hour of our death;" followed by the Salve, with its "mourning and weeping in this vale of tears;" and finally, the Creed. On reaching "The resurrection of the flesh and life everlasting" the people sensed that their saint had yielded up his soul to God. It was not necessary to close his eyes even, for he died with them closed. When an attempt was made to wake Blasillo, it was found that he, too, had fallen asleep in the Lord forever. So that later there were two bodies to be buried.

The village immediately repaired en masse to the house of the saint to carry away holy relics, to divide up pieces of his garments among themselves, to carry off whatever they could find as a memento of the blessed martyr. My brother preserved his breviary, between the pages of which he discovered a carnation, dried as in a herbarium and mounted on a piece of paper, and upon the paper a cross and a certain date.

No one in the village seemed able to believe that Don Emmanuel was dead; everyone expected to see him — perhaps some of them did — taking his daily walk along the side of the lake, his figure mirrored in the water, or silhouetted against the background of the mountain. They continued to hear his voice, and they all visited his grave, around which a veritable cult sprang up, old women "possessed by devils" came to touch the cross of walnut, made with his own hands from the tree which had yielded the six planks of his casket.

The ones who least of all believed in his death were my brother and I. Lazarus carried on the tradition of the saint, and he began to compile a record of the priest's words. Some of the conversations in this account of mine were made possible by his notes.

"It was he," said my brother, "who made me into a new man. I was a true Lazarus whom he raised from the dead. He gave me faith."

"Ah, faith . . ."

"Yes, faith, faith in the charity of life, in life's joy. It was he who cured me of my delusion of 'progress,' of my belief in its political implications. For there are, Angela, two types of dangerous and harmful men: those who, convinced of life beyond the grave, of the resurrection of the flesh, torment other people — like the inquisitors they are — so that they will despise this life as a transitory thing and

work for the other life; and then, there are those who, believing only in this life . . ."

"Like you, perhaps . . ."

"Yes, and like Don Emmanuel. Believing only in this world, this second group looks forward to some vague future society and exerts every effort to prevent the populace finding consoling joy from belief in another world . . ."

"And so . . ."

"The people should be allowed to live with their illusion."

The poor priest who came to the parish to replace Don Emmanuel found himself overwhelmed in Valverde de Lucerna by the memory of the saint, and he put himself in the hands of my brother and myself for guidance. He wanted only to follow in the footsteps of the saint. And my brother told him: "Very little theology, Father, very little theology. Religion, religion, religion." Listening to him, I smiled to myself, wondering if this was not a kind of theology, too.

I had by now begun to fear for my poor brother. From the time Don Emmanuel died it could scarcely be said that he lived. Daily he went to the priest's tomb; for hours on end he stood gazing into the lake. He was filled with nostalgia for deep, abiding peace.

"Don't stare into the lake so much," I begged him.

"Don't worry. It's not this lake which draws me, nor the mountains. Only, I cannot live without his help."

"And the joy of living, Lazarus, what about the joy of living?"

"That's for others. Not for those of us who have seen God's face, those of us on whom the Dream of Life has gazed with His eyes."

"What; are you preparing to go and see Don Emmanuel?"

"No, sister, no. Here at home now, between the two of us, the whole truth — bitter as it may be, bitter as the sea into which the sweet waters of our lake flow — the whole truth for you, who are so set against it . . .''

No, no, Lazarus. You are wrong. Your truth is not the truth.''

"It's my truth."

"Yours, perhaps, but surely not . . .''

"His, too."

"No, Lazarus. Not now, it isn't. Now, he must believe otherwise; now he must believe . . .''

"Listen, Angela, once Don Emmanuel told me that there are truths which, though one reveals them to oneself, must be kept from others; and I told him that telling me was the same as telling himself. And then he said, he confessed to me, that he thought that more than one of the great saints, perhaps the very greatest himself, had died without believing in the other life."

"Is it possible?''

"All too possible! And now, sister, you must be careful that here, among the people, no one even suspects our secret . . .''

"Suspect it?'' I cried in amazement. "Why even if I were to try, in a fit of madness, to explain it to them, they wouldn't understand it. The people do not understand your words, they understand your actions much better. To try and explain all this to them would be like reading some pages from Saint Thomas Aquinas to eight-year-old children, in Latin.''

"All the better. In any case, when I am gone, pray for me and for him and for all of us.''

At length, his own time came. A sickness which had been eating away at his robust nature seemed to flare with the death of Don Emmanuel.

"I don't so much mind dying,'' he said to me in his last days, "as the fact that with me another piece of Don Emmanuel dies too. The remainder of him must live on with you. Until, one day, even we dead will die forever.''

When he lay in the throes of death, the people of the village came in to bid him farewell (as is customary in our towns) and they commended his soul to the care of Don Emmanuel the Good, Martyr. My brother said nothing to them; he had nothing more to say. He had already said everything there was to say. He had become a link between the two Valverde de Lucernas — the one at the bottom of the lake and the one reflected in its surface. He was already one more of us who had died of life, and, in his way, one more of our saints.

I was desolate, more than desolate; but I was, at least, among my own people, in my own village. Now, having lost my Saint Emmanuel, the father of my soul, and my own Lazarus, my more than carnal brother, my spiritual brother, now it is I realize that I have aged. But, have I really lost them then? Have I grown old? Is my death approaching?

I must live! And he taught me to live, he taught us to live, to feel life, to feel the meaning of life, to merge with the soul of the mountain, with the soul of the lake, with the soul of the village, to lose ourselves in them so as to remain in them forever. He taught me by his life to lose myself in the life of the people of my village, and I no longer felt the passing of the hours, and the days, and the years, any more than I felt the passage of the water in the lake. It began to seem that my life would always be thus. I no longer felt myself growing old. I no longer lived in myself, but in my people, and my people lived in me. I tried to speak as they spoke, as they spoke without trying. I went into the street — it was the one highway — and, since I knew everyone, I lived in them and forgot myself (while, on the other hand, in Madrid, where I went once with my brother, I had felt a terrible loneliness, since I knew no one, and had been tortured by the sight of so many unknown people).

Now, as I write this memoir, this confession of my experience with saintliness, with a saint, I am of the opinion that Don Emmanuel the Good, my Don Emmanuel, and my brother, too, died believing they did not believe, but that, without believing in their belief, they actually believed, with resignation and in desolation.

But why, I have asked myself repeatedly, did not Don Emmanuel attempt to convert my brother deceitfully, with a lie, pretending to be a believer himself without being one? And I have finally come to think that Don Emmanuel realized he would not be able to delude him, that with him a fraud would not do, that only through the truth, with his truth, would he be able to convert him; that he knew he would accomplish nothing if he attempted to enact the comedy — the tragedy, rather — which he played out for the benefit of the people. And thus did he win him over, in effect, to his pious fraud; thus did he win him over to the cause of life with the truth of death. And thus did he win me, who never permitted anyone to see through his divine, his most saintly, game. For I believed then, and I believe now, that God — as part of I know not what sacred and inscrutable purpose — caused them to believe they were unbelievers. And that at the moment of their passing, perhaps, the blindfold was removed.

And I, do I believe?

As I write this — here in my mother's old house, and I past my fiftieth year and my memories growing as dim and blanched as my hair — outside it is snowing, snowing upon the lake, snowing upon the mountain, upon the memory of my father, the stranger, upon the memory of my mother, my brother Lazarus, my people, upon the memory of my Saint Emmanuel, and even on the memory of the poor fool Blasillo, my Saint Blasillo — and may he help me in heaven! The snow effaces corners and blots out shadows, for even in the night it shines and illuminates. Truly, I do not know what is true and what is false, nor what I saw and what I merely dreamt — or rather, what I dreamt and what I merely saw —, nor what I really knew or what I merely believed true. Neither do I know whether or not I am transferring to this paper, white as the snow outside, my consciousness, for it to remain in writing, leaving me without it. But why, any longer, cling to it?

Do I really understand any of it? Do I really believe in any of it? Did what I am writing about here actually take place, and did it take place in just the way I tell it? Is it possible for such things to happen? Is it possible that all this is more than a dream dreamed within another dream? Can it be that I, Angela Carballino, a woman in her fifties, am the only one in this village to be assailed by far-fetched thoughts, thoughts unknown to everyone else? And the others, those around me, do they believe? And what does it mean, to believe? At least they go on living. And now they believe in Saint Emmanuel the Good, Martyr, who, with no hope of immortality for himself, preserved their hope in it.

It appears that our most illustrious bishop, who set in motion the process for beatifying our saint from Valverde de Lucerna, is intent on writing an account of Don Emmanuel's life, something which would serve as a guide for the perfect parish priest, and with this end in mind he is gathering information of every sort. He has repeatedly solicited information from me; more than once he has come to see me; and I have supplied him with all sorts of facts. But I have never revealed the tragic secret of Don Emmanuel and my brother. And it is curious that he has never suspected. I trust that what I have set down here will never come to his knowledge. For, all temporal authorities are to be avoided; I fear all authorities on this earth — even when they are church authorities.

But this is an end to it. Let its fate be what it will . . .

How, you ask, did this document, this memoir of Angela Carballino fall into my hands? That, reader, is something I must keep secret. I have transcribed it for you just as it is written, just as it came to me, with only a few, a very few editorial emendations. It recalls to you other things I have written? This fact does not gainsay its objectivity, its originality. Moreover, for all I know, perhaps I created real, actual beings, independent of me, beyond my control, characters with immortal souls. For all I know, Augusto Perez in my novel *Mist*[2] was right when he claimed to be more real, more objective than I myself, who had thought to have invented him. As for the reality of this Saint Emmanuel the Good, Martyr — as he is revealed to me by his disciple and spiritual daughter Angela Carballino — of his reality it has not occurred to me to doubt. I believe in it more than the saint himself did. I believe in it more than I do in my own reality.

And now, before I bring this epilogue to a close, I wish to recall to your mind, patient reader, the ninth verse of the Epistle of the forgotten Apostle, Saint Judas — what power in a name! — where we are told how my heavenly patron, St. Michael Archangel (Michael means "Who such as

2. In the denouement of *Mist*, the protagonist Augusto Perez turns on Unamuno, and tells him that he, a creation of human thought and genius, is more real than his author, a product of blind animality.

God?" and archangel means archmessenger) disputed with the Devil (Devil means accuser, prosecutor,) over the body of Moses, and would not allow him to carry it off as a prize, to damnation. Instead, he told the Devil: "May the Lord rebuke thee." And may he who wishes to understand, understand!

I would like also, since Angela Carballino injected her own feelings into her narrative — I don't know how it could have been otherwise — to comment on her statement to the effect that if Don Emmanuel and his disciple Lazarus had confessed their convictions to the people, they, the people, would not have understood. Nor, I should like to add, would they have believed the pair. They would have believed in their works and not their words. And works stand by themselves, and need no words to back them up. In a village like Valverde de Lucerna one makes one's confession by one's conduct.

And as for faith, the people scarce know what it is, and care less.

I am well aware of the fact that no action takes place in this narrative, this *novelistic* narrative, if you will — the novel is, after all, the most intimate, the truest history, so that I scarcely understand why some people are outraged to have the Bible called a novel, when such a designation actually sets it above some mere chronicle or other. In short, nothing happens. But I hope that this is because everything that takes place happens, and, instead of coming to pass, and passing away, remains forever, like the lakes and the mountains and the blessed simple souls fixed firmly beyond faith and despair, the blessed souls who, in the lakes and the mountains, outside history, in their divine novel, take refuge.

For Consideration

1. What is your initial conception of Don Emmanuel, based on the opening paragraph?

2. What does Angela hope to gain from Don Emmanuel when she returns to Valverde de Lucerna from the convent?

3. Don Emmanuel is, early in the account, explicitly compared to Jesus. How extensive is the similarity? What characteristic of Don Emmanuel most forcefully promotes the comparison?

4. What are the initial "clues" about the "secret" of Don Emmanuel? Why does the narrator tell of the secret before telling you what it is? Is this narrative device effective? Is it annoying? The narrator describes Don Emmanuel's "secret" and its bearing on his role as a priest "as if a caravan crossing the desert lost its leader as they approached the goal of their trek, whereupon his people lifted him on their shoulders to bring his lifeless body into the promised land." To what is this passage an allusion? What is its significance?

5. Don Emmanuel is said to have "fled relentlessly from idleness and solitude." Later he admits that "solitude would crush my soul." Why is this conflict so intense? What value is traditionally given to solitude and meditation in the priestly role?

6. What are the "new" values that Lazarus introduces into the village life? Why do the villagers anticipate a "duel" between Lazarus and Don Emmanuel? Immediately after Lazarus receives Communion the first time, a cock crows. To what incident does this allude? What does it mean here?

7. The story, in the title and elsewhere, contains implicit definitions of "saintliness." What characteristics are traditionally attached to the word? What is Lazarus' view of Don Emmanuel's sainthood?

8. How does the relationship between Don Emmanuel and Angela change in the story? Do they reverse roles or simply assume different ones?

9. Isolate the bases for and characteristics of Don Emmanuel's priestly role. Why does he continue to minister? What, for him, is the role of religion? What does he mean, in saying to Angela, "Pray for us all . . . pray, too, for our Lord Jesus Christ"?

10. What is the significance of names in the story? (Lazarus? Angela? Emmanuel?) In what sense has Don Emmanuel given Lazarus faith?

11. What is the significance of the lake in the story? What does it symbolize?

12. Why, at the end of the story, does the author step in and speak to his readers? Does the action add credibility or detract from it? Does it emphasize or lessen the importance of Don Emmanuel's secret?

tone and irony

In the previous section we considered the two narrators of "Saint Emmanuel the Good, Martyr": the sympathetic, involved participant, Angela, and the more distant, more objective author, Unamuno. In describing the two narrators in this way we are describing the **tone** of the narrative of each, the kind of attitude each brings to the subject. Similarly, when we speak of the tone of a story we refer to the author's attitude toward the subject — or at least the attitude that we, as readers, perceive.

The tone of a story should be kept distinct from the attitudes and emotions of characters within the story. Malamud's Leo Finkle in "The Magic Barrel" is intense and serious, almost humorless in his pursuit of an appropriate mate. But the tone of the story is much lighter; Malamud depicts his protagonist sympathetically, but with enough humor to poke fun at some of his foibles. In "The Maypole of Merry Mount," the tone of the story stands somewhere between the extreme merrymaking of the revelers in the forest and the excessive harshness of the Puritan intruders. The author's attitude is revealed most clearly in his sympathetic treatment of the Lord and Lady of the May, whose love seems deeper than the frivolity of the revelers and much more humane than the cold dogmatism of the Puritans.

In perceiving tone and attitude, both of characters and of the author, we must be alert to the possibilities of **irony**. Broadly speaking, actions, speech, and situations are either straightforward or ironic. They either mean what they appear to mean, or something different or opposite. Irony adds interest and complexity for it enables the artist to portray an action or situation in one light while implying the possibility of quite a different interpretation.

Irony in fiction is of three types: verbal irony, situational irony, and dramatic irony. A character who says one thing but means another has engaged in verbal irony. Near the end of "Saint Emmanuel the Good, Martyr," Lazarus comments that St. Emmanuel "gave me faith." Lazarus is not referring to religious faith in any conventional sense, and though he goes on to describe the "faith" he has, the statement itself is highly ironic. The final lines of "Hills Like White Elephants" are the girl's affirmation, " 'I feel fine . . . There's nothing wrong with me. I feel fine.' " The reader knows, however, that the statement is far from true; most of the story shows us how upset she is.

Situational irony is apparent in action or circumstances which appear to mean one thing but mean another. The story of St. Emmanuel is filled with situational irony for the priest consistently appears conventionally pious while being tormented by the loss of key elements of his faith. The end of "The Magic Barrel" presents another good example. Malamud describes the excitement and hope of Leo Finkle as he meets the young girl whom he has come to love through a picture:

> She waited uneasily and shyly. From afar he saw that her eyes — clearly her father's — were filled with desperate innocence. He pictured, in her, his own redemption. Violins and lit candles revolved in the sky. Leo ran forward with flowers outthrust.

The sense of hope and the anticipation of joy is, however, effectively and ironically undercut by Malamud in the final words of the story. He describes the girl's father, Salzman, who, "leaning against a wall, chanted prayers for the dead." The juxtaposition of the hopeful union and the prayers for the dead confirms that we should not take the final event at face value.

In some stories the reader may know the reality of a situation before or more fully than a character does, and this is termed dramatic irony. In "Revelation," the principal character, Mrs. Turpin, sees herself as a superior individual: pious, devout, properly discriminating; the reader, however, begins to understand the true stature of Mrs. Turpin before she does and is thus better prepared for the accurate "revelation" of her character at the end. Each type of irony adds to the complexity of a story because it forces the reader to understand both the surface meaning of conversation or action and the more accurate meaning beneath the surface.

James Thurber's "Mr. Preble Gets Rid of His Wife" is a short, witty piece whose effectiveness is largely a result of the light and surprising tone with which the story is told.

As suggested above, Flannery O'Connor's "Revelation" reveals the way irony is used to counteract surface attitudes and ideas. In the process it reveals some key distinctions between the attitudes of a character and the attitudes of the author. Mrs. Turpin believes herself pious and superior; O'Connor frequently undercuts that view, however, and lets us see the real Mrs. Turpin as a result.

In Albert Camus' "The Guest" irony is pervasive. From the title to the final line, we are reminded that actions and situations do not always mean what they appear to mean. In the world of Camus' story, actions motivated by concern and good will may result in a death threat, as they do for the principal character Daru.

JAMES THURBER (1894—1961)
Mr. Preble Gets Rid of His Wife

Mr. Preble was a plump middle-aged lawyer in Scarsdale. He used to kid with his stenographer about running away with him. "Let's run away together," he would say, during a pause in dictation. "All righty," she would say.

One rainy Monday afternoon, Mr. Preble was more serious about it than usual.

"Let's run away together," said Mr. Preble.

"All righty," said his stenographer. Mr. Preble jingled the keys in his pocket and looked out the window.

"My wife would be glad to get rid of me," he said.

"Would she give you a divorce?" asked the stenographer.

"I don't suppose so," he said. The stenographer laughed.

"You'd have to get rid of your wife," she said.

Mr. Preble was unusually silent at dinner that night. About half an hour after coffee, he spoke without looking up from his paper.

"Let's go down in the cellar," Mr. Preble said to his wife.

"What for?" she said, not looking up from her book.

"Oh, I don't know," he said. "We never go down in the cellar any more. The way we used to."

"We never did go down in the cellar that I remember," said Mrs. Preble. "I could rest easy the balance of my life if I never went down in the cellar." Mr. Preble was silent for several minutes.

"Supposing I said it meant a whole lot to me," began Mr. Preble.

"What's come over you?" his wife demanded. "It's cold down there and there is absolutely nothing to do."

"We could pick up pieces of coal," said Mr. Preble. "We might get up some kind of a game with pieces of coal."

"I don't want to," said his wife. "Anyway, I'm reading."

"Listen," said Mr. Preble, rising and walking up and down. "Why won't you come down in the cellar? You can read down there, as far as that goes."

"There isn't a good enough light down there," she said, "and anyway, I'm not going to go down in the cellar. You may as well make up your mind to that."

"Gee whiz!" said Mr. Preble, kicking at the edge of a rug. "Other people's wives go down in the cellar. Why is it you never want to do anything? I come home worn out from the office and you won't even go down in the cellar with me. God knows it isn't very far — it isn't as if I was asking you to go to the movies or some place."

"I don't want to *go!*" shouted Mrs. Preble. Mr. Preble sat down on the edge of a davenport.

"All right, all *right*," he said. He picked up the newspaper again. "I wish you'd let me tell you more about it. It's — kind of a surprise."

"Will you quit harping on that subject?" asked Mrs. Preble.

"Listen," said Mr. Preble, leaping to his feet. "I might as well tell you the truth instead of beating around the bush. I want to get rid of you so I can marry my stenographer. Is there anything especially wrong about that? People do it every day. Love is something you can't control ——"

"We've been all over that," said Mrs. Preble. "I'm not going to go all over that again."

"I just wanted you to know how things are," said Mr. Preble. "But you have to take everything so literally. Good Lord, do you suppose I really wanted to go down in the cellar and make up some silly game with pieces of coal?"

"I never believed that for a minute," said Mrs. Preble. "I knew all along you wanted to get me down there and bury me."

"You can say that now — after I told you," said Mr. Preble. "But it would never have occurred to you if I hadn't."

"You didn't tell me; I got it out of you," said Mrs. Preble. "Anyway, I'm always two steps ahead of what you're thinking."

"You're never within a mile of what I'm thinking," said Mr. Preble.

"Is that so? I knew you wanted to bury me the minute you set foot in this house tonight." Mrs. Preble held him with a glare.

"Now that's just plain damn exaggeration," said Mr. Preble, considerably annoyed. "You knew nothing of the sort. As a matter of fact, I never thought of it till just a few minutes ago."

"It was in the back of your mind," said Mrs. Preble. "I suppose this filing woman put you up to it."

"You needn't get sarcastic," said Mr. Preble. "I have plenty of people to file without having her file. She doesn't know anything about this. She isn't in on it. I was going to tell her you had gone to visit some friends and fell over a cliff. She wants me to get a divorce."

"That's a laugh," said Mrs. Preble. "*That's* a laugh. You may bury me, but you'll never get a divorce."

"She knows that! I told her that," said Mr. Preble. "I mean — I told her I'd never get a divorce."

"Oh, you probably told her about burying me, too," said Mrs. Preble.

"That's not true," said Mr. Preble, with dignity. "That's between you and me. I was never going to tell a soul."

"You'd blab it to the whole world; don't tell me," said Mrs. Preble. "I know you." Mr. Preble puffed at his cigar.

"I wish you were buried now and it was all over with," he said.

"Don't you suppose you would get caught, you crazy thing?" she said. "They always get caught. Why don't you go to bed? You're just getting yourself all worked up over nothing."

"I'm not going to bed," said Mr. Preble. "I'm going to bury you in the cellar. I've got my mind made up to it. I don't know how I could make it any plainer."

"Listen," cried Mrs. Preble, throwing her book down, "will you be satisfied and shut up if I go down in the cellar? Can I have a little peace if I go down in the cellar? Will you let me alone then?"

"Yes," said Mr. Preble. "But you spoil it by taking that attitude."

"Sure, sure, I always spoil everything. I stop reading right in the middle of a chapter. I'll never know how the story comes out — but that's nothing to you."

"Did I make you start reading the book?" asked Mr. Preble. He opened the cellar door. "Here, you go first."

"Brrr," said Mrs. Preble, starting down the steps. "It's *cold* down here! You *would* think of this, at this time of year! Any other husband would have buried his wife in the summer."

"You can't arrange those things just whenever you want to," said Mr. Preble. "I didn't fall in love with this girl till late fall."

"Anybody else would have fallen in love with her long before that. She's been around for years. Why is it you always let other men get in ahead of you? Mercy, but it's dirty down here! What have you got there?"

"I was going to hit you over the head with this shovel," said Mr. Preble.

"You were, huh?" said Mrs. Preble.

"Well, get that out of your mind. Do you want to leave a great big clue right here in the middle of everything where the first detective that comes snooping around will find it? Go out in the street and find some piece of iron or something — something that doesn't belong to you."

"Oh, all right," said Mr. Preble. "But there won't be any piece of iron in the street. Women always expect to pick up a piece of iron anywhere."

"If you look in the right place you'll find it," said Mrs. Preble. "And don't be gone long. Don't you dare stop in at the cigarstore. I'm not going to stand down here in this cold cellar all night and freeze."

"All right," said Mr. Preble. "I'll hurry."

"And shut that *door* behind you!" she screamed after him. "Where were you born — in a barn?"

For Consideration

1. The light tone of this piece is juxtaposed against the "serious" subject of a man trying to get rid of his wife. What is the effect of this juxtaposition?

2. What feelings and responses dominate the relationship between the Prebles? What is Mrs. Preble's attitude toward her husband's attempt to get rid of her? Is this in any sense a "typical" couple in modern society? In what ways?

FLANNERY O'CONNOR (1925—1964)

Revelation

The doctor's waiting room, which was very small, was almost full when the Turpins entered and Mrs. Turpin, who was very large, made it look even smaller by her presence. She stood looming at the head of the magazine table set in the center of it, a living demonstration that the room was inadequate and ridiculous. Her little bright black eyes took in all the patients as she sized up the seating situation There was one vacant chair and a place on the sofa occupied by a blond child in a dirty blue romper who should have been told to move over and make room for the lady. He was five or six, but Mrs. Turpin saw at once that no one was going to tell him to move over. He was slumped down in the seat, his arms idle at his sides and his eyes idle in his head; his nose ran unchecked.

Mrs. Turpin put a firm hand on Claud's shoulder and said in a voice that included anyone who wanted to listen, "Claud, you sit in that chair there," and gave him a push down into the vacant one. Claud was florid and bald and sturdy, somewhat shorter than Mrs. Turpin, but he sat down as if he were accustomed to doing what she told him to.

Mrs. Turpin remained standing. The only man in the room besides Claud was a lean stringy old fellow with a rusty hand spread out on each knee, whose eyes were closed as if he were asleep or dead or pretending to be so as not to get up and offer her his seat. Her gaze settled agreeably on a well-dressed gray-haired lady whose eyes met hers and whose expression said: if that child belonged to me, he would have some manners and move over — there's plenty of room there for you and him too.

Claud looked up with a sigh and made as if to rise.

"Sit down," Mrs. Turpin said. "You know you're not supposed to stand on that leg. He has an ulcer on his leg," she explained.

Claud lifted his foot onto the magazine table and rolled his trouser leg up to reveal a purple swelling on a plump marble-white calf.

"My!" the pleasant lady said. "How did you do that?"

"A cow kicked him," Mrs. Turpin said.

"Goodness!" said the lady.

Claud rolled his trouser leg down.

"Maybe the little boy would move over," the lady suggested, but the child did not stir.

"Somebody will be leaving in a minute," Mrs. Turpin said. She could not understand why a doctor — with as much money as they made charging five dollars a day to just stick their head in the hospital door and look at you — couldn't afford a decent-sized waiting room. This one was hardly bigger than a garage. The table was cluttered with limp-looking magazines and at one end of it there was a big green glass ash tray full of cigarette butts and cotton wads with little blood spots on them. If she had had anything to do with the running of the place, that would have been emptied every so often. There were no chairs against the wall at the head of the room. It had a rectangular-shaped panel in it that permitted a view of the office where the nurse came and went and the secretary listened to the radio. A plastic fern in a gold pot sat in the opening and trailed its fronds down almost to the floor. The radio was softly playing gospel music.

Just then the inner door opened and a nurse with the highest stack of yellow hair Mrs. Turpin had ever seen put her face in the crack and called for the next patient. The woman sitting beside Claud grasped the two arms of her chair and hoisted herself up; she pulled her dress free from her legs and lumbered through the door where the nurse had disappeared.

Mrs. Turpin eased into the vacant chair, which held her tight as a corset. "I wish I could reduce," she said, and rolled her eyes and gave a comic sigh.

"Oh, *you* aren't fat," the stylish lady said.

"Ooooo I am too," Mrs. Turpin said. "Claud he eats all he wants to and never weighs over one hundred and seventy-five pounds, but me I just look at something good to eat and I gain some weight," and her stomach and shoulders shook with laughter. "You can eat all you want to, can't you, Claud?" she asked, turning to him.

Claud only grinned.

"Well, as long as you have such a good disposition," the stylish lady said, "I don't think it makes a bit of difference what size you are. You just can't beat a good disposition."

Next to her was a fat girl of eighteen or nineteen, scowling into a thick blue book which Mrs. Turpin saw was entitled *Human Development*. The girl raised her head and directed her scowl at Mrs. Turpin as if she did not like her looks. She appeared annoyed that anyone should speak while she tried to read. The poor girl's face was blue with acne and Mrs. Turpin thought how pitiful it was to have a face like that at that age. She gave the girl a friendly smile but the girl only scowled the harder. Mrs. Turpin herself was fat but she had always had good skin, and, though

she was forty-seven years old, there was not a wrinkle in her face except around her eyes from laughing too much.

Next to the ugly girl was the child, still in exactly the same position, and next to him was a thin leathery old woman in a cotton print dress. She and Claud had three sacks of chicken feed in their pump house that was in the same print. She had seen from the first that the child belonged with the old woman. She could tell by the way they sat — kind of vacant and white-trashy, as if they would sit there until Doomsday if nobody called and told them to get up. And at right angles but next to the well-dressed pleasant lady was a lank-faced woman who was certainly the child's mother. She had on a yellow sweat shirt and wine-colored slacks, both gritty-looking, and the rims of her lips were stained with snuff. Her dirty yellow hair was tied behind with a little piece of red paper ribbon. Worse than niggers any day, Mrs. Turpin thought.

The gospel hymn playing was, "When I looked up and He looked down," and Mrs. Turpin, who knew it, supplied the last line mentally, "And wona these days I know I'll we-eara crown."

Without appearing to, Mrs. Turpin always noticed people's feet. The well-dressed lady had on red and gray suede shoes to match her dress. Mrs. Turpin had on her good black patent leather pumps. The ugly girl had on Girl Scout shoes and heavy socks. The old woman had on tennis shoes and the white-trashy mother had on what appeared to be bedroom slippers, black straw with gold braid threaded through them — exactly what you would have expected her to have on.

Sometimes at night when she couldn't go to sleep, Mrs. Turpin would occupy herself with the question of who she would have chosen to be if she couldn't have been herself. If Jesus had said to her before he made her, "There's only two places available for you. You can either be a nigger or white-trash," what would she have said? "Please, Jesus, please," she would have said, "just let me wait until there's another place available," and he would have said, "No, you have to go right now and I have only those two places so make up your mind." She would have wiggled and squirmed and begged and pleaded but it would have been no use and finally she would have said, "All right, make me a nigger then — but that don't mean a trashy one." And he would have made her a neat clean respectable Negro woman, herself but black.

Next to the child's mother was a red-headed youngish woman, reading one of the magazines and working a piece of chewing gum, hell for leather, as Claud would say. Mrs. Turpin could not see the woman's feet. She was not white-trash, just common. Sometimes Mrs. Turpin occupied herself at night naming the classes of people. On the bottom of the heap were most colored people, not the kind she would have been if she had been one, but most of them; then next to them — not above, just away from — were the white-trash; then above them were the home-owners, and above them the home-and-land owners, to which she and Claude belonged. Above she and Claude were people with a lot of money and much bigger houses and much more land. But here the complexity of it would begin to bear in on her, for some of the people with a lot of money were common and ought to be below she and Claud and some of the people who had good blood had lost their money and had to rent and then there were colored people who owned their homes and land as well. There was a colored dentist in town who had two red Lincolns and a swimming pool and a farm with registered white-face cattle on it. Usually by the time she had fallen asleep all the classes of people were moiling and roiling around in her head, and she would dream they were all crammed in together in a box car, being ridden off to be put in a gas oven.

"That's a beautiful clock," she said and nodded to her right. It was a big wall clock, the face encased in a brass sunburst.

"Yes, it's very pretty," the stylish lady said agreeably. "And right on the dot too," she added, glancing at her watch.

The ugly girl beside her cast an eye upward at the clock, smirked, then looked directly at Mrs. Turpin and smirked again. Then she returned her eyes to her book. She was obviously the lady's daughter because, although they didn't look anything alike as to disposition, they both had the same shape of face and the same blue eyes. On the lady they sparkled pleasantly but in the girl's seared face they appeared alternately to smolder and to blaze.

What if Jesus had said, "All right, you can be white-trash or a nigger or ugly"!

Mrs. Turpin felt an awful pity for the girl, though she thought it was one thing to be ugly and another to act ugly.

The woman with the snuff-stained lips turned around in her chair and looked up at the clock. Then she turned back and appeared to look a little to the side of Mrs. Turpin. There was a cast in one of her eyes. "You want to know wher you can get you one of themther clocks?" she asked in a loud voice.

"No, I already have a nice clock," Mrs. Turpin said. Once somebody like her got a leg in the conversation, she would be all over it.

"You can get you one with green stamps," the woman said. "That's most likely wher he got hisn. Save you up enough, you can get you most anythang. I got me some joo'ry."

Ought to have got you a wash rag and some soap, Mrs. Turpin thought.

"I get contour sheets with mine," the pleasant lady said.

The daughter slammed her book shut. She looked straight in front of her, directly through Mrs. Turpin and on through the yellow curtain and the plate glass window which made the wall behind her. The girl's eyes seemed lit all of a sudden with a peculiar light, an unnatural light like night road signs give. Mrs. Turpin turned her head to see if there was anything going on outside that she should see, but she could not see anything. Figures passing cast only a pale shadow through the curtain. There was no reason the girl should single her out for her ugly looks.

"Miss Finley," the nurse said, cracking the door. The gum-chewing woman got up and passed in front of her and Claud and went into the office. She had on red high-heeled shoes.

Directly across the table, the ugly girl's eyes were fixed on Mrs. Turpin as if she had some very special reason for disliking her.

"This is wonderful weather, isn't it?" the girl's mother said.

"It's good weather for cotton if you can get the niggers to pick it," Mrs. Turpin said, "but niggers don't want to pick cotton any more. You can't get the white folks to pick it and now you can't get the niggers — because they got to be right up there with the white folks."

"They gonna *try* anyways," the white-trash woman said, leaning forward.

"Do you have one of the cotton-picking machines?" the pleasant lady asked.

"No," Mrs. Turpin said, "they leave half the cotton in the field. We don't have much cotton anyway. If you want to make it farming now, you have to have a little of everything. We got a couple of acres of cotton and a few hogs and chickens and just enough white-face that Claud can look after them himself."

"One thang I don't want," the white-trash woman said, wiping her mouth with the back of her hand. "Hogs. Nasty stinking things, a-gruntin and a-rootin all over the place."

Mrs. Turpin gave her the merest edge of her attention. "Our hogs are not dirty and they don't stink," she said. "They're cleaner than some children I've seen. Their feet never touch the ground. We have a pig-parlor — that's where you raise them on concrete," she explained to the pleasant lady, "and Claud scoots them down with the hose every afternoon and washes off the floor." Cleaner by far than that child right there, she thought. Poor nasty little thing. He had not moved except to put the thumb of his dirty hand into his mouth.

The woman turned her face away from Mrs. Turpin. "I know I wouldn't scoot down no hog with no hose," she said to the wall.

You wouldn't have no hog to scoot down, Mrs. Turpin said to herself.

"A-gruntin and a-rootin and a-groanin," the woman muttered.

"We got a little of everything," Mrs. Turpin said to the pleasant lady. "It's no use in having more than you can handle yourself with help like it is. We found enough niggers to pick our cotton this year but Claud he has to go after them and take them home again in the evening. They can't walk that half a mile. No they can't. I tell you," she said and laughed merrily, "I sure am tired of buttering up niggers, but you got to love em if you want em to work for you. When they come in the morning, I run out and I say, 'Hi yawl this morning?' and when Claud drives them off to the field I just wave to beat the band and they just wave back." And she waved her hand rapidly to illustrate.

"Like you read out of the same book," the lady said, showing she understood perfectly.

"Child, yes," Mrs. Turpin said. "And when they come in from the field, I run out with a bucket of icewater. That's the way it's going to be from now on," she said. "You may as well face it."

"One thang I know," the white-trash woman said. "Two thangs I ain't going to do: love no niggers or scoot down no hog with no hose." And she let out a bark of contempt.

The look that Mrs. Turpin and the pleasant lady exchanged indicated they both understood that you had to *have* certain things before you could *know* certain things. But every time Mrs. Turpin exchanged a look with the lady, she was aware that the ugly girl's peculiar eyes were still on her, and she had trouble bringing her attention back to the conversation.

"When you got something," she said, "you got to look after it." And when you ain't got a thing but breath and britches, she added to herself, you can afford to come to town every morning and just sit on the Court House coping and spit.

A grotesque revolving shadow passed across the curtain behind her and was thrown palely on the opposite wall. Then a bicycle clattered down against the outside of the building. The door opened and a colored boy glided in with a tray from the drugstore. It had two large red and white paper cups on it with tops on them. He was a tall, very black boy in discolored white pants and a green nylon shirt. He was chewing gum slowly, as if to music. He set the tray down in the office opening next to the fern and stuck his head through to look for the secretary. She was not in there. He rested his arms on the ledge and waited, his narrow bottom stuck out, swaying to the left and right. He raised a hand over his head and scratched the base of his skull.

"You see that button there, boy?" Mrs. Turpin said. "You can punch that and she'll come. She's probably in the back somewhere."

"Is thas right?" the boy said agreeably, as if he had never seen the button before. He leaned to the right and put his finger on it. "She sometime out," he said and twisted around to face his audience, his elbows behind him on the counter. The nurse appeared and he twisted back again. She handed him a dollar and he rooted in his pocket and made the change and counted it out to her. She gave him fifteen cents for a tip and he went out with the empty tray. The heavy door swung to slowly and closed at length with the sound of suction. For a moment no one spoke.

"They ought to send all them niggers back to Africa," the white-trash woman said. "That's wher they come from in the first place."

"Oh, I couldn't do without my good colored friends," the pleasant lady said.

"There's a heap of things worse than a nigger," Mrs. Turpin agreed. "It's all kinds of them just like it's all kinds of us."

"Yes, and it takes all kinds to make the world go round," the lady said in her musical voice.

As she said it, the raw-complexioned girl snapped her teeth together. Her lower lip turned downwards and inside out, revealing the pale pink inside of her mouth. After a second it rolled back up. It was the ugliest face Mrs. Turpin had ever seen anyone make and for a moment she was certain that the girl had made it at her. She was looking at her as if she had known and disliked her all her life — all of Mrs. Turpin's life, it seemed too, not just all the girl's life. Why, girl, I don't even know you, Mrs. Turpin said silently.

She forced her attention back to the discussion. "It wouldn't be practical to send them back to Africa," she said. "They wouldn't want to go. They got it too good here."

"Wouldn't be what they wanted — if I had anythang to do with it," the woman said.

"It wouldn't be a way in the world you could get all the niggers back over there," Mrs. Turpin said. "They'd be hiding out and lying down and turning sick on you and wailing and hollering and raring and pitching. It wouldn't be a way in the world to get them over there."

"They got over here," the trashy woman said. "Get back like they got over."

"It wasn't so many of them then," Mrs. Turpin explained.

The woman looked at Mrs. Turpin as if here was an idiot indeed but Mrs. Turpin was not bothered by the look, considering where it came from.

"Nooo," she said, "they're going to stay here where they can go to New York and marry white folks and improve their color. That's what they all want to do, every one of them, improve their color."

"You know what comes of that, don't you?" Claud asked.

"No, Claud, what?" Mrs. Turpin said.

Claud's eyes twinkled. "White-faced niggers," he said with never a smile.

Everybody in the office laughed except the white-trash and the ugly girl. The girl gripped the book in her lap with white fingers. The trashy woman looked around her from face to face as if she thought they were all idiots. The old woman in the feed sack dress continued to gaze expressionless across the floor at the high-top shoes of the man opposite her, the one who had been pretending to be asleep when the Turpins came in. He was laughing heartily, his hands still spread out on his knees. The child had fallen to the side and was lying now almost face down in the old woman's lap.

While they recovered from their laughter, the nasal chorus on the radio kept the room from silence.

> "You go to blank blank
> And I'll go to mine
> But we'll all blank along
> To-geth-ther,
> And all along the blank
> We'll hep eachother out
> Smile-ling in any kind of
> Weath-ther!"

Mrs. Turpin didn't catch every word but she caught enough to agree with the spirit of the song and it turned her thoughts sober. To help anybody out that needed it was her philosophy of life. She never spared herself when she found somebody in need, whether they were white or black, trash or decent. And of all she had to be thankful for, she was most thankful that this was so. If Jesus had said, "You can be high society and have all the money you want and be thin and svelte-like, but you can't be a good woman with it," she would have had to say, "Well don't make me that then. Make me a good woman and it don't matter what else, how fat or how ugly or how poor!" Her heart rose. He had not made her a nigger or white-trash or ugly! He had made her herself and given her a little of everything. Jesus, thank you! she said. Thank you thank you thank you! Whenever she counted her blessings she felt as buoyant as if she weighed one hundred and twenty-five pounds instead of one hundred and eighty.

"What's wrong with your little boy?" the pleasant lady asked the white-trashy woman.

"He has a ulcer," the woman said proudly. "He ain't give me a minute's peace since he was born. Him and her are just alike," she said, nodding at the old woman, who was running her leathery fingers through the child's pale hair. "Look like I can't get nothing down them two but Co' Cola and candy."

That's all you try to get down em, Mrs. Turpin said to herself. Too lazy to light the fire. There was nothing you could tell her about people like them that she didn't know already. And it was not just that they didn't have anything. Because if you gave them everything, in two weeks it would all be broken or filthy or they would have chopped it up for lightwood. She knew all this from her own experience. Help them you must, but help them you couldn't.

All at once the ugly girl turned her lips inside out again. Her eyes fixed like two drills on Mrs. Turpin. This time there was no mistaking that there was something urgent behind them.

Girl, Mrs. Turpin exclaimed silently, I haven't done a thing to you! The girl might be confusing her with somebody else. There was no need to sit by and let herself be intimidated. "You must be in college," she said boldly, looking directly at the girl. "I see you reading a book there."

The girl continued to stare and pointedly did not answer.

Her mother blushed at this rudeness. "The lady asked you a question, Mary Grace," she said under her breath.

"I have ears," Mary Grace said.

The poor mother blushed again. "Mary Grace goes to Wellesley College," she explained. She twisted one of the buttons on her dress. "In Massachusetts," she added with a grimace. "And in the summer she just keeps right on studying. Just reads all the time, a real book worm. She's done real well at Wellesley; she's taking English and Math and History and Psychology and Social Studies," she rattled on, "and I think it's too much. I think she ought to get out and have fun."

The girl looked as if she would like to hurl them all through the plate glass window.

"Way up north," Mrs. Turpin murmured and thought, well, it hasn't done much for her manners.

"I'd almost rather to have him sick," the white-trash woman said, wrenching the attention back to herself. "He's so mean when he ain't. Look like some children just take natural to meanness. It's some gets bad when they get sick but he was the opposite. Took sick and turned good. He don't give me no trouble now. It's me waitin to see the doctor," she said.

If I was going to send anybody back to Africa, Mrs. Turpin thought, it would be your kind, woman. "Yes, indeed," she said

aloud, but looking up at the ceiling, "it's a heap of things worse than a nigger." And dirtier than a hog, she added to herself.

"I think people with bad dispositions are more to be pitied than anyone on earth," the pleasant lady said in a voice that was decidedly thin.

"I thank the Lord he has blessed me with a good one," Mrs. Turpin said. "The day has never dawned that I couldn't find something to laugh at."

"Not since she married me anyways," Claud said with a comical straight face.

Everybody laughed except the girl and the white-trash.

Mrs. Turpin's stomach shook. "He's such a caution," she said, "that I can't help but laugh at him."

The girl made a loud ugly noise through her teeth.

Her mother's mouth grew thin and tight. "I think the worst thing in the world," she said, "is an ungrateful person. To have everything and not appreciate it. I know a girl," she said, "who has parents who would give her anything, a little brother who loves her dearly, who is getting a good education, who wears the best clothes, but who can never say a kind word to anyone, who never smiles, who just criticizes and complains all day long."

"Is she too old to paddle?" Claud asked.

The girl's face was almost purple.

"Yes," the lady said, "I'm afraid there's nothing to do but leave her to her folly. Some day she'll wake up and it'll be too late."

"It never hurt anyone to smile," Mrs. Turpin said. "It just makes you feel better all over."

"Of course," the lady said sadly, "but there are just some people you can't tell anything to. They can't take criticism."

"If it's one thing I am," Mrs. Turpin said with feeling, "it's grateful. When I think who all I could have been besides myself and what all I got, a little of everything, and a good disposition besides, I just feel like shouting, 'Thank you, Jesus, for making everything the way it is!' It could have been different!" For one thing, somebody else could have got Claud. At the thought of this, she was flooded with gratitude and a terrible pang of joy ran through her. "Oh thank you, Jesus, Jesus, thank you!" she cried aloud.

The book struck her directly over her left eye. It struck almost at the same instant that she realized the girl was about to hurl it. Before she could utter a sound, the raw face came crashing across the table toward her, howling. The girl's fingers sank like clamps into the soft flesh of her neck. She heard the mother cry out and Claud shout, "Whoa!" There was an instant when she was certain that she was about to be in an earthquake.

All at once her vision narrowed and she saw everything as if it were happening in a small room far away, or as if she were looking at it through the wrong end of a telescope. Claud's face crumpled and fell out of sight. The nurse ran in, then out, then in again. Then the gangling figure of the doctor rushed out of the inner door. Magazines flew this way and that as the table turned over. The girl fell with a thud and Mrs. Turpin's vision suddenly reversed itself and she saw everything large instead of small. The eyes of the white-trashy woman were staring hugely at the floor. There the girl, held down on one side by the nurse and on the other by her mother, was wrenching and turning in their grasp. The doctor was kneeling astride her, trying to hold her arm down. He managed after a second to sink a long needle into it.

Mrs. Turpin felt entirely hollow except for her heart which swung from side to side as if it were agitated in a great empty drum of flesh.

"Somebody that's not busy call for the ambulance," the doctor said in the offhand voice young doctors adopt for terrible occasions.

Mrs. Turpin could not have moved a finger. The old man who had been sitting next to her skipped nimbly into the office and made the call, for the secretary still seemed to be gone.

"Claud!" Mrs. Turpin called.

He was not in his chair. She knew she must jump up and find him but she felt like some one trying to catch a train in a dream, when everything moves in slow motion and the faster you try to run the slower you go.

"Here I am," a suffocated voice, very unlike Claud's, said.

He was doubled up in the corner on the floor, pale as paper, holding his leg. She wanted to get up and go to him but she could not move. Instead, her gaze was drawn slowly downward to the churning face on the floor, which she could see over the doctor's shoulder.

The girl's eyes stopped rolling and focused on her. They seemed a much lighter blue than before, as if a door that had been tightly closed behind them was now open to admit light and air.

Mrs. Turpin's head cleared and her power of motion returned. She leaned forward until she was looking directly into the fierce brilliant eyes. There was no doubt in her mind that the girl did know her, knew her in some intense and personal way, beyond time and place and condition. "What you got to say to me?" she asked hoarsely and held her breath, waiting, as for a revelation.

The girl raised her head. Her gaze locked with Mrs. Turpin's. "Go back to hell where you came from, you old wart hog," she whispered. Her voice was low but clear. Her eyes burned for a moment as if she saw with pleasure that her message had struck its target.

Mrs. Turpin sank back in her chair.

After a moment the girl's eyes closed and she turned her head wearily to the side.

The doctor rose and handed the nurse the empty syringe. He leaned over and put both hands for a moment on the mother's shoulders, which were shaking. She was sitting on the floor, her lips pressed together, holding Mary Grace's hand in her lap. The girl's fingers were gripped like a baby's around her thumb. "Go on to the hospital," he said. "I'll call and make the arrangements."

"Now let's see that neck," he said in a jovial voice to Mrs. Turpin. He began to inspect her neck with his first two fingers. Two little moon-shaped lines like pink fish bones were indented over her windpipe. There was the beginning of an angry red swelling above her eye. His fingers passed over this also.

"Lea' me be," she said thickly and shook him off. "See about Claud. She kicked him."

"I'll see about him in a minute," he said and felt her pulse. He was a thin gray-haired man, given to pleasantries. "Go home and have yourself a vacation the rest of the day," he said and patted her on the shoulder.

Quit your pattin me, Mrs. Turpin growled to herself.

"And put an ice pack over that eye," he said. Then he went and squatted down beside Claud and looked at his leg. After a moment he pulled him up and Claud limped after him into the office.

Until the ambulance came, the only sounds in the room were the tremulous moans of the girl's mother, who continued to sit on the floor. The white-trash woman did not take her eyes off the girl. Mrs. Turpin looked straight ahead at nothing. Presently the ambulance drew up, a long dark shadow, behind the curtain. The attendants came in and set the stretcher down beside the girl and lifted her expertly onto it and carried her out. The nurse helped the mother gather up her things. The shadow of the ambulance moved silently away and the nurse came back in the office.

"That ther girl is going to be a lunatic, ain't she?" the white-trash woman asked the nurse, but the nurse kept on to the back and never answered her.

"Yes, she's going to be a lunatic," the white-trash woman said to the rest of them.

"Po' critter," the old woman murmured. The child's face was still in her lap. His eyes looked idly out over her knees. He had not moved during the disturbance except to draw one leg up under him.

"I thank Gawd," the white-trash woman said fervently, "I ain't a lunatic."

Claud came limping out and the Turpins went home.

As their pick-up truck turned into their own dirt road and made the crest of the hill, Mrs. Turpin gripped the window ledge and looked out suspiciously. The land sloped gracefully down through a field dotted with lavender weeds and at the start of the rise their small yellow frame house, with its little flower beds spread out around it like a fancy apron, sat primly in its accustomed place between two giant hickory trees. She would not have been startled to see a burnt wound between two blackened chimneys.

Neither of them felt like eating so they put on their house clothes and lowered the shade in the bedroom and lay down, Claud with his leg on a pillow and herself with a damp washcloth over her eye. The instant she was flat on her back, the image of a razor-backed hog with warts on its face and horns coming out behind its ears snorted into her head. She moaned, a low quiet moan.

"I am not," she said tearfully, "a wart hog. From hell." But the denial had no force. The girl's eyes and her words, even the tone of her voice, low but clear, directed only to her, brooked no repudiation. She had been singled out for the message, though there was trash in the room to whom it might justly have been applied. The full force of this fact struck her only now. There was a woman there who was neglecting her own child but she had been overlooked. The message had been given to Ruby Turpin, a respectable, hard-working, church-going woman. The tears dried. Her eyes began to burn instead with wrath.

She rose on her elbow and the washcloth fell into her hand. Claud was lying on his back, snoring. She wanted to tell him what the girl had said. At the same time, she did not wish to put the image of herself as a wart hog from hell into his mind.

"Hey, Claud," she muttered and pushed his shoulder.

Claud opened one pale baby blue eye.

She looked into it warily. He did not think about anything. He just went his way.

"Wha, whasit?" he said and closed the eye again.

"Nothing," she said. "Does you leg pain you?"

"Hurts like hell," Claud said.

"It'll quit terreckly," she said and lay back down. In a moment Claud was snoring again. For the rest of the afternoon they lay there. Claud slept. She scowled at the ceiling. Occasionally she raised her fist and made a small stabbing motion over her chest as if she was defending her innocence to invisible guests who were like the comforters of Job, reasonable-seeming but wrong.

About five-thirty Claud stirred. "Got to go after those niggers," he sighed, not moving.

She was looking straight up as if there were unintelligible handwriting on the ceiling. The protuberance over her eye had turned a greenish-blue. "Listen here," she said.

"What?"

"Kiss me."

Claud leaned over and kissed her loudly on the mouth. He pinched her side and their hands interlocked. Her expression of ferocious concentration did not change. Claud got up, groaning and growling, and limped off. She continued to study the ceiling.

She did not get up until she heard the pick-up truck coming back with the Negroes. Then she rose and thrust her feet in her brown oxfords, which she did not bother to lace, and stumped out onto the back porch and got her red plastic bucket. She emptied a tray of ice cubes into it and filled it half full of water and went out into the back yard. Every afternoon after Claud brought the hands in, one of the boys helped him put out hay and the rest waited in the back of the truck until he was ready to take them home. The truck was parked in the shade under one of the hickory trees.

"Hi yawl this evening?" Mrs. Turpin asked grimly, appearing with the bucket and the dipper. There were three women and a boy in the truck.

"Us doin nicely," the oldest woman said. "Hi you doin?" and her gaze stuck immediately on the dark lump on Mrs. Turpin's forehead. "You done fell down, ain't you?" she asked in a solicitous voice. The old woman was dark and almost toothless. She had on an old felt hat of Claud's set back on her head. The other two women were younger and lighter and they both had new bright green sunhats. One of them had hers on her head; the other had taken hers off and the boy was grinning beneath it.

Mrs. Turpin set the bucket down on the floor of the truck. "Yawl hep yourselves," she said. She looked around to make sure Claud had gone. "No, I didn't fall down," she said, folding her arms. "It was something worse than that."

"Ain't nothing bad happen to you!" the old woman said. She said it as if they all knew that Mrs. Turpin was protected in some special way by Divine Providence. "You just had you a little fall."

"We were in town at the doctor's office for where the cow kicked Mr. Turpin," Mrs. Turpin said in a flat tone that indicated they could leave off their foolishness. "And there was this girl there. A big fat girl with her face all broke out. I could look at that girl and tell she was peculiar but I couldn't tell how. And me and her mama was just talking and going along and all of a sudden WHAM! She throws this big book she was reading at me and . . ."

"Naw!" the old woman cried out.

"And then she jumps over the table and commences to choke me."

"Naw!" they all exclaimed, "naw!"

"Hi come she do that?" the old woman asked. "What ail her?"

Mrs. Turpin only glared in front of her.

"Somethin ail her," the old woman said.

"They carried her off in an ambulance," Mrs. Turpin continued, "But before she went she was rolling on the floor and they were trying to hold her down to give her a shot and she said something to me." She paused. "You know what she said to me?"

"What she say?" they asked.

"She said," Mrs. Turpin began, and stopped, her face very dark and heavy. The sun was getting whiter and whiter, blanching the sky overhead so that the leaves of the hickory tree were black in the face of it. She could not bring forth the words. "Something real ugly," she muttered.

"She sho shouldn't said nothin ugly to you," the old woman said. "You so sweet. You the sweetest lady I know."

"She pretty too," the one with the hat on said.

"And stout," the other one said. "I never knowed no sweeter white lady."

"That's the truth befo' Jesus," the old woman said. "Amen! You des as sweet and pretty as you can be."

Mrs. Turpin knew exactly how much Negro flattery was worth and it added to her rage. "She said," she began again and finished this time with a fierce rush of breath, "that I was an old wart hog from hell."

There was an astounded silence.

"Where she at?" the youngest woman cried in a piercing voice.

"Lemme see her. I'll kill her!"

"I'll kill her with you!" the other one cried.

"She b'long in the sylum," the old woman said emphatically. "You the sweetest white lady I know."

"She pretty too," the other two said. "Stout as she can be and sweet. Jesus satisfied with her!"

"Deed he is," the old woman declared.

Idiots! Mrs. Turpin growled to herself. You could never say anything intelligent to a nigger. You could talk at them but not with them. "Yawl ain't drunk your water," she said shortly. "Leave the bucket in the truck when you're finished with it. I got more to do than just stand around and pass the time of day," and she moved off and into the house.

She stood for a moment in the middle of the kitchen. The dark protuberance over her eye looked like a miniature tornado cloud which might any moment sweep across the horizon of her brow. Her lower lip protruded dangerously. She squared her massive shoulders. Then she marched into the front of the house and out the side door and started down the road to the pig parlor. She had the look of a woman going single-handed, weaponless, into battle.

The sun was a deep yellow now like a

harvest moon and was riding westward very fast over the far tree line as if it meant to reach the hogs before she did. The road was rutted and she kicked several good-sized stones out of her path as she strode along. The pig parlor was on a little knoll at the end of a lane that ran off from the side of the barn. It was a square of concrete as large as a small room, with a board fence about four feet high around it. The concrete floor sloped slightly so that the hog wash could drain off into a trench where it was carried to the field for fertilizer. Claud was standing on the outside, on the edge of the concrete, hanging onto the top board, hosing down the floor inside. The hose was connected to the faucet of a water trough nearby.

Mrs. Turpin climbed up beside him and glowered down at the hogs inside. There were seven long-snouted bristly shoats in it — tan with liver-colored spots — and an old sow a few weeks off from farrowing. She was lying on her side grunting. The shoats were running about shaking themselves like idiot children, their little slit pig eyes searching the floor for anything left. She had read that pigs were the most intelligent animal. She doubted it. They were supposed to be smarter than dogs. There had even been a pig astronaut. He had performed his assignment perfectly but died of a heart attack afterwards because they left him in his electric suit, sitting upright throughout his examination when naturally a hog should be on all fours.

A-gruntin and a-rootin and a-groanin.

"Gimme that hose," she said, yanking it away from Claud. "Go on and carry them niggers home and then get off that leg."

"You look like you might have swallowed a mad dog," Claud observed, but he got down and limped off. He paid no attention to her humors.

Until he was out of earshot, Mrs. Turpin stood on the side of the pen, holding the hose and pointing the stream of water at the hind quarters of any shoat that looked as if it might try to lie down. When he had had time to get over the hill, she turned her head slightly and her wrathful eyes scanned the path. He was nowhere in sight. She turned back again and seemed to gather herself up. Her shoulders rose and she drew in her breath.

"What do you send me a message like that for?" she said in a low fierce voice, barely above a whisper but with the force of a shout in its concentrated fury. "How am I a hog and me both? How am I saved and from hell too?" Her free fist was knotted and with the other she gripped the hose, blindly pointing the stream of water in and out of the eye of the old sow whose outraged squeal she did not hear.

The pig parlor commanded a view of the back pasture where their twenty beef cows were gathered around the hay-bales Claud and the boy had put out. The freshly cut pasture sloped down to the highway. Across it was their cotton field and beyond that a dark green dusty wood which they owned as well. The sun was behind the wood, very red, looking over the paling of trees like a farmer inspecting his own hogs.

"Why me?" she rumbled. "It's no trash around here, black or white, that I haven't given to. And break my back to the bone every day working. And do for the church."

She appeared to be the right size woman to command the arena before her. "How am I a hog?" she demanded. "Exactly how am I like them?" and she jabbed the stream of water at the shoats. "There was plenty of trash there. It didn't have to be me.

"If you like trash better, go get yourself some trash then," she railed. "You could have made me trash. Or a nigger. If trash is what you wanted why didn't you make me trash?" She shook her fist with the hose in it and a watery snake appeared momentarily in the air. "I could quit working and take it easy and be filthy," she growled. "Lounge about the sidewalks all day drinking root beer. Dip snuff and spit in every puddle and have it all over my face. I could be nasty.

"Or you could have made me a nigger. It's too late for me to be a nigger," she said with deep sarcasm, "but I could act like one. Lay down in the middle of the road and stop traffic. Roll on the ground."

In the deepening light everything was taking on a mysterious hue. The pasture was growing a peculiar glassy green and the streak of highway had turned lavender. She braced herself for a final assault and this time her voice rolled out over the pasture. "Go on," she yelled, "call me a hog! Call me a hog again. From hell. Call me a wart hog from hell. Put that bottom rail on top. There'll still be a top and bottom!"

A garbled echo returned to her.

A final surge of fury shook her and she roared, "Who do you think you are?"

The color of everything, field and crimson sky, burned for a moment with a transparent intensity. The question carried over the pasture and across the highway and the cotton field and returned to her clearly like an answer from beyond the wood.

She opened her mouth but no sound came out of it.

A tiny truck, Claud's, appeared on the highway, heading rapidly out of sight. Its gears scraped thinly. It looked like a child's toy. At any moment a bigger truck might smash into it and scatter Claud's and the niggers' brains all over the road.

Mrs. Turpin stood there, her gaze fixed on the highway, all her muscles rigid, until in five or six minutes the truck reappeared, returning. She waited until it had had time to turn into their own road. Then like a monumental statue coming to life, she bent her head slowly and gazed, as if through the very heart of the mystery, down into the pig parlor at the hogs. They had settled all in one corner around the old sow who was grunting softly. A red glow suffused them. They appeared to pant with a secret life.

Until the sun slipped finally behind the tree line, Mrs. Turpin remained there with her gaze bent to them as if she were absorbing some abysmal life-giving knowledge. At last she lifted her head. There was only a purple streak in the sky, cutting through a field of crimson and leading, like an extension of the highway, into the descending dusk. She raised her hands from the side of the pen in a gesture hieratic and profound. A visionary light settled in her eyes. She saw the streak as a vast swinging bridge extending upward from the earth through a field of living fire. Upon it a vast horde of souls were rumbling toward heaven. There were whole companies of white-trash, clean for the first time in their lives, and bands of black niggers in white robes, and battalions of freaks and lunatics shouting and clapping and leaping like frogs. And bringing up the end of the procession was a tribe of people whom she recognized at once as those who, like herself and Claud, had always had a little of everything and the God-given wit to use it right. She leaned forward to observe them closer. They were marching behind the others with great dignity, accountable as they had always been for good order and common sense and respectable behavior. They alone were on key. Yet she could see by their shocked and altered faces that even their virtues were being burned away. She lowered her hands and gripped the rail of the hog pen, her eyes small but fixed unblinkingly on what lay ahead. In a moment the vision faded but she remained where she was, immobile.

At length she got down and turned off the faucet and made her slow way on the darkening path to the house. In the woods around her the invisible cricket choruses had struck up, but what she heard were the voices of the souls climbing upward into the starry field and shouting hallelujah.

For Consideration

1. Mrs. Turpin would seem to be an observant person, perhaps excessively so. What might that reveal about her? What features of other people does she focus on?

2. Why would Mrs. Turpin choose to be a black woman rather than "white-trash"? On what basis does she discriminate between the two groups? Between the several classes of people she identifies?

3. Mrs. Turpin sees sharp differences between herself and the "white-trashy" woman. What are they? Are the differences as clear as Mrs. Turpin believes? How do you know?

4. What is the significance of Mrs. Turpin's recognition (revelation?) that "the girl did know her, knew her in some intense and personal way, beyond time and place and condition" and of the girl's response to her immediately after, "Go back to hell where you came from, you old wart hog?"

5. Why is Mrs. Turpin unable to repudiate the girl's accusation? Since she believes that "you could never say anything intelligent to a nigger," why is Mrs. Turpin so anxious to tell the black workers what happened to her in the doctor's office?

6. When Mrs. Turpin goes toward the pig parlor she has "the look of a woman going single-handed, weaponless, into battle," and when she is there she uses the water hose as a weapon against the pigs and talks fiercely to herself. Is she addressing anyone else? (God? Satan? the pigs?) For what purpose?

7. When her rage subsides, Mrs. Turpin looks down into the pig parlor, "as if through the very heart of mystery," to see the sow and the pigs together, appearing "to pant with a secret life." What is the mystery, the secret life which she observes? Are the pig parlor and its occupants a symbol? Of what?

8. What is the significance of the vision Mrs. Turpin experiences? Who leads the "vast horde of souls" rumbling toward heaven? Who brings up the rear? What is the meaning of this final scene? What, finally, is the "revelation" Mrs. Turpin experiences?

ALBERT CAMUS   (1913—1960)

The Guest

Translated by Justin O'Brien

The schoolmaster was watching the two men climb toward him. One was on horseback, the other on foot. They had not yet tackled the abrupt rise leading to the schoolhouse built on the hillside. They were toiling onward, making slow progress in the snow, among the stones, on the vast expanse of the high, deserted plateau. From time to time the horse stumbled. Without hearing anything yet, he could see the breath issuing from the horse's nostrils. One of the men, at least, knew the region. They were following the trail although it had disappeared days ago under a layer of dirty white snow. The schoolmaster calculated that it would take them half an hour to get onto the hill. It was cold; he went back into the school to get a sweater.

He crossed the empty, frigid classroom. On the blackboard the four rivers of France, drawn with four different colored chalks, had been flowing toward their estuaries for the past three days. Snow had suddenly fallen in mid-October after eight months of drought without the transition of rain, and the twenty pupils, more or less, who lived in the villages scattered over the plateau had stopped coming. With fair weather they would return. Daru now heated only the single room that was his lodging, adjoining the classroom and giving also onto the plateau to the east. Like the class windows, his window looked to the south too. On that side the school was a few kilometers from the point where the plateau began to slope toward the south. In clear weather could be seen the purple mass of the mountain range where the gap opened onto the desert.

Somewhat warmed, Daru returned to the window from which he had first seen the two men. They were no longer visible. Hence they must have tackled the rise. The sky was not so dark, for the snow had stopped falling during the night. The morning had opened with a dirty light which had scarcely become brighter as the ceiling of clouds lifted. At two in the afternoon it seemed as if the day were merely beginning. But still this was better than those three days when the thick snow was falling amidst unbroken darkness with little gusts of wind that rattled the double door of the classroom. Then Daru had spent long hours in his room, leaving it only to go to the shed and feed the chickens or get some coal. Fortunately the delivery truck from Tadjid, the nearest village to the north, had brought his supplies two days before the blizzard. It would return in forty-eight hours.

Besides, he had enough to resist a siege, for the little room was cluttered with bags of wheat that the administration left as a stock to distribute to those of his pupils whose families had suffered from the drought. Actually they had all been victims because they were all poor. Every day Daru would distribute a ration to the children. They had missed it, he knew, during these bad days. Possibly one of the fathers or big brothers would come this afternoon and he could supply them with grain. It was just a matter of carrying them over to the next harvest. Now shiploads of wheat were arriving from France and the worst was over. But it would be hard to forget that poverty, that army of ragged ghosts wandering in the sunlight, the plateaus burned to a cinder month after month, the earth shriveled up little by little, literally scorched, every stone bursting into dust under one's foot. The sheep had died then by thousands and even a few men, here and there, sometimes without anyone's knowing.

In contrast with such poverty, he who lived almost like a monk in his remote schoolhouse, nonetheless satisfied with the little he had and with the rough life, had felt like a lord with his white-washed walls, his narrow couch, his unpainted shelves, his well, and his weekly provision of water and food. And suddenly this snow, without warning, without the foretaste of rain. This is the way the region was, cruel to live in, even without men — who didn't help matters either. But Daru had been born here. Everywhere else, he felt exiled.

He stepped out onto the terrace in front of the schoolhouse. The two men were now halfway up the slope. He recognized the horseman as Balducci, the old gendarme he had known for a long time. Balducci was holding on the end of a rope an Arab who was walking behind him with hands bound and head lowered. The gendarme waved a greeting to which Daru did not reply, lost as he was in contemplation of the Arab dressed in a faded blue jellaba, his feet in sandals but covered with socks of heavy raw wool, his head surmounted by a narrow, short *chèche*. They were approaching. Balducci was holding back his horse in order not to hurt the Arab, and the group was advancing slowly.

Within earshot, Balducci shouted: "One hour to do the three kilometers from El Ameur!" Daru did not answer. Short and square in his thick sweater, he watched them climb. Not once had the Arab raised his head. "Hello," said Daru when they got up onto the terrace. "Come in and

warm up." Balducci painfully got down from his horse without letting go the rope. From under his bristling mustache he smiled at the schoolmaster. His little dark eyes, deep-set under a tanned forehead, and his mouth surrounded with wrinkles made him look attentive and studious. Daru took the bridle, led the horse to the shed, and came back to the two men, who were now waiting for him in the school. He led them into his room. "I am going to heat up the classroom," he said. "We'll be more comfortable there." When he entered the room again, Balducci was on the couch. He had undone the rope tying him to the Arab, who had squatted near the stove. His hands still bound, the *chèche* pushed back on his head, he was looking toward the window. At first Daru noticed only his huge lips, fat, smooth, almost Negroid; yet his nose was straight, his eyes were dark and full of fever. The *chèche* revealed an obstinate forehead and, under the weathered skin now rather discolored by the cold, the whole face had a restless and rebellious look that struck Daru when the Arab, turning his face toward him, looked him straight in the eyes. "Go into the other room," said the schoolmaster, "and I'll make you some mint tea." "Thanks," Balducci said. "What a chore! How I long for retirement." And addressing his prisoner in Arabic: "Come on, you." The Arab got up and, slowly, holding his bound wrists in front of him, went into the classroom.

With the tea, Daru brought a chair. But Balducci was already enthroned on the nearest pupil's desk and the Arab had squatted against the teacher's platform facing the stove, which stood between the desk and the window. When he held out the glass of tea to the prisoner, Daru hesitated at the sight of his bound hands. "He might perhaps be untied." "Sure," said Balducci. "That was for the trip." He started to get to his feet. But Daru, setting the glass on the floor, had knelt beside the

Arab. Without saying anything, the Arab watched him with his feverish eyes. Once his hands were free, he rubbed his swollen wrists against each other, took the glass of tea, and sucked up the burning liquid in swift little sips.

"Good," said Daru. "And where are you headed?"

Balducci withdrew his mustache from the tea. "Here, son."

"Odd pupils! And you're spending the night?"

"No. I'm going back to El Ameur. And you will deliver this fellow to Tinguit. He is expected at police headquarters."

Balducci was looking at Daru with a friendly little smile.

"What's this story?" asked the schoolmaster. "Are you pulling my leg?"

"No, son. Those are the orders."

"The orders? I'm not . . ." Daru hesitated, not wanting to hurt the old Corsican. "I mean, that's not my job."

"What! What's the meaning of that? In wartime people do all kinds of jobs."

"Then I'll wait for the declaration of war!"

Balducci nodded.

"O.K. But the orders exist and they concern you too. Things are brewing, it appears. There is talk of a forthcoming revolt. We are mobilized, in a way."

Daru still had his obstinate look.

"Listen, son," Balducci said. "I like you and you must understand. There's only a dozen of us at El Ameur to patrol throughout the whole territory of a small department and I must get back in a hurry. I was told to hand this guy over to you and return without delay. He couldn't be kept there. His village was beginning to stir; they wanted to take him back. You must take him to Tinguit tomorrow before the day is over. Twenty kilometers shouldn't faze a husky fellow like you. After that, all will be over. You'll come back to your pupils and your comfortable life."

Behind the wall the horse could be heard snorting and pawing the earth. Daru was looking out the window. Decidedly, the weather was clearing and the light was increasing over the snowy plateau. When all the snow was melted, the sun would take over again and once more would burn the fields of stone. For days, still, the unchanging sky would shed its dry light on the solitary expanse where nothing had any connection with man.

"After all," he said, turning around toward Balducci, "what did he do?" And, before the gendarme had opened his mouth, he asked: "Does he speak French?"

"No, not a word. We had been looking for him for a month, but they were hiding him. He killed his cousin."

"Is he against us?"

"I don't think so. But you can never be sure."

"Why did he kill?"

"A family squabble, I think. One owed the other grain, it seems. It's not at all clear. In short, he killed his cousin with a billhook. You know, like a sheep, *kreezk!*"

Balducci made the gesture of drawing a blade across his throat and the Arab, his attention attracted, watched him with a sort of anxiety. Daru felt a sudden wrath against the man, against all men with their rotten spite, their tireless hates, their blood lust.

But the kettle was singing on the stove. He served Balducci more tea, hesitated, then served the Arab again, who, a second time, drank avidly. His raised arms made the jellaba fall open and the schoolmaster saw his thin, muscular chest.

"Thanks, kid," Balducci said. "And now, I'm off."

He got up and went toward the Arab, taking a small rope from his pocket.

"What are you doing?" Daru asked dryly.

Balducci, disconcerted, showed him the rope.

"Don't bother."

The old gendarme hesitated. "It's up to you. Of course, you are armed?"

"I have my shotgun."

"Where?"

"In the trunk."

"You ought to have it near your bed."

"Why? I have nothing to fear."

"You're crazy, son. If there's an uprising, no one is safe, we're all in the same boat."

"I'll defend myself. I'll have time to see them coming."

Balducci began to laugh, then suddenly the mustache covered the white teeth.

"You'll have time? O.K. That's just what I was saying. You have always been a little cracked. That's why I like you, my son was like that."

At the same time he took out his revolver and put it on the desk.

"Keep it; I don't need two weapons from here to El Ameur."

The revolver shone against the black paint of the table. When the gendarme turned toward him, the schoolmaster caught the smell of leather and horse-flesh.

"Listen, Balducci," Daru said suddenly, "every bit of this disgusts me, and first of all your fellow here. But I won't hand him over. Fight, yes, if I have to. But not that."

The old gendarme stood in front of him and looked at him severely.

"You're being a fool," he said slowly. "I don't like it either. You don't get used to putting a rope on a man even after years of it, and you're even ashamed — yes, ashamed. But you can't let them have their way."

"I won't hand him over," Daru said again.

"It's an order, son, and I repeat it."

"That's right. Repeat to them what I've said to you: I won't hand him over."

Balducci made a visible effort to reflect. He looked at the Arab and at Daru. At last he decided.

"No, I won't tell them anything. If you

want to drop us, go ahead; I'll not denounce you. I have an order to deliver the prisoner and I'm doing so. And now you'll just sign this paper for me."

"There's no need. I'll not deny that you left him with me."

"Don't be mean with me. I know you'll tell the truth. You're from hereabouts and you are a man. But you must sign, that's the rule."

Daru opened his drawer, took out a little square bottle of purple ink, the red wooden penholder with the "sergeant-major" pen he used for making models of penmanship, and signed. The gendarme carefully folded the paper and put it into his wallet. Then he moved toward the door.

"I'll see you off," Daru said.

"No," said Balducci. "There's no use being polite. You insulted me."

He looked at the Arab, motionless in the same spot, sniffed peevishly, and turned away toward the door. "Good-by, son," he said. The door shut behind him. Balducci appeared suddenly outside the window and then disappeared. His footsteps were muffled by the snow. The horse stirred on the other side of the wall and several chickens fluttered in fright. A moment later Balducci reappeared outside the window leading the horse by the bridle. He walked toward the little rise without turning around and disappeared from sight with the horse following him. A big stone could be heard bouncing down. Daru walked back toward the prisoner, who, without stirring, never took his eyes off him. "Wait," the schoolmaster said in Arabic and went toward the bedroom. As he was going through the door, he had a second thought, went to the desk, took the revolver, and stuck it in his pocket. Then, without looking back, he went into his room.

For some time he lay on his couch watching the sky gradually close over, listening to the silence. It was this silence that had seemed painful to him during the first days here, after the war. He had requested a post in the little town at the base of the foothills separating the upper plateaus from the desert. There, rocky walls, green and black to the north, pink and lavender to the south, marked the frontier of eternal summer. He had been named to a post farther north, on the plateau itself. In the beginning, the solitude and the silence had been hard for him on these wastelands peopled only by stones. Occasionally, furrows suggested cultivation, but they had been dug to uncover a certain kind of stone good for building. The only plowing here was to harvest rocks. Elsewhere a thin layer of soil accumulated in the hollows would be scraped out to enrich paltry village gardens. This is the way it was: bare rock covered three quarters of the region. Towns sprang up, flourished, then disappeared; men came by, loved one another or fought bitterly, then died. No one in this desert, neither he nor his guest, mattered. And yet, outside this desert neither of them, Daru knew, could have really lived.

When he got up, no noise came from the classroom. He was amazed at the unmixed joy he derived from the mere thought that the Arab might have fled and that he would be alone with no decision to make. But the prisoner was there. He had merely stretched out between the stove and the desk. With eyes open, he was staring at the ceiling. In that position, his thick lips were particularly noticeable, giving him a pouting look. "Come," said Daru. The Arab got up and followed him. In the bedroom, the schoolmaster pointed to a chair near the table under the window. The Arab sat down without taking his eyes off Daru.

"Are you hungry?"

"Yes," the prisoner said.

Daru set the table for two. He took flour and oil, shaped a cake in a frying-pan, and lighted the little stove that functioned on bottled gas. While the cake was cooking, he went out to the shed to get cheese, eggs, dates, and condensed milk. When the cake was done he set it on the window sill to cool, heated some condensed milk diluted with water, and beat up the eggs into an omelette. In one of his motions he knocked against the revolver stuck in his right pocket. He set the bowl down, went into the classroom, and put the revolver in his desk drawer. When he came back to the room, night was falling. He put on the light and served the Arab. "Eat," he said. The Arab took a piece of the cake, lifted it eagerly to his mouth, and stopped short.

"And you?" he asked.

"After you. I'll eat too."

The thick lips opened slightly. The Arab hesitated, then bit into the cake determinedly.

The meal over, the Arab looked at the schoolmaster. "Are you the judge?"

"No, I'm simply keeping you until tomorrow."

"Why do you eat with me?"

"I'm hungry."

The Arab fell silent. Daru got up and went out. He brought back a folding bed from the shed, set it up between the table and the stove, perpendicular to his own bed. From a large suitcase which, upright in a corner, served as a shelf for papers, he took two blankets and arranged them on the camp bed. Then he stopped, felt useless, and sat down on his bed. There was nothing more to do or to get ready. He had to look at this man. He looked at him, therefore, trying to imagine his face bursting with rage. He couldn't do so. He could see nothing but the dark yet shining eyes and the animal mouth.

"Why did you kill him?" he asked in a voice whose hostile tone surprised him.

The Arab looked away.

"He ran away. I ran after him."

He raised his eyes to Daru again and they were full or a sort of woeful interrogation. "Now what will they do to me?"

"Are you afraid?"

He stiffened, turning his eyes away.

"Are you sorry?"

The Arab stared at him openmouthed. Obviously he did not understand. Daru's annoyance was growing. At the same time he felt awkward and selfconscious with his big body wedged between the two beds.

"Lie down there," he said impatiently. "That's your bed."

The Arab didn't move. He called to Daru:

"Tell me!"

The schoolmaster looked at him.

"Is the gendarme coming back tomorrow?"

"I don't know."

"Are you coming with us?"

"I don't know. Why?"

The prisoner got up and stretched out on top of the blankets, his feet toward the window. The light from the electric bulb shone straight into his eyes and he closed them at once.

"Why?" Daru repeated, standing beside the bed.

The Arab opened his eyes under the blinding light and looked at him, trying not to blink.

"Come with us," he said.

In the middle of the night, Daru was still not asleep. He had gone to bed after undressing completely; he generally slept naked. But when he suddenly realized that he had nothing on, he hesitated. He felt vulnerable and the temptation came to him to put his clothes back on. Then he shrugged his shoulders; after all, he wasn't a child and, if need be, he could break his adversary in two. From his bed he could observe him, lying on his back, still motionless with his eyes closed under the harsh light. When Daru turned out the light, the darkness seemed to coagulate all of a sudden. Little by little, the night came

back to life in the window where the starless sky was stirring gently. The schoolmaster soon made out the body lying at his feet. The Arab still did not move, but his eyes seemed open. A faint wind was prowling around the schoolhouse. Perhaps it would drive away the clouds and the sun would reappear.

During the night the wind increased. The hens fluttered a little and then were silent. The Arab turned over on his side with his back to Daru, who thought he heard him moan. Then he listened for his guest's breathing, become heavier and more regular. He listened to that breath so close to him and mused without being able to go to sleep. In this room where he had been sleeping alone for a year, this presence bothered him. But it bothered him also by imposing on him a sort of brotherhood he knew well but refused to accept in the present circumstances. Men who share the same rooms, soldiers or prisoners, develop a strange alliance as if, having cast off their armor with their clothing, they fraternized every evening, over and above their differences, in the ancient community of dream and fatigue. But Daru shook himself; he didn't like such musings, and it was essential to sleep.

A little later, however, when the Arab stirred slightly, the schoolmaster was still not asleep. When the prisoner made a second move, he stiffened, on the alert. The Arab was lifting himself slowly on his arms with almost the motion of a sleepwalker. Seated upright in bed, he waited motionless without turning his head toward Daru, as if he were listening attentively. Daru did not stir; it had just occurred to him that the revolver was still in the drawer of his desk. It was better to act at once. Yet he continued to observe the prisoner, who, with the same slithery motion, put his feet on the ground, waited again, then began to stand up slowly. Daru was about to call out to him when the Arab began to walk, in a quite natural but extraordinarily silent way. He was heading toward the door at the end of the room that opened into the shed. He lifted the latch with precaution and went out, pushing the door behind him but without shutting it. Daru had not stirred. "He is running away," he merely thought. "Good riddance!" Yet he listened attentively. The hens were not fluttering; the guest must be on the plateau. A faint sound of water reached him, and he didn't know what it was until the Arab again stood framed in the doorway, closed the door carefully, and came back to bed without a sound. Then Daru turned his back on him and fell asleep. Still later he seemed, from the depths of his sleep, to hear furtive steps around the schoolhouse. "I'm dreaming! I'm dreaming!" he repeated to himself. And he went on sleeping.

When he awoke, the sky was clear; the loose window let in a cold, pure air. The Arab was asleep, hunched up under the blankets now, his mouth open, utterly relaxed. But when Daru shook him, he started dreadfully, staring at Daru with wild eyes as if he had never seen him and such a frightened expression that the schoolmaster stepped back. "Don't be afraid. It's me. You must eat." The Arab nodded his head and said yes. Calm had returned to his face, but his expression was vacant and listless.

The coffee was ready. They drank it seated together on the folding bed as they munched their pieces of the cake. Then Daru led the Arab under the shed and showed him the faucet where he washed. He went back into the room, folded the blankets and the bed, made his own bed and put the room in order. Then he went through the classroom and out onto the terrace. The sun was already rising in the blue sky; a soft, bright light was bathing the deserted plateau. On the ridge the snow was melting in spots. The stones were about to reappear. Crouched on the edge of the plateau, the schoolmaster looked at the deserted expanse. He thought of Balducci. He had hurt him, for he had sent him off in a way as if he didn't want to be associated with him. He could still hear the gendarme's farewell and, without knowing why, he felt strangely empty and vulnerable. At that moment, from the other side of the schoolhouse, the prisoner coughed. Daru listened to him almost despite himself and then, furious, threw a pebble that whistled through the air before sinking into the snow. That man's stupid crime revolted him, but to hand him over was contrary to honor. Merely thinking of it made him smart with humiliation. And he cursed at one and the same time his own people who had sent him this Arab and the Arab too who had dared to kill and not managed to get away. Daru got up, walked in a circle on the terrace, waited motionless, and then went back into the schoolhouse.

The Arab, leaning over the cement floor of the shed, was washing his teeth with two fingers. Daru looked at him and said: "Come." He went back into the room ahead of the prisoner. He slipped a hunting-jacket on over his sweater and put on walking-shoes. Standing, he waited until the Arab had put on his *chèche* and sandals. They went into the classroom and the schoolmaster pointed to the exit, saying: "Go ahead." The fellow didn't budge. "I'm coming," said Daru. The Arab went out. Daru went back into the room and made a package of pieces of rusk, dates, and sugar. In the classroom, before going out, he hesitated a second in front of his desk, then crossed the threshold and locked the door. "That's the way," he said. He started toward the east, followed by the prisoner. But, a short distance from the schoolhouse, he thought he heard a slight sound behind them. He retraced his steps and examined the surroundings of the house; there was no one there. The Arab watched him without seeming to understand. "Come on," said Daru.

They walked for an hour and rested beside a sharp peak of limestone. The snow was melting faster and faster and the sun was drinking up the puddles at once, rapidly cleaning the plateau, which gradually dried and vibrated like the air itself. When they resumed walking, the ground rang under their feet. From time to time a bird rent the space in front of them with a joyful cry. Daru breathed in deeply the fresh morning light. He felt a sort of rapture before the vast familiar expanse, now almost entirely yellow under its dome of blue sky. They walked an hour more, descending toward the south. They reached a level height made up of crumbly rocks. From there on, the plateau sloped down, eastward, toward a low plain where there were a few spindly trees and, to the south, toward outcroppings of rock that gave the landscape a chaotic look.

Daru surveyed the two directions. There was nothing but the sky on the horizon. Not a man could be seen. He turned toward the Arab, who was looking at him blankly. Daru held out the package to him. "Take it," he said. "There are dates, bread, and sugar. You can hold out for two days. Here are a thousand francs too." The Arab took the package and the money but kept his full hands at chest level as if he didn't know what to do with what was being given him. "Now look," the schoolmaster said as he pointed in the direction of the east, "there's the way to Tinguit. You have a two-hour walk. At Tinguit you'll find the administration and the police. They are expecting you." The Arab looked toward the east, still holding the package and the money against his chest. Daru took his elbow and turned him rather roughly toward the south. At the foot of the height on which they stood could be

seen a faint path. "That's the trail across the plateau. In a day's walk from here you'll find pasturelands and the first nomads. They'll take you in and shelter you according to their law." The Arab had now turned toward Daru and a sort of panic was visible in his expression. "Listen," he said. Daru shook his head: "No, be quiet. Now I'm leaving you." He turned his back on him, took two long steps in the direction of the school, looked hesitantly at the motionless Arab, and started off again. For a few minutes he heard nothing but his own step resounding on the cold ground and did not turn his head. A moment later, however, he turned around. The Arab was still there on the edge of the hill, his arms hanging now, and he was looking at the schoolmaster. Daru felt something rise in his throat. But he swore with impatience, waved vaguely, and started off again. He had already gone some distance when he again stopped and looked. There was no longer anyone on the hill.

Daru hesitated. The sun was now rather high in the sky and was beginning to beat down on his head. The schoolmaster retraced his steps, at first somewhat uncertainly, then with decision. When he reached the little hill, he was bathed in sweat. He climbed it as fast as he could and stopped, out of breath, at the top. The rock-fields to the south stood out sharply against the blue sky, but on the plain to the east a steamy heat was already rising. And in that slight haze, Daru, with heavy heart, made out the Arab walking slowly on the road to prison.

A little later, standing before the window of the classroom, the schoolmaster was watching the clear light bathing the whole surface of the plateau, but he hardly saw it. Behind him on the blackboard, among the winding French rivers, sprawled the clumsily chalked-up words he had just read: "You handed over our brother. You will pay for this." Daru looked at the sky, the plateau, and, beyond, the invisible lands stretching all the way to the sea. In this vast landscape he had loved so much, he was alone.

For Consideration

1. What is the setting of the story? What kind of atmosphere does it contribute? Daru, who was born in the area, is said to have "felt exiled" everywhere else. Why?

2. What is Balducci's attitude toward his duty regarding the prisoner? How does it differ from Daru's?

3. At one point Daru thinks that "no one in this desert, neither he nor his guest, mattered. And yet, outside this desert neither of them, Daru knew, could have really lived." What explains Daru's ambivalent response to his and the Arab's condition?

4. Daru's feelings toward the Arab change as the story progresses. How does he feel at the beginning? What happens to cause changes in his attitude? Why doesn't Daru want a rope put on the prisoner when Balducci leaves? Where and why do feelings of trust between Daru and the Arab begin to come more apparent?

5. Why does Daru let the Arab decide whether or not to turn himself in? Why, given this choice, does the Arab take the road which will lead to prison?

6. Explain the irony of the final scene, when Daru sees the threatening note written on the blackboard. What is the meaning of the final sentence in the story: "In this vast landscape he had loved so much, he was alone."? Is the concern here only with Daru's physical isolation?

7. Why is the story titled "The Guest" instead of, possibly, "The Captive" or "The Prisoner"?

symbol

Our understanding of a story is dependent, to varying degrees, on our comprehension of plot, character, setting, point of view, tone, and irony. It may also depend on our perception of certain features of a story which have been invested with a unique significance. Authors invent and reinforce **symbols** when they want to present an object or action realistically and, at the same time, give it meaning beyond its literal appearance. Symbolism is one form of **imagery**, that is, language which appeals to one of the senses (see the discussion under Poetry, pp. 271–477).

At this point in interpretation some readers have difficulty because, for them, identifying symbols implies finding "hidden meanings" which (as the disclaimer sometimes goes) an author may never have intended in the first place. The key to answering this objection is to be found within the story itself. However, it is prudent to have a healthy skepticism about the reading of symbols in a story, for undoubtedly anyone can force personal meanings into something he or she has read. After finishing "The Open Boat," a reader may decide that the boat ride represents or symbolizes the joy and freedom to be found in life at sea, away from the frustrations of civilization, where one can be in harmony with nature. That "interpretation" may be appropriate for the raft ride of Huckleberry Finn and Jim, but it ignores and, in fact, contradicts, much of the context of "The Open Boat." Symbolic interpretations can be wrong-headed, but not all of them are. In the case of "The Open Boat" it is surely right to believe that Crane is not simply writing a good adventure story about four shipwrecked men. One clue to this belief is to be found in the constant reveries of the correspondent, who deliberates often and profoundly about the meaning of life. Another clue is seen in the conception of the universe and nature, which, while seeming to be antagonistic to the survival of the men, is finally judged by the narrator to be "flatly indifferent" to their plight. Based on this and other evidence *in the story itself*, the sea journey may be seen as a microcosm of life as the author conceived it. It is symbolic, not of joy and freedom, but of the vicissitudes and uncertainties of life in which the universe as a whole is indifferent to the individual. A key to understanding the story is therefore a willingness to believe that the sea is a sea and something more, that the boat is a boat but also represents something else. Objects or actions such as the maypole in Hawthorne's story, the rescue of Mabel Pervin in "The Horse Dealer's Daughter," or the lake in "St. Emmanuel the Good, Martyr" should be understood in the same way. The stories themselves encourage a symbolic reading. The recognition of this other level of meaning ought neither to distort nor to "ruin" a good story but to add to our appreciation of it.

Occasionally, the symbolic representation is so thorough that there is virtually a one-to-one correspondence between objects, actions, or characters in a story and what they represent on another level. Literature of this type is called **allegory**, to distinguish it from the less exact, less thorough use of symbolism in other forms. In the medieval allegorical play *Everyman* the principal character (named Everyman) meets various companions on his way to death. Their names — Fellowship, Good Deeds, Beauty — suggest immediately the quality with which each is identified. Indeed, in this and other allegories there is hardly a "realistic" level at all; the importance of the piece lies in the values and qualities the characters stand for.

The three stories which follow include a symbolic level, but in different ways and with different effects. "The Horse Dealer's Daughter" includes one central symbolic action, but symbolism is not otherwise pervasive in the story. When Lawrence describes the near-drowning and rescue of Mabel Pervin, he does so in terms which encourage a view of the action as a symbolic death and resurrection. Both Mabel and her rescuer, Jack Fergusson, have been experiencing a death-like existence. After the episode in the water, each is revived and reborn, a change reflected most noticeably in their new attitudes toward each other.

Crane's "The Open Boat," as suggested above, describes the sea, the land, and the entire experience of the men in the boat in terms that point to an important symbolic level running throughout the story. The realistic level of the action remains, at the same time, vivid and convincing.

Jackson's "The Lottery" cannot be judged simply in terms of realistic fiction. Although the characters seem ordinary enough, the action they pursue must be read symbolically if it is to have its greatest impact. Some readers have viewed the story as a modern allegory, with a close correspondence between the action depicted and the meaning it is intended to convey.

D. H. LAWRENCE   (1885—1930)
The Horse Dealer's Daughter

"Well, Mabel, and what are you going to do with yourself?" asked Joe, with foolish flippancy. He felt quite safe himself. Without listening for an answer, he turned aside, worked a grain of tobacco to the tip of his tongue, and spat it out. He did not care about anything, since he felt safe himself.

The three brothers and the sister sat round the desolate breakfast-table, attempting some sort of desultory consultation. The morning's post had given the final tap to the family fortunes, and all was over. The dreary dining-room itself, with its heavy mahogany furniture, looked as if it were waiting to be done away with.

But the consultation amounted to nothing. There was a strange air of ineffectuality about the three men, as they sprawled at table, smoking and reflecting vaguely on their own condition. The girl was alone, a rather short, sullen-looking young woman of twenty-seven. She did not share the same life as her brothers. She would have been good-looking, save for the impressive fixity of her face, 'bull-dog', as her brothers called it.

There was a confused tramping of horses' feet outside. The three men all sprawled round in their chairs to watch. Beyond the dark holly bushes that separated the strip of lawn from the high-road, they could see a cavalcade of shire horses swinging out of their own yard, being taken for exercise. This was the last time. These were the last horses that would go through their hands. The young men watched with critical, callous looks. They were all frightened at the collapse of their lives, and the sense of disaster in which they were involved left them no inner freedom.

Yet they were three fine, well-set fellows enough. Joe, the eldest, was a man of thirty-three, broad and handsome in a hot, flushed way. His face was red, he twisted his black moustache over a thick finger, his eyes were shallow and restless. He had a sensual way of uncovering his teeth when he laughed, and his bearing was stupid. Now he watched the horses with a glazed look of helplessness in his eyes, a certain stupor of downfall.

The great draught-horses swung past. They were tied head to tail, four of them, and they heaved along to where a lane branched off from the high-road, planting their great hoofs floutingly in the fine black mud, swinging their great rounded haunches sumptuously, and trotting a few sudden steps as they were led into the lane, round the corner. Every movement showed a massive, slumbrous strength, and a stupidity which held them in subjection. The groom at the head looked back, jerking the leading rope. And the cavalcade moved out of sight up the lane, the tail of the last horse, bobbed up tight and stiff, held out taut from the swinging great haunches as they rocked behind the hedges in a motion-like sleep.

Joe watched with glazed hopeless eyes. The horses were almóst like his own body to him. He felt he was done for now. Luckily he was engaged to a woman as old as himself, and therefore her father, who was steward of a neighbouring estate, would provide him with a job. He would marry and go into harness. His life was over, he would be a subject animal now.

He turned uneasily aside, the retreating steps of the horses echoing in his ears. Then, with foolish restlessness, he reached for the scraps of bacon-rind from the plates, and making a faint whistling sound, flung them to the terrier that lay against the fender. He watched the dog swallow them, and waited till the creature looked into his eyes. Then a faint grin came on his face, and in a high, foolish voice he said:

"You won't get much more bacon, shall you, you little b ——?"

The dog faintly and dismally wagged its tail, then lowered its haunches, circled round, and lay down again.

There was another helpless silence at the table. Joe sprawled uneasily in his seat, not willing to go till the family conclave was dissolved. Fred Henry, the second brother, was erect, clean-limbed, alert. He had watched the passing of the horses with more *sang-froid*. If he was an animal, like Joe, he was an animal which controls, not one which is controlled. He was master of any horse, and he carried himself with a well-tempered air of mastery. But he was not master of the situations of life. He pushed his coarse brown moustache upwards, off his lip, and glanced irritably at his sister, who sat impassive and inscrutable.

"You'll go and stop with Lucy for a bit, shan't you?" he asked. The girl did not answer.

"I don't see what else you can do," persisted Fred Henry.

"Go as a skivvy," Joe interpolated laconically.

The girl did not move a muscle.

"If I was her, I should go in for training for a nurse," said Malcolm, the youngest of them all. He was the baby of the family, a young man of twenty-two, with a fresh, jaunty *museau*.

But Mabel did not take any notice of him. They had talked at her and round her for so many years, that she hardly heard them at all.

The marble clock on the mantelpiece softly chimed the half-hour, the dog rose uneasily from the hearth-rug and looked at the party at the breakfast-table. But still they sat on in ineffectual conclave.

"Oh, all right," said Joe suddenly, apropos of nothing. "I'll get a move on."

He pushed back his chair, straddled his knees with a downward jerk, to get them free, in horsey fashion, and went to the fire. Still he did not go out of the room; he was curious to know what the others would do or say. He began to charge his pipe, looking down at the dog and saying in a high, affected voice:

"Going wi' me? Going wi' me are ter? Tha'rt goin' further than tha counts on just now, dost hear?"

The dog faintly wagged its tail, the man stuck out his jaw and covered his pipe with his hands, and puffed intently, losing himself in the tobacco, looking down all the while at the dog with an absent brown eye. The dog looked up at him in mournful distrust. Joe stood with his knees stuck out, in real horsey fashion.

"Have you had a letter from Lucy?" Fred Henry asked of his sister.

"Last week," came the neutral reply.

"And what does she say?"

There was no answer.

"Does she *ask* you to go and stop there?" persisted Fred Henry.

"She says I can if I like."

"Well, then, you'd better. Tell her you'll come on Monday."

This was received in silence.

"That's what you'll do then, is it?" said Fred Henry, in some exasperation.

But she made no answer. There was a silence of futility and irritation in the room. Malcolm grinned fatuously.

"You'll have to make up your mind between now and next Wednesday," said Joe loudly, "or else find yourself lodgings on the kerbstone."

The face of the young woman darkened, but she sat on immutable.

"Here's Jack Fergusson!" exclaimed Malcolm, who was looking aimlessly out of the window.

"Where?" exclaimed Joe loudly.

"Just gone past."

"Coming in?"

Malcolm craned his neck to see the gate.

"Yes," he said.

There was a silence. Mabel sat on like one condemned, at the head of the table. Then a whistle was heard from the kitchen. The dog got up and barked sharply. Joe opened the door and shouted:

"Come on."

After a moment a young man entered. He was muffled up in overcoat and a purple woollen scarf, and his tweed cap, which he did not remove, was pulled down on his head. He was of medium height, his face was rather long and pale, his eyes looked tired.

"Hello, Jack! Well, Jack!" exclaimed Malcolm and Joe. Fred Henry merely said: "Jack."

"What's doing?" asked the newcomer, evidently addressing Fred Henry.

"Same. We've got to be out by Wednesday. Got a cold?"

"I have — got it bad, too."

"Why don't you stop in?"

"*Me* stop in? When I can't stand on my legs, perhaps I shall have a chance." The young man spoke huskily. He had a slight Scotch accent.

"It's a knock-out, isn't it," said Joe, boisterously, "if a doctor goes round croaking with a cold. Looks bad for the patients, doesn't it?"

The young doctor looked at him slowly.

"Anything the matter with *you*, then?" he asked sarcastically.

"Not as I know of. Damn your eyes, I hope not. Why?"

"I thought you were very concerned about the patients, wondered if you might be one yourself."

"Damn it, no, I've never been patient to no flaming doctor, and hope I never shall be," returned Joe.

At this point Mabel rose from the table, and they all seemed to become aware of her existence. She began putting the dishes together. The young doctor looked at her, but did not address her. He had not greeted her. She went out of the room with the tray, her face impassive and unchanged.

"When are you off then, all of you?" asked the doctor.

"I'm catching the eleven-forty," replied Malcolm. "Are you goin' down wi' th' trap, Joe?"

"Yes, I've told you I'm going down wi' th' trap, haven't I?"

"We'd better be getting her in then. So long, Jack, if I don't see you before I go," said Malcolm, shaking hands.

He went out, followed by Joe, who seemed to have his tail between his legs.

"Well, this is the devil's own," exclaimed the doctor, when he was left alone with Fred Henry. "Going before Wednesday, are you?"

"That's the orders," replied the other.

"Where, to Northampton?"

"That's it."

"The devil!" exclaimed Fergusson, with quiet chagrin.

And there was silence between the two.

"All settled up, are you?" asked Fergusson.

"About."

There was another pause.

"Well, I shall miss yer, Freddy, boy," said the young doctor.

"And I shall miss thee, Jack," returned the other.

"Miss you like hell," mused the doctor.

Fred Henry turned aside. There was nothing to say. Mabel came in again, to finish clearing the table.

"What are *you* going to do, then, Miss Pervin?" asked Fergusson. "Going to your sister's, are you?"

Mabel looked at him with her steady, dangerous eyes, that always made him uncomfortable, unsettling his superficial ease.

"No," she said.

"Well, what in the name of fortune *are* you going to do? Say what you mean to do," cried Fred Henry, with futile intensity.

But she only averted her head, and continued her work. She folded the white table-cloth, and put on the chenille cloth.

"The sulkiest bitch that ever trod!" muttered her brother.

But she finished her task with perfectly impassive face, the young doctor watching her interestedly all the while. Then she went out.

Fred Henry stared after her, clenching his lips, his blue eyes fixing in sharp antagonism, as he made a grimace of sour exasperation.

"You could bray her into bits, and that's all you'd get out of her," he said, in a small, narrowed tone.

The doctor smiled faintly.

"What's she *going* to do, then?" he asked.

"Strike me if *I* know!" returned the other.

There was a pause. Then the doctor stirred.

"I'll be seeing you to-night, shall I?" he said to his friend.

"Ay — where's it to be? Are we going over to Jessdale?"

"I don't know. I've got such a cold on me. I'll come round to the 'Moon and Stars,' anyway."

"Let Lizzie and May miss their night for once, eh?"

"That's it — if I feel as I do now."

"All's one ——"

The two young men went through the passage and down to the back door together. The house was large, but it was servantless now, and desolate. At the back was a small bricked house-yard and beyond that a big square, gravelled fine and red, and having stables on two sides. Sloping, dank, winter-dark fields stretched away on the open sides.

But the stables were empty. Joseph Pervin, the father of the family, had been a man of no education, who had become a fairly large horse dealer. The stables had been full of horses, there was a great turmoil and come-and-go of horses and of dealers and grooms. Then the kitchen was full of servants. But of late things had declined. The old man had married a second time, to retrieve his fortunes. Now he was dead and everything was gone to the dogs, there was nothing but debt and threatening.

For months, Mabel had been servantless in the big house, keeping the home together in penury for her ineffectual brothers. She had kept house for ten years. But previously it was with unstinted means. Then, however brutal and coarse everything was, the sense of money had kept her proud, confident. The men might be foul-mouthed, the women in the kitchen might have bad reputations, her brothers might have illegitimate children. But so long as there was money, the girl felt herself established, and brutally proud, reserved.

No company came to the house, save dealers and coarse men. Mabel had no associates of her own sex, after her sister went away. But she did not mind. She went regularly to church, she attended to her father. And she lived in the memory of her mother, who had died when she was fourteen, and whom she had loved. She had loved her father, too, in a different way, depending upon him, and feeling secure in him, until at the age of fifty-four he married again. And then she had set hard against him. Now he had died and left them all hopelessly in debt.

She had suffered badly during the period of poverty. Nothing, however, could shake the curious, sullen, animal pride that dominated each member of the family. Now, for Mabel, the end had come. Still she would not cast about her. She would follow her own way just the same. She would always hold the keys of her own situation. Mindless and persistent, she endured from day to day. Why should she think? Why should she answer anybody? It was enough that this was the end, and there was no way out. She need not pass any more darkly along the main street of the small town, avoiding every eye. She need not demean herself any more, going into the shops and buying the cheapest food. This was at an end. She thought of nobody, not even of herself. Mindless and persistent, she seemed in a sort of ecstasy to be coming nearer to her fulfilment, her own glorification, approaching her dead mother, who was glorified.

In the afternoon she took a little bag, with shears and sponge and a small scrubbing-brush, and went out. It was a grey, wintry day, with saddened, dark green fields and an atmosphere blackened by the smoke of foundries not far off. She went quickly, darkly along the causeway, heeding nobody, through the town to the churchyard.

There she always felt secure, as if no one could see her, although as a matter of fact she was exposed to the stare of everyone who passed along under the churchyard wall. Nevertheless, once under the shadow of the great looming church, among the graves, she felt immune from the world, reserved within the thick churchyard wall as in another country.

Carefully she clipped the grass from the grave, and arranged the pinky white, small chrysanthemums in the tin cross. When this was done, she took an empty jar from a neighbouring grave, brought water, and carefully, most scrupulously sponged the marble headstone and the coping-stone.

It gave her sincere satisfaction to do this. She felt in immediate contact with the world of her mother. She took minute pains, went through the park in a state bordering on pure happiness, as if in performing this task she came into a subtle, intimate connection with her mother. For the life she followed here in the world was far less real than the world of death she inherited from her mother.

The doctor's house was just by the church. Fergusson, being a mere hired assistant, was slave to the country-side. As he hurried now to attend to the out-patients in the surgery, glancing across the graveyard with his quick eye, he saw the girl at her task at the grave. She seemed so intent and remote, it was like looking into another world. Some mystical element was touched in him. He slowed down as he walked, watching her as if spellbound.

She lifted her eyes, feeling him looking. Their eyes met. And each looked again at once, each feeling, in some way, found out by the other. He lifted his cap and passed on down the road. There remained distinct in his consciousness, like a vision, the memory of her face, lifted from the tombstone in the churchyard, and looking at him with slow, large, portentous eyes. It *was* portentous, her face. It seemed to mesmerise him. There was a heavy power in her eyes which laid hold of his whole being, as if he had drunk some powerful drug. He had been feeling weak and done before. Now the life came back into him, he felt delivered from his own fretted, daily self.

He finished his duties at the surgery as quickly as might be, hastily filling up the bottles of the waiting people with cheap drugs. Then, in perpetual haste, he set off again to visit several cases in another part of his round, before tea-time. At all times he preferred to walk if he could, but particularly when he was not well. He fancied the motion restored him.

The afternoon was falling. It was grey, deadened, and wintry, with a slow, moist, heavy coldness sinking in and deadening all the faculties. But why should he think or notice? He hastily climbed the hill and turned across the dark green fields, following the black cinder-track. In the distance, across a shallow dip in the country, the small town was clustered like smouldering ash, a tower, a spire, a heap of low, raw, extinct houses. And on the nearest fringe of the town, sloping into the dip, was Oldmeadow, the Pervins' house. He could see the stables and the outbuildings distinctly, as they lay towards him on the slope. Well, he would not go there many more times! Another resource would be lost to him, another place gone: the only company he cared for in the alien, ugly little town he was losing. Nothing but work, drudgery, constant hastening from dwelling to dwelling among the colliers and the iron-workers. It wore him out, but at the same time he had a craving for it. It was a stimulant to him to be in the homes of the working people, moving, as it were, through the innermost body of their life. His nerves were excited and gratified. He could come so near, into the very lives of the rough, inarticulate, powerfully emotional men and women. He grumbled, he said he hated the hellish hole. But as a matter of fact it excited him, the contact with the rough, strongly-feeling people was a stimulant applied direct to his nerves.

Below Oldmeadow, in the green, shallow, soddened hollow of fields, lay a square, deep pond. Roving across the landscape, the doctor's quick eye detected a figure in black passing through the gate of the field, down towards the pond. He looked again. It would be Mabel Pervin. His mind suddenly became alive and attentive.

Why was she going down there? He pulled up on the path on the slope above, and stood staring. He could just make sure of the small black figure moving in the hollow of the failing day. He seemed to see her in the midst of such obscurity, that he was like a clairvoyant, seeing rather with the mind's eye than with ordinary sight. Yet he could see her positively enough, whilst he kept his eye attentive. He felt, if he looked away from her, in the thick, ugly falling dusk, he would lose her altogether.

He followed her minutely as she moved, direct and intent, like something transmitted rather than stirring in voluntary activity, straight down the field towards the pond. There she stood on the bank for a moment. She never raised her head. Then she waded slowly into the water.

He stood motionless as the small black figure walked slowly and deliberately towards the centre of the pond, very slowly, gradually moving deeper into the motionless water, and still moving forward as the water got up to her breast. Then he could see her no more in the dusk of the dead afternoon.

"There!" he exclaimed. "Would you believe it?"

And he hastened straight down, running over the wet, soddened fields, pushing through the hedges, down into the depression of callous wintry obscurity. It took him several minutes to come to the pond. He stood on the bank, breathing heavily. He could see nothing. His eyes seemed to penetrate the dead water. Yes, perhaps that was the dark shadow of her black clothing beneath the surface of the water.

He slowly ventured into the pond. The bottom was deep, soft clay, he sank in, and the water clasped dead cold round his legs. As he stirred he could smell the cold, rotten clay that fouled up into the water. It was objectionable in his lungs. Still, repelled and yet not heeding, he moved deeper into the pond. The cold water rose over his thighs, over his loins, upon his abdomen. The lower part of his body was all sunk in the hideous cold element. And the bottom was so deeply soft and uncertain, he was afraid of pitching with his mouth underneath. He could not swim, and was afraid.

He crouched a little, spreading his hands under the water and moving them round, trying to feel for her. The dead cold pond swayed upon his chest. He moved again, a little deeper, and again, with his hands underneath, he felt all around under the water. And he touched her clothing. But it evaded his fingers. He made a desperate effort to grasp it.

And so doing he lost his balance and went under, horribly, suffocating in the foul earthy water, struggling madly for a few moments. At last, after what seemed an eternity, he got his footing, rose again into the air and looked around. He gasped, and knew he was in the world. Then he looked at the water. She had risen near him. He grasped her clothing, and drawing her nearer, turned to take his way to land again.

He went very slowly, carefully, absorbed in the slow progress. He rose higher, climbing out of the pond. The water was now only about his legs; he was thankful, full of relief to be out of the clutches of the pond. He lifted her and staggered on to the bank, out of the horror of wet, grey clay.

He laid her down on the bank. She was quite unconscious and running with water. He made the water come from her mouth, he worked to restore her. He did not have to work very long before he could feel the breathing begin again in her; she was breathing naturally. He worked a little

longer. He could feel her live beneath his hands; she was coming back. He wiped her face, wrapped her in his overcoat, looked round into the dim, dark grey world, then lifted her and staggered down the bank and across the fields.

It seemed an unthinkably long way, and his burden so heavy he felt he would never get to the house. But at last he was in the stable-yard, and then in the house-yard. He opened the door and went into the house. In the kitchen he laid her down on the hearth-rug and called. The house was empty. But the fire was burning in the grate.

Then again he kneeled to attend to her. She was breathing regularly, her eyes were wide open and as if conscious, but there seemed something missing in her look. She was conscious in herself, but unconscious of her surroundings.

He ran upstairs, took blankets from a bed, and put them before the fire to warm. Then he removed her saturated, earthy-smelling clothing, rubbed her dry with a towel, and wrapped her naked in the blankets. Then he went into the dining-room, to look for spirits. There was a little whisky. He drank a gulp himself, and put some into her mouth.

The effect was instantaneous. She looked full into his face, as if she had been seeing him for some time, and yet had only just become conscious of him.

"Dr. Fergusson?" she said.

"What?" he answered.

He was divesting himself of his coat, intending to find some dry clothing upstairs. He could not bear the smell of the dead, clayey water, and he was mortally afraid for his own health.

"What did I do?" she asked.

"Walked into the pond," he replied. He had begun to shudder like one sick, and could hardly attend to her. Her eyes remained full on him, he seemed to be going dark in his mind, looking back at her helplessly. The shuddering became quieter in him, his life came back to him, dark and unknowing, but strong again.

"Was I out of my mind?" she asked, while her eyes were fixed on him all the time.

"Maybe, for the moment," he replied. He felt quiet, because his strength had come back. The strange fretful strain had left him.

"Am I out of my mind now?" she asked.

"Are you?" he reflected a moment. "No," he answered truthfully, "I don't see that you are." He turned his face aside. He was afraid now, because he felt dazed, and felt dimly that her power was stronger than his, in this issue. And she continued to look at him fixedly all the time. "Can you tell me where I shall find some dry things to put on?" he asked.

"Did you dive into the pond for me?" she asked.

"No," he answered. "I walked in. But I went in overhead as well."

There was silence for a moment. He hesitated. He very much wanted to go upstairs to get into dry clothing. But there was another desire in him. And she seemed to hold him. His will seemed to have gone to sleep, and left him, standing there slack before her. But he felt warm inside himself. He did not shudder at all, though his clothes were sodden on him.

"Why did you?" she asked.

"Because I didn't want you to do such a foolish thing," he said.

"It wasn't foolish," she said, still gazing at him as she lay on the floor, with a sofa cushion under her head. "It was the right thing to do. *I* knew best, then."

"I'll go and shift these wet things," he said. But still he had not the power to move out of her presence, until she sent him. It was as if she had the life of his body in her hands, and he could not extricate himself. Or perhaps he did not want to.

Suddenly she sat up. Then she became aware of her own immediate condition. She felt the blankets about her, she knew her own limbs. For a moment it seemed as if her reason were going. She looked round, with wild eye, as if seeking something. He stood still with fear. She saw her clothing lying scattered.

"Who undressed me?" she asked, her eyes resting full and inevitable on his face.

"I did," he replied, "to bring you round."

For some moments she sat and gazed at him awfully, her lips parted.

"Do you love me, then?" she asked.

He only stood and stared at her, fascinated. His soul seemed to melt.

She shuffled forward on her knees, and put her arms round him, round his legs, as he stood there, pressing her breasts against his knees and thighs, clutching him with strange, convulsive certainty, pressing his thighs against her, drawing him to her face, her throat, as she looked up at him with flaring, humble eyes of transfiguration, triumphant in first possession.

"You love me," she murmured, in strange transport, yearning and triumphant and confident. "You love me. I know you love me, I know."

And she was passionately kissing his knees, through the wet clothing, passionately and indiscriminately kissing his knees, his legs, as if unaware of everything.

He looked down at the tangled wet hair, the wild, bare, animal shoulders. He was amazed, bewildered, and afraid. He had never thought of loving her. He had never wanted to love her. When he rescued her and restored her, he was a doctor, and she was a patient. He had had no single personal thought of her. Nay, this introduction of the personal element was very distasteful to him, a violation of his professional honour. It was horrible to have her there embracing his knees. It was horrible. He revolted from it, violently. And yet — and yet — he had not the power to break away.

She looked at him again, with the same supplication of powerful love, and that same transcendent, frightening light of triumph. In view of the delicate flame which seemed to come from her face like a light, he was powerless. And yet he had never intended to love her. He had never intended. And something stubborn in him could not give way.

"You love me," she repeated, in a murmur of deep, rhapsodic assurance. "You love me."

Her hands were drawing him, drawing him down to her. He was afraid, even a little horrified. For he had, really, no intention of loving her. Yet her hands were drawing him towards her. He put out his hand quickly to steady himself, and grasped her bare shoulder. A flame seemed to burn the hand that grasped her soft shoulder. He had no intention of loving her: his whole will was against his yielding. It was horrible. And yet wonderful was the touch of her shoulders, beautiful the shining of her face. Was she perhaps mad? He had a horror of yielding to her. Yet something in him ached also.

He had been staring away at the door, away from her. But his hand remained on her shoulder. She had gone suddenly very still. He looked down at her. Her eyes were now wide with fear, with doubt, the light was dying from her face, a shadow of terrible greyness was returning. He could not bear the touch of her eyes' question upon him, and the look of death behind the question.

With an inward groan he gave way, and let his heart yield towards her. A sudden gentle smile came on his face. And her eyes, which never left his face, slowly,

slowly filled with tears. He watched the strange water rise in her eyes, like some slow fountain coming up. And his heart seemed to burn and melt away in his breast.

He could not bear to look at her any more. He dropped on his knees and caught her head with his arms and pressed her face against his throat. She was very still. His heart, which seemed to have broken, was burning with a kind of agony in his breast. And he felt her slow, hot tears wetting his throat. But he could not move.

He felt the hot tears wet his neck and the hollows of his neck, and he remained motionless, suspended through one of man's eternities. Only now it had become indispensable to him to have her face pressed close to him; he could never let her go again. He could never let her head go away from the close clutch of his arm. He wanted to remain like that for ever, with his heart hurting him in a pain that was also life to him. Without knowing, he was looking down on her damp, soft brown hair.

Then, as it were suddenly, he smelt the horrid stagnant smell of that water. And at the same moment she drew away from him and looked at him. Her eyes were wistful and unfathomable. He was afraid of them, and he fell to kissing her, not knowing what he was doing. He wanted her eyes not to have that terrible, wistful, unfathomable look.

When she turned her face to him again, a faint delicate flush was glowing, and there was again dawning that terrible shining of joy in her eyes, which really terrified him, and yet which he now wanted to see, because he feared the look of doubt still more.

"You love me?" she said, rather faltering.

"Yes." The word cost him a painful effort. Not because it wasn't true. But because it was too newly true, the *saying* seemed to tear open again his newly-torn heart. And he hardly wanted it to be true, even now.

She lifted her face to him, and he bent forward and kissed her on the mouth, gently, with the one kiss that is an eternal pledge. And as he kissed her his heart strained again in his breast. He never intended to love her. But now it was over. He had crossed over the gulf to her, and all that he had left behind had shrivelled and become void.

After the kiss, her eyes again slowly filled with tears. She sat still, away from him, with her face drooped aside, and her hands folded in her lap. The tears fell very slowly. There was complete silence. He too sat there motionless and silent on the hearth-rug. The strange pain of his heart that was broken seemed to consume him. That he should love her? That this was love! That he should be ripped open in this way! Him, a doctor! How they would all jeer if they knew! It was agony to him to think they might know.

In the curious naked pain of the thought he looked again to her. She was sitting there drooped into a muse. He saw a tear fall, and his heart flared hot. He saw for the first time that one of her shoulders was quite uncovered, one arm bare, he could see one of her small breasts; dimly, because it had become almost dark in the room.

"Why are you crying?" he asked, in an altered voice.

She looked up at him, and behind her tears the consciousness of her situation for the first time brought a dark look of shame to her eyes.

"I'm not crying, really," she said, watching him, half frightened.

He reached his hand, and softly closed it on her bare arm.

"I love you! I love you!" he said in a soft, low vibrating voice, unlike himself.

She shrank, and dropped her head. The soft, penetrating grip of his hand on her arm distressed her. She looked up at him.

"I want to go," she said. "I want to go and get you some dry things."

"Why?" he said. "I'm all right."

"But I want to go," she said. "And I want you to change your things."

He released her arm, and she wrapped herself in the blanket, looking at him rather frightened. And still she did not rise.

"Kiss me," she said wistfully.

He kissed her, but briefly, half in anger.

Then, after a second, she rose nervously, all mixed up in the blanket. He watched her in her confusion as she tried to extricate herself and wrap herself up so that she could walk. He watched her relentlessly, as she knew. And as she went, the blanket trailing, and as he saw a glimpse of her feet and her white leg, he tried to remember her as she was when he had wrapped her in the blanket. But then he didn't want to remember, because she had been nothing to him then, and his nature revolted from remembering her as she was when she was nothing to him.

A tumbling, muffled noise from within the dark house startled him. Then he heard her voice: "There are clothes." He rose and went to the foot of the stairs, and gathered up the garments she had thrown down. Then he came back to the fire, to rub himself down and dress. He grinned at his own appearance when he had finished.

The fire was sinking, so he put on coal. The house was now quite dark, save for the light of a street-lamp that shone in faintly from beyond the holly trees. He lit the gas with matches he found on the mantelpiece. Then he emptied the pockets of his own clothes, and threw all his wet things in a heap into the scullery. After which he gathered up her sodden clothes, gently, and put them in a separate heap on the copper-top in the scullery.

It was six o'clock on the clock. His own watch had stopped. He ought to go back to the surgery. He waited, and still she did not come down. So he went to the foot of the stairs and called:

"I shall have to go."

Almost immediately he heard her coming down. She had on her best dress of black voile, and her hair was tidy, but still damp. She looked at him — and in spite of herself, smiled.

"I don't like you in those clothes," she said.

"Do I look a sight?" he answered.

They were shy of one another.

"I'll make you some tea," she said.

"No, I must go."

"Must you?" And she looked at him again with the wide, strained, doubtful eyes. And again, from the pain of his breast, he knew how he loved her. He went and bent to kiss her, gently, passionately, with his heart's painful kiss.

"And my hair smells so horrible," she murmured in distraction. "And I'm so awful, I'm so awful! Oh no, I'm too awful." And she broke into bitter, heart-broken sobbing. "You can't want to love me, I'm horrible."

"Don't be silly, don't be silly," he said, trying to comfort her, kissing her, holding her in his arms. "I want you, I want to marry you, we're going to be married, quickly, quickly — to-morrow if I can."

But she only sobbed terribly, and cried:

"I feel awful. I feel awful. I feel I'm horrible to you."

"No, I want you, I want you," was all he answered, blindly, with that terrible intonation which frightened her almost more than her horror lest he should *not* want her.

For Consideration

1. Notice the opening descriptions of the Pervin family and their surroundings. What do they suggest about the kind and quality of life of the family? What is the point of the animal-like descriptions of several of the family members?

2. What is Mabel's relationship to her father and brothers? What is her relationship to her mother? Why does she find more real "the world of death she inherited from her mother"? What does this suggest about her?

3. On three occasions in the story Jack and Mabel meet. How do those occasions reveal a changing relationship between the two?

4. What is Jack's response to his life and surroundings? How does he find his circumstances both hateful and exciting?

5. The near-drowning and rescue is the climactic action of the story. How does it function beyond its literal importance? After that incident both Mabel and Jack have changed. Why, and in what ways? Why does Mabel say, so abruptly, "Do you love me, then?" Is the relationship between the two at the end one based on love? How do you explain their almost tormented responses to each other? What is meant by the final words of the story, that the intonation of Jack's voice frightened her "almost more than her horror lest he should *not* want her?"

For Comparison

Mabel Pervin and Anya in "An Anna Round His Neck" (p. 30) both come from depressed family situations. Each has lost a mother and each is the only woman in a family dominated by males. In what other ways are their situations comparable? To what extent is each delivered from her misery?

STEPHEN CRANE   (1871–1900)

The Open Boat

A Tale intended to be after the Fact: Being the Experience of Four Men from the Sunk Steamer Commodore

I

None of them knew the colour of the sky. Their eyes glanced level, and were fastened upon the waves that swept toward them. These waves were of the hue of slate, save for the tops, which were of foaming white, and all of the men knew the colours of the sea. The horizon narrowed and widened, and dipped and rose, and at all times its edge was jagged with waves that seemed thrust up in points like rocks.

Many a man ought to have a bathtub larger than the boat which here rode upon the sea. These waves were most wrongfully and barbarously abrupt and tall, and each froth-top was a problem in small-boat navigation.

The cook squatted in the bottom, and looked with both eyes at the six inches of gunwale which separated him from the ocean. His sleeves were rolled over his fat forearms, and the two flaps of his unbuttoned vest dangled as he bent to bail out the boat. Often he said, "Gawd! that was a narrow clip." As he remarked it he invariably gazed eastward over the broken sea.

The oiler, steering with one of the two oars in the boat, sometimes raised himself suddenly to keep clear of the water that swirled in over the stern. It was a thin little oar, and it seemed often ready to snap.

The correspondent, pulling at the other oar, watched the waves and wondered why he was there.

The injured captain, lying in the bow, was at this time buried in that profound dejection and indifference which come, temporarily at least, to even the bravest and most enduring when, willy-nilly, the firm fails, the army loses, the ship goes down. The mind of the master of a vessel is rooted deep in the timbers of her, though he command for a day or a decade; and this captain had on him the stern impression of a scene in the greys of dawn of seven turned faces, and later a stump of a topmast with a white ball on it, that slashed to and fro at the waves, went low and lower, and down. Thereafter there was something strange in his voice. Although steady, it was deep with mourning, and of a quality beyond oration or tears.

"Keep 'er a little more south, Billie," said he.

"A little more south, sir," said the oiler in the stern.

A seat in this boat was not unlike a seat upon a bucking broncho, and by the same token a broncho is not much smaller. The craft pranced and reared and plunged like an animal. As each wave came, and she rose for it, she seemed like a horse making at a fence outrageously high. The manner of her scramble over these walls of water is a mystic thing, and, moreover, at the top of them were ordinarily these problems in white water, the foam racing down from the summit of each wave requiring a new leap, and a leap from the air. Then, after scornfully bumping a crest, she would slide and race and splash down a long incline, and arrive bobbing and nodding in front of the next menace.

A singular disadvantage of the sea lies in the fact that after successfully surmounting one wave you discover that there is another behind it just as important and just as nervously anxious to do something effective in the way of swamping boats. In a ten-foot dinghy one can get an idea of the resources of the sea in the line of waves that is not probable to the average experience which is never at sea in a dinghy. As each slaty wall of water approached, it shut all else from the view of the men in the boat, and it was not difficult to imagine that this particular wave was the final outburst of the ocean, the last effort of the grim water. There was a terrible grace in the move of the waves, and they came in silence, save for the snarling of the crests.

In the wan light the faces of the men must have been grey. Their eyes must have glinted in strange ways as they gazed steadily astern. Viewed from a balcony, the whole thing would doubtless have been weirdly picturesque. But the men in the boat had no time to see it, and if they had had leisure, there were other things to occupy their minds. The sun swung steadily up the sky, and they knew it was broad day because the colour of the sea changed from slate to emerald green streaked with amber lights, and the foam was like tumbling snow. The process of the breaking day was unknown to them. They were aware only of this effect upon the colour of the waves that rolled toward them.

In disjointed sentences the cook and the correspondent argued as to the difference between a life-saving station and a house of refuge. The cook had said: "There's a house of refuge just north of the Mosquito Inlet Light, and as soon as they see us they'll come off in their boat and pick us up."

"As soon as who see us?" said the correspondent.

"The crew," said the cook.

"Houses of refuge don't have crews," said the correspondent. "As I understand them, they are only places where clothes and grub are stored for the benefit of shipwrecked people. They don't carry crews."

"Oh, yes, they do," said the cook.

"No, they don't," said the correspondent.

"Well, we're not there yet, anyhow," said the oiler, in the stern.

"Well," said the cook, "perhaps it's not a house of refuge that I'm thinking of as being near Mosquito Inlet Light, perhaps it's a life-saving station."

"We're not there yet," said the oiler in the stern.

II

As the boat bounced from the top of each wave the wind tore through the hair of the hatless men, and as the craft plopped her stern down again the spray slashed past them. The crest of each of these waves was a hill, from the top of which the men surveyed for a moment a broad tumultuous expanse, shining and wind-riven. It was probably splendid, it was probably glorious, this play of the free sea, wild with lights of emerald and white and amber.

"Bully good thing it's an on-shore wind," said the cook. "If not, where would we be? Wouldn't have a show."

"That's right," said the correspondent.

The busy oiler nodded his assent.

Then the captain, in the bow, chuckled in a way that expressed humour, contempt, tragedy, all in one. "Do you think

we've got much of a show now, boys?"
said he.

Whereupon the three were silent, save
for a trifle of hemming and hawing. To express any particular optimism at this time
they felt to be childish and stupid, but
they all doubtless possessed this sense of
the situation in their minds. A young man
thinks doggedly at such times. On the
other hand, the ethics of their condition
was decidedly against any open suggestion
of hopelessness. So they were silent.

"Oh, well," said the captain, soothing
his children, "we'll get ashore all right."

But there was that in his tone which
made them think; so the oiler quoth, "Yes!
if this wind holds."

The cook was bailing. "Yes! if we don't
catch hell in the surf."

Canton-flannel gulls flew near and far.
Sometimes they sat down on the sea, near
patches of brown seaweed that rolled over
the waves with a movement like carpets on
a line in a gale. The birds sat comfortably
in groups, and they were envied by some
in the dinghy, for the wrath of the sea was
no more to them than it was to a covey of
prairie chickens a thousand miles inland.
Often they came very close and stared at
the men with black bead-like eyes. At
these times they were uncanny and sinister
in their unblinking scrutiny, and the men
hooted angrily at them, telling them to be
gone. One came, and evidently decided to
alight on the top of the captain's head. The
bird flew parallel to the boat and did not
circle, but made short sidelong jumps in
the air in chicken-fashion. His black eyes
were wistfully fixed upon the captain's
head. "Ugly brute," said the oiler to the
bird. "You look as if you were made with a
jackknife." The cook and the correspondent swore darkly at the creature. The captain naturally wished to knock it away with
the end of the heavy painter, but he did
not dare do it, because anything resembl-
ing an emphatic gesture would have cap-

sized this freighted boat; and so, with his
open hand, the captain gently and carefully waved the gull away. After it had been
discouraged from the pursuit the captain
breathed easier on account of his hair, and
others breathed easier because the bird
struck their minds at this time as being
somehow gruesome and ominous.

In the meantime the oiler and the correspondent rowed. And also they rowed.
They sat together in the same seat, and
each rowed an oar. Then the oiler took
both oars; then the correspondent took
both oars; then the oiler; then the correspondent. They rowed and they rowed.
The very ticklish part of the business was
when the time came for the reclining one
in the stern to take his turn at the oars. By
the very last star of truth, it is easier to
steal eggs from under a hen than it was to
change seats in the dinghy. First the man
in the stern slid his hand along the thwart
and moved with care, as if he were of
Sèvres. Then the man in the rowing-seat
slid his hand along the other thwart. It was
all done with the most extraordinary care.
As the two sidled past each other, the
whole party kept watchful eyes on the
coming wave, and the captain cried:
"Look out, now! Steady, there!"

The brown mats of seaweed that
appeared from time to time were like
islands, bits of earth. They were traveling,
apparently, neither one way nor the other.
They were, to all intents, stationary. They
informed the men in the boat that it was
making progress slowly toward the land.

The captain, rearing cautiously in the
bow after the dinghy soared on a great
swell, said that he had seen the lighthouse
at Mosquito Inlet. Presently the cook
remarked that he had seen it. The correspondent was at the oars then, and for
some reason he too wished to look at the
lighthouse; but his back was toward the far
shore, and the waves were important, and
for some time he could not seize an oppor-

tunity to turn his head. But at last there came a wave more gentle than the others, and when at the crest of it he swiftly scoured the western horizon.

"See it?" said the captain.

"No," said the correspondent, slowly; "I didn't see anything."

"Look again," said the captain. He pointed. "It's exactly in that direction."

At the top of another wave the correspondent did as he was bid, and this time his eyes chanced on a small, still thing on the edge of the swaying horizon. It was precisely like the point of a pin. It took an anxious eye to find a lighthouse so tiny.

"Think we'll make it, Captain?"

"If this wind holds and the boat don't swamp, we can't do much else," said the captain.

The little boat, lifted by each towering sea and splashed viciously by the crests, made progress that in the absence of seaweed was not apparent to those in her. She seemed just a wee thing wallowing, miraculously top up, at the mercy of five oceans. Occasionally a great spread of water, like white flames, swarmed into her.

"Bail her, cook," said the captain, serenely.

"All right, Captain," said the cheerful cook.

III

It would be difficult to describe the subtle brotherhood of men that was here established on the seas. No one said that it was so. No one mentioned it. But it dwelt in the boat, and each man felt it warm him. They were a captain, an oiler, a cook, and a correspondent, and they were friends — friends in a more curiously iron-bound degree than may be common. The hurt captain, lying against the water-jar in the bow, spoke always in a low voice and calmly; but he could never command a more ready and swiftly obedient crew than the motley three of the dinghy. It was more than a mere recognition of what was best for the common safety. There was surely in it a quality that was personal and heart-felt. And after this devotion to the commander of the boat, there was this comradeship, that the correspondent, for instance, who had been taught to be cynical of men, knew even at the time was the best experience of his life. But no one said that it was so. No one mentioned it.

"I wish we had a sail," remarked the captain. "We might try my overcoat on the end of an oar, and give you two boys a chance to rest." So the cook and the correspondent held the mast and spread wide the overcoat; the oiler steered; and the little boat made good way with her new rig. Sometimes the oiler had to scull sharply to keep a sea from breaking into the boat, but otherwise sailing was a success.

Meanwhile the lighthouse had been growing slowly larger. It had now almost assumed colour, and appeared like a little grey shadow on the sky. The man at the oars could not be prevented from turning his head rather often to try for a glimpse of this little grey shadow.

At last, from the top of each wave, the men in the tossing boat could see land. Even as the lighthouse was an upright shadow on the sky, this land seemed but a long black shadow on the sea. It certainly was thinner than paper. "We must be about opposite New Smyrna," said the cook, who had coasted this shore often in schooners. "Captain, by the way, I believe they abandoned that life-saving station there about a year ago."

"Did they?" said the captain.

The wind slowly died away. The cook and the correspondent were not now obliged to slave in order to hold high the oar. But the waves continued their old impetuous swooping at the dinghy, and the little craft, no longer under way, struggled woundily over them. The oiler or the correspondent took the oars again.

Shipwrecks are *àpropos* of nothing. If men could only train for them and have them occur when the men had reached pink condition, there would be less drowning at sea. Of the four in the dinghy none had slept any time worth mentioning for two days and two nights previous to embarking in the dinghy, and in the excitement of clambering about the deck of a foundering ship they had also forgotten to eat heartily.

For these reasons, and for others, neither the oiler nor the correspondent was fond of rowing at this time. The correspondent wondered ingenuously how in the name of all that was sane could there be people who thought it amusing to row a boat. It was not an amusement; it was a diabolical punishment, and even a genius of mental aberrations could never conclude that it was anything but a horror to the muscles and a crime against the back. He mentioned to the boat in general how the amusement of rowing struck him, and the weary-faced oiler smiled in full sympathy. Previously to the foundering, by the way, the oiler had worked a double watch in the engine-room of the ship.

"Take her easy now, boys," said the captain. "Don't spend yourselves. If we have to run a surf you'll need all your strength, because we'll sure have to swim for it. Take your time."

Slowly the land arose from the sea. From a black line it became a line of black and line of white — trees and sand. Finally the captain said that he could make out a house on the shore. "That's the house of refuge, sure," said the cook. "They'll see us before long, and come out after us."

The distant lighthouse reared high. "The keeper ought to be able to make us out now, if he's looking through a glass," said the captain. "He'll notify the life-saving people."

"None of those other boats could have got ashore to give word of this wreck," said the oiler, in a low voice, "else the life-boat would be out hunting us."

Slowly and beautifully the land loomed out of the sea. The wind came again. It had veered from the north-east to the south-east. Finally a new sound struck the ears of the men in the boat. It was the low thunder of the surf on the shore. "We'll never be able to make the lighthouse now," said the captain. "Swing her head a little more north, Billie."

"A little more north, sir," said the oiler.

Whereupon the little boat turned her nose once more down the wind, and all but the oarsman watched the shore grow. Under the influence of this expansion doubt and direful apprehension were leaving the minds of the men. The management of the boat was still most absorbing, but it could not prevent a quiet cheerfulness. In an hour, perhaps, they would be ashore.

Their backbones had become thoroughly used to balancing in the boat, and they now rode this wild colt of a dinghy like circus men. The correspondent thought that he had been drenched to the skin, but happening to feel in the top pocket of his coat, he found therein eight cigars. Four of them were soaked with sea-water; four were perfectly scatheless. After a search, somebody produced three dry matches; and thereupon the four waifs rode impudently in their little boat and, with an assurance of an impending rescue shining in their eyes, puffed at the big cigars, and judged well and ill of all men. Everybody took a drink of water.

IV

"Cook," remarked the captain, "there don't seem to be any signs of life about your house of refuge."

"No," replied the cook. "Funny they don't see us!"

A broad stretch of lowly coast lay before the eyes of the men. It was of low dunes topped with dark vegetation. The roar of the surf was plain, and sometimes they could see the white lip of a wave as it spun up the beach. A tiny house was blocked out black upon the sky. Southward, the slim lighthouse lifted its little grey length.

Tide, wind, and waves were swinging the dinghy northward. "Funny they don't see us," said the men.

The surf's roar was here dulled, but its tone was nevertheless thunderous and mighty. As the boat swam over the great rollers the men sat listening to this roar. "We'll swamp sure," said everybody.

It is fair to say here that there was not a life-saving station within twenty miles in either direction; but the men did not know this fact, and in consequence they made dark and opprobrious remarks concerning the eyesight of the nation's life-savers. Four scowling men sat in the dinghy and surpassed records in the invention of epithets.

"Funny they don't see us."

The light-heartedness of a former time had completely faded. To their sharpened minds it was easy to conjure pictures of all kinds of incompetency and blindness and, indeed, cowardice. There was the shore of the populous land, and it was bitter and bitter to them that from it came no sign.

"Well," said the captain, ultimately, "I suppose we'll have to make a try for ourselves. If we stay out here too long, we'll none of us have strength left to swim after the boat swamps."

And so the oiler, who was at the oars, turned the boat straight for the shore. There was a sudden tightening of muscles. There was some thinking.

"If we don't all get ashore," said the captain — "if we don't all get ashore, I suppose you fellows know where to send news of my finish?"

They then briefly exchanged some addresses and admonitions. As for the reflections of the men, there was a great deal of rage in them. Perchance they might be formulated thus: "If I am going to be drowned — if I am going to be drowned — if I am going to be drowned, why, in the name of the seven mad gods who rule the sea, was I allowed to come thus far and contemplate sand and trees? Was I brought here merely to have my nose dragged away as I was about to nibble the sacred cheese of life? It is preposterous. If this old ninny-woman, Fate, cannot do better than this, she should be deprived of the management of men's fortunes. She is an old hen who knows not her intention. If she has decided to drown me, why did she not do it in the beginning and save me all this trouble? The whole affair is absurd. — But no; she cannot mean to drown me. She dare not drown me. She cannot drown me. Not after all this work." Afterward the man might have had an impulse to shake his fist at the clouds. "Just you drown me, now, and then hear what I call you!"

The billows that came at this time were more formidable. They seemed always just about to break and roll over the little boat in a turmoil of foam. There was a preparatory and long growl in the speech of them. No mind unused to the sea would have concluded that the dinghy could ascend these sheer heights in time. The shore was still afar. The oiler was a wily surfman. "Boys," he said swiftly, "she won't live three minutes more, and we're too far out to swim. Shall I take her to sea again, Captain?"

"Yes; go ahead!" said the captain.

This oiler, by a series of quick miracles and fast and steady oarsmanship, turned the boat in the middle of the surf and took her safely to sea again.

There was a considerable silence as the boat bumped over the furrowed sea to deeper water. Then somebody in gloom spoke: "Well, anyhow, they must have seen us from the shore by now."

The gulls went in slanting flight up the

wind toward the grey, desolate east. A squall, marked by dingy clouds and clouds brick-red like smoke from a burning building, appeared from the south-east.

"What do you think of those life-saving people? Ain't they peaches?"

"Funny they haven't seen us."

"Maybe they think we're out here for sport! Maybe they think we're fishin'. Maybe they think we're damned fools."

It was a long afternoon. A changed tide tried to force them southward, but wind and wave said northward. Far ahead, where coast-line, sea, and sky formed their mighty angle, there were little dots which seemed to indicate a city on the shore.

"St. Augustine?"

The captain shook his head. "Too near Mosquito Inlet."

And the oiler rowed, and then the correspondent rowed; then the oiler rowed. It was a weary business. The human back can become the seat of more aches and pains than are registered in books for the composite anatomy of a regiment. It is a limited area, but it can become the theatre of innumerable muscular conflicts, tangles, wrenches, knots, and other comforts.

"Did you ever like to row, Billie?" asked the correspondent.

"No," said the oiler; "hang it!"

When one exchanged the rowing-seat for a place in the bottom of the boat, he suffered a bodily depression that caused him to be careless of everything save an obligation to wiggle one finger. There was cold seawater swashing to and fro in the boat, and he lay in it. His head, pillowed on a thwart, was within an inch of the swirl of a wavecrest, and sometimes a particularly obstreperous sea came inboard and drenched him once more. But these matters did not annoy him. It is almost certain that if the boat had capsized he would have tumbled comfortably out upon the ocean as if he felt sure that it was a great soft mattress.

"Look! There's a man on the shore!"

"Where?"

"There! See 'im? See 'im?"

"Yes, sure! He's walking along."

"Now he's stopped. Look! He's facing us!"

"He's waving at us!"

"So he is! By thunder!"

"Ah, now we're all right! Now we're all right! There'll be a boat out here for us in half an hour."

"He's going on. He's running. He's going up to that house there."

The remote beach seemed lower than the sea, and it required a searching glance to discern the little black figure. The captain saw a floating stick, and they rowed to it. A bath towel was by some weird chance in the boat, and tying this on the stick, the captain waved it. The oarsman did not dare turn his head, so he was obliged to ask questions.

"What's he doing now?"

"He's standing still again. He's looking, I think. — There he goes again — toward the house. — Now he's stopped again."

"Is he waving at us?"

"No, not now; he was, though."

"Look! There comes another man!"

"He's running."

"Look at him go, would you!"

"Why, he's on a bicycle. Now he's met the other man. They're both waving at us. Look!"

"There comes something up the beach."

"What the devil is that thing?"

"Why, it looks like a boat."

"Why, certainly, it's a boat."

"No; it's on wheels."

"Yes, so it is. Well, that must be the life-boat. They drag them along shore on a wagon."

"That's the life-boat, sure."

"No, by God, it's — it's an omnibus."

"I tell you it's a life-boat."

"It is not! It's an omnibus. I can see it

plain. See? One of these big hotel omnibuses."

"By thunder, you're right. It's an omnibus, sure as fate. What do you suppose they are doing with an omnibus? Maybe they are going around collecting the life-crew, hey?"

"That's it, likely. Look! There's a fellow waving a little black flag. He's standing on the steps of the omnibus. There come those other two fellows. Now they're all talking together. Look at the fellow with the flag. Maybe he ain't waving it!"

"That ain't a flag, is it? That's his coat. Why, certainly, that's his coat."

"So it is; it's his coat. He's taken it off and is waving it around his head. But would you look at him swing it!"

"Oh, say, there isn't any life-saving station there. That's just a winter-resort hotel omnibus that has brought over some of the boarders to see us drown."

"What's that idiot with the coat mean? What's he signaling, anyhow?"

"It looks as if he were trying to tell us to go north. There must be a life-saving station up there."

"No; he thinks we're fishing. Just giving us a merry hand. See? Ah, there, Willie!"

"Well, I wish I could make something out of those signals. What do you suppose he means?"

"He don't mean anything; he's just playing."

"Well, if he'd just signal us to try the surf again, or to go to sea and wait, or go north, or go south, or go to hell, there would be some reason in it. But look at him! He just stands there and keeps his coat revolving like a wheel. The ass!"

"There come more people."

"Now there's quite a mob. Look! Isn't that a boat?"

"Where? Oh, I see where you mean. No, that's no boat."

"That fellow is still waving his coat."

"He must think we like to see him do that. Why don't he quit it? It don't mean anything."

"I don't know. I think he is trying to make us go north. It must be that there's a life-saving station there somewhere."

"Say, he ain't tired yet. Look at 'im wave!"

"Wonder how long he can keep that up. He's been revolving his coat ever since he caught sight of us. He's an idiot. Why aren't they getting men to bring a boat out? A fishing-boat — one of those big yawls — could come out here all right. Why don't he do something?"

"Oh, it's all right now."

"They'll have a boat out here for us in less than no time, now that they've seen us."

A faint yellow tone came into the sky over the low land. The shadows on the sea slowly deepened. The wind bore coldness with it, and the men began to shiver.

"Holy smoke!" said one, allowing his voice to express his impious mood, "if we keep on monkeying out here! If we've got to flounder out here all night!"

"Oh, we'll never have to stay here all night! Don't you worry. They've seen us now, and it won't be long before they'll come chasing out after us."

The shore grew dusky. The man waving a coat blended gradually into this gloom, and it swallowed in the same manner the omnibus and the group of people. The spray, when it dashed uproariously over the side, made the voyagers shrink and swear like men who were being branded.

"I'd like to catch the chump who waved the coat. I feel like socking him one, just for luck."

"Why? What did he do?"

"Oh, nothing, but then he seemed so damned cheerful."

In the meantime the oiler rowed, and then the correspondent rowed, and then the oiler rowed. Grey-faced and bowed forward, they mechanically, turn by turn, plied the leaden oars. The form of the lighthouse had vanished from the southern horizon, but finally a pale star appeared, just lifting from the sea. The streaked saffron in the west passed before the all-merging darkness, and the sea to the east was black. The land had vanished, and was expressed only by the low and drear thunder of the surf.

"If I am going to be drowned — if I am going to be drowned — if I am going to be drowned, why, in the name of the seven mad gods who rule the sea, was I allowed to come thus far and contemplate sand and trees? Was I brought here merely to have my nose dragged away as I was about to nibble the sacred cheese of life?"

The patient captain, drooped over the water-jar, was sometimes obliged to speak to the oarsman.

"Keep her head up! Keep her head up!"

"Keep her head up, sir." The voices were weary and low.

This was surely a quiet evening. All save the oarsman lay heavily and listlessly in the boat's bottom. As for him, his eyes were just capable of noting the tall black waves that swept forward in a most sinister silence, save for an occasional subdued growl of a crest.

The cook's head was on a thwart, and he looked without interest at the water under his nose. He was deep in other scenes. Finally he spoke, "Billie," he murmured, dreamfully, "what kind of pie do you like best?"

V

"Pie!" said the oiler and the correspondent, agitatedly, "Don't talk about those things, blast you!"

"Well," said the cook, "I was just thinking about ham sandwiches and —"

A night on the sea in an open boat is a long night. As darkness settled finally, the shine of the light, lifting from the sea in the south, changed to full gold. On the northern horizon a new light appeared, a small bluish gleam on the edge of the waters. These two lights were the furniture of the world. Otherwise there was nothing but waves.

Two men huddled in the stern, and distances were so magnificent in the dinghy that the rower was enabled to keep his feet partly warm by thrusting them under his companions. Their legs indeed extended far under the rowing-seat until they touched the feet of the captain forward. Sometimes, despite the efforts of the tired oarsman, a wave came piling into the boat, an icy wave of the night, and the chilling water soaked them anew. They would twist their bodies for a moment and groan, and sleep the dead sleep once more, while the water in the boat gurgled about them as the craft rocked.

The plan of the oiler and the correspondent was for one to row until he lost the ability, and then arouse the other from his sea-water couch in the bottom of the boat.

The oiler plied the oars until his head drooped forward and the overpowering sleep blinded him; and he rowed yet afterward. Then he touched a man in the bottom of the boat, and called his name. "Will you spell me for a little while?" he said, meekly.

"Sure, Billie," said the correspondent, awaking and dragging himself to a sitting position. They exchanged places carefully, and the oiler, cuddling down in the sea-water at the cook's side, seemed to go to sleep instantly.

The particular violence of the sea had ceased. The waves came without snarling. The obligation of the man at the oars was to keep the boat headed so that the tilt of the rollers would not capsize her, and to preserve her from filling when the crests rushed past. The black waves were silent and hard to be seen in the darkness. Often one was almost upon the boat before the oarsman was aware.

In a low voice the correspondent addressed the captain. He was not sure that the captain was awake, although this iron man seemed to be always awake. "Captain, shall I keep her making for that light north, sir?"

The same steady voice answered him. "Yes. Keep it about two points off the port bow."

The cook had tied a life-belt around himself in order to get even the warmth which this clumsy cork contrivance could donate, and he seemed almost stove-like when a rower, whose teeth invariably chattered wildly as soon as he ceased his labour, dropped down to sleep.

The correspondent, as he rowed, looked down at the two men sleeping underfoot. The cook's arm was around the oiler's shoulders, and, with their fragmentary clothing and haggard faces, they were the babes of the sea — a grotesque rendering of the old babes in the wood.

Later he must have grown stupid at his work, for suddenly there was a growling of water, and a crest came with a roar and a swash into the boat, and it was a wonder that it did not set the cook afloat in his lifebelt. The cook continued to sleep, but the oiler sat up, blinking his eyes and shaking with the new cold.

"Oh, I'm awfully sorry, Billie," said the correspondent, contritely.

"That's all right, old boy," said the oiler, and lay down again and was asleep.

Presently it seemed that even the captain dozed, and the correspondent thought that he was the one man afloat on all the oceans. The wind had a voice as it came over the waves, and it was sadder than the end.

There was a long, loud swishing astern of the boat, and a gleaming trail of phosphorescence, like blue flame, was furrowed on the black waters. It might have

been made by a monstrous knife.

Then there came a stillness, while the correspondent breathed with open mouth and looked at the sea.

Suddenly there was another swish and another long flash of bluish light, and this time it was alongside the boat, and might almost have been reached with an oar. The correspondent saw an enormous fin speed like a shadow through the water, hurling the crystalline spray and leaving the long glowing trail.

The correspondent looked over his shoulder at the captain. His face was hidden, and he seemed to be asleep. He looked at the babes of the sea. They certainly were asleep. So, being bereft of sympathy, he leaned a little way to one side and swore softly into the sea.

But the thing did not then leave the vicinity of the boat. Ahead or astern, on one side or the other, at intervals long or short, fled the long sparkling streak, and there was to be heard the *whirroo* of the dark fin. The speed and power of the thing was greatly to be admired. It cut the water like a gigantic and keen projectile.

The presence of this biding thing did not affect the man with the same horror that it would if he had been a picnicker. He simply looked at the sea dully and swore in an undertone.

Nevertheless, it is true that he did not wish to be alone with the thing. He wished one of his companions to awake by chance and keep him company with it. But the captain hung motionless over the water-jar, and the oiler and cook in the bottom of the boat were plunged in slumber.

VI

"If I am going to be drowned — if I am going to be drowned — if I am going to be drowned, why, in the name of the seven mad gods who rule the sea, was I allowed to come thus far and contemplate sand and trees?"

During this dismal night, it may be remarked that a man would conclude that it was really the intention of the seven mad gods to drown him, despite the abominable injustice of it. For it was certainly an abominable injustice to drown a man who had worked so hard, so hard. The man felt it would be a crime most unnatural. Other people had drowned at sea since galleys swarmed with painted sails, but still —

When it occurs to a man that nature does not regard him as important, and that she feels she would not maim the universe by disposing of him, he at first wishes to throw bricks at the temple, and he hates deeply the fact that there are no bricks and no temples. Any visible expression of nature would surely be pelleted with his jeers.

Then, if there be no tangible thing to hoot, he feels, perhaps, the desire to confront a personification and indulge in pleas, bowed to one knee, and with hands supplicant, saying, "Yes, but I love myself."

A high cold star on a winter's night is the word he feels that she says to him. Thereafter he knows the pathos of his situation.

The men in the dinghy had not discussed these matters, but each had, no doubt, reflected upon them in silence and according to his mind. There was seldom any expression upon their faces save the general one of complete weariness. Speech was devoted to the business of the boat.

To chime the notes of his emotion, a verse mysteriously entered the correspondent's head. He had even forgotten that he had forgotten this verse, but it suddenly was in his mind.

> A soldier of the Legion lay dying in
> Algiers;
> There was lack of woman's nursing,
> there was dearth of woman's tears;
> But a comrade stood beside him, and
> he took that comrade's hand,
> And he said, "I never more shall see
> my own, my native land."

In his childhood the correspondent had been made acquainted with the fact that a soldier of the Legion lay dying in Algiers, but he had never regarded the fact as important. Myriads of his school-fellows had informed him of the soldier's plight, but the dinning had naturally ended by making him perfectly indifferent. He had never considered it his affair that a soldier of the Legion lay dying in Algiers, nor had it appeared to him as a matter for sorrow. It was less to him than the breaking of a pencil's point.

Now, however, it quaintly came to him as a human, living thing. It was no longer merely a picture of a few throes in the breast of a poet, meanwhile drinking tea and warming his feet at the grate; it was an actuality — stern, mournful, and fine.

The correspondent plainly saw the soldier. He lay on the sand with his feet out straight and still. While his pale left hand was upon his chest in an attempt to thwart the going of his life, the blood came between his fingers. In the far Algerian distance, a city of low square forms was set against a sky that was faint with the last sunset hues. The correspondent, plying the oars and dreaming of the slow and slower movements of the lips of the soldier, was moved by a profound and perfectly impersonal comprehension. He was sorry for the soldier of the Legion who lay dying in Algiers.

The thing which had followed the boat and waited had evidently grown bored at the delay. There was no longer to be heard the slash of the cut-water, and there was no longer the flame of the long trail. The light in the north still glimmered, but it was apparently no nearer to the boat. Sometimes the boom of the surf rang in the correspondent's ears, and he turned the craft seaward then and rowed harder. Southward, some one had evidently built a watch-fire on the beach. It was too low and too far to be seen, but it made a shimmering, roseate reflection upon the bluff in back of it, and this could be discerned from the boat. The wind came stronger, and sometimes a wave suddenly raged out like a mountain cat, and there was to be seen the sheen and sparkle of a broken crest.

The captain, in the bow, moved on his water-jar and sat erect. "Pretty long night," he observed to the correspondent. He looked at the shore. "Those life-saving people take their time."

"Did you see that shark playing around?"

"Yes, I saw him. He was a big fellow, all right."

"Wish I had known you were awake."

Later the correspondent spoke into the bottom of the boat. "Billie!" There was a slow and gradual disentanglement. "Billie, will you spell me?"

"Sure," said the oiler.

As soon as the correspondent touched the cold, comfortable sea-water in the bottom of the boat and had huddled close to the cook's life-belt he was deep in sleep, despite the fact that his teeth played all the popular airs. This sleep was so good to him that it was but a moment before he heard a voice call his name in a tone that demonstrated the last stages of exhaustion. "Will you spell me?"

"Sure, Billie."

The light in the north had mysteriously vanished, but the correspondent took his course from the wide-awake captain.

Later in the night they took the boat farther out to sea, and the captain directed the cook to take one oar at the stern and keep the boat facing the seas. He was to call out if he should hear the thunder of the surf. This plan enabled the oiler and the correspondent to get respite together.

"We'll give those boys a chance to get into shape again," said the captain. They curled down and, after a few preliminary chatterings and trembles, slept once more the dead sleep. Neither knew they had bequeathed to the cook the company of another shark, or perhaps the same shark.

As the boat caroused on the waves, spray occasionally bumped over the side and gave them a fresh soaking, but this had no power to break their repose. The ominous slash of the wind and the water affected them as it would have affected mummies.

"Boys," said the cook, with the notes of every reluctance in his voice, "she's drifted in pretty close. I guess one of you had better take her to sea again." The correspondent, aroused, heard the crash of the toppled crests.

As he was rowing, the captain gave him some whisky-and-water, and this steadied the chills out of him. "If I ever get ashore and anybody shows me even a photograph of an oar—"

At last there was a short conversation.

"Billie! — Billie, will you spell me?"

"Sure," said the oiler.

VII

When the correspondent again opened his eyes, the sea and the sky were each of the grey hue of the dawning. Later, carmine and gold was painted upon the waters. The morning appeared finally, in its splendour, with a sky of pure blue, and the sunlight flamed on the tips of the waves.

On the distant dunes were set many little black cottages, and a tall white windmill reared above them. No man, nor dog, nor bicycle appeared on the beach. The cottages might have formed a deserted village.

The voyagers scanned the shore. A conference was held in the boat. "Well," said the captain, "if no help is coming, we might better try a run through the surf right away. If we stay out here much longer we will be too weak to do anything for ourselves at all." The others silently acquiesced in this reasoning. The boat was headed for the beach. The correspondent wondered if none ever ascended the tall wind-tower, and if then they never looked seaward. This tower was a giant, standing with its back to the plight of the ants. It represented in a degree, to the correspondent, the serenity of nature amid the struggles of the individual — nature in the wind, and nature in the vision of men. She did not seem cruel to him then, nor beneficent, nor treacherous, nor wise. But she was indifferent, flatly indifferent. It is, perhaps, plausible that a man in this situation, impressed with the unconcern of the universe, should see the innumerable flaws of his life, and have them taste wickedly in his mind, and wish for another chance. A distinction between right and wrong seems absurdly clear to him, then, in this new ignorance of the grave-edge, and he understands that if he were given another opportunity he would mend his conduct and his words, and be better and brighter during an introduction or at a tea.

"Now, boys," said the captain, "she is going to swamp sure. All we can do is to work her in as far as possible, and then when she swamps, pile out and scramble for the beach. Keep cool now, and don't jump until she swamps sure."

The oiler took the oars. Over his shoulders he scanned the surf. "Captain," he said, "I think I'd better bring her about and keep her head-on to the seas and back her in."

"All right, Billie," said the captain. "Back her in." The oiler swung the boat then, and, seated in the stern, the cook and the correspondent were obliged to look over their shoulders to contemplate the lonely and indifferent shore.

The monstrous inshore rollers heaved the boat high until the men were again enabled to see the white sheets of water scudding up the slanted beach. "We won't get in very close," said the captain. Each time a man could wrest his attention from the rollers, he turned his glance toward the shore, and in the expression of the eyes during this contemplation there was a singular quality. The correspondent, observing the others, knew that they were not afraid, but the full meaning of their glances was shrouded.

As for himself, he was too tired to grapple fundamentally with the fact. He tried to coerce his mind into thinking of it, but the mind was dominated at this time by the muscles, and the muscles said they did not care. It merely occurred to him that if he should drown it would be a shame.

There were no hurried words, no pallor, no plain agitation. The men simply looked at the shore. "Now, remember to get well clear of the boat when you jump," said the captain.

Seaward the crest of a roller suddenly fell with a thunderous crash, and the long white comber came roaring down upon the boat.

"Steady now," said the captain. The men were silent. They turned their eyes from the shore to the comber and waited. The boat slid up the incline, leaped at the furious top, bounced over it, and swung down the long back of the wave. Some water had been shipped, and the cook bailed it out.

But the next crest crashed also. The tumbling, boiling flood of white water caught the boat and whirled it almost perpendicular. Water swarmed in from all sides. The correspondent had his hands on the gunwale at this time, and when the water entered at that place he swiftly withdrew his fingers, as if he objected to wetting them.

The little boat, drunken with this weight of water, reeled and snuggled deeper into the sea.

"Bail her out, cook! Bail her out!" said the captain.

"All right, Captain," said the cook.

"Now, boys, the next one will do for us sure," said the oiler. "Mind to jump clear of the boat."

The third wave moved forward, huge, furious, implacable. It fairly swallowed the dinghy, and almost simultaneously the men tumbled into the sea. A piece of life-belt had lain in the bottom of the boat, and as the correspondent went overboard he held this to his chest with his left hand.

The January water was icy, and he reflected immediately that it was colder than he had expected to find it off the coast of Florida. This appeared to his dazed mind as a fact important enough to be noted at the time. The coldness of the water was sad; it was tragic. This fact was somehow mixed and confused with his opinion of his own situation, so that it seemed almost a proper reason for tears. The water was cold.

When he came to the surface he was conscious of little but the noisy water. Afterward he saw his companions in the sea. The oiler was ahead in the race. He was swimming strongly and rapidly. Off to the correspondent's left, the cook's great white and corked back bulged out of the water; and in the rear the captain was hanging with his one good hand to the keel of the overturned dinghy.

There is a certain immovable quality to a shore, and the correspondent wondered at it amid the confusion of the sea.

It seemed also very attractive; but the correspondent knew that it was a long journey, and he paddled leisurely. The piece of life-preserver lay under him, and sometimes he whirled down the incline of a wave as if he were on a hand-sled.

But finally he arrived at a place in the sea where travel was beset with difficulty. He did not pause swimming to inquire what manner of current had caught him, but there his progress ceased. The shore was set before him like a bit of scenery on a stage, and he looked at it and understood with his eyes each detail of it.

As the cook passed, much farther to the left, the captain was calling to him. "Turn over on your back, cook! Turn over on your back and use the oar."

"All right, sir." The cook turned on his back, and, paddling with an oar, went ahead as if he were a canoe.

Presently the boat also passed to the left of the correspondent, with the captain clinging with one hand to the keel. He would have appeared like a man raising himself to look over a board fence if it were not for the extraordinary gymnastics of the boat. The correspondent marvelled that the captain could still hold to it.

They passed on nearer to the shore — the oiler, the cook, the captain — and following them went the water-jar, bouncing gaily over the seas.

The correspondent remained in the grip of this strange new enemy — a current. The shore, with its white slope of sand and its green bluff topped with little silent cottages, was spread like a picture before him. It was very near to him then, but he was impressed as one who, in a gallery, looks at a scene from Brittany or Algiers.

He thought: "I am going to drown? Can it be possible? Can it be possible? Can it be possible?" Perhaps an individual must consider his own death to be the final phenomenon of nature.

But later a wave perhaps whirled him out of his small deadly current, for he found suddenly that he could again make progress toward the shore. Later still he was aware that the captain, clinging with one hand to the keel of the dinghy, had his face turned away from the shore and toward him, and was calling his name. "Come to the boat! Come to the boat!"

In his struggle to reach the captain and the boat, he reflected that when one gets properly wearied drowning must really be a comfortable arrangement — a cessation of hostilities accompanied by a large degree of relief; and he was glad of it, for the main thing in his mind for some moments had been horror of the temporary agony. He did not wish to be hurt.

Presently he saw a man running along the shore. He was undressing with most remarkable speed. Coat, trousers, shirt, everything flew magically off him.

"Come to the boat!" called the captain.

"All right, Captain." As the correspondent paddled, he saw the captain let himself down to bottom and leave the boat. Then the correspondent performed his one little marvel of the voyage. A large wave caught him and flung him with ease and supreme speed completely over the boat and far beyond it. It struck him even then as an event in gymnastics and a true miracle of the sea. An overturned boat in the surf is not a plaything to a swimming man.

The correspondent arrived in water that reached only to his waist, but his condition did not enable him to stand for more than a moment. Each wave knocked him into a heap, and the undertow pulled at him.

Then he saw the man who had been running and undressing, and undressing and running, come bounding into the water. He dragged ashore the cook, and then waded toward the captain; but the captain waved him away and sent him to the correspondent. He was naked — naked as a tree in winter; but a halo was about his head, and he shone like a saint. He gave a strong pull, and a long drag, and a bully heave at the correspondent's hand. The correspondent, schooled in the minor formulae, said "Thanks, old man." But suddenly the man cried, "What's that?" He pointed a swift finger. The correspondent said, "Go."

In the shallows, face downward, lay the oiler. His forehead touched sand that was periodically, between each wave, clear of the sea.

The correspondent did not know all that transpired afterward. When he achieved safe ground he fell, striking the sand with each particular part of his body. It was as if he had dropped from a roof, but the thud was grateful to him.

It seemed that instantly the beach was populated with men with blankets, clothes, and flasks, and women with coffee-pots and all the remedies sacred to their minds. The welcome of the land to the men from the sea was warm and generous; but a still and dripping shape was carried slowly up the beach, and the land's welcome for it could only be the different and sinister hospitality of the grave.

When it came night, the white waves paced to and fro in the moonlight, and the wind brought the sound of the great sea's voice to the men on the shore, and they felt that they could then be interpreters.

For Consideration

1. This story is drawn from an experience Crane actually had at sea and which he wrote about in a journalistic piece for an American newspaper. How in this fictional account does Crane create the illusion of reality? What in the story suggests that it is more than an adventure at sea?

2. The point of view is third-person but limited. Through whose mind do we perceive most of the action? What can Crane accomplish through this point of view that he could not accomplish through another form of narration?

3. What is the condition of the men at sea? Does that condition change as the story unfolds? How do the men respond to their predicament? To each other? What is the significance of the "subtle brotherhood" they have established? How does this brotherhood relate to the correspondent's sympathetic response to the story of the dying soldier in Algiers?

4. What kind of values and qualities does the sea represent in the story? The land? Are those values static or changing in the story? Compare the inhabitants on land to the men at sea.

5. What conception of the universe is implied in the two passages on the "seven mad gods who rule the sea"? What is the relative position of humankind in these passages and in the story in general?

6. The correspondent thinks frequently about the character and role of nature. What does "nature" mean here? What kind of force is it finally seen to be?

7. Is the ending of the story a confirmation or denial of the correspondent's recognition of a "flatly indifferent" universe? In what sense are the three survivors "interpreters"? Interpreters of what?

SHIRLEY JACKSON (1919–1965)

The Lottery

The morning of June 27th was clear and sunny, with the fresh warmth of a full-summer day; the flowers were blossoming profusely and the grass was richly green. The people of the village began to gather in the square, between the post office and the bank, around ten o'clock; in some towns there were so many people that the lottery took two days and had to be started on June 26th, but in this village, where there were only about three hundred people, the whole lottery took less than two hours, so it could begin at ten o'clock in the morning and still be through in time to allow the villagers to get home for noon dinner.

The children assembled first, of course. School was recently over for the summer, and the feeling of liberty sat uneasily on most of them; they tended to gather together quietly for a while before they broke into boisterous play, and their talk was still of the classroom and the teacher, of books and reprimands. Bobby Martin had already stuffed his pockets full of stones, and the other boys soon followed his example, selecting the smoothest and roundest stones; Bobby and Harry Jones and Dickie Delacroix — the villagers pronounced this name "Dellacroy" — eventually made a great pile of stones in one corner of the square and guarded it against the raids of the other boys. The girls stood aside, talking among themselves, looking over their shoulders at the boys, and the very small children rolled in the dust or clung to the hands of their older brothers or sisters.

Soon the men began to gather, surveying their own children, speaking of planting and rain, tractors and taxes. They stood together, away from the pile of stones in the corner, and their jokes were quiet and they smiled rather than laughed. The women, wearing faded house dresses and sweaters, came shortly after their menfolk. They greeted one another and exchanged bits of gossip as they went to join their husbands. Soon the women, standing by their husbands, began to call to their children, and the children came reluctantly, having to be called four or five times. Bobby Martin ducked under his mother's grasping hand and ran, laughing, back to the pile of stones. His father spoke up sharply, and Bobby came quickly and took his place between his father and his oldest brother.

The lottery was conducted — as were

the square dances, the teen-age club, the Halloween program — by Mr. Summers, who had time and energy to devote to civic activities. He was a round-faced, jovial man and he ran the coal business, and people were sorry for him, because he had no children and his wife was a scold. When he arrived in the square, carrying the black wooden box, there was a murmur of conversation among the villagers, and he waved and called, "Little late today, folks." The postmaster, Mr. Graves, followed him, carrying a three-legged stool, and the stool was put in the center of the square and Mr. Summers set the black box down on it. The villagers kept their distance, leaving a space between themselves and the stool, and when Mr. Summers said, "Some of you fellows want to give me a hand?" there was a hesitation before two men, Mr. Martin and his oldest son, Baxter, came forward to hold the box steady on the stool while Mr. Summers stirred up the papers inside it.

The original paraphernalia for the lottery had been lost long ago, and the black box now resting on the stool had been put into use even before Old Man Warner, the oldest man in town, was born. Mr. Summers spoke frequently to the villagers about making a new box, but no one liked to upset even as much tradition as was represented by the black box. There was a story that the present box had been made with some pieces of the box that had preceded it, the one that had been constructed when the first people settled down to make a village here. Every year, after the lottery, Mr. Summers began talking again about a new box, but every year the subject was allowed to fade off without anything's being done. The black box grew shabbier each year; by now it was no longer completely black but splintered badly along one side to show the original wood color, and in some places faded or stained.

Mr. Martin and his oldest son, Baxter, held the black box securely on the stool until Mr. Summers had stirred the papers thoroughly with his hand. Because so much of the ritual had been forgotten or discarded, Mr. Summers had been successful in having slips of paper substituted for the chips of wood that had been used for generations. Chips of wood, Mr. Summers had argued, had been all very well when the village was tiny, but now that the population was more than three hundred and likely to keep on growing, it was necessary to use something that would fit more easily into the black box. The night before the lottery, Mr. Summers and Mr. Graves made up the slips of paper and put them in the box, and it was then taken to the safe of Mr. Summers' coal company and locked up until Mr. Summers was ready to take it to the square next morning. The rest of the year, the box was put away, sometimes one place, sometimes another; it had spent one year in Mr. Graves's barn and another year underfoot in the post office, and sometimes it was set on a shelf in the Martin grocery and left there.

There was a great deal of fussing to be done before Mr. Summers declared the lottery open. There were the lists to make up — of heads of families, heads of households in each family, members of each household in each family. There was the proper swearing-in of Mr. Summers by the postmaster, as the official of the lottery; at one time, some people remembered, there had been a recital of some sort, performed by the official of the lottery, a perfunctory, tuneless chant that had been rattled off duly each year; some people believed that the official of the lottery used to stand just so when he said or sang it, others believed that he was supposed to walk among the people, but years and years ago this part of the ritual had been allowed to lapse. There had been,

also, a ritual salute, which the official of the lottery had had to use in addressing each person who came up to draw from the box, but this also had changed with time, until now it was felt necessary only for the official to speak to each person approaching. Mr. Summers was very good at all this; in his clean white shirt and blue jeans, with one hand resting carelessly on the black box, he seemed very proper and important as he talked interminably to Mr. Graves and the Martins.

Just as Mr. Summers finally left off talking and turned to the assembled villagers, Mrs. Hutchinson came hurriedly along the path to the square, her sweater thrown over her shoulders, and slid into place in the back of the crowd. "Clean forgot what day it was," she said to Mrs. Delacroix, who stood next to her, and they both laughed softly. "Thought my old man was out back stacking wood," Mrs. Hutchinson went on, "and then I looked out the window and the kids was gone, and then I remembered it was the twenty-seventh and came a-running." She dried her hands on her apron, and Mrs. Delacroix said, "You're in time, though. They're still talking away up there."

Mrs. Hutchinson craned her neck to see through the crowd and found her husband and children standing near the front. She tapped Mrs. Delacroix on the arm as a farewell and began to make her way through the crowd. The people separated good-humoredly to let her through; two or three people said, in voices just loud enough to be heard across the crowd, "Here comes your Missus, Hutchinson," and "Bill, she made it after all." Mrs. Hutchinson reached her husband, and Mr. Summers, who had been waiting, said cheerfully, "Thought we were going to have to get on without you, Tessie." Mrs. Hutchinson said, grinning, "Wouldn't have me leave m'dishes in the sink, now, would you, Joe?", and soft laughter ran through the crowd as the people stirred back into position after Mrs. Hutchinson's arrival.

"Well, now," Mr. Summers said soberly, "guess we better get started, get this over with, so's we can go back to work. Anybody ain't here?"

"Dunbar," several people said. "Dunbar, Dunbar."

Mr. Summers consulted his list. "Clyde Dunbar," he said. "That's right. He's broke his leg, hasn't he? Who's drawing for him?"

"Me, I guess," a woman said, and Mr. Summers turned to look at her. "Wife draws for her husband," Mr. Summers said. "Don't you have a grown boy to do it for you, Janey?" Although Mr. Summers and everyone else in the village knew the answer perfectly well, it was the business of the official of the lottery to ask such questions formally. Mr. Summers waited with an expression of polite interest while Mrs. Dunbar answered.

"Horace's not but sixteen yet," Mrs. Dunbar said regretfully. "Guess I gotta fill in for the old man this year."

"Right," Mr. Summers said. He made a note on the list he was holding. Then he asked, "Watson boy drawing this year?"

A tall boy in the crowd raised his hand. "Here," he said. "I'm drawing for m'mother and me." He blinked his eyes nervously and ducked his head as several voices in the crowd said things like "Good fellow, Jack," and "Glad to see your mother's got a man to do it."

"Well," Mr. Summers said, "guess that's everyone. Old Man Warner make it?"

"Here," a voice said, and Mr. Summers nodded.

A sudden hush fell on the crowd as Mr. Summers cleared his throat and looked at the list. "All ready?" he called. "Now, I'll read the names — heads of families first — and the men come up and take a paper out of the box. Keep the paper folded in your hand without looking at it until everyone has had a turn. Everything clear?"

The people had done it so many times that they only half listened to the directions; most of them were quiet, wetting their lips, not looking around. Then Mr. Summers raised one hand high and said, "Adams." A man disengaged himself from the crowd and came forward. "Hi, Steve," Mr. Summers said, and Mr. Adams said, "Hi, Joe." They grinned at one another humorlessly and nervously. Then Mr. Adams reached into the black box and took out a folded paper. He held it firmly by one corner as he turned and went hastily back to his place in the crowd, where he stood a little apart from his family, not looking down at his hand.

"Allen," Mr. Summers said. "Anderson. . . . Bentham."

"Seems like there's no time at all between lotteries any more," Mrs. Delacroix said to Mrs. Graves in the back row. "Seems like we got through with the last one only last week."

"Time sure goes fast," Mrs. Graves said.

"Clark. . . . Delacroix."

"There goes my old man," Mrs. Delacroix said. She held her breath while her husband went forward.

"Dunbar," Mr. Summers said, and Mrs. Dunbar went steadily to the box while one of the women said, "Go on, Janey," and another said, "There she goes."

"We're next," Mrs. Graves said. She watched while Mr. Graves came around from the side of the box, greeted Mr. Summers gravely, and selected a slip of paper from the box. By now, all through the crowd there were men holding the small folded papers in their large hands, turning them over and over nervously. Mrs. Dunbar and her two sons stood together, Mrs. Dunbar holding the slip of paper.

"Harburt. . . . Hutchinson."

"Get up there, Bill," Mrs. Hutchinson said, and the people near her laughed.

"Jones."

"They do say," Mr. Adams said to Old Man Warner, who stood next to him, "that over in the north village they're talking of giving up the lottery."

Old Man Warner snorted. "Pack of crazy fools," he said. "Listening to the young folks, nothing's good enough for *them*. Next thing you know, they'll be wanting to go back to living in caves, nobody work any more, live *that* way for a while. Used to be a saying about 'Lottery in June, corn be heavy soon.' First thing you know, we'd all be eating stewed chickweed and acorns. There's *always* been a lottery," he added petulantly. "Bad enough to see young Joe Summers up there joking with everybody."

"Some places have already quit lotteries," Mrs. Adams said.

"Nothing but trouble in *that*," Old Man Warner said stoutly. "Pack of young fools."

"Martin." And Bobby Martin watched his father go forward. "Overdyke. . . . Percy."

"I wish they'd hurry," Mrs. Dunbar said to her older son. "I wish they'd hurry."

"They're almost through," her son said.

"You get ready to run tell Dad," Mrs. Dunbar said.

Mr. Summers called his own name and then stepped forward precisely and selected a slip from the box. Then he called, "Warner."

"Seventy-seventh year I been in the lottery," Old Man Warner said as he went through the crowd. "Seventy-seventh time."

"Watson." The tall boy came awkwardly through the crowd. Someone said, "Don't be nervous, Jack," and Mr. Summers said, "Take your time, son."

"Zanini."

After that, there was a long pause, a breathless pause, until Mr. Summers, holding his slip of paper in the air, said, "All right, fellows." For a minute, no one moved, and then all the slips of paper were opened. Suddenly, all the women began to speak at once, saying, "Who is it?," "Who's got it?," "Is it the Dunbars?," "Is it the Watsons?" Then the voices began to say, "It's Hutchinson. It's Bill," "Bill Hutchinson's got it."

"Go tell your father," Mrs. Dunbar said to her older son.

People began to look around to see the Hutchinsons. Bill Hutchinson was standing quiet, staring down at the paper in his hand. Suddenly, Tessie Hutchinson shouted to Mr. Summers, "You didn't give him time enough to take any paper he wanted. I saw you. It wasn't fair!"

"Be a good sport, Tessie," Mrs. Delacroix called, and Mrs. Graves said, "All of us took the same chance."

"Shut up, Tessie," Bill Hutchinson said.

"Well, everyone," Mr. Summers said, "that was done pretty fast, and now we've got to be hurrying a little more to get done in time." He consulted his next list. "Bill," he said, "you draw for the Hutchinson family. You got any other households in the Hutchinsons?"

"There's Don and Eva," Mrs. Hutchinson yelled. "Make *them* take their chance!"

"Daughters draw with their husbands' families, Tessie," Mr. Summers said gently. "You know that as well as anyone else."

"It wasn't *fair*," Tessie said.

"I guess not, Joe," Bill Hutchinson said regretfully. "My daughter draws with her husband's family, that's only fair. And I've got no other family except the kids."

"Then, as far as drawing for families is concerned, it's you," Mr. Summers said in explanation, "and as far as drawing for households is concerned, that's you, too. Right?"

"Right," Bill Hutchinson said.

"How many kids, Bill?" Mr. Summers asked formally.

"Three," Bill Hutchinson said. "There's Bill, Jr., and Nancy, and little Dave. And Tessie and me."

"All right, then," Mr. Summers said. "Harry, you got their tickets back?"

Mr. Graves nodded and held up the slips of paper. "Put them in the box, then," Mr. Summers directed. "Take Bill's and put it in."

"I think we ought to start over," Mrs. Hutchinson said, as quietly as she could. "I tell you it wasn't *fair*. You didn't give him time enough to choose. *Every*body saw that."

Mr. Graves had selected the five slips and put them in the box, and he dropped all the papers but those onto the ground, where the breeze caught them and lifted them off.

"Listen, everybody," Mrs. Hutchinson was saying to the people around her.

"Ready, Bill?" Mr. Summers asked, and Bill Hutchinson, with one quick glance around at his wife and children, nodded.

"Remember," Mr. Summers said, "take the slips and keep them folded until each person has taken one. Harry, you help little Dave." Mr. Graves took the hand of the little boy, who came willingly with him up to the box. "Take a paper out of the box, Davy," Mr. Summers said. Davy put his hand into the box and laughed. "Take just *one* paper," Mr. Summers said. "Harry, you hold it for him." Mr. Graves took the child's hand and removed the folded paper from the tight fist and held it while little Dave stood next to him and looked up at him wonderingly.

"Nancy next," Mr. Summers said. Nancy was twelve, and her school friends breathed heavily as she went forward, switching her skirt, and took a slip daintily from the box. "Bill, Jr.," Mr. Summers said, and Billy, his face red and his feet overlarge, nearly knocked the box over as he got a paper out. "Tessie," Mr. Summers said. She hesitated for a minute, looking around defiantly, and then set her lips and went up to the box. She snatched a paper out and held it behind her.

"Bill," Mr. Summers said, and Bill Hutchinson reached into the box and felt around, bringing his hand out at last with the slip of paper in it.

The crowd was quiet. A girl whispered, "I hope it's not Nancy," and the sound of the whisper reached the edges of the crowd.

"It's not the way it used to be," Old Man Warner said clearly. "People ain't the way they used to be."

"All right," Mr. Summers said. "Open the papers. Harry, you open little Dave's."

Mr. Graves opened the slip of paper and there was a general sigh through the crowd as he held it up and everyone could see that it was blank. Nancy and Bill, Jr., opened theirs at the same time, and both beamed and laughed, turning around to the crowd and holding their slips of paper above their heads.

"Tessie," Mr. Summers said. There was a pause, and then Mr. Summers looked at Bill Hutchinson, and Bill unfolded his paper and showed it. It was blank.

"It's Tessie," Mr. Summers said, and his voice was hushed. "Show us her paper, Bill."

Bill Hutchinson went over to his wife and forced the slip of paper out of her hand. It had a black spot on it, the black spot Mr. Summers had made the night before with the heavy pencil in the coal-company office. Bill Hutchinson held it up, and there was a stir in the crowd.

"All right, folks," Mr. Summers said. "Let's finish quickly."

Although the villagers had forgotten the

ritual and lost the original black box, they still remembered to use stones. The pile of stones the boys had made earlier was ready; there were stones on the ground with the blowing scraps of paper that had come out of the box. Mrs. Delacroix selected a stone so large she had to pick it up with both hands and turned to Mrs. Dunbar. "Come on," she said. "Hurry up."

Mrs. Dunbar had small stones in both hands, and she said, gasping for breath, "I can't run at all. You'll have to go ahead and I'll catch up with you."

The children had stones already, and someone gave little Davy Hutchinson a few pebbles.

Tessie Hutchinson was in the center of a cleared space by now, and she held her hands out desperately as the villagers moved in on her. "It isn't fair," she said. A stone hit her on the side of the head.

Old Man Warner was saying, "Come on, come on, everyone." Steve Adams was in the front of the crowd of villagers, with Mrs. Graves beside him.

"It isn't fair, it isn't right," Mrs. Hutchinson screamed, and then they were upon her.

For Consideration

1. What is the tone of this story? How does it keep hidden the full impact of the event being described?

2. There is emphasis throughout on the ritual quality, the tradition which accompanies the lottery (e.g., the same old box is used because "no one liked to upset even as much tradition as was represented by the black box"). How closely do the villagers adhere to set action? What does the concern with ritual suggest about their response to the lottery?

3. What do the villagers talk about as the lottery progresses? What attitudes are expressed toward the event itself? The oldest participant is Old Man Warner. How does he feel about the lottery?

4. At what point does it become evident that the lottery is in reality a very grim affair? What is the purpose of withholding such information from the reader until late in the story?

5. A "scapegoat" is someone who, though innocent, is punished in order to alleviate the sense of guilt in others. Is Mrs. Hutchinson a scapegoat here? If so, for what purpose?

6. What theme is worked out through the story? Can the story be seen as an allegory? If so, of what?

stories for further reading

LUIGI PIRANDELLO (1867–1936)
The Captive

Translated by Arthur and Henrie Mayne

It looked as if old Vicè Guarnotta were walking along the road — so regularly did his body sway from side to side with the movements of the little donkey on which he sat. His legs dangled outside the stirrups and nearly dragged along the dusty highway. He was returning, as he did every day at that hour, from his holding on the edge of the plateau, almost overhanging the sea. The aged donkey, even more tired and melancholy than her master, had begun to pant from the effort of ascending the interminable road, which wound its way up the mountain in a succession of steep curves and hair-pin bends. At the summit of the spur stood the ramshackle houses of the little town, huddled closely together, one above another. It was so late that the peasants had all returned home from the country-side and the road was deserted. If Guarnotta did happen to meet anyone, he always received a friendly greeting, for — God be thanked — they all thought well of him.

In the old man's eyes, the whole world was now as lonely as that highway, and his own life grey as that twilight. He glanced at the bare branches projecting over the low, cracked walls, the tall dusty cacti, and the heaps of road-metal lying here and there — which some one really might have thought of spreading over the numerous holes and ruts. Everything about him was still, silent and deserted, as if, like him, oppressed by a sense of infinite boredom and futility. Even the silence seemed to have turned into dust — dust that lay so thick that he could not hear the footsteps of his donkey.

What quantities of that road-dust had the old man carried home every evening! Whenever he took off his coat, his wife seized it and held it out at arm's length. To relieve her feelings, she displayed it round the room — to the chairs and the wardrobe, the bed and the coffer, exclaiming:—

"Just look at it! Look! Why, you could write on it with your finger!"

If only he would yield to her persuasion and not wear his black suit of broadcloth out on the farm. Hadn't she ordered three corduroy suits for him, for that very purpose — three of them? And while she raged and angrily gesticulated, Guarnotta, sitting in his shirt-sleeves, often felt tempted to sink his teeth into the three stumpy fingers which she brandished in front of his eyes; but, like a well-behaved dog, he confined himself to giving her a side-glance of dissatisfaction and let her continue her nagging. Fifteen years before — on the death of his only son — had he not vowed that he would dress in black for the rest of his life? So, therefore . . .

"But why d'you want to wear black out in the fields? I'll put crepe bands on the sleeves of your corduroy coats. That and a black tie will be quite enough — after fifteen years!"

He let her nag. Was he not out on his holding by the sea the whole blessed day? For years past, he had never been seen in the town. Therefore, if he did not wear mourning for his son out on the country-side, where was he to wear it? Why, in God's name, didn't she think a little before opening her mouth — then she would leave him in peace. . . . Oh! so he was to wear mourning in his heart, was he? Indeed! And who said that he didn't wear it in his heart? But he wanted people to see some external sign of it. Let the trees see it, and the birds of the air — since the boy, alas! was unable to see that he wore it for him. . . . Why on earth was his wife grumbling so about it? Was it because she had to shake and brush the clothes every evening? Why not let the servants do it? There were three of them to wait upon only two persons. Was it for economy's sake? Come, what nonsense! One black suit a year cost only eighty or ninety lire. She ought to realise that it wasn't right — it wasn't kind of her to go on like that. She was his second wife: the son, who had died, had been by the first one. He had no

other relatives — even distant ones; therefore, on his death, all his property (and it was no small amount) would pass to her and to her nephews and nieces. She should keep quiet then, if only for decency's sake. . . . Ah well! Being the sort of woman she was, she didn't, of course, see it in that way.

So that was why he stayed out all day, alone on his land, alone with his trees and the panorama of the sea spread just below him; and, as he listened to the continuous gentle rustling of the foliage and the sad little song of the waves — which seemed to float up to him from an endless distance — his soul was constantly oppressed by a sense of the vanity of all things and the insufferable boredom of life.

He had reached a point less than half-a-mile from the little town and could hear the soft chimes of the *Ave Maria* from the chapel of the *Addolorata* on the top of the hill, when, at a sharp bend in the road, there came a shout:—

"Face to the ground!"

Three men, who had lain ambushed in the shadow, sprang out upon him; he noticed that they wore masks and carried guns. One seized his ass's bridle, while the others, in the twinkling of an eye, dragged him from the saddle and threw him on the road; one man knelt on his legs and fastened his wrists together, the other meanwhile bandaging his eyes with a folded handkerchief tied tightly round his head.

He had barely time to say: "But what do you want, my lads?" — when he was forced to his feet, pushed and hustled off the road, and dragged violently down the stony hill-side towards the valley.

"But, my lads . . ."

"Silence or you're a dead man!"

He was frightened by their rough handling, but still more so by the state of terror that the three men were in —

Luigi Pirandello / **175**

obviously on account of their deed of violence. He could hear them panting like wild beasts. They were going to do something horrible to him.

But perhaps they did not mean to kill him — at any rate not at once. If they had been paid to murder him, or were carrying out a vendetta, they would have dispatched him up there on the high-road, from their ambush in the shadows. So it must be that they were carrying him off for a ransom.

"My lads . . ."

They gripped his arms more tightly, shook him, and told him again to be silent.

"But at least loosen the bandage a little. It's very tight on my eyes. . . . I can't . . ."

"Go on! Move. . . ."

First down, then up, now straight on, then turning back: down again, then up and up and up. Where could they be taking him?

Sinister imaginings haunted his mind on that terrible, blind march over rocks and thorns, pushed and pulled along in total darkness. And then, suddenly, he saw the lights — the lights of the little town on top of the ridge — the oil lamps shining from the houses and streets — just as he had seen them round the bend a moment before he was attacked, just as he had seen them again and again on his way home from his holding at that evening hour. How strange! He saw them plainly through the tight bandage over his eyes — as clearly as before when his eyes were open. How strange. . . . As he stumbled on and on, savagely pulled and pushed by his captors, so that his heart filled with terror, he took the little lamps with him; and not only those soft, sad little lamps, but the whole of the mountain spur with the town on its summit — the town whose other in-habitants went safely and peacefully about their business, unconscious of his horrible adventure.

At one point he caught the sound of the

hurried patter of his ass's hoofs.

Oh! So they were dragging his weary old donkey along, too! She, poor beast, could not understand. All she would notice would be the unwonted hurry and rough treatment, but she would go where she was taken, without any idea of what had happened. If only they would stop a mo-ment and let him speak, he would tell them quietly that he was ready to pay whatever they demanded. He had not long now to live, and it really was not worth while suffering such hideous treatment just for the sake of a little money — money which brought him no satisfaction.

"My lads . . ."

"Silence! Go on!"

"I can't manage it. . . . Why are you do-ing this to me? I'm ready to . . ."

"Silence! We'll talk later. Go on!"

They made him trudge like that for what seemed eternity. At last, overcome by weariness and sick and giddy from the tight bandage, he fainted and remained unconscious.

He recovered his senses next morning and found himself lying, utterly ex-hausted, in a low cavern.

A strong, musty smell seemed to emanate from the first light of dawn, which entered wanly through the winding entrance to the chalky grotto. Faint though it was, that light comforted him in his pain — the pain he felt from the rough handling he had undergone. He remem-bered that brutal violence as if it had been a nightmare — remembered how, when he had been unable to keep on his feet, he had been carried, first on one man's back and then on another's, dropped on the ground and dragged along, then held up by his arms and legs.

Where was he now? He listened atten-tively: from the stillness outside, he im-agined that he was high on some lofty peak. The idea made him feel quite giddy. He was unable to move, for his hands and feet were tied, and he lay stretched on the ground like a dead animal. His limbs and head were so heavy that they seemed made of lead. He wondered whether he was wounded. Perhaps they had left him there for dead.

No. There they were, discussing something outside the cave. So his fate was not yet settled. . . . He considered what had happened, and found that he had no longer any thought of attempting to escape from his position of danger. He knew that he could not escape, and he had almost lost the will to do so. The disaster was accomplished — it was as if it had happened a long time ago, almost in a previous life. That life had been a miserable affair, and he had left it far, far away, down below in the valley, where they had captured him. Now he had only the silence of that high place — a void in which the past was forgotten. Even if they set him free, he no longer had the strength, perhaps not even the desire, to go down and restart the old life.

Suddenly a wave of self-pity swept over him, and he began to shudder with horror at the fate awaiting him, as he saw one of his captors crawling into the cave on all fours. The man's face was concealed by a red handkerchief with holes made in front for the eyes. Guarnotta looked quickly at his hands. They carried no weapon, only a new pencil — the kind you buy for a halfpenny — not yet sharpened. In his other hand was a crumpled sheet of common note-paper, with an envelope held in its fold.

The old man felt reassured. He smiled involuntarily. At that moment, the other two — also masked — entered the cave on their hands and knees. One of them came up to him and undid his hands, but not his feet. Then the first to enter spoke: —

"Now have some sense! You must write as we tell you."

Guarnotta thought he recognised the voice. Yes, of course! It was Manuzza —

so-called because he had one arm shorter than the other. But was it really he? A glance at the man's left arm confirmed his suspicion. He felt sure that he would recognise the other two, if they removed their masks, for he knew everyone in the town. He replied: —

"Have some sense, indeed! It's you, my lads, who ought to have some sense. To whom do you want me to write? And what am I to write with? That thing?"

He pointed to the pencil.

"Why not? It's a pencil, isn't it?"

"Yes, it's a pencil, all right. But you don't even understand how such things are used."

"What d'you mean?"

"Why! You must sharpen it first!"

"Sharpen it?"

"Yes, sharpen it, with a pen-knife, there — at the tip."

"Pen-knife — I haven't got one," said Manuzza, and added: "Have some sense now — here, have some sense!" followed by a string of oaths.

"Yes, I've got sense, all right, Manuzza. . . ."

"Oh!" shouted the fellow. "So you've recognised me?"

"What else can you expect, when you hide your face and leave your left arm exposed? Take off that handkerchief and look me straight in the eyes. Why are you doing this . . . to me?"

"Stop all that chatter!" bellowed Manuzza, pulling the handkerchief from his face. "I've told you to have some sense. Either you write or I'll kill you!"

"Yes, yes! I'm ready to write," rejoined Guarnotta, "when you've sharpened the pencil. But — if you don't mind my asking — it's money you want, my lads, isn't it? How much?"

"Three thousand florins!"

"Three thousand? That's no small sum."

"You're worth that much! Let's have no nonsense about it!"

Luigi Pirandello / **177**

"Three thousand florins?"

"Yes, and more too! More than that!"

"Quite true. I am worth more than that, but I've not got that sum at home, in ready money. I should have to sell some houses and fields. D'you think that can be done at a day's notice and without my presence there?"

"Tell them to borrow the money!"

"Tell who?"

"Your wife and nephews!"

Guarnotta smiled bitterly and tried to raise himself up on one of his elbows.

"That's just the point I wanted to explain," he answered. "My lads, you have made a great mistake. Are you counting on my wife and her nephews? If you're bent on killing me, kill me. Here I am! Kill me and no more said about it. But if it's money you're after, you can only get the money from me, on condition that you let me return home."

"What are you talking about? Let you go home? Do you think we're mad? You're joking!"

"Well, then . . ." began Guarnotta, with a sigh.

Manuzza snatched the sheet of writing paper angrily from his companion's hand and repeated: —

"Stop all that chatter, as I told you — just you write! The pencil. . . . Oh God, yes! . . . it has to be sharpened. . . . How's that done?"

Guarnotta explained the way and the men exchanged glances and left the cave. As he saw them crawl out, on all fours — looking like three animals — he could not refrain from smiling once more. He reflected that they were now engaged in trying to sharpen that pencil, and that perhaps, by dint of pruning it like a branch of a tree, they would fail in their attempts. That was what might well happen, and he smiled at the idea, at the thought that, at that moment, his life depended on the absurd difficulty which those three men would be up against, in trying to carry out

an operation they had never performed before. Perhaps, when they saw the pencil growing smaller and smaller, they would be so annoyed that, on their next entry, they would show him that though their knives might be no good for sharpening a pencil, they were quite good for cutting his throat. . . . He had been a fool and had committed an unpardonable mistake in letting that fellow Manuzza know that he recognised him. . . . Yes, he could hear them all talking at once — outside the cave, shouting and cursing. He was sure they were passing that wretched halfpenny pencil from one to another and that it was growing shorter and shorter under their clumsy treatment. Heaven knows what kind of knives they held in their great chalky fists. . . . There they were, crawling back in single file, having failed in their endeavour.

"The wood's rotten," said Manuzza. "That pencil's no good. As *you* know how to write, haven't you by any chance got a decent pencil in your pocket, properly sharpened?"

"No, I haven't, my lads," replied Guarnotta. "And anyhow it would be useless, I assure you. I would have written if you'd given me a pencil and paper. But to whom should I write? To my wife and nephews? They are her nephews, not mine — d'you understand that? You may be quite sure that none of them would have answered. They'd have pretended that they never received the threatening letter, and wash their hands of me. If you want money from them, you shouldn't have begun by falling on me. You should have gone and made terms with them — say a thousand florins — for killing me. But they wouldn't even have paid that much. . . . I quite admit that they look forward to my death, but — you see — I'm an old man, and they expect that God will very soon grant it to them free of expense and in that way there'll be no feeling of remorse. You surely don't imagine they'd pay you a centesimo, one single centesimo, to *save* my life? You have muddled the whole business. My life is only of interest to myself; and it isn't of much interest even to me — that's the truth. Still, I admit, I don't want to die like this — it's a horrible death. And therefore, simply to escape that kind of end, I promise and swear to you, by the soul of my dear son, that, as soon as I possibly can — within two or three days — I myself will bring you the money to the place you appoint."

"Yes! After you've already reported us!"

"I swear that I will not do so. I swear that I will not breathe a word of this matter to anyone. Remember, my life is at stake!"

"It is at present, but will it be when you are free? Why, even before going home, you'll report us to the police!"

"I swear to you that I will not! You really ought to trust me. Remember that I go out every day into the country, and my life, out there, is in your hands. And have I not always been a father to you boys? God knows, you have always looked up to me and respected me. . . . Do you think that I'm anxious to expose myself to the danger of a vendetta? No, you ought to trust my word and let me return home, and you can be sure that you'll have the money."

They said no more to him, but exchanged glances and left the cave, crawling away on hands and knees.

All day long he did not see them again. At first he could hear them engaged in discussion outside; after a while, no further sound reached him.

He lay there, turning over in his mind all the probabilities, and wondering what decision they would come to. One thing seemed clear to him — that he had fallen into the hands of three stupid fellows, mere amateurs, and that this was probably their first essay in crime. They had entered on it blindly, thinking solely of his money, without giving any previous consideration

to their position as married men with families. Now that they realised their blunder, they did not know what to do next, and could see no way out of their difficulties. As for his oath that he would not denounce them, none of the three would trust in it, least of all Manuzza, who had been recognised. What was to happen then?

His only hope was that it would not occur to any one of them to feel repentance for their stupid, unreasonable act, and a consequent desire to wipe out every trace of this first offence. If they decided to continue brigandage as outlaws, they might as well spare his life and set him free, without worrying about his denouncing them; but, if they repented and wanted to return to an honest livelihood, they must necessarily prevent the denunciation which they were convinced would follow on his freedom, and therefore they must murder him.

It followed from this that God might, he hoped, come to his assistance by enlightening them — by bringing them to see that it would not profit them to live an honest life. It should not be difficult to persuade them of this, seeing that they had already shown, by kidnapping him, that they were prepared to imperil their immortal souls. But he was very anxious about the disillusionment which they must have experienced when their eyes were opened to the great blunder they had committed, at the outset of a career of crime: for disillusionment is very apt to turn into repentance and into a desire to abandon a path which has begun badly. To withdraw from it, obliterating every trace of their previous steps, they might logically hold that they had no alternative but to commit a crime; for, if they were willing to set him free, would they not, with equal logic, be forced to go on committing crimes? They would conclude then that it was better to commit that one crime at the outset — a deed which would remain secret, entirely untraced — than to commit any number of crimes, done openly as outlaws. At the cost of one misdeed, they could still hope to save themselves, not indeed as far as their consciences were concerned, but in the sight of men: if they were to release him — they would argue — they would be irretrievably lost.

As a result of these harassing reflections, he arrived at the conclusion that on that day or on the morrow, perhaps that very night while he slept, they would assassinate him.

He waited until it grew dark inside the cave. Then, overcome with terror at the thought of falling asleep in that silent and dreadful place, he determined to crawl outside the cave, even though his hands and feet were still tied. He moved forward with infinite difficulty, wriggling along like a worm, restraining his instinctive fears in an endeavour to make the least possible noise. What could he possibly hope for, in trying to poke his head out, like a glow-worm from its hole? Nothing. But at least he would see the sky and meet his death in the open, face to face, and not have it come upon him treacherously in his sleep. That was something.

Ah! there he was, at last. . . . Quietly. . . . Was that moonlight? Yes, there was the young moon, and countless stars. . . . What a splendid night! Where was he? . . . On some mountain-top — the air and the silence proved that. . . . Perhaps that was Monte Caltafaraci over there, or San Benedetto. . . . Then what was that valley? Either the plain of Consolida or the valley of Clerici? Yes, and that mountain to the west must be the Carapezza. But if so, what were those twinkling lights over there, glittering like clusters of fire-flies in the opal moonlight? Were they the lights of Girgenti? Why then — Good God! — then he was quite near! And it had seemed as if they had made him walk so far, so far. . . .

He looked anxiously round him, as if the possibility that they might have gone off, leaving him there, aroused his fear rather than hope. Dark and motionless, squatting like a great owl on a bank of chalk, sat one of the three men, left on guard; he showed plainly in the faint, pale light of the moon. Was he asleep?

The old man tried to squirm his way out a little farther, but all at once his arms lost all their power, as he heard a voice saying quite calmly: —

"I'm watching you, Don Vicè. Back you go, or I shoot!"

He held his breath and lay motionless, looking out. Perhaps the man might think that he had made a mistake.

"I am watching you."

"Let me have a breath of fresh air," he then begged. "I'm suffocated inside there. D'you mean to keep me like this? I'm thirsty — I'm dying of thirst——"

The man made a threatening gesture:—

"Well, you can stay there, but only on condition you don't utter a sound. I'm hungry and thirsty too, as well as you. Keep silent or I make you go back inside."

Silence. . . . But at least he had the moon, revealing all those quiet valleys and mountains . . . and the relief of the fresh air . . . and the sad glimmer of those distant lights shining from his native town.

Where had the other two gone? Had they left to this third man the task of dispatching him during the night. If so, why did he not do it at once? What was he waiting for? Was he perhaps waiting for the other two to come back that night?

Again he felt tempted to speak, but restrained himself. Well, if that was what they had decided to do . . .

He looked again at the bank where the man had been squatting and saw that he had resumed his former position. Judging from his voice and accent, Guarnotta concluded that he came from Grotte, a large village among the sulphur mines. Could it possibly be Fillico, a quiet, kindly fellow, a regular beast of burden, strong as a horse. If it really was he — if that silent, hard-working man had left the straight path, it was a bad business.

He could not stand it any longer, but spoke almost automatically, not as a question, in fact without any clear intention — it seemed as if he meant the name to sound as if uttered by some one else:—

"Fillico. . . ."

The man did not stir.

Guarnotta waited, then repeated it in the same tone, as if it were some other person talking; as he spoke, he gazed intently at his finger with which he was drawing marks on the sand.

"Fillico."

This time a shudder ran down his spine at the thought that his obstinacy in repeating that name — almost involuntarily — was likely to be paid for by a gunshot in return.

But again the man made no movement. Then Guarnotta gave a loud sigh of despair; suddenly his head was a dead weight which he could no longer support. He lay like a dying animal, with his face in the sand — the sand running into his open mouth — and, in spite of the prohibition against speaking and the threat of shooting, he began to rave — to rave interminably. He spoke of the beautiful moon — he cried a farewell to it, for it had by this time set —; he spoke of the stars which God had created and placed in the distant heavens, so that the brute creation could not know that they were really countless worlds, much larger than this earth; he spoke of the earth, saying that everyone who is not a brute — a mere animal — knows that it spins like a top; it seemed to relieve his feelings to declare that at that very moment there were men on it with their heads pointing downwards, and that they did not fall off into the sky for reasons which everyone ought to take the trouble

to find out, unless he were the lowest of the low — a mere clod into which our Lord God has not breathed the divine spirit.

In the midst of all his wild raving, he suddenly found that he was talking astronomy, expounding it like a professor; and the man, who had gradually drawn nearer to him, was now sitting beside him there, close to the mouth of the cave; and that it actually was as he had guessed — Fillico from Grotte; and that it so happened that Fillico had wanted to know about these matters for many years — all about the zodiac, the milky way, the nebulae. . . . But he was not easy to convince; he did not think the explanations given were true.

It was a strange situation. It was strange, too, that though he was at the end of his strength, exhausted by despair, though he had a gun-barrel pointing at him — yet he was able to devote great attention to cleaning his finger-nails with a stalk of grass, taking care that it did not break or bend. He also examined his remaining teeth — only three incisors and one canine — and devoted much consideration to the problem whether his neighbour, the maker of wine-jars, who had lost his wife a fortnight back, was left with three children or with four. . . .

"Now, let's talk seriously. Just tell me, what d'you think I am? By the Madonna! D'you think I am a blade of grass — that blade of grass, there, which you can pluck like this, just as if it were nothing? Feel me! By the Madonna, I'm made of flesh and blood, and I have a soul, which God gave me, just as He has given you one. Yet you mean to cut my throat while I'm asleep? No . . . don't go. . . . Wait here . . . listen to me . . . what? You're not going? Oh! I see — as long as I was speaking of the stars. . . . Listen to what I've got to say. Cut my throat here while I'm awake — not treacherously while I'm asleep. . . . D'you hear? What d'you say to that? You won't answer? But why are you putting it off? What are you waiting for, I want to know? If it's money you're after, you won't get it. You can't keep me here and you don't want to let me go. . . . You mean to kill me? Well, for God's sake do it and get it over!"

But he was talking to empty space. The man had gone off and was again squatting like an owl on the bank, to show him that it was quite useless to speak on that subject — he would not listen to a word.

After all, thought Guarnotta, how stupid it was to worry like that. If he had to be murdered, was it not better to be murdered during his sleep? He even decided that if he was still awake when he heard them crawl into the cave later on, he would shut his eyes and pretend to be sleeping. Not that there was any need to shut his eyes, really — it would be dark and he could keep them open. All he had to do was to make no movement when they came close and were feeling for his throat, to cut it like a sheep's.

So he simply said "Good-night" and crawled away inside the cave.

They did not, however, murder him. They admitted their blunder; but were unwilling either to set him free or to kill him. They would keep him there.

"What! For ever?"

For as long as God saw fit. They placed themselves in His hands. The captivity would terminate sooner or later, according as He wished to impose upon them a short or a long expiation for their fault in taking Guarnotta captive.

What was their intention then? That he should die a natural death up there? Could that be their intention — he asked.

Yes, that was it.

"But by all that is holy, can't you silly idiots see that it's not God, in the least, who is going to kill me, it's you who will be doing it, keeping me here in this cave, dy-ing of hunger and thirst and cold, tied up like an animal, sleeping on the ground, easing myself here on the ground like an animal."

His protest was in vain: they had placed the matter in God's hands and their prisoner might as well have been talking to the stones. They pointed out to him, however, that as for dying of starvation, it was not true; neither was it true that he would have to sleep on the ground. They had brought him up three bundles of straw for his bed and, to keep off the cold, there was an old cloak padded with cotton-wool, which belonged to one of them. And, moreover, there would be his daily bread and something to eat with it. They took it out of their own mouths and from the mouths of their wives and children to give it to him. It was bread which would cost them much toil to procure, for one of them would have to keep guard over him, taking it in turns, while the other two went out to work. In the earthen pitcher was drinking water — and God only knew how hard it was to find water in that thirsty tract. As for his having to ease himself on the floor of his cave, he could go outside at night and do it in the open.

"What? With you watching me?"

"Do it. I won't look at you."

When he found that he could make no impression on this stupid obduracy, he began to stamp his feet like a child. Were they brutes, then, with hearts of stone?

"Look here! Do you admit that you've made a grave mistake — yes or no?"

Yes, they admitted it.

"Do you admit that you've got to pay for that mistake?"

Yes, they would pay for it by refraining from killing him, by waiting till God granted them his death and by endeavouring to alleviate, to the utmost of their power, the sufferings which they had brought upon him.

"Very good — Oh! very good indeed!

That's your expiation — you block-heads — for the sin you yourselves confess that you've committed. But what about me? Where do I come in? What sin did I commit? Am I, or am I not, the victim of your mistake? Why should you make me pay the penalty for the sin which you committed? Since I had nothing to do with it, why should I have to suffer in this way — for your fault? How can you attempt to justify that?"

No, they did not attempt any justification, but simply listened to him — their harsh, chalk-stained features impassive, their eyes dull and fixed. *There* was the straw — *there* was the overcoat . . . and *there* the pitcher of water . . . and the bread which they had earned with the sweat of their brows . . . and he could come outside to defecate.

They persisted in their expiation, taking it in turns to remain behind on guard over him. When keeping him company, they made him tell them about the stars and about all manner of things in town and country — what splendid harvests there were in former times when people were truly religious, and how certain diseases of plants were not known in those good old days when there was more religion. They brought him an old almanac, picked up somewhere, so that he could beguile his leisure by reading it, and stood round him watching, full of envy at his good fortune in being able to read.

"Do tell us what it means — this printed sheet with that moon and the scales and those fish and the scorpion?"

His words stimulated their curiosity and they were gluttons for further knowledge, listening to him with child-like wonder and uttering low grunts of amazement. Little by little, he came to enjoy his talks with them. In telling of so much that was new to them, it almost seemed to be new to him too, as if something alive were stirring within him, as if his soul were awakening after long years of torpor in his former distressful existence. Once his anger had subsided, he found that a new life was beginning for him and tried to adapt himself to it. As time passed, he bowed before the inevitable, though his surroundings were strange and devoid of interest, he was not longer under the threat of a horrible end.

By this time, he reflected, he was already dead to everyone, on his distant farm overlooking the sea and in the town whose lights he could see at night. Perhaps no one had bothered to search for him after his mysterious disappearance; even if they had searched, they would not have put much energy into the task, as there was nobody keenly interested in finding him.

Since his heart had withered long years ago, what object was there now in returning to life — to that life which he had been leading? He felt that he had no real ground for complaint at his deprivations; for if he could recover his former comfort, he would recover also the terrible depression of his former life — a life that dragged its weary way through years of intolerable boredom! There was this to be said for his captivity, that although he spent his time merely lying on the ground, he did not feel the hours drag so wearily. Day followed day on that silent mountain spur, devoid of all sense and purpose, and it seemed to him as if time had ceased. In that extreme seclusion, even the consciousness of his own existence dropped away from him. He would look round at his shoulders and the chalk wall of the cave beside him, as the only things which had a real existence; or his hand, if his eyes rested on it — yes, that too was real and lived just on its own account; or it might be that rock or twig — they existed in a world of frightful isolation.

As the old man's anger at his unjust

treatment died down, and he came gradually to the conclusion that what had befallen him was not such a disaster as had at first appeared, he began to perceive that it was indeed a very severe punishment that those three men had inflicted upon themselves — the task of keeping him there as a prisoner. Dead though he already was to everyone else, he remained alive solely for them, and they had taken on the entire burden of his support. They could have freed themselves from that burden without the slightest difficulty, since his person no longer possessed value to anyone, since nobody took any interest in him. But, on the contrary, they continued to bear it, and carried through with resignation their self-imposed punishment. Not only did they never complain, but they even did their best to render their task still more arduous by the little attentions which they lavished on him. For, quite apart from the duty imposed by their consciences, they had, all three of them, become genuinely attached to the old man, regarding him as their own private property in which no one else had any claim. In some mysterious manner, they derived a great satisfaction from this — a satisfaction which they would miss for the rest of their lives, when the time came to lose him.

One day, Fillico brought his wife to the cave. She had a baby at her breast and was holding a little girl by the hand; the child had carried up a fine home-made cake as a gift for 'grand-dad.'

How they stared at him — the mother and daughter. He reflected that by then he must have been several months in captivity and present a lamentable appearance — dirty, ragged, and with tufts of bushy hair on his chin and cheeks. Pleased at their visit, he received them with a friendly smile. Perhaps it was the sight of a smile on the emaciated face which so startled the good woman and her daughter.

"Don't be afraid, my darling! Come here, little one . . . that's right. See, there's a bit for you. Yes, you eat it. So Mummy made it, did she?"

"Mummy."

"That's lovely. Have you got any little brothers? . . . Three? Oh! Poor Fillico! Four children already. . . . Bring the boys up here to me. I'd like to see them. Next week, yes, that's right — only I hope there won't be any next week for me. . . ."

The next week duly arrived: in truth God wished the three men's expiation to last a long time, for it dragged on for over two months more.

He died on a Sunday, on a splendid evening when it was still bright as day, up on the heights. Fillico had brought his children to see old grand-dad and Manuzza his also. He died while he was playing with the children, behaving like a boy himself, wearing a red handkerchief over his head to cloak his bushy hair. Whilst amusing the children and laughing at his own antics, he suddenly collapsed on the ground; the men rushed forward to pick him up and found him dead.

They put the children on one side and sent them and the women down from the mountain. Kneeling round the corpse, the three men burst into floods of tears, with fervent prayers for his soul and for their own salvation. Then they buried him in the cave.

During the rest of their lives, if anyone happened to mention Guarnotta in their presence and speak of his mysterious disappearance, they would say:—

"He was a saint, that man. . . . I'm sure he was admitted straight to paradise."

For Consideration

1. What impressions do the opening paragraphs give about Vicè Guarnotta's life? What seems to be his relationship with his wife? Is there a connection between his mourning for his son and his "sense of the vanity for all things and the insufferable boredom of life"?

2. What are Guarnotta's initial reactions to his capture? Why does he quickly lose his will to escape?

3. What is Guarnotta's motive for offering to get the three thousand florins? Why isn't his offer accepted? Is Guarnotta's anticipation that he will be killed based on reason or illogical paranoia?

4. When do the men begin to become interested in Guarnotta as other than a captive? What is the basis for that interest? In what sense is their decision not to kill him expiation for them?

5. In talking to the captors Guarnotta finds "his soul . . . awakening after long years of torpor in his former distressful existence." What is happening to Guarnotta? What kind of awakening is this?

6. What do you understand the ending to mean? Are the men's comments about Guarnotta's saintliness to be taken facetiously or seriously? In what sense might he be a saint to them?

For Comparison

The description of Guarnotta's soul "awakening after long years of torpor in his former distressful existence" provides a basis for comparing his experience to that of Anya ("An Anna round his Neck") and, perhaps, Jack Fergusson and Mabel Pervin ("The Horse Dealer's Daughter") and Leo Finkle ("The Magic Barrel"). Each person has experienced a "distressful existence" from which he or she is, at least momentarily or superficially, delivered. Extend the comparisons and indicate the contrasts further.

JAMES JOYCE (1882–1941)
Araby

North Richmond Street, being blind, was a quiet street except at the hour when the Christian Brothers' School set the boys free. An uninhabited house of two storeys stood at the blind end, detached from its neighbours in a square ground. The other houses of the street, conscious of decent lives within them, gazed at one another with brown imperturbable faces.

The former tenant of our house, a priest, had died in the back drawing-room. Air, musty from having been long enclosed, hung in all the rooms, and the waste room behind the kitchen was littered with old useless papers. Among these I found a few paper-covered books, the pages of which were curled and damp: *The Abbot*, by Walter Scott, *The Devout Communicant* and *The Memoirs of Vidocq*. I liked the last best because its leaves were yellow. The wild garden behind the house contained a central apple-tree and a few straggling bushes under one of which I found the late tenant's rusty bicycle-pump. He had been a very charitable priest; in his will he had left all his money to institutions and the furniture of his house to his sister.

When the short days of winter came dusk fell before we had well eaten our dinners. When we met in the street the houses had grown sombre. The space of sky above us was the colour of ever-changing violet and towards it the lamps of the street lifted their feeble lanterns. The cold air stung us and we played till our bodies glowed. Our shouts echoed in the silent street. The career of our play brought us through the dark muddy lanes behind the houses where we ran the gantlet of the rough tribes from the cottages, to the back doors of the dark dripping gardens where odours arose from the ashpits, to the dark odorous stables where a coachman smoothed and combed the horse or shook music from the buckled harness. When we returned to the street light from the kitchen windows had filled the areas. If my uncle was seen turning the corner we hid in the shadow until we had seen him safely housed. Or if Mangan's sister came out on the doorstep to call her brother in to his tea we watched her from

our shadow peer up and down the street. We waited to see whether she would remain or go in and, if she remained, we left our shadow and walked up to Mangan's steps resignedly. She was waiting for us, her figure defined by the light from the half-opened door. Her brother always teased her before he obeyed and I stood by the railing looking at her. Her dress swung as she moved her body and the soft rope of her hair tossed from side to side.

Every morning I lay on the floor in the front parlour watching her door. The blind was pulled down to within an inch of the sash so that I could not be seen. When she came out on the doorstep my heart leaped. I ran to the hall, seized my books and followed her. I kept her brown figure always in my eye and, when we came near the point at which our ways diverged, I quickened my pace and passed her. This happened morning after morning. I had never spoken to her, except for a few casual words, and yet her name was like a summons to all my foolish blood.

Her image accompanied me even in places the most hostile to romance. On Saturday evenings when my aunt went marketing I had to go to carry some of the parcels. We walked through the flaring streets, jostled by drunken men and bargaining women, amid the curses of labourers, the shrill litanies of shop-boys who stood on guard by the barrels of pigs' cheeks, the nasal chanting of street-singers, who sang a *come-all-you* about O'Donovan Rossa, or a ballad about the troubles in our native land. These noises converged in a single sensation of life for me: I imagined that I bore my chalice safely through a throng of foes. Her name sprang to my lips at moments in strange prayers and praises which I myself did not understand. My eyes were often full of tears (I could not tell why) and at times a flood from my heart seemed to pour itself out into my bosom. I thought little of the future. I did not know whether I would ever speak to her or not or, if I spoke to her, how I could tell her of my confused adoration. But my body was like a harp and her words and gestures were like fingers running upon the wires.

One evening I went into the back drawing-room in which the priest had died. It was a dark rainy evening and there was no sound in the house. Through one of the broken panes I heard the rain impinge upon the earth, the fine incessant needles of water playing in the sodden beds. Some distant lamp or lighted window gleamed below me. I was thankful that I could see so little. All my senses seemed to desire to veil themselves and, feeling that I was about to slip from them, I pressed the palms of my hands together until they trembled, murmuring: *O love! O love!* many times.

At last she spoke to me. When she addressed the first words to me I was so confused that I did not know what to answer. She asked me was I going to *Araby*. I forget whether I answered yes or no. It would be a splendid bazaar, she said; she would love to go.

—And why can't you? I asked.

While she spoke she turned a silver bracelet round and round her wrist. She could not go, she said, because there would be a retreat that week in her convent. Her brother and two other boys were fighting for their caps and I was alone at the railing. She held one of the spikes, bowing her head towards me. The light from the lamp opposite our door caught the white curve of her neck, lit up her hair that rested there and, falling, lit up the hand upon the railing. It fell over one side of her dress and caught the white border of a petticoat, just visible as she stood at ease.

—It's well for you, she said.

—If I go, I said, I will bring you something.

What innumerable follies laid waste my waking and sleeping thoughts after that evening! I wished to annihilate the tedious intervening days. I chafed against the work of school. At night in my bedroom and by day in the classroom her image came between me and the page I strove to read. The syllables of the word *Araby* were called to me through the silence in which my soul luxuriated and cast an Eastern enchantment over me. I asked for leave to go to the bazaar on Saturday night. My aunt was surprised and hoped it was not some Freemason affair. I answered few questions in class. I watched my master's face pass from amiability to sternness; he hoped I was not beginning to idle. I could not call my wandering thoughts together. I had hardly any patience with the serious work of life which, now that it stood between me and my desire, seemed to me child's play, ugly monotonous child's play.

On Saturday morning I reminded my uncle that I wished to go to the bazaar in the evening. He was fussing at the hallstand, looking for the hat-brush, and answered me curtly:

—Yes, boy, I know.

As he was in the hall I could not go into the front parlour and lie at the window. I left the house in bad humour and walked slowly towards the school. The air was pitilessly raw and already my heart misgave me.

When I came home to dinner my uncle had not yet been home. Still it was early. I sat staring at the clock for some time and, when its ticking began to irritate me, I left the room. I mounted the staircase and gained the upper part of the house. The high cold empty gloomy rooms liberated me and I went from room to room singing. From the front window I saw my companions playing below in the street. Their cries reached me weakened and indistinct and, leaning my forehead against the cool glass, I looked over at the dark house where she lived. I may have stood there for an hour, seeing nothing but the brown-clad figure cast by my imagination, touched discreetly by the lamplight at the curved neck, at the hand upon the railings and at the border below the dress.

When I came downstairs again I found Mrs Mercer sitting at the fire. She was an old garrulous woman, a pawnbroker's widow, who collected used stamps for some pious purpose. I had to endure the gossip of the tea-table. The meal was prolonged beyond an hour and still my uncle did not come. Mrs Mercer stood up to go: she was sorry she couldn't wait any longer, but it was after eight o'clock and she did not like to be out late, as the night air was bad for her. When she had gone I began to walk up and down the room, clenching my fists. My aunt said:

—I'm afraid you may put off your bazaar for this night of Our Lord.

At nine o'clock I heard my uncle's latchkey in the halldoor. I heard him talking to himself and heard the hallstand rocking when it had received the weight of his overcoat. I could interpret these signs. When he was midway through his dinner I asked him to give me the money to go to the bazaar. He had forgotten.

—The people are in bed and after their first sleep now, he said.

I did not smile. My aunt said to him energetically:

—Can't you give him the money and let him go? You've kept him late enough as it is.

My uncle said he was very sorry he had forgotten. He said he believed in the old saying: *All work and no play makes Jack a dull boy*. He asked me where I was going and, when I had told him a second time he asked me did I know *The Arab's Farewell to his Steed*. When I left the kitchen he was about to recite the opening lines of the piece to my aunt.

I held a florin tightly in my hand as I strode down Buckingham Street towards the station. The sight of the streets thronged with buyers and glaring with gas recalled to me the purpose of my journey. I took my seat in a third-class carriage of a deserted train. After an intolerable delay the train moved out of the station slowly. It crept onward among ruinous houses and over the twinkling river. At Westland Row Station a crowd of people pressed to the carriage doors; but the porters moved them back, saying that it was a special train for the bazaar. I remained alone in the bare carriage. In a few minutes the train drew up beside an improvised wooden platform. I passed out on to the road and saw by the lighted dial of a clock that it was ten minutes to ten. In front of me was a large building which displayed the magical name.

I could not find any sixpenny entrance and, fearing that the bazaar would be closed, I passed in quickly through a turnstile, handing a shilling to a weary-looking man. I found myself in a big hall girdled at half its height by a gallery. Nearly all the stalls were closed and the greater part of the hall was in darkness. I recognised a silence like that which pervades a church after a service. I walked into the centre of the bazaar timidly. A few people were gathered about the stalls which were still open. Before a curtain, over which the words *Café Chantant* were written in coloured lamps, two men were counting money on a salver. I listened to the fall of the coins.

Remembering with difficulty why I had come I went over to one of the stalls and examined porcelain vases and flowered tea-sets. At the door of the stall a young lady was talking and laughing with two young gentlemen. I remarked their English accents and listened vaguely to their conversation.

—O, I never said such a thing!

—O, but you did!

—O, but I didn't!

—Didn't she say that?

—Yes. I heard her.

—O, there's a . . . fib!

Observing me the young lady came over and asked me did I wish to buy anything. The tone of her voice was not encouraging; she seemed to have spoken to me out of a sense of duty. I looked humbly at the great jars that stood like eastern guards at either side of the dark entrance to the stall and murmured:

—No, thank you.

The young lady changed the position of one of the vases and went back to the two young men. They began to talk of the same subject. Once or twice the young lady glanced at me over her shoulder.

I lingered before her stall, though I knew my stay was useless, to make my interest in her wares seem the more real. Then I turned away slowly and walked down the middle of the bazaar. I allowed the two pennies to fall against the sixpence in my pocket. I heard a voice call from one end of the gallery that the light was out. The upper part of the hall was now completely dark.

Gazing up into the darkness I saw myself as a creature driven and derided by vanity; and my eyes burned with anguish and anger.

For Consideration

1. What qualities are suggested by the opening description of North Richmond Street?

2. What is the basis of the narrator's relationship to Mangan's sister? Why isn't she ever given a name?

3. What, besides his feelings of romance, is suggested by the narrator's response to the noise and jostling of the crowd at the market ("I imagined that I bore my chalice safely through a throng of foes.")? What is the source of the image here? In what ways has his romance had a demonstrable effect on other areas of his life?

4. What does the young narrator experience at the bazaar? Why is the sound or feel of money mentioned several times during the episode? What does the conversation mean?

5. Why, after the experience at Araby, does the boy see himself "as a creature driven and derided by vanity"? What has caused this apparent change in his view of himself?

EUDORA WELTY (1909–   )

A Still Moment

Lorenzo Dow rode the Old Natchez Trace at top speed upon a race horse, and the cry of the itinerant Man of God, "I must have souls! And souls I must have!" rang in his own windy ears. He rode as if never to stop, toward his night's appointment.

It was the hour of sunset. All the souls that he had saved and all those he had not took dusky shapes in the mist that hung between the high banks, and seemed by their great number and density to block his way, and showed no signs of melting or changing back into mist, so that he feared his passage was to be difficult forever. The poor souls that were not saved were darker and more pitiful than those that were, and still there was not any of the radiance he would have hoped to see in such a congregation.

"Light up, in God's name!" he called, in the pain of his disappointment.

Then a whole swarm of fireflies instantly flickered all around him, up and down, back and forth, first one golden light and then another, flashing without any of the weariness that had held back the souls. These were the signs sent from God that he had not seen the accumulated radiance of saved souls because he was not able, and that his eyes were more able to see the fireflies of the Lord than His blessed souls.

"Lord, give me the strength to see the angels when I am in Paradise," he said. "Do not let my eyes remain in this failing proportion to my loving heart always."

He gasped and held on. It was that day's complexity of horse-trading that had left him in the end with a Spanish race horse for which he was bound to send money in November from Georgia. Riding faster on the beast and still faster until he felt as if he were flying he sent thoughts of love with matching speed to his wife Peggy in Massachusetts. He found it effortless to love at a distance. He could look at the flowering trees and love Peggy in fullness, just as he could see his visions and love God. And Peggy, to whom he had not spoken until he could speak fateful words ("Would she accept of such an object as him?"), Peggy, the bride, with whom he had spent a few hours of time, showing of herself a small round handwriting, declared all in one letter, her first, that she felt the same as he, and that the fear was never of separation, but only of death.

Lorenzo well knew that it was Death that opened underfoot, that rippled by at night, that was the silence the birds did their singing in. He was close to death, closer than any animal or bird. On the back of one horse after another, winding them all, he was always riding toward it or away from it, and the Lord sent him directions with protection in His mind.

Just then he rode into a thicket of Indians taking aim with their new guns. One stepped out and took the horse by the bridle, it stopped at a touch, and the rest made a closing circle. The guns pointed.

"Incline!" The inner voice spoke sternly and with its customary lightning-quickness.

Lorenzo inclined all the way forward and put his head to the horse's silky mane, his body to its body, until a bullet meant for him would endanger the horse and make his death of no value. Prone he rode out through the circle of Indians, his obedience to the voice leaving him almost fearless, almost careless with joy.

But as he straightened and pressed ahead, care caught up with him again. Turning half-beast and half-divine, dividing himself like a heathen Centaur, he had escaped his death once more. But was it to be always by some metamorphosis of himself that he escaped, some humiliation of his faith, some admission to strength and argumentation and not frailty? Each time when he acted so it was at the command of an instinct that he took at once as the word of an angel, until too late, when he knew it was the word of the devil. He had roared like a tiger at Indians, he had submerged himself in water blowing the savage bubbles of the alligator, and they skirted him by. He had prostrated himself to appear dead, and deceived bears. But all the time God would have protected him in His own way, less hurried, more divine.

Even now he saw a serpent crossing the Trace, giving out knowing glances.

He cried, "I know you now!", and the serpent gave him one look out of which all the fire had been taken, and went away in two darts into the tangle.

He rode on, all expectation, and the voices in the throats of the wild beasts went, almost without his noticing when, into words. "Praise God," they said. "Deliver us from one another." Birds especially sang of divine love which was the one ceaseless protection. "Peace, in peace," were their words so many times when they spoke from the briars, in a courteous sort of inflection, and he turned his countenance toward all perched creatures with a benevolence striving to match their own.

He rode on past the little intersecting trails, letting himself be guided by voices and by lights. It was battlesounds he heard most, sending him on, but sometimes ocean sounds, that long beat of waves that would make his heart pound and retreat as heavily as they, and he despaired again in his failure in Ireland when he took a voyage and persuaded with the Catholics with his back against the door, and then ran away to their cries of "Mind the white hat!" But when he heard singing it was not the militant and sharp sound of Wesley's hymns, but a soft, tireless and tender air that had no beginning and no end, and the softness of distance, and he had pleaded with the Lord to find out if all this meant that it was wicked, but no answer had come.

Soon night would descend, and a camp-meeting ground ahead would fill with its sinners like the sky with its stars. How he hungered for them! He looked in prescience with a longing of love over the throng that waited while the flames of the torches threw change, change, change over their faces. How could he bring them enough, if it were not divine love and sufficient warning of all that could threaten them? He rode on faster. He was a filler of appointments, and he filled more and more, until his journeys up and down creation were nothing but a shuttle, driving back and forth upon the rich expanse of his vision. He was homeless by his own choice, he must be everywhere at some time, and somewhere soon. There hastening in the wilderness on his flying horse he gave the night's torch-lit crowd a premature benediction, he could not wait. He spread his arms out, one at a time for safety, and he wished, when they would all be gathered in by his tin horn blasts and the inspired words would go out over their heads, to brood above the entire and passionate life of the wide world, to become its rightful part.

He peered ahead. "Inhabitants of Time! The wilderness is your souls on earth!" he shouted ahead into the treetops. "Look about you, if you would view the conditions of your spirit, put here by the good Lord to show you and afright you. These wild places and these trails of awesome loneliness lie nowhere, nowhere, but in your heart."

A dark man, who was James Murrell the outlaw, rode his horse out of a cane brake and began going along beside Lorenzo without looking at him. He had the alternately proud and aggrieved look of a man believing himself to be an instrument in the hands of a power, and when he was young he said at once to strangers that he was being used by Evil, or sometimes he stopped a traveler by shouting, "Stop! I'm the Devil!" He rode along now talking and drawing out his talk, by some deep control of the voice gradually slowing the speed of Lorenzo's horse down until both the horses were softly trotting. He would have wondered that nothing he said was heard, not knowing that Lorenzo listened only to voices of whose heavenly origin he was more certain.

Murrell riding along with his victim-to-be, Murrell riding, was Murrell talking. He told away at his long tales, with always a distance and a long length of time flowing through them, and all centered about a silent man. In each the silent man would have done a piece of evil, a robbery or a murder, in a place of long ago, and it was all made for the revelation in the end that the silent man was Murrell himself, and the long story had happened yesterday, and the place *here* — the Natchez Trace. It would only take one dawning look for the victim to see that all of this was another story and he himself had listened his way into it, and that he too was about to recede in time (to where the dread was forgotten) for some listener and to live for a listener in the long ago. Destroy the present! — that must have been the first thing that was whispered in Murrell's heart — the living moment and the man

that lives in it must die before you can go on. It was his habit to bring the journey — which might even take days — to a close with a kind of ceremony. Turning his face at last into the face of the victim, for he had never seen him before now, he would tower up with the sudden height of a man no longer the tale teller but the speechless protagonist, silent at last, one degree nearer the hero. Then he would murder the man.

But it would always start over. This man going forward was going backward with talk. He saw nothing, observed no world at all. The two ends of his journey pulled at him always and held him in a nowhere, half asleep, smiling and witty, dangling his predicament. He was a murderer whose final stroke was over-long postponed, who had to bring himself through the greatest tedium to act, as if the whole wilderness, where he was born, were his impediment. But behind him and before him he kept in sight a victim, he saw a man fixed and stayed at the point of death — no matter how the man's eyes denied it, a victim, hands spreading to reach as if for the first time for life. Contempt! That is what Murrell gave that man.

Lorenzo might have understood, if he had not been in haste, that Murrell in laying hold of a man meant to solve his mystery of being. It was as if other men, all but himself, would lighten their hold on the secret, upon assault, and let it fly free at death. In his violence he was only treating of enigma. The violence shook his own body first, like a force gathering, and now he turned in the saddle.

Lorenzo's despair had to be kindled as well as his ecstasy, and could not come without that kindling. Before the awe-filled moment when the faces were turned up under the flares, as though an angel hand tipped their chins, he had no way of telling whether he would enter the sermon by sorrow or by joy. But at this moment the face of Murrell was turned toward him, turning at last, all solitary, in its full, and Lorenzo would have seized the man at once by his black coat and shaken him like prey for a lost soul, so instantly was he certain that the false fire was in his heart instead of the true fire. But Murrell, quick when he was quick, had put his own hand out, a restraining hand, and laid it on the wavelike flesh of the Spanish race horse, which quivered and shuddered at the touch.

They had come to a great live-oak tree at the edge of a low marsh-land. The burning sun hung low, like a head lowered on folded arms, and over the long reaches of violet trees the evening seemed still with thought. Lorenzo knew the place from having seen it among many in dreams, and he stopped readily and willingly. He drew rein, and Murrell drew rein, he dismounted and Murrell dismounted, he took a step, and Murrell was there too; and Lorenzo was not surprised at the closeness, how Murrell in his long dark coat and over it his dark face darkening still, stood beside him like a brother seeking light.

But in that moment instead of two men coming to stop by the great forked tree, there were three.

From far away, a student, Audubon, had been approaching lightly on the wilderness floor, disturbing nothing in his lightness. The long day of beauty had led him this certain distance. A flock of purple finches that he tried for the first moment to count went over his head. He made a spelling of the soft *pet* of the ivory-billed woodpecker. He told himself always: remember.

Coming upon the Trace, he looked at the high cedars, azure and still as distant smoke overhead, with their silver roots trailing down on either side like the veins of deepness in this place, and he noted some fact to his memory — this earth that wears but will not crumble or slide or turn to dust, they say it exists in one other spot in the world, Egypt — and then forgot it. He walked quietly. All life used this Trace, and he liked to see the animals move along it in direct, oblivious journeys, for they had begun it and made it, the buffalo and deer and the small running creatures before man ever knew where he wanted to go, and birds flew a great mirrored course above. Walking beneath them Audubon remembered how in the cities he had seen these very birds in his imagination, calling them up whenever he wished, even in the hard and glittering outer parlors where if an artist were humble enough to wait, some idle hand held up promised money. He walked lightly and he went as carefully as he had started at two that morning, crayon and paper, a gun, and a small bottle of spirits disposed about his body. (*Note: "The mocking birds so gentle that they would scarcely move out of the way."*) He looked with care; great abundance had ceased to startle him, and he could see things one by one. In Natchez they had told him of many strange and marvelous birds that were to be found here. Their descriptions had been exact, complete, and wildly varying, and he took them for inventions and believed that like all the worldly things that came out of Natchez, they would be disposed of and shamed by any man's excursion into the reality of Nature.

In the valley he appeared under the tree, a sure man, very sure and tender, as if the touch of all the earth rubbed upon him and the stains of the flowery swamp had made him so.

Lorenzo welcomed him and turned fond eyes upon him. To transmute a man into an angel was the hope that drove him all over the world and never let him flinch from a meeting or withhold good-byes for long. This hope insistently divided his life into only two parts, journey and rest.

There could be no night and day and love and despair and longing and satisfaction to make partitions in the single ecstasy of this alternation. All things were speech.

"God created the world," said Lorenzo, "and it exists to give testimony. Life is the tongue: speak."

But instead of speech there happened a moment of deepest silence.

Audubon said nothing because he had gone without speaking a word for days. He did not regard his thoughts for the birds and animals as susceptible, in their first change, to words. His long playing on the flute was not in its origin a talking to himself. Rather than speak to order or describe, he would always draw a deer with a stroke across it to communicate his need of venison to an Indian. He had only found words when he discovered that there is much otherwise lost that can be noted down each item in its own day, and he wrote often now in a journal, not wanting anything to be lost the way it had been, all the past, and he would write about a day, "Only sorry that the Sun Sets."

Murrell, his cheated hand hiding the gun, could only continue to smile at Lorenzo but he remembered in malice that he had disguised himself once as an Evangelist, and his final words to this victim would have been, "One of my disguises was what you are."

Then in Murrell Audubon saw what he thought of as "acquired sorrow" — that cumbrousness and darkness from which the naked Indian, coming just as he was made from God's hand, was so lightly free. He noted the eyes — the dark kind that loved to look through chinks, and saw neither closeness nor distance, light nor shade, wonder nor familiarity. They were narrowed to contract the heart, narrowed to make an averting plan. Audubon knew the finest-drawn tendons of the body and the working of their power, for he had touched them, and he supposed then that

in man the enlargement of the eye to see started a motion in the hands to make or do, and that the narrowing of the eye stopped the hand and contracted the heart. Now Murrell's eyes followed an ant on a blade of grass, up the blade and down, many times in the single moment. Audubon had examined the Cave-In Rock where one robber had lived his hiding life, and the air in the cave was the cavelike air that enclosed this man, the same odor, flinty and dark. O secret life, he thought — is it true that the secret is withdrawn from the true disclosure, that man is a cave man, and that the openness I see, the ways through forests, the rivers brimming light, the wide arches where the birds fly, are dreams of freedom? If my origin is withheld from me, is my end to be unknown too? Is the radiance I see closed into an interval between two darks, or can it not illuminate them both and discover at last, though it cannot be spoken, what was thought hidden and lost?

In that quiet moment a solitary snowy heron flew down not far away and began to feed beside the marsh water.

At the single streak of flight, the ears of the race horse lifted, and the eyes of both horses filled with the soft lights of sunset, which in the next instant were reflected in the eyes of the men too as they all looked into the west toward the heron, and all eyes seemed infused with a sort of wildness.

Lorenzo gave the bird a triumphant look, such as a man may bestow upon his own vision, and thought, Nearness is near, lighted in a marsh-land, feeding at sunset. Praise God, His love has come visible.

Murrell, in suspicion pursuing all glances, blinking into a haze, saw only whiteness ensconced in darkness, as if it were a little luminous shell that drew in and held the eyesight. When he shaded his eyes, the brand "H.T." on his thumb thrust itself into his own vision, and he looked at the bird with the whole plan of the Mystic Rebellion darting from him as if in rays of the bright reflected light, and he stood looking proudly, leader as he was bound to become of the slaves, the brigands and outcasts of the entire Natchez country, with plans, dates, maps burning like a brand into his brain, and he saw himself proudly in a moment of prophecy going down rank after rank of successively bowing slaves to unroll and flaunt an awesome great picture of the Devil colored on a banner.

Audubon's eyes embraced the object in the distance and he could see it as carefully as if he held it in his hand. It was a snowy heron alone out of its flock. He watched it steadily, in his care noting the exact inevitable things. When it feeds it muddies the water with its foot. . . . It was as if each detail about the heron happened slowly in time, and only once. He felt again the old stab of wonder — what structure of life bridged the reptile's scale and the heron's feather? That knowledge too had been lost. He watched without moving. The bird was defenseless in the world except for the intensity of its life, and he wondered, how can heat of blood and speed of heart defend it? Then he thought, as always as if it were new and unbelievable, it has nothing in space or time to prevent its flight. And he waited, knowing that some birds will wait for a sense of their presence to travel to men before they will fly away from them.

Fixed in its pure white profile it stood in the precipitous moment, a plumicorn on its head, its breeding dress extended in rays, eating steadily the little water creatures. There was a little space between each man and the others, where they stood overwhelmed. No one could say the three had ever met, or that this moment of intersection had ever come in their lives, or its promise fulfilled. But before them the white heron rested in the grasses with the evening all around it, lighter and more serene than the evening, flight closed in its body, the circuit of its beauty closed, a bird seen and a bird still, its motion calm as if it were offered: Take my flight. . . .

What each of them had wanted was simply *all*. To save all souls, to destroy all men, to see and to record all life that filled this world — all, all — but now a single frail yearning seemed to go out of the three of them for a moment and to stretch toward this one snowy, shy bird in the marshes. It was as if three whirlwinds had drawn together at some center, to find there feeding in peace a snowy heron. Its own slow spiral of flight could take it away in its own time, but for a little it held them still, it laid quiet over them, and they stood for a moment unburdened. . . .

Murrell wore no mask, for his face was that, a face that was aware while he was somnolent, a face that watched for him, and listened for him, alert and nearly brutal, the guard of a planner. He was quick without that he might be slow within, he staved off time, he wandered and plotted, and yet his whole desire mounted in him toward the end (was this the end — the sight of a bird feeding at dusk?), toward the instant of confession. His incessant deeds were thick in his heart now, and flinging himself to the ground he thought wearily, when all these trees are cut down, and the Trace lost, then my Conspiracy that is yet to spread itself will be disclosed, and all the stone-loaded bodies of murdered men will be pulled up, and all everywhere will know poor Murrell. His look pressed upon Lorenzo, who stared upward, and Audubon, who was taking out his gun, and his eyes squinted up to them in pleading, as if to say, "How soon may I speak, and how soon will you pity me?" Then he looked back to the bird, and he thought if it would look at him a dread penetration would fill and gratify his heart.

Audubon in each act of life was aware of the mysterious origin he half-concealed and half-sought for. People along the way asked him in their kindness or their rudeness if it were true, that he was born a prince, and was the Lost Dauphin, and some said it was his secret, and some said that that was what he wished to find out before he died. But if it was his identity that he wished to discover, or if it was what a man had to seize beyond that, the way for him was by endless examination, by the care for every bird that flew in his path and every serpent that shone underfoot. Not one was enough; he looked deeper and deeper, on and on, as if for a particular beast or some legendary bird. Some men's eyes persisted in looking outward when they opened to look inward, and to their delight, there outflung was the astonishing world under the sky. When a man at last brought himself to face some mirror-surface he still saw the world looking back at him, and if he continued to look, to look closer and closer, what then? The gaze that looks outward must be trained without rest, to be indomitable. It must see as slowly as Murrell's ant in the grass, as exhaustively as Lorenzo's angel of God, and then, Audubon dreamed, with his mind going to his pointed brush, it must see like this, and he tightened his hand on the trigger of the gun and pulled it, and his eyes went closed. In memory the heron was all its solitude, its total beauty. All its whiteness could be seen from all sides at once, its pure feathers were as if counted and known and their array one upon the other would never be lost. But it was not from that memory that he could paint.

His opening eyes met Lorenzo's, close and flashing, and it was on seeing horror deep in them, like fires in abysses, that he recognized it for the first time. He had never seen horror in its purity and clarity until now, in bright blue eyes. He went and picked up the bird. He had thought it to be a female, just as one sees the moon as female; and so it was. He put it in his bag, and started away. But Lorenzo had already

gone on, leaning a-tilt on the horse which went slowly.

Murrell was left behind, but he was proud of the dispersal, as if he had done it, as if he had always known that three men in simply being together and doing a thing can, by their obstinacy, take the pride out of one another. Each must go away alone, each send the others away alone. He himself had purposely kept to the wildest country in the world, and would have sought it out, the loneliest road. He looked about with satisfaction, and hid. Travelers were forever innocent, he believed: that was his faith. He lay in wait; his faith was in innocence and his knowledge was of ruin; and had these things been shaken? Now, what could possibly be outside his grasp? Churning all about him like a cloud about the sun was the great folding descent of his thought. Plans of deeds made his thoughts, and they rolled and mingled about his ears as if he heard a dark voice that rose up to overcome the wilderness voice, or was one with it. The night would soon come; and he had gone through the day.

Audubon, splattered and wet, turned back into the wilderness with the heron warm under his hand, his head still light in a kind of trance. It was undeniable, on some Sunday mornings, when he turned over and over his drawings they seemed beautiful to him, through what was dramatic in the conflict of life, or what was exact. What he would draw, and what he had seen, became for a moment one to him then. Yet soon enough, and it seemed to come in that same moment, like Lorenzo's horror and the gun's firing, he knew that even the sight of the heron which surely he alone had appreciated, had not been all his belonging, and that never could any vision, even any simple sight, belong to him or to any man. He knew that the best he could make would be, after it was apart from his hand, a dead thing and not a live thing, never the essence, only a sum of parts; and that it would always meet with a stranger's sight, and never be one with the beauty in any other man's head in the world. As he had seen the bird most purely at its moment of death, in some fatal way, in his care for looking outward, he saw his long labor most revealingly at the point where it met its limit. Still carefully, for he was trained to see well in the dark, he walked on into the deeper woods, noting all sights, all sounds, and was gentler than they as he went.

In the woods that echoed yet in his ears, Lorenzo riding slowly looked back. The hair rose on his head and his hands began to shake with cold, and suddenly it seemed to him that God Himself, just now, thought of the Idea of Separateness. For surely He had never thought of it before, when the little white heron was flying down to feed. He could understand God's giving Separateness first and then giving Love to follow and heal in its wonder; but God had reversed this, and given Love first and then Separateness, as though it did not matter to Him which came first. Perhaps it was that God never counted the moments of Time; Lorenzo did that, among his tasks of love. Time did not occur to God.

Therefore — did He even know of it? How to explain Time and Separateness back to God, Who had never thought of them, Who could let the whole world come to grief in a scattering moment?

Lorenzo brought his cold hands together in a clasp and stared through the distance at the place where the bird had been as if he saw it still; as if nothing could really take away what had happened to him, the beautiful little vision of the feeding bird. Its beauty had been greater than he could account for. The sweat of rapture poured down from his forehead, and then he shouted into the marshes.

"Tempter!"

He whirled forward in the saddle and began to hurry the horse to its high speed. His camp ground was far away still, though even now they must be lighting the torches and gathering in the multitudes, so that at the appointed time he would duly appear in their midst, to deliver his address on the subject of "In that day when all hearts shall be disclosed."

Then the sun dropped below the trees, and the new moon, slender and white, hung shyly in the west.

For Consideration

1. The story concerns three distinct men who are forced by circumstances to confront each other. What kind of life and values does each represent? How does each respond to the others?

2. Lorenzo is frequently associated with light (especially with the fireflies), Murrell, the "dark man," with darkness. Are these associations symbolic? Of what? When Lorenzo and Murrell dismount they act as one, with Murrell as the shadow of Lorenzo as the author describes it: "He drew rein, and Murrell drew rein, he dismounted and Murrell dismounted, he took a step, and Murrell was there too; and Lorenzo was not surprised at the closeness, how Murrell in his long dark coat and over it his dark face darkening still, stood beside him like a brother seeking light." What is the

significance of this description? Can Murrell be seen, in psychological terms, as Lorenzo's alter-ego?

3. What interests does each of the three have in the Trace? How does each react to natural occurrences? During "a still moment" in their encounter a "solitary snowy heron" flies over. How does each man view the bird? How is that reaction representative of the values each man has?

4. Why does Audubon kill the heron? Is the action compatible with his appearance as a nature-lover?

5. What is Lorenzo's response to the heron's death? What is the basis of the horror which Audubon sees deep within his eyes? What is Murrell's reaction to Audubon's deed? Why, after the men depart, is he "proud of the dispersal, as if he had done it"?

6. What is the meaning of Lorenzo's colloquy on Love and Separateness? What is meant by each term in this context? Why does Lorenzo shout "Tempter!" before leaving the area in great speed?

DORIS LESSING (1919–   )
Notes for a Case History

Maureen Watson was born at 93 Nelson's Way, N.1., in 1942. She did not remember the war, or rather, when people said "The War," she thought of Austerity: couponed curtains, traded clothes, the half pound of butter swapped for the quarter of tea. (Maureen's parents preferred tea to butter.) Further back, at the roots of her life, she *felt* a movement of fire and shadow, a leaping and a subsidence of light. She did not know whether this was a memory or a picture she had formed, perhaps from what her parents had told her of the night the bomb fell two streets from Nelson's Way and they had all stood among piles of smoking rubble for a day and night, watching firemen hose the flames. This feeling was not only of danger, but of fatality, of being helpless before great impersonal forces; and was how she most deeply felt, saw, or thought an early childhood which the social viewer would describe perhaps like this: "Maureen Watson, conceived by chance on an unexpected granted-at-the-last-minute leave, at the height of the worst war in history, infant support of a mother only occasionally upheld (the chances of war deciding) by a husband she had met in a bomb shelter during an air raid: poor baby, born into a historical upheaval which destroyed forty million and might very well have destroyed her."

As for Maureen, her memories and the reminiscences of her parents made her dismiss the whole business as boring, and nothing to do with her.

It was at her seventh birthday party she

first made this clear. She wore a mauve organdy frock with a pink sash, and her golden hair was in ringlets. One of the mothers said: "This is the first unrationed party dress my Shirley has had. It's a shame, isn't it?" And her own mother said: "Well of course these war children don't know what they've missed." At which Maureen said: "*I* am not a war child." "What are you then, love?" said her mother, fondly exchanging glances.

"I'm Maureen," said Maureen.

"And I'm Shirley," said Shirley, joining cause.

Shirley Banner was Maureen's best friend. The Watsons and the Banners were better than the rest of the street. The Watsons lived in an end house, at higher weekly payments. The Banners had a sweets-paper-and-tobacco shop.

Maureen and Shirley remembered (or had they been told?) that once Nelson's Way was a curved terrace of houses. Then the ground-floor level had broken into shops: a grocer's, a laundry, a hardware, a baker, a dairy. It seemed as if every second family in the street ran a shop to supply certain defined needs of the other families. What other needs were there? Apparently none; for Maureen's parents applied for permission to the Council, and the ground floor of their house became a second grocery shop, by way of broken-down walls, new shelves, a deepfreeze. Maureen remembered two small rooms, each with flowered curtains where deep shadows moved and flickered from the two small fires that burned back to back in the centre wall that divided them. These two rooms disappeared in clouds of dust from which sweet-smelling planks of wood stuck out. Strange but friendly men paid her compliments on her golden corkscrews and asked her for kisses, which they did not get. They gave her sips of sweet tea from their canteens (filled twice a day by her mother) and made her bracelets of the spiralling fringes of yellow wood. Then

they disappeared. There was the new shop. Maureen's Shop. Maureen went with her mother to the sign shop to arrange for these two words to be written in yellow paint on a blue ground.

Even without the name, Maureen would have known that the shop was connected with hopes for her future; and that her future was what her mother lived for.

She was pretty. She had always known it. Even where the shadows of fire and dark were, they had played over a pretty baby. "You were such a pretty baby, Maureen." And at the birthday parties: "Maureen's growing really pretty, Mrs. Watson." But all babies and little girls are pretty, she knew that well enough . . . no, it was something more. For Shirley was plump, dark — pretty. Yet their parents' — or rather, their mothers' — talk had made it clear from the start that Shirley was not in the same class as Maureen.

When Maureen was ten there was an episode of importance. The two mothers were in the room above Maureen's Shop and they were brushing their little girls' hair out. Shirley's mother said: "Maureen could do really well for herself, Mrs. Watson." And Mrs. Watson nodded, but sighed deeply. The sigh annoyed Maureen, because it contradicted the absolute certainty that she felt (it had been bred into her) about her future. Also because it had to do with the *boring* era which she remembered, or thought she did, as a tiger-striped movement of fire. *Chance:* Mrs. Watson's sigh was like a prayer to the gods of Luck: it was the sigh of a small helpless thing being tossed about by big seas and gales. Maureen made a decision, there and then, that she had nothing in common with the little people who were prepared to be helpless and tossed about. For she was going to be quite different. She was already different. Not only The War but the shadows of war had long gone, except for talk in the newspapers which had nothing to do with her. The shops were full of everything. The Banners' sweets-tobacco-paper shop had just been done up; and Maureen's was short of nothing. Maureen and Shirley, two pretty little girls in smart mother-made dresses, were children of plenty, and knew it, because their parents kept saying (apparently they did not care how tedious they were): "These kids don't lack for anything, do they? They don't know what it can be like, do they?" This, with the suggestion that they ought to be grateful for not lacking anything, always made the children sulky, and they went off to flirt their full many-petticoated skirts where the neighbours could see them and pay them compliments.

Eleven years. Twelve years. Already Shirley had subsided into her role of pretty girl's plainer girl friend, although of course she was not plain at all. Fair girl, dark girl, and Maureen by mysterious birthright was the "pretty one," and there was no doubt in either of their minds which girl the boys would try first for a date. Yet this balance was by no means as unfair as it seemed. Maureen, parrying and jesting on street corners, at bus stops, knew she was doing battle for two, because the boys she discarded Shirley got: Shirley got far more boys than she would have done without Maureen who, for her part, needed — more, *had* to have — a foil. Her role demanded one.

They both left school at fifteen, Maureen to work in the shop. She was keeping her eyes open: her mother's phrase. She wore a slim white overall, pinned her fair curls up, was neat and pretty in her movements. She smiled calmly when customers said: "My word, Mrs. Watson, your Maureen's turned out, hasn't she?"

About that time there was a second moment of consciousness. Mrs. Watson was finishing a new dress for Maureen, and the fitting was taking rather long. Maureen fidgeted and her mother said: "Well, it's your capital, isn't it? You've got to see that, love." And she added the deep unconscious sigh. Maureen said: "Well don't go on about it, it's not very nice, is it?" And what she meant was, not that the idea was not very nice, but that she had gone beyond needing to be reminded about it; she was feeling the irritated embarrassment of a child when it is reminded to clean its teeth after this habit has become second nature. Mrs. Watson saw and understood this, and sighed again; and this time it was the maternal sigh which means: Oh dear, you are growing up fast! "Oh *Mum*," said Maureen, "sometimes you just make me tired, you do really."

Sixteen. She was managing her capital perfectly. Her assets were a slight delicate prettiness, and a dress sense that must have been a gift from God, or more probably because she had been reading the fashion magazines since practically before consciousness. Shirley had put in six months of beehive hair, pouting scarlet lips, and an air of sullen disdain; but Maureen's sense of herself was much finer. She modelled herself on film stars, but with an understanding of how far she could go — of what was allowable to Maureen. So the experience of being Bardot, Monroe, or whoever it was, refined her: she took from it an essence, which was learning to be a vehicle for other people's fantasies. So while Shirley had been a dozen stars, but really *been* them, in violent temporary transmogrifications, from which she emerged (often enough with a laugh) Shirley — plump, good-natured, and herself — Maureen remained herself through every role, but creating her appearance, like an alter ego, to meet the expression in people's eyes.

Round about sixteen, another incident: prophetic. Mrs. Watson had a cousin who worked in the dress trade, and this man, unthought-of for many years, was met at a wedding. He commented on Maureen, a vision in white gauze. Mrs. Watson worked secretly on this slender material for some weeks; then wrote to him: Could Maureen be a model? He had only remote connections with the world of expensive clothes and girls, but he dropped into the shop with frankly personal aims. Maureen in a white wrapper was still pretty, very; but her remote air told this shrewd man that she would certainly not go out with him. She was saving herself; he knew that air of self-esteem very well from other exemplars. Such girls do not go out with middle-aged cousins, except as a favour or to get something. However, he told Mrs. Watson that Maureen was definitely model material, but that she would have to do something about her voice. (He meant her accent of course; and so Mrs. Watson understood him.) He left addresses and advice, and Mrs. Watson was in a state of quivering ambition. She said so to Maureen: "This is your chance, girl. Take it." What Maureen heard was: "This is *my* chance."

Maureen, nothing if not alert for her Big Chance, for which her whole life had prepared her, accepted her mother's gift of a hundred pounds (she did not thank her, no thanks were due) and actually wrote to the school where she would be taught voice training.

Then she fell into sullen withdrawal, which she understood so little that a week had gone by before she said she must be sick — or something. She was rude to her mother: very rare, this. Her father chided her for it: even rarer. But he spoke in such a way that Maureen understood for the first time that this drive, this push, this family effort to gain her a glamorous future, came from her mother, her father was not implicated. For him, she was a pretty-enough girl, spoiled by a silly woman.

Maureen slowly understood she was not sick, she was growing up. For one thing: if she changed her "voice" so as to be good enough to mix with new people, she would no longer be part of this street, she would no longer be *Our Maureen*. What would she be then? Her mother knew: she would marry a duke and be whisked off to Hollywood. Maureen examined her mother's ideas for her and shrank with humiliation. She was above all no fool, but she had been very foolish. For one thing: when she used her eyes, with the scales of illusion off them, she saw that the million streets of London blossomed with girls as pretty as she. What, then, had fed the illusion in herself and in other people? What accounted for the special tone, the special looks that always greeted her? Why, nothing more than that she, Maureen, because of her mother's will behind her, had carried herself from childhood as something special, apart, destined for a great future.

Meanwhile (as she clearly saw) she was in 93 Nelson's Way, serving behind the counter of Maureen's Shop. (She now wondered what the neighbours had thought — before they got used to it — about her mother's fondness so terribly displayed.) She was dependent on nothing less than that a duke or a film producer would walk in to buy a quarter of tea and some sliced bread.

Maureen sulked. So her father said. So her mother complained. Maureen was — thinking? Yes. But more, a wrong had been done her, she knew it, and the sulking was more of a protective silence while she grew a scab over a wound.

She emerged demanding that the hundred pounds should be spent on sending her to secretarial school. Her parents complained that she could have learned how to be a secretary for nothing if she had stayed on at school another year. She said: "Yes, but you didn't have the sense to make me, did you? What did you think — I was going to sell butter like you all my life?" Unfair, on the face of it; but deeply fair, in view of what they had done to her. In their different ways they knew it. (Mr. Watson knew in his heart, for instance, that he should never have allowed his wife to call the shop "Maureen's.") Maureen went, then, to secretarial school for a year. Shirley went with her: she had been selling cosmetics in the local branch of a big chain store. To raise the hundred pounds was difficult for Shirley's parents: the shop had done badly, had been bought by a big firm; her father was an assistant in it. For that matter, it wasn't all that easy for the Watsons: the hundred pounds was the result of small savings and pinchings over years.

This was the first time Maureen had thought of the word capital in connection with money, rather than her own natural assets: it was comparatively easy for the Watsons to raise money, because they had capital: the Banners had no capital. (Mrs. Watson said the Banners had had *bad luck.*) Maureen strengthened her will; and as a result the two families behaved even more as if the girls would have different futures — or, to put it another way, that while the two sums of a hundred pounds were the same, the Watsons could be expected to earn more on theirs than the Banners.

This was reflected directly in the two girls' discussions about boys. Shirley would say: "I'm more easygoing than you."

Maureen would reply: "*I* only let them go so far."

Their first decisions on this almighty subject had taken place years before, when they were thirteen. Even then Shirley went further ("let them go further") than Maureen. It was put down, between them, to Shirley's warmer temperament — charitably; for both knew it was because of Maureen's higher value in the market.

At the secretarial school they met boys they had not met before. Previously boys had been from the street or the neighbourhood, known from birth, and for this reason not often gone out with — that would have been boring (serious, with possibilities of marriage). Or boys picked up after dances or at the pictures. But now there were new boys met day after day in the school. Shirley went out with one for weeks, thought of getting engaged, changed her mind, went out with another. Maureen went out with a dozen, chosen carefully. She knew what she was doing — and scolded Shirley for being so *soft.* "You're just stupid, Shirl — I mean, you've got to get on. Why don't you do like me?"

What Maureen did was to allow herself to be courted, until she agreed at last, as a favour, to be taken out. First, lunch — a word she began to use now. She would agree to go out to lunch two or three times with one boy, while she was taken out to supper (dinner) by another. The dinner partner, having been rewarded by a closed-mouth kiss for eight, ten, twelve nights, got angry or sulky or reproachful, according to his nature. He dropped her, and the lunch partner was promoted to dinner partner.

Maureen ate free for the year of her training. It wasn't that she planned it like this: but when she heard other girls say they paid their way or liked to be independent, it seemed to Maureen wrongheaded. To pay for herself would be to let herself be undervalued: even the idea of it made her nervous and sulky.

At the end of the training Maureen got a job in a big architect's office. She was a junior typist. She stuck out for a professional office because the whole point of the training was to enable her to meet a better class of people. Of course she had already learned not to use the phrase, and when her mother did snubbed her with: "I don't know what you mean, better *class,* but it's not much point my going into that hardware stuck upstairs in an office by myself if I can get a job where there's some life about."

Shirley went into a draper's shop where there was one other typist (female) and five male assistants.

In Maureen's place there were six architects, out most of the time, or invisible in large offices visited only by the real secretaries; a lower stratum of young men in training, designers, draftsmen, managers, etc., and a pool of typists.

The young men were mostly of her own class. For some months she ate and was entertained at their expense; and at each week's end there was a solemn ceremony, the high point of the week, certainly the most exciting moment in it, when she divided her wage. It was seven pounds (rising to ten in three years) and she allocated two pounds for clothes, four for the post office, and one pound for the week's odd expenses.

At the end of a year she understood two things. That she had saved something like two hundred pounds. That there was not a young man in the office who would take her out again. They regarded her, according to their natures, with resentment or with admiration for her cool management of them. But there was nothing doing *there* — so they all knew.

Maureen thought this over. If she were not taken out to meals and entertainment, she must pay for herself and save no money, or she must never go out at all. If she was going to be taken out, then she must give something in return. What she gave was an open mouth, and freedom to the waist. She calculated that because of her prettiness she could give much less than other girls.

She was using her *capital* with even more intelligence than before. A good part of her time — all not spent in the office or being taken out — went in front of her looking glass, or with the better-class fashion magazines. She studied them with formidable concentration. By now she knew she could have gone anywhere in these islands, except for her voice. Whereas, months before, she had sulked in a sort of fright at the idea of cutting herself off from her street and the neighbours, now she softened and shaped her voice, listening to the clients and the senior architects in the office. She knew her voice had changed when Shirley said: "You're talking nice, Maureen, much nicer than me."

There was a boy in the office who teased her about it. His name was Tony Head. He was in training to be an accountant for the firm, and was very much from her own background. After having taken her out twice to lunch, he had never asked her again. She knew why: he had told her. "Can't afford you, Maureen," he said. He earned not much more than she did. He was nineteen, ambitious, serious, and she liked him.

Then she was nineteen. Shirley was engaged to one of the assistants in her shop, and would be married next Christmas.

Maureen took forty pounds out of her savings and went on a tour to Italy. It was her first time out of England. She hated it: not Italy, but the fact that half the sixty people on the tour were girls, like herself, looking for a good time, and the other half elderly couples. In Rome, Pisa, Florence, Venice, the Italians mooned over Maureen, courted her with melting eyes, while she walked past them, distant as a starlet. They probably thought she was one. The courier, a sharp young man, took Maureen out to supper one night after he had finished his duties, and made it clear that her mouth, even if opened, and her breasts, were not enough. Maureen smiled at him sweetly through the rest of the trip. No one paid for her odd coffees, ices and drinks. On the last night of the trip, in a panic because the forty-pound investment had yielded so little, she went out with an Italian boy who spoke seven words of English. She thought him crude, and left him after an hour.

But she had learned a good deal for her forty pounds. Quietly, in her lunch hour, she went off to the National Gallery and to the Tate. There she looked, critical and respectful, at pictures, memorising their subjects, or main colours, learning names. When invited out, she asked to be taken to "foreign" films, and when she got back home wrote down the names of the director and the stars. She looked at the book page of the *Express* (she made her parents buy it instead of the *Mirror*) and sometimes bought a recommended book, if it was a best seller.

Twenty. Shirley was married and had a baby. Maureen saw little of her — both girls felt they had a new world of knowledge the other couldn't appreciate.

Maureen was earning ten pounds a week, and saved six.

There came to the office, as an apprentice architect, Stanley Hunt, from grammar school and technical college. Tallish, well-dressed, fair, with a small moustache. They took each other's measure, knowing they were the same kind. It was some weeks before he asked her out. She knew, by putting herself in his place, that he was looking for a wife with a little money or a house of her own, if he couldn't get a lady. (She smiled when she heard him using this word about one of the clients.) He tried to know clients socially, to be accepted by them as they accepted the senior architects. All this Maureen watched, her cool little face saying nothing.

One day, after he had invited a Miss Plast (Chelsea, well-off, investing money in houses) to coffee, and been turned down, he asked Maureen to join him in a sandwich lunch. Maureen thanked him delightfully, but said she already had an engagement. She went off to the National

Gallery, sat on the steps, froze off wolves and pickups, and ate a sandwich by herself.

A week later, invited to lunch by Stanley, she suggested the Trattoria Siciliana which was more expensive, as she knew quite well, than he had expected. But this meal was a success. He was impressed with her, though he knew (how could he not, when his was similar?) her background.

She was careful to be engaged for two weeks. Then she agreed to go to the pictures — "a foreign film, if you don't mind, I think the American films are just boring." She did not offer to pay, but remarked casually that she had nearly six hundred pounds in the post office. "I'm thinking of buying a little business, sometime. A dress shop. I've got a cousin in the trade."

Stanley agreed that "with your taste" it would be a sure thing.

Maureen no longer went to the Palais, or similar places (though she certainly did not conceal from Stanley that she had "once"), but she loved to dance. Twice they went to the West End together and danced at a Club which was "a nice place." They danced well together. On the second occasion she offered to pay her share, for the first time in her life. He refused, as she had known he would, but she could see he liked her for offering: more, was relieved; in the office they said she was mean, and he must have heard them. On that night, taken home lingeringly, she opened her mouth for him and let his hands go down to her thighs. She felt a sharp sexuality which made her congratulate herself that she had never, like Shirley, gone "halfway" before. Well of course, girls were going to get married to just anybody if they let themselves be all worked up every time they were taken out!

But Stanley was not at all caught. He was too cool a customer, as she was. He was still looking for something better.

He would be an architect in a couple of

years; he would be in a profession; he was putting down money for a house; he was good-looking, attractive to women, and with these assets he ought to do better than marry Maureen. Maureen agreed with him.

But meanwhile he took her out. She was careful often to be engaged elsewhere. She was careful always to be worth taking somewhere expensive. When he took her home, while she did not go so far as "nearly the whole way," she went "everything but"; and she was glad she did not like him better, because otherwise she would have been lost. She knew quite well she did not really like him, although her mind was clouded by her response to his hands, his moustache, his clothes and his new car.

She knew, because meanwhile a relationship she understood very well, and regretted, had grown up with Tony. He, watching this duel between the well-matched pair, would grin and drop remarks at which Maureen coloured and turned coldly away. He often asked her out — but only for a "Dutch treat" — expecting her to refuse. "How's your savings account, Maureen? I can't save, you girls get it all spent on you." Tony took out a good many girls: Maureen kept a count of them. She hated him; yet she liked him, and knew she did. She relied on him above all for this grinning, honest understanding of her: he did not approve of her, but perhaps (she felt in her heart) he was right? During this period she several times burst into tears when alone, without apparent reason; afterwards she felt that life had no flavour. Her future was narrowing down to Stanley; and at these times she viewed it through Tony Head's eyes.

One night the firm had a party for the senior members of the staff. Stanley was senior, Maureen and Tony were not. Maureen knew that Stanley had previously asked another girl to go, and when he asked herself, was uncertain whether she could make it until the very last moment:

particularly as his inviting her, a junior, meant that he was trying out on the senior members the idea of Maureen as a wife. But she acquitted herself very well. First, she was the best-looking woman in the room by far, and the best-dressed. Everyone looked at her and commented: they were used to her as a pretty typist; but tonight she was using all her will to make them look at her, to make her face and body reflect what they admired. She made no mistakes. When the party was over Stanley and two of the younger architects suggested they drive out to London airport for breakfast, and they did. The two other girls were middle-class. Maureen kept silent for the most part, smiling serenely. She had been to Italy, she remarked, when a plane rose to go to Italy. Yes, she had liked it, though she thought the Italians were too noisy; what she had enjoyed best was the Sistine Chapel and a boat trip on the Adriatic. She hadn't cared for Venice much, it was beautiful, but the canals smelled, and there were far too many people; perhaps it would be better to go in winter? She said all this, having a right to it, and it came off. As she spoke she remembered Tony, who had once met her on her way to the National Gallery. "Getting yourself an education, Maureen? That's right, it'll pay off well, that will."

She knew, thinking it all over afterwards, that the evening had been important for her with Stanley. Because of this, she did not go out with him for a week, she said she was busy talking to her cousin about the possibilities of a dress shop. She sat in her room thinking about Stanley, and when thoughts of Tony came into her mind, irritatedly pushed them away. If she could succeed with Stanley, why not with someone better? The two architects from that evening had eyed her all the following week: they did not, however, ask her out. She then found that both were engaged to marry the girls they had been with. It was bad luck: she was sure that otherwise they would have asked her out. How to meet more like them? Well, that was the trouble — the drive to the airport was a bit of a fluke; it was the first time she had actually met the seniors socially.

Meanwhile Stanley showed an impatience in his courtship — and for the first time. As for her, she was getting on for twenty-one, and all the girls she had grown up with were married and had their first or even their second babies.

She went out with Stanley to a dinner in the West End at an Italian restaurant. Afterwards they were both very passionate. Maureen, afterwards, was furious with herself: some borderline had been crossed (she supposed she still could be called a virgin?) and now decisions would have to be made.

Stanley was in love with her. She was in love with Stanley. A week later he proposed to her. It was done with a violent moaning intensity that she knew was due to his conflicts over marrying her. She was not good enough. He was not good enough. They were second-best for each other. They writhed and moaned and bit in the car, and agreed to marry. Her eight hundred pounds would make it easier to buy the house in a good suburb. He would formally meet her parents next Sunday.

"So you're engaged to Stanley Hunt?" said Tony.

"Looks like it, doesn't it?"

"Caught him — good for you!"

"He's caught me, more like it!"

"Have it your way."

She was red and angry. He was serious.

"Come and have a bite?" he said. She went.

It was a small restaurant, full of office workers eating on luncheon vouchers. She ate fried plaice ("No chips, please") and he ate steak-and-kidney pudding. He joked, watched her, watched her intently, said finally: "Can't you do better than that?" He meant, and she knew it, better

in the sense she would use herself, in her heart: he meant *nice*. Like himself. But did that mean that Tony thought *she* was nice? Unlike Stanley? She did not think she was, she was moved to tears (concealed) that he did. "What's wrong with him then?" she demanded, casual. "What's wrong with *you*? You need your head examined." He said it seriously, and they exchanged a long look. The two of them sat looking goodbye at each other: the extremely pretty girl at whom everyone in the room kept glancing and remarking on, and the good-looking, dark, rather fat young accountant who was brusque and solemn with disappointment in her. With love for her? Very likely.

She went home silent, thinking of Tony. When she thought of him she needed to cry. She also needed to hurt him.

But she told her parents she was engaged to Stanley, who would be an architect. They would have their own house, in (they thought) Hemel Hampstead. He owned a car. He was coming to tea on Sunday. Her mother forgot the dukes and the film producers before the announcement ended: her father listened judiciously, then congratulated her. He had been going to a football match on Sunday, but agreed, after persuasion, that this was a good-enough reason to stay home.

Her mother then began discussing, with deference to Maureen's superior knowledge, how to manage next Sunday to best advantage. For four days she went on about it. But she was talking to herself. Her husband listened, said nothing. And Maureen listened, critically, like her father. Mrs. Watson began clamouring for a definite opinion on what sort of cake to serve on Sunday. But Maureen had no opinion. She sat, quiet, looking at her mother, a largish ageing woman, her exfair hair dyed yellow, her flesh guttering. She was like an excited child, and it was not attractive. *Stupid, stupid, stupid* — that's all you are, thought Maureen.

As for Maureen, if anyone had made the comparison, she was "sulking" as she had before over being a model and having to be drilled out of her "voice." She said nothing but: "It'll be all right, Mum, don't get so worked up." Which was true, because Stanley knew what to expect: he knew why he had not been invited to meet her parents until properly hooked. He would have done the same in her place. He *was* doing the same: she was going to meet his parents the week after. What Mrs. Watson, Mr. Watson, wore on Sunday; whether sandwiches or cake were served; whether there were fresh or artificial flowers — none of it mattered. The Watsons were part of the bargain: what he was paying in return for publicly owning the most covetable woman anywhere they were likely to be; and for the right to sleep with her after the public display.

Meanwhile Maureen said not a word. She sat on her bed looking at nothing in particular. Once or twice she examined her face in the mirror, and even put cream on it. And she cut out a dress, but put it aside.

On Sunday Mrs. Watson laid tea for four, using her own judgement since Maureen was too deeply in love (so she told everyone) to notice such trifles. At four Stanley was expected, and at 3:55 Maureen descended to the living room. She wore: a faded pink dress from three summers before; her mother's cretonne overall used for housework; and a piece of cloth tied round her hair that might very well have been a duster. At any rate, it was a faded grey. She had put on a pair of her mother's old shoes. She could not be called plain; but she looked like her own faded elder sister, dressed for a hard day's spring cleaning.

Her father, knowledgeable, said nothing: he lowered the paper, examined her, let out a short laugh, and lifted it again.

Mrs. Watson, understanding at last that this was a real crisis, burst into tears. Stanley arrived before Mrs. Watson could stop herself crying. He nearly said to Mrs. Watson: "I didn't know Maureen had an older sister." Maureen sat listless at one end of the table; Mr. Watson sat grinning at the other, and Mrs. Watson sniffed and wiped her eyes between the two.

Maureen said: "Hello, Stanley, meet my father and mother." He shook their hands and stared at her. She did not meet his eyes: rather, the surface of her blue gaze met the furious, incredulous, hurt pounce of his glares at her. Maureen poured tea, offered him sandwiches and cake, and made conversation about the weather, and the prices of food, and the dangers of giving even good customers credit in the shop. He sat there, a well-set-up young man, with his brushed hair, his brushed moustache, his checked brown cloth jacket, and a face flaming with anger and affront. He said nothing, but Maureen talked on, her voice trailing and cool. At five o'clock, Mrs. Watson again burst into tears, her whole body shaking, and Stanley brusquely left.

Mr. Watson said: "Well, why did you lead him on, then?" and turned on the television. Mrs. Watson went to lie down. Maureen, in her own room, took off the various items of her disguise, and returned them to her mother's room. "Don't cry, Mum. What are you carrying on like that for? What's the matter?" Then she dressed extremely carefully in a new white linen suit, brown shoes, beige blouse. She did her hair and her face, and sat looking at herself. The last two hours (or week) hit her, and her stomach hurt so that she doubled up. She cried; but the tears smeared her makeup, and she stopped herself with the side of a fist against her mouth.

It now seemed to her that for the last week she had simply not been Maureen;

she had been someone else. What had she done it for? Why? Then she knew it was for Tony: during all that ridiculous scene at the tea table, she had imagined Tony looking on, grinning, but understanding her.

She now wiped her face quite clear of tears, and went quietly out of the house so as not to disturb her father and mother. There was a telephone booth at the corner. She stepped calm and aloof along the street, her mouth held (as it always was) in an almost smile. Bert from the grocer's shop said: "Hey, Maureen, that's a smasher. Who's it for?" And she gave him the smile and the toss of the head that went with the street and said: "You, Bert, it's all for you." She went to the telephone booth thinking of Tony. She felt as if he already knew what had happened. She would say: "Let's go and dance, Tony." He would say: "Where shall I meet you?" She dialled his number, and it rang and it rang and it rang. She stood holding the receiver, waiting. About ten minutes — more. Slowly she replaced it. *He had let her down.* He had been telling her, in words and without, to be something, to stay something, and now he did not care, he had let her down.

Maureen quietened herself and telephoned Stanley.

All right then, if that's how you want it, she said to Tony.

Stanley answered, and she said amiably: "Hello."

Silence. She could hear him breathing, fast. She could see his affronted face.

"Well, aren't you going to say anything?" She tried to make this casual, but she could hear the fear in her voice. Oh yes, she could lose him and probably had. To hide the fear she said: "Can't you take a joke, Stanley?" and laughed.

"A joke!"

She laughed. Not bad, it sounded all right.

"I thought you'd gone off your nut,

clean off your rocker. . . ." He was breathing in and out, a rasping noise. She was reminded of his hot breathing down her neck and her arms. Her own breath quickened, even while she thought: I don't like him, I really don't like him at all . . . and she said softly: "Oh Stan, I was having a bit of a giggle, that's all."

Silence. Now, this was the crucial moment.

"Oh Stan, can't you see — I thought it was all just boring, that's all it was." She laughed again.

He said: "Nice for your parents, I don't think."

"Oh they don't mind — they laughed after you'd left, though first they were cross." She added hastily, afraid he might think they were laughing at him: "They're used to me, that's all it is."

Another long silence. With all her willpower she insisted that he should soften. But he said nothing, merely breathed in and out, into the receiver.

"Stanley, it was only a joke, you aren't really angry, are you, Stanley?" The tears sounded in her voice now, and she judged it better that they should.

He said, after hesitation: "Well, Maureen, I just didn't like it, I don't like that kind of thing, that's all." She allowed herself to go on crying, and after a while he said, forgiving her in a voice that was condescending and irritated: "Well, all right, all right, there's no point in crying, is there?"

He was annoyed with himself for giving in, she knew that, because she would have been. He had given her up, thrown her over, during the last couple of hours: he was pleased, really, that something from outside had forced him to give her up. Now he could be free for the something better that would turn up — someone who would not strike terror into him by an extraordinary performance like this afternoon's.

"Let's go off to the pictures, Stan. . . ."

Even now, he hesitated. Then he said, quick and reluctant: "I'll meet you at Leicester Square, outside the Odeon, at seven o'clock." He put down the receiver.

Usually he came to pick her up in the car from the corner of the street.

She stood smiling, the tears running down her face. She knew she was crying because of the loss of Tony, who had let her down. She walked back to her house to make up again, thinking that she was in Stanley's power now: there was no balance between them, the advantage was all his.

For Consideration

1. Characterize Maureen's childhood. What is her relationship to her family, especially her mother?

2. Distinguish as fully as possible the values and characteristics associated with Shirley and those associated with Maureen. How does Lessing avoid stereotyping the two? Where does each character fall on the scale of flat to round?

3. What is the basis of Maureen's relationships with boys? What does she seek to gain from those associations?

4. Increasingly, Maureen's values and aims are divided between Tony Head and Stanley Hunt. What does she see in each? Why, as she becomes further attached to Stanley, does she find thoughts of Tony gnawing at her?

5. How do you account for Maureen's bizarre dress and action on the day of Stanley's meeting with her parents? Why is her attire described as a "disguise"? In what sense, as she admits, was her action done for Tony? Why, later, does she accuse Tony of having let her down?

6. Why are these "notes for a case history"? What does the title suggest about Maureen?

For Comparison

What similarities are there between Maureen and the young woman in "How I Contemplated the World from the Detroit House of Correction and Began My Life Over Again" (p. 11)? How alike are their associations with family? With other women? With men? Oates' story originates in part from the Detroit House of Correction; the present story is said to be "notes for a case history." What does each title suggest about the principal character?

JAMES BALDWIN   (1924–   )
Sonny's Blues

I read about it in the paper, in the subway, on my way to work. I read it, and I couldn't believe it, and I read it again. Then perhaps I just stared at it, at the newsprint spelling out his name, spelling out the story. I stared at it in the swinging lights of the subway car, and in the faces and bodies of the people, and in my own face, trapped in the darkness which roared outside.

It was not to be believed and I kept telling myself that, as I walked from the subway station to the high school. And at the same time I couldn't doubt it. I was scared, scared for Sonny. He became real to me again. A great block of ice got settled in my belly and kept melting there slowly all day long, while I taught my classes algebra. It was a special kind of ice. It kept melting, sending trickles of ice water all up and down my veins, but it never got less. Sometimes it hardened and seemed to expand until I felt my guts were going to come spilling out or that I was going to choke or scream. This would always be at a moment when I was remembering some specific thing Sonny had once said or done.

When he was about as old as the boys in my classes his face had been bright and open, there was a lot of copper in it; and he'd had wonderfully direct brown eyes, and great gentleness and privacy. I wondered what he looked like now. He had been picked up, the evening before, in a raid on an apartment downtown, for peddling and using heroin.

I couldn't believe it: but what I mean by that is that I couldn't find any room for it anywhere inside me. I had kept it outside me for a long time. I hadn't wanted to know. I had had suspicions, but I didn't name them, I kept putting them away. I told myself that Sonny was wild, but he wasn't crazy. And he'd always been a good boy, he hadn't ever turned hard or evil or disrespectful, the way kids can, so quick, so quick, especially in Harlem. I didn't want to believe that I'd ever see my brother going down, coming to nothing, all that light in his face gone out, in the condition I'd already seen so many others. Yet it had happened and here I was, talking about algebra to a lot of boys who might, every one of them for all I knew, be popping off needles every time they went to the head. Maybe it did more for them than algebra could.

I was sure that the first time Sonny had ever had horse, he couldn't have been much older than these boys were now. These boys, now, were living as we'd been living then, they were growing up with a rush and their heads bumped abruptly against the low ceiling of their actual possibilities. They were filled with rage. All they really knew were two darknesses, the darkness of their lives, which was now closing in on them, and the darkness of the movies, which had blinded them to that other darkness, and in which they now, vindictively, dreamed, at once more together than they were at any other time, and more alone.

When the last bell rang, the last class ended, I let out my breath. It seemed I'd been holding it for all that time. My clothes were wet — I may have looked as though I'd been sitting in a steam bath, all dressed up, all afternoon. I sat alone in the classroom a long time. I listened to the boys outside, downstairs, shouting and cursing and laughing. Their laughter struck me for perhaps the first time. It was not the joyous laughter which — God knows why — one associates with children. It was mocking and insular, its intent was to denigrate. It was disenchanted, and in this, also, lay the authority of their curses. Perhaps I was listening to them because I was thinking about my brother and in them I heard my brother. And myself.

One boy was whistling a tune, at once very complicated and very simple, it seemed to be pouring out of him as though he were a bird, and it sounded very cool and moving through all that harsh, bright air, only just holding its own through all those other sounds.

I stood up and walked over to the window and looked down into the courtyard. It was the beginning of the spring and the sap was rising in the boys. A teacher passed through them every now and again, quickly, as though he or she couldn't wait to get out of that courtyard, to get those boys out of their sight and off their minds. I started collecting my stuff. I thought I'd better get home and talk to Isabel.

The courtyard was almost deserted by the time I got downstairs. I saw this boy standing in the shadow of a doorway, looking just like Sonny. I almost called his name. Then I saw that it wasn't Sonny, but somebody we used to know, a boy from around our block. He'd been Sonny's friend. He'd never been mine, having been too young for me, and, anyway, I'd never liked him. And now, even though he was a grown-up man, he still hung around that block, still spent hours on the street corners, was always high and raggy. I used to run into him from time to time and he'd often work around to asking me for a quarter or fifty cents. He always had some real good excuse, too, and I always gave it to him, I don't know why.

But now, abruptly, I hated him. I couldn't stand the way he looked at me, partly like a dog, partly like a cunning child. I wanted to ask him what the hell he was doing in the school courtyard.

He sort of shuffled over to me, and he said, "I see you got the papers. So you already know about it."

"You mean about Sonny? Yes, I already know about it. How come they didn't get you?"

He grinned. It made him repulsive and it also brought to mind what he'd looked like as a kid. "I wasn't there. I stay away from them people."

"Good for you." I offered him a cigarette and I watched him through the smoke. "You come all the way down here just to tell me about Sonny?"

"That's right." He was sort of shaking his head and his eyes looked strange, as though they were about to cross. The bright sun deadened his damp dark brown skin and it made his eyes look yellow and showed up the dirt in his kinked hair. He smelled funky. I moved a little away from him and I said, "Well, thanks. But I already know about it and I got to get home."

"I'll walk you a little ways," he said. We started walking. There were a couple of kids still loitering in the courtyard and one of them said goodnight to me and looked strangely at the boy beside me.

"What're you going to do?" he asked me. "I mean, about Sonny?"

"Look. I haven't seen Sonny for over a year, I'm not sure I'm going to do anything. Anyway, what the hell can I do?"

"That's right," he said quickly, "ain't nothing you can do. Can't much help old Sonny no more, I guess."

It was what I was thinking and so it seemed to me he had no right to say it.

"I'm surprised at Sonny, though," he went on — he had a funny way of talking, he looked straight ahead as though he were talking to himself — "I thought Sonny was a smart boy, I thought he was too smart to get hung."

"I guess he thought so too," I said sharply, "and that's how he got hung. And how about you? You're pretty goddamn smart, I bet."

Then he looked directly at me, just for a minute. "I ain't smart," he said. "If I was smart, I'd have reached for a pistol a long time ago."

"Look. Don't tell *me* your sad story, if it was up to me, I'd give you one." Then I felt guilty — guilty, probably, for never having supposed that the poor bastard *had* a story of his own, much less a sad one, and I asked, quickly, "What's going to happen to him now?"

He didn't answer this. He was off by himself some place. "Funny thing," he said, and from his tone we might have been discussing the quickest way to get to Brooklyn, "when I saw the papers this morning, the first thing I asked myself was if I had anything to do with it. I felt sort of responsible."

I began to listen more carefully. The subway station was on the corner, just before us, and I stopped. He stopped, too. We were in front of a bar and he ducked slightly, peering in, but whoever he was looking for didn't seem to be there. The juke box was blasting away with something black and bouncy and I half watched the barmaid as she danced her way from the juke box to her place behind the bar. And I watched her face as she laughingly responded to something someone said to her, still keeping time to the music. When she smiled one saw the little girl, one sensed the doomed, still-struggling woman beneath the battered face of the semi-whore.

"I never *give* Sonny nothing," the boy said finally, "but a long time ago I come to school high and Sonny asked me how it felt." He paused, I couldn't bear to watch him, I watched the barmaid, and I listened to the music which seemed to be causing the pavement to shake. "I told him it felt great." The music stopped, the barmaid paused and watched the juke box until the music began again. "It did."

All this was carrying me some place I didn't want to go. I certainly didn't want to know how it felt. It filled everything, the people, the houses, the music, the dark, quicksilver barmaid, with menace; and this menace was their reality.

"What's going to happen to him now?" I asked again.

"They'll send him away some place and they'll try to cure him." He shook his head. "Maybe he'll even think he's kicked the habit. Then they'll let him loose" — he gestured, throwing his cigarette into the gutter. "That's all."

"What do you mean, that's *all*?"

But I knew what he meant.

"I *mean*, that's *all*." He turned his head and looked at me, pulling down the corners of his mouth. "Don't you know what I mean?" he asked, softly.

"How the hell *would* I know what you mean?" I almost whispered it, I don't know why.

"That's right," he said to the air, "how would *he* know what I mean?" He turned toward me again, patient and calm, and yet I somehow felt him shaking, shaking as though he were going to fall apart. I felt that ice in my guts again, the dread I'd felt all afternoon; and again I watched the barmaid, moving about the bar, washing glasses, and singing. "Listen. They'll let him out and then it'll just start all over again. That's what I mean."

"You mean — they'll let him out. And then he'll just start working his way back in again. You mean he'll never kick the habit. Is that what you mean?"

"That's right," he said cheerfully. "*You* see what I mean."

"Tell me," I said at last, "why does he want to die? He must want to die, he's killing himself, why does he want to die?"

He looked at me in surprise. He licked his lips. "He don't want to die. He wants to live. Don't nobody want to die, ever."

Then I wanted to ask him — too many things. He could not have answered, or if he had, I could not have borne the answers. I started walking. "Well, I guess it's none of my business."

"It's going to be rough on old Sonny," he said. We reached the subway station. "This is your station?" he asked. I nodded. I took one step down. "Damn!" he said, suddenly. I looked up at him. He grinned again. "Damn it if I didn't leave all my money home. You ain't got a dollar on you, have you? Just for a couple of days, is all."

All at once something inside gave and threatened to come pouring out of me. I didn't hate him any more. I felt that in another moment I'd start crying like a child.

"Sure," I said. "Don't sweat." I looked in my wallet and didn't have a dollar, I only had a five. "Here," I said. "That hold you?"

He didn't look at it — he didn't want to look at it. A terrible, closed look came over his face, as though he were keeping the number on the bill a secret from him and me. "Thanks," he said, and now he was dying to see me go. "Don't worry about Sonny. Maybe I'll write him or something."

"Sure," I said. "You do that. So long."

"Be seeing you," he said. I went on down the steps.

And I didn't write Sonny or send him anything for a long time. When I finally did, it was just after my little girl died, he wrote me back a letter which made me feel like a bastard.

Here's what he said:

Dear brother,

You don't know how much I needed to hear from you. I wanted to write you many a time but I dug how much I must have hurt you and so I didn't write. But now I feel like a man who's been trying to climb up out of some deep, real deep and funky hole and just saw the sun up there, outside. I got to get outside.

I can't tell you much about how I got here. I mean I don't know how to tell you. I guess I was afraid of something or I was trying to escape from something and you know I have never been very strong in the head (smile). I'm glad Mama and Daddy are dead and can't see what's happened to their son and I swear if I'd known what I was doing I would never have hurt you so, you and a lot of other fine people who were nice to me and who believed in me.

I don't want you to think it had anything to do with me being a musician. It's more than that. Or maybe less than that. I can't get anything straight in my head down here and I try not to think about what's going to happen to me when I get outside again. Sometime I think I'm going to flip and *never* get outside and sometime I think I'll come straight back. I tell you one thing, though, I'd rather blow my brains out than go through this again. But that's what they all say, so they tell me. If I tell you when I'm coming to New York and if you could meet me, I sure would appreciate it. Give my love to Isabel and the kids and I was sure sorry to hear about little Gracie. I wish I could be like Mama and say the Lord's will be done, but I don't know it seems to me that trouble is the one thing that never does get stopped and I don't know what good it does to blame it on the Lord. But maybe it does some good if you believe it.

Your brother,
Sonny

Then I kept in constant touch with him and I sent him whatever I could and I went to meet him when he came back to New York. When I saw him many things I thought I had forgotten came flooding back to me. This was because I had begun, finally, to wonder about Sonny, about the life that Sonny lived inside. This life, whatever it was, had made him older and thinner and it had deepened the distant stillness in which he had always moved. He looked very unlike my baby brother. Yet, when he smiled, when we shook hands, the baby brother I'd never known looked out from the depths of his private life, like an animal waiting to be coaxed into the light.

"How you been keeping?" he asked me.

"All right. And you?"

"Just fine." He was smiling all over his face. "It's good to see you again."

"It's good to see you."

The seven years' difference in our ages lay between us like a chasm: I wondered if these years would ever operate between us as a bridge. I was remembering, and it made it hard to catch my breath, that I had been there when he was born; and I had heard the first words he had ever spoken. When he started to walk, he walked from our mother straight to me. I caught him just before he fell when he took the first steps he ever took in this world.

"How's Isabel?"

"Just fine. She's dying to see you."

"And the boys?"

"They're fine, too. They're anxious to see their uncle."

"Oh, come on. You know they don't remember me."

"Are you kidding? Of course they remember you."

He grinned again. We got into a taxi. We had a lot to say to each other, far too much to know how to begin.

As the taxi began to move, I asked, "You still want to go to India?"

He laughed. "You still remember that. Hell, no. This place is Indian enough for me."

"It used to belong to them," I said.

And he laughed again. "They damn sure knew what they were doing when they got rid of it."

Years ago, when he was around fourteen, he'd been all hipped on the idea of going to India. He read books about people sitting on rocks, naked, in all kinds of weather, but mostly bad, naturally, and walking barefoot through hot coals and arriving at wisdom. I used to say that it sounded to me as though they were getting away from wisdom as fast as they could. I think he sort of looked down on me for that.

"Do you mind," he asked, "if we have the driver drive alongside the park? On the west side — I haven't seen the city in so long."

"Of course not," I said. I was afraid that I might sound as though I were humoring him, but I hoped he wouldn't take it that way.

So we drove along, between the green of the park and the stony, lifeless elegance of hotels and apartment buildings, toward the vivid, killing streets of our childhood. These streets hadn't changed, though housing projects jutted up out of them now like rocks in the middle of a boiling sea. Most of the houses in which we had grown up had vanished, as had the stores from which we had stolen, the basements in which we had first tried sex, the rooftops from which we had hurled tin cans and bricks. But houses exactly like the houses of our past yet dominated the landscape, boys exactly like the boys we once had been found themselves smothering in these houses, came down into the streets for light and air and found themselves encircled by disaster. Some escaped the trap, most didn't. Those who got out always left something of themselves behind, as some animals amputate a leg and leave it in the trap. It might be said, perhaps, that I had escaped, after all, I was a school teacher; or that Sonny had, he hadn't lived in Harlem for years. Yet, as the cab moved uptown through streets which seemed, with a rush, to darken with dark people, and as I covertly studied Sonny's face, it came to me that what we both were seeking through our separate cab windows was that part of ourselves which had been left behind. It's always at the hour of trouble and confrontation that the missing member aches.

We hit 110th Street and started rolling up Lenox Avenue. And I'd known this avenue all my life, but it seemed to me again, as it had seemed on the day I'd first heard about Sonny's trouble, filled with a hidden menace which was its very breath of life.

"We almost there," said Sonny.

"Almost." We were both too nervous to say anything more.

We live in a housing project. It hasn't been up long. A few days after it was up it seemed uninhabitably new, now, of course, it's already rundown. It looks like a parody of the good, clean, faceless life — God knows the people who live in it do their best to make it a parody. The beat-looking grass lying around isn't enough to make their lives green, the hedges will never hold out the streets, and they know it. The big windows fool no one, they aren't big enough to make space out of no space. They don't bother with the windows, they watch the TV screen instead. The playground is most popular with the children who don't play at jacks, or skip rope, or roller skate, or swing, and they can be found in it after dark. We moved in partly because it's not too far from where I teach, and partly for the kids; but it's really just like the houses in which Sonny and I grew up. The same things happen, they'll have the same things to remember. The moment Sonny and I started into the house I had the feeling that I was simply bringing him back into the danger he had almost died trying to escape.

Sonny has never been talkative. So I don't know why I was sure he'd be dying to talk to me when supper was over the first night. Everything went fine, the oldest boy remembered him, and the youngest boy liked him, and Sonny had remembered to bring something for each of them; and Isabel, who is really much nicer than I am, more open and giving, had gone to a lot of trouble about dinner and was genuinely glad to see him. And she's always been able to tease Sonny in a way that I haven't. It was nice to see her face so vivid again and to hear her laugh and watch her make Sonny laugh. She wasn't, or, anyway, she didn't seem to be, at all uneasy or embarrassed. She chatted as though there were no subject which had to be avoided and she got Sonny past his first, faint stiffness. And thank God she was there, for I was filled with that icy dread again. Everything I did seemed awkward to me, and everything I said sounded freighted with hidden meaning. I was trying to remember everything I'd heard about dope addiction and I couldn't help watching Sonny for signs. I wasn't doing it out of malice. I was trying to find out something about my brother. I was dying to hear him tell me he was safe.

"Safe!" my father grunted, whenever Mama suggested trying to move to a neighborhood which might be safer for children. "Safe, hell! Ain't no place safe for kids, nor nobody."

He always went on like this, but he wasn't, ever, really as bad as he sounded, not even on weekends, when he got drunk. As a matter of fact, he was always on the lookout for "something a little better," but he died before he found it. He died suddenly, during a drunken weekend in the middle of the war, when Sonny was fifteen. He and Sonny hadn't ever got on too well. And this was partly because Sonny was the apple of his father's eye. It was because he loved Sonny so much and was frightened for him, that he was always fighting with him. It doesn't do any good to fight with Sonny. Sonny just moves back, inside himself, where he can't be reached. But the principal reason that they never hit it off is that they were so much alike. Daddy was big and rough and loud-talking, just the opposite of Sonny, but they both had — that same privacy.

Mama tried to tell me something about this, just after Daddy died. I was home on leave from the army.

This was the last time I ever saw my mother alive. Just the same, this picture gets all mixed up in my mind with pictures I had of her when she was younger. The way I always see her is the way she used to be on a Sunday afternoon, say, when the old folks were talking after the big Sunday dinner. I always see her wearing pale blue. She'd be sitting on the sofa. And my father would be sitting in the easy chair, not far from her. And the living room would be full of church folks and relatives. There they sit, in chairs all around the living room, and the night is creeping up outside, but nobody knows it yet. You can see the darkness growing against the window-panes and you hear the street noises every now and again, or maybe the jangling beat of a tambourine from one of the churches close by, but it's real quiet in the room. For a moment nobody's talking, but every face looks darkening, like the sky outside. And my mother rocks a little from the waist, and my father's eyes are closed. Everyone is looking at something a child can't see. For a minute they've forgotten the children. Maybe a kid is lying on the rug, half asleep. Maybe somebody's got a kid in his lap and is absent-mindedly strok-ing the kid's head. Maybe there's a kid, quiet and big-eyed, curled up in a big chair in the corner. The silence, the darkness coming, and the darkness in the faces frightens the child obscurely. He hopes that the hand which strokes his forehead will never stop — will never die. He hopes that there will never come a time when the old folks won't be sitting around the living room, talking about where they've come from, and what they've seen, and what's happened to them and their kinfolk.

But something deep and watchful in the child knows that this is bound to end, is already ending. In a moment someone will get up and turn on the light. Then the old folks will remember the children and they won't talk any more that day. And when light fills the room, the child is filled with darkness. He knows that every time this happens he's moved just a little closer to that darkness outside. The darkness outside is what the old folks have been talking about. It's what they've come from. It's what they endure. The child knows that they won't talk any more because if he knows too much about what's happened to *them*, he'll know too much too soon, about what's going to happen to *him*.

The last time I talked to my mother, I remember I was restless. I wanted to get out and see Isabel. We weren't married then and we had a lot to straighten out between us.

There Mama sat, in black, by the window. She was humming an old church song, *Lord, you brought me from a long ways off.* Sonny was out somewhere. Mama kept watching the streets.

"I don't know," she said, "if I'll ever see you again, after you go off from here. But I hope you'll remember the things I tried to teach you."

"Don't talk like that," I said, and smiled. "You'll be here a long time yet."

She smiled, too, but she said nothing.

She was quiet for a long time. And I said, "Mama, don't you worry about nothing. I'll be writing all the time, and you be getting the checks. . . ."

"I want to talk to you about your brother," she said, suddenly. "If anything happens to me he ain't going to have nobody to look out for him."

"Mama," I said, "ain't nothing going to happen to you *or* Sonny. Sonny's all right. He's a good boy and he's got good sense."

"It ain't a question of his being a good boy," Mama said, "nor of his having good sense. It ain't only the bad ones, nor yet the dumb ones that gets sucked under." She stopped, looking at me. "Your Daddy once had a brother," she said, and she smiled in a way that made me feel she was in pain. "You didn't never know that, did you?"

"No," I said, "I never knew that," and I watched her face.

"Oh, yes," she said, "your Daddy had a brother. She looked out of the window again. "I know you never saw your Daddy cry. But *I* did — many a time, through all these years."

I asked her, "What happened to his brother? How come nobody's ever talked about him?"

This was the first time I ever saw my mother look old.

"His brother got killed," she said, "when he was just a little younger than you are now. I knew him. He was a fine boy. He was maybe a little full of the devil, but he didn't mean nobody no harm."

Then she stopped and the room was silent, exactly as it had sometimes been on those Sunday afternoons. Mama kept looking out into the streets.

"He used to have a job in the mill," she said, "and, like all young folks, he just liked to perform on Saturday nights. Saturday nights, him and your father would drift around to different places, go to dances and things like that, or just sit around with people they knew, and your father's brother would sing, he had a fine voice, and play along with himself on his guitar. Well, this particular Saturday night, him and your father was coming home from some place, and they were both a little drunk and there was a moon that night, it was bright like day. Your father's brother was feeling kind of good, and he was whistling to himself, and he had his guitar slung over his shoulder. They was coming down a hill and beneath them was a road that turned off from the highway. Well, your father's brother, being always kind of frisky, decided to run down this hill, and he did, with that guitar banging and clanging behind him, and he ran across the road, and he was making water behind a tree. And your father was sort of amused at him and he was still coming down the hill, kind of slow. Then he heard a car motor and that same minute his brother stepped from behind the tree, into the road, in the moonlight. And he started to cross the road. And your father started to run down the hill, he says he don't know why. This car was full of white men. They was all drunk, and when they seen your father's brother they let out a great whoop and holler and they aimed the car straight at him. They was having fun, they just wanted to scare him, the way they do sometimes, you know. But they was drunk. And I guess the boy, being drunk, too, and scared, kind of lost his head. By the time he jumped it was too late. Your father says he heard his brother scream when the car rolled over him, and he heard the wood of that guitar when it give, and he heard them strings go flying, and he heard them white men shouting, and the car kept on a-going and it ain't stopped till this day. And, time your father got down the hill, his brother weren't nothing but blood and pulp."

Tears were gleaming on my mother's face. There wasn't anything I could say.

"He never mentioned it," she said, "because I never let him mention it before you children. Your Daddy was like a crazy man that night and for many a night thereafter. He says he never in his life seen anything as dark as that road after the lights of that car had gone away. Weren't nothing, weren't nobody on that road, just your Daddy and his brother and that busted guitar. Oh, yes, Your Daddy never did really get right again. Till the day he died he weren't sure but that every white man he saw was the man that killed his brother."

She stopped and took out her handkerchief and dried her eyes and looked at me.

"I ain't telling you all this," she said, "to make you scared or bitter or to make you hate nobody. I'm telling you this because you got a brother. And the world ain't changed."

I guess I didn't want to believe this. I guess she saw this in my face. She turned away from me, toward the window again, searching those streets.

"But I praise my Redeemer," she said at last, "that He called your Daddy home before me. I ain't saying it to throw no flowers at myself, but, I declare, it keeps me from feeling too cast down to know I helped your father get safely through this world. Your father always acted like he was the roughest, strongest man on earth. And everybody took him to be like that. But if he hadn't had *me* there — to see his tears!"

She was crying again. Still, I couldn't move. I said, "Lord, Lord, Mama, I didn't know it was like that."

"Oh, honey," she said, "there's a lot that you don't know. But you are going to find it out." She stood up from the window and came over to me. "You got to hold on to your brother," she said, "and don't let him fall, no matter what it looks like is happening to him and no matter how evil you gets with him. You going to be evil with him many a time. But don't you forget what I told you, you hear?"

"I won't forget," I said. "Don't you worry, I won't forget. I won't let nothing happen to Sonny."

My mother smiled as though she were amused at something she saw in my face. Then, "You may not be able to stop nothing from happening. But you got to let him know you's *there*."

Two days later I was married, and then I was gone. And I had a lot of things on my mind and I pretty well forgot my promise to Mama until I got shipped home on a special furlough for her funeral.

And, after the funeral, with just Sonny and me alone in the empty kitchen, I tried to find out something about him.

"What do you want to do?" I asked him.

"I'm going to be a musician," he said.

For he had graduated, in the time I had been away, from dancing to the juke box to finding out who was playing what, and what they were doing with it, and he had bought himself a set of drums.

"You mean, you want to be a drummer?" I somehow had the feeling that being a drummer might be all right for other people but not for my brother Sonny.

"I don't think," he said, looking at me very gravely, "that I'll ever be a good drummer. But I think I can play a piano."

I frowned. I'd never played the role of the older brother quite so seriously before, had scarcely ever, in fact, *asked* Sonny a damn thing. I sensed myself in the presence of something I didn't really know how to handle, didn't understand. So I made my frown a little deeper as I asked: "What kind of musician do you want to be?"

He grinned. "How many kinds do you think there are?"

"Be *serious*," I said.

He laughed, throwing his head back, and then looked at me. "I *am* serious."

"Well, then, for Christ's sake, stop kidding around and answer a serious question. I mean, do you want to be a concert pianist, you want to play classical music and all that, or — or what?" Long before I finished he was laughing again. "For Christ's *sake*, Sonny!"

He sobered, but with difficulty. "I'm sorry. But you sound so — *scared!*" and he was off again.

"Well, you may think it's funny now, baby, but it's not going to be so funny when you have to make your living at it, let me tell you *that*." I was furious because I knew he was laughing at me and I didn't know why.

"No," he said, very sober now, and afraid, perhaps, that he'd hurt me, "I don't want to be a classical pianist. That isn't what interests me. I mean" — he paused, looking hard at me, as though his eyes would help me to understand, and then gestured helplessly, as though perhaps his hand would help — "I mean, I'll have a lot of studying to do, and I'll have to study *everything*, but, I mean, I want to play *with* — jazz musicians." He stopped. "I want to play jazz," he said.

Well, the word had never before sounded as heavy, as real, as it sounded that afternoon in Sonny's mouth. I just looked at him and I was probably frowning a real frown by this time. I simply couldn't see why on earth he'd want to spend his time hanging around nightclubs, clowning around on bandstands, while people pushed each other around a dance floor. It seemed — beneath him, somehow. I had never thought about it before, had never been forced to, but I suppose I had always put jazz musicians in a class with what Daddy called "good-time people."

"Are you *serious*?"

"Hell, *yes*, I'm serious."

He looked more helpless than ever, and annoyed, and deeply hurt.

I suggested, helpfully: "You mean — like Louis Armstrong?"

His face closed as though I'd struck him. "No. I'm not talking about none of that old-time, down home crap."

"Well, look, Sonny, I'm sorry, don't get mad. I just don't altogether get it, that's all. Name somebody — you know, a jazz musician you admire."

"Bird."

"Who?"

"Bird! Charlie Parker! Don't they teach you nothing in the goddamn army?"

I lit a cigarette. I was surprised and then a little amused to discover that I was trembling. "I've been out of touch," I said. "You'll have to be patient with me. Now. Who's this Parker character?"

"He's just one of the greatest jazz musicians alive," said Sonny, sullenly, his hands in his pockets, his back to me. "Maybe *the* greatest," he added, bitterly, "that's probably why *you* never heard of him."

"All right," I said, "I'm ignorant. I'm sorry. I'll go out and buy all the cat's records right away, all right?"

"It don't," said Sonny, with dignity, "make any difference to me. I don't care what you listen to. Don't do me no favors."

I was beginning to realize that I'd never seen him so upset before. With another part of my mind I was thinking that this would probably turn out to be one of those things kids go through and that I shouldn't make it seem important by pushing it too hard. Still, I didn't think it would do any harm to ask: "Doesn't all this take a lot of time? Can you make a living at it?"

He turned back to me and half leaned, half sat, on the kitchen table. "Everything takes time," he said, "and — well, yes, sure, I can make a living at it. But what I don't seem to be able to make you understand is that it's the only thing I want to do."

"Well, Sonny," I said, gently, "you know people can't always do exactly what they *want* to do —"

"*No*, I don't know that," said Sonny, surprising me. "I think people *ought* to do what they want to do, what else are they alive for?"

"You getting to be a big boy," I said desperately, "it's time you started thinking about your future."

"I'm thinking about my future," said Sonny, grimly. "I think about it all the time."

I gave up. I decided, if he didn't change his mind, that we could always talk about it later. "In the meantime," I said, "you got to finish school." We had already decided that he'd have to move in with Isabel and her folks. I knew this wasn't the ideal arrangement because Isabel's folks are inclined to be dicty and they hadn't especially wanted Isabel to marry me. But I didn't know what else to do. "And we have to get you fixed up at Isabel's."

There was a long silence. He moved from the kitchen table to the window. "That's a terrible idea. You know it yourself."

"Do you have a *better* idea?"

He just walked up and down the kitchen for a minute. He was as tall as I was. He had started to shave. I suddenly had the feeling that I didn't know him at all.

He stopped at the kitchen table and picked up my cigarettes. Looking at me with a kind of mocking, amused defiance, he put one between his lips. "You mind?"

"You smoking already?"

He lit the cigarette and nodded, watching me through the smoke. "I just wanted to see if I'd have the courage to smoke in front of you." He grinned and blew a great cloud of smoke to the ceiling. "It was easy." He looked at my face.

"Come on, now. I bet you was smoking at my age, tell the truth."

I didn't say anything but the truth was on my face, and he laughed. But now there was something very strained in his laugh. "Sure. And I bet that ain't all you was doing."

He was frightening me a little. "Cut the crap," I said. "We already decided that you was going to go and live at Isabel's. Now what's got into you all of a sudden?"

"*You* decided it," he pointed out. "*I* didn't decide nothing." He stopped in front of me, leaning against the stove, arms loosely folded. "Look, brother. I don't want to stay in Harlem no more, I really don't." He was very earnest. He looked at me, then over toward the kitchen window. There was something in his eyes I'd never seen before, some thoughtfulness, some worry all his own. He rubbed the muscle of one arm. "It's time I was getting out of here."

"Where do you want to *go*, Sonny?"

"I want to join the army. Or the navy, I don't care. If I say I'm old enough, they'll believe me."

Then I got mad. It was because I was so scared. "You must be crazy. You goddamn fool, what the hell do you want to go and join the *army* for?"

"I just told you. To get out of Harlem."

"Sonny, you haven't even finished *school*. And if you really want to be a musician, how do you expect to study if you're in the *army*?"

He looked at me, trapped, and in anguish. "There's ways. I might be able to work out some kind of deal. Anyway, I'll have the G.I. Bill when I come out."

"*If* you come out." We stared at each other. "Sonny, please. Be reasonable. I know the setup is far from perfect. But we got to do the best we can."

"I ain't learning nothing in school," he said. "Even when I go." He turned away from me and opened the window and threw his cigarette out into the narrow alley. I watched his back. "At least, I ain't learning nothing you'd want me to learn." He slammed the window so hard I thought the glass would fly out, and turned back to me. "And I'm sick of the stink of these garbage cans!"

"Sonny," I said, "I know how you feel. But if you don't finish school now, you're going to be sorry later that you didn't." I grabbed him by the shoulders. "And you only got another year. It ain't so bad. And I'll come back and I swear I'll help you do *whatever* you want to do. Just try to put up with it till I come back. Will you please do that? For me?"

He didn't answer and he wouldn't look at me.

"Sonny. You hear me?"

He pulled away. "I hear you. But you never hear anything *I* say."

I didn't know what to say to that. He looked out of the window and then back at me. "OK," he said, and sighed. "I'll try."

Then I said, trying to cheer him up a little, "They got a piano at Isabel's. You can practice on it."

And as a matter of fact, it did cheer him up for a minute. "That's right," he said to himself. "I forgot that." His face relaxed a little. But the worry, the thoughtfulness, played on it still, the way shadows play on a face which is staring into the fire.

But I thought I'd never hear the end of that piano. At first, Isabel would write me, saying how nice it was that Sonny was so serious about his music and how, as soon as he came in from school, or wherever he had been when he was supposed to be at school, he went straight to that piano and stayed there until suppertime. And, after supper, he went back to that piano and stayed there until everybody went to bed. He was at the piano all day Saturday and all day Sunday. Then he bought a record player and started playing records. He'd play one record over and over again, all day long sometimes, and he'd improvise along with it on the piano. Or he'd play one section of the record, one chord, one change, one progression, then he'd do it on the piano. Then back to the record. Then back to the piano.

Well, I really don't know how they stood it. Isabel finally confessed that it wasn't like living with a person at all, it was like living with sound. And the sound didn't make any sense to her, didn't make any sense to any of them — naturally. They began, in a way, to be afflicted by this presence that was living in their home. It was as though Sonny was some sort of god, or monster. He moved in an atmosphere which wasn't like theirs at all. They fed him and he ate, he washed himself, he walked in and out of their door; he certainly wasn't nasty or unpleasant or rude, Sonny isn't any of those things; but it was as though he were all wrapped up in some cloud, some fire, some vision all his own; and there wasn't any way to reach him.

At the same time, he wasn't really a man yet, he was still a child, and they had to watch out for him in all kinds of ways. They certainly couldn't throw him out. Neither did they dare to make a great scene about that piano because even they dimly sensed, as I sensed, from so many thousands of miles away, that Sonny was at that piano playing for his life.

But he hadn't been going to school. One day a letter came from the school board and Isabel's mother got it — there had, apparently, been other letters but Sonny had torn them up. This day, when Sonny came in, Isabel's mother showed him the letter and asked where he'd been spending his time. And she finally got it out of him that he'd been down in Greenwich Village, with musicians and other characters, in a white girl's apartment. And this scared her and she started to scream at him and what came up, once she began — though she denies it to this day — was what sacrifices they were making to give Sonny a decent home and how little he appreciated it.

Sonny didn't play the piano that day. By evening, Isabel's mother had calmed down but then there was the old man to deal with, and Isabel herself. Isabel says she did her best to be calm but she broke down and started crying. She says she just watched Sonny's face. She could tell, by watching him, what was happening with him. And what was happening was that they penetrated his cloud, they had reached him. Even if their fingers had been a thousand times more gentle than human fingers ever are, he could hardly help feeling that they had stripped him naked and were spitting on that nakedness. For he also had to see that his presence, that music, which was life or death to him, had been torture for them and that they had endured it, not at all for his sake, but only for mine. And Sonny couldn't take that. He can take it a little better today than he could then but he's still not very good at it and, frankly, I don't know anybody who is.

The silence of the next few days must have been louder than the sound of all the music ever played since time began. One morning, before she went to work, Isabel was in his room for something and she suddenly realized that all of his records were gone. And she knew for certain that he was gone. And he was. He went as far as the navy would carry him. He finally sent me a postcard from some place in Greece and that was the first I knew that Sonny was still alive. I didn't see him any more until we were both back in New York and the war had long been over.

He was a man by then, of course, but I wasn't willing to see it. He came by the house from time to time, but we fought almost every time we met. I didn't like the way he carried himself, loose and dream-like all the time, and I didn't like his friends, and his music seemed to be merely an excuse for the life he led. It sounded just that weird and disordered.

Then we had a fight, a pretty awful fight, and I didn't see him for months. By and by I looked him up, where he was living, in a furnished room in the Village, and I tried to make it up. But there were lots of other people in the room and Sonny just lay on his bed, and he wouldn't come downstairs with me, and he treated these other people as though they were his family and I weren't. So I got mad and then he got mad, and then I told him that he might just as well be dead as live the way he was living. Then he stood up and he told me not to worry about him any more in life, that he *was* dead as far as I was concerned. Then he pushed me to the door and the other people looked on as though nothing were happening, and he slammed the door behind me. I stood in the hallway, staring at the door. I heard somebody laugh in the room and then the tears came to my eyes. I started down the steps, whistling to keep from crying, I kept whistling to myself, *You going to need me, baby, one of these cold, rainy days.*

I read about Sonny's trouble in the spring. Little Grace died in the fall. She was a beautiful little girl. But she only lived a little over two years. She died of polio and she suffered. She had a slight fever for a couple of days, but it didn't seem like anything and we just kept her in bed. And we would certainly have called the doctor, but the fever dropped, she seemed to be all right. So we thought it had just been a cold. Then, one day, she was up, playing, Isabel was in the the kitchen fixing lunch for the two boys when they'd come in from school, and she heard Grace fall down in the living room. When you have a lot of children you don't always start running when one of them falls, unless they start screaming or something.

And, this time, Grace was quiet. Yet, Isabel says that when she heard that *thump* and then that silence, something happened in her to make her afraid. And she ran to the living room and there was little Grace on the floor, all twisted up, and the reason she hadn't screamed was that she couldn't get her breath. And when she did scream, it was the worst sound, Isabel says, that she'd ever heard in all her life, and she still hears it sometimes in her dreams. Isabel will sometimes wake me up with a low, moaning, strangled sound and I have to be quick to awaken her and hold her to me and where Isabel is weeping against me seems a mortal wound.

I think I may have written Sonny the very day that little Grace was buried. I was sitting in the living room in the dark, by myself, and I suddenly thought of Sonny. My trouble made his real.

One Saturday afternoon, when Sonny had been living with us, or, anyway, been in our house, for nearly two weeks, I found myself wandering aimlessly about the living room, drinking from a can of beer, and trying to work up the courage to search Sonny's room. He was out, he was usually out whenever I was home, and Isabel had taken the children to see their grand-parents. Suddenly I was standing still in front of the living room window, watching Seventh Avenue. The idea of searching Sonny's room made me still. I scarcely dared to admit to myself what I'd be searching for. I didn't know what I'd do if I found it. Or if I didn't.

On the sidewalk across from me, near the entrance to a barbecue joint, some people were holding an old-fashioned revival meeting. The barbecue cook, wearing a dirty white apron, his conked hair reddish and metallic in the pale sun, and a cigarette between his lips, stood in the doorway, watching them. Kids and older people paused in their errands and stood there, along with some older men and a

couple of very tough-looking women who watched everything that happened on the avenue, as though they owned it, or were maybe owned by it. Well, they were watching this, too. The revival was being carried on by three sisters in black, and a brother. All they had were their voices and their Bibles and a tambourine. The brother was testifying and while he testified two of the sisters stood together, seeming to say, amen, and the third sister walked around with the tambourine outstretched and a couple of people dropped coins into it. Then the brother's testimony ended and the sister who had been taking up the collection dumped the coins into her palm and transferred them to the pocket of her long black robe. Then she raised both hands, striking the tambourine against the air, and then against one hand, and she started to sing. And the two other sisters and the brother joined in.

It was strange, suddenly, to watch, though I had been seeing these street meetings all my life. So, of course, had everybody else down there. Yet, they paused and watched and listened and I stood still at the window. "*Tis the old ship of Zion,*" they sang, and the sister with the tambourine kept a steady, jangling beat, "*it has rescued many a thousand!*" Not a soul under the sound of their voices was hearing this song for the first time, not one of them had been rescued. Nor had they seen much in the way of rescue work being done around them. Neither did they especially believe in the holiness of the three sisters and the brother, they knew too much about them, knew where they lived, and how. The woman with the tambourine, whose voice dominated the air, whose face was bright with joy, was divided by very little from the woman who stood watching her, a cigarette between her heavy, chapped lips, her hair a cuckoo's nest, her face scarred and swollen from many beatings, and her black eyes glittering like coal. Perhaps they both knew this, which was why, when, as rarely, they addressed each other, they addressed each other as Sister. As the singing filled the air the watching, listening faces underwent a change, the eyes focusing on something within; the music seemed to soothe a poison out of them; and time seemed, nearly, to fall away from the sullen, belligerent, battered faces, as though they were fleeing back to their first condition, while dreaming of their last. The barbecue cook half shook his head and smiled, and dropped his cigarette and disappeared into his joint. A man fumbled in his pockets for change and stood holding it in his hand impatiently, as though he had just remembered a pressing appointment further up the avenue. He looked furious. Then I saw Sonny, standing on the edge of the crowd. He was carrying a wide, flat notebook with a green cover, and it made him look, from where I was standing, almost like a schoolboy. The coppery sun brought out the copper in his skin, he was very faintly smiling, standing very still. Then the singing stopped, the tambourine turned into a collection plate again. The furious man dropped in his coins and vanished, so did a couple of the women, and Sonny dropped some change in the plate, looking directly at the woman with a little smile. He started across the avenue, toward the house. He has a slow, loping walk, something like the way Harlem hipsters walk, only he's imposed on this his own half-beat. I had never really noticed it before.

I stayed at the window, both relieved and apprehensive. As Sonny disappeared from my sight, they began singing again. And they were still singing when his key turned in the lock.

"Hey," he said.

"Hey, yourself. You want some beer?"

"No. Well, maybe." But he came up to the window and stood beside me, looking out. "What a warm voice," he said.

They were singing *If I could only hear my mother pray again!*

"Yes," I said, "and she can sure beat that tambourine."

"But what a terrible song," he said, and laughed. He dropped his notebook on the sofa and disappeared into the kitchen. "Where's Isabel and the kids?"

"I think they went to see their grandparents. You hungry?"

"No." He came back into the living room with his can of beer. "You want to come some place with me tonight?"

I sensed, I don't know how, that I couldn't possibly say no. "Sure. Where?"

He sat down on the sofa and picked up his notebook and started leafing through it. "I'm going to sit in with some fellows in a joint in the Village."

"You mean, you're going to play, tonight?"

"That's right." He took a swallow of his beer and moved back to the window. He gave me a sidelong look. "If you can stand it."

"I'll try," I said.

He smiled to himself and we both watched as the meeting across the way broke up. The three sisters and the brother, heads bowed, were singing *God be with you till we meet again.* The faces around them were very quiet. Then the song ended. The small crowd dispersed. We watched the three women and the lone man walk slowly up the avenue.

"When she was singing before," said Sonny, abruptly, "her voice reminded me for a minute of what heroin feels like sometimes — when it's in your veins. It makes you feel sort of warm and cool at the same time. And distant. And — and sure." He sipped his beer, very deliberately not looking at me. I watched his face. "It makes you feel — in control. Sometimes you've got to have that feeling."

"Do you?" I sat down slowly in the easy chair.

"Sometimes." He went to the sofa and

picked up his notebook again. "Some people do."

"In order," I asked, "to play?" And my voice was very ugly, full of contempt and anger.

"Well" — he looked at me with great, troubled eyes, as though, in fact, he hoped his eyes would tell me things he could never otherwise say — "they *think* so. And *if* they think so — !"

"And what do *you* think?" I asked.

He sat on the sofa and put his can of beer on the floor. "I don't know," he said, and I couldn't be sure if he were answering my question or pursuing his thoughts. His face didn't tell me. "It's not so much to *play*. It's to *stand* it, to be able to make it at all. On any level." He frowned and smiled: "In order to keep from shaking to pieces."

"But these friends of yours," I said, "they seem to shake themselves to pieces pretty goddamn fast."

"Maybe." He played with the notebook. And something told me that I should curb my tongue, that Sonny was doing his best to talk, that I should listen. "But of course you only know the ones that've gone to pieces. Some don't — or at least they haven't *yet* and that's just about all *any* of us can say." He paused. "And then there are some who just live, really, in hell, and they know it and they see what's happening and they go right on. I don't know." He sighed, dropped the notebook, folded his arms. "Some guys, you can tell from the way they play, they on something *all* the time. And you can see that, well, it makes something real for them. But of course," he picked up his beer from the floor and sipped it and put the can down again, "they *want* to, too, you've got to see that. Even some of them that say they don't — *some*, not all."

"And what about you?" I asked — I couldn't help it. "What about you? Do *you* want to?"

He stood up and walked to the window and remained silent for a long time. Then he sighed. "Me," he said. Then: "While I was downstairs before, on my way here, listening to that woman sing, it struck me all of a sudden how much suffering she must have had to go through — to sing like that. It's *repulsive* to think you have to suffer that much."

I said: "But there's no way not to suffer — is there, Sonny?"

"I believe not," he said and smiled, "but that's never stopped anyone from trying." He looked at me. "Has it?" I realized, with this mocking look, that there stood between us, forever, beyond the power of time or forgiveness, the fact that I had held silence — so long! — when he had needed human speech to help him. He turned back to the window. "No, there's no way not to suffer. But you try all kinds of ways to keep from drowning in it, to keep on top of it, and to make it seem — well, like *you*. Like you did something, all right, and now you're suffering for it. You know?" I said nothing. "Well you know," he said, impatiently, "why *do* people suffer? Maybe it's better to do something to give it a reason, *any* reason."

"But we just agreed," I said, "that there's no way not to suffer. Isn't it better, then, just to — take it?"

"But nobody just takes it," Sonny cried, "that's what I'm telling you! *Everybody* tries not to. You're just hung up on the *way* some people try — it's not *your* way!"

The hair on my face began to itch, my face felt wet. "That's not true," I said, "that's not true. I don't give a damn what other people do, I don't even care how they suffer. I just care how *you* suffer." And he looked at me. "Please believe me," I said, "I don't want to see you — die — trying not to suffer."

"I won't," he said, flatly, "die trying not to suffer. At least, not any faster than anybody else."

"But there's no need," I said, trying to laugh, "is there? in killing yourself."

I wanted to say more, but I couldn't. I wanted to talk about will power and how life could be — well, beautiful. I wanted to say that it was all within; but was it? or, rather, wasn't that exactly the trouble? And I wanted to promise that I would never fail him again. But it would all have sounded — empty words and lies.

So I made the promise to myself and prayed that I would keep it.

"It's terrible sometimes, inside," he said, "that's what's the trouble. You walk these streets, black and funky and cold, and there's not really a living ass to talk to, and there's nothing shaking, and there's no way of getting it out — that storm inside. You can't talk it and you can't make love with it, and when you finally try to get with it and play it, you realize *nobody's* listening. So *you've* got to listen. You got to find a way to listen."

And then he walked away from the window and sat on the sofa again, as though all the wind had suddenly been knocked out of him. "Sometimes you'll do *anything* to play, even cut your mother's throat." He laughed and looked at me. "Or your brother's." Then he sobered. "Or your own." Then: "Don't worry. I'm all right now and I think I'll *be* all right. But I can't forget — where I've been. I don't mean just the physical place I've been, I mean where I've *been*. And *what* I've been."

"What have you been, Sonny?" I asked.

He smiled — but sat sideways on the sofa, his elbow resting on the back, his fingers playing with his mouth and chin, not looking at me. "I've been something I didn't recognize, didn't know I could be. Didn't know anybody could be." He stopped, looking inward, looking helplessly young, looking old. "I'm not talking about it now because I feel *guilty* or anything like that — maybe it would be better if I did, I don't know. Anyway, I can't really talk about it. Not to you, not to

anybody," and now he turned and faced me. "Sometimes, you know, and it was actually when I was most *out* of the world, I felt that I was in it, that I was *with* it, really, and I could play or I didn't really have to *play*, it just came out of me, it was there. And I don't know how I played, thinking about it now, but I know I did awful things, those times, sometimes, to people. Or it wasn't that I *did* anything to them — it was that they weren't real." He picked up the beer can; it was empty; he rolled it between his palms: "And other times — well, I needed a fix, I needed to find a place to lean, I needed to clear a space to *listen* — and I couldn't find it, and I — went crazy, I did terrible things to *me*, I was terrible *for* me." He began pressing the beer can between his hands, I watched the metal begin to give. It glittered, as he played with it, like a knife, and I was afraid he would cut himself, but I said nothing. "Oh well. I can never tell you. I was all by myself at the bottom of something, stinking and sweating and crying and shaking, and I smelled it, you know? *my* stink, and I thought I'd die if I couldn't get away from it and yet, all the same, I knew that everything I was doing was just locking me in with it. And I didn't know," he paused, still flattening the beer can, "I didn't know, I still *don't* know, something kept telling me that maybe it was good to smell your own stink, but I didn't think that *that* was what I'd been trying to do — and — who can stand it?" and he abruptly dropped the ruined beer can, looking at me with a small, still smile, and then rose, walking to the window as though it were the lodestone rock. I watched his face, he watched the avenue. "I couldn't tell you when Mama died — but the reason I wanted to leave Harlem so bad was to get away from drugs. And then, when I ran away, that's what I was running from — really. When I came back, nothing had changed, *I* hadn't changed, I was just —

older." And he stopped, drumming with his fingers on the windowpane. The sun had vanished, soon darkness would fall. I watched his face. "It can come again," he said, almost as though speaking to himself. Then he turned to me. "It can come again," he repeated. "I just want you to know that."

"All right," I said, at last. "So it can come again, All right."

He smiled, but the smile was sorrowful. "I had to try to tell you," he said.

"Yes," I said. "I understand that."

"You're my brother," he said, looking straight at me, and not smiling at all.

"Yes," I repeated, "yes. I understand that."

He turned back to the window, looking out. "All that hatred down there," he said, "all that hatred and misery and love. It's a wonder it doesn't blow the avenue apart."

We went to the only nightclub on a short, dark street, downtown. We squeezed through the narrow, chattering, jampacked bar to the entrance of the big room, where the bandstand was. And we stood there for a moment, for the lights were very dim in this room and we couldn't see. Then, "Hello, boy," said a voice and an enormous black man, much older than Sonny or myself, erupted out of all that atmospheric lighting and put an arm around Sonny's shoulder. "I been sitting right here," he said, "waiting for you."

He had a big voice, too, and heads in the darkness turned toward us.

Sonny grinned and pulled a little away, and said, "Creole, this is my brother. I told you about him."

Creole shook my hand. "I'm glad to meet you, son," he said, and it was clear that he was glad to meet me *there*, for Sonny's sake. And he smiled, "You got a real musician in *your* family," and he took his arm from Sonny's shoulder and slapped him, lightly, affectionately, with the back of his hand.

"Well. Now I've heard it all," said a voice behind us. This was another musician, and a friend of Sonny's, a coal-black, cheerful-looking man, built close to the ground. He immediately began confiding to me, at the top of his lungs, the most terrible things about Sonny, his teeth gleaming like a lighthouse and his laugh coming up out of him like the beginning of an earthquake. And it turned out that everyone at the bar knew Sonny, or almost everyone; some were musicians, working there, or nearby, or not working, some were simply hangers-on, and some were there to hear Sonny play. I was introduced to all of them and they were all very polite to me. Yet, it was clear that, for them, I was only Sonny's brother. Here, I was in Sonny's world. Or, rather: his kingdom. Here, it was not even a question that his veins bore royal blood.

They were going to play soon and Creole installed me, by myself, at a table in a dark corner. Then I watched them, Creole, and the little black man, and Sonny, and the others, while they horsed around, standing just below the bandstand. The light from the bandstand spilled just a little short of them and, watching them laughing and gesturing and moving about, I had the feeling that they, nevertheless, were being most careful not to step into that circle of light too suddenly: that if they moved into the light too suddenly, without thinking, they would perish in flame. Then, while I watched, one of them, the small, black man, moved into the light and crossed the bandstand and started fooling around with his drums. Then — being funny and being, also, extremely ceremonious — Creole took Sonny by the arm and led him to the piano. A woman's voice called Sonny's name and a few hands started clapping. And Sonny, also being funny and being ceremonious, and so touched, I think, that he could have cried, but neither hiding it nor showing it, riding it like a man, grinned, and put both hands to his heart and bowed from the waist.

Creole then went to the bass fiddle and a lean, very bright-skinned brown man jumped up on the bandstand and picked up his horn. So there they were, and the atmosphere on the bandstand and in the room began to change and tighten. Someone stepped up to the microphone and announced them. Then there were all kinds of murmurs. Some people at the bar shushed others. The waitress ran around, frantically getting in the last orders, guys and chicks got closer to each other, and the lights on the bandstand, on the quartet, turned to a kind of indigo. Then they all looked different there. Creole looked about him for the last time, as though he were making certain that all his chickens were in the coop, and then he — jumped and struck the fiddle. And there they were.

All I know about music is that not many people ever really hear it. And even then, on the rare occasions when something opens within, and the music enters, what we mainly hear, or hear corroborated, are personal, private, vanishing evocations. But the man who creates the music is hearing something else, is dealing with the roar rising from the void and imposing order on it as it hits the air. What is evoked in him, then, is of another order, more terrible because it has no words, and triumphant, too, for that same reason. And his triumph, when he triumphs, is ours. I just watched Sonny's face. His face was troubled, he was working hard, but he wasn't with it. And I had the feeling that, in a way, everyone on the bandstand was waiting for him, both waiting for him and pushing him along. But as I began to watch Creole, I realized that it was Creole who held them all back. He had them on a short rein. Up there, keeping the beat with

his whole body, wailing on the fiddle, with his eyes half closed, he was listening to everything, but he was listening to Sonny. He was having a dialogue with Sonny. He wanted Sonny to leave the shoreline and strike out for the deep water. He was Sonny's witness that deep water and drowning were not the same thing — he had been there, and he knew. And he wanted Sonny to know. He was waiting for Sonny to do the things on the keys which would let Creole know that Sonny was in the water.

And, while Creole listened, Sonny moved, deep within, exactly like someone in torment. I had never before thought of how awful the relationship must be between the musician and his instrument. He has to fill it, this instrument, with the breath of life, his own. He has to make it do what he wants it to do. And a piano is just a piano. It's made out of so much wood and wires and little hammers and big ones, and ivory. While there's only so much you can do with it, the only way to find this out is to try; to try and make it do everything.

And Sonny hadn't been near a piano for over a year. And he wasn't on much better terms with his life, not the life that stretched before him now. He and the piano stammered, started one way, got scared, stopped; started another way, panicked, marked time, started again; then seemed to have found a direction, panicked again, got stuck. And the face I saw on Sonny I'd never seen before. Everything had been burned out of it, and, at the same time, things usually hidden were being burned in, by the fire and fury of the battle which was occurring in him up there.

Yet, watching Creole's face as they neared the end of the first set, I had the feeling that something had happened, something I hadn't heard. Then they finished, there was scattered applause, and then, without an instant's warning, Creole started into something else, it was almost sardonic, it was *Am I Blue*. And, as though he commanded, Sonny began to play. Something began to happen. And Creole let out the reins. The dry, low, black man said something awful on the drums, Creole answered, and the drums talked back. Then the horn insisted, sweet and high, slightly detached perhaps, and Creole listened, commenting now and then, dry, and driving, beautiful and calm and old. Then they all came together again, and Sonny was part of the family again. I could tell this from his face. He seemed to have found, right there beneath his fingers, a damn brand-new piano. It seemed that he couldn't get over it. Then, for awhile, just being happy with Sonny, they seemed to be agreeing with him that brand-new pianos certainly were a gas.

Then Creole stepped forward to remind them that what they were playing was the blues. He hit something in all of them, he hit something in me, myself, and the music tightened and deepened, apprehension began to beat the air. Creole began to tell us what the blues were all about. They were not about anything very new. He and his boys up there were keeping it new, at the risk of ruin, destruction, madness, and death, in order to find new ways to make us listen. For, while the tale of how we suffer, and how we are delighted, and how we may triumph is never new, it always must be heard. There isn't any other tale to tell, it's the only light we've got in all this darkness.

And this tale, according to that face, that body, those strong hands on those strings, has another aspect in every country, and a new depth in every generation. Listen, Creole seemed to be saying, listen. Now these are Sonny's blues. He made the little black man on the drums know it, and the bright, brown man on the horn. Creole wasn't trying any longer to get Sonny in the water. He was wishing him Godspeed.

Then he stepped back, very slowly, filling the air with the immense suggestion that Sonny speak for himself.

Then they all gathered around Sonny and Sonny played. Every now and again one of them seemed to say, amen. Sonny's fingers filled the air with life, his life. But that life contained so many others. And Sonny went all the way back, he really began with the spare, flat statement of the opening phrase of the song. Then he began to make it his. It was very beautiful because it wasn't hurried and it was no longer a lament. I seemed to hear with what burning he had made it his, with what burning we had yet to make it ours, how we could cease lamenting. Freedom lurked around us and I understood, at last, that he could help us to be free if we would listen, that he would never be free until we did. Yet, there was no battle in his face now. I heard what he had gone through, and would continue to go through until he came to rest in earth. He had made it his: that long line, of which we knew only Mama and Daddy. And he was giving it back, as everything must be given back, so that, passing through death, it can live forever. I saw my mother's face again, and felt, for the first time, how the stones of the road she had walked on must have bruised her feet. I saw the moonlit road where my father's brother died. And it brought something else back to me, and carried me past it, I saw my little girl again and felt Isabel's tears again, and I felt my own tears begin to rise. And I was yet aware that this was only a moment, that the world waited outside, as hungry as a tiger, and that trouble stretched above us, longer than the sky.

Then it was over. Creole and Sonny let out their breath, both soaking wet, and grinning. There was a lot of applause and some of it was real. In the dark, the girl came by and I asked her to take drinks to the bandstand. There was a long pause, while they talked up there in the indigo light and after awhile I saw the girl put a Scotch and milk on top of the piano for Sonny. He didn't seem to notice it, but just before they started playing again, he sipped from it and looked toward me, and nodded. Then he put it back on top of the piano. For me, then, as they began to play again, it glowed and shook above my brother's head like the very cup of trembling.

For Consideration

1. Catalogue the differing values and concerns implicit in the respective lifestyles of Sonny and the narrator. What does the narrator imply about Sonny when he thinks of "the distant stillness in which he had always moved" and of "the depths of his private life"? Isolate the various factors which either promote or weaken the relationship between the two.

2. Light and darkness are prominent symbols in the story. What values, beyond the literalness of each, are associated with the related images? What is the "darkness outside" toward which, in the narrator's recollection of his past life, a child inevitably moves?

3. What is the significance for Sonny of his music? What does the narrator mean when he says about Sonny's earlier efforts at the piano that "Sonny was at that piano playing for his life"?

4. What does the narrator learn about Sonny from the dialogue before the final scene? How much understanding is there between the two?

5. What is the significance of the blues in the story? Why that particular form of music? Why does the narrator call the blues "the only light we've got in all this darkness"? What is Sonny's accomplishment in the final scene? How fully does the narrator respond to his brother's action?

JOHN UPDIKE (1932–   )
A & P

In walks these three girls in nothing but bathing suits. I'm in the third checkout slot, with my back to the door, so I don't see them until they're over by the bread. The one that caught my eye first was the one in the plaid green two-piece. She was a chunky kid, with a good tan and a sweet broad soft-looking can with those two crescents of white just under it, where the sun never seems to hit, at the top of the backs of her legs. I stood there with my hand on a box of HiHo crackers trying to remember if I rang it up or not. I ring it up again and the customer starts giving me hell. She's one of these cash-register-watchers, a witch about fifty with rouge on her cheekbones and no eyebrows, and I know it made her day to trip me up. She'd been watching cash registers for fifty years and probably never seen a mistake before.

By the time I got her feathers smoothed and her goodies into a bag — she gives me a little snort in passing, if she'd been born at the right time they would have burned her over in Salem — by the time I get her on her way the girls had circled around the bread and were coming back, without a pushcart, back my way along the counters, in the aisle between the checkouts and the Special bins. They didn't even have shoes on. There was this chunky one, with the two-piece — it was bright green and the seams on the bra were still sharp and her belly was still pretty pale so I guessed she just got it (the suit) — there was this one, with one of those chubby berry-faces, the lips all bunched together under her nose, this one, and a tall one, with black hair that hadn't quite frizzed right, and one of these sunburns right across under the eyes, and a chin that was too long — you know, the kind of girl other girls think is very "striking" and "attractive" but never quite makes it, as they very well know, which is why they like her so much — and then the third one, that wasn't quite so tall. She was the queen. She kind of led them, the other two peeking around and making their shoulders round. She didn't look around, not this queen, she just walked straight on slowly, on these long white prima-donna legs. She came down a little hard on her heels, as if she didn't

walk in her bare feet that much, putting down her heels and then letting the weight move along to her toes as if she was testing the floor with every step, putting a little deliberate extra action into it. You never know for sure how girls' minds work (do you really think it's a mind in there or just a little buzz like a bee in a glass jar?) but you got the idea she had talked the other two into coming in here with her, and now she was showing them how to do it, walk slow and hold yourself straight.

She had on a kind of dirty-pink — beige maybe, I don't know — bathing suit with a little nubble all over it and, what got me, the straps were down. They were off her shoulders looped loose around the cool tops of her arms, and I guess as a result the suit had slipped a little on her, so all around the top of the cloth there was this shining rim. If it hadn't been there you wouldn't have known there could have been anything whiter than those shoulders. With the straps pushed off, there was nothing between the top of the suit and the top of her head except just *her*, this clean bare plane of the top of her chest down from the shoulder bones like a dented sheet of metal tilted in the light. I mean, it was more than pretty.

She had sort of oaky hair that the sun and salt had bleached, done up in a bun that was unravelling, and a kind of prim face. Walking into the A & P with your straps down, I suppose it's the only kind of face you *can* have. She held her head so high her neck, coming up out of those white shoulders, looked kind of stretched, but I didn't mind. The longer her neck was, the more of her there was.

She must have felt in the corner of her eye me and over my shoulder Stokesie in the second slot watching, but she didn't tip. Not this queen. She kept her eyes moving across the racks, and stopped, and turned so slow it made my stomach rub the inside of my apron, and buzzed to the other two, who kind of huddled against her for relief, and then they all three of them went up the cat-and-dog-food-break-fast-cereal-macaroni-rice-raisins-season-ings-spreads-spaghetti-soft-drinks-crackers-and-cookies aisle. From the third slot I look straight up this aisle to the meat counter, and I watched them all the way. The fat one with the tan sort of fumbled with the cookies, but on second thought she put the package back. The sheep pushing their carts down the aisle — the girls were walking against the usual traffic (not that we have one-way signs or any-thing) — were pretty hilarious. You could see them, when Queenie's white shoulders dawned on them, kind of jerk, or hop, or hiccup, but their eyes snapped back to their own baskets and on they pushed. I bet you could set off dynamite in an A & P and the people would by and large keep reaching and checking oatmeal off their lists and muttering "Let me see, there was a third thing, began with A, asparagus, no, ah, yes, applesauce!" or whatever it is they do mutter. But there was no doubt, this jiggled them. A few houseslaves in pin curlers even looked around after pushing their carts past to make sure what they had seen was correct.

You know, it's one thing to have a girl in a bathing suit down on the beach, where what with the glare nobody can look at each other much anyway, and another thing in the cool of the A & P, under the fluorescent lights, against all those stacked packages, with her feet paddling along naked over our checkerboard green-and-cream rubber-tile floor.

"Oh Daddy," Stokesie said beside me. "I feel so faint."

"Darling," I said. "Hold me tight." Stokesie's married, with two babies chalked up on his fuselage already, but as far as I can tell that's the only difference. He's twenty-two, and I was nineteen this April.

"Is it done?" he asks, the responsible married man finding his voice. I forgot to say he thinks he's going to be manager some sunny day, maybe in 1990 when it's called the Great Alexandrov and Pet-rooshki Tea Company or something.

What he meant was, our town is five miles from a beach, with a big summer colony out on the Point, but we're right in the middle of town, and the women generally put on a shirt or shorts or something before they get out of the car into the street. And anyway these are usually women with six children and varicose veins mapping their legs and nobody, including them, could care less. As I say, we're right in the middle of town, and if you stand at our front doors you can see two banks and the Congregational church and the newspaper store and three real-estate offices and about twenty-seven old freeloaders tearing up Central Street because the sewer broke again. It's not as if we're on the Cape; we're north of Boston and there's people in this town haven't seen the ocean for twenty years.

The girls had reached the meat counter and were asking McMahon something. He pointed, they pointed, and they shuffled out of sight behind a pyramid of Diet Delight peaches. All that was left for us to see was old McMahon patting his mouth and looking after them sizing up their joints. Poor kids, I began to feel sorry for them, they couldn't help it.

Now here comes the sad part of the story, at least my family says it's sad, but I don't think it's so sad myself. The store's pretty empty, it being Thursday after-noon, so there was nothing much to do ex-cept lean on the register and wait for the girls to show up again. The whole store was like a pinball machine and I didn't know which tunnel they'd come out of. After a while they come around out of the far aisle, around the light bulbs, records at discount of the Caribbean Six or Tony Martin Sings or some such gunk you wonder they waste the wax on, sixpacks of candy bars, and plastic toys done up in cellophane that fall apart when a kid looks at them anyway. Around they come, Queenie still leading the way, and holding a little gray jar in her hand. Slots Three through Seven are unmanned and I could see her wondering between Stokes and me, but Stokesie with his usual luck draws an old party in baggy gray pants who stumbles up with four giant cans of pineapple juice (what do these bums *do* with all that pineapple juice? I've often asked myself) so the girls come to me. Queenie puts down the jar and I take it into my fingers icy cold. Kingfish Fancy Herring Snacks in Pure Sour Cream: 49⁴. Now her hands are empty, not a ring or a bracelet, bare as God made them, and I wonder where the money's coming from. Still with that prim look she lifts a folded dollar bill out of the hollow at the center of her nubbled pink top. The jar went heavy in my hand. Really, I thought that was so cute.

Then everybody's luck begins to run out. Lengel comes in from haggling with a truck full of cabbages on the lot and is about to scuttle into that door marked MANAGER behind which he hides all day when the girls touch his eye. Lengel's pretty dreary, teaches Sunday school and the rest, but he doesn't miss that much. He comes over and says, "Girls, this isn't the beach."

Queenie blushes, though maybe it's just a brush of sunburn I was noticing for the first time, now that she was so close. "My mother asked me to pick up a jar of herring snacks." Her voice kind of startled me, the way voices do when you see the people first, coming out so flat and dumb yet kind of tony, too, the way it ticked over "pick up" and "snacks." All of a sudden I slid right down her voice into her living room. Her father and the other men were stand-

ing around in ice-cream coats and bow ties and the women were in sandals picking up herring snacks on toothpicks off a big glass plate and they were all holding drinks the color of water with olives and sprigs of mint in them. When my parents have somebody over they get lemonade and if it's a real racy affair Schlitz in tall glasses with "They'll Do It Every Time" cartoons stencilled on.

"That's all right," Lengel said. "But this isn't the beach." His repeating this struck me as funny, as if it had just occurred to him, and he had been thinking all these years the A & P was a great big dune and he was the head lifeguard. He didn't like my smiling — as I say he doesn't miss much — but he concentrates on giving the girls that sad Sunday-school-superintendent stare.

Queenie's blush is no sunburn now, and the plump one in plaid, that I liked better from the back — a really sweet can — pipes up, "We weren't doing any shopping. We just came in for the one thing."

"That makes no difference," Lengel tells her, and I could see from the way his eyes went that he hadn't noticed she was wearing a two-piece before. "We want you decently dressed when you come in here."

"We *are* decent," Queenie says suddenly, her lower lip pushing, getting sore now that she remembers her place, a place from which the crowd that runs the A & P must look pretty crummy. Fancy Herring Snacks flashed in her very blue eyes.

"Girls, I don't want to argue with you. After this come in here with your shoulders covered. It's our policy." He turns his back. That's policy for you. Policy is what the kingpins want. What the others want is juvenile delinquency.

All this while, the customers had been showing up with their carts but, you know, sheep, seeing a scene they had all bunched up on Stokesie, who shook open a paper bag as gently as peeling a peach, not wanting to miss a word. I could feel in the silence everybody getting nervous, most of all Lengel, who asks me, "Sammy, have you rung up their purchase?"

I thought and said "No" but it wasn't about that I was thinking. I go through the punches, 4, 9, GROC, TOT — it's more complicated than you think, and after you do it often enough, it begins to make a little song, that you hear words to, in my case "Hello (*bing*) there, you (*gung*) hap-py *pee*-pul (*splat*)!" — the *splat* being the drawer flying out. I uncrease the bill, tenderly as you may imagine, it just having come from between the two smoothest scoops of vanilla I had ever known were there, and pass a half and a penny into her narrow pink palm, and nestle the herrings in a bag and twist its neck and hand it over, all the time thinking.

The girls, and who'd blame them, are in a hurry to get out, so I say "I quit" to Lengel quick enough for them to hear, hoping they'll stop and watch me, their unsuspected hero. They keep right on going, into the electric eye; the door flies open and they flicker across the lot to their car, Queenie and Plaid and Big Tall Goony-Goony (not that as raw material she was so bad), leaving me with Lengel and a kink in his eyebrow.

"Did you say something, Sammy?"

"I said I quit."

"I thought you did."

"You didn't have to embarrass them."

"It was they who were embarrassing us."

I started to say something that came out "Fiddle-de-doo." It's a saying of my grandmother's, and I know she would have been pleased.

"I don't think you know what you're saying," Lengel said.

"I know you don't," I said. "But I do." I pull the bow at the back of my apron and start shrugging it off my shoulders. A couple customers that had been heading for my slot begin to knock against each other, like scared pigs in a chute.

Lengel sighs and begins to look very patient and old and gray. He's been a friend of my parents for years. "Sammy, you don't want to do this to your Mom and Dad," he tells me. It's true, I don't. But it seems to me that once you begin a gesture it's fatal not to go through with it. I fold the apron, "Sammy" stitched in red on the pocket, and put it on the counter, and drop the bow tie on top of it. The bow tie is theirs, if you've ever wondered. "You'll feel this for the rest of your life," Lengel says, and I know that's true, too, but remembering how he made that pretty girl blush makes me so scrunchy inside I punch the No Sale tab and the machine whirs "pee-pul" and the drawer splats out. One advantage to this scene taking place in summer, I can follow this up with a clean exit, there's no fumbling around getting your coat and galoshes, I just saunter into the electric eye in my white shirt that my mother ironed the night before, and the door heaves itself open, and outside the sunshine is skating around on the asphalt.

I look around for my girls, but they're gone, of course. There wasn't anybody but some young married screaming with her children about some candy they didn't get by the door of a powder-blue Falcon station wagon. Looking back in the big windows, over the bags of peat moss and aluminum lawn furniture stacked on the pavement, I could see Lengel in my place in the slot, checking the sheep through. His face was dark gray and his back stiff, as if he'd just had an injection of iron, and my stomach kind of fell as I felt how hard the world was going to be to me hereafter.

For Consideration

1. The young narrator has some distinct characterizations of most of the people who come into the store. How, for example, does he characterize the shoppers in general? What might these responses suggest about him?

2. Why does he give so much attention to Queenie? How much of his attraction to her is simply physical? How does he see himself in relationship to her?

3. Why does Sammy quit his job? Near the end he observes that "once you begin a gesture it's fatal not go through with it." What kind of gesture is indicated in his action? What does Lengel mean in saying to Sammy, "You'll feel this for the rest of your life"?

4. Looking back at the store from the outside, Sammy "felt how hard the world was going to be to me hereafter." Is the event so momentous or is he simply exaggerating? In what ways might the conflict be larger than a mere incident in a store?

5. Why is the story titled "A & P"?

For Comparison

How do the experiences described here compare to those described in "Araby" (p. 185)? In what respects are the two narrators alike? The experience of each focuses on a girl and the outcome shows us a less naive, less optimistic person than we saw at the beginning. What other similarities and differences do you see?

DONALD BARTHELME (1933–)
The Sandman

Dear Dr. Hodder, I realize that it is probably wrong to write a letter to one's girl friend's shrink but there are several things going on here that I think ought to be pointed out to you. I thought of making a personal visit but the situation then, as I'm sure you understand, would be completely untenable — I would be *visiting a psychiatrist*. I also understand that in writing to you I am in some sense interfering with the process but you don't have to discuss with Susan what I have said. Please consider this an "eyes only" letter. Please think of it as personal and confidential.

You must be aware, first, that because Susan is my girl friend pretty much everything she discusses with you she also discusses with me. She tells me what she said and what you said. We have been seeing each other for about six months now and I am pretty familiar with her story, or stories. Similarly, with your responses, or at least the general pattern. I know, for example, that my habit of referring to you as "the sandman" annoys you but let me assure you that I mean nothing unpleasant by it. It is simply a nickname. The reference is to the old rhyme: "Sea-sand does the sandman bring/Sleep to end the day/He dusts the children's eyes with sand/And steals their dreams away." (This is a variant; there are other versions, but this is the one I prefer.) I also understand that you are a little bit shaky because the prestige of analysis is now, as I'm sure you know far better than I, at a nadir. This must tend to make you nervous and who can blame you? One always tends to get a little bit shook when one's methodology is in question. Of course! (By the bye, let me say that I am very pleased that you are one of the ones that talk, instead of just sitting there. I think that's a good thing, an excellent thing, I congratulate you.)

To the point. I fully understand that Susan's wish to terminate with you and buy a piano instead has disturbed you. You have every right to be disturbed and to say that she is not electing the proper course, that what she says conceals something else, that she is evading reality, etc., etc. Go ahead. But there is one possibility here that you might be, just might be, missing. Which is that she means it.

Susan says: "I want to buy a piano."

You think: She wishes to terminate the analysis and escape into the piano.

Or: Yes, it is true that her father wanted her to be a concert pianist and that she studied for twelve years with Goetzmann. But she does not really want to reopen that can of maggots. She wants me to disapprove.

Or: Having failed to achieve a career as a concert pianist, she wishes to fail again. She is now too old to achieve the original objective. The spontaneous organization of defeat!

Or: She is flirting again.

Or:

Or:

Or:

Or:

The one thing you cannot consider, by the nature of your training and of the discipline itself, is that she really might want to terminate the analysis and buy a piano. That the piano might be more necessary and valuable to her than the analysis.[1]

What we really have to consider here is the locus of hope. Does hope reside in the analysis or rather in the piano? As a shrink rather than a piano salesman you would naturally tend to opt for the analysis. But there are differences. The piano salesman can stand behind his product; you, unfortunately, cannot. A Steinway is a known quantity, whereas an analysis can succeed or fail. I don't reproach you for this, I simply note it. (An interesting question: Why do laymen feel such a desire to, in plain language, fuck over shrinks? As I am doing here, in a sense? I don't mean hostility in the psychoanalytic encounter, I mean in general. This is an interesting phenomenon and should be investigated by somebody.)

It might be useful if I gave you a little taste of my own experience of analysis. I only went five or six times. Dr. Behring was a tall thin man who never said anything much. If you could get a "What comes to mind?" out of him you were doing splendidly. There was a little incident that is, perhaps, illustrative. I went for my hour one day and told him about some-

1. For an admirable discussion of this sort of communication failure and many other matters of interest see Percy, "Toward a Triadic Theory of Meaning," *Psychiatry*, Vol. 35 (February 1972), pp. 6-14 *et seq.*

thing I was worried about. (I was then working for a newspaper down in Texas.) There was a story that four black teenagers had come across a little white boy, about ten, in a vacant lot, sodomized him repeatedly and then put him inside a refrigerator and closed the door (this was before they had that requirement that abandoned refrigerators had to have their doors removed) and he suffocated. I don't know to this day what actually happened, but the cops had picked up *some* black kids and were reportedly beating the shit out of them in an effort to make them confess. I was not on the police run at that time but one of the police reporters told me about it and I told Dr. Behring. A good liberal, he grew white with anger and said what was I doing about it? It was the first time he had talked. So I was shaken — it hadn't occurred to me that I was required to do something about it, he was right — and after I left I called my then sister-in-law, who was at that time secretary to a City Councilman. As you can imagine, such a position is a very powerful one — the councilmen are mostly off making business deals and the executive secretaries run the office — and she got on to the chief of police with an inquiry as to what was going on and if there was any police brutality involved and if so, how much. The case was a very sensational one, you see; *Ebony* had a writer down there trying to cover it but he couldn't get in to see the boys and the cops had roughed him up some, they couldn't understand at that time that there could be such a thing as a black reporter. They understood that they had to be a little careful with the white reporters, but a black reporter was beyond them. But my sister-in-law threw her weight (her Councilman's weight) around a bit and suggested to the chief that if there was a serious amount of brutality going on the cops had better stop it, because there was too much outside interest in the

case and it would be extremely bad PR if the brutality stuff got out. I also called a guy I knew pretty high up in the sheriff's department and suggested that *he* suggest to his colleagues that they cool it. I hinted at unspeakable political urgencies and he picked it up. The sheriff's department was separate from the police department but they both operated out of the Courthouse Building and they interacted quite a bit, in the normal course. So the long and short of it was that the cops decided to show the four black kids at a press conference to demonstrate that they weren't really beat all to rags, and that took place at four in the afternoon. I went and the kids looked O.K., except for one whose teeth were out and who the cops said had fallen down the stairs. Well, we all know the falling-down-the-stairs story but the point was the *degree* of mishandling and it was clear that the kids had not been half-killed by the cops, as the rumor stated. They were walking and talking naturally, although scared to death, as who would not be? There weren't any TV pictures because the newspaper people always pulled out the plugs of the TV people, at important moments, in those days — it was a standard thing. Now while I admit it sounds callous to be talking about the degree of brutality being minimal, let me tell you that it was no small matter, in that time and place, to force the cops to show the kids to the press at all. It was an achievement, of sorts. So about eight o'clock I called Dr. Behring at home, I hope interrupting his supper, and told him that the kids were O.K., relatively, and he said that was fine, he was glad to hear it. They were later no-billed and I stopped seeing him. That was my experience of analysis and that it may have left me a little sour, I freely grant. Allow for this bias.

To continue. I take exception to your remark that Susan's "openness" is a form of voyeurism. This remark interested me for a while, until I thought about it. Voyeurism I take to be an eroticized expression of curiosity whose chief phenomenological characteristic is the distance maintained between the voyeur and the object. The tension between the desire to draw near the object and the necessity to maintain the distance becomes a libidinous energy nondischarge, which is what the voyeur seeks.[2] The tension. But your remark indicates, in my opinion, a radical misreading of the problem. Susan's "openness" — a willingness of the heart, if you will allow such a term — is not at all comparable to the activities of the voyeur. Susan draws near. Distance is not her thing — not by a long chalk. Frequently, as you know, she gets burned, but she always tries again. What is operating here, I suggest, is an attempt on your part to "stabilize" Susan's behavior in reference to a state-of-affairs that you feel should obtain. Susan gets married and lives happily ever after. Or: There is within Susan a certain amount of creativity which should be liberated and actualized. Susan becomes an artist and lives happily ever after.

But your norms are, I suggest, skewing your view of the problem, and very badly.

Let us take the first case. You reason: If Susan is happy or at least functioning in the present state of affairs (that is, moving from man to man as a silver dollar moves from hand to hand), then why is she seeing a shrink? Something is wrong. New behavior is indicated. Susan is to get married and live happily ever after. May I offer another view? That is, that "seeing a shrink" might be precisely a maneuver in a situation in which Susan *does not want* to get married and live happily ever after? That getting married and living happily ever after might be, for Susan, the worst of fates, and that in order to validate her non-

acceptance of this norm she defines herself to herself as shrink-needing? That you are actually certifying the behavior which you seek to change? (When she says to you that she's not shrinkable, you should listen.)

Perhaps, Dr. Hodder, my logic is feeble, perhaps my intuitions are frail. It is, God knows, a complex and difficult question. Your perception that Susan is an artist of some kind *in potentia* is, I think, an acute one. But the proposition "Susan becomes an artist and lives happily ever after" is ridiculous. (I realize that I am couching the proposition in such terms — "happily ever after" — that it is ridiculous on the face of it, but there is ridiculousness piled upon ridiculousness.) Let me point out, if it has escaped your notice, that what an artist does, is fail. Any reading of the literature[3] (I mean the theory of artistic creation), however summary, will persuade you instantly that the paradigmatic artistic experience is that of failure. The actualization fails to meet, equal, the intuition. There is something "out there" which cannot be brought "here." This is standard. I don't mean bad artists, I mean good artists. There is no such thing as a "successful artist" (except, of course, in worldly terms). The proposition should read, "Susan becomes an artist and lives unhappily ever after." This is the case. Don't be deceived.

What I am saying is, that the therapy of choice is not clear. I deeply sympathize. You have a dilemma.

I ask you to note, by the way, that Susan's is not a seeking after instant gratification as dealt out by so-called encounter or sensitivity groups, nude marathons, or dope. None of this is what is going down. "Joy" is not Susan's bag. I praise her for seeking out you rather than getting involved with any of this other idiocy. Her

2. See, for example, Straus, "Shame As a Historiological Problem," in *Phenomenological Psychology* (New York: Basic Books, 1966), p. 219.

3. Especially, perhaps, Ehrenzweig, *The Hidden Order of Art* (University of California Press, 1966), pp. 234-9.

forte, I would suggest, is mind, and if there are games being played they are being conducted with taste, decorum, and some amount of intellectual rigor. Not-bad games. When I take Susan out to dinner she does not order chocolate-covered ants, even if they are on the menu. (Have you, by the way, tried Alfredo's, at the corner of Bank and Hudson streets? It's wonderful.) (Parenthetically, the problem of analysts sleeping with their patients is well known and I understand that Susan has been routinely seducing you — a reflex, she can't help it — throughout the analysis. I understand that there is a new splinter group of therapists, behaviorists of some kind, who take this to be some kind of ethic? Is this true? Does this mean that they do it only when they want to, or whether they want to or not? At a dinner party the other evening a lady analyst was saying that three cases of this kind had recently come to her attention and she seemed to think that this was rather a lot. The problem of maintaining mentorship is, as we know, not easy. I think you have done very well in this regard, and God knows it must have been difficult, given those skirts Susan wears that unbutton up to the crotch and which she routinely leaves unbuttoned to the third button.)

Am I wandering too much for you? Bear with me. The world is waiting for the sunrise.

We are left, I submit, with the problem of her depressions. They are, I agree, terrible. Your idea that I am not "supportive" enough is, I think, wrong. I have found, as a practical matter, that the best thing to do is to just do ordinary things, read the newspaper for example, or watch basketball, or wash the dishes. That seems to allow her to come out of it better than any amount of so-called "support." (About the *chasmus hystericus* or hysterical yawning I don't worry any more. It is masking behavior, of course, but after all, you must allow us our tics. The world is waiting for the sunrise.) What do you do with a patient who finds the world unsatisfactory? The world *is* unsatisfactory; only a fool would deny it. I know that your own ongoing psychic structuralization is still going on — you are thirty-seven and I am forty-one — but you must be old enough by now to realize that shit is shit. Susan's perception that America has somehow got hold of the greed ethic and that the greed ethic has turned America into a tidy little hell is not, I think, wrong. What do you do with such a perception? Apply Band-Aids, I suppose. About her depressions, I wouldn't do anything. I'd leave them alone. Put on a record.[4]

Let me tell you a story.

One night we were at her place, about three a.m., and this man called, another lover, quite a well-known musician who is very good, very fast — a good man. He asked Susan "Is he there?," meaning me, and she said "Yes," and he said "What are you doing?," and she said, "What do you think?," and he said, "When will you be finished?," and she said, "Never." Are you, Doctor dear, in a position to appreciate the beauty of this reply, in this context?

What I am saying is that Susan is wonderful. *As is.* There are not so many things around to which that word can be accurately applied. Therefore I must view your efforts to improve her with, let us say, a certain amount of ambivalence. If this makes me a negative factor in the analysis, so be it. I will be a negative factor until the cows come home, and cheerfully. I can't help it, Doctor, I am voting for the piano.

With best wishes,

4. For example, Harrison, "Wah Wah," Apple Records STCH 639, Side One, Track 3.

For Consideration

1. The epistolary novel is a long piece of prose fiction which consists mainly or entirely of letters. In that context "The Sandman" might be called an epistolary short story. Why has Barthelme adopted the form here? What are its advantages? Its limitations?

2. Why does the writer think of the psychiatrist as "the sandman"? What are the implications of the old rhyme?

3. What are the differences between the writer's and the psychiatrist's reactions to Susan's wish to buy the piano? Why are the reactions appropriate for each person?

4. Why does the writer include footnotes in his letter? Are they for the psychiatrist or the reader (you)?

5. On what grounds might it be true that the piano is "more necessary and valuable to her [Susan] than the analysis"?

6. What is the purpose of telling the story of the black kids and the police in Texas? This could be seen as a long digression — is it?

7. What are the bases for the writer's objections to the "get married" or the "become an artist" solutions? Is his contention that Susan "is wonderful. *As is*" selfish or sound? Can it be both? What implicit values guide the psychiatrist to want to change Susan and the writer to want to keep her as she is?

For Comparison

"The Sandman" and "The Magic Barrel" (p. 76) concern love situations in which the woman is judged unstable in some way, either spiritually (Salzman's daughter) or mentally (Susan). Yet Leo Finkle and the letter writer here both affirm their intention to pursue the love affairs, in spite of a father or a psychiatrist. What point about love or human behavior are the authors making?

JAMES ALAN McPHERSON   (1943–   )
A Matter of Vocabulary

Thomas Brown stopped going to church at twelve after one Sunday morning when he had been caught playing behind the minister's pulpit by several deacons who had come up into the room early to count the money they had collected from the other children in the Sunday school downstairs. Thomas had seen them putting some of the change in their pockets and they had seen him trying to hide behind the big worn brown pulpit with the several black Bibles and the pitcher of ice water and the glass used by the minister in the more passionate parts of his sermons. It was a Southern Baptist Church.

"Come on down off of that, little Brother Brown," one of the fat, black-suited deacons had told him. "We see you tryin' to hide. Ain't no use tryin' to hide in God's House."

Thomas had stood up and looked at them; all three of them, big-bellied, severe and religiously righteous. "I wasn't tryin' to hide," he said in a low voice.

"Then what was you doin' behind Reverend Stone's pulpit?"

"I was praying," Thomas had said coolly.

After that he did not like to go to church. Still, his mother would make him go every Sunday morning; and since he was only thirteen and very obedient, he could find no excuse not to leave the house. But after leaving with his brother Edward, he would not go all the way to church again. He would make Edward, who was a year younger, leave him at a certain corner a few blocks away from the church where Saturday-night drunks were sleeping or waiting in misery for the bars to open on Monday morning. His own father had been that way and Thomas knew that the waiting was very hard. He felt good toward the men, being almost one of them, and liked to listen to them curse and threaten each other lazily in the hot Georgia sun. He liked to look into their faces and wonder what was in their minds that made them not care about anything except the bars opening on Monday morning. He liked to try to distinguish the different shades of black in their hands and arms and faces. And he liked the smell

of them. But most of all he liked it when they talked to him and gave him an excuse for not walking down the street two blocks to the Baptist Church.

"Don' you ever get married, boy," Arthur, one of the meaner drunks with a missing eye, told him on several occasions.

The first time he had said it the boy had asked: "Why not?"

"Cause a bitch ain't shit, man. You mind you don' get married now, hear? A bitch'll take all yo' money and then throw you out *in the street!*"

"Damn straight!" Leroy, another drunk much darker than Arthur and a long-shoreman, said. "That's all they fit for, takin' a man's money and runnin' around."

Thomas would sit on the stoop of an old deserted house with the men lying on the ground below him, too lazy to brush away the flies that came at them from the urine-soaked dirt on the hot Sunday mornings, and he would look and listen and consider. And after a few weeks of this he found himself very afraid of girls.

Things about life had always come to Thomas Brown by listening and being quiet. He remembered how he had learned about being black, and about how some other people were not. And the difference it made. He felt at home sitting with the waiting drunks because they were black and he knew that they liked him because for months before he had stopped going to church, he had spoken to them while passing, and they had returned his greeting. His mother had always taught him to speak to people in the streets because Southern blacks do not know how to live without neighbors who exchange greetings. He had noted, however, when he was nine, that certain people did not return his greetings. At first he had thought that their silence was due to his own low voice: he had gone to a Catholic school for three years where the black-caped nuns put an academic premium on silence. He had learned that in complete silence lay his safety from being slapped or hit on the flat of the hand with a wooden ruler. And he had been a model student. But even when he raised his voice, intentionally, to certain people in the street they still did not respond. Then he had noticed that while they had different faces like the nuns, whom he never thought of as real people, these non-speakers were completely different in dress and color from the people he knew. But still, he wondered why they would not speak.

He never asked his mother or anyone else about it: ever since those three years with the nuns he did not like to talk much. And he began to consider certain things about his own person as possible reasons for these slights. He began to consider why it was necessary for one to go to the bathroom. He began to consider whether only people like him had to go to the toilet and whether or not this thing was the cause of his complexion; and whether the other people could know about the bathroom merely by looking at his skin, and did not speak because they knew he did it. This bothered him a lot; but he never asked anyone about it. Not even his brother Edward, with whom he shared a bed and from whom, in the night and dark closeness of the bed, there should have been kept no secret thoughts. Nor did he speak of it to Leroy, the most talkative drunk, who wet the dirt behind the old house where they sat with no shame in his face and always shook himself in the direction of the Baptist Church, two blocks down the street.

"You better go to church," his mother told him when he was finally discovered. "If you don' go, you goin' to hell for sure."

"I don't think I wanna go back," he said.

"You'll be a *sinner* if you don' go," she said, pointing her finger at him with great gravity. "You'll go to hell, sure enough."

Thomas felt doomed already. He had told the worst lie in the world in the worst place in the world and he knew that going back to church would not save him now. He knew that there was a hell because the nuns had told him about it, and he knew that he would end up in one of the little rooms in that place. But he still hoped for some time in Purgatory, with a chance to move into a better room later, if he could be very good for a while before he died. He wanted to be very good and he tried all the time very hard not to have to go to the bathroom. But when his mother talked about hell, he thought again that perhaps he would have to spend all his time, after death, in that great fiery hot burning room she talked about. She had been raised in the Southern Baptist Church and had gone to church, to the same minister, all her life; up until the time she had to start working on Sundays. But she still maintained her faith and never talked, in her conception of hell and how it would be for sinners, about the separate rooms for certain people. Listening to his mother talk about hell in the kitchen while she cooked supper and sweated, Thomas thought that perhaps she did know more than the nuns because there were so many people who believed like her, including the bald Reverend Stone in their church, in that one great burning room, and the Judgment Day.

"The hour's gonna come when the Horn will blow," his mother told him while he cowered in the corner behind her stove, feeling the heat from it on his face. "The Horn's gonna blow all through the world on that Great Morning and all them in the graves will hear it and be raised up," she continued.

"Even Daddy?"

His mother paused, and let the spoon stand still in the pot on the stove. "Everybody," she said, "both the Quick and the Dead and everybody that's alive. Then the stars are gonna fall and all the sinners will be cryin' and tryin' to hide in the corners and under houses. But it won't do no good to hide. You can't hide from God. Then they gonna call the Roll with everybody's name on it and the sheeps are gonna be divided from the goats, the Good on the Right and the Bad on the Left. And then the ground's gonna open up and all them on the Left are gonna fall right into a burnin' pool of fire and brimstone and they're gonna be cryin' and screamin' for mercy but there won't be none because it will be too late. Especially for those who don't repent and go to church."

Then his mother stood over him, her eyes almost red with emotion, her face wet from the stove, and shining black, and very close to tears.

Thomas felt the heat from the stove where he sat in the corner next to the broom. He was scared. He thought about being on the Left with Leroy and Arthur, and all the men who sat on the corner two blocks away from the Baptist Church. He did not think it was at all fair.

"Won't there be no rooms for different people?" he asked her.

"What kind of rooms?" his mother said.

"Rooms for people who ain't done too much wrong."

"There ain't gonna be no separate rooms for any Sinners on the *Left*! Everybody on the Left is gonna fall right into the same fiery pit and the ones on the Right will be raised up into glory."

Thomas felt very hot in the corner.

"Where do you want to be, Tommy?" his mother asked.

He could think of nothing to say.

"You want to be on the Right or on the Left?"

"I don't know."

"What do you mean?" she said. "You still got time, son."

"I don't know if I can ever get over on the Right," Thomas said.

His mother looked down at him. She was a very warm person and sometimes she hugged him or touched him on the face when he least expected it. But sometimes she was severe.

"You can still get on the Right side Tommy, if you go to church."

"I don't see how I can," he said again.

"Go on back to church, son," his mother said.

"I'll go," Tommy said. But he was not sure whether he could ever go back again after what he had done right behind the pulpit. But to please her, and to make her know that he was really sorry and that he would really try to go back to church, and to make certain in her mind that he genuinely wanted to have a place on the Right on Judgment Day, he helped her cook dinner and then washed the dishes afterwards.

II

They lived on the top floor of a gray wooden house next to a funeral parlor. Thomas and Edward could look out of the kitchen window and down into the rear door of the funeral parlor, which was always open, and watch Billy Herbs, the mortician, working on the bodies. Sometimes the smell of the embalming fluid would float through the open door and up to them, leaning out the window. It was not a good smell. Sometimes Billy Herbs would come to the back door of the embalming room in his white coat and look up at them, and laugh, and wave for them to come down. They never went down. And after a few minutes of getting fresh air, Billy Herbs would look at them again and go back to his work.

Down the street, almost at the corner, was a police station. There were always two fat, white-faced, red-nosed, blue-suited policemen who never seemed to go anywhere sitting in the small room. These two men had never spoken to Thomas except on one occasion when he was doing some hard thinking about getting on the Right Side on Judgment Day.

He had been on his way home from school in the afternoon. It was fall and he was kicking leaves. His eyes fell upon a green five-dollar bill on the black sand sidewalk, just a few steps away from the station. At first he did not know what to do; he had never found money before. But finding money on the ground was a good feeling. He had picked up the bill and carried it home, to a house that needed it, to his mother. It was not a great amount of money to lose, but theirs was a very poor street and his mother had directed him, without any hesitation, to turn in the lost five dollars at the police station. And he had done this, going to the station himself and telling the men, in a scared voice, how he had found the money, where he had found it, and how his mother had directed him to bring it to the station in case the loser should come in looking for it. The men had listened; they smiled at him and then at each other, and a policeman with a long red nose assured him, still smiling, that if the owner did not call for the five dollars in a week, they would bring the money to his house and it would be his. But the money never came back to his house, and when he saw the red-nosed policeman coming out of the station much, much more than a week later, the man did not even look at him, and Thomas had known that he should not ask what had happened to the money. Instead, in his mind, he credited it against the Judgment Time when, perhaps, there would be some uncertainty about whether he should stand on the Right Side, or whether he should cry with Leroy and Arthur and the other sinners, on the Left.

There was another interesting place on that street. It was across from his house, next to the Michelob Bar on the corner.

It was an old brown house and an old woman, Mrs. Quick, lived there. Every morning, on their way to school, Thomas and Edward would see her washing her porch with potash and water in a steel tub and a little stiff broom. The boards on her porch were very white from so much washing and he could see no reason why she should have to wash it every morning. She never had any visitors to track it except the Crab Lady who, even though she stopped to talk with Mrs. Quick every morning on her route, never went up on the porch. Sometimes the Crab Lady's call would awaken Thomas and his brother in the big bed they shared. *"Crabs! Buy my crabs!"* she would sing, like a big, loud bird, because the words all ran together in her song and it sounded to them like: *"Crabbonnieee crabs!"* They both would race to the window in their underwear and watch her walking on the other side of the street, an old wicker basket balanced on her head and covered with a bright red cloth that moved up and down with the bouncing of the crabs under it as she walked. She was a big, dull-black woman and wore a checkered apron over her dress, and she always held one hand up to the basket on her head as she swayed down the black dirt sidewalk. She did not sell many crabs on that street; they were too plentiful in the town. But still she came, every morning, with her song: *"Crabbonniee crabs!"*

"Wonder why she comes every morning," Thomas said to his brother once. "Nobody never buys crabs here."

"Maybe somebody down the street buys from her," Edward answered.

"Ain't nobody going to buy crabs this early in the morning. She oughta come at night when the guys are over at Michelob."

"Maybe she just comes by to talk to Mrs. Quick," Edward said.

And that was true enough. For every morning the Crab Lady would stop and talk to Mrs. Quick while she washed down her porch. She would never set the basket on the ground while she talked, but always stood with one hand on her wide hip and the other balancing the basket on her head, talking. And Mrs. Quick would continue to scrub her porch. Thomas and his brother would watch them until their mother came in to make them wash and dress for school. Leaving the window, Thomas would try to get a last look at Mrs. Quick, her head covered by a white bandanna, her old back bent in scrubbing, still talking to the Crab Lady. He would wonder what they talked about every morning. Not knowing this bothered him and he began to imagine their morning conversations. Mrs. Quick was West Indian and knew all about roots and voodoo, and Thomas was very afraid of her. He suspected that they talked about voodoo and who in the neighborhood had been fixed. Roots were like voodoo, and knowing about them made Mrs. Quick something to be feared. Thomas thought that she must know everything about him and everyone in the world, because once he and Edward and Luke, a fat boy who worked in the fish market around the corner, had put some salt and pepper and brown sand in a small tobacco pouch, and had thrown it on her white-wood porch, next to the screen door. They had done it as a joke and had run away afterwards, into an alley between his house and the funeral parlor across the street, and waited for her to come out and discover the pouch. They had waited for almost fifteen minutes and still she did not come out; and after all that time waiting it was not such a good joke any more and so they had gone off to the graveyard to gather green berries for their slingshots. But the next morning, on his way to school, Mrs. Quick had looked up from scrubbing her porch and called him over, across the dirt street.

"You better watch yourself, boy," she had said. "You hear me?"

"Why?" Thomas had asked, very frightened and eager to be running away to join his brother who was still walking in the wet spring morning, still safe and on his way to school.

Mrs. Quick had looked at him, very intensely. Her face was very black and wrinkled and her hair was white where it was not covered by the white bandanna. Her mouth was small and tight and deliberate and her eyes were dark and red where they should have been white. "You left-handed, ain't you?"

"Yes ma'am."

"Then watch yourself. Watch yourself good, 'less you get fixed."

"I ain't done nothin'," he said. But he knew that she was aware that he was lying.

"You left-handed, ain't you?"

He nodded.

"Then you owe the Devil a day's work and you better keep watch on yourself 'less you get fixed." Upon the last word in this pronouncement she had locked her eyes on his and seemed to look right into his soul. It was as if she knew that he was doomed to stand on the Left Side on that Day, no matter what good he still might do in life. He had said nothing, but her eyes looked so deep into his own that he had no other choice but to hold his head down. He looked away, and far up the street he could see the Crab Lady, swaying along in the dirt. Then he had run.

Late in the night there was another sound Thomas could hear in his bed, next to his brother. This sound did not come every night, but it was a steady sound and it made him shiver when it did come. He would be lying close and warm against his brother's back and the sound would bring him away from sleep.

"*Mr. Jones! I love you, Mr. Jones!*"

This was the horrible night sound of the Barefoot Lady, who came whenever she was drunk to rummage through the neighborhood garbage cans for scraps of food, and to stand before the locked door of the Herbert L. Jones Funeral Parlor and wake the neighborhood with her cry: "*Mr. Jones! I love you, Mr. Jones!*"

"Eddie, wake up!" He would push his brother's back. "It's the Barefoot Lady again."

Fully awake, they would listen to her pitiful moans, like a lonely dog at midnight or the faraway low whistle of a night train pushing along the edge of the town, heading north.

"She scares me," he would say to his brother.

"Yeah, Tommy," his brother would say.

There were certain creaking sounds about the old house that were only audible on the nights when she screamed.

"Why does she love Mr. Jones? He's a undertaker," he would ask his brother. But there would be no answer because his brother was younger and still knew how to be very quiet when he was afraid.

"*Mr. Jones! I love you, Mr. Jones!*"

"It's nighttime," Thomas would go on, talking to himself. "She ought to be scared by all the bodies he keeps in the back room. But maybe it ain't the bodies. Maybe Mr. Jones buried somebody for her a long time ago for free and she likes him for it. Maybe she never gets no chance to see him in the daytime so she comes at night. I bet she remembers that person Mr. Jones buried for her for free and gets drunk and comes in the night to thank him."

"Shut up, Tommy, please," Edward said in the dark. "I'm scared." Edward moved closer to him in the bed and then lay very quiet. But he still made the covers move with his trembling.

"*Mr. Jones! I love you, Mr. Jones!*"

Thomas thought about the back room of the Herbert L. Jones Funeral Parlor and the blue-and-white neon sign above its door and the Barefoot Lady, with feet caked with dirt and long yellow and black toenails, standing under that neon light. He had only seen her once in the day; but that once had been enough. She wore rags and an old black hat, and her nose and lips were huge and pink, and her hair was long and stringy and hanging far below her shoulders, and she had been drooling. He had come across her one morning digging into their garbage can for scraps. He had felt sorry for her because he and his brother and his mother threw out very few scraps, and had gone back up the stairs to ask his mother for something to give her. His mother had sent down some fresh biscuits and fried bacon, and watching her eat it with her dirty hands with their long black fingernails had made him sick. Now, in his bed, he could still see her eating the biscuits, flakes of the dough sticking to the bacon grease around her mouth. It was a bad picture to see above his bed in the shadows on the ceiling. And it did not help to close his eyes; because then he could see her more vividly, with all the horrible dirty colors of her rags and face and feet made sharper in his mind. He could see her the way he could see the bad men and monsters from *The Shadow* and *Suspense* and *Gangbusters* and *Inner Sanctum* every night after his mother had made him turn off the big brown radio in the living room. He could see these figures, men with long faces and humps in their backs and old women with streaming hair dressed all in black and cats with yellow eyes and huge rats, on the walls in the living room when it was dark there; and when he got into bed and closed his eyes they really came alive and frightened him, the way the present picture in his mind of the Barefoot Lady, her long toenails scratching on the thirty-two stairs as she came up to make him give her more biscuits and bacon, was frightening him. He did not know what to do, and so he moved closer to his brother, who was asleep now. Thomas wanted to wake him up so that he would have help against the Barefoot Lady. He wanted to cut on the light but he was afraid the light would show her where he was. He sweated, and waited. And downstairs, from below the blue-and-white lighted sign above the locked door to the funeral parlor, he heard her scream again; a painful sound, lonely, desperate, threatening, impatient, angry, hungry, he had no word to place it.

"*Mr. Jones! I love you, Mr. Jones!*"

III

Thomas Brown got his first job when he was thirteen. Both he and his brother worked at the Feinberg Super Market, owned by Milton Feinberg and his sister, Sarah Feinberg. Between the two of them they made a good third of a man's salary. Thomas had worked himself up from carry-out boy and was now in the Produce Department, while Edward, who was still new, remained a carry-out boy. Thomas enjoyed the status he had over the other boys. He enjoyed not having to be put outside on the street like the other boys up front whenever business was slow and Milton Feinberg wanted to save money. He enjoyed being able to work all week after school while the boys up front had to wait for weekends when there would be sales and a lot of shoppers. He especially liked being a regular boy because then he had to help mop and wax the floors of the store every Sunday morning and could not go to church. He knew that his mother was not pleased when he had been taken into the mopping crew because now he had an excuse not to attend church. But being on the crew meant making an extra three dollars and he knew that she was pleased with the money. Still, she made him pray at night, and especially on Sunday.

His job was bagging potatoes. It was very simple. Every day after school and all day Saturday he would come in the air-conditioned produce room, put on a blue smock, take a fifty-pound sack of potatoes off a huge stack of sacks, slit open the sack and let the potatoes fall into a shopping cart next to a scale, and proceed to put them into five- and ten-pound plastic bags. It was very simple; he could do it in his sleep. Then he would spend the rest of the day bagging potatoes and looking out of the big window, which separated the produce room from the rest of the store, at the customers. They were mostly white, and he had finally learned why they did not speak to him in the street. He had learned that after he came to the supermarket and now he did not mind going to the bathroom, knowing, when he did go, that all of them had to go, just as he did, in the secret places they called home. They had been speaking to him for a long time now, on this business level, and he had formed some small friendships grounded in this.

He knew Fred Burke, the vet who had got a war injury in his back and walked funny. Fred Burke was the butcher's helper who made hamburger from scraps of fat and useless meat cuttings and red powder in the back of the produce room, where the customers could not see. He liked to laugh when he mixed the red powder into the ground white substance, holding gobs of the soft stuff up over the big tub and letting it drip, and then dunking his hands down into the tub again. Sometimes he threw some of it at Thomas, in fun, and

Thomas had to duck. But it was all in fun and he did not mind it except when the red and white meat splattered the window and Thomas had to clean it off so that his view of the customers, as he bagged potatoes, would not be obstructed.

He thought of the window as a one-way mirror which allowed him to examine the people who frequented the store without being noticed himself. And it seemed as though he was never really noticed by any of them; no one ever stared back at him as he stood, only his head and shoulders visible behind the glass, looking out at the way certain hands fingered items and the way certain feet moved and the way some faces were set and determined while others laughed with mouths that moved in seemingly pleasant conversation. But none of them ever looked up from what they were about or even casually glanced in his direction. It was as if they could not see beyond the glass.

His line of vision covered the entire produce aisle and he could see the customers who entered the store making their way down that aisle, pushing their carts and stopping, selectively, first at the produce racks, then at the meat counter, then off to the side, beyond his view, to the canned goods and frozen foods and toilet items to the unseen right of him. He began to invent names for certain of the regular customers, the ones who came at a special time each week. One man, a gross fat person with a huge belly and the rough red neck and face of a farmer, who wheeled one shopping cart before him while he pulled another behind, Thomas called Big Funk because, he thought, no one could be that fat and wear the same faded dungaree suit each week without smelling bad. Another face he called The Rich Old Lady, because she was old and pushed her cart along slowly, with a dignity shown by none of the other shoppers. She always

bought parsley, and once, when Thomas was wheeling a big cart of bagged potatoes out to the racks, he passed her and smelled a perfume that was light and very fine to smell for just an instant. It did not linger in the air like most other perfumes he had smelled. And it seemed to him that she must have had it made just for her and that it was so expensive that it stayed with her body and would never linger behind her when she had passed a place. He liked that about her. Also, he had heard from the boys up front that she would never carry her own groceries to her house, no more than half a block from the store, and that no matter how small her purchases were, she would require a boy to carry them for her and would always tip a quarter. Thomas knew that there was a general fight among the carry-out boys whenever she checked out. Such a fight seemed worthy of her. And after a while of watching her, he would make a special point of wheeling a cart of newly bagged potatoes out to the racks when he saw her come in the store, just to smell the perfume. But she never noticed him either.

"You make sure you don't go over on them scales now," Miss Hester, the produce manager, would remind him whenever she saw him looking for too long a time out of the window. "Mr. Milton would git mad if you went over ten pounds."

Thomas always knew when she was watching him and just when she would speak. He had developed an instinct for this from being around her. He knew that it worried her when he was silent because she could not know what he was thinking. He knew, even at that age, that he was brighter than she was; and he thought that she must know it too because he could sense her getting uncomfortable when she stood in back of him in her blue smock, watching him lift the potatoes to the plastic bag until it was almost full, and then the plastic bag up to the gray metal scale, and then watching the red arrow fly across to 10. Somehow it almost always stopped wavering at exactly ten pounds. Filling the bags was automatic with him, a conditioned reflex, and he could do it quite easily, without breaking his concentration on things beyond the window. And he knew that this bothered her a great deal; so much so, in fact, that she constantly asked him questions, standing by the counter or the sink behind him, to make him aware that she was in the room. She was always nervous when he did not say anything for a long time and he knew this too, and was sometimes silent, even when he had something to say, so that she could hear the thud and swish of the potatoes going into the bag, rhythmically, and the sound of the bags coming down on the scale, and after a second, the sound, sputtering and silken, of the tops of the bags being twisted and sealed in the tape machine. Edward liked to produce these sounds for her because he knew she wanted something more.

Miss Hester had toes like the Barefoot Lady, except that her nails were shorter and cleaner, and except that she was white. She always wore sandals, was hefty like a man, and had hair under her arms. Whenever she smiled he could not think of her face or smile as that of a woman. It was too tight. And her laugh was too loud and came from too far away inside her. And the huge crates of lettuce or cantaloupes or celery she could lift very easily made her even less a woman. She had short red-brown hair, and whenever he got very close to her it seemed very much unlike the Rich Old Lady's smell.

"What you daydreamin' about so much all the time?" she asked him once.

"I was just thinking, Miss Hester," he had said.

"What about?"

"School and things."

He could sense her standing behind him at the sink, letting her hands pause on the knife and the celery she was trimming.

"You gonna finish high school?"

"I guess so."

"You must be pretty smart, huh Tommy?"

"No. I ain't so smart," he said.

"But you sure do think a lot."

"Maybe I just daydream," Thomas told her.

Her knife had started cutting into the celery branches again. He kept up his bagging.

"Well, anyway, you a good worker. You a good boy, Tommy."

Thomas did not say anything.

"Your brother, he's a good worker too. But he ain't like you, though."

"I know," he said.

"He talks a lot up front. All the cashiers like him a lot."

"Eddie likes to talk," Thomas said.

"Yeah," said Miss Hester. "Maybe he talks too much. Mr. Milton and Miss Sarah are watchin' him."

"What for?"

She stopped cutting the celery again. "I donno," she said. "I reckon it's jest that he talks a lot."

IV

On Saturday nights Thomas and his brother would buy the family groceries in the Feinberg Super Market. Checking the list made out by his mother gave Thomas a feeling of responsibility that he liked. He was free to buy things not even on the list and he liked this too. They paid for the groceries out of their own money, and doing this, with some of the employees watching, made an especially good feeling for him. Sometimes they bought ice cream or a pie or something special for their mother. This made them exceptional. The other black employees, the carry-out boys, the stock clerks, the bag boys, would have no immediate purpose in mind for their money beyond eating a big meal on Saturday nights or buying whiskey from a bootlegger because they were minors, or buying a new pair of brightly colored pants or pointed shoes to wear into the store on their day off, as if to make all the other employees see that they were above being, at least on this one day, what they were all the rest of the week.

Thomas and his brother did not have a day off: they worked straight through the week, after school, and they worked all day on Saturdays. But Edward did not mop on Sunday mornings and he still went to church. Thomas felt relieved that his brother was almost certain to be on the Right Side on That Day because he had stayed in the church and would never be exposed to all the stealing the mopping crew did when they were alone in the store on Sunday mornings with Benny Bills, the manager, who looked the other way when they stole packages of meat and soda and cartons of cigarettes. Thomas suspected that Mr. Bills was stealing bigger things himself, after they had finished mopping and waxing and after he had locked the crew out of the store just after twelve o'clock each Sunday. Thomas also suspected that Milton Feinberg, a big-boned man who wore custom-made shoes and smoked very strong bad-smelling green cigars, knew just what everyone was stealing and was only waiting for a convenient time to catch certain people. He could see it in the way he smiled and rolled the cigar around in his mouth whenever he talked to certain of the bigger stealers; and seeing this, Thomas never stole. At first he thought it was because he was afraid of Milton Feinberg, who had green eyes that

could look as deep as Mrs. Quick's; and then he thought to himself that he could not do it because the opportunity only came on Sunday mornings when, if he had never told that first lie, he should have been in church.

Milton and his sister, Sarah Feinberg, liked him. He could tell it by the way Sarah Feinberg always called him up to her office to clean. There were always rolls of coins on her desk, and scattered small change on the floor when he swept. But he never touched any of it. Instead, he would gather what was on the floor and stack the coins very neatly on her desk. And when she came back into the office after he had swept and mopped and waxed and dusted and emptied her wastebaskets, Sarah Feinberg would smile at Thomas from behind her little glasses and say: "You're a good boy, Tommy."

He could tell that Milton Feinberg liked him because whenever he went to the bank for money he would always ask Thomas to come out to the car to help him bring the heavy white sacks into the store, and sometimes up to his office. On one occasion, he had picked Thomas up on the street, after school, when Thomas was running in order to get to work on time. Milton Feinberg had driven him to the store.

"I like you," Milton Feinberg told Thomas. "You're a good worker."

Thomas could think of nothing to say.

"When you quit school, there'll be a place in the store for you."

"I ain't gonna quit school," Thomas had said.

Milton Feinberg smiled and chewed on his green cigar. "Well, when you finish high school you can come on to work full time. Miss Hester says you're a good worker."

"Bagging potatoes is easy," said Thomas.

Milton Feinberg smiled again as he

drove the car. "Well, we can get you in the stockroom, if you can handle it. Think you can handle it?"

"Yeah," said Thomas. But he was not thinking of the stockroom and unloading trucks and stacking cases of canned goods and soap in the big, musty upstairs storeroom. He was thinking of how far away he was from finishing high school and how little that long time seemed to matter to Milton Feinberg.

V

Thomas was examining a very ugly man from behind his window one afternoon when Miss Hester came into the produce room from the front of the store. As usual, she stood behind him. Thomas was aware of her eyes on his back. He could feel them on his shoulders as he pushed potatoes into the plastic bags. Miss Hester was silent. And Thomas went on with his work and watching the very ugly man. This man was bald and had a long, thin red nose that twisted down unnaturally, almost to the same level as his lower lip. The man had no chin, but only three layers of skin that lapped down onto his neck like a red cloth necklace. Harry Jackson, one of the stock clerks who occasionally passed through the produce room to steal an apple or a banana, had christened the very ugly man "*Do-funny*," just as he had christened Thomas "Little Brother" soon after he had come to the job when he was thirteen. Looking at Do-funny made Thomas sad: he wondered how the man had lost his chin. Perhaps, he thought, Do had lost it in the war, or perhaps in a car accident. He was trying to picture just how Do-funny would look after the accident when he realized that his chin was gone forever, when Miss Hester spoke from behind him.

"Your brother's in a lotta trouble up front," she said.

Thomas turned to look at her. "What's the matter?"

Miss Hester smiled at him in that way she had, like a man.

"He put a order in the wrong car."

"Did the people bring it back?"

"Yeah," she said. "But some folks is still missin' their groceries. They're out there now mad as hell."

"Was it Eddie lost them?"

"Yeah. Miss Sarah is mad as hell. Everybody's standin' round up there."

He looked through the glass window and up the produce aisle and saw his brother coming toward him from the front of the store. His brother was untying the knot in his blue smock when he came in the swinging door of the air-conditioned produce room. His brother did not speak to him but walked directly over to the sink next to Miss Hester and began to suck water from the black hose. He looked very hot but only his nose was sweating. Thomas turned completely away from the window and stood facing his brother.

"What's the matter up front, Eddie?" he said.

"Nothing," his brother replied, his jaws tight.

"I heard you put a order in the wrong car and the folks cain't git it back," said Miss Hester.

"Yeah," said Eddie.

"Why you tryin' to hide back here?" she said.

"I ain't tryin' to hide," said Eddie.

Thomas watched them and said nothing.

"You best go on back up front there," Miss Hester said.

At that moment Miss Sarah Feinberg pushed through the door. She had her hands in the pockets of her blue sweater and she walked to the middle of the small, cool room and glared at Edward Brown. The door continued swinging back and forth and making a clicking sound in the time she stood there, silent, short of breath and angry. Thomas dropped a half-filled bag of potatoes down into the cart and waited with his brother.

"Why are you back here?" Miss Sarah Feinberg asked Edward.

"I come back for some water."

"You know you lost twenty-seven dollars' worth of groceries up there?"

"It wasn't my fault," said Eddie.

"If you kept your mind on what you're supposed to do this wouldn't have happened. But no! You're always talking, always smiling around, always running your mouth with everybody."

"The people who got the wrong bags might bring them back," Eddie said. His nose was still sweating in the cool room. "Evidently somebody took my cart by mistake."

"*Evidently! Evidently!*" said Miss Sarah Feinberg. "Miss Hester, you should please listen to *that! Evidently*. You let them go to school and they think they know everything. *Evidently*, you say?"

"Yeah," said Eddie. Thomas saw that he was about to cry.

Miss Hester was still smiling like a man.

Miss Sarah Feinberg stood with her hands in her sweater pockets and braced on her hips, looking Eddie in the face. Eddie did not hold his eyes down and Thomas felt really good but sad that he did not.

"You get back up front," said Miss Sarah Feinberg. And she shoved her way through the door again and out of the cool produce room.

"Evidently, evidently, that sure was funny," said Miss Hester when the fat woman was halfway down the produce aisle. "Lord, was she mad. I ain't never seen her git so mad."

Neither Thomas nor Eddie said anything.

Then Miss Hester stopped smiling.

"You best git on back up front, Eddie."

"No," said Eddie. "I'm goin' home."

"You ain't quittin'?" said Miss Hester.

"Yeah."

"What for?"

"I donno. I just gotta go home."

"But don't your folk need the money?"

"No," Eddie said.

He took off his blue smock and laid it on the big pile of fifty-pound potato sacks. "I'm goin' home," he said again. He did not look at his brother. He walked through the door and Thomas watched him walk slowly down the produce aisle and then out the front door, without looking at anything at all.

Then Thomas went over to the stack of potato sacks and pushed the blue smock off the top sack and into a basket on the floor next to the stack. He picked up a fifty-pound sack and lugged it over to the cart and tore it open with his fingers, spilling its contents of big and small dirty brown potatoes into the cart. He could feel Miss Hester's eyes on him, on his arms and shoulders and hands as they moved. He changed the weights on the scale and began to put the potatoes into five-pound bags. He could feel Miss Hester's eyes on his back as he worked. He worked very quickly and looked out the window into the store. Big Funk was supposed to come this afternoon. Thomas had finished seven five-pound bags before Miss Hester moved from where she had been standing behind him, and he knew she was about to speak.

"You going to quit too, Tommy?"

"No," he said.

"I guess your folk *do* need the money now, huh?"

"No," he said. "We don't need the money."

She did not say anything else. Thomas was thinking about Big Funk and what could be done with the time if he did not come. He did not want to think about his brother or his mother or the money, or even the good feeling he got when Milton Feinberg saw them buying the Saturday night groceries. If Big Funk did not come, then perhaps he could catch another glimpse of Do-funny before he left the store. The Rich Old Lady would not come again until next week. He decided that it would be necessary to record the faces and bodies of new people as they wandered, selectively, with their shopping carts beyond the big window glass. He liked it very much now that none of them ever looked up and saw him watching. That way he did not ever have to feel embarrassed or guilty. That way he would never have to feel compelled to nod his head or move his mouth or eyes, or make any indication of a greeting to them. That way he would never have to feel bad when they did not speak back.

VI

In his bed that night, lying very close to his brother's breathing back, Thomas thought again very seriously about the Judgment Day and the Left Side. Now, there were certain people he would like to have with him on the Left Side, on That Day. He thought about church and how he could never go back because of the place where the deacons had made him tell his first great lie. He wondered whether it was because he did not want to have to go back to church on Sunday mornings that he had not quit. He wondered if it was because of the money or going to church or because of the window that he had not walked out of the store with his brother. That would have been good: the two of them walking out together. But he had not done it and now he could not make himself know why. Suddenly, in the night, he heard the

Barefoot Lady, under the blue-and-white Herbert L. Jones sign, screaming.

"Mr. Jones! I love you, Mr. Jones!"

But the sound did not frighten him now. He pushed against his brother's back.

"Eddie? *Eddie.*"

"Yeah?"

"Wonder why she does it?"

"I donno."

"I wonder why," he said again.

Eddie did not answer. But after the sound of the woman came again his brother turned over in the bed and said to Thomas:

"You gonna quit?"

"No."

"Why not? We could always carry papers."

"I dunno. I just ain't gonna quit. Not now."

"Well *I* ain't goin' back. I'll go back in there one day when I'm rich. I'm gonna go in and buy everything but hamburger."

"Yeah," said Thomas. But he was not listening to his brother.

"Mr. Jones! I love you, Mr. Jones!"

"And I'm gonna learn all the big words in the world too," his brother went on. "When I go back in there I'm gonna be talking so big that fat old Miss Sarah won't even be able to understand me."

"That'll be good," said Thomas. But he was thinking to himself now.

"You'll see," said Eddie. "I'll do it, too."

But Thomas did not answer him. He was waiting for the sound to come again.

"Mr. Jones! I love you, Mr. Jones!"

And then he knew why the Barefoot Lady came to that place almost every night to cry where there was no one alive in the building to hear or care about her sound. He felt what she must feel. And he knew now why the causes of the sound had always bothered him and would always bother him. There was a word in his mind now, a big word, that made good sense of her sound and the burning feeling thing he felt inside himself. It was all very clear, and now he understood that the Barefoot Lady came in the night not because she really loved Mr. Jones or because he had once buried someone for her for free, or even because she liked the blue-and-white lighted sign. She came always in the night to scream because she, like himself, was in misery, and did not know what else to do.

For Consideration

1. The early part of the story sets the scene of Thomas' home and family life in vivid terms. What is his relationship with his mother? With his brother? What effect is created by the characterizations of Mrs. Quick, the Crab Lady, and the Barefoot Lady? Of what significance is the close proximity of the Herbert A. Jones Funeral Parlor?

2. What connections are there between the circumstances of Thomas' home surroundings and his work at the supermarket? What is his relative position in each environment? How does the author provide a transition between the two locales?

3. Contemplating his decision to keep his job though his brother has quit, Thomas "could not make himself know why" he stayed. Why do you think he stayed on? What is the source of the misery he feels at the end of the story? Is it more than a sibling association with his brother's plight?

4. What is the significance of Thomas' final sympathy with the Barefoot Lady? What is the matter of vocabulary, the "big word," that gives the story its title?

TONI CADE BAMBARA   (1939–   )

My Man Bovanne

Blind people got a hummin jones if you notice. Which is understandable completely once you been around one and notice what no eyes will force you into to see people, and you get past the first time, which seems to come out of nowhere, and it's like you in church again with fat-chest ladies and old gents gruntin a hum low in the throat to whatever the preacher be saying. Shakey Bee bottom lip all swole up with

Sweet Peach and me explainin how come the sweet-potato bread was a dollar-quarter this time stead of dollar regular and he say uh huh he understand, then he break into this *thizzin* kind of hum which is quiet, but fiercesome just the same, if you ain't ready for it. Which I wasn't. But I got used to it and the onliest time I had to say somethin bout it was when he was playin checkers on the stoop one time and he commenst to hummin quite churchy seem to me. So I says, "Look here Shakey Bee, I can't beat you and Jesus too," He stop.

So that's how come I asked My Man Bovanne to dance. He ain't my man mind you, just a nice ole gent from the block that we all know cause he fixes things and the kids like him. Or used to fore Black Power got hold their minds and mess em around till they can't be civil to ole folks. So we at this benefit for my niece's cousin who's runnin for somethin with this Black party somethin or other behind her. And I press up close to dance with Bovanne who blind and I'm hummin and he hummin, chest to chest like talkin. Not jammin my breasts into the man. Wasn't bout tits. Was bout vibrations. And he dug it and asked me what color dress I had on and how my hair was fixed and how I was doin without a man, not nosy but nice-like, and who was at this affair and was the canapés dainty-stingy or healthy enough to get hold of proper. Comfy and cheery is what I'm tryin to get across. Touch talkin like the heel of the hand on the tambourine or on a drum.

But right away Joe Lee come up on us and frown for dancing so close to the man. My own son who knows what kind of warm I am about; and don't grown men call me long distance and in the middle of the night for a little Mama comfort? But he frown. Which ain't right since Bovanne can't see and defend himself. Just a nice old man who fixes toasters and busted irons and bicycles and things and changes the lock on my door when my men friends get messy. Nice man. Which is not why they invited him. Grass roots you see. Me and Sister Taylor and the woman who does heads at Mamies and the man from the barber shop, we all there on account of we grass roots. And I ain't never been souther than Brooklyn Battery and no more country than the window box on my fire escape. And just yesterday my kids tellin me to take them countrified rags off my head and be cool. And now can't get Black enough to suit em. So everybody passin sayin My Man Bovanne. Big deal, keep steppin and don't even stop a minute to get the man a drink or one of them cute sandwiches or tell him what's goin on. And him standin there with a smile ready case someone do speak he want to be ready. So that's how come I pull him on the dance floor and we dance squeezin past the tables and chairs and all them coats and people standin round up in each other face talkin bout this and that but got no use for this blind man who mostly fixed skates and skooters for all these folks when they was just kids. So I'm pressed up close and we touch talkin with the hum. And here come my daughter cuttin her eye at me like she do when she tell me about my "apolitical" self like I got hoof and mouf disease and there ain't no hope at all. And I don't pay her no mind and just look up in Bovanne shadow face and tell him his stomach like a drum and he laugh. Laugh real loud. And here come my youngest, Task, with a tap on my elbow like he the third-grade monitor and I'm cuttin up on the line to assembly.

"I was just talkin on the drums," I explained when they hauled me into the kitchen. I figured drums was my best defense. They can get ready for drums what with all this heritage business. And

Bovanne stomach just like that drum Task give me when he come back from Africa. You just touch it and it hum thizzm, thizzm. So I stuck to the drum story. "Just drummin that's all."

"Mama, what are you talkin about?"

"She had too much to drink," say Elo to Task cause she don't hardly say nuthin to me direct no more since that ugly argument about my wigs.

"Look here Mama," say Task, the gentle one. "We just tryin to pull your coat. You were makin a spectacle of youself out there dancing like that."

"Dancin like what?"

Task run a hand over his left ear like his father for the world and his father before that.

"Like a bitch in heat," say Elo.

"Well uhh, I was goin to say like one of them sex-starved ladies gettin on in years and not too discriminating. Know what I mean?"

I don't answer cause I'll cry. Terrible thing when your own children talk to you like that. Pullin me out the party and hustlin me into some stranger's kitchen in the back of a bar just like the damn police. And ain't like I'm old old. I can still wear me some sleeveless dresses without the meat hangin off my arm. And I keep up with some things through my kids. Who ain't kids no more. To hear them tell it. So I don't say nuthin.

"Dancin with that tom," say Elo to Joe Lee, who leanin on the folks' freezer. "His feet can smell a cracker a mile away and go into their shuffle number post haste. And them eyes. He could be a little considerate and put on some shades. Who wants to look into them blown-out fuses that — "

"Is this what they call the generation gap?" I say.

"Generation gap," spits Elo, like I suggested castor oil and fricassee possum in the milk-shakes or somethin. "That's a

white concept for a white phenomenon. There's no generation gap among Black people. We are a col — "

"Yeh, well never mind," says Joe Lee. "The point is Mama . . . well, it's pride. You embarrass yourself and us too dancin like that."

"I wasn't shame." Then nobody say nuthin. Them standin there in they pretty clothes with drinks in they hands and gangin up on me, and me in the third-degree chair and nary a olive to my name. Felt just like the police got hold to me.

"First of all," Task say, holding up his hand and tickin off the offenses, "the dress. Now that dress is too short, Mama, and too low-cut for a woman your age. And Tamu's going to make a speech tonight to kick off the campaign and will be introducin you and expecting you to organize the council of elders — "

"Me? Didn nobody ask me nuthin. You mean Nisi? She change her name?"

"Well, Norton was supposed to tell you about it. Nisi wants to introduce you and then encourage the older folks ass. And people'll say, 'Ain't that the horny bitch that was to form a Council of the Elders to act as an advisory — ' "

"And you going to be standing there with your boobs out and that wig on your head and that hem up to your grindin with the blind dude?"

"Elo, be cool a minute," say Task, gettin to the next finger. "And then there's the drinkin. Mama, you know you can't drink cause next thing you know you be laughin loud and carryin on," and he grab another finger for the loudness. "And then there's the dancin. You been tattooed on the man for four records straight and slow draggin even on the fast numbers. How you think that look for a woman your age?"

"What's my age?"

"What?"

"I'm axin you all a simple question. You keep talkin bout what's proper for a woman my age. How old am I anyhow?" And Joe Lee slams his eyes shut and squinches up his face to figure. And Task run a hand over his ear and stare into his glass like the ice cubes goin calculate for him. And Elo just starin at the top of my head like she goin rip the wig off any minute now.

"Is your hair braided up under that thing? If so, why don't you take it off? You always did do a neat cornroll."

"Uh huh," cause I'm thinkin how she couldn't undo her hair fast enough talking bout cornroll so countrified. None of which was the subject. "How old, I say?"

"Sixtee-one or —"

"You a damn lie Joe Lee Peoples."

"And that's another thing," say Task on the fingers.

"You know what you all can kiss," I said, gettin up and brushin the wrinkles out my lap.

"Oh, Mama," Elo say, puttin a hand on my shoulder like she hasn't done since she left home and the hand landin light and not sure it supposed to be there. Which hurt me to my heart. Cause this was the child in our happiness fore Mr. Peoples die. And I carried that child strapped to my chest till she was nearly two. We was close is what I'm tryin to tell you. Cause it was more me in the child than the others. And even after Task it was the girlchild I covered in the night and wept over for no reason at all less it was she was a chub-chub like me and not very pretty, but a warm child. And how did things get to this, that she can't put a sure hand on me and say Mama we love you and care about you and you entitled to enjoy yourself cause you a good woman?

"And then there's Reverend Trent," say Task, glancin from left to right like they hatchin a plot and just now lettin me in

on it. "You were suppose to be talking with him tonight, Mama, about giving us his basement for campaign headquarters and —"

"Didn nobody tell me nuthin. If grass roots mean you kept in the dark I can't use it. I really can't. And Reven Trent a fool anyway the way he tore into the widow man up there on Edgecomb cause he wouldn't take in three of them foster children and the woman not even comfy in the ground yet and the man's mind messed up and —"

"Look here," say Task. "What we need is a family conference so we can get all this stuff cleared up and laid out on the table. In the meantime I think we better get back into the other room and tend to business. And in the meantime, Mama, see if you can't get to Reverend Trent and —"

"You want me to belly rub with the Reven, that it?"

"Oh damn," Elo say and go through the swingin door.

"We'll talk about all this at dinner. How's tomorrow night, Joe Lee?" While Joe Lee being self-important I'm wonderin who's doin the cookin and how come nobody ax me if I'm free and do I get a corsage and things like that. Then Joe nod that it's O.K. and he go through the swingin door and just a little hubbub come through from the other room. Then Task smile his smile, looking just like his daddy, and he leave. And it just me in this stranger's kitchen, which was a mess I wouldn't never let my kitchen look like. Poison you just to look at the pots. Then the door swing the other way and it's My Man Bovanne standin there sayin Miss Hazel but lookin at the deep fry and then at the steam table, and most surprised when I come up on him from the other direction and take him on out of there. Pass the folks pushin up towards the stage where Nisi and some other people settin and ready to talk, and folks gettin to the last of the sandwiches and the booze fore they settle down in one spot and listen serious. And I'm thinkin bout tellin Bovanne what a lovely long dress Nisi got on and the earrings and her hair piled up in a cone and the people bout to hear how we all gettin screwed and gotta form our own party and everybody there listenin and lookin. But instead I just haul the man on out of there, and Joe Lee and his wife look at me like I'm terrible, but they ain't said boo to the man yet. Cause he blind and old and don't nobody there need him since they grown up and don't need they skates fixed no more.

"Where we goin, Miss Hazel?" Him knowin all the time.

"First we gonna buy you some dark sunglasses. Then you comin with me to the supermarket so I can pick up tomorrow's dinner, which is goin to be a grand thing proper and you invited. Then we goin to my house."

"That be fine. I surely would like to rest my feet." Bein cute, but you got to let men play out they little show, blind or not. So he chat on bout how tired he is and how he appreciate me takin him in hand this way. And I'm thinkin I'll have him change the lock on my door first thing. Then I'll give the man a nice warm bath with jasmine leaves in the water and a little Epsom salt on the sponge to do his back. And then a good rubdown with rose water and olive oil. Then a cup of lemon tea with a taste in it. And a little talcum, some of that fancy stuff Nisi mother sent over last Christmas. And then a massage, a good face massage round the forehead which is the worryin part. Cause you gots to take care of the older folks. And let them know they still needed to run the mimeo machine and keep the spark plugs clean and fix the mailboxes for folks who might help us get the breakfast program goin, and the school for the little kids and the campaign and all. Cause old folks is the nation. That what Nisi was sayin and I mean to do my part.

"I imagine you are a very pretty woman, Miss Hazel."

"I surely am," I say just like the hussy my daughter always say I was.

For Consideration

1. What do you know about the narrator after reading a few paragraphs? What is the advantage of having the story told with first-person point of view?

2. What is revealed about conflicts between generations? What is the narrator's attitude toward those conflicts?

3. Why are Mama's children concerned about her? Is their interest selfish or selfless?

4. Why does Mama persist in relating to "my man Bovanne"? What is her motive for doing so?

5. Mama thinks that "old folks is the nation." What does she mean? Is she necessarily correct?

6. What does the ending lead us to conclude about Mama? Who controls her life?

DAVID BLACK (1945–   )
Laud

When my father was fifty-eight years old, after reading Henri Troyat's biography of Tolstoy, he ran away from home. Having packed a red wool shirt, a faded pair of Levi's, a change of underwear, and three pairs of gray ski socks, he walked the mile from his house on Maplewood Terrace to Route 91 north, and sticking out his thumb, hitched a ride with a Friendly Ice Cream Shop manager to West Springfield, where after a wait of half an hour he picked up a second ride with a teen-aged boy traveling from Staten Island to Warwick, Massachusetts, to visit a religious commune called the Brotherhood of the Spirit.

"They sleep during the day," my father later explained to us, his eyes squinting in the dim light of the single sixty-watt bulb that swung above our kitchen table through clouds of insects, "and farm at night. Their leader is twenty-two years old, twenty-two, twenty-three, Michael somebody, a Greek name, and he also sings in a rock band. These communities interest me. . . ."

A third ride with a dairy farmer along Route 116 to Route 47 brought my father within seven miles of the farmhouse which Maxie and I had rented.

"I asked the farmer about these communes," my father said. "He seemed to like them. He kept saying over and over that his two sons couldn't wait to go to New York or San Francisco and that he admired the kids who left the cities to farm. It made me proud of you. . . ."

Before leaving Springfield, my father had written a letter which he gave to me with a warning not to read until after he'd gone. His destination was unclear. Nova Scotia perhaps, Wyoming, Mexico. The letter said:

Dear Dennis, when you were seven under an influence we were never able to determine — Hopalong Cassidy, Tom Corbett and His Space Cadets, probably one of your television heroes — you ran away from home.

We found you around the corner, pushing along on your scooter. Since you hadn't left in anger, you evidently thought when you saw us that we'd come to give you a cheerful send-off.

You were enraged when we demanded that you turn your scooter around. We were being unreasonable in trying to abort your adventure.

I have no doubt that I will be as unsuccessful now as you were then. The terribly embarrassing thing is not being able to explain why one left in the first place.

I left your mother an inadequate note. Undoubtedly she'll also see this one, which won't explain anything either.

I didn't leave because I was unhappy. I wasn't angry. I wasn't suffocating. But I am running away. From what? Nothing.

I may not be able to tell you these things — not that any of them are particularly revealing — when I see you, but I did want to leave you with some kind of comment. At least an intimate gesture.

When we meet, both of us I'm sure will be too disturbed (or embarrassed) to make any kind of peace with each other.

For twenty-eight years, my father had

taught English in the Springfield public school system with the passionate conviction that he was saving souls, although, because he was an atheist, he would never have phrased it that way. He had been raised in the Mount Sinai Orphanage in Boston as an orthodox Jew and had early abandoned Yahweh to the adults in the home who beat him when he misbehaved and ignored him when he didn't.

His father, my grandfather, Aaron, deserted his children in 1921, freeing himself to scheme for various unattained fortunes. The few times he showed up at the orphanage to take my father on outings, after delicatessen lunches — whitefish with lemon, knockwurst and sauerkraut, lox, knishes, pirogi — he would give my father bootleg gin to deliver. His most horrible childhood experience, my father once told me, was when he tripped climbing onto a trolley and smashed a bottle. Terror of police and shame at having failed overwhelmed him. He watched the trolley clatter away and then, sneaking through alleys and yards, raced to the orphanage, convinced that he would be sent to the reformatory.

His second most horrible childhood experience, he said, was when he was angry with his older brother, Abraham, for beating him up in the school yard. While Abraham was showering, my father threw a canful of lye at him. Abraham, screaming, shot flat against the shower wall, his back and right side puffing like burning marshmallow. My father rushed into the orphanage kitchen, stole a half-pound slab of butter — for which he was later thrashed — and crouching in the fetid, gray, dormitory shower, smeared the butter over his brother's quivering body.

Abraham goaded the orphanage kids to fight the Catholic gangs in the neighborhood. In a side street behind a kosher butcher shop, he was knifed in the chest. My father, although shorter and younger than the others, fought for and gained control of the Mount Sinai gang, to lead them in a war against those who'd killed his brother, to prove he was tougher than his brother had been.

To reinforce his leadership, my father staged a raid on the food stores in the orphanage cellar, escaping punishment by hiding in a flour barrel when he heard one of the cooks coming down the stairs. He led his cronies to the fourth-floor laundry shoot, down which he jumped, sixty feet. The expected billowing pile of sheets was not waiting for him below. My father shattered his leg, driving the bone two inches into his hip. Terrified of punishment, my father hobbled on his smashed limb for the rest of the day, twisted in a white pain through the night, and fainted at the washroom sink the following morning.

While in the hospital, he did chin-ups on a bar that he had placed across his bed and, once on his feet, learned to throw his crutch; so when back on the street he was taunted by gang members who stood just out of reach, he was able to turn the crutch into a successful weapon. After cracking one tormentor's spine and permanently paralyzing him, my father was sent into a special disciplinary ward, where he learned woodwork, printing, and how to play the trumpet.

One of his teachers, a twenty-six-year-old wire manufacturer's daughter who had insisted on working with the incorrigibles, having been attracted by my father's intelligence, spent hours with him after classes, giving him books, playing him scratchy 78's of Bix Beiderbecke. On a rainy afternoon, while listening to "Mississippi Mud" with Bing Crosby and Frank Trambauer on vocals, my father ran his hand up her skirt.

She slapped him. He slapped her back just as her boyfriend, a Harvard graduate student in mathematics, walked in the door. To escape what he assumed would be a stretch in the reformatory, my father left the orphanage that night. He was seventeen, a fair trumpet player with a love for jazz and a determination to go to college.

He got a job in New York at a club called the Blue Room, sitting in for the regular trumpet player, a man called D'Agostino, who was dead drunk when he wasn't gambling and gambling when he should have been performing at the club. One night in a poker game with D'Agostino and Larry Craft, a gangster with a bad stomach who drank alternately from a tumbler of rye and one of cream, my father exploited a remarkable luck and won three thousand dollars. After the game, he taxied home and, before going to bed, wrote a letter asking for an application for admission to Boston University.

He conned and wheedled his way into the B.A. program. Between the money he'd saved and the money he'd won, he had enough to pay for tuition and living expenses for two years. He did well, skidded from scholarship to scholarship for eleven years, during which time he collected a dozen languages, an uneasy but extensive acquaintance with English literature, a library of over two thousand books, three degrees, and a wife.

He met my mother while he was living in Gloucester, Massachusetts, with four other members of the World Socialist Party, a pure Marxist conspiracy so innocent that they were not banned from agitating on Boston Common during World War II. The five of them had rented three cabins near the beach. My father lived alone. One Saturday, he cleaned house, threw the trash into the fireplace to burn, and having left some records stacked on the mantel, walked down the road for a swim.

Ethel Diamond, the twenty-four-year-old social worker who in two years would become my mother, was visiting her sister and her new brother-in-law. She threw (accidentally? on purpose? she claims it was a mistake) a beach ball at my father, who was stalking out of the water. He tossed it back. They introduced themselves. He wooed her with an economy of words and well-placed hands. She agreed to walk to his cabin for coffee and cake. On the path they met the postman, who said, "Do you live in the number two cabin up that way?"

My father said, "Yes."

"Well," said the postman, walking on and looking at the letters he was shuffling, "it's burning to the ground."

When I was a child and my father would sit in the twilight on the edge of my bed telling me the story, at this point I would bolt up with a knot in my chest as though I had swallowed a hard ball of cold water and say, "The records caught on fire, didn't they?"

He would nod and stand, making the mattress bounce, and say as he walked through the gloom to my bedroom door. "That's right. They were made of shellac and caught on fire from the trash in the fireplace."

And once, when I was older, almost too old to be told bedtime stories, I said, "That was pretty stupid, leaving them on the mantel, wasn't it?"

My father paused in the door, a dark shape against the hall dusk.

"Yes," he said, "it was stupid." And then half in anger, half in puzzlement, he added, "Don't you know most of life is made up of stupid mistakes?"

I said, "It isn't."

"Good night," said my father.

"It isn't," I repeated; and, as I felt my hold on my father weakening — he was backing into the hall, making calm-down gestures with his hands — I screamed, "It isn't. It isn't. It isn't."

My father stopped his retreat and reentered the bedroom.

"You're in a nice rage," he said.

"No, I'm not," I said, throwing myself back on the bed.

"That's all right," he said. "It's all right to be in a rage. If I hadn't been in a rage, I never would have gone to college. And I'm glad I went." He stood, staring down at me. I twisted like the grubs I used to impale in the backyard. "But save the rage for something worthwhile," he said at last, "because you can use it up on worthless things; and when you need it for something important, it's gone."

The evening my father arrived at our farmhouse, Maxie and I were in the garden. I was squatting by the pole beans, pulling up pigweed and witchgrass. Maxie was kneeling over the carrots, thinning the row.

She straightened and, stepping over the line of feathery stalks, said, "Some old man just walked up our front porch." She turned to me. "Dennis?"

I came down the path between the furrows. My father, still carrying his suitcase, had circled back into sight around the corner of the house. He strolled, glancing up at the second-floor porch, where a Mexican hammock hung. Abandoned books, our current fancies (*Vikram and the Vampire*, Hammett's *Red Harvest*, Father Brown, Lovecraft's map of local western Massachusetts horrors, what else, some books on education, some books on garden insects, a book of popular astronomy with which Maxie and I tried to decipher the night sky), made human-looking lumps — buttocks, shoulder, elbow — in the hammock's blue web. My father put down his suitcase and called up at the shape he assumed was a resting body.

"Hello," he shouted. "Dennis? Maxie?"

The books in the hammock did not resolve themselves into some head, arms, and torso; did not sit up and peer down at my father; did not answer.

"Hey," my father called, "wake up,

Dennis, greet your prodigal pop. I've suddenly become a dropout."

The sun was behind us, balanced on the horizon, large and round as a yawn. When I shouted to him, my father turned and put his hand to his forehead in a salute to shade his eyes.

Bluff and grinning — the bared teeth occasionally turning into a manic grimace — my father described his day's adventures.

"Running away was the climax," he said. "The rest will be an extended, increasingly painful denouement."

Later at dinner, his elbows propped up on the table, my father continued to sketch his running away as though it were a neatly, already completed play. His voice vibrated with the same wheedling urgency that balanced his lectures on a nice edge of curiosity. When I was a freshman in college, one vacation I sat in on his class, partly to judge him with the mean, keen eye of a nineteen-year-old son, partly to probe into the eager pride he roused in me.

He started the class by saying — I wrote it down, irked at having been nudged from my role as critical son into that of appreciative student — "By lumping certain of Shakespeare's plays together under the title of tragedies, you imaginatively annihilate the great differences among them. *Macbeth* touches our scorn as much as our pity. *Hamlet* moves us to an ecstasy of frustration. But it's impossible to read *Lear* without weeping."

That struck me as extraordinary: "It's impossible to read *Lear* without weeping."

I had just read it for a Humanities course and hadn't wept. I was sure none of my father's students had wept. My friends at college had dutifully venerated it, but as far as I knew no one had wept. I was half-sure my father hadn't wept when reading it, that his speech was merely showmanship.

But there was something in the certainty

with which he said it, the absolute conviction that one could not really read the play, understand it, and believe in the old king's despair without shedding tears, which sprung some valve of respect.

At home, my father faltered from one decision to another: should he buy a new car, put up the screens, call so-and-so on the school committee to protest the exclusion of *A Connecticut Yankee in King Arthur's Court* from the list of books to be bought for the following year, wear a white or a pale blue shirt to a retirement dinner. . . . At home, when I would confront him with a bristling assertion which I knew contradicted his opinion ("Wolfe wasn't a very good writer, was he, Dad?"), he would clear his throat, hesitate, temporize, shrug.

In class, there he was, speaking *ex cathedra!* And he seemed to be right.

That evening and for weeks thereafter, I tried to elicit the same sureness from him — about books, music, politics, flavors of ice cream, anything. But he would squint his eyes in pain and, my insistence prickling up against him, step back, step back again, dropping *maybe*'s and *perhaps*'s along the path of his retreat, as though he were both trying to escape and to leave a trail for me to follow.

I couldn't follow him, however — at least, not into his blinking, shrugging insecurity, not even into smiling, cautious ambiguity. I wanted him to be certain, to be absolute, to slam his fist onto a tabletop and say, "Look, kid, you're wrong." But he refused to give me any further demonstration of what I assumed to be his rigid and correct self.

The night he arrived, trying to sound casual, but giddy at the prospect of rupturing the traditional membrane of polite ignorance of each other's intimate motives or excuses which separated us, I asked him why he had always evaded my questions.

"Your questions?" my father mur-mured. "Your questions? Did you ever really want to know what I thought? I always felt you were throwing some kind of noose over my head, and if I had resisted the rope would slip tighter."

"Did you think that?" I asked, apparently surprised, but feeling that he was right and that I had known it all along. "Did you really think I was trying to trap you?"

"Weren't you?" he asked, the pained furtive glance slipping into his eyes like sizzling drops of water skittering onto a hot skillet.

We both flinched, paused at the moment when only anger or love would have carried us into each other's sealed worlds. I tapped my knees with fingers that abruptly seemed large and clumsy. My father crossed his legs and thrust his hands deep into his pockets. His chin touched his chest; and, blinking up over the tops of his glasses, he exchanged one dangerous subject for another.

"Well," he said in an innocent treble, "when am I going to be a grandfather?"

"What do you want to be a grandfather for?" I said. "Isn't being a father hard enough?"

"Hard?" he asked.

"Are you in a hurry to be one?" Maxie leaned back stiffly in her chair, the same way she tenses herself when we're in the car and I take a curve too fast.

Unsure whether Maxie was joking or provoking him, he said, "You've been married three years. I was a father nine months after the vows."

"Marvelous," said Maxie, "how did you manage that?"

"Should I explain the facts of life?" my father asked.

"I know all about them," said Maxie. "You find babies under cabbages. That's what we're growing in our garden. Dennis, why are you shaking your head at me?"

"Why are you being unpleasant?" I asked.

My father, trying to appease Maxie by defending her, accused me.

"You're always finding something wrong," he said. "She's just having a joke."

"I'm not *she*," said Maxie. "Call me by my name."

"What are you yelling at me for?" said my father. "I'm on your side."

"My side?" she said. "What are you talking about? I don't have a side."

Desperately attempting not to be misunderstood, terrified that my father would dismiss her anger as something that he, as a male, could charm away, she grabbed his hands and pulled him toward her.

The contact was not sexual, but an effort to make him know the hungry something in her which wielded her femininity like a weapon. My father became tensed attention, sensing the merely erotic.

"I want a baby," she said.

"Then why don't you have one?" my father asked.

"Because I'm not ready," I said.

The emotional acceleration stopped. There was a noticeable lag in our responses. None of us was sure what had happened. My father untangled his hands from Maxie's grasp and folded them on the table.

"Dennis has this thing about fatherhood," said Maxie, her voice flat, although her neutral tone had set up a flag: this is where I can be hurt; don't hurt me. "Dennis thinks that fathers have to choose between destroying their children or being destroyed by them."

"What about us?" my father asked me. "Do you think I destroyed you?"

Suddenly exposed by his assumption — "Do you think *I* destroyed *you*?" — he started shaking his head no, as though to cue me; and in doing so he was typically offering himself for the sacrifice. He was saying: given the choice between your destruction or my destruction, let us agree upon doing me in.

"Well," he said, "do you think you destroyed me?"

The question was rhetorical. Neither of us was prepared to admit the answer. My father quickly said, "We were talking about babies." But it sounded as though he had said: let's talk about something less important than this male struggle of ours; let's talk about some trifling woman's complaint — "We were talking about babies . . ."

Maxie spilled her coffee over the table. My father grabbed a napkin and began mopping up the mess. When finished, he stuffed the dripping napkin into a glass.

"It's bedtime," he said. "I'm tired." At the bottom of the stairs, he half turned. "Ah, Dennis, I haven't quite settled where I'm going yet. Would it be too much of an inconvenience if I stayed here for a day or two?"

I said, "No. I'd like that."

"Good." He started to go.

"Stay as long as you want."

"Good," he repeated.

"This is as good a place to run away to as any other," I said, realizing as I spoke that willfully, although unconsciously, I had maimed him as surely as if I had just laid a hot poker across his face.

He made a noise halfway between a snort and a guffaw and, having said a gloomy good night, climbed the stairs to his bedroom.

"Are you afraid your son will hate you as much as you hate him?" Maxie asked. She was testing me: if I could hate him, couldn't I also hate her?

"I don't want to have to be a model," I said.

"Do you think we could have a baby in a year?" she said, invoking one of our catechisms. We had fixed scripts for exorcising all the devils of anxiety, anger, love, lust, all the insistent affects that threatened to crowd habit and security from our lives. By varying the old questions and answers slightly every time, we walked through our roles, we safely sneaked forward toward being the people we wanted to become. When Maxie asked, "Do you think we could have a baby in a year?" she was saying, "I'm frightened. I don't recognize you. Play your role."

"Yes, in a year," I should say.

"Yes, in a year we should be settled enough . . ." I should say.

"Yes, in a year. Of course, it depends . . ." I should say.

As in a guessing game, you must try one variation after the other until you find the one that fits, the correct answer.

I said: "I don't want a baby."

"I don't believe you," said Maxie. "You're lying. Aren't you? Aren't you?" Her need had claws. I had not been lying. I had been exploring a growing panic. In bed, when she put her hands flat against my back and asked again, "Weren't you lying?" I gave her, instead of love, the devious gift of a soothing answer: "I was lying, yes."

Maxie and I slept in a large room behind the kitchen to take advantage during cold weather of the fireplace across from which we had placed our bed. Sometime before dawn, a noise woke me; and peering into the dark kitchen, I found my father, luridly lit by the blue and yellow ring of flame on the gas stove.

He wore only his tan slacks, no shirt or shoes, and was whistling Kate Smith's theme song, "When the Moon Comes Over the Mountain." As he poured steaming water from a tea kettle over the coffee in the Melita filter bag, he began singing in a low, nasal, Vaughn Monroe style. The piddling stream of dripping coffee accompanied him. After clanking the kettle back onto the stove and turning off the gas, he switched to a Bing Crosby version of "Because My Baby Don't Mean Maybe Now."

It was too dark to see him, but I heard him shuffling in an easy soft-shoe to his own music. I gauged the distance between our worlds as the difference between Crosby's chorus, nonsense sounds that slid from his mouth like water dribbling through parted lips — "Buh buh ba la, buh buh ba la, ba la" — and the music I would have babbled in the dark, a fierce spray of sound, Little Richard Penniman's "A wop bop a loo mop a lam bam boom . . ."

Not that different after all, because somehow the relaxed syllables of my father's song and the angry syllables of mine both slipped a wedge between the singer and seriousness. Neither chorus meant anything. Or rather, both choruses meant something more than words could have expressed. They were magic chants to invoke some spook of youth. Standing in the dark and letting "Tutti Frutti" bop in my mind beside the music my father was making, I for the first time felt old.

Up until that moment, I had still thought of myself as, say, nineteen. Perhaps twenty or twenty-one at the most. I was stunned. I could slide my imagination back a decade and discover myself as essentially the same person that was standing in the dark kitchen, secretly listening to my father jolt through a repertoire of early jazz and swing. I had a history! I felt like a lucky archaeologist who stumbles onto a terrain fertile with artifacts of an unknown civilization: intact temples buried under soil pocked with pottery, weapons, primitive games, uncrushed skulls, tools, coins, bracelets . . .

The screen door creaked open and banged shut, and I saw a hole in the dark move across the lawn. I followed, letting the screen door bang to alert my father to my presence.

"Maxie?" he asked. "Dennis?"

"Dennis," I said. "You're up early."

"I couldn't sleep," he said. "Sorry I disturbed you."

"I couldn't sleep either," I lied, trying to force an intimacy by admitting to a similar complaint. I couldn't say I was sorry for hurting him earlier, because by acknowledging the injury I would only enlarge it. To establish contact, I had to make myself vulnerable, but I couldn't think of anything sufficiently sensitive. Ever since we had left New York and moved to the farm, my life had been remarkably uneventful, happy. The slight annoyances of the past year were not substantial enough to offer up as a token of my defenselessness. It was like finding yourself at the altar of some blood-thirsty god with only a chipmunk to slaughter and a knife too frail for suicide.

So I lied again, sketching a general anxiety to explain my insomnia. My father rose to the bait, gave the lie flesh by making connections I had not implied.

"Are you having problems with Maxie?" he asked.

Since his question had a slight tremor of intimacy — the father probing the son's misery with the same delicacy used to tease out a splinter with a needle and the same possibility of having to dig painfully into the flesh — I assumed my father felt he'd found a sensitive spot.

"Yes," I said, "a little."

Ready to jab a nerve, he asked, "Is she unfaithful?"

We were exchanging hostages. I won't hurt you if you won't hurt me. I hoped we would make more exchanges, inching closer to each other with each revelation.

It would be painful to admit that Maxie was unfaithful (even though as far as I knew she wasn't), but I supposed my father would not make any deadly attacks. And even if I were wrong and he did, my confidence was a fraud. I wasn't ready to trust my father that entirely. So once more I lied.

"Yes," I said.

He said, "I'm sorry."

"It's nothing serious," I said.

My father laughed, I think, sympathetically.

"You don't sound convincing," he said, and after a pause added, "Well, she's a very attractive woman. Are you going to separate?"

"I don't know," I said.

"Look, Dennis," he said, "you can talk to me." Without stopping, however, to let me talk, he continued, "That would have some kind of neatness to it. Both of us leaving our wives in the same summer. We could become hoboes together." There was another pause. When he laughed again, he had changed his position. I turned quickly around, chilled, as though I feared he'd attack me if I let him get behind me.

"Do you want a drink?" I asked.

"What do you have?"

"Jack Daniel's?"

"OK," he said.

I walked back into the house to get the bottle. On my way out, I hesitated, tiptoed to my bedroom, and feeling in the dark for Maxie's head, kissed her on the cheek. She murmured something and flung an arm up over my neck, pulling me down to kiss me on the side of the mouth. Feeling reassured — I didn't want my lies to conjure up some infidelity — I went outside into the chilly morning. The dark had become gray, and I could make out my father's face.

I offered him the bottle. He drank, wiped his lips with the back of his hand, and handed the liquor back. I drank, gave him the bottle, which he held at his side.

"That's some garden," he said. "That's some garden you've got back there."

"Yeah," I said, slowly moving in that direction beside him. "It's the thing which makes sense out of this place. We're very proud of it." My throat tightened. Here was a revelation, although I wasn't sure that my father would understand. "When we came here," I said, "I was very unsure about giving up a lot of things. Ambition. You know, trying to be a success. Making it in New York. It was like all that was the bone in my life. All winter I'd get these flashes of desperation. I felt completely abandoned. We left this place only a dozen times between October and March — except to drive into the Piggly-Wiggly for food. No one ever came out here. Too far.

"It got so I couldn't read a paper or watch TV without getting terrified and angry. Running scared. Things were happening. I thought they were important. We didn't even know about the invasion of Laos until months afterward. Funny. It was like being stuck in a dream and not being able to get out. Even though it was a fairly pleasant dream. I wanted to go back to New York. Maxie wanted to stay here."

"So that's where the trouble started," said my father.

Yes, I thought, there had been trouble between Maxie and me. Not the kind my father had assumed and I had pretended, but just as serious. Being vulnerable to others, it seemed, was also being vulnerable to yourself. And the real revelations surprise both of you.

"It wasn't true what I said before about Maxie," I said.

My father grunted. I'm not sure he believed me.

"Not in the way I meant it, at least," I added. "But there was . . ."

"Was?"

"Is . . . a little, I guess . . . is a breach. I only said that other thing because — because it seemed like you wanted to believe it and . . ."

"Like I want to believe it?" my father interrupted. "Why would I want to believe Maxie was unfaithful?"

"I don't know," I said. "Why would you?"

It had gotten much lighter. We were standing on the edge of the garden. My father tipped back the bottle and took a long drink after which he handed it to me. I drank, capped the bottle. My father said:

"I envy you, Dennis. I envy you your age, the times in which you grew up, your generation, the fact that you could escape New York, ambition, whatever, I envy you this." He waved to the garden. "Yeah," he said, "this."

We were walking around the garden. I said:

"In the spring, when we planted, all the terrors vanished. It was like watching things grow, having helped them grow, healed all the raw things inside."

"Yes," said my father, "and when winter comes?"

I sighed.

"That," I said, "terrifies me. It's like thinking about death."

"I think about death a lot," said my father. "I figure I've got a decade left. Ten years. Can you imagine that? Ten years." He made a noise that was the beginning of a laugh. "Next year it'll be nine years. Then eight. Then seven. Can you imagine that?"

"Yes," I said.

"No, you can't. No, you can't. What are you? Thirty. You're still invulnerable. Nothing can hurt you."

I started to say something, but he interrupted:

"Shut up. You don't know . . . You don't know . . ." He put a hand over his eyes. "Wouldn't that be remarkable? If I started to cry. God, I envy you. How were you able to do this? How?" He reached up and grabbed an overhanging branch with both hands. "Goddamn me," he said. "Goddamn me, but I want to do something outrageous."

My father went in to bed. I stayed up, made two soft-boiled eggs, which I ate while sitting in the porch rocker and listening to the birds, and an hour later left for Martin's Stables, where I worked three days a week in the barn, shoveling up manure which I spread in the fields to fertilize the grass which was cut, bailed, and carted back into the barn for the horses to eat. Once I asked Mr. Martin why he didn't let the horses graze in the fields and in the natural course of events spread the manure themselves. Tipping his red bald head to the side and opening his eyes wide, he said:

"But, my friend, that wouldn't make sense, would it?"

When I returned home at six-thirty, Maxie dropped her hoe and ran around the tomato plants toward me. She was pointing behind herself at the woods.

"I want him to leave," she said. "I want him to leave tonight." Her face was sunburned, and there was a dried spot of blood on her forehead where she'd squashed a mosquito. "He tried to make love to me today. I was swimming in the stream. He'd followed me down. I guess, since I didn't have any clothes on, he took that as some sort of invitation . . ." She waved her hands in front of her face to brush away bugs. A drop of sweat slid from her right temple down her smudged cheek and trembled on her chin. She slapped at it. "Damn flies," she said.

"Where is he?" I asked, some Oedipal nerve lighting up like a pinball machine.

She gestured. I circled around the garden and climbed the hill into the woods. The path twisted through thick pines, some hickory, birch, beech, red and silver maple . . . After peeling a curl from a black birch, I put the bark under my tongue and let the taste of wintergreen fill my mouth. That and the smell of the purple milkweed blossoms which hung on the top of the knee-high stalks in sunny patches fixed the moment for me. There was an awful joy seeping through the locks in my brain. If I'd found my father then, I would have killed him.

I walked for fifteen minutes until I came to the slope that led down to the stream. Floating in the shallow water, face up, eyes closed, his mouth warped into a miserable grin, my father looked very old. Having stopped at the edge of the bank, I said, "Put your clothes on."

My father opened his eyes.

"I've been waiting for you," he said. "I stayed down here after Maxie left. I couldn't bear to be with her after what I did."

I said, "Get out of the water and get dressed."

"At first," he said, still not moving, just floating there, "I was terrified of what would happen when you got back. It was a curious feeling, to be terrified of one's son. I had all sorts of strange thoughts. If we fought, I figured you'd have the advantage; and I even felt bad that I hadn't beat the shit out of you when you were a kid. You know? To make up for whatever you might do to me today. Then I thought, What the hell. This is what we've both been waiting for. All that talk this morning. You didn't want to get close to me because you loved me. You wanted to get close enough to . . ."

"If I'm going to beat the shit out of you," I said, "I'd rather do it when you're dressed, but if you don't get dressed I'll do it when you're naked."

"Then I thought," my father said, standing, the water running down his body, "that if we fought, maybe it wouldn't be such an uneven match after all." He picked up his shirt and wiped himself off, threw the shirt into the grass, climbed into his slacks. "You've had a pretty soft life, Dennis. You've never fought for blood. I have."

"Do you think I'm afraid of you?" I asked.

"No," he said. We were standing face to face, and I could see the muscles in his shoulders and chest tensing. "But I'm not afraid of you either."

For a long time neither of us said, did anything. A frog started croaking right by our feet. My father licked his lips. I cleared my throat and said:

"You're going to leave tonight, aren't you?"

He said, "Yes."

"Are you going home?"

"Not right away." He blinked, momentarily bringing back the same vacant expression I used to hate, but then he narrowed his eyes and peered very hard at my face. "If I could figure out a way to hurt you," he said, "I would. You condescend. We're not going to be able to know each other until you realize in what way we're equal."

"Good-bye," I said.

He held out his hand. "Good-bye."

I left my father and walked back to the house. It was beginning to get dark. Maxie had set the table for two, and the absence of the third place oppressed me. I left most of my food. The meat loaf smelled stale, rancid. Maxie cleared the table, carried out the garbage, and screamed. I ran onto the porch. Maxie stood at the rocker, the garbage pail spilled on the ground beside her.

In the garden my father was dragging up pole beans, kicking over cabbages, tearing down tomato plants.

"Aren't you going to do anything?" Maxie wailed.

I leaned against the kitchen door and, ready to welcome hate or the rigid fusing of respect to love, watched my father rage.

For Consideration

1. What characteristics of the father are revealed in the opening of the story? What is the relationship between father and son? What is implied in the father's running away from home?

2. What are the consequences of the father's intrusion into the marriage of his son? Is he a threat? Why?

3. What distinction does Dennis make between the two songs that his father and he would sing? How do those songs represent themselves or their lives? Why does Dennis lie to his father a number of times?

4. What promotes the confrontation between Dennis and his father? Is it more than the father's aborted seduction of Maxie? What are the implications of that action? Can it be seen as something other than indecorous or perverse?

5. What is the significance of the father's action at the end of the story? What seems to be Dennis' dominant response — "hate" or "the rigid fusing of respect to love"? Why doesn't he stop his father from destroying the garden?

6. What does "laud" refer to here? Is the title ironic or serious?

For Comparison

Compare Dennis' father to Mama in "My Man Bovanne." Neither fits the stereotype of the older, more sedate, more conservative parent. What motivates the action of each? Their conduct might easily be labeled senile or irresponsible. Do those labels seems satisfactory?

Both "Laud" and "Sonny's Blues" (p. 210) focus on family members who have become isolated from each other. Are the bases for the alienation similar? To what extent does the alienation seem resolved in each story?

David Black / **269**

⩺ POETRY ⩹

introduction

MARIANNE MOORE   (1887–1972)

Poetry

I, too, dislike it: there are things that are important beyond all this
      fiddle.
  Reading it, however, with a perfect contempt for it, one discovers
      in
it after all, a place for the genuine.
  Hands that can grasp, eyes
  that can dilate, hair that can rise   5
    if it must, these things are important not because a

high-sounding interpretation can be put upon them but because they
      are
useful. When they become so derivative as to become
      unintelligible,
the same thing may be said for all of us, that we
  do not admire what   10
    we cannot understand: the bat
      holding on upside down or in quest of something to

eat, elephants pushing, a wild horse taking a roll, a tireless wolf
      under
a tree, the immovable critic twitching his skin like a horse that feels
      a flea, the base-
ball fan, the statistician —   15
    nor is it valid
      to discriminate against 'business documents and

school-books'; all these phenomena are important. One must make a
      distinction
  however: when dragged into prominence by half poets, the result
      is not poetry,
nor till the poets among us can be   20
    'literalists of
  the imagination' — above
      insolence and triviality and can present

for inspection, 'imaginary gardens with real toads in them', shall we
      have
  it. In the meantime, if you demand on the one hand,   25
the raw material of poetry in
  all its rawness and
  that which is on the other hand
    genuine, you are interested in poetry.

Marianne Moore begins "Poetry" with the surprising and significant
pronouncement: "I, too, dislike it." One imagines that Moore has in
mind any number of audiences who have just told her how much they
dislike poetry. The unexpressed disclaimer to which she responds
appears, in fact, to be taken for granted by the poet. We may rightly
assume with her that if most readers (and most students) like a good
story, most would testify that they don't like poetry. As a poet, Moore
does not, of course, simply dismiss poetry as one of any number of un-
liked things. She goes on to persuade her readers, gently and effectively, that there is in poetry a "place for the genuine" and that if one is
interested both in the "raw material" of poetry — which is surely the

18. *business documents and school books* The quotation is taken from the *Diaries of Tolstoy,*
published in 1917. Tolstoy refers to distinctions between poetry and prose but admits his own
uncertainty about differences between the two forms. He adds: "Poetry is verse: prose is not
verse. Or else poetry is everything with the exception of business documents and school
books." **22.** *literalists of the imagination* from Yeats' essay on Blake, whom he criticizes for being "a too literal realist of imagination."

varieties of life itself — and in that which is genuine, one is interested in poetry.

While it is doubtful that many readers who dislike poetry will be immediately converted by Moore's observations, her poem convincingly points to both the problems and the pleasures of reading poetry. Poetry is difficult. Even the most experienced readers, when confronted with a new poem, may find it difficult to read and comprehend the words before them. Poetry is concentrated. It is difficult, at least in part, because it is concentrated. It is usually not the more relaxed language of conversation (though it can be of course), and we are therefore forced to read with extraordinary care and attention. If we daydream while reading part of a story or while seeing part of a play, we may revive in time to understand the essential storyline or plot. But if we daydream while reading a poem we will very likely have to start over again. Because of its usual brevity and concentration, poetry is demanding for a reader. The language of poetry, in addition to being concise (and perhaps in order to be concise), is rich in associations and images; it is, for the most part, a highly figurative language which demands still more of an alert and sensitive reader. Because of its language, poetry is often given over to a "high-sounding interpretation" which Moore refers to with less than great admiration. Many teachers and even more students would confirm that high-sounding interpretations frequently produce skepticism and outright cynicism from the new student of literature. They too often imply that only the privileged few can understand and appreciate poetry, and, admittedly, too often the interpretations begin to take on lives of their own far removed from the poem at hand. At the same time, most readers would admit that without a conscious effort at interpretation, some poems would be more confusing than insightful.

In light of such associations with poetry it is not surprising that any of us might say with Marianne Moore and her imagined audience: "I, too, dislike it."

The balance to this objection, much of which is explored in the remainder of Moore's poem, is that poetry, while demanding a lot from its readers, also rewards them. Its very concentration, one source of its difficulty, is equally a source of richness and precision not found in any other literary form. The nineteenth-century poet and critic Samuel Taylor Coleridge spoke of this precision when he defined prose as "words in their best order" and poetry as "the best words in their best order." The imaged and figurative language of poetry forces a reader to work hard, but it yields insights and pleasures not discovered without the use of such language. Most important of all, poems give us perspectives on life that are, quite simply, not found through any other medium. Just as there is no replacing a story, a drama, a film, or a painting for the unique perspective each brings to its subject, so poetry is equally irreplaceable. No other form captures so briefly and so richly the varieties of life and experience. Those varieties, "the raw material of poetry," are evident in the array of poems in this collection. And the poems provide evidence, too, that poetry is interested in truth, is interested, finally, in that which is "genuine."

"Poetry"   For Consideration

1. What, in spite of her "dislike" of poetry, does the poet find "genuine" in it?

2. Although not wishing to discriminate against "business documents and school-books," the poet confirms that one must make a distinction. Between what?

3. What view of poetry's subject matter is emphasized here? What is the meaning of references to "literalists of the imagination" and "gardens with real toads"? What is the "raw material of poetry"?

Here are some further poems on poetry and the arts. What similarities and differences do you find in the sentiments expressed? How do they relate to your own conception of poetry?

ALFRED, LORD TENNYSON   (1809–1892)
The Poet

The poet in a golden clime was born,
   With golden stars above;
Dower'd with the hate of hate, the scorn of scorn,
   The love of love.

He saw thro' life and death, thro' good and ill,　　　　　　5
　　　He saw thro' his own soul.
The marvel of the everlasting will,
　　　An open scroll,

Before him lay; with echoing feet he threaded
　　　The secretest walks of fame:　　　　　　　　　　10
The viewless arrows of his thoughts were headed
　　　And wing'd with flame,

Like Indian reeds blown from his silver tongue,
　　　And of so fierce a flight,
From Calpe unto Caucasus they sung,　　　　　　　　15
　　　Filling with light

And vagrant melodies the winds which bore
　　　Them earthward till they lit;
Then, like the arrow-seeds of the field flower,
　　　The fruitful wit　　　　　　　　　　　　　　20

Cleaving took root, and springing forth anew
　　　Where'er they fell, behold,
Like to the mother plant in semblance, grew
　　　A flower all gold,

And bravely furnish'd all abroad to fling　　　　　　　25
　　　The winged shafts of truth,
To throng with stately blooms the breathing spring
　　　Of Hope and Youth.

So many minds did gird their orbs with beams,
　　　Tho' one did fling the fire;　　　　　　　　　　30
Heaven flow'd upon the soul in many dreams
　　　Of high desire.

Thus truth was multiplied on truth, the world
　　　Like one great garden show'd,
And thro' the wreaths of floating dark upcurl'd,　　　35
　　　Rare sunrise flow'd.

And Freedom rear'd in that august sunrise
　　　Her beautiful bold brow,
When rites and forms before his burning eyes
　　　Melted like snow.　　　　　　　　　　　　　40

There was no blood upon her maiden robes
　　　Sunn'd by those orient skies;

15. *From Calpe unto Caucasus* From Gibraltar to the Caucasus Mountains, the western and eastern boundaries of the ancient world.

But round about the circles of the globes
     Of her keen eyes

And in her raiment's hem was traced in flame   45
     WISDOM, a name to shake
All evil dreams of power — a sacred name.
     And when she spake,

Her words did gather thunder as they ran,
     And as the lightning to the thunder   50
Which follows it, riving the spirit of man,
     Making earth wonder,

So was their meaning to her words. No sword
     Of wrath her right arm whirl'd,
But one poor poet's scroll, and with *his* word   55
     She shook the world.

For Consideration

1. The poem presents the poet's role as an exalted and prophetic one. What is suggested about a poet's abilities to feel and perceive in the opening two stanzas?

2. Through what image do we see the fruition and influence of his poetry? What particular values does his art promote?

3. What concept of power is enunciated in lines 37–53? Why is there no blood on Freedom's robes?

4. What do the last lines imply about the poet's effect on the world?

WILLIAM CARLOS WILLIAMS (1883–1963)

The Artist

Mr. T.
      bareheaded
            in a soiled undershirt
his hair standing out
      on all sides   5
            stood on his toes
heels together
      arms gracefully
            for the moment
curled above his head.   10
      Then he whirled about
            bounded
into the air
      and with an *entrechat*
            perfectly achieved   15
completed the figure.
      My mother
            taken by surprise
where she sat
      in her invalid's chair   20
            was left speechless.
Bravo! she cried at last
      and clapped her hands.
            The man's wife
came from the kitchen: 25
      What goes on here? she said.
            But the show was over.

For Consideration

1.   The poem is marked by incongruities, particularly the action of the un-kempt man. If the poem, judging from the title, is supposed to be a serious look at the artist, what is it saying?

14. *Entrechat* a ballet jump in which a dancer crosses his or her feet several times while in the air.

2. Why is the man's disgraceful appearance emphasized and juxtaposed against his graceful dance?

3. How does the audience respond? Is the artist's effort seen and appreciated by everyone there? What might be implied about the artistic act itself in the poem?

For Comparison

How do Williams' and Tennyson's conceptions of the artist differ? How does each treat the artist? The art? The audience? Is Williams' view a disparaging one?

ARCHIBALD MacLEISH (1892–)
Ars Poetica

A poem should be palpable and mute
As a globed fruit,

Dumb
As old medallions to the thumb,

Silent as the sleeve-worn stone   5
Of casement ledges where the moss has grown—

A poem should be wordless
As the flight of birds.

A poem should be motionless in time
As the moon climbs,   10

Leaving, as the moon releases
Twig by twig the night-entangled trees,

Leaving, as the moon behind the winter leaves,
Memory by memory the mind—

Title. *Ars Poetica* the art of poetry.

A poem should be motionless in time 15
As the moon climbs.

A poem should be equal to:
Not true.

For all the history of grief
An empty doorway and a maple leaf. 20

For love
The leaning grasses and two lights above the sea—

A poem should not mean
But be.

For Consideration

1. Since a poem is made up of words how can it be "wordless"? What point about poetry is MacLeish making here?

2. How is a poem "motionless in time"?

3. What does the final part of the poem say about poetry's aim? Why is it equal to "not true"? What do the references to grief and love mean in this context?

4. The consummate statement of the poem is the last. Is the poet saying that poems have no meaning? Does this poem have a meaning?

GWENDOLYN BROOKS (1917–   )
The Chicago Picasso

August 15, 1967

"Mayor Daley tugged a white ribbon, loosing the blue percale wrap. A hearty cheer went up as the covering slipped off the big steel sculpture that looks at once like a bird and a woman."

—Chicago *Sun-Times*

(Seiji Ozawa leads the Symphony.
The Mayor smiles.
And 50,000 See.)

Does man love Art? Man visits Art, but squirms.
Art hurts. Art urges voyages—
and it is easier to stay at home,
the nice beer ready.
    In commonrooms   5
we belch, or sniff, or scratch.
Are raw.

But we must cook ourselves and style ourselves for Art, who
is a requiring courtesan.
We squirm.   10
We do not hug the Mona Lisa.
We
may touch or tolerate
an astounding fountain, or a horse-and-rider.

At most, another Lion.   15

Observe the tall cold of a Flower
which is as innocent and as guilty,
as meaningful and as meaningless as any
other flower in the western field.

For Consideration

1.   What is man's relationship to art as portrayed in the poem? What does art
     demand of its audience?

2. The occasion is the unveiling of a sculpture especially designed by Picasso for the city of Chicago; thus the Chicago Picasso is public art. What does the poem say about the likely response of the public to it?

3. What does the final reference to the Flower mean? Why is it at once innocent and guilty, meaningful and meaningless? Is it, in this context, art?

poetic forms

Broadly speaking, poetry may be divided into three species or classes: the **narrative**, the **lyric**, and the **dramatic** poem. The narrative poem, like narrative prose, tells a story. The preeminent example of the narrative poem is the **epic**, a long tale of a great historical or mythical event with heroes and heroines of equal magnitude. Homer's *The Odyssey*, Virgil's *The Aeneid*, Dante's *The Divine Comedy*, and Milton's *Paradise Lost* are four important examples of the epic. Epics are essentially an older narrative form, although a briefer form of narrative poetry, the **ballad**, remains actively produced. Ballads such as "Lord Randal," "The Unquiet Grave," and "Bonny Barbara Allan" are from medieval tradition; "Frankie and Johnny" is more recent in origin but is also anonymous and rooted in popular folk tradition. In a modern vein, songwriters such as Kris Kristofferson ("Sunday Mornin' Comin' Down," "Me and Bobby McGee") or Bob Dylan ("A Hard Rain's A-Gonna Fall," "Desolation Row") continue the ballad tradition. Already we can see that distinctions among the classes of poetry are blurred. The ballad, as a narrative, tells a story in essentially chronological form; as a lyric, it is relatively brief and intended to be sung.

The literary ballad, as distinct from the popular ballad, retains the importance of narrative but aims for more significance in its treatment of theme or image. Keats' "La Belle Dame sans Merci," for example, is based on a popular myth which is freshly worked out by the poet.

ANONYMOUS SCOTTISH BALLAD
(15th CENTURY)

Lord Randal

1

"O where ha' you been, Lord Randal, my son?
And where ha' you been, my handsome young man?"
"I ha' been at the greenwood; mother, mak my bed soon,
For I'm wearied wi' huntin', and fain wad lie down."

2

"And wha met ye there, Lord Randal, my son?   5
And wha met you there, my handsome young man?"
"O I met wi' my true-love; mother, mak my bed soon,
For I'm wearied wi' huntin', and fain wad lie down."

3

"And what did she give you, Lord Randal, my son?
And what did she give you, my handsome young man?"   10
"Eels fried in a pan; mother, mak my bed soon,
For I'm wearied wi' huntin', and fain wad lie down."

4

"And wha gat your leavin's, Lord Randal, my son?
And wha gat your leavin's, my handsome young man?"
"My hawks and my hounds; mother, mak my bed soon,   15
For I'm wearied wi' huntin', and fain wad lie down."

5

"And what becam of them, Lord Randal, my son?
And what becam of them, my handsome young man?"
"They stretched their legs out and died; mother, mak my bed soon,
For I'm wearied wi' huntin', and fain wad lie down."   20

4. *wad* would.   13. *leavin's* remains of the food.

6

"O I fear you are poisoned, Lord Randal, my son!
I fear you are poisoned, my handsome young man!"
"O yes, I am poisoned; mother, mak my bed soon,
For I'm sick at the heart, and I fain wad lie down."

7

"What d' ye leave to your mother, Lord Randal, my son?   25
What d' ye leave to your mother, my handsome young man?"
"Four and twenty milk kye; mother, mak my bed soon,
For I'm sick at the heart, and I fain wad lie down."

8

"What d' ye leave to your sister, Lord Randal, my son?
What d' ye leave to your sister, my handsome young man?"   30
"My gold and my silver; mother, mak my bed soon,
For I'm sick at the heart, and I fain wad lie down."

9

"What d' ye leave to your brother, Lord Randal, my son?
What d' ye leave to your brother, my handsome young man?"
"My houses and my lands; mother, mak my bed soon,   35
For I'm sick at the heart, and I fain wad lie down."

10

"What d' ye leave to your true-love, Lord Randal, my son?
What d' ye leave to your true-love, my handsome young man?"
"I leave her hell and fire; mother, mak my bed soon,
For I'm sick at the heart, and I fain wad lie down."   40

27. *kye* cattle.

For Consideration

1..   Notice the occasions when the ballad makes a slight change in a frequently repeated phrase. What is the effect of these alterations?

2..   The gift bestowed on the "true-love" is left until the end. Why?

ANONYMOUS ENGLISH BALLAD
(15th CENTURY)

The Unquiet Grave

1

"The wind doth blow today, my love,
   And a few small drops of rain;
I never had but one true-love,
   In cold grave she was lain.

2

"I'll do as much for my true-love   5
   As any young man may;
I'll sit and mourn all at her grave
   For a twelvemonth and a day."

3

The twelvemonth and a day being up,
   The dead began to speak: 10
"Oh who sits weeping on my grave,
   And will not let me sleep?"

4

" 'T is I, my love, sits on your grave,
   And will not let you sleep;

For I crave one kiss of your clay-cold lips, 15
    And that is all I seek."

5

"You crave one kiss of my clay-cold lips,
    But my breath smells earthy strong;
If you have one kiss of my clay-cold lips,
    Your time will not be long. 20

6

" 'T is down in yonder garden green,
    Love, where we used to walk,
The finest flower that e'er was seen
    Is withered to a stalk.

7

"The stalk is withered dry, my love, 25
    So will our hearts decay;
So make yourself content, my love,
    Till God calls you away."

For Consideration

1. What prevents the ballad from being a morbid or sentimental look at the death of a loved one?

2. Which of the speakers is the more reasonable?

ANONYMOUS SCOTTISH BALLAD
(15th CENTURY)
Bonny Barbara Allan

It was in and about the Martinmas time,
  When the green leaves were afalling,
That Sir John Graeme, in the West Country,
  Fell in love with Barbara Allan.

He sent his men down through the town,   5
  To the place where she was dwelling:
"O haste and come to my master dear,
  Gin ye be Barbara Allan."

O hooly, hooly rose she up,
  To the place where he was lying,   10
And when she drew the curtain by:
  "Young man, I think you're dying."

"O it's I'm sick, and very, very sick,
  And 'tis a' for Barbara Allan." —
"O the better for me ye's never be,   15
  Tho your heart's blood were aspilling.

"O dinna ye mind, young man," said she,
  "When ye was in the tavern adrinking,
That ye made the health gae round and round,
  And slighted Barbara Allan?"   20

He turned his face unto the wall,
  And death was with him dealing:
"Adieu, adieu, my dear friends all,
  And be kind to Barbara Allan."

And slowly, slowly raise she up,   25
  And slowly, slowly left him.
And sighing said she could not stay,
  Since death of life had reft him.

She had not gane a mile but twa,

8. *Gin* if.   9. *hooly* slowly.   17. *dinna ye mind* don't you remember.   19. *health* toasts.   29. *twa* two.

When she heard the dead-bell ringing, 30
And every jow that the dead-bell geid,
    It cried, "Woe to Barbara Allan!"

"O mother, mother, make my bed!
    O make it saft and narrow!
Since my love died for me today, 35
    I'll die for him tomorrow."

For Consideration

1. Why is Barbara Allan's response so cold to the dying man? What has he done that she still remembers?

2. Why, at the end of the ballad, is Barbara willing to "die for him"? Has she changed within the poem? Where? Why?

JOHN KEATS   (1795—1821)
La Belle Dame sans Merci

O what can ail thee, Knight at arms,
    Alone and palely loitering?
The sedge has withered from the Lake
    And no birds sing!

O what can ail thee, Knight at arms, 5
    So haggard, and so woebegone?
The squirrel's granary is full
    And the harvest's done.

I see a lily on thy brow
    With anguish moist and fever dew, 10
And on thy cheeks a fading rose
    Fast withereth too.

31. *jow* stroke.   **Title.** the beautiful lady without mercy.

"I met a Lady in the Meads,
    Full beautiful, a faery's child,
Her hair was long, her foot was light   15
    And her eyes were wild.

"I made a Garland for her head,
    And bracelets too, and fragrant Zone;
She looked at me as she did love
    And made sweet moan.   20

"I set her on my pacing steed
    And nothing else saw all day long,
For sidelong would she bend and sing
    A faery's song.

"She found me roots of relish sweet,   25
    And honey wild, and manna dew,
And sure in language strange she said
    'I love thee true.'

"She took me to her elfin grot
    And there she wept and sighed full sore,   30
And there I shut her wild wild eyes
    With kisses four.

"And there she lullèd me asleep,
    And there I dreamed, Ah Woe betide!
The latest dream I ever dreamt   35
    On the cold hill side.

"I saw pale Kings, and Princes too,
    Pale warriors, death-pale were they all;
They cried, 'La belle dame sans merci
    Thee hath in thrall!'   40

"I saw their starved lips in the gloam
    With horried warning gapéd wide,
And I awoke, and found me here
    On the cold hill's side.

"And this is why I sojourn here,   45
    Alone and palely loitering;
Though the sedge is withered from the Lake
    And no birds sing."

18. *zone* girdle. 29. *grot* a cavern, but associated too with a crypt. 35. *latest* last.

For Consideration

1. What kind of atmosphere is advanced in the poem? What is the condition of the knight at the beginning?

2. What associations exist between the condition of the knight and the external world?

3. What is the meaning of the knight's dream? What is the warning he receives? How does his subsequent condition show the truth of the warning?

ANONYMOUS AMERICAN BALLAD
(20th CENTURY)

Frankie and Johnny

Frankie she was a good woman, Johnny he was her man,
And every silver dollar Frankie made went straight to her Johnny's
   hand.
He was her man, but he done her wrong.

Frankie and Johnny went walking, Johnny in a brand new suit.
"Cost me a hundred," says Frankie, "but don't my Johnny look
   cute?"   5
He was her man, but he done her wrong.

Frankie went down to the corner, she called for a thimble of gin,
She says to the fat bartender, "Has my lovin' Johnny been in?"
I can't believe he's been doing me wrong."

"Ain't going to tell you no story, ain't going to tell you no lie, 10
Mister Johnny was in here 'bout an hour ago with a floozy named
   Ella Fly.
He is your man, but I believe he's doing you wrong."

Frankie ran down to the pawn shop, she didn't go there for fun.
She turned in her doorknob diamonds, she took out a forty-four gun.
He was her man, but he done her wrong.   15

Frankie ran down to the parlor-house, she leaned on the parlor-house
  bell.
"Stand out of my way, you floozies, or I'll splash you all over Hell!
I want my man, he's been doing me wrong."

Frankie looked over the transom, the tears ran out of her eyes.
There was her lovin' Johnny a-lovin' up Ella Fly.   20
He was her man, but he was doing her wrong.

She threw back her red silk kimono, she whipped out that old
  forty-four
Rooty-toot-toot, three times she did shoot, right through that hardwood
  door.
He was her man, but he done her wrong.

Johnny grabbed off his Stetson, "O Lord no, Frankie, don't shoot!"   25
But Frankie squeezed the trigger three times more and he fell down
  like a stick of wood.
He was her man, but he done her wrong.

The first shot, Johnny staggered; the second shot, he fell;
The third shot took him through the heart and his face started
  coming out in Hell.
He was her man, but he done her wrong.   30

"O roll me over easy, roll me over slow,
Roll me over on my right side, honey, so my heart don't overflow.
I was your man, but I done you wrong."

Bring on your rubber-tired hearses, bring on your rubber-tired hacks.
There's eight men going to the burying yard and only seven of 'em
  coming back.
He was her man, but he done her wrong.   35

The judge look hard at the jury, says, "It's plain as plain can be,
This woman put some daylight through her man, it's murder in the
  second degree.
He was her man, and she done him wrong."   40

Now it wasn't murder in the second degree, it wasn't murder in the
  third,
All Frankie did was drop her man like a hunter drops a bird.
He was her man, but he done her wrong.

The jury went out on Frankie, sat under an electric fan,
Came back and said, "You're a free woman, go kill yourself another
  man   45
If he does you wrong, if he does you wrong."

"O put me away in a dungeon, put me in a cold, cold cell,
Put me where the north wind blows from the southeast corner of
     Hell.
I shot my man, 'cause he done me wrong."

Frankie she heard a rumbling, away down under the ground.   50
Maybe it was little Johnny where she had shot him down.
He was her man, but he done her wrong.

Frankie went out to the burying yard, just to look her Johnny in
     the face.
"Ain't it hard to see you, Johnny, in this lonesome place?"
He was her man, but he done her wrong.   55

Well, I looked down the lonesome street, Lord, as far off as I could
     see,
All I could hear was a two-string fiddle playing, "Nearer, My God, to
     Thee."
He was her man, but he done her wrong.

For Consideration

1. What is the tone of the narrative? Where is it best revealed?

2. Note the line repeated at the end of each stanza. How do the changes in
    the line help carry the story forward?

3. What is suggested about the environment or atmosphere within which
    the events occur? How does the atmosphere add to the narrative?

JOHN LENNON (1940–   )
PAUL McCARTNEY (1942–   )

Eleanor Rigby

Ah, look at all the lonely people!
Ah, look at all the lonely people!

Eleanor Rigby
Picks up the rice in the church where a wedding has been,
Lives in a dream,   5
Waits at the window
Wearing the face that she keeps in a jar by the door.
Who is it for?

All the lonely people,
Where do they all come from?   10
All the lonely people
Where do they all belong?

Father McKenzie,
Writing the words of a sermon that no one will hear,
No one comes near   15
Look at him working,
Darning his socks in the night where there's nobody there.
What does he care?

All the lonely people
Where do they all come from?   20
All the lonely people
Where do they all belong?

Eleanor Rigby
Died in the church and was buried along with her name.
Nobody came.   25
Father McKenzie,
Wiping the dirt from his hands as he walks from the grave,
No one was saved.

All the lonely people,
Where do they all come from?   30
All the lonely people,
Where do they all belong?

Ah, look at all the lonely people!
Ah, look at all the lonely people!

For Consideration

1. How are the lives of Eleanor Rigby and Father McKenzie similar? How are
    they different? How is each representative of "all the lonely people"?

For Comparison

How is this contemporary song similar to the earlier ballads? How can it be distinguished from them?

The **lyric**, as the word suggests, was originally a song intended to be sung to the accompaniment of a stringed instrument called a lyre, a musical association we still retain when we speak of the lyrics of a song. More generally, however, it refers to any poem that is relatively brief and that gives expression to an emotion, a thought, or in a dramatic situation, a reaction. The lyric is, for modern readers, the form most immediately identified with poetry, and is the form for which the comments in the introduction are most applicable. Hence, the lyric occupies most of the attention of this book. The simplest lyric is that which expresses an emotion, a mood, or a single idea.

WILLIAM BLAKE (1757-1827)

Eternity

He who bends to himself a joy
Does the winged life destroy;
But he who kisses the joy as it flies
Lives in eternity's sun rise.

For Consideration

1. What concept of joy is Blake describing in each couplet? Why does the action in the first couplet "destroy" while that in the second gives life?

Most lyrics are not, of course, as short and neat as Blake's poem. Still, we can usually deal with a lyric in one sitting and understand the way it works within a fairly short time.

ANONYMOUS ENGLISH LYRIC   (15th CENTURY)
I Have a Young Sister

I have a young sister
  Far beyond the sea;
Many be the drowries
  That she sente me.

She sente me the cherry   5
  Withouten any stone,
And so she did the dove
  Withouten any bone.

She sente me the briar
  Withouten any rind;   10
She bade me love my leman
  Without longing.

How should any cherry
  Be withoute stone?
And how should any dove   15
  Be withoute bone?

3. *drowries* tokens.   10. *rind* bark.   11. *leman* loved one.

How should any briar
 Be withoute rind?
How should I love my leman
 Without longing?   20

When the cherry was a flower,
 Then hadde it no stone.
When the dove was an egg,
 Then hadde it no bone.

When the briar was unbred,   25
 Then hadde it no rind.
When the maiden hath that she loveth,
 She is without longing.

For Consideration

1. The song is built on several contradictions which turn out to be true. How does the subject of love relate to these?

2. If you know a modern version of this song, jot it down, noting the differences between the two versions.

ANONYMOUS ENGLISH LYRIC (15th CENTURY)
A God and Yet a Man?

A god and yet a man?
 A maid and yet a mother?
Wit wonders what wit can
 Conceive this or the other.

A god and can he die?   5
 A dead man, can he live?

25. *unbred* not grown, still in the seed.

What wit can well reply?
  What reason reason give?

God, truth itself, doth teach it.
  Man's wit sinks too far under
By reason's power to reach it.
  Believe and leave to wonder.

10

For Consideration

1. Like the secular song "I Have a Young Sister," this religious lyric is built on paradoxes, apparent contradictions that turn out to be true. What is the religious basis for the paradoxes here?

2. What is the final admonition to the reader?

GEORGE GORDON, LORD BYRON (1788—1824)

When We Two Parted

When we two parted
  In silence and tears,
Half broken-hearted
  To sever for years,
Pale grew thy cheek and cold,
  Colder thy kiss;
Truly that hour foretold
  Sorrow to this.

The dew of the morning
  Sunk chill on my brow—
It felt like the warning
  Of what I feel now.
Thy vows are all broken,

5

10

12. *leave* cease.

And light is thy fame;
I hear thy name spoken,   15
  And share in its shame.

They name thee before me,
  A knell to mine ear;
A shudder comes o'er me—
  Why wert thou so dear?   20
They know not I knew thee,
  Who knew thee too well—
Long, long shall I rue thee,
  Too deeply to tell.

In secret we met—   25
  In silence I grieve,
That thy heart could forget,
  Thy spirit deceive.
If I should meet thee
  After long years,   30
How should I greet thee?—
  With silence and tears.

For Consideration

1. The poem gives little detail about the former relationship alluded to or about the woman herself, focusing instead on the man's past and present emotions. What type of relationship was it? Who seems to have been responsible for its end?

2. What is the woman doing now? What is suggested by the broken vows, light fame, and shame? What evidence is there that the speaker still feels strongly about the woman?

3. The end of the poem comes full circle, emphasizing the response of "silence and tears." Does it imply the same as the "silence and tears" of line two? What differences might be involved?

EMILY DICKINSON   (1830–1886)
To Make a Prairie

To make a prairie it takes a clover and one bee,
One clover, and a bee,
And revery.
The revery alone will do,
If bees are few.

For Consideration

1.   The poem begins with a quasi-scientific focus. How is it possible for one bee and one clover to make a prairie?

2.   The mention of "revery" alters the emphasis to the extent that the poet finally implies that revery alone is enough to "make a prairie." How has the concept of a prairie shifted in the poem? What qualities are associated with it at the end?

MURIEL RUKEYSER   (1913–   )
This Place in the Ways

Having come to this place
I set out once again
On the dark and marvelous way
From where I began:
Belief in the love of the world,   5
Woman, spirit, and man.

Having failed in all things
I enter a new age

Seeing the old ways as toys,
The houses of a stage   10
Painted and long forgot;
And I find love and rage.

Rage for the world as it is
But for what it may be
More love now than last year.   15
And always less self-pity
Since I know in a clearer light
The strength of the mystery.

And at this place in the ways
I wait for song,   20
My poem-hand still, on the paper,
All night long.
Poems in throat and hand, asleep,
And my storm beating strong!

For Consideration

1. The "place in the ways" represents some kind of turning point or new beginning for the speaker. What values are re-affirmed? In what ways has the speaker come to a "new age"?

2. Why does the speaker feel both rage and love? What is the mystery which lessens her self-pity?

3. What connections does the closing stanza make between the speaker's role as poet and the important point she has reached in her life?

As a generic description, the lyric includes a number of other and more specific forms which, while still lyrical in mode, have characteristics of their own. Three of the important forms are the ode, the elegy, and the sonnet.

An **ode** is usually a longer lyric, rather elaborate and traditionally on some lofty theme. The Greek ode was originally a choral piece, intended as a lengthy song of praise to the gods or heroes. The English ode has included less emphasis on the specific subject of the poem and has assumed no particular length, but it has retained the quality of praise. Poems such as Wordsworth's "Ode: Intimations of Immortality," Shelley's "Ode to the West Wind," and Keats' "Ode to a Nightingale" are fairly long and are clearly set in the ode tradition. Here are two briefer examples.

JOHN KEATS (1795–1821)

Ode on a Grecian Urn

1

Thou still unravished bride of quietness,
   Thou foster child of silence and slow time,
Sylvan historian, who canst thus express
   A flowery tale more sweetly than our rhyme:
What leaf-fringed legend haunts about thy shape   5
   Of deities or mortals, or of both,
      In Tempe or the dales of Arcady?
   What men or gods are these? What maidens loath?
What mad pursuit? What struggle to escape?
     What pipes and timbrels? What wild ecstasy?   10

2

Heard melodies are sweet, but those unheard
   Are sweeter; therefore, ye soft pipes, play on;
Not to the sensual ear, but, more endeared,
   Pipe to the spirit ditties of no tone:
Fair youth, beneath the trees, thou canst not leave   15
   Thy song, nor ever can those trees be bare;
     Bold Lover, never, never canst thou kiss,
Though winning near the goal — yet, do not grieve;
     She cannot fade, though thou hast not thy bliss,
   Forever wilt thou love, and she be fair!   20

---

3. *Sylvan* rustic, of a woodland scene. 7. *Tempe or the dales of Arcady* Tempe is a valley in Greece, associated with rural beauty. Arcady is a reference to Arcadia, a region of Greece which stood as a symbol of the pastoral ideal.

3

Ah, happy, happy boughs! that cannot shed
  Your leaves, nor ever bid the Spring adieu;
And, happy melodist, unweariéd,
  Forever piping songs forever new;
More happy love! more happy, happy love!   25
  Forever warm and still to be enjoyed,
    Forever panting, and forever young;
All breathing human passion far above,
  That leaves a heart high-sorrowful and cloyed,
    A burning forehead, and a parching tongue.   30

4

Who are these coming to the sacrifice?
  To what green altar, O mysterious priest,
Lead'st thou that heifer lowing at the skies,
  And all her silken flanks with garlands dressed?
What little town by river or sea shore,   35
  Or mountain-built with peaceful citadel,
    Is emptied of this folk, this pious morn?
And, little town, thy streets forevermore
  Will silent be; and not a soul to tell
    Why thou art desolate, can e'er return.   40

5

O Attic shape! Fair attitude! with brede
  Of marble men and maidens overwrought,
With forest branches and the trodden weed;
  Thou, silent form, dost tease us out of thought
As doth eternity: Cold Pastoral!   45
  When old age shall this generation waste,
    Thou shalt remain, in midst of other woe
  Than ours, a friend to man, to whom thou say'st,
"Beauty is truth, truth beauty," — that is all
  Ye know on earth, and all ye need to know.   50

41. *Attic* Greek; *brede* braid, interwoven pattern.

For Consideration

1. The poem focuses on an urn depicting several scenes of people frozen in action. In his address to the urn, the poet notes, among other things, this art's ability to freeze and thus make permanent its subjects. Why, specifically, is the urn a "foster child of silence and slow time"?

2. What scenes are described in stanzas two and four? How does the poet emphasize the timeless quality of what he sees?

3. How does the urn "tease us out of thought"? What does the poet learn from the urn?

4. The final two lines have caused much discussion and difficulty, partly because uncertain punctuation makes it unclear whether the urn speaks all of the last two lines or the poet responds to the urn after the remarks on beauty and truth. How might an interpretation of the lines differ depending on punctuation? What truth about art are the lines affirming?

JOHN KEATS   (1795–1821)

To Autumn

I

Season of mists and mellow fruitfulness,
  Close bosom-friend of the maturing sun;
Conspiring with him how to load and bless
  With fruit the vines that round the thatch-eves run;
To bend with apples the mossed cottage-trees,   5
  And fill all fruit with ripeness to the core;
    To swell the gourd, and plump the hazel shells
With a sweet kernel; to set budding more,
  And still more, later flowers for the bees,
  Until they think warm days will never cease,   10
    For Summer has o'er-brimmed their clammy cells.

II

Who hath not seen thee oft amid thy store?
  Sometimes whoever seeks abroad may find
Thee sitting careless on a granary floor,

Thy hair soft-lifted by the winnowing wind;   15
Or on a half-reaped furrow sound asleep,
  Drowsed with the fume of poppies, while thy hook
    Spares the next swath and all its twinèd flowers;
And sometimes like a gleaner thou dost keep
  Steady thy laden head across a brook;   20
Or by a cider-press, with patient look,
    Thou watchest the last oozings hours by hours.

III

Where are the songs of Spring? Aye, where are they?
  Think not of them, thou hast thy music too,—
While barred clouds bloom the soft-dying day,   25
  And touch the stubble-plains with rosy hue;
Then in a wailful choir the small gnats mourn
  Among the river sallows, borne aloft
    Or sinking as the light wind lives or dies;
And full-grown lambs loud bleat from hilly bourn;   30
  Hedge-crickets sing; and now with treble soft
  The red-breast whistles from a garden-croft;
    And gathering swallows twitter in the skies.

For Consideration

1. What does Autumn bring in stanza one? By what means does the poet move to a personification of Autumn in stanza two?

2. What various roles does Autumn assume in the second stanza? How do those relate to the season itself?

3. What are the songs of Autumn? What qualities of the season does the poet celebrate here?

    As an ode is usually a hymn of praise, so by contrast an **elegy** is mournful and melancholy, and its frequent subject is death. This was not always the case, particularly in Greek and Latin poetry which identified the elegy by its form (alternate lines of dactylic hexameter and dactylic pentameter) rather than by its tone or subject. Now, however, "elegy" is a designation usually limited to verse which is meditative or lamenting.

28. *sallows* willows.

JOHN CROWE RANSOM (1888–1974)
Bells for John Whiteside's Daughter

There was such speed in her little body,
And such lightness in her footfall,
It is no wonder her brown study
Astonishes us all.

Her wars were bruited in our high window.   5
We looked among orchard trees and beyond
Where she took arms against her shadow,
Or harried unto the pond

The lazy geese, like a snow cloud
Dripping their snow on the green grass,   10
Tricking and stopping, sleepy and proud,
Who cried in goose, Alas,

For the tireless heart within the little
Lady with rod that made them rise
From their noon apple-dreams and scuttle   15
Goose-fashion under the skies!

But now go the bells, and we are ready,
In one house we are sternly stopped
To say we are vexed at her brown study,
Lying so primly propped.   20

For Consideration

1. What is the "brown study" which astonishes all witnesses? How does it
    relate to the speed and lightness which have characterized the girl?

2. Why does the poet describe her activities as "wars" and as taking arms?
    Why is so much attention (two full stanzas) given to a description of her
    harrying the geese to the pond?

3. The final stanza has come full circle, being closely related to the first, but
    it is not mere repetition. How has the tone of the poem changed? In the

5. *bruited* sounded.

first stanza there is astonishment, in the last vexation. What differing connotations do the two words have? How does the description of the mourners ("we are sternly stopped") and of the girl's body ("Lying so primly propped") reinforce the mood and meaning of the final stanza?

THEODORE ROETHKE (1908–1963)
Elegy for Jane

My Student, Thrown by a Horse

I remember the neckcurls, limp and damp as tendrils;
And her quick look, a sidelong pickerel smile;
And how, once startled into talk, the light syllables leaped for her,
And she balanced in the delight of her thought,
A wren, happy, tail into the wind,   5
Her song trembling the twigs and small branches.
The shade sang with her;
The leaves, their whispers turned to kissing;
And the mold sang in the bleached valleys under the rose.

Oh, when she was sad, she cast herself down into such a pure depth,   10
Even a father could not find her:
Scraping her cheek against straw;
Stirring the clearest water.

My sparrow, you are not here,
Waiting like a fern, making a spiny shadow.   15
The sides of wet stones cannot console me,
Nor the moss, wound with the last light.

If only I could nudge you from this sleep,
My maimed darling, my skittery pigeon.
Over this damp grave I speak the words of my love: 20
I, with no rights in this matter,
Neither father nor lover.

For Consideration

1. What do we know of the girl eulogized from the opening stanza? What characteristics did she possess? What image does the poet focus on in the second half of the stanza? How does it enhance the portrait of the girl?

2. What characteristic is emphasized in the second stanza? How does it relate to the focus of the first? What do references to "straw" and "clearest water" mean?

3. The third stanza is cast in the negative, confirming that the girl is not like a fern and that neither wet stones nor moss console the poet. How are these images related? What unrealized hope or consolation do they refer to?

4. There is an intentional ambivalence in the fourth stanza, which focuses on the poet himself. Although "neither father nor lover," he speaks "the words of my love." What effect does this acknowledgement of his feelings and of his relationship to the girl have on our reading of the elegy?

While the elegy, once distinguished by its form, is now distinguished by tone and subject, the **sonnet** is a poem on any subject and with any tone but in a fairly exact form. The sonnet is a poem of fourteen lines with a meter that is (usually) iambic pentameter. The English (or Shakespearean) sonnet is divided into three sections of four lines each (quatrains) and a final couplet; the standard rhyme scheme is *a b a b, c d c d, e f e f, g g* though there are, of course, many variations. The Italian (or Petrarchan) sonnet has two basic divisions of eight lines and six lines, an octave and a sestet. The sonnet was most popular during the Renaissance when a number of poets wrote collections of sonnets, called sonnet sequences, on related themes. Although no longer so prominent, the sonnet is still a form which interests many poets. Of the following four examples, the first two are built on the Shakespearean model, the second two on the Petrarchan model. The cummings poem is a good example of the way a modern poet can both rely on and vary from the traditional form.

WILLIAM SHAKESPEARE (1564–1616)

When, in Disgrace with Fortune and Men's Eyes

When, in disgrace with Fortune and men's eyes,
I all alone beweep my outcast state,
And trouble deaf heaven with my bootless cries,
And look upon myself and curse my fate,
Wishing me like to one more rich in hope,   5
Featured like him, like him with friends possessed,
Desiring this man's art and that man's scope,
With what I most enjoy contented least;
Yet in these thoughts myself almost despising
Haply I think on thee, and then my state,   10
Like to the lark at break of day arising
From sullen earth, sings hymns at heaven's gate:
   For thy sweet love remembered such wealth brings
   That then I scorn to change my state with kings.

For Consideration

1. What is the mood of the speaker at the opening? What does he want that he does not have?

2. What causes the change in his mood? How is the image of lines 11 and 12 appropriate for that change?

3. In what sense are the last two lines a reversal of the first lines of the poem?

1. *disgrace* disfavor. **3.** *bootless* pointless. **7.** *scope* mental capabilities. **10.** *Haply* by chance.

e. e. cummings (1894—1962)

i thank You God

i thank You God for most this amazing
day:for the leaping greenly spirits of trees
and a blue true dream of sky;and for everything
which is natural which is infinite which is yes

(i who have died am alive again today,   5
and this is the sun's birthday;this is the birth
day of life and of love and wings:and of the gay
great happening illimitably earth)

how should tasting touching hearing seeing
breathing any—lifted from the no   10
of all nothing—human merely being
doubt unimaginable You?

(now the ears of my ears awake and
now the eyes of my eyes are opened)

For Consideration

1. For what does the poet thank God? What characteristics of the day does
    he identify as praiseworthy? What time of the day is it?

2. On what basis does the poet affirm his faith in an "unimaginable You"?
    What are the ears of his ears and the eyes of his eyes?

JOHN MILTON (1608–1674)
When I Consider How My Light Is Spent

When I consider how my light is spent
  Ere half my days, in this dark world and wide,
  And that one talent which is death to hide
  Lodged with me useless, though my soul more bent
To serve therewith my Maker, and present   5
  My true account, lest he returning chide;
  "Doth God exact day-labor, light denied?"
  I fondly ask; but Patience to prevent
That murmur, soon replies, "God doth not need
  Either man's work or his own gifts; who best   10
  Bear his mild yoke, they serve him best. His state
Is kingly. Thousands at his bidding speed
  And post o'er land and ocean without rest:
  They also serve who only stand and wait."

For Consideration

1. What is the source of the reference in lines 3–7? What is the attitude of the speaker toward his debility?

2. What is the impact of the response of Patience? Why is it Patience which answers?

3. Characterize the two groups described in the last three lines. What is the speaker's position among them?

Title. a reference to Milton's blindness, which became total in 1651. 8. *fondly* foolishly.

GERARD MANLEY HOPKINS   (1844–1889)

Spring

Nothing is so beautiful as Spring —
　　When weeds, in wheels, shoot long and lovely and lush;
　　Thrush's eggs look little low heavens, and thrush
Through the echoing timber does so rinse and wring
The ear, it strikes like lightnings to hear him sing;　　　　　　5
　　The glassy peartree leaves and blooms, they brush
　　The descending blue; that blue is all in a rush
With richness; the racing lambs too have fair their fling.

What is all this juice and all this joy?
　　A strain of the earth's sweet being in the beginning　　　　10
In Eden garden. — Have, get, before it cloy,
　　Before it cloud, Christ, lord, and sour with sinning,
Innocent mind and Mayday in girl and boy,
　　Most, O maid's child, thy choice and worthy the winning.

For Consideration

1.　Hopkins is noted for his alliterations (see p. 393), and they are evident here. Does the prominence of the technique add to or detract from the aim of the poem?

2.　What qualities of Spring does the poet call attention to? Why is it appropriate to compare Spring to "the beginning/In Eden garden"?

3.　In the last four lines the poem acquires a more specifically religious aim (Hopkins himself was a Jesuit priest), yet the imagery allows an effective transition. How do "cloy" and "sour" relate both to Spring and to the innocence of the girl and boy mentioned in line 13? What is the meaning of Mayday? How does it also relate to Spring and to the children?

11. *cloy* surfeit with an excess, but usually of something initially pleasing.

It might be argued that all lyric poems are **dramatic** since all have a speaker of some sort who is in some kind of situation. Often, however, the situation is not readily identified and we can only assume that the speaker is the poet. Blake's "Eternity" and Dickinson's "To Make a Prairie," for example, set no scene with any precision; the lyrical outpouring is made without regard to a specific situation. In some poems, though, we understand rather exactly the type of person who is speaking and the situation which gives rise to the poem. Wordsworth's "It is a Beauteous Evening" presents a man and a woman walking in the evening, near a sea, with the man reflecting on the meaning of the experience for him. Thomas Kinsella's "Mirror in February" sets an equally exact scene: a man looking at himself in the mirror after shaving and contemplating his own existence. In neither of these examples is the speaker identified as someone necessarily distinct from the poet, but in each a reader understands that the poem is created out of a concrete situation. Hence, poems which set a specific scene can also be called dramatic poems.

WILLIAM WORDSWORTH   (1770–1850)

It Is a Beauteous Evening

It is a beauteous evening, calm and free,
The holy time is quiet as a Nun
Breathless with adoration; the broad sun
Is sinking down in its tranquility;
The gentleness of heaven broods o'er the Sea: 5
Listen! the mighty Being is awake,
And doth with his eternal motion make
A sound like thunder — everlastingly.
Dear Child! dear Girl! that walkest with me here,
If thou appear untouched by solemn thought,   10
Thy nature is not therefore less divine:
Thou liest in Abraham's bosom all the year,
And worship'st at the Temple's inner shrine,
God being with thee when we know it not.

9. *Dear Child* the girl with Wordsworth is Caroline, his daughter by Annette Vallon.
12. *Abraham's bosom* the resting place of souls destined for heaven (*see* Luke 16).

1.   How does the poet describe the evening? How does he associate it with the "mighty Being"?

2.   How does the girl's reaction differ from the poet's? What does it mean for her soul to lie in Abraham's bosom all the year? What are the characteristics of the divine nature that the poem calls attention to?

THOMAS KINSELLA   (1928–   )
Mirror in February

The day dawns with scent of must and rain,
Of opened soil, dark trees, dry bedroom air.
Under the fading lamp, half dressed — my brain
Idling on some compulsive fantasy —
I towel my shaven lip and stop, and stare,   5
Riveted by a dark exhausted eye,
A dry downturning mouth.

It seems again that it is time to learn,
In this untiring, crumbling place of growth
To which, for the time being, I return.   10
Now plainly in the mirror of my soul
I read that I have looked my last on youth
And little more; for they are not made whole
That reach the age of Christ.

Below my window the awakening trees,   15
Hacked clean for better bearing, stand defaced
Suffering their brute necessities,
And how should the flesh not quail that span for span
Is mutilated more? In slow distaste
I fold my towel with what grace I can,   20
Not young and not renewable, but man.

For Consideration

1. This poem focuses on the physical effects of aging and then moves to the emotional and psychological effects. What image allows for a smooth transition here?

2. There is an implicit comparison between the trees "hacked clean for better bearing" and the speaker. What point is the speaker making about himself? Why is the tree image an effective one?

3. What is the force of the final action and the final line? What attitude is implicit in the final words?

A particular kind of dramatic poem, the **dramatic monologue**, not only sets a scene but is composed of the words of one of the imagined participants in that scene. In a dramatic monologue, the speaker is not to be identified with the poet, even though he or she may occasionally (or frequently) express the poet's views. In one of Robert Browning's longer dramatic monologues, "Fra Lippo Lippi," the views of life and art expressed by the speaker are compatible with Browning's, but those views remain, within the poem, the expressions of the poetic character, not the author. Examples of the dramatic monologue in this book include the two poems which follow, as well as Tennyson's "Ulysses" and Eliot's "The Love Song of J. Alfred Prufrock." Each involves a created speaker whose words form the poem. It is therefore essential that a reader bring to a dramatic monologue the same discrimination demanded by a stage drama. As a theatre-goer cannot be certain that any one character in a play fully expresses the author's viewpoint so a reader cannot assume that the one character in a dramatic monologue is to be identified with the author.

ROBERT BROWNING (1812–1889)

My Last Duchess

Ferrara

That's my last duchess painted on the wall,
Looking as if she were alive. I call
That piece a wonder, now: Frà Pandolf's hands
Worked busily a day, and there she stands.
Will't please you sit and look at her? I said   5
"Frà Pandolf" by design, for never read
Strangers like you that pictured countenance,
The depth and passion of its earnest glance,
But to myself they turned (since none puts by
The curtain I have drawn for you, but I)   10
And seemed as they would ask me, if they durst,
How such a glance came there; so, not the first
Are you to turn and ask thus. Sir, 'twas not
Her husband's presence only, called that spot
Of joy into the Duchess' cheek: perhaps   15
Frà Pandolf chanced to say "Her mantle laps
"Over my lady's wrist too much," or "Paint
"Must never hope to reproduce the faint
"Half-flush that dies along her throat": such stuff
Was courtesy, she thought, and cause enough   20
For calling up that spot of joy. She had
A heart — how shall I say? — too soon made glad,
Too easily impressed; she liked whate'er
She looked on, and her looks went everywhere.
Sir, 'twas all one! My favor at her breast,   25
The dropping of the daylight in the West,
The bough of cherries some officious fool
Broke in the orchard for her, the white mule
She rode with round the terrace — all and each
Would draw from her alike the approving speech,   30
Or blush, at least. She thanked men — good! but thanked
Somehow — I know not how — as if she ranked
My gift of a nine-hundred-years-old name
With anybody's gift. Who'd stoop to blame
This sort of trifling? Even had you skill   35

Title. the words here are spoken by the Duke of Ferrara (born 1533), whose first wife, whom he
married when she was fourteen, died three years later under suspicious circumstances. Browning's interest, of course, is not primarily in historical accuracy. **3.** *Fra Pandolf* not a historical
artist but, like *Claus of Innsbruck* (line 56), one created for the poem.

In speech — which I have not — to make your will
Quite clear to such an one, and say, "Just this
"Or that in you disgusts me; here you miss,
"Or there exceed the mark" — and if she let
Herself be lessoned so, nor plainly set   40
Her wits to yours, forsooth, and made excuse,
—E'en then would be some stooping; and I choose
Never to stoop. Oh sir, she smiled, no doubt,
Whene'er I passed her; but who passed without
Much the same smile? This grew; I gave commands;   45
Then all smiles stopped together. There she stands
As if alive. Will 't please you rise? We'll meet
The company below, then. I repeat,
The Count your master's known munificence
Is ample warrant that no just pretense   50
Of mine for dowry will be disallowed;
Though his fair daughter's self, as I avowed
At starting, is my object. Nay, we'll go
Together down, sir. Notice Neptune, though,
Taming a sea-horse, thought a rarity,   55
Which Claus of Innsbruck cast in bronze for me!

For Consideration

1. What is the Duke's attitude toward his former duchess? How are his values revealed in his response to her? What about her attitude toward others most disturbs him?

2. Why does the Duke reveal himself so clearly to the representative of the Count, the father of his duchess-to-be? Is the self-revelation conscious or unintentional?

3. What has happened to the last duchess?

4. What are the Duke's wishes regarding the new duchess and her dowry?

5. Why does the poem end with the comment about the bronze art piece? How does that final comment fit the portrait of the Duke we have already seen?

6. The poem is made up of rhymed couplets throughout, but they are so unobtrusive that a first-time reader often misses them. How does Browning mask the regular rhyme and rhythm pattern of the poem?

RANDALL JARRELL (1914−1965)

Next Day

Moving from Cheer to Joy, from Joy to All,
I take a box
And add it to my wild rice, my Cornish game hens.
The slacked or shorted, basketed, identical
Food-gathering flocks   5
Are selves I overlook. Wisdom, said William James,

Is learning what to overlook. And I am wise
If that is wisdom.
Yet somehow, as I buy All from these shelves
And the boy takes it to my station wagon,   10
What I've become
Troubles me even if I shut my eyes.

When I was young and miserable and pretty
And poor, I'd wish
What all girls wish: to have a husband,   15
A house and children. Now that I'm old, my wish
Is womanish:
That the boy putting groceries in my car

See me. It bewilders me he doesn't see me.
For so many years   20
I was good enough to eat: the world looked at me
And its mouth watered. How often they have undressed me,
The eyes of strangers!
And, holding their flesh within my flesh, their vile

Imaginings within my imagining,   25
I too have taken
The chance of life. Now the boy pats my dog
And we start home. Now I am good.
The last mistaken,
Ecstatic, accidental bliss, the blind   30

Happiness that, bursting, leaves upon the palm
Some soap and water —
It was so long ago, back in some Gay
Twenties, Nineties, I don't know . . . Today I miss

My lovely daughter   35
Away at school, my sons away at school,

My husband away at work — I wish for them.
The dog, the maid,
And I go through the sure unvarying days
At home in them. As I look at my life,   40
I am afraid
Only that it will change, as I am changing:

I am afraid, this morning, of my face.
It looks at me
From the rear-view mirror, with the eyes I hate,   45
The smile I hate. Its plain, lined look
Of gray discovery
Repeats to me: "You're old." That's all, I'm old.

And yet I'm afraid, as I was at the funeral
I went to yesterday.   50
My friend's cold made-up face, granite among its flowers,
Her undressed, operated-on, dressed body
Were my face and body.
As I think of her I hear her telling me

How young I seem, I *am* exceptional;   55
I think of all I have.
But really no one is exceptional,
No one has anything, I'm anybody,
I stand beside my grave
Confused with my life, that is commonplace and solitary.   60

For Consideration

1. What is the occasion for the poem? Why is the speaker troubled?

2. What does the speaker wish for? Why does she call it "womanish"? What
    is the "chance of life" that she has previously taken?

3. The poem begins with a familiar setting in a grocery store and ends with
    an imagined watch over the speaker's own grave. What are the stages
    through which the speaker passes in building to that climactic scene?

4. One tension created in the poem is that between the speaker's belief that
    she is "exceptional" and her recognition that her life is "commonplace
    and solitary." How does the poet lend force to both portraits? Which
    view of her life dominates the poem?

5. Why is the poem titled "Next Day"? What has precipitated the reflections here?

For Comparison

"Mirror in February" (p. 312) and "Next Day" both include the reactions of a person to his or her appearance in a mirror. How are the reactions similar? How are they different? Compare the final view of the woman in "Next Day" to that of the man in "Mirror in February."

persona, tone, irony

One of the first questions a reader needs to ask about a poem is: Who is speaking? The speaker, or **persona**, may be radically removed from or closely aligned with the poet, but in either instance we need to know. We should not make the mistake of assuming that the speaker of a poem is simply the author. In concert with our determination about the speaker's relationship to the author's voice, we need also to identify the speaker's situation — the occasion which gives rise to his or her remarks. Sometimes, as in a dramatic monologue, the occasion is quite specific: Browning's Duke, for example, is in his chambers speaking to a representative of the father of his duchess-to-be. For most poems, the occasion is less definite though it may still be significant. The following poem is written in response to the hearing of a bird's song; otherwise we know of the occasion with little exactness.

THEODORE ROETHKE (1908—1963)

The Reply

Bird, bird don't edge me in;
    I've had enough today
    Of your fine-honed lay
That prickles my coarse skin.

I'm neither out nor in   5
    Before that simple tune
    As cryptic as a rune,
    As round and pure as the moon,
And fresh as salt-drenched skin.

This shivers me; I swear   10
    A tune so bold and bare,
    Yet fine as maidenhair,
Shakes every sense. I'm five
Times five a man; I breathe
    This sudden random song,   15
    And, like you, bird, I sing,
    A man, a man alive.

For Consideration

1.   What is the speaker's response to the bird's song? What qualities are implied in its being "As cryptic as a rune, As round and pure as the moon, And fresh as salt-drenched skin"?

2.   How is the song at once "bold and bare" and yet "fine as maidenhair"?

3.   Each succeeding stanza is longer than the one which precedes it. How does that complete the focus of each stanza?

4.   Obviously the bird's song can have no "message" in the usual sense, yet the poet is moved to respond to it. What does his "reply" suggest about the mood and temperament of the experience?

Regardless of the speaker or the occasion, we need to evaluate the **tone** of a poem, the attitude of the speaker toward the subject. The attitude may be one of scorn, delight, hatred, or praise, but it will inevitably affect a reader's response to the poem. Consider the following two poems that deal, at least in part, with the subject of growing old. Arnold's poem reflects sarcasm and bitterness toward "the hollow ghost" which results from aging; Tennyson's Ulysses, however, is assertive, confident, even optimistic about the opportunities which still lie before him, opportunities "To strive, to seek, to find, and not to yield." There are many other differences between the two poems, of course, including the important fact that Tennyson's poem is a dramatic monologue, and Arnold's is not. One key to relating the two poems remains, nonetheless, our ability to perceive differences in tone between them.

MATTHEW ARNOLD   (1822–1888)

Growing Old

What is it to grow old?
Is it to lose the glory of the form,
The lustre of the eye?
Is it for beauty to forego her wreath?
— Yes, but not this alone.   5

Is it to feel our strength —
Not our bloom only, but our strength — decay?
Is it to feel each limb
Grow stiffer, every function less exact,
Each nerve more loosely strung?   10

Yes, this, and more; but not
Ah, 'tis not what in youth we dreamed 'twould be!
'Tis not to have our life
Mellowed and softened as with sunset-glow,
A golden day's decline.   15

'Tis not to see the world
As from a height, with rapt prophetic eyes,

And heart profoundly stirred;
And weep, and feel the fulness of the past,
The years that are no more.

It is to spend long days
And not once feel that we were ever young;
It is to add, immured
In the hot prison of the present, month
To month with weary pain.

It is to suffer this,
And feel but half, and feebly, what we feel.
Deep in our hidden heart
Festers the dull remembrance of a change,
But no emotion — none.

It is — last stage of all —
When we are frozen up within, and quite
The phantom of ourselves,
To hear the world applaud the hollow ghost
Which blamed the living man.

For Consideration

1. This poem was apparently written as an ironic response to the optimism expressed toward old age by Browning ("Rabbi Ben Ezra") and others. What is the attitude expressed here?

2. The poem creates a certain tension by focusing initially on half-truths about growing old and then on untruths about the experience. Beginning in the fifth stanza the poet comments more directly on the experience itself. Does this order of thought enhance or diminish the point the poet wants to make?

3. How does the "truth" of stanzas 5, 6, and 7 contrast with the "untruths" of stanzas 3 and 4? (Note some of the specific contrasts: e.g., the "heart profoundly stirred" and the "hidden heart"; the "rapt prophetic eyes" and "the hollow ghost.")

4. Where in the poem are the physical effects of growing old emphasized? Where are the emotional or spiritual effects stressed? What relationships between the two are implied?

35. *blamed* censured, but in this context, brought discredit to.

ALFRED, LORD TENNYSON (1809–1892)

Ulysses

It little profits that an idle king,
By this still hearth, among these barren crags,
Matched with an aged wife, I mete and dole
Unequal laws unto a savage race,
That hoard, and sleep, and feed, and know not me.   5

I cannot rest from travel; I will drink
Life to the lees. All times I have enjoyed
Greatly, have suffered greatly, both with those
That loved me, and alone; on shore, and when
Through scudding drifts the rainy Hyades   10
Vexed the dim sea. I am become a name;
For always roaming with a hungry heart
Much have I seen and known — cities of men
And manners, climates, councils, governments,
Myself not least, but honored of them all —   15
And drunk delight of battle with my peers,
Far on the ringing plains of windy Troy.
I am a part of all that I have met;
Yet all experience is an arch wherethrough
Gleams that untraveled world whose margin fades   20
Forever and forever when I move.
How dull it is to pause, to make an end,
To rust unburnished, not to shine in use!
As though to breathe were life! Life piled on life
Were all too little, and of one to me   25
Little remains; but every hour is saved
From that eternal silence, something more,
A bringer of new things; and vile it were
For some three suns to store and hoard myself,
And this gray spirit yearning in desire   30
To follow knowledge like a sinking star,
Beyond the utmost bound of human thought.

This is my son, mine own Telemachus,
To whom I leave the scepter and the isle —
Well-loved of me, discerning to fulfill   35
This labor, by slow prudence to make mild
A rugged people, and through soft degrees
Subdue them to the useful and the good.

Most blameless is he, centered in the sphere
Of common duties, decent not to fail   40
In offices of tenderness, and pay
Meet adoration to my household gods,
When I am gone. He works his work, I mine.

     There lies the port; the vessel puffs her sail;
There gloom the dark, broad seas. My mariners,   45
Souls that have toiled, and wrought, and thought with me —
That ever with a frolic welcome took
The thunder and the sunshine, and opposed
Free hearts, free foreheads — you and I are old;
Old age hath yet his honor and his toil.   50
Death closes all; but something ere the end,
Some work of noble note, may yet be done,
Not unbecoming men that strove with Gods.
The lights begin to twinkle from the rocks;
The long day wanes; the slow moon climbs; the deep   55
Moans round with many voices. Come, my friends,
'Tis not too late to seek a newer world.
Push off, and sitting well in order smite
The sounding furrows; for my purpose holds
To sail beyond the sunset, and the baths   60
Of all the western stars, until I die.
It may be that the gulfs will wash us down;
It may be we shall touch the Happy Isles,
And see the great Achilles, whom we knew.
Though much is taken, much abides; and though   65
We are not now that strength which in old days
Moved earth and heaven, that which we are, we are —
One equal temper of heroic hearts,
Made weak by time and fate, but strong in will
To strive, to seek, to find, and not to yield.   70

For Consideration

1. The poem is a monologue spoken by the aging Ulysses, long after his
    return to Ithaca following his voyage from Troy (the subject of Homer's
    The Odyssey). He expresses his intention to leave the life of an "idle
    king" in order to travel and explore once again. The speech is directed to
    some of his former mariners and followers. What is Ulysses' view of his
    people? Why does he wish to leave them and his family?

2. What is the view of life and experience espoused in lines 19–26? How do
    Ulysses' life and goals contrast with those of his son?

3. In what direction will Ulysses sail? Why is that appropriate? How does he respond to old age and death?

4. Not all readers see Ulysses' view of life as a positive one. What are its virtues? What are its limitations?

For Comparison

"Mirror in February" (p. 312) and "Next Day" (p. 316) also present individuals who are confronting the fact that they are growing older. How do the tones of those two poems compare to the tones and attitudes of the speakers of "Growing Old" and "Ulysses"?

A speaker may, of course, appear to have one attitude toward his subject while, in fact, having an attitude that is quite different or opposite. Or he may have an attitude that, in light of the subject, is surprising or unexpected. In either instance the tone is marked by **irony**. Irony can work at all levels in a poem, from individual words to the poem as a whole, but it is particularly important when it controls the tone of a poem.

Describe the tone of each of the following poems. What relationship does there seem to be between tone and subject? In which poems is irony important?

JOHN DONNE   (1572–1631)

Batter My Heart, Three-Personed God

Batter my heart, three-personed God; for You
As yet but knock, breathe, shine, and seek to mend;
That I may rise and stand, o'erthrow me, 'and bend
Your force to break, blow, burn, and make me new.
I, like an usurped town, to'another due,   5
Labor to'admit You, but O, to no end;

Reason, Your viceroy'in me, me should defend,
But is captíved, and proves weak or untrue.
Yet dearly'I love You,'and would be lovéd fain,
But am betrothed unto Your enemy.   10
Divorce me,'untie or break that knot again;
Take me to You, imprison me, for I,
Except You'enthrall me, never shall be free,
Nor ever chaste, except You ravish me.

For Consideration

1. Why is God "three-personed"? How are the three persons identified in lines 2 and 4 (note the verbs "knock, breathe, shine" and "break, blow, burn")?

2. What is the basic image identified in line 5? What roles do God and the speaker occupy in that image? Why is Reason the "viceroy" of God?

3. What metaphor is introduced in line 9? Who is the enemy to whom the speaker is betrothed?

4. The final couplet of the poem contains two striking paradoxes, freedom only through slavery, chastity only through rape. What do they mean here? What effect do images of physical violence and sexual violation have in this poem about God's relationship to a man?

X. J. KENNEDY (1929–   )
First Confession

Blood thudded in my ears. I scuffed,
   Steps stubborn, to the telltale booth
Beyond whose curtained portal coughed
   The robed repositor of truth.

The slat shot back. The universe   5
   Bowed down his cratered dome to hear

7. *viceroy* a governor of a province, ruling as the representative of his king.

Enumerated my each curse,
   The sip snitched from my old man's beer,

My sloth pride envy lechery,
   The dime held back from Peter's Pence   10
With which I'd bribed my girl to pee
   That I might spy her instruments.

Hovering scale-pans when I'd done
   Settled their balance slow as silt
While in the restless dark I burned   15
   Bright as a brimstone in my guilt

Until as one feeds birds he doled
   Seven Our Fathers and a Hail
Which I to double-scrub my soul
   Intoned twice at the altar rail   20

Where Sunday in seraphic light
   I knelt, as full of grace as most,
And stuck my tongue out at the priest:
   A fresh roost for the Holy Ghost.

For Consideration

1. What is the effect of the elevated language in the poem (e.g., "robed repositor of truth," "Bowed down his cratered dome")? The boy is apparently young since this is his "first confession." Is the language in harmony with his age? Why is it used?

2. How serious are the young boy's sins? What are the "hovering scale-pans"? What impressions do we receive of the priest who hears the confession?

3. Line 23 is intentionally ambiguous in its implications. What seems to be the dominant attitude of the boy during the confessional? Does he take it seriously or not?

4. The tone here is obviously a light one. How else would you describe it? Is it mocking? Good-humored? Does it seem an appropriate tone for its subject?

NIKKI GIOVANNI (1943–   )

Ego Tripping
(there may be
a reason why)

I was born in the congo
I walked to the fertile crescent and built
   the sphinx
I designed a pyramid so tough that a star
   that only glows every one hundred years falls   5
   into the center giving divine perfect light
I am bad

I sat on the throne
   drinking nectar with allah
I got hot and sent an ice age to europe   10
   to cool my thirst
My oldest daughter is nefertiti
   the tears from my birth pains
   created the nile
I am a beautiful woman   15

I gazed on the forest and burned
   out the sahara desert
   with a packet of goat's meat
   and a change of clothes
I crossed it in two hours   20
I am a gazelle so swift
   so swift you can't catch me

   For a birthday present when he was three
I gave my son hannibal an elephant
   He gave me rome for mother's day   25
My strength flows ever on

My son noah built new/ark and
I stood proudly at the helm
   as we sailed on a soft summer day

12. *Nefertiti* Queen of Egypt in the early 14th century B.C. 24. *hannibal* the Carthaginian soldier and general.

I turned myself into myself and was 30
    jesus
    men intone my loving name
    All praises All praises
I am the one who would save

I sowed diamonds in my back yard 35
My bowels deliver uranium
    the filings from my fingernails are
    semi-precious jewels
    On a trip north
I caught cold and blew 40
My nose giving oil to the arab world
I am so hip even my errors are correct
I sailed west to reach east and had to round off
    the earth as I went
    The hair from my head thinned and gold was laid 45
    across three continents

I am so perfect so divine so ethereal so surreal
I cannot be comprehended
    except by my permission

I mean ... . I . . . can fly 50
    like a bird in the sky . . .

For Consideration

1.   The poem depends throughout on hyperbole. What point about herself or about woman is the poet making? "Ego tripping" can be equivalent to mere self-indulgence. Does the poem escape that negative judgment? What does the sub-title mean?

2.   A historical sense dominates the poem. Why does the poet focus on great events in the world's making and its history?

3.   The last image seems almost modest in comparison to the ones which preceded it. What is the effect of that more concrete, less far-reaching image?

4.   The poet is a black woman. Does that affect your reading of the poem?

ALLEN GINSBERG (1926–   )

Uptown

Yellow-lit Budweiser signs over oaken bars,
"I've seen everything" — the bartender handing me change of $10,
I stared at him amiably thru an obvious Adamic beard —
with Montana musicians homeless in Manhattan, teen age
curly hair themselves — we sat at the antique booth & gossiped,   5
Madame Grady's literary salon a curious value in New York —
"If I had my way, I'd cut off your hair and send you to Vietnam" —
"Bless you then" I replied to a hatted thin citizen hurrying to the
                barroom door
upon wet dark Amsterdam Avenue decades later —
"And if I couldn't do that I'd cut your throat" he snarled farewell,   10
and "Bless you sir" I added as he went to his fate in the rain,
                dapper Irishman.

For Consideration

1. What is the speaker's relationship to the barroom society described here?
    What characteristics does he give himself in the poem?

2. Physical appearance receives considerable attention in this short poem.
    Why? What levels of society are represented here?

EMILY DICKINSON (1830–1886)

Because I Could Not Stop for Death

Because I could not stop for Death —
He kindly stopped for me —
The Carriage held but just Ourselves —
And Immortality.

3. *Adamic* relating to the fallen Adam, unregenerate.

We slowly drove — He knew no haste   5
And I had put away
My labor and my leisure too,
For His Civility —

We passed the School, where Children strove
At Recess — in the Ring —   10
We passed the Fields of Gazing Grain —
We passed the Setting Sun —

Or rather — He passed Us —
The Dews drew quivering and chill —
For only Gossamer, my Gown —   15
My Tippet — only Tulle —

We paused before a House that seemed
A Swelling of the Ground —
The Roof was scarcely visible —
The Cornice — in the Ground —   20

Since then — 'tis Centuries — and yet
Feels shorter than the Day
I first surmised the Horses Heads
Were toward Eternity —

For Consideration

1. How is Death portrayed in the poem? How does the poet give Death the appearance of an associate rather than an antagonist?

2. What meaning lies behind the objects passed in stanza three? Why a school, then fields of grain, and finally the setting sun?

3. What is the House of stanza five?

4. From what point of view and from what time is the poem written? What appears to be the speaker's situation at the beginning of the poem? Is the speaker's point of view at the end (looking back on an event centuries ago) surprising or expected?

15. *Gossamer* light material. **16.** *Tippet* cape or scarf; *Tulle* a sheer net

imagery: figurative language

ROBERT FROST (1874–1963)
Dust of Snow

The way a crow
Shook down on me
The dust of snow
From a hemlock tree

Has given my heart   5
A change of mood
And saved some part
Of a day I had rued.

A discussion of this brief poem of Robert Frost might begin with any of several observations: the poet's experience in a natural setting, the "change of mood" the experience promotes, the sense of expectation with which the poem concludes. Quite possibly, though, we would first notice and remark on the concrete description which opens the poem. Frost first wishes us to imagine the experience before he goes on to comment on its importance. Poets frequently rely on such **images** to add concreteness and appeal to a poem. Although the term "image" is associated most specifically with a pictorial appeal, in poetry it identifies a part of a poem which appeals to any of the senses. The prominent images are the **visual** (or pictorial) and the **auditory** (or aural), the appeals being, respectively, to sight and to hearing. Frost's poem relies primarily on visual imagery, as does this poem written in response to a painting.

ANNE SEXTON (1928–1974)

The Starry Night

*That does not keep me from having a terrible need of — shall I say the word —
religion. Then I go out at night to paint the stars.*

Vincent Van Gogh in a letter to his brother

The town does not exist
except where one black-haired tree slips
up like a drowned woman into the hot sky.
The town is silent. The night boils with eleven stars
Oh starry starry night! This is how   5
I want to die.

It moves. They are all alive.
Even the moon bulges in its orange irons
to push children, like a god, from its eye.
The old unseen serpent swallows up the stars.   10
Oh starry starry night! This is how
I want to die:

into that rushing beast of the night,
sucked up by that great dragon, to split
from my life with no flag,   15
no belly,
no cry.

For Consideration

1. The poem sets a scene from Van Gogh's painting, *Starry Night*, and then establishes a connection between that scene and death. How do the night and town appear in the poem?

2. The second stanza describes a changing scene, focusing especially on the personified, deified moon and the "old unseen serpents." What do these images represent in the poem?

3. The last stanza makes clearer the relationship between the scene and "how I want to die." What kind of death does the poet desire? What is it to be "sucked up by that great dragon"?

Epigraph. *Van Gogh* the Dutch painter who became insane in his thirties and later committed suicide. One of his paintings is entitled *Starry Night*.

William Blake's "London" appeals especially to our sense of hearing by emphasizing the sounds from the city. In addition to the auditory imagery in such words as "cry," "sigh," and "Blasts," the poem also contains an example of **synesthesia** (the description of one sense experience in terms of another), as when "the hapless soldier's sigh" (auditory) "Runs in blood down palace walls" (visual).

WILLIAM BLAKE   (1757–1827)

London

I wander through each chartered street,
Near where the chartered Thames does flow,
And mark in every face I meet
Marks of weakness, marks of woe.

In every cry of every man,   5
In every infant's cry of fear,
In every voice, in every ban,
The mind-forged manacles I hear.

How the chimney-sweeper's cry
Every black'ning church appalls,   10
And the hapless soldier's sigh
Runs in blood down the palace walls.

But most through midnight streets I hear
How the youthful harlot's curse
Blasts the new-born infant's tear   15
And blights with plagues the marriage hearse.

For Consideration

1.   What are the features of this society? What is the source of the despair which is so prominent? Why are the streets and the river Thames "chartered"? In what sense are the inhabitants also "chartered"?

2. "Manacles," like "chartered," suggests the presence of restrictions and limitations on man and society. Why are the manacles "mind-forged"?

3. The auditory imagery functions, in part, to emphasize the desperation of the scenes. What is the effect of poetically joining the chimney-sweeper's cry to the church, the soldier's sigh to the palace walls, and the harlot's curse to the birth of an infant and a marriage?

4. Line 15 probably refers to the effects of venereal disease on an infant, received from parental contact with a prostitute. How does the harlot's curse plague the marriage? Why a marriage "hearse"?

Other forms of imagery appear less frequently but are occasionally important. The final stanza of Tennyson's "The Eagle" includes an example of **kinetic** imagery, or imagery of motion, as it invites us both to see the bird and to experience movement as he leaves his lofty perch:

> The wrinkled sea beneath him crawls:
> He watches from his mountain walls,
> And like a thunderbolt he falls.

An image may also appeal to the sense of touch (a **tactile** image), the sense of smell (an **olfactory** image), the sense of taste (a **gustatory** image), or to senses other than the traditional five or six. For rather obvious reasons, however, the imagery of poetry is predominately visual or auditory.

ALFRED, LORD TENNYSON (1809–1892)

The Eagle: A Fragment

He clasps the crag with crooked hands;
Close to the sun in lonely lands,
Ringed with the azure world, he stands.

The wrinkled sea beneath him crawls;
He watches from his mountain walls,
And like a thunderbolt he falls.   5

For Consideration

1. Little is said about specific qualities associated with the eagle, yet we receive a vivid picture of him standing and falling. What virtues does the poem implicitly identify with the eagle?

2. Although effectively presented in its own right, the poem also depends on traditional values associated with the eagle. (In the Renaissance, for example, it was the highest form of bird, analogous to the king as the highest ruler of man or the Sun as the greatest of solar objects.) Would the poem have been as effective if it had been written about a sparrow or a pelican?

URI ZVI GREENBERG   (1895−   )

With My God the Blacksmith

Translated from the Hebrew by Arieh Sachs

Like chapters of prophecy, my days burn in all their revelations,
My body among them like a lump of metal to be forged.
And over me stands my God the blacksmith and hammers with
      might:
Each wound time has cut in me opens like a crack for Him
And emits in sparks of moments the pent-up fire.   5

This is my destiny-sentence till evening come upon the road.
And when I return to throw my beaten lump on the bed,
My mouth is a gaping wound.
And *naked* I speak to my God: "Yours has been hard labor.
Now night has fallen; come — let us both rest."   10

For Consideration

1. One biblical verse which is pertinent here is Jeremiah 23:29 — "Is not my word like as a fire? saith the Lord; and like a hammer that breaketh the rock in pieces?" How does the image of God the blacksmith join the references to fire and hammer?

2. What defines the relationship between God and man in the poem? Why, in line 9, does the speaker describe God's work as having been "hard labor"? What does he mean when he says that, with evening, both he and God will be able to rest? Why is he naked when he says this?

For Comparison

How are God in this poem and God in Donne's "Batter My Heart" (p. 324) alike? How does each act to perfect a relationship with a human being?

ROBERT BROWNING (1812–1889)

Meeting at Night

1

The gray sea and the long black land;
And the yellow half-moon large and low;
And the startled little waves that leap,
In fiery ringlets from their sleep,
As I gain the cove with pushing prow,   5
And quench its speed i' the slushy sand.

2

Then a mile of warm sea-scented beach;
Three fields to cross till a farm appears;
A tap at the pane, the quick sharp scratch
And blue spurt of a lighted match,   10
And a voice less loud, through its joys and fears,
Than the two hearts beating each to each!

ROBERT BROWNING (1812–1889)

Parting at Morning

Round the cape of a sudden came the sea,
And the sun looked over the mountain's rim:
And straight was a path of gold for him,
And the need of a world of men for me.

For Consideration

1. What effect do the opening descriptions have? What is their source in the first poem? What is happening?

2. The first poem ends at the climactic moment. Is that effective?

3. What does the second poem tell us about the needs of the man? What does it suggest about his night and day experiences?

For Comparison

These two poems originally appeared under the single title, "Night and Morning." How do they present contrasting views of the experience and the people involved?

ELIZABETH BISHOP (1911–   )

The Fish

I caught a tremendous fish
and held him beside the boat
half out of water, with my hook
fast in a corner of his mouth.

He didn't fight.   5
He hadn't fought at all.
He hung a grunting weight,
battered and venerable
and homely. Here and there
his brown skin hung in strips   10
like ancient wallpaper,
and its pattern of darker brown
was like wallpaper:
shapes like full-blown roses
stained and lost through age.   15
He was speckled with barnacles,
fine rosettes of lime,
and infested
with tiny white sea-lice,
and underneath two or three   20
rags of green weed hung down.
While his gills were breathing in
the terrible oxygen
— the frightening gills,
fresh and crisp with blood,   25
that can cut so badly —
I thought of the coarse white flesh
packed in like feathers,
the big bones and the little bones,
the dramatic reds and blacks   30
of his shiny entrails,
and the pink swim-bladder
like a big peony.
I looked into his eyes
which were far larger than mine   35
but shallower, and yellowed,
the irises backed and packed
with tarnished tinfoil
seen through the lenses
of old scratched isinglass.   40
They shifted a little, but not
to return my stare.
— It was more like the tipping
of an object toward the light.
I admired his sullen face,   45
the mechanism of his jaw,
and then I saw
that from his lower lip
— if you could call it a lip —

40. *isinglass* semi-transparent gelatin prepared from the air bladders of fish.

grim, wet, and weaponlike,   50
hung five old pieces of fish-line,
or four and a wire leader
with the swivel still attached,
with all their five big hooks
grown firmly in his mouth.   55
A green line, frayed at the end
where he broke it, two heavier lines,
and a fine black thread
still crimped from the strain and snap
when it broke and he got away.   60
Like medals with their ribbons
frayed and wavering,
a five-haired beard of wisdom
trailing from his aching jaw.
I stared and stared   65
and victory filled up
the little rented boat,
from the pool of bilge
where oil had spread a rainbow
around the rusted engine   70
to the bailer rusted orange,
the sun-cracked thwarts,
the oarlocks on their strings,
the gunnels — until everything
was rainbow, rainbow, rainbow!   75
And I let the fish go.

For Consideration

1. How is the fish described in the opening lines? What are its distinct features?

2. How do the eyes and jaws reinforce the earlier depiction of the fish?

3. Why is the speaker filled with a sense of victory, culminating in everything becoming "rainbow, rainbow, rainbow!" Why, then, does she let the fish go?

Images are usually created when a poet engages in the use of **figurative language**, that is, language which enables a speaker to say something important but in a non-literal way, or to comment on one thing in terms of something else. Figurative language also allows the abstract or theoretical to be expressed concretely. We recognize figures of speech in our own conversation when we say, for example, "I felt light as a feather," "That idea hit me like a two-ton truck," or "I'll wait here until hell freezes over." Unlike these examples, of course, a skillful poet avoids clichés, but like these examples, figures of speech are used to give emphasis or to focus on the suggestive quality of language. In figures of speech, in other words, we are not so concerned with the **denotation** of a word, its dictionary, literal meaning, as with its **connotation**, qualities, emotions, or values associated with it. When Tennyson asks us to think of the eagle falling "like a thunderbolt," he is not concentrating on the thunderbolt as "a single discharge of lightning with the accompanying thunder," but rather on the thunderbolt's association with immediate power and awesomeness. Connotations depend on denotative meanings but go beyond them.

The **metaphor** and the **simile** are the two most familiar figures of speech. The simile states an explicit comparison by using some connective term (usually "like" or "as"):

> one black-haired tree slips
> up like a drowned woman into the hot sky.
>
> Sexton, "The Starry Night"

> O my luve is like a red, red rose
>
> Burns, "A Red, Red Rose"

> I met her as a blossom on a stem
> Before she ever breathed
>
> Roethke, "The Dream"

The metaphor omits the connecting term, implying an identity between the two objects compared:

> I am a gazelle so swift
>
> Giovanni, "Ego Tripping"

> She was a Phantom of delight
>
> Wordsworth, "She Was a Phantom of Delight"

Increasingly the term metaphor is used to describe either of the two forms here, so that the term "metaphorical language" encompasses the simile as well as the metaphor.

SIR WALTER RALEGH (ca. 1552–1618)

What Is Our Life?

What is our life? a play of passion,
Our mirth the music of division;
Our mothers' wombs the tiring-houses be
Where we are dressed for this short comedy;
Heaven the judicious, sharp spectator is   5
That sits and marks still who doth act amiss;
Our graves that hide us from the searching sun
Are like drawn curtains when the play is done:
Thus march we, playing, to our latest rest,
Only we die in earnest, that's no jest.   10

For Consideration

1. The poem rests on the basic metaphor of the world as a stage, a fairly prominent image in Renaissance England. What kind of play is being performed? What role do people play in it?

2. Describe the tone of the poem. What is the effect of compressing the human life into 10 lines?

1. *a play of passion* a pun on "passion play," a medieval religious drama. 2. *music of division* a musical variation on a theme. 3. *tiring-houses* dressing areas for actors and actresses.

ANONYMOUS ZUNI PRAYER
Presenting an Infant to the Sun

Now this is the day.
Our child,
Into the daylight
You will go out standing.
Preparing for your day,   5
We have passed our days.
When all your days were at an end,
When eight days were past,
Our sun father
Went in to sit down at his sacred place.   10
And our night fathers
Having come out standing to their sacred place,
Passing a blessed night
We came today.
Now this day   15
Our fathers,
Dawn priests,
Have come out standing to their sacred place.
Our sun father,
Having come out standing to his sacred place,   20
Our child, it is your day.
This day,
The flesh of the white corn,
Prayer meal,
To our sun father   25
This prayer meal we offer.
May your road be fulfilled
Reaching to the road of your sun father,
When your road is fulfilled
In your thoughts may we live,   30
May we be the ones whom your thoughts will embrace,
For this, on this day
To our sun father,
We offer prayer meal.
To this end: 35
May you help us all to finish our roads.

For Consideration

1. The poem focuses on the ceremonious presentation of a newborn child. Who is the speaker here? What is the tone of the prayer?

2. Who are the "sun father," "night fathers," and "dawn priests"?

3. What is the effect of the repeated description of the "fathers" going to their sacred place?

4. The prayer for the child does not begin until line 27. What is the effect of the preparatory comments? What does the speaker pray for?

5. The "road of life" is a familiar metaphor, almost a cliché, but it is effectively presented here. How does the child's "road" (lines 27 and 29) relate to the multiple "roads" at the end of the poem?

PSALM 23

The Lord is My Shepherd

The Lord is my shepherd; I shall not want.
He maketh me to lie down in green pastures:
He leadeth me beside the still waters.
He restoreth my soul:
He leadeth me in the paths of righteousness   5
For his name's sake.
Yea, though I walk through the valley of the shadow of death,
I will fear no evil: for thou art with me;
Thy rod and thy staff they comfort me.
Thou preparest a table before me   10
In the presence of mine enemies:
Thou anointest my head with oil;
My cup runneth over.
Surely goodness and mercy shall follow me
All the days of my life: 15
And I will dwell in the house of the Lord for ever.

For Consideration

1. One difficulty in studying this poem is that it is for many too familiar and thus effortlessly recited, yet, as a poem, the biblical verses are rich in poetic techniques. What is the initial metaphor in the poem? What image takes over in line 10?

2. The two metaphors are related both through the benevolent action of the Lord and through the provisions he makes available. What pleasures does the sheep receive from the shepherd (lines 1—9)? What does the guest receive from his host (lines 10—16)?

ROBERT BURNS (1759—1796)

A Red, Red Rose

O my luve is like a red, red rose,
  That's newly sprung in June:
O my luve is like a melodie,
  That's sweetly played in tune.

As fair art thou, my bonie lass,   5
  So deep in luve am I;
And I will luve thee still, my dear,
  Till a' the seas gang dry.

Till a' the seas gang dry, my dear,
  And the rocks melt wi' the sun: 10
And I will luve thee still, my dear,
  While the sands o' life shall run.

And fare thee weel, my only luve!
  And fare thee weel a while!
And I will come again, my luve,   15
  Tho' it were ten thousand mile.

For Consideration

1. What virtues are implied in the metaphors which compare the poet's love to a rose and to a melody?

2. What are the sources of the images in the poem? What might they indicate about the speaker's background and society?

3. The final two stanzas confirm the speaker's love in hyperbolic terms. With what effect? Are the final two lines a hyperbole? Why or why not?

ANONYMOUS AZTEC POEM

A Woman's Complaint

What shall I do? My man compares me
to a wild red flower.
When I have withered in his hands,
he will leave me.

For Consideration

This lament might have been written as a response to the first two lines of Burns' poem (it wasn't, of course). What questions does it raise about the use of metaphors? Is the response here an appropriate one? Why or why not?

RUTH HERSCHBERGER (1917–   )

So If You Love Me

So if you love me you will tolerant
Be of the nature that is with me sent.
  I cannot be a different thing although
  For your sake, to win you, I would grow
      Wings and shed thorns,   5
      Be weed, or newly born,
  Anything so to please you,
  But I'm myself and cannot ease you.

Come kindly to me then, forgiveness use,
Do not heap on my patent-wrongs abuse,   10
  For your sake I'd be different but am not,
  For your sake I'd have other needs forgot,
    But I am one
    And they are of the sum
  Of me, and will not set me free   15
  From my desires, which still follow me.

Oh choose, and choose me wholly, so we be
All of imperfectness, but summary.
  Be sum, no fraction, though a fraction may
  Marvelous wonder easily convey,   20
    Yet it's but part
    And may not be the heart,
  The whole is all of us, if we use not
  All strata, love's geology's forgot.

For Consideration

1.   What distinctions is the speaker drawing between what she would do for her lover and what she can do? There is a mention of "patent-wrongs" and frequent references to an imperfect nature, but specific faults are not identified. Why not?

2.   The final stanza deals with imagery of wholeness and parts, occasionally with an almost mathematical precision. What concept of wholeness refers

to the speaker herself? What is the "sum" which she refers to? How does she relate it to the "whole" which "is all of us"? The final lines introduce a geological image. How does it relate to what has been said of the two lovers?

JOHN DONNE (1572–1631)
A Valediction: Forbidding Mourning

As virtuous men pass mildly away,
  And whisper to their souls to go,
Whilst some of their sad friends do say
  The breath goes now, and some say, No;

So let us melt, and make no noise,   5
  No tear-floods, nor sigh-tempests move,
'Twere profanation of our joys
  To tell the laity our love.

Moving of th' earth brings harms and fears,
  Men reckon what it did and meant;   10
But trepidation of the spheres,
  Though greater far, is innocent.

Dull sublunary lovers' love
  (Whose soul is sense) cannot admit
Absence, because it doth remove   15
  Those things which elemented it.

But we by'a love so much refined
  That our selves know not what it is,
Inter-assuréd of the mind,
  Care less, eyes, lips, and hands to miss.   20

Our two souls therefore, which are one,
  Though I must go, endure not yet

11. *trepidation* a term from Ptolemaic astronomy, referring to movement attributed to the ninth sphere, hence, "greater far."

A breach, but an expansion,
    Like gold to airy thinness beat.

If they be two, they are two so   25
    As stiff twin compasses are two;
Thy soul, the fixed foot, makes no show
    To move, but doth, if th' other do.

And though it in the center sit,
    Yet when the other far doth roam,   30
It leans and hearkens after it,
    And grows erect, as that comes home.

Such wilt thou be to me, who must
    Like th' other foot, obliquely run;
Thy firmness makes my circle just,   35
    And makes me end where I begun.

For Consideration

1.   Is this poem about the death of one of a pair of lovers, or only a temporary separation? What scene is described in the opening stanza? How is it related to the situation of the man and woman in the poem?

2.   Stanzas three to five introduce astronomical imagery in an attempt to distinguish between two types of lovers: "dull sublunary lovers" and the speaker and his love. On what is the love of the former based? Why does separation threaten their love? In what sense is the love of the latter "so much refined"? How do these two kinds of love relate to the two astronomical movements mentioned in stanza three?

3.   What does the image of beaten gold emphasize about the man and woman? How does it fit into the separation the two are about to experience?

4.   The seventh stanza introduces one of the best known images in English poetry, the comparison of the lovers to the two feet of a compass. How does the poet use the image to comment on their relationship? What role does each have in maintaining their love?

Metonymy and **synecdoche** are closely related as figures of speech. As the term "metaphor" sometimes designates both simile and metaphor, the term "metonymy" is used increasingly to encompass synecdoche as well. In metonymy an object is used in place of something — another object, a profession, an action and so on — which it is closely related to or which it suggests. In Shelley's "Ozymandias" the poet, describing the work of the sculptor and the passions of his subject, refers to "the hand that mocked them [the passions], and the heart that fed." Neither hand nor heart is to be taken literally, of course; each is a substitute, respectively, for the artist who made the figure and the passionate man he represented. Synecdoche is the figure of speech in which a part of something is substituted for the whole or the whole is used in reference to a part. A "roof" may mean house and "engine" may mean automobile. T. S. Eliot's "The Love Song of J. Alfred Prufrock" uses synecdoche when a lobster is referred to as "a pair of ragged claws."

Endowing an object, animal, or abstract concept with human characteristics is the poetic use of **personification**. Keats' "To Autumn" personifies that season throughout, as in these lines:

> Sometimes whoever seeks abroad may find
> Thee sitting careless on a granary floor,
> Thy hair soft-lifted by the winnowing wind.

Similarly, Emily Dickinson personifies Death in "Because I Could Not Stop for Death" and Tennyson personifies the eagle in "The Eagle." A particular form of personification is the **apostrophe**, an address to an inanimate or non-human object or to a person who is understood not to be literally listening. The opening of "The Sun Rising" by Donne includes an apostrophe:

> Busy old fool, unruly sun,

as does Roethke's "The Reply"

> Bird, bird don't edge me in.

Saying more than what one actually means — in other words, exaggeration — is overstatement or **hyperbole**; saying less than what one means is understatement. Giovanni's poem "Ego Tripping" is built on hyperboles:

> I walked to the fertile crescent and built the sphinx.

> The hair from my head thinned and gold was laid across three
>   continents

I mean . . . I . . . can fly
   like a bird in the sky . . .

Marvell's "To His Coy Mistress" contains an effective and ironic understatement. It is used in the context of his attempt to convince his mistress that now, not later, is the time for love:

The grave's a fine and private place,
But none, I think, do there embrace.

Paradox and **oxymoron** are both ways of saying things that are, or appear to be, contradictory. A paradox is a statement that seems necessarily false but is, in an important way, true. Donne's poem "Batter My Heart, Three-Personed God" includes the paradoxical plea to God:

I,
Except You 'enthrall me, never shall be free,
Nor ever chaste, except You ravish me.

Freedom through slavery or chastity through rape are patently impossible — except as the poet works out his meaning here. An oxymoron is, in essence, a condensed paradox, usually made up of an adjective and a noun which are contradictory — e.g., living death, fiery cold. Blake's reference to "the marriage hearse" in the last line of "London" is oxymoronic in its impact.

MARGE PIERCY (1936–   )

Community

Loving feels lonely in a violent world,
irrelevant to people burning like last year's weeds
with bellies distended, with fish throats agape
and flesh melting down to glue.
We can no longer shut out the screaming   5
that leaks through the ventilation system,
the small bits of bone in the processed bread,
so we are trying to make a community
warm, loose as hair but shaped like a weapon.

Caring, we must use each other to death.   10
Love is arthritic. Mistrust swells like a prune.
Perhaps we gather so they may dig one big cheap grave.
From the roof of the Pentagon which is our Bastille
the generals armed like Martians watch through binoculars
the campfires of draftcards and barricades on the grass.   15
All summer helicopters whine over the ghetto.
Casting up jetsam of charred fingers and torn constitutions
the only world breaks on the door of morning.
We have to build our city, our camp
from used razorblades and bumpers and aspirin boxes   20
in the shadow of the nuclear plant that kills the fish
with coke bottle lamps flickering
on the chemical night.

For Consideration

1. What is the basis for the "community" promoted in the poem? What
    qualities about it are evident in line 9 ("warm, loose as hair but shaped
    like a weapon")? Why is love "lonely" and "arthritic"?

2. There are at least two societies evident in the poem — a larger one ("a
    violent world") and the smaller community formed in reaction to the first.
    How are the two different? How are they alike?

JOHN DONNE (1572–1631)
The Sun Rising

Busy old fool, unruly sun,
    Why dost thou thus,
Through windows and through curtains call on us?
Must to thy motions lovers' seasons run?

13. *Bastille* a fortress and prison in Paris, stormed on July 14, 1789 by an angry mob in an action regarded as the outbreak of the French Revolution.

Saucy pedantic wretch, go chide 5
 Late school boys and sour prentices,
Go tell court huntsmen that the king will ride,
 Call country ants to harvest offices;
Love, all alike, no season knows nor clime,
Nor hours, days, months, which are the rags of time. 10

Thy beams, so reverend and strong
 Why shouldst thou think?
I could eclipse and cloud them with a wink,
But that I would not lose her sight so long;
 If her eyes have not blinded thine, 15
 Look, and tomorrow late tell me,
Whether both th' Indias of spice and mine
Be where thou leftst them, or lie here with me.
Ask for those kings whom thou saw'st yesterday,
And thou shalt hear, All here in one bed lay. 20

She's all states, and all princes, I,
 Nothing else is.
Princes do but play us; compared to this,
All honor's mimic, all wealth alchemy.
 Thou, sun, art half as happy as we, 25
 In that the world's contracted thus;
Thine age asks ease, and since thy duties be
 To warm the world, that's done in warming us.
Shine here to us, and thou art everywhere;
This bed thy center is, these walls, thy sphere. 30

For Consideration

1. Donne is known for the abrupt openings to many of his poems. What effect does the abruptness have here?

2. What is the poet's request of the sun? Why does he stress that love is not controlled by time?

3. How does the poet emphasize the value of the woman beside him?

4. The final stanza equates the world at large with the world of the lovers. Why would both the lovers and the sun be happy "that the world's contracted thus"?

17. *Indias* India and the West Indies, both sources of valuable goods. 24. *alchemy* an early and unorthodox predecessor of chemistry, used here in the sense of fraudulent.

STANLEY KUNITZ (1905–   )

The War Against the Trees

The man who sold his lawn to standard oil
Joked with his neighbors come to watch the show
While the bulldozers, drunk with gasoline,
Tested the virtue of the soil
Under the branchy sky   5
By overthrowing first the privet-row.

Forsythia-forays and hydrangea-raids
Were but preliminaries to a war
Against the great-grandfathers of the town,
So freshly lopped and maimed.   10
They struck and struck again,
And with each elm a century went down.

All day the hireling engines charged the trees,
Subverting them by hacking underground
In grub-dominions, where dark summer's mole   15
Rampages through his halls,
Till a northern seizure shook
Those crowns, forcing the giants to their knees.

I saw the ghosts of children at their games
Racing beyond their childhood in the shade,   20
And while the green world turned its death-foxed page
And a red wagon wheeled,
I watched them disappear
Into the suburbs of their grievous age.

Ripped from the craters much too big for hearts   25
The club-roots bared their amputated coils,
Raw gorgons matted blind, whose pocks and scars
Cried Moon! on a corner lot
One witness-moment, caught
In the rear-view mirrors of the passing cars.   30

6. *privet-row* a row of shrubs. **21.** *death-foxed* aged and discolored with death. **27.** *gorgons*
the three snaky-haired sisters in Greek mythology whose glance turned the observer to stone.

For Consideration

1. What image lies behind the descriptions of the bulldozer and the soil in the first stanza? To what effect?

2. What metaphor controls the poem beginning in the second stanza? Who are the "great-grandfathers of the town"? What values are identified with the trees? What characteristics are associated with the tree-destroyers?

3. Where do the ghosts of the children disappear to? Why is theirs a "grievous age"?

4. What are the "gorgons" of the trees? Why are they "matted blind"? Why do the pocks and scars cry "Moon"? What does the last reference suggest, with the scene caught only a moment "in the rear-view mirrors of the passing cars"?

ANDREW MARVELL (1621–1678)

To His Coy Mistress

Had we but world enough, and time,
This coyness, Lady, were no crime.
We would sit down and think which way
To walk and pass our long love's day.
Thou by the Indian Ganges' side   5
Shouldst rubies find; I by the tide
Of Humber would complain. I would
Love you ten years before the Flood,
And you should, if you please, refuse
Till the conversion of the Jews.   10
My vegetable love would grow
Vaster than empires, and more slow;
An hundred years would go to praise
Thine eyes and on thy forehead gaze;
Two hundred to adore each breast,   15
But thirty thousand to the rest;

---

7. *Humber* a river on which Marvell's hometown was located. **10.** *conversion of the Jews* implying the last days of history. In the Christian tradition, it was thought to be one of the final events before the end of the world.

An age at least to every part,
And the last age should show your heart.
For, Lady, you deserve this state,
Nor would I love at lower rate.   20

But at my back I always hear
Time's winged chariot hurrying near;
And yonder all before us lie
Deserts of vast eternity.
Thy beauty shall no more be found,   25
Nor, in thy marble vault, shall sound
My echoing song; then worms shall try
That long preserved virginity,
And your quaint honor turn to dust,
And into ashes all my lust: 30
The grave's a fine and private place,
But none, I think, do there embrace.

Now therefore, while the youthful hue
Sits on thy skin like morning dew,
And while thy willing soul transpires   35
At every pore with instant fires,
Now let us sport us while we may,
And now, like amorous birds of prey,
Rather at once our time devour
Than languish in his slow-chapped power.   40
Let us roll all our strength and all
Our sweetness up into one ball,
And tear our pleasures with rough strife
Through the iron gates of life:
Thus, though we cannot make our sun   45
Stand still, yet we will make him run.

For Consideration

1. The opening section of the poem (lines 1–20) focuses on a conditional
    acceptance of the lady's coyness. On what condition is the acceptance
    based? The poet devotes a number of lines to a description of what he
    would do if there were "world enough, and time." What effect does this
    have?

2. The transitional "But" (line 21) brings us away from the conditional
    statements of the preceding lines. What does the poet affirm the situation

40. *slow-chapped power* the powerful closing of the jaws.

to be in reality? What is the tone of his comments on her continuing virginity and honor?

3.   Line 33 begins the direct appeal. How does the speaker wish himself and his lover to act? How, in this section, will they use time to their advantage? The poet speaks of the two devouring time and of making the sun run, though they cannot make it stand still. What relationship between time and action is he presenting?

JOHN DONNE   (1572–1631)
Death, Be Not Proud

Death, be not proud, though some have callèd thee
Mighty and dreadful, for thou are not so;
For those whom thou think'st thou dost overthrow
Die not, poor Death, nor yet canst thou kill me.
From rest and sleep, which but thy pictures be,   5
Much pleasure; then from thee much more must flow,
And soonest our best men with thee do go,
Rest of their bones, and soul's delivery.
Thou'art slave to fate, chance, kings, and desperate men,
And dost with poison, war, and sickness dwell,   10
And poppy'or charms can make us sleep as well
And better than thy stroke; why swell'st thou then?
One short sleep past, we wake eternally
And death shall be no more; Death, thou shalt die.

For Consideration

1.   The opening four lines of the poem present an opposition to Death's pride and a reason for that opposition, which subsequent lines go on to explore in greater detail. Why does the poet introduce "rest and sleep" in line 5? How are they death's pictures? Why would the "best men" choose to go with death?

2.   Lines 9–12 continue the personification of death and attack death for several reasons, describing it as a slave, citing its unfavorable companions,

and suggesting that others perform its work as well or better. What, on a literal level, is the poet saying about death in each instance?

3. The poem ends with the paradox of death dying. How and when does this happen? Donne was a Christian clergyman; is it helpful or necessary to know that?

An **allusion** is a special kind of figure of speech, a reference to something — usually from history, literature, or myth — outside the context of the poem itself. All figures of speech, of course, add to the immediate context of a poem by encouraging a comparison or an otherwise witty perception of a situation. An allusion, though, is a unique addition, for it assumes knowledge which the poem itself may not supply. The poems which follow both utilize allusion. In Bly's poem, the allusion is a single one; in some respects, in fact, the poem communicates satisfactorily even if the allusion is not perceived. In Eliot's poem, however, allusions are scattered throughout and are a key to much of the meaning of the poem.

Other poems in which allusions are important include Yeats' "The Second Coming," Giovanni's "Ego Tripping," and Sexton's "The Starry Night."

ROBERT BLY (1926–)

The Great Society

Dentists continue to water their lawns even in the rain;
Hands developed with terrible labor by apes
Hang from the sleeves of evangelists;
There are murdered kings in the light-bulbs outside movie theatres;
The coffins of the poor are hibernating in piles of new tires.   5

The janitor sits troubled by the boiler,
And the hotel keeper shuffles the cards of insanity.
The President dreams of invading Cuba.

Bushes are growing over the outdoor grills,
Vines over the yachts and the leather seats.   10

The city broods over ash cans and darkening mortar.
On the far shore, at Coney Island, dark children
Play on the chilling beach: a sprig of black seaweed,
Shells, a skyful of birds,
While the mayor sits with his head in his hands.   15

For Consideration

1. What were the values Lyndon Johnson envisioned for his "great society"?
    What values and characteristics are apparent in the society of the poem?

2. The tone of the poem has surface qualities of being cold, analytical, ob-
    jective. But irony is also important, as each line shows something wrong
    with "the great society." What characteristics tie the various images
    together? Who are the "murdered kings"? What are the "coffins of the
    poor"? The "cards of insanity"?

T. S. ELIOT (1888–1965)

The Love Song of J. Alfred Prufrock

*S'io credessi che mia risposta fosse
a persona che mai tornasse al mondo,
questa fiamma staria senza più scosse.
Ma per ciò che giammai di questo fondo
non tornò vivo alcun, s'i'odo il vero,
senza tema d'infamia ti rispondo.*

Let us go then, you and I,
When the evening is spread out against the sky
Like a patient etherised upon a table;
Let us go, through certain half-deserted streets,

Epigraph. From Dante's *Inferno*, Canto 27, lines 61–66. These words are spoken by a damned
soul encountered by Dante and Virgil. Thinking that his words will never reach the living world,
he says: "If I believed my answer were to a person who would ever return to the world, this
flame would move no more. But since from this depth no one has ever returned alive, if what I
hear is true, without fear of infamy, I answer you."

The muttering retreats   5
Of restless nights in one-night cheap hotels
And sawdust restaurants with oyster-shells:
Streets that follow like a tedious argument
Of insidious intent
To lead you to an overwhelming question. . .   10
Oh, do not ask, 'What is it?'
Let us go and make our visit.

In the room the women come and go
Talking of Michelangelo.

The yellow fog that rubs its back upon the window-panes,   15
The yellow smoke that rubs its muzzle on the window-panes,
Licked its tongue into the corners of the evening,
Lingered upon the pools that stand in drains,
Let fall upon its back the soot that falls from chimneys,
Slipped by the terrace, made a sudden leap,   20
And seeing that it was a soft October night,
Curled once about the house, and fell asleep.

And indeed there will be time
For the yellow smoke that slides along the street
Rubbing its back upon the window-panes;   25
There will be time, there will be time
To prepare a face to meet the faces that you meet;
There will be time to murder and create,
And time for all the works and days of hands
That lift and drop a question on your plate;   30
Time for you and time for me,
And time yet for a hundred indecisions,
And for a hundred visions and revisions,
Before the taking of a toast and tea.

In the room the women come and go   35
Talking of Michaelangelo.

And indeed there will be time
To wonder, 'Do I dare?' and, 'Do I dare?'
Time to turn back and descend the stair,
With a bald spot in the middle of my hair —   40
(They will say: 'How his hair is growing thin!')
My morning coat, my collar mounting firmly to the chin,
My necktie rich and modest, but asserted by a simple pin —
(They will say: 'But how his arms and legs are thin!')
Do I dare   45

29. *works and days* the title of a poem on agricultural life by the Greek poet Hesiod.

Disturb the universe?
In a minute there is time
For decisions and revisions which a minute will reverse.

For I have known them all already, known them all —
Have known the evenings, mornings, afternoons,   50
I have measured out my life with coffee spoons;
I know the voices dying with a dying fall
Beneath the music from a farther room.
    So how should I presume?

And I have known the eyes already, known them all —   55
The eyes that fix you in a formulated phrase,
And when I am formulated, sprawling on a pin,
When I am pinned and wriggling on the wall,
Then how should I begin
To spit out all the butt-ends of my days and ways?   60
    And how should I presume?

And I have known the arms already, known them all —
Arms that are braceleted and white and bare
(But in the lamplight, downed with light brown hair!)
Is it perfume from a dress   65
That makes me so digress?
Arms that lie along a table, or wrap about a shawl.
    And should I then presume?
    And how should I begin?

  . . . .
Shall I say, I have gone at dusk through narrow streets   70
And watched the smoke that rises from the pipes
Of lonely men in shirt-sleeves, leaning out of windows? . . .

I should have been a pair of ragged claws
Scuttling across the floors of silent seas.

  . . . . .
And the afternoon, the evening, sleeps so peacefully!   75
Smoothed by long fingers,
Asleep . . . tired . . . or it malingers,
Stretched on the floor, here beside you and me.
Should I, after tea and cakes and ices,
Have the strength to force the moment to its crisis?   80
But though I have wept and fasted, wept and prayed,
Though I have seen my head (grown slightly bald) brought in upon a
          platter,
I am no prophet — and here's no great matter;

52. *dying fall* echoing a speech from Shakespeare's *Twelfth Night* (I.i.4).

I have seen the moment of my greatness flicker,
And I have seen the eternal Footman hold my coat, and snicker,   85
And in short, I was afraid.

And would it have been worth it, after all,
After the cups, the marmalade, the tea,
Among the porcelain, among some talk of you and me,
Would it have been worth while,   90
To have bitten off the matter with a smile,
To have squeezed the universe into a ball
To roll it towards some overwhelming question,
To say: 'I am Lazarus, come from the dead,
Come back to tell you all, I shall tell you all' —   95
If one, settling a pillow by her head,
   Should say: 'That is not what I meant at all.
   That is not it, at all.'

And would it have been worth it, after all,
Would it have been worth while,   100
After the sunsets and the dooryards and the sprinkled streets,
After the novels, after the teacups, after the skirts that trail along the
               floor —
And this, and so much more? —
It is impossible to say just what I mean!
But as if a magic lantern threw the nerves in patterns on a screen: 105
Would it have been worth while
If one, settling a pillow or throwing off a shawl,
And turning toward the window, should say:
   'That is not it at all,
   That is not what I meant, at all.'   110

            . . . . .

No! I am not Prince Hamlet, nor was meant to be;
Am an attendant lord, one that will do
To swell a progress, start a scene or two,
Advise the prince; no doubt, an easy tool,
Deferential, glad to be of use,   115
Politic, cautious, and meticulous;
Full of high sentence, but a bit obtuse;
At times, indeed, almost ridiculous —
Almost, at times, the Fool.

I grow old . . . I grow old . . .   120
I shall wear the bottoms of my trousers rolled.

92. *To have squeezed the universe into a ball* drawn from Marvell's "To His Coy Mistress"
(lines 41–42). **94–95.** *Lazarus* raised from the dead by Jesus as described in the Gospels. Eliot
may also be alluding to Luke 16:19–31, an account of the life and afterlife of Lazarus and the
rich man. **118.** *Full of high sentence* from the description of the Clerk of Oxford in Chaucer's
The Canterbury Tales.

Shall I part my hair behind? Do I dare to eat a peach?
I shall wear white flannel trousers, and walk upon the beach.
I have heard the mermaids singing, each to each.

I do not think that they will sing to me.   125

I have seen them riding seaward on the waves
Combing the white hair of the waves blown back
When the wind blows the water white and black.

We have lingered in the chambers of the sea
By sea-girls wreathed with seaweed red and brown   130
Till human voices wake us, and we drown.

For Consideration

1. What is the association between the epigraph from Dante and the poem
    proper?

2. Characterize Prufrock as fully as possible. What is his conception of
    himself? Who are the "you and I" at the beginning of the poem? There
    are several indications of the kind of society in which Prufrock finds
    himself. What are its features?

3. Prufrock is apparently on his way to an afternoon or evening tea where
    he will ask "some overwhelming question" (perhaps an avowal of love) to
    a woman present. The poem itself, however, follows the thoughts of
    Prufrock himself (a kind of poetic stream of consciousness technique)
    rather than relying on objective description. What connections are there
    among the various thoughts Prufrock expresses?

4. Adding to the difficulty of the poem are the several allusions, some
    familiar, some not. Besides the verbal references identified in the notes,
    there are allusions to the beheading of John the Baptist (lines 81–83), to
    Hamlet and Polonius (and possibly others) from *Hamlet* (lines 111 ff) and,
    perhaps, to the Fool from *King Lear* (Line 119). What purposes are served
    by these allusions? How is Prufrock's situation comparable to that in
    Marvell's poem? How is he unlike Hamlet but like an "attendant lord" in
    the play?

5. What do the mermaids represent at the end of the poem? What is
    suggested by the last line, "Till human voices wake us, and we drown"?

imagery: symbol and allegory

As can be seen from the previous examples, imagery is an encompassing term. Metaphors, similes, personifications — as well as many literal references and allusions — all appeal to our sensory perception. An image need not be figurative (e.g., the tree in "The Starry Night" or the eagle falling in "The Eagle") but, as we have seen, a figure of speech usually creates an image.

We see another type of image at work in these examples.

WILLIAM BLAKE (1757–1827)
The Lamb

Little Lamb, who made thee?
  Dost thou know who made thee?
Gave thee life & bid thee feed,
By the stream & o'er the mead;
Gave thee clothing of delight,   5
Softest clothing wooly bright;
Gave thee such a tender voice,
Making all the vales rejoice!
  Little Lamb who made thee?
  Dost thou know who made thee?   10

  Little Lamb I'll tell thee,
  Little Lamb I'll tell thee!
He is called by thy name,

For he calls himself a Lamb:
He is meek & he is mild,   15
He became a little child:
I a child & thou a lamb,
We are callèd by his name.
   Little Lamb God bless thee.
   Little Lamb God bless thee.   20

WILLIAM BLAKE (1757–1827)
The Tyger

Tyger! Tyger! burning bright
In the forests of the night,
What immortal hand or eye
Could frame thy fearful symmetry?

In what distant deeps or skies   5
Burnt the fire of thine eyes?
On what wings dare he aspire?
What the hand, dare seize the fire?

And what shoulder, & what art,
Could twist the sinews of thy heart?   10
And when thy heart began to beat,
What dread hand? & what dread feet?

What the hammer? what the chain?
In what furnace was thy brain?
What the anvil? what dread grasp   15
Dare its deadly terrors clasp?

When the stars threw down their spears,
And water'd heaven with their tears,
Did he smile his work to see?
Did he who made the Lamb make thee?   20

Tyger! Tyger! burning bright

In the forests of the night,
What immortal hand or eye
Dare frame thy fearful symmetry?

"The Lamb" For Consideration

1. Who is the speaker here? Beyond the identification in line 17, what characteristics of the poem help identify the speaker?

2. What is the relationship between the subject, the lamb, and the speaker? What qualities in each does the poem call attention to?

"The Tyger" For Consideration

1. What qualities are associated with the "tyger"? What portrait is created by terms such as "fearful symmetry," "distant deeps," "dread hand," "dread feet," "dread grasp," and "deadly terrors"? Does the tiger seem to be "real"?

2. What qualities are associated with the creator of the tiger? Are they the same as those associated with the tiger?

Neither of the creatures addressed in these companion poems is the object of a metaphor; in neither poem is there an explicit comparison of the lamb to something else or the tiger to something else. At the same time, most readers would agree that the poems are not simply about a white, fluffy creature called a lamb and a larger, more ferocious creature called a tiger. Meanings and associations reverberate from each poem, but they are not tied to an exact metaphor. We have, rather, the creatures operating as **symbols** of qualities and values beyond themselves. A symbol, as we see in these examples, is an object or action so loaded with significance that its meaning transcends its literal appearance. The distinction between metaphor and symbol is often a blurry one; generally, though, a metaphor refers to something other than itself, a symbol refers to itself and something more. The lamb is a lamb but something more, the tiger is a tiger but more than that as well. The lamb and the tiger are conventional symbols; that is, they have, through a number of centuries, acquired certain associations that continue to the present, the lamb associated with childlike innocence and delight, the tiger with strength and ferocity. Similarly, a cross is a traditional symbol of the Christian religion, a rose is a usual symbol of love, fire is a conventional symbol of purification or, alternately, of destruction. We cannot merely stop with conventional associations, of course, for we need to see how the poet works out his aim in each poem. The conventional qualities, though, give us a firm starting point. A poet may also invent a personal symbol for use in a particular poem; such a creation relies, not on traditional associations acquired through long use, but on the particular qualities attached to an object or action during the course of a work. The symbolism in such modern poems as Eliot's "The Love Song of J. Alfred Prufrock" or Yeats' "The Second Coming" is largely of the poet's own making.

If the symbolic level conveys a story in which each object or character stands for something other than itself, we refer to the selection as an **allegory**. One difference between symbol and allegory is the matter of exactness. In spite of their importance as conventional symbols, we cannot say with certainty what the lamb and the tiger of Blake's poems represent. That is, we cannot circumscribe a fence around the "meaning" of each and say, "This is what it means, and nothing more." Allegory allows us to perceive more rigid relationships between object and meaning. The difference between symbol and allegory can be further illustrated by looking at two poems of George Herbert, a seventeenth-century English poet and Anglican priest.

GEORGE HERBERT (1593–1633)

Life

I made a posy, while the day ran by:
"Here will I smell my remnant out, and tie
       My life within this band."
But Time did beckon to the flowers, and they
By noon most cunningly did steal away,   5
       And withered in my hand.

My hand was next to them, and then my heart;
I took, without more thinking, in good part

                    Time's gentle admonition;
Who did so sweetly death's sad taste convey,   10
Making my mind to smell my fatal day,
                    Yet sugaring the suspicion.

Farewell dear flowers, sweetly your time ye spent,
Fit, while ye lived, for smell or ornament,
                    And after death for cures.   15
I follow straight without complaints or grief,
Since, if my scent be good, I care not if
                    It be as short as yours.

GEORGE HERBERT (1593–1633)

Redemption

Having been tenant long to a rich lord,
    Not thriving, I resolvéd to be bold,
    And make a suit unto him, to afford
A new small-rented lease, and cancel the old.

In heaven at his manor I him sought;   5
    They told me there that he was lately gone
    About some land, which he had dearly bought
Long since on earth, to take possessiön.

I straight returned, and knowing his great birth,
    Sought him accordingly in great resorts;   10
    In cities, theaters, gardens, parks, and courts;
At length I heard a ragged noise and mirth
    Of thieves and murderers; there I him espied,
    Who straight, *Your suit is granted*, said, and died.

In the poem "Life" the poet has consciously made the flowers a symbol so that he can, as he says, "tie/My life within this band." The flowers remain flowers throughout but are invested with additional significance because of the poet's aim in the poem. Each stage in the life of the flowers allows the poet to understand his own life and his own future better. "Redemption" encourages us to see a one-to-one relationship between the story told and its meaning in terms of the Christian concept of redemption. From the initial reference to a "rich lord" to the final description of the lord's death — each action mentioned has an additional meaning within the framework of the Christian religion. Both poems lead us beyond the literal level, one symbolically, the other allegorically.

The following poems include objects or actions which can be read symbolically. Do any encourage an allegorical reading?

WALT WHITMAN (1819–1892)

I Saw in Louisiana a Live-oak Growing

I saw in Louisiana a live-oak growing,
All alone stood it and the moss hung down from the branches,
Without any companion it grew there uttering joyous leaves of dark
      green,
And its look, rude, unbending, lusty, made me think of myself,
But I wonder'd how it could utter joyous leaves standing alone there
      without its friend near, for I knew I could not,   5
And I broke off a twig with a certain number of leaves upon it, and
      twined around it a little moss,
And brought it away, and I have placed it in sight in my room,
It is not needed to remind me as of my own dear friends,
(For I believe lately I think of little else than of them,)
Yet it remains to me a curious token, it makes me think of manly love;   10
For all that, and though the live-oak glistens there in Louisiana solitary
      in a wide flat space,
Uttering joyous leaves all its life without a friend a lover near,
I know very well I could not.

For Consideration

1. The poet here consciously makes a symbol ("a curious token") of the tree and the twig he breaks from it. Why does it make him think of himself? Why does he disassociate himself from it?

2. What is the "manly love" which the twig reminds him of? What might be the traditional values associated with "manliness" which the poet is thinking of here?

WILLIAM BLAKE (1757–1827)

A Poison Tree

I was angry with my friend:
I told my wrath, my wrath did end.
I was angry with my foe:
I told it not, my wrath did grow.

And I waterd it in fears,   5
Night & morning with my tears;
And I sunnéd it with smiles,
And with soft deceitful wiles.

And it grew both day and night,
Till it bore an apple bright.   10
And my foe beheld it shine,
And he knew that it was mine,

And into my garden stole,
When the night had veild the pole;
In the morning glad I see   15
My foe stretched beneath the tree.

For Consideration

1.   What two responses are indicated in lines 2 and 4 of stanza one? What differing effects do they have?

2.   What literal actions are implied by each of the imaginative actions in the poem? What is the point of the poem?

ROBERT FROST   (1874—1963)
The Subverted Flower

She drew back; he was calm:
"It is this that had the power."
And he lashed his open palm
With the tender-headed flower.
He smiled for her to smile,   5
But she was either blind
Or willfully unkind.
He eyed her for a while
For a woman and a puzzle.
He flicked and flung the flower,   10
And another sort of smile
Caught up like fingertips
The corners of his lips
And cracked his ragged muzzle.
She was standing to the waist   15
In goldenrod and brake,
Her shining hair displaced.
He stretched her either arm
As if she made it ache
To clasp her — not to harm;   20
As if he could not spare
To touch her neck and hair.
"If this has come to us
And not to me alone ——"
So she thought she heard him say;   25
Though with every word he spoke
His lips were sucked and blown
And the effort made him choke

Like a tiger at a bone.
She had to lean away. 30
She dared not stir a foot,
Lest movement should provoke
The demon of pursuit
That slumbers in a brute.
It was then her mother's call 35
From inside the garden wall
Made her steal a look of fear
To see if he could hear
And would pounce to end it all
Before her mother came. 40
She looked and saw the shame:
A hand hung like a paw,
An arm worked like a saw
As if to be persuasive,
An ingratiating laugh 45
That cut the snout in half,
An eye become evasive.
A girl could only see
That a flower had marred a man,
But what she could not see 50
Was that the flower might be
Other than base and fetid:
That the flower had done but part,
And what the flower began
Her own too meager heart 55
Had terribly completed.
She looked and saw the worst.
And the dog or what it was,
Obeying bestial laws,
A coward save at night, 60
Turned from the place and ran.
She heard him stumble first
And use his hands in flight.
She heard him bark outright.
And oh, for one so young 65
The bitter words she spit
Like some tenacious bit
That will not leave the tongue.
She plucked her lips for it,
And still the horror clung. 70
Her mother wiped the foam
From her chin, picked up her comb,
And drew her backward home.

52. *fetid* having a heavy smell.

For Consideration

1. What are the beginning attitudes of the man and woman in the poem? What is the man intending by his use of the flower to strike his hand? Of what might the flower be a symbol?

2. The first twenty-four lines focus mainly on the point of view of the man, the remainder, the point of view of the woman. What differences are there in their perspectives?

3. What does the woman fear? What image does she associate with the man?

4. At what point do we see the poet's attitude toward the experience described? Where do his sympathies lie?

5. What image is associated with the man at the end? From whose point of view do we see him? What image is associated with the woman? From whose point of view do we see her?

D. H. LAWRENCE   (1885–1930)

Snake

A snake came to my water-trough
On a hot, hot day, and I in pyjamas for the heat,
To drink there.

In the deep, strange-scented shade of the great dark carob-tree
I came down the steps with my pitcher   5
And must wait, must stand and wait, for there he was at the trough
        before me.

He reached down from a fissure in the earth-wall in the gloom
And trailed his yellow-brown slackness soft-bellied down, over the
        edge of the stone trough
And rested his throat upon the stone bottom,
And where the water had dripped from the tap, in a small clearness,   10
He sipped with his straight mouth,
Softly drank through his straight gums, into his slack long body,
Silently.

Someone was before me at my water-trough,
And I, like a second comer, waiting.   15

He lifted his head from his drinking, as cattle do,
And looked at me vaguely, as drinking cattle do,
And flickered his two-forked tongue from his lips, and mused
        a moment,
And stooped and drank a little more,
Being earth-brown, earth-golden from the burning bowels of the earth   20
On the day of Sicilian July, with Etna smoking.

The voice of my education said to me
He must be killed,
For in Sicily the black, black snakes are innocent, the gold are
        venomous.

And voices in me said, If you were a man   25
You would take a stick and break him now, and finish him off.

But must I confess how I liked him,
How glad I was he had come like a guest in quiet, to drink
        at my water-trough
And depart peaceful, pacified, and thankless,
Into the burning bowels of this earth?   30

Was it cowardice, that I dared not kill him?
Was it perversity, that I longed to talk to him?
Was it humility, to feel so honoured?
I felt so honoured.

And yet those voices: 35
If you were not afraid, you would kill him!

And truly I was afraid, I was most afraid,
But even so, honoured still more
That he should seek my hospitality
From out the dark door of the secret earth.   40

He drank enough
And lifted his head, dreamily, as one who has drunken,
And flickered his tongue like a forked night on the air, so black;
Seeming to lick his lips,
And looked around like a god, unseeing, into the air,   45
And slowly turned his head,
And slowly, very slowly, as if thrice adream,
Proceeded to draw his slow length curving round
And climb again the broken bank of my wall-face.

And as he put his head into that dreadful hole,   50
And as he slowly drew up, snake-easing his shoulders, and
        entered farther,

A sort of horror, a sort of protest against his withdrawing
          into that horrid black hole,
Deliberately going into the blackness, and slowly drawing
          himself after,
Overcame me now his back was turned.

I looked round, I put down my pitcher,   55
I picked up a clumsy log
And threw it at the water-trough with a clatter.

I think it did not hit him,
But suddenly that part of him that was left behind convulsed
          in undignified haste,
Writhed like lightning, and was gone   60
Into the black hole, the earth-lipped fissure in the wall-front,
At which, in the intense still noon, I stared with fascination.

And immediately I regretted it.
I thought how paltry, how vulgar, what a mean act!
I despised myself and the voices of my accursed human education.   65

And I thought of the albatross,
And I wished he would come back, my snake.

For he seemed to me again like a king,
Like a king in exile, uncrowned in the underworld,
Now due to be crowned again.   70

And so, I missed my chance with one of the lords
Of life.
And I have something to expiate;
A pettiness.

For Consideration

1. What is the initial response of the speaker to the snake's appearance?
    Why does he give so much attention to the physical qualities and actions
    of the snake?

2. What are the "voice of my education" and the other voices which urge
    the man to kill the snake and mock him for not doing so? What is the
    source of the speaker's admiration for the snake?

66. *albatross* a large seabird. It was for killing an albatross that Coleridge's ancient mariner
("The Rime of the Ancient Mariner") was cursed.

3. Why does the man throw the log at the snake in spite of his earlier reaction? How does he feel after he has done it?

4. Why is the snake seen as "a king in exile" and as "one of the lords/of life"? What is the "pettiness" which the speaker must now expiate?

For Comparison

"The Fish" (p. 337) and "Snake" depict creatures considered either unattractive or frightening, yet each speaker gains something significant from the contact. In what ways are the responses similar? How are they different?

ROBERT FROST   (1874—1963)

Birches

When I see birches bend to left and right
Across the lines of straighter darker trees,
I like to think some boy's been swinging them.
But swinging doesn't bend them down to stay
As ice storms do. Often you must have seen them   5
Loaded with ice a sunny winter morning
After a rain. They click upon themselves
As the breeze rises, and turn many-colored
As the stir cracks and crazes their enamel.
Soon the sun's warmth makes them shed crystal shells   10
Shattering and avalanching on the snow crust —
Such heaps of broken glass to sweep away
You'd think the inner dome of heaven had fallen.
They are dragged to the withered bracken by the load,
And they seem not to break; though once they are bowed   15
So low for long, they never right themselves:
You may see their trunks arching in the woods
Years afterwards, trailing their leaves on the ground
Like girls on hands and knees that throw their hair
Before them over their heads to dry in the sun.   20
But I was going to say when Truth broke in

14. *bracken* overgrowth of plants.

With all her matter of fact about the ice storm,
I should prefer to have some boy bend them
As he went out and in to fetch the cows —
Some boy too far from town to learn baseball,   25
Whose only play was what he found himself,
Summer or winter, and could play alone.
One by one he subdued his father's trees
By riding them down over and over again
Until he took the stiffness out of them,   30
And not one but hung limp, not one was left
For him to conquer. He learned all there was
To learn about not launching out too soon
And so not carrying the tree away
Clear to the ground. He always kept his poise   35
To the top branches, climbing carefully
With the same pains you use to fill a cup
Up to the brim, and even above the brim.
Then he flung outward, feet first, with a swish,
Kicking his way down through the air to the ground.   40
So was I once myself a swinger of birches.
And so I dream of going back to be.
It's when I'm weary of considerations,
And life is too much like a pathless wood
Where your face burns and tickles with the cobwebs   45
Broken across it, and one eye is weeping
From a twig's having lashed across it open.
I'd like to get away from earth awhile
And then come back to it and begin over.
May no fate willfully misunderstand me   50
And half grant what I wish and snatch me away
Not to return. Earth's the right place for love:
I don't know where it's likely to go better.
I'd like to go by climbing a birch tree,
And climb black branches up a snow-white trunk   55
Toward heaven, till the tree could bear no more,
But dipped its top and set me down again.
That would be good both going and coming back.
One could do worse than be a swinger of birches.

For Consideration

1. Where does Truth break into the poet's thoughts? How does he react to
   it? Why does he prefer his own account, even if untrue?

2. What does the swinger of birches get from his experience (lines 23–40)? Why does the speaker "dream of going back to be" a swinger?

3. Lines 50–58 qualify the poet's desire "to get away from earth awhile." Why does he not wish to be misunderstood? The poem focuses on two types of experiences in life, one producing weariness, the other exuberance. What are the characteristics associated with life "like a pathless wood"? With the swinging of birches? Which type of experience is the more permanent in the poem?

rhythm, rhyme, and sound

The most obvious difference between poetry and prose is in form. Prose is written in sentences, poetry in lines; prose is in paragraphs, poetry in stanzas. Because of this, a thorough study of poetry involves principles related to the formal presentation of language in verse, in other words, principles of metrics or versification. **Prosody**, the study of technical matters of verse, need not, and in most instances should not, be an end in itself. Rather, rhythm, rhyme, and sound, like other elements of poetry, can make important contributions to the meaning of a poem.

    Rhythm (from a Greek word meaning "flow") refers to the total metrical effect of the pattern of stressed and unstressed syllables, the pauses, the length of the lines — all that goes into creating the movement and flow of the poem. The basic starting point in assessing rhythm is **meter**, which, in English verse, is the more or less regular pattern of stressed and unstressed syllables in a line. Paul Fussell has suggested in *Poetic Meter and Poetic Form* that meter and rhythm can "mean" in at least three ways. First, because meter is a convention, it calls immediate attention to the poem itself. When we see even a brief poem written with meter, lines, and stanzas, we understand immediately that a concentrated, figurative, or symbolic portrait will emerge. If we go to an ornithological lecture on the eagle or begin to read an essay titled "The Eagle" we bring to each experience certain assumptions or expectations. When we see Tennyson's poem titled "The Eagle," however, we realize, as Fussell claims, that we will not experience the "real object" but the object "transmuted into symbolic form." Thus we are prepared when Tennyson's eagle looks like this:

He clasps the crag with crooked hands;
Close to the sun in lonely lands,
Ringed with the azure world, he stands.

The wrinkled sea beneath him crawls;
He watches from his mountain walls,
And like a thunderbolt he falls.

Second, because there are standard and regular meters, marked deviations from the norm can produce striking emotional effects. Poets occasionally use a regular meter to produce certain expectations about rhythm or mood and then abruptly alter the meter at a point which coincides with a significant change in mood or meaning. The first six lines of Yeats' "The Second Coming" provide a brief example of this effect:

Turning and turning in the widening gyre
The falcon cannot hear the falconer;
Things fall apart; the center cannot hold;
Mere anarchy is loosed upon the world,
The blood-dimmed tide is loosed, and everywhere
The ceremony of innocence is drowned;

The first two lines, which focus on the image of the falcon and the falconer, are regular and rhythmic, easily and smoothly read. The movement and turning described are reflected in the easy flow of the lines. Beginning in the third line, however, where the subject is the falling apart of order and society, the meter also "falls apart"; the lines are abrupt and jerky, reinforcing the disorder. The regularity of the first two lines thus emphasizes the deviations which characterize the next four lines.

Fussell suggests, third, that because meters are frequently associated with certain emotions or qualities, they can enhance those qualities regardless of the subject. In this regard Fussell notes that the form and meter of the limerick, regardless of its subject, connote impudence or indecency. Here are two examples. What emotions do the form and meter evoke as you read the limericks?

A tutor who tooted the flute
Tried to tutor two tooters to toot.
    Said the two to the tutor,
    "Is it harder to toot or
To tutor two tooters to toot?"

There was a young woman named Lynn
Whose physique was so terribly thin
    That when she essayed

To drink lemonade
She slipped through the straw and fell in.

W. H. Auden's poem on the death of his fellow-poet W. B. Yeats
is a more complex and, certainly, more important example of the
association between emotion and rhythm.

W. H. AUDEN (1907–1973)

In Memory of W. B. Yeats

(d. Jan. 1939)

I

He disappeared in the dead of winter:
The brooks were frozen, the airports almost deserted,
And snow disfigured the public statues;
The mercury sank in the mouth of the dying day.
What instruments we have agree   5
The day of his death was a dark cold day.

Far from his illness
The wolves ran on through the evergreen forests,
The peasant river was untempted by the fashionable quays;
By mourning tongues   10
The death of the poet was kept from his poems.

But for him it was his last afternoon as himself,
An afternoon of nurses and rumours;
The provinces of his body revolted,
The squares of his mind were empty,   15
Silence invaded the suburbs,
The current of his feeling failed; he became his admirers.

Now he is scattered among a hundred cities
And wholly given over to unfamiliar affections,
To find his happiness in another kind of wood   20

9. *quays* paved banks or artificial landing points on a river.

And be punished under a foreign code of conscience.
The words of a dead man
Are modified in the guts of the living.

But in the importance and noise of to-morrow
When the brokers are roaring like beasts on the floor of the Bourse,   25
And the poor have the sufferings to which they are fairly
      accustomed,
And each in the cell of himself is almost convinced of his freedom,
A few thousand will think of this day
As one thinks of a day when one did something slightly unusual.
What instruments we have agree   30
The day of his death was a dark cold day.

II

You were silly like us; your gift survived it all:
The parish of rich women, physical decay,
Yourself. Mad Ireland hurt you into poetry.
Now Ireland has her madness and her weather still,   35
For poetry makes nothing happen: it survives
In the valley of its making where executives
Would never want to tamper, flows on south
From ranches of isolation and the busy griefs,
Raw towns that we believe and die in; it survives,   40
A way of happening, a mouth.

III

Earth, receive an honoured guest:
William Yeats is laid to rest.
Let the Irish vessel lie
Emptied of its poetry.   45

In the nightmare of the dark
All the dogs of Europe bark,
And the living nations wait,
Each sequestered in its hate;

Intellectual disgrace   50
Stares from every human face,
And the seas of pity lie
Locked and frozen in each eye.

25. *Bourse* European stock exchange.

Follow, poet, follow right
To the bottom of the night,   55
With your unconstraining voice
Still persuade us to rejoice;

With the farming of a verse
Make a vineyard of the curse,
Sing of human unsuccess   60
In a rapture of distress;

In the deserts of the heart
Let the healing fountain start,
In the prison of his days
Teach the free man how to praise.   65

For Consideration

1. How does Auden use the time of Yeats' death as an image in his poem?

2. The second stanza focuses on others, the third on Yeats himself. What is happening "far from his illness"? How was "the death of the poet . . . kept from his poems"? What does Auden mean in saying that the dead poet "became his admirers"?

3. What do the third and fourth stanzas suggest about the poet's audience of admirers? How do they represent the words and thoughts of Yeats? What is the tone of these stanzas? Is the intent to disparage or praise the few who are affected by Yeats' death?

4. The second part is addressed to Yeats but deals more with a conception of poetry. What is poetry here? Why does it make "nothing happen"?

5. The rhythm and rhyme of Part III have changed dramatically. How do they reinforce the meaning of the poem in this part? Stanzas two and three refer to the oncoming of World War II but they portray more generally the situation of human beings at the time. What kind of society does Auden describe? What is the attitude of individuals? What, in the final three stanzas especially, is the poet's role and his response to the situation? How will he "rejoice," "sing," and "praise"?

The poem begins by emphasizing the dreary and cold day on which Yeats died and the accompanying mood of dreariness and melancholy. There is a speech-like quality to the poem at that point; it is slow, without any regular metrical beat, in keeping with the somber tone and subject. The final section of the poem, however, as a contrast to the earlier emphasis on dying and mourning, focuses on Yeats' role as a poet and emphasizes the qualities of healing and of praise which are implicit in the poet's role. Significantly, the meter of the poem is regular and fast, almost lilting in its effect. We can isolate and mark the rhythm of a stanza in the last section and see its consistent pattern (∪ = unaccented syllable, ∕ = accented syllable):

Earth, receive an honoured guest:

William Yeats is laid to rest.

Let the Irish vessel lie

Emptied of its poetry.

In spite of the death which gives occasion to the poem, Auden clearly wants us to read the final section of his elegy with a spirited joy, a joy ironic in light of the "nightmare" of stanzas two and three but in keeping with the poet's own efforts to "persuade us to rejoice."

In some verse, meter is based on the length of time required to pronounce syllables (quantitative verse) or on the number of syllables per line (syllabic verse), but in most English verse, meter is based on **stress** or **accent**. A particular meter is judged to be a more or less regular pattern of stressed and unstressed syllables. The basic unit of measurement in a line of poetry is called a **foot**. A foot nearly always consists of two or three syllables, one of which is stressed. The particular pattern of stressed and unstressed syllables and the number of such combinations (the number of feet) per line becomes the usual way of indicating the meter of a poem. The most common feet in English poetry are:

iamb (iambic) — one unstressed syllable followed by one stressed (∪∕)

trochee (trochaic) — one stressed syllable followed by one unstressed (∕∪)

anapest (anapestic) — two unstressed syllables followed by one stressed (∪∪∕)

dactyl (dactylic) — one stressed syllable followed by two unstressed (∕∪∪)

spondee (spondaic) — two stressed syllables (∕∕)

The feet themselves can suggest certain moods or emotions. Most noticeably, the two stressed syllables of the spondee hint at importance or special emphasis to that part of the line. The number of feet per line are indicated by the following terms:

monometer — one foot

dimeter — two feet

trimeter — three feet

tetrameter — four feet

pentameter — five feet

hexameter — six feet

heptameter — seven feet

octameter — eight feet

The analysis or scansion of the meter of a given poem may lead to the conclusion that it is composed of four feet of an unstressed syllable followed by a stressed syllable — hence, iambic tetrameter. The meter of the following line from Robert Herrick's "Delight in Disorder" is an example:

An erring lace, which here and there

It is unusual, of course, for an entire poem to be made up of a single, unvarying meter. Herrick's poem is dominated by one meter, but, as we see below, there are several variations:

ROBERT HERRICK   (1591–1674)
Delight in Disorder

A sweet| disor|der in| the dress

Kindles| in clothes| a wan|tonness.

A lawn| about| the shoul|ders thrown

Into | a fine | distrac | tion;°

An err | ing lace, | which here | and there   5

Enthralls | the crim | son stom | acher;

A cuff | neglect | ful, and | thereby

Ribbons | to flow | confus | edly;

A win | ning wave, | deserv | ing note,

In the | tempest | uous pet | ticoat;   10

A care | less shoe | string, in | whose tie

I see | a wild | civil | ity;

Do more | bewitch | me than | when art

Is too | precise | in ev | ery part.

Herrick's poem is marked by a basic rhythm pattern, dominated by the iambic tetrameter. But the several exceptions to this pattern illustrate some important principles of scansion. As you scan a poem you should look for the stress pattern which recognizes the best meaning and the best sound of the words; do not be fooled into thinking that the recurring meter must be followed resolutely. Variations such as those seen in lines 4 and 10 or in words such as "kindles" or "ribbons" establish a counter-rhythm which is set against the expected rhythm of the regular iambic tetrameter pattern. Furthermore, the variations are more consistent with the syntactical emphasis of given words and phrases; "kindles" and "ribbons," in poetry or out, are not pronounced "kin-dles" or "rib-bóns." It is appropriate, too, that there be some "disorder" in the meter, since the subject of the poem is disorder of other types. The last two lines, which call attention to "precise" art, are appropriately regular in their rhythm pattern. All of this is to suggest that reading poetry, while not simply like reading prose, need not be overly strained or artificial.

The temptation to read "poetically" also spills over to the reading of sentences and phrases. Because poems are written in lines, we

° Herrick would probably have pronounced this word with four syllables to fill out the line. The last foot (˘ ˘) is called a pyrrhic and is uncommon in English verse.

sometimes mistakenly believe that we should pause at the end of each line, catch a breath, and then go on to the next line. This is an appropriate way of reading only if the line is an end-stopped line, if there is, in other words, a definite pause in syntax. The punctuation of lines 2, 4, 6, 8, 9, 10, and 12 in Herrick's poem indicates the value of a pause; the syntax of lines 1, 3, and 5 may justify a briefer pause though there is no punctuation. We would do wrong, though, to separate the last two lines in the same way. A key phrase, in fact, is "when art/Is too precise"; we should therefore read it for its best meaning. Line 13 is an example of a run-on line; the meter and rhyme are important, but they should not distort the appropriate syntactical emphasis.

Metrical anaylsis is not, of course, an exact science. A sentence of prose may be given several different emphases; so may a line of poetry. You may quite properly disagree with certain of my accentual markings of Herrick's poem. Generally speaking, though, the discrepancies between two readings of the same line will not be great. The aim is not to arrive at the single correct analysis but to promote a reasonable and effective one.

A few other metrical terms deserve mention. If there is a complete pause in the middle of a line we have a **caesura**, but it does not affect the meter of the line:

> Things fall apart; the center cannot hold
>
> Yeats, "The Second Coming"

Lines which end (and possibly rhyme) on unaccented syllables are said to have a feminine ending:

> Into a fine distraction
>
> Enthralls the crimson stomacher.

Lines which end on accented syllables are said to have a masculine ending:

> A winning wave, deserving note,
> In the tempestuous petticoat.

A **stanza** of poetry is a unit consisting of several lines, usually with the same metrical pattern. A **couplet** is a stanza (or a distinct grouping) of two lines, usually rhymed. The heroic couplet is a rhyming couplet of iambic pentameter, usually containing a complete thought and with a noticeable emphasis at the end of each line. Its name derives from its frequent use in heroic or epic poems, particularly in eighteenth-century England. The triplet or **tercet** is a three-line stanza, usually of one rhyme. The **quatrain** is a four-line stanza, whether rhymed or un-rhymed.

We should conclude this discussion of rhythm in poetry by emphasizing that not all poetry is rhythmical. Much modern poetry is written as **free verse**; that is, it is free of metrical restrictions. It may include rhyme though ordinarily it does not. Free verse should not be confused with **blank verse**, which is metrical poetry composed of lines of unrhymed iambic pentameter.

For the following poems try some experimenting. Read them silently, then aloud. If there is a regular rhythm pattern, try over-emphasizing it; then go back and read the poem in light of syntax and meaning. If the poem is not a metrical one, what determines stress and accent? Note how rhythm and meaning cohere in some of the poems.

ALEXANDER POPE (1688–1744)

From An Essay on Man

Know then thyself, presume not God to scan;
The proper study of Mankind is Man.
Plac'd on this isthmus of a middle state,
A Being darkly wise, and rudely great:
With too much knowledge for the Sceptic side,　　　　5
With too much weakness for the Stoic's pride,
He hangs between; in doubt to act, or rest;
In doubt to deem himself a God, or Beast;
In doubt his Mind or Body to prefer;
Born but to die, and reas'ning but to err;　　　　10
Alike in ignorance, his reason such,
Whether he thinks too little, or too much:
Chaos of Thought and Passion, all confus'd;
Still by himself abus'd, or disabus'd;
Created half to rise, and half to fall;　　　　15
Great lord of all things, yet a prey to all;
Sole judge of Truth, in endless Error hurl'd:
The glory, jest, and riddle of the world!

For Consideration

1. What conception of man governs this poem? What are the various ways in which he occupies a "middle state"? What is the purpose of such oxymoronic phrases as "darkly wise" and "rudely great"? Why is the persona here neither Sceptic nor Stoic?

2. What is the tone of the poem? What is the knowledge of oneself that the poet urges?

W. B. YEATS (1865–1939)
The Second Coming

Turning and turning in the widening gyre
The falcon cannot hear the falconer;
Things fall apart; the center cannot hold;
Mere anarchy is loosed upon the world,
The blood-dimmed tide is loosed, and everywhere   5
The ceremony of innocence is drowned;
The best lack all conviction, while the worst
Are full of passionate intensity.

Surely some revelation is at hand;
Surely the Second Coming is at hand;   10
The Second Coming! Hardly are those words out
When a vast image out of *Spiritus Mundi*
Troubles my sight: somewhere in sands of the desert
A shape with lion body and the head of a man,
A gaze blank and pitiless as the sun,   15
Is moving its slow thighs, while all about it
Reel shadows of the indignant desert birds.
The darkness drops again; but now I know
That twenty centuries of stony sleep
Were vexed to nightmare by a rocking cradle,   20
And what rough beast, its hour come round at last,
Slouches towards Bethlehem to be born?

1. *gyre* spiral. The term relates both to the immediate image and to Yeats' cyclic view of history. 12. *Spiritus Mundi* soul of the world, i.e., the collective unconscious, the racial memory of human kind.

For Consideration

1. The poem is based on Yeats' mythic conception of the history of the world. Yeats believed that human history could be charted on a Great Wheel, with each turning of the wheel marking a two thousand year period (see line 19). At the end of each period a significant action, the beginning of a new civilization, a "second coming," would occur.

2. How is present society portrayed in the first stanza? What values have been lost?

3. The second stanza contains allusions to the first and second coming of Christ. How Christ-like does the deity in this poem appear to be? What vision of the future does the poem promote?

W. H. AUDEN (1907—1973)
The Unknown Citizen

(To JS/07/M/378
This Marble Monument
Is Erected by the State)

He was found by the Bureau of Statistics to be
One against whom there was no official complaint,
And all the reports on his conduct agree
That, in the modern sense of an old-fashioned word, he was a saint,
For in everything he did he served the Greater Community.   5
Except for the War till the day he retired
He worked in a factory and never got fired,
But satisfied his employers, Fudge Motors Inc.
Yet he wasn't a scab or odd in his views,
For his Union reports that he paid his dues,   10
(Our report on his Union shows it was sound)
And our Social Psychology workers found
That he was popular with his mates and liked a drink.
The Press are convinced that he bought a paper every day
And that his reactions to advertisements were normal in every way.   15
Policies taken out in his name prove that he was fully insured,
And his Health-card shows he was once in hospital but left it cured.
Both Producers Research and High-Grade Living declare
He was fully sensible to the advantages of the Instalment Plan

And had everything necessary to the Modern Man, 20
A phonograph, a radio, a car and a frigidaire.
Our researchers into Public Opinion are content
That he held the proper opinions for the time of year;
When there was peace, he was for peace; when there was war,
      he went.
He was married and added five children to the population, 25
Which our Eugenist says was the right number for a parent of his
      generation,
And our teachers report that he never interfered with their
      education.
Was he free? Was he happy? The question is absurd:
Had anything been wrong, we should certainly have heard.

For Consideration

1.   Why is the citizen deemed "a saint"? What characterizes the life of the citizen? His job? His habits? His possessions? His political thought?

2.   What can we conclude about the characteristics of the society of which the unknown citizen is a part? Why, in this society, are questions about freedom and happiness absurd?

GEORGE HERBERT (1593−1633)
The Collar

I struck the board and cried, "No more;
   I will abroad!
What? shall I ever sigh and pine?
My lines and life are free, free as the road,
  Loose as the wind, as large as store. 5
     Shall I be still in suit?
Have I no harvest but a thorn
To let me blood, and not restore

6. *in suit* brought under the law, prosecuted. Perhaps also a reference to the clerical garb.

What I have lost with cordial fruit?
      Sure there was wine
  Before my sighs did dry it; there was corn
    Before my tears did drown it.
  Is the year only lost to me?
    Have I no bays to crown it,
No flowers, no garlands gay? All blasted?
      All wasted?
  Not so, my heart; but there is fruit,
    And thou hast hands.
  Recover all thy sigh-blown age
On double pleasures: leave thy cold dispute
Of what is fit and not. Forsake thy cage,
    Thy rope of sands,
Which petty thoughts have made, and made to thee
  Good cable, to enforce and draw,
    And be thy law,
  While thou didst wink and wouldst not see.
    Away! take heed;
    I will abroad.
Call in thy death's-head there; tie up thy fears.
    He that forbears
  To suit and serve his need,
    Deserves his load."
But as I raved and grew more fierce and wild
    At every word,
Methought I heard one calling, *Child!*
    And I replied, *My Lord.*

10

15

20

25

30

35

For Consideration

1.   The title is intentionally ambiguous. The "collar" is at once the clerical collar and a collar which restricts or binds (a noose, for example). In "collar" we perhaps are also to hear "caller," a reference to the exclamations of the speaker in the poem.

2.   The speaker is apparently a minister of God. (Herbert himself was an Anglican priest.) What characteristics are associated with that function in the opening lines?

3.   Lines 7–13 introduce images that have meaning both in terms of the poet's cry for freedom and in terms of the religious office he holds. How does "thorn" carry a double meaning? "Wine"? "Corn"?

---

14. *bayes* laurels, given as a prize for victory or excellence.

4. We are to understand that the poet becomes "more fierce and wild" as the poem progresses. Read the poem aloud. Do rhythm and stress contribute to a wild effect? Read aloud lines 33—36. Have the rhythm and stress changed?

5. What does the ending of the poem mean? How does it relate to the raving in most of the poem?

LUCILLE CLIFTON (1937–   )
Good Times

My Daddy has paid the rent
and the insurance man is gone
and the lights is back on
and my uncle Brud has hit
for one dollar straight   5
and they is good times
good times
good times

My Mama has made bread
and Grampaw has come   10
and everybody is drunk
and dancing in the kitchen
and singing in the kitchen
oh these is good times
good times   15
good times

oh children think about the
good times

For Consideration

1. The poem has a song-like quality, particularly with the repetition of "good times." How do the rhythm and emphasis reinforce the meaning of the poem?

2.   What do you know of the social standing of the family described? What is the reason for the "good times"?

PAUL BLACKBURN   (1926—1971)
Good Morning Love!

Rise at 7:15
study the
artifacts
         (2 books
         1 photo   5
         1 gouache sketch
         2 unclean socks
perform the neces-
sary ablutions
         hands   10
         face
         feet
         crotch)
even answer the door with good grace, even
if it's the light & gas man   15
announcing himself as "EDISON!
Readjer meter mister?"
For Christ sake yes
read my meter
Nothing can alter the euphoria   20
The blister is still on one finger
         There just are
some mornings worth getting up
         & making a cup
of coffee that's all   25

6. *gouache* method of painting with opaque watercolors.

For Consideration

1. What experience is described in the poem? Why are the objects mentioned described as "artifacts?" Why is the washing "necessary ablutions"?
Why does the poet cite the exact words of the meter-reader?

2. Does the poem suggest a reason for the "euphoria" which is maintained
here?

As children, most of us associated poetry with **rhyme** to the extent
that we may have believed that anything that rhymed was poetry and
that all poetry rhymed. The untruth of that assumption is evident
throughout this book, but it remains true that rhyme can be important
in poetry — to add pleasure and pleasant sounds or, perhaps, to call
attention to two words of similar sound and associated meanings. True
or exact rhymes involve words with different consonant sounds
followed by identical vowel sounds (toe—blow—go, book—look—took).
Spelling is not the criterion; sound is. In half-rhyme only the final consonant sounds are the same (mirth—forth, pretty—slutty). In masculine
rhyme the final syllables of the words are stressed and are identical
(map—lap, confuse—bemuse). In feminine rhyme unstressed but identical final syllables follow stressed and rhyming syllables (building—gilding, collection—detection). End-rhyme places the rhyming
word at the end of the line; internal rhyme places a rhyming word in
the middle of the line.

Various terms identify several other sound patterns in verse, not
necessarily associated with rhyme. **Alliteration** is the repetition of initial
sounds in words:

The hulk of him is like hills heaving.

Merwin, "Leviathan"

As we have seen with other examples, technique — here, alliteration —
reinforces meaning. The point of the line is to emphasize the size of
leviathan, a hugeness emphasized by the repeated heavy h sound of
"hulk," "him," "hills," and "heaving." **Assonance** is the repetition of
identical vowel sounds accompanied by different consonant sounds
(him—fit, boat—goal). **Consonance** is the repetition of identical consonant sounds with differing vowels (bitter—batter—butter, role—rail).
Onomatopoeia is the use of a word the sound of which suggests its
meaning (hiss, tinkle).

In the following poems sound patterns, frequently rhyme, are important. As you read and react to the poems, notice the different ways a poet may utilize these elements of poetry.

JONATHAN SWIFT (1667–1745)

A Description of the Morning

Now hardly here and there a hackney-coach
Appearing, showed the ruddy morn's approach.
Now Betty from her master's bed had flown,
And softly stole to discompose her own.
The slipshod 'prentice from his master's door   5
Had pared the dirt and sprinkled round the floor.
Now Moll had whirled her mop with dext'rous airs,
Prepared to scrub the entry and the stairs.
The youth with broomy stumps began to trace
The kennel-edge where wheels had worn the place.   10
The small-coal man was heard with cadence deep,
'Till drowned in shriller notes of chimney-sweep.
Duns at his Lordship's gate began to meet,
And brick-dust Moll had screamed through half the street.
The turnkey now his flock returning sees,   15
Duly let out a-nights to steal for fees.
The watchful bailiffs take their silent stands,
And schoolboys lag with satchels in their hands.

For Consideration

1. The title implies a straight forward and objective portrayal of early morning activities, but the poem, at least occasionally, hints that not all is open and agreeable in this society. What evidence is there of irony in Swift's description?

2. How does the tone of the poem enhance the irony?

10. *kennel-edge* gutter. **13.** *duns* bill collectors. **15.** *turnkey* jailer. **17.** *bailiffs* officials of the law, empowered to arrest violators and here silently waiting to do so.

ANONYMOUS DRINKING SONG
(15th CENTURY)
Bring Us In Good Ale

Bring us in good ale, and bring us in good ale!
For our blessed Lady's sake, bring us in good ale!

Bring us in no brown bread, for that is made of bran.
Nor bring us in no white bread, for therein is no game,
   But bring us in good ale!   5

Bring us in no beef, for there is many bones,
But bring us in good ale, for that goth down at ones,
   And bring us in good ale!

Bring us in no bacon, for that is passing fat,
But bring us in good ale, and give us enough of that,
   And bring us in good ale!   10

Bring us in no mutton, for that is often lean,
Nor bring us in no tripes, for they be seldom clean,
   But bring us in good ale!

Bring us in no eggs, for there are many shells,   15
But bring us in good ale, and give us nothing else,
   And bring us in good ale!

Bring us in no butter, for therein are many hores,
Nor bring us in no pigs' flesh, for that will make us boars,
   But bring us in good ale!   20

Bring us in no capons' flesh, for that is often dear,
Nor bring us in no ducks' flesh, for they slobber in the mere,
   But bring us in good ale!

---

4. *game* pleasure. 7. *ones* once. 13. *tripes* the stomach of an ox, prepared as food. 18. *hores* hairs. 21. *capons* chicken; *dear* very expensive. 22. *slobber in the mere* befoul themselves in the water.

ROBERT HERRICK   (1591−1674)

Upon Julia's Voice

So smooth, so sweet, so silv'ry is thy voice,
As, could they hear, the Damn'd would make no noise,
But listen to thee, (walking in thy chamber)
Melting melodious words, to Lutes of Amber.

For Consideration

1. How do the form and movement of the poem help suggest the quality of Julia's voice?

GERARD MANLEY HOPKINS   (1844−1889)

God's Grandeur

The world is charged with the grandeur of God.
  It will flame out, like shining from shook foil;
  It gathers to a greatness, like the ooze of oil

Crushed. Why do men then now not reck his rod?
Generations have trod, have trod, have trod;   5
   And all is seared with trade; bleared, smeared with toil;
   And wears man's smudge and shares man's smell: the soil
Is bare now, nor can foot feel, being shod.

And for all this, nature is never spent;
   There lives the dearest freshness deep down things;   10
And though the last lights off the black West went
   Oh, morning, at the brown brink eastward, springs —
Because the Holy Ghost over the bent
   World broods with warm breast and with ah! bright wings.

For Consideration

1.   How do sound and rhythm reinforce meaning in the poem? Where does the poet use alliteration? To what effect? Why does he repeat the phrase of line 5?

2.   What contrast is developed between the generations of men and the world "charged with the grandeur of God"? What words and values are attached to each?

3.   What image controls the last two lines of the poem?

4. *crushed* e.g., as when olives are crushed for their oil.

poems for further reading

Some Final Comments

At the end of his statement on the art of poetry ("Ars Poetica"), Archibald MacLeish declares:

A poem should not mean
But be.

The implications of MacLeish's pronouncement notwithstanding, most readers of poetry are interested in what it says, what its significance is, what it means. MacLeish may be cautioning against the tendency to turn poetry into some didactic message, some way by which a poet tells us how to think or act. Clearly, poetry does not have this kind of "meaning." Some of the poems included thus far and a number which follow deal with society, and several are an indictment of the society which exists contemporaneous with the poem, (e.g., the poems of Bly, Piercy, and Randall). None, however, is at all like a political or sociological tract which urges certain precise correctives for society. Poems "teach" us, but not about sociological or political values; instead, they remain essentially human by teaching us more about ourselves.

The effort to understand a poem, to form an interpretation of a poem, ideally includes identifying all those elements which make a poem what it is. The responsibilities of the good reader of poetry are both to respond to all the ingredients in a poem — words, images, rhythm, form — and to recognize those ingredients in a given poem which are most important. While, as suggested earlier, the form of the sonnet is important, this element is not equally significant in all poems. Likewise, in Auden's "In Memory of W. B. Yeats," the meter and rhythm are important to the meaning; in other poems they are given less emphasis. It is safe to say that words — images, symbols, figures of speech — will be the principal concern of an interpretation, for poetry remains, fundamentally, a communication using words. But words, particularly in a poetic context, cannot exist in isolation. They are related to other words, to the form of the presentation, and to the speech patterns with which they are spoken or read. So we come back to a frequent assertion in these remarks. All elements of poetry are, potentially, at the disposal of the poet, and each must be considered by the thorough reader.

Students frequently ask about an upcoming examination or paper on poetry, "Do you want our opinion?" I usually tell them that I want an interpretation. The difference between the two terms may be largely one of connotation, but it is important. Too often "opinion" implies a too-personal, too-esoteric reaction to poetry, a kind of "It means anything I want it to mean" approach. Interpretation connotes a more judicious, more responsible activity. It is still an individual assignment, of course; two interpretations of the same poem need not be the same in all respects. The interpretations ought, however, to rely on the poem being considered, not primarily on one's own experience or what one has read elsewhere, even though these experiences are valuable.

Within this context an interpretation can be a creative as well as a critical reaction. Criticism involves analysis, the legitimate taking apart of a poem to see how it works. Few of us, however, would be content if the experience stopped there, if we could go no further than dissecting a poem to find, say, two metaphors, one synecdoche, two caesuras, and a meter of dactylic pentameter. To be complete our action must involve synthesis, bringing the parts back together into the whole. Doing this, with the understanding we have gained through analysis, can be an imaginative and fulfilling experience. It should be, as has been said before, an experience which brings the reader both insight and pleasure.

As you read poems from the collection which follows, be open to all of the elements of poetry discussed in preceding pages. The questions which follow the poems point you to some ideas and techniques, but they are by no means exhaustive. Ideally, they will give you a start toward your own delight in and understanding of the poetry.

an arrangement by theme

the human condition:
individuals and communities

ETHERIDGE KNIGHT   (1933–   )

Hard Rock Returns to Prison from the Hospital for the Criminal Insane

Hard Rock was "known not to take no shit
From nobody," and he had the scars to prove it:
Split purple lips, lumped ears, welts above
His yellow eyes, and one long scar that cut
Across his temple and plowed through a thick   5
Canopy of kinky hair.

The WORD was that Hard Rock wasn't a mean nigger
Anymore, that the doctors had bored a hole in his head,
Cut out part of his brain, and shot electricity
Through the rest. When they brought Hard Rock back,   10
Handcuffed and chained, he was turned loose,
Like a freshly gelded stallion, to try his new status.
And we all waited and watched, like indians at a corral,
To see if the WORD was true.

As we waited we wrapped ourselves in the cloak 15
Of his exploits: "Man, the last time, it took eight
Screws to put him in the Hole." "Yeah, remember when he
Smacked the captain with his dinner tray?" "He set
The record for time in the Hole — 67 straight days!"
"Ol Hard Rock! man, that's one crazy nigger." 20
And then the jewel of a myth that Hard Rock had once bit
A screw on the thumb and poisoned him with syphilitic spit.

The testing came, to see if Hard Rock was really tame.
A hillbilly called him a black son of a bitch
And didn't lose his teeth, a screw who knew Hard Rock 25
From before shook him down and barked in his face.
And Hard Rock did *nothing*. Just grinned and looked silly,
His eyes empty like knot holes in a fence.

And even after we discovered that it took Hard Rock
Exactly 3 minutes to tell you his first name, 30
We told ourselves that he had just wised up,
Was being cool; but we could not fool ourselves for long,
And we turned away, our eyes on the ground. Crushed.
He had been our Destroyer, the doer of things
We dreamed of doing but could not bring ourselves to do, 35
The fears of years, like a biting whip,
Had cut grooves too deeply across our backs.

For Consideration

1. What kind of person was Hard Rock before the operation? What kind of person is he after? What is the operation mentioned here?

2. Why the typographical emphasis on WORD?

3. What has been the importance of Hard Rock for the men around him? What is their reaction now?

4. What image of the individual and society does the poem promote?

THOM GUNN (1929–   )

Human Condition

Now it is fog, I walk
Contained within my coat;
No castle more cut off
By reason of its moat:
Only the sentry's cough,   5
The mercenaries' talk.

The street lamps, visible,
Drop no light on the ground,
But press beams painfully
In a yard of fog around.   10
I am condemned to be
An individual.

In the established border
There balances a mere
Pinpoint of consciousness.   15
I stay, or start from, here:
No fog makes more or less
The neighbouring disorder.

Particular, I must
Find out the limitation   20
Of mind and universe,
To pick thought and sensation
And turn to my own use
Disordered hate or lust.

I seek, to break, my span.   25
I am my one touchstone.
This is a test more hard
Than any ever known.
And thus I keep my guard
On that which makes me man.   30

Much is unknowable.
No problem shall be faced
Until the problem is;
I, born to fog, to waste,
Walk through hypothesis,   35
An individual.

For Consideration

1. What is the atmosphere of the poem at the opening? What is the occasion?

2. How does the poet emphasize the sense of isolation? What images promote his aloneness?

3. Why, in the second stanza, is his individuality seen as a negative force ("condemned to be/An individual")? What is a "touchstone" (line 26)? Why does the persona call himself his own touchstone?

4. Why, in the next-to-last line, does the poet say that he walks "through hypothesis"? What is the force of the last line, "an individual"? What attitude toward the "human condition" governs this poem?

W. B. YEATS (1865–1939)

A Prayer for My Daughter

Once more the storm is howling, and half hid
Under this cradle-hood and coverlid
My child sleeps on. There is no obstacle
But Gregory's wood and one bare hill
Whereby the haystack- and roof-levelling wind,   5
Bred on the Atlantic, can be stayed;
And for an hour I have walked and prayed
Because of the great gloom that is in my mind.

I have walked and prayed for this young child an hour
And heard the sea-wind scream upon the tower,   10
And under the arches of the bridge, and scream
In the elms above the flooded stream;
Imagining in excited reverie
That the future years had come,
Dancing to a frenzied drum.   15
Out of the murderous innocence of the sea.

May she be granted beauty and yet not
Beauty to make a stranger's eye distraught,
Or hers before a looking-glass, for such,
Being made beautiful overmuch,   20
Consider beauty a sufficient end,
Lose natural kindness and maybe

The heart-revealing intimacy
That chooses right, and never find a friend.

Helen being chosen found life flat and dull   25
And later had much trouble from a fool,
While that great Queen, that rose out of the spray,
Being fatherless could have her way
Yet chose a bandy-leggèd smith for man.
It's certain that fine women eat   30
A crazy salad with their meat
Whereby the Horn of Plenty is undone.

In courtesy I'd have her chiefly learned;
Hearts are not had as a gift but hearts are earned
By those that are not entirely beautiful;   35
Yet many, that have played the fool
For beauty's very self, has charm made wise,
And many a poor man that has roved,
Loved and thought himself beloved,
From a glad kindness cannot take his eyes.   40

May she become a flourishing hidden tree
That all her thoughts may like the linnet be,
And have no business but dispensing round
Their magnanimities of sound,
Nor but in merriment begin a chase,   45
Nor but in merriment a quarrel.
O may she live like some green laurel
Rooted in one dear perpetual place.

My mind, because the minds that I have loved,
The sort of beauty that I have approved,   50
Prosper but little, has dried up of late,
Yet knows that to be choked with hate
May well be of all evil chances chief.
If there's no hatred in a mind
Assault and battery of the wind   55
Can never tear the linnet from the leaf.

An intellectual hatred is the worst,
So let her think opinions are accursed.
Have I not seen the loveliest woman born

25. *Helen* Helen, wife of Menelaus, kidnapped and taken to Troy by Paris (*a fool*). **27.** *That great Queen* Aphrodite, born from the sea, made Vulcan (*bandy-leggèd smith*) her husband. **59.** *the loveliest woman* Maud Gonne, an Irish nationalist and revolutionary and a love of Yeats' life. He believed that her beauty and potential were wasted in her extreme political stands.

Out of the mouth of Plenty's horn,   60
Because of her opinionated mind
Barter that horn and every good
By quiet natures understood
For an old bellows full of angry wind?

Considering that, all hatred driven hence,   65
The soul recovers radical innocence
And learns at last that it is self-delighting,
Self-appeasing, self-affrighting,
And that its own sweet will is Heaven's will;
She can, though every face should scowl   70
And every windy quarter howl
Or every bellows burst, be happy still.

And may her bridegroom bring her to a house
Where all's accustomed, ceremonious;
For arrogance and hatred are the wares   75
Peddled in the thoroughfares.
How but in custom and in ceremony
Are innocence and beauty born?
Ceremony's a name for the rich horn,
And custom for the spreading laurel tree.   80

For Consideration

1. What is the occasion of the poem? How does that occasion reinforce the "great gloom" in the poet's mind? What is the source of the gloom?

2. What is the meaning of the "Horn of Plenty" mentioned in line 32? Where else in the poem is the image found?

3. What does the poet wish for his daughter? What does he wish her to avoid?

4. Stanza six compares the daughter to "a flourishing hidden tree," a "linnet," and "some green laurel." What attributes are associated with each figure?

5. Why, of characteristics to be avoided, is "intellectual hatred" the worst? What is the "radical innocence" which can be recovered when hatred is "driven hence"?

6. What values do ceremony and custom have in the last stanza? Both terms, in certain contexts, imply a habitual but superficial ritual or action. How does the poet avoid those connotations here?

PERCY BYSSHE SHELLEY (1792–1822)

Ozymandias

I met a traveler from an antique land
Who said: Two vast and trunkless legs of stone
Stand in the desert . . . Near them, on the sand,
Half sunk, a shattered visage lies, whose frown,
And wrinkled lip, and sneer of cold command, 5
Tell that its sculptor well those passions read
Which yet survive, stamped on these lifeless things,
The hand that mocked them, and the heart that fed:
And on the pedestal these words appear:
"My name is Ozymandias, king of kings: 10
Look on my works, ye Mighty, and despair!"
Nothing beside remains. Round the decay
Of that colossal wreck, boundless and bare
The lone and level sands stretch far away.

For Consideration

1.   What impressions of the "two vast and trunkless legs of stone," and the person they once represented, are created by the opening lines? What is suggested by the "shattered visage"?

2.   How does the poet enhance the irony of Ozymandias' words? Why does the poem conclude with a description of the "lone and level sands" which stretch far away from the "colossal wreck"?

For Comparison

What distinguishes the "ego-tripping" implied in Ozymandias' words from Giovanni's "Ego Tripping" (p. 327)? How are attitudes and tones in the two poems different?

BYRON BLACK (1940–   )

I, the Fake Mad Bomber and Walking It Home Again

First comes the cold,
and puffing as classes change
fast as the frames of a film
and dried old sarcophagi of professors reel on
trot placidly Latin with its dust and their rot.   5

Then dives the red sun
crashes like the stock market, in black
"the day was fine" as Wm. says
and the Tower stands impudent, one wants to slap it down
before the blast-off into stone-gray space.   10

Brisk bright day
Wm. and I walking fast,
we smile at lurid tales which shock like adders

Dark people with the faces of bulldogs
gruffly waddle past, Chryslers with the scream of a rocket   15
charge us jousting, we hurry fast
to the flap and claw of the Night Hawk

where dark hamburgers from the heart of a living vulture
are served by an Aztec princess
"the hamburger don't come with onions"   20
(pimples as jewels, and the pop of gum)
And the white bourgeois, slimy smiles
slide in with assuredness of talkative slugs, to music of the bank

outside the brightwork of their gaudy Cadillacs
wails like a chrome banshee toward the cool evening, and sad glass
        eyes,   25

And I thanking Wm. we part
he for home
and I full of cheer and good meat

4. *sarcophagi* stone coffins.

head for my place, legs flashing
the power of wet muscles   30
sends an electric orgasm,
and as approaching Red River, now dry
beside the stadium where Christians are devourers
the night breaks
I know myself as the Fake Mad Bomber   35
and light a black cigar in the dark to prove it.

For Consideration

1. Where is the speaker as the poem begins? What is his estimation of the professors?

2. Who is Wm.? Whom do Wm. and the speaker encounter on their walk and at the Night Hawk?

3. What is the effect of the animal imagery in the poem? What portrait of society does it encourage?

4. What has made the speaker "full of cheer and good meat"? If he is the Fake Mad Bomber, what does he want to bomb? Why is he a "fake"?

5. The poem describes several landmarks at the University of Texas, a university Black attended. Where does the poem focus on the university community? How might it be seen as representative of society in general?

For Comparison

"Uptown" (p. 329) and "I, the Fake Mad Bomber and Walking It Home Again" involve speakers who are, to varying degrees, alienated from the societies in which they find themselves; Auden's "Unknown Citizen," (p. 388), on the other hand, fits comfortably into his society. He even has a monument erected to him by the state. What distinguishes these relationships to society? What are the causes of the alienation in the Ginsberg and Black poems?

LUIS MUNOZ MARIN (1898–)

Pamphlet

I have broken the rainbow
against my heart
as one breaks a useless sword against a knee.
I have blown the clouds of rose colour and blood colour
beyond the farthest horizons.   5
I have drowned my dreams
in order to glut the dreams that sleep for me in the veins
of men who sweated and wept and raged
to season my coffee . . .

The dream that sleeps in breasts stifled by tuberculosis   10
    (A little air, a little sunshine!);
the dream that dreams in stomachs strangled by hunger
    (A bit of bread, a bit of white bread!);
the dream of bare feet
    (Fewer stones on the road, Lord, fewer broken bottles!);   15
the dream of calloused hands
    (Moss . . . clean cambric . . . things smooth, soft, soothing!);
The dream of trampled hearts
    (Love . . . Life . . . Life! . . .)

I am the pamphleteer of God,   20
God's agitator,
and I go with the mob of stars and hungry men
toward the great dawn . . .

For Consideration

1. What is implied in the metaphoric action of breaking the rainbow, blowing away the clouds, and drowning the dreams? There is intentional ambiguity in the word "glut," meaning both to choke up or stop, and to satisfy fully. Which seems the more appropriate meaning here?

2. Who are the people whose dreaming is recognized here? What can you tell of their place in society, their work, their morale?

3. The "pamphleteer" was (perhaps *is*) usually a spokesman for a certain cause, often a controversial one — hence an "agitator." What is the pamphleteer agitating for in the poem? Why are both "stars" and "hungry men" in the mob he joins? What is the "great dawn"?

DUDLEY RANDALL (1914–   )

Roses and Revolutions

Musing on roses and revolutions,
I saw night close down on the earth like a great dark wing,
and the lighted cities were like tapers in the night,
and I heard the lamentations of a million hearts
regretting life and crying for the grave,   5
and I saw the Negro lying in the swamp with his face blown off,
and in northern cities with his manhood maligned and felt the
        writhing
of his viscera like that of the hare hunted down or the bear at bay,
and I saw men working and taking no joy in their work
and embracing the hard-eyed whore with joyless excitement   10
and lying with wives and virgins in impotence.

And as I groped in darkness
and felt the pain of millions,
gradually, like day driving night across the continent,
I saw dawn upon them like the sun a vision   15
of a time when all men walk proudly through the earth
and the bombs and missiles lie at the bottom of the ocean
like the bones of dinosaurs buried under the shale of eras,
and men strive with each other not for power or the accumulation
        of paper
but in joy create for others the house, the poem, the game of
        athletic beauty.   20

Then washed in the brightness of this vision,
I saw how in its radiance would grow and be nourished and suddenly
burst into terrible and splendid bloom
the blood-red flower of revolution.

For Consideration

1.   Imagery of light and darkness controls the atmosphere of the poem, in
part because the poem apparently grows out of a night-time reflection.
What values are attached to light and dark here? Which stanza is
dominated by darkness? Which by light?

2. What are the characteristics of the society envisioned in the poem? How does it differ from the one which presently exists?

3. The poem opens with "roses and revolutions" and closes with "the blood-red flower of revolution." What changes have occurred in the force of the image?

LAWRENCE FERLINGHETTI (1919–   )
Crazy

crazy
     to be alive in such a strange
          world
with the band playing schmaltz
        in the classic bandshell
            and the people   5
  on the benches under the clipped trees
         and girls
   on the grass
     and the breeze blowing and the streamers   10
streaming
    and a fat man with a graflex
    and a dark woman with a dark dog she called Lucia
    and a cat on a leash
    and a pekinese with a blond baby   15
    and a cuban in a fedora
    and a bunch of boys posing for a group
          picture
  and just then
      while the band went right on playing   20
         schmaltz
a midget ran past shouting and waving his hat
        at someone
    and a young man with a gay campaignbutton
came up and said
      Are you by any chance a registered
         DEMOCRAT?

For Consideration

1. How do the descriptions of the people in the park reinforce the strangeness, the craziness of this world?

2. What is the force of "crazy" here? Is the judgment of this society a serious one? Is it a negative judgment?

the world outside

RICHARD WILBUR   (1921–   )

Love Calls Us to the Things of This World

The eyes open to a cry of pulleys,
And spirited from sleep, the astounded soul
Hangs for a moment bodiless and simple
As false dawn.
                    Outside the open window
The morning air is all awash with angels.   5

Some are in bed-sheets, some are in blouses,
Some are in smocks: but truly there they are.
Now they are rising together in calm swells
Of halcyon feeling, filling whatever they wear
With the deep joy of their impersonal breathing;   10

Now they are flying in place, conveying
The terrible speed of their omnipresence, moving
And staying like white water; and now of a sudden
They swoon down into so rapt a quiet
That nobody seems to be there.
                        The soul shrinks   15

From all that it is about to remember,
From the punctual rape of every blessèd day,
And cries,
   "Oh, let there be nothing on earth but laundry,
Nothing but rosy hands in the rising steam
And clear dances done in the sight of heaven."   20

  Yet, as the sun acknowledges
With a warm look the world's hunks and colors,
The soul descends once more in bitter love
To accept the waking body, saying now
In a changed voice as the man yawns and rises,   25

  "Bring them down from their ruddy gallows;
Let there be clean linen for the backs of thieves;
Let lovers go fresh and sweet to be undone,
And the heaviest nuns walk in a pure floating
Of dark habits,
    keeping their difficult balance."   30

For Consideration

1. The poem opens with an imagined experience of a soul momentarily separated from its body in the early morning. What vision does it have of the world outside?

2. What is meant by the soul's prayer for "laundry," "rosy hands," and "clear dances"?

3. Why is the soul's descent to the body made with "bitter love"? How has its plea changed at the end of the poem? What meaning is implied by the conjunction of thieves, lovers, and nuns?

WALLACE STEVENS (1879–1955)

Not Ideas About the Thing
But the Thing Itself

At the earliest ending of winter,
In March, a scrawny cry from outside
Seemed like a sound in his mind.

He knew that he heard it,
A bird's cry, at daylight or before,   5
In the early March wind.

The sun was rising at six,
No longer a battered panache above snow . . .
It would have been outside.

It was not from the vast ventriloquism   10
Of sleep's faded papier-mâché . . .
The sun was coming from outside.

That scrawny cry — it was
A chorister whose c preceded the choir.
It was part of the colossal sun,   15

Surrounded by its choral rings,
Still far away. It was like
A new knowledge of reality.

For Consideration

1. What is the season here? How does it enhance the experience described?

2. The person awakening seems initially uncertain of the source of the sound he hears, for it seems "like a sound in his mind." What does "The vast ventriloquism/Of sleep's faded papier-mâché" refer to?

3. Stanza five contains a noticeable alliteration ("scrawny cry . . . chorister . . . choir . . . colossal . . . choral"). What is its effect here?

8. *panache* an ornamental plume or decoration.

4. How is the "scrawny cry" a part of the "colossal sun"? Why is it like "a new knowledge of reality"?

For Comparison

Compare this poem to Roethke's "The Reply" (p. 319) which also treats the song of a bird. How are the occasions and responses different in the poems? What similarities do you see?

RALPH WALDO EMERSON   (1803–1882)

Hamatreya

Bulkeley, Hunt, Willard, Hosmer, Meriam, Flint,
Possessed the land which rendered to their toil
Hay, corn, roots, hemp, flax, apples, wool and wood.
Each of these landlords walked amidst his farm,
Saying, ' 'T is mine, my children's and my name's.   5
How sweet the west wind sounds in my own trees!
How graceful climb those shadows on my hill!
I fancy these pure waters and the flags
Know me, as does my dog: we sympathize;
And, I affirm, my actions smack of the soil.'   10

Where are these men? Asleep beneath their grounds:
And strangers, fond as they, their furrows plough.
Earth laughs in flowers, to see her boastful boys
Earth proud, proud of the earth which is not theirs;
Who steer the plough, but cannot steer their feet   15
Clear of the grave.
They added ridge to valley, brook to pond,
And sighed for all that bounded their domain;
'This suits me for a pasture, that's my park;
We must have clay, lime, gravel, granite-ledge,   20
And misty lowland, where to go for peat.

Title. *Hamatreya* Variant on the Hindu name Maitreya. In Emerson's journal there is reference to a passage from the Hindu *Vishner Purana.* Included is an "Earth song" recited to Maitreya. **1.** *Bulkeley . . . Flint* early settlers of Concord, Massachusetts. **8.** *flags* plants.

The land is well — lies fairly to the south.
'T is good, when you have crossed the sea and back,
To find the sitfast acres where you left them.'
Ah! the hot owner sees not Death, who adds   25
Him to his land, a lump of mould the more.
Hear what the Earth says:

Earth-song

Mine and yours;
Mine, not yours.
Earth endures;   30
Stars abide —
Shine down in the old sea;
Old are the shores;
But where are old men?
I who have seen much,   35
Such have I never seen.

The lawyer's deed
Ran sure,
In tail,
To them, and to their heirs   40
Who shall succeed,
Without fail,
Forevermore.

Here is the land,
Shaggy with wood,   45
With its old valley,
Mound and flood.
But the heritors?
Fled like the flood's foam.
The lawyer, and the laws,   50
And the kingdom,
Clean swept herefrom.

They called me theirs.
Who so controlled me;
Yet every one   55
Wished to stay, and is gone,
How am I theirs,
If they cannot hold me,
But I hold them?

39. *in tail* the legal limitation of an estate to a specified person and his heirs.

When I heard the Earth-song,
I was no longer brave;
My avarice cooled
Like lust in the chill of the grave.

For Consideration

1. What is the attitude of the settlers of Concord toward their land? (Note the repetition of "mine ... my children's ... my name's ... my own trees" etc. in lines 5–10).

2. Why does Earth laugh? Why "in flowers"?

3. What is mistaken about a possessive attitude toward the land? Who turns out to be the ultimate possessor in the poem? What is the effect of the Earth-song on the poet? How does the final stanza bring together several images which have been important in the poem?

ROBERT BRIDGES (1844–1930)
London Snow

When men were all asleep the snow came flying,
In large white flakes falling on the city brown,
Stealthily and perpetually settling and loosely lying,
 Hushing the latest traffic of the drowsy town;
Deadening, muffling, stifling its murmurs failing;   5
Lazily and incessantly floating down and down:
 Silently sifting and veiling road, roof and railing;
Hiding difference, making unevenness even,
Into angles and crevices softly drifting and sailing.
 All night it fell, and when full inches seven   10
It lay in the depth of its uncompacted lightness,
The clouds blew off from a high and frosty heaven;
 And all woke earlier for the unaccustomed brightness
Of the winter dawning, the strange unheavenly glare:
The eye marvelled — marvelled at the dazzling whiteness;   15

The ear hearkened to the stillness of the solemn air;
No sound of wheel rumbling nor of foot falling,
And the busy morning cries came thin and spare.
  Then boys I heard, as they went to school, calling,
They gathered up the crystal manna to freeze   20
Their tongues with tasting, their hands with snowballing;
  Or rioted in a drift, plunging up to the knees;
Or peering up from under the white-mossed wonder,
'O look at the trees!' they cried, 'O look at the trees!'
  With lessened load a few carts creak and blunder,   25
Following along the white deserted way,
A country company long dispersed asunder:
  When now already the sun, in pale display
Standing by Paul's high dome, spread forth below
His sparkling beams, and awoke the stir of the day.   30
  For now doors open, and war is waged with the snow;
And trains of sombre men, past tale of number,
Tread long brown paths, as toward their toil they go:
  But even for them awhile no cares encumber
Their minds diverted; the daily word is unspoken,   35
The daily thoughts of labour and sorrow slumber
  At the sight of the beauty that greets them, for the charm they have
          broken.

For Consideration

1. What effects does the falling snow have on the city before it awakens? Do
    those effects appear to be positive or negative?

2. How does the city react to the snow? What are the sources of the excite-
    ment it brings? What is the source of the allusion, in line 20, to "crystal
    manna"?

3. After the initial excitement over the snow, why is "war" waged against it?
    With what mood is the war carried out?

29. *Paul's high dome* the dome of St. Paul's Cathedral.

e. e. cummings   (1894−1962)

O sweet spontaneous

O sweet spontaneous
earth how often have
the
doting

      fingers of
prurient philosophers pinched
and
poked

thee
, has the naughty thumb
of science prodded
thy

     beauty   how
often have religions taken
thee upon their scraggy knees
squeezing and

buffeting thee that thou mightest conceive
gods
      (but
true

to the incomparable
couch of death thy
rhythmic
lover

      thou answerest

them only with
         spring)

For Consideration

1. Why is earth "sweet spontaneous"? What is it personified as here? How is that image appropriate to the final emphasis on spring?

2. Why are philosophers, scientists, and religionists criticized for their responses to the earth? What has each tried to do to it? How has religion attempted to make earth conceive gods?

3. In what sense is death the "rhythmic lover" of the earth? What relationship between earth, death, and spring is the poet conveying?

For Comparison

What characteristics of spring do "Spring" (p. 310) and "O sweet spontaneous" both identify? How are their emphases different? Since cummings objected to religion "squeezing and buffeting" the earth, do you think he would object to the ending of Hopkins' poem?

D. H. LAWRENCE   (1885–1930)

The Wild Common

The quick sparks on the gorse-bushes are leaping
Little jets of sunlight texture imitating flame;
Above them, exultant, the peewits are sweeping:
They have triumphed again o'er the ages, their screamings proclaim.

Rabbits, handfuls of brown earth, lie   5
Low-rounded on the mournful turf they have bitten down to the
　　　　quick.
Are they asleep? — are they living? — Now see, when I
Lift my arms, the hill bursts and heaves under their spurting kick!

The common flaunts bravely; but below, from the rushes
Crowds of glittering king-cups surge to challenge the blossoming
　　　　bushes;
There the lazy streamlet pushes   10
His bent course mildly; here wakes again, leaps, laughs, and gushes

Into a deep pond, an old sheep-dip,
Dark, overgrown with willows, cool, with the brook ebbing through
        so slow;
Naked on the steep, soft lip   15
Of the turf I stand watching my own white shadow quivering to
        and fro.

What if the gorse-flowers shrivelled, and I were gone?
What if the waters ceased, where were the marigolds then, and the
        gudgeon?
What is this thing that I look down upon?
White on the water wimples my shadow, strains like a dog on a string,
        to run on.   20

How it looks back, like a white dog to its master!
I on the bank all substance, my shadow all shadow looking up to me,
        looking back!
And the water runs, and runs faster, runs faster,
And the white dog dances and quivers, I am holding his cord
        quite slack.

But how splendid it is to be substance, here!   25
My shadow is neither here nor there; but I, I am royally here!
I am here! I am here! screams the peewit; the may-blobs burst out
        in a laugh as they hear!
Here! flick the rabbits. Here! pants the gorse. Here! say the insects far
        and near.

Over my skin in the sunshine, the warm, clinging air
Flushed with the songs of seven larks singing at once, goes kissing me
        glad.   30
You are here! You are here! We have found you! Everywhere
We sought you substantial, you touchstone of caresses, you naked lad!

Oh but the water loves me and folds me,
Plays with me, sways me, lifts me and sinks me, murmurs: Oh
        marvellous stuff!
No longer shadow! — and it holds me   35
Close, and it rolls me, enfolds me, touches me, as if never it could
        touch me enough.

Sun, but in substance, yellow water-blobs!
Wings and feathers on the crying, mysterious ages, peewits wheeling!
All that is right, all that is good, all that is God takes substance!
        a rabbit lobs
In confirmation, I hear sevenfold lark-songs pealing.   40

13. *sheep-dip* a liquid into which sheep are immersed to destroy parasites. 18. *gudgeon* a
small European fish.

For Consideration

1. The opening three stanzas include a number of strong verbal forms ("leaping ... sweeping ... triumphed ... proclaim ... bursts and heaves ... spurting ... flaunts ... surge ... pushes ... leaps, laughs, and gushes"). What images do these terms create? How do they enhance the portrait of a *wild* common?

2. Why is the speaker naked? What is he doing in the common?

3. What distinctions does the speaker make between substance and shadow? Why does he find it "splendid ... to be substance"? How do the environs confirm his judgment that "all that is right, all that is good, all that is God takes substance!"?

4. What connections are made in the poem between the speaker's response to the common and his response to himself? How does one amplify and reinforce the other?

For Comparison

Compare Lawrence's poem to others in which a speaker reacts to an experience in Nature (e.g., "The Reply" (p. 319), "Dust of Snow" (p. 321), "The Darkling Thrush" (p. 434)). In what ways does Lawrence give his poem a physical, rather than an emotional or psychological, emphasis?

JOHN CLARE (1793–1864)

Poets Love Nature

Poets love nature, and themselves are love,
The scorn of fools, and mock of idle pride.
The vile in nature worthless deeds approve,
They court the vile and spurn all good beside.
Poets love nature; like the calm of heaven,   5
Her gifts like heaven's love spread far and wide:
In all her works there are no signs of leaven,
Sorrow abashes from her simple pride.

7. *leaven* here meaning to mingle or interfere with, or spoil.

Her flowers, like pleasures, have their season's birth,
And bloom through regions here below;   10
They are her very scriptures upon earth,
And teach us simple mirth where'er we go.
Even in prison they can solace me,
For where they bloom God is, and I am free.

For Consideration

1. The poem speaks both of Nature and of poets. What connection between the two is made in the first four lines?

2. What is the value of Nature in lines 5—12? What does it teach the poet?

3. This is a sonnet and, characteristically, an important part of the theme is withheld until the couplet at the end. Here that couplet focuses on a paradox. What does it mean? What is its source?

JOHN WAIN (1925–   )

Reason for Not Writing Orthodox Nature Poetry

The January sky is deep and calm.
The mountain sprawls in comfort, and the sea
Sleeps in the crook of that enormous arm.

And Nature from a simple recipe —
Rocks, water, mist, a sunlit winter's day —   5
Has brewed a cup whose strength has dizzied me.

So little beauty is enough to pay;
The heart so soon yields up its store of love,
And where you love you cannot break away.

So sages never found it hard to prove   10
Nor prophets to declare in metaphor
That God and Nature must be hand in glove.

And this became the basis of their lore.
Then later poets found it easy going
To give the public what they bargained for,   15

And like a spectacled curator showing
The wares of his museum to the crowd,
They yearly waxed more eloquent and knowing

More slick, more photographic, and more proud:
From Tennyson with notebook in his hand   20
(His truth to Nature fits him like a shroud)

To moderns who devoutly hymn the land.
So be it: each is welcome to his voice;
They are a gentle, if a useless, band.

But leave me free to make a sterner choice;   25
Content, without embellishment, to note
How little beauty bids the heart rejoice,

How little beauty catches at the throat,
Simply, I love this mountain and this bay
With love that I can never speak by rote,   30

And where you love you cannot break away.

For Consideration

1. The opening three stanzas make it clear that the poet is not unaffected by
   the scene before him, yet for a "reason" he does not write an orthodox
   nature poem. What are the implied characteristics of the type of poem he
   will not write? What is his reason for not doing so?

2. The speaker mentions sages, prophets, later poets (including Tennyson)
   and moderns. What does he find wrong with their responses? What is the
   "sterner choice" that he makes?

3. The poem is made up of triplets. How does the rhyme pattern reinforce
   unity both within each triplet and from one triplet to another?

For Comparison

What poems included in this section might fall under the indictment of Wain? He implies that orthodox nature poetry is excessive, too slick, too proud. Do other poems here fit that description in your judgment? Do you think Wain would like a poem such as Clare's "Poets Love Nature"?

forms of joy

ROBERT HERRICK (1591–1674)

To Live Merrily, and to Trust to Good Verses

Now is the time for mirth,
   Nor cheek or tongue be dumb;
For with the flow'ry earth
   The golden pomp is come.

The golden pomp is come;   5
   For now each tree does wear,
Made of her pap and gum,
   Rich beads of amber here.

Now reigns the rose, and now
   Th' Arabian dew besmears   10
My uncontrollèd brow
   And my retorted hairs.

Homer, this health to thee,
   In sack of such a kind

12. *retorted* tossed backwards.

That it would make thee see   15
  Though thou wert ne'er so blind.

Next, Virgil I'll call forth
  To pledge this second health
In wine, whose each cup's worth
  An Indian commonwealth.   20

A goblet next I'll drink
  To Ovid, and suppose,
Made he the pledge, he'd think
  The world had all one nose.

Then this immensive cup   25
  Of aromatic wine,
Catullus, I quaff up
  To that terse muse of thine.

Wild I am now with heat;
  O Bacchus! cool thy rays!   30
Or frantic, I shall eat
  Thy thyrse, and bite the bays.

Round, round the roof does run;
  And being ravished thus,
Come, I will drink a tun   35
  To my Propertius.

Now, to Tibullus, next,
  This flood I drink to thee;
But stay, I see a text
  That this presents to me.   40

Behold, Tibullus lies
  Here burnt, whose small return
Of ashes scarce suffice
  To fill a little urn.

Trust to good verses then;   45
  They only will aspire,
When pyramids, as men,
  Are lost i' th' funeral fire.

And when all bodies meet,

---

24. *one nose* punning on Ovid's full name, Publius Ovidius Naso. 32. *thyrse* Bacchus' rod.
39. *text* from Ovid's *Amores* III. 9. 39–40, translated in the next stanza.

In Lethe to be drowned,   50
Then only numbers sweet
    With endless life are crowned.

For Consideration

1. What time of year is it? Why is that season appropriate for the mood and theme of the poem?

2. How does the mood of the poet change from stanza to stanza? Where is it evident that he is becoming increasingly merry in his drinking and toasting?

3.. Line 39 seems to call a halt to the merriment in order to consider a text from Ovid on Tibullus. What is the point of the following stanza? Why does it lead the speaker to conclude that only "good verses" can be trusted?

BEN JONSON (1573–1637)
Inviting a Friend to Supper

Tonight, grave sir, both my poor house, and I
Do equally desire your company;
Not that we think us worthy such a guest,
But that your worth will dignify our feast
With those that come, whose grace may make that seem   5
Something, which else could hope for no esteem.
It is the fair acceptance, sir, creates
The entertainment perfect, not the cates.
Yet shall you have, to rectify your palate,
An olive, capers, or some better salad   10
Ushering the mutton; with a short-legged hen,
If we can get her, full of eggs, and then
Lemons, and wine for sauce; to these a cony

---

50. *Lethe* the River of Forgetfulness in Hades. **51.** *numbers* poems. A volume of Herrick's religious poetry was titled *Noble Numbers*. **8.** *cates* dainty food, delicacies. **13.** *cony* rabbit.

Is not to be despaired of, for our money;
And, though fowl now be scarce, yet there are clerks, 15
The sky not falling, think we may have larks.
I'll tell you of more, and lie, so you will come:
Of partridge, pheasant, woodcock, of which some
May yet be there, and godwit, if we can;
Knot, rail, and ruff too. Howsoe'er, my man 20
Shall read a piece of Virgil, Tacitus,
Livy, or of some better book to us,
Of which we'll speak our minds, amidst our meat;
And I'll profess no verses to repeat.
To this, if aught appear which I not know of, 25
That will the pastry, not my paper, show of.
Digestive cheese and fruit there sure will be;
But that which most doth take my Muse and me,
Is a pure cup of rich Canary wine,
Which is the Mermaid's now, but shall be mine; 30
Of which had Horace, or Anacreon tasted,
Their lives, as do their lines, till now had lasted.
Tobacco, nectar, or the Thespian spring,
Are all but Luther's beer to this I sing.
Of this we will sup free, but moderately, 35
And we will have no Pooley, or Parrot by,
Nor shall our cups make any guilty men;
But, at our parting we will be as when
We innocently met. No simple word
That shall be uttered at our mirthful board, 40
Shall make us sad next morning or affright
The liberty that we'll enjoy tonight.

For Consideration

1. What are the sources of the pleasure in this poem? What, according to
    the poet, is the greatest pleasure to be had from the evening? What does
    he give most of his attention to here?

2. What is the meaning of lines 37–39? What do innocence and guilt refer
    to?

19–20. *godwit . . . knot, rail . . . ruff* edible birds.   30. *Mermaid* a London tavern.   36. *Pooley,
or Parrot* Robert Poley and Henry Parrot, infamous spies for the government.

Jonson's poem emphasizes the importance of a decorous and "mirthful board."
How does the experience anticipated here compare to the experience in "To
Live Merrily, and to Trust to Good Verses" and in "Bring Us In Good Ale"
(p. 395)? What sources of pleasure exist in one poem but not in the others?

WILLIAM WORDSWORTH   (1770–1850)
The Solitary Reaper

Behold her, single in the field,
Yon solitary Highland Lass!
Reaping and singing by herself;
Stop here, or gently pass!
Alone she cuts and binds the grain,   5
And sings a melancholy strain;
O listen! For the Vale profound
Is overflowing with the sound.

No Nightingale did ever chaunt
More welcome notes to weary bands   10
Of travellers in some shady haunt,
Among Arabian sands:
A voice so thrilling ne'er was heard
In spring-time from the Cuckoo-bird,
Breaking the silence of the seas   15
Among the farthest Hebrides.

Will no one tell me what she sings?—
Perhaps the plaintive numbers flow
For old, unhappy, far-off things,
And battles long ago: 20
Or is it some more humble lay,
Familiar matter of today?
Some natural sorrow, loss, or pain,
That has been, and may be again?

16. *Hebrides* islands off western Scotland.

Whate'er the theme, the Maiden sang   25
As if her song could have no ending;
I saw her singing at her work,
And o'er the sickle bending: —
I listened, motionless and still;
And, as I mounted up the hill,   30
The music in my heart I bore,
Long after it was heard no more.

For Consideration

1. The poet moves from the girl in the first stanza to the images of the
    Nightingale and the Cuckoo-bird in the second. How do they reinforce
    the importance of the girl and her song? What effect do the birds' songs
    have on those who hear them?

2. As is evident from the third stanza, the poet does not know the language
    in which the girl sings. What does he speculate may be the subject of her
    song? Finally, do the words themselves really matter?

3. What makes evident the lasting impact of the experience?

WALLACE STEVENS   (1879–1955)
The Idea of Order at Key West

She sang beyond the genius of the sea.
The water never formed to mind or voice,
Like a body wholly body, fluttering
Its empty sleeves; and yet its mimic motion
Made constant cry, caused constantly a cry,   5
That was not ours although we understood,
Inhuman, of the veritable ocean.

The sea was not a mask. No more was she.
The song and water were not medleyed sound

1. *genius* attendant spirit.

Even if what she sang was what she heard,   10
Since what she sang was uttered word by word.
It may be that in all her phrases stirred
The grinding water and the gasping wind;
But it was she and not the sea we heard.

For she was the maker of the song she sang.   15
The ever-hooded, tragic-gestured sea
Was merely a place by which she walked to sing.
Whose spirit is this? we said, because we knew
It was the spirit that we sought and knew
That we should ask this often as she sang.   20

If it was only the dark voice of the sea
That rose, or even colored by many waves;
If it was only the outer voice of sky
And cloud, of the sunken coral water-walled,
However clear, it would have been deep air,   25
The heaving speech of air, a summer sound
Repeated in a summer without end
And sound alone. But it was more than that,
More even than her voice, and ours, among
The meaningless plungings of water and the wind,   30
Theatrical distances, bronze shadows heaped
On high horizons, mountainous atmospheres
Of sky and sea.
                        It was her voice that made
The sky acutest at its vanishing.
She measured to the hour its solitude.   35
She was the single artificer of the world
In which she sang. And when she sang, the sea,
Whatever self it had, became the self
That was her song, for she was the maker. Then we,
As we beheld her striding there alone,   40
Knew that there never was a world for her
Except the one she sang and, singing, made.

Ramon Fernandez, tell me, if you know,
Why, when the singing ended and we turned
Toward the town, tell why the glassy lights,   45
The lights in the fishing boats at anchor there,
As the night descended, tilting in the air,
Mastered the night and portioned out the sea,

44. *Ramon Fernandez* Stevens indicated that he made up this name for his poem and only later
discovered that Ramon Fernandez was the name of a French literary critic (1894–1944).

Fixing emblazoned zones and fiery poles,
Arranging, deepening, enchanting night. 50

Oh! Blessed rage for order, pale Ramon,
The maker's rage to order words of the sea,
Words of the fragrant portals, dimly-starred,
And of ourselves and of our origins,
In ghostlier demarcations, keener sounds. 55

For Consideration

1. This poem is a difficult one, the ideas and phrasing complex and searching. What is the immediate occasion for the poem?

2. One help in understanding the poem is to recognize that both "she" (a girl, a mermaid?) and the sea have a song. How does the motion and "constant cry" of the sea in the first stanza mimic the girl's song? Which song is dominant according to the poet?

3. The poem seems to be searching for some higher principle, a "spirit," or order which governs the girl's song and the sea's. Why does the poet conclude that "it" (the spirit presumably) is more than the voice of the sea, "more even than her voice, and ours"?

4. In what sense is the girl a maker, an artificer of her own world? How is the sea affected by her song in lines 37–39?

5. As the singing ends the poet and his companion see the lights of the fishing boats blazing against the darkness. How does the scene reemphasize the "idea of order" gained from hearing the girl's song?

6. How in the final stanza does the poet relate the maker's "rage to order" and the rage for order "of ourselves and of our origins"?

For Comparison

This poem is often compared to Wordsworth's "The Solitary Reaper." What characteristics do they have in common? How are the responses to the experience described similar? How are they different? Which poem elaborates more on the meaning of the experience? Which of the poems do you find more effective?

ROBERT CREELEY (1926–   )
A Wicker Basket

Comes the time when it's later
and onto your table the headwaiter
puts the bill, and very soon after
rings out the sound of lively laughter —

Picking up change, hands like a walrus,   5
and a face like a barndoor's,
a head without an apparent size,
nothing but two eyes —

So that's you, man,
or me. I make it as I can,   10
I pick up, I go
faster than they know —

Out the door, the street like a night,
any night, and no one in sight,
but then, well, there she is,   15
old friend Liz —

And she opens the door of her cadillac,
I step in back,
and we're gone.
She turns me on —   20

There are very huge stars, man, in the sky,
and from somewhere very far off someone hands me a slice of
        apple pie,
with a gob of white, white ice cream on top of it,
and I eat it —

Slowly. And while certainly   25
they are laughing at me, and all around me is racket
of these cats not making it, I make it

in my wicker basket.

For Consideration

1. How does the speaker describe himself in the opening stanzas? Why are his hands like a walrus, his face like a barndoor's?

2. What lifestyle is described in lines 10–12? Who are "they" referred to twice in the poem? Why at the end are "they" laughing at the speaker?

3. What is the "wicker basket"? What does the speaker mean when he says, "I make it in my wicker basket"?

the importance of creatures

THOMAS HARDY (1840–1928)
The Darkling Thrush

I leant upon a coppice gate
    When Frost was spectre-gray,
And Winter's dregs made desolate
    The weakening eye of day.
The tangled bine-stems scored the sky   5
    Like strings of broken lyres,
And all mankind that haunted nigh
    Had sought their household fires.

The land's sharp features seemed to be
    The Century's corpse outleant,   10
His crypt the cloudy canopy,
    The wind his death-lament.
The ancient pulse of germ and birth
    Was shrunken hard and dry,
And every spirit upon earth   15
    Seemed fervourless as I.

At once a voice arose among
    The bleak twigs overhead
In a full-hearted evensong
    Of joy illimited;   20
An aged thrush, frail, gaunt, and small,
    In blast-beruffled plume,
Had chosen thus to fling his soul
    Upon the growing gloom.

So little cause for carolings   25
    Of such ecstatic sound
Was written on terrestrial things
    Afar or nigh around,
That I could think there trembled through
    His happy good-night air   30
Some blessed Hope, whereof he knew
    And I was unaware.

For Consideration

1. What characteristics does the poet initially assign to himself and his
    world? The poem was written in December of 1900. How does the time
    add to the mood of the opening stanzas?

2. What appearance has the thrush who breaks through the gloom "in a
    full-hearted evensong"? What effect does the song have on the speaker?

3. The bird is apparently aware of "some blessed Hope." Is the speaker? Has
    he been changed by the song he has heard?

RICHARD EBERHART   (1904—   )

Sea-Hawk

The six-foot nest of the sea-hawk,
Almost inaccessible,
Surveys from the headland the lonely, the violent waters.

I have driven him off,
Somewhat foolhardily,   5
And look into the fierce eye of the offspring.

It is an eye of fire,
An eye of icy crystal,
A threat of ancient purity,

Power of an immense reserve,   10
An agate-well of purpose,
Life before man, and maybe after.

How many centuries of sight
In this piercing, inhuman perfection
Stretch the gaze off the rocky promontory,   15

To make the mind exult
At the eye of a sea-hawk,
A blaze of grandeur, permanence of the impersonal.

For Consideration

1. This poem, like "The Fish," focuses on the eyes of the creature observed. What qualities are held by the "fierce eye" of the young sea-hawks?

2. Where does the poet use alliteration? How does that technique tie together the qualities inherent in the sea-hawk?

3. What value to the bird is implied in the phrases "ancient purity," "Life before man, and maybe after," and "permanence of the impersonal"?

W. S. MERWIN (1927–   )

Leviathan

This is the black sea-brute bulling through wave-wrack,
Ancient as ocean's shifting hills, who in sea-toils
Travelling, who furrowing the salt acres

Heavily, his wake hoary behind him,
Shoulders spouting, the fist of his forehead   5
Over wastes gray-green crashing, among horses unbroken
From bellowing fields, past bone-wreck of vessels,
Tide-ruin, wash of lost bodies bobbing
No longer sought for, and islands of ice gleaming,
Who ravening the rank flood, wave-marshalling,   10
Overmastering the dark sea-marches, finds home
And harvest. Frightening to foolhardiest
Mariners, his size were difficult to describe:
The hulk of him is like hills heaving,
Dark, yet as crags of drift-ice, crowns cracking in thunder,   15
Like land's self by night black-looming, surf churning and trailing
Along his shores' rushing, shoal-water boding
About the dark of his jaws; and who should moor at his edge
And fare on afoot would find gates of no gardens,
But the hill of dark underfoot diving,   20
Closing overhead, the cold deep, and drowning.
He is called Leviathan, and named for rolling,
First created he was of all creatures,
He has held Jonah three days and nights,
He is that curling serpent that in ocean is,   25
Sea-fright he is, and the shadow under the earth.
Days there are, nonetheless, when he lies
Like an angel, although a lost angel
On the waste's unease, no eye of man moving,
Bird hovering, fish flashing, creature whatever   30
Who after him came to herit earth's emptiness.
Froth at flanks seething soothes to stillness,
Waits; with one eye he watches
Dark of night sinking last, with one eye dayrise
As at first over foaming pastures. He makes no cry   35
Though that light is a breath. The sea curling,
Star-climbed, wind-combed, cumbered with itself still
As at first it was, is the hand not yet contented
Of the Creator. And he waits for the world to begin.

For Consideration

1. Where does the first sentence of the poem end? Read it aloud. How does
    the aural effect help capture the image and movement of the leviathan?

22. *named for rolling* In *Moby-Dick*, Melville cites *Webster's Dictionary*: "This animal is named
from roundness or rolling." **23.** *first created* Genesis 1:21.

2. The description of the leviathan, like those of Tennyson's eagle and Eberhart's sea-hawk, is enhanced by alliteration. How does the technique enhance the sense of danger and majesty associated with the beast?

3. What different image of the leviathan commences in line 27? What qualities are associated with him in the later lines? What is the association between the leviathan and the rest of creation?

N. SCOTT MOMADAY (1934–)
The Bear

What ruse of vision,
escarping the wall of leaves,
   rending incision
into countless surfaces,

   would cull and color   5
his somnolence, whose old age
   has outworn valor,
all but the fact of courage?

   Seen, he does not come,
move, but seems forever there,   10
   dimensionless, dumb,
in the windless noon's hot glare.

   More scarred than others
these years since the trap maimed him,
   pain slants his withers,   15
drawing up the crooked limb.

   Then he is gone, whole,
without urgency, from sight,
   as buzzards control,
imperceptibly, their flight.   20

2. *escarping* cutting down.

For Consideration

1. What are the prominent features of this bear? Why does he have only the "fact of courage" left? How does the poet suggest the bear's poor vision?

2. Is the bear frightened by the intruder? How do we know? How does the poem hint at features of the bear which are more than, or more important than, physical?

JAMES WRIGHT (1927–   )

A Blessing

Just off the highway to Rochester, Minnesota,
Twilight bounds softly forth on the grass.
And the eyes of those two Indian ponies
Darken with kindness.
They have come gladly out of the willows   5
To welcome my friend and me.
We step over the barbed wire into the pasture
Where they have been grazing all day, alone.
They ripple tensely, they can hardly contain their happiness
That we have come.   10
They bow shyly as wet swans. They love each other.
There is no loneliness like theirs.
At home once more,
They begin munching the young tufts of spring in the darkness.
I would like to hold the slenderer one in my arms,   15
For she has walked over to me
And nuzzled my left hand.
She is black and white,
Her mane falls wild on her forehead,
And the light breeze moves me to caress her long ear   20
That is delicate as the skin over a girl's wrist.
Suddenly I realize
That if I stepped out of my body I would break
Into blossom.

For Consideration

1. Two reactions are described here: that of the ponies to the people and that of the people to the ponies. How do the ponies react? What is the reason for their happiness?

2. What image governs the last ten lines of the poem? What is the basis for the speaker's attraction to the slenderer pony?

3. What about the speaker's feelings is implied in the last two lines? What is important about his response to the horse?

ROBERT FROST   (1874—1963)

Two Look at Two

Love and forgetting might have carried them
A little further up the mountainside
With night so near, but not much further up.
They must have halted soon in any case
With thoughts of the path back, how rough it was   5
With rock and washout, and unsafe in darkness;
When they were halted by a tumbled wall
With barbed-wire binding. They stood facing this,
Spending what onward impulse they still had
In one last look the way they must not go,   10
On up the failing path, where, if a stone
Or earthslide moved at night, it moved itself;
No footstep moved it. "This is all," they sighed,
"Good-night to woods." But not so; there was more.
A doe from round a spruce stood looking at them   15
Across the wall, as near the wall as they.
She saw them in their field, they her in hers.
The difficulty of seeing what stood still,
Like some up-ended boulder split in two,
Was in her clouded eyes: they saw no fear there.   20
She seemed to think that, two thus, they were safe.
Then, as if they were something that, though strange,
She could not trouble her mind with too long,
She sighed and passed unscared along the wall.

"*This*, then, is all. What more is there to ask?" 25
But no, not yet. A snort to bid them wait.
A buck from round the spruce stood looking at them
Across the wall, as near the wall as they.
This was an antlered buck of lusty nostril,
Not the same doe come back into her place. 30
He viewed them quizzically with jerks of head,
As if to ask, "Why don't you make some motion?
Or give some sign of life? Because you can't.
I doubt if you're as living as you look."
Thus till he had them almost feeling dared 35
To stretch a proffering hand — and a spell-breaking.
Then he too passed unscared along the wall.
Two had seen two, whichever side you spoke from.
"This *must* be all." It was all. Still they stood,
A great wave from it going over them, 40
As if the earth in one unlooked-for favor
Had made them certain earth returned their love.

For Consideration

1. What is the condition of the two people who are described at the opening of the poem? What do they seem to be looking for in the woods?

2. How does the doe respond to the appearance of the couple? How are they affected by her? What meaning does the buck add to the scene? What is the source of the spell the couple does not wish to break?

3. Early in the poem, having witnessed the scene, the human lovers conclude, " 'This is all.' " Later they observe, " '*This*, then, is all,' " and finally, " 'This *must* be all.' " How do these reactions relate to the organization and development of the poem?

4. What exactly is the "unlooked-for favor" which makes the couple "certain earth returned their love"? What kind of love is the poem referring to at the end?

For Comparison

Frost's poem and "A Blessing" portray two looking at two, and love, of some type, seems to be important in each poem. How are the two experiences related? Is the insight or pleasure gained by the two human couples the same?

death and life

W. B. YEATS (1865—1939)

Easter 1916

I have met them at close of day
Coming with vivid faces
From counter or desk among grey
Eighteenth-century houses.
I have passed with a nod of the head   5
Or polite meaningless words,
Or have lingered awhile and said
Polite meaningless words,
And thought before I had done
Of a mocking tale or a gibe   10
To please a companion
Around the fire at the club,
Being certain that they and I
But lived where motley is worn:
All changed, changed utterly: 15
A terrible beauty is born.

That woman's days were spent
In ignorant good-will,
Her nights in argument
Until her voice grew shrill.   20
What voice more sweet than hers
When, young and beautiful,

Title. The title refers to a rebellion by Irish nationalists in Dublin which took place on April 24, 1916. The leaders of the rebellion, several of whom are described here, were later executed. **14.** *motley* diverse in color or appearance.   **17.** *that woman's* Countess Markiewicz, a participant in the rebellion.

She rode to harriers?
This man had kept a school
And rode our wingèd horse;   25
This other his helper and friend
Was coming into his force;
He might have won fame in the end,
So sensitive his nature seemed,
So daring and sweet his thought.   30
This other man I had dreamed
A drunken, vainglorious lout.
He had done most bitter wrong
To some who are near my heart,
Yet I number him in the song;   35
He, too, has resigned his part
In the casual comedy;
He, too, has been changed in his turn,
Transformed utterly:
A terrible beauty is born.   40

Hearts with one purpose alone
Through summer and winter seem
Enchanted to a stone
To trouble the living stream.
The horse that comes from the road,   45
The rider, the birds that range
From cloud to tumbling cloud,
Minute by minute they change;
A shadow of cloud on the stream
Changes minute by minute;   50
A horse-hoof slides on the brim,
And a horse plashes within it;
The long-legged moor-hens dive,
And hens to moor-cocks call;
Minute by minute they live: 55
The stone's in the midst of all.

Too long a sacrifice
Can make a stone of the heart.
O when may it suffice?
That is Heaven's part, our part   60
To murmur name upon name,
As a mother names her child
When sleep at last has come

24. *this man* Patrick Pearse, the leader of the insurrection. He was a schoolmaster and poet, hence the reference to the winged horse, Pegasus, identified with poetic inspiration. **26.** *This other* Thomas MacDonagh, a dramatist and, like Pearse, a poet. **31.** *This other man* Major John MacBride, who had married Maud Gonne, the ideal love of Yeats' earlier years. MacBride had separated from his wife, in part because of his heavy drinking.

On limbs that had run wild.
What is it but nightfall?   65
No, no, not night but death;
Was it needless death after all?
For England may keep faith
For all that is done and said.
We know their dream; enough   70
To know they dreamed and are dead;
And what if excess of love
Bewildered them till they died?
I write it out in a verse —
MacDonagh and MacBride   75
And Connolly and Pearse
Now and in time to be,
Wherever green is worn,
Are changed, changed utterly:
A terrible beauty is born.   80

For Consideration

1. What characterizes the society described in the opening stanza? What is
   the poet's association with the people he describes?

2. What has brought on the change and the "terrible beauty"? How has it
   affected the former "casual comedy"?

3. What image controls the third stanza? What comment is the poet making
   about the unity and action of the rebels?

4. What is the controlling response of the poet to the people and their
   deaths? What ambivalence is suggested by the metaphor of the mother
   and child in lines 60–64? Why may the deaths have been needless? Does
   that possibility affect the poet's judgment here?

DYLAN THOMAS (1914–1953)

Do Not Go Gentle into That Good Night

Do not go gentle into that good night,
Old age should burn and rave at close of day;
Rage, rage against the dying of the light.

Though wise men at their end know dark is right,
Because their words had forked no lightning they   5
Do not go gentle into that good night.

Good men, the last wave by, crying how bright
Their frail deeds might have danced in a green bay,
Rage, rage against the dying of the light.

Wild men who caught and sang the sun in flight,   10
And learn, too late, they grieved it on its way,
Do not go gentle into that good night.

Grave men, near death, who see with blinding sight
Blind eyes could blaze like meteors and be gay,
Rage, rage against the dying of the light.   15

And you, my father, there on the sad height,
Curse, bless, me now with your fierce tears, I pray.
Do not go gentle into that good night.
Rage, rage against the dying of the light.

For Consideration

1. What is the basic admonition of the poem? What would it be to "go gentle into that good night" rather than "rage against the dying of the light"?

2. After the opening stanzas the poet describes four types of men who for various reasons "do not go gentle" into their deaths. What kind of persons are represented by the "wise men," the "good men," "the wild men," and the "grave men"? Why does each resist death when it comes? What errors or failures have marked their lives?

Title. The poem was written about Thomas' father, during the latter's final illness.

3. From the final stanza what appears to be the relationship between the poet and his dying father? What personal response does the poet seek to gain from his father?

JOHN BERRYMAN (1914–1972)
A Strut for Roethke

Westward, hit a low note, for a roarer lost
across the Sound but north from Bremerton,
hit a way down note.
And never cadenza again of flowers, or cost.
Him who could really do that cleared his throat   5
& staggered on.

The bluebells, pool-shallows, saluted his over-needs,
while the clouds growled, heh-heh, & snapped, & crashed.

No stunt he'll ever unflinch once more will fail
(O lucky fellow, eh Bones?) — drifted off upstairs,   10
downstairs, somewheres.
No more daily, trying to hit the head on the nail:
thirstless: without a think in his head:
back from wherever, with it said.

Hit a high long note, for a lover found   15
needing a lower into friendlier ground
to bug among worms no more
around um jungles where ah blurt 'What for?'
Weeds, too, he favoured as   most men don't favour men.
The Garden Master's gone.   20

2. *across the Sound* . . . the reference is to the location of the poet Roethke's death. He died of a heart attack in August, 1963, on Bainbridge Island off Puget Sound, Washington. **4.** *cadenza* a brilliant flourish or solo passage near the close of a concerto. **10.** *Bones* with reference to bones as a result of death. More importantly, though, the title Bones, or Mr. Bones, was given to the last performer in a minstrel show. The final act usually included a performance with bones.

For Consideration

1. The syntax of the poem makes it difficult to follow but fits in with the conception of a "strut." What qualities and attitudes does the title connote?

2. The reference to "westward" alludes to the location of Roethke's death. How does it function as an image in the poem? What tribute to Roethke is implied in the reference to a "cadenza" of flowers and in the line which follows?

3. There is a good deal of garden and flower imagery in the poem, ultimately attributable to the fact that Roethke's father was a commercial gardener and so Roethke frequently included garden imagery in his poetry. What relationship exists between the dead poet and the vegetation? What happened when "the clouds growled, heh-heh, & snapped, & crashed"?

4. The third stanza, like the first, alludes to facts in Roethke's life but hints at a larger, controlling image. Roethke was a victim of alcoholism and had several breakdowns which threatened his career and his associations. How do these facts relate to the reference to a "stunt" and the address to Bones, the title of a performer in a minstrel show? Do the lines disparage the poet eulogized?

5. Why does the speaker at the last "hit a high long note"? How does the reference to ground relate both to the death and the garden imagery? The final praise of Roethke as a "Garden Master," important metaphorically, is not to be taken literally. In what sense might Berryman be referring to Roethke as a master?

doubt and faith

EMILY DICKINSON   (1830–1886)
I Know That He Exists

I know that He exists.
Somewhere — in Silence —
He has hid his rare life
From our gross eyes.

'Tis an instant's play.   5
'Tis a fond Ambush —
Just to make Bliss
Earn her own surprise!

But — should the play
Prove piercing earnest —   10
Should the glee — glaze —
In Death's — stiff — stare —

Would not the fun
Look too expensive!
Would not the jest —   15
Have crawled too far!

For Consideration

1.   The poem begins with a definite declaration of God's existence, but then
     goes on to elaborate on the roles played by God and humanity. Does the
     rest of the poem reinforce the confidence of the first line or detract from
     it?

2. The basic metaphor of the poem is that of a game played by God and humanity. What kind of game is it? What role does each play?

3. Define the overall tone of the poem. Where does it appear to change?

MATTHEW ARNOLD (1822–1888)
Dover Beach

The sea is calm tonight.
The tide is full, the moon lies fair
Upon the straits — on the French coast the light
Gleams and is gone; the cliffs of England stand,
Glimmering and vast, out in the tranquil bay. 5
Come to the window, sweet is the night air!
Only, from the long line of spray
Where the sea meets the moon-blanched land,
Listen! you hear the grating roar
Of pebbles which the waves draw back, and fling, 10
At their return, up the high strand,
Begin, and cease, and then again begin,
With tremulous cadence slow, and bring
The eternal note of sadness in.

Sophocles long ago 15
Heard it on the Aegean, and it brought
Into his mind the turbid ebb and flow
Of human misery; we
Find also in the sound a thought,
Hearing it by this distant northern sea. 20

The Sea of Faith
Was once, too, at the full, and round earth's shore
Lay like the folds of a bright girdle furled.
But now I only hear
Its melancholy, long, withdrawing roar, 25
Retreating, to the breath

15–18. *Sophocles* . . . *Antigone*, lines 583 ff.

Of the night wind, down the vast edges drear
And naked shingles of the world.

Ah, love, let us be true
To one another! for the world, which seems   30
To lie before us like a land of dreams,
So various, so beautiful, so new,
Hath really neither joy, nor love, nor light,
Nor certitude, nor peace, nor help for pain;
And we are here as on a darkling plain   35
Swept with confused alarms of struggle and flight,
Where ignorant armies clash by night.

For Consideration

1. What characteristics of the evening does the poet focus on (lines 1—14)? Why does he refer to the reactions of the Greek Sophocles?

2. How does the poet metaphorically relate the sea he observes to the Sea of Faith? How did it once appear? How does it appear now?

3. What response does the poet have to his companion in light of his reflections on faith? What comfort does the world, as he describes it, afford?

GERARD MANLEY HOPKINS (1844—1889)
Thou Art Indeed Just, Lord, If I Contend

Justus quidem tu es, Domine, si disputem tecum: verumtamen justa loquar ad te: Quare via impiorum prosperatur? etc.

Thou art indeed just, Lord, if I contend
With thee; but, sir, so what I plead is just.
Why do sinners' ways prosper? and why must
Disappointment all I endeavor end?

28. *shingles* seashores. **37.** *ignorant armies* a topical allusion, the exact source of which is debatable. **Epigraph.** *Justus quidem tu es* . . . from the Latin Vulgate version of Jeremiah 12:1, translated by Hopkins in the first three lines of the poem.

Wert thou my enemy, O thou my friend,   5
How wouldst thou worse, I wonder, than thou dost
Defeat, thwart me? Oh, the sots and thralls of lust
Do in spare hours more thrive than I that spend,
Sir, life upon thy cause. See, banks and brakes
Now, leavèd how thick! lacèd they are again   10
With fretty chervil, look, and fresh wind shakes
Them; birds build — but not I build; no, but strain,
Time's eunuch, and not breed one work that wakes.
Mine, O thou lord of life, send my roots rain.

For Consideration

1. Why is the speaker questioning God's response to him at the beginning of the poem?

2. What kind of life and person are depicted as "the sobs and thralls of lust"?

3. What image controls the final six lines of the poem? What connection exists between the image and the two types of life thus far described, the speakers' and sinners'? Why does the speaker describe himself as "Time's eunuch"? What response and what results does he wish for in his final plea?

For Comparison

Compare the attitudes of the speakers in this poem and Donne's "Batter My Heart" (p. 324). Each appears to be contending with God in some sense. Why?

11. *chervil* a leafy herb, often used in salads.

WILLIAM CARLOS WILLIAMS (1883–1963)
The Gift

As the wise men of old brought gifts
    guided by a star
        to the humble birthplace

of the god of love,
    the devils   5
        as an old print shows
retreated in confusion.

    What could a baby know
        of gold ornaments
or frankincense and myrrh,   10
    of priestly robes
        and devout genuflections?

But the imagination
    knows all stories
        before they are told   15
and knows the truth of this one
    past all defection

The rich gifts
    so unsuitable for a child
        though devoutly proffered,   20
stood for all that love can bring.

    The men were old
        how could they know
of a mother's needs
    or a child's   25
    appetite?

But as they kneeled
    the child was fed.
        They saw it
and   30
    gave praise!

    A miracle
had taken place,

                    hard gold to love,
a mother's milk!   35
            before
                        their wondering eyes.

The ass brayed
            the cattle lowed.
                        It was their nature.   40

All men by their nature give praise.
            It is all
                        they can do.

The very devils
            by their flight give praise.   45
                        What is death,
beside this?

            Nothing. The wise men
                        came with gifts
and bowed down   50
            to worship
            this perfection.

For Consideration

1.   The poem initially admits the incongruity of the rich gifts delivered to the
     infant Jesus, "the god of love," but goes on to affirm their ap-
     propriateness. What does the poet mean by saying that the "imagination"
     knows stories before they are told and knows the truth of this story?

2.   What essential human responses does the poem focus on? Why are the
     gifts themselves so important?

3.   Why does the poet say, on the matter of giving praise, that it is all that
     men can do? The specific occasion here is the birth of Jesus. Is the
     poem's meaning limited to that incident?

PHILIP LARKIN (1922–   )

Church Going

Once I am sure there's nothing going on
I step inside, letting the door thud shut.
Another church: matting, seats, and stone,
And little books; sprawlings of flowers, cut
For Sunday, brownish now; some brass and stuff   5
Up at the holy end; the small neat organ;
And a tense, musty, unignorable silence,
Brewed God knows how long. Hatless, I take off
My cycle-clips in awkward reverence,

Move forward, run my hand around the font.   10
From where I stand, the roof looks almost new —
Cleaned, or restored? Someone would know: I don't.
Mounting the lectern, I peruse a few
Hectoring large-scale verses, and pronounce
"Here endeth" much more loudly than I'd meant.   15
The echoes snigger briefly. Back at the door
I sign the book, donate an Irish sixpence,
Reflect the place was not worth stopping for.

Yet stop I did: in fact I often do,
And always end much at a loss like this,   20
Wondering what to look for; wondering, too,
When churches fall completely out of use
What we shall turn them into, if we shall keep
A few cathedrals chronically on show,
Their parchment, plate and pyx in locked cases,   25
And let the rest rent-free to rain and sheep.
Shall we avoid them as unlucky places?

Or, after dark, will dubious women come
To make their children touch a particular stone;
Pick simples for a cancer; or on some   30
Advised night see walking a dead one?
Power of some sort or other will go on
In games, in riddles, seemingly at random;
But superstition, like belief, must die,

14. *hectoring* swaggering, blustery. 25. *pyx* container for the Eucharist. 30. *simples* medicinal plants.

And what remains when disbelief has gone? 35
Grass, weedy pavement, brambles, buttress, sky,

A shape less recognizable each week,
A purpose more obscure. I wonder who
Will be the last, the very last, to seek
This place for what it was; one of the crew 40
That tap and jot and know what rood-lofts were?
Some ruin-bibber, randy for antique,
Or Christmas-addict, counting on a whiff
Of gown-and-bands and organ-pipes and myrrh?
Or will he be my representative, 45

Bored, uninformed, knowing the ghostly silt
Dispersed, yet tending to this cross of ground
Through suburb scrub because it held unspilt
So long and equably what since is found
Only in separation — marriage, and birth, 50
And death, and thoughts of these — for whom was built
This special shell? For, though I've no idea
What this accoutred frowsty barn is worth,
It pleases me to stand in silence here;

A serious house on serious earth it is, 55
In whose blent air all our compulsions meet,
Are recognized, and robed as destinies.
And that much never can be obsolete,
Since someone will forever be surprising
A hunger in himself to be more serious, 60
And gravitating with it to this ground,
Which, he once heard, was proper to grow wise in,
If only that so many dead lie round.

For Consideration

1. What kind of person does the speaker appear to be? Is his activity in the church traditional?

2. Stanzas 3–6 anticipate a time when churches fall into disuse and when certain people will still be attracted to them. What attitudes are exhibited? What are the several reasons why some will still seek out churches?

41. *rood-lofts* large crucifixes affixed to beams, especially at the entrance to a medieval church. 42. *ruin-bibber* one addicted to ruins. 53. *accoutred frowsty* furnished musty. 56. *blent* blended.

3. What characterizes the observer whom the speaker labels his "representative"? Why does he tend to "this cross of ground"? Why, taking on his own voice again, does the speaker confirm his pleasure in standing in the church? What is it about the church that "never can be obsolete"? Of what truths in the human situation is the church taken to be a symbol? Describe the tone of the poem. Is it ironic?

the ways of love

WILLIAM SHAKESPEARE (1564—1616)
Let Me Not to the Marriage of True Minds

Let me not to the marriage of true minds
Admit impediments: love is not love
Which alters when it alteration finds.
Or bends with the remover to remove.
Oh no! it is an ever-fixèd mark   5
That looks on tempests and is never shaken;
It is the star to every wandering bark,
Whose worth's unknown although his height be taken.
Love's not Time's fool, though rosy lips and cheeks
Within his bending sickle's compass come;   10
Love alters not with his brief hours and weeks,
But bears it out even to the edge of doom.
    If this be error and upon me proved,
    I never writ, nor no man ever loved.

For Consideration

1. Through what images does the poet emphasize the steadfastness of love? What are the "impediments" which will not be allowed?

2. In what sense is love not "Time's fool"?

3. What is the tone of the last two lines? What point is the poet making?

CHRISTOPHER MARLOWE (1564–1593)

The Passionate Shepherd to His Love

Come live with me and be my love,
And we will all the pleasures prove
That valleys, groves, hills, and fields,
Woods, or steepy mountain yields.

And we will sit upon the rocks,   5
Seeing the shepherds feed their flocks,
By shallow rivers to whose falls
Melodious birds sing madrigals.

And I will make thee beds of roses
And a thousand fragrant posies,   10
A cap of flowers, and a kirtle
Embroidered all with leaves of myrtle.

A gown made of the finest wool
Which from our pretty lambs we pull;
Fair lined slippers for the cold,   15
With buckles of the purest gold;

A belt of straw and ivy buds,
With coral clasps and amber studs;
And if these pleasures may thee move,
Come live with me, and be my love.   20

11. *kirtle* gown or dress.

The shepherd swains shall dance and sing ²¹
For thy delight each May morning
If these delights thy mind may move,
Then live with me and be my love.

For Consideration

1. What kind of pleasures does the poet describe in order to win his love? How prominent is the woman in this love poem?

2. The speaker is identified as "passionate"? Does he appear to feel passionately? For what, the woman or his pleasures?

SIR WALTER RALEGH (ca. 1552—1618)
The Nymph's Reply to the Shepherd

If all the world and love were young,
And truth in every shepherd's tongue,
These pretty pleasures might me move
To live with thee and be thy love.

Time drives the flocks from field to fold ⁵
When rivers rage and rocks grow cold,
And Philomel becometh dumb;
The rest complains of cares to come.

The flowers do fade, and wanton fields
To wayward winter reckoning yields; ¹⁰
A honey tongue, a heart of gall,
Is fancy's spring, but sorrow's fall.

Thy gowns, thy shoes, thy beds of roses,
Thy cap, thy kirtle, and thy posies

21. *swains* rustics, usually young boys. 7. *Philomel* the nightingale. 14. *kirtle* gown or dress (see Marlowe's poem, line 11).

Soon break, soon wither, soon forgotten — 15
In folly ripe, in reason rotten.

Thy belt of straw and ivy buds,
Thy coral clasps and amber studs,
All these in me no means can move
To come to thee and be thy love. 20

But could youth last and love still breed,
Had joys no date nor age no need,
Then these delights my mind might move
To live with thee and be thy love.

For Consideration

1. This was one of several poems written in response to Marlowe's and hence written from the viewpoint of the woman. The first stanza gives a conditional acceptance of the proposal, which the remainder of the poem goes on more thoroughly to question. Under what conditions might the woman here be moved to accept the shepherd's proposal?

2. What conception of Time controls stanzas 2–5? What happens to the pleasures previously introduced by the shepherd?

3. The final stanza restates a conditional acceptance. What is its effect now? How is the tone of the final stanza different from the first?

For Comparison

The two poems, Marlowe's and Ralegh's, are intended to be compared, the second written in response to the first. Consider the following: the voices of the speakers, the tones of the poems, their attitudes toward love and the lover. Which of the two poems do you consider more effective?

ROBERT DUNCAN (1919–   )

Such Is the Sickness of Many a Good Thing

Was he then Adam of the Burning Way?
hid away in the heat like wrath
    conceald in Love's face,
or the seed, Eris in Eros,
    key and lock   5
of what I was?   I could not speak
    the releasing
word.   For into a dark
    matter he came
and askt me to say what   10
    I could not say.   "I ."

All the flame in me stopt
    against my tongue.
My heart was a stone, a dumb
    unmanageable thing in me,   15
a darkness that stood athwart
    his need
for the enlightening, the
    "I love you" that has
only this one quick in time,   20
    this one start
when its moment is true.

Such is the sickness of many a good thing
that now into my life from long ago this
refusing to say I love you has bound   25
the weeping, the yielding, the
    yearning to be taken again,
into a knot, a waiting, a string

so taut it taunts the song,
it resists the touch. It grows dark   30
to draw down the lover's hand
from its lightness to what's
    underground.

4. *Eris in Eros* discord in love. The names are from Greek mythology.

1. What past situation does the poem call attention to? What had the speaker done at that time?

2. What does the image of the "flame" indicate about the speaker's feelings at that occasion?

3. How does the past event affect the speaker now? What does the binding of weeping, yielding, and yearning to be taken refer to? What mood or reaction is indicated in the final image of the poem?

GREGORY CORSO (1930–   )

Marriage

Should I get married? Should I be good?
Astound the girl next door
with my velvet suit and faustus hood?
Don't take her to movies but to cemeteries
tell all about werewolf bathtubs and forked clarinets   5
then desire her and kiss her and all the preliminaries
and she going just so far and I understanding why
not getting angry saying You must feel! It's beautiful to feel!
Instead take her in my arms
lean against an old crooked tombstone   10
and woo her the entire night the constellations in the sky —

When she introduces me to her parents
back straightened, hair finally combed, strangled by a tie,
should I sit knees together on their 3rd degree sofa
and not ask Where's the bathroom?   15
How else to feel other than I am,
often thinking Flash Gordon soap —
O how terrible it must be for a young man
seated before a family and the family thinking
We never saw him before! He wants our Mary Lou!   20
After tea and homemade cookies they ask
What do you do for a living?
Should I tell them? Would they like me then?

Say All right get married, we're not losing a daughter
we're gaining a son —   25
And should I then ask Where's the bathroom?

O God, and the wedding! All her family and her friends
and only a handful of mine all scroungy and bearded
just wait to get at the drinks and food — .
And the priest! he looking at me as if I masturbated   30
asking me Do you take this woman
for your lawful wedded wife!
And I trembling what to say say Pie Glue!
I kiss the bride all those corny men slapping me on the back
She's all yours, boy! Ha-ha-ha!   35
And in their eyes you could see
some obscene honeymoon going on —
Then all that absurd rice and clanky cans and shoes
Niagara Falls! Hordes of us!
Husbands! Wives! Flowers! Chocolates!   40
All streaming into cosy hotels
All going to do the same thing tonight
The indifferent clerk he knowing what was going to happen
The lobby zombies they knowing what
The whistling elevator man he knowing   45
The winking bellboy knowing
Everybody knowing!
I'd be almost inclined not to do anything!
Stay up all night! Stare that hotel clerk in the eye!
Screaming: I deny honeymoon! I deny honeymoon!   50
running rampant into those almost climactic suites
yelling Radio belly! Cat shovel!
O I'd live in Niagara forever! in a dark cave beneath the Falls
I'd sit there the Mad Honeymooner
devising ways to break marriages, a scourge of bigamy   55
a saint of divorce —

But I should get married I should be good
How nice it'd be to come home to her
and sit by the fireplace and she in the kitchen
aproned young and lovely wanting my baby   60
and so happy about me she burns the roast beef
and comes crying to me and I get up from my big papa chair
saying Christmas teeth! Radiant brains! Apple deaf!
God what a husband I'd make! Yes, I should get married!
So much to do! like sneaking into Mr. Jones' house late at night   65
and cover his golf clubs with 1920 Norwegian books
Like hanging a picture of Rimbaud on the lawnmower

67. *Rimbaud* a nineteenth-century French poet.

Like pasting Tannu Tuva postage stamps
all over the picket fence
Like when Mrs Kindhead comes to collect   70
for the Community Chest
grab her and tell her There are unfavourable omens in the sky!
And when the mayor comes to get my vote tell him
When are you going to stop people killing whales!
And when the milkman comes leave him a note in the bottle   75
Penguin dust, bring me penguin dust, I want penguin dust —

Yet if I should get married and it's Connecticut and snow
and she gives birth to a child and I am sleepless, worn,
up for nights, head bowed against a quiet window
the past behind me,   80
finding myself in the most common of situations
a trembling man knowledged with responsibility
not twig-smear nor Roman coin soup —
O what would that be like!
Surely I'd give it for a nipple a rubber Tacitus   85
For a rattle a bag of broken Bach records
Tack Della Francesca all over its crib
Sew the Greek alphabet on its bib
And build for its playpen a roofless Parthenon

No, I doubt I'd be that kind of father   90
not rural not snow no quiet window
but hot smelly tight New York City
seven flights up, roaches and rats in the walls
a fat Reichian wife screeching over potatoes Get a job!
And five nose running brats in love with Batman   95
And the neighbours all toothless and dry haired
like those hag masses of the 18th century
all wanting to come in and watch TV
The landlord wants his rent
Grocery store Blue Cross Gas & Electric Knights of Columbus   100
Impossible to lie back and dream
Telephone snow, ghost parking —
No! I should not get married I should never get married!
But — imagine if I were married
to a beautiful sophisticated woman   105
tall and pale wearing an elegant black dress
and long black gloves
holding a cigarette holder in one hand
and a highball in the other

---

68. *Tannu Tuva* a remote area of the U.S.S.R. 85. *Tacitus* a Roman historian. 87. *Della Francesca* an Italian Renaissance painter. 94. *Reichian* a reference to Wilhelm Reich, a controversial psychiatrist and biophysicist.

and we lived high up in a penthouse with a huge window 110
from which we could see all of New York
and even farther on clearer days
No, can't imagine myself married to that pleasant prison dream —

O but what about love? I forget love
not that I am incapable of love 115
it's just that I see love as odd as wearing shoes —
I never wanted to marry a girl who was like my mother
And Ingrid Bergman was always impossible
And there's maybe a girl now but she's already married
And I don't like men and — 120
but there's got to be somebody!
Because what if I'm 60 years old and not married,
all alone in a furnished room with pee stains on my underwear
and everybody else is married!
All the universe married but me! 125

Ah, yet well I know that were a woman possible as I am possible
then marriage would be possible —
Like SHE in her lonely alien gaud waiting her Egyptian lover
so I wait — bereft of 2,000 years and the bath of life.

For Consideration

1. The poem follows the traditional courtship pattern from dating to propos-
    ing to wedding and to marriage. But the perspective on those events is
    not at all traditional. What kind of person appears to be speaking? What
    are his attitudes toward these imagined events?

2. The fourth stanza appears to begin more conventionally, with a reaffirma-
    tion of some conventional pleasures in marriage. Soon, though, the
    speaker's point of view is clearly unconventional. Why, in the second half
    of the stanza, does he think he ought to get married?

3. What lies behind and connects those things the speaker wants to do (e.g.,
    the Norwegian books, Rimbaud, Tanna Tuva, Tacitus, Bach, Della
    Francesca, Parthenon)?

4. What types of marriage does the speaker consider? Does any attract him?
    Does love have importance in his considerations?

128. *SHE* the heroine of H. Rider Haggard's play *She*. She achieves eternal youth by bathing in
a pillar of flame, waiting thousands of years for her Egyptian lover to return; *gaud* something
gaudy or showy.

DENISE LEVERTOV (1923–   )

The Wife

A frog under you,
knees drawn up
ready to leap out of time,

a dog beside you,
snuffing at you, seeking   5
scent of you, an idea unformulated,

I give up on
trying to answer my question,
Do I love you enough?

It's enough to be   10
so much here. And
certainly when I catch

your mind in the
act of plucking
truth from the dark surrounding nowhere   15

as a swallow skims a
gnat from the
deep sky,

I don't stop to ask myself
Do I love him? but   20
laugh for joy.

For Consideration

1. What appears to be the occasion for the poem? What are the husband and wife doing?

2. What does the man do which causes the woman's final reaction? Why does she no longer ask herself questions but "laugh for joy"?

e. e. cummings   (1894–1962)

if i have made, my lady

if i have made,my lady,intricate
imperfect various things chiefly which wrong
your eyes (frailer than most deep dreams are frail)
songs less firm than your body's whitest song
upon my mind — if i have failed to snare   5
the glance too shy — if through my singing slips
the very skilful strangeness of your smile
the keen primeval silence of your hair

— let the world say "his most wise music stole
nothing from death" —
                              you only will create   10
(who are so perfectly alive) my shame:
lady through whose profound and fragile lips
the sweet small clumsy feet of April came

into the ragged meadow of my soul.

For Consideration

1.   The poem describes the efforts of the speaker in trying to capture, par-
     ticularly in an artistic form, the essences of his lady. The specific
     references to singing may also hint at efforts to capture the woman in the
     song of a poem. How does the poet describe his efforts? How do they
     relate to the woman herself?

2.   What response to his efforts, even if partially successful, will the world
     make? In what sense will only the woman create his shame?

3.   What does the final image of April and "ragged meadow" mean? What is
     the poet saying about the woman's effect on him?

WILLIAM WORDSWORTH (1770–1850)
She Was a Phantom of Delight

She was a Phantom of delight
When first she gleamed upon my sight;
A lovely Apparition, sent
To be a moment's ornament;
Her eyes as stars of Twilight fair;   5
Like Twilight's, too, her dusky hair;
But all things else about her drawn
From May-time and the cheerful Dawn;
A dancing Shape, an Image gay,
To haunt, to startle, and way-lay.   10

I saw her upon nearer view,
A Spirit, yet a Woman too!
Her household motions light and free,
And steps of virgin-liberty;
A countenance in which did meet   15
Sweet records, promises as sweet;
A Creature not too bright or good
For human nature's daily food;
For transient sorrows, simple wiles,
Praise, blame, love, kisses, tears, and smiles.   20

And now I see with eye serene
The very pulse of the machine;
A Being breathing thoughtful breath,
A Traveler between life and death;
The reason firm, the temperate will,   25
Endurance, foresight, strength, and skill;
A perfect Woman, nobly planned,
To warn, to comfort, and command;
And yet a Spirit still, and bright
With something of angelic light.   30

1. *Phantom* with usual implications of incorporeal, but also suggesting something ideal or complete.

For Consideration

1. What characteristics in the woman's appearance are emphasized in the first stanza? What is the effect of words such as Phantom, Apparition, ornament, Twilight, May-time, Dawn, haunt, startle, and so on?

2. How has the description of the woman changed in the second stanza? What characteristics are emphasized there?

3. By the third stanza the woman has become "perfect." What qualities newly mentioned here lead to that conclusion? What is the consummate view of the woman in the poem?

THEODORE ROETHKE   (1908–1963)

The Dream

1

I met her as a blossom on a stem
Before she ever breathed, and in that dream
The mind remembers from a deeper sleep:
Eye learned from eye, cold lip from sensual lip.
My dream divided on a point of fire;   5
Light hardened on the water where we were;
A bird sang low; the moonlight sifted in;
The water rippled, and she rippled on.

2

She came toward me in the flowing air,
A shape of change, encircled by its fire.   10
I watched her there, between me and the moon;
The bushes and the stones danced on and on;
I touched her shadow when the light delayed;
I turned my face away, and yet she stayed.
A bird sang from the center of a tree;   15
She loved the wind because the wind loved me.

3

Love is not love until love's vulnerable.
She slowed to sigh, in that long interval.
A small bird flew in circles where we stood;
The deer came down, out of the dappled wood.   20
All who remember, doubt. Who calls that strange?
I tossed a stone, and listened to its plunge.
She knew the grammar of least motion, she
Lent me one virtue, and I live thereby.

4

She held her body steady in the wind;   25
Our shadows met, and slowly swung around;
She turned the field into a glittering sea;
I played in flame and water like a boy
And I swayed out beyond the white seafoam;
Like a wet log, I sang within a flame   30
In that last while, eternity's confine,
I came to love, I came into my own.

For Consideration

1. The simile of line 1 ("as a blossom on a stem") is joined with the image of
    the dream to introduce the woman in the first stanza. What is her effect
    on the scene?

2. Stanzas 2 and 3 imply interrelationships among her appearance, the ac-
    tions of nature, and the responses of the speaker. How are the speaker
    and nature responding to her presence?

3. What does the speaker mean in saying that "Love is not love until love's
    vulnerable"? How does the statement relate to the portrait of the woman
    in the third stanza?

4. Each stanza makes explicit reference to the image of fire; all but the sec-
    ond refer to water. What effect do the images have in the poem? The
    final stanza brings them together, with the swaying "beyond the white
    seafoam" and the singing "within a flame." How do the images reinforce
    the realization of love, especially as expressed in the last line?

For Comparison

On the surface Roethke's poem and Wordsworth's are similar, each describing a woman who is apparitional in appearance. How similar are the poems otherwise? Are similar virtues apparent in both women? Do they affect the speakers in similar or different ways?

poetry and the arts

W. B. YEATS (1865–1939)
Sailing to Byzantium

I

That is no country for old men. The young
In one another's arms, birds in the trees
— Those dying generations — at their song,
The salmon-falls, the mackerel-crowded seas,
Fish, flesh, or fowl, commend all summer long   5
Whatever is begotten, born, and dies.
Caught in that sensual music all neglect
Monuments of unageing intellect.

II

An aged man is but a paltry thing,
A tattered coat upon a stick, unless   10
Soul clap its hands and sing, and louder sing
For every tatter in its mortal dress,
Nor is there singing school but studying
Monuments of its own magnificence;
And therefore I have sailed the seas and come   15
To the holy city of Byzantium.

16. *Byzantium* an ancient Greek city, but specifically suggesting for Yeats a time when art and intellect were at their height. He once said that if given a month to spend in antiquity he would spend it in Byzantium.

III

O sages standing in God's holy fire
As in the gold mosaic of a wall,
Come from the holy fire, perne in a gyre,
And be the singing-masters of my soul.   20
Consume my heart away; sick with desire
And fastened to a dying animal
It knows not what it is; and gather me
Into the artifice of eternity.

IV

Once out of nature I shall never take   25
My bodily form from any natural thing,
But such a form as Grecian goldsmiths make
Of hammered gold and gold enamelling
To keep a drowsy Emperor awake;
Or set upon a golden bough to sing   30
To lords and ladies of Byzantium
Of what is past, or passing, or to come.

For Consideration

1. What kind of society is depicted in stanza one? What distinguishes the characteristics of "sensual music" from those of the "Monuments of unageing intellect"?

2. What are the monuments of the soul's own magnificence in stanza two? How do they relate to Yeats' journey to Byzantium, for him a historical center of art and culture?

3. How does stanza three emphasize the poet's desire for permanence? Why does he wish to be gathered into the "artifice of eternity"?

4. What "unnatural" object will the poet become when he is "out of nature"?

5. Throughout the poem, the poet draws distinctions between permanence and impermanence, sensuality and intellect, the natural and the artistic. What characteristics and values are associated with the conflicting qualities?

---

19. *perne in a gyre* whirl down in a spiral, i.e., descend to the poet.

ROBERT DUNCAN   (1919–   )

Poetry, A Natural Thing

     Neither our vices nor our virtues
further the poem. "They came up
     and died
just like they do every year
     on the rocks."   5

     The poem
feeds upon thought, feeling, impulse,
     to breed itself,
a spiritual urgency at the dark ladders leaping.

This beauty is an inner persistence   10
     toward the source
striving against (within) down-rushet of the river,
     a call we heard and answer
in the lateness of the world
     primordial bellowings   15
from which the youngest world might spring,

salmon not in the well where the
     hazelnut falls
but at the falls battling, inarticulate,
     blindly making it.   20

This is one picture apt for the mind.

A second: a moose painted by Stubbs,
where last year's extravagant antlers
     lie on the ground.
The forlorn moosey-faced poem wears   25
     new antler-buds,
     the same,

"a little heavy, a little contrived",

his only beauty to be
     all moose.   30

22. *Stubbs* the eighteenth-century artist, George Stubbs, who often painted animals.

For Consideration

1. What image controls the opening quotation and the opening several stanzas? How is it related to the conception of poetry presented here? What is meant by the emphasis on "spiritual urgency," "inner persistence," and "primordial bellowings"?

2. What is the metaphoric relationship between the painting of the moose and a "forlorn moosey-faced poem"? What is the source of beauty emphasized here?

3. What view of poetry is indicated by the two images taken together? How is poetry a "natural thing" here?

WALLACE STEVENS (1879–1955)

Of Modern Poetry

The poem of the mind in the act of finding
What will suffice. It has not always had
To find: the scene was set; it repeated what
Was in the script.
             Then the theatre was changed
To something else. Its past was a souvenir.   5
It has to be living, to learn the speech of the place.
It has to face the men of the time and to meet
The women of the time. It has to think about war
And it has to find what will suffice. It has
To construct a new stage. It has to be on that stage   10
And, like an insatiable actor, slowly and
With meditation, speak words that in the ear,
In the delicatest ear of the mind, repeat,
Exactly, that which it wants to hear, at the sound
Of which, an invisible audience listens,   15
Not to the play, but to itself, expressed
In an emotion as of two people, as of two
Emotions becoming one. The actor is
A metaphysician in the dark, twanging
An instrument, twanging a wiry string that gives   20
Sounds passing through sudden rightnesses, wholly

Containing the mind, below which it cannot descend,
Beyond which it has no will to rise.
                                        It must
Be the finding of a satisfaction, and may
Be of a man skating, a woman dancing, a woman   25
Combing. The poem of the act of the mind.

For Consideration

1. Why is modern poetry "the poem of the mind"? Why, in the past, has poetry not had to "find/what will suffice"? What kind of sufficiency is meant here?

2. What does the poem say about the contemporaneity and immediacy of poetry? What is the relationship between poem and audience as seen through the metaphor of the stage?

3. What value and worth in poetry does this poem emphasize?

suggestions for cross-listing

poetic forms

persona, tone, irony

imagery: figurative language

imagery: symbol and allegory

rhythm, rhyme, and sound

❧ DRAMA ❧

introduction

More than any other literary form, drama encourages the immediate involvement of an audience with the human characters portrayed. No other form of literature can provide such intense possibilities. Though the characters are the products of the writer's imagination, if the drama is successful we do not see them as such, but as human beings, somehow related to ourselves. Even if we know subconsciously that the writer is present, that his or her views are being expressed through the characters, we nonetheless consciously witness that the persons before us on the stage are talking and acting and thinking and loving. It is King Lear who conveys the agony and joy of living, not Shakespeare; it is Professor Borg who reflects on his past and present life, not Bergman.

By contrast, fiction or poetry, no matter how effective or powerful, softens our direct engagement with other human beings. The characters of a story or novel remain, to a greater or lesser extent, controlled by the author who created them. Even in the much-hailed "stream-of-consciousness" novels, authors stand between the reader and the subject, however much they may wish to project only the words and thoughts of the subjects themselves. Poetry even more certainly involves us with the perspective of an author or an author's created persona. (Exceptions are the dramatic monologue and the dramatic poem which, by their very descriptions, are as dramatic as they are poetic.) In poetry, the contact with human emotions and thoughts is frequent, but with fully-drawn human beings, rare.

None of these comments is meant to imply the superiority of

drama over other literary forms. Quite the contrary, the very characteristics that give drama its power and appeal yield limitations as well. If we are closely involved with human beings, their number must remain small. The stage requires limitations of character and setting that are unknown to the novelist or poet. And the presence of an audience stipulates that the action must be performed during a reasonable length of time. One cannot simply mark the book at chapter seven. Time and space are terrible enemies of all artists, but especially the dramatist. Drama also involves a limitation for the audience. One listens and watches and is affected, but after the curtains close, the play itself and one's response to it begin to fade. There is no going back (unless one sees the whole play again) to pick up at chapter seven. But even with these limitations the immediacy and impact of our involvement in other human lives is unmistakable and unique. No other form can match this particular feature.

What I have said thus far is appropriate for drama acted, but what about drama read? No doubt drama intended to be acted has less immediate impact when read from a text. Nothing replaces the value of good acting in making a dramatic character live vividly for us. The important dimension of *seeing* another human being is lost when, even as we read a story or novel, we must imagine the person whose lines we read from the dramatic text. Gestures, facial expressions, changes and modulations of voice and emotions — all are either lost or confined to occasional stage directions.

But this apparent liability has its compensations. If dramatic characters live through good acting, they may die through poor acting. In reading we run no such risk with the ability, preparation, or temperament of another participant. And there is another and more important asset to be realized from reading a play. An actor or actress, whether skilled or incompetent, is inevitably an interpreter and, as such, necessarily interposes a perspective between our own and that of the play. It may be, in other words, that a given representation of a character on stage is false to our reading and interpretation of the character. There is value in this, of course, for another's interpretation may enhance our own. Nonetheless, we often find that, to confirm our judgment of a character or our response to an actor's playing of it, we return to the text itself. At that moment no one — neither author nor actor — stands between us and the person whose words we read. Another theater, a theater of our own making and imagination, becomes the stage for the drama, and it is up to us to make it work.

JOHN MILLINGTON SYNGE (1871–1909)

Riders to the Sea

Characters

MAURYA, an old woman

BARTLEY, her son

CATHLEEN, her daughter

NORA, a younger daughter

MEN and WOMEN

Scene: An Island off the West of Ireland. Cottage kitchen, with nets, oilskins, spinning-wheel, some new boards standing by the wall, etc. CATHLEEN, *a girl of about twenty, finishes kneading cake, and puts it down in the pot-oven by the fire; then wipes her hands, and begins to spin at the wheel.* NORA, *a young girl, puts her head in at the door.*

NORA (*in a low voice*): Where is she?

CATHLEEN: She's lying down, God help her, and maybe sleeping, if she's able.

(NORA *comes in softly, and takes a bundle from under her shawl.*)

CATHLEEN (*spinning the wheel rapidly*): What is it you have?

NORA: The young priest is after bringing them. It's a shirt and a plain stocking were got off a drowned man in Donegal.

(CATHLEEN *stops her wheel with a sudden movement, and leans out to listen.*)

NORA: We're to find out if it's Michael's they are, some time herself will be down looking by the sea.

CATHLEEN: How would they be Michael's, Nora? How would he go the length of that way to the far north?

NORA: The young priest says he's known the like of it. "If it's Michael's they are," says he, "you can tell herself he's got a clean burial by the grace of God, and if they're not his, let no one say a word about them, for she'll be getting her death," says he, "with crying and lamenting."

(*The door which* NORA *half closed is blown open by a gust of wind.*)

CATHLEEN (*looking out anxiously*): Did you ask him would he stop Bartley going this day with the horses to the Galway fair?

NORA: "I won't stop him," says he, "but let you not be afraid. Herself does be saying prayers half through the night, and the Almighty God won't leave her destitute," says he, "with no son living."

CATHLEEN: Is the sea bad by the white rocks, Nora?

NORA: Middling bad, God help us. There's a great roaring in the west, and it's worse it'll be getting when the tide's turned to the wind. (*She goes over to the table with the bundle.*) Shall I open it now?

CATHLEEN: Maybe she'd wake up on us, and come in before we'd done. (*Coming to the table.*) It's a long time we'll be, and the two of us crying.

NORA (*goes to the inner door and listens*): She's moving about on the bed. She'll be coming in a minute.

CATHLEEN: Give me the ladder, and I'll put them up in the turf-loft, the way she won't know of them at all, and maybe when the tide turns she'll be going down to see would he be floating from the east.

(*They put the ladder against the gable of the chimney;* CATHLEEN *goes up a few steps and hides the bundle in the turf-loft.* MAURYA *comes from the inner room.*)

MAURYA (*looking up at* CATHLEEN *and speaking querulously*): Isn't it turf enough you have for this day and evening?

CATHLEEN: There's a cake baking at the fire for a short space (*throwing down the turf*), and Bartley will want it when the tide turns if he goes to Connemara.

(NORA *picks up the turf and puts it round the pot-oven.*)

MAURYA (*sitting down on a stool at the fire*): He won't go this day with the wind rising from the south and west. He won't go this day, for the young priest will stop him surely.

NORA: He'll not stop him, mother, and I heard Eamon Simon and Stephen Pheety and Colum Shawn saying he would go.

MAURYA: Where is he itself?

NORA: He went down to see would there be another boat sailing in the week, and I'm thinking· it won't be long till he's here now, for the tide's turning at the green head, and the hooker's¹ tacking from the east.

CATHLEEN: I hear some one passing the big stones.

NORA (*looking out*): He's coming now, and he in a hurry.

BARTLEY (*comes in and looks round the room. Speaking sadly and*

1. *hooker* a sailing vessel.

quietly): Where is the bit of new rope, Cathleen, was bought in Connemara?

CATHLEEN (*coming down*): Give it to him, Nora; it's on a nail by the white boards. I hung it up this morning, for the pig with the black feet was eating it.

NORA (*giving him a rope*): Is that it, Bartley?

MAURYA: You'd do right to leave that rope, Bartley, hanging by the boards. (*Bartley takes the rope.*) It will be wanting in this place, I'm telling you, if Michael is washed up to-morrow morning, or the next morning, or any morning in the week, for it's a deep grave we'll make him by the grace of God.

BARTLEY (*beginning to work with the rope*): I've no halter the way I can ride down on the mare, and I must go now quickly. This is the one boat going for two weeks or beyond it, and the fair will be a good fair for horses I heard them saying below.

MAURYA: It's a hard thing they'll be saying below if the body is washed up and there's no man in it to make the coffin, and I after giving a big price for the finest white boards you'd find in Connemara.

(*She looks round at the boards.*)

BARTLEY: How would it be washed up, and we after looking each day for nine days, and a strong wind blowing a while back from the west and south?

MAURYA: If it isn't found itself, that wind is raising the sea, and there was a star up against the moon, and it rising in the night. If it was a hundred horses, or a thousand horses you had itself, what is the price of a thousand horses against a son where there is one son only?

BARTLEY (*working at the halter, to* CATHLEEN): Let you go down each day, and see the sheep aren't jumping in on the rye, and if the jobber comes you can sell the pig with the black feet if there is a good price going.

MAURYA: How would the like of her get a good price for a pig?

BARTLEY (*to* CATHLEEN): If the west wind holds with the last bit of the moon let you and Nora get up weed[2] enough for another cock[3] for the kelp.[4] It's hard set we'll be from this day with no one in it but one man to work.

MAURYA: It's hard set we'll be surely the day you're drownd'd with the rest. What way will I live and the girls with me, and I an old woman looking for the grave?

---

2. *weed* sea weed.   **3.** *cock* a cone-shaped pile.   **4.** *kelp* the ash of seaweed, a source of potash and iodine.

(BARTLEY *lays down the halter, takes off his old coat, and puts on a newer one of the same flannel.*)

BARTLEY (*to* NORA): Is she coming to the pier?

NORA (*looking out*): She's passing the green head and letting fall her sails.

BARTLEY (*getting his purse and tobacco*): I'll have half an hour to go down, and you'll see me coming again in two days, or in three days, or maybe in four days if the wind is bad.

MAURYA (*turning round to the fire, and putting her shawl over her head*): Isn't it a hard and cruel man won't hear a word from an old woman, and she holding him from the sea?

CATHLEEN: It's the life of a young man to be going on the sea, and who would listen to an old woman with one thing and she saying it over?

BARTLEY (*taking the halter*): I must go now quickly. I'll ride down on the red mare, and the gray pony'll run behind me. . . . The blessing of God on you.

(*He goes out.*)

MAURYA (*crying out as he is in the door*): He's gone now, God spare us, and we'll not see him again. He's gone now, and when the black night is falling I'll have no son left me in the world.

CATHLEEN: Why wouldn't you give him your blessing and he looking round in the door? Isn't it sorrow enough is on every one in this house without your sending him out with an unlucky word behind him, and a hard word in his ear?

(MAURYA *takes up the tongs and begins raking the fire aimlessly without looking round.*)

NORA (*turning towards her*): You're taking away the turf from the cake.

CATHLEEN (*crying out*): The Son of God forgive us, Nora; we're after forgetting his bit of bread.

(*She comes over to the fire.*)

NORA: And it's destroyed he'll be going till dark night, and he after eating nothing since the sun went up.

CATHLEEN (*turning the cake out of the oven*): It's destroyed he'll be, surely. There's no sense left on any person in a house where an old woman will be talking for ever.

(MAURYA *sways herself on her stool.*)

CATHLEEN (*cutting off some of the bread and rolling it in a cloth; to* MAURYA): Let you go down now to the spring well and give him this and he passing. You'll see him then and the dark word will be broken, and you can say "God speed you," the way he'll be easy in his mind.

MAURYA (*taking the bread*): Will I be in it as soon as himself?

CATHLEEN: If you go now quickly.

MAURYA (*standing up unsteadily*): It's hard set I am to walk.

CATHLEEN (*looking at her anxiously*): Give her the stick, Nora, or maybe she'll slip on the big stones

NORA: What stick?

CATHLEEN: The stick Michael brought from Connemara.

MAURYA (*taking a stick* NORA *gives her*): In the big world the old people do be leaving things after them for their sons and children, but in this place it is the young men do be leaving things behind for them that do be old.

(*She goes out slowly.* NORA *goes over to the ladder.*)

CATHLEEN: Wait, Nora, maybe she'd turn back quickly. She's that sorry, God help her, you wouldn't know the thing she'd do.

NORA: Is she gone round by the bush?

CATHLEEN (*looking out*): She's gone now. Throw it down quickly, for the Lord knows when she'll be out of it again.

NORA (*getting the bundle from the loft*): The young priest said he'd be passing to-morrow, and we might go down and speak to him below if it's Michael's they are surely.

CATHLEEN (*taking the bundle*): Did he say what way they were found?

NORA (*coming down*): "There were two men," says he, "and they rowing round with poteen[5] before the cocks crowed, and the oar of one of them caught the body, and they passing the black cliffs of the north."

CATHLEEN (*trying to open the bundle*): Give me a knife, Nora, the string's perished with the salt water, and there's a black knot on it you wouldn't loosen in a week.

NORA (*giving her a knife*): I've heard tell it was a long way to Donegal.

CATHLEEN (*cutting the string*): It is surely. There was a man here a while ago — the man sold us that knife — and he said if you set off walking from the rocks beyond, it would be in seven days you'd be in Donegal.

NORA: And what time would a man take, and he floating?

5. *poteen* illegal whiskey.

(CATHLEEN *opens the bundle and takes out a bit of a stocking. They look at them eagerly.*)

CATHLEEN (*in a low voice*): The Lord spare us, Nora! isn't it a queer hard thing to say if it's his they are surely?

NORA: I'll get his shirt off the hook the way we can put the one flannel on the other. (*She looks through some clothes hanging in the corner.*) It's not with them, Cathleen, and where will it be?

CATHLEEN: I'm thinking Bartley put it on him in the morning, for his own shirt was heavy with the salt in it. (*Pointing to the corner.*) There's a bit of a sleeve was of the same stuff. Give me that and it will do.

(NORA *brings it to her and they compare the flannel.*)

CATHLEEN: It's the same stuff, Nora; but if it is itself aren't there great rolls of it in the shops of Galway, and isn't it many another man may have a shirt of it as well as Michael himself?

NORA (*who has taken up the stocking and counted the stitches, crying out*): It's Michael, Cathleen, it's Michael; God spare his soul, and what will herself say when she hears this story, and Bartley on the sea?

CATHLEEN (*taking the stocking*): It's a plain stocking.

NORA: It's the second one of the third pair I knitted, and I put up three score stitches, and I dropped four of them.

CATHLEEN (*counts the stitches*): It's that number is in it. (*Crying out.*) Ah, Nora, isn't it a bitter thing to think of him floating that way to the far north, and no one to keen[6] him but the black hags that do be flying on the sea?

NORA (*swinging herself half round, and throwing out her arms on the clothes*): And isn't it a pitiful thing when there is nothing left of a man who was a great rower and fisher, but a bit of an old shirt and a plain stocking?

CATHLEEN (*after an instant*): Tell me is herself coming, Nora? I hear a little sound on the path.

NORA (*looking out*): She is, Cathleen. She's coming up to the door.

CATHLEEN: Put these things away before she'll come in. Maybe it's easier she'll be after giving her blessing to Bartley, and we won't let on we've heard anything the time he's on the sea.

NORA (*helping CATHLEEN to close the bundle*): We'll put them here in the corner.

6. *keen* lament

(*They put them into a hole in the chimney corner.* CATHLEEN *goes back to the spinning-wheel.*)

NORA: Will she see it was crying I was?

CATHLEEN: Keep your back to the door the way the light'll not be on you.

(NORA *sits down at the chimney corner, with her back to the door.* MAURYA *comes in very slowly, without looking at the girls, and goes over to her stool at the other side of the fire. The cloth with the bread is still in her hand. The girls look at each other, and* NORA *points to the bundle of bread.*)

CATHLEEN (*after spinning for a moment*): You didn't give him his bit of bread?

(MAURYA *begins to keen softly, without turning round.*)

CATHLEEN: Did you see him riding down?

(MAURYA *goes on keening.*)

CATHLEEN (*a little impatiently*): God forgive you; isn't it a better thing to raise your voice and tell what you seen, than to be making lamentation for a thing that's done? Did you see Bartley, I'm saying to you.

MAURYA (*with a weak voice*): My heart's broken from this day.

CATHLEEN (*as before*): Did you see Bartley?

MAURYA: I seen the fearfulest thing.

CATHLEEN (*leaves her wheel and looks out*): God forgive you; he's riding the mare now over the green head, and the gray pony behind him.

MAURYA (*starts, so that her shawl falls back from her head and shows her white tossed hair. With a frightened voice*): The gray pony behind him. . . .

CATHLEEN (*coming to the fire*): What is it ails you, at all?

MAURYA (*speaking very slowly*): I've seen the fearfulest thing any person has seen, since the day Bride Dara seen the dead man with the child in his arms.

CATHLEEN AND NORA: Uah.

(*They crouch down in front of the old woman at the fire.*)

NORA: Tell us what it is you seen.

MAURYA: I went down to the spring well, and I stood there saying a prayer to myself. Then Bartley came along, and he riding on the red mare with the gray pony behind him. (*She puts up her hands, as if to hide something from her eyes.*) The Son of God spare us, Nora!

CATHLEEN: What is it you seen?

MAURYA: I seen Michael himself.

CATHLEEN (*speaking softly*): You did not, mother. It wasn't Michael you seen, for his body is after being found in the far north, and he's got a clean burial by the grace of God.

MAURYA (*a little defiantly*): I'm after seeing him this day, and he riding and galloping. Bartley came first on the red mare; and I tried to say "God speed you," but something choked the words in my throat. He went by quickly; and "the blessing of God on you," says he, and I could say nothing. I looked up then, and I crying, at the gray pony, and there was Michael upon it — with fine clothes on him, and new shoes on his feet.

CATHLEEN (*begins to keen*): It's destroyed we are from this day. It's destroyed, surely.

NORA: Didn't the young priest say the Almighty God won't leave her destitute with no son living?

MAURYA (*in a low voice, but clearly*): It's little the like of him knows of the sea. . . . Bartley will be lost now, and let you call in Eamon and make me a good coffin out of the white boards, for I won't live after them. I've had a husband, and a husband's father, and six sons in this house — six fine men, though it was a hard birth I had with every one of them and they coming to the world — and some of them were found and some of them were not found, but they're gone now the lot of them. . . . There were Stephen, and Shawn, were lost in the great wind, and found after in the Bay of Gregory of the Golden Mouth, and carried up the two of them on one plank, and in by that door.

(*She pauses for a moment, the girls start as if they heard something through the door that is half open behind them.*)

NORA (*in a whisper*): Did you hear that, Cathleen? Did you hear a noise in the north-east?

CATHLEEN (*in a whisper*): There's some one after crying out by the seashore.

MAURYA (*continues without hearing anything*): There was Sheamus and his father, and his own father again, were lost in a dark night, and not a stick or sign was seen of them when the sun went up. There was Patch after was drowned out of a curagh[7] that turned over. I was sitting here with Bartley, and he a baby, lying on my two knees, and I seen two women, and three women, and four women coming in, and they crossing themselves, and not saying a word. I looked out then,

---

7. *curagh* a light boat.

and there were men coming after them, and they holding a thing in the half of a red sail, and water dripping out of it — it was a dry day, Nora — and leaving a track to the door.

(*She pauses again with her hand stretched out towards the door. It opens softly and old women begin to come in, crossing themselves on the threshold, and kneeling down in front of the stage with their backs to the people, and the white waist-bands of the red petticoats they wear over their heads just seen from behind.*)

MAURYA (*half in a dream, to* CATHLEEN): Is it Patch, or Michael, or what is it at all?

CATHLEEN: Michael is after being found in the far north, and when he is found there how could he be here in this place?

MAURYA: There does be a power of young men floating round in the sea, and what way would they know if it was Michael they had, or another man like him, for when a man is nine days in the sea, and the wind blowing, it's hard set his own mother would be to say what man was in it.

CATHLEEN: It's Michael, God spare him, for they're after sending us a bit of his clothes from the far north.

(*She reaches out and hands* MAURYA *the clothes that belonged to Michael.* MAURYA *stands up slowly, and takes them in her hands.* NORA *looks out.*)

NORA: They're carrying a thing among them and there's water dripping out of it and leaving a track by the big stones.

CATHLEEN (*in a whisper to the women who have come in*): Is it Bartley it is?

ONE OF THE WOMEN: It is surely, God rest his soul.

(*Two younger women come in and pull out the table. Then men carry in the body of* BARTLEY, *laid on a plank, with a bit of a sail over it, and lay it on the table.*)

CATHLEEN (*to the women, as they are doing so*): What way was he drowned?

ONE OF THE WOMEN: The gray pony knocked him over into the sea, and he was washed out where there is a great surf on the white rocks.

(MAURYA *has gone over and knelt down at the head of the table. The women are keening softly and swaying themselves with a slow movement.* CATHLEEN *and* NORA *kneel at the other end of the table. The men kneel near the door.*)

MAURYA (*raising her head and speaking as if she did not see the people around her*): They're all gone now, and there isn't anything more the sea can do to me. . . . I'll have no call now to be up crying and praying when the wind breaks from the south, and you can hear the surf is in the east, and the surf is in the west, making a great stir with the two noises, and they hitting one on the other. I'll have no call now to be going down and getting Holy Water in the dark nights after Samhain,[8] and I won't care what way the sea is when the other women will be keening. (*To* NORA.) Give me the Holy Water, Nora, there's a small cup still on the dresser.

(NORA *gives it to her.*)

MAURYA (*drops Michael's clothes across* BARTLEY's *feet, and sprinkles the Holy Water over him*): It isn't that I haven't prayed for you, Bartley, to the Almighty God. It isn't that I haven't said prayers in the dark night till you wouldn't know what I'd be saying; but it's a great rest I'll have now, and it's time surely. It's a great rest I'll have now, and great sleeping in the long nights after Samhain, if it's only a bit of wet flour we do have to eat, and maybe a fish that would be stinking.

(*She kneels down again, crossing herself, and saying prayers under her breath.*)

CATHLEEN (*to an old man*): Maybe yourself and Eamon would make a coffin when the sun rises. We have fine white boards herself bought, God help her, thinking Michael would be found, and I have a new cake you can eat while you'll be working.

THE OLD MAN (*looking at the boards*): Are there nails with them?

CATHLEEN: There are not, Colum; we didn't think of the nails.

ANOTHER MAN: It's a great wonder she wouldn't think of the nails, and all the coffins she's seen made already.

CATHLEEN: It's getting old she is, and broken.

(MAURYA *stands up again very slowly and spreads out the pieces of Michael's clothes beside the body, sprinkling them with the last of the Holy Water.*)

NORA (*in a whisper to* CATHLEEN): She's quiet now and easy; but the day Michael was drowned you could hear her crying out from this to the spring well. It's fonder she was of Michael, and would any one have thought that?

CATHLEEN (*slowly and clearly*): An old woman will be soon tired with anything she will do, and isn't it nine days herself is after crying and keening, and making great sorrow in the house?

MAURYA (*puts the empty cup mouth downwards on the table, and lays her hands together on* BARTLEY's *feet*): They're all together this time, and

8. *Samhain* All Saints' Day, November 1.

the end is come. May the Almighty God have mercy on Bartley's soul, and on Michael's soul, and on the souls of Sheamus and Patch, and Stephen and Shawn (*bending her head*); and may He have mercy on my soul, Nora, and on the soul of every one is left living in the world.

(*She pauses, and the keen rises a little more loudly from the women, then sinks away.*)

MAURYA (*continuing*): Michael has a clean burial in the far north, by the grace of the Almighty God. Bartley will have a fine coffin out of the white boards, and a deep grave surely. What more can we want than that? No man at all can be living for ever, and we must be satisfied.

(*She kneels down again and the curtain falls slowly.*)

For Consideration

1. Synge's play is based on his visits to the Aran Islands (off the coast of Ireland) beginning in 1898. He wrote about his visits in *The Aran Islands*, an account which includes references to some of the events and folkloric beliefs central in the play (e.g., a woman's vision of a drowned son riding a horse, an account of a coffin intended for one person but used for another). What qualities and values does the atmosphere of the play promote?

2. What are the attitudes of Cathleen and Nora when they receive the bundle which may contain Michael's clothing? Why do they keep its existence from Maurya?

3. Why is Bartley going to Galway fair? Why does Maurya want to prevent his going? Why is she so convinced that he will not survive his journey? (E.g., "He's gone now, and when the black night is falling I'll have no son left me in the world.")

4. What are the implications of the vision Maurya has of both Bartley and Michael riding horses to the sea? How does Michael appear in the vision?

5. How does Maurya take the news of the discovery of Michael's body? Of Bartley's death? Why does she say that "it's a great rest I'll have now, and it's time surely"?

6. To what extent is Maurya's final attitude characterized by resignation? Is she "quiet now and easy" because she has given up or for some other reason? Why does she pray for mercy on the souls of each of her sons, on her own soul, and then "on the soul of every one is left living in the world"?

7. What is the source of the final satisfaction Maurya professes? Is her profession convincing?

Plot and Theme

The action of a drama must lead somewhere and its various stages must, to be comprehensible, be causally related. Even in a contemporary absurdist play we can discern some relationships among the various actions, even though the actions themselves may seem silly or absurd. The **plot** of a drama, the arrangement and presentation of the action, is the basic level of communication; unless we understand what is going on and why it is happening, we cannot pick up the subtleties of theme and characterization which a playwright strives for. Synge's *Riders to the Sea* is a brief play, but the important elements of drama — including plot — are present. Were we to describe what the play is about we might include such information as the following: The setting is an island off Ireland. An old woman, while waiting to learn the fate of a son apparently lost in the sea north of the island, tries unsuccessfully to convince a final son not to leave on a journey which will also involve travel at sea. He ignores her request and is subsequently drowned; his body is returned to his mother at the same time that she learns that her other son's body has been found in the sea in the north.

This summary adequately captures most of the important action of the play, but it should be obvious that it fails to emphasize the care with which the events are selected and arranged. Of particular importance in Synge's presentation is the way he builds on two key concerns of the drama: the attempt to identify the clothing, and therefore the fate, of Michael, and Maurya's attempt to protect her surviving son. These parallel concerns are climactically brought together in Maurya's vision of Bartley and Michael both riding horses to the sea, and in the final scene of the drama, where Bartley's drowned body represents not only his death, but Michael's death, and the deaths of all the other male members of the family as well. The plot is not, therefore, merely the story; a discussion of plot focuses on *how* the story is presented to us.

The action of Synge's play, and of most dramas, conveniently falls into three basic stages: **rising action, climax,** and **falling action.** The rising action introduces characters and sets up the tension or conflict around which the action revolves. In *Riders to the Sea*, the rising action introduces each of the principal characters, including the dead Michael, and presents the conflict between Maurya and Bartley and the tension resulting from doubts about Michael's death. There is, at the same time, the larger conflict between people and the sea which runs throughout the play and which Maurya, especially, confronts at several key points. The tension builds until Bartley's body is brought in, a climatic occasion which coincides with Maurya's realization of Michael's fate in the north. The climax of the action then gives way to a conscious falling-off, an easing of the tension, as Maurya quietly, even prayerfully, acknowledges what has happened and its decisive effect on her and her family. The falling action, and the play, concludes with a

resolution or **dénouement** (literally, "unknotting"). Maurya's final words and actions not only reveal the painful resolution of the external conflict between humans and the sea but also suggest that the conflict within Maurya herself has yielded to a quiet determination:

> Michael has a clean burial in the far north, by the grace of the Almighty God. Bartley will have a fine coffin out of the white boards, and a deep grave surely. What more can we want than that? No man at all can be living for ever, and we must be satisfied.

As we might expect, the plot of *Riders to the Sea* is more easily described and divided than the plot of, say, *King Lear*. There would likely be considerable disagreement about where the climax of Shakespeare's play occurs; most would probably admit that there is not one but several climaxes, each a culmination of a particular tension or conflict presented in the play. In spite of the added length and complexity of *King Lear*, however, certain characteristics of its plot, and of the plots of all the plays collected here, correspond to the divisions described above.

Having said this much about the plot of *Riders to the Sea*, having attempted, particularly, to understand the effects of the particular arrangement of events, we have inevitably begun to touch on the **theme** of the drama. First some words of caution. The theme of a play is not its message or its moral; it is not the reduction of a work of literature to a one-sentence statement. Any good piece of literature, in fact, defies that kind of simplistic attempt. The fiction writer Flannery O'Connor expressed an author's inevitable outrage at this treatment of theme:

> People talk about the theme of a story as if the theme were like the string that a sack of chicken feed is tied with. They think that if you can pick out the theme, the way you pick the right thread in the chicken-feed sack, you can rip the story open and feed the chickens. But this is not the way meaning works in fiction.

Clearly, this is not the way meaning works in drama either. Still, there are concerns and patterns — universal, human, and profound — around which works of literature are built and which are revealed within the work itself, not merely, to pick up on O'Connor's metaphor, tied to it.

Riders to the Sea is fundamentally concerned with conflict, both between members of a family and between individuals and forces outside themselves. The sea surrounds the island on which Synge's characters live and is a force which they must always confront. At the opening of the play Michael has apparently been lost to the sea, and, very shortly, Bartley reveals his intentions to go to a fair across the sea in spite of his mother's plea for him to stay. Maurya speaks of her attempt to protect Bartley as one of "holding him from the sea," and Cathleen replies, "It's the life of a young man to be going on the sea." Later, when she realizes that she has lost all of her men, Maurya sees the sea as a kind of victorious opponent: "They're all gone now, and there isn't anything more the sea can do with me." Balancing the sense of the sea's victory over man is the strength and endurance seen in Maurya, especially at the end. Her action has ritual and religious qualities, and Nora observes the change in her: "She's quiet now and easy." Even the "clean burial" for Michael and the "fine coffin" for Bartley bring a measure of solace to her, and her final words, as noted before, reveal her own resolve: "What more can we want than that? No man at all can be living for ever, and we must be satisfied." *Riders to the Sea* has as one theme the struggle of people against extra-human forces, showing both the victory those forces may achieve and the inner strength of those who must endure.

As with plot, the theme of a short or relatively simple play is much easier to determine and discuss than that of a long or complex play. Two plays included in this book, Ionesco's *The Leader* and Shakespeare's *King Lear* are contrasting examples. *The Leader* contains a few themes which can be distinctly isolated — the vapid quality of love in contemporary society, the naive hero-worship of the crowd — and above all stands the figure of the leader himself, headless and mindless, a symbol of the best, and worst, in society. The complexity of *King Lear* makes an attempt to capture its theme in a few words quite difficult. It is not wrong to note that the play is concerned with "filial ingratitude" or excessive pride in a man or, as in *Riders to the Sea*, a universe which may be alien to the wishes and well-being of people in general. It is about all of these and more; to emphasize any one at the expense of the others is likely to do an injustice to the play as a whole. We may profitably speak of the theme(s) of *King Lear* but we must consistently recognize its complex treatment of the human situation depicted.

Characterization

Because dramatists do not have the luxury of speaking between the lines of their characters and because they cannot depend on description, explanation, or elaboration of their own to convey their intentions (with the exception of some directions), they must rely fully on their characters to work for them. **Characterization** is thus particularly important in a drama, and playwrights utilize a number of techniques to reveal the concerns and values of their characters. Most obviously, characters will reveal themselves to us by what they say and do. We need not always accept given statements as being true for, as in any human situation, characters may speak falsely because of the person they are addressing. The cumulative effects of characters' speeches, however, are the surest way of understanding who they are and what they stand for. We understand Maurya, for example — her initial doubt and distress and her final quiet determination — as she is revealed in her own utterances. We may also know more about characters by what others say about them, though again a reader must exercise an appropriate caution before automatically believing such comments. One character may, of course, lie about another, as in *King Lear* the villain Edmund deceives Gloucester into believing that his son Edgar intends to kill him. We need to understand the qualities of the characters who speak before we accept too quickly what they say.

Occasionally characters are revealed, not just by what they say or do or by what others say about them, but by an implicit contrast to another character in the drama. One character set against another in this way is called a **dramatic foil**. Recognizing dramatic foils is particularly important when we see characters in comparable situations reacting differently. Dramatic foils do not function importantly in *Riders to the Sea*, largely because of the singular dominance of Maurya. In several of the other plays here, however, they are important. Early in *Antigone*, for example, Antigone and Ismene face almost exactly the same dilemma — whether to disobey Creon and thereby risk their lives by burying the body of their dead brother, or obey the law and be safe. Antigone's firm resolve to bury the body, and the danger inherent in such action, are enhanced by Ismene's decision not to act. Simply because they act differently we perceive the characters better.

Throughout a drama we are interested in the **motivation** of characters, the purpose and intent which guide their actions. It is largely the matter of motivation that allows us to separate the principal character of a play, the **protagonist**, from an opponent, an **antagonist**. Traditionally, the protagonist is the sympathetic hero, the antagonist a villainous or unscrupulous foe. The protagonist need not be so virtuous, however; Shakespeare's Richard III and Macbeth are two examples of unheroic protagonists who dominate the action of their respective plays. Few dramas — even those with the traditional conflict of hero and foe — allow us to pigeon-hole characters too easily. We can say that in *King Lear*, Cordelia is essentially good and Edmund essentially evil, but between those two are many characters who seem sometimes well meaning, sometimes selfish or proud. Lear himself, the sympathetic protagonist, nonetheless acts mistakenly, even cruelly, at times.

Riders to the Sea may seem to be without this traditional conflict between a protagonist and an antagonist, since Maurya is the only dominant character. There is an antagonist however, a non-human one, revealed in the conflict between Maurya and the sea, the one fighting to protect what is left of her family, the other seeking to destroy it. Maurya's recognition of her powerful foe is seen in the line quoted earlier: "They're all gone now, and there isn't anything more the sea can do to me." Although the conflict in this play is not the usual one of human against human, it is no less crucial or consequential.

To sum up, responding to characters in a drama is not so different from responding to people we do not know. We come with an open mind, hear them talk, see them act, and listen to what others say about them. We do not have the luxury of talking to them and asking them questions, but if we use what we have, prudently and intelligently, we will know much about them, and thus much about the play, just the same.

Dramatic Conventions

Much of what has been said about drama thus far is true, to varying degrees, for other forms of literature as well. A short story, a novel, or a narrative poem has a plot and it may correspond to the three-part division of plot described above. Each work may have a theme and in each — certainly in fiction — characterization may be important. The unique feature of drama is, of course, that it is intended for presentation on a stage, and includes the additional trappings peculiar to that format. Even when a play is read, there exist a number of dramatic elements which have particular pertinence to a stage setting. These elements may be unrealistic in the strictest sense, but an audience accepts them in order to let the drama work. These features, **dramatic conventions**, include even matters so quickly accepted as setting or language. *Riders to the Sea* is set on an island and in a cottage kitchen; if we saw the play performed we would know that the stage remained a stage but we would accept the dramatic designations nonetheless. The entire question of setting is, in fact, a convention that almost any audience, no matter how new to drama, accepts. The performance of plays on a modern stage often aids our imagination, for the scenery and stage construction may be designed to resemble a palace or an apartment or a mountain area. All we have, though, is help; we still have to accept the unreal as real, to submit ourselves to what Coleridge described, in a different context, as the "willing suspension of disbelief."

Time is another matter treated almost indifferently by many playwrights. There was a period in the history of English literature when some writers believed that the time taken to perform a play should approximate the time consumed by all the action presented. Few writers or audiences have ever paid allegiance to that rigid assumption. Between two scenes or acts, hours, days, even years may pass, and an audience, waiting only five or ten minutes, accepts the transition quite easily. *Riders to the Sea* has only one uninterrupted scene, played on stage for less than an hour. Yet we are asked to believe that in that time Bartley comes in the kitchen, (after the elapse of several minutes at the opening), leaves to get his horses, rides off toward the sea, drowns, and is brought back before his mother. It cannot happen, but for the playwright and audience it can, of course, and does.

Two other conventions, more specific in nature and less frequently encountered, are the **soliloquy** and the **aside**. The soliloquy is a monologue spoken by a character alone on stage. Were this a real life situation we would find the practice strange; few of us talk aloud to ourselves — or at least few of us admit that we do. Because the characters are speaking to themselves, or to the audience, we can usually assume that they speak the truth as they understand it. This is the case especially in Shakespearean drama, where a soliloquy reveals characters, even evil ones, speaking honestly to themselves. In *King Lear*, Edmund's opening soliloquy of Act I, scene ii, reveals his bitter nature; a moment later, when his father comes in, Edmund's attitude and character change, but because of our understanding of the importance of the soliloquy we can see that the monologue reveals Edmund as he really is, the dialogue as he pretends to be. The aside is a speech uttered in the middle of dialogue but intended only for the speaker and the audience. Like the soliloquy, the aside is a more honest revelation of a character's thoughts and dispositions. It is a speech not intended for, and thus not influenced by, another character in the play.

The concern with convention leads us back to the emphasis of the earlier introduction: the audience's vital participation in the drama if the meaning and impact are fully to be realized. Drama is a public form of literature. An audience which is blind to conventions, or resistant to characters who speak in poetry or who are portrayed allegorically, can effectively squelch the point and impact of a play. But an audience which accepts these dramatic trappings and allows them to contribute to the working of the play as a whole, assures itself of the fullest possible involvement with the action and characters presented.

tragedy and comedy

Drama is ordinarily divided into tragedy and comedy, but having recognized those classes we ought quickly to dispel certain simplistic notions connected with them. It is not enough to say, and sometimes not even right to say, that tragedy is sad, comedy happy, or that tragedy ends pessimistically, comedy optimistically. There is enough truth in the associations to keep them alive, but enough falsehood to make them misleading. A comedy is not necessarily funny; it may, in fact, focus significantly on bittersweet experiences of unhappy people; conversely, a tragedy may bring deep and abiding pleasure and provide resolutions which are satisfying and fulfilling, if not happy. Important distinctions ought, however, to be made.

Tragedy usually focuses on an individual rather than society; in Shakespearean tragedy we see this focus further emphasized in the titles of the tragedies (*Hamlet, Othello, King Lear, Macbeth*), which suggest the importance of the tragic figure. In a tragedy the tragic figure experiences some kind of downfall, some personal misfortune or calamity, which results in death or despair. Death is a crucial ingredient of tragedies though it does not always come to the tragic figure. At the end of *King Lear* — and all other Shakespearean tragedies — the tragic hero dies. At the end of *Antigone*, however, Creon is still alive though we understand clearly that, with the deaths of nearly all members of his family, he is experiencing a death-in-life. *Oedipus the King* is another well-known Greek tragedy which allows the hero to live at the end of the drama; as with Creon, however, Oedipus is in such misery because of what he has learned during the play (he has unknowingly killed his father and married his mother) that we feel his continuing to live is, in some measure, only an added punishment.

Most comments about tragedy still owe much to the observations of Aristotle who, in his *Poetics*, elevated the tragedy to the highest form of literature. Aristotle emphasized the importance of tragedy by defining it as "an imitation of an action that is serious, complete, and of a certain magnitude"; Aristotle further emphasized that a tragic figure should be a basically good person who is "above the common level."

That is, in classical and Shakespearean tragedy, especially, there is a conscious elevation of the tragic figure to a position above that of ordinary human beings. The tragedy, therefore, usually focuses on a person who is, at the beginning of the play, deemed successful and important (e.g., Creon in *Antigone* and King Lear in *King Lear*). To make the play a tragedy and to give it its unmatched impact, that elevated personage must experience misfortune or disaster. At the heart of most tragedies, therefore, is irony, for we see an important and happy person lose his or her fortunate position and fall to misery and, possibly, death.

A particular form of irony is the reversal of intention (Aristotle's term: *peripeteia*). The irony of a tragic fall is made even more pronounced if the misfortune arises from an action which was intended to bring happiness and well-being. We see such reversals in both *Antigone* and *King Lear*. In the former, Creon institutes a decree which he believes will bring him more power and prestige, but it eventually results in death for his family and a total loss of position for him. King Lear intends, by dividing up his kingdom among his daughters, to make his final days easier and more pleasant; in fact, the action divides his family and leads to his own ostracism.

In tragedy the hero falls at least in part as a result of personal weakness or error. This tragic error (Aristotle's term: *hamartia*) need not be a permanent frailty in the character, as the more familiar term "tragic flaw" would suggest. The tragic error may simply be a mistake which the hero makes in a given circumstance, but it will, of course, have consequences serious enough to lead to his or her downfall. One of the most frequent failings which leads to a tragic fall is excessive pride, or **hubris**. Pride is, of course, in keeping with the exalted position of tragic figures; they not only have wealth and power beyond that of ordinary people, but also believe themselves to be better or more important or more respected. The fall which results in a tragedy is therefore a humbling experience for a person once considered great.

Most of the above emphasizes the downward movement of tragedy, the fall to death or despair. That fall is usually accompanied, however, by the tragic heroes' recognition of their misdeeds and responsibilities (Aristotle's term: *anagnorisis*). In a tragedy, therefore, we do not simply see a person commit a grievous mistake for which a severe penalty must be paid; we also see the development of a fuller self-understanding. In both *Antigone* and *King Lear* the audience perceives the errors (both a result of hubris) of Creon and Lear early in each drama. The principal characters, however, come to an understanding of what they have done only very late in the action. When the full impact of his wrong is felt, each king responds with a strikingly humble conception of himself. Creon, in his last speech, alludes to the deaths of his wife and son and to his recognition that he must assume responsibility for their deaths:

Lead me away. I have been rash and foolish.
I have killed my son and wife.
I look for comfort; my comfort lies here dead.
Whatever my hands have touched has come to nothing.
Fate has brought all my pride to a thought of dust.

Lear's recognition of past mistakes is equally humbling. At the end of Act IV, in the presence of the daughter whom he has most wronged, he speaks of himself as a "very foolish fond old man, / Fourscore and upward, not an hour more nor less; / And to deal plainly, I fear I am not in my perfect mind."

The element of recognition and the attendant affirmation which it suggests for the sensitive human being is one ingredient which balances the otherwise negative features of a tragedy. There is considerable debate over the degree of hope or affirmation which can be found in a tragedy, and the issues are various and complex. It would seem, though, that the presence of affirmative qualities is necessary in order for us to feel the full tension between affirmation and negation in a tragedy. Some degree of affirmation, such as the hero's recognition, ought also to be present if we are to experience the catharsis, or cleansing, which Aristotle emphasized as a part of the audience's response to a tragedy. Aristotle noted that tragedy arouses "pity and fear" in an audience but added that the aim of tragedy is to effect "the proper purgation of these emotions." Finally, some balance between the negative and affirmative is surely what makes tragedy so compelling and so serious as literature. Few of us respond to the human situation as either fully joyful or completely despairing. Tragedy, which proposes to look at life seriously, reflects a similar balance. Arthur Miller, a contemporary American playwright, focused on this characteristic in his attempt to emphasize the more hopeful qualities of tragedy.

> Tragedy requires a . . . balance between what is possible and what is impossible. And it is curious, although edifying, that the plays we revere, century after century, are the tragedies. In them, and in them alone, lies the belief — optimistic, if you will — in the perfectability of man.
>
> "Tragedy and the Common Man"

You do not have to accept Miller's view of tragedy, but you may find it a useful balance to impressions you have had previously.

Comedy is easier to talk about than tragedy; it is ordinarily lighter in its portrayal of humanity and human frailties, and, it is safe to say, is usually less gripping that the tragedy. In contrast to tragedy, comedy seldom focuses on an individual; it is almost always concerned with communities and relationships, the family or the society at large. There are essentially two types of comedy: the **romantic** comedy and the **satiric** comedy. The former emphasizes love, usually the struggle of a young and idealistic couple to gain each other and to gain acceptance of their relationship. There may be many threats and obstacles to their union, but in a comedy, as distinct from a love tragedy (e.g., *Romeo and Juliet* or *Antony and Cleopatra*), the threats and obstacles never seem too serious and are never allowed to overcome the young lovers. Some of the best known romantic comedies are Shakespeare's, and the titles of many of his plays suggest the lightness of the form (e.g., *As You Like It; Twelfth Night, or, What You Will; A Midsummer Night's Dream*). The satiric comedy is often more biting in tone, having as its aim the exposure of an individual's or society's weaknesses. Tragedy, as we have seen, also deals fundamentally with human weakness, but satire, whether in poetry or in a play, attempts to poke fun at and ridicule the weakness, not to show its progression toward a tragic conclusion. *Happy Ending*, included in this book, is a satiric comedy, for it lays bare the problems of relationships between blacks and whites, between the haves and the have-nots, in contemporary American society. Even the title has a satiric thrust, for after reading the play we understand that the ending is happy only within the limits imposed by society; the society itself remains grossly imperfect.

Comedy, then, focuses on society and encourages us to look on people's foibles with a detached laughter. We are not caught up by the seriousness of the play nor do we feel so involved with the characters. Rather, while they may speak to what we know of ourselves or of others, we remain detached from them in important ways. The detachment is absent from our response to a tragedy. There, involvement is a key. The popularity of *Hamlet* is a testimony to the fact that audiences have seen their own humanity reflected in the young prince; we are part of the tragic action as we are not part of, say, the action of one of Shakespeare's romantic comedies or even of *Happy Ending*. A full response to either form should produce understanding, but in a comedy it is reached from the perspective of the detached observer, in a tragedy, from the perspective of the involved participant.

SOPHOCLES   (496–406 B.C.)

Antigone[1]

An English Version by Dudley Fitts and Robert Fitzgerald

The Characters

ANTIGONE

ISMENE

EURYDICE

CREON

HAIMON

TEIRESIAS

A SENTRY

A MESSENGER

CHORUS

SCENE: *Before the palace of Creon, King of Thebes. A central double door, and two lateral doors. A platform extends the length of the facade, and from this platform three steps lead down into the 'orchestra,' or chorus-ground.*

TIME: *dawn of the day after the repulse of the Argive army from the assault on Thebes.*

1. *Title* A Greek audience would have known of the legendary incidents alluded to in this play, but since most modern audiences do not, it is necessary to set forth some background information. The principal characters here are all related to Oedipus, the former King of Thebes. On learning that he had unknowingly killed his father and married his mother, Oedipus blinded himself and went into exile. He left behind two daughters, Antigone and Ismene, and two sons, Eteocles and Polyneices. After the latter two fought over the kingship, Polyneices was driven into exile, only to return later with an army (the Argives) which aligned his forces with those of other Greek princes. During the battle which ensued between Eteocles' forces and Polyneices', the two brothers fought and killed each other. Ascending to the throne, then, was Créon, brother of Jocasta and uncle to the brothers, Antigone, and Ismene. As a first act Creon decreed that the body of Polyneices was to remain unburied. Antigone, as the play commences, opposes that decree.

Prologue

(ANTIGONE *and* ISMENE *enter from the central door of the Palace.*)

ANTIGONE: Ismenê, dear sister,
   You would think that we had already suffered enough
   For the curse on Oedipus:
   I cannot imagine any grief
   That you and I have not gone through. And now—⁣   5
   Have they told you of the new decree of our King Creon?

ISMENE: I have heard nothing: I know
   That two sisters lost two brothers, a double death
   In a single hour; and I know that the Argive army
   Fled in the night; but beyond this, nothing.   10

ANTIGONE: I thought so. And that is why I wanted you
   To come out here with me. There is something we must do.

ISMENE: Why do you speak so strangely?

ANTIGONE: Listen, Ismenê:
   Creon buried our brother Eteoclês   15
   With military honours, gave him a soldier's funeral,
   And it was right that he should; but Polyneicês,
   Who fought as bravely and died as miserably,—
   They say that Creon has sworn
   No one shall bury him, no one mourn for him,   20
   But his body must lie in the fields, a sweet treasure
   For carrion birds to find as they search for food.
   That is what they say, and our good Creon is coming here
   To announce it publicly; and the penalty—
   Stoning to death in the public square!
                                       There it is,   25
   And now you can prove what you are:
   A true sister, or a traitor to your family.

ISMENE: Poor Antigonê! But what can I do about it?

ANTIGONE: You must decide whether you will help me or not.

ISMENE: I don't understand you. Help you in what?   30

ANTIGONE: Ismenê, I am going to bury him. Will you come?

ISMENE: Bury him! You have just said the new law forbids it.

ANTIGONE: He is my brother. And he is your brother, too.

ISMENE: But think of the danger! Think what Creon will do!

ANTIGONE: Creon is not strong enough to stand in my way.   35

ISMENE: Ah sister!
　　　　Oedipus died, everyone hating him
　　　For what his own search brought to light, his eyes
　　　Ripped out by his own hand; and Iocastê died,
　　　His mother and wife at once: she twisted the cords　　　　　　40
　　　That strangled her life; and our two brothers died,
　　　Each killed by the other's sword. And we are left:
　　　But oh, Antigonê,
　　　Think how much more terrible than these
　　　Our own death would be if we should go against Creon　　　45
　　　And do what he has forbidden! We are only women,
　　　We cannot fight with men, Antigonê!
　　　The law is strong, we must give in to the law
　　　In this thing, and in worse. I beg the Dead
　　　To forgive me, but I am helpless: I must yield　　　　　　　50
　　　To those in authority. And I think it is dangerous business
　　　To be always meddling.

ANTIGONE:　　　　　　　　　If that is what you think,
　　　I should not want you, even if you asked to come.
　　　You have made your choice, you can be what you want to be.
　　　But I will bury him; and if I must die,　　　　　　　　　　55
　　　I say that this crime is holy: I shall lie down
　　　With him in death, and I shall be as dear
　　　To him as he to me.
　　　　　　　　It is the dead,
　　　Not the living, who make the longest demands:
　　　We die for ever . . .
　　　　　　　　You may do as you like,　　　　　　　　　60
　　　Since apparently the laws of the gods mean nothing to you.

ISMENE: They mean a great deal to me; but I have no strength
　　　To break laws that were made for the public good.

ANTIGONE: That must be your excuse, I suppose. But as for me,
　　　I will bury the brother I love.

ISMENE:　　　　　　　　　Antigonê,　　　　　　　　　　　　65
　　　I am so afraid for you!

ANTIGONE:　　　　　　　You need not be:
　　　You have yourself to consider, after all.

ISMENE: But no one must hear of this, you must tell no one!
　　　I will keep it a secret, I promise!

ANTIGONE:　　　　　　　　Oh tell it! Tell everyone!
　　　Think how they'll hate you when it all comes out　　　　　70
　　　If they learn that you knew about it all the time!

ISMENE: So fiery! You should be cold with fear.

ANTIGONE: Perhaps. But I am doing only what I must.

ISMENE: But can you do it? I say that you cannot.

ANTIGONE: Very well: when my strength gives out, I shall do no more. 75

ISMENE: Impossible things should not be tried at all.

ANTIGONE: Go away, Ismenê:
 I shall be hating you soon, and the dead will too,
 For your words are hateful. Leave me my foolish plan:
 I am not afraid of the danger; if it means death, 80
 It will not be the worst of deaths — death without honour.

ISMENE: Go then, if you feel that you must.
 You are unwise,
 But a loyal friend indeed to those who love you.

(*Exit into the Palace.* ANTIGONE *goes off, L. Enter the* CHORUS.)

Parodos[2]

Strophe I

CHORUS: Now the long blade of the sun, lying
 Level east to west, touches with glory
 Thebes of the Seven Gates. Open, unlidded
 Eye of golden day! O marching light
 Across the eddy and rush of Dircê's[3] stream, 5
 Striking the white shields of the enemy
 Thrown headlong backward from the blaze of morning!

CHORAGOS:[4] Polyneicês their commander
 Roused them with windy phrases,
 He the wild eagle screaming 10
 Insults above our land,
 His wings their shields of snow,
 His crest their marshalled helms.

2. *Parodos* the song chanted by the chorus as it enters the acting area. The chorus, in this play representing Theban elders, is on stage during the remainder of the drama. Strophe and Antistrophe ("turn" and "counter-turn") indicate the movement of the chorus as it walks from one side of the stage to the other. 3. *Dirce* A stream named after a queen of Thebes. 4. *Choragos* the spokesman for the chorus, the choral leader.

Antistrophe I

CHORUS: Against our seven gates in a yawning ring
       The famished spears came onward in the night;   15
       But before his jaws were sated with our blood,
       Or pinefire took the garland of our towers,
       He was thrown back; and as he turned, great Thebes—
       No tender victim for his noisy power—
       Rose like a dragon behind him, shouting war.   20

CHORAGOS: For God hates utterly
       The bray of bragging tongues;
       And when he beheld their smiling,
       Their swagger of golden helms,
       The frown of his thunder blasted   25
       Their first man from our walls.

Strophe 2

CHORUS: We heard his shout of triumph high in the air
       Turn to a scream; far out in a flaming arc
       He fell with his windy torch, and the earth struck him.
       And others storming in fury no less than his   30
       Found shock of death in the dusty joy of battle.

CHORAGOS: Seven captains at seven gates
       Yielded their clanging arms to the god
       That bends the battle-line and breaks it.
       These two only, brothers in blood,   35
       Face to face in matchless rage,
       Mirroring each the other's death,
       Clashed in long combat.

Antistrophe 2

CHORUS: But now in the beautiful morning of victory
       Let Thebes of the many chariots sing for joy!   40
       With hearts for dancing we'll take leave of war:
       Our temples shall be sweet with hymns of praise,
       And the long night shall echo with our chorus.

Scene I

CHORAGOS: But now at last our new King is coming:
    Creon of Thebes, Menoiceus' son.
    In this auspicious dawn of his reign
    What are the new complexities
    That shifting Fate has woven for him?   5
    What is his counsel? Why has he summoned
    The old men to hear him?

(*Enter* CREON *from the Palace, C. He addresses the* CHORUS *from the top step.*)

CREON: Gentlemen: I have the honour to inform you that our Ship of State, which recent storms have threatened to destroy, has come safely to harbour at last, guided by the merciful wisdom of Heaven. 10 I have summoned you here this morning because I know that I can depend upon you: your devotion to King Laïos was absolute; you never hesitated in your duty to our late ruler Oedipus; and when Oedipus died, your loyalty was transferred to his children. Unfortunately, as you know, his two sons, the princes Eteoclês and 15 Polyneicês, have killed each other in battle; and I, as the next in blood, have succeeded to the full power of the throne.

I am aware, of course, that no Ruler can expect complete loyalty from his subjects until he has been tested in office. Nevertheless, I say to you at the very outset that I have nothing but contempt for 20 the kind of Governor who is afraid, for whatever reason, to follow the course that he knows is best for the State; and as for the man who sets private friendship above the public welfare, — I have no use for him, either. I call God to witness that if I saw my country headed for ruin, I should not be afraid to speak out plainly; and I 25 need hardly remind you that I would never have any dealings with an enemy of the people. No one values friendship more highly than I; but we must remember that friends made at the risk of wrecking our Ship are not real friends at all.

These are my principles, at any rate, and that is why I have made 30 the following decision concerning the sons of Oedipus: Eteoclês, who died as a man should die, fighting for his country, is to be buried with full military honours, with all the ceremony that is usual when the greatest heroes die; but his brother Polyneices, who broke his exile to come back with fire and sword against his native city and the shrines of his fathers' gods, whose one idea was to spill the blood of his blood and sell his own people into slavery — Polyneices, I say, is to have no burial: no man is to touch him or say the least prayer for him; he shall lie on the plain, unburied; and the birds and the scavenging dogs can do with him whatever they like.   40

This is my command, and you can see the wisdom behind it. As long as I am King, no traitor is going to be honoured with the loyal man. But whoever shows by word and deed that he is on the side of the State, — he shall have my respect while he is living, and my reverence when he is dead. 45

CHORAGOS: If that is your will, Creon son of Menoiceus,
You have the right to enforce it: we are yours.

CREON: That is my will. Take care that you do your part.

CHORAGOS: We are old men: let the younger ones carry it out.

CREON: I do not mean that: the sentries have been appointed. 50

CHORAGOS: Then what is it that you would have us do?

CREON: You will give no support to whoever breaks this law.

CHORAGOS: Only a crazy man is in love with death!

CREON: And death it is; yet money talks, and the wisest
Have sometimes been known to count a few coins too many. 55

(*Enter* SENTRY *from L.*)

SENTRY: I'll not say that I'm out of breath from running, King, because every time I stopped to think about what I have to tell you, I felt like going back. And all the time a voice kept saying, 'You fool, don't you know you're walking straight into trouble?'; and then another voice: 'Yes, but if you let somebody else get the news to 60 Creon first, it will be even worse than that for you!' But good sense won out, at least I hope it was good sense, and here I am with a story that makes no sense at all; but I'll tell it anyhow, because, as they say, what's going to happen's going to happen, and—

CREON: Come to the point. What have you to say? 65

SENTRY: I did not do it. I did not see who did it. You must not punish me for what someone else has done.

CREON: A comprehensive defence! More effective, perhaps,
If I knew its purpose. Come: what is it?

SENTRY: A dreadful thing . . . I don't know how to put it— 70

CREON: Out with it!

SENTRY: Well, then;
The dead man—
                Polyneices—

(*Pause. The* SENTRY *is overcome, fumbles for words.* CREON *waits impassively.*)

out there—

someone,—

New dust on the slimy flesh!

(*Pause. No sign from* CREON.)

Someone has given it burial that way, and
Gone . . .   75

(*Long pause.* CREON *finally speaks with deadly control:*)

CREON: And the man who dared do this?

SENTRY: I swear I
Do not know! You must believe me!

. Listen:

The ground was dry, not a sign of digging, no,
Not a wheeltrack in the dust, no trace of anyone.
It was when they relieved us this morning: and one of them,   80
The corporal, pointed to it.

There it was,

The strangest—

Look:

The body, just mounded over with light dust: you see?
Not buried really, but as if they'd covered it
Just enough for the ghost's peace.[5] And no sign   85
Of dogs or any wild animal that had been there.

And then what a scene there was! Every man of us
Accusing the other: we all proved the other man did it,
We all had proof that we could not have done it.
We were ready to take hot iron in our hands,   90
Walk through fire, swear by all the gods,
It was not I!
I do not know who it was, but it was not I!

(CREON'S *rage has been mounting steadily, but the* SENTRY *is too intent
upon his story to notice it.*)

And then, when this came to nothing, someone said
A thing that silenced us and made us stare   95
Down at the ground: you had to be told the news,
And one of us had to do it! We threw the dice,
And the bad luck fell to me. So here I am,
No happier to be here than you are to have me:
Nobody likes the man who brings bad news.   100

---

5. *ghost's peace* the Greeks believed that the spirit of a dead person whose body was unburied
would not be at peace; hence, one reason Antigone is determined to bury Polyneices.

CHORAGOS: I have been wondering, King: can it be that the gods have
    done this?

CREON (*Furiously*): Stop!
    Must you doddering wrecks
    Go out of your heads entirely? 'The gods!'   105
    Intolerable!
    The gods favour this corpse? Why? How had he served them?
    Tried to loot their temples, burn their images,
    Yes, and the whole State, and its laws with it!
    Is it your senile opinion that the gods love to honour bad men?   110
    A pious thought!—
                    No, from the very beginning
    There have been those who have whispered together,
    Stiff-necked anarchists, putting their heads together,
    Scheming against me in alleys. These are the men,
    And they have bribed my own guard to do this thing.   115

    Money! (*Sententiously*)
    There's nothing in the world so demoralising as money.
    Down go your cities,
    Homes gone, men gone, honest hearts corrupted,
    Crookedness of all kinds, and all for money!

(*To* SENTRY)

                                But you—!   120
    I swear by God and by the throne of God,
    The man who has done this thing shall pay for it!
    Find that man, bring him here to me, or your death
    Will be the least of your problems: I'll string you up
    Alive, and there will be certain ways to make you   125
    Discover your employer before you die;
    And the process may teach you a lesson you seem to have missed:
    The dearest profit is sometimes all too dear:
    That depends on the source. Do you understand me?
    A fortune won is often misfortune.   130

SENTRY: King, may I speak?

CREON: Your very voice distresses me.

SENTRY: Are you sure that it is my voice, and not your conscience?

CREON: By God, he wants to analyse me now!

SENTRY: It is not what I say, but what has been done, that hurts you.

CREON: You talk too much.

SENTRY: Maybe, but I've done nothing.   135

CREON: Sold your soul for some silver: that's all you've done.

SENTRY: How dreadful it is when the right judge judges wrong!

CREON: Your figures of speech
    May entertain you now; but unless you bring me the man,
    You will get little profit from them in the end.   140

(*Exit* CREON *into the Palace.*)

SENTRY: 'Bring me the man'—!
    I'd like nothing better than bringing him the man!
    But bring him or not, you have seen the last of me here.
    At any rate, I am safe!

(*Exit* SENTRY)

Ode I

Strophe I

CHORUS: Numberless are the world's wonders, but none
    More wonderful than man; the stormgrey sea
    Yields to his prows, the huge crests bear him high;
    Earth, holy and inexhaustible, is graven
    With shining furrows where his plows have gone   5
    Year after year, the timeless labour of stallions.

Antistrophe I

    The lightboned birds and beasts that cling to cover,
    The lithe fish lighting their reaches of dim water,
    All are taken, tamed in the net of his mind;
    The lion on the hill, the wild horse windy-maned,   10
    Resign to him; and his blunt yoke has broken
    The sultry shoulders of the mountain bull.

Strophe 2

    Words also, and thought as rapid as air,
    He fashions to his good use; statecraft is his,
    And his the skill that deflects the arrows of snow,   15
    The spears of winter rain: from every wind
    He has made himself secure — from all but one:
    In the late wind of death he cannot stand.

Antistrophe 2

O clear intelligence, force beyond all measure!
O fate of man, working both good and evil! 20
When the laws are kept, how proudly his city stands!
When the laws are broken, what of his city then?
Never may the anárchic man find rest at my hearth,
Never be it said that my thoughts are his thoughts.

Scene II

(*Re-enter* SENTRY *leading* ANTIGONE.)

CHORAGOS: What does this mean? Surely this captive woman
    Is the Princess, Antigonê. Why should she be taken?

SENTRY: Here is the one who did it! We caught her
    In the very act of burying him. — Where is Creon?

CHORAGOS: Just coming from the house.

(*Enter* CREON, *C.*)

CREON: What has happened? 5
    Why have you come back so soon?

SENTRY (*Expansively*):   O King,
    A man should never be too sure of anything:
    I would have sworn
    That you'd not see me here again: your anger
    Frightened me so, and the things you threatened me with; 10
    But how could I tell then
    That I'd be able to solve the case so soon?

    No dice-throwing this time: I was only too glad to come!

    Here is this woman. She is the guilty one:
    We found her trying to bury him. 15

    Take her, then; question her; judge her as you will.
    I am through with the whole thing now, and glád óf it.

CREON: But this is Antigonê! Why have you brought her here?

SENTRY: She was burying him, I tell you!

CREON (*Severely*):   Is this the truth?

SENTRY: I saw her with my own eyes. Can I say more? 20

CREON: The details: come, tell me quickly!

SENTRY: It was like this:
    After those terrible threats of yours, King,
    We went back and brushed the dust away from the body.
    The flesh was soft by now, and stinking,
    So we sat on a hill to windward and kept guard. 25
    No napping this time! We kept each other awake.
    But nothing happened until the white round sun
    Whirled in the centre of the round sky over us:
    Then, suddenly,
    A storm of dust roared up from the earth, and the sky 30
    Went out, the plain vanished with all its trees
    In the stinging dark. We closed our eyes and endured it.
    The whirlwind lasted a long time, but it passed;
    And then we looked, and there was Antigonê!

    I have seen 35
    A mother bird come back to a stripped nest, heard
    Her crying bitterly a broken note or two
    For the young ones stolen. Just so, when this girl
    Found the bare corpse, and all her love's work wasted,
    She wept, and cried on heaven to damn the hands 40
    That had done this thing.
                       And then she brought more dust
    And sprinkled wine three times for her brother's ghost.

    We ran and took her at once. She was not afraid,
    Not even when we charged her with what she had done.
    She denied nothing.
                   And this was a comfort to me, 45
    And some uneasiness: for it is a good thing
    To escape from death, but it is no great pleasure
    To bring death to a friend.
                  Yet I always say
    There is nothing so comfortable as your own safe skin!

CREON (*Slowly, dangerously*): And you, Antigonê, 50
    You with your head hanging, — do you confess this thing?

ANTIGONE: I do. I deny nothing.

CREON (*To* SENTRY):   You may go.

(*Exit* SENTRY)

(*To* ANTIGONE)

    Tell me, tell me briefly:

Had you heard my proclamation touching this matter?

ANTIGONE: It was public. Could I help hearing it? 55

CREON: And yet you dared defy the law.

ANTIGONE: I dared.
It was not God's proclamation. That final Justice
That rules the world below makes no such laws.

Your edict, King, was strong,
But all your strength is weakness itself against 60
The immortal unrecorded laws of God.
They are not merely now: they were, and shall be,
Operative for ever, beyond man utterly.

I knew I must die, even without your decree:
I am only mortal. And if I must die 65
Now, before it is my time to die,
Surely this is no hardship: can anyone
Living, as I live, with evil all about me,
Think Death less than a friend? This death of mine
Is of no importance; but if I had left my brother 70
Lying in death unburied, I should have suffered.
Now I do not.
You smile at me. Ah Creon,
Think me a fool, if you like; but it may well be
That a fool convicts me of folly.

CHORAGOS: Like father, like daughter: both headstrong, deaf to reason! 75
She has never learned to yield.

CREON: She has much to learn.
The inflexible heart breaks first, the toughest iron
Cracks first, and the wildest horses bend their necks
At the pull of the smallest curb.
Pride? In a slave?
This girl is guilty of a double insolence, 80
Breaking the given laws and boasting of it.
Who is the man here,
She or I, if this crime goes unpunished?
Sister's child, or more than sister's child,
Or closer yet in blood — she and her sister 85
Win bitter death for this!

(*To* SERVANTS)

Go, some of you,
Arrest Ismenê. I accuse her equally.
Bring her: you will find her sniffling in the house there.

Her mind's a traitor: crimes kept in the dark
Cry for light, and the guardian brain shudders;   90
But how much worse than this
Is brazen boasting of barefaced anarchy!

ANTIGONE: Creon, what more do you want than my death?

CREON: Nothing.
    That gives me everything.

ANTIGONE: Then I beg you: kill me.
    This talking is a great weariness: your words   95
    Are distasteful to me, and I am sure that mine
    Seem so to you. And yet they should not seem so:
    I should have praise and honour for what I have done.
    All these men here would praise me
    Were their lips not frozen shut with fear of you.   100

(*Bitterly*)

    Ah the good fortune of kings,
    Licensed to say and do whatever they please!

CREON: You are alone here in that opinion.

ANTIGONE: No, they are with me. But they keep their tongues in leash.

CREON: Maybe. But you are guilty, and they are not.   105

ANTIGONE: There is no guilt in reverence for the dead.

CREON: But Eteoclês — was he not your brother too?

ANTIGONE: My brother too.

CREON: And you insult his memory?

ANTIGONE (*Softly*): The dead man would not say that I insult it.

CREON: He would: for you honour a traitor as much as him.   110

ANTIGONE: His own brother, traitor or not, and equal in blood.

CREON: He made war on his country. Eteoclês defended it.

ANTIGONE: Nevertheless, there are honours due all the dead.

CREON: But not the same for the wicked as for the just.

ANTIGONE: Ah Creon, Creon,   115
    Which of us can say what the gods hold wicked?

CREON: An enemy is an enemy, even dead.

ANTIGONE: It is my nature to join in love, not hate.

CREON (*Finally losing patience*): Go join them, then; if you must have
        your love,

Find it in hell! 120

CHORAGOS: But see, Ismenê comes:

(*Enter* ISMENE, *guarded*.)

Those tears are sisterly, the cloud
That shadows her eyes rains down gentle sorrow.

CREON: You too, Ismenê,
Snake in my ordered house, sucking my blood 125
Stealthily — and all the time I never knew
That these two sisters were aiming at my throne!

Ismene,
Do you confess your share in this crime, or deny it?
Answer me.

ISMENE: Yes, if she will let me say so. I am guilty. 130

ANTIGONE (*Coldly*): No, Ismenê. You have no right to say so.
You would not help me, and I will not have you help me.

ISMENE: But now I know what you meant; and I am here
To join you, to take my share of punishment.

ANTIGONE: The dead man and the gods who rule the dead 135
Know whose act this was. Words are not friends.

ISMENE: Do you refuse me, Antigonê? I want to die with you:
I too have a duty that I must discharge to the dead.

ANTIGONE: You shall not lessen my death by sharing it.

ISMENE: What do I care for life when you are dead? 140

ANTIGONE: Ask Creon. You're always hanging on his opinions.

ISMENE: You are laughing at me. Why, Antigonê?

ANTIGONE: It's a joyless laughter, Ismenê.

ISMENE: But can I do nothing?

ANTIGONE: Yes. Save yourself. I shall not envy you.
There are those who will praise you; I shall have honour, too. 145

ISMENE: But we are equally guilty!

ANTIGONE: No more, Ismenê.
You are alive, but I belong to Death.

CREON (*To the* CHORUS): Gentlemen, I beg you to observe these girls:
One has just now lost her mind; the other,
It seems, has never had a mind at all. 150

ISMENE: Grief teaches the steadiest minds to waver, King.

CREON: Yours certainly did, when you assumed guilt with the guilty!

ISMENE: But how could I go on living without her?

CREON: You are.
    She is already dead.

ISMENE: But your own son's bride!

CREON: There are places enough for him to push his plow.   155
    I want no wicked women for my sons!

ISMENE: O dearest Haimon, how your father wrongs you!

CREON: I've had enough of your childish talk of marriage!

CHORAGOS: Do you really intend to steal this girl from your son?

CREON: No; Death will do that for me.

CHORAGOS: Then she must die?   160

CREON (*Ironically*): You dazzle me.
                        —But enough of this talk!

(*To* GUARDS:)

    You, there, take them away and guard them well:
    For they are but women, and even brave men run
    When they see Death coming.

(*Exeunt* ISMENE, ANTIGONE, *and* GUARDS.)

Ode II

Strophe I

CHORUS: Fortunate is the man who has never tasted God's vengeance!
    Where once the anger of heaven has struck, that house is shaken
    For ever: damnation rises behind each child
    Like a wave cresting out of the black northeast,
    When the long darkness under sea roars up   5
    And bursts drumming death upon the windwhipped sand.

Antistrophe I

    I have seen this gathering sorrow from time long past
    Loom upon Oedipus' children: generation from generation

Takes the compulsive rage of the enemy god.
So lately this last flower of Oedipus' line   10
Drank the sunlight! but now a passionate word
And a handful of dust have closed up all its beauty.

Strophe 2

What mortal arrogance
Transcends the wrath of Zeus?
Sleep cannot lull him, nor the effortless long months   15
Of the timeless gods: but he is young for ever,
And his house is the shining day of high Olympos.
    All that is and shall be,
    And all the past, is his.
No pride on earth is free of the curse of heaven.   20

Antistrophe 2

The straying dreams of men
May bring them ghosts of joy:
But as they drowse, the waking embers burn them;
Or they walk with fixed eyes, as blind men walk.
But the ancient wisdom speaks for our own time: 25
    Fate works most for woe
    With Folly's fairest show.
Man's little pleasure is the spring of sorrow.

Scene III

CHORAGOS: But here is Haimon, King, the last of all your sons.
    Is it grief for Antigonê that brings him here,
    And bitterness at being robbed of his bride?

(*Enter* HAIMON)

CREON: We shall soon see, and no need of diviners.
                                                        —Son,
    You have heard my final judgment on that girl: 5
    Have you come here hating me, or have you come
    With deference and with love, whatever I do?

HAIMON: I am your son, father. You are my guide.

You make things clear for me, and I obey you.
No marriage means more to me than your continuing wisdom. 10

CREON: Good. That is the way to behave: subordinate
Everything else, my son, to your father's will.
This is what a man prays for, that he may get
Sons attentive and dutiful in his house,
Each one hating his father's enemies, 15
Honouring his father's friends. But if his sons
Fail him, if they turn out unprofitably,
What has he fathered but trouble for himself
And amusement for the malicious?
                                        So you are right
Not to lose your head over this woman. 20
Your pleasure with her would soon grow cold, Haimon,
And then you'd have a hellcat in bed and elsewhere.
Let her find her husband in Hell!
Of all the people in this city, only she
Has had contempt for my law and broken it. 25

Do you want me to show myself weak before the people?
Or to break my sworn word? No, and I will not.
The woman dies.

I suppose she'll plead 'family ties.' Well, let her.
If I permit my own family to rebel, 30
How shall I earn the world's obedience?
Show me the man who keeps his house in hand,
He's fit for public authority.
                                    I'll have no dealings
With law-breakers, critics of the government:
Whoever is chosen to govern should be obeyed— 35
Must be obeyed, in all things, great and small,
Just and unjust! O Haimon,
The man who knows how to obey, and that man only,
Knows how to give commands when the time comes.
You can depend on him, no matter how fast 40
The spears come: he's a good soldier, he'll stick it out.

Anarchy, anarchy! Show me a greater evil!
This is why cities tumble and the great houses rain down,
This is what scatters armies!

No, no: good lives are made so by discipline. 45
We keep the laws then, and the lawmakers,
And no woman shall seduce us. If we must lose,
Let's lose to a man, at least! Is a woman stronger than we?

CHORAGOS: Unless time has rusted my wits,
What you say, King, is said with point and dignity.   50

HAIMON (*Boyishly earnest*): Father:
Reason is God's crowning gift to man, and you are right
To warn me against losing mine. I cannot say—
I hope that I shall never want to say! — that you
Have reasoned badly. Yet there are other men   55
Who can reason, too; and their opinions might be helpful.
You are not in a position to know everything
That people say or do, or what they feel.
Your temper terrifies them — everyone
Will tell you only what you like to hear.   60
But I, at any rate, can listen; and I have heard them
Muttering and whispering in the dark about this girl.
They say no woman has ever, so unreasonably,
Died so shameful a death for a generous act:
'She covered her brother's body. Is this indecent?   65
'She kept him from dogs and vultures. Is this a crime?
'Death? — She should have all the honour that we can give her!'

This is the way they talk out there in the city.

You must believe me:
Nothing is closer to me than your happiness   70
What could be closer? Must not any son
Value his father's fortune as his father does his?
I beg you, do not be unchangeable:
Do not believe that you alone can be right.
The man who thinks that,   75
The man who maintains that only he has the power
To reason correctly, the gift to speak, the soul—
A man like that, when you know him, turns out empty.

It is not reason never to yield to reason!

In flood time you can see how some trees bend,   80
And because they bend, even their twigs are safe,
While stubborn trees are torn up, roots and all.
And the same thing happens in sailing:
Make your sheet fast, never slacken,—and over you go,
Head over heels and under: and there's your voyage.   85

Forget you are angry! Let yourself be moved!
I know I am young; but please let me say this:
The ideal condition
Would be, I admit, that men should be right by instinct;

But since we are all too likely to go astray,   90
The reasonable thing is to learn from those who can teach.

CHORAGOS: You will do well to listen to him, King,
If what he says is sensible. And you, Haimon,
Must listen to your father. — Both speak well.

CREON: You consider it right for a man of my years and experience   95
To go to school to a boy?

HAIMON: It is not right
If I am wrong. But if I am young, and right,
What does my age matter?

CREON: You think it right to stand up for an anarchist?

HAIMON: Not at all. I pay no respect to criminals.   100

CREON: Then she is not a criminal?

HAIMON: The City would deny it, to a man.

CREON: And the City proposes to teach me how to rule?

HAIMON: Ah. Who is it that's talking like a boy now?

CREON: My voice is the one voice giving orders in this City!   105

HAIMON: It is no City if it takes orders from one voice.

CREON: The State is the King!

HAIMON: Yes, if the State is a desert.

(*Pause*)

CREON: This boy, it seems, has sold out to a woman.

HAIMON: If you are a woman: my concern is only for you.

CREON: So? Your 'concern'! In a public brawl with your father!   110

HAIMON: How about you, in a public brawl with justice?

CREON: With justice, when all that I do is within my rights?

HAIMON: You have no right to trample on God's right.

CREON (*Completely out of control*): Fool, adolescent fool! Taken in
by a woman!

HAIMON: You'll never see me taken in by anything vile.   115

CREON: Every word you say is for her!

HAIMON (*Quietly, darkly*):   And for you.
And for me. And for the gods under the earth.

CREON: You'll never marry her while she lives.

HAIMON: Then she must die. — But her death will cause another.

CREON: Another? 120
Have you lost your senses? Is this an open threat?

HAIMON: There is no threat in speaking to emptiness.

CREON: I swear you'll regret this superior tone of yours!
You are the empty one!

HAIMON: If you were not my father,
I'd say you were perverse. 125

CREON: You girlstruck fool, don't play at words with me!

HAIMON: I am sorry. You prefer silence.

CREON: Now, by God—!
I swear, by all the gods in heaven above us,
You'll watch it, I swear you shall!

(*To the* SERVANTS:)

Bring her out!
Bring the woman out! Let her die before his eyes! 130
Here, this instant, with her bridegroom beside her!

HAIMON: Not here, no; she will not die here, King.
And you will never see my face again.
Go on raving as long as you've a friend to endure you.

(*Exit* HAIMON.)

CHORAGOS: Gone, gone. 135
Creon, a young man in a rage is dangerous!

CREON: Let him do, or dream to do, more than a man can.
He shall not save these girls from death.

CHORAGOS: These girls?
You have sentenced them both?

CREON: No, you are right.
I will not kill the one whose hands are clean. 140

CHORAGOS: But Antigonê?

CREON (*Sombrely*): I will carry her far away
Out there in the wilderness, and lock her
Living in a vault of stone. She shall have food,
As the custom is, to absolve the State of her death.
And there let her pray to the gods of hell: 145
They are her only gods:
Perhaps they will show her an escape from death,

Or she may learn,
                        though late,
That piety shown the dead is pity in vain.

(*Exit* CREON.)

Ode III

Strophe

CHORUS: Love, unconquerable
        Waster of rich men, keeper
        Of warm lights and all-night vigil
        In the soft face of a girl:
        Sea-wanderer, forest-visitor!   5
        Even the pure Immortals cannot escape you,
        And mortal man, in his one day's dusk,
        Trembles before your glory.

Antistrophe

        Surely you swerve upon ruin
        The just man's consenting heart,   10
        As here you have made bright anger
        Strike between father and son—
        And none has conquered but Love!
        A girl's glance working the will of heaven:
        Pleasure to her alone who mocks us,   15
        Merciless Aphroditê.[6]

Scene IV

CHORAGOS (*As* ANTIGONE *enters guarded*):
        But I can no longer stand in awe of this,
        Nor, seeing what I see, keep back my tears.   1
        Here is Antigonê, passing to that chamber
        Where all find sleep at last.

6. *Aphrodite* goddess of love and beauty.

Strophe I

ANTIGONE: Look upon me, friends, and pity me   5
        Turning back at the night's edge to say
        Goodbye to the sun that shines for me no longer;
        Now sleepy Death
        Summons me down to Acheron,[7] that cold shore:
        There is no bridesong there, nor any music.   10

CHORUS: Yet not unpraised, not without a kind of honour,
        You walk at last into the underworld;
        Untouched by sickness, broken by no sword.
        What woman has ever found your way to death?

Antistrophe I

ANTIGONE: How often I have heard the story of Niobé,[8]   15
        Tantalos' wretched daughter, how the stone
        Clung fast about her, ivy-close: and they say
        The rain falls endlessly
        And sifting soft snow; her tears are never done.
        I feel the loneliness of her death in mine.   20

CHORUS: But she was born of heaven, and you
        Are woman, woman-born. If her death is yours,
        A mortal woman's, is this not for you
        Glory in our world and in the world beyond?

Strophe 2

ANTIGONE: You laugh at me. Ah, friends, friends,   25
        Can you not wait until I am dead? O Thebes,
        O men many-charioted, in love with Fortune,
        Dear springs of Dircê, sacred Theban grove,
        Be witnesses for me, denied all pity,
        Unjustly judged! and think a word of love   30
        For her whose path turns
        Under dark earth, where there are no more tears.

CHORUS: You have passed beyond human daring and come at last
        Into a place of stone where Justice sits.

7. *Acheron* a river in Hades. 8. *Niobe* daughter of Tantalus and wife of Amphion of Thebes. After her children were killed, she was turned into a statue by Zeus, and in that state she continued to weep.

I cannot tell

35

What shape of your father's guilt appears in this.

Antistrophe 2

ANTIGONE: You have touched it at last: that bridal bed
    Unspeakable, horror of son and mother mingling:
    Their crime, infection of all our family!
    O Oedipus, father and brother! 40
    Your marriage strikes from the grave to murder mine.
    I have been a stranger here in my own land:
    All my life
    The blasphemy of my birth has followed me.

CHORUS: Reverence is a virtue, but strength 45
    Lives in established law: that must prevail.
    You have made your choice,
    Your death is the doing of your conscious hand.

Epode

ANTIGONE: Then let me go, since all your words are bitter,
    And the very light of the sun is cold to me. 50
    Lead me to my vigil, where I must have
    Neither love nor lamentation; no song, but silence.

(CREON *interrupts impatiently.*)

CREON: If dirges and planned lamentations could put off death,
    Men would be singing for ever.

(*To the* SERVANTS):

                        Take her, go!
    You know your orders: take her to the vault 55
    And leave her alone there. And if she lives or dies,
    That's her affair, not ours: our hands are clean.

ANTIGONE: O tomb, vaulted bride-bed in eternal rock,
    Soon I shall be with my own again
    Where Persephonê[9] welcomes the thin ghosts underground: 60
    And I shall see my father again, and you, mother,
    And dearest Polyneicês—
                  dearest indeed

9. *Persephone* queen of Hadès, the underworld.

To me, since it was my hand
That washed him clean and poured the ritual wine:
And my reward is death before my time!   65

And yet, as men's hearts know, I have done no wrong,
I have not sinned before God. Or if I have,
I shall know the truth in death. But if the guilt
Lies upon Creon who judged me, then, I pray,
May his punishment equal my own.

CHORAGOS: O passionate heart,   70
        Unyielding, tormented still by the same winds!

CREON: Her guards shall have good cause to regret their delaying.

ANTIGONE: Ah! That voice is like the voice of death!

CREON: I can give you no reason to think you are mistaken.

ANTIGONE: Thebes, and you my fathers' gods,   75
        And rulers of Thebes, you see me now, the last
        Unhappy daughter of a line of kings,
        Your kings, led away to death. You will remember
        What things I suffer, and at what men's hands,
        Because I would not transgress the laws of heaven. 80

(*To the* GUARDS, *simply:*)

        Come: let us wait no longer.

(*Exit* ANTIGONE, *L., guarded.*)

Ode IV

Strophe I

CHORUS: All Danaê's[10] beauty was locked away
        In a brazen cell where the sunlight could not come:
        A small room, still as any grave, enclosed her.
        Yet she was a princess too,
        And Zeus in a rain of gold poured love upon her.   5
        O child, child,
        No power in wealth or war

10. *Danae* imprisoned by her father to prevent her from having a son, she was visited by Zeus in the form of a shower of gold. From that union was conceived Perseus.

Or tough sea-blackened ships
Can prevail against untiring Destiny!

Antistrophe I

And Dryas' son[11] also, that furious king,   10
Bore the god's prisoning anger for his pride:
Sealed up by Dionysos in deaf stone,
His madness died among echoes.
So at the last he learned what dreadful power
His tongue had mocked: 15
For he had profaned the revels,
And fired the wrath of the nine
Implacable Sisters[12] that love the sound of the flute.

Strophe 2

And old men tell a half-remembered tale[13]
Of horror done where a dark ledge splits the sea   20
And a double surf beats on the gréy shóres:
How a king's new woman, sick
With hatred for the queen he had imprisoned,
Ripped out his two sons' eyes with her bloody hands
While grinning Arês[14] watched the shuttle plunge   25
Four times: four blind wounds crying for revenge,

Antistrophe 2

Crying, tears and blood mingled.—Piteously born,
Those sons whose mother was of heavenly birth!
Her father was the god of the North Wind
And she was cradled by gales,   30
She raced with young colts on the glittering hills
And walked untrammeled in the open light:
But in her marriage deathless Fate found means
To build a tomb like yours for all her joy.

11. *Dryas son* Lycurgus, a King of Thrace, who was imprisoned by Dionysus in a rocky cave and driven mad. 12. *nine Implacable Sisters* the nine Muses. 13. *half-remembered tale* Phineus, King of Thrace, imprisoned his first wife, Cleopatra, daughter of Boreas, god of the North Wind. His second wife blinded the two sons Cleopatra had borne him. 14. *Ares* god of war.

Scene V

(*Enter blind* TEIRESIAS,[15] *led by a boy. The opening speeches of* TEIRESIAS *should be in singsong contrast to the realistic lines of* CREON.)

TEIRESIAS: This is the way the blind man comes, Princes, Princes,
　　Lock-step, two heads lit by the eyes of one.

CREON: What new thing have you to tell us, old Teiresias?

TEIRESIAS: I have much to tell you: listen to the prophet, Creon.

CREON: I am not aware that I have ever failed to listen.　　　　5

TEIRESIAS: Then you have done wisely, King, and ruled well.

CREON: I admit my debt to you. But what have you to say?

TEIRESIAS: This, Creon: you stand once more on the edge of fate.

CREON: What do you mean? Your words are a kind of dread.

TEIRESIAS: Listen, Creon:　　　　　　　　　　　　　　　　10
　　I was sitting in my chair of augury,[16] at the place
　　Where the birds gather about me. They were all a-chatter,
　　As is their habit, when suddenly I heard
　　A strange note in their jangling, a scream, a
　　Whirring fury; I knew that they were fighting,　　　　15
　　Tearing each other, dying
　　In a whirlwind of wings clashing. And I was afraid.
　　I began the rites of burnt-offering at the altar,
　　But Hephaistos[17] failed me: instead of bright flame,
　　There was only the sputtering slime of the fat thigh-flesh　　20
　　Melting: the entrails dissolved in grey smoke,
　　The bare bone burst from the welter. And no blaze!

　　This was a sign from heaven. My boy described it,
　　Seeing for me as I see for others.

　　I tell you, Creon, you yourself have brought　　　　25
　　This new calamity upon us. Our hearths and altars
　　Are stained with the corruption of dogs and carrion birds
　　That glut themselves on the corpse of Oedipus' son.
　　The gods are deaf when we pray to them, their fire
　　Recoils from our offering, their birds of omen　　　　30
　　Have no cry of comfort, for they are gorged
　　With the thick blood of the dead.

---

15. *Teiresias* a celebrated blind prophet in Greek mythology. **16.** *chair of augury* place of divination or prophecy, usually the location of omens or other signs. **17.** *Hephaistos* god of fire and metalworking.

O my son,

These are no trifles! Think: all men make mistakes,
But a good man yields when he knows his course is wrong,
And repairs the evil. The only crime is pride.   35

Give in to the dead man, then: do not fight with a corpse—
What glory is it to kill a man who is dead?
Think, I beg you:
It is for your own good that I speak as I do.
You should be able to yield for your own good.   40

CREON: It seems that prophets have made me their especial province.
    All my life long
    I have been a kind of butt for the dull arrows
    Of doddering fortune-tellers!

No, Teiresias:

    If your birds — if the great eagles of God himself   45
    Should carry him stinking bit by bit to heaven,
    I would not yield. I am not afraid of pollution:
    No man can defile the gods.

Do what you will,

    Go into business, make money, speculate
    In India gold or that synthetic gold from Sardis,[18]   50
    Get rich — you will not buy my consent to bury him.
    Teiresias, it is a sorry thing when a wise man
    Sells his wisdom, lets out his words for hire!

TEIRESIAS: Ah Creon! Is there no man left in the world—

CREON: To do what? — Come, let's have the aphorism!   55

TEIRESIAS: No man who knows that wisdom outweighs any wealth?

CREON: As surely as bribes are baser than any baseness.

TEIRESIAS: You are sick, Creon! You are deathly sick!

CREON: As you say: it is not my place to challenge a prophet.

TEIRESIAS: Yet you have said my prophecy is for sale.   60

CREON: The generation of prophets has always loved gold.

TEIRESIAS: The generation of kings has always loved brass.

CREON: You forget yourself! You are speaking to your King.

TEIRESIAS: I know it. You are a king because of me.

CREON: You have a certain skill; but you have sold out.   65

TEIRESIAS: King, you will drive me to words that—

---

18. *Sardis* ancient city of West Asia Minor.

CREON: You would have me do this?
    Only remember: I will not pay you for them.

TEIRESIAS: No, you will find them too costly.

CREON: No doubt. Speak:
    Whatever you say, you will not change my will.

TEIRESIAS: Then take this, and take it to heart!   70
    The time is not far off when you shall pay back
    Corpse for corpse, flesh of your own flesh.
    You have thrust the child of this world into living night,
    You have kept from the gods below the child that is theirs:
    The one in a grave before her death, the other,   75
    Dead, denied the grave. This is your crime:
    And the Furies and the dark gods of Hell
    Are swift with terrible punishment for you.

    Do you want to buy me now, Creon?
                          Not many days,
    And your house will be full of men and women weeping,   80
    And curses will be hurled at you from far
    Cities grieving for sons unburied, left to rot
    Before the walls of Thebes.

    These are my arrows, Creon: they are all for you.

(*To* BOY:)

    But come, child: lead me home.   85
    Let him waste his fine anger upon younger men.
    Maybe he will learn at last
    To control a wiser tongue in a better head.

(*Exit* TEIRESIAS)

CHORAGOS: The old man has gone, King, but his words
    Remain to plague us. I am old, too,   90
    But I cannot remember that he was ever false.

CREON: That is true. . . . It troubles me.
    Oh it is hard to give in! but it is worse
    To risk everything for stubborn pride.

CHORAGOS: Creon: take my advice.

CREON: What shall I do?   95

CHORAGOS: Go quickly: free Antigonê from her vault
    And build a tomb for the body of Polyneicês.

CREON: You would have me do this?

CHORAGOS: Creon, yes!
　　And it must be done at once: God moves
　　Swiftly to cancel the folly of stubborn men.   100

CREON: It is hard to deny the heart! But I
　　Will do it: I will not fight with destiny.

CHORAGOS: You must go yourself, you cannot leave it to others.

CREON: I will go.
　　　　　　—Bring axes, servants:
　　Come with me to the tomb. I buried her, I   105
　　Will set her free.
　　　　　　　　Oh quickly!
　　My mind misgives—
　　The laws of the gods are mighty, and a man must serve them
　　To the last day of his life!

(*Exit* CREON)

Paean[19]

Strophe I

CHORAGOS: God of many names[20]

CHORUS: O Iacchos
　　　　　　　　　　　　　　　son
　　of Cadmeian Sémelê
　　　　　　　　　　　O born of the Thunder!
　　Guardian of the West
　　　　　　　　　　Regent
　　of Eleusis' plain
　　　　　　　　O Prince of maenad Thebes
　　and the Dragon Field by rippling Ismenos: 5

Antistrophe I

CHORAGOS: God of many names

19. *Paean* generally, a hymn of joy and praise, but here an invocation for aid and comfort. 20. *God of many names* Iacchus (also known as Dionysus and Bacchus), the god of wine. The chorus emulates Dionysian rites performed at the plain of Eleusis.

CHORUS: the flame of torches
    flares on our hills
                         the nymphs of Iacchos
    dance at the spring of Castalia:[21]

    from the vine-close mountain
                                come ah come in ivy:
    Evohé evohé! sings through the streets of Thebes   10

Strophe 2

CHORAGOS: God of many names

CHORUS: Iacchos of Thebes
    heavenly Child
                    of Semele bride of the Thunderer!
    The shadow of plague is upon us:
                                      come
    with clement feet
                       oh come from Parnasos
    down the long slopes
                         across the lamenting water   15

Antistrophe 2

CHORAGOS: Iô Fire! Chorister of the throbbing stars!
    O purest among the voices of the night!
    Thou son of God, blaze for us!

CHORUS: Come with choric rapture of circling Maenads
    Who cry *Iô Iacche!*
                         God of many names!   20

Exodus[22]

(*Enter* MESSENGER, *L.*)

MESSENGER: Men of the line of Cadmos,[23] you who live

---

21. *Castalia* a spring on Mount Parnassus (or Parnasos). Both spring and mount were sacred to the gods.   **22.** *Exodus* the final scene of the drama.   **23.** *Cadmos* or Cadmus, the founder and first king of Thebes. One of his daughters was Semele, mother of Dionysus.

Near Amphion's[24] citadel:
                          I cannot say
Of any condition of human life 'This is fixed,
This is clearly good, or bad'. Fate raises up,
And Fate casts down the happy and unhappy alike: 5
No man can foretell his Fate.
                          Take the case of Creon:
Creon was happy once, as I count happiness:
Victorious in battle, sole governor of the land,
Fortunate father of children nobly born.
And now it has all gone from him! Who can say   10
That a man is still alive when his life's joy fails?
He is a walking dead man. Grant him rich,
Let him live like a king in his great house:
If his pleasure is gone, I would not give
So much as the shadow of smoke for all he owns.   15

CHORAGOS: Your words hint at sorrow: what is your news for us?

MESSENGER: They are dead. The living are guilty of their death.

CHORAGOS: Who is guilty? Who is dead? Speak!

MESSENGER: Haimon.
        Haimon is dead; and the hand that killed him
        Is his own hand.

CHORAGOS: His father's? or his own?   20

MESSENGER: His own, driven mad by the murder his father had done.

CHORAGOS: Teiresias, Teiresias, how clearly you saw it all!

MESSENGER: This is my news: you must draw what conclusions you can
        from it.

CHORAGOS: But look: Eurydicê, our Queen:
        Has she overheard us?   25

(*Enter* EURYDICE *from the Palace, C.*)

EURYDICE: I have heard something, friends:
        As I was unlocking the gate of Pallas'[25] shrine,
        For I needed her help today, I heard a voice
        Telling of some new sorrow. And I fainted
        There at the temple with all my maidens about me.   30
        But speak again: whatever it is, I can bear it:
        Grief and I are no strangers.

24. *Amphion* a gifted musician who built a part of Thebes by moving the stones with his music. 25. *Pallas* Athena, goddess of wisdom and reason.

MESSENGER: Dearest Lady,
I will tell you plainly all that I have seen.
I shall not try to comfort you: what is the use,
Since comfort could lie only in what is not true?   35
The truth is always best.
                         I went with Creon
To the outer plain where Polyneicês was lying,
No friend to pity him, his body shredded by dogs.
We made our prayers in that place to Hecatê[26]
And Pluto,[27] that they would be merciful. And we bathed   40
The corpse with holy water, and we brought
Fresh-broken branches to burn what was left of it,
And upon the urn we heaped up a towering barrow
Of the earth of his own land.
                         When we were done, we ran
To the vault where Antigonê lay on her couch of stone.   45
One of the servants had gone ahead,
And while he was yet far off he heard a voice
Grieving within the chamber, and he came back
And told Creon. And as the King went closer,
The air was full of wailing, the words lost,   50
And he begged us to make all haste. 'Am I a prophet?'
He said, weeping, 'And must I walk this road,
'The saddest of all that I have gone before?
'My son's voice calls me on. Oh quickly, quickly!
'Look through the crevice there, and tell me   55
'If it is Haimon, or some deception of the gods!'

We obeyed; and in the cavern's farthest corner
We saw her lying:
She had made a noose of her fine linen veil
And hanged herself. Haimon lay beside her,   60
His arms about her waist, lamenting her,
His love lost under ground, crying out
That his father had stolen her away from him.
When Creon saw him the tears rushed to his eyes
And he called to him: 'What have you done, child? Speak
     to me.   65
'What are you thinking that makes your eyes so strange?
'O my son, my son, I come to you on my knees!'
But Haimon spat in his face. He said not a word,
Staring—
          And suddenly drew his sword
And lunged. Creon shrank back, the blade missed; and the boy,   70
Desperate against himself, drove it half its length

26. *Hecate* goddess of night.   27. *Pluto* god of the underworld or Hades.

Into his own side, and fell. And as he died
He gathered Antigonê close in his arms again,
Choking, his blood bright red on her white cheek.
And now he lies dead with the dead, and she is his   75
At last, his bride in the houses of the dead.

(*Exit* EURYDICE *into the Palace.*)

CHORAGOS: She has left us without a word. What can this mean?

MESSENGER: It troubles me, too; yet she knows what is best,
      Her grief is too great for public lamentation,
      And doubtless she has gone to her chamber to weep   80
      For her dead son, leading her maidens in his dirge.

CHORAGOS: It may be so: but I fear this deep silence.

(*Pause*)

MESSENGER: I will see what she is doing. I will go in.

(*Exit* MESSENGER *into the Palace. Enter* CREON *with attendants, bearing* HAIMON'S *body.*)

CHORAGOS: But here is the King himself: oh look at him,
      Bearing his own damnation in his arms.   85

CREON: Nothing you say can touch me any more.
      My own blind heart has brought me
      From darkness to final darkness. Here you see
      The father murdering, the murdered son—
      And all my civic wisdom!   90

      Haimon my son, so young, so young to die,
      I was the fool, not you; and you died for me.

CHORAGOS: That is the truth; but you were late in learning it.

CREON: This truth is hard to bear. Surely a god
      Has crushed me beneath the hugest weight of heaven,   95
      And driven me headlong a barbaric way
      To trample out the thing I held most dear.

      The pains that men will take to come to pain!

(*Enter* MESSENGER *from the Palace.*)

MESSENGER: The burden you carry in your hands is heavy,
      But it is not all: you will find more in your house.   100

CREON: What burden worse than this shall I find there?

MESSENGER: The Queen is dead.

CREON: O port of death, deaf world,

Is there no pity for me? And you, Angel of evil,
I was dead, and your words are death again.   105
Is it true, boy? Can it be true?
Is my wife dead? Has death bred death?

MESSENGER: You can see for yourself.

(*The doors are opened, and the body of* EURYDICE *is disclosed within.*)

CREON: Oh pity!
All true, all true, and more than I can bear!   110
O my wife, my son!

MESSENGER: She stood before the altar, and her heart
Welcomed the knife her own hand guided,
And a great cry burst from her lips for Megareus[28] dead,
And for Haimon dead, her sons; and her last breath   115
Was a curse for their father, the murderer of her sons.
And she fell, and the dark flowed in through her closing eyes

CREON: O God, I am sick with fear.
Are there no swords here? Has no one a blow for me?

MESSENGER: Her curse is upon you for the deaths of both.   120

CREON: It is right that it should be. I alone am guilty.
I know it, and I say it. Lead me in,
Quickly, friends.
I have neither life nor substance. Lead me in.

CHORAGOS: You are right, if there can be right in so much wrong.   125
The briefest way is best in a world of sorrow.

CREON: Let it come,
Let death come quickly, and be kind to me.
I would not ever see the sun again.

CHORAGOS: All that will come when it will; but we, meanwhile,   130
Have much to do. Leave the future to itself.

CREON: All my heart was in that prayer!

CHORAGOS: Then do not pray any more: the sky is deaf.

CREON: Lead me away. I have been rash and foolish.
I have killed my son and my wife.   135
I look for comfort; my comfort lies here dead.
Whatever my hands have touched has come to nothing.
Fate has brought all my pride to a thought of dust.

---

28. *Megareus* or Menoeceus, Creon's younger son, who sacrificed himself in the battle over
Thebes in order to secure the victory for the Thebans.

(*As* CREON *is being led into the house, the* CHORAGOS *advances and speaks directly to the audience.*)

CHORAGOS: There is no happiness where there is no wisdom;
No wisdom but in submission to the gods.   140
Big words are always punished,
And proud men in old age learn to be wise.

For Consideration

1. Assess the differing reactions of Antigone and Ismene to the burial of Polyneices. Why does Ismene choose not to join Antigone in the action? What justification is there for Antigone's judgment that her "crime is holy"?

2. The opening Parados of the chorus is in part a recapitulation of events that occurred prior to the opening of the play. What other purpose does it serve? What is its significance immediately following Antigone's pronouncement and immediately preceding Creon's entry?

3. What is the impact of Creon's opening speech? What is his conception of the ideal ruler? What is the relationship between that conception and his decision not to allow Polyneices to be buried? How does Choragos, as the spokesman for the Chorus of Theban elders, respond to the decree?

4. There is some obvious humor in the presentation of the sentry. What is its purpose? What function does it serve in contrast to the increasing rage of Creon? How does Creon react to Choragos' suggestion that "the gods" might have sprinkled the dust on the body of Polyneices?

5. What conception of man is promoted in the first Ode? What is the relationship between man and law in Antistrophe 2? What is the significance of these observations for the play at this point?

6. What is Antigone's defense before Creon of her defiance of his law? What are some of the issues inherent in the debate over God's law and man-made law? Is their conflict a simple one of right vs. wrong?

7. What is the theme of Ode II? What lies behind talk of vengeance, curse, and fate? Why is "Oedipus' line" of concern here?

8. To what concerns does Haimon appeal in arguing with his father? How does his conception of the State and justice differ from Creon's? Who appears the more mature, the more reasonable in his argument?

9. What is Teiresias' contribution to the play? Why is it significant that he is blind? That he is a prophet?

10. One important element in this play is what Aristotle would have called a peripeteia or reversal. That is, Creon acts decisively so as to bring about a

certain result, and quite the opposite happens. How does the Messenger account for that reversal in the opening speech of the Exodus?

11. Creon, like most tragic figures, comes to a recognition of his wrong, albeit too late to save Antigone, Haimon, and Eurydice. What exactly does he now realize, that he did not see before, about himself? About life in general?

12. Who is the tragic hero in the play, Antigone or Creon? Is it possible that they share that role? With whom does your greater sympathy lie?

WILLIAM SHAKESPEARE (1564—1616)

The Tragedy of King Lear

Dramatis Personae

LEAR, King of Britain

KING OF FRANCE

DUKE OF BURGUNDY

DUKE OF CORNWALL, husband to Regan

DUKE OF ALBANY, husband to Goneril

EARL OF KENT

EARL OF GLOUCESTER

EDGAR, son to Gloucester

EDMUND, bastard son to Gloucester

CURAN, a courtier

OSWALD, steward to Goneril

OLD MAN, tenant to Gloucester

DOCTOR

LEAR'S FOOL

A CAPTAIN, subordinate to Edmund

GENTLEMEN, attending on Cordelia

A HERALD

SERVANTS to Cornwall

GONERIL
REGAN } daughters to Lear
CORDELIA

KNIGHTS attending on Lear   OFFICERS

MESSENGERS SOLDIERS ATTENDANTS

SCENE: *Britain*

Act I

Scene I.

(*King Lear's palace.*)

(*Enter* KENT, GLOUCESTER, *and* EDMUND.)

KENT: I thought the king had more affected[1] the Duke of Albany[2] than Cornwall.

GLOUCESTER: It did always seem so to us; but now, in the division of the kingdom, it appears not which of the dukes he values most, for equalities are so weighed that curiosity in neither can make choice of either's moiety.[3]   5

KENT: Is not this your son, my lord?

GLOUCESTER: His breeding,[4] sir, hath been at my charge. I have so often blushed to acknowledge him that now I am brazed[5] to't.

KENT: I cannot conceive[6] you.   10

GLOUCESTER: Sir, this young fellow's mother could; whereupon she grew round-wombed, and had indeed, sir, a son for her cradle ere she had a husband for her bed. Do you smell a fault?

KENT: I cannot wish the fault undone, the issue[7] of it being so proper.[8]

GLOUCESTER: But I have a son, sir, by order of law, some year elder than   15
this, who yet is no dearer in my account:[9] though this knave[10] came something saucily[11] to the world before he was sent for, yet was his mother fair, there was good sport at his making, and the whoreson[12] must be acknowledged. Do you know this noble gentleman, Edmund?   20

EDMUND: No, my lord.

GLOUCESTER: My Lord of Kent. Remember him hereafter as my honorable friend.

EDMUND: My services to your lordship.

KENT: I must love you, and sue[13] to know you better.   25

EDMUND: Sir, I shall study deserving.

I.i. 1 *affected* loved. 2. *Albany* Albanacte, whose domain extended "from the river Humber to the point of Caithness" (Holinshed). 3. *equalities . . . moiety* shares are so balanced against one another that careful examination by neither can make him wish the other's portion. 4. *breeding* upbringing. 5. *brazed* made brazen, hardened. 6. *conceive* understand (pun follows). 7. *issue* result (child). 8. *proper* handsome. 9. *account* estimation. 10. *knave* fellow (without disapproval); 11. *saucily* (1) insolently (2) lasciviously. 12. *whoreson* fellow (literally, son of a whore). 13. *sue* entreat.

GLOUCESTER: He hath been out[14] nine years, and away he shall again. The
    king is coming.

(*Sound a sennet.*[15] *Enter one bearing a coronet,*[16] *then King* LEAR, *then the
Dukes of* CORNWALL *and* ALBANY, *next* GONERIL, REGAN, CORDELIA, *and*
ATTENDANTS.)

LEAR: Attend the lords of France and Burgundy, Gloucester.

GLOUCESTER: I shall, my lord. (*Exit, with* EDMUND.)   30

LEAR: Meantime we shall express our darker purpose.[17]
    Give me the map there. Know that we have divided
    In three our kingdom; and 'tis our fast[18] intent
    To shake all cares and business from our age,
    Conferring them on younger strengths, while we   35
    Unburthened crawl toward death. Our son of Cornwall,
    And you our no less loving son of Albany,
    We have this hour a constant will to publish[19]
    Our daughters' several[20] dowers, that future strife
    May be prevented[21] now. The princes, France and Burgundy,   40
    Great rivals in our youngest daughter's love,
    Long in our court have made their amorous sojourn,
    And here are to be answered. Tell me, my daughters
    (Since now we will divest us both of rule,
    Interest[22] of territory, cares of state),   45
    Which of you shall we say doth love us most,
    That we our largest bounty may extend
    Where nature doth with merit challenge.[23] Goneril,
    Our eldest-born, speak first.

GONERIL: Sir, I love you more than word can wield[24] the matter;   50
    Dearer than eyesight, space,[25] and liberty;
    Beyond what can be valued, rich or rare;
    No less than life, with grace, health, beauty, honor;
    As much as child e'er loved, or father found;
    A love that makes breath[26] poor, and speech unable:[27]   55
    Beyond all manner of so much[28] I love you.

CORDELIA (*Aside*): What shall Cordelia speak? Love, and be silent.

LEAR: Of all these bounds, even from this line to this,
    With shadowy forests, and with champains riched,[29]
    With plenteous rivers, and wide-skirted meads,[30]   60

14. *out* away, abroad. 15. s.d. *sennet* set of notes played on a trumpet, signaling the entrance
or departure of a procession. 16. *coronet* small crown, intended for Cordelia. 17. *darker purpose* hidden intention. 18. *fast* fixed. 19. *constant . . . publish* fixed intention to proclaim. 20. *several* separate. 21. *prevented* forestalled. 22. *Interest* legal right. 23. *nature
. . . challenge* natural affection contends with desert for (or lays claim to) bounty. 24. *wield*
handle. 25. *space* scope. 26. *breath* language. 27. *unable* impotent. 28. *Beyond . . . much*
beyond all these comparisons. 29. *champains riched* enriched plains. 30. *wide-skirted meads*
extensive grasslands.

We make thee lady. To thine and Albany's issues[31]
Be this perpetual.[32] What says our second daughter,
Our dearest Regan, wife of Cornwall? Speak.

REGAN: I am made of that self mettle[33] as my sister,
And prize me at her worth.[34] In my true heart   65
I find she names my very deed of love;[35]
Only she comes too short, that[36] I profess
Myself an enemy to all other joys
Which the most precious square of sense professes,[37]
And find I am alone felicitate[38]   70
In your dear highness' love.

CORDELIA (*Aside*):   Then poor Cordelia!
And yet not so, since I am sure my love's
More ponderous[39] than my tongue.

LEAR: To thee and thine hereditary ever
Remain this ample third of our fair kingdom,   75
No less in space, validity,[40] and pleasure
Than that conferred on Goneril. Now, our joy,
Although our last and least,[41] to whose young love
The vines of France and milk[42] of Burgundy
Strive to be interest,[43] what can you say to draw   80
A third more opulent than your sisters? Speak.

CORDELIA: Nothing my lord.

LEAR: Nothing?

CORDELIA: Nothing.

LEAR: Nothing will come of nothing. Speak again.   85

CORDELIA: Unhappy that I am, I cannot heave
My heart into my mouth. I love your majesty
According to my bond,[44] no more nor less.

LEAR: How, how, Cordelia? Mend your speech a little,
Lest you may mar your fortunes.

CORDELIA: Good my lord,   90
You have begot me, bred me, loved me. I
Return those duties back as are right fit,[45]
Obey you, love you, and most honor you.

---

31. *issues* descendants. 32. *perpetual* in perpetuity. 33. *self mettle* same material or temperament. 34. *prize . . . worth* value me the same (imperative). 35. *my . . . love* what my love really is (a legalism). 36. *that* in that. 37. *Which . . . professes* which the choicest estimate of sense avows. 38. *felicitate* made happy. 39. *ponderous* weighty. 40. *validity* value. 41. *least* youngest, smallest. 42. *milk* i.e., pastures. 43. *interest* closely connected, as interested parties. 44. *bond* filial obligation. 45. *Return . . . fit* i.e., am correspondingly dutiful.

Why have my sisters husbands, if they say
They love you all? Haply,[46] when I shall wed, 95
That lord whose hand must take my plight[47] shall carry
Half my love with him, half my care and duty.
Sure I shall never marry like my sisters,
To love my father all.

LEAR: But goes thy heart with this?

CORDELIA   Ay, my good lord. 100

LEAR: So young, and so untender?

CORDELIA: So young, my lord, and true.

LEAR: Let it be so, thy truth then be thy dower!
For, by the sacred radiance of the sun,
The mysteries of Hecate[48] and the night, 105
By all the operation of the orbs[49]
From whom we do exist and cease to be,
Here I disclaim all my paternal care,
Propinquity and property of blood,[50]
And as a stranger to my heart and me 110
Hold thee from this for ever. The barbarous Scythian,[51]
Or he that makes his generation messes[52]
To gorge his appetite, shall to my bosom
Be as well neighbored, pitied, and relieved,
As thou my sometime[53] daughter.

KENT: Good my liege— 115

LEAR: Peace, Kent!
Come not between the dragon[54] and his wrath.
I loved her most, and thought to set my rest[55]
On her kind nursery.[56] Hence and avoid my sight!
So be my grave my peace, as here I give 120
Her father's heart from her! Call France. Who stirs?
Call Burgundy. Cornwall and Albany,
With my two daughters' dowers digest[57] the third;
Let pride, which she calls plainness, marry her.[58]
I do invest you jointly with my power, 125
Preeminence, and all the large effects
That troop with majesty.[59] Ourself,[60] by monthly course,

---

46. *Haply* perhaps. 47. *plight* troth plight. 48. *mysteries of Hecate* secret rites of Hecate (goddess of the infernal world, and of witchcraft). 49. *operation . . . orbs* astrological influence. 50. *Propinquity . . . blood* relationship and common blood. 51. *Scythian* type of the savage. 52. *makes . . . messes* eats his own offspring. 53. *sometime* former. 54. *dragon* (1) heraldic device of Britain (2) emblem of ferocity. 55. *set my rest* (1) stake my all (a term from the card game of primero) (2) find my rest. 56. *nursery* care, nursing. 57. *digest* absorb. 58. *Let . . . her* let her pride be her dowry and gain her a husband. 59. *effects . . . majesty* accompaniments that go with kingship. 60. *Ourself* the royal "we."

With reservation[61] of an hundred knights,
By you to be sustained, shall our abode
Make with you by due turn. Only we shall retain   130
The name, and all th' addition[62] to a king. The sway,
Revenue, execution of the rest,
Beloved sons, be yours; which to confirm.
This coronet[63] part between you.

KENT: Royal Lear,
Whom I have ever honored as my king,   135
Loved as my father, as my master followed,
As my great patron thought on in my prayers —

LEAR: The bow is bent and drawn; make from the shaft.[64]

KENT: Let it fall[65] rather, though the fork[66] invade
The region of my heart. Be Kent unmannerly   140
When Lear is mad. What wouldst thou do, old man?
Thinkst thou that duty shall have dread to speak
When power to flattery bows? To plainness honor's bound
When majesty falls to folly. Reserve thy state,[67]
And in thy best consideration[68] check   145
This hideous rashness. Answer my life my judgment,[69]
Thy youngest daughter does not love thee least,
Nor are those empty-hearted whose low sounds
Reverb[70] no hollowness.[71]

LEAR: Kent, on thy life, no more!

KENT: My life I never held but as a pawn[72]   150
To wage[73] against thine enemies; nor fear to lose it,
Thy safety being motive.[74]

LEAR: Out of my sight!

KENT: See better, Lear, and let me still[75] remain
The true blank[76] of thine eye.

LEAR: Now by Apollo —

KENT: Now by Apollo, king,   155
Thou swear'st thy gods in vain.

LEAR: O vassal! Miscreant![77]

---

61. *reservation* the action of reserving a privilege (a legalism). **62.** *addition* titles and
honors. **63.** *coronet* the crown that was to have been Cordelia's. **64.** *make . . . shaft* avoid the
arrow. **65.** *fall* strike. **66.** *fork* forked head of the arrow. **67.** *Reserve thy state* retain your
kingly authority. **68.** *best consideration* most careful reflection. **69.** *Answer . . . judgment* I
will stake my life on my opinion. **70.** *Reverb* reverberate. **71.** *hollowness* (1) emptiness (2) insincerity. **72.** *pawn* stake in a wager. **73.** *wage* (1) wager (2) carry on war. **74.** *motive* moving cause. **75.** *still* always. **76.** *blank* the white spot in the center of the target (at which Lear
should aim). **77.** *vassal! Miscreant!* base wretch! Misbeliever.

(*Laying his hand on his sword.*)

ALBANY, CORNWALL: Dear sir, forbear!

KENT: Kill thy physician, and the fee bestow
    Upon the foul disease. Revoke thy gift,
    Or, whilst I can vent clamor[78] from my throat,   160
    I'll tell thee thou dost evil.

LEAR: Hear me, recreant![79]
    On thine allegiance,[80] hear me!
    That thou hast sought to make us break our vows,
    Which we durst never yet, and with strained[81] pride
    To come betwixt our sentence[82] and our power,   165
    Which nor our nature nor our place can bear,
    Our potency made good,[83] take thy reward.
    Five days we do allot thee for provision[84]
    To shield thee from diseases[85] of the world,
    And on the sixth to turn thy hated back   170
    Upon our kingdom. If, on the tenth day following,
    Thy banished trunk[86] be found in our dominions,
    The moment is thy death. Away! By Jupiter,
    This shall not be revoked.

KENT: Fare thee well, king. Sith[87] thus thou wilt appear,   175
    Freedom lives hence, and banishment is here.

(*To* CORDELIA.)

    The gods to their dear shelter take thee, maid,
    That justly think'st, and hast most rightly said.

(*To* REGAN *and* GONERIL.)

    And your large speeches may your deeds approve,[88]
    That good effects[89] may spring from words of love.   180
    Thus Kent, O princes, bids you all adieu;
    He'll shape his old course[90] in a country new.   (*Exit.*)

(*Flourish.*[91] *Enter* GLOUCESTER, *with* FRANCE *and* BURGUNDY; ATTENDANTS.)

GLOUCESTER: Here's France and Burgundy, my noble lord.

LEAR: My Lord of Burgundy,
    We first address toward you, who with this king   185
    Hath rivaled for our daughter. What in the least

---

78. *vent clamor* utter a cry.   **79.** *recreant* traitor.   **80.** *On thine allegiance* to forswear, which is to commit high treason.   **81.** *strained* forced (and so excessive).   **82.** *sentence* judgment, decree.   **83.** *Our . . . good* my royal authority being now asserted.   **84.** *for provision* for making preparation.   **85.** *diseases* troubles.   **86.** *trunk* body.   **87.** *Sith* since.   **88.** *approve* prove true.   **89.** *effects* results.   **90.** *shape . . . course* pursue his customary way.   **91.** *s.d. Flourish* trumpet fanfare.

Will you require in present[92] dower with her,
Or cease your quest of love?

BURGUNDY: Most royal majesty,
I crave no more than hath your highness offered,
Nor will you tender[93] less.

LEAR: Right noble Burgundy,   190
When she was dear[94] to us, we did hold her so;
But now her price is fallen. Sir, there she stands.
If aught within that little seeming substance,[95]
Or all of it, with our displeasure pieced,[96]
And nothing more, may fitly like[97] your grace,   195
She's there, and she is yours.

BURGUNDY: I know no answer.

LEAR: Will you, with those infirmities she owes,[98]
Unfriended, new adopted to our hate,
Dow'red with our curse, and strangered[99] with our oath,
Take her, or leave her?

BURGUNDY: Pardon me, royal sir.   200
Election makes not up[100] on such conditions.

LEAR: Then leave her, sir; for, by the pow'r that made me,
I tell you all her wealth. (To FRANCE.) For you, great king,
I would not from your love make such a stray
To[101] match you where I hate; therefore beseech[102] you   205
T' avert your liking a more worthier way[103]
Than on a wretch whom nature is ashamed
Almost t'acknowledge hers.

FRANCE: This is most strange,
That she whom even but now was your best object,[104]
The argument[105] of your praise, balm of your age,   210
The best, the dearest, should in this trice of time
Commit a thing so monstrous to dismantle[106]
So many folds of favor. Sure her offense
Must be of such unnatural degree
That monsters it,[107] or your fore-vouched[108] affection   215
Fall into taint;[109] which to believe of her

92. *present* immediate. 93. *tender* offer. 94. *dear* (1) beloved (2) valued at a high price. 95. *little seeming substance* person who is (1) inconsiderable (2) outspoken. 96. *pieced* added to it. 97. *fitly like* please by its fitness. 98. *owes* possess. 99. *strangered* made a stranger. 100. *Election ... up* no one can choose. 101. *make ... To* stray so far as to. 102. *beseech* I beseech. 103. *avert ... way* turn your affections from her and bestow them on a better person. 104. *your best object* the one you loved most. 105. *argument* subject. 106. *dismantle* strip off. 107. *That monsters it* as makes it monstrous, unnatural. 108. *fore-vouched* previously sworn. 109. *Fall into taint* must be taken as having been unjustified all along; i.e., Cordelia was unworthy of your love from the first.

Must be a faith that reason without miracle
Should never plant in me.[110]

CORDELIA: I yet beseech your majesty,
If for[111] I want that glib and oily art
To speak and purpose not,[112] since what I well intend   220
I'll do't before I speak, that you make known
It is no vicious blot, murder, or foulness,
No unchaste action or dishonored step,
That hath deprived me of your grace and favor;
But even for want of that for which I am richer,   225
A still-soliciting[113] eye, and such a tongue
That I am glad I have not, though not to have it
Hath lost[114] me in your liking.

LEAR: Better thou
Hadst not been born than not t' have pleased me better.

FRANCE: Is it but this? A tardiness in nature[115]   230
Which often leaves the history unspoke[116]
That it intends to do. My Lord of Burgundy,
What say you[117] to the lady? Love's not love
When it is mingled with regards[118] that stands
Aloof from th' entire point.[119] Will you have her?   235
She is herself a dowry.

BURGUNDY: Royal king,
Give but that portion which yourself proposed,
And here I take Cordelia by the hand,
Duchess of Burgundy.

LEAR: Nothing. I have sworn. I am firm.   240

BURGUNDY: I am sorry then you have so lost a father
That you must lose a husband.

CORDELIA: Peace be with Burgundy.
Since that respects of fortune[120] are his love,
I shall not be his wife.

FRANCE: Fairest Cordelia, that art most rich being poor,   245
Most choice forsaken, and most loved despised,
Thee and thy virtues here I seize upon.
Be it lawful I take up what's cast away.
Gods, gods! 'Tis strange that from their cold'st neglect

110. *reason . . . me* my reason would have to be supported by a miracle to make me believe.
111. *for* because. 112. *purpose not* not mean to do what I promise. 113. *still-soliciting* always
begging. 114. *lost* ruined. 115. *tardiness in nature* natural reticence. 116. *leaves . . . unspoke* does not announce the action. 117. *What say you* i.e., will you have. 118. *regards* considerations (the dowry). 119. *stands . . . point* have nothing to do with the essential question
(love). 120. *respects of fortune* mercenary considerations.

My love should kindle to inflamed respect.[121]   250
Thy dow'rless daughter, king, thrown to my chance,[122]
Is queen of us, of ours, and our fair France.
Not all the dukes of wat'rish[123] Burgundy
Can buy this unprized precious[124] maid of me.
Bid them farewell, Cordelia, though unkind.   255
Thou losest here,[125] a better where[126] to find.

LEAR: Thou hast her, France; let her be thine, for we
Have no such daughter, nor shall ever see
That face of hers again. Therefore be gone,
Without our grace, our love, our benison.[127]   260
Come, noble Burgundy.

(*Flourish. Exeunt* LEAR, BURGUNDY, CORNWALL, ALBANY, GLOUCESTER,
and ATTENDANTS.)

FRANCE: Bid farewell to your sisters.

CORDELIA: The jewels of our father,[128] with washed[129] eyes
Cordelia leaves you. I know you what you are,
And, like a sister,[130] am most loath to call   265
Your faults as they are named.[131] Love well our father.
To your professèd[132] bosoms I commit him.
But yet, alas, stood I within his grace,
I would prefer[133] him to a better place.
So farewell to you both.   270

REGAN: Prescribe not us our duty.

GONERIL: Let your study
Be to content your lord, who hath received you
At Fortune's alms.[134] You have obedience scanted,[135]
And well are worth the want that you have wanted.[136]

CORDELIA: Time shall unfold what plighted[137] cunning hides,   275
Who covers faults, at last shame them derides.[138]
Well may you prosper.

FRANCE: Come, my fair Cordelia.

(*Exit* FRANCE *and* CORDELIA.)

121. *inflamed respect* more ardent affection. 122. *chance* lot. 123. *wat'rish* (1) with many
rivers (2) weak, diluted. 124. *unprized precious* unappreciated by others, and yet precious. 125. *here* in this place. 126. *where* other place. 127. *benison* blessing. 128. *The
jewels . . . father* you creatures prized by our father; 129. *washed* (1) weeping (2) clear-
sighted. 130. *like a sister* because I am a sister, i.e., loyal, affectionate. 131. *as . . . named* by
their right and ugly names. 132. *professed* pretending to love.   133. *prefer* recommend. 134. *At Fortune's alms* as a charitable bequest from Fortune (and so, by extension, as
one beggared or cast down by Fortune). 135. *scanted* stinted. 136. *worth . . . wanted* deserve
to be denied, even as you have denied. 137. *plighted* pleated, enfolded. 138. *Who . . .
derides* Those who hide their evil are finally exposed and shamed ("He that hideth his sins, shall
not prosper").

GONERIL: Sister, it is not little I have to say of what most nearly appertains to us both. I think our father will hence tonight.

REGAN: That's most certain, and with you; next month with us. 280

GONERIL: You see how full of changes his age is. The observation we have made of it hath not been little. He always loved our sister most, and with what poor judgment he hath now cast her off appears too grossly.[139]

REGAN: 'Tis the infirmity of his age; yet he hath ever but slenderly known 285 himself.

GONERIL: The best and soundest of his time[140] hath been but rash; then must we look from his age to receive not alone the imperfections of long-ingrafted[141] condition,[142] but therewithal[143] the unruly waywardness that infirm and choleric years bring with them. 290

REGAN: Such unconstant starts[144] are we like to have from him as this of Kent's banishment.

GONERIL: There is further compliment[145] of leave-taking between France and him. Pray you, let's hit[146] together; if our father carry authority with such disposition as he bears,[147] this last surrender[148] of his will 295 but offend[149] us.

REGAN: We shall further think of it.

GONERIL: We must do something, and i' th' heat.[150]

(*Exeunt.*)

Scene II.

(*The Earl of Gloucester's castle.*)

(*Enter* EDMUND *with a letter.*)

EDMUND: Thou, Nature,[1] art my goddess; to thy law
My services are bound. Wherefore should I
Stand in the plague of custom,[2] and permit
The curiosity[3] of nations to deprive me,
For that[4] I am some twelve or fourteen moonshines[5] 5
Lag of[6] a brother? Why bastard? Wherefore base?

---

139. *grossly* obviously. 140. *of his time* period of his life up to now. 141. *long-ingrafted* implanted for a long time. 142. *condition* disposition. 143. *therewithal* with them. 144. *unconstant starts* impulsive whims. 145. *compliment* formal courtesy. 146. *hit* agree. 147. *carry . . . bears* continues, and in such frame of mind, to wield the sovereign power. 148. *last surrender* recent abdication. 149. *offend* vex. 150. *i' th' heat* while the iron is hot. I.ii. 1. *Nature* Edmund's conception of Nature accords with our description of a bastard as a natural child. 2. *Stand . . . custom* respect hateful convention. 3. *curiosity* nice distinctions. 4. *For that* because. 5. *moonshines* months. 6. *Lag of* short of being (in age).

When my dimensions are as well compact,[7]
My mind as generous,[8] and my shape as true,
As honest[9] madam's issue? Why brand they us
With base? With baseness? Bastardy? Base? Base?   10
Who, in the lusty stealth of nature, take
More composition[10] and fierce[11] quality
Than doth, within a dull, stale, tired bed,
Go to th' creating a whole tribe of fops[12]
Got[13] 'tween asleep and wake? Well then,   15
Legitimate Edgar, I must have your land.
Our father's love is to the bastard Edmund
As to th' legitimate. Fine word, "legitimate."
Well, my legitimate, if this letter speed,[14]
And my invention[15] thrive, Edmund the base   20
Shall top th' legitimate. I grow, I prosper.
Now, gods, stand up for bastards.

(*Enter* GLOUCESTER.)

GLOUCESTER: Kent banished thus? and France in choler parted?
And the king gone tonight? prescribed[16] his pow'r?
Confined to exhibition?[17] All this done   25
Upon the gad?[18] Edmund, how now? What news?

EDMUND: So please your lordship, none.

GLOUCESTER: Why so earnestly seek you to put up[19] that letter?

EDMUND: I know no news, my lord.

GLOUCESTER: What paper were you reading?   30

EDMUND: Nothing, my lord.

GLOUCESTER: No? What needed then that terrible dispatch[20] of it into your
pocket? The quality of nothing hath not such need to hide itself.
Let's see. Come, if it be nothing, I shall not need spectacles.

EDMUND: I beseech you, sir, pardon me. It is a letter from my brother   35
that I have not all o'er-read; and for so much as I have perused, I
find it not fit for your o'erlooking.[21]

GLOUCESTER: Give me the letter, sir.

EDMUND: I shall offend, either to detain or give it. The contents, as in part
I understand them, are to blame.[22]   40

GLOUCESTER: Let's see, let's see.

7. *compact* framed. 8. *generous* gallant. 9. *honest* chaste. 10. *composition* complete-
ness. 11. *fierce* energetic. 12. *fops* fools. 13. *Got* begot. 14. *speed* prosper. 15. *invention* plan. 16. *prescribed* limited. 17. *exhibition* an allowance or pension. 18. *Upon the gad*
on the spur of the moment (as if pricked by a gad or goad). 19. *put up* put away, conceal. 20. *terrible dispatch* hasty putting away. 21. *o'erlooking* inspection. 22. *to blame*
blameworthy.

EDMUND: I hope, for my brother's justification, he wrote this but as an essay or taste[23] of my virtue.

GLOUCESTER (*Reads.*): "This policy and reverence[24] of age makes the world bitter to the best of our times;[25] keeps our fortunes from us till our oldness cannot relish[26] them. I begin to find an idle and fond[27] bondage in the oppression of aged tyranny, who sways, not as it hath power, but as it is suffered.[28] Come to me, that of this I may speak more. If our father would sleep till I waked him, you should enjoy half his revenue[29] for ever, and live the beloved of your brother, Edgar."
Hum! Conspiracy? "Sleep till I waked him, you should enjoy half his revenue." My son Edgar! Had he a hand to write this? A heart and brain to breed it in? When came you to this? Who brought it?

EDMUND: It was not brought me, my lord; there's the cunning of it. I found it thrown in at the casement of my closet.[30]

GLOUCESTER: You know the character[31] to be your brother's?

EDMUND: If the matter were good, my lord, I durst swear it were his; but in respect of that,[32] I would fain[33] think it were not.

GLOUCESTER: It is his.

EDMUND: It is his hand, my lord; but I hope his heart is not in the contents.

GLOUCESTER: Has he never before sounded[34] you in this business?

EDMUND: Never, my lord. But I have heard him oft maintain it to be fit that, sons at perfect[35] age, and fathers declined, the father should be as ward to the son, and the son manage his revenue.

GLOUCESTER: O villain, villain! His very opinion in the letter. Abhorred villain, unnatural, detested,[36] brutish villain; worse than brutish! Go, sirrah,[37] seek him. I'll apprehend him. Abominable villain! Where is he?

EDMUND: I do not well know, my lord. If it shall please you to suspend your indignation against my brother till you can derive from him better testimony of his intent, you should run a certain course,[38] where, if you violently proceed against him, mistaking his purpose, it would make a great gap[39] in your own honor and shake in pieces the heart of his obedience. I dare pawn down[40] my life for him that he

---

23. *essay or taste* test. **24.** *policy and reverence* policy of reverencing (hendiadys). **25.** *best ... times* best years of our lives (i.e., our youth). **26.** *relish* enjoy; **27.** *idle and fond* foolish. **28.** *who ... suffered* which rules, not from its own strength, but from our allowance. **29.** *revenue* income. **30.** *casement ... closet* window of my room. **31.** *character* handwriting. **32.** *in ... that* in view of what it is. **33.** *fain* prefer to. **34.** *sounded* sounded you out. **35.** *perfect* mature. **36.** *detested* detestable. **37.** *sirrah* sir (familiar form of address). **38.** *run ... course* proceed safely, know where you are going. **39.** *gap* breach. **40.** *pawn down* stake.

hath writ this to feel[41] my affection to your honor, and to no other pretense of danger.[42]

GLOUCESTER: Think you so?

EDMUND: If your honor judge it meet,[43] I will place you where you shall   80 hear us confer of this, and by an auricular assurance[44] have your satisfaction, and that without any further delay than this very evening.

GLOUCESTER: He cannot be such a monster.

EDMUND: Nor is not, sure.   85

GLOUCESTER: To his father, that so tenderly and entirely loves him. Heaven and earth! Edmund, seek him out; wind me into him,[45] I pray you; frame[46] the business after your own wisdom. I would unstate myself to be in a due resolution.[47]

EDMUND: I will seek him, sir, presently;[48] convey[49] the business as I shall   90 find means, and acquaint you withal.[50]

GLOUCESTER: These late[51] eclipses in the sun and moon portend no good to us. Though the wisdom of nature[52] can reason[53] it thus and thus, yet nature finds itself scourged by the sequent effects.[54] Love cools, friendship falls off,[55] brothers divide. In cities, mutinies;[56] in coun-   95 tries, discord; in palaces, treason; and the bond cracked 'twixt son and father. This villain of mine comes under the prediction,[57] there's son against father; the king falls from bias of nature,[58] there's father against child. We have seen the best of our time.[59] Machinations, hollowness,[60] treachery, and all ruinous disorders follow us disqui-   100 etly[61] to our graves. Find out this villain, Edmund; it shall lose thee nothing.[62] Do it carefully. And the noble and true-hearted Kent banished; his offense, honesty. 'Tis strange.   (*Exit.*)

EDMUND: This is the excellent foppery[63] of the world, that when we are sick in fortune, often the surfeits of our own behavior,[64] we make   105 guilty of our disasters the sun, the moon, and stars; as if we were villains on[65] necessity; fools by heavenly compulsion; knaves, thieves, and treachers by spherical predominance;[66] drunkards, liars, and

---

41. *feel* test. 42. *pretense of danger* dangerous purpose. 43. *meet* fit. 44. *auricular assurance* proof heard with your own ears. 45. *wind . . . him* insinuate yourself into his confidence for me. 46. *frame* manage. 47. *unstate . . . resolution* forfeit my earldom to know the truth. 48. *presently* at once. 49. *convey* manage. 50. *withal* with it. 51. *late* recent. 52. *wisdom of nature* scientific learning. 53. *reason* explain. 54. *yet . . . effects* nonetheless our world is punished with subsequent disasters. 55. *falls off* revolts. 56. *mutinies* riots. 57. *This . . . prediction* my son's villainous behavior is included in these portents, and bears them out. 58. *bias of nature* natural inclination (the metaphor is from the game of bowls). 59. *best . . . time* our best days. 60. *hollowness* insincerity. 61. *disquietly* unquietly. 62. *it . . . nothing* you will not lose by it. 63. *foppery* folly. 64. *often . . . behavior* often caused by our own excesses. 65. *on* of. 66. *treachers . . . predominance* traitors because of the ascendancy of a particular star at our birth.

adulterers by an enforced obedience of planetary influence;[67] and all
that we are evil in, by a divine thrusting on.[68] An admirable evasion 110
of whoremaster[69] man, to lay his goatish[70] disposition on the charge
of a star. My father compounded[71] with my mother under the
Dragon's Tail,[72] and my nativity[73] was under Ursa Major,[74] so that it
follows I am rough and lecherous. Fut![75] I should have been that[76] I
am, had the maidenliest star in the firmament twinkled on my 115
bastardizing. Edgar —

(*Enter* EDGAR.)

and pat he comes, like the catastrophe[77] of the old comedy. My cue
is villainous melancholy, with a sigh like Tom o' Bedlam[78] — O,
these eclipses do portend these divisions. Fa, sol, la, mi.[79]

EDGAR: How now, brother Edmund; what serious contemplation are you 120
in?

EDMUND: I am thinking, brother, of a prediction I read this other day,
what should follow these eclipses.

EDGAR: Do you busy yourself with that?

EDMUND: I promise you, the effects he writes of succeed[80] unhappily: as of 125
unnaturalness[81] between the child and the parent, death, dearth,
dissolutions of ancient amities,[82] divisions in state, menaces and
maledictions against king and nobles, needless diffidences,[83] banishment of friends, dissipation of cohorts,[84] nuptial breaches, and I
know not what. 130

EDGAR: How long have you been a sectary astronomical?[85]

EDMUND: Come, come, when saw you my father last?

EDGAR: Why, the night gone by.

EDMUND: Spake you with him?

EDGAR: Ay, two hours together. 135

EDMUND: Parted you in good terms? Found you no displeasure in him by
word nor countenance?[86]

EDGAR: None at all.

67. *by . . . influence* because we had to submit to the influence of our star. **68.** *divine thrusting on* supernatural compulsion. **69.** *whoremaster* lecherous. **70.** *goatish* lascivious. **71.** *compounded* (1) made terms (2) formed (a child). **72.** *Dragon's Tail* the constellation Draco. **73.** *nativity* birthday. **74.** *Ursa Major* the Great Bear. **75.** *Fut* 's foot (an impatient oath). **76.** *that* what. **77.** *catastrophe* conclusion. **78.** *My . . . Bedlam* I must be doleful, like a lunatic beggar out of Bethlehem (Bedlam) Hospital, the London madhouse. **79.** *Fa, sol, la, mi* Edmund's humming of the musical notes is perhaps prompted by his use of the word *division*, which describes a musical variation. **80.** *succeed* follow. **81.** *unnaturalness* unkindness. **82.** *amities* friendships. **83.** *diffidences* distrusts. **84.** *dissipation of cohorts* falling away of supporters. **85.** *sectary astronomical* believer in astrology. **86.** *countenance* expression.

EDMUND: Bethink yourself wherein you may have offended him; and at my entreaty forbear his presence[87] until some little time hath 140 qualified[88] the heat of his displeasure, which at this instant so rageth in him that with the mischief of your person it would scarcely allay.[89]

EDGAR: Some villain hath done me wrong.

EDMUND: That's my fear, brother. I pray you have a continent forbearance[90] till the speed of his rage goes slower; and, as I say, retire with 145 me to my lodging, from whence I will fitly[91] bring you to hear my lord speak. Pray ye, go; there's my key. If you do stir abroad, go armed.

EDGAR: Armed, brother?

EDMUND: Brother, I advise you to the best. Go armed. I am no honest 150 man if there be any good meaning toward you. I have told you what I have seen and heard; but faintly, nothing like the image and horror[92] of it. Pray you, away.

EDGAR: Shall I hear from you anon?[93]

EDMUND: I do serve you in this business.   155

(*Exit* EDGAR.)

> A credulous father, and a brother noble,
> Whose nature is so far from doing harms
> That he suspects none; on whose foolish honesty
> My practices[94] ride easy. I see the business.
> Let me, if not by birth, have lands by wit.   160
> All with me's meet[95] that I can fashion fit.[96] (*Exit.*)

Scene III.

(*The Duke of Albany's palace.*)

(*Enter* GONERIL, *and* OSWALD, *her steward.*)

GONERIL: Did my father strike my gentleman for chiding of his Fool?[1]

OSWALD: Ay, madam.

GONERIL: By day and night he wrongs me. Every hour
He flashes into one gross crime[2] or other
That sets us all at odds. I'll not endure it.   5
His knights grow riotous,[3] and himself upbraids us

---

87. *forbear his presence* keep away from him. 88. *qualified* lessened. 89. *with . . . allay* even an injury to you would not appease his anger. 90. *have . . . forbearance* be restrained and keep yourself withdrawn. 91. *fitly* at a fit time. 92. *image and horror* true horrible picture. 93. *anon* in a little while. 94. *practices* plots. 95. *meet* proper. 96. *fashion fit* shape to my purpose. I.iii. 1. *Fool* court jester. 2. *crime* offense. 3. *riotous* dissolute.

On every trifle. When he returns from hunting,
I will not speak with him. Say I am sick.
If you come slack of former services,[4]
You shall do well; the fault of it I'll answer.[5]   10

(*Horns within.*)

OSWALD: He's coming, madam; I hear him.

GONERIL: Put on what weary negligence you please,
You and your fellows. I'd have it come to question.[6]
If he distaste[7] it, let him to my sister,
Whose mind and mine I know in that are one,   15
Not to be overruled. Idle[8] old man,
That still would manage those authorities
That he hath given away. Now, by my life,
Old fools are babes again, and must be used
With checks as flatteries, when they are seen abused.[9]   20
Remember what I have said.

OSWALD: Well, madam.

GONERIL: And let his knights have colder looks among you.
What grows of it, no matter; advise your fellows so.
I would breed from hence occasions, and I shall,
That I may speak.[10] I'll write straight[11] to my sister   25
To hold my course. Go, prepare for dinner. (*Exeunt.*)

Scene IV.

(*A hall in the same.*)

(*Enter* KENT *disguised.*)

KENT: If but as well I other accents borrow
That can my speech defuse,[1] my good intent
May carry through itself to that full issue[2]
For which I razed my likeness.[3] Now, banished Kent,
If thou canst serve where thou dost stand condemned,   5
So may it come,[4] thy master whom thou lov'st
Shall find thee full of labors.

(*Horns within.[5] Enter* LEAR, KNIGHTS, *and* ATTENDANTS.)

---

4. *come . . . services* are less serviceable to him than formerly. 5. *answer* answer for. 6. *come to question* be discussed openly. 7. *distaste* dislike. 8. *Idle* foolish. 9. *With . . . abused* with restraints as well as soothing words when they are misguided. 10. *breed . . . speak* find in this opportunities for speaking out. 11. *straight* at once. I.iv. 1. *defuse* disguise. 2. *full issue* perfect result. 3. *razed my likeness* shaved off, disguised my natural appearance. 4. *So . . . come* so may it fall out. 5. *s.d. within* offstage.

LEAR: Let me not stay[6] a jot for dinner; go, get it ready. (*Exit an* ATTENDANT.) How now, what art thou?

KENT: A man, sir.

LEAR: What dost thou profess?[7] What wouldst thou with us?

KENT: I do profess[8] to be no less than I seem, to serve him truly that will put me in trust, to love him that is honest, to converse with him that is wise and says little, to fear judgment,[9] to fight when I cannot choose, and to eat no fish.[10]

LEAR: What art thou?

KENT: A very honest-hearted fellow and as poor as the king.

LEAR: If thou be'st as poor for a subject as he's for a king, thou art poor enough. What wouldst thou?

KENT: Service.

LEAR: Who wouldst thou serve?

KENT: You.

LEAR: Dost thou know me, fellow?

KENT: No, sir, but you have that in your countenance[11] which I would fain[12] call master.

LEAR: What's that?

KENT: Authority.

LEAR: What services canst thou do?

KENT: I can keep honest counsel,[13] ride, run, mar a curious tale in telling it,[14] and deliver a plain message bluntly. That which ordinary men are fit for, I am qualified in, and the best of me is diligence.

LEAR: How old art thou?

KENT: Not so young, sir, to love a woman for singing, nor so old to dote on her for anything. I have years on my back forty-eight.

LEAR: Follow me; thou shalt serve me. If I like thee no worse after dinner, I will not part from thee yet. Dinner, ho, dinner! Where's my knave?[15] my Fool? Go you and call my Fool hither.

(*Exit an* ATTENDANT.)

(*Enter* OSWALD.)

---

6. *stay* wait. **7.** *What . . . profess* What do you do? **8.** *profess* claim. **9.** *judgment* by a heavenly or earthly judge. **10.** *eat no fish* i.e., (1) I am no Catholic, but a loyal Protestant (2) I am no weakling (3) I use no prostitutes. **11.** *countenance* bearing. **12.** *fain* like to. **13.** *honest counsel* honorable secrets. **14.** *mar . . . it* i.e., I cannot speak like an affected courtier ("curious" = elaborate, as against plain). **15.** *knave* boy.

You, you, sirrah, where's my daughter?

OSWALD: So please you — (*Exit.*)

LEAR: What says the fellow there? Call the clotpoll[16] back. (*Exit a* KNIGHT.)   40
Where's my Fool? Ho, I think the world's asleep.

(*Reenter* KNIGHT.)

How now? Where's that mongrel?

KNIGHT: He says, my lord, your daughter is not well.

LEAR: Why came not the slave back to me when I called him?

KNIGHT: Sir, he answered me in the roundest[17] manner, he would not.   45

LEAR: He would not?

KNIGHT: My lord, I know not what the matter is; but to my judgment
your highness is not entertained[18] with that ceremonious affection as
you were wont. There's a great abatement of kindness appears as
well in the general dependents[19] as in the duke himself also and your   50
daughter.

LEAR: Ha? Say'st thou so?

KNIGHT: I beseech you pardon me, my lord, if I be mistaken; for my duty
cannot be silent when I think your highness wronged.

LEAR: Thou but rememb'rest[20] me of mine own conception.[21] I have per-   55
ceived a most faint neglect[22] of late, which I have rather blamed as
mine own jealous curiosity[23] than as a very pretense[24] and purpose of
unkindness. I will look further into't. But where's my Fool? I have
not seen him this two days.

KNIGHT: Since my young lady's going into France, sir, the Fool hath much   60
pined away.

LEAR: No more of that; I have noted it well. Go you and tell my daughter
I would speak with her. Go you, call hither my Fool. (*Exit an*
ATTENDANT.)

(*Enter* OSWALD.)

O, you, sir, you! Come you hither, sir. Who am I, sir?

OSWALD: My lady's father.   65

LEAR: "My lady's father"? My lord's knave, you whoreson dog, you slave,
you cur!

OSWALD: I am none of these, my lord; I beseech your pardon.

16. *clotpoll* Clodpoll, blockhead. 17. *roundest* rudest. 18. *entertained* treated. 19. *depen-dants* servants. 20. *rememb'rest* remindest. 21. *conception* idea. 22. *faint neglect* i.e., "weary negligence" (I.iii.13). 23. *mine ... curiosity* suspicious concern for my own dignity. 24. *very pretense* actual intention.

LEAR: Do you bandy²⁵ looks with me, you rascal?

(*Striking him.*)

OSWALD: I'll not be strucken,²⁶ my lord.   70

KENT: Nor tripped neither, you base football²⁷ player.

(*Tripping up his heels.*)

LEAR: I thank thee, fellow. Thou serv'st me, and I'll love thee.

KENT: Come, sir, arise, away. I'll teach you differences.²⁸ Away, away. If
you will measure your lubber's²⁹ length again, tarry; but away. Go
to!³⁰ Have you wisdom?³¹ So.³² (*Pushes* OSWALD *out.*)   75

LEAR: Now, my friendly knave, I thank thee. There's earnest³³ of thy
service.

(*Giving* KENT *money.*).

(*Enter* FOOL.)

FOOL: Let me hire him too. Here's my coxcomb.³⁴

(*Offering* KENT *his cap.*)

LEAR: How now, my pretty knave? How dost thou?

FOOL: Sirrah, you were best³⁵ take my coxcomb.   80

KENT: Why, Fool?

FOOL: Why? For taking one's part that's out of favor. Nay, an³⁶ thou canst
not smile as the wind sits,³⁷ thou'lt catch cold shortly. There, take
my coxcomb. Why, this fellow has banished³⁸ two on's daughters,
and did the third a blessing against his will. If thou follow him, thou 85
must needs wear my coxcomb. — How now, nuncle?³⁹ Would I had
two coxcombs and two daughters.

LEAR: Why, my boy?

FOOL: If I gave them all my living,⁴⁰ I'd keep my coxcombs myself.
There's mine; beg another of thy daughters.   90

LEAR: Take heed, sirrah — the whip.

FOOL: Truth's a dog must to kennel; he must be whipped out, when Lady
the Brach⁴¹ may stand by th' fire and stink.

---

25. *bandy* exchange insolently (metaphor from tennis). **26.** *strucken* struck. **27.** *football* a low
game played by idle boys, to the scandal of sensible men. **28.** *differences* of rank. **29.** *lubber's* lout's. **30.** *Go to* expression of derisive incredulity. **31.** *Have you wisdom* i.e., Do you
know what's good for you? **32.** *So* good. **33.** *earnest* money for services rendered. **34.** *coxcomb* professional fool's cap, shaped like a coxcomb. **35.** *you were best* you had
better. **36.** *an* if. **37.** *smile . . . sits* ingratiate yourself with those in power. **38.** *banished*
alienated (by making them independent). **39.** *nuncle* contracton of "mine uncle." **40.** *living*
property. **41.** *Brach* bitch.

LEAR: A pestilent gall[42] to me.

FOOL: Sirrah, I'll teach thee a speech.   95

LEAR: Do.

FOOL: Mark it, nuncle.
 Have more than thou showest,
 Speak less than thou knowest,
 Lend less than thou owest,[43]   100
 Ride more than thou goest,[44]
 Learn more than thou trowest,[45]
 Set less than thou throwest;[46]
 Leave thy drink and thy whore,
 And keep in-a-door,   105
 And thou shalt have more
 Than two tens to a score.[47]

KENT: This is nothing, Fool.

FOOL: Then 'tis like the breath of an unfee'd[48] lawyer — you gave me
nothing for't. Can you make no use of nothing, nuncle?   110

LEAR: Why, no, boy. Nothing can be made out of nothing.

FOOL (*To* KENT.): Prithee tell him, so much the rent of his land comes to;
he will not believe a fool.

LEAR: A bitter[49] fool.

FOOL: Dost thou know the difference, my boy, between a bitter fool and a   115
sweet one?

LEAR: No, lad; teach me.

FOOL: That lord that counseled thee
 To give away thy land,
 Come place him here by me,   120
 Do thou for him stand.
 The sweet and bitter fool
 Will presently appear;
 The one in motley[50] here,
 The other found out[51] there.[52]   125

LEAR: Dost thou call me fool, boy?

FOOL: All thy other titles thou hast given away; that thou wast born with.

KENT: This is not altogether fool, my lord.

42. *gall* sore. **43.** *owest* ownest. **44.** *goest* walkest. **45.** *trowest* knowest. **46.** *Set . . . throwest* bet less than you play for (get odds from your opponent). **47.** *have . . . score* i.e., come away with more than you had (two tens, or twenty shillings, make a score, or one pound). **48.** *unfee'd* unpaid for. **49.** *bitter* satirical. **50.** *motley* the costume of the professional jester. **51.** *found out* revealed. **52.** *there* the Fool points at Lear, as a fool in the grain.

FOOL: No, faith; lords and great men will not let me.[53] If I had a monopoly[54] out, they would have part on't. And ladies too, they will not 130
let me have all the fool to myself; they'll be snatching. Nuncle, give
me an egg, and I'll give thee two crowns.

LEAR: What two crowns shall they be?

FOOL: Why, after I have cut the egg i' the middle and eat up the meat,
the two crowns of the egg. When thou clovest thy crown i' th' mid- 135
dle and gav'st away both parts, thou bor'st thine ass on thy back o'er
the dirt.[55] Thou hadst little wit in thy bald crown when thou gav'st
thy gold one away. If I speak like myself[56] in this, let him be
whipped[57] that first finds it so. (*Singing.*)
        Fools had ne'er less grace in a year, 140
          For wise men are grown foppish,
        And know not how their wits to wear,
          Their manners are so apish.[58]

LEAR: When were you wont to be so full of songs, sirrah?

FOOL: I have used[59] it, nuncle, e'er since thou mad'st thydaughters thy 145
mothers; for when thou gav'st them the rod, and put'st down thine
own breeches, (*Singing.*)
        Then they for sudden joy did weep,
          And I for sorrow sung,
        That such a king should play bo-peep[60] 150
          And go the fools among.
Prithee, nuncle, keep a schoolmaster that can teach thy Fool to lie. I
would fain learn to lie.

LEAR: And[61] you lie, sirrah, we'll have you whipped.

FOOL: I marvel what kin thou and thy daughters are. They'll have me 155
whipped for speaking true; thou'lt have me whipped for lying; and
sometimes I am whipped for holding my peace. I had rather be any
kind o' thing than a fool, and yet I would not be thee, nuncle; thou
hast pared thy wit o' both sides and left nothing i' th' middle. Here
comes one o' the parings. 160

(*Enter* GONERIL.)

LEAR: How now, daughter? What makes that frontlet[62] on? Methinks you
are too much of late i' th' frown.

---

53. *let me* i.e., let me have all the folly to myself. **54.** *monopoly* James I gave great scandal by
granting to his "snatching" courtiers royal patents to deal exclusively in some com-
modity. **55.** *bor'st . . . dirt* like the foolish and unnatural countryman in Aesop's
fable. **56.** *like myself* like a fool. **57.** *let . . . whipped* i.e., let the man be whipped for a fool
who thinks my true saying to be foolish. **58.** *Fools . . . apish* i.e., fools were never in less favor
than now, and the reason is that wise men, turning foolish, and not knowing how to use their intelligence, imitate the professional fools and so make them unnecessary. **59.** *used* practiced. **60.** *play bo-peep* (1) act like a child (2) blind himself. **61.** *And* if. **62.** *frontlet* frown
(literally, ornamental band).

FOOL: Thou wast a pretty fellow when thou hadst no need to care for her frowning. Now thou art an O without a figure.[63] I am better than thou art now: I am a fool, thou art nothing. (*To* GONERIL.) Yes, forsooth, I will hold my tongue. So your face bids me, though you say nothing. Mum, mum,

> He that keeps nor crust nor crum,[64]
> Weary of all, shall want[65] some.

(*Pointing to* LEAR.)

> That's a shealed peascod.[66]

GONERIL: Not only, sir, this your all-licensed[67] Fool,
But other[68] of your insolent retinue
Do hourly carp and quarrel, breaking forth
In rank[69] and not-to-be-endurèd riots. Sir,
I had thought by making this well known unto you
To have found a safe[70] redress, but now grow fearful,
By what yourself too late[71] have spoke and done,
That you protect this course, and put it on
By your allowance;[72] which if you should, the fault
Would not 'scape censure, nor the redresses sleep,[73]
Which, in the tender of[74] a wholesome weal,[75]
Might in their working do you that offense,
Which else were shame, that then necessity
Will call discreet proceeding.[76]

FOOL: For you know, nuncle,

> The hedge-sparrow fed the cuckoo[77] so long
> That it had it head bit off by it[78] young.

So out went the candle, and we were left darkling.[79]

LEAR: Are you our daughter?

GONERIL: Come sir,
I would you would make use of your good wisdom
Whereof I know you are fraught[80] and put away
These dispositions[81] which of late transport you
From what you rightly are.

FOOL: May not an ass know when the cart draws the horse? Whoop, Jug,[82] I love thee!

---

63. *figure* digit, to give value to the cipher (Lear is a nought).   **64.** *crum* soft bread inside the loaf.   **65.** *want* lack.   **66.** *shealed peascod* empty pea pod.   **67.** *all-licensed* privileged to take any liberties.   **68.** *other* others.   **69.** *rank* gross.   **70.** *safe* sure.   **71.** *too late* lately.   **72.** *put . . . allowance* promote it by your approval;   *allowance* approval.   **73.** *redresses sleep* correction fail to follow.   **74.** *tender of* desire for.   **75.** *weal* state.   **76.** *Might . . . proceeding* as I apply it, the correction might humiliate you; but the need to take action cancels what would otherwise be unfilial conduct in me.   **77.** *cuckoo* which lays its eggs in the nests of other birds.   **78.** *it* its.   **79.** *darkling* in the dark.   **80.** *fraught* endowed.   **81.** *dispositions* moods.   **82.** *Jug* Joan (a quotation from a popular song?).

LEAR: Does any here know me? This is not Lear.
    Does Lear walk thus? Speak thus? Where are his eyes?
    Either his notion[83] weakens, or his discernings[84]
    Are lethargied[85] — Ha! Waking? 'Tis not so.   200
    Who is it that can tell me who I am?

FOOL: Lear's shadow.

LEAR: I would learn that; for, by the marks of sovereignty,[86] knowledge,
    and reason, I should be false[87] persuaded I had daughters.

FOOL: Which[88] they will make an obedient father.   205

LEAR: Your name, fair gentlewoman?

GONERIL: This admiration,[89] sir, is much o' th' savor[90]
    Of other your[91] new pranks. I do beseech you
    To understand my purposes aright.
    As you are old and reverend, should be wise.   210
    Here do you keep a hundred knights and squires,
    Men so disordered, so deboshed,[92] and bold,
    That this our court, infected with their manners,
    Shows[93] like a riotous inn. Epicurism[94] and lust
    Makes it more like a tavern or a brothel   215
    Than a graced[95] palace. The shame itself doth speak
    For instant remedy. Be then desired[96]
    By her, that else will take the thing she begs,
    A little to disquantity your train,[97]
    And the remainders[98] that shall still depend,[99]   220
    To be such men as may besort[100] your age,
    Which know themselves, and you.

LEAR: Darkness and devils!
    Saddle my horses; call my train together.
    Degenerate[101] bastard, I'll not trouble thee:
    Yet have I left a daughter.   225

GONERIL: You strike my people, and your disordered rabble
    Make servants of their betters.

(*Enter* ALBANY.)

LEAR: Woe, that too late repents. O, sir, are you come?
    Is it your will? Speak, sir. Prepare my horses.

---

83. *notion* understanding. 84. *discernings* faculties. 85. *lethargied* paralyzed. 86. *marks of sovereignty* i.e., tokens that Lear is king, and hence father to his daughters. 87. *false* falsely. 88. *Which* whom (Lear). 89. *admiration* (affected) wonderment. 90. *is . . . savor* smacks much. 91. *other your* others of your. 92. *deboshed* debauched. 93. *Shows* appears. 94. *Epicurism* riotous living. 95. *graced* dignified. 96. *desired* requested. 97. *disquantity your train* reduce the number of your dependents. 98. *remainders* those who remain. 99. *depend* attend on you. 100. *besort* befit. 101. *Degenerate* unnatural.

Ingratitude! thou marble-hearted fiend, 230
More hideous when thou show'st thee in a child
Than the sea-monster.

ALBANY: Pray, sir, be patient.

LEAR: Detested kite,[102] thou liest.
My train are men of choice and rarest parts,[103]
That all particulars of duty know, 235
And, in the most exact regard,[104] support
The worships[105] of their name. O most small fault,
How ugly didst thou in Cordelia show!
Which, like an engine,[106] wrenched my frame of nature
From the fixed place,[107] drew from my heart all love, 240
And added to the gall.[108] O Lear, Lear, Lear!
Beat at this gate that let thy folly in

(*Striking his head.*)

And thy dear judgment out. Go, go, my people.

ALBANY: My lord, I am guiltless, as I am ignorant
Of what hath moved you.

LEAR: It may be so, my lord. 245
Hear, Nature, hear; dear goddess, hear:
Suspend thy purpose if thou didst intend
To make this creature fruitful.
'Into her womb convey sterility,
Dry up in her the organs of increase,[109] 250
And from her derogate[110] body never spring
A babe to honor her. If she must teem,[111]
Create her child of spleen,[112] that it may live
And be a thwart disnatured[113] torment to her.
Let it stamp wrinkles in her brow of youth, 255
With cadent[114] tears fret[115] channels in her cheeks,
Turn all her mother's pains and benefits[116]
To laughter and contempt, that she may feel
How sharper than a serpent's tooth it is
To have a thankless child. Away, away! (*Exit*) 260

ALBANY: Now, gods that we adore, whereof comes this?

GONERIL: Never afflict yourself to know the cause,

---

102. *kite* scavenging bird of prey. 103. *parts* accomplishments. 104. *exact regard* strict attention to detail. 105. *worships* honor. 106. *engine* destructive contrivance. 107. *wrenched . . . place* i.e., disorders my natural self. 108. *gall* bitterness. 109. *increase* childbearing. 110. *derogate* degraded. 111. *teem* conceive. 112. *spleen* ill humor. 113. *thwart disnatured* perverse unnatural. 114. *cadent* falling. 115. *fret* wear. 116. *benefits* the mother's beneficent care of her child.

But let his disposition[117] have that scope
As[118] dotage gives it.

(*Enter* LEAR.)

LEAR: What, fifty of my followers at a clap?[119]   265
With fortnight?

ALBANY: What's the matter, sir?

LEAR: I'll tell thee. (*To* GONERIL.) Life and death, I am ashamed   265
That thou hast power to shake my manhood[120] thus!
That these hot tears, which break from me perforce,[121]
Should make thee worth them. Blasts and fogs upon thee!
Th' untented woundings[122] of a father's curse
Pierce every sense about thee! Old fond[123] eyes,   270
Beweep[124] this cause again, I'll pluck ye out
And cast you, with the waters that you loose,[125]
To temper[126] clay. Yea, is it come to this?
Ha! Let it be so. I have another daughter,
Who I am sure is kind and comfortable.[127]   275
When she shall hear this of thee, with her nails
She'll flay thy wolvish visage. Thou shalt find
That I'll resume the shape[128] which thou dost think
I have cast off for ever.

(*Exit* LEAR, *with* KENT *and* ATTENDANTS.)

GONERIL: Do you mark that?

ALBANY: I cannot be so partial, Goneril,   280
To the great love I bear you[129] —

GONERIL: Pray you, content. What, Oswald, ho!

(*To the* FOOL.)

You, sir, more knave than fool, after your master!

FOOL: Nuncle Lear, nuncle Lear, tarry. Take the Fool[130] with thee.
A fox, when one has caught her,   285
And such a daughter,
Should sure to the slaughter,
If my cap would buy a halter.[131]
So the Fool follows after.[132] (*Exit.*)

GONERIL: This man hath had good counsel. A hundred knights!   290

117. *disposition* mood. 118. *As* that. 119. *at a clap* at one stroke. 120. *shake my manhood*
i.e., with tears. 121. *perforce* involuntarily, against my will. 122. *untented woundings*
wounds too deep to be probed with a tent (roll of lint). 123. *fond* foolish. 124. *Beweep* if you
weep over. 125. *loose* (1) let loose (2) lose, as of no avail. 126. *temper* mix with and soften.
127. *comfortable* ready to comfort. 128. *shape* i.e., kingly role. 129. *I cannot . . . you* i.e.,
even though my love inclines me to you, I must protest. 130. *Fool* (1) the Fool himself (2) the
epithet or character of "fool" 131, 132. *halter, after* pronounced "hauter," "auter."

'Tis politic[133] and safe to let him keep
At point[134] a hundred knights: yes, that on every dream,
Each buzz,[135] each fancy, each complaint, dislike,
He may enguard[136] his dotage with their pow'rs
And hold our lives in mercy.[137] Oswald, I say!   295

ALBANY: Well, you may fear too far.

GONERIL: Safer than trust too far.
Let me still take away the harms I fear,
Not fear still to be taken.[138] I know his heart.
What he hath uttered I have writ my sister.
If she sustain him and his hundred knights,   300
When I have showed th' unfitness —

(*Enter* OSWALD.)

                                    How now, Oswald?
What, have you writ that letter to my sister?

OSWALD: Ay, madam.

GONERIL: Take you some company,[139] and away to horse.
Inform her full of my particular[140] fear,   305
And thereto add such reasons of your own
As may compact[141] it more. Get you gone,
And hasten your return. (*Exit* OSWALD.) No, no, my lord,
This milky gentleness and course[142] of yours
Though I condemn not,[143] yet under pardon,   310
You are much more attasked[144] for want of wisdom
Than praised for harmful mildness.[145]

ALBANY: How far your eyes may pierce I cannot tell;
Striving to better, oft we mar what's well.

GONERIL: Nay then —   315

ALBANY: Well, well, th' event.[146] (*Exeunt.*)

Scene V.

(*Court before the same.*)

(*Enter* LEAR, KENT, *and* FOOL.)

133. *politic* good policy. 134. *At point* armed. 135. *buzz* rumor. 136. *enguard* protect. 137. *in mercy* at his mercy. 138. *Not . . . taken* rather than remain fearful of being overtaken by them. 139. *company* escort. 140. *particular* own. 141. *compact* strengthen. 142. *milky . . . course* mild and gentle way (hendiadys). 143. *condemn not* condemn it not. 144. *attasked* taken to task, blamed. 145. *harmful mildness* dangerous indulgence. 146. *th' event* i.e., we'll see what happens.

LEAR: Go you before to Gloucester with these letters. Acquaint my daughter no further with anything you know than comes from her demand out of the letter.[1] If your diligence be not speedy, I shall be there afore you.

KENT: I will not sleep, my lord, till I have delivered your letter. (*Exit.*)   5

FOOL: If a man's brains were in's heels, were't[2] not in danger of kibes?[3]

LEAR: Ay, boy.

FOOL: Then I prithee be merry. Thy wit shall not go slipshod.[4]

LEAR: Ha, ha, ha.

FOOL: Shalt[5] see thy other daughter will use thee kindly;[6] for though she's   10
as like this as a crab's[7] like an apple, yet I can tell what I can tell.

LEAR: Why, what canst thou tell, my boy?

FOOL: She will taste as like this as a crab does to a crab. Thou cans't tell why one's nose stands i' th' middle on's[8] face?

LEAR: No.   15

FOOL: Why, to keep one's eyes of[9] either side's nose, that what a man cannot smell out, he may spy into.

LEAR: I did her wrong.

FOOL: Canst tell how an oyster makes his shell?

LEAR: No.   20

FOOL: Nor I neither; but I can tell why a snail has a house.

LEAR: Why?

FOOL: Why, to put's head in; not to give it away to his daughters, and leave his horns[10] without a case.

LEAR: I will forget my nature.[11] So kind a father! Be my horses ready?   25

FOOL: Thy asses are gone about 'em. The reason why the seven stars[12] are no moe[13] than seven is a pretty[14] reason.

LEAR: Because they are not eight.

FOOL: Yes indeed. Thou wouldst make a good fool.

LEAR: To take't again perforce![15] Monster ingratitude!   30

I.v. **1.** *than . . . letter* than her reading of the letter brings her to ask. **2.** *were't* i.e., the brains. **3.** *kibes* chilblains. **4.** *Thy . . . slipshod* Your brains shall not go in slippers (because you have no brains to be protected from chilblains). **5.** *Shalt* thou shalt. **6.** *kindly* (1) affectionately (2) after her kind or nature. **7.** *crab* crab apple. **8.** *on's* of his. **9.** *of* on. **10.** *horns* (1) snail's horns (2) cuckold's horns. **11.** *nature* paternal instincts. **12.** *seven stars* the Pleiades. **13.** *moe* more. **14.** *pretty* apt. **15.** *To . . . perforce* (1) of Goneril, who has forcibly taken away Lear's privileges; or (2) of Lear, who meditates a forcible resumption of authority

FOOL: If thou wert my fool, nuncle, I'd have thee beaten for being old before thy time.

LEAR: How's that?

FOOL: Thou shouldst not have been old till thou hadst been wise.

LEAR: O, let me not be mad, not mad, sweet heaven! 35
Keep me in temper;[16] I would not be mad!

(*Enter* GENTLEMAN.)

How now, are the horses ready?

GENTLEMAN: Ready, my lord.

LEAR: Come, boy.

FOOL: She that's a maid now, and laughs at my departure, 40
Shall not be a maid long, unless things be cut shorter.[17]

(*Exeunt.*)

Act II

Scene I.

(*The Earl of Gloucester's castle.*)

(*Enter* EDMUND *and* CURAN, *severally*[1])

EDMUND: Save[2] thee, Curan.

CURAN: And you, sir. I have been with your father, and given him notice that the Duke of Cornwall and Regan his duchess will be here with him this night.

EDMUND: How comes that? 5

CURAN: Nay, I know not. You have heard of the news abroad? I mean the whispered ones, for they are yet but ear-kissing arguments.[3]

EDMUND: Not I. Pray you, what are they?

CURAN: Have you heard of no likely[4] wars toward,[5] 'twixt the Dukes of Cornwall and Albany? 10

EDMUND: Not a word.

16. *in temper* sane. 17. *She . . . shorter* The maid who laughs, missing the tragic implications of this quarrel, will not have sense enough to preserve her virginity ("things" = penises). **II.i. 1. s.d.** *severally* separately (from different entrances onstage). **2.** *Save* God save. **3.** *ear-kissing arguments* subjects whispered in the ear. **4.** *likely* probable. **5.** *toward* impending.

CURAN: You may do, then, in time. Fare you well, sir. (*Exit.*)

EDMUND: The duke be here tonight? The better![6] best!
    This weaves itself perforce[7] into my business.
    My father hath set guard to take my brother,   15
    And I have one thing of a queasy question[8]
    Which I must act. Briefness[9] and Fortune, work!
    Brother, a word; descend. Brother, I say!

(*Enter* EDGAR.)

    My father watches. O sir, fly this place.
    Intelligence[10] is given where you are hid.   20
    You have now the good advantage of the night.
    Have you not spoken 'gainst the Duke of Cornwall?
    He's coming hither, now i' th' night, i' th' haste,[11]
    And Regan with him. Have you nothing said
    Upon his party[12] 'gainst the Duke of Albany?   25
    Advise yourself.[13]

EDGAR: I am sure on't,[14] not a word.

EDMUND: I hear my father coming. Pardon me:
    In cunning[15] I must draw my sword upon you.
    Draw, seem to defend yourself; now quit you[16] well.
    Yield! Come before my father! Light ho, here!   30
    Fly, brother. Torches, torches! — So farewell.

(*Exit* EDGAR.)

    Some blood drawn on me would beget opinion[17]

(*Wounds his arm.*)

    Of my more fierce endeavor. I have seen drunkards
    Do more than this in sport. Father, father!
    Stop, stop! No help?   35

(*Enter* GLOUCESTER, *and* SERVANTS *with torches.*)

GLOUCESTER: Now, Edmund, where's the villain?

EDMUND: Here stood he in the dark, his sharp sword out,
    Mumbling of wicked charms, conjuring the moon
    To stand auspicious mistress.

GLOUCESTER: But where is he?

EDMUND: Look, sir, I bleed.

---

6. *The better* So much the better.   7. *perforce* necessarily.   8. *of . . . question* that requires delicate handling (to be "queasy" is to be on the point of vomiting).   9. *Briefness* speed.   10. *Intelligence* information.   11. *i' th' haste* in great haste.   12. *Upon his party* censuring his enmity.   13. *Advise yourself* Reflect.   14. *on't* of it.   15. *In cunning* as a pretense.   16. *quit you* acquaint yourself.   17. *beget opinion* create the impression.

GLOUCESTER: Where is the villain, Edmund?   40

EDMUND: Fled this way, sir, when by no means he could —

GLOUCESTER: Pursue him, ho! Go after. (*Exeunt some* SERVANTS.) By no
    means what?

EDMUND: Persuade me to the murder of your lordship;
    But that I told him the revenging gods
    'Gainst parricides did all the thunder bend;[18]   45
    Spoke with how manifold and strong a bond
    The child was bound to th' father. Sir, in fine[19]
    Seeing how loathly opposite[20] I stood
    To his unnatural purpose, in fell[21] motion[22]
    With his preparèd sword he charges home   50
    My unprovided[23] body, latched[24] mine arm;
    But when he saw my best alarumed[25] spirits
    Bold in the quarrel's right,[26] roused to th' encounter,
    Or whether gasted[27] by the noise I made,
    Full suddenly he fled.

GLOUCESTER: Let him fly far.   55
    Not in this land shall he remain uncaught;
    And found — dispatch.[28] The noble duke my master,
    My worthy arch[29] and patron, comes tonight.
    By his authority I will proclaim it,
    That he which finds him shall deserve our thanks,   60
    Bringing the murderous coward to the stake.
    He that conceals him, death.[30]

EDMUND: When I dissuaded him from his intent,
    And found him pight[31] to do it, with curst[32] speech
    I threatened to discover[33] him. He replied,   65
    Thou unpossessing[34] bastard, dost thou think,
    If I would stand against thee, would the reposal[35]
    Of any trust, virtue, or worth in thee
    Make thy words faithed?[36] No. What I should deny —
    As this I would, ay, though thou didst produce   70
    My very character[37] — I'd turn it all
    To thy suggestion,[38] plot, and damnèd practice.[39]
    And thou must make a dullard of the world,[40]
    If they not thought[41] the profits of my death

18. *bend* aim. **19.** *in fine* finally. **20.** *loathly opposite* bitterly opposed. **21.** *fell* deadly. **22.** *motion* thrust (a term from fencing). **23.** *unprovided* unprotected. **24.** *latched* wounded (lanced). **25.** *best alarumed* wholly aroused. **26.** *Bold . . . right* confident in the rightness of my cause. **27.** *gasted* struck aghast. **28.** *dispatch* i.e., he will be killed. **29.** *arch* chief. **30.** *death* the same elliptical form that characterizes "dispatch." **31.** *pight* determined. **32.** *curst* angry. **33.** *discover* expose. **34.** *unpossessing* beggarly (landless). **35.** *reposal* placing. **36.** *faithed* believed. **37.** *character* handwriting. **38.** *suggestion* instigation. **39.** *practice* device. **40.** *make . . . world* think everyone stupid. **41.** *not thought* did not think.

Were very pregnant[42] and potential spirits[43]
To make thee seek it."

GLOUCESTER: O strange and fastened[44] villain!
Would he deny his letter, said he? I never got[45] him.

(*Tucket*[46] *within*.)

Hark, the duke's trumpets. I know not why he comes.
All ports[47] I'll bar; the villain shall not 'scape;
The duke must grant me that. Besides, his picture   80
I will send far and near, that all the kingdom
May have due note of him; and of my land,
Loyal and natural[48] boy, I'll work the means
To make thee capable.[49]

(*Enter* CORNWALL, REGAN, *and* ATTENDANTS.)

CORNWALL: How now, my noble friend! Since I came hither,   85
Which I can call but now, I have heard strange news.

REGAN: If it be true, all vengeance comes too short
Which can pursue th' offender. How dost, my lord?

GLOUCESTER: O madam, my old heart is cracked, it's cracked.

REGAN: What, did my father's godson seek your life?   90
He whom my father named, your Edgar?

GLOUCESTER: O lady, lady, shame would have it hid.

REGAN: Was he not companion with the riotous knights
That tended upon my father?

GLOUCESTER: I know not, madam. 'Tis too bad, too bad.   95

EDMUND: Yes, madam, he was of that consort.[50]

REGAN: No marvel then, though he were ill affected.[51]
'Tis they have put[52] him on the old man's death,
To have th' expense and waste[53] of his revenues.
I have this present evening from my sister   100
Been well informed of them, and with such cautions
That, if they come to sojourn at my house,
I'll not be there.

CORNWALL: Nor I, assure thee, Regan.
Edmund, I hear that you have shown your father
A childlike[54] office.

42. *pregnant* teeming with incitement. 43. *potential spirits* powerful evil spirits. 44. *fastened*
hardened. 45. *got* begot. 46. s.d. *Tucket* Cornwall's special trumpet call. 47. *ports* exits, of
whatever sort. 48. *natural* (1) kind (filial) (2) illegitimate. 49. *capable* able to inherit. 50. *consort* company. 51. *ill affected* disposed to evil. 52. *put* set. 53. *expense and
waste* squandering. 54. *childlike* filial.

EDMUND: It was my duty, sir.

GLOUCESTER: He did bewray his practice,[55] and received
    This hurt you see, striving to apprehend him.

CORNWALL: Is he pursued?

GLOUCESTER: Ay, my good lord.

CORNWALL: If he be taken, he shall never more
    Be feared of doing[56] harm. Make your own purpose,
    How in my strength you please.[57] For you, Edmund,
    Whose virtue and obedience[58] doth this instant
    So much commend itself, you shall be ours.
    Natures of such deep trust we shall much need;
    You we first seize on.

EDMUND: I shall serve you, sir,
    Truly, however else.

GLOUCESTER: For him I thank your grace.

CORNWALL: You know not why we came to visit you?

REGAN: Thus out of season, threading dark-eyed night.
    Occasions, noble Gloucester, of some prize,[59]
    Wherein we must have use of your advice.
    Our father he hath writ, so hath our sister,
    Of differences,[60] which[61] I best thought it fit
    To answer from[62] our home. The several messengers
    From hence attend dispatch.[63] Our good old friend,
    Lay comforts to your bosom,[64] and bestow
    Your needful[65] counsel to our businesses,
    Which craves the instant use.[66]

GLOUCESTER: I serve you, madam.
    Your graces are right welcome. (*Exeunt. Flourish.*)

Scene II.

(*Before Gloucester's castle.*)

(*Enter* KENT *and* OSWALD, *severally.*)

OSWALD: Good dawning[1] to thee, friend. Art of this house?[2]

---

55. *bewray his practice* disclose his plot. 56. *of doing* because he might do. 57. *Make . . . please* Use my power freely, in carrying out your plans for his capture. 58. *virtue and obedience* virtuous obedience. 59. *prize* importance. 60. *differences* quarrels. 61. *which* referring not to "differences," but to the letter Lear has written. 62. *from* away from. 63. *attend dispatch* are waiting to be sent off. 64. *Lay . . . bosom* console yourself (about Edgar's supposed treason). 65. *needful* needed. 66. *craves . . . use* demands immediate transaction. **II.ii.** 1. *dawning* dawn is impending, but not yet arrived. 2. *Art . . . house* Do you live here?

KENT: Ay.

OSWALD: Where may we set our horses?

KENT: I' th' mire.

OSWALD: Prithee, if thou lov'st me, tell me. 5

KENT: I love thee not.

OSWALD: Why then, I care not for thee.

KENT: If I had thee in Lipsbury Pinfold,[3] I would make thee care for me.

OSWALD: Why dost thou use me thus? I know thee not.

KENT: Fellow, I know thee. 10

OSWALD: What dost thou know me for?

KENT: A knave, a rascal, an eater of broken meats;[4] a base, proud, shallow, beggarly, three-suited,[5] hundred-pound,[6] filthy worsted-stocking[7] knave; a lily-livered, action-taking,[8] whoreson, glass-gazing,[9] super-serviceable,[10] finical[11] rogue; one-trunk-inheriting[12] slave; one that 15 wouldst be a bawd in way of good service,[13] and art nothing but the composition[14] of a knave, beggar, coward, pander, and the son and heir of a mongrel bitch; one whom I will beat into clamorous whining if thou deniest the least syllable of thy addition.[15]

OSWALD: Why, what a monstrous fellow art thou, thus to rail on one that 20 is neither known of thee nor knows thee!

KENT: What a brazen-faced varlet art thou to deny thou knowest me! Is it two days since I tripped up thy heels and beat thee before the king? (*Drawing his sword.*) Draw, you rogue, for though it be night, yet the moon shines. I'll make a sop o' th' moonshine[16] of you. You 25 whoreson cullionly barbermonger,[17] draw!

OSWALD: Away, I have nothing to do with thee.

KENT: Draw, you rascal. You come with letters against the king, and take Vanity the puppet's[18] part against the royalty of her father. Draw, you rogue, or I'll so carbonado[19] your shanks. Draw, you rascal. 30 Come your ways.[20]

3. *Lipsbury Pinfold* a pound or pen in which strayed animals are enclosed ("Lipsbury" may denote a particular place, or may be slang for "between my teeth"). 4. *broken meats* scraps of food. 5. *three-suited* the wardrobe permitted to a servant or "knave." 6. *hundred-pound* the extent of Oswald's wealth, and thus a sneer at his aspiring to gentility. 7. *worsted-stocking* worn by servants. 8. *action-taking* one who refuses a fight and goes to law instead. 9. *glass-gazing* conceited. 10. *superserviceable* sycophantic, serving without principle. 11. *finical* overfastidious. 12. *one-trunk-inheriting* possessing only a trunkful of goods. 13. *bawd . . . service* pimp, to please his master. 14. *composition* compound. 15. *addition* titles. 16. *sop . . . moonshine* i.e., Oswald will admit the moonlight, and so sop it up, through the open wounds Kent is preparing to give him. 17. *cullionly barbermonger* base patron of hairdressers (effeminate man). 18. *Vanity the puppet's* Goneril, here identified with one of the personified characters in the morality plays, which were sometimes put on as puppet shows. 19. *carbonado* cut across, like a piece of meat before cooking. 20. *Come your ways* Get along!

OSWALD: Help, ho! Murder! Help!

KENT: Strike, you slave! Stand, rogue! Stand, you neat[21] slave! Strike!

(*Beating him.*)

OSWALD: Help, ho! Murder, murder!

(*Enter* EDMUND, *with his rapier drawn,* CORNWALL, REGAN, GLOUCESTER, SERVANTS.)

EDMUND: How now? What's the matter? Part!   35

KENT: With you,[22] goodman boy,[23] if you please! Come, I'll flesh[24] ye, come on, young master.

GLOUCESTER: Weapons? Arms? What's the matter here?

CORNWALL: Keep peace, upon your lives. He dies that strikes again. What is the matter?   40

REGAN: The messengers from our sister and the king.

CORNWALL: What is your difference?[25] Speak.

OSWALD: I am scarce in breath, my lord.

KENT: No marvel, you have so bestirred[26] your valor. You cowardly rascal, nature disclaims in thee.[27] A tailor made thee.[28]   45

CORNWALL: Thou art a strange fellow. A tailor make a man?

KENT: A tailor, sir. A stonecutter or a painter could not have made him so ill, though they had been but two years o' th' trade.

CORNWALL: Speak yet, how grew your quarrel?

OSWALD: This ancient ruffian, sir, whose life I have spared at suit of[29] his   50
gray beard —

KENT: Thou whoreson zed,[30] thou unnecessary letter! My lord, if you will give me leave, I will tread this unbolted[31] villain into mortar and daub the wall of a jakes[32] with him. Spare my gray beard, you wagtail![33]   55

CORNWALL: Peace, sirrah!
You beastly[34] knave, know you no reverence?

KENT: Yes, sir, but anger hath a privilege.

---

21. *neat* (1) foppish (2) unmixed, as in "neat wine." **22.** *With you* i.e., the quarrel is with you. **23.** *goodman boy* young man (peasants are "goodmen"; "boy" is a term of contempt). **24.** *flesh* introduce to blood (term from hunting). **25.** *difference* quarrel. **26.** *bestirred* exercised. **27.** *nature . . . thee* nature renounces any part in you. **28.** *A tailor made thee* from the proverb "The tailor makes the man." **29.** *at suit of* out of pity for. **30.** *zed* the letter Z, generally omitted in contemporary dictionaries. **31.** *unbolted* unsifted, i.e., altogether a villain. **32.** *jakes* privy. **33.** *wagtail* a bird that bobs its tail up and down, and thus suggests obsequiousness. **34.** *beastly* irrational.

CORNWALL: Why art thou angry?

KENT: That such a slave as this should wear a sword, 60
    Who wears no honesty. Such smiling rogues as these,
    Like rats, oft bite the holy cords[35] atwain
    Which are too intrince[36] t' unloose; smooth[37] every passion
    That in the natures of their lords rebel,
    Being oil to fire, snow to the colder moods; 65
    Renege,[38] affirm, and turn their halcyon beaks[39]
    With every gale and vary[40] of their masters,
    Knowing naught, like dogs, but following.
    A plague upon your epileptic[41] visage!
    Smile you[42] my speeches, as I were a fool? 70
    Goose, if I had you upon Sarum Plain,[43]
    I'd drive ye cackling home to Camelot.[44]

CORNWALL: What, art thou mad, old fellow?

GLOUCESTER: How fell you out? Say that.

KENT: No contraries[45] hold more antipathy 75
    Than I and such a knave.

CORNWALL: Why dost thou call him knave? What is his fault?

KENT: His countenance likes[46] me not.

CORNWALL: No more perchance does mine, nor his, nor hers.

KENT: Sir, 'tis my occupation to be plain: 80
    I have seen better faces in my time
    Than stands on any shoulder that I see
    Before me at this instant.

CORNWALL: This is some fellow
    Who, having been praised for bluntness, doth affect
    A saucy roughness, and constrains the garb 85
    Quite from his nature.[47] He cannot flatter, he;
    An honest mind and plain, he must speak truth.
    And[48] they will take it, so; if not, he's plain.
    These kind of knaves I know, which in this plainness
    Harbor more craft and more corrupter ends 90

---

35. *holy cords* sacred bonds of affection (as between husbands and wives, parents and children).
36. *intrince* entangled, intricate. 37. *smooth* appease. 38. *Renege* deny. 39. *halcyon beaks* the halcyon or kingfisher serves here as a type of the opportunist because, when hung up by the tail or neck, it was supposed to turn with the wind, like a weathervane. 40. *gale and vary* varying gale (hendiadys). 41. *epileptic* distorted by grinning. 42. *Smile you* do you smile at. 43. *Sarum Plain* Salisbury Plain. 44. *Camelot* the residence of King Arthur (presumably a particular point, now lost, is intended here). 45. *contraries* opposites. 46. *likes* pleases. 47. *constrains . . . nature* forces the manner of candid speech to be a cloak, not for candor but for craft. 48. *And* if.

Than twenty silly-duckling observants[49]
That stretch their duties nicely.[50]

KENT: Sir, in good faith, in sincere verity,
Under th' allowance[51] of your great aspect,[52]
Whose influence,[53] like the wreath of radiant fire   95
On flick'ring Phoebus' front[54] —

CORNWALL: What mean'st by this?

KENT: To go out of my dialect,[55] which you discommend so much. I know,
sir, I am no flatterer. He[56] that beguiled you in a plain accent was a
plain knave, which, for my part, I will not be, though I should win
your displeasure to entreat me to't.[57]   100

CORNWALL: What was th' offense you gave him?

OSWALD: I never gave him any.
It pleased the king his master very late[58]
To strike at me, upon his misconstruction;[59]
When he, compact,[60] and flattering his displeasure,   105
Tripped me behind; being down, insulted, railed,
And put upon him such a deal of man[61]
That worthied him,[62] got praises of the king
For him attempting who was self-subdued;[63]
And, in the fleshment[64] of this dread exploit,   110
Drew on me here again.

KENT: None of these rogues and cowards
But Ajax is their fool.[65]

CORNWALL: Fetch forth the stocks!
You stubborn[66] ancient knave, you reverent[67] braggart,
We'll teach you.

KENT: Sir, I am too old to learn.
Call not your stocks for me, I serve the king,   115
On whose employment I was sent to you.
You shall do small respect, show too bold malice

49. *silly-ducking observants* ridiculously obsequious attendants. 50. *nicely* punctiliously. 51. *allowance* approval. 52. *aspect* (1) appearance (2) position of the heavenly bodies. 53. *influence* astrological power. 54. *Phoebus' front* forehead of the sun. 55. *dialect* customary manner of speaking. 56. *He* i.e., the sort of candid-crafty man Cornwall has been describing. 57. *though . . . to't* even if I were to succeed in bringing your graceless person ("displeasure" personified, and in lieu of the expected form, "your grace") to beg me to be a plain knave. 58. *very late* recently. 59. *misconstruction* misunderstanding. 60. *compact* in league with the king. 61. *put . . . man.* pretended such manly behavior. 62. *worthied him* made him seem heroic. 63. *For . . . self-subdued* for attacking a man (Oswald) who offered no resistance. 64. *fleshment* the blood-thirstiness excited by his first success or "fleshing." 65. *None . . . fool* i.e., cowardly rogues like Oswald always impose on fools like Cornwall (who is likened to Ajax: [1] the braggart Greek warrior [2] a jakes or privy). 66. *stubborn* rude. 67. *reverent* old.

Against the grace and person[68] of my master,
Stocking his messenger.

CORNWALL: Fetch forth the stocks. As I have life and honor, 120
There shall he sit till noon.

REGAN: Till noon? Till night, my lord, and all night too.

KENT: Why, madam, if I were your father's dog,
You should not use me so.

REGAN: Sir, being his knave, I will.

CORNWALL: This is a fellow of the selfsame color[69] 125
Our sister speaks of. Come, bring away[70] the stocks.

(*Stocks brought out.*)

GLOUCESTER: Let me beseech your grace not to do so.
His fault is much, and the good king his master
Will check[71] him for't. Your purposed[72] low correction
Is such as basest and contemnèd'st[73] wretches 130
For pilf'rings and most common trespasses
Are punished with.
The king his master needs must take it ill
That he, so slightly valued in[74] his messenger,
Should have him thus restrained.

CORNWALL: I'll answer[75] that. 135

REGAN: My sister may receive it much more worse,
To have her gentleman abused, assaulted,
For following her affairs. Put in his legs.
(KENT *is put in the stocks.*)

Come, my good lord, away!

(*Exeunt all but* GLOUCESTER *and* KENT.)

GLOUCESTER: I am sorry for thee, friend. 'Tis the duke's pleasure, 140
Whose disposition[76] all the world well knows
Will not be rubbed[77] nor stopped. I'll entreat for thee.

KENT: Pray do not, sir. I have watched[78] and traveled hard.
Some time I shall sleep out, the rest I'll whistle.
A good man's fortune may grow out at heels.[79] 145
Give[80] you good morrow.

GLOUCESTER: The duke's to blame in this. 'Twill be ill taken.[81] (*Exit.*)

68. *grace and person* i.e., Lear as sovereign and in his personal character. **69.** *color* kind. **70.** *away* out. **71.** *check* correct. **72.** *purposed* intended. **73.** *contemnèd'st* most despised. **74.** *slightly valued in* little honored in the person of. **75.** *answer* answer for. **76.** *disposition* inclination. **77.** *rubbed* diverted (metaphor from the game of bowls). **78.** *watched* gone without sleep. **79.** *A . . . heels* Even a good man may have bad fortune. **80.** *Give* God give. **81.** *taken* received.

KENT: Good king, that must approve⁸² the common saw,⁸³
        Thou out of heaven's benediction com'st
        To the warm sun.⁸⁴   150
        Approach, thou beacon to this under globe,⁸⁵
        That by thy comfortable⁸⁶ beams I may
        Peruse this letter. Nothing almost sees miracles
        But misery.⁸⁷ I know 'tis from Cordelia,
        Who hath most fortunately been informed   155
        Of my obscurèd⁸⁸ course. And shall find time
        From this enormous state, seeking to give
        Losses their remedies.⁸⁹ All weary and o'erwatched,
        Take vantage,⁹⁰ heavy eyes, not to behold
        This shameful lodging. Fortune, good night;   160
        Smile once more, turn thy wheel.⁹¹

(*Sleeps.*)

Scene III.

(*A wood.*)

(*Enter* EDGAR.)

EDGAR: I heard myself proclaimed,
        And by the happy¹ hollow of a tree
        Escaped the hunt. No port is free, no place
        That guard and most unusual vigilance
        Does not attend my taking.² Whiles I may 'scape,   5
        I will preserve myself; and am bethought³
        To take the basest and most poorest shape
        That ever penury, in contempt of man,
        Brought near to beast,⁴ my face I'll grime with filth,
        Blanket my loins, elf⁵ all my hairs in knots,   10
        And with presented⁶ nakedness outface⁷
        The winds and persecutions of the sky.
        The country gives me proof⁸ and precedent
        Of Bedlam⁹ beggars, who, with roaring voices,

---

82. *approve* confirm. **83.** *saw* proverb. **84.** *Thou . . . sun* i.e., Lear goes from better to worse, from heaven's blessing or shelter to lack of shelter. **85.** *beacon . . . globe* i.e., the sun, whose rising Kent anticipates. **86.** *comfortable* comforting. **87.** *Nothing . . . misery* i.e., True perception belongs only to the wretched. **88.** *obscurèd* disguised. **89.** *shall . . . remedies* a possible reading: Cordelia, away from this monstrous state of things, will find occasion to right the wrongs we suffer. **90.** *vantage* advantage (of sleep). **91.** *turn thy wheel* i.e., so that Kent, who is at the bottom, may climb upward. **II.iii. 1.** *happy* lucky. **2.** *attend my taking* watch to capture me. **3.** *am bethought* have decided. **4.** *penury . . . beast* poverty, to show how contemptible man is, reduced to the level of a beast. **5.** *Blanket* cover only with a blanket; *elf* tangle (into "elflocks," supposed to be caused by elves). **6.** *presented* the show of. **7.** *outface* brave. **8.** *proof* example. **9.** *Bedlam* see I.ii.118.

Strike[10] in their numbed and mortified[11] bare arms   15
Pins, wooden pricks,[12] nails, sprigs of rosemary;
And with this horrible object[13] from low[14] farms,
Poor pelting[15] villages, sheepcotes, and mills,
Sometimes with lunatic bans,[16] sometime with prayers,
Enforce their charity. Poor Turlygod, Poor Tom,[17]   20
That's something yet: Edgar I nothing am.[18] (*Exit.*)

Scene IV.

(*Before Gloucester's castle.* KENT *in the stocks.*)

(*Enter* LEAR, FOOL, *and* GENTLEMAN.)

LEAR: 'Tis strange that they should so depart from home,
And not send back my messenger.

GENTLEMAN: As I learned,
The night before there was no purpose[1] in them
Of this remove.[2]

KENT: Hail to thee, noble master.

LEAR: Ha!   5
Mak'st thou this shame thy pastime?[3]

KENT: No, my lord.

FOOL: Ha, ha, he wears cruel[4] garters. Horses are tied by the heads, dogs
and bears by th' neck, monkeys by th' loins, and men by th' legs.
When a man's overlusty at legs,[5] then he wears wooden nether-
stocks.[6]   10

LEAR: What's he that hath so much thy place mistook
To set thee here?

KENT: It is both he and she,
Your son and daughter.

LEAR: No.

KENT: Yes.   15

LEAR: No, I say.

---

10. *Strike* stick. **11.** *mortified* not alive to pain. **12.** *pricks* skewers. **13.** *object* spectacle. **14.** *low* humble. **15.** *pelting* paltry. **16.** *bans* curses. **17.** *Poor . . . Tom* Edgar recites
the names a Bedlam beggar gives himself. **18.** *That's . . . am* There's a chance for me in that I
am no longer known for myself. **II.iv. 1.** *purpose* intention. **2.** *remove* removal. **3.** *Mak'st
. . . pastime* Are you doing this to amuse yourself? **4.** *cruel* (1) painful (2) "crewel," a worsted
yarn used in garters. **5.** *overlusty at legs* (1) a vagabond (2) sexually promiscuous (?)
6. *netherstocks* stockings (as opposed to knee breeches, or upperstocks).

KENT: I say yea.

LEAR: No, no, they would not.

KENT: Yes, they have.

LEAR: By Jupiter, I swear no! 20

KENT: By Juno, I swear ay!

LEAR: They durst not do't;
They could not, would not do't. 'Tis worse than murder
To do upon respect[7] such violent outrage.
Resolve[8] me with all modest[9] haste which way
Thou mightst deserve or they impose this usage, 25
Coming from us.

KENT: My lord, when at their home
I did commend[10] your highness' letters to them,
Ere I was risen from the place that showed
My duty kneeling, came there a reeking post,[11]
Stewed[12] in his haste, half breathless, panting forth 30
From Goneril his mistress salutations,
Delivered letters, spite of intermission,[13]
Which presently[14] they read; on[15] whose contents
They summoned up their meiny,[16] straight took horse,
Commanded me to follow and attend 35
The leisure of their answer, gave me cold looks,
And meeting here the other messenger,
Whose welcome I perceived had poisoned mine,
Being the very fellow which of late
Displayed[17] so saucily against your highness, 40
Having more man than wit[18] about me, drew;
He raised[19] the house, with loud and coward cries.
Your son and daughter found this trespass worth[20]
The shame which here it suffers.

FOOL: Winter's not gone yet, if the wild geese fly that way.[21] 45
      Fathers that wear rags
        Do make their children blind,[22]
      But fathers that bear bags[23]
        Shall see their children kind.
      Fortune, that arrant whore, 50

7. *upon respect* (1) on the respect due to the king (2) deliberately. 8. *Resolve* inform. 9. *modest* becoming. 10. *commend* deliver. 11. *reeking post* sweating messenger. 12. *stewed* steaming. 13. *spite of intermission* in spite of the interrupting of my business. 14. *presently* at once. 15. *on* on the strength of. 16. *meiny* retinue. 17. *Displayed* showed off. 18. *more ... wit* more manhood than sense. 19. *raised* aroused. 20. *worth* deserving. 21. *Winter's ... way* More trouble is to come, since Cornwall and Regan act so ("geese" is used contemptuously as in Kent's quarrel with Oswald, II.ii.71-72). 22. *blind* i.e., indifferent. 23. *bags* moneybags.

Ne'er turns the key[24] to th' poor.
But for all this, thou shalt have as many dolors[25] for thy daughters as thou canst tell[26] in a year.

LEAR: O, how this mother swells up toward my heart!
Hysterica passio,[27] down, thou climbing sorrow,   55
Thy element's[28] below. Where is this daughter?

KENT: With the earl, sir, here within.

LEAR: Follow me not;
Stay here. (*Exit.*)

GENTLEMAN: Made you no more offense but what you speak of?

KENT: None.   60
How chance[29] the king comes with so small a number?

FOOL: And[30] thou hadst been set i' th' stocks for that question, thou'dst well deserved it.

KENT: Why, Fool?

FOOL: We'll set thee to school to an ant, to teach thee there's no laboring   65
i' th' winter.[31] All that follow their noses are led by their eyes but
blind men, and there's not a nose among twenty but can smell him
that's stinking.[32] Let go thy hold when a great wheel runs down a
hill, lest it break thy neck with following. But the great one that
goes upward, let him draw thee after. When a wise man gives thee   70
better counsel, give me mine again. I would have none but knaves
follow it since a fool gives it.
    That sir, which serves and seeks for gain,
        And follows but for form,[33]
    Will pack,[34] when it begins to rain,   75
        And leave thee in the storm.
    But I will tarry; the Fool will stay,
        And let the wise man fly.
    The knave turns Fool that runs away,
        The Fool no knave,[35] perdy.[36]   80

KENT: Where learned you this, Fool?

FOOL: Not i' th' stocks, fool.

---

24. *turns the key* i.e., opens the door. 25. *dolors* (1) sorrows (2) dollars (English name for Spanish and German coins). 26. *tell* (1) tell about (2) count. 27. *mother . . . Hysterica passio* hysteria, causing suffocation or choking. 28. *element* proper place. 29. *How chance* how does it happen that. 30. *And* if. 31. *We'll . . . winter* in the popular fable the ant, unlike the improvident grasshopper, anticipates the winter when none can labor by laying up provisions in the summer; Lear, trusting foolishly to summer days, finds himself unprovided for, and unable to provide, now that "winter" has come. 32. *All . . . stinking* i.e., all can smell out the decay of Lear's fortunes. 33. *form* show. 34. *pack* be off. 35. *The . . . knave* i.e., the faithless man is the true fool, for wisdom requires fidelity; Lear's Fool, who remains faithful, is at least no knave. 36. *perdy* by God (French *par Dieu*).

(*Enter* LEAR *and* GLOUCESTER.)

LEAR: Deny[37] to speak with me? They are sick, they are weary,
They have traveled all the night? Mere fetches,[38]
The images[39] of revolt and flying off![40]   85
Fetch me a better answer.

GLOUCESTER: My dear lord,
You know the fiery quality[41] of the duke,
How unremovable and fixed he is
In his own course.

LEAR: Vengeance, plague, death, confusion!
Fiery? What quality? Why, Gloucester, Gloucester,   90
I'd speak with the Duke of Cornwall and his wife.

GLOUCESTER: Well, my good lord, I have informed them so.

LEAR: Informed them? Dost thou understand me, man?

GLOUCESTER: Ay, my good lord.

LEAR: The king would speak with Cornwall. The dear father   95
Would with his daughter speak, commands — tends[42] — service.
Are they informed of this? My breath and blood!
Fiery? The fiery duke, tell the hot duke that —
No, but not yet. May be he is not well.
Infirmity doth still neglect all office   100
Whereto our health is bound.[43] We are not ourselves
When nature, being oppressed, commands the mind
To suffer with the body. I'll forbear;
And am fallen out[44] with my more headier will[45]
To take the indisposed and sickly fit   105
For the sound man. (*Looking on* KENT.) Death on my state![46]
    Wherefore
Should he sit here? This act persuades me
That this remotion[47] of the duke and her
Is practice[48] only. Give me my servant forth.[49]
Go tell the duke and's wife I'd speak with them!   110
Now, presently![50] Bid them come forth and hear me,
Or at their chamber door I'll beat the drum
Till it cry sleep to death.[51]

GLOUCESTER: I would have all well betwixt you. (*Exit.*)

37. *Deny* refuse. 38. *fetches* subterfuges, acts of tacking (nautical metaphor). 39. *images* exact likenesses. 40. *flying off* desertion. 41. *quality* temperament. 42. *tends* attends (i.e., awaits); with, possibly, an ironic second meaning, "tenders," or "offers." 43. *Whereto* ... *bound* duties which we are required to perform, when in health. 44. *fallen out* angry. 45. *headier will* headlong inclination. 46. *state* royal condition. 47. *remotion* (1) removal (2) remaining aloof. 48. *practice* pretense. 49. *forth* i.e., out of the stocks. 50. *presently* at once. 51. *cry* ... *death* follow sleep, like a cry or pack of hounds, until it kills it.

LEAR: O me, my heart, my rising heart! But down! 115

FOOL: Cry to it, nuncle, as the cockney[52] did to the eels when she put 'em
i' th' paste[53] alive. She knapped[54] 'em o' th' coxcombs[55] with a stick
and cried, "Down, wantons,[56] down!" 'Twas her brother that, in
pure kindness to his horse, buttered his hay.[57]

(*Enter* CORNWALL, REGAN, GLOUCESTER, SERVANTS.)

LEAR: Good morrow to you both.

CORNWALL: Hail to your grace. 120

(KENT *here set at liberty.*)

REGAN: I am glad to see your highness.

LEAR: Regan, I think you are. I know what reason
I have to think so. If thou shouldst not be glad,
I would divorce me from thy mother's tomb,
Sepulchring an adultress.[58] (*To* KENT.) O, are you free? 125
Some other time for that. Beloved Regan,
Thy sister's naught.[59] O Regan, she hath tied
Sharp-toothed unkindness, like a vulture, here.

(*Points to his heart.*)

I can scarce speak to thee. Thou'lt not believe
With how depraved a quality[60] — O Regan! 130

REGAN: I pray you, sir, take patience. I have hope.
You less know how to value her desert
Than she to scant her duty.[61]

LEAR: Say? how is that?

REGAN: I cannot think my sister in the least
Would fail her obligation. If, sir, perchance 135
She have restrained the riots of your followers,
'Tis on such ground, and to such wholesome end,
As clears her from all blame.

LEAR: My curses on her!

REGAN: O, sir, you are old,
Nature in you stands on the very verge 140
Of his confine.[62] You should be ruled, and led

52. *cockney* Londoner (ignorant city dweller). 53. *paste* pastry pie. 54. *knapped*
rapped. 55. *coxcombs* heads. 56. *wantons* i.e., playful things (with a sexual implication). 57. *buttered his hay* i.e., the city dweller does from ignorance what the dishonest
ostler does from craft: greases the hay the traveler has paid for, so that the horse will not
eat. 58. *divorce . . . adultress* i.e., repudiate your dead mother as having conceived you by
another man. 59. *naught* wicked. 60. *quality* nature. 61. *I have . . . duty* despite the double
negative, the passage means, "I believe that you fail to give Goneril her due, rather than that
she fails to fulfill her duty." 62. *Nature . . . confine* i.e., you are nearing the end of your life.

By some discretion that discerns your state
Better than you yourself.[63] Therefore I pray you
That to our sister you do make return,
Say you have wronged her.

LEAR: Ask her forgiveness?   145
Do you but mark how this becomes the house:[64]
"Dear daughter, I confess that I am old.

(*Kneeling.*)

Age is unnecessary. On my knees I beg
That you'll vouchsafe me raiment, bed, and food."

REGAN: Good sir, no more. These are unsightly tricks.   150
Return you to my sister!

LEAR: (*Rising.*) Never, Regan.
She hath abated[65] me of half my train,
Looked black upon me, struck me with her tongue,
Most serpentlike, upon the very heart.
All the stored vengeances of heaven fall   155
On her ingrateful top![66] Strike her young bones,[67]
You taking[68] airs, with lameness.

CORNWALL: Fie, sir, fie!

LEAR: You nimble lightnings, dart your blinding flames
Into her scornful eyes! Infect her beauty,
You fen-sucked[69] fogs, drawn by the pow'rful sun,   160
To fall and blister[70] her pride.

REGAN: O the blest gods!
So will you wish on me when the rash mood is on.

LEAR: No, Regan, thou shalt never have my curse.
Thy tender-hefted[71] nature shall not give
Thee o'er to harshness. Her eyes are fierce, but thine   165
Do comfort, and not burn. 'Tis not in thee
To grudge my pleasures, to cut off my train,
To bandy[72] hasty words, to scant my sizes,[73]
And, in conclusion, to oppose the bolt[74]
Against my coming in. Thou better know'st   170
The offices of nature, bonds of childhood,[75]
Effects[76] of courtesy, dues of gratitude.

63. *some . . . yourself* some. discreet person who understands your condition more than you do.
64. *becomes the house* suits my royal and paternal position. 65. *abated* curtailed. 66. *top* head. 67. *young bones* the reference may be to unborn children, rather than to Goneril herself. 68. *taking* infecting. 69. *fen-sucked* drawn up from the swamps by the sun. 70. *fall and blister* fall upon and raise blisters. 71. *tender-hefted* gently framed. 72. *bandy* volley (metaphor from tennis). 73. *scant my sizes* reduce my allowances. 74. *oppose the bolt* bar the door. 75. *offices . . . childhood* natural duties, a child's duty to its parent. 76. *Effects* manifestations.

Thy half o' th' kingdom hast thou not forgot,
Wherein I thee endowed.

REGAN: Good sir, to th' purpose.[77]

(*Tucket within.*)

LEAR: Who put my man i' th' stocks?

CORNWALL: What trumpet's that?   175

REGAN: I know't — my sister's. This approves[78] her letter,
That she would soon be here.

(*Enter* OSWALD.)

                              Is your lady come?

LEAR: This is a slave, whose easy borrowed[79] pride
Dwells in the fickle grace[80] of her he follows.
Out, varlet,[81] from my sight.

CORNWALL: What means your grace?   180

LEAR: Who stocked my servant? Regan, I have good hope
Thou didst not know on't.

(*Enter* GONERIL.)

                              Who comes here? O heavens!
If you do love old men, if your sweet sway
Allow[82] obedience, if you yourselves are old,
Make it[83] your cause. Send down, and take my part.   185

(*To* GONERIL.)

Art not ashamed to look upon this beard?
O Regan, will you take her by the hand?

GONERIL: Why not by th' hand, sir? How have I offended?
All's not offense that indiscretion finds[84]
And dotage terms so.

LEAR: O sides,[85] you are too tough!   190
Will you yet hold? How came my man i' th' stocks?

CORNWALL: I set him there, sir; but his own disorders[86]
Deserved much less advancement.[87]

LEAR: You? Did you?

REGAN: I pray you, father, being weak, seem so.[88]

77. *to th' purpose* come to the point. 78. *approves* confirms. 79. *easy borrowed* (1) facile and
taken from another (2) acquired without anything to back it up (like money borrowed without
security). 80. *grace* favor. 81. *varlet* base fellow. 82. *Allow* approve of. 83. *it* my
cause. 84. *finds* judges. 85. *sides* breast. 86. *disorders* misconduct. 87. *advancement* promotion. 88. *seem so* act weak.

If till the expiration of your month   195
You will return and sojourn with my sister,
Dismissing half your train, come then to me.
I am now from home, and out of that provision
Which shall be needful for your entertainment.[89]

LEAR: Return to her, and fifty men dismissed?   200
No, rather I abjure all roofs, and choose
To wage[90] against the enmity o' th' air,
To be a comrade with the wolf and owl,
Necessity's sharp pinch.[91] Return with her?
Why, the hot-blooded[92] France, that dowerless took   205
Our youngest born, I could as well be brought
To knee[93] his throne, and, squirelike,[94] pension beg
To keep base life afoot. Return with her?
Persuade me rather to be slave and sumpter[95]
To this detested groom. (*Pointing at* OSWALD.)

GONERIL: At your choice, sir.   210

LEAR: I prithee, daughter, do not make me mad.
I will not trouble thee, my child; farewell.
We'll no more meet, no more see one another.
But yet thou art my flesh, my blood, my daughter,
Or rather a disease that's in my flesh,   215
Which I must needs call mine. Thou art a boil,
A plague-sore, or embossèd carbuncle[96]
In my corrupted blood. But I'll not chide thee.
Let shame come when it will, I do not call it.
I do not bid the Thunder-bearer[97] shoot,   220
Nor tell tales of thee to high-judging[98] Jove.
Mend when thou canst, be better at thy leisure,
I can be patient, I can stay with Regan,
I and my hundred knights.

REGAN: Not altogether so.
I looked not for you yet, nor am provided   225
For your fit welcome. Give ear, sir, to my sister,
For those that mingle reason with your passion[99]
Must be content to think you old, and so —
But she knows what she does.

LEAR: Is this well spoken?

REGAN: I dare avouch[100] it, sir. What, fifty followers?   230

89. *entertainment* maintenance. 90. *wage* fight. 91. *Necessity's sharp pinch* a summing up of
the hard choice he has just announced. 92. *hot-blooded* passionate. 93. *knee* kneel
before. 94. *squirelike* like a retainer. 95. *sumpter* pack horse. 96. *embossed carbuncle*
swollen boil. 97. *Thunder-bearer* Jupiter. 98. *high-judging* (1) supreme (2) judging from
heaven. 99. *mingle . . . passion* i.e., consider your turbulent behavior coolly and reasonably. 100. *avouch* swear by.

Is it not well? What should you need of more?
Yea, or so many, sith that[101] both charge[102] and danger
Speak 'gainst so great a number? How in one house
Should many people, under two commands,
Hold[103] amity? 'Tis hard, almost impossible.   235

GONERIL: Why might not you, my lord, receive attendance
From those that she calls servants, or from mine?

REGAN: Why not, my lord? If then they chanced to slack[104] ye,
We could control them. If you will come to me
(For now I spy a danger), I entreat you   240
To bring but five-and-twenty. To no more
Will I give place or notice.[105]

LEAR: I gave you all.

REGAN: And in good time you gave it.

LEAR: Made you my guardians, my depositaries,[106]
But kept a reservation[107] to be followed   245
With such a number. What, must I come to you
With five-and-twenty? Regan, said you so?

REGAN: And speak't again, my lord. No more with me.

LEAR: Those wicked creatures yet do look well-favored[108]
When others are more wicked; not being the worst   250
Stands in some rank of praise.[109] (*To* GONERIL.) I'll go with thee.
Thy fifty yet doth double five-and-twenty,
And thou art twice her love.[110]

GONERIL: Hear me, my lord.
What need you five-and-twenty? ten? or five?
To follow[111] in a house where twice so many   255
Have a command to tend you?

REGAN: What need one?

LEAR: O reason[112] not the need! Our basest beggars
Are in the poorest thing superfluous.[113]
Allow not nature more than nature needs,[114]
Man's life is cheap as beast's. Thou art a lady: 260
If only to go warm were gorgeous,
Why, nature needs not what thou gorgeous wear'st,

---

101. *sith that* since. 102. *charge* expense. 103. *Hold* preserve. 104. *slack* neglect. 105. *notice* recognition. 106. *depositaries* trustees. 107. *reservation* condition. 108. *well-favored* handsome. 109. *not . . . praise* i.e., that Goneril is not so bad as Regan is one thing in her favor. 110. *her love* i.e., as loving as she. 111. *follow* attend on you. 112. *reason* scrutinize. 113. *Are . . . superfluous* have some trifle not absolutely necessary. 114. *needs* i.e., to sustain life.

Which scarcely keeps thee warm.[115] But, for true need —
You heavens, give me that patience, patience I need.
You see me here, you gods, a poor old man,   265
As full of grief as age, wretched in both.
If it be you that stirs these daughters' hearts
Against their father, fool[116] me not so much
To bear[117] it tamely; touch me with noble anger,
And let not women's weapons, water drops,   270
Stain my man's cheeks. No, you unnatural hags!
I will have such revenges on you both
That all the world shall — I will do such things —
What they are, yet I know not; but they shall be
The terrors of the earth. You think I'll weep.   275
No, I'll not weep.

(*Storm and tempest.*)

I have full cause of weeping, but this heart
Shall break into a hundred thousand flaws[118]
Or ere[119] I'll weep. O Fool, I shall go mad!

(*Exeunt* LEAR, GLOUCESTER, KENT, *and* FOOL.)

CORNWALL: Let us withdraw, 'twill be a storm.   280

REGAN: This house is little; the old man and's people
Cannot be well bestowed.[120]

GONERIL: 'Tis his own blame; hath[121] put himself from rest[122]
And must needs taste his folly.

REGAN: For his particular,[123] I'll receive him gladly,   285
But not one follower.

GONERIL: So am I purposed.[124]
Where is my Lord of Gloucester?

CORNWALL: Followed the old man forth.

(*Enter* GLOUCESTER.)

                                        He is returned.

GLOUCESTER: The king is in high rage.

CORNWALL: Whither is he going?

GLOUCESTER: He calls to horse, but will I know not whither.   290

115. *If . . . warm* If to satisfy the need for warmth were to be gorgeous, you would not need the
clothing you wear, which is worn more for beauty than warmth. 116. *fool* humiliate. 117. *To
bear* as to make me bear. 118. *flaws* (1) pieces (2) cracks (3) gusts of passion. 119. *Or ere*
before. 120. *bestowed* lodged. 121. *hath* he hath. 122. *rest* (1) place of residence (2) repose
of mind. 123. *his particular* himself personally. 124. *purposed* determined.

CORNWALL: 'Tis best to give him way, he leads himself.[125]

GONERIL: My lord, entreat him by no means to stay.

GLOUCESTER: Alack, the night comes on, and the high winds
Do sorely ruffle.[126] For many miles about
There's scarce a bush.

REGAN: O, sir, to willful men   295
The injuries that they themselves procure
Must be their schoolmasters. Shut up your doors.
He is attended with a desperate train,
And what they may incense[127] him to, being apt
To have his ear abused,[128] wisdom bids fear.   300

CORNWALL: Shut up your doors, my lord; 'tis a wild night.
My Regan counsels well. Come out o' th' storm.

(*Exeunt.*)

Act III

Scene I.

(*A heath.*)

(*Storm still.*[1] *Enter* KENT *and a* GENTLEMAN *severally.*)

KENT: Who's there besides foul weather?

GENTLEMAN: One minded like the weather most unquietly.[2]

KENT: I know you. Where's the king?

GENTLEMAN: Contending with the fretful elements;
Bids the wind blow the earth into the sea,   5
Or swell the curled waters 'bove the main,[3]
That things might change[4] or cease; tears his white hair,
Which the impetuous blasts, with eyeless[5] rage,
Catch in their fury, and make nothing of;
Strives in his little world of man[6] to outscorn   10
The to-and-fro-conflicting wind and rain.
This night, wherein the cub-drawn[7] bear would couch,[8]

125. *give . . . himself* let him go; he insists on his own way. 126. *ruffle* rage. 127. *incense* incite. 128. *being . . . abused* he being inclined to harken to bad counsel. III.i. 1. *still* continually. 2. *minded . . . unquietly* disturbed in mind, like the weather. 3. *main* land. 4. *change* (1) be destroyed (2) be exchanged (i.e., turned upside down) (3) change for the better. 5. *eyeless* (1) blind (2) invisible. 6. *little . . . man* the microcosm, as opposed to the universe or macrocosm, which it copies in little. 7. *cub-drawn* sucked dry by her cubs, and so ravenously hungry. 8. *couch* take shelter in its lair.

The lion, and the belly-pinchèd[9] wolf
Keep their fur dry, unbonneted[10] he runs,
And bids what will take all.[11]

KENT: But who is with him?   15

GENTLEMAN: None but the Fool, who labors to outjest
His heart-struck injuries.

KENT: Sir, I do know you,
And dare upon the warrant of my note[12]
Commend a dear thing[13] to you. There is division,
Although as yet the face of it is covered   20
With mutual cunning, 'twixt Albany and Cornwall;
Who have — as who have not, that[14] their great stars
Thronèd[15] and set high? — servants, who seem no less,[16]
Which are to France the spies and speculations
Intelligent[17] of our state. What hath been seen,   25
Either in snuffs and packings[18] of the dukes,
Or the hard rein which both of them hath borne[19]
Against the old kind king, or something deeper,
Whereof, perchance, these are but furnishings[20] —
But, true it is, from France there comes a power[21]   30
Into this scattered[22] kingdom, who already,
Wise in our negligence, have secret feet
In some of our best ports, and are at point[23]
To show their open banner. Now to you:
If on my credit you dare build[24] so far   35
To[25] make your speed to Dover, you shall find
Some that will thank you, making[26] just[27] report
Of how unnatural and bemadding[28] sorrow
The king hath cause to plain.[29]
I am a gentleman of blood and breeding,[30]   40
And from some knowledge and assurance[31] offer
This office[32] to you.

GENTLEMAN: I will talk further with you.

KENT: No, do not.
For confirmation that I am much more
Than my out-wall,[33] open this purse and take   45

9. *belly-pinched* starved. 10. *unbonneted* hatless. 11. *take all* like the reckless gambler, staking all he has left. 12. *warrant . . . note* strength of what I have taken note (of you). 13. *Commend . . . thing* entrust important business. 14. *that* whom. 15. *stars Thronèd* destinies have throned. 16. *seem no less* seem to be so. 17. *speculations Intelligent* giving intelligence. 18. *snuffs and packings* quarrels and plots. 19. *hard . . . borne* close and cruel control they have exercised. 20. *furnishings* excuses. 21. *power* army. 22. *scattered* disunited. 23. *at point* ready. 24. *If . . . build* if you can trust me, proceed. 25. *To* as to. 26. *making* for making. 27. *just* accurate. 28. *bemadding* maddening. 29. *plain* complain of. 30. *blood and breeding* noble family. 31. *knowledge and assurance* sure and trustworthy information. 32. *office* service (i.e., the trip to Dover). 33. *out-wall* superficial appearance.

What it contains. If you shall see Cordelia,
As fear not but you shall, show her this ring,
And she will tell you who that fellow[34] is
That yet you do not know. Fie on this storm!
I will go seek the king.   50

GENTLEMAN: Give me your hand. Have you no more to say?

KENT: Few words, but, to effect,[35] more than all yet:
That when we have found the king — in which your pain[36]
That way, I'll this — he that first lights on him,
Holla the other. (*Exeunt severally.*)   55

Scene II.

(*Another part of the heath.*)

(*Storm still. Enter* LEAR *and* FOOL.)

LEAR: Blow, winds, and crack your cheeks. Rage, blow!
You cataracts and hurricanoes,[1] spout
Till you have drenched our steeples, drowned the cocks.[2]
You sulph'rous and thought-executing[3] fires,
Vaunt-couriers[4] of oak-cleaving thunderbolts,   5
Singe my white head. And thou, all-shaking thunder,
Strike flat the thick rotundity[5] o' th' world,
Crack Nature's molds,[6] all germains spill[7] at once,
That makes ingrateful[8] man.

FOOL: O nuncle, court holy-water[9] in a dry house is better than this rain 10
water out o' door. Good nuncle, in; ask thy daughters blessing.
Here's a night pities neither wise man nor fools.

LEAR: Rumble thy bellyful. Spit, fire. Spout, rain!
Nor rain, wind, thunder, fire are my daughters.
I tax[10] not you, you elements, with unkindness.   15
I never gave you kingdom, called you children,
You owe me no subscription.[11] Then let fall
Your horrible pleasure.[12] Here I stand your slave,
A poor, infirm, weak, and despised old man.
But yet I call you servile ministers,[13]   20

34. *fellow* companion. 35. *to effect* in their importance. 36. *pain* labor. **III.ii.** 1.
hurricanoes waterspouts. 2. *cocks* weathercocks. 3. *thought-executing* (1) doing execution as
quick as thought (2) executing or carrying out the thought of him who hurls the
lightning. 4. *Vaunt-couriers* heralds, scouts who range before the main body of the army. 5. *rotundity* i.e., not only the sphere of the globe, but the roundness of gestation
(Delius). 6. *Nature's molds* the molds or forms in which men are made. 7. *all germains spill*
destroy the basic seeds of life. 8. *ingrateful* ungrateful. 9. *court holy-water* flattery. 10. *tax*
accuse. 11. *subscription* allegiance, submission. 12. *pleasure* will. 13. *ministers* agents.

That will with two pernicious daughters join
Your high-engendered battles[14] 'gainst a head
So old and white as this. O, ho! 'tis foul.

FOOL: He that has a house to put's head in has a good headpiece.[15]
    The codpiece[16] that will house   **25**
      Before the head as any,
    The head and he[17] shall louse:
      So beggars marry many.[18]
    The man that makes his toe
      What he his heart should make   **30**
    Shall of a corn cry woe,
      And turn his sleep to wake.[19]
For there was never yet fair woman but she made mouths in a glass.[20]

(*Enter* KENT.)

LEAR: No, I will be the pattern of all patience,   **35**
    I will say nothing.

KENT: Who's there?

FOOL: Marry,[21] here's grace and a codpiece; that's a wise man and a fool.[22]

KENT: Alas, sir, are you here? Things that love night
    Love not such nights as these. The wrathful skies   **40**
    Gallow[23] the very wanderers of the dark
    And make them keep[24] their caves. Since I was man,
    Such sheets of fire, such bursts of horrid[25] thunder,
    Such groans of roaring wind and rain, I never
    Remember to have heard. Man's nature cannot carry[26]   **45**
    Th' affliction nor the fear.

LEAR: Let the great gods
    That keep this dreadful pudder[27] o'er our heads
    Find out their enemies now.[28] Tremble, thou wretch,
    That hast within thee undivulgèd crimes
    Unwhipped of justice. Hide thee, thou bloody hand,   **50**
    Thou perjured,[29] and thou simular[30] of virtue

14. *high-engendered battles* armies formed in the heavens. 15. *headpiece* (1) helmet (2) brain. 16. *codpiece* penis (literally, padding worn at the crotch of a man's hose). 17. *he* it. 18. *many* i.e., lice; *The . . . many* The man who gratifies his sexual appetites before he has a roof over his head will end up a lousy beggar. 19. *The . . . wake* The man who, ignoring the fit order of things, elevates what is base above what is noble, will suffer for it as Lear has, in banishing Cordelia and enriching her sisters. 20. *made . . . glass* posed before a mirror (irrelevant nonsense, except that it calls to mind the general theme of vanity and folly). 21. *Marry* a mild oath, from "By the Virgin Mary." 22. *here's . . . fool* Kent's question is answered: the king ("grace") is here, as well as the Fool — who customarily wears an exaggerated codpiece; but which is left ambiguous, since Lear has previously been called a codpiece. 23. *Gallow* frighten. 24. *keep* remain inside. 25. *horrid* horrible. 26. *carry* endure. 27. *pudder* turmoil. 28. *Find . . . now* i.e., discover sinners by the terror they reveal. 29. *perjured* perjurer. 30. *simular* counterfeiter.

That art incestuous. Caitiff,[31] to pieces shake,
That under covert and convenient seeming[32]
Has practiced on[33] man's life. Close[34] pent-up guilts,
Rive[35] your concealing continents [36] and cry   55
These dreadful summoners grace.[37] I am a man
More sinned against than sinning.

KENT: Alack, bareheaded?
Gracious my lord,[38] hard by here is a hovel;
Some friendship will it lend you 'gainst the tempest.
Repose you there, while I to this hard house   60
(More harder than the stones whereof 'tis raised,
Which even but now, demanding after[39] you,
Denied me to come in) return, and force
Their scanted[40] courtesy.

LEAR: My wits begin to turn.
Come on, my boy. How dost, my boy? Art cold?   65
I am cold myself. Where is this straw, my fellow?
The art[41] of our necessities is strange,
That can make vile things precious. Come, your hovel.
Poor Fool and knave, I have one part in my heart
That's sorry yet for thee.   70

FOOL (*Singing.*):
          He that has and a little tiny wit,
              With heigh-ho, the wind and the rain,
          Must make content with his fortunes fit,[42]
              Though the rain it raineth every day.

LEAR: True, my good boy. Come, bring us to this hovel. (*Exit, with* KENT.)   75

FOOL: This is a brave[43] night to cool a courtesan. I'll speak a prophecy ere
     I go:
          When priests are more in word than matter;
          When brewers mar their malt with water;
          When nobles are their tailors' tutors,   80
          No heretics burned, but wenches' suitors;[44]
          When every case in law is right,
          No squire in debt nor no poor knight;

31. *Caitiff* wretch. 32. *seeming* hypocrisy. 33. *practiced on* plotted against. 34. *Close* hidden. 35. *Rive* split open. 36. *continents* containers. 37. *cry . . . grace* beg mercy from the vengeful gods (here figured as officers who summoned a man charged with immorality before the ecclesiastical court). 38. *Gracious my lord* my gracious lord. 39. *demanding after* asking for. 40. *scanted* stinted. 41. *art* magic powers of the alchemists, who sought to transmute base metals into precious. 42. *Must . . . fit* must be satisfied with a fortune as tiny as his wit. 43. *brave* fine. 44. *When . . . suitors* the first four prophecies are fulfilled already, and hence "confusion" has come to England: the priest does not suit his action to his words; the brewer adulterates his beer; the nobleman is subservient to his tailor (i.e., cares only for fashion); religious heretics escape, and only those burn (i.e., suffer) who are afflicted with venereal disease.

When slanders do not live in tongues;
Nor cutpurses come not to throngs;
When usurers tell their gold i' th' field,[45]   85
And bawds and whores do churches build,[46]
Then shall the realm of Albion[47]
Come to great confusion.
Then comes the time, who lives to see't,   90
That going shall be used with feet.[48]
    This prophecy Merlin[49] shall make, for I live before his time. (*Exit.*)

Scene III.

(*Gloucester's castle.*)

(*Enter* GLOUCESTER *and* EDMUND.)

GLOUCESTER: Alack, alack, Edmund, I like not this unnatural dealing.
When I desired their leave that I might pity[1] him, they took from
me the use of mine own house, charged me on pain of perpetual displeasure neither to speak of him, entreat for him, or any way sustain[2]
him.   5

EDMUND: Most savage and unnatural.

GLOUCESTER: Go to; say you nothing. There is division[3] between the dukes,
and a worse[4] matter than that. I have received a letter this night —
'tis dangerous to be spoken[5] — I have locked the letter in my closet.[6]
These injuries the king now bears will be revenged home;[7] there is   10
part of a power[8] already footed;[9] we must incline to[10] the king. I will
look[11] him and privily[12] relieve him. Go you and maintain talk with
the duke, that my charity be not of[13] him perceived. If he ask for
me, I am ill and gone to bed. If I die for it, as no less is threatened
me, the king my old master must be relieved. There is strange things   15
toward,[14] Edmund; pray you be careful. (*Exit.*)

EDMUND: This courtesy forbid[15] thee shall the duke
    Instantly know, and of that letter too.
    This seems a fair deserving,[16] and must draw me
    That which my father loses — no less than all.   20
    The younger rises when the old doth fall. (*Exit.*)

---

45. *tell . . . field* count their money in the open.   **46.** *When . . . build* the last six prophecies, as
they are Utopian, are meant ironically; they will never be fulfilled.   **47.** *Albion*
England.   **48.** *going . . . feet* people will walk on their feet.   **49.** *Merlin* King Arthur's great
magician who, according to Holinshed's *Chronicles*, lived later than Lear.   **III.iii. 1.** *pity* show
pity to.   **2.** *sustain* care for.   **3.** *division* falling out.   **4.** *worse* more serious (i.e., the French
invasion).   **5.** *spoken* spoken of.   **6.** *closet* room.   **7.** *home* to the utmost.   **8.** *power* army.   **9.** *footed* landed.   **10.** *incline to* take the side of.   **11.** *look* search for.   **12.** *privily*
secretly.   **13.** *of* by.   **14.** *toward* impending.   **15.** *courtesy forbid* kindness forbidden (i.e., to
Lear).   **16.** *fair deserving* an action deserving reward.

Scene IV.

(*The heath. Before a hovel.*)

(*Enter* LEAR, KENT, *and* FOOL.)

KENT: Here is the place, my lord. Good my lord, enter.
The tyranny of the open night's too rough
For nature to endure. (*Storm still.*)

LEAR: Let me alone.

KENT: Good my lord, enter here.

LEAR: Wilt break my heart?[1]

KENT: I had rather break mine own. Good my lord, enter.   5

LEAR: Thou think'st 'tis much that this contentious storm
Invades us to the skin: so 'tis to thee;
But where the greater malady is fixed,[2]
The lesser is scarce felt. Thou'dst shun a bear;
But if thy flight lay toward the roaring sea,   10
Thou'dst meet the bear i' th' mouth.[3] When the mind's free,[4]
The body's delicate. The tempest in my mind
Doth from my senses take all feeling else,
Save what beats there. Filial ingratitude,
Is it not as[5] this mouth should tear this hand   15
For lifting food to't? But I will punish home.[6]
No, I will weep no more. In such a night
To shut me out! Pour on, I will endure.
In such a night as this! O Regan, Goneril,
Your old kind father, whose frank[7] heart gave all —   20
O, that way madness lies; let me shun that.
No more of that!

KENT: Good my lord, enter here.

LEAR: Prithee go in thyself; seek thine own ease.
This tempest will not give me leave to ponder
On things would hurt me more, but I'll go in.   25

(*To the* FOOL.)

In, boy; go first. You houseless poverty[8] —
Nay, get thee in. I'll pray, and then I'll sleep.

(*Exit* FOOL.)

III.iv. **1.** *break my heart* i.e., by shutting out the storm which distracts me from thinking. **2.** *fixed* lodged (in the mind). **3.** *i' th' mouth* in the teeth. **4.** *free* i.e., from care. **5.** *as* as if. **6.** *home* to the utmost. **7.** *frank* liberal (magnanimous). **8.** *houseless poverty* the unsheltered poor, abstracted.

Poor naked wretches, wheresoe'er you are,
That bide[9] the pelting of this pitiless storm,
How shall your houseless heads and unfed sides, 30
Your looped and windowed[10] raggedness, defend you
From seasons such as these? O, I have ta'en
Too little care of this! Take physic, pomp;[11]
Expose thyself to feel what wretches feel,
That thou mayest shake the superflux[12] to them, 35
And show the heavens more just.

EDGAR (*Within.*): Fathom and half, fathom and half![13] Poor Tom!

(*Enter* FOOL.)

FOOL: Come not in here, nuncle, here's a spirit. Help me, help me!

KENT: Give me thy hand. Who's there?

FOOL: A spirit, a spirit. He says his name's Poor Tom. 40

KENT: What art thou that dost grumble there i' th' straw? Come forth.

(*Enter* EDGAR *disguised as a madman.*)

EDGAR: Away! the foul fiend follows me. Through the sharp hawthorn blows the cold wind.[14] Humh! Go to thy cold bed, and warm thee.[15]

LEAR: Didst thou give all to thy daughters? And art thou come to this?

EDGAR: Who gives anything to Poor Tom? Whom the foul fiend hath led 45
through fire and through flame, through ford and whirlpool, o'er
bog and quagmire; that hath laid knives under his pillow and halters
in his pew,[16] set ratsbane[17] by his porridge,[18] made him proud of
heart, to ride on a bay trotting horse over four-inched bridges,[19] to
course[20] his own shadow for[21] a traitor. Bless thy five wits,[22] Tom's a- 50
cold. O, do, de, do, de, do, de. Bless thee from whirlwinds, star-
blasting,[23] and taking.[24] Do Poor Tom some charity, whom the foul
fiend vexes. There could I have him now — and there — and there
again — and there.

(*Storm still.*)

LEAR: What, has his daughters brought him to this pass?[25] Couldst thou 55
save nothing? Wouldst thou give 'em all?

9. *bide* endure. **10.** *looped and windowed* full of holes. **11.** *Take physic, pomp* Take
medicine to cure yourselves, you great men. **12.** *superflux* superfluity. **13.** *Fathom and half*
Edgar, because of the downpour, pretends to take soundings. **14.** *Through ... wind* a line
from the ballad of "The Friar of Orders Gray." **15.** *Go ... thee* a reminiscence of *The Taming
of the Shrew*, Induction, lines 9–10, which themselves are an echo of a line in Thomas Kyd's
The Spanish Tragedy. **16.** *pew* gallery or balcony outside a window. **17.** *knives ... halters
... ratsbane* the fiend tempts Poor Tom to suicide. **18.** *porridge* broth. **19.** *ride ... bridges*
i.e., risk his life. **20.** *course* chase. **21.** *for* as. **22.** *five wits* common wit, imagination, fantasy, estimation, memory. **23.** *star-blasting* the evil caused by malignant stars. **24.** *taking* pernicious influences. **25.** *pass* wretched condition.

FOOL: Nay, he reserved a blanket,²⁶ else we had been all shamed.

LEAR: Now all the plagues that in the pendulous²⁷ air
Hang fated o'er²⁸ men's faults light on thy daughters!

KENT: He hath no daughters, sir. 60

LEAR: Death, traitor; nothing could have subdued²⁹ nature
To such a lowness but his unkind daughters.
Is it the fashion that discarded fathers
Should have thus little mercy on³⁰ their flesh?
Judicious punishment — 'twas this flesh begot 65
Those pelican³¹ daughters.

EDGAR: Pillicock sat on Pillicock Hill.³² Alow, alow, loo, loo!³³

FOOL: This cold night will turn us all to fools and madmen.

EDGAR: Take heed o' th' foul fiend; obey thy parents; keep thy word's
justice;³⁴ swear not; commit not³⁵ with man's sworn spouse; set not 70
thy sweet heart on proud array. Tom's a-cold.

LEAR: What has thou been?

EDGAR: A servingman, proud in heart and mind; that curled my hair, wore
gloves in my cap;³⁶ served the lust of my mistress' heart, and did the
act of darkness with her; swore as many oaths as I spake words, and 75
broke them in the sweet face of heaven. One that slept in the con-
triving of lust, and waked to do it. Wine loved I deeply, dice dearly;
and in woman outparamoured the Turk.³⁷ False of heart, light of
ear,³⁸ bloody of hand; hog in sloth, fox in stealth, wolf in greediness,
dog in madness, lion in prey.³⁹ Let not the creaking⁴⁰ of shoes nor 80
the rustling of silks betray thy poor heart to woman. Keep thy foot
out of brothels, thy hand out of plackets,⁴¹ thy pen from lenders'
books,⁴² and defy the foul fiend. Still through the hawthorn blows
the cold wind; says suum, mun, nonny.⁴³ Dolphin⁴⁴ my boy, boy,
sessa!⁴⁵ let him trot by. 85

(*Storm still.*)

LEAR: Thou wert better in a grave than to answer⁴⁶ with thy uncovered

---

26. *blanket* i.e., to cover his nakedness. **27.** *pendulous* overhanging. **28.** *fated o'er* destined to punish. **29.** *subdued* reduced. **30.** *on* i.e., shown to. **31.** *pelican* supposed to feed on its parent's blood. **32.** *Pillicock . . . Hill* probably quoted from a nursery rhyme, and suggested by "pelican"; "pillicock" is a term of endearment and the phallus. **33.** *Alow . . . loo* a hunting call, or the refrain of the song (?). **34.** *keep . . . justice* i.e., do not break thy word. **35.** *commit not* i.e., adultery. **36.** *gloves . . . cap* i.e., as a pledge from his mistress. **37.** *outparamoured the Turk* had more concubines than the sultan. **38.** *light of ear* ready to hear flattery and slander. **39.** *prey* preying. **40.** *creaking* deliberately cultivated, as fashionable. **41.** *plackets* opening in skirts. **42.** *pen . . . books* i.e., do not enter your name in the moneylender's account book. **43.** *suum, mun, nonny* the noise of the wind. **44.** *Dolphin* the French dauphin (identified by the English with the devil; Poor Tom is presumably quoting from a ballad). **45.** *sessa* an interjection: "Go on!" **46.** *answer* confront, bear the brunt of body this extremity[47] of the skies. Is man no more than this? Consider him well. Thou ow'st[48] the worm no silk, the beast no hide, the sheep no wool, the cat[49] no perfume. Ha! here's three on's[50] are sophisticated.[51] Thou art the thing itself; unaccommodated[52] man is no more but such a poor, bare, forked[53] animal as thou art. Off, off, you lendings.[54] Come, unbutton here.

(Tearing off his clothes.)

FOOL: Prithee, nuncle, be contented, 'tis a naughty[55] night to swim in. Now a little fire in a wild[56] field were like an old lecher's heart — a small spark, all the rest on's[57] body, cold. Look, here comes a walking fire.

(Enter GLOUCESTER with a torch.)

EDGAR: This is the foul fiend Flibbertigibbet.[58] He begins at curfew,[59] and walks till the first cock.[60] He gives the web and the pin,[61] squints[62] the eye, and makes the harelip; mildews the white[63] wheat, and hurts the poor creature of earth.
Swithold footed thrice the old;[64]
He met the nightmare,[65] and her nine fold;[66]
Bid her alight[67]
And her troth plight,[68]
And aroint[69] thee, witch, aroint thee!

KENT: How fares your grace?

LEAR: What's he?

KENT: Who's there? What is't you seek?

GLOUCESTER: What are you there? Your names?

EDGAR: Poor Tom, that eats the swimming frog, the toad, the todpole, the wall-newt and the water;[70] that in the fury of his heart, when the foul fiend rages, eats cow-dung for sallets,[71] swallows the old rat and the ditch-dog,[72] drinks the green mantle[73] of the standing[74] pool; who is whipped from tithing[75] to tithing, and stocked, punished, and imprisoned; who hath had three suits to his back, six shirts to his body, Horse to ride, and weapon to wear,

---

47. *extremity* extreme severity.   **48.** *ow'st* have taken from.   **49.** *cat* civet cat, whose glands yield perfume.   **50.** *on's* of us.   **51.** *sophisticated* adulterated, made artificial.   **52.** *unaccommodated* uncivilized.   **53.** *forked* i.e., two-legged.   **54.** *lendings* borrowed garments.   **55.** *naughty* wicked.   **56.** *wild* barren.   **57.** *on's* of his.   **58.** *Flibbertigibbet* a figure from Elizabethan demonology.   **59.** *curfew* 9 P.M.   **60.** *first cock* midnight.   **61.** *web* ... *pin* cataract.   **62.** *squints* crosses.   **63.** *white* ripening.   **64.** *Swithold* ... *old* Withold (an Anglo-Saxon saint who subdued demons) walked three times across the open country.   **65.** *nightmare* demon.   **66.** *fold* offspring.   **67.** *alight* i.e., from the horse she had possessed.   **68.** *her troth plight* pledge her word.   **69.** *aroint* be gone.   **70.** *todpole* ... *water* tadpole, wall lizard, water newt.   **71.** *sallets* salads.   **72.** *ditch-dog* dead dog in a ditch.   **73.** *mantle* scum.   **74.** *standing* stagnant.   **75.** *tithing* a district comprising ten families.

But mice and rats, and such small deer,[76]
Have been Tom's food for seven long year.[77]
Beware my follower![78] Peace, Smulkin,[79] peace, thou fiend!

GLOUCESTER: What, hath your grace no better company?   120

EDGAR: The Prince of Darkness is a gentleman.
    Modo[80] he's called, and Mahu.[81]

GLOUCESTER: Our flesh and blood, my lord, is grown so vile
    That it doth hate what gets[82] it.

EDGAR: Poor Tom's a-cold.   125

GLOUCESTER: Go in with me. My duty cannot suffer[83]
    T' obey in all your daughters' hard commands.
    Though their injunction be to bar my doors
    And let this tyrannous night take hold upon you,
    Yet have I ventured to come seek you out   130
    And bring you where both fire and food is ready.

LEAR: First let me talk with this philosopher.
    What is the cause of thunder?

KENT: Good my lord, take his offer; go into th' house.

LEAR: I'll talk a word with this same learnéd Theban.[84]   135
    What is your study?[85]

EDGAR: How to prevent[86] the fiend, and to kill vermin.

LEAR: Let me ask you one word in private.

KENT: Importune him once more to go, my lord.
    His wits begin t' unsettle.

GLOUCESTER: Canst thou blame him?   140

(Storm still.)

    His daughters seek his death. Ah, that good Kent,
    He said it would be thus, poor banished man!
    Thou say'st the king grows mad — I'll tell thee, friend,
    I am almost mad myself. I had a son,
    Now outlawed from my blood,[87] he sought my life   145
    But lately, very late.[88] I loved him, friend,
    No father his son dearer. True to tell thee,
    The grief hath crazed my wits. What a night's this!
    I do beseech your grace —

76. *deer* game. 77. *But ... year* adapted from a popular romance, "Bevis of Hampton." 78. *follower* familiar. 79. *Smulkin;* 80. *Modo;* 81. *Mahu* Elizabethan devils, from Samuel Harsnett's *Declaration* of 1603. 82. *gets* begets. 83. *suffer* permit me. 84. *Theban* i.e., Greek philosopher. 85. *study* particular scientific study. 86. *prevent* balk. 87. *outlawed ... blood* disowned and tainted, like a carbuncle in the corrupted blood. 88. *late* recently.

LEAR: O, cry you mercy,[89] sir.
Noble philosopher, your company.   150

EDGAR: Tom's a-cold.

GLOUCESTER: In, fellow, there, into th' hovel; keep thee warm.

LEAR: Come, let's in all.

KENT: This way, my lord.

LEAR: With him!
I will keep still with my philosopher.

KENT: Good my lord, soothe[90] him; let him take the fellow.   155

GLOUCESTER: Take him you on.[91]

KENT: Sirrah, come on; go along with us.

LEAR: Come, good Athenian.[92]

GLOUCESTER: No words, no words! Hush.

EDGAR: Child Rowland to the dark tower came,[93]   160
His word was still,[94] "Fie, foh, and fum,
I smell the blood of a British man."[95] (*Exeunt.*)

Scene V.

(*Gloucester's castle.*)

(*Enter* CORNWALL *and* EDMUND.)

CORNWALL: I will have my revenge ere I depart his house.

EDMUND: How, my lord, I may be censured,[1] that nature thus gives way to
loyalty, something fears[2] me to think of.

CORNWALL: I now perceive it was not altogether your brother's evil disposition made him seek his death; but a provoking merit, set a-work by
a reprovable badness in himself.[3]

EDMUND: How malicious is my fortune that I must repent to be just! This
is the letter which he spoke of, which approves[4] him an intelligent
party[5] to the advantages[6] of France. O heavens, that his treason were
not! or not I the detector!   10

89. *cry you mercy* I beg your pardon. 90. *soothe* humor. 91. *you on* with you. 92. *Athenian* i.e., philosopher (like "Theban"). 93. *Child . . . came* from a lost ballad (?); "child" = a
candidate for knighthood; "Rowland" was Charlemagne's nephew, the hero of *The Song of
Roland*. 94. *His . . . still* his motto was always. 95. *Fie . . . man* a deliberately absurd linking
of the chivalric hero with the nursery tale of Jack the Giant-Killer. III.v. 1. *censured*
judged. 2. *something fears* somewhat frightens. 3. *a provoking . . . himself* a stimulating
goodness in Edgar, brought into play by a blamable badness in Gloucester. 4. *approves*
proves. 5. *intelligent party* (1) spy (2) well-informed person. 6. *to the advantages* on behalf
of.

CORNWALL: Go with me to the duchess.

EDMUND: If the matter of this paper be certain, you have mighty business in hand.

CORNWALL: True or false, it hath made thee Earl of Gloucester. Seek out where thy father is, that he may be ready for our apprehension.[7]   15

EDMUND (*Aside.*): If I find him comforting[8] the king, it will stuff his suspicion more fully. — I will persever[9] in my course of loyalty, though the conflict be sore between that and my blood.[10]

CORNWALL: I will lay trust upon[11] thee, and thou shalt find a dearer father in my love. (*Exeunt.*)   20

Scene VI.

(*A chamber in a farmhouse adjoining the castle.*)

(*Enter* KENT *and* GLOUCESTER.)

GLOUCESTER: Here is better than the open air; take it thankfully. I will piece out the comfort with what addition I can. I will not be long from you.

KENT: All the power of his wits have given way to his impatience.[1] The gods reward your kindness.   5

(*Exit* GLOUCESTER.)

(*Enter* LEAR, EDGAR, *and* FOOL.)

EDGAR: Frateretto[2] calls me, and tells me Nero[3] is an angler in the lake of darkness. Pray, innocent,[4] and beware the foul fiend.

FOOL: Prithee, nuncle, tell me whether a madman be a gentleman or a yeoman.[5]

LEAR: A king, a king.   10

FOOL: No, he's a yeoman that has a gentleman to his son; for he's a mad yeoman that sees his son a gentleman before him.

LEAR: To have a thousand with red burning spits
Coming hizzing[6] in upon 'em —

---

7. *apprehension* arrest. 8. *comforting* supporting (a legalism). 9. *persever* persevere. 10. *blood* natural feelings. 11. *lay trust upon* (1) trust (2) advance. III.vi. 1. *impatience* raging. 2. *Frateretto* Elizabethan devil, from Harsnett's *Declaration*. 3. *Nero* who is mentioned by Harsnett, and whose angling is reported by Chaucer in "The Monk's Tale." 4. *innocent* fool. 5. *yeoman* farmer (just below a gentleman in rank; the Fool asks what class of man has most indulged his children, and thus been driven mad). 6. *hizzing* hissing.

EDGAR: The foul fiend bites my back.   ¹⁵

FOOL: He's mad that trusts in the tameness of a wolf, a horse's health, a
    boy's love, or a whore's oath.

LEAR: It shall be done; I will arraign[7] them straight.[8]

(*To* EDGAR.)

    Come, sit thou here, most learned justice.[9]

(*To the* FOOL.)

    Thou, sapient[10] sir, sit here. Now, you she-foxes —   ²⁰

EDGAR: Look, where he[11] stands and glares. Want'st thou eyes at trial,
    madam?[12]
    Come o'er the bourn,[13] Bessy, to me.

FOOL: Her boat hath a leak,
       And she must not speak   ²⁵
    Why she dares not come over to thee.[14]

EDGAR: The foul fiend haunts Poor Tom in the voice of a nightingale.[15]
    Hoppedance[16] cries in Tom's belly for two white herring.[17] Croak[18]
    not, black angel; I have no food for thee.

KENT: How do you, sir? Stand you not so amazed.[19]   ³⁰
    Will you lie down and rest upon the cushions?

LEAR: I'll see their trial first. Bring in their evidence.[20]

(*To* EDGAR.)

    Thou, robed man of justice, take thy place.

(*To the* FOOL.)

    And thou, his yokefellow of equity,[21]
    Bench[22] by his side. (*To* KENT.) You are o' th' commission;[23]   ³⁵
    Sit you too.

EDGAR: Let us deal justly.
       Sleepest or wakest thou, jolly shepherd?
        Thy sheep be in the corn;[24]
    And for one blast of thy minikin[25] mouth   ⁴⁰

---

7. *arraign* bring to trial. 8. *straight* straightaway. 9. *justice* justicer, judge. 10. *sapient* wise. 11. *he* i.e., a fiend. 12. *Want'st . . . madam* (to Goneril) i.e., Do you want eyes to look at you during your trial? The fiend serves that purpose. 13. *bourn* brook (Edgar quotes from a popular ballad. 14. *Her . . . thee* the Fool parodies the ballad. 15. *nightingale* i.e., the Fool's singing. 16. *Hoppedance* Hoberdidance (another devil from Harsnett's *Declaration*). 17. *white herring* unsmoked (as against the black and sulfurous devil?). 18. *Croak* rumble (because his belly is empty). 19. *amazed* astonished. 20. *evidence* the evidence of witnesses against them. 21. *yokefellow of equity* partner in justice. 22. *Bench* sit on the bench. 23. *commission* those commissioned as king's justices. 24. *corn* wheat. 25. *minikin* shrill.

Thy sheep shall take no harm.[26]
Purr, the cat is gray.[27]

LEAR: Arraign her first. 'Tis Goneril, I here take my oath before this
honorable assembly, she kicked the poor king her father.

FOOL: Come hither, mistress. Is your name Goneril?   45

LEAR: She cannot deny it.

FOOL: Cry you mercy, I took you for a joint stool.[28]

LEAR: And here's another, whose warped looks proclaim
What store[29] her heart is made on. Stop her there!
Arms, arms, sword, fire! Corruption in the place![30]   50
False justicer, why hast thou let her 'scape?

EDGAR: Bless thy five wits!

KENT: O pity! Sir, where is the patience now
That you so oft have boasted to retain?

EDGAR (*Aside.*): My tears begin to take his part so much   55
They mar my counterfeiting.[31]

LEAR: The little dogs and all,
Tray, Blanch, and Sweetheart — see, they bark at me.

EDGAR: Tom will throw his head at them. Avaunt, you curs.
Be thy mouth or black or[32] white,   60
Tooth that poisons if it bite;
Mastiff, greyhound, mongrel grim,
Hound or spaniel, brach[33] or lym,[34]
Or bobtail tike, or trundle-tail[35] —
Tom will make him weep and wail;   65
For, with throwing[36] thus my head,
Dogs leaped the hatch,[37] and all are fled.
Do, de, de, de. Sessa![38] Come, march to wakes[39] and fairs and market
towns. Poor Tom, thy horn[40] is dry.

LEAR: Then let them anatomize Regan. See what breeds about her heart.[41]   70

---

26. *Sleepest . . . harm* probably quoted or adapted from an Elizabethan song. **27.** *gray* devils were thought to assume the shape of a gray cat. **28.** *Cry . . . stool* proverbial and deliberately impudent apology for overlooking a person; a joint stool was a low stool made by a joiner, perhaps here a stage property to represent Goneril and Regan, "joint stool" can also suggest the judicial bench; hence Goneril may be identified by the Fool, ironically, with those in power, who judge. **29.** *store* stuff. **30.** *Corruption . . . place* bribery in the court. **31.** *counterfeiting* i.e., feigned madness. **32.** *or . . . or* either . . . or. **33.** *brach* bitch. **34.** *lym* bloodhound (from the liam or leash with which he was led). **35.** *bobtail . . . trundle-tail* short-tailed or long-tailed cur. **36.** *throwing* jerking (as a hound lifts its head from the ground, the scent having been lost). **37.** *leaped the hatch* leaped over the lower half of a divided door (i.e., left in a hurry). **38.** *Sessa* Be off!. **39.** *wakes* feasts attending the dedication of a church. **40.** *horn* horn bottle which the Bedlam used in begging a drink (Edgar is suggesting that he is unable to play his role any longer). **41.** *Then . . . heart* i.e., If the Bedlam's horn is dry, let Regan, whose heart has become as hard as horn, be dissected.

Is there any cause in nature that make[42] these hard hearts? (*To*
EDGAR.) You, sir, I entertain[43] for one of my hundred;[44] only I do not
like the fashion of your garments. You will say they are Persian,[45] but
let them be changed.

KENT: Now, good my lord, lie here and rest awhile.   75

LEAR: Make no noise, make no noise; draw the curtains.[46]
    So, so. We'll go to supper i' th' morning.

FOOL: And I'll go to bed at noon.[47]

(*Enter* GLOUCESTER.)

GLOUCESTER: Come hither, friend. Where is the king my master?

KENT: Here, sir, but trouble him not; his wits are gone.   80

GLOUCESTER: Good friend, I prithee take him in thy arms.
    I have o'erheard a plot of death upon him.
    There is a litter ready; lay him in't
    And drive toward Dover, friend, where thou shalt meet
    Both welcome and protection. Take up thy master.   85
    If thou shouldst dally half an hour, his life,
    With thine and all that offer to defend him,
    Stand in assurèd loss. Take up, take up,
    And follow me, that will to some provision[48]
    Give thee quick conduct.[49]

KENT: Oppressèd nature sleeps.   90
    This rest might yet have balmed thy broken sinews,[50]
    Which, if convenience[51] will not allow,
    Stand in hard cure.[52] (*To the* FOOL.) Come, help to bear thy master.
    Thou must not stay behind.

GLOUCESTER: Come, come, away!

(*Exeunt all but* EDGAR.)

EDGAR: When we our betters see bearing our woes,   95
    We scarcely think our miseries our foes.[53]
    Who alone suffers suffers most i' th' mind,
    Leaving free[54] things and happy shows[55] behind;
    But then the mind much sufferance[56] doth o'erskip
    When grief hath mates, and bearing fellowship.[57]   100
    How light and portable[58] my pain seems now,

---

42. *make* subjunctive. 43. *entertain* engage. 44. *hundred* i.e., Lear's hundred
knights. 45. *Persian* gorgeous (ironically of Edgar's rags). 46. *curtains* Lear imagines himself
in bed. 47. *And ... noon* the Fool's last words. 48. *provision* maintenance. 49. *conduct*
direction. 50. *balmed ... sinews* soothed thy racked nerves. 51. *convenience* fortunate occasion. 52. *Stand ... cure* will be hard to cure. 53. *our foes* enemies peculiar to
ourselves. 54. *free* carefree. 55. *shows* scenes. 56. *sufferance* suffering. 57. *bearing fellowship* suffering has company. 58. *portable* able to be supported or endured.

When that which makes me bend makes the king bow.
He childed as I fathered. Tom, away.
Mark the high noises,⁵⁹ and thyself bewray⁶⁰
When false opinion, whose wrong thoughts⁶¹ defile thee,   105
In thy just proof repeals and reconciles thee.⁶²
What will hap more⁶³ tonight, safe 'scape the king!
Lurk,⁶⁴ lurk. (*Exit.*)

Scene VII.

(*Gloucester's castle.*)

(*Enter* CORNWALL, REGAN, GONERIL, EDMUND, *and* SERVANTS.)

CORNWALL (*To* GONERIL.): Post speedily to my lord your husband; show
   him this letter. The army of France is landed. (*To* SERVANTS.) Seek
   out the traitor Gloucester. (*Exeunt some of the* SERVANTS.)

REGAN: Hang him instantly.

GONERIL: Pluck out his eyes.   5

CORNWALL: Leave him to my displeasure. Edmund, keep you our sister
   company. The revenges we are bound¹ to take upon your traitorous
   father are not fit for your beholding. Advise the duke where you are
   going, to a most festinate² preparation. We are bound to the like.
   Our posts³ shall be swift and intelligent⁴ betwixt us. Farewell, dear 10
   sister; farewell, my Lord of Gloucester.⁵

(*Enter* OSWALD.)

   How now? Where's the king?

OSWALD: My Lord of Gloucester hath conveyed him hence.
   Some five or six and thirty of his knights,
   Hot questrists⁶ after him, met him at gate;   15
   Who, with some other of the lords dependants,⁷
   Are gone with him toward Dover, where they boast
   To have well-armed friends.

CORNWALL: Get horses for your mistress.

(*Exit* OSWALD.)

GONERIL: Farewell, sweet lord, and sister.

59. *Mark . . . noises* observe the rumors of strife among those in power. **60.** *bewray* reveal. **61.** *wrong thoughts* misconceptions. **62.** *In . . . thee* on the manifesting of your innocence recalls you from outlawry and restores amity between you and your father. **63.** *What . . . more* whatever else happens. **64.** *Lurk* hide. **III.vii. 1.** *bound* (1) forced (2) purposing to. **2.** *festinate* speedy. **3.** *posts* messengers. **4.** *intelligent* full of information. **5.** *Lord of Gloucester* Edmund, now elevated to the title. **6.** *questrists* searchers. **7.** *lords dependants* attendant lords (members of Lear's retinue).

CORNWALL: Edmund, farewell. (*Exeunt* GONERIL *and* EDMUND.)
                                    Go seek the traitor Gloucester,   20
          Pinion him like a thief, bring him before us.

(*Exeunt other* SERVANTS.)

          Though well we may not pass upon[8] his life
          Without the form of justice, yet our power
          Shall do a court'sy to[9] our wrath, which men
          May blame, but not control.

(*Enter* GLOUCESTER, *brought in by two or three*.)

                                    Who's there, the traitor?   25

REGAN: Ingrateful fox, 'tis he.

CORNWALL: Bind fast his corky[10] arms.

GLOUCESTER: What means your graces? Good my friends, consider
          You are my guests. Do me no foul play, friends.

CORNWALL: Bind him, I say. (SERVANTS *bind him*.)

REGAN: Hard, hard! O filthy traitor.   30

GLOUCESTER: Unmerciful lady as you are, I'm none.

CORNWALL: To this chair bind him. Villain, thou shalt find —

(REGAN *plucks his beard*[11].)

GLOUCESTER: By the kind gods, 'tis most ignobly done
          To pluck me by the beard.

REGAN: So white, and such a traitor?

GLOUCESTER: Naughty[12] lady,   35
          These hairs which thou dost ravish from my chin
          Will quicken[13] and accuse thee. I am your host.
          With robber's hands my hospitable favors[14]
          You should not ruffle[15] thus. What will you do?

CORNWALL: Come, sir, what letters had you late[16] from France?   40

REGAN: Be simple-answered,[17] for we know the truth.

CORNWALL: And what confederacy have you with the traitors
          Late footed in the kingdom?

REGAN: To whose hands you have sent the lunatic king:
          Speak.   45

8. *pass upon* pass judgment on. 9. *do . . . to* indulge. 10. *corky* sapless (because old). 11.
s.d. *plucks his beard* a deadly insult. 12. *Naughty* wicked. 13. *quicken* come to
life. 14. *hospitable favors* face of your host. 15. *ruffle* tear at violently. 16. *late* recently.
17. *simple-answered* straightforward in answering.

GLOUCESTER: I have a letter guessingly[18] set down,
Which came from one that's of a neutral heart,
And not from one opposed.

CORNWALL: Cunning.

REGAN: And false.

CORNWALL: Where hast thou sent the king?

GLOUCESTER: To Dover.   50

REGAN: Wherefore to Dover? Wast thou not charged at peril[19] —

CORNWALL: Wherefore to Dover? Let him answer that.

GLOUCESTER: I am tied to th' stake, and I must stand the course.[20]

REGAN: Wherefore to Dover?

GLOUCESTER: Because I would not see thy cruel nails   55
Pluck out his poor old eyes; nor thy fierce sister
In his anointed[21] flesh rash[22] boarish fangs.
The sea, with such a storm as his bare head
In hell-black night endured, would have buoyed[23] up
And quenched the stellèd[24] fires.   60
Yet, poor old heart, he holp[25] the heavens to rain.
If wolves had at thy gate howled that dearn[26] time,
Thou shouldst have said, "Good porter, turn the key."[27]
All cruels else subscribe.[28] But I shall see
The wingèd[29] vengeance overtake such children.   65

CORNWALL: See't shalt thou never. Fellows, hold the chair.
Upon these eyes of thine I'll set my foot.

GLOUCESTER: He that will think[30] to live till he be old,
Give me some help. — O cruel! O you gods!

REGAN: One side will mock[31] another. Th' other too.   70

CORNWALL: If you see vengeance —

FIRST SERVANT: Hold your hand, my lord!
I have served you ever since I was a child;
But better service have I never done you
Than now to bid you hold.

REGAN: How now, you dog?

18. *guessingly* without certain knowledge. 19. *charged at peril* ordered under penalty. 20. *course* coursing (in which a relay of dogs baits a bull or bear tied in the pit). 21. *anointed* holy (because king). 22. *rash* strike with the tusk, like a boar. 23. *buoyed* risen. 24. *stellèd* (1) fixed (as opposed to the planets or wandering stars) (2) starry. 25. *holp* helped. 26. *dearn* dread. 27. *turn the key* i.e., unlock the gate. 28. *All ... subscribe* All cruel creatures but man are compassionate. 29. *wingèd* (1) heavenly (2) swift. 30. *will think* expects. 31. *mock* make ridiculous (because of the contrast).

FIRST SERVANT: If you did wear a beard upon your chin,
    I'd shake it[32] on this quarrel. What do you mean![33]

CORNWALL: My villain![34]

(*Draw and fight.*)

FIRST SERVANT: Nay, then, come on, and take the chance of anger.

REGAN: Give me thy sword. A peasant stand up thus?

(*She takes a sword and runs at him behind, kills him.*)

FIRST SERVANT: O, I am slain! my lord, you have one eye left
    To see some mischief[35] on him. O!

CORNWALL: Lest it see more, prevent it. Out, vile jelly.
    Where is thy luster now?

GLOUCESTER: All dark and comfortless. Where's my son Edmund?
    Edmund, enkindle all the sparks of nature[36]
    To quit[37] this horrid act.

REGAN: Out, treacherous villain,
    Thou call'st on him that hates thee. It was he
    That made the overture[38] of thy treasons to us;
    Who is too good to pity thee.

GLOUCESTER: O my follies! Then Edgar was abused.[39]
    Kind gods, forgive me that, and prosper him.

REGAN: Go thrust him out at gates, and let him smell
    His way to Dover. (*Exit one, with* GLOUCESTER.)

               How is't, my lord? How look you?[40]

CORNWALL: I have received a hurt. Follow me, lady.
    Turn out that eyeless villain. Throw this slave
    Upon the dunghill. Regan, I bleed apace.
    Untimely comes this hurt. Give me your arm. (*Exeunt.*)

SECOND SERVANT: I'll never care what wickedness I do,
    If this man come to good.

THIRD SERVANT: If she live long,
    And in the end meet the old course of death,[41]
    Women will all turn monsters.

SECOND SERVANT: Let's follow the old earl, and get the Bedlam

---

32. *shake it* an insult comparable to Regan's plucking of Gloucester's beard. **33.** *What . . . mean* i.e., What terrible things are you doing? **34.** *villain* serf (with a suggestion of the modern meaning). **35.** *mischief* injury. **36.** *enkindle . . . nature* fan your natural feeling into flame. **37.** *quit* requite. **38.** *overture* disclosure. **39.** *abused* wronged. **40.** *How look you* How are you?. **41.** *meet . . . death* die the customary death of old age.

To lead him where he would. His roguish madness
Allows itself to anything.[42]

THIRD SERVANT: Go thou. I'll fetch some flax and whites of eggs   105
To apply to his bleeding face. Now heaven help him.

(*Exeunt severally.*)

Act IV

Scene 1.

(*The heath.*)

(*Enter* EDGAR.)

EDGAR: Yet better thus, and known to be contemned,[1]
Than still contemned and flattered. To be worst,
The lowest and most dejected[2] thing of fortune,
Stands still in esperance,[3] lives not in fear:
The lamentable change is from the best,   5
The worst returns to laughter.[4] Welcome then,
Thou unsubstantial air that I embrace!
The wretch that thou hast blown unto the worst
Owes[5] nothing to thy blasts.

(*Enter* GLOUCESTER, *led by an* OLD MAN.)

                              But who comes here?
My father, poorly led?[6] World, world, O world!   10
But that thy strange mutations make us hate thee,
Life would not yield to age.[7]

OLD MAN: O, my good lord,
I have been your tenant, and your father's tenant,
These fourscore years.

GLOUCESTER: Away, get thee away; good friend, be gone: 15
Thy comforts[8] can do me no good at all;
Thee they may hurt.[9]

OLD MAN: You cannot see your way.

GLOUCESTER: I have no way and therefore want[10] no eyes;

---

42. *His . . . anything* his lack of all self-control leaves him open to any suggestion. **IV.i.**
1. *known . . . contemned* conscious of being despised. 2. *dejected* abased. 3. *esperance* hope. 4. *returns to laughter* changes for the better. 5. *Owes* is in debt for. 6. *poorly led* (1) led like a poor man, with only one attendant (2) led by a poor man. 7. *But . . . age* We should not agree to grow old and hence die, except for the hateful mutability of life. 8. *comforts* ministrations. 9. *hurt* injure. 10. *want* require.

I stumbled when I saw. Full oft 'tis seen,
Our means secure us, and our mere defects 20
Prove our commodities.[11] Oh, dear son Edgar,
The food[12] of thy abusèd[13] father's wrath!
Might I but live to see thee in[14] my touch,
I'd say I had eyes again!

OLD MAN: How now! Who's there?

EDGAR (*Aside.*): O gods! Who is't can say, "I am at the worst"? 25
I am worse than e'er I was.

OLD MAN: 'Tis poor mad Tom.

EDGAR (*Aside.*): And worse I may be yet: the worst is not
So long as we can say, "This is the worst."[15]

OLD MAN: Fellow, where goest?

GLOUCESTER: Is it a beggar-man?

OLD MAN: Madman and beggar too. 30

GLOUCESTER: He has some reason,[16] else he could not beg.
I' th' last night's storm I such a fellow saw,
Which made me think a man a worm. My son
Came then into my mind, and yet my mind
Was then scarce friends with him. I have heard more since. 35
As flies to wanton[17] boys, are we to th' gods,
They kill us for their sport.

EDGAR: (*Aside.*) How should this be?[18]
Bad is the trade that must play fool to sorrow,
Ang'ring[19] itself and others. Bless thee, master!

GLOUCESTER: Is that the naked fellow?

OLD MAN: Ay, my lord. 40

GLOUCESTER: Then, prithee, get thee gone: if for my sake
Thou wilt o'ertake us hence a mile or twain
I' th' way toward Dover, do it for ancient[20] love,
And bring some covering for this naked soul,
Which I'll entreat to lead me.

OLD MAN: Alack, sir, he is mad. 45

GLOUCESTER: 'Tis the time's plague,[21] when madmen lead the blind.

11. *Our . . . commodities* Our resources make us overconfident, while our afflictions make for
our advantage. 12. *food* i.e., the object on which Gloucester's anger fed. 13. *abused*
deceived 14. *in* i.e., with, by means of 15. *the . . . worst* so long as a man continues to suffer
(i.e., is still alive), even greater suffering may await him. 16. *reason* faculty of
reasoning. 17. *wanton* (1) playful (2) reckless. 18. *How . . . be* i.e., How can this horror
be? 19. *Ang'ring* offending. 20. *ancient* (1) the love the Old Man feels, by virtue of his long
tenancy (2) the love that formerly obtained between master and man. 21. *time's plague*
characteristic disorder of this time.

Do as I bid thee, or rather do thy pleasure;[22]
Above the rest,[23] be gone.

OLD MAN: I'll bring him the best 'parel[24] that I have,
Come on't what will. (*Exit.*) 50

GLOUCESTER: Sirrah, naked fellow —

EDGAR: Poor Tom's a-cold. (*Aside.*) I cannot daub it[25] further.

GLOUCESTER: Come hither, fellow.

EDGAR (*Aside.*): And yet I must. — Bless thy sweet eyes, they bleed.

GLOUCESTER: Know'st thou the way to Dover? 55

EDGAR: Both stile and gate, horse-way and footpath.
Poor Tom hath been scared out of his good wits.
Bless thee, good man's son, from the foul fiend!
Five fiends have been in Poor Tom at once; of lust, as Obidicut,[26]
Hobbididence, prince of dumbness;[27] Mahu, of stealing; Modo, of 60
murder; Flibbertigibbet, of mopping and mowing;[28] who since
possesses chamber-maids and waiting-women. So, bless thee, master!

GLOUCESTER: Here, take this purse, thou whom the heavens' plagues
Have humbled to all strokes:[29] that I am wretched
Makes thee the happier. Heavens, deal so still!
Let the superfluous[30] and lust-dieted[31] man, 65
That slaves[32] your ordinance,[33] that will not see
Because he does not feel, feel your pow'r quickly;
So distribution should undo excess,[34]
And each man have enough. Dost thou know Dover? 70

EDGAR: Ay, master.

GLOUCESTER: There is a cliff whose high and bending[35] head
Looks fearfully[36] in the confinèd deep:[37]
Bring me but to the very brim of it,
And I'll repair the misery thou dost bear
With something rich about me: from that place 75
I shall no leading need.

EDGAR: Give me thy arm:
Poor Tom shall lead thee. (*Exeunt.*)

22. *thy pleasure* as you like it. 23. *the rest* all. 24. *parel* apparel. 25. *daub it* lay it on (figure from plastering mortar). 26. *Obidicut* Hoberdicut, a devil (like the four that follow, from Harsnett's *Declaration*). 27. *dumbness* muteness (like the crimes and afflictions in the next lines, the result of diabolic possession). 28. *mopping and mowing* grimacing and making faces. 29. *humbled ... strokes* brought so low as to bear anything humbly. 30. *superfluous* possessed of superfluities. 31. *lust-dieted* whose lust is gratified (like Gloucester's). 32. *slaves* (1) tramples, spurns like a slave (2) tears, rends (Old English *slaefan*) (?). 33. *ordinance* law. 34. *So ... excess* Then the man with too much wealth would distribute it among those with too little. 35. *bending* overhanging. 36. *fearfully* occasioning fear. 37. *confined deep* the sea, hemmed in below.

Scene II.

(*Before the Duke of Albany's palace.*)

(*Enter* GONERIL *and* EDMUND.)

GONERIL: Welcome, my lord: I marvel our mild husband
    Not met[1] us on the way.

(*Enter* OSWALD.)

                    Now, where's your master?

OSWALD: Madam, within; but never man so changed.
    I told him of the army that was landed:
    He smiled at it. I told him you were coming;   5
    His answer was, "The worse." Of Gloucester's treachery,
    And of the loyal service of his son
    When I informed him, then he called me sot,[2]
    And told me I had turned the wrong side out:
    What most he should dislike seems pleasant to him;   10
    What like,[3] offensive.

GONERIL (*To* EDMUND.): Then shall you go no further.
    It is the cowish[4] terror of his spirit,
    That dares not undertake:[5] he'll not feel wrongs,
    Which tie him to an answer.[6] Our wishes on the way   15
    May prove effects.[7] Back, Edmund, to my brother;
    Hasten his musters[8] and conduct his pow'rs.[9]
    I must change names[10] at home and give the distaff[11]
    Into my husband's hands. This trusty servant
    Shall pass between us: ere long you are like to hear,   20
    If you dare venture in your own behalf,
    A mistress's[12] command. Wear this; spare speech;

(*Giving a favor.*)

    Decline your head.[13] This kiss, if it durst speak,
    Would stretch thy spirits up into the air:
    Conceive[14] and fare thee well.   25

EDMUND: Yours in the ranks of death.

GONERIL: My most dear Gloucester!

IV.ii **1.** *Not met* did not meet. **2.** *sot* fool. **3.** *What like* what he should like. **4.** *cowish* cowardly. **5.** *undertake* venture. **6.** *tie . . . answer* oblige him to retaliate. **7.** *Our . . . effects* Our desires (that you might be my husband), as we journeyed here, may be fulfilled. **8.** *musters* collecting of troops. **9.** *conduct his pow'rs* lead his army. **10.** *change names* i.e., exchange the name of "mistress" for that of "master." **11.** *distaff* spinning stick (wifely symbol). **12.** *mistress's* lover's (and also, Albany having been disposed of, lady's or wife's). **13.** *Decline your head* i.e., that Goneril may kiss him. **14.** *Conceive* understand (with a sexual implication, that includes "stretch thy spirits," line 24; and "death," line 26: "to die," meaning "to experience sexual intercourse").

(*Exit* EDMUND.)

> O, the difference of man and man!
> To thee a woman's services are due:
> My fool usurps my body.[15]

OSWALD: Madam, here comes my lord. (*Exit.*)

(*Enter* ALBANY.)

GONERIL: I have been worth the whistle[16]

ALBANY: O Goneril!   30
> You are not worth the dust which the rude wind
> Blows in your face. I fear your disposition:[17]
> That nature which contemns[18] its origin
> Cannot be bordered certain in itself;[19]
> She that herself will sliver and disbranch[20]   35
> From her material sap,[21] perforce must wither
> And come to deadly use.[22]

GONERIL: No more; the text[23] is foolish.

ALBANY: Wisdom and goodness to the vile seem vile:
> Filths savor but themselves.[24] What have you done?   40
> Tigers, not daughters, what have you performed?
> A father, and a gracious aged man,
> Whose reverence even the head-lugged bear[25] would lick,
> Most barbarous, most degenerate, have you madded.[26]
> Could my good brother suffer you to do it?   45
> A man, a prince, by him so benefited!
> If that the heavens do not their visible spirits[27]
> Send quickly down to tame these vile offenses,
> It will come,
> Humanity must perforce prey on itself,   50
> Like monsters of the deep.

GONERIL: Milk-livered[28] man!
> That bear'st a cheek for blows, a head for wrongs;
> Who hast not in thy brows an eye discerning
> Thine honor from thy suffering,[29] that not know'st
> Fools do those villains pity who are punished   55

15. *My . . . body* My husband wrongfully enjoys me. 16. *I . . . whistle* i.e., Once you valued me (the proverb is implied, "It is a poor dog that is not worth the whistling"). 17. *disposition* nature. 18. *contemns* despises. 19. *bordered . . . itself* kept within its normal bounds. 20. *sliver and disbranch* cut off. 21. *material sap* essential and life-giving sustenance. 22. *come . . . use* i.e., be as a dead branch for the burning. 23. *text* i.e., on which your sermon is based. 24. *Filths . . . themselves* the filthy relish only the taste of filth. 25. *head-lugged bear* bear-baited by the dogs, and hence enraged. 26. *madded* made mad. 27. *visible spirits* avenging spirits in material form. 28. *Milk-livered* lily-livered (hence cowardly, the liver being regarded as the seat of courage). 29. *discerning . . . suffering* able to distinguish between insults that ought to be resented, and ordinary pain that is to be borne.

Ere they have done their mischief.[30] Where's thy drum?
France spreads his banners in our noiseless[31] land,
With plumèd helm[32] thy state begins to threat,[33]
Whilst thou, a moral[34] fool, sits still and cries,
"Alack, why does he so?"

ALBANY: See thyself, devil!   60
Proper[35] deformity seems not in the fiend
So horrid as in woman.

GONERIL: O vain fool!

ALBANY: Thou changèd and self-covered[36] thing, for shame,
Be-monster not thy feature.[37] Were't my fitness[38]
To let these hands obey my blood,[39]   65
They are apt enough to dislocate and tear
Thy flesh and bones: howe'er[40] thou art a fiend,
A woman's shape doth shield thee.

GONERIL: Marry, your manhood mew.[41]

(*Enter a* MESSENGER.)

ALBANY: What news?   70

MESSENGER: O, my good lord, the Duke of Cornwall's dead
Slain by his servant, going to[42] put out
The other eye of Gloucester.

ALBANY: Gloucester's eyes!

MESSENGER: A servant that he bred,[43] thrilled with remorse,[44]
Opposed against the act, bending his sword   75
To his great master, who thereat enraged
Flew on him, and amongst them felled[45] him dead,
But not without that harmful stroke which since
Hath plucked him after.[46]

ALBANY: This shows you are above,
You justicers,[47] that these our nether[48] crimes   80
So speedily can venge.[49] But, O poor Gloucester!
Lost he his other eye?

30. *Fools . . . mischief* Only fools are sorry for criminals whose intended criminality is prevented by punishment. 31. *noiseless* i.e., the drum, signifying preparation for war, is silent. 32. *helm* helmet. 33. *thy . . . threat* France begins to threaten Albany's realm. 34. *moral* moralizing; but also with the implication that morality and folly are one. 35. *Proper* (1) natural (to a fiend) (2) fair-appearing. 36. *changèd and self-covered* i.e., transformed, by the contorting of her woman's face, on which appears the fiendish behavior she has allowed herself (Goneril has disguised nature by wickedness). 37. *Be-monster . . . feature* do not change your appearance into a fiend's. 38. *my fitness* appropriate for me. 39. *blood* passion. 40. *howe'er* but even if. 41. *your manhood mew* (1) coop up or confine (pretended) manhood (2) molt or shed it, if that is what is supposed to "shield" me from you. 42. *going to* as he was about to. 43. *bred* reared. 44. *thrilled with remorse* pierced by compassion. 45. *amongst them felled* others assisting, they felled. 46. *plucked him after* i.e., brought Cornwall to death with his servant. 47. *justicers* judges. 48. *nether* committed below (on earth). 49. *venge* avenge.

MESSENGER: Both, both, my lord.
    This letter, madam, craves⁵⁰ a speedy answer;
    'Tis from your sister.

GONERIL: (*Aside.*) One way I like this well;
    But being widow, and my Gloucester with her,   85
    May all the building in my fancy pluck
    Upon my hateful life.⁵¹ Another way,⁵²
    The news is not so tart.⁵³ — I'll read, and answer. (*Exit.*)

ALBANY: Where was his son when they did take his eyes?

MESSENGER: Come with my lady hither.

ALBANY: He is not here.   90

MESSENGER: No, my good lord; I met him back⁵⁴ again.

ALBANY: Knows he the wickedness?

MESSENGER: Ay, my good lord; 'twas he informed against him,
    And quit the house on purpose, that their punishment
    Might have the freer course.

ALBANY: Gloucester, I live   95
    To thank thee for the love thou showed'st the king,
    And to revenge thine eyes. Come hither, friend:
    Tell me what more thou know'st. (*Exeunt.*)

Scene III.

(*The French camp near Dover.*)

(*Enter* KENT *and a* GENTLEMAN.)

KENT: Why the King of France is so suddenly gone back, know you no
    reason?

GENTLEMAN: Something he left imperfect in the state,¹ which since his
    coming forth is thought of, which imports² to the kingdom so much
    fear and danger that his personal return was most required and   5
    necessary.

KENT: Who hath he left behind him general?

GENTLEMAN: The Marshal of France, Monsieur La Far.

KENT: Did your letters pierce³ the queen to any demonstration of grief?

GENTLEMAN: Ay, sir; she took them, read them in my presence,   10

---

50. *craves* demands. **51.** *May . . . life* These things may send my future hopes, my castles in
air, crashing down upon the hateful (married) life I lead now. **52.** *Another way* looked at
another way. **53.** *tart* sour. **54.** *back* going back. **IV.iii. 1.** *imperfect . . . state* unsettled in
his own kingdom. **2.** *imports* portends. **3.** *pierce* impel.

And now and then an ample tear trilled[4] down
Her delicate cheek: it seemed she was a queen
Over her passion, who most rebel-like
Sought to be king o'er her.

KENT: O, then it moved her.

GENTLEMAN: Not to a rage: patience and sorrow strove   15
Who should express her goodliest.[5] You have seen
Sunshine and rain at once: her smiles and tears
Were like a better way:[6] those happy smilets[7]
That played on her ripe lip seemed not to know
What guests were in her eyes, which parted thence   20
As pearls from diamonds dropped. In brief,
Sorrow would be a rarity most belovèd,
If all could so become it.[8]

KENT: Made she no verbal question?

GENTLEMAN: Faith, once or twice she heaved[9] the name of "father"
Pantingly forth, as if it pressed her heart;   25
Cried, "Sisters! Sisters! Shame of ladies! Sisters!
Kent! Father! Sisters! What, i' th' storm? i' th' night?
Let pity not be believed!"[10] There she shook
The holy water from her heavenly eyes,
And clamor moistened:[11] then away she started   30
To deal with grief alone.

KENT: It is the stars,
The stars above us, govern our conditions;[12]
Else one self mate and make could not beget
Such different issues.[13] You spoke not with her since?

GENTLEMAN: No.   35

KENT: Was this before the king returned?

GENTLEMAN: No, since.

KENT: Well, sir, the poor distressèd Lear's i' th' town;
Who sometime in his better tune[14] remembers
What we are come about, and by no means
Will yield to see his daughter.

GENTLEMAN: Why, good sir?   40

4. *trilled* trickled. 5. *Who ... goodliest* which should give her the most becoming expression. 6. *Were ... way* i.e., improved on that spectacle. 7. *smilets* little
smiles. 8. *Sorrow ... it* sorrow would be a coveted jewel if it became others as it does
her. 9. *heaved* expressed with difficulty. 10. *Let ... believed* Let it not be believed for
pity. 11. *clamor moistened* moistened clamor, i.e., mixed (and perhaps assuaged) her outcries
with tears. 12. *govern our conditions* determine what we are. 13. *Else ... issues* otherwise
the same husband and wife could not produce such different children. 14. *better tune* composed, less jangled intervals.

KENT: A sovereign[15] shame so elbows[16] him: his own unkindness
That stripped her from his benediction, turned her
To foreign casualties,[17] gave her dear rights
To his dog-hearted daughters: these things sting
His mind so venomously that burning shame   45
Detains him from Cordelia.

GENTLEMAN: Alack, poor gentleman!

KENT: Of Albany's and Cornwall's powers you heard not?

GENTLEMAN: 'Tis so,[18] they are afoot.

KENT: Well, sir, I'll bring you to our master Lear,
And leave you to attend him: some dear cause[19]   50
Will in concealment wrap me up awhile;
When I am known aright, you shall not grieve
Lending me this acquaintance. I pray you, go
Along with me. (*Exeunt.*)

Scene IV.

(*The same. A tent.*)

(*Enter, with drum and colors,* CORDELIA, DOCTOR *and* SOLDIERS.)

CORDELIA: Alack, 'tis he: why, he was met even now
As mad as the vexed sea; singing aloud;
Crowned with rank femiter and furrow-weeds,
With hardocks, hemlock, nettles, cuckoo-flow'rs,
Darnel,[1] and all the idle weeds that grow   5
In our sustaining corn.[2] A century[3] send forth;
Search every acre in the high-grown field,
And bring him to our eye. (*Exit an* OFFICER.) What can man's
     wisdom[4]
In the restoring his bereavèd[5] sense?
He that helps him take all my outward[6] worth.   10

DOCTOR: There is means, madam:
Our foster-nurse[7] of nature is repose,
The which he lacks: that to provoke[8] in him,

---

15. *sovereign* overpowering. **16.** *elbows* jogs his elbow (i.e., reminds him). **17.** *casualties* chances. **18.** *'Tis so* i.e., I have heard of them. **19.** *dear cause* important reason. **IV.iv.** **1.** *femiter . . . Darnel: femiter* fumitory, whose leaves and juice are bitter; *furrow-weeds* weeds that grow in the furrow, or plowed land; *hardocks* hoar or white docks (?), burdocks, harlocks; *hemlock* a poison; *nettles* plants that sting and burn; *cuckoo-flow'rs* identified with a plant employed to remedy diseases of the brain; *Darnel* tares, noisome weeds. **2.** *sustaining corn* life-maintaining wheat. **3.** *century* sentry (?); troop of a hundred soldiers. **4.** *What . . . wisdom* what can science accomplish. **5.** *bereavèd* impaired. **6.** *outward* material. **7.** *foster-nurse* fostering nurse. **8.** *provoke* induce.

Are many simples operative,[9] whose power
Will close the eye of anguish.

CORDELIA: All blest secrets,   15
All you unpublished virtues[10] of the earth,
Spring with my tears! be aidant and remediate[11]
In the good man's distress! Seek, seek for him,
Lest his ungoverned rage dissolve the life
That wants the means to lead it.[12]

(*Enter* MESSENGER.)

MESSENGER: News, madam;   20
The British pow'rs are marching hitherward.

CORDELIA: 'Tis known before. Our preparation stands
In expectation of them. O dear father,
It is thy business that I go about;
Therefore[13] great France   25
My mourning and importuned[14] tears hath pitied.
No blown[15] ambition doth our arms incite,
But love, dear love, and our aged father's right:
Soon may I hear and see him! (*Exeunt.*)

Scene V.

(*Gloucester's castle.*)

(*Enter* REGAN *and* OSWALD.)

REGAN: But are my brother's pow'rs set forth?

OSWALD: Ay, madam.

REGAN: Himself in person there?

OSWALD: Madam, with much ado:[1]
Your sister is the better soldier.

REGAN: Lord Edmund spake not with your lord at home?

OSWALD: No, madam.   5

REGAN: What might import[2] my sister's letter to him?

OSWALD: I know not, lady.

REGAN: Faith, he is posted[3] hence on serious matter.

9. *simples operative* efficacious medicinal herbs.   10. *unpublished virtues* i.e., secret remedial
herbs.   11. *remediate* remedial.   12. *wants . . . it* i.e., lacks the reason to control the
rage.   13. *Therefore* because of that.   14. *importuned* importunate.   15. *blown* puffed up.
IV.v. 1. *ado* bother and persuasion.   2. *import* purport, carry as its message.   3. *is posted* has
ridden speedily.

It was great ignorance,[4] Gloucester's eyes being out,
To let him live. Where he arrives he moves   10
All hearts against us: Edmund, I think, is gone,
In pity of his misery, to dispatch
His nighted[5] life; moreover, to descry
The strength o' th' enemy.

OSWALD: I must needs after him, madam, with my letter.   15

REGAN: Our troops set forth tomorrow: stay with us;
The ways are dangerous.

OSWALD: I may not, madam:
My lady charged my duty[6] in this business.

REGAN: Why should she write to Edmund? Might not you
Transport her purposes[7] by word? Belike,[8]   20
Some things I know not what. I'll love thee much,
Let me unseal the letter.

OSWALD: Madam, I had rather —

REGAN: I know your lady does not love her husband:
I am sure of that: and at her late[9] being here
She gave strange eliads[10] and most speaking looks   25
To noble Edmund. I know you are of her bosom.[11]

OSWALD: I, madam?

REGAN: I speak in understanding: y' are; I know't:
Therefore I do advise you, take this note:[12]
My lord is dead; Edmund and I have talked;   30
And more convenient[13] is he for my hand
Than for your lady's: you may gather more.[14]
If you do find him, pray you, give him this;[15]
And when your mistress hears thus much from you,
I pray, desire her call[16] her wisdom to her.   35
So, fare you well.
If you do chance to hear of that blind traitor,
Preferment[17] falls on him that cuts him off.

OSWALD: Would I could meet him, madam! I should show
What party I do follow.

REGAN: Fare thee well. (*Exeunt.*)   40

---

4. *ignorance* folly. 5. *nighted* (1) darkened, because blinded (2) benighted. 6. *charged my duty* ordered me as a solemn duty. 7. *Transport her purposes* convey her intentions. 8. *Belike* probably. 9. *late* recently. 10. *eliads* amorous looks. 11. *of her bosom* in her confidence. 12. *take this note* take note of this. 13. *convenient* fitting. 14. *gather more* surmise more yourself. 15. *this* this advice. 16. *call* recall. 17. *Preferment* promotion.

Scene VI.

(Fields near Dover.)

(Enter GLOUCESTER *and* EDGAR.)

GLOUCESTER: When shall I come to th' top of that same hill?

EDGAR: You do climb up it now. Look, how we labor.

GLOUCESTER: Methinks the ground is even.

EDGAR: Horrible steep.
Hark, do you hear the sea?

GLOUCESTER: No, truly.

EDGAR: Why then your other senses grow imperfect   5
By your eyes' anguish.[1]

GLOUCESTER: So may it be indeed.
Methinks thy voice is altered, and thou speak'st
In better phrase and matter than thou didst.

EDGAR: Y' are much deceived: in nothing am I changed
But in my garments.

GLOUCESTER: Methinks y' are better spoken.   10

EDGAR: Come on, sir; here's the place: stand still. How fearful
And dizzy 'tis to cast one's eyes so low!
The crows and choughs[2] that wing the midway air[3]
Show scarce so gross[4] as beetles. Half way down
Hangs one that gathers sampire,[5] dreadful trade!   15
Methinks he seems no bigger than his head.
The fishermen that walk upon the beach
Appear like mice; and yond tall anchoring[6] bark
Diminished to her cock;[7] her cock, a buoy
Almost too small for sight. The murmuring surge   20
That on th' unnumb'red idle pebble[8] chafes
Cannot be heard so high. I'll look no more,
Lest my brain turn and the deficient sight
Topple[9] down headlong.

GLOUCESTER: Set me where you stand.

EDGAR: Give me your hand: you are now within a foot   25

IV.vi. 1. *anguish* pain. **2.** *choughs* a kind of crow. **3.** *midway air* i.e., halfway down the cliff. **4.** *gross* large. **5.** *sampire* samphire, an aromatic herb associated with Dover Cliffs. **6.** *anchoring* anchored. **7.** *cock* cockboat, a small boat usually towed behind the ship. **8.** *unnumb'red idle pebble* innumerable pebbles, moved to and fro by the waves to no purpose. **9.** *the . . . Topple* my failing sight topple me.

Of th' extreme verge: for all beneath the moon
Would I not leap upright.[10]

GLOUCESTER: Let go my hand.
Here, friend, 's another purse; in it a jewel
Well worth a poor man's taking. Fairies[11] and gods
Prosper it with thee! Go thou further off;   30
Bid me farewell, and let me hear thee going.

EDGAR: Now fare ye well, good sir.

GLOUCESTER: With all my heart.

EDGAR (*Aside*.): Why I do trifle thus with his despair
Is done to cure it.[12]

GLOUCESTER: O you mighty gods!

(*He kneels.*)

This world I do renounce, and in your sights   35
Shake patiently my great affliction off:
If I could bear it longer and not fall
To quarrel with[13] your great opposeless[14] wills,
My snuff[15] and loathèd part of nature should
Burn itself out. If Edgar lives, O bless him!   40
Now, fellow, fare thee well. (*He falls.*)

EDGAR: Gone, sir, farewell.
And yet I know not how[16] conceit[17] may rob
The treasury of life, when life itself
Yields to[18] the theft. Had he been where he thought,
By this had thought been past. Alive or dead?   45
Ho, you sir! friend! Hear you, sir! speak!
Thus might he pass[19] indeed: yet he revives.
What are you, sir?

GLOUCESTER: Away, and let me die.

EDGAR: Hadst thou been aught but gossamer, feathers, air,
So many fathom down precipitating,[20]   50
Thou'dst shivered like an egg: but thou dost breathe;
Hast heavy substance; bleed'st not; speak'st; art sound.
Ten masts at each[21] make not the altitude
Which thou hast perpendicularly fell:
Thy life's[22] a miracle. Speak yet again.   55

---

10. *upright* i.e., even up in the air, to say nothing of forward, over the cliff.   **11.** *Fairies* who are supposed to guard and multiply hidden treasure.   **12.** *Why . . . it* I ᵢlay on his despair in order to cure it.   **13.** *fall . . . with* rebel against.   **14.** *opposeless* not to be, and not capable of being, opposed.   **15.** *snuff* the guttering (and stinking) wick of a burnt-out candle.   **16.** *how* but what.   **17.** *conceit* imagination.   **18.** *Yields to* allows.   **19.** *pass* die.   **20.** *precipitating* falling.   **21.** *at each* one on top of the other.   **22.** *life's* survival.

GLOUCESTER: But have I fall'n, or no?

EDGAR: From the dread summit of this chalky bourn.[23]
Look up a-height;[24] the shrill-gorged[25] lark so far
Cannot be seen or heard: do but look up.

GLOUCESTER: Alack, I have no eyes.   60
Is wretchedness deprived that benefit,
To end itself by death? 'Twas yet some comfort,
When misery could beguile[26] the tyrant's rage
And frustrate his proud will.

EDGAR: Give me your arm.
Up, so. How is't? Feel you[27] your legs? You stand.   65

GLOUCESTER: Too well, too well.

EDGAR: This is above all strangeness.
Upon the crown o' th' cliff, what thing was that
Which parted from you?

GLOUCESTER: A poor unfortunate beggar.

EDGAR: As I stood here below, methought his eyes
Were two full moons; he had a thousand noses,   70
Horns whelked[28] and waved like the enridgèd[29] sea:
It was some fiend; therefore, thou happy father,[30]
Think that the clearest[31] gods, who make them honors
Of men's impossibilities,[32] have preserved thee.

GLOUCESTER: I do remember now: henceforth I'll bear   75
Affliction till it do cry out itself,
"Enough, enough," and die. That thing you speak of,
I took it for a man; often 'twould say,
"The fiend, the fiend" — he led me to that place.

EDGAR: Bear free[33] and patient thoughts.

(*Enter* LEAR *fantastically dressed with wild flowers.*)

                                              But who comes here?   80
The safer[34] sense will ne'er accommodate[35]
His master thus.

LEAR: No, they cannot touch me for coining,[36] I am the king himself.

EDGAR: O thou side-piercing sight!

---

23. *bourn* boundary. **24.** *a-height* on high. **25.** *gorged* throated, voiced. **26.** *beguile* cheat (i.e., by suicide). **27.** *Feel you* have you any feeling in. **28.** *whelked* twisted. **29.** *enridgèd* i.e., furrowed into waves. **30.** *happy father* fortunate old man. **31.** *clearest* purest. **32.** *who . . . impossibilities* who cause themselves to be honored and revered by performing miracles of which men are incapable. **33.** *free* i.e., emancipated from grief and despair, which fetter the soul. **34.** *safer* sounder, saner. **35.** *accommodate* dress, adorn. **36.** *touch . . . coining* arrest me for minting coins (the king's prerogative).

LEAR: Nature's above art in that respect.[37] There's your press-money.[38] 85
That fellow handles his bow like a crow-keeper;[39] draw me a clothier's yard.[40] Look, look, a mouse! Peace, peace; this piece of
toasted cheese will do't. There's my gauntlet;[41] I'll prove it on[42] a
giant. Bring up the brown bills.[43] O, well flown,[44] bird! i' th' clout, i'
th' clout.[45] hewgh![46] Give the word.[47] 90

EDGAR: Sweet marjoram.[48]

LEAR: Pass.

GLOUCESTER: I know that voice.

LEAR: Ha! Goneril, with a white beard! They flattered me like a dog,[49]
and told me I had white hairs in my beard ere the black ones were 95
there.[50] To say "ay" and "no" to everything that I said! "Ay" and
"no" too was no good divinity.[51] When the rain came to wet me
once and the wind to make me chatter; when the thunder would not
peace at my bidding; there I found 'em, there I smelt 'em out. Go
to, they are not men o' their words; they told me I was everything; 100
'tis a lie, I am not ague-proof.[52]

GLOUCESTER: The trick[53] of that voice I do well remember:
Is't not the king?

LEAR: Ay, every inch a king.
When I do stare, see how the subject quakes.
I pardon that man's life. What was thy cause?[54] 105
Adultery?
Thou shalt not die: die for adultery! No:
The wren goes to't, and the small gilded fly
Does lecher[55] in my sight.
Let copulation thrive; for Gloucester's bastard son 110
Was kinder to his father than my daughters
Got[56] 'tween the lawful sheets.
To't, luxury,[57] pell-mell! for I lack soldiers.[58]

37. *Nature's . . . respect* i.e., a born king is superior to legal (and hence artificial) inhibition;
there is also a glance here at the popular Renaissance debate concerning the relative importance
of nature (inspiration) and art (training). 38. *press-money* paid to conscripted
soldiers. 39. *crowkeeper* a farmer scaring away crows. 40. *clothier's yard* the standard English
arrow was a cloth-yard long; here the injunction is to draw the arrow back, like a powerful
archer, a full yard to the ear. 41. *gauntlet* armored glove, thrown down as a
challenge. 42. *prove it on* maintain my challenge even against. 43. *brown bills* halberds var-
nished to prevent rust (here the reference is to the soldiers who carry them). 44. *well flown*
falconer's cry; and perhaps a reference to the flight of the arrow. 45. *clout* the target shot
at. 46. *hewgh* imitating the whizzing of the arrow (?). 47. *word* password. 48. *Sweet marjoram* herb, used as a remedy for brain disease. 49. *like a dog* as a dog flatters. 50. *I . . .
there* I was wise before I had even grown a beard. 51. *no good divinity* bad theology, because
contrary to the biblical saying (II. Corinthians 1:18), "Our word toward you was not yea and
nay"; see also James 5:12, "But let your yea be yea, and your nay, nay; lest ye fall into condemnation"; and Matthew 5:36–37. 52. *ague-proof* secure against fever. 53. *trick* intonation. 54. *cause* offense. 55. *lecher* copulate. 56. *Got* begot. 57. *luxury* lechery. 58. *for
. . . soldiers* i.e., (1) whom copulation will supply (?) (2) and am therefore powerless (?).

Behold yond simp'ring dame,
Whose face between her forks presages snow,[59]   115
That minces[60] virtue and does shake the head
To hear of pleasure's name.[61]
The fitchew,[62] nor the soilèd[63] horse, goes to't
With a more riotous appetite.
Down from the waist they are Centaurs,[64]   120
Though women all above:
But to the girdle[65] do the gods inherit,[66]
Beneath is all the fiend's.
There's hell, there's darkness, there is the sulphurous pit, burning,
scalding, stench, consumption; fie, fie, fie! pah, pah! Give me an   125
ounce of civet,[67] good apothecary, sweeten my imagination: there's
money for thee.

GLOUCESTER: O, let me kiss that hand!

LEAR: Let me wipe it first; it smells of mortality.[68]

GLOUCESTER: O ruined piece of nature! This great world   130
Shall so wear out to nought.[69] Dost thou know me?

LEAR: I remember thine eyes well enough. Dost thou squiny[70] at me? No,
do thy worst, blind Cupid;[71] I'll not love. Read thou this challenge;[72]
mark but the penning of it.

GLOUCESTER: Were all thy letters suns, I could not see.   135

EDGAR: I would not take[73] this from report: it is,
And my heart breaks at it.

LEAR: Read.

GLOUCESTER: What, with the case[74] of eyes?

LEAR: O, ho, are you there with me?[75] No eyes in your head, nor no   140
money in your purse? Your eyes are in a heavy case,[76] your purse in
a light,[77] yet you see how this world goes.

GLOUCESTER: I see it feelingly.[78]

LEAR: What, art mad? A man may see how this world goes with no eyes.
Look with thine ears: see how yond justice rails upon yond simple[79]   145

59. *Whose . . . snow* whose cold demeanor seems to promise chaste behavior ("forks" =
legs). 60. *minces* squeamishly pretends to. 61. *pleasure's name* the very name of sexual
pleasure. 62. *fitchew* polecat (and slang for prostitute). 63. *soilèd* put to pasture, and hence
wanton with feeding. 64. *Centaurs* lustful creatures, half man and half horse. 65. *girdle*
waist. 66. *inherit* possess. 67. *civet* perfume. 68. *mortality* (1) death (2) existence. 69. *This . . . nought* i.e., The universe (macrocosm) will decay to nothing in the same
way as the little world of man (microcosm). 70. *squiny* squint, look sideways, like a
prostitute. 71. *blind Cupid* the sign hung before a brothel. 72. *challenge* a reminiscence of
lines 87–88. 73. *take* believe. 74. *case* empty sockets. 75. *are . . . me* is that what you tell
me. 76. *heavy case* sad plight (pun on line 139). 77. *light* i.e., empty. 78. *feelingly* (1) by
touch (2) by feeling pain (3) with emotion. 79. *simple* common, of low estate.

thief. Hark, in thine ear: change places, and, handy-dandy,[80] which is the justice, which is the thief? Thou hast seen a farmer's dog bark at a beggar?

GLOUCESTER: Ay, sir.

LEAR: And the creature run from the cur? There thou mightst behold the 150
great image of authority[81] a dog's obeyed in office.[82]
Thou rascal beadle,[83] hold thy bloody hand!
Why dost thou lash that whore? Strip thy own back;
Thou hotly lusts to use her in that kind[84]
For which thou whip'st her. The userer hangs the cozener.[85] 155
Through tattered clothes small vices do appear;
Robes and furred gowns[86] hide all. Plate sin with gold,
And the strong lance of justice hurtless[87] breaks;
Arm it in rags, a pygmy's straw does pierce it.
None does offend, none, I say, none; I'll able[88] 'em: 160
Take that[89] of me, my friend, who have the power
To seal th' accuser's lips. Get thee glass eyes,[90]
And, like a scurvy politician,[91] seem
To see the things thou dost not. Now, now, now, now.
Pull off my boots: harder, harder: so. 165

EDGAR: O, matter and impertinency[92] mixed!
Reason in madness!

LEAR: If thou wilt weep my fortunes, take my eyes.
I know thee well enough; thy name is Gloucester:
Thou must be patient; we came crying hither: 170
Thou know'st, the first time that we smell the air
We wawl and cry. I will preach to thee: mark.

GLOUCESTER: Alack, alack the day!

LEAR: When we are born, we cry that we are come
To this great stage of fools. This[93] a good block.[94] 175
It were a delicate[95] strategem, to shoe

80. *handy-dandy* i.e., choose, guess (after the children's game — "Handy-dandy, prickly prandy" — of choosing the correct hand). 81. *image of authority* symbol revealing the true meaning of authority. 82. *a dog's . . . office* i.e., whoever has power is obeyed. 83. *beadle* parish constable. 84. *kind* i.e., sexual act. 85. *The userer . . . cozener* i.e., The powerful moneylender, in his role as judge, puts to death the petty cheat. 86. *Robes . . . gowns* worn by a judge. 87. *hurtless* i.e., without hurting the sinner. 88. *able* vouch for. 89. *that* the immunity just conferred (line 160). 90. *glass eyes* spectacles. 91. *scurvy politician* vile politic man. 92. *matter and impertinency* sense and nonsense. 93. *This'* this is. 94. *block* various meanings have been suggested, for example, the stump of a tree, on which Lear is supposed to climb; a mounting-block, which suggests "horse" (line 177); a hat (which Lear or another must be made to wear), from the block on which a felt hat is molded, and which would suggest a "felt" (line 177); the proposal here is that "block" be taken to denote the quintain, whose function is to bear blows, "a mere lifeless block" (*As You Like It*, I.ii.247), an object shaped like a man and used for tilting practice; see also *Much Ado About Nothing*, II.i.231–232, "She misused me past the endurance of a block!" and, in the same passage, the associated reference, "I stood like a man at a mark [target]" (lines 237–38). 95. *delicate* subtle.

A troop of horse with felt: I'll put't in proof;[96]
And when I have stol'n upon these son-in-laws,
Then, kill, kill, kill, kill, kill, kill!

(*Enter a* GENTLEMAN, *with* ATTENDANTS.)

GENTLEMAN: O, here he is: lay hand upon him. Sir,   180
    Your most dear daughter —

LEAR: No rescue? What, a prisoner? I am even
    The natural fool[97] of fortune. Use me well;
    You shall have ransom. Let me have surgeons;
    I am cut[98] to th' brains.

GENTLEMAN: You shall have anything.   185

LEAR: No seconds?[99] all myself?
    Why, this would make a man a man of salt,[100]
    To use his eyes for garden water-pots,
    Ay, and laying autumn's dust.

GENTLEMAN: Good sir —   190

LEAR: I will die bravely,[101] like a smug[102] bridegroom.[103] What!
    I will be jovial: come, come; I am a king;
    Masters, know you that?

GENTLEMAN: You are a royal one, and we obey you.

LEAR: Then there's life in't.[104] Come, and you get it,   195
    you shall get it by running. Sa, sa, sa, sa.[105]

(*Exit running;* ATTENDANTS *follow.*)

GENTLEMAN: A sight most pitiful in the meanest wretch,
    Past speaking of in a king! Thou hast one daughter
    Who redeems Nature from the general curse
    Which twain have brought her to.[106]   200

EDGAR: Hail, gentle[107] sir.

GENTLEMAN: Sir, speed[108] you: what's your will?

EDGAR: Do you hear aught, sir, of a battle toward?[109]

GENTLEMAN: Most sure and vulgar:[110] every one hears that,
    Which can distinguish sound.

---

96. *put't in proof* test it. **97.** *natural fool* born sport (with pun on "natural" = imbecile). **98.** *cut* wounded. **99.** *seconds* supporters. **100.** *man of salt* i.e., all (salt) tears. **101.** *bravely* (1) smartly attired (2) courageously. **102.** *smug* spick and span. **103.** *bridegroom* whose "brave" sexual feats are picked up in the pun on "die." **104.** *there's life in't* there's still hope. **105.** *Sa . . . sa* hunting and rallying cry; also an interjection of defiance. **106.** *general . . . to* (1) universal condemnation which Goneril and Regan have made for (2) damnation incurred by the original sin of Adam and Eve. **107.** *gentle* noble. **108.** *speed* Godspeed. **109.** *toward* impending. **110.** *vulgar* common knowledge.

EDGAR: But, by your favor,
    How near's the other army?   205

GENTLEMAN: Near and on speedy foot; the main descry
    Stands on the hourly thought.[111]

EDGAR: I thank you, sir: that's all.

GENTLEMAN: Though that the queen on special cause is here,
    Her army is moved on.

EDGAR: I thank you, sir. (*Exit* GENTLEMAN.)

GLOUCESTER: You ever-gentle gods, take my breath from me;   210
    Let not my worser spirit[112] tempt me again
    To die before you please.

EDGAR: Well pray you, father.

GLOUCESTER: Now, good sir, what are you?

EDGAR: A most poor man, made tame[113] to fortune's blows;
    Who, by the art of known and feeling sorrows,[114]   215
    Am pregnant[115] to good pity. Give me your hand,
    I'll lead you to some biding.[116]

GLOUCESTER: Hearty thanks;
    The bounty and the benison[117] of heaven
    To boot, and boot.[118]

(*Enter* OSWALD.)

OSWALD: A proclaimed prize![119] Most happy![120]
    That eyeless head of thine was first framed[121] flesh   220
    To raise my fortunes. Thou old unhappy traitor,
    Briefly thyself remember:[122] the sword is out
    That must destroy thee.

GLOUCESTER: Now let thy friendly[123] hand
    Put strength enough to't. (EDGAR *interposes.*)

OSWALD: Wherefore, bold peasant,
    Dar'st thou support a published[124] traitor? Hence!   225
    Lest that th' infection of his fortune take
    Like hold on thee. Let go his arm.

---

111. *the main . . . thought* we expect to see the main body of the army any hour. 112. *worser spirit* bad angel, evil side of my nature. 113. *tame* submissive. 114. *art . . . sorrows* instruction of sorrows painfully experienced. 115. *pregnant* disposed. 116. *biding* place of refuge. 117. *benison* blessing. 118. *To . . . boot* also, and in the highest degree. 119. *proclaimed prize* i.e., one with a price on his head. 120. *happy* fortunate (for Oswald). 121. *framed* created. 122. *thyself remember* i.e., pray, think of your sins. 123. *friendly* i.e., because it offers the death Gloucester covets. 124. *published* proclaimed.

EDGAR: Chill[125] not let go, zir, without vurther 'casion.[126]

OSWALD: Let go, slave, or thou diest!

EDGAR: Good gentleman, go your gait,[127] and let poor volk[128] pass. And 230
chud ha' bin zwaggered[129] out of my life, 'twould not ha' bin zo long
as 'tis by a vortnight. Nay, come not near th' old man; keep out, che
vor' ye,[130] or I'se[131] try whether your costard[132] or my ballow[133] be the
harder: chill be plain with you.

OSWALD: Out, dunghill!   235

(*They fight.*)

EDGAR: Chill pick your teeth,[134] zir: come; no matter vor your foins.[135]

(OSWALD *falls.*)

OSWALD: Slave, thou hast slain me. Villain, take my purse:
If ever thou wilt thrive, bury my body,
And give the letters which thou find'st about[136] me
To Edmund Earl of Gloucester; seek him out   240
Upon the English party.[137] O, untimely death!
Death! (*He dies.*)

EDGAR: I know thee well. A serviceable[138] villain,
As duteous[139] to the vices of thy mistress
As badness would desire.

GLOUCESTER: What, is he dead?   245

EDGAR: Sit you down, father; rest you.
Let's see these pockets: the letters that he speaks of
May be my friends. He's dead; I am only sorry
He had no other deathsman.[140] Let us see:
Leave,[141] gentle wax;[142] and, manners, blame us not: 250
To know our enemies' minds, we rip their hearts;
Their papers[143] is more lawful.

(*Reads the letter.*)

"Let our reciprocal vows be remembered. You have many opportunities to cut him off: if your will want not,[144] time and place will be
fruitfully offered. There is nothing done, if he return the conquerer: 255
then am I the prisoner, and his bed my jail; from the loathed
warmth whereof deliver me, and supply the place for your labor.

125. *Chill* I will (Edgar speaks in rustic dialect). **126.** *vurther 'casion* further occasion. **127.** *gait* way. **128.** *volk* folk. **129.** *And . . . zwaggered* if I could have been
swaggered. **130.** *che vor' ye* I warrant you. **131.** *I'se* I shall. **132.** *costard* head (literally,
"apple"). **133.** *ballow* cudgel. **134.** *Chill . . . teeth* I will knock your teeth out. **135.** *foins*
thrusts. **136.** *about* upon. **137.** *party* side. **138.** *serviceable* ready to be used. **139.** *duteous*
obedient. **140.** *deathsman* executioner. **141.** *Leave* by your leave. **142.** *wax* with which the
letter is sealed. **143.** *Their papers* i.e., to rip their papers. **144.** *if . . . not* if your desire (and
lust) be not lacking.

"Your — wife, so I would[145] say — affectionate servant, and for
you her own for venture,[146]

                                                          Goneril." 260

O indistinguished space of woman's will![147]
A plot upon her virtuous husband's life;
And the exchange[148] my brother! Here in the sands
Thee I'll rake up,[149] the post unsanctified[150]
Of murderous lechers; and in the mature[151] time,   265
With this ungracious paper[152] strike[153] the sight
Of the death-practiced[154] duke: for him 'tis well
That of thy death and business I can tell.

GLOUCESTER: The king is mad: how stiff[155] is my vile sense,[156]
That I stand up, and have ingenious[157] feeling   270
Of my huge sorrows! Better I were distract:[158]
So should my thoughts be severed from my griefs,
And woes by wrong imaginations[159] lose
The knowledge of themselves. (*Drum afar off.*)

EDGAR: Give me your hand:
Far off, methinks, I hear the beaten drum   275
Come, father, I'll bestow[160] you with a friend. (*Exeunt.*)

Scene VII.

(*A tent in the French camp.*)

(*Enter* CORDELIA, KENT, DOCTOR, *and* GENTLEMAN.)

CORDELIA: O thou good Kent, how shall I live and work,
To match thy goodness? My life will be too short,
And every measure fail me.

KENT: To be acknowledged, madam, is o'erpaid.
All my reports go[1] with the modest truth,   5
Nor more nor clipped,[2] but so.

CORDELIA: Be better suited:[3]
These weeds[4] are memories[5] of those worser hours:
I prithee, put them off.

---

145. *would* would like to. 146. *and . . . venture* i.e., and one who holds you her own for ven-
turing (Edmund had earlier been promised union by Goneril, "If you dare venture in your own
behalf," IV.ii.21). 147. *indistinguished . . . will* unlimited range of woman's lust. 148. *exchange* substitute. 149. *rake up* cover up, bury. 150. *post unsanctified* unholy messenger. 151. *mature* ripe. 152. *ungracious paper* wicked letter. 153. *strike* blast. 154. *death-
practiced* whose death is plotted. 155. *stiff* unbending. 156. *vile sense* hateful capacity for
feeling. 157. *ingenious* conscious. 158. *distract* distracted, mad. 159. *wrong imaginations*
delusions. 160. *bestow* lodge. IV.vii. 1. *go* conform. 2. *clipped* curtailed. 3. *suited* attired. 4. *weeds* clothes. 5. *memories* reminders.

KENT: Pardon, dear madam;
        Yet to be known shortens my made intent:[6]
        My boon I make it,[7] that you know me not   10
        Till time and I think meet.[8]

CORDELIA: Then be't so, my good lord. (*To the* DOCTOR.) How does the
        king?

DOCTOR: Madam, sleeps still.

CORDELIA: O you kind gods!
        Cure this great breach in his abusèd[9] nature.   15
        Th' untuned and jarring senses, O, wind up[10]
        Of this child-changèd[11] father.

DOCTOR: So please your majesty
        That we may wake the king: he hath slept long.

CORDELIA: Be governed by your knowledge, and proceed
        I' th' sway of[12] your own will. Is he arrayed?   20

(*Enter* LEAR *in a chair carried by* SERVANTS.)

GENTLEMAN: Ay, madam; in the heaviness of sleep
        We put fresh garments on him.

DOCTOR: Be by, good madam, when we do awake him;
        I doubt not of his temperance.[13]

CORDELIA: Very well.

DOCTOR: Please you, draw near. Louder the music there!   25

CORDELIA: O my dear father, restoration hang
        Thy medicine on my lips, and let this kiss
        Repair those violent harms that my two sisters
        Have in thy reverence[14] made.

KENT: Kind and dear princess.

CORDELIA: Had you not been their father, these white flakes[15]   30
        Did challenge[16] pity of them. Was this a face
        To be opposed against the warring winds?
        To stand against the deep dread-bolted[17] thunder?
        In the most terrible and nimble stroke
        Of quick, cross[18] lightning to watch — poor perdu![19] —   35
        With this thin helm?[20] Mine enemy's dog,

6. *Yet . . . intent* to reveal myself just yet interferes with the plan I have made. 7. *My . . . it* I
ask this reward. 8. *meet* fitting. 9. *abusèd* disturbed. 10. *wind up* tune. 11. *child-changèd*
changed, deranged (and also, reduced to a child) by the cruelty of his children. 12. *I' . . . of*
according to. 13. *temperance* sanity. 14. *reverence* revered person. 15. *flakes* hairs (in long
strands). 16. *challenge* claim. 17. *deep dread-bolted* deep-voiced and furnished with the
dreadful thunderbolt. 18. *cross* zigzag. 19. *perdu* (1) sentry in a forlorn position (2) lost
one. 20. *helm* helmet (his scanty hair).

Though he had bit me, should have stood that night
Against my fire; and wast thou fain,[21] poor father,
To hovel thee with swine and rogues[22] forlorn,
In short[23] and musty straw?[24] Alack, alack!   40
'Tis wonder that thy life and wits at once
Had not concluded all.[25] He wakes; speak to him.

DOCTOR: Madam, do you; 'tis fittest.

CORDELIA: How does my royal lord? How fares your majesty?

LEAR: You do me wrong to take me out o' th' grave: 45
Thou art a soul in bliss; but I am bound
Upon a wheel of fire,[26] that mine own tears
Do scald like molten lead.

CORDELIA: Sir, do you know me?

LEAR: You are a spirit, I know. Where did you die?

CORDELIA: Still, still, far wide.[27]   50

DOCTOR: He's scarce awake: let him alone awhile.

LEAR: Where have I been? Where am I? Fair daylight?
I am mightily abused.[28] I should ev'n die with pity,
To see another thus. I know not what to say.
I will not swear these are my hands: let's see;   55
I feel this pin prick. Would I were assured
Of my condition.

CORDELIA: O, look upon me, sir,
And hold your hand in benediction o'er me.
You must not kneel.

LEAR: Pray, do not mock me:
I am a very foolish fond[29] old man,   60
Fourscore and upward, not an hour more or less;
And, to deal plainly,
I fear I am not in my perfect mind.
Methinks I should know you and know this man,
Yet I am doubtful; for I am mainly[30] ignorant   65
What place this is, and all the skill I have
Remembers not these garments, nor I know not
Where I did lodge last night. Do not laugh at me,

---

21. *fain* pleased. 22. *rogues* vagabonds. 23–24. *short* when straw is freshly cut, it is long, and suitable for bedding, given its flexibility and crispness; as it is used, it becomes musty, shreds into pieces, is "short"; in contemporary Maine usage, "short manure" refers to dung mixed with straw that has been broken up, "long manure" to dung mixed with coarse new straw. 25. *concluded all* come to a complete end. 26. *wheel of fire* torment associated by the Middle Ages with hell, where Lear thinks he is. 27. *wide* i.e., of the mark (of sanity). 28. *abused* deluded. 29. *fond* in dotage. 30. *mainly* entirely.

For, as I am a man, I think this lady
To be my child Cordelia.

CORDELIA: And so I am, I am.   70

LEAR: Be your tears wet? Yes, faith. I pray, weep not.
If you have poison for me, I will drink it.
I know you do not love me; for your sisters
Have, as I do remember, done me wrong.
You have some cause, they have not.

CORDELIA: No cause, no cause.   75

LEAR: Am I in France?

KENT: In your own kingdom, sir.

LEAR: Do not abuse[31] me.

DOCTOR: Be comforted, good madam: the great rage,[32]
You see, is killed in him: and yet it is danger
To make him even o'er[33] the time he has lost.   80
Desire him to go in; trouble him no more
Till further settling.[34]

CORDELIA: Will't please your highness walk?[35]

LEAR: You must bear with me.
Pray you now, forget and forgive. I am old and foolish. (*Exeunt.
Manent*[36] KENT *and* GENTLEMAN.)

GENTLEMAN: Holds it true, sir, that the Duke of Cornwall was so slain?   85

KENT: Most certain, sir.

GENTLEMAN: Who is conductor of his people?

KENT: As 'tis said, the bastard son of Gloucester.

GENTLEMAN: They say Edgar, his banished son, is with the Earl of Kent in
Germany.   90

KENT: Report is changeable.[37] 'Tis time to look about; the powers[38] of the
kingdom approach apace.

GENTLEMAN: The arbitrement[39] is like to be bloody.
Fare you well, sir. (*Exit.*)

KENT: My point and period will be thoroughly wrought[40]   100
Or well or ill, as this day's battle fought (*Exit.*)

---

31. *abuse* deceive. 32. *rage* frenzy. 33. *even o'er* smooth over by filling in; and hence, "recollect." 34. *settling* calming. 35. *walk* perhaps in the sense of "withdraw." 36. s.d. *Manent* remain. 37. *Report is changeable* rumors are unreliable. 38. *powers* armies. 39. *arbitrement* deciding encounter. 40. *My . . . wrought* the aim and end, the close of my life, will be
completely worked out.

Act V

Scene I.

(*The British camp near Dover.*)

(*Enter, with drum and colors,* EDMUND, REGAN, GENTLEMEN, *and* SOLDIERS.)

EDMUND: Know[1] of the duke if his last purpose hold,[2]
    Or whether since he is advised[3] by aught
    To change the course: he's full of alteration
    And self-reproving: bring his constant pleasure.[4]

(*To a* GENTLEMAN, *who goes out.*)

REGAN: Our sister's man is certainly miscarried.[5]   5

EDMUND: 'Tis to be doubted,[6] madam.

REGAN: Now, sweet lord,
    You know the goodness I intend upon you:
    Tell me, but truly, but then speak the truth,
    Do you not love my sister?

EDMUND: In honored[7] love.

REGAN: But have you never found my brother's way   10
    To the forfended[8] place?

EDMUND: That thought abuses[9] you.

REGAN: I am doubtful that you have been conjunct
    And bosomed with her, as far as we call hers.[10]

EDMUND: No, by mine honor, madam.

REGAN: I shall never endure her: dear my lord,   15
    Be not familiar with her.

EDMUND: Fear[11] me not. —
    She and the duke her husband!

(*Enter, with drum and colors,* ALBANY, GONERIL, [*and*] SOLDIERS.)

GONERIL (*Aside*): I had rather lose the battle than that sister
    Should loosen[12] him and me.

ALBANY: Our very loving sister, well be-met.[13]   20
    Sir, this I heard, the king is come to his daughter,

V.i. **1.** *Know* learn. **2.** *last purpose hold* most recent intention (to fight) be maintained. **3.** *advised* induced. **4.** *constant pleasure* fixed (final) decision. **5.** *miscarried* come to grief. **6.** *doubted* feared. **7.** *honored* honorable. **8.** *forfended* forbidden. **9.** *abuses* (1) deceives (2) demeans, is unworthy of. **10.** *I . . . hers* I fear that you have united with her intimately, in the fullest possible way. **11.** *Fear* distrust. **12.** *loosen* separate. **13.** *be-met* met.

With others whom the rigor of our state[14]
Forced to cry out. Where I could not be honest,[15]
I never yet was valiant: for this business,
It touches us, as[16] France invades our land, 25
Not bolds the king, with others, whom, I fear,
Most just and heavy causes make oppose.[17]

EDMUND: Sir, you speak nobly.

REGAN: Why is this reasoned?[18]

GONERIL: Combine together 'gainst the enemy;
For these domestic and particular broils[19] 30
Are not the question[20] here.

ALBANY: Let's then determine.
With th' ancient of war[21] on our proceeding.

EDMUND: I shall attend you presently at your tent.

REGAN: Sister, you'll go with us?[22]

GONERIL: No. 35

REGAN: 'Tis most convenient;[23] pray you, go with us.

GONERIL (Aside): O, ho, I know the riddle.[24] — I will go.

(Exeunt both the ARMIES.)

(Enter EDGAR disguised.)

EDGAR: If e'er your grace had speech with man so poor,
Hear me one word.

ALBANY (To those going out.): I'll overtake you.(To EDGAR.) Speak. 40

(Exeunt all but ALBANY and EDGAR.)

EDGAR: Before you fight the battle, ope this letter.
If you have victory, let the trumpet sound
For[25] him that brought it: wretched though I seem,
I can produce a champion that will prove[26]
What is avouchèd[27] there. If you miscarry, 45
Your business of[28] the world hath so an end,
And machination[29] ceases. Fortune love you.

ALBANY: Stay till I have read the letter.

14. rigor . . . state tyranny of our government. 15. honest honorable. 16. touches us, as concerns me, only in that. 17. Not . . . oppose and not in that France emboldens the king and others, who have been led, by real and serious grievances, to take up arms against us. 18. reasoned argued. 19. particular broils private quarrels. 20. question issue. 21. th' ancient of war experienced commanders. 22. us me, (rather than Edmund). 23. convenient fitting, desirable. 24. riddle real reason (for Regan's curious request). 25. sound For summon. 26. prove i.e., by trial of combat. 27. avouchèd maintained. 28. of in. 29. machination plotting.

EDGAR: I was forbid it.
　　　When time shall serve, let but the herald cry,
　　　And I'll appear again.   **50**

ALBANY: Why, fare thee well: I will o'erlook[30] thy paper.

(*Exit* EDGAR.)

(*Enter* EDMUND.)

EDMUND: The enemy's in view: draw up your powers.
　　　Here is the guess[31] of their true strength and forces
　　　By diligent discovery;[32] but your haste
　　　Is now urged on you.

ALBANY: We will greet[33] the time. (*Exit.*)   **55**

EDMUND: To both these sisters have I sworn my love;
　　　Each jealous[34] of the other, as the stung
　　　Are of the adder. Which of them shall I take?
　　　Both? One? Or neither? Neither can be enjoyed,
　　　If both remain alive: to take the widow   **60**
　　　Exasperates, makes mad her sister Goneril;
　　　And hardly[35] shall I carry out my side,[36]
　　　Her husband being alive. Now then, we'll use
　　　His countenance[37] for the battle; which being done,
　　　Let her who would be rid of him devise   **65**
　　　His speedy taking off. As for the mercy
　　　Which he intends to Lear and to Cordelia,
　　　The battle done, and they within our power,
　　　Shall never see his pardon; for my state
　　　Stands on me to defend, not to debate.[38] (*Exit.*)   **70**

Scene II.

(*A field between the two camps.*)

(*Alarum*[1] *within. Enter, with drum and colors,* LEAR, CORDELIA, *and* SOLDIERS, *over the stage; and exeunt.*)

(*Enter* EDGAR *and* GLOUCESTER.)

EDGAR: Here, father,[2] take the shadow of this tree
　　　For your good host; pray that the right may thrive.

---

30. *o'erlook* read over. **31.** *guess* estimate. **32.** *By diligent discovery* obtained by careful reconnoitering. **33.** *greet* i.e., meet the demands of. **34.** *jealous* suspicious. **35.** *hardly* with difficulty. **36.** *carry . . . side* (1) satisfy my ambition (2) fulfill my bargain (with Goneril). **37.** *countenance* authority. **38.** *for . . . debate* my position requires me to act, not to reason about right and wrong. **V.ii. s.d.** *Alarum* a trumpet call to battle. **2.** *father* i.e., venerable old man (Edgar has not yet revealed his identity).

If ever I return to you again,
I'll bring you comfort.

GLOUCESTER: Grace go with you, sir.

(*Exit* EDGAR.)

(*Alarum and retreat*[3] *within. Reenter* EDGAR.)

EDGAR: Away, old man; give me thy hand; away!   5
King Lear hath lost, he and his daughter ta'en:[4]
Give me thy hand; come on.

GLOUCESTER: No further, sir; a man may rot even here.

EDGAR: What, in ill thoughts again? Men must endure
Their going hence, even as their coming hither: 10
Ripeness[5] is all. Come on.

GLOUCESTER: And that's true too. (*Exeunt.*)

Scene III.

(*The British camp near Dover.*)

(*Enter, in conquest, with drum and colors,* EDMUND; LEAR *and* CORDELIA, *as prisoners;* SOLDIERS, CAPTAIN.)

EDMUND: Some officers take them away: good guard,[1]
Until their greater pleasures[2] first be known
That are to censure[3] them.

CORDELIA: We are not the first
Who with best meaning[4] have incurred the worst.
For thee, oppressèd king, I am cast down;   5
Myself could else out-frown false Fortune's frown.
Shall we not see these daughters and these sisters?

LEAR: No, no, no, no! Come, let's away to prison:
We two alone will sing like birds i' th' cage:
When thou dost ask me blessing, I'll kneel down   10
And ask of thee forgiveness: so we'll live,
And pray, and sing, and tell old tales, and laugh
At gilded butterflies,[5] and hear poor rogues
Talk of court news; and we'll talk with them too,
Who loses and who wins, who's in, who's out;   15
And take upon's the mystery of things,

---

3. s.d. *retreat* signaled by a trumpet. **4.** *ta'en* captured. **5.** *Ripeness* maturity, as of fruit that is ready to fall. **V.iii. 1.** *good guard* let them be well guarded. **2.** *their greater pleasures* the will of those in command, the great ones. **3.** *censure* pass judgment on. **4.** *meaning* intentions. **5.** *gilded butterflies* i.e., gorgeously attired courtiers, fluttering after nothing.

As if we were God's spies:[6] and we'll wear out,[7]
In a walled prison, packs and sects of great ones
The ebb and flow by th' moon.[8]

EDMUND: Take them away.

LEAR: Upon such sacrifices, my Cordelia,   20
    The gods themselves throw incense.[9] Have I caught thee?
    He that parts us shall bring a brand from heaven,
    And fire us hence like foxes.[10] Wipe thine eyes;
    The good years[11] shall devour them,[12] flesh and fell,[13]
    Ere they shall make us weep. We'll see 'em starved first.   25
    Come. (*Exeunt* LEAR *and* CORDELIA, *guarded*.)

EDMUND: Come hither, captain; hark.
    Take thou this note: go follow them to prison:
    One step I have advanced thee; if thou dost
    As this instructs thee, thou dost make thy way   30
    To noble fortunes: know thou this, that men
    Are as the time is:[14] to be tender-minded
    Does not become a sword:[15] thy great employment
    Will not bear question;[16] either say thou'lt do't,
    Or thrive by other means.

CAPTAIN: I'll do't, my lord.   35

EDMUND: About it; and write happy[17] when th' hast done.
    Mark; I say, instantly, and carry it so[18]
    As I have set it down.

CAPTAIN: I cannot draw a cart, nor eat dried oats;
    If it be man's work, I'll do't. (*Exit* CAPTAIN.)   40

(*Flourish. Enter* ALBANY, GONERIL, REGAN, *another* CAPTAIN, *and* SOLDIERS.)

ALBANY: Sir, you have showed today your valiant strain,[19]
    And fortune led you well: you have the captives
    Who were the opposites of[20] this day's strife:
    I do require them of you, so to use them
    As we shall find their merits[21] and our safety   45
    May equally determine.

6. *take . . . spies* profess to read the riddle of existence, as if endowed with divine omniscience. 7. *wear out* outlast. 8. *packs . . . moon* intriguing and partisan cliques of those in
high station, whose fortunes change every month. 9. *Upon . . . incense* i.e., the gods approve
our renunciation of the world. 10. *He . . . foxes* No human agency can separate us, but only
divine interposition, as of a heavenly torch parting us like foxes that are driven from their place
of refuge by fire and smoke. 11. *good years* plague and pestilence ("undefined malefic power
or agency," N.E.D.). 12. *them* the enemies of Lear and Cordelia. 13. *fell* skin. 14. *as . . . is*
i.e., absolutely determined by the exigencies of the moment. 15. *become a sword* befit a
soldier. 16. *bear question* admit of discussion. 17. *write happy* style yourself fortunate. 18. *carry it so* manage the affair in exactly that manner (as if Cordelia had taken her
own life). 19. *strain* (1) stock (2) character. 20. *opposites of* opponents in. 21. *merits*
deserts.

EDMUND: Sir, I thought it fit
To send the old and miserable king
To some retention and appointed guard;[22]
Whose[23] age had charms in it, whose title more,
To pluck the common bosom on his side,[24]   50
And turn our impressed lances in our eyes[25]
Which do command them. With him I sent the queen:
My reason all the same; and they are ready
Tomorrow, or at further space[26] t'appear
Where you shall hold your session.[27] At this time   55
We sweat and bleed: the friend hath lost his friend;
And the best quarrels, in the heat, are cursed
By those that feel their sharpness.[28]
The question of Cordelia and her father
Requires a fitter place.

ALBANY: Sir, by your patience,   60
I hold you but a subject of[29] this war,
Not as a brother.

REGAN: That's as we list to grace[30] him.
Methinks our pleasure might have been demanded,
Ere you had spoke so far. He led our powers,
Bore the commission of my place and person;   65
The which immediacy may well stand up
And call itself your brother.[31]

GONERIL: Not so hot:
In his own grace he doth exalt himself
More than in your addition.[32]

REGAN: In my rights,
By me invested, he compeers[33] the best.   70

GONERIL: That were the most,[34] if he should husband you.[35]

REGAN: Jesters do oft prove prophets.

GONERIL: Holla, holla!
That eye that told you so looked but a-squint.[36]

REGAN: Lady, I am not well; else I should answer

---

22. *retention ... guard* confinement under duly appointed guard. **23.** *Whose* i.e.,
Lear's. **24.** *pluck ... side* win the sympathy of the people to himself. **25.** *turn ... eyes* turn
our conscripted lancers against us. **26.** *further space* a later time. **27.** *session* trial. **28.** *best
... sharpness* worthiest causes may be judged badly by those who have been affected painfully
by them, and whose passion has not yet cooled. **29.** *subject of* subordinate in. **30.** *list to
grace* wish to honor. **31.** *Bore ... brother* was authorized, as my deputy, to take command; his
present status, as my immediate representative, entitles him to be considered your
equal. **32.** *your addition* honors you have bestowed on him. **33.** *compeers* equals. **34.** *most*
most complete investing in your rights. **35.** *husband you* become your husband. **36.** *a-squint*
cross-eyed.

From a full-flowing stomach.[37] General,
Take thou my soldiers, prisoners, patrimony;[38]
Dispose of them, of me; the walls is thine:[39]
Witness the world, that I create thee here
My lord, and master.

GONERIL: Mean you to enjoy him?

ALBANY: The let-alone[40] lies not in your good will.

EDMUND: Nor in thine, lord.

ALBANY: Half-blooded[41] fellow, yes.

REGAN (*To* EDMUND.): Let the drum strike, and prove my title thine.[42]

ALBANY: Stay yet; hear reason. Edmund, I arrest thee
On capital treason; and in thy attaint[43]
This gilded serpent (*pointing to* GONERIL.) For your claim, fair sister,
I bar it in the interest of my wife.
'Tis she is subcontracted[44] to this lord,
And I, her husband, contradict your banes.[45]
If you will marry, make your loves[46] to me;
My lady is bespoke.[47]

GONERIL: An interlude![48]

ALBANY: Thou art armed, Gloucester: let the trumpet sound:
If none appear to prove upon thy person
Thy heinous, manifest, and many treasons,
There is my pledge,[49] (*throwing down a glove*): I'll make[50] it on
    thy heart,
Ere I taste bread, thou art in nothing less
Than I have here proclaimed thee.

REGAN: Sick, O, sick!

GONERIL (*Aside.*): If not, I'll ne'er trust medicine.[51]

EDMUND (*Throwing down a glove.*): There's my exchange,[52] what in
    the world he is
That names me traitor, villainlike he lies:[53]
Call by the trumpet:[54] he that dares approach,

75

80

85

90

95

100

---

37. *From . . . stomach* angrily.   38. *patrimony* inheritance.   39. *walls is thine* i.e., Regan's person, which Edmund has stormed and won.   40. *let-alone* power to prevent.   41. *Half-blooded* bastard, and so only half noble.   42. *prove . . . thine* prove by combat your entitlement to my rights.   43. *in thy attaint* as a sharer in the treason for which you are impeached.   44. *subcontracted* pledged by a contract which is called into question by the existence of a previous contract (Goneril's marriage).   45. *contradict your banes* forbid your announced intention to marry (by citing the precontract).   46. *loves* love-suits.   47. *bespoke* already pledged.   48. *interlude* play.   49. *pledge* gage.   50. *make* prove.   51. *medicine* poison.   52. *exchange* technical term, denoting the glove Edmund throws down.   53. *villainlike he lies* the lie direct, a challenge to mortal combat.   54. *trumpet* trumpeter.

On him, on you — who not? — I will maintain
My truth and honor firmly.

ALBANY: A herald, ho!

EDMUND: A herald, ho, a herald!

ALBANY: Trust to thy single virtue;[55] for thy soldiers,
All levied in my name, have in my name   105
Took their discharge.

REGAN: My sickness grows upon me.

ALBANY: She is not well; convey her to my tent.

(*Exit* REGAN, *led.*)

(*Enter a* HERALD.)

Come hither, herald. Let the trumpet sound —
And read out this.

CAPTAIN: Sound, trumpet!   110

(*A trumpet sounds.*)

HERALD (*Reads.*): "If any man of quality or degree[56] within the lists[57] of
the army will maintain upon Edmund, supposed Earl of Gloucester,
that he is a manifold traitor, let him appear by the third sound of
the trumpet: he is bold in his defense."

EDMUND: Sound!   115

(*First trumpet.*)

HERALD: Again!

(*Second trumpet.*)

HERALD: Again!

(*Third trumpet.*)

(*Trumpet answers within. Enter* EDGAR, *at the third sound, armed, a
trumpet before him.*[58])

ALBANY: Ask him his purposes, why he appears
Upon this call o' th' trumpet.

HERALD: What are you?
Your name, your quality,[59] and why you answer   120
This present summons?

EDGAR: Know, my name is lost;

---

55. *single virtue* unaided valor. **56.** *quality or degree* rank or position. **57.** *lists* rolls. **58.**
s.d. *trumpet before him* trumpeter preceding him. **59.** *quality* rank.

By treason's tooth bare-gnawn and canker-bit:[60]
Yet am I noble as the adversary
I come to cope.[61]

ALBANY: Which is that adversary?

EDGAR: What's he that speaks for Edmund, Earl of Gloucester?   125

EDMUND: Himself: what say'st thou to him?

EDGAR8:   Draw thy sword,
That if my speech offend a noble heart,
Thy arm do thee justice: here is mine.
Behold it is my privilege,
The privilege of mine honors,   130
My oath, and my profession.[62] I protest,
Maugre[63] thy strength, place, youth, and eminence,
Despite thy victor sword and fire-new[64] fortune,
Thy valor and thy heart,[65] thou art a traitor,
False to thy gods, thy brother, and thy father,   135
Conspirant[66] 'gainst this high illustrious prince,
And from th' extremest upward[67] of thy head
To the descent and dust below thy foot,[68]
A most toad-spotted traitor.[69] Say thou "No,"
This sword, this arm and my best spirits are bent[70]   140
To prove upon thy heart, whereto I speak,[71]
Thou liest.

EDMUND: In wisdom[72] I should ask thy name,
But since thy outside looks so fair and warlike,
And that thy tongue some say[73] of breeding breathes,   145
What safe and nicely[74] I might well delay[75]
By rule of knighthood, I disdain and spurn:
Back do I toss these treasons[76] to thy head;
With the hell-hated[77] lie o'erwhelm thy heart;
Which for they yet glance by and scarcely bruise,   150
This sword of mine shall give them instant way,
Where they shall rest for ever.[78] Trumpets, speak!

---

60. *canker-bit* eaten by the caterpillar. **61.** *cope* encounter. **62.** *it . . . profession* my knighthood entitles me to challenge you, and to have my challenge accepted. **63.** *Maugre* despite. **64.** *fire-new* fresh from the forge or mint. **65.** *heart* courage. **66.** *Conspirant* conspiring, a conspirator. **67.** *extremest upward* the very top. **68.** *the . . . foot* your lowest part (sole) and the dust beneath it. **69.** *toad-spotted traitor* spotted with treason (and hence venomous, as the toad is allegedly marked with spots that exude venom). **70.** *bent* directed. **71.** *whereto I speak* Edgar speaks from the heart, and speaks to the heart of Edmund. **72.** *wisdom* prudence (since he is not obliged to fight with one of lesser rank). **73.** *say* assay (i.e., touch, sign). **74.** *safe and nicely* cautiously and punctiliously. **75.** *delay* i.e., avoid. **76.** *treasons* accusations of treason. **77.** *hell-hated* hated like hell. **78.** *Which . . . ever* which accusations of treason, since as yet they do no harm, even though I have hurled them back, I now thrust upon you still more forcibly, with my sword, so that they may remain with you permanently.

(*Alarums. They fight.* EDMUND *falls.*)

ALBANY: Save[79] him, save him!

GONERIL: This is practice,[80] Gloucester:
    By th' law of war thou wast not bound to answer
    An unknown opposite;[81] thou art not vanquished,   155
    But cozened and beguiled.

ALBANY: Shut your mouth, dame,
    Or with this paper shall I stop it. Hold, sir;[82]
    Thou[83] worse than any name, read thine own evil.
    No tearing, lady; I perceive you know it.

GONERIL: Say, if I do, the laws are mine, not thine: 160
    Who can arraign me for't?

ALBANY: Most monstrous! O!
    Know'st thou this paper?

GONERIL: Ask me not what I know. (*Exit.*)

ALBANY: Go after her; she's desperate; govern[84] her.

EDMUND: What you have charged me with, that have I done;
    And more, much more; the time will bring it out.   165
    'Tis past, and so am I. But what art thou
    That hast this fortune on[85] me? If thou'rt noble,
    I do forgive thee.

EDGAR: Let's exchange charity.[86]
    I am no less in blood[87] than thou art, Edmund;
    If more,[88] the more th' hast wronged me.   170
    My name is Edgar, and thy father's son.
    The gods are just, and of our pleasant[89] vices
    Make instruments to plague us:
    The dark and vicious place[90] where thee he got[91]
    Cost him his eyes.

EDMUND: Th' hast spoken right, 'tis true;   175
    The wheel is come full circle; I am here.[92]

ALBANY: Methought thy very gait did prophesy[93]
    A royal nobleness: I must embrace thee:
    Let sorrow split my heart, if ever I
    Did hate thee or thy father!

---

79. *Save* spare. **80.** *practice* trickery. **81.** *opposite* opponent. **82.** *Hold, sir* to Edmund: "Just a moment!" **83.** *Thou* probably Goneril. **84.** *govern* control. **85.** *fortune on* victory over. **86.** *charity* forgiveness and love. **87.** *blood* lineage. **88.** *If more* if I am more noble (since legitimate). **89.** *of our pleasant* out of our pleasurable. **90.** *place* i.e., the adulterous bed. **91.** *got* begot. **92.** *wheel . . . here* i.e., Fortune's wheel, on which Edmund ascended, has now, in its downward turning, deposited him at the bottom, whence he began. **93.** *gait did prophesy* carriage did promise.

EDGAR: Worthy[94] prince, I know't.   180

ALBANY: Where have you hid yourself?
How have you known the miseries of your father?

EDGAR: By nursing them, my lord. List a brief tale;
And when 'tis told, O, that my heart would burst!
The bloody proclamation to escape[95]   185
That followed me so near — O, our lives' sweetness,
That we the pain of death would hourly die
Rather than die at once![96] — taught me to shift
Into a madman's rags, t' assume a semblance
That very dogs disdained: and in this habit[97]   190
Met I my father with his bleeding rings,[98]
Their precious stones new lost; became his guide,
Led him, begged for him, saved him from despair;
Never — O fault! — revealed myself unto him,
Until some half-hour past, when I was armed,   195
Not sure, though hoping, of this good success,
I asked his blessing, and from first to last
Told him of our pilgrimage.[99] But his flawed[100] heart —
Alack, too weak the conflict to support —
'Twixt two extremes of passion, joy and grief,   200
Burst smilingly.

EDMUND: This speech of yours hath moved me,
And shall perchance do good: but speak you on;
You look as you had something more to say.

ALBANY: If there be more, more woeful, hold it in;
For I am almost ready to dissolve,[101]   205
Hearing of this.

EDGAR: This would have seemed a period[102]
To such as love not sorrow; but another,
To amplify too much, would make much more,
And top extremity.[103]
Whilst I was big in clamor,[104] came there in a man,   210
Who, having seen me in my worst estate,[105]
Shunned my abhorred[106] society; but then, finding
Who 'twas that so endured, with his strong arms
He fastened on my neck, and bellowed out
As he'd burst heaven; threw him on my father;   215

---

94. *Worthy* honorable. **95.** *to escape* (my wish) to escape the sentence of death. **96.** *O . . . once* How sweet is life, that we choose to suffer death every hour rather than make an end at once. **97.** *habit* attire. **98.** *rings* sockets. **99.** *our pilgrimage* of our (purgatorial) journey. **100.** *flawed* cracked. **101.** *dissolve* i.e., into tears. **102.** *period* limit. **103.** *but . . . extremity* just one woe more, described too fully, would go beyond the extreme limit. **104.** *big in clamor* loud in lamentation. **105.** *estate* condition. **106.** *abhorred* abhorrent.

Told the most piteous tale of Lear and him
That ever ear received: which in recounting
His grief grew puissant,[107] and the strings of life
Began to crack: twice then the trumpets sounded,
And there I left him tranced.[108]

ALBANY: But who was this? 220

EDGAR: Kent, sir, the banished Kent; who in disguise
Followed his enemy[109] king, and did him service
Improper for a slave.

(*Enter a* GENTLEMAN, *with a bloody knife.*)

GENTLEMAN: Help, help, O, help!

EDGAR: What kind of help?

ALBANY: Speak, man.

EDGAR: What means this bloody knife?

GENTLEMAN: 'Tis hot, it smokes;[110] 225
It came even from the heart of — O, she's dead!

ALBANY: Who dead? Speak, man.

GENTLEMAN: Your lady, sir, your lady: and her sister
By her is poisoned; she confesses it.

EDMUND: I was contracted[111] to them both: all three 230
Now marry[112] in an instant.

EDGAR: Here comes Kent.

ALBANY: Produce the bodies, be they alive or dead.

(*Exit* GENTLEMAN.)

This judgment of the heavens, that makes us tremble,
Touches us not with pity.

(*Enter* KENT.)

O, is this he?
The time will not allow the compliment[113] 235
Which very manners[114] urges.

KENT: I am come
To bid my king and master aye[115] good night;
Is he not here?

ALBANY: Great thing of[116] us forgot!

---

107. *puissant* overmastering. **108.** *tranced* insensible. **109.** *enemy* hostile. **110.** *smokes* steams. **111.** *contracted* betrothed. **112.** *marry* i.e., unite in death. **113.** *compliment* ceremony. **114.** *very manners* ordinary civility. **115.** *aye* forever. **116.** *thing of* matter by.

Speak, Edmund, where's the king? and where's Cordelia?
See'st thou this object,[117] Kent?   240

(*The bodies of* GONERIL *and* REGAN *are brought in.*)

KENT: Alack, why thus?

EDMUND: Yet[118] Edmund was beloved:
The one the other poisoned for my sake,
And after slew herself.

ALBANY: Even so. Cover their faces.

EDMUND: I pant for life:[119] some good I mean to do,   245
Despite of mine own nature. Quickly send,
Be brief in it, to th' castle; for my writ[120]
Is on the life of Lear and on Cordelia:
Nay, send in time.

ALBANY: Run, run, O, run!

EDGAR: To who, my lord? Who has the office?[121] Send   250
Thy token of reprieve.[122]

EDMUND: Well thought on: take my sword,
Give it the captain.

EDGAR: Haste thee, for thy life.

(*Exit* MESSENGER.)

EDMUND: He hath commission from thy wife and me
To hang Cordelia in the prison, and   255
To lay the blame upon her own despair,
That she fordid[123] herself.

ALBANY: The gods defend her! Bear him hence awhile.

(EDMUND *is borne off.*)

(*Enter* LEAR, *with* CORDELIA *in his arms,* GENTLEMAN, *and others following.*)

LEAR: How, howl, howl, howl! O, you are men of stones:
Had I your tongues and eyes, I'd use them so   260
That heaven's vault should crack. She's gone for ever.
I know when one is dead and when one lives;
She's dead as earth. Lend me a looking-glass;
If that her breath will mist or stain the stone,[124]
Why, then she lives.

KENT: Is this the promised end?[125]   265

117. *object* sight (the bodies of Goneril and Regan).   118. *Yet* in spite of all.   119. *pant for life* gasp for life.   120. *writ* command (ordering the execution).   121. *office* commission.   122. *token of reprieve* sign that they are reprieved.   123. *fordid* destroyed.   124. *stone* i.e., the surface of the crystal looking-glass.   125. *promised end* doomsday.

EDGAR: Or image[126] of that horror?

ALBANY: Fall and cease.[127]

LEAR: This feather stirs; she lives. If it be so,
It is a chance which does redeem[128] all sorrows
That ever I have felt.

KENT: O my good master.

LEAR: Prithee, away.

EDGAR: 'Tis noble Kent, your friend.   270

LEAR: A plague upon you, murderers, traitors all!
I might have saved her; now she's gone for ever.
Cordelia, Cordelia, stay a little. Ha,
What is't thou say'st? Her voice was ever soft,
Gentle and low, an excellent thing in woman.   275
I killed the slave that was a-hanging thee.

GENTLEMAN: 'Tis true, my lords, he did.

LEAR: Did I not, fellow?
I have seen the day, with my good biting falchion[129]
I would have made them skip: I am old now,
And these same crosses[130] spoil me.[131] Who are you?   280
Mine eyes are not o' th' best: I'll tell you straight.[132]

KENT: If Fortune brag of two[133] she loved and hated,
One of them we behold.

LEAR: This is a dull sight.[134] Are you not Kent?

KENT: The same,
Your servant Kent. Where is your servant Caius?[135]   285

LEAR: He's a good fellow, I can tell you that;
He'll strike, and quickly too: he's dead and rotten.

KENT: No, my good lord; I am the very man.

LEAR: I'll see that straight.[136]

KENT: That from your first of difference and decay[137]   290
Have followed your sad steps.

LEAR: You are welcome hither.

126. *image* exact likeness. 127. *Fall and cease* i.e., Let the heavens fall, and all things
finish. 128. *redeem* make good. 129. *falchion* small curved sword. 130. *crosses*
troubles. 131. *spoil me* i.e., my prowess as a swordsman. 132. *tell you straight* recognize you
straightaway. 133. *two* i.e., Lear, and some hypothetical second, who is also a prime example
of Fortune's inconstancy ("loved and hated"). 134. *dull sight* (1) melancholy spectacle (2) faul-
ty eyesight (Lear's own, clouded by weeping). 135. *Caius* Kent's name, in disguise. 136. *see
that straight* attend to that in a moment. 137. *your ... decay* beginning of your decline in fortune.

KENT: Nor no man else:[138] all's cheerless, dark and deadly.
　　Your eldest daughters have fordone[139] themselves,
　　And desperately[140] are dead.

LEAR:　　　　　　　　　　　Ay, so I think.

ALBANY: He knows not what he says, and vain is it　　　　　　295
　　That we present us to him.

EDGAR:　　　　　　　　　Very bootless.[141]

(*Enter a* MESSENGER.)

MESSENGER: Edmund is dead, my lord.

ALBANY:　　　　　　　　　　That's but a trifle here.
　　You lords and noble friends, know our intent.
　　What comfort to this great decay may come[142]
　　Shall be applied. For us, we[143] will resign,　　　　　　300
　　During the life of this old majesty,
　　To him our absolute power: (*to* EDGAR *and* KENT) you, to your rights;
　　With boots,[144] and such addition[145] as your honors
　　Have more than merited. All friends shall taste
　　The wages of their virtue, and all foes　　　　　　　　305
　　The cup of their deservings. O, see, see!

LEAR: And my poor fool[146] is hanged: no, no, no life?
　　Why should a dog, a horse, a rat, have life,
　　And thou no breath at all? Thou'lt come no more,
　　Never, never, never, never, never.　　　　　　　　　310
　　Pray you, undo this button.[147] Thank you, sir.
　　Do you see this? Look on her. Look, her lips,
　　Look there, look there. (*He dies.*)

EDGAR:　　　　　　　He faints. My lord, my lord!

KENT: Break, heart; I prithee, break.

EDGAR:　　　　　　　　　Look up, my lord.

KENT: Vex not his ghost:[148] O, let him pass! He hates him　　315
　　That would upon the rack[149] of this tough world
　　Stretch him out longer.[150]

EDGAR:　　　　　　　　He is gone indeed.

138. *Nor ... else* no, I am not welcome, nor is anyone else. 139. *fordone* destroyed. 140. *desperately* in despair. 141. *bootless* fruitless. 142. *What ... come* whatever aid may present itself to this great ruined man. 143. *us, we* the royal "we." 144. *boot* good measure. 145. *addition* additional titles and rights. 146. *fool* Cordelia ("fool" being a term of endearment; but it is perfectly possible to take the word as referring also to the Fool). 147. *undo this button* i.e., to ease the suffocation Lear feels. 148. *Vex ... ghost* do not trouble his departing spirit. 149. *rack* instrument of torture, stretching the victim's joints to dislocation. 150. *longer* (1) in time (2) in bodily length.

KENT: The wonder is he hath endured so long:
      He but usurped[151] his life.

ALBANY: Bear them from hence. Our present business   320
        Is general woe. (*To* KENT *and* EDGAR.) Friends of my soul, you twain,
        Rule in this realm and the gored state sustain.

KENT: I have a journey, sir, shortly to go;
      My master calls me, I must not say no.

EDGAR: The weight of this sad time we must obey,[152]   325
       Speak what we feel, not what we ought to say.
       The oldest hath borne most: we that are young
       Shall never see so much, nor live so long.
                                        (*Exeunt, with a dead march.*)

For Consideration

Act I

1. To a Renaissance audience the opening scene would have raised some
   disturbing questions. A king was generally thought to be an agent of God
   on earth and, as such, he could not resign or neglect his office. Furthermore, the resignation or overthrow of a king posed a serious threat to the
   order and harmony which, ideally, existed in the country. Yet Lear is plan-
   ning to forego his responsibilities, retaining only "the name, and all th'
   addition to a king." What are his reasons? What is his motive for forcing
   his daughters to proclaim their love? Why does Lear react so harshly to
   Cordelia's "Nothing" response?

2. As many have noted, the main plot involving Lear and his daughters and
   the sub-plot involving Gloucester and his sons mirror each other. How
   close is the parallel? There would be little artistic reason for constructing
   this mirror relationship if it involved only a repetition of the same theme.
   How does Shakespeare use one plot, not only to repeat, but to enhance,
   clarify, or qualify the themes of the other plot?

3. The play is fundamentally about the ironic development and maturation
   — ironic because Lear is an old man — of the king as he comes to know
   himself and his relationships better. Based on your reading of the first
   scene, what qualities does Lear lack?

4. Cordelia, Kent, Edgar, and the Fool might be seen as the "loyalists" in the
   play, yet Cordelia is banished, Kent and Edgar must assume disguises, and
   the Fool is a "fool." What does this suggest about the state of the
   kingdom and about Lear's rule of it?

151. *usurped* possessed beyond the allotted term. 152. *obey* submit to.

Act II

5. One of the most provocative and enigmatic relationships in *King Lear* is that between the king and the fool. On what is it based? What sustains it when Lear's world in general seems to be crumbling? Renaissance attitudes toward mental incapacity or insanity, like modern ones, varied. It was not unusual, however, for the royalty to employ a "fool" or court jester to entertain and amuse family and guests. In the process of entertaining, the fool might well get by with arrogant or offensive remarks because he was judged as no threat. How well does this fool fit that portrait? In what ways does his role go beyond that of an amusing court jester?

6. When Lear becomes particularly angry he appeals to natural forces to aid him (see I.i.103ff, II.iv.158ff, III.ii.1ff). What is the significance of such appeals? What do they tell us about Lear?

Act III

7. The storm scene of Act III is one of the most famous in Shakespeare. What is significant about the storm itself? What is its relationship to Lear's discontent at this point? How is it appropriate as setting and as symbol?

8. Does Lear go mad as he fears he will? How does he respond to the appearance of Edgar disguised as a madman? Scene vi involves Gloucester, Lear, Kent, the Fool and Edgar. Of this group who is mad and who is not?

9. What is the significance of the mock-trial in scene vi?

Act IV

10. This play, more than any of the others presented here, delves consistently and agonizingly into questions concerning the nature of humanity and its relationship to the world around it and the forces above it. Isolate the answers to these questions as developed by the various characters. (Edmund, for example, sees humanity — or at least himself — under the control of natural and base desires (only one of the several definitions of "Nature" implicit in the play). How credible is his judgment? Are we inclined to accept this view as the perspective of the play as a whole? Gloucester's expressed view of the human condition, though different in kind, is not a happy one either: "As flies to wanton boys, are we to th' gods, / They kill us for their sport" (IV.i.36–37). What are the judgments of Edgar? Albany? Cordelia? What is Lear's perspective on humanity, the gods and the world?)

11. Act IV, scene vii is important, for it shows Lear awakening after his torment on the heath. How does he appear here in contrast to the earlier torment? Where does he think he is? How does he now compare to the powerful and arrogant man we saw at the beginning of the play?

Act V

12. How do you respond to Lear's speech to Cordelia, V.iii.8—19? What are his intentions?

13. The last appearance of Lear and Cordelia is troubling to many readers. Are both deaths — particularly Cordelia's — necessary for the tragic effect? Does the ending give you any sense of hope? What effect does it have on you?

For Comparison

Compare King Lear and Creon as tragic heroes. It is generally assumed that, while tragic figures may err even grievously, they are never so evil that we cannot respond to them with some degree of human sympathy and understanding. Are you able to respond sympathetically to both Lear and Creon throughout the two plays? At what points are you least in sympathy with their actions? When are you most responsive to them? What distinguishes their wrong action from the action and motives of someone like Edmund? Which play do you like better? Why?

DOUGLAS TURNER WARD (1931–   )
Happy Ending

Cast of Characters (in order of appearance)

ELLIE

VI

JUNIE

ARTHUR

TIME: *The present, an early weekday evening around five or six p.m.*

PLACE: *The spotless kitchen of a Harlem tenement apartment. At stage-left is a closed door providing entry to the outside hallway. On the opposite side of the stage is another door leading into the interior of the railroad flat. Sandwiched between this door and a window facing the brick walls of the apartment's inner shaft is a giant, dazzling white refrigerator. Positioned center-stage is a gleaming, porcelain-topped oval table. Directly behind is a modern stove-range. To the left of the stove, another window looks out upon a backyard court. The window is flanked on its left by a kitchen sink. Adjacent to the refrigerator, upstage-right, a bathroom door completes the setting.*

As curtain rises, waning rays of daylight can be seen streaming through the courtyard window. Two handsome women, both in their late thirties or early forties, are sitting at opposite ends of the kitchen table. They are dressed as if recently entered from work. Hats and coats are still worn, handbags lie on floor propped against legs of respective chairs. They remain in dejected poses, weeping noiselessly.

ELLIE: Let me have your handkerchief, Vi. . . . (*Vi hands it to her absently. Ellie daubs eyes, then rests hankie on table. It lies there until Vi motions for it to be handed back.*)

VI: What we go'n' do, Ellie?

ELLIE: Don' know. . . . Don't seem like there's much more we kin do. . . .

VI: This time it really might happen. . . .

ELLIE: I know. . . .

VI: Persons kin go but just so far. . . .

ELLIE: Lord, this may be the limit. . . .

VI: End of the line. . . .

ELLIE: Hear us, Savior!

VI: . . . Think it might help if I prayed a novena to Him first thing tomorrow morning?

ELLIE: . . . Certainly couldn't do no harm. . . . (*They lapse into silence once again, passing hankie back and forth on request. Suddenly, Junie, a tall, slender, sharply handsome, tastefully dressed youth in his early twenties, bursts upon the scene, rushing through hallway door.*)

JUNIE: (*Rapidly crossing, shedding coat in transit.*): Hey, Vi, Ellie . . . (*Exits through interior door, talking offstage.*) Ellie, do I have any more pleated shirts clean . . . ? Gotta make fast impression on new chick tonight. . . . (*Thrusting head back into view.*) One of them foxy, black "Four-Hundred" debutantes, you dig! All class and manners, but nothing underneath but a luscious, V-8 chassis! — Which is A-O-reet wit' me since that's all I'm after. You hear me talking to ya! Now, tell me what I say! Hah, hah, hah! (*Withdraws head back offstage.*) . . . Sure got them petty tyrants straight at the unemployment office today. (*Dripping contempt.*) Wanted me to snatchup one of them jive jobs they try to palm off on ya. I told 'em no, thanks! — SHOVE IT! (*Reentering, busily buttoning elegantly pleated shirt.*) If they can't find me something in my field, up to my standards, forget it! . . . Damn, act like they paying you money out their own pockets. . . . Whatcha got to eat, Ellie? . . . I'm scarfy as a bear. In fact — with little salt 'n' pepper, I could devour one of you — or both between a doubledecker! (*Descends upon them to illustrate playfully. Pulls up short on noticing their tears for the first time.*) Hey? . . . What'sa matter . . . ? What's up? (*They fail to respond.*) Is it the kids? (*They shake heads negatively.*) Somebody sick down home? (*Fearfully.*) Nothing's wrong wit' mother?!!! (*They shake heads again.*) Roy or Jim in jail? . . . Arthur or Ben lose their jobs? (*Another double headshake.*) Tell me, I wanta know! Everything was fine this morning. Som'um musta happened since. Come on, what is it?!

ELLIE: Should we tell him, Vi?

VI: I don't know. . . . No use gitting him worried and upset. . . .

ELLIE (*Sighing heavily.*) Maybe we better. He's got to find out sooner or later.

JUNIE: What are you crying for?

ELLIE: . . . Our bosses — Mr. and Mrs. Harrison, Junie. . . .

JUNIE: ???Mr. and Mrs. Harrison . . . ? (*Suddenly relieved, amused and sardonic.*) What happened? They escaped from a car wreck — UNHURT?

ELLIE (*Failing to grasp sarcasm.*): No.

JUNIE (*Returning to shirt-buttoning.*): Did you just git disappointing news flashes they go'n' live forever?

VI (*Also misreading him.*): No, Junie.

JUNIE: Well, what then? . . . I don't get it.

ELLIE: They's getting a divorce. . . .

JUNIE: ???A what — ?

VI: A divorce.

JUNIE: ???Why?

ELLIE: 'Cause Mr. Harrison caught her wit' a man.

JUNIE: Well, it's not the first time 'cording to you.

ELLIE: The other times wasn't wit' his best friend.

JUNIE: His best friend? WHEEE! Boy, she really did it up this time. . . . Her previous excursions were restricted to his casual acquaintances! . . . But why the hell should he be so upset? He's put up wit' all the rest. This only means she's gitting closer to home. Maybe next time it'll be him, ha, ha, ha. . . .

ELLIE (*Reprimandingly.*): It's no joke, Junie.

JUNIE (*Exiting into bathroom.*): How'd it happen?

ELLIE (*Flaring at the memory.*): Just walked in and caught 'em in his own bedroom!

VI (*Even more outraged.*): Was that dirty dog, Mr. Heller, lives on the 19th floor of the same building!

ELLIE (*Anger mounting.*): I warned her to be careful when she first started messing with him. I told her Mr. Harrison was really gon' kick her out if he found out, but she'd have the snake sneak in sometimes soon as Mr. Harrison left! Even had nerve to invite him to chaperone his own wife back later in the evening for a li'l' after-dinner snack!

JUNIE (*Re-entering, merrily.*): What's a little exchange of pleasantries among rich friends, bosom buddies? Now, all Harrison has to do is return the favor and even things up.

VI: She really cooked her goose this time.

JUNIE: Good for her.

ELLIE: Good . . . ?

JUNIE: Sure — what'd she 'spect? To wait 'till she hauled some cat into bed right next to her old man befo' he got the message?

VI: They is gitting a *divorce*, Junie!

JUNIE (*Sauntering over to fruit bowl atop refrigerator.*): That's all? . . . I'm surprised I didn't read headlines 'bout a double murder and one suicide. . . . But I forgot! — that's our colored folk's method of clearing up little gummy problems like that — that is, MINUS the suicide bit.

ELLIE: *They's breaking up their home, Junie!*

JUNIE (*Biting into apple selected from bowl.*): They'll learn to live wit' it. . . . Might even git to like the idea.

VI: And the chillun?

JUNIE: Delicate li'l' boobies will receive nice fat allowances to ease the pain until they grow up to take over the world.

ELLIE: ???Is that all you feel at a time like this, boy?

VI: Disastrous, that's what it is!

ELLIE: Tragicull 'n' unfair!

JUNIE: Is this what you boohooing 'bout?!!!

ELLIE: Could you think of anything worser?

JUNIE: But, why?! (*Exits into interior.*)

ELLIE: 'Cause this time we KNOW HE MEANS BUSINESS, JUNIE! Ain't no false alarm like them other times. We were there, right there! . . . Had a feeling somp'um was go'n' happen soon as I answered the door and let Mr. Heller in! Like chilly pneumonia on top a breeze. . . . Miss Harrison tole me she didn't wanta be disturbed for the rest of the afternoon. Well, she was disturbed all right! They musta fell asleep 'cause Mr. Harrison even got home late and still caught 'em. . . .

JUNIE (*Returns with tie, etc., to continue dressing.*): Couldn't you have interrupted their togetherness and sounded a timely danger warning?

ELLIE: We didn't hear him. I was in the kitchen, Vi down in basement ironing. I didn't know Mr. Harrison had come in 'till I heard screaming from the bedroom. But soon as I did, I called Vi and me and her tipped down the hall and heard Mr. Harrison order Mr. Heller to put his clothes back on and stop considering hisself a friend for the rest of his life! " 'N' you — slut! Pack up and git out soon as you find a suitable apartment." . . . Then he invited me and Vi into the room and told us he was divorcing her. . . . That man was hurt, Junie, hurt deep! Could see it in his eyes. . . . Like a little boy, so sad he made you wanta grab hold his head and rock him in your arms like a baby.

VI: Miss Harrison looked a sight herself, po' thing! Like a li'l' girl caught stealing crackers out the cookie jar.

ELLIE: I almost crowned ole back-stabber Heller! Come brushing up 'gainst *me* on his way out!

JUNIE (*Almost cracking up with laughter.*): Shoulda pinned medal on him as he flew by. Escaping wit' head still on shoulder and no bullet-holes dotting through his chest.

ELLIE (*Once again taking him literally.*): The skunk really left us all too high and dry for that, Junie. . . . Oh, don't think it wouldn't broke your heart, too, nephew. . . . Sneaky rascal gone, rest of us in sorrow, tears pouring down our faces 'n' me and Vi jist begging and begging. . . . (*As if to Harrisons.*) "Y'all please think twice befo' you do anything you'll be sorry for. You love each other — and who's in better position than Vi and me to know how much you love each other — " (*Junie ceases dressing to listen closely.*)

VI: 'Course she love him, just can't help herself.

ELLIE: " — When two hearts love each other as much as we know y'all do, they better take whole lots of time befo' doing something so awful as breaking up a marriage — even if it ain't hunert-percent perfect. Think about your reputation and the scandal this will cause Mr. Harrison. Jist 'bout kill your po' mother — her wit' her blood pressure, artritis, gout, heart tickle 'n' everything. But most of all, don't orphan the kids! Kids come first. Dear li'l' angels! Just innocents looking on gitting hurt in ways they can't understand."

JUNIE (*Incredulous.*): You told 'em this, Ellie?

ELLIE: Love conquers all, Junie!

JUNIE: Wit' your assistance, Vi?

VI: As much as I could deliver, Junie.

JUNIE: And what impression did your tender concern have on the bereaved couple?

ELLIE: Mr. Harrison said he understood 'n' appreciated our feelings and was very grateful for our kindly advice — but he was sorry, his mind was made up. She'd gone too far and he couldn't forgive her — not EVER! . . . We might judge him a harsh, vindicty man, he said, but he couldn't bring hisself to do it. Even apologized to us for being so cruel.

JUNIE (*Continuing his slow boil.*): You accepted his apology, Vi?

VI: I should say not. I pleaded wit' him agin to think it over for sake of home, family and good name!

JUNIE: Well of all the goddamn things I ever heard!

ELLIE (*Heartened by his misread support.*): I'm telling ya!

VI: I knew it was go'n' happen if she kept on like she did!

ELLIE: Just wouldn't listen!

JUNIE: It's a disgrace!

ELLIE: Ain't the word!

VI: Lot worse than that!

JUNIE: Did you both plop down on your knees begging him to give her another chance?

VI: NO! — But we woulda if we'd thought about it! Why didn't we, Ellie?!

ELLIE: Things happened so fast —

JUNIE: Never have I been so humiliated in all my life — !

VI (*Self-disgusted by their glaring omission.*): No excuse not thinking 'bout it, Ellie!

ELLIE: Certainly ain't.

JUNIE: What about your pride — !?

VI: You right! Musta been false pride kept us from dropping to our knees!

JUNIE: Acting like imbeciles! Crying your heart out 'cause Massa and Mistress are go'n' break up housekeeping!!! Maybe I oughta go beat up the adulterous rat crawling in between the sheets!!! (*Pacing up and down in angry indignation as they sit stunned.*) Here we are — Africa rising to its place in the sun wit' Prime Ministers and other dignitaries taking seats around the international conference table — us here fighting for our rights like never before, changing the whole image, dumping stereotypes behind us and replacing 'em wit' new images of dignity and dimension — and I come home and find my own aunts, sisters of my mother, daughters of my grandpa who never took crap off no cracker even though he did live on a plantation — DROWNING themselves in tears jist 'cause boss man is gonna kick bosslady out on her nose . . . !!! Maybe *Gone With The Wind* was accurate! Maybe we jist can't help "Miss Scarrrrrrlet-ing" and "Oh Lawdying" every time mistress white gets a splinter in her pinky. That's what *I'm* talking about.

VI: Ain't you got no feelings, boy?

JUNIE: Feelings?!!! . . . So you work every day in their kitchen, Ellie, and every Thursday you wash their stinky clothes, Vi. But that don't mean they're paying you to bleed from their scratches! . . . Look — don't get me wrong — I'm not blaming you for being domestics. It's an honorable job. It's the only kind available sometimes, and it carries no stigma in itself — but that's all it is, A JOB! An exchange of work for pay! BAD PAY AT THAT! Which is all the more reason why you shouldn't give a damn whether the Harrisons kick, kill or mangle each other!

ELLIE: You gotta care, Junie —

JUNIE: "Breaking up home and family!" — Why, I've seen both of you ditch two husbands apiece and itching to send third ones packing if they don't toe the line. You don't even cry over that!

ELLIE: Don't have time to —

JUNIE: Boy, if some gray cat was peeping in on you, he'da sprinted back home and wrote five Uncle Toms Cabins and ten Old Black Joes!

ELLIE: Wait a minute, now —

JUNIE: I never heard you shedding such tragic tears when your own li'l' crumbcrushers suffered through fatherless periods! All you grumbled was "good riddance, they better off wit'out the sonsabitches!" . . . Maybe Harrison tots will make out just as well. They got puny li'l' advantages of millions of dollars and slightly less parched skins!

VI: Show some tenderness, boy. Ain't human not to trouble over our bosses' sorrows —

JUNIE: That's what shames me. I gave you credit for more integrity. Didn't figger you had chalk streaks in ya. You oughta be shamed for *yourselves!*

ELLIE: And done what?

JUNIE: NOTHING! — Shoulda told 'em their sticky mess is their own mud puddle. You neutrals. Just work there. Aren't interested in what they do!

ELLIE: That wouldn't be expressing our deepest sentiments —

JUNIE: I'm ashamed you even had any "sentiments!" . . . Look, it's hopeless, I'm not getting anywhere trying to make you understand. . . . I'm going out for a whiff of fresh air! (*Rushes to exit.*)

ELLIE: COME BACK HERE, BOY!

JUNIE (*Stopping at door.*): What? To watch you blubber over Massa? No, thanks!

ELLIE: I said come here, you hear me talking to you!

VI: You still ain't too big to git yourself slapped down!

ELLIE: Your ma gave us right any time we saw fit! (*He returns reluctantly. Stands aside. An uneasy silence prevails. They commence a sweet, sly, needling attack.*) . . . Better git yourself somp'um to eat. (*Rises, taking off coat.*)

JUNIE (*Sulking.*): I lost my appetite.

ELLIE (*Hanging coat up.*): What you want?

JUNIE: I told you I'm not hungry anymore.

VI: *We* made you lose your appetite . . . ? (*He doesn't reply.*)

ELLIE: What did you crave befo' you lost it?

JUNIE: Anything you had cooked. Didn't have anything special in mind. . . .

ELLIE (*Off-handedly.*): Steak? . . . T-Bone? . . . Porterhouse? . . . Filet . . . ?

JUNIE: No. . . . I didn't particularly have steak in mind.

VI: Been eating too many lately, huh? (*Stands at table exchanging goods from Ellie's shopping bag into her own.*)

JUNIE: Just kinda tired of 'em, that's all.

ELLIE: How 'bout some chicken then . . . ? Roast beef? . . . Lobster? . . . Squab? Duck, or something?

JUNIE (*Nettled.*): All I wanted was some food, Ellie! . . . In fact, I really had a hankering for some plain ole collard greens, neck bones or ham hocks. . . .

ELLIE: Good eatin', boy. Glad to hear that. Means that high-class digestion hasn't spoiled your taste buds yet. . . But if you want that rich, choice food, you welcome to it —

JUNIE: I know that, Ellie!

ELLIE: It's in the freezer for you, go and look.

JUNIE: I don't hafta, Ellie, I know —

ELLIE: Go look anyway.

JUNIE (*Goes and opens refrigerator door.*): It's there, Ellie, I didn't need look.

VI: Come here for a second, Junie, got something on your pants leg. (*He obeys. She picks a piece of lint off trousers, then rubs material admiringly.*) Pants to your suit, ain't they? . . . Sure is a fine suit to be trotting off to the unemployment office. . . . Which one-'r the other you gon' wear tonight when you try to con that girl out her virginity — if she still got it? — The gray one? Brown one? The tweed? Or maybe you go'n' git sporty and strut that snazzy plaid jacket and them tight light pants? If not — which jacket and which pants?

ELLIE: Slept good last night, nephew? Or maybe you gitting tired of that foam rubber mattress and sheepfur blanket?

VI: How do them fine college queens and snooty office girls like the furniture they half-see when you sneak 'em in here late at night? Surprised to see such fancy stuff in a beat-up ole flat, ain't they? But it helps you put 'em at ease, don't it? I bet even those sweet li'l' white ones are impressed by your class?

JUNIE (*Indignantly.*): That's not fair, Vi —

ELLIE: When last time you bought any food in this house, boy?

JUNIE: Ellie, you know —

ELLIE: When, Junie?

JUNIE: Not since I been here, but —

VI: And your last piece of clothes?

JUNIE (*More indignant.*): I bought some underwear last week, Vi!

VI: I mean clothes you wear on top, Junie. Shirts, pants, jackets, coats?

JUNIE (*Squirming.*): You — you know I haven't, Vi —

ELLIE (*Resists.*): Buy anything else in your room besides that tiny, midget frame for your ma's picture?

JUNIE: All right. I know I'm indebted to ya. You don't have to rub it in. I'll make it up to you when I git on my feet and *fulfill* my potential. . . . But that's not the point!

ELLIE: You ain't indebted to us, Junie.

JUNIE: Yes, I am, I know it, I thank you for it.

ELLIE: Don't hafta thank us —

JUNIE: But that's not the issue! Despite your benevolence, I refuse to let you blackmail my principle, slapping me in the face wit' how good you been to me during my temporary outta work period! I'm talking to you now, 'bout something above our personal relationship. Pride — Race — Dignity —

ELLIE: What's go'n' happen to me and Vi's dignity if Mr. Harrison throws Mrs. Harrison out on her nose as you put it?

JUNIE: Git another job! You not dependent on them. You young, healthy, in the prime of life. . . . In fact — I've always wondered why you stagnate as domestics when you're trained and qualified to do something better and more dignified.

ELLIE: Glad you brought that up. Know why I'm not breaking my back as a practical nurse and Vi's not frying hair — 'cept on the side? . . . 'Cause the work's too hard, the money ain't worth it and there's not much room for advancement —

JUNIE: Where kin you advance as a domestic? From kitchen to closet?! (*Vi has moved to fridge to deposit meats etc.*)

ELLIE (*Refusing to be provoked, continuing evenly.*): Besides, when I started working for the Harrisons, Junie, Mr. Harrison vowed that he would support me for life if I stayed with 'em until his daughter Sandy, his oldest child, reached ten years old.

JUNIE: Bully for him! He'll build ya a little cottage backa the penthouse garage!

ELLIE (*Still unruffled.*): Mr. Harrison is strictly a man of his word, Junie. Which means that even if I left one day after Sandy made ten, he owes me some money every week or every month as long as I live. . . . Sandy is *nine*, Junie, EN-EYE-EN-EE! If I don't last another year, the deal is off.

JUNIE: Don't need no handouts! Even hearing you say you want any makes me shame!

ELLIE: Done used that word quite a lot, boy. You shamed of us? . . . Well, git slapped in the face wit' this? How shame you go'n' be when you hafta git outta here and hustle yourself a job! — ANY JOB?!!!

JUNIE: Huh?

ELLIE: How shame you go'n' be when you start gitting raggedy and all them foxy girls are no longer impressed 'bout how slick, smooth and pretty you look? When you stop being one-'r the best-dressed black boys in New York City?

JUNIE: Don't get you, Ellie?

ELLIE: I know you went to college for a coupler years, boy, but I thought you still had some sense, or I woulda told you. . . .

VI (*Standing at Junie's right as Ellie sits to his left.*): Every time you bite into one of them big tender juicy steaks and chaw it down into your belly, ever think where it's coming from?

ELLIE: The Harrisons.

VI: Every time you lay one of them young gals down in that plush soft bed of yours and hear her sigh in luxury, ever think 'bout who you owe it to?

ELLIE: The Harrisons.

VI: When you swoop down home to that rundown house your ma and pa
rent, latch eyes on all that fine furniture there, you ever think who's
responsible?

ELLIE: The Harrisons.

VI: You ain't bought a suit or piece of clothes in five years and none of
the other four men in this family have. . . . Why not?

ELLIE: Mr. Harrison.

VI: Junie, you is a fine, choice hunk of chocolate pigmeat, pretty as a
new-minted penny and slick 'nuff to suck sugar outta gingerbread
wit'out it losing its flavor — but the Harrisons ain't hardly elected
you no favorite pin-up boy to introduce to Santa Claus. Took a heap
of pow'ful coaxing to win you such splendid sponsorship and wealthy
commissions, 'cause waiting for the Harrisons to voluntarily *donate*
their Christian charity is one sure way of landing head-first in the
poor-house dungeon. . . . Who runs the Harrisons' house, Junie?
(*Moves to sit at table.*)

JUNIE: ??? . . . Ellie . . . I guess . . . ?

ELLIE: *From top to bottom.* I cook the food, scrub the floor, open the
doors, serve the tables, answer the phones, dust the furniture, raise
the children, lay out the clothes, greet the guests, fix the drinks and
dump the garbage — all for bad pay as you said. . . . You right,
Junie, money I git in my envelope ain't worth the time 'n' the
headache. . . . *But — God Helps Those Who Help Themselves.* . . . I
also ORDER the food, estimate the credit, PAY the bills and
BALANCE the budget. Which means that each steak I order for
them, befo' butcher carves cow, I done reserved TWO for myself.
Miss Harrison wouldn't know how much steak cost and Mr. Harrison
so loaded, he writes me a check wit'out even looking. . . . Every once
in a full moon they git so good-hearted and tell me take some
leftovers home, but by that time my freezer and pantry is already
fuller than theirs. . . . Every one of them high price suits I lay on
you haven't been worn more than once and some of 'em not at all.
You lucky to be same size as Mr. Harrison, Junie. He don't know
how much clothes he got in his wardrobe, which is why *yours* is as
big as *his.* Jim, Roy, Arthur and Ben can't even fit into the man's
clothes, but that still don't stop 'em from cutting, shortening, altering and stretching 'em to fit. Roy almost ruined his feet trying to
wear the man's shoes. . . . Now, I've had a perfect record keeping
y'all elegantly dressed and stylishly-fashion-plated — 'cept that time
Mr. Harrison caught me off-guard asking: "Ellie, where's my brown
suit?" "In the cleaners," I told him and had to snatch it off your
hanger and smuggle it back — temporarily.

VI: If y'all warn't so lucky and *Mrs. Harrison* so tacky flashy Ellie and I would also be best dressed domestics of the year.

ELLIE: Which, if you didn't notice, is what your Aunt Doris was — rest her soul — when we laid her in her grave, decked out in the costliest, ritziest, most expensest nightgown the good Lord ever waited to feast his eyes on. . . . As for furniture, we could move out his whole house in one day if we had to.

VI: Which is what we did when they moved from the old penthouse and we hired us a moving van to haul 'nuff pieces to furnish both our own apartments and still had enough to ship a living room set down home to your ma. Mr. Harrison told us to donate the stuff to charity. We did — US!

ELLIE: Add all *our* bills I add on to *their* bills — Jim even tried to git me to sneak in his car note, but that was going too far — all the deluxe plane tickets your ma jets up here on every year, weekly prescriptions filled on their tab, tons of laundry cleaned along wit' theirs and a thousand other services and I'm earning me quite a bonus along with my bad pay. It's the BONUS that counts, Junie. Total it up for nine years and I'd be losing money on any other job. Now Vi and I, after cutting cane, picking rice and shucking corn befo' we could braid our hair in pigtails, figure we just gitting back what's owed us. . . . But, if Mr. Harrison boots Mrs. Harrison out on her tocus, the party's over. He's not go'n' need us. Miss Harrison ain't got a copper cent of her own. Anyway, the set-up won't be as ripe for picking. My bonus is suddenly cut off and out the window go my pension.

VI: Suppose we did git us another job wit' one-'r them penny-pinching old misers hiding behind cupboards watching whether you stealing sugar cubes? Wit' our fringe benefits choked off, we'd fall down so quick to a style of living we ain't been used to for a long time, it would make your head swim. I don't think we could stand it. . . . Could you?

ELLIE: So when me and Vi saw our pigeons scampering out the window for good today, tears started flowing like rain. The first tear trickle out my eyes had a roast in it.

VI: Mine was a chicken.

ELLIE: Second had a crate of eggs.

VI: Mine a whole pig.

ELLIE: Third an oriental rug.

VI: A continental couch.

ELLIE: An overcoat for Arthur.

VI: A bathrobe for Ben.

ELLIE: My gas, electric and telephone bills in it.

VI: Three months' rent, Lord!

ELLIE: The faster the stream started gushing, the faster them nightmares crowded my eyes until I coulda flooded 'em 'nuff water to swim in. Every time I pleaded "Think of your love! — "

VI: She meant think 'bout our bills.

ELLIE: Every time I begged "Don't crack up the home! — "

VI: It meant please keep *ours* cemented together!

ELLIE: "Don't victim the chillun! — "

VI: By all means insure the happiness of *our* li'l' darlings!

ELLIE: They didn't know 'bout these eyeball visions — they only see what they see 'n' hear what they hear — and that's okey-doke wit' me — but I was gitting these watery pictures in my mind 'n' feeling a giant-size sickness in my gut! Few seconds longer and I woulda been down on my knees wit'out even thinking 'bout it!

VI: If I didn't beat ya to the floor!

ELLIE: Junie — maybe we shoulda given a little more thought to that — watchamacallit? — "image" of yours. Maybe we did dishonor Africa, embarrass the NAACP, are hopelessly behind time and scandalously outdated. But we didn't have too much time to think. . . . Now that you know the whole truth, you have a right to disown us. We hardly worthy of your respect. . . . But when I thought 'bout that new top-coat wit' the velvet-trimmed collar I just packed to bring you . . . (*Tears begin to re-form.*) . . . coupler new cashmere sweaters, brand-new slacks, a shiny new attache case for your appointments, and a scrumptious new collapsible swimming pool I promised your ma for her backyard — I couldn't help but cry. (*Vi has joined her in a double torrent.*)

JUNIE (*Who has been standing stoically throughout, says*): . . . Vi?

VI: . . . What?

JUNIE: . . . Pass me the handkerchief. . . . (*He receives it and joins the table — a moist-faced trio. Arthur, Ellie's husband, walks in, finding them thus.*)

ARTHUR (*Beelining for bathroom.*): Even', everybody. . . . (*Hearing no response, stops before entering john.*) Hey, what's the matter? What you three looking like somebody died for?

ELLIE: It's the Harrisons, Arthur. Mr. Harrison gitting a divorce.

ARTHUR: Aww, not ag'in!

VI: He really means it this time, Arthur.

ARTHUR: . . . He does?

ELLIE: Yes, Jesus.

ARTHUR: You sure?

VI: Caught her dead to rights.

ARTHUR (*Indignant.*): But he can't do that!

VI: He is.

ARTHUR: What 'bout us?!

JUNIE: What you think we grieving 'bout?

ARTHUR: Well, just don't sit there! What we go'n do?

ELLIE: Done it, didn't work.

ARTHUR: Not at all?

ELLIE: Nope.

ARTHUR: Not even a little bit?

ELLIE: Not one lousy inch.

ARTHUR (*Crestfallen.*): Make room for me. (*They provide space. He sits, completing the depressed quartet.*)

JUNIE (*Suddenly jolted with an idea.*): Ellie! Wait! Why don't you tell him to take her on a private ocean cruise, just the two of 'em, so they kin recapture the thrill for one another!

ELLIE: He did that already, until somebody told him she was cuddling up with the ship stoker in the engine room.

JUNIE (*Undaunted.*): Advise him to spend less time wit' his business and more with her. She wouldn't need look outside for satisfaction!

ELLIE: Tried that too, but his business like to fell apart and he caught her making eyes at the messenger bringing him the news.

JUNIE (*Desperate.*): Convince him she's sick! It's not her fault, he should send her to a psychiatrist!

ELLIE: Already did . . . till he found out she was doing more than talking on the couch.

JUNIE: What 'bout a twenty-four hour guard on her? That won't give her so many opportunities?!

ELLIE: What about guards? They men, too.

JUNIE (*In angry frustration.*): Well, damn, git her a chastity belt and lock her up!

ELLIE: Locks, also, have been known to be picked.

ARTHUR (*Inspired by a brilliant solution.*): WAIT! I GOT IT! I GOT IT! . . . Tell him you know of some steady-ready goofer dust . . . or jooger-mooger saltpeter to cool her down. And you'll slip it in her food every day!

ELLIE: Wouldn't work. . . . Way her glands function, probably jazz her up like a Spanish fly.

VI: Let's face it, it's all over. We just gotta tuck in our belts, stare the future square in the eye and git ready for a depression. It's not go'n' do us no good to whine over spilt clabber. . . . You jist better start scrounging 'round for that job, Junie. Befo' you git chance to sneeze, we will have had it! And call up — NO! Write your ma and tell her not to come up this year.

ELLIE: Arthur, best you scrape up another job to moonlight wit' the one you got. We facing some scuffling days 'head us.

VI: Well. . . . I better git out of here and go warn my own crew 'bout Satan's retribution. . . . Well . . . it was good while it lasted. Ellie. . . .

ELLIE: Real good. (*They glance at each other and another deluge starts. The phone interrupts, but no one bothers to answer. Finally, Arthur rises and exits in the direction of peals. During his absence, the disconsolate trio remains silent.*)

ARTHUR (*Re-entering slowly, treading each step with the deliberateness of a man fearful of cracking eggs.*): That — was — Mr. Harrison — he said — thank both of you for desperately trying to — shock him to his senses — pry open his eyes to the light — and rescue his house from collapsing — he and Mrs. Harrison, after stren'ous consideration, are gonna stick it out together! (*A stunned moment of absolute silence prevails, finally broken by an earsplitting, exultant whoop which erupts simultaneously from each member of the quartet. They spring to feet, embracing and prancing around the room, crying through laughter. Arthur simmers down first, shhushes to recapture their attention.*) ELLIE . . . Ellie, Mr. Harrison requests if it's not too much trouble, he'd like for you to come over and stay wit' Sandy and Snookie while he and Mrs. Harrison go out and celebrate their reunion and it's too late to git a baby-sitter.

ELLIE: If it's all right?!!! . . . Tell him I'm climbing on a broomstick, then shuttling to a jet! (*Arthur starts to exit.*) Wait a minute! Waaaait a minute! Hold on! — I must be crazy. Don't tell him that. . . . Tell him he knows very well it's after my working hours and I'm not paid to baby-sit and since I've already made plans for the evening, I'll be glad to do it for double-over-time, two extra days' pay and triple-time off to recuperate from the imposition. ... And, Arthur! ... Kinda suggest that *you* is a little peeved 'cause he's interrupting me from taking care of something important for you. He might toss in a day for your suffering.

ARTHUR: He'll swear he was snatching you away from my death-bed, guarding my door 'gainst Lucifer busting through! (*Exits.*)

ELLIE: I'd better throw on some more clothes. (*Exits.*)

JUNIE: Vi, what you s'pose grandpa would say 'bout his chillun if he got a breathing-spell in between dodging pitchforks and sidestepping the fiery flames?

VI: Shame on you, boy, Papa ain't near'bouts doing no ducking 'n' dodging. Why, he's right up there plunked down safe, snuggled up tight beside the good Lord's righteous throne.

ARTHUR (*Re-entering.*): He was real sorry. "If it wasn't such a special occasion, he wouldn't bother us!" (*They guffaw heartily.*)

JUNIE: This IS a special occasion! ... (*Grandly.*) Arthur, Arthur, break out a flagon of the latest champagne Ellie brought us.

ARTHUR: At your service, massa Junie.

JUNIE: The nineteen-forty-seven! That was a good year. Not the fifty, which was bad!

ARTHUR: No kidding?! (ARTHUR *moves to refrigerator.* ELLIE *returns, ready to depart.*)

JUNIE: Wait for a drink, auntie. We've gotta celebrate OUR resurrection. A Toast of Deliverance. (ARTHUR *presents* JUNIE *with champagne, points out '47 label, then gets goblets from shelf.* JUNIE *pours, they lift goblets.*) First! ... To the victors and the vanquished, top-dog and the bottom-dog! Sometimes it's hard to tell which is which ... !

VI: If nothing else, boy, education did teach you how to sling around some GAB.

ARTHUR: Ain't hardly the way I heard the slinging described. (*They all laugh.*)

JUNIE: Second! ... To my two cagey aunts. May they continue to prevail in times of distress!

ARTHUR: May they!

JUNIE: ... Third! ... To the Harrisons! ... May they endure forever in marital bliss! Cheers to 'em! (*All cheer. After finishing drink,* ELLIE *moves to exit through hallway door.* JUNIE *stops her.*) Oh, Ellie . . . why don't you start fattening Mr. Harrison up? Please slip some more potatoes and starch onto his menu. I've gained a few pounds and the clothes are gitting a little tight. Don't you think it's time for him to plumpen up a bit, stick on a little weight?

ELLIE: Would ten pounds do?

JUNIE: Perfect! (*Another round of laughter. Again she moves to exit.*) . . . AND ELLIE! . . . Kinda hint 'round to him that fashions is changing. I wouldn't want him to fall behind in the latest styles. . . .

VI (*Lifting goblet, along with* ARTHUR *and* ELLIE, *in a final toast.*): There's hope, Junie. You'll make it, boy, you'll make it. . . . (*Laughter rings as lights fade.*)

(*Curtain.*)

For Consideration

1. What are the sources of the humor in this play? The play is categorized as a satiric comedy. Why?

2. What appears initially to motivate Vi and Ellie's concern for the Harrisons? How does their reaction contrast with Junie's? What lies behind the latter's response to the impending divorce of the white couple?

3. When Vi and Ellie plead with the Harrisons not to break up their marriage, what do they appeal to? Is there ever any hint of self-interest in their appeal? How does Junie respond to their portrait of themselves with the Harrisons?

4. In the earlier part of the play, Junie plays the role of the knowledgeable, proud, and independent "new" black, while Vi and Ellie appear to fit the stereotype of the "old" black, working in menial jobs and, as Junie puts it, "crying your heart out, 'cause Massa and Mistress are go'n' break up housekeeping!" How accurate are those impressions? When do you begin to see the characters in a different light?

5. How do Ellie and Vi go about enlightening Junie about the advantages to be had from their work with the Harrisons? How does he respond to their attempt?

6. How stereotyped do Vi and Ellie appear by the end of the play? What have they done to alter their image?

7. The impact of the play is at least in part dependent on its biting social commentary. What are the forces at work in the society portrayed? Does the play seem limited in its impact to a given social situation in a given era? (Does it, in other words, have the ingredient of "universality" which is judged necessary for great literature?) Why or why not? Does the play have a purpose, a theme? What is it?

plays for further reading

A Note on Other Forms

Since good playwrights do not write with prescriptive formulas for a play in mind, it is not surprising that many plays do not fit comfortably into the mold of either tragedy or comedy. The other forms discussed here offer some significant variations on the basic modes of comedy and tragedy.

The **tragicomedy** is, as its label implies, aligned with both tragedy and comedy, and yet fully with neither. In general terms it is perhaps accurate to say that it is a play which has a comic resolution — i.e., the ending is more or less happy, no one of consequence dies, the threats to happiness are either gone or diminished — but which has the overtones of tragedy throughout — a greater seriousness, a deeper reflection on humankind and its failings. The modern screenplay by Ingmar Bergman, *Wild Strawberries*, is usually classified as a tragicomedy, and embodies the characteristics mentioned above. Like a tragedy — in fact, notably like *King Lear* — *Wild Strawberries* focuses on an individual, Professor Borg, and his reflections on life. The mistakes of Professor Borg are serious ones and the deliberations on his past life seem always to have the potential for tragedy. That potential, though, is never realized. No one dies in the play, and no one is left in despair. While it may be going too far to say that all trouble is resolved or that the ending of *Wild Strawberries* is completely happy, it is nearer the conclusion of comedy than tragedy.

The **allegory**, in dramatic form, presents a series of characters who are not so much human beings as they are limited facets of the human personality. While the aim of most playwrights is to convey full-blooded human beings, the aim of the allegorist is to portray distinct types who act in predictable ways. The titles of several medieval morality plays suggest their allegorical qualities: *Mankind, Everyman, The Castle of Perseverance*. The characters who perform in these dramas are likewise allegorical types; in *The Castle of Perseverance*, for example, the characters include Folly, Pleasure, Backbiter, and Lust-Liker. There is no pretense in these plays that the experiences are true to ordinary life or that the characters are human beings.

The allegory is an example of **expressionistic** drama, a form which is unlike the realistic drama of *Riders to the Sea* or *King Lear*, to cite only two. The playwright does not pretend that the setting or the characters are true to "reality" as we know it; rather, "unreal" happenings are portrayed to express a certain truth about the human situation. A contemporary example of expressionistic drama is the **absurdist** play, so named because it emphasizes and dramatizes the absurdities in life and humanity. As with the allegory — and absurdist plays are sometimes quite similar to allegories — the dramatist aims toward a truth about life and humanity, but without the conventional trappings of a realistic setting in a distinct social environment. *The Leader*, an absurdist play by Eugene Ionesco, presents characters who have no names and who run around on stage with no clear sense of purpose or meaning. They are awaiting the arrival of a "leader," but both the waiting and the result are filled with absurdities. The action of the play is absurd, but the play itself need not be. To put it in other terms: one point of a drama like *The Leader* may be to suggest that life, or much of life, is filled with meaningless talk or action, but that does not make the play itself meaningless. A "meaning" is conveyed through a dramatic emphasis on meaninglessness.

HENRIK IBSEN (1828–1906)

Hedda Gabler

Translated by Edmund Gosse and William Archer

Characters

GEORGE TESMAN
HEDDA TESMAN, his wife
MISS JULIANA TESMAN, his aunt
MRS. ELVSTED
JUDGE BRACK
EILERT LÖVBORG
BERTA, servant at the Tesmans'

The scene of the action is Tesman's villa, in the west end of Christiania.

Act I

SCENE: *A spacious, handsome, and tastefully furnished drawing room, decorated in dark colors. In the back, a wide doorway with curtains drawn back, leading into a smaller room decorated in the same style as the drawing room. In the right-hand wall of the front room, a folding door leading out to the hall. In the opposite wall, on the left, a glass door, also with curtains drawn back. Through the panes can be seen part of a verandah outside, and trees covered with autumn foliage. An oval table, with a cover on it, and surrounded by chairs, stands well forward. In front, by the wall on the right, a wide stove of dark porcelain, a high-backed armchair, a cushioned footrest, and two footstools. A settee, with a small round table in front of it, fills the upper right-hand corner. In front, on the left, a little way from the wall, a sofa. Farther back than the glass door, a piano. On either side of the doorway at the back a whatnot with terra-cotta and majolica ornaments. Against the back wall of the inner room a sofa, with a table, and one or two chairs. Over the sofa hangs the portrait of a handsome elderly man in a General's uniform. Over the table a hanging lamp, with an opal glass shade. A number of bouquets are arranged about the drawing room, in vases and glasses. Others lie upon the tables. The floors in both rooms are covered with thick carpets. Morning light. The sun shines in through the glass door.*

    MISS JULIANA TESMAN, *with her bonnet on and carrying a parasol, comes in from the hall, followed by* BERTA, *who carries a bouquet wrapped in paper.* MISS TESMAN *is a comely and pleasant-looking lady of about sixty-*

five. She is nicely but simply dressed in a gray walking costume. BERTA *is a middle-aged woman of plain and rather countrified appearance.*

MISS TESMAN (*stops close to the door, listens, and says softly*): Upon my word, I don't believe they are stirring yet!

BERTA (*also softly*): I told you so, Miss. Remember how late the steamboat got in last night. And then, when they got home! — good Lord, what a lot the young mistress had to unpack before she could get to bed.

MISS TESMAN: Well, well — let them have their sleep out. But let us see that they get a good breath of the fresh morning air when they do appear. (*She goes to the glass door and throws it open.*)

BERTA (*beside the table, at a loss what to do with the bouquet in her hand*): I declare there isn't a bit of room left. I think I'll put it down here, Miss. (*She places it on the piano.*)

MISS TESMAN: So you've got a new mistress now, my dear Berta. Heaven knows it was a wrench to me to part with you.

BERTA (*on the point of weeping*): And do you think it wasn't hard for me too, Miss? After all the blessed years I've been with you and Miss Rina.

MISS TESMAN: We must make the best of it, Berta. There was nothing else to be done. George can't do without you, you see — he absolutely can't. He has had you to look after him ever since he was a little boy.

BERTA: Ah, but, Miss Julia, I can't help thinking of Miss Rina lying helpless at home there, poor thing. And with only that new girl, too! She'll never learn to take proper care of an invalid.

MISS TESMAN: Oh, I shall manage to train her. And of course, you know, I shall take most of it upon myself. You needn't be uneasy about my poor sister, my dear Berta.

BERTA: Well, but there's another thing, Miss. I'm so mortally afraid I shan't be able to suit the young mistress.

MISS TESMAN: Oh, well — just at first there may be one or two things ——

BERTA: Most like she'll be terrible grand in her ways.

MISS TESMAN: Well, you can't wonder at that — General Gabler's daughter! Think of the sort of life she was accustomed to in her father's time. Don't you remember how we used to see her riding down the road along with the General? In that long black habit — and with feathers in her hat?

BERTA: Yes, indeed — I remember well enough — ! But good Lord, I should never have dreamt in those days that she and Master George would make a match of it.

MISS TESMAN: Nor I. But, by-the-bye, Berta — while I think of it: in future you mustn't say Master George. You must say Dr. Tesman.

BERTA: Yes, the young mistress spoke of that too — last night — the moment they set foot in the house. Is it true, then, Miss?

MISS TESMAN: Yes, indeed it is. Only think, Berta — some foreign university has made him a doctor — while he has been abroad, you understand. I hadn't heard a word about it, until he told me himself upon the pier.

BERTA: Well, well, he's clever enough for anything, he is. But I didn't think he'd have gone in for doctoring people too.

MISS TESMAN: No, no, it's not that sort of doctor he is. (*Nods significantly.*) But let me tell you, we may have to call him something still grander before long.

BERTA: You don't say so! What can that be, Miss?

MISS TESMAN (*smiling*): H'm — wouldn't you like to know! (*With emotion.*) Ah, dear, dear — if my poor brother could only look up from his grave now, and see what his little boy has grown into! (*Looks around.*) But bless me, Berta — why have you done this? Taken the chintz covers off all the furniture?

BERTA: The mistress told me to. She can't abide covers on the chairs, she says.

MISS TESMAN: Are they going to make this their everyday sitting room then?

BERTA: Yes, that's what I understood — from the mistress. Master George — the doctor — he said nothing.

(GEORGE TESMAN *comes from the right into the inner room, humming to himself, and carrying an unstrapped empty portmanteau. He is a middle-sized, young-looking man of thirty-three, rather stout, with a round, open, cheerful face, fair hair and beard. He wears spectacles, and is somewhat carelessly dressed in comfortable indoor clothes.*)

MISS TESMAN: Good morning, good morning, George.

TESMAN (*in the doorway between the rooms*): Aunt Julia! Dear Aunt Julia! (*Goes up to her and shakes hands warmly.*) Come all this way — so early! Eh?

MISS TESMAN: Why of course I had to come and see how you were getting on.

TESMAN: In spite of your having had no proper night's rest?

MISS TESMAN: Oh, that makes no difference to me.

TESMAN: Well, I suppose you got home all right from the pier? Eh?

MISS TESMAN: Yes, quite safely, thank goodness. Judge Brack was good enough to see me right to my door.

TESMAN: We were so sorry we couldn't give you a seat in the carriage. But you saw what a pile of boxes Hedda had to bring with her.

MISS TESMAN: Yes, she had certainly plenty of boxes.

BERTA (*to* TESMAN): Shall I go in and see if there's anything I can do for the mistress?

TESMAN: No, thank you, Berta — you needn't. She said she would ring if she wanted anything.

BERTA (*going towards the right*): Very well.

TESMAN: But look here — take this portmanteau with you.

BERTA (*taking it*): I'll put it in the attic. (*She goes out by the hall door.*)

TESMAN: Fancy, Aunty — I had the whole of that portmanteau chock full of copies of documents. You wouldn't believe how much I have picked up from all the archives I have been examining — curious old details that no one has had any idea of ——

MISS TESMAN: Yes, you don't seem to have wasted your time on your wedding trip, George.

TESMAN: No, that I haven't. But do take off your bonnet, Auntie. Look here! Let me untie the strings — eh?

MISS TESMAN (*while he does so*): Well, well — this is just as if you were still at home with us.

TESMAN (*with the bonnet in his hand, looks at it from all sides*): Why, what a gorgeous bonnet you've been investing in!

MISS TESMAN: I bought it on Hedda's account.

TESMAN: On Hedda's account? Eh?

MISS TESMAN: Yes, so 'that Hedda needn't be ashamed of me if we happened to go out together.

TESMAN (*patting her cheek*): You always think of everything, Aunt Julia. (*Lays the bonnet on a chair beside the table.*) And now, look here — suppose we sit comfortably on the sofa and have a little chat, till Hedda comes.

(*They seat themselves. She places her parasol in the corner of the sofa.*)

MISS TESMAN (*takes both his hands and looks at him*): What a delight it is to have you again, as large as life, before my very eyes, George! My George — my poor brother's own boy!

TESMAN: And it's a delight for me, too, to see you again, Aunt Julia! You, who have been father and mother in one to me.

MISS TESMAN: Oh, yes, I know you will always keep a place in your heart for your old aunts.

TESMAN: And what about Aunt Rina? No improvement — eh!

MISS TESMAN: Oh, no — we can scarcely look for any improvement in her case, poor thing. There she lies, helpless, as she has lain for all these years. But heaven grant I may not lose her yet awhile! For if I did, I don't know what I should make of my life, George — especially now that I haven't you to look after any more.

TESMAN (*patting her back*): There, there, there —— !

MISS TESMAN (*suddenly changing her tone*): And to think that here you are a married man, George! — And that you should be the one to carry off Hedda Gabler, the beautiful Hedda Gabler! Only think of it — she, that was so beset with admirers!

TESMAN (*hums a little and smiles complacently*): Yes, I fancy I have several good friends about town who would like to stand in my shoes — eh?

MISS TESMAN: And then this fine long wedding tour you have had! More than five — nearly six months ——

TESMAN: Well, for me it has been a sort of tour of research as well. I have had to do so much grubbing among old records — and to read no end of books too, Auntie.

MISS TESMAN: Oh, yes, I suppose so. (*More confidentially, and lowering her voice a little.*) But listen now, George — have you nothing — nothing special to tell me?

TESMAN: As to our journey?

MISS TESMAN: Yes.

TESMAN: No, I don't know of anything except what I have told you in my letters. I had a doctor's degree conferred on me — but that I told you yesterday.

MISS TESMAN: Yes, yes, you did. But what I mean is — haven't you any — any — expectations —— ?

TESMAN: Expectations?

MISS TESMAN: Why, you know, George — I'm your old auntie!

TESMAN: Why, of course I have expectations.

MISS TESMAN: Ah!

TESMAN: I have every expectation of being a professor one of these days.

MISS TESMAN: Oh, yes, a professor ——

TESMAN: Indeed, I may say I am certain of it. But my dear Auntie — you know all about that already!

MISS TESMAN (*laughing to herself*): Yes, of course I do. You are quite right there. (*Changing the subject.*) But we were talking about your journey. It must have cost a great deal of money, George?

TESMAN: Well, you see — my handsome traveling scholarship went a good way.

MISS TESMAN: But I can't understand how you can have made it go far enough for two.

TESMAN: No, that's not so easy to understand — eh?

MISS TESMAN: And especially traveling with a lady — they tell me that makes it ever so much more expensive.

TESMAN: Yes, of course — it makes it a little more expensive. But Hedda had to have this trip, Auntie! She really had to. Nothing else would have done.

MISS TESMAN: No, no, I suppose not. A wedding tour seems to be quite indispensable nowadays. But tell me now — have you gone thoroughly over the house yet?

TESMAN: Yes, you may be sure I have. I have been afoot ever since daylight.

MISS TESMAN: And what do you think of it all?

TESMAN: I'm delighted! Quite delighted! Only I can't think what we are to do with the two empty rooms between this inner parlor and Hedda's bedroom.

MISS TESMAN (*laughing*): Oh, my dear George, I dare say you may find some use for them — in the course of time.

TESMAN: Why of course you are quite right, Aunt Julia! You mean as my library increases — eh?

MISS TESMAN: Yes, quite so, my dear boy. It was your library I was thinking of.

TESMAN: I am specially pleased on Hedda's account. Often and often, before we were engaged, she said that she would never care to live anywhere but in Secretary Falk's villa.

MISS TESMAN: Yes, it was lucky that this very house should come into the market, just after you had started.

TESMAN: Yes, Aunt Julia, the luck was on our side, wasn't it — eh?

MISS TESMAN: But the expense, my dear George! You will find it very expensive, all this.

TESMAN (*looks at her, a little cast down*): Yes, I suppose I shall, Aunt!

MISS TESMAN: Oh, frightfully!

TESMAN: How much do you think? In round numbers? — Eh?

MISS TESMAN: Oh, I can't even guess until all the accounts come in.

TESMAN: Well, fortunately, Judge Brack has secured the most favorable terms for me — so he said in a letter to Hedda.

MISS TESMAN: Yes, don't be uneasy, my dear boy. Besides, I have given security for the furniture and all the carpets.

TESMAN: Security? You? My dear Aunt Julia — what sort of security could you give?

MISS TESMAN: I have given a mortgage on our annuity.

TESMAN (*jumps up*): What! On your — and Aunt Rina's annuity!

MISS TESMAN: Yes, I knew of no other plan, you see.

TESMAN (*placing himself before her*): Have you gone out of your senses, Auntie! Your annuity — it's all that you and Aunt Rina have to live upon.

MISS TESMAN: Well, well, don't get so excited about it. It's only a matter of form you know — Judge Brack assured me of that. It was he that was kind enough to arrange the whole affair for me. A mere matter of form, he said.

TESMAN: Yes, that may be all very well. But nevertheless —

MISS TESMAN: You will have your own salary to depend upon now. And, good heavens, even if we did have to pay up a little — ! To eke things out a bit at the start — ! Why, it would be nothing but a pleasure to us.

TESMAN: Oh, Auntie — will you never be tired of making sacrifices for me!

MISS TESMAN (*rises and lays her hands on his shoulders*): Have I had any other happiness in this world except to smooth your way for you, my dear boy? You, who have had neither father nor mother to depend on. And now we have reached the goal, George! Things have looked black enough for us, sometimes; but, thank heaven, now you have nothing to fear.

TESMAN: Yes, it is really marvelous how everything has turned out for the best.

MISS TESMAN: And the people who opposed you — who wanted to bar the way for you — now you have them at your feet. They have fallen, George. Your most dangerous rival — his fall was the worst. And now he has to lie on the bed he has made for himself — poor misguided creature.

TESMAN: Have you heard anything of Eilert? Since I went away, I mean.

MISS TESMAN: Only that he is said to have published a new book.

TESMAN: What! Eilert Lövborg! Recently — eh?

MISS TESMAN: Yes, so they say. Heaven knows whether it can be worth anything! Ah, when your new book appears — that will be another story, George! What is it to be about?

TESMAN: It will deal with the domestic industries of Brabant during the Middle Ages.

MISS TESMAN: Fancy — to be able to write on such a subject as that.

TESMAN: However, it may be some time before the book is ready. I have all these collections to arrange first, you see.

MISS TESMAN: Yes, collecting and arranging — no one can beat you at that. There you are my poor brother's own son.

TESMAN: I am looking forward eagerly to setting to work at it; especially now that I have my own delightful home to work in.

MISS TESMAN: And, most of all, now that you have got the wife of your heart, my dear George.

TESMAN (*embracing her*): Oh, yes, yes, Aunt Julia. Hedda — she is the best part of all! (*Looks towards the doorway.*) I believe I hear her coming — eh?

(HEDDA *enters from the left through the inner room. She is a woman of nine-and-twenty. Her face and figure show refinement and distinction. Her complexion is pale and opaque. Her steel-gray eyes express a cold, unruffled repose. Her hair is of an agreeable medium brown, but not particularly abundant. She is dressed in a tasteful, somewhat loose-fitting morning gown.*)

MISS TESMAN (*going to meet* HEDDA): Good morning, my dear Hedda! Good morning, and a hearty welcome.

HEDDA (*holds out her hand*): Good morning, dear Miss Tesman! So early a call! That is kind of you.

MISS TESMAN (*with some embarrassment*): Well — has the bride slept well in her new home?

HEDDA: Oh yes, thanks. Passably.

TESMAN (*laughing*): Passably! Come, that's good, Hedda! You were sleeping like a stone when I got up.

HEDDA: Fortunately. Of course one has always to accustom one's self to new surroundings, Miss Tesman — little by little. (*Looking towards the left.*) Oh — there the servant has gone and opened the verandah door, and let in a whole flood of sunshine.

MISS TESMAN (*going towards the door*): Well, then, we will shut it.

HEDDA: No, no, not that! Tesman, please draw the curtains. That will give a softer light.

TESMAN (*at the door*): All right — all right. There now, Hedda, now you have both shade and fresh air.

HEDDA: Yes, fresh air we certainly must have, with all these stacks of flowers —— But — won't you sit down, Miss Tesman?

MISS TESMAN: No, thank you. Now that I have seen that everything is all right here — thank heaven! I must be getting home again. My sister is lying longing for me, poor thing.

TESMAN: Give her my very best love, Auntie; and say I shall look in and see her later in the day.

MISS TESMAN: Yes, yes, I'll be sure to tell her. But by-the-bye, George — (*feeling in her dress pocket*) — I have almost forgotten — I have something for you here.

TESMAN: What is it, Auntie? Eh?

MISS TESMAN (*produces a flat parcel wrapped in newspaper and hands it to him*): Look here, my dear boy.

TESMAN (*opening the parcel*): Well, I declare! Have you really saved them for me, Aunt Julia! Hedda! isn't this touching — eh?

HEDDA (*beside the whatnot on the right*): Well, what is it?

TESMAN: My old morning shoes! My slippers.

HEDDA: Indeed. I remember you often spoke of them while we were abroad.

TESMAN: Yes, I missed them terribly. (*Goes up to her.*) Now you shall see them, Hedda!

HEDDA (*going towards the stove*): Thanks, I really don't care about it.

TESMAN (*following her*): Only think — ill as she was, Aunt Rina embroidered these for me. Oh, you can't think how many associations cling to them.

HEDDA (*at the table*): Scarcely for me.

MISS TESMAN: Of course not for Hedda, George.

TESMAN: Well, but now that she belongs to the family, I thought ——

HEDDA (*interrupting*): We shall never get on with this servant, Tesman.

MISS TESMAN: Not get on with Berta?

TESMAN: Why, dear, what puts that in your head? Eh?

HEDDA (*pointing*): Look there! She has left her old bonnet lying about on a chair.

TESMAN (*in consternation, drops the slippers on the floor*): Why, Hedda ——

HEDDA: Just fancy, if any one should come in and see it.

TESMAN: But Hedda — that's Aunt Julia's bonnet.

HEDDA: Is it!

MISS TESMAN (*taking up the bonnet*): Yes, indeed it's mine. And what's more, it's not old, Madame Hedda.

HEDDA: I really did not look closely at it, Miss Tesman.

MISS TESMAN (*trying on the bonnet*): Let me tell you it's the first time I have worn it — the very first time.

TESMAN: And a very nice bonnet it is too — quite a beauty!

MISS TESMAN: Oh, it's no such great thing, George. (*Looks around her.*) My parasol —— ? Ah, here. (*Takes it.*) For this is mine too — (*mutters*) — not Berta's.

TESMAN: A new bonnet and a new parasol! Only think, Hedda!

HEDDA: Very handsome indeed.

TESMAN: Yes, isn't it? But Auntie, take a good look at Hedda before you go! See how handsome she is!

MISS TESMAN: Oh, my dear boy, there's nothing new in that. Hedda was always lovely. (*She nods and goes towards the right.*)

TESMAN (*following*): Yes, but have you noticed what splendid condition she is in? How she has filled out on the journey?

HEDDA (*crossing the room*): Oh, do be quiet —— !

MISS TESMAN (*who has stopped and turned*): Filled out?

TESMAN: Of course you don't notice it so much now that she has that dress on. But I, who can see ——

HEDDA (*at the glass door, impatiently*): Oh, you can't see anything.

TESMAN: It must be the mountain air in the Tyrol ——

HEDDA (*curtly, interrupting*): I am exactly as I was when I started.

TESMAN: So you insist; but I'm quite certain you are not. Don't you agree with me, Auntie?

MISS TESMAN (*who has been gazing at her with folded hands*): Hedda is lovely — lovely — lovely. (*Goes up to her, takes her head between both hands, draws it downwards, and kisses her hair.*) God bless and preserve Hedda Tesman — for George's sake.

HEDDA (*gently freeing herself*): Oh! Let me go.

MISS TESMAN (*in quiet emotion*): I shall not let a day pass without coming to see you.

TESMAN: No you won't, will you, Auntie? Eh?

MISS TESMAN: Good-by — good-by!

(*She goes out by the hall door.* TESMAN *accompanies her. The door remains half open.* TESMAN *can be heard repeating his message to Aunt Rina and his thanks for the slippers.*
In the meantime, HEDDA *walks about the room raising her arms and clenching her hands as if in desperation. Then she flings back the curtains from the glass door, and stands there looking out.*
Presently TESMAN *returns and closes the door behind him.*)

TESMAN (*picks up the slippers from the floor*): What are you looking at, Hedda?

HEDDA (*once more calm and mistress of herself*): I am only looking at the leaves. They are so yellow — so withered.

TESMAN (*wraps up the slippers and lays them on the table*): Well you see, we are well into September now.

HEDDA (*again restless*): Yes, to think of it! Already in — in September.

TESMAN: Don't you think Aunt Julia's manner was strange, dear? Almost solemn? Can you imagine what was the matter with her? Eh?

HEDDA: I scarcely know her, you see. Is she often like that?

TESMAN: No, not as she was today.

HEDDA (*leaving the glass door*): Do you think she was annoyed about the bonnet?

TESMAN: Oh, scarcely at all. Perhaps a little, just at the moment ——

HEDDA: But what an idea, to pitch her bonnet about in the drawing room! No one does that sort of thing.

TESMAN: Well you may be sure Aunt Julia won't do it again.

HEDDA: In any case, I shall manage to make my peace with her.

TESMAN: Yes, my dear, good Hedda, if you only would.

HEDDA: When you call this afternoon, you might invite her to spend the evening here.

TESMAN: Yes, that I will. And there's one thing more you could do that would delight her heart.

HEDDA: What is it?

TESMAN: If you could only prevail on yourself to say *du*[1] to her. For my sake, Hedda? Eh?

HEDDA: No, no, Tesman — you really musn't ask that of me. I have told you so already. I shall try to call her "Aunt"; and you must be satisfied with that.

TESMAN: Well, well. Only I think now that you belong to the family, you ——

HEDDA: H'm — I can't in the least see why ——

(*She goes up towards the middle doorway.*)

TESMAN (*after a pause*): Is there anything the matter with you, Hedda? Eh?

HEDDA: I'm only looking at my old piano. It doesn't go at all well with all the other things.

TESMAN: The first time I draw my salary, we'll see about exchanging it.

HEDDA: No, no — no exchanging. I don't want to part with it. Suppose we put it there in the inner room, and then get another here in its place. When it's convenient, I mean.

TESMAN (*a little taken aback*): Yes — of course we could do that.

HEDDA (*takes up the bouquet from the piano*): These flowers were not here last night when we arrived.

TESMAN: Aunt Julia must have brought them for you.

HEDDA (*examining the bouquet*): A visiting card. (*Takes it out and reads.*) "Shall return later in the day." Can you guess whose card it is?

TESMAN: No. Whose? Eh?

HEDDA: The name is "Mrs. Elvsted."

TESMAN: Is it really? Sheriff Elvsted's wife? Miss Rysing that was.

HEDDA: Exactly. The girl with the irritating hair, that she was always showing off. An old flame of yours, I've been told.

---

1. *Du* thou, the familiar form of the pronoun *you*.

TESMAN (*laughing*): Oh, that didn't last long; and it was before I knew you, Hedda. But fancy her being in town!

HEDDA: It's odd that she should call upon us. I have scarcely seen her since we left school.

TESMAN: I haven't seen her either for — heaven knows how long. I wonder how she can endure to live in such an out-of-the-way hole — eh?

HEDDA (*after a moment's thought says suddenly*): Tell me, Tesman — isn't it somewhere near there that he — that — Eilert Lövborg is living?

TESMAN: Yes, he is somewhere in that part of the country.

(BERTA *enters by the hall door.*)

BERTA: That lady, ma'am, that brought some flowers a little while ago, is here again. (*Pointing.*) The flowers you have in your hand, ma'am.

HEDDA: Ah, is she? Well, please show her in.

(BERTA *opens the door for* MRS. ELVSTED, *and goes out herself.* MRS. ELVSTED *is a woman of fragile figure, with pretty, soft features. Her eyes are light blue, large, round, and somewhat prominent, with a startled, inquiring expression. Her hair is remarkably light, almost flaxen, and unusually abundant and wavy. She is a couple of years younger than* HEDDA. *She wears a dark visiting dress, tasteful, but not quite in the latest fashion.*)

HEDDA (*receives her warmly*): How do you do, my dear Mrs. Elvsted? It's delightful to see you again.

MRS. ELVSTED (*nervously, struggling for self-control*): Yes, it's a very long time since we met.

TESMAN (*gives her his hand*): And we too — eh?

HEDDA: Thanks for your lovely flowers ——

MRS. ELVSTED: Oh, not at all —— I would have come straight here yesterday afternoon; but I heard that you were away ——

TESMAN: Have you just come to town? Eh?

MRS. ELVSTED: I arrived yesterday, about midday. Oh, I was quite in despair when I heard that you were not at home.

HEDDA: In despair! How so?

TESMAN: Why, my dear Mrs. Rysing — I mean Mrs. Elvsted ——

HEDDA: I hope that you are not in any trouble?

MRS. ELVSTED: Yes, I am. And I don't know another living creature here that I can turn to.

HEDDA (*laying the bouquet on the table*): Come — let us sit here on the sofa ——

MRS. ELVSTED: Oh, I am too restless to sit down.

HEDDA: Oh no, you're not. Come here. (*She draws* MRS. ELVSTED *down upon the sofa and sits at her side.*)

TESMAN: Well? What is it, Mrs. Elvsted?

HEDDA: Has anything particular happened to you at home?

MRS. ELVSTED: Yes — and no. Oh — I am so anxious you should not misunderstand me ——

HEDDA: Then your best plan is to tell us the whole story, Mrs. Elvsted.

TESMAN: I suppose that's what you have come for — eh?

MRS. ELVSTED: Yes, yes — of course it is. Well then, I must tell you — if you don't already know — that Eilert Lövborg is in town, too.

HEDDA: Lövborg —— !

TESMAN: What! Has Eilert Lövborg come back? Fancy that, Hedda!

HEDDA: Well, well — I hear it.

MRS. ELVSTED: He has been here a week already. Just fancy — a whole week! In this terrible town, alone! With so many temptations on all sides.

HEDDA: But my dear Mrs. Elvsted — how does he concern you so much?

MRS. ELVSTED (*looks at her with a startled air, and says rapidly*): He was the children's tutor.

HEDDA: Your children's?

MRS. ELVSTED: My husband's. I have none.

HEDDA: Your step-children's, then?

MRS. ELVSTED: Yes.

TESMAN (*somewhat hesitatingly*): Then was he — I don't know how to express it — was he — regular enough in his habits to be fit for the post? Eh?

MRS. ELVSTED: For the last two years his conduct has been irreproachable.

TESMAN: Has it indeed? Fancy that, Hedda!

HEDDA: I hear it.

MRS. ELVSTED: Perfectly irreproachable, I assure you! In every respect. But all the same — now that I know he is here — in this great town —

and with a large sum of money in his hands — I can't help being in mortal fear for him.

TESMAN: Why did he not remain where he was? With you and your husband? Eh?

MRS. ELVSTED: After his book was published he was too restless and unsettled to remain with us.

TESMAN: Yes, by-the-bye, Aunt Julia told me he had published a new book.

MRS. ELVSTED: Yes, a big book, dealing with the march of civilization — in broad outline, as it were. It came out about a fortnight ago. And since it has sold so well, and been so much read — and made such a sensation —

TESMAN: Has it indeed? It must be something he has had lying by since his better days.

MRS. ELVSTED: Long ago, you mean?

TESMAN: Yes.

MRS. ELVSTED: No, he has written it all since he has been with us — within the last year.

TESMAN: Isn't that good news, Hedda? Think of that.

MRS. ELVSTED: Ah, yes, if only it would last!

HEDDA: Have you seen him here in town?

MRS. ELVSTED: No, not yet. I have had the greatest difficulty in finding out his address. But this morning I discovered it at last.

HEDDA (*looks searchingly at her*): Do you know, it seems to me a little odd of your husband — h'm ——

MRS. ELVSTED (*starting nervously*): Of my husband! What?

HEDDA: That he should send you to town on such an errand — that he does not come himself and look after his friend.

MRS. ELVSTED: Oh no, no — my husband has no time. And besides, I — I had some shopping to do.

HEDDA (*with a slight smile*): Ah, that is a different matter.

MRS. ELVSTED (*rising quickly and uneasily*): And now I beg and implore you, Mr. Tesman — receive Eilert Lövborg kindly if he comes to you! And that he is sure to do. You see you were such great friends in the old days. And then you are interested in the same studies — the same branch of science — so far as I can understand.

TESMAN: We used to be, at any rate.

MRS. ELVSTED: That is why I beg so earnestly that you — you too — will keep a sharp eye upon him. Oh, you will promise me that, Mr. Tesman — won't you?

TESMAN: With the greatest of pleasure, Mrs. Rysing ——

HEDDA: Elvsted.

TESMAN: I assure you I shall do all I possibly can for Eilert. You may rely upon me.

MRS. ELVSTED: Oh, how very, very kind of you! (*Presses his hands.*) Thanks, thanks, thanks! (*Frightened.*) You see, my husband is very fond of him!

HEDDA (*rising*): You ought to write to him, Tesman. Perhaps he may not care to come to you of his own accord.

TESMAN: Well, perhaps it would be the right thing to do, Hedda? Eh?

HEDDA: And the sooner the better. Why not at once?

MRS. ELVSTED (*imploringly*): Oh, if you only would!

TESMAN: I'll write this moment. Have you his address, Mrs. — Mrs. Elvsted?

MRS. ELVSTED: Yes. (*Takes a slip of paper from her pocket, and hands it to him.*) Here it is.

TESMAN: Good, good. Then I'll go in —— (*Looks about him.*) By-the-bye — my slippers? Oh, here. (*Takes the packet, and is about to go.*)

HEDDA: Be sure you write him a cordial, friendly letter. And a good long one too.

TESMAN: Yes, I will.

MRS. ELVSTED: But please, please don't say a word to show that I have suggested it.

TESMAN: No, how could you think I would? Eh? (*He goes out to the right, through the inner room.*)

HEDDA (*goes up to* MRS. ELVSTED, *smiles, and says in a low voice*): There. We have killed two birds with one stone.

MRS. ELVSTED: What do you mean?

HEDDA: Could you not see that I wanted him to go?

MRS. ELVSTED: Yes, to write the letter ——

HEDDA: And that I might speak to you alone.

MRS. ELVSTED (*confused*): About the same thing?

HEDDA: Precisely.

MRS. ELVSTED (*apprehensively*): But there is nothing more, Mrs. Tesman! Absolutely nothing!

HEDDA: Oh, yes, but there is. There is a great deal more — I can see that. Sit here — and we'll have a cosy, confidential chat. (*She forces* MRS. ELVSTED *to sit in the easy chair beside the stove, and seats herself on one of the footstools.*)

MRS. ELVSTED (*anxiously, looking at her watch*): But, my dear Mrs. Tesman — I was really on the point of going.

HEDDA: Oh, you can't be in such a hurry. Well? Now tell me something about your life at home.

MRS. ELVSTED: Oh, that is just what I care least to speak about.

HEDDA: But to me, dear —— ? Why, weren't we schoolfellows?

MRS. ELVSTED: Yes, but you were in the class above me. Oh, how dreadfully afraid of you I was then!

HEDDA: Afraid of me?

MRS. ELVSTED: *Yes*, dreadfully. For when we met on the stairs you used always to pull my hair.

HEDDA: Did I, really?

MRS. ELVSTED: Yes, and once you said you would burn it off my head.

HEDDA: Oh, that was all nonsense, of course.

MRS. ELVSTED: Yes, but I was so silly in those days. And since then, too — we have drifted so far — far apart from each other. Our circles have been so entirely different.

HEDDA: Well then, we must try to drift together again. Now listen! At school we said *du* to each other; and we called each other by our Christian names ——

MRS. ELVSTED: No, I am sure you must be mistaken.

HEDDA: No, not at all! I can remember quite distinctly. So now we are going to renew our old friendship. (*Draws the footstool closer to* MRS. ELVSTED.) There now! (*Kisses her cheek.*) You must say *du* to me and call me Hedda.

MRS. ELVSTED (*presses and pats her hands*): Oh, how good and kind you are! I am not used to such kindness.

HEDDA: There, there, there! And I shall say *du* to you, as in the old days, and call you my dear Thora.

MRS. ELVSTED: My name is Thea.

HEDDA: Why, of course! I meant Thea. (*Looks at her compassionately.*) So you are not accustomed to goodness and kindness, Thea? Not in your own home?

MRS. ELVSTED: Oh, if I only had a home! But I haven't any; I have never had a home.

HEDDA (*looks at her for a moment*): I almost suspected as much.

MRS. ELVSTED (*gazing helplessly before her*): Yes — yes — yes.

HEDDA: I don't quite remember — was it not as housekeeper that you first went to Mr. Elvsted's?

MRS. ELVSTED: I really went as governess. But his wife — his late wife — was an invalid — and rarely left her room. So I had to look after the housekeeping as well.

HEDDA: And then — at last — you became mistress of the house.

MRS. ELVSTED (*sadly*): Yes, I did.

HEDDA: Let me see — about how long ago was that?

MRS. ELVSTED: My marriage?

HEDDA: Yes.

MRS. ELVSTED: Five years ago.

HEDDA: To be sure; it must be that.

MRS. ELVSTED: Oh, those five years ——— ! Or at all events the last two or three of them! Oh, if you[2] could only imagine ———

HEDDA (*giving her a little slap on the hand*): De? Fie, Thea!

MRS. ELVSTED: Yes, yes, I will try ——— Well if — you could only imagine and understand ———

HEDDA (*lightly*): Eilert Lövborg has been in your neighborhood about three years, hasn't he?

MRS. ELVSTED (*looks at her doubtfully*): Eilert Lövborg? Yes — he has.

HEDDA: Had you known him before, in town here?

MRS. ELVSTED: Scarcely at all. I mean — I knew him by name of course.

HEDDA: But you saw a good deal of him in the country?

MRS. ELVSTED: Yes, he came to us every day. You see, he gave the children lessons; for in the long run I couldn't manage it all myself.

2. Mrs. Elvsted here uses the formal pronoun *De*, whereupon Hedda rebukes her. In her next speech Mrs. Elvsted says *du*.

HEDDA: No, that's clear. And your husband —— ? I suppose he is often away from home?

MRS. ELVSTED: Yes. Being Sheriff, you know, he has to travel about a good deal in his district.

HEDDA (*leaning against the arm of the chair*): Thea — my poor, sweet Thea — now you must tell me everything — exactly as it stands.

MRS. ELVSTED: Well then, you must question me.

HEDDA: What sort of a man is your husband, Thea? I mean — you know — in everyday life. Is he kind to you?

MRS. ELVSTED (*evasively*): I am sure he means well in everything.

HEDDA: I should think he must be altogether too old for you. There is at least twenty years' difference between you, is there not?

MRS. ELVSTED (*irritably*): Yes, that is true, too. Everything about him is repellent to me! We have not a thought in common. We have no single point of sympathy — he and I.

HEDDA: But is he not fond of you all the same? In his own way?

MRS. ELVSTED: Oh, I really don't know. I think he regards me simply as a useful property. And then it doesn't cost much to keep me. I am not expensive.

HEDDA: That is stupid of you.

MRS. ELVSTED (*shakes her head*): It cannot be otherwise — not with him. I don't think he really cares for any one but himself — and perhaps a little for the children.

HEDDA: And for Eilert Lövborg, Thea.

MRS. ELVSTED (*looking at her*): For Eilert Lövborg? What puts that into your head?

HEDDA: Well, my dear — I should say, when he sends you after him all the way to town —— (*Smiling almost imperceptibly.*) And besides, you said so yourself, to Tesman.

MRS. ELVSTED (*with a little nervous twitch*): Did I? Yes, I suppose I did. (*Vehemently, but not loudly.*) No — I may just as well make a clean breast of it at once! For it must all come out in any case.

HEDDA: Why, my dear Thea —— ?

MRS. ELVSTED: Well, to make a long story short: My husband did not know that I was coming.

HEDDA: What! Your husband didn't know it!

MRS. ELVSTED: No, of course not. For that matter, he was away from home himself — he was traveling. Oh, I could bear it no longer, Hedda! I couldn't indeed — so utterly alone as I should have been in future.

HEDDA: Well? And then?

MRS. ELVSTED: So I put together some of my things — what I needed most — as quietly as possible. And then I left the house.

HEDDA: Without a word?

MRS. ELVSTED: Yes — and took the train straight to town.

HEDDA: Why, my dear, good Thea — to think of you daring to do it!

MRS. ELVSTED (*rises and moves about the room*): What else could I possibly do?

HEDDA: But what do you think your husband will say when you go home again?

MRS. ELVSTED (*at the table, looks at her*): Back to him.

HEDDA: Of course.

MRS. ELVSTED: I shall never go back to him again.

HEDDA (*rising and going towards her*): Then you have left your home — for good and all?

MRS. ELVSTED: Yes. There was nothing else to be done.

HEDDA: But then — to take flight so openly.

MRS. ELVSTED: Oh, it's impossible to keep things of that sort secret.

HEDDA: But what do you think people will say of you, Thea?

MRS. ELVSTED: They may say what they like for aught *I* care. (*Seats herself wearily and sadly on the sofa.*) I have done nothing but what I had to do.

HEDDA (*after a short silence*): And what are your plans now? What do you think of doing?

MRS. ELVSTED: I don't know yet. I only know this, that I must live here, where Eilert Lövborg is — if I am to live at all.

HEDDA (*takes a chair from the table, seats herself beside her, and strokes her hands*): My dear Thea — how did this — this friendship — between you and Eilert Lövborg come about?

MRS. ELVSTED: Oh, it grew up gradually. I gained a sort of influence over him.

HEDDA: Indeed?

MRS. ELVSTED: He gave up his old habits. Not because I asked him to, for I never dared do that. But of course he saw how repulsive they were to me; and so he dropped them.

HEDDA (*concealing an involuntary smile of scorn*): Then you have reclaimed him — as the saying goes — my little Thea.

MRS. ELVSTED: So he says himself, at any rate. And he, on his side, has made a real human being of me — taught me to think, and to understand so many things.

HEDDA: Did he give you lessons too, then?

MRS. ELVSTED: No, not exactly lessons. But he talked to me — talked about such an infinity of things. And then came the lovely, happy time when I began to share in his work — when he allowed me to help him!

HEDDA: Oh, he did, did he?

MRS. ELVSTED: Yes! He never wrote anything without my assistance.

HEDDA: You were two good comrades, in fact?

MRS. ELVSTED (*eagerly*): Comrades! Yes, fancy, Hedda — that is the very word he used! Oh, I ought to feel perfectly happy; and yet I cannot; for I don't know how long it will last.

HEDDA: Are you no surer of him than that?

MRS. ELVSTED (*gloomily*): A woman's shadow stands between Eilert Lövborg and me.

HEDDA (*looks at her anxiously*): Who can that be?

MRS. ELVSTED: I don't know. Some one he knew in his — in his past. Some one he has never been able wholly to forget.

HEDDA: What has he told you — about this?

MRS. ELVSTED: He has only once — quite vaguely — alluded to it.

HEDDA: Well! And what did he say?

MRS. ELVSTED: He said that when they parted, she threatened to shoot him with a pistol.

HEDDA (*with cold composure*): Oh, nonsense! No one does that sort of thing here.

MRS. ELVSTED: No. And that is why I think it must have been that redhaired singing woman whom he once ——

HEDDA: Yes, very likely.

MRS. ELVSTED: For I remember they used to say of her that she carried loaded firearms.

HEDDA: Oh — then of course it must have been she.

MRS. ELVSTED (*wringing her hands*): And now just fancy, Hedda — I hear that this singing woman — that she is in town again! Oh, I don't know what to do ——

HEDDA (*glancing towards the inner room*): Hush! Here comes Tesman. (*Rises and whispers.*) Thea — all this must remain between you and me.

MRS. ELVSTED (*springing up*): Oh, yes, yes! for heaven's sake —— !

(GEORGE TESMAN, *with a letter in his hand, comes from the right through the inner room.*)

TESMAN: There now — the epistle is finished.

HEDDA: That's right. And now Mrs. Elvsted is just going. Wait a moment — I'll go with you to the garden gate.

TESMAN: Do you think Berta could post the letter, Hedda dear?

HEDDA (*takes it*): I will tell her to.

(BERTA *enters from the hall.*)

BERTA: Judge Brack wishes to know if Mrs. Tesman will receive him.

HEDDA: Yes, ask Judge Brack to come in. And look here — put this letter in the post.

BERTA (*taking the letter*): Yes, ma'am.

(*She opens the door for* JUDGE BRACK *and goes out herself.* BRACK *is a man of forty-five; thickset, but well built and elastic in his movements. His face is roundish with an aristocratic profile. His hair is short, still almost black, and carefully dressed. His eyes are lively and sparkling. His eyebrows thick. His moustaches are also thick, with short-cut ends. He wears a well-cut walking suit, a little too youthful for his age. He uses an eyeglass, which he now and then lets drop.*)

JUDGE BRACK (*with his hat in his hand, bowing*): May one venture to call so early in the day?

HEDDA: Of course one may.

TESMAN (*presses his hand*): You are welcome at any time. (*Introducing him.*) Judge Brack — Miss Rysing ——

HEDDA: Oh —— !

BRACK (*bowing*): Ah — delighted ——

HEDDA (*looks at him and laughs*): It's nice to have a look at you by daylight, Judge!

BRACK: Do you find me — altered?

HEDDA: A little younger, I think.

BRACK: Thank you so much.

TESMAN: But what do you think of Hedda — eh? Doesn't she look flourishing? She has actually ——

HEDDA: Oh, do leave me alone. You haven't thanked Judge Brack for all the trouble he has taken ——

BRACK: Oh, nonsense — it was a pleasure to me ——

HEDDA: Yes, you are a friend indeed. But here stands Thea all impatience to be off — so *au revoir*, Judge. I shall be back again presently. (*Mutual salutations.* MRS. ELVSTED *and* HEDDA *go out by the hall door.*)

BRACK: Well, is your wife tolerably satisfied ——

TESMAN: Yes, we can't thank you sufficiently. Of course she talks of a little rearrangement here and there; and one or two things are still wanting. We shall have to buy some additional trifles.

BRACK: Indeed!

TESMAN: But we won't trouble you about these things. Hedda says she herself will look after what is wanting. —— Shan't we sit down? Eh?

BRACK: Thanks, for a moment. (*Seats himself beside the table.*) There is something I wanted to speak to you about, my dear Tesman.

TESMAN: Indeed? Ah, I understand! (*Seating himself.*) I suppose it's the serious part of the frolic that is coming now. Eh?

BRACK: Oh, the money question is not so very pressing; though, for that matter, I wish we had gone a little more economically to work.

TESMAN: But that would never have done, you know! Think of Hedda, my dear fellow! You, who know her so well —— I couldn't possibly ask her to put up with a shabby style of living!

BRACK: No, no — that is just the difficulty.

TESMAN: And then — fortunately — it can't be long before I receive my appointment.

BRACK: Well, you see — such things are often apt to hang fire for a time.

TESMAN: Have you heard anything definite? Eh?

BRACK: Nothing exactly definite —— (*Interrupting himself.*) But, by-the-bye — I have one piece of news for you.

TESMAN: Well?

BRACK: Your old friend, Eilert Lövborg, has returned to town.

TESMAN: I know that already.

BRACK: Indeed! How did you learn it?

TESMAN: From that lady who went out with Hedda.

BRACK: Really? What was her name? I didn't quite catch it.

TESMAN: Mrs. Elvsted.

BRACK: Aha — Sheriff Elvsted's wife? Of course — he has been living up in their regions.

TESMAN: And fancy — I'm delighted to hear that he is quite a reformed character!

BRACK: So they say.

TESMAN: And then he has published a new book — eh?

BRACK: Yes, indeed he has.

TESMAN: And I hear it has made some sensation!

BRACK: Quite an unusual sensation.

TESMAN: Fancy — isn't that good news! A man of such extraordinary talents —— I felt so grieved to think that he had gone irretrievably to ruin.

BRACK: That was what everybody thought.

TESMAN: But I cannot imagine what he will take to now! How in the world will he be able to make his living? Eh?

(*During the last words,* HEDDA *has entered by the hall door.*)

HEDDA (*to* BRACK, *laughing with a touch of scorn*): Tesman is forever worrying about how people are to make their living.

TESMAN: Well, you see, dear — we were talking about poor Eilert Lövborg.

HEDDA (*glancing at him rapidly*): Oh, indeed? (*Seats herself in the armchair beside the stove and asks indifferently.*) What is the matter with him?

TESMAN: Well — no doubt he has run through all his property long ago; and he can scarcely write a new book every year — eh? So I really can't see what is to become of him.

BRACK: Perhaps I can give you some information on that point.

TESMAN: Indeed!

BRACK: You must remember that his relations have a good deal of influence.

TESMAN: Oh, his relations, unfortunately, have entirely washed their hands of him.

BRACK: At one time, they called him the hope of the family.

TESMAN: At one time, yes! But he has put an end to all that.

HEDDA: Who knows? (*With a slight smile.*) I hear they have reclaimed him up at Sheriff Elvsted's ——

BRACK: And then this book that he has published ——

TESMAN: Well, well, I hope to goodness they may find something for him to do. I have just written to him. I asked him to come and see us this evening, Hedda dear.

BRACK: But, my dear fellow, you are booked for my bachelors' party this evening. You promised on the pier last night.

HEDDA: Had you forgotten, Tesman?

TESMAN: Yes, I had utterly forgotten.

BRACK: But it doesn't matter, for you may be sure he won't come.

TESMAN: What makes you think that? Eh?

BRACK (*with a little hesitation, rising and resting his hands on the back of his chair*): My dear Tesman — and you too, Mrs. Tesman — I think I ought not to keep you in the dark about something that — that —

TESMAN: That concerns Eilert —— ?

BRACK: Both you and him.

TESMAN: Well, my dear Judge, out with it.

BRACK: You must be prepared to find your appointment deferred longer than you desired or expected.

TESMAN (*jumping up uneasily*): Is there some hitch about it? Eh?

BRACK: The nomination may perhaps be made conditional on the result of a competition ——

TESMAN: Competition! Think of that, Hedda!

HEDDA (*leans farther back in the chair*): Aha — aha!

TESMAN: But who can my competitor be? Surely not —— ?

BRACK: Yes, precisely — Eilert Lövborg.

TESMAN (*clasping his hands*): No, no — it's quite inconceivable! Quite impossible! Eh?

BRACK: H'm — that is what it may come to, all the same.

TESMAN: Well but, Judge Brack — it would show the most incredible lack of consideration for me. (*Gesticulates with his arms.*) For — just think — I'm a married man. We have been married on the strength of these prospects, Hedda and I; and run deep into debt; and borrowed money from Aunt Julia too. Good heavens, they had as good as promised me the appointment. Eh?

BRACK: Well, well, well — no doubt you will get it in the end; only after a contest.

HEDDA (*immovable in her armchair*): Fancy, Tesman, there will be a sort of sporting interest in that.

TESMAN: Why, my dearest Hedda, how can you be so indifferent about it.

HEDDA (*as before*): I am not at all indifferent. I am most eager to see who wins.

BRACK: In any case, Mrs. Tesman, it is best that you should know how matters stand. I mean — before you set about the little purchases I hear you are threatening.

HEDDA: This can make no difference.

BRACK: Indeed! Then I have no more to say. Good-by! (*To* TESMAN.) I shall look in on my way back from my afternoon walk, and take you home with me.

TESMAN: Oh yes, yes — your news has quite upset me.

HEDDA (*reclining, holds out her hand*): Good-by, Judge; and be sure you call in the afternoon.

BRACK: Many thanks. Good-by, good-by!

TESMAN (*accompanying him to the door*): Good-by, my dear Judge! You must really excuse me —— (JUDGE BRACK *goes out by the hall door.*)

TESMAN (*crosses the room*): Oh, Hedda — one should never rush into adventures. Eh?

HEDDA (*looks at him, smiling*): Do you do that?

TESMAN: Yes, dear — there is no denying — it was adventurous to go and marry and set up house upon mere expectations.

HEDDA: Perhaps you are right there.

TESMAN: Well — at all events, we have our delightful home, Hedda! Fancy, the home we both dreamed of — the home we were in love with, I may almost say. Eh?

HEDDA (*rising slowly and wearily*): It was part of our compact that we were to go into society — to keep open house.

TESMAN: Yes, if you only knew how I had been looking forward to it! Fancy — to see you as hostess — in a select circle? Eh? Well, well well — for the present we shall have to get on without society, Hedda — only to invite Aunt Julia now and then. Oh, I intended you to lead such an utterly different life, dear —— !

HEDDA: Of course I cannot have my man in livery just yet.

TESMAN: Oh no, unfortunately. It would be out of the question for us to keep a footman, you know.

HEDDA: And the saddle horse I was to have had ——

TESMAN (*aghast*): The saddle horse!

HEDDA: —— I suppose I must not think of that now.

TESMAN: Good heavens, no! — that's as clear as daylight.

HEDDA (*goes up the room*): Well, I shall have one thing at least to kill time with in the meanwhile.

TESMAN (*beaming*): Oh, thank heaven for that! What is it, Hedda? Eh?

HEDDA (*in the middle doorway, looks at him with covert scorn*): My pistols, George.

TESMAN (*in alarm*): Your pistols!

HEDDA (*with cold eyes*): General Gabler's pistols. (*She goes out through the inner room, to the left.*)

TESMAN (*rushes up to the middle doorway and calls after her*): No, for heaven's sake, Hedda darling — don't touch those dangerous things! For my sake, Hedda! Eh?

Act II

SCENE: *The room at the* TESSMANS' *as in the first Act, except that the piano has been removed, and an elegant little writing table with bookshelves put in its place. A smaller table stands near the sofa at the left. Most of the bouquets have been taken away.* MRS. ELVSTED'S *bouquet is upon the large table in front. It is afternoon.*

HEDDA, *dressed to receive callers, is alone in the room. She stands by the open glass door, loading a revolver. The fellow to it lies in an open pistol case on the writing table.*

HEDDA (*looks down the garden, and calls*): So you are here again, Judge!

BRACK (*is heard calling from a distance*): As you see, Mrs. Tesman!

HEDDA (*raises the pistol and points*): Now I'll shoot you, Judge Brack!

BRACK (*calling unseen*): No, no, no! Don't stand aiming at me!

HEDDA: This is what comes of sneaking in by the back way.[1] (*She fires.*)

BRACK (*nearer*): Are you out of your senses —— !

HEDDA: Dear me — did I happen to hit you?

BRACK (*still outside*): I wish you would let these pranks alone!

HEDDA: Come in then, Judge.

(JUDGE BRACK, *dressed as though for a men's party, enters by the glass door. He carries a light overcoat over his arm.*)

BRACK: What the deuce — haven't you tired of that sport, yet? What are you shooting at?

HEDDA: Oh, I am only firing in the air.

BRACK (*gently takes the pistol out of her hand*): Allow me, madam! (*Looks at it.*) Ah — I know this pistol well! (*Looks around.*) Where is the case? Ah, here it is. (*Lays the pistol in it, and shuts it.*) Now we won't play at that game any more today.

HEDDA: Then what in heaven's name would you have me do with myself?

BRACK: Have you had no visitors?

HEDDA (*closing the glass door*): Not one. I suppose all our set are still out of town.

BRACK: And is Tesman not at home either?

HEDDA (*at the writing table, putting the pistol case in a drawer which she shuts*): No. He rushed off to his aunt's directly after lunch; he didn't expect you so early.

BRACK: H'm — how stupid of me not to have thought of that!

HEDDA (*turning her head to look at him*): Why stupid?

BRACK: Because if I had thought of it I should have come a little — earlier.

HEDDA (*crossing the room*): Then you would have found no one to receive you; for I have been in my room changing my dress ever since lunch.

BRACK: And is there no sort of little chink that we could hold a parley through?

1. *Bagveje* means both "back ways" and "underhanded courses."

HEDDA: You have forgotten to arrange one.

BRACK: That was another piece of stupidity.

HEDDA: Well, we must just settle down here — and wait. Tesman is not likely to be back for some time yet.

BRACK: Never mind; I shall not be impatient.

(HEDDA *seats herself in the corner of the sofa.* BRACK *lays his overcoat over the back of the nearest chair, and sits down, but keeps his hat in his hand. A short silence. They look at each other.*)

HEDDA: Well?

BRACK (*in the same tone*): Well?

HEDDA: I spoke first.

BRACK (*bending a little forward*): Come, let us have a cozy little chat, Mrs. Hedda.

HEDDA (*leaning further back in the sofa*): Does it not seem like a whole eternity since our last talk? Of course I don't count those few words yesterday evening and this morning.

BRACK: You mean since our last confidential talk? Our last tete-a-tete?

HEDDA: Well, yes — since you put it so.

BRACK: Not a day has passed but I have wished that you were home again.

HEDDA: And I have done nothing but wish the same thing.

BRACK: You? Really, Mrs. Hedda? And I thought you had been enjoying your tour so much!

HEDDA: Oh, yes, you may be sure of that!

BRACK: But Tesman's letters spoke of nothing but happiness.

HEDDA: Oh, Tesman! You see, he thinks nothing so delightful as grubbing in libraries and making copies of old parchments, or whatever you call them.

BRACK (*with a spice of malice*): Well, that is his vocation in life — or part of it at any rate.

HEDDA: Yes, of course; and no doubt when it's your vocation —— But *I!* Oh, my dear Mr. Brack, how mortally bored I have been.

BRACK (*sympathetically*): Do you really say so? In downright earnest?

HEDDA: Yes, you can surely understand it —— ! To go for six whole months without meeting a soul that knew anything of our circle, or could talk about the things we are interested in.

BRACK: Yes, yes — I too should feel that a deprivation.

HEDDA: And then, what I found most intolerable of all ——

BRACK: Well?

HEDDA: —— was being everlastingly in the company of — one and the same person ——

BRACK (*with a nod of assent*): Morning, noon, and night, yes — at all possible times and seasons.

HEDDA: I said "everlastingly."

BRACK: Just so. But I should have thought, with our excellent Tesman, one could ——

HEDDA: Tesman is — a specialist, my dear Judge.

BRACK: Undeniably.

HEDDA: And specialists are not at all amusing to travel with. Not in the long run at any rate.

BRACK: Not even — the specialist one happens to love?

HEDDA: Faugh — don't use that sickening word!

BRACK (*taken aback*): What do you say, Mrs. Hedda?

HEDDA (*half laughing, half irritated*): You should just try it! To hear of nothing but the history of civilization, morning, noon, and night —

BRACK: Everlastingly.

HEDDA: Yes, yes, yes! And then all this about the domestic industry of the middle ages —— ! That's the most disgusting part of it!

BRACK (*looks searchingly at her*): But tell me — in that case, how am I to understand your —— ? H'm ——

HEDDA: My accepting George Tesman, you mean?

BRACK: Well, let us put it so.

HEDDA: Good heavens, do you see anything so wonderful in that?

BRACK: Yes and no — Mrs. Hedda.

HEDDA: I had positively danced myself tired, my dear Judge. My day was done —— (*With a slight shudder.*) Oh no — I won't say that; nor think it either!

BRACK: You have assuredly no reason to.

HEDDA: Oh, reasons —— (*Watching him closely.*) George Tesman — after all, you must admit that he is correctness itself.

BRACK: His correctness and respectability are beyond all question.

HEDDA: And I don't see anything absolutely ridiculous about him. Do you?

BRACK: Ridiculous? N — no — I shouldn't exactly say so ——

HEDDA: Well — and his powers of research, at all events, are untiring. I see no reason why he should not one day come to the front, after all.

BRACK (*looks at her hesitatingly*): I thought that you, like every one else, expected him to attain the highest distinction.

HEDDA (*with an expression of fatigue*): Yes, so I did. — And then, since he was bent, at all hazards, on being allowed to provide for me — I really don't know why I should not have accepted his offer?

BRACK: No — if you look at it in that light ——

HEDDA: It was more than my other adorers were prepared to do for me, my dear Judge.

BRACK (*laughing*): Well, I can't answer for all the rest; but as for myself, you know quite well that I have always entertained a — a certain respect for the marriage tie — for marriage as an institution, Mrs. Hedda.

HEDDA (*jestingly*): Oh, I assure you I have never cherished any hopes with respect to you.

BRACK: All I require is a pleasant and intimate interior, where I can make myself useful in every way, and am free to come and go as — as a trusted friend ——

HEDDA: Of the master of the house, do you mean?

BRACK (*bowing*): Frankly — of the mistress first of all; but of course of the master, too, in the second place. Such a triangular friendship — if I may call it so — is really a great convenience for all parties, let me tell you.

HEDDA: Yes, I have many a time longed for some one to make a third on our travels. Oh — those railway-carriage tête-à-têtes —— !

BRACK: Fortunately your wedding journey is over now.

HEDDA (*shaking her head*): Not by a long — long way. I have only arrived at a station on the line.

BRACK: Well, then the passengers jump out and move about a little, Mrs. Hedda.

HEDDA: I never jump out.

BRACK: Really?

HEDDA: No — because there is always some one standing by to ——

BRACK (*laughing*): To look at your ankles, do you mean?

HEDDA: Precisely.

BRACK: Well but, dear me ——

HEDDA (*with a gesture of repulsion*): I won't have it. I would rather keep my seat where I happen to be — and continue the tête-à-tête.

BRACK: But suppose a third person were to jump in and join the couple.

HEDDA: Ah — that is quite another matter!

BRACK: A trusted, sympathetic friend ——

HEDDA: —— with a fund of conversation on all sorts of lively topics ——

BRACK: —— and not the least bit of a specialist!

HEDDA (*with an audible sigh*): Yes, that would be a relief indeed.

BRACK (*hears the front door open, and glances in that direction*): The triangle is completed.

HEDDA (*half aloud*): And on goes the train.

(GEORGE TESMAN, *in a gray walking suit, with a soft felt hat, enters from the hall. He has a number of unbound books under his arm and in his pockets.*)

TESMAN (*goes up to the table beside the corner settee*): Ouf — what a load for a warm day — all these books. (*Lays them on the table.*) I'm positively perspiring, Hedda. Hallo — are you there already, my dear Judge? Eh? Berta didn't tell me.

BRACK (*rising*): I came in through the garden.

HEDDA: What books have you got there?

TESMAN (*stands looking them through*): Some new books on my special subjects — quite indispensable to me.

HEDDA: Your special subjects?

BRACK: Yes, books on his special subjects, Mrs. Tesman. (BRACK *and* HEDDA *exchange a confidential smile.*)

HEDDA: Do you need still more books on your special subjects?

TESMAN: Yes, my dear Hedda, one can never have too many of them. Of course one must keep up with all that is written and published.

HEDDA: Yes, I suppose one must.

TESMAN (*searching among his books*): And look here — I have got hold of Eilert Lövborg's new book too. (*Offering it to her.*) Perhaps you would like to glance through it, Hedda? Eh?

HEDDA: No, thank you. Or rather — afterwards perhaps.

TESMAN: I looked into it a little on the way home.

BRACK: Well, what do you think of it — as a specialist?

TESMAN: I think it shows quite remarkable soundness of judgment. He never wrote 'like that before. (*Putting the books together.*) Now I shall take all these into my study. I'm longing to cut the leaves —— ! And then I must change my clothes. (*To* BRACK.) I suppose we needn't start just yet? Eh?

BRACK: Oh, dear no — there is not the slightest hurry.

TESMAN: Well then, I will take my time. (*Is going with his books, but stops in the doorway and turns.*) By-the-bye, Hedda — Aunt Julia is not coming this evening.

HEDDA: Not coming? Is it that affair of the bonnet that keeps her away?

TESMAN: Oh, not at all. How could you think such a thing of Aunt Julia? Just fancy —— ! The fact is, Aunt Rina is very ill.

HEDDA: She always is.

TESMAN: Yes, but today she is much worse than usual, poor dear.

HEDDA: Oh, then it's only natural that her sister should remain with her. I must bear my disappointment.

TESMAN: And you can't imagine, dear, how delighted Aunt Julia seemed to be — because you had come home looking so flourishing!

HEDDA (*half aloud, rising*): Oh, those everlasting aunts!

TESMAN: What?

HEDDA (*going to the glass door*): Nothing.

TESMAN: Oh, all right. (*He goes through the inner room, out to the right.*)

BRACK: What bonnet were you talking about?

HEDDA: Oh, it was a little episode with Miss Tesman this morning. She had laid down her bonnet on the chair there — (*Looks at him and smiles.*) — and I pretended to think it was the servant's.

BRACK (*shaking his head*): Now my dear Mrs. Hedda, how could you do such a thing? To that excellent old lady, too!

HEDDA (*nervously crossing the room*): Well, you see — these impulses come over me all of a sudden; and I cannot resist them. (*Throws herself down in the easy chair by the stove.*) Oh, I don't know how to explain it.

BRACK (*behind the easy chair*): You are not really happy — that is at the bottom of it.

HEDDA (*looking straight before her*): I know of no reason why I should be — happy. Perhaps you can give me one?

BRACK: Well — amongst other things, because you have got exactly the home you had set your heart on.

HEDDA (*looks up at him and laughs*): Do you too believe in that legend?

BRACK: Is there nothing in it, then?

HEDDA: Oh, yes, there is something in it.

BRACK: Well?

HEDDA: There is this in it, that I made use of Tesman to see me home from evening parties last summer ——

BRACK: I, unfortunately, had to go quite a different way.

HEDDA: That's true. I know you were going a different way last summer.

BRACK (*laughing*): Oh fie, Mrs. Hedda! Well, then — you and Tesman —— ?

HEDDA: Well, we happened to pass here one evening; Tesman, poor fellow, was writhing in the agony of having to find conversation; so I took pity on the learned man ——

BRACK (*smiles doubtfully*): You took pity? H'm ——

HEDDA: Yes, I really did. And so — to help him out of his torment — I happened to say, in pure thoughtlessness, that I should like to live in this villa.

BRACK: No more than that?

HEDDA: Not that evening.

BRACK: But afterwards?

HEDDA: Yes, my thoughtlessness had consequences, my dear Judge.

BRACK: Unfortunately that too often happens, Mrs. Hedda.

HEDDA: Thanks! So you see it was this enthusiasm for Secretary Falk's villa that first constituted a bond of sympathy between George Tesman and me. From that came our engagement and our marriage, and our wedding journey, and all the rest of it. Well, well, my dear Judge — as you make your bed so you must lie, I could almost say.

BRACK: This is exquisite! And you really cared not a rap about it all the time.

HEDDA: No, heaven knows I didn't.

BRACK: But now? Now that we have made it so homelike for you?

HEDDA: Uh — the rooms all seem to smell of lavender and dried rose leaves. — But perhaps it's Aunt Julia that has brought that scent with her.

BRACK (*laughing*): No, I think it must be a legacy from the late Mrs. Secretary Falk.

HEDDA: Yes, there is an odor of mortality about it. It reminds me of a bouquet — the day after the ball. (*Clasps her hands behind her head, leans back in her chair and looks at him.*) Oh, my dear Judge — you cannot imagine how horribly I shall bore myself here.

BRACK: Why should not you, too, find some sort of vocation in life, Mrs. Hedda?

HEDDA: A vocation — that should attract me?

BRACK: If possible, of course.

HEDDA: Heaven knows what sort of a vocation that could be. I often wonder whether —— (*Breaking off.*) But that would never do either.

BRACK: Who can tell? Let me hear what it is.

HEDDA: Whether I might not get Tesman to go into politics, I mean.

BRACK (*laughing*): Tesman? No, really now, political life is not the thing for him — not at all in his line.

HEDDA: No, I daresay not. But if I could get him into it all the same?

BRACK: Why — what satisfaction could you find in that? If he is not fitted for that sort of thing, why should you want to drive him into it?

HEDDA: Because I am bored, I tell you! (*After a pause.*) So you think it quite out of the question that Tesman should ever get into the ministry?

BRACK: H'm — you see, my dear Mrs. Hedda — to get into the ministry, he would have to be a tolerably rich man.

HEDDA (*rising impatiently*): Yes, there we have it! It is this genteel poverty I have managed to drop into —— ! (*Crosses the room.*) That is what makes life so pitiable! So utterly ludicrous! For that's what it is.

BRACK: Now *I* should say the fault lay elsewhere.

HEDDA: Where, then?

BRACK: You have never gone through any really stimulating experience.

HEDDA: Anything serious, you mean?

BRACK: Yes, you may call it so. But now you may perhaps have one in store.

HEDDA (*tossing her head*): Oh, you're thinking of the annoyances about this wretched professorship! But that must be Tesman's own affair. I assure you I shall not waste a thought upon it.

BRACK: No, no, I daresay not. But suppose now that what people call — in elegant language — a solemn responsibility were to come upon you? (*Smiling.*) A new responsibility, Mrs. Hedda?

HEDDA (*angrily*): Be quiet! Nothing of that sort will ever happen!

BRACK (*warily*): We will speak of this again a year hence — at the very outside.

HEDDA (*curtly*): I have no turn for anything of the sort, Judge Brack. No responsibilities for me!

BRACK: Are you so unlike the generality of women as to have no turn for duties which —— ?

HEDDA (*beside the glass door*): Oh, be quiet, I tell you! I often think there is only one thing in the world I have any turn for.

BRACK (*drawing near to her*): And what is that, if I may ask?

HEDDA (*stands looking out*): Boring myself to death. Now you know it. (*Turns, looks towards the inner room, and laughs.*) Yes, as I thought! Here comes the Professor.

BRACK (*softly, in a tone of warning*): Come, come, come, Mrs. Hedda!

(GEORGE TESMAN, *dressed for the party, with his gloves and hat in his hand, enters from the right through the inner room.*)

TESMAN: Hedda, has no message come from Eilert Lövborg? Eh?

HEDDA: No.

TESMAN: Then you'll see he'll be here presently.

BRACK: Do you really think he will come?

TESMAN: Yes, I am almost sure of it. For what you were telling us this morning must have been a mere floating rumor.

BRACK: You think so?

TESMAN: At any rate, Aunt Julia said she did not believe for a moment that he would ever stand in my way again. Fancy that!

BRACK: Well then, that's all right.

TESMAN (*placing his hat and gloves on a chair on the right*): Yes, but you must really let me wait for him as long as possible.

BRACK: We have plenty of time yet. None of my guests will arrive before seven or half-past.

TESMAN: Then meanwhile we can keep Hedda company, and see what happens. Eh?

HEDDA (*placing* BRACK'S *hat and overcoat upon the corner settee*): And at the worst Mr. Lövborg can remain here with me.

BRACK (*offering to take his things*): Oh, allow me, Mrs. Tesman! What do you mean by "At the worst"?

HEDDA: If he won't go with you and Tesman.

TESMAN (*looks dubiously at her*): But, Hedda dear — do you think it would quite do for him to remain with you? Eh? Remember, Aunt Julia can't come.

HEDDA: No, but Mrs. Elvsted is coming. We three can have a cup of tea together.

TESMAN: Oh, yes, that will be all right.

BRACK (*smiling*): And that would perhaps be the safest plan for him.

HEDDA: Why so?

BRACK: Well, you know, Mrs. Tesman, how you used to gird at my little bachelor parties. You declared they were adapted only for men of the strictest principles.

HEDDA: But no doubt Mr. Lövborg's principles are strict enough now. A converted sinner —— (BERTA *appears at the hall door.*)

BERTA: There's a gentleman asking if you are at home, ma'am ——

HEDDA: Well, show him in.

TESMAN (*softly*): I'm sure it is he! Fancy that!

(EILERT LÖVBORG *enters from the hall. He is slim and lean; of the same age as* TESMAN, *but looks older and somewhat worn-out. His hair and beard are of a blackish brown, his face long and pale, but with patches of color on the cheekbones. He is dressed in a well-cut black visiting suit, quite new. He has dark gloves and a silk hat. He stops near the door, and makes a rapid bow, seeming somewhat embarrassed.*)

TESMAN (*goes up to him and shakes him warmly by the hand*): Well, my dear Eilert — so at last we meet again!

LÖVBORG (*speaks in a subdued voice*): Thanks for your letter, Tesman. (*Approaching* HEDDA.) Will you too shake hands with me, Mrs. Tesman?

HEDDA (*taking his hand*): I am glad to see you, Mr. Lövborg. (*With a motion of her hand.*) I don't know whether you two gentlemen —— ?

LÖVBORG (*bowing slightly*): Judge Brack, I think.

BRACK (*doing likewise*): Oh, yes, in the old days ——

TESMAN (*to* LÖVBORG, *with his hands on his shoulders*): And now you must make yourself entirely at home, Eilert! Mustn't he, Hedda? For I hear you are going to settle in town again? Eh?

LÖVBORG: Yes, I am.

TESMAN: Quite right, quite right. Let me tell you, I have got hold of your new book; but I haven't had time to read it yet.

LÖVBORG: You may spare yourself the trouble.

TESMAN: Why so?

LÖVBORG: Because there is very little in it.

TESMAN: Just fancy — how can you say so?

BRACK: But it has been very much praised, I hear.

LÖVBORG: That was what I wanted; so I put nothing into the book but what every one would agree with.

BRACK: Very wise of you.

TESMAN: Well but, my dear Eilert —— !

LÖVBORG: For now I mean to win myself a position again — to make a fresh start.

TESMAN (*a little embarrassed*): Ah, that is what you wish to do? Eh?

LÖVBORG (*smiling, lays down his hat, and draws a packet, wrapped in paper, from his coat pocket*): But when this one appears, George Tesman, you will have to read it. For this is the real book — the book I have put my true self into.

TESMAN: Indeed? And what is it?

LÖVBORG: It is the continuation.

TESMAN: The continuation? Of what?

LÖVBORG: Of the book.

TESMAN: Of the new book?

LÖVBORG: Of course.

TESMAN: Why, my dear Eilert — does it not come down to our own days?

LÖVBORG: Yes, it does; and this one deals with the future.

TESMAN: With the future! But, good heavens, we know nothing of the future!

LÖVBORG: No; but there is a thing or two to be said about it all the same. (*Opens the packet.*) Look here ——

TESMAN: Why, that's not your handwriting.

LÖVBORG: I dictated it. (*Turning over the pages.*) It falls into two sections. The first deals with the civilizing forces of the future. And here is the second — (*running through the pages towards the end*) — forecasting the probable line of development.

TESMAN: How odd now! I should never have thought of writing anything of that sort.

HEDDA (*at the glass door, drumming on the pane*): H'm — I daresay not.

LÖVBORG (*replacing the manuscript in its paper and laying the packet on the table*): I brought it, thinking I might read you a little of it this evening.

TESMAN: That was very good of you, Eilert. But this evening —— ? (*Looking at* BRACK.) I don't quite see how we can manage it ——

LÖVBORG: Well then, some other time. There is no hurry.

BRACK: I must tell you, Mr. Lövborg — there is a little gathering at my house this evening — mainly in honor of Tesman, you know ——

LÖVBORG (*looking for his hat*): Oh — then I won't detain you ——

BRACK: No, but listen — will you not do me the favor of joining us?

LÖVBORG (*curtly and decidedly*): No, I can't — thank you very much.

BRACK: Oh, nonsense — do! We shall be quite a select little circle. And I assure you we shall have a "lively time," as Mrs. Hed — as Mrs. Tesman says.

LÖVBORG: I have no doubt of it. But nevertheless ——

BRACK: And then you might bring your manuscript with you, and read it to Tesman at my house. I could give you a room to yourselves.

TESMAN: Yes, think of that, Eilert, — why shouldn't you? Eh?

HEDDA (*interposing*): But, Tesman, if Mr. Lövborg would really rather not! I am sure Mr. Lövborg is much more inclined to remain here and have supper with me.

LÖVBORG (*looking at her*): With you, Mrs. Tesman?

HEDDA: And with Mrs. Elvsted.

LÖVBORG: Ah —— (*Lightly.*) I saw her for a moment this morning.

HEDDA: Did you? Well, she is coming this evening. So you see you are almost bound to remain, Mr. Lövborg, or she will have no one to see her home.

LÖVBORG: That's true. Many thanks, Mrs. Tesman — in that case I will remain.

HEDDA: Then I have one or two orders to give the servant ——

(*She goes to the hall door and rings.* BERTA *enters.* HEDDA *talks to her in a whisper, and points toward the inner room.* BERTA *nods and goes out again.*)

TESMAN (*at the same time, to* LÖVBORG): Tell me, Eilert — is it this new subject — the future — that you are going to lecture about?

LÖVBORG: Yes.

TESMAN: They told me at the bookseller's, that you are going to deliver a course of lectures this autumn.

LÖVBORG: That is my intention. I hope you won't take it ill, Tesman.

TESMAN: Oh no, not in the least! But —— ?

LÖVBORG: I can quite understand that it must be disagreeable to you.

TESMAN (*cast down*): Oh, I can't expect you, out of consideration for me, to ——

LÖVBORG: But I shall wait till you have received your appointment.

TESMAN: Will you wait? Yes, but — yes, but — are you not going to compete with me? Eh?

LÖVBORG: No; it is only the moral victory I care for.

TESMAN: Why, bless me — then Aunt Julia was right after all! Oh yes — I knew it! Hedda! Just fancy — Eilert Lövborg is not going to stand in our way!

HEDDA (*curtly*): Our way? Pray leave me out of the question.

(*She goes up towards the inner room, where* BERTA *is placing a tray with decanters and glasses on the table.* HEDDA *nods approval, and comes forward again.* BERTA *goes out.*)

TESMAN (*at the same time*): And you, Judge Brack — what do you say to this? Eh?

BRACK: Well, I say that a moral victory — h'm — may be all very fine ——

TESMAN: Yes, certainly. But all the same ——

HEDDA (*looking at* TESMAN *with a cold smile*): You stand there looking as if you were thunderstruck ——

TESMAN: Yes — so I am — I almost think ——

BRACK: Don't you see, Mrs. Tesman, a thunderstorm has just passed over?

HEDDA (*pointing towards the inner room*): Will you not take a glass of cold punch, gentlemen?

BRACK (*looking at his watch*): A stirrup cup? Yes, it wouldn't come amiss.

TESMAN: A capital idea, Hedda! Just the thing! Now that the weight has been taken off my mind ——

HEDDA: Will you not join them, Mr. Lovborg?

LÖVBORG (*with a gesture of refusal*): No, thank you. Nothing for me.

BRACK: Why, bless me — cold punch is surely not poison.

LÖVBORG: Perhaps not for every one.

HEDDA: I will keep Mr. Lövborg company in the meantime.

TESMAN: Yes, yes, Hedda dear, do.

(*He and* BRACK *go into the inner room, seat themselves, drink punch, smoke cigarettes, and carry on a lively conversation during what follows.* EILERT LÖVBORG *remains beside the stove.* HEDDA *goes to the writing table.*)

HEDDA (*raising her voice a little*): Do you care to look at some photographs, Mr. Lövborg? You know Tesman and I made a tour in the Tyrol on our way home?

(*She takes up an album, and places it on the table beside the sofa, in the further corner of which she seats herself.* EILERT LÖVBORG *approaches, stops, and looks at her. Then he takes a chair and seats himself at her left, with his back towards the inner room.*)

HEDDA (*opening the album*): Do you see this range of mountains, Mr. Lovborg? It's the Ortler group. Tesman has written the name underneath. Here it is: "The Ortler group near Meran."

LÖVBORG (*who has never taken his eyes off her, says softly and slowly*): Hedda — Gabler!

HEDDA (*glancing hastily at him*): Ah! Hush!

LÖVBORG (*repeats softly*): Hedda Gabler!

HEDDA (*looking at the album*): That was my name in the old days — when we two knew each other.

LÖVBORG: And I must teach myself never to say Hedda Gabler again — never, as long as I live.

HEDDA (*still turning over the pages*): Yes, you must. And I think you ought to practice in time. The sooner the better, I should say.

LÖVBORG (*in a tone of indignation*): Hedda Gabler married? And married to — George Tesman!

HEDDA: Yes — so the world goes.

LÖVBORG: Oh, Hedda, Hedda — how could you[2] throw yourself away!

HEDDA (*looks sharply at him*): What? I can't allow this!

LÖVBORG: What do you mean? (TESMAN *comes into the room and goes toward the sofa.*)

HEDDA (*hears him coming and says in an indifferent tone*): And this is a view from the Val d'Ampezzo, Mr. Lövborg. Just look at these peaks! (*Looks affectionately up at* TESMAN.) What's the name of these curious peaks, dear?

TESMAN: Let me see? Oh, those are the Dolomites.

HEDDA: Yes, that's it! Those are the Dolomites, Mr. Lövborg.

TESMAN: Hedda dear, I only wanted to ask whether I shouldn't bring you a little punch after all? For yourself at any rate — eh?

HEDDA: Yes, do, please; and perhaps a few biscuits.

TESMAN: No cigarettes?

HEDDA: No.

TESMAN: Very well.

(*He goes into the inner room and out to the right.* BRACK *sits in the inner room, and keeps an eye from time to time on* HEDDA *and* LÖVBORG.)

LÖVBORG (*softly, as before*): Answer me, Hedda — how could you go and do this?

HEDDA (*apparently absorbed in the album*): If you continue to say *du* to me I won't talk to you.

LÖVBORG: May I say *du* when we are alone?

HEDDA: No. You may think it; but you mustn't say it.

LÖVBORG: Ah, I understand. It is an offense against George Tesman, whom you[3] — love.

HEDDA (*glances at him and smiles*): Love? What an idea!

LÖVBORG: You don't love him then!

HEDDA: But I won't hear of any sort of unfaithfulness! Remember that.

LÖVBORG: Hedda — answer me one thing ——

HEDDA: Hush! (TESMAN *enters with a small tray from the inner room.*)

TESMAN: Here you are! Isn't this tempting? (*He puts the tray on the table.*)

---

2. He uses the familiar *du*.   3. From this point onward Lövborg uses the formal *De*.

HEDDA: Why do you bring it yourself?

TESMAN (*filling the glasses*): Because I think it's such fun to wait upon you, Hedda.

HEDDA: But you have poured out two glasses. Mr. Lövborg said he wouldn't have any ——

TESMAN: No, but Mrs. Elvsted will soon be here, won't she?

HEDDA: Yes, by-the-bye — Mrs. Elvsted ——

TESMAN: Had you forgotten her? Eh?

HEDDA: We were so absorbed in these photographs. (*Shows him a picture.*) Do you remember this little village?

TESMAN: Oh, it's that one just below the Brenner Pass. It was there we passed the night ——

HEDDA: —— and met that lively party of tourists.

TESMAN: Yes, that was the place. Fancy — if we could only have had you with us, Eilert! Eh? (*He returns to the inner room and sits beside* BRACK.)

LÖVBORG: Answer me this one thing, Hedda ——

HEDDA: Well?

LÖVBORG: Was there no love in your friendship for me either? Not a spark — not a tinge of love in it?

HEDDA: I wonder if there was? To me it seems as though we were two good comrades — two thoroughly intimate friends. (*Smilingly.*) You especially were frankness itself.

LÖVBORG: It was you that made me so.

HEDDA: As I look back upon it all, I think there was really something beautiful, something fascinating — something daring —in — in that secret intimacy — that comradeship which no living creature so much as dreamed of.

LÖVBORG: Yes, yes, Hedda! Was there not? When I used to come to your father's in the afternoon — and the General sat over at the window reading his papers — with his back towards us ——

HEDDA: And we two on the corner sofa ——

LÖVBORG: Always with the same illustrated paper before us ——

HEDDA: For want of an album, yes.

LÖVBORG: Yes, Hedda, and when I made my confessions to you — told you about myself, things that at that time no one else knew! There I would sit and tell you of my escapades — my days and nights of devilment. Oh, Hedda — what was the power in you that forced me to confess these things?

HEDDA: Do you think it was any power in me?

LÖVBORG: How else can I explain it? And all those — those roundabout questions you used to put to me ——

HEDDA: Which you understood so particularly well ——

LÖVBORG: How could you sit and question me like that? Question me quite frankly ——

HEDDA: In roundabout terms, please observe.

LÖVBORG: Yes, but frankly nevertheless. Cross-question me about — all that sort of thing?

HEDDA: And how could you answer, Mr. Lövborg?

LÖVBORG: Yes, that is just what I can't understand — in looking back upon it. But tell me now, Hedda — was there not love at the bottom of our friendship? On your side, did you not feel as though you might purge my stains away if I made you my confessor? Was it not so?

HEDDA: No, not quite.

LÖVBORG: What was your motive, then?

HEDDA: Do you think it quite incomprehensible that a young girl — when it can be done — without any one knowing ——

LÖVBORG: Well?

HEDDA: —— should be glad to have a peep, now and then, into a world which ——

LÖVBORG: Which —— ?

HEDDA: —— which she is forbidden to know anything about?

LÖVBORG: So that was it?

HEDDA: Partly. Partly — I almost think.

LÖVBORG: Comradeship in the thirst for life. But why should not that, at any rate, have continued?

HEDDA: The fault was yours.

LÖVBORG: It was you that broke with me.

HEDDA: Yes, when our friendship threatened to develop into something more serious. Shame upon you, Eilert Lövborg! How could you think of wronging your — your frank comrade?

LÖVBORG (clenching his hands): Oh, why did you not carry out your threat? Why did you not shoot me down?

HEDDA: Because I have such a dread of scandal.

LÖVBORG: Yes, Hedda, you are a coward at heart.

HEDDA: A terrible coward. (*Changing her tone.*) But it was a lucky thing for you. And now you have found ample consolation at the Elvsteds'.

LÖVBORG: I know what Thea has confided to you.

HEDDA: And perhaps you have confided to her something about us?

LÖVBORG: Not a word. She is too stupid to understand anything of that sort.

HEDDA: Stupid?

LÖVBORG: She is stupid about matters of that sort.

HEDDA: And I am cowardly. (*Bends over towards him, without looking him in the face, and says more softly.*) But now I will confide something to you.

LÖVBORG (*eagerly*): Well?

HEDDA: The fact that I dared not shoot you down ——

LÖVBORG: Yes!

HEDDA: —— that was not my most arrant cowardice — that evening.

LÖVBORG (*looks at her a moment, understands, and whispers passionately*): Oh, Hedda! Hedda Gabler! Now I begin to see a hidden reason beneath our comradeship! You[4] and I —— ! After all, then, it was your craving for life ——

HEDDA (*softly, with a sharp glance*): Take care! Believe nothing of the sort!

(*Twilight has begun to fall. The hall door is opened from without by* BERTA.)

HEDDA (*closes the album with a bang and calls smilingly*): Ah, at last! My darling Thea, come along!

(MRS. ELVSTED *enters from the hall. She is in evening dress. The door is closed behind her.*)

HEDDA (*on the sofa, stretches out her arms towards her*): My sweet Thea — you can't think how I have been longing for you!

(MRS. ELVSTED, *in passing, exchanges slight salutations with the gentlemen in the inner room, then goes up to the table and gives* HEDDA *her hands.* EILERT LÖVBORG *has risen. He and* MRS. ELVSTED *greet each other with a silent nod.*)

4. In this speech he once more says *du*. Hedda addresses him throughout as *De*.

MRS. ELVSTED: Ought I to go in and talk to your husband for a moment?

HEDDA: Oh, not at all. Leave those two alone. They will soon be going.

MRS. ELVSTED: Are they going out?

HEDDA: Yes, to a supper party.

MRS. ELVSTED (*quickly, to* LÖVBORG): Not you?

LÖVBORG: No.

HEDDA: Mr. Lövborg remains with us.

MRS. ELVSTED (*takes a chair and is about to seat herself at his side*): Oh, how nice it is here!

HEDDA: No, thank you, my little Thea! Not there! You'll be good enough to come over here to me. I will sit between you.

MRS. ELVSTED: Yes, just as you please.

(*She goes round the table and seats herself on the sofa on* HEDDA'S *right.* LÖVBORG *reseats himself on his chair.*)

LÖVBORG (*after a short pause, to* HEDDA): Is not she lovely to look at?

HEDDA (*lightly stroking her hair*): Only to look at?

LÖVBORG: Yes. For we two — she and I —we are two real comrades. We have absolute faith in each other; so we can sit and talk with perfect frankness ——

HEDDA: Not round about, Mr. Lövborg?

LÖVBORG: Well ——

MRS. ELVSTED (*softly clinging close to* HEDDA): Oh, how happy I am, Hedda; for, only think, he says I have inspired him too.

HEDDA (*looks at her with a smile*): Ah! Does he say that, dear?

LÖVBORG: And then she is so brave, Mrs. Tesman!

MRS. ELVSTED: Good heavens — am I brave?

LÖVBORG: Exceedingly — where your comrade is concerned.

HEDDA: Ah, yes — courage! If one only had that!

LÖVBORG: What then? What do you mean?

HEDDA: Then life would perhaps be liveable, after all. (*With a sudden change of tone.*) But now, my dearest Thea, you really must have a glass of cold punch.

MRS. ELVSTED: No, thanks — I never take anything of that kind.

HEDDA: Well then, you, Mr. Lövborg.

LÖVBORG: Nor I, thank you.

MRS. ELVSTED: No, he doesn't either.

HEDDA (*looks fixedly at him*): But if I say you shall?

LÖVBORG: It would be no use.

HEDDA (*laughing*): Then I, poor creature, have no sort of power over you?

LÖVBORG: Not in that respect.

HEDDA: But seriously, I think you ought to — for your own sake.

MRS. ELVSTED: Why, Hedda —— !

LOVBORG: How so?

HEDDA: Or rather on account of other people.

LÖVBORG: Indeed?

HEDDA: Otherwise people might be apt to suspect that — in your heart of hearts — you did not feel quite secure — quite confident of yourself.

MRS. ELVSTED (*softly*): Oh please, Hedda ——

LÖVBORG: People may suspect what they like — for the present.

MRS. ELVSTED (*joyfully*): Yes, let them!

HEDDA: I saw it plainly in Judge Brack's face a moment ago.

LÖVBORG: What did you see?

HEDDA: His contemptuous smile, when you dared not go with them into the inner room.

LÖVBORG: Dared not? Of course I preferred to stop here and talk to you.

MRS. ELVSTED: What could be more natural, Hedda?

HEDDA: But the Judge could not guess that. And I saw, too, the way he smiled and glanced at Tesman when you dared not accept his invitation to this wretched little supper party of his.

LÖVBORG: Dared not! Do you say I dared not?

HEDDA: *I* don't say so. But that was how Judge Brack understood it.

LÖVBORG: Well, let him.

HEDDA: Then you are not going with them?

LÖVBORG: I will stay here with you and Thea.

MRS. ELVSTED: Yes, Hedda — how can you doubt that?

HEDDA (*smiles and nods approvingly to* LÖVBORG): Firm as a rock! Faithful to your principles, now and forever! Ah, that is how a man should be! (*Turns to* MRS. ELVSTED *and caresses her.*) Well now, what did I tell you, when you came to us this morning in such a state of distraction ——

LÖVBORG (*surprised*): Distraction!

MRS. ELVSTED (*terrified*): Hedda — oh Hedda —— !

HEDDA: You can see for yourself; you haven't the slightest reason to be in such mortal terror —— (*Interrupting herself.*) There! Now we can all three enjoy ourselves!

LÖVBORG (*who has given a start*): Ah — what is all this, Mrs. Tesman?

MRS. ELVSTED: Oh my God, Hedda! What are you saying? What are you doing?

HEDDA: Don't get excited! That horrid Judge Brack is sitting watching you.

LÖVBORG: So she was in mortal terror! On my account!

MRS. ELVSTED (*softly and piteously*): Oh, Hedda — now you have ruined everything!

LÖVBORG (*looks fixedly at her for a moment. His face is distorted*): So that was my comrade's frank confidence in me?

MRS. ELVSTED (*imploringly*): Oh, my dearest friend — only let me tell you ——

LÖVBORG (*takes one of the glasses of punch, raises it to his lips, and says in a low, husky voice*): Your health, Thea!

(*He empties the glass, puts it down and takes the second.*)

MRS. ELVSTED (*softly*): Oh, Hedda, Hedda — how could you do this?

HEDDA: *I* do it? *I?* Are you crazy?

LÖVBORG: Here's to your health too, Mrs. Tesman. Thanks for the truth. Hurrah for the truth!

(*He empties the glass and is about to refill it.*)

HEDDA (*lays her hand on his arm*): Come, come — no more for the present. Remember you are going out to supper.

MRS. ELVSTED: No, no, no!

HEDDA: Hush! They are sitting watching you.

LÖVBORG (*putting down the glass*): Now, Thea — tell me the truth ——

MRS. ELVSTED: Yes.

LÖVBORG: Did your husband know that you had come after me?

MRS. ELVSTED (*wringing her hands*): Oh, Hedda — do you hear what he is asking?

LÖVBORG: Was it arranged between you and him that you were to come to town and look after me? Perhaps it was the Sheriff himself that urged you to come? Aha, my dear — no doubt he wanted my help in his office! Or was it at the card table that he missed me?

MRS. ELVSTED (*softly, in agony*): Oh, Lövborg, Lövborg —— !

LÖVBORG (*seizes a glass and is on the point of filling it*): Here's a glass for the old Sheriff too!

HEDDA (*preventing him*): No more just now. Remember you have to read your manuscript to Tesman.

LÖVBORG (*calmly, putting down the glass*): It was stupid of me all this, Thea — to take it in this way, I mean. Don't be angry with me, my dear, dear comrade. You shall see — both you and the others — that if I was fallen once — now I have risen again! Thanks to you, Thea.

MRS. ELVSTED (*radiant with joy*): Oh, heaven be praised —— !

(BRACK *has in the meantime looked at his watch. He and* TESMAN *rise and come into the drawing room.*)

BRACK (*takes his hat and overcoat*): Well, Mrs. Tesman, our time has come.

HEDDA: I suppose it has.

LÖVBORG (*rising*): Mine too, Judge Brack.

MRS. ELVSTED (*softly and imploringly*): Oh, Lövborg, don't do it!

HEDDA (*pinching her arm*): They can hear you!

MRS. ELVSTED (*with a suppressed shriek*): Ow!

LÖVBORG (*to* BRACK): You were good enough to invite me.

BRACK: Well, are you coming after all?

LÖVBORG: Yes, many thanks.

BRACK: I'm delighted ——

LÖVBORG (*to* TESMAN, *putting the parcel of MS. in his pocket*): I should like to show you one or two things before I send it to the printer's.

TESMAN: Fancy — that will be delightful. But, Hedda dear, how is Mrs. Elvsted to get home? Eh?

HEDDA: Oh, that can be managed somehow.

LÖVBORG (*looking towards the ladies*): Mrs. Elvsted? Of course, I'll come again and fetch her. (*Approaching.*) At ten or thereabouts, Mrs. Tesman? Will that do?

HEDDA: Certainly. That will do capitally.

TESMAN: Well, then, that's all right. But you must not expect me so early, Hedda.

HEDDA: Oh, you may stop as long — as long as ever you please.

MRS. ELVSTED (*trying to conceal her anxiety*): Well then, Mr. Lövborg — I shall remain here until you come.

LÖVBORG (*with his hat in his hand*): Pray do, Mrs. Elvsted.

BRACK: And now off goes the excursion train, gentlemen! I hope we shall have a lively time, as a certain fair lady puts it.

HEDDA: Ah, if only the fair lady could be present unseen —— !

BRACK: Why unseen?

HEDDA: In order to hear a little of your liveliness at first hand, Judge Brack.

BRACK (*laughing*): I should not advise the fair lady to try it.

TESMAN (*also laughing*): Come, you're a nice one, Hedda! Fancy that!

BRACK: Well, good-by, good-by, ladies.

LÖVBORG (*bowing*): About ten o'clock, then.

(BRACK, LÖVBORG, *and* TESMAN *go out by the hall door. At the same time* BERTA *enters from the inner room with a lighted lamp, which she places on the dining room table; she goes out by the way she came.*)

MRS. ELVSTED (*who has risen and is wandering restlessly about the room*): Hedda — Hedda — what will come of all this?

HEDDA: At ten o'clock — he will be here. I can see him already — with vine leaves in his hair — flushed and fearless ——

MRS. ELVSTED: Oh, I hope he may.

HEDDA: And then, you see — then he will have regained control over himself. Then he will be a free man for all his days.

MRS. ELVSTED: Oh God! — if he would only come as you see him now!

HEDDA: He will come as I see him — so, and not otherwise! (*Rises and approaches* THEA.) You may doubt him as long as you please; I believe in him. And now we will try ——

MRS. ELVSTED: You have some hidden motive in this, Hedda!

HEDDA: Yes, I have. I want for once in my life to have power to mold a human destiny.

MRS. ELVSTED: Have you not the power?

HEDDA: I have not — and have never had it.

MRS. ELVSTED: Not your husband's?

HEDDA: Do you think that is worth the trouble? Oh, if you could only understand how poor I am. And fate has made you so rich! (*Clasps her passionately in her arms.*) I think I must burn your hair off, after all.

MRS. ELVSTED: Let me go! Let me go! I am afraid of you, Hedda!

BERTA (*in the middle doorway*): Tea is laid in the dining room, ma'am.

HEDDA: Very well. We are coming.

MRS. ELVSTED: No, no, no! I would rather go home alone! At once!

HEDDA: Nonsense! First you shall have a cup of tea, you little stupid. And then — at ten o'clock — Eilert Lövborg will be here — with vine leaves in his hair. (*She drags* MRS. ELVSTED *almost by force towards the middle doorway.*)

Act III

SCENE: *The room at the* TESMANS' *The curtains are drawn over the middle doorway, and also over the glass door. The lamp, half turned down, and with a shade over it, is burning on the table. In the stove, the door of which stands open, there has been a fire, which is now nearly burnt out.* MRS. ELVSTED, *wrapped in a large shawl, and with her feet upon a footrest, sits close to the stove, sunk back in the armchair.* HEDDA, *fully dressed, lies sleeping upon the sofa, with a sofa blanket over her.*

MRS. ELVSTED (*after a pause, suddenly sits up in her chair, and listens eagerly. Then she sinks back again wearily, moaning to herself*): Not yet! — Oh God — oh God — not yet!

(BERTA *slips in by the hall door. She has a letter in her hand.*)

MRS. ELVSTED (*turns and whispers eagerly*): Well — has any one come?

BERTA (*softly*): Yes, a girl has brought this letter.

MRS. ELVSTED (*quickly, holding out her hand*): A letter! Give it to me!

BERTA: No, it's for Dr. Tesman, ma'am.

MRS. ELVSTED: Oh, indeed.

BERTA: It was Miss Tesman's servant that brought it. I'll lay it here on the table.

MRS. ELVSTED: Yes, do.

BERTA (*laying down the letter*): I think I had better put out the lamp. It's smoking.

MRS. ELVSTED: Yes, put it out. It must soon be daylight now.

BERTA (*putting out the lamp*): It is daylight already, ma'am.

MRS. ELVSTED: Yes, broad day! And no one come back yet —— !

BERTA: Lord bless you, ma'am! I guessed how it would be.

MRS. ELVSTED: You guessed?

BERTA: Yes, when I saw that a certain person had come back to town — and that he went off with them. For we've heard enough about that gentleman before now.

MRS. ELVSTED: Don't speak so loud. You will waken Mrs. Tesman.

BERTA (*looks towards the sofa and sighs*): No, no — let her sleep, poor thing. Shan't I put some wood on the fire?

MRS. ELVSTED: Thanks, not for me.

BERTA: Oh, very well. (*She goes softly out by the hall door.*)

HEDDA (*is awakened by the shutting of the door, and looks up*): What's that —— ?

MRS. ELVSTED: It was only the servant ——

HEDDA (*looking about her*): Oh, we're here —— ! Yes, now I remember. (*Sits erect upon the sofa, stretches herself, and rubs her eyes.*) What o'clock is it, Thea?

MRS. ELVSTED (*looks at her watch*): It's past seven.

HEDDA: When did Tesman come home?

MRS. ELVSTED: He has not come.

HEDDA: Not come home yet?

MRS. ELVSTED (*rising*): No one has come.

HEDDA: Think of our watching and waiting here till four in the morning ——

MRS. ELVSTED (*wringing her hands*): And how I watched and waited for him!

HEDDA (*yawns, and says with her hand before her mouth*): Well, well — we might have spared ourselves the trouble.

MRS. ELVSTED: Did you get a little sleep?

HEDDA: Oh yes; I believe I have slept pretty well. Have you not?

MRS. ELVSTED: Not for a moment. I couldn't, Hedda — not to save my life.

HEDDA (*rises and goes towards her*): There, there, there! There's nothing to be so alarmed about. I understand quite well what has happened.

MRS. ELVSTED: Well, what do you think? Won't you tell me?

HEDDA: Why, of course it has been a very late affair at Judge Brack's ——

MRS. ELVSTED: Yes, yes, that is clear enough. But all the same ——

HEDDA: And then, you see, Tesman hasn't cared to come home and ring us up in the middle of the night. (*Laughing.*) Perhaps he wasn't inclined to show himself either — immediately after a jollification.

MRS. ELVSTED: But in that case — where can he have gone?

HEDDA: Of course he has gone to his aunts' and slept there. They have his old room ready for him.

MRS. ELVSTED: No, he can't be with them; for a letter has just come for him from Miss Tesman. There it lies.

HEDDA: Indeed? (*Looks at the address.*) Why yes, it's addressed in Aunt Julia's own hand. Well then, he has remained at Judge Brack's. And as for Eilert Lövborg — he is sitting, with vine leaves in his hair, reading his manuscript.

MRS. ELVSTED: Oh Hedda, you are just saying things you don't believe a bit.

HEDDA: You really are a little blockhead, Thea.

MRS. ELVSTED: Oh yes, I suppose I am.

HEDDA: And how mortally tired you look.

MRS. ELVSTED: Yes, I am mortally tired.

HEDDA: Well then, you must do as I tell you. You must go into my room and lie down for a little while.

MRS. ELVSTED: Oh no, no — I shouldn't be able to sleep.

HEDDA: I am sure you would.

MRS. ELVSTED: Well, but your husband is certain to come soon now; and then I want to know at once ——

HEDDA: I shall take care to let you know when he comes.

MRS. ELVSTED: Do you promise me, Hedda?

HEDDA: Yes, rely upon me. Just you go in and have a sleep in the meantime.

MRS. ELVSTED: Thanks; then I'll try to. (*She goes off through the inner room.*)

(HEDDA *goes up to the glass door and draws back the curtains. The broad daylight streams into the room. Then she takes a little hand glass from the writing table, looks at herself in it, and arranges her hair. Next she goes to the hall door and presses the bell button.* BERTA *presently appears at the hall door.*)

BERTA: Did you want anything, ma'am?

HEDDA: Yes; you must put some more wood in the stove. I am shivering.

BERTA: Bless me — I'll make up the fire at once. (*She rakes the embers together and lays a piece of wood upon them; then stops and listens.*) That was a ring at the front door, ma'am.

HEDDA: Then go to the door. I will look after the fire.

BERTA: It'll soon burn up. (*She goes out by the hall door.*)

(HEDDA *kneels on the footrest and lays some more pieces of wood in the stove. After a short pause,* GEORGE TESMAN *enters from the hall. He looks tired and rather serious. He steals on tiptoe towards the middle doorway and is about to slip through the curtains.*)

HEDDA (*at the stove, without looking up*): Good morning.

TESMAN (*turns*): Hedda! (*Approaching her.*) Good heavens — are you up so early? Eh?

HEDDA: Yes, I am up very early this morning.

TESMAN: And I never doubted you were still sound asleep! Fancy that, Hedda!

HEDDA: Don't speak so loud. Mrs. Elvsted is resting in my room.

TESMAN: Has Mrs. Elvsted been here all night?

HEDDA: Yes, since no one came to fetch her.

TESMAN: Ah, to be sure.

HEDDA (*closes the door of the stove and rises*): Well, did you enjoy yourself at Judge Brack's?

TESMAN: Have you been anxious about me? Eh?

HEDDA: No, I should never think of being anxious. But I asked if you had enjoyed yourself.

TESMAN: Oh yes — for once in a way. Especially the beginning of the evening; for then Eilert read me part of his book. We arrived more than an hour too early — fancy that! And Brack had all sorts of arrangements to make — so Eilert read to me.

HEDDA (*seating herself by the table on the right*): Well? Tell me, then ——

TESMAN (*sitting on a footstool near the stove*): Oh Hedda, you can't conceive what a book that is going to be! I believe it is one of the most remarkable things that have ever been written. Fancy that!

HEDDA: Yes, yes; I don't care about that ——

TESMAN: I must make a confession to you, Hedda. When he had finished reading — a horrid feeling came over me.

HEDDA: A horrid feeling?

TESMAN: I felt jealous of Eilert for having had it in him to write such a book. Only think, Hedda!

HEDDA: Yes, yes, I am thinking!

TESMAN: And then how pitiful to think that he — with all his gifts — should be irreclaimable after all.

HEDDA: I suppose you mean that he has more courage than the rest?

TESMAN: No, not at all — I mean that he is incapable of taking his pleasures in moderation.

HEDDA: And what came of it all — in the end?

TESMAN: Well, to tell the truth, I think it might best be described as an orgy, Hedda.

HEDDA: Had he vine leaves in his hair?

TESMAN: Vine leaves? No, I saw nothing of the sort. But he made a long, rambling speech in honor of the woman who had inspired him in his work — that was the phrase he used.

HEDDA: Did he name her?

TESMAN: No, he didn't; but I can't help thinking he meant Mrs. Elvsted. You may be sure he did.

HEDDA: Well — where did you part from him?

TESMAN: On the way to town. We broke up — the last of us at any rate — all together; and Brack came with us to get a breath of fresh air. And then, you see, we agreed to take Eilert home; for he had had far more than was good for him.

HEDDA: I daresay.

TESMAN: But now comes the strange part of it, Hedda; or, I should rather say, the melancholy part of it. I declare I am almost ashamed — on Eilert's account — to tell you ——

HEDDA: Oh, go on ——

TESMAN: Well, as we were getting near town, you see, I happened to drop a little behind the others. Only for a minute or two — fancy that!

HEDDA: Yes, yes, yes, but —— ?

TESMAN: And then, as I hurried after them — what do you think I found by the wayside? Eh?

HEDDA: Oh, how should I know!

TESMAN: You mustn't speak of it to a soul, Hedda! Do you hear! Promise me, for Eilert's sake. (*Draws a parcel, wrapped in paper, from his coat pocket.*) Fancy, dear — I found this.

HEDDA: Is not that the parcel he had with him yesterday?

TESMAN: Yes, it is the whole of his precious, irreplaceable manuscript! And he had gone and lost it, and knew nothing about it. Only fancy, Hedda! So deplorably ——

HEDDA: But why did you not give him back the parcel at once?

TESMAN: I didn't dare to — in the state he was then in ——

HEDDA: Did you not tell any of the others that you had found it?

TESMAN: Oh, far from it! You can surely understand that, for Eilert's sake, I wouldn't do that.

HEDDA: So no one knows that Eilert Lovbörg's manuscript is in your possession?

TESMAN: No. And no one must know it.

HEDDA: Then what did you say to him afterwards?

TESMAN: I didn't talk to him again at all; for when we got in among the streets, he and two or three of the others gave us the slip and disappeared. Fancy that!

HEDDA: Indeed! They must have taken him home then.

TESMAN: Yes, so it would appear. And Brack, too, left us.

HEDDA: And what have you been doing with yourself since?

TESMAN: Well, I and some of the others went home with one of the party, a jolly fellow, and took our morning coffee with him; or perhaps I should rather call it our night coffee — eh? But now, when I have rested a little, and given Eilert, poor fellow, time to have his sleep out, I must take this back to him.

HEDDA (*holds out her hand for the packet*): No — don't give it to him! Not in such a hurry, I mean. Let me read it first.

TESMAN: No, my dearest Hedda, I mustn't, I really mustn't.

HEDDA: You must not?

TESMAN: No — for you can imagine what a state of despair he will be in when he awakens and misses the manuscript. He has no copy of it, you must know! He told me so.

HEDDA (*looking searchingly at him*): Can such a thing not be reproduced? Written over again?

TESMAN: No, I don't think that would be possible. For the inspiration, you see ——

HEDDA: Yes, yes — I suppose it depends on that. (*Lightly.*) But, by-the-bye — here is a letter for you.

TESMAN: Fancy —— !

HEDDA (*handing it to him*): It came early this morning.

TESMAN: It's from Aunt Julia! What can it be? (*He lays the packet on the other footstool, opens the letter, runs his eye through it, and jumps up.*) Oh, Hedda — she says that poor Aunt Rina is dying!

HEDDA: Well, we were prepared for that.

TESMAN: And that if I want to see her again, I must make haste. I'll run in to them at once.

HEDDA (*suppressing a smile*): Will you run?

TESMAN: Oh, dearest Hedda — if you could only make up your mind to come with me! Just think!

HEDDA (*rises and says wearily, repelling the idea*): No, no, don't ask me. I will not look upon sickness and death. I loathe all sorts of ugliness.

TESMAN: Well, well, then —— ! (*Bustling around.*) My hat — my overcoat —— ? Oh, in the hall — I do hope I mayn't come too late, Hedda! Eh?

HEDDA: Oh, if you run ——

(BERTA *appears at the hall door.*)

BERTA: Judge Brack is at the door, and wishes to know if he may come in.

TESMAN: At this time! No, I can't possibly see him.

HEDDA: But I can. (*To* BERTA.) Ask Judge Brack to come in. (BERTA *goes out.*)

HEDDA (*quickly whispering*): The parcel, Tesman! (*She snatches it up from the stool.*)

TESMAN: Yes, give it to me!

HEDDA: No, no, I will keep it till you come back.

(*She goes to the writing table and places it in the bookcase.* TESMAN *stands in a flurry of haste, and cannot get his gloves on.* JUDGE BRACK *enters from the hall.*)

HEDDA (*nodding to him*): You are an early bird, I must say.

BRACK: Yes, don't you think so? (*To* TESMAN.) Are you on the move, too?

TESMAN: Yes, I must rush off to my aunts'. Fancy — the invalid one is lying at death's door, poor creature.

BRACK: Dear me, is she indeed? Then on no account let me detain you. At such a critical moment ——

TESMAN: Yes, I must really rush —— Good-by! Good-by! (*He hastens out by the hall door.*)

HEDDA (*approaching*): You seem to have made a particularly lively night of it at your rooms, Judge Brack.

BRACK: I assure you I have not had my clothes off, Mrs. Hedda.

HEDDA: Not you, either?

BRACK: No, as you may see. But what has Tesman been telling you of the night's adventures?

HEDDA: Oh, some tiresome story. Only that they went and had coffee somewhere or other.

BRACK: I have heard about that coffee-party already. Eilert Lovbörg was not with them, I fancy?

HEDDA: No, they had taken him home before that.

BRACK: Tesman, too?

HEDDA: No, but some of the others, he said.

BRACK (*smiling*): George Tesman is really an ingenuous creature, Mrs. Hedda.

HEDDA: Yes, heaven knows he is. Then is there something behind all this?

BRACK: Yes, perhaps there may be.

HEDDA: Well then, sit down, my dear Judge, and tell your story in comfort.

(*She seats herself to the left of the table.* BRACK *sits near her, at the long side of the table.*)

HEDDA: Now then?

BRACK: I had special reasons for keeping track of my guests — or rather of some of my guests — last night.

HEDDA: Of Eilert Lövborg among the rest, perhaps?

BRACK: Frankly, yes.

HEDDA: Now you make me really curious ——

BRACK: Do you know where he and one or two of the others finished the night, Mrs. Hedda?

HEDDA: If it is not quite unmentionable, tell me.

BRACK: Oh no, it's not at all unmentionable. Well, they put in an appearance at a particularly animated soiree.

HEDDA: Of the lively kind?

BRACK: Of the very liveliest ——

HEDDA: Tell me more of this, Judge Brack ——

BRACK: Lövborg, as well as the others, had been invited in advance. I knew all about it. But he had declined the invitation; for now, as you know, he has become a new man.

HEDDA: Up at the Elvsteds', yes. But he went after all, then?

BRACK: Well, you see, Mrs. Hedda — unhappily the spirit moved him at my rooms last evening ——

HEDDA: Yes, I hear he found inspiration.

BRACK: Pretty violent inspiration. Well, I fancy that altered his purpose; for we men folk are unfortunately not always so firm in our principles as we ought to be.

HEDDA: Oh, I am sure you are an exception, Judge Brack. But as to Lövborg —— ?

BRACK: To make a long story short — he landed at last in Mademoiselle Diana's rooms.

HEDDA: Mademoiselle Diana's?

BRACK: It was Mademoiselle Diana that was giving the soiree, to a select circle of her admirers and her lady friends.

HEDDA: Is she a red-haired woman?

BRACK: Precisely.

HEDDA: A sort of a — singer?

BRACK: Oh yes — in her leisure moments. And moreover a mighty huntress — of men — Mrs. Hedda. You have no doubt heard of her. Eilert Lovborg was one of her most enthusiastic protectors — in the days of his glory.

HEDDA: And how did all this end?

BRACK: Far from amicably, it appears. After a most tender meeting, they seem to have come to blows ——

HEDDA: Lövborg and she?

BRACK: Yes. He accused her or her friends of having robbed him. He declared that his pocketbook had disappeared — and other things as well. In short, he seems to have made a furious disturbance.

HEDDA: And what came of it all?

BRACK: It came to a general scrimmage, in which the ladies as well as the gentlemen took part. Fortunately the police at last appeared on the scene.

HEDDA: The police too?

BRACK: Yes. I fancy it will prove a costly frolic for Eilert Lövborg, crazy being that he is.

HEDDA: How so?

BRACK: He seems to have made a violent resistance — to have hit one of the constables on the head and torn the coat off his back. So they had to march him off to the police station with the rest.

HEDDA: How have you learnt all this?

BRACK: From the police themselves.

HEDDA (*gazing straight before her*): So that is what happened. Then he had no vine leaves in his hair.

BRACK: Vine leaves, Mrs. Hedda?

HEDDA (*changing her tone*): But tell me now, Judge — what is your real reason for tracking out Eilert Lövborg's movements so carefully?

BRACK: In the first place, it could not be entirely indifferent to me if it should appear in the police court that he came straight from my house.

HEDDA: Will the matter come into court, then?

BRACK: Of course. However, I should scarcely have troubled so much about that. But I thought that, as a friend of the family, it was my duty to supply you and Tesman with a full account of his nocturnal exploits.

HEDDA: Why so, Judge Brack?

BRACK: Why, because I have a shrewd suspicion that he intends to use you as a sort of blind.

HEDDA: Oh, how can you think such a thing!

BRACK: Good heavens, Mrs. Hedda — we have eyes in our head. Mark my words! This Mrs. Elvsted will be in no hurry to leave town again.

HEDDA: Well, even if there should be anything between them, I suppose there are plenty of other places where they could meet.

BRACK: Not a single home. Henceforth, as before, every respectable house will be closed against Eilert Lövborg.

HEDDA: And so ought mine to be, you mean?

BRACK: Yes. I confess it would be more than painful to me if this personage were to be made free of your house. How superfluous, how intrusive, he would be, if he were to force his way into ——

HEDDA: —— into the triangle?

BRACK: Precisely. It would simply mean that I should find myself homeless.

HEDDA (*looks at him with a smile*): So you want to be the one cock in the basket — that is your aim.

BRACK (*nods slowly and lowers his voice*): Yes, that is my aim. And for that I will fight — with every weapon I can command.

HEDDA (*her smile vanishing*): I see you are a dangerous person — when it comes to the point.

BRACK: Do you think so?

HEDDA: I am beginning to think so. And I am exceedingly glad to think — that you have no sort of hold over me.

BRACK (*laughing equivocally*): Well, well, Mrs. Hedda — perhaps you are right there. If I had, who knows what I might be capable of?

HEDDA: Come, come now, Judge Brack. That sounds almost like a threat.

BRACK (*rising*): Oh, not at all! The triangle, you know, ought, if possible, to be spontaneously constructed.

HEDDA: There I agree with you.

BRACK: Well, now I have said all I had to say; and I had better be getting back to town. Good-by, Mrs. Hedda. (*He goes towards the glass door.*)

HEDDA (*rising*): Are you going through the garden?

BRACK: Yes, it's a short cut for me.

HEDDA: And then it is the back way, too.

BRACK: Quite so. I have no objection to back ways. They may be piquant enough at times.

HEDDA: When there is ball practice going on, you mean?

BRACK (*in the doorway, laughing to her*): Oh, people don't shoot their tame poultry, I fancy.

HEDDA (*also laughing*): Oh no, when there is only one cock in the basket ——

(*They exchange laughing nods of farewell. He goes. She closes the door behind him.*

HEDDA, *who has become quite serious, stands for a moment looking out. Presently she goes and peeps through the curtain over the middle doorway. Then she goes to the writing table, takes* LÖVBORG'S *packet out of the bookcase, and is on the point of looking through its contents.* BERTA *is heard speaking loudly in the hall.* HEDDA *turns and listens. Then she hastily locks up the packet in the drawer, and lays the key on the inkstand.*

EILERT LÖVBORG, *with his great coat on and his hat in his hand, tears open the hall door. He looks somewhat confused and irritated.*)

LÖVBORG (*looking towards the hall*): And I tell you I must and will come in! There!

(*He closes the door, turns and sees* HEDDA, *at once regains his self-control, and bows.*)

HEDDA (*at the writing table*): Well, Mr. Lövborg, this is rather a late hour to call for Thea.

LÖVBORG: You mean rather an early hour to call on you. Pray pardon me.

HEDDA: How do you know that she is still here?

LÖVBORG: They told me at her lodgings that she had been out all night.

HEDDA (*going to the oval table*): Did you notice anything about the people of the house when they said that?

LÖVBORG (*looks inquiringly at her*): Notice anything about them?

HEDDA: I mean, did they seem to think it odd?

LÖVBORG (*suddenly understanding*): Oh yes, of course! I am dragging her down with me! However, I didn't notice anything. — I suppose Tesman is not up yet?

HEDDA: No — I think not ——

LÖVBORG: When did he come home?

HEDDA: Very late.

LÖVBORG: Did he tell you anything?

HEDDA: Yes, I gathered that you had had an exceedingly jolly evening at Judge Brack's.

LÖVBORG: Nothing more?

HEDDA: I don't think so. However, I was so dreadfully sleepy ——

(MRS. ELVSTED *enters through the curtains of the middle doorway.*)

MRS. ELVSTED (*going towards him*): Ah, Lövborg! At last —— !

LÖVBORG: Yes, at last. And too late!

MRS. ELVSTED (*looks anxiously at him*): What is too late?

LÖVBORG: Everything is too late now. It is all over with me.

MRS. ELVSTED: Oh no, no — don't say that!

LÖVBORG: You will say the same when you hear ——

MRS. ELVSTED: I won't hear anything!

HEDDA: Perhaps you would prefer to talk to her alone! If so, I will leave you.

LÖVBORG: No, stay — you too. I beg you to stay.

MRS. ELVSTED: Yes, but I won't hear anything, I tell you.

LÖVBORG: It is not last night's adventures that I want to talk about.

MRS. ELVSTED: What is it then —— ?

LÖVBORG: I want to say that now our ways must part.

MRS. ELVSTED: Part!

HEDDA (*involuntarily*): I knew it!

LÖVBORG: You can be of no more service to me, Thea.

MRS. ELVSTED: How can you stand there and say that! No more service to you! Am I not to help you now, as before? Are we not to go on working together?

LÖVBORG: Henceforward I shall do no work.

MRS. ELVSTED (*despairingly*): Then what am I to do with my life?

LÖVBORG: You must try to live your life as if you had never known me.

MRS. ELVSTED: But you know I cannot do that!

LÖVBORG: Try if you cannot, Thea. You must go home again ——

MRS. ELVSTED (*in vehement protest*): Never in this world! Where you are, there will I be also! I will not let myself be driven away like this! I will remain here! I will be with you when the book appears.

HEDDA (*half aloud, in suspense*): Ah yes — the book!

LÖVBORG (*looks at her*): My book and Thea's; for that is what it is.

MRS. ELVSTED: Yes, I feel that it is. And that is why I have a right to be with you when it appears! I will see with my own eyes how respect and honor pour in upon you afresh. And the happiness — the happiness — oh, I must share it with you!

LÖVBORG: Thea — our book will never appear.

HEDDA: Ah!

MRS. ELVSTED: Never appear!

LÖVBORG: Can never appear.

MRS. ELVSTED (*in agonized foreboding*): Lövborg — what have you done with the manuscript?

HEDDA (*looks anxiously at him*): Yes, the manuscript —— ?

MRS. ELVSTED: Where is it?

LÖVBORG: Oh Thea — don't ask me about it!

MRS. ELVSTED: Yes, yes, I will know. I demand to be told at once.

LÖVBORG: The manuscript — Well then — I have torn the manuscript into a thousand pieces.

MRS. ELVSTED (*shrieks*): Oh no, no —— !

HEDDA (*involuntarily*): But that's not ——

LÖVBORG (*looks at her*): Not true, you think?

HEDDA (*collecting herself*): Oh well, of course — since you say so. But it sounded so improbable ——

LÖVBORG: It is true, all the same.

MRS. ELVSTED (*wringing her hands*): Oh God — oh God, Hedda — torn his own work to pieces!

LÖVBORG: I have torn my own life to pieces. So why should I not tear my lifework too —— ?

MRS. ELVSTED: And you did this last night?

LÖVBORG: Yes, I tell you! Tore it into a thousand pieces and scattered them on the fiord — far out. There there is cool sea water at any rate — let them drift upon it — drift with the current and the wind. And then presently they will sink — deeper and deeper — as I shall, Thea.

MRS. ELVSTED: Do you know, Lövborg, that what you have done with the book — I shall think of it to my dying day as though you had killed a little child.

LÖVBORG: Yes, you are right. It is a sort of child murder.

MRS. ELVSTED: How could you, then —— ! Did not the child belong to me too?

HEDDA (almost inaudibly): Ah, the child ——

MRS. ELVSTED (breathing heavily): It is all over then. Well, well, now I will go, Hedda.

HEDDA: But you are not going away from town?

MRS. ELVSTED: Oh, I don't know what I shall do. I see nothing but darkness before me. (She goes out by the hall door.)

HEDDA (stands waiting for a moment): So you are not going to see her home, Mr. Lövborg?

LÖVBORG: I? Through the streets? Would you have people see her walking with me?

HEDDA: Of course I don't know what else may have happened last night. But is it so utterly irretrievable?

LÖVBORG: It will not end with last night — I know that perfectly well. And the thing is that now I have no taste for that sort of life either. I won't begin it anew. She has broken my courage and my power of braving life out.

HEDDA (looking straight before her): So that pretty little fool has had her fingers in a man's destiny. (Looks at him.) But all the same, how could you treat her so heartlessly?

LÖVBORG: Oh, don't say that it was heartless!

HEDDA: To go and destroy what has filled her whole soul for months and years! You do not call that heartless!

LÖVBORG: To you I can tell the truth, Hedda.

HEDDA: The truth?

LÖVBORG: First promise me — give me your word — that what I now confide to you Thea shall never know.

HEDDA: I give you my word.

LÖVBORG: Good. Then let me tell you that what I said just now was untrue.

HEDDA: About the manuscript?

LÖVBORG: Yes. I have not torn it to pieces — nor thrown it into the fiord.

HEDDA: No, n — But — where is it then!

LÖVBORG: I have destroyed it none the less — utterly destroyed it, Hedda!

HEDDA: I don't understand.

LÖVBORG: Thea said that what I had done seemed to her like a child murder.

HEDDA: Yes, so she said.

LÖVBORG: But to kill his child — that is not the worst thing a father can do to it.

HEDDA: Not the worst?

LÖVBORG: No. I wanted to spare Thea from hearing the worst.

HEDDA: Then what is the worst?

LÖVBORG: Suppose now, Hedda, that a man — in the small hours of the morning — came home to his child's mother after a night of riot and debauchery, and said: "Listen — I have been here and there — in this place and in that. And I have taken our child with me — to this place and to that. And I have lost the child — utterly lost it. The devil knows into what hands it may have fallen — who may have had their clutches on it."

HEDDA: Well — but when all is said and done, you know — that was only a book ——

LÖVBORG: Thea's pure soul was in that book.

HEDDA: Yes, so I understand.

LÖVBORG: And you can understand, too, that for her and me together no future is possible.

HEDDA: What path do you mean to take then?

LÖVBORG: None. I will only try to make an end of it all — the sooner the better.

HEDDA (*a step nearer to him*): Eilert Lövborg — listen to me. Will you not try to — to do it beautifully?

LÖVBORG: Beautifully? (*Smiling.*) With vine leaves in my hair, as you used to dream in the old days —— ?

HEDDA: No, no. I have lost my faith in the vine leaves. But beautifully, nevertheless! For once in a way! — Good-by! You must go now — and do not come here any more.

LÖVBORG: Good-by, Mrs. Tesman. And give George Tesman my love. (*He is on the point of going.*)

HEDDA: No, wait! I must give you a memento to take with you.

(*She goes to the writing table and opens the drawer and the pistol case; then returns to* LÖVBORG *with one of the pistols.*)

LÖVBORG: Good-by, Hedda Gabler. (*He goes out by the hall door.*)

HEDDA (*nodding slowly*): Do you recognize it? It was aimed at you once.

LÖVBORG: You should have used it then.

HEDDA: Take it — and do you use it now.

LÖVBORG (*puts the pistol in his breast pocket*): Thanks!

HEDDA: And beautifully, Eilert Lövborg. Promise me that!

LÖVBORG: Good-by, Hedda Gabler. (*He goes out by the hall door.*)

(HEDDA *listens for a moment at the door. Then she goes up to the writing table, takes out the packet of manuscript, peeps under the cover, draws a few of the sheets half out, and looks at them. Next she goes over and seats herself in the armchair beside the stove, with the packet in her lap. Presently she opens the stove door, and then the packet.*)

HEDDA (*throws one of the quires into the fire and whispers to herself*): Now I am burning your child, Thea! — Burning it, curlylocks! (*Throwing one or two more quires into the stove.*) Your child and Eilert Lövborg's. (*Throws the rest in.*) I am burning — I am burning your child.

Act IV

SCENE: *The same rooms at the* TESMANS'. *It is evening. The drawing room is in darkness. The back room is lighted by the hanging lamp over the table. The curtains over the glass door are drawn close.*

HEDDA, *dressed in black, walks to and fro in the dark room. Then she goes into the back room and disappears, for a moment to the left. She is heard to strike a few chords on the piano. Presently she comes in sight again, and returns to the drawing room.*

BERTA *enters from the right, through the inner room, with a lighted lamp, which she places on the table in front of the corner settee in the drawing room. Her eyes are red with weeping, and she has black ribbons in her cap. She goes quietly and circumspectly out to the right.*

HEDDA *goes up to the glass door, lifts the curtain a little aside, and looks out into the darkness.*

Shortly afterwards, MISS TESMAN, *in mourning, with a bonnet and veil on, comes in from the hall.* HEDDA *goes towards her and holds out her hand.*

MISS TESMAN: Yes, Hedda, here I am, in mourning and forlorn; for now my poor sister has at last found peace.

HEDDA: I have heard the news already, as you see. Tesman sent me a card.

MISS TESMAN: Yes, he promised me he would. But nevertheless I thought that to Hedda — here in the house of life — I ought myself to bring the tidings of death.

HEDDA: That was very kind of you.

MISS TESMAN: Ah, Rina ought not to have left us just now. This is not the time for Hedda's house to be a house of mourning.

HEDDA (*changing the subject*): She died quite peacefully, did she not, Miss Tesman?

MISS TESMAN: Oh, her end was so calm, so beautiful. And then she had the unspeakable happiness of seeing George once more — and bidding him good-by. Has he come home yet?

HEDDA: No. He wrote that he might be detained. But won't you sit down?

MISS TESMAN: No thank you, my dear, dear Hedda. I should like to, but I have so much to do. I must prepare my dear one for her rest as well as I can. She shall go to her grave looking her best.

HEDDA: Can I not help you in any way?

MISS TESMAN: Oh, you must not think of it! Hedda Tesman must have no hand in such mournful work. Nor let her thoughts dwell on it either — not at this time.

HEDDA: One is not always mistress of one's thoughts ——

MISS TESMAN (*continuing*): Ah yes, it is the way of the world. At home we shall be sewing a shroud; and here there will soon be sewing too, I suppose — but of another sort, thank God!

(GEORGE TESMAN *enters by the hall door.*)

HEDDA: Ah, you have come at last!

TESMAN: You here, Aunt Julia? With Hedda? Fancy that!

MISS TESMAN: I was just going, my dear boy. Well, have you done all you promised?

TESMAN: No; I'm really afraid I have forgotten half of it. I must come to you again tomorrow. Today my brain is all in a whirl. I can't keep my thoughts together.

MISS TESMAN: Why, my dear George, you mustn't take it in this way.

TESMAN: Mustn't —— ? How do you mean?

MISS TESMAN: Even in your sorrow you must rejoice, as I do — rejoice that she is at rest.

TESMAN: Oh yes, yes — you are thinking of Aunt Rina.

HEDDA: You will feel lonely now, Miss Tesman.

MISS TESMAN: Just at first, yes. But that will not last very long, I hope. I daresay I shall soon find an occupant for poor Rina's little room.

TESMAN: Indeed? Who do you think will take it? Eh?

MISS TESMAN: Oh, there's always some poor invalid or other in want of nursing, unfortunately.

HEDDA: Would you really take such a burden upon you again?

MISS TESMAN: A burden! Heaven forgive you, child — it has been no burden to me.

HEDDA: But suppose you had a total stranger on your hands ——

MISS TESMAN: Oh, one soon makes friends with sick folk; and it's such an absolute necessity for me to have some one to live for. Well, heaven be praised, there may soon be something in this house, too, to keep an old aunt busy.

HEDDA: Oh, don't trouble about anything here.

TESMAN: Yes, just fancy what a nice time we three might have together, if —— ?

HEDDA: If —— ?

TESMAN (uneasily): Oh, nothing. It will all come right. Let us hope so — eh?

MISS TESMAN: Well, well, I daresay you two want to talk to each other. (Smiling.) And perhaps Hedda may have something to tell you too, George. Good-by! I must go home to Rina. (Turning at the door.) How strange it is to think that now Rina is with me and with my poor brother as well!

TESMAN: Yes, fancy that, Aunt Julia! Eh?

(MISS TESMAN goes out by the hall door.)

HEDDA (follows TESMAN coldly and searchingly with her eyes): I almost believe your Aunt Rina's death affects you more than it does your Aunt Julia.

TESMAN: Oh, it's not that alone. It's Eilert I am so terribly uneasy about.

HEDDA (*quickly*): Is there anything new about him?

TESMAN: I looked in at his rooms this afternoon, intending to tell him the manuscript was in safe keeping.

HEDDA: Well, did you not find him?

TESMAN: No. He wasn't at home. But afterwards I met Mrs. Elvsted, and she told me that he had been here early this morning.

HEDDA: Yes, directly after you had gone.

TESMAN: And he said that he had torn his manuscript to pieces — eh?

HEDDA: Yes, so he declared.

TESMAN: Why, good heavens, he must have been completely out of his mind! And I suppose you thought it best not to give it back to him, Hedda?

HEDDA: No, he did not get it.

TESMAN: But of course you told him that we had it?

HEDDA: No. (*Quickly.*) Did you tell Mrs. Elvsted?

TESMAN: No, I thought I had better not. But you ought to have told him. Fancy, if, in desperation, he should go and do himself some injury! Let me have the manuscript, Hedda! I will take it to him at once. Where is it?

HEDDA (*cold and immovable, leaning on the armchair*): I have not got it.

TESMAN: Have not got it? What in the world do you mean?

HEDDA: I have burnt it — every line of it.

TESMAN (*with a violent movement of terror*): Burnt! Burnt Eilert's manuscript!

HEDDA: Don't scream so. The servant might hear you.

TESMAN: Burnt! Why, good God —— ! No, no, no! It's impossible!

HEDDA: It is so, nevertheless.

TESMAN: Do you know what you have done, Hedda? It's unlawful appropriation of lost property. Fancy that! Just ask Judge Brack, and he'll tell you what it is.

HEDDA: I advise you not to speak of it — either to Judge Brack, or to any one else.

TESMAN: But how could you do anything so unheard-of? What put it into your head? What possessed you? Answer me that — eh?

HEDDA (*suppressing an almost imperceptible smile*): I did it for your sake, George.

TESMAN: For my sake!

HEDDA: This morning, when you told me about what he had read to you ——

TESMAN: Yes, yes — what then?

HEDDA: You acknowledged that you envied him his work.

TESMAN: Oh, of course I didn't mean that literally.

HEDDA: No matter — I could not bear the idea that any one should throw you into the shade.

TESMAN (*in an outburst of mingled doubt and joy*): Hedda! Oh, is this true? But — but — I never knew you to show your love like that before. Fancy that!

HEDDA: Well, I may as well tell you that — just at this time —— (*Impatiently, breaking off.*) No, no; you can ask Aunt Julia. She will tell you, fast enough.

TESMAN: Oh, I almost think I understand you, Hedda! (*Clasps his hands together.*) Great heavens! do you really mean it! Eh?

HEDDA: Don't shout so. The servant might hear.

TESMAN (*laughing in irrepressible glee*): The servant! Why, how absurd you are, Hedda. It's only my old Berta! Why, I'll tell Berta myself.

HEDDA (*clenching her hands together in desperation*): Oh, it is killing me — it is killing me, all this!

TESMAN: What is, Hedda? Eh?

HEDDA (*coldly, controlling herself*): All this — absurdity — George.

TESMAN: Absurdity! Do you see anything absurd in my being overjoyed at the news! But after all perhaps I had better not say anything to Berta.

HEDDA: Oh — why not that too?

TESMAN: No, no, not yet! But I must certainly tell Aunt Julia. And then that you have begun to call me George too! Fancy that! Oh, Aunt Julia will be so happy — so happy.

HEDDA: When she hears that I have burnt Eilert Lövborg's manuscript — for your sake?

TESMAN: No, by-the-bye — that affair of the manuscript — of course nobody must know about that. But that you love me so much.

Hedda — Aunt Julia must really share my joy in that! I wonder, now, whether this sort of thing is usual in young wives? Eh?

HEDDA: I think you had better ask Aunt Julia that question too.

TESMAN: I will indeed, some time or other. (*Looks uneasy and downcast again.*) And yet the manuscript — the manuscript! Good God! It is terrible to think what will become of poor Eilert now.

(MRS. ELVSTED, *dressed as in the first Act, with hat and cloak, enters by the hall door.*)

MRS. ELVSTED (*greets them hurriedly, and says in evident agitation*): Oh, dear Hedda, forgive my coming again.

HEDDA: What is the matter with you, Thea?

TESMAN: Something about Eilert Lövborg again — eh?

MRS. ELVSTED: Yes! I am dreadfully afraid some misfortune has happened to him.

HEDDA (*seizes her arm*): Ah, do you think so?

TESMAN: Why, good Lord — what makes you think that, Mrs. Elvsted?

MRS. ELVSTED: I heard them talking of him at my boarding house — just as I came in. Oh, the most incredible rumors are afloat about him today.

TESMAN: Yes, fancy, so I heard too! And I can bear witness that he went straight home to bed last night. Fancy that!

HEDDA: Well, what did they say at the boarding house?

MRS. ELVSTED: Oh, I couldn't make out anything clearly. Either they knew nothing definite, or else —— They stopped talking when they saw me; and I did not dare to ask.

TESMAN (*moving about uneasily*): We must hope — we must hope that you misunderstood them, Mrs. Elvsted.

MRS. ELVSTED: No, no; I am sure it was of him they were talking. And I heard something about the hospital or ——

TESMAN: The hospital?

HEDDA: No — surely that cannot be!

MRS. ELVSTED: Oh, I was in such mortal terror! I went to his lodgings and asked for him there.

HEDDA: You could make up your mind to that, Thea!

MRS. ELVSTED: What else could I do? I really could bear the suspense no longer.

TESMAN: But you didn't find him either — eh?

MRS. ELVSTED: No. And the people knew nothing about him. He hadn't been home since yesterday afternoon, they said.

TESMAN: Yesterday! Fancy, how could they say that?

MRS. ELVSTED: Oh, I am sure something terrible must have happened to him.

TESMAN: Hedda dear — how would it be if I were to go and make inquiries —— ?

HEDDA: No, no — don't you mix yourself up in this affair.

(JUDGE BRACK, *with his hat in his hand, enters by the hall door, which* BERTA *opens, and closes behind him. He looks grave and bows in silence.*)

TESMAN: Oh, is that you, my dear Judge? Eh?

BRACK: Yes. It was imperative I should see you this evening.

TESMAN: I can see you have heard the news about Aunt Rina.

BRACK: Yes, that among other things.

TESMAN: Isn't it sad — eh?

BRACK: Well, my dear Tesman, that depends on how you look at it.

TESMAN (*looks doubtfully at him*): Has anything else happened?

BRACK: Yes.

HEDDA (*in suspense*): Anything sad, Judge Brack?

BRACK: That, too, depends on how you look at it, Mrs. Tesman.

MRS. ELVSTED (*unable to restrain her anxiety*): Oh! it is something about Eilert Lövborg!

BRACK (*with a glance at her*): What makes you think that, Madam? Perhaps you have already heard something —— ?

MRS. ELVSTED (*in confusion*): No, nothing at all, but ——

TESMAN: Oh, for heaven's sake, tell us!

BRACK (*shrugging his shoulders*): Well, I regret to say Eilert Lövborg has been taken to the hospital. He is lying at the point of death.

MRS. ELVSTED (*shrieks*): Oh God! Oh God ——

TESMAN: To the hospital! And at the point of death.

HEDDA (*involuntarily*): So soon then ——

MRS. ELVSTED (*wailing*): And we parted in anger, Hedda!

HEDDA (*whispers*): Thea — Thea — be careful!

MRS. ELVSTED (*not heeding her*): I must go to him! I must see him alive!

BRACK: It is useless, Madam. No one will be admitted.

MRS. ELVSTED: Oh, at least tell me what has happened to him? What is it?

TESMAN: You don't mean to say that he has himself —— Eh?

HEDDA: Yes, I am sure he has.

TESMAN: Hedda, how can you —— ?

BRACK (*keeping his eyes fixed upon her*): Unfortunately you have guessed quite correctly, Mrs. Tesman.

MRS. ELVSTED: Oh, how horrible!

TESMAN: Himself, then! Fancy that!

HEDDA: Shot himself!

BRACK: Rightly guessed again, Mrs. Tesman.

MRS. ELVSTED (*with an effort at self-control*): When did it happen, Mr. Brack?

BRACK: This afternoon — between three and four.

TESMAN: But, good Lord, where did he do it? Eh?

BRACK (*with some hesitation*): Where? Well — I suppose at his lodgings.

MRS. ELVSTED: No, that cannot be; for I was there between six and seven.

BRACK: Well, then, somewhere else. I don't know exactly. I only know that he was found —— . He had shot himself — in the breast.

MRS. ELVSTED: Oh, how terrible! That he should die like that!

HEDDA (*to* BRACK): Was it in the breast?

BRACK: Yes — as I told you.

HEDDA: Not in the temple?

BRACK: In the breast, Mrs. Tesman.

HEDDA: Well, well — the breast is a good place, too.

BRACK: How do you mean, Mrs. Tesman?

HEDDA (*evasively*): Oh, nothing — nothing.

TESMAN: And the wound is dangerous, you say — eh?

BRACK: Absolutely mortal. The end has probably come by this time.

MRS. ELVSTED: Yes, yes, I feel it. The end! The end! Oh, Hedda —— !

TESMAN: But tell me, how have you learnt all this?

BRACK (*curtly*): Through one of the police. A man I had some business with.

HEDDA (*in a clear voice*): At last a deed worth doing!

TESMAN (*terrified*): Good heavens, Hedda! What are you saying?

HEDDA: I say there is beauty in this.

BRACK: H'm, Mrs. Tesman ——

TESMAN: Beauty! Fancy that!

MRS. ELVSTED: Oh, Hedda, how can you talk of beauty in such an act!

HEDDA: Eilert Lövborg has himself made up his account with life. He has had the courage to do — the one right thing.

MRS. ELVSTED: No, you must never think that was how it happened! It must have been in delirium that he did it.

TESMAN: In despair!

HEDDA: That he did not. I am certain of that.

MRS. ELVSTED: Yes, yes! In delirium! Just as when he tore up our manuscript.

BRACK (*starting*): The manuscript? Has he torn that up?

MRS. ELVSTED: Yes, last night.

TESMAN (*whispers softly*): Oh, Hedda, we shall never get over this.

BRACK: H'm, very extraordinary.

TESMAN (*moving about the room*): To think of Eilert going out of the world in this way! And not leaving behind him the book that would have immortalized his name ——

MRS. ELVSTED: Oh, if only it could be put together again!

TESMAN: Yes, if it only could! I don't know what I would not give ——

MRS. ELVSTED: Perhaps it can, Mr. Tesman.

TESMAN: What do you mean?

MRS. ELVSTED (*searches in the pocket of her dress*): Look here. I have kept all the loose notes he used to dictate from.

HEDDA (*a step forward*): Ah —— !

TESMAN: You have kept them, Mrs. Elvsted! Eh?

MRS. ELVSTED: Yes, I have them here. I put them in my pocket when I left home. Here they still are ——

TESMAN: Oh, do let me see them!

MRS. ELVSTED (*hands him a bundle of papers*): But they are in such disorder — all mixed up.

TESMAN: Fancy, if we could make something out of them, after all! Perhaps if we two put our heads together ——

MRS. ELVSTED: Oh, yes, at least let us try ——

TESMAN: We will manage it! We must! I will dedicate my life to this task.

HEDDA: You, George? Your life?

TESMAN: Yes, or rather all the time I can spare. My own collections must wait in the meantime. Hedda — you understand, eh? I owe this to Eilert's memory.

HEDDA: Perhaps.

TESMAN: And so, my dear Mrs. Elvsted, we will give our whole minds to it. There is no use in brooding over what can't be undone — eh? We must try to control our grief as much as possible, and ——

MRS. ELVSTED: Yes, yes, Mr. Tesman, I will do the best I can.

TESMAN: Well then, come here. I can't rest until we have looked through the notes. Where shall we sit? Here? No, in there, in the back room. Excuse me, my dear Judge. Come with me, Mrs. Elvsted.

MRS. ELVSTED: Oh, if only it were possible!

(TESMAN *and* MRS. ELVSTED *go into the back room. She takes off her hat and cloak. They both sit at the table under the hanging lamp, and are soon deep in an eager examination of the papers.* HEDDA *crosses to the stove and sits in an armchair. Presently* BRACK *goes up to her.*)

HEDDA (*in a low voice*): Oh, what a sense of freedom it gives one, this act of Eilert Lövborg's.

BRACK: Freedom, Mrs. Hedda? Well, of course, it is a release for him ——

HEDDA: I mean for me. It gives me a sense of freedom to know that a deed of deliberate courage is still possible in this world — a deed of spontaneous beauty.

BRACK (*smiling*): H'm — my dear Mrs. Hedda ——

HEDDA: Oh, I know what you are going to say. For you are a kind of a specialist too, like — you know!

BRACK (*looking hard at her*): Eilert Lövborg was more to you than perhaps you are willing to admit to yourself. Am I wrong?

HEDDA: I don't answer such questions. I only know Eilert Lövborg has had the courage to live his life after his own fashion. And then — the last great act, with its beauty! Ah! that he should have the will and the strength to turn away from the banquet of life — so early.

BRACK: I am sorry, Mrs. Hedda — but I fear I must dispel an amiable illusion.

HEDDA: Illusion?

BRACK: Which could not have lasted long in any case.

HEDDA: What do you mean?

BRACK: Eilert Lövborg did not shoot himself voluntarily.

HEDDA: Not voluntarily?

BRACK: No. The thing did not happen exactly as I told it.

HEDDA (*in suspense*): Have you concealed something? What is it?

BRACK: For poor Mrs. Elvsted's sake I idealized the facts a little.

HEDDA: What are the facts?

BRACK: First, that he is already dead.

HEDDA: At the hospital?

BRACK: Yes — without regaining consciousness.

HEDDA: What more have you concealed?

BRACK: This — the event did not happen at his lodgings.

HEDDA: Oh, that can make no difference.

BRACK: Perhaps it may. For I must tell you — Eilert Lövborg was found shot in — in Mademoiselle Diana's boudoir.

HEDDA (*makes a motion as if to rise, but sinks back again*): That is impossible, Judge Brack! He cannot have been there again today.

BRACK: He was there this afternoon. He went there, he said, to demand the return of something which they had taken from him. Talked wildly about a lost child ——

HEDDA: Ah — so that was why ——

BRACK: I thought probably he meant his manuscript; but now I hear he destroyed that himself. So I suppose it must have been his pocket-book.

HEDDA: Yes, no doubt. And there — there he was found?

BRACK: Yes, there. With a pistol in his breast-pocket, discharged. The ball had lodged in a vital part.

HEDDA: In the breast — yes.

BRACK: No — in the bowels.

HEDDA (*looks up at him with an expression of loathing*): That too! Oh what curse is it that makes everything I touch turn ludicrous and mean?

BRACK: There is one point more, Mrs. Hedda — another disagreeable feature in the affair.

HEDDA: And what is that?

BRACK: The pistol he carried ——

HEDDA (*breathless*): Well? What of it?

BRACK: He must have stolen it.

HEDDA (*leaps up*): Stolen it! That is not true! He did not steal it!

BRACK: No other explanation is possible. He must have stolen it —— Hush!

(TESMAN *and* MRS. ELVSTED *have risen from the table in the back room, and come into the drawing room.*)

TESMAN (*with the papers in both his hands*): Hedda dear, it is almost impossible to see under that lamp. Think of that!

HEDDA: Yes, I am thinking.

TESMAN: Would you mind our sitting at your writing table — eh?

HEDDA: If you like. (*Quickly.*) No, wait! Let me clear it first!

TESMAN: Oh, you needn't trouble, Hedda. There is plenty of room.

HEDDA: No, no; let me clear it, I say! I will take these things in and put them on the piano. There! (*She has drawn out an object, covered with sheet music, from under the bookcase, places several other pieces of music upon it, and carries the whole into the inner room, to the left.* TESMAN *lays the scraps of paper on the writing table, and moves the lamp there from the corner table.* HEDDA *returns.*)

HEDDA (*behind* MRS. ELVSTED'S *chair, gently ruffling her hair*): Well, my sweet Thea, how goes it with Eilert Lövborg's monument?

MRS. ELVSTED (*looks dispiritedly up at her*): Oh, it will be terribly hard to put in order.

TESMAN: We must manage it. I am determined. And arranging other people's papers is just the work for me.

(HEDDA *goes over to the stove, and seats herself on one of the footstools.* BRACK *stands over her, leaning on the armchair.*)

HEDDA (*whispers*): What did you say about the pistol?

BRACK (*softly*): That he must have stolen it.

HEDDA: Why stolen it?

BRACK: Because every other explanation ought to be impossible, Mrs. Hedda.

HEDDA: Indeed?

BRACK (*glances at her*): Of course Eilert Lövborg was here this morning. Was he not?

HEDDA: Yes.

BRACK: Were you alone with him?

HEDDA: Part of the time.

BRACK: Did you not leave the room whilst he was here?

HEDDA: No.

BRACK: Try to recollect. Were you not out of the room a moment?

HEDDA: Yes, perhaps just a moment — out in the hall.

BRACK: And where was your pistol case during that time?

HEDDA: I had it locked up in ——

BRACK: Well, Mrs. Hedda?

HEDDA: The case stood there on the writing table.

BRACK: Have you looked since, to see whether both the pistols are there?

HEDDA: No.

BRACK: Well, you need not. I saw the pistol found in Lövborg's pocket, and I knew it at once as the one I had seen yesterday — and before, too.

HEDDA: Have you it with you?

BRACK: No; the police have it.

HEDDA: What will the police do with it?

BRACK: Search till they find the owner.

HEDDA: Do you think they will succeed?

BRACK (*bends over her and whispers*): No, Hedda Gabler — not so long as I say nothing.

HEDDA (*looks frightened at him*): And if you do not say nothing — what then?

BRACK (*shrugs his shoulders*): There is always the possibility that the pistol was stolen.

HEDDA (*firmly*): Death rather than that.

BRACK (*smiling*): People say such things — but they don't do them.

HEDDA (*without replying*): And supposing the pistol was stolen, and the owner is discovered? What then?

BRACK: Well, Hedda — then comes the scandal.

HEDDA: The scandal!

BRACK: Yes, the scandal — of which you are mortally afraid. You will, of course, be brought before the court — both you and Mademoiselle Diana. She will have to explain how the thing happened — whether it was an accidental shot or murder. Did the pistol go off as he was trying to take it out of his pocket, to threaten her with? Or did she tear the pistol out of his hand, shoot him, and push it back into his pocket? That would be quite like her; for she is an able-bodied young person, this same Mademoiselle Diana.

HEDDA: But *I* have nothing to do with all this repulsive business.

BRACK: No. But you will have to answer the question: Why did you give Eilert Lövborg the pistol? And what conclusions will people draw from the fact that you did give it to him?

HEDDA (*lets her head sink*): That is true. I did not think of that.

BRACK: Well, fortunately, there is no danger, so long as I say nothing.

HEDDA (*looks up at him*): So I am in your power, Judge Brack. You have me at your beck and call, from this time forward.

BRACK (*whispers softly*): Dearest Hedda — believe me — I shall not abuse my advantage.

HEDDA: I am in your power none the less. Subject to your will and your demands. A slave, a slave then! (*Rises impetuously.*) No, I cannot endure the thought of that! Never!

BRACK (*looks half-mockingly at her*): People generally get used to the inevitable.

HEDDA (*returns his look*): Yes, perhaps. (*She crosses to the writing table. Suppressing an involuntary smile, she imitates* TESMAN'S *intonations.*) Well? Are you getting on, George? Eh?

TESMAN: Heaven knows, dear. In any case it will be the work of months.

HEDDA (*as before*): Fancy that! (*Passes her hands softly through* MRS. ELVSTED'S *hair.*) Doesn't it seem strange to you, Thea? Here are you sitting with Tesman — just as you used to sit with Eilert Lövborg?

MRS. ELVSTED: Ah, if I could only inspire your husband in the same way.

HEDDA: Oh, that will come too — in time.

TESMAN: Yes, do you know, Hedda — I really think I begin to feel something of the sort. But won't you go and sit with Brack again?

HEDDA: Is there nothing I can do to help you two?

TESMAN: No, nothing in the world. (*Turning his head.*) I trust to you to keep Hedda company, my dear Brack.

BRACK (*with a glance at* HEDDA): With the very greatest of pleasure.

HEDDA: Thanks. But I am tired this evening. I will go in and lie down a little on the sofa.

TESMAN: Yes, do dear — eh?

(HEDDA *goes into the back room and draws the curtains. A short pause. Suddenly she is heard playing a wild dance on the piano.*)

MRS. ELVSTED (*starts from her chair*): Oh — what is that?

TESMAN (*runs to the doorway*): Why, my dearest Hedda — don't play dance music tonight! Just think of Aunt Rina! And of Eilert too!

HEDDA (*puts her head out between the curtains*): And of Aunt Julia. And of all the rest of them. After this, I will be quiet. (*Closes the curtains again.*)

TESMAN (*at the writing table*): It's not good for her to see us at this distressing work. I'll tell you what, Mrs. Elvsted, you shall take the empty room at Aunt Julia's, and then I will come over in the evenings, and we can sit and work there — eh?

HEDDA (*in the inner room*): I hear what you are saying, Tesman. But how am *I* to get through the evenings out here?

TESMAN (*turning over the papers*): Oh, I daresay Judge Brack will be so kind as to look in now and then, even though I am out.

BRACK (*in the armchair, calls out gaily*): Every blessed evening, with all the pleasure in life, Mrs. Tesman! We shall get on capitally together, we two!

HEDDA (*speaking loud and clear*): Yes, don't you flatter yourself we will, Judge Brack? Now that you are the one cock in the basket ——

(*A shot is heard within.* TESMAN, MRS. ELVSTED, *and* BRACK *leap to their feet.*)

TESMAN: Oh, now she is playing with those pistols again.

(*He throws back the curtains and runs in, followed by* MRS. ELVSTED. HEDDA *lies stretched on the sofa, lifeless. Confusion and cries.* BERTA *enters in alarm from the right.*)

TESMAN (*shrieks to* BRACK): Shot herself! Shot herself in the temple! Fancy that!

BRACK (*half-fainting in the armchair*): Good God! — people don't do such things.

For Consideration

Act I

1. What has been Aunt Julia's past relationship to George? What are her several reactions to Hedda and Hedda's new role in the family?
2. Aunt Julia, commenting on George's work, observes: "Collecting and arranging — no one can beat you at that." To what extent does collecting and arranging characterize George's response to other areas of his life?
3. Describe Hedda as she first appears on stage. How does her dress reinforce her personality and values?
4. Mrs. Elvsted observes that Hedda, as a schoolmate, frightened her: "When we met on the stairs you used always to pull my hair." Is Hedda's present action toward Mrs. Elvsted an analogous kind of cruelty?
5. Act I includes considerable foreshadowing of events and relationships to be revealed later. What are some of the matters about which suggestions or hints are mentioned?

Act II

6. Act I ends with Hedda and her guns; Act II begins with the same pairing. How do those scenes further reveal Hedda to us?
7. Why did Hedda marry George? What does she wish to gain from the relationship?
8. What kind of triangular arrangement do Hedda and Judge Brack seek?
9. The subject of future children for Hedda and George is hinted at by several characters but is never explicitly mentioned. Why?
10. Lövborg speaks of the power in Hedda that forced him to confess his secret thoughts and actions. Do we see that power elsewhere in the play? What is its source?
11. Her friendship with Lövborg, according to Hedda, was broken off when it "threatened to develop into something more serious." Does Hedda have any serious attachments in the play? On what basis does she establish relationships?
12. Why does Hedda reveal to Lövborg Mrs. Elvsted's concern for him?

Act III

13. What is Judge Brack's motive in telling Hedda of Lövborg's nocturnal escapades?
14. When Lövborg, Hedda, and Mrs. Elvsted speak of Lövborg's manuscript, they refer to it as a "child." What is the importance of the image? What does it suggest about Lövborg and Mrs. Elvsted? Why doesn't Hedda tell Lövborg the truth about the manuscript? Why does she encourage him to kill himself "beautifully"?

Act IV

15. Two deaths are important in Act IV, Aunt Rina's and Lövborg's. What are the reactions to the deaths? Whose is treated with greater importance?

16. The circumstances of Lövborg's death are not at all those initially described by Judge Brack. In what respects is the true account a more fitting —
though less "beautiful" — end?
17. What exactly does Hedda fear as a result of Judge Brack's knowledge of
the gun? Is her suicide surprising or appropriate for her? What does it tell
us about her character and values?
18. Is Hedda Gabler a tragic figure? Why or why not?

INGMAR BERGMAN (1918–   )
Wild Strawberries

The Cast

PROFESSOR ISAK BORG	Victor Sjöström
SARA	Bibi Andersson
MARIANNE	Ingrid Thulin
EVALD	Gunnar Björnstrand
AGDA	Jullan Kindahl
ANDERS	Folke Sundquist
VIKTOR	Björn Bjelvenstam
ISAK's MOTHER	Naima Wifstrand
MRS. ALMAN	Gunnel Broström
ISAK's WIFE	Gertrud Fridh
HER LOVER	Ake Fridell
AUNT	Sif Ruud
ALMAN	Gunnar Sjöberg
AKERMAN	Max von Sydow
UNCLE ARON	Yngve Nordwall
SIGFRID	Per Sjöstrand
SIGBRITT	Gio Petré
CHARLOTTA	Gunnel Lindblom
ANGELICA	Maud Hansson
MRS. AKERMAN	Anne-Mari Wiman
ANNA	Eva Norée
THE TWINS	Lena Bergman
	Monica Ehrling
HAGBART	Per Skogsberg
BENJAMIN	Göran Lundquist
PROMOTER	Professor Helge Wulff

NOTE: There are no cast listings for Tiger and Jakob because the scene in which these characters appear did not appear in the finished film.

The Credits

Screenplay	Ingmar Bergman
Director	Ingmar Bergman
Assistant director	Gösta Ekman
Director of photography	Gunnar Fischer
Assistant cameraman	Björn Thermenius
Music	Erik Nordgren
Music directed by	E. Eckert-Lundin
Sets	Gittan Gustafsson
Costumes	Millie Ström
Make-up	Nils Nittel (of Carl M. Lundh, Inc.)
Sound	Aaby Wedin and Lennart Wallin
Editor	Oscar Rosander
Production supervisor	Allan Ekelund

Running time: 90 minutes

Produced by Svensk Filmindustri; distributed in the United States by Janus Films, Inc., and in Great Britain by Contemporary Films Ltd.

At the age of seventy-six, I feel that I'm much too old to lie to myself. But of course I can't be too sure. My complacent attitude toward my own truthfulness could be dishonesty in disguise, although I don't quite know what I might want to hide. Nevertheless, if for some reason I would have to evaluate myself, I am sure that I would do so without shame or concern for my reputation. But if I should be asked to express an opinion about someone else, I would be considerably more cautious. There is the greatest danger in passing such judgment. In all probability one is guilty of errors, exaggerations, even tremendous lies. Rather than commit such follies, I remain silent.

As a result, I have of my own free will withdrawn almost completely from society, because one's relationship with other people consists mainly of discussing and evaluating one's neighbor's conduct. Therefore I have found myself rather alone in my old age. This is not a regret but a statement of fact. All I ask of life is to be left alone and to have the opportunity to devote myself to the few things which continue to interest me, however superficial they may be. For example, I derive pleasure from keeping up with the steady progress made in my profession (I once taught bacteriology), I find relaxation in a game of golf, and now and then I read some memoirs or a good detective story.

My life has been filled with work, and for that I am grateful. It began with a struggle for daily bread and developed into the continuous pursuit of a beloved science. I have a son living in Lund who is a physician and has been married for many years. He has no children. My mother is still living and quite active despite her advanced age (she is ninety-six). She lives in the vicinity of Huskvarna. We seldom see each other. My nine sisters and brothers are dead, but they left a number of children and grandchildren. I have very little contact with my relatives. My wife Karin died many years ago. Our marriage was quite unhappy. I am fortunate in having a good housekeeper.

This is all I have to say about myself. Perhaps I ought to add that I am an old pedant, and at times quite trying, both to myself and to the people who have to be around me. I detest emotional outbursts, women's tears and the crying of children. On the whole, I find loud noises and sudden startling occurrences most disconcerting.

Later I will come back to the reason for writing this story, which is, as nearly as I can make it, a true account of the events, dreams and thoughts which befell me on a certain day.

In the early morning of Saturday, the first of June, I had a strange and very unpleasant dream. I dreamed that I was taking my usual morning stroll through the streets. It was quite early and no human being was in sight. This was a bit surprising to me. I also noted that there were no vehicles parked along the curbs. The city seemed strangely deserted, as if it were a holiday morning in the middle of summer.

The sun was shining brightly and made sharp black shadows, but it gave off no warmth. Even though I walked on the sunny side, I felt chilly.

The stillness was also remarkable. I usually stroll along a broad, tree-lined boulevard, and even before sunrise the sparrows and crows are as a rule extremely noisy. Besides, there is always the perpetual roar from the center of the city. But this morning nothing was heard, the silence was absolute, and my footsteps echoed almost anxiously against the walls of the buildings. I began to wonder what had happened.

Just at that moment I passed the shop of a watchmaker-optometrist, whose sign had always been a large clock that gave the exact time. Under this clock hung a picture of a pair of giant eyeglasses with staring eyes. On my morning walks I had always smiled to myself at this slightly grotesque detail in the street scene.

To my amazement, the hands of the clock had disappeared. The dial was blank, and below it someone had smashed both of the eyes so that they looked like watery, infected sores.

Instinctively I pulled out my own watch to check the time, but I found that my old reliable gold timepiece had also lost its hands. I held it to my ear to find out if it was still ticking. Then I heard my heart beat. It was pounding very fast and irregularly. I was overwhelmed by an inexplicable feeling of frenzy.

I put my watch away and leaned for a few moments against the wall of a building until the feeling had passed. My heart calmed down and I decided to return home.

To my joy, I saw that someone was standing on the street corner. His back was toward me. I rushed up to him and touched his arm. He turned quickly and to my horror I found that the man had no face under his soft felt hat.

I pulled my hand back and in the same moment the entire figure collapsed as if it were made of dust or frail splinters. On the sidewalk lay a pile of clothes. The person himself had disappeared without a trace.

I looked around in bewilderment and realized that I must have lost my way. I was in a part of the city where I had never been before.

I stood on an open square surrounded by high, ugly apartment buildings. From this narrow square, streets spread out in all directions. Everyone was dead; there was not a sign of a living soul.

High above me the sun shone completely white, and light forced its way down between the houses as if it were the blade of a razor-sharp knife. I was so cold that my entire body shivered.

Finally I found the strength to move again and chose one of the narrow streets at random. I walked as quickly as my pounding heart allowed, yet the street seemed to be endless.

Then I heard the tolling of bells and suddenly I was standing on another open square near an unattractive little church of red brick. There was no graveyard next to it and the church was surrounded on all sides by gray-walled buildings.

Not far from the church a funeral procession was wending its way slowly through the streets, led by an ancient hearse and followed by some old-fashioned hired carriages. These were pulled by pairs of meager-looking horses, weighed down under enormous black shabracks.

I stopped and uncovered my head. It was an intense relief to see living creatures, hear the sound of horses trotting and church bells ringing.

Then everything happened very quickly and so frighteningly that even as I write this I still feel a definite uneasiness.

The hearse was just about to turn in front of the church gate when suddenly it began to sway and rock like a ship in a storm. I saw that one of the wheels had come loose and was rolling toward me with a loud clatter. I had to throw myself to one side to avoid being hit. It struck the church wall right behind me and splintered into pieces.

The other carriages stopped at a distance but no one got out or came to help. The huge hearse swayed and teetered on its three wheels. Suddenly the coffin was thrown out and fell into the street. As if relieved, the hearse straightened and rolled on toward a side street, followed by the other carriages.

The tolling of the church bells had stopped and I stood alone with the overturned, partly smashed coffin. Gripped by a fearful curiosity, I approached. A hand stuck out from the pile of splintered boards. When I leaned forward, the dead hand clutched my arm and pulled me down toward the casket with enormous force. I struggled helplessly against it as the corpse slowly rose from the coffin. It was a man dressed in a frock coat.

To my horror, I saw that the corpse was myself. I tried to free my arm, but he held it in a powerful grip. All this time he stared at me without emotion and seemed to be smiling scornfully.

In this moment of senseless horror, I awakened and sat up in my bed. It was three in the morning and the sun was already reflecting from the rooftops opposite my window. I closed my eyes and I muttered words of reality against my dream — against all the evil and frightening dreams which have haunted me these last few years.

ISAK: My name is Isak Borg. I am still alive. I am seventy-six years old. I really feel quite well.

When I had muttered these words I felt calmer, drank a glass of water, and lay down to ponder on the day which was ahead of me. I knew immediately what I should do. I got out of bed, pulled open the curtains, found the weather radiant, and breathed in the fine morning air. Then I put on my robe and went through the apartment (where the clocks were striking three) to the room of my old housekeeper. When I opened the door she sat up immediately, wide awake.

AGDA: Are you ill, Professor?

ISAK: Listen, Miss Agda, will you please prepare some breakfast? I'm taking the car.

AGDA: You're taking the car, Professor?

ISAK: Yes, I'll drive down to Lund with my own two hands. I've never believed in airplanes.

AGDA: Dear Professor! Go back to sleep and I'll bring you coffee at nine o'clock and then we'll start at ten, as was decided.

ISAK: Very well then, I'll go without eating.

AGDA: And who's going to pack the frock coat?

ISAK: I'll do that myself.

AGDA: And what will become of me?

ISAK: Miss Agda, you can go with me in the car or take the airplane — that's up to you.

AGDA: For an entire year I've been looking forward to being present at the ceremony when you become a Jubilee Doctor, and everything was perfectly organized. Now you come and tell me that you're going to drive down instead of going by plane.

ISAK: The presentation is not until five o'clock, and if I leave at once I'll have fourteen hours in which to get there.

AGDA: Everything will be ruined that way. Your son will be waiting at Malmo airport. What will he say?

ISAK: You can make some explanation, Miss Agda.

AGDA: If you take the car, I won't be with you at the ceremony.

ISAK: Now listen, Miss Agda.

AGDA: You can take the car and drive there and destroy the most solemn day of my life . . .

ISAK: We are not married, Miss Agda.

AGDA: I thank God every night that we're not. For seventy-four years I have acted according to my own principles, and they won't fail me today.

ISAK: Is that your last word on this matter, Miss Agda?

AGDA: That is my last word. But I'll be saying a lot to myself about mean old gentlemen who think only of themselves and never about the feelings of others who have served them faithfully for forty years.

ISAK: I really don't know how I've been able to stand your immense hunger for power all these years.

AGDA: Just tell me and it can be ended tomorrow.

ISAK: Anyway, I'm going to drive, and you may do whatever the hell you want to. I'm a grown man and I don't have to put up with your bossiness.

Our last words, I must admit, were spoken rather loudly, partly because of Miss Agda's unruly temper and partly because I had gone to the bathroom, where I shaved and completed my morning toilet. When I came out of the bathroom, I found to my surprise that Miss Agda was busy packing my frock coat and other necessities. She seemed to have come to her senses and I tried a friendly pat on the back to make her understand that I had forgiven her.

ISAK: There is no one who can pack like you.

AGDA: Is that so.

ISAK: Old sourpuss.

I was very angry that she didn't answer. True, my last words weren't very well chosen, but Miss Agda has a way of being cross which would try the patience of a saint.

AGDA: Should I boil a couple of eggs to go with the coffee, sir?

ISAK: Yes, thank you, that's very kind of you, Miss Agda. Thank you, dear Miss Agda.

Without noticing my efforts to be nice in spite of everything, the old lady disappeared into the kitchen.

ISAK: Jubilee Doctor! Damn stupidity. The faculty could just as well make me jubilee idiot. I'm going to buy something for the old sourpuss to sweeten her up a little. I hate people who are slow to forget. I can't even hurt a fly; how could I ever hurt Miss Agda?

Then she appeared in the doorway.

AGDA: Do you want toast?

ISAK: No, thank you for everything. Don't trouble yourself over me.

AGDA: Why are *you* sour?

I didn't have time to answer before the door closed in my face. I dressed and went into the dining room, where my breakfast was waiting. The morning sun threw a bright stripe across the dining-room table. Miss Agda puttered about quietly with a coffee pot and poured steaming coffee into my personal cup.

ISAK: Won't you have a cup too?

AGDA: No, thanks.

Miss Agda went over to water the flowers in the window and turned her back to me quite naturally but in a very definite way. Then the door of a nearby room opened and my daughter-in-law, Marianne, entered. She was still wearing pajamas and was smoking a cigarette.

ISAK: May I ask why my esteemed daughter-in-law is out of bed at this hour of the morning?

MARIANNE: It's a little difficult to sleep when you and Miss Agda are shouting at each other loud enough to shake the walls.

ISAK: Surely no one here has been shouting.

AGDA: Of course not, no one here has been shouting.

MARIANNE: You're going by car to Lund.

ISAK: Yes, I think so.

MARIANNE: May I go with you?

ISAK: What? You want to go home?

MARIANNE: Yes, I want to go home.

ISAK: Home to Evald?

MARIANNE: That's it. You don't have to ask my reasons. If I could afford it, I would take the train.

ISAK: Of course you can go with me.

MARIANNE: I'll be ready in about ten minutes.

Marianne put out her cigarette in an ash tray on the table, went into her room and closed the door. Agda brought another cup but said nothing. We were both surprised but had to remain silent about Marianne's sudden decision to go home to my son Evald. Nevertheless, I felt obliged to shake my head.

AGDA: Good Lord!

Shortly after half past three, I drove my car out of the garage. Marianne came out through the front gate dressed in slacks and a short jacket (she is a stately young woman). I looked up toward the window to see if Agda was standing there. She was. I waved to her but she did not wave back. Angrily I got into the car, slammed the door and started the engine. Silently we left the quiet, sleeping city. Marianne was about to light a cigarette.

ISAK: Please don't smoke.

MARIANNE: Of course.

ISAK: I can't stand cigarette smoke.

MARIANNE: I forgot.

ISAK: Besides, cigarette smoking is both expensive and unhealthy. There should be a law against women smoking.

MARIANNE: The weather is nice.

ISAK: Yes, but oppressive. I have a feeling that we'll have a storm.

MARIANNE: So do I.

ISAK: Now take the cigar. Cigars are an expression of the fundamental idea of smoking. A stimulant and a relaxation. A manly vice.

MARIANNE: And what vices may a woman have?

ISAK: Crying, bearing children, and gossiping about the neighbors.

MARIANNE: How old are you really, Father Isak?

ISAK: Why do you want to know?

MARIANNE: No real reason. Why?

ISAK: I know why you asked.

MARIANNE: Oh.

ISAK: Don't pretend. You don't like me and you never have.

MARIANNE: I know you only as a father-in-law.

ISAK: Why are you going home again?

MARIANNE: An impulse. That's all.

ISAK: Evald happens to be my son.

MARIANNE: Yes, I'm sure he is.

ISAK: So, it may not be so strange that I ask you.

MARIANNE: This is something which really does not concern you.

ISAK: Do you want to hear my opinion?

She provoked me with her unshakable calm and remoteness. Besides, I was very curious and a little worried.

ISAK: Evald and I are very much alike. We have our principles.

MARIANNE: You don't have to tell me.

ISAK: This *loan* for example. Evald got a loan from me with which to complete his studies. He was to have paid it back when he became a lecturer at the university. It became a matter of honor for him to pay it back at the rate of five thousand per year. Although I realize that it's difficult for him, a bargain is a bargain.

MARIANNE: For us it means that we can never have a holiday together and that your son works himself to death.

ISAK: You have an income of your own.

MARIANNE: . . . Especially when you're stinking rich and have no need for the money.

ISAK: A bargain is a bargain, my dear Marianne. And I know that Evald understands and respects me.

MARIANNE: That may be true, but he also hates you.

Her calm, almost matter-of-fact tone startled me. I tried to look into her eyes, but she stared straight ahead and her face remained expressionless.

ISAK: Evald and I have never coddled each other.

MARIANNE: I believe you.

ISAK: I'm sorry that you dislike me, because I rather like you.

MARIANNE: That's nice.

ISAK: Tell me, what do you really have against me?

MARIANNE: Do you want me to be frank?

ISAK: Please.

MARIANNE: You are an old egotist, Father. You are completely inconsiderate and you have never listened to anyone but yourself. All this is well hidden behind your mask of old-fashioned charm and your friendliness. But you are hard as nails, even though everyone depicts you as a great humanitarian. We who have seen you at close range, we know what you really are. You can't fool us. For instance, do you remember when I came to you a month ago? I had some idiotic idea that you would help Evald and me. So I asked to stay with you for a few weeks. Do you remember what you said?

ISAK: I told you that you were most cordially welcome.

MARIANNE: This is what you really said, but I'm sure you've forgotten: Don't try to pull me into your marital problems because I don't give a damn about them, and everyone has his own troubles.

ISAK: Did I say that?

MARIANNE: You said more than that.

ISAK: That was the worst, I hope.

MARIANNE: This is what you said, word for word: I have no respect for suffering of the soul, so don't come to me and complain. But if you need spiritual masturbation, I can make an appointment for you with some good quack, or perhaps with a minister, it's so popular these days.

ISAK: Did I say that?

MARIANNE: You have rather inflexible opinions, Father. It would be terrible to have to depend on you in any way.

ISAK: Is that so. Now, if I am honest, I must say that I've enjoyed having you around the house.

MARIANNE: Like a cat.

ISAK: Like a cat, or a human being, it's the same thing. You are a fine young woman and I'm sorry that you dislike me.

MARIANNE: I don't dislike you.

ISAK: Oh.

MARIANNE: I feel sorry for you.

I could hardly keep from laughing at her odd tone of voice and lack of logic. She herself laughed, by the way, and it cleared the air a bit.

ISAK: I really would like to tell you about a dream I had this morning.

MARIANNE: I'm not very interested in dreams.

ISAK: No, perhaps not.

We drove for a while in silence. The sun stood high in the sky and the road was brilliantly white. Suddenly I had an impulse. I slowed down and swung the car into a small side road on the left, leading down to the sea. It was a twisting, forest road, bordered by piles of newly cut timber which smelled strongly in the heat of the sun. Marianne looked up, a bit surprised, but remained silent. I parked the car in a curve of the road.

ISAK: Come, I'll show you something.

She sighed quietly and followed me down the little hill to the gate. Now we could see the large yellow house set among the birch trees, with its terrace facing the bay. The house slept behind closed doors and drawn blinds.

ISAK: Every summer for the first twenty years of my life we lived out here. There were ten of us children. Yes, you probably know that.

MARIANNE: What a ridiculous old house.

ISAK: It is an antique.

MARIANNE: Do people live here now?

ISAK: Not this summer.

MARIANNE: I'll go down to the water and take a dip if you don't mind. We have lots of time.

ISAK: I'll go over to the wild-strawberry patch for a moment.

I suddenly found that I was speaking without a listener. Marianne was lazily making her way down to the beach.

ISAK: The old strawberry patch. . . .

I went toward the house and immediately found the spot, but it seemed to be much smaller and less impressive than I had remembered.

There were still many wild strawberries, however. I sat down next to an old apple tree that stood alone and ate the berries, one by one. I may very well have become a little sentimental. Perhaps I was a little tired and somewhat melancholy. It's not unlikely that I began to think about one thing or another that was associated with my childhood haunts.

I had a strange feeling of solemnity, as if this were a day of decision. (It was not the only time that day that I was to feel that way.) The quietness of the summer morning. The calm bay. The birds' brilliant concert in the foliage. The old sleeping house. The aromatic apple tree which leaned slightly, supporting my back. The wild strawberries.

I don't know how it happened, but the day's clear reality flowed into dreamlike images. I don't even know if it was a dream, or memories which arose with the force of real events. I do not know how it began either, but I think that it was when I heard the playing of a piano.

Astonished, I turned my head and looked at the house, a short distance up the hill. It had been transformed in a strange way. The facade, which only a few moments ago was so blind and shut, was now alive and the sun glittered on the open windows. White curtains swayed in the warm summer breeze. The gaudy awnings were rolled halfway down; smoke came from the chimney. The old summerhouse seemed to be bursting with life. You could hear the music of the piano (it was something by Waldteufel), happy voices echoing through the open windows, laughter, footsteps, the cries of children, the squeaking of the pump. Someone started to sing up there on the second floor. It was a strong, almost Italian *bel-canto* tenor. In spite of all this, not a human being was in sight. For a few moments the scene still had a feeling of unreality, like a mirage which could instantly evaporate and be lost in silence.

Suddenly I saw her. When I turned around after looking at the strangely transformed house I discovered her where she was kneeling in her sun-yellow cotton dress, picking wild strawberries. I recognized her immediately and I became excited. She was so close to me that I could touch her, but my lingering feeling of the evanescence of the situation prevented me from making her notice my presence. (I was amused. Mental image or dream or whatever this was, she looked just as I remembered her: a girl in a yellow summer dress, freckled and tanned and glowing with light-hearted young womanhood.)

I sat for a few minutes and silently looked at her. Finally I couldn't help calling out her name, rather quietly but nevertheless quite audibly. She didn't react. I tried once more, a little louder.

ISAK: Sara . . . It's me, your cousin Isak. . . . I've become a little old, of course, and do not quite look as I used to. But you haven't changed the slightest bit. Little cousin, can't you hear me?

She didn't hear me, but eagerly continued to pick the wild strawberries, putting them into a small straw basket. I understood then that one cannot easily converse with one's memories. This discovery did not make me particularly sad. I decided to keep quiet and hoped that this unusual and pleasant situation would last as long as possible.

Then, a boy came strolling down the hill. He was already growing a small mustache despite the fact that he couldn't have been more than eighteen or nineteen years old. He was dressed in a shirt and trousers and wore his student's cap pushed way back on his head. He stepped right behind Sara, took off his glasses and wiped them with a large white handkerchief. (I recognized him as my brother Sigfrid, one year older than myself. We shared many happy moments and troubles. He died, by the way, relatively young, of pyclitis. He was a lecturer in Slavic languages at Uppsala University.)

SIGFRID: Good morning, sweet cousin. What are you doing?

SARA: Can't you see that I'm picking wild strawberries, stupid?

SIGFRID: And who shall be favored with these tasty berries, plucked in the morning watch by a dulcet young maiden?

SARA: Oh you! Don't you know that Uncle Aron's birthday is today? I forgot to prepare a present for him. So, he gets a basket of wild strawberries. That's good enough, isn't it?

SIGFRID: I'll help you.

SARA: You know, Charlotta and Sigbritt have sewn a sampler for him and Angelica has baked a cake and Anna has painted a really pretty picture and Kristina and Birgitta have written a song which they'll sing.

SIGFRID: That's the best of all, because Uncle Aron is stone deaf.

SARA: He will be very happy and you are stupid.

SIGFRID: And the nape of your neck is deuced pretty.

Sigfrid quickly bent over the girl and rather gallantly kissed her on her downy neck. Sara became rather annoyed.

SARA: You know that you're not allowed to do that.

SIGFRID: Who said so?

SARA: I said so. Besides, you are a particularly unbearable little snot who thinks he's something.

SIGFRID: I'm your cousin, and you're sweet on me.

SARA: On you!

SIGFRID: Come here and I'll kiss you on the mouth.

SARA: If you don't keep away I'll tell Isak that you try to kiss me all the time.

SIGFRID: Little Isak. I can beat him easily with one hand tied behind my back.

SARA: Isak and I are secretly engaged. You know that very well.

SIGFRID: Yes, your engagement is so secret that the whole house knows about it.

SARA: Could I help it if the twins ran around and blabbered everything?

SIGFRID: Then when are you going to get married? When are you going to get married? When are you going to get married? When are you going to get married?

SARA: I'll tell you one thing, of your four brothers I can't decide which is the least vain. But I think it's Isak. In any case, he's the kindest. And you are the most awful, the most unbearable, the most stupid, the most idiotic, the most ridiculous, the most cocky — I can't think of enough names to call you.

SIGFRID: Admit that you're a little sweet on me.

SARA: Besides, you smoke smelly cigars.

SIGFRID: That's a man's smell, isn't it?

SARA: Besides, the twins, who know *everything*, say that you've done *rather* nasty things with the oldest Berglund girl. And she's not a *really nice* girl, the twins say. And I believe them.

SIGFRID: If you only knew how pretty you are when you blush like that. Now you must kiss me. I can't stand it any more. I'm completely in love with you, now that I think about it.

SARA: Oh, that's only talk. The twins say that you're crazy about girls. Is it really true?

Suddenly he kissed her hard and rather skillfully. She was carried away by this game and returned his kiss with a certain fierceness. But then she was conscience-stricken and threw herself down on the ground, knocking over the basket of wild strawberries. She was very angry and began crying with excitement.

SIGFRID: Don't scream. Someone might come.

SARA: Look at the wild strawberries, all spilled. And what will Isak say? He is so kind and really loves me. Oh, how sorry I am, oh, what you've done to me. You've turned me into a bad woman, at least *nearly*. Go away. I don't want to see you any more, at least not before breakfast. I have to hurry. Help me pick up the strawberries. And look, I have a spot on my gown.

Then the gong suddenly sounded, announcing that breakfast was being served. The sound seemed to bring forth many human beings not far from where I stood, an astonished onlooker.

The flag with the Swedish-Norwegian Union emblem went up and instantly stiffened against the light summer clouds; big brother Hagbart, dressed in his cadet uniform, handled the ropes expertly. From the bathhouse one could hear wild laughter, and through the louvered door tumbled two redheaded girls about thirteen years old, as identical as two wild strawberries. They laughed so hard they could hardly walk, and they whispered things to each other that were apparently both very secret and quite amusing. Sigbritt, tall and lanky, with thick hair in heavy rolls across her forehead, came out carrying the baby's bassinet and placed it in the shadow of the arbor. Charlotta (the diligent, self-sacrificing sister who carried the responsibilities of the household on her round shoulders) rushed out on the veranda and shouted to Sara and Sigfrid to hurry. Seventeen-year-old Benjamin dived out of some bushes, his pimply face red from the sun, and looked around with an annoyed expression. In his hand he held a thick, open book. Angelica (the beauty of the family) came skipping out of the woods, joined the twins, and was immediately made part of some hilarious secret. Finally, fifteen-year-old Anna came running out of the house, asked Hagbart about something, then raised her voice and started to shout for Isak. I arose, surprised and worried, unable to answer her cry.

TWINS (*in unison*): I think that Isak is out fishing with Father and they probably can't hear the gong. And Father said, by the way, that we shouldn't wait to eat. That's what Father said, I definitely remember.

Oh, yes, Father and I were out fishing together. I felt a secret and completely inexplicable happiness at this message, and I stood for a long while wondering what I should do in this new old world which I was suddenly given the opportunity to visit.

The rest of the family had entered the house and something was being discussed quite loudly inside. Only Sigbritt's little child remained on the terrace, sleeping in the shadows of the tall lilac bushes.

Curiosity overwhelmed me. I went slowly up the slope toward the house and soon found myself in the long, dark corridor which was connected with the foyer by glass doors. From there I had a good view into the large, sunlit dining room with its white table already set for breakfast, the light furniture, the wallpaper, the figurines, the palms, the airy summer curtains, the scoured white wooden floor with its broad planks and blue rag rugs, the pictures and the sampler, the large, crownlike chandelier.

There they were now, my nine brothers and sisters, my aunt, and Uncle Aron. The only ones missing were Father, Mother and I.

Everyone was standing behind his chair, with lowered head, and hands clenched together. Aunt recited the prayer "In Jesus' name to the table we go/, Bless You for the food You bestow." After which the whole troop sat down with much chatter and scraping of chairs. My aunt (a stately woman in her best years, endowed with a powerful sense of authority and a resonant voice) demanded silence.

AUNT: Benjamin will immediately go and wash his hands. How long is it going to take you to learn cleanliness?

BENJAMIN: I *have* washed my hands.

AUNT: Sigbritt, pass the porridge to Angelica and give the twins their portions. Your fingernails are coal-black. Pass me the bread, Hagbart. Who taught you to spread so much butter on the bread? Can you do that at the military academy? Charlotta, the salt shaker is stopped up. How often have I told you that it shouldn't be left out in the open, because the salt gets humid.

BENJAMIN: *I have washed my hands,* but I have paint under my nails.

UNCLE ARON: Who has picked wild strawberries for me?

SARA: I have. (*Louder*) I have.

AUNT: You have to speak up, my child. You know that Uncle Aron is a bit hard of hearing.

SARA (*thunderously*): *I have!*

ARON: Oh my, you remembered Uncle Aron's birthday. That was really very kind of you.

HAGBART: Couldn't Uncle Aron have a little drink for breakfast in honor of the day?

AUNT: A drink at breakfast when Father isn't home is completely out of the question.

TWINS (*in unison*): Uncle Aron has already had three drinks. I know. I know. We saw him at eight o'clock when we went down to the bathhouse.

AUNT: The twins should hold their tongues and eat. Besides, you haven't made your beds and as punishment you'll have to dry the dinner silverware. Benjamin must not bite his nails. Don't sit and jump on the chair, Anna. You aren't a child any more.

ANNA: I want to give Uncle Aron my picture, please, Auntie. Can't we give him our presents now, right away?

AUNT: Where is your picture?

ANNA: Here under the table.

AUNT: You'll have to wait until we've eaten.

SIGFRID: It's a very advanced work of art, I'd say. It's a picture of Tristan and Isolde, but you can't tell for sure which one is Tristan.

SARA: Oh, he always spoils things, the little fop! Now he's making Anna unhappy. See if she doesn't start to cry.

ANNA: Not at all. I can overlook Sigfrid's faults.

TWINS (*together*): By the way, what were Sara and Sigfrid up to in the wild-strawberry patch this morning? We saw everything from the bathhouse.

SIGBRITT: Calm down now, children!

CHARLOTTA: Someone should put gags on the twins.

AUNT: Twins, keep still or leave the table.

BENJAMIN: Doesn't a person have freedom of expression, eh?

SIGFRID: Shut up, you snotnoses.

ANGELICA: Sara is blushing, Sara is blushing, Sara is blushing.

TWINS: Sigfrid is blushing, too. Ha-ha! Sigfrid and Sara! Sigfrid and Sara! Sigfrid and Sara!

AUNT (*thunderously*): Quiet! We'll have quiet at the table!

ARON: What did you say? Of course we shall be happy.

The twins snicker in the silence. Sara throws the porridge spoon at her tormentors.

CHARLOTTA: But, Sara!

SARA: They're just lying. They're liars!

Sara rose from the table so violently that her chair turned over. She stood hesitantly for a moment, her face red and tears splashing down her cheeks. Then she ran away furiously, throwing herself at the door and out into the foyer.

She opened the glass door and disappeared out on the porch, where I could hear her sobbing violently. Gentle Charlotta came out of the dining room and went past me on her way to console Sara.

I could hear their voices from the darkness of the foyer and I came closer stealthily. Sara sat on a red stool (which Grandmother once used, when she wanted to take off her rubber boots) while Charlotta stood in front of her, patting her gently on the head. The miserable girl pressed her tear-stained face against Charlotta's skirt over and over again. The tinted light from the stained-glass windows of the outer door painted the whole picture in a strange way.

SARA: Isak is so refined. He is so enormously refined and moral and sensitive and he wants us to read poetry together and he talks about the after-life and wants to play duets on the piano and he likes to kiss only in the dark and he talks about sinfulness. I think he is extremely intellectual and morally aloof and I feel so worthless, and I *am* so worthless, you can't deny that. But sometimes I get the feeling that I'm much older than Isak, do you know what I mean? And then I think he's a child even if we are the same age, and then Sigfrid is so fresh and exciting and I want to go home. I don't want to be here all summer, to be a laughingstock for the twins and the rest of you — *no, I don't want that.*

CHARLOTTA: I'll talk to Sigfrid, I will! If he doesn't leave you alone I'll see to it that he gets a few more chores to do. Father will arrange that without any trouble. He also thinks Sigfrid is nasty and needs a little work to keep him out of mischief.

SARA: Poor little Isak, he is so kind to me. Oh, how unfair everything is.

CHARLOTTA: Everything will work out for the best, you'll see. Listen, now they're singing for Uncle Aron.

SARA: Isn't it crazy to write a song for a deaf man! That's typical of the twins.

Then two girlish voices sang a song that could be heard throughout the house. Charlotta placed her arm around Sara's shoulders, and Sara blew her nose quite loudly. Both girls returned to the dining room, where the mood had become very lively. Uncle Aron had arisen, his round perspiring face lit like a lantern, and he had tears in his eyes. He held a sheet of music before him while the twins stood nearby and sang with all their might. When they had finished everyone applauded, and Uncle Aron kissed them on the forehead and wiped his face with a napkin. My aunt rose from the table and proposed a quadruple cheer. Everyone got up and hurrahed. Suddenly Anna shouted and pointed out the window. Everyone turned to look.

ANNA: Look, here comes Father.

AUNT: Well, finally! Sigbritt, take out the porridge bowl and have it warmed. Charlotta, you bring up more milk from the cellar.

The women fussed around, but Sara ran out of the house, down the slope, and disappeared behind the small arbor which stood on the edge of the birch-tree pasture. I followed her with curiosity, but lost her. Suddenly I stood alone at the wild-strawberry patch. A feeling of emptiness and sadness came over me. I was awakened by a girl's voice asking me something. I looked up.

In front of me stood a young lady in shorts and a boy's checked shirt. She was very tanned, and her blond hair was tangled and bleached by the sun and the sea. She sucked on an unlit pipe, wore wooden sandals on her feet and dark glasses on her nose.

SARA: Is this your shack?

ISAK: No, it isn't.

SARA: It's a good thing you're the truthful type. My old man owns the whole peninsula . . . including the shack.

ISAK: I lived here once. Two hundred years ago.

SARA: Uh huh. Is that your jalopy standing up at the gate?

ISAK: It's my jalopy, yes.

SARA: Looks like an antique.

ISAK: It *is* an antique, just like its owner.

SARA: You've got a sense of humor about yourself, too. That's fantastic. Where are you heading, by the way? In which direction, I mean.

ISAK: I'm going to Lund.

SARA: What a fantastic coincidence. I'm on my way to Italy.

ISAK: I'd feel very honored if you came along.

SARA: My name is Sara. Silly name, isn't it?

ISAK: My name is Isak. Rather silly too.

SARA: Weren't they married?

ISAK: Unfortunately not. It was Abraham and Sara.

SARA: Shall we take off?

ISAK: I have another lady with me. Here she comes. This is Sara, and this is Marianne. We'll have company to Lund. Sara is going to Italy but she has agreed to travel part way with us.

SARA: Now you're being ironic again, but it suits you.

We began walking toward the car. Marianne and I exchanged amused glances, the first contact between us. When we came to the car, two young men with round blond crew-cut heads popped up. They were also wearing checked shirts, shorts, wooden sandals and sunglasses. Each carried a rucksack.

SARA: Hey, fellows. I've got a lift nearly all the way to Italy. This is Anders, and this one with the glasses is Viktor, called Vicke . . . and this is Father Isak.

VIKTOR: Hello.

ISAK: Hello.

ANDERS: How do you do, sir.

ISAK: Hello.

SARA: That cookie you're staring at so hard, her name is Marianne.

MARIANNE: Hello.

BOYS (*together*): Hello.

SARA: It's a pretty big car.

ISAK: Just jump in. There's room for everybody. We can put the baggage in the trunk, if you don't mind.

We packed things away, and then we all got into the car. I drove carefully, leaving my childhood world behind. Sara took off her sunglasses and laughed. She was very much like her namesake of the past.

SARA: Of course I have to tell Isak that Anders and I are going steady. We are crazy about each other. Viktor is with us as a chaperon. That was decided by the old man. Viktor is also in love with me and is watching Anders like a madman. This was a brilliant idea of my old man. I'll probably have to seduce Viktor to get him out of the way. I'd better tell Isak that I'm a virgin. That's why I can talk so brazenly.

I looked at her through the rear-view mirror. She was sitting comfortably with her legs on the backs of the folding seats. Anders had a proprietary arm around her shoulders and looked rather angry, for which I could hardly blame him. Viktor, on the other hand, seemed completely disinterested and stared fixedly at the nape of Marianne's neck — and whatever else he could glimpse of her figure.

SARA: I smoke a pipe. Viktor says it's healthier. He's crazy about everything that's healthy.

No one answered, or considered any comment necessary. We continued our trip in a silence which was by no means unpleasant, just a little shy. The weather had become quite warm, almost oppressive, and we had opened all the windows. The road was broad and straight. I was in a spirited mood. The day had been full of stimulating surprises.

Ingmar Bergman / 771

ISAK: I had a first love whose name was Sara.

SARA: She was like me, of course.

ISAK: As a matter of fact, she was rather like you.

SARA: What happened to her?

ISAK: She married my brother Sigfrid and had six children. Now she's seventy-five years old and a rather beautiful little old lady.

SARA: I can't imagine anything worse than getting old. Oh, excuse me. I think I said something stupid.

Her tone was so sincerely repentant that everyone burst into laughter. And then it happened.

We were on a broad, blind right curve. I kept hard to the left and at that moment a little black car came speeding straight toward us. I had time to see Marianne brace her right hand against the windshield and I heard Sara scream. Then I slammed on the brakes with all my strength. Our big car skidded to the left and went off the road into a pasture. The black car disappeared with a squeal, rolled over and fell into a deep ditch to the right of the road. Startled, we stared at one another, we had escaped without a scratch. Some thick black tire tracks and several big marks on the road surface were the only signs of the other car. A short distance away, a couple of rotating front wheels stuck up from the ditch.

All of us began running toward it and then stopped in astonishment. The overturned car's radio sang a morning hymn. Two people crawled out of the ditch, a man and a woman, in the midst of a violent quarrel which was on the verge of coming to blows. When they saw us watching they immediately stopped and the man limped toward me.

ALMAN: How are you? There's nothing for me to say. The blame is completely ours. We have no excuses. It was my wife who was driving. Are you all right? Everyone safe and sound? Thank God for that.

He mumbled nervously, took off his eyeglasses and put them on again, and looked at us with frightened glances.

ALMAN: The would-be murderers should introduce themselves. Alman is my name. I'm an engineer at the Stockholm electric power plant. Back there is my wife, Berit. She used to be an actress, and it was that fact we were discussing when . . . when . . . when . . .

He interrupted himself with an artificial laugh and waved at his wife. When she remained motionless, he took a few limping steps toward her.

ISAK: How is your leg?

ALMAN: It's not from this. I've been crippled for years. Unfortunately it's not only my leg that's crippled, according to my wife. Come here now, Berit, and make your apologies.

The woman mustered her courage. She moved jerkily in spite of her rotund body.

BERIT: Please, pretty please forgive me, as children say. It was my fault, everything. I was just going to hit my husband when that curve appeared. One thing is obvious: God punishes some people immediately — or what do you think, Sten? You're a Catholic.

ISAK: Perhaps we should take a look at your car and see if we can't put it right side up again.

ALMAN: Please don't trouble yourself over us. I beg of you.

BERIT: Shut up now, Sten darling. Some people do have completely unselfish intentions, even if you don't believe it.

ALMAN: My wife is a little nervous, I think. But we've had a shock. That's the word. A shock.

He laughed once more and tore off his glasses and put them on again. The young men had already jumped down into the ditch and were trying to lift the little car. Marianne ran back to our car and backed it down the road. With the help of a rope which I always carry in the trunk, we succeeded in getting the other car on an even keel. Mr. Alman suddenly cheered up, threw off his jacket and rolled up his shirt sleeves. Then he put his shoulder alongside Sara, Viktor and Anders and began to push.

BERIT: Now watch the engineer closely, see how he matches his strength with the young boys, how he tenses his feeble muscles to impress the pretty girl. Sten darling, watch out that you don't have a hemorrhage.

ALMAN: My wife loves to embarrass me in front of strangers. I let her — it's psychotherapy.

We towed and shoved and pushed and suddenly the little car was standing on the road. By then, of course, its radio had gone dead. Alman sat down behind the wheel of the dented car and got the motor started. The car had gone a few feet when one of the front wheels rolled off abruptly and slid far down into the ravine.

BERIT: A true picture of our marriage.

Alman stood hesitantly on the gleaming white road, perspiring nervously. Marianne, who had stayed out of the whole scene, was still sitting behind the wheel of our car. The youngsters sat down at the edge of the road. All of us were a little upset.

ISAK: I can't see any other way out. The lady and the gentleman must ride with us to the nearest gas station. There you can telephone for help.

ALMAN: Don't trouble yourself over us. We'll have a refreshing walk. Won't we, Berit?

BERIT: With his leg. Dear Lord, that would be a scream.

ALMAN: In her delightful way my wife has just said thank you for both of us.

Silently we climbed into the car, which was suddenly completely filled. (Marianne drove; I sat beside her. Mr. and Mrs. Alman were on the folding seats. The three youngsters occupied the back seat.) Alman whistled some popular tune softly but soon fell silent. No one had any particular desire to converse. Marianne drove very calmly and carefully.

Suddenly Berit Alman started to cry. Her husband carefully put his arm around her shoulders, but she drew away and pulled out a handkerchief, which she began tearing with her fingernails.

ALMAN: I can never tell if my wife is really crying or putting on an act. Dammit, I think these are real tears. Well, that's the way it is when you see death staring you in the face.

BERIT: Can't you shut up?

ALMAN: My wife has unusual powers of the imagination. For two years she made me believe that she had cancer and pestered all our friends with all kinds of imaginary symptoms, despite the fact that the doctors couldn't find anything the matter. She was so convincing that we believed her more than the doctors. That's pretty clever, admit it. It's such stuff that saints are made of! Look, now she's crying about a death scare. It's a pity we don't have a movie camera around. Lights! Action! Camera! It's a "take," as they say in the film world.

MARIANNE: It's understandable that you're upset, Mr. Alman, but how about leaving your wife alone for a little while?

ALMAN: A woman's tears are meant for women. Don't criticize a woman's tears; they're holy. You are beautiful, dear Miss whatever your name is. But Berit here is beginning to get a little shabby. That's why you can afford to defend her.

MARIANNE: Allow me to feel compassion for your wife for different reasons.

ALMAN: Very sarcastic! Still, you don't seem to be at all hysterical. But Berit is a genius at hysterics. Do you know what that means from my point of view?

MARIANNE: You're a Catholic, aren't you? That's what your wife said.

ALMAN: Quite right. That is my way of enduring. I ridicule my wife and she ridicules me. She has her hysterics and I have my Catholicism. But we need each other's company. It's only out of pure selfishness that we haven't murdered each other by now.

Berit turned toward her husband and slapped his face. He dropped his glasses, which he had fortunately just taken off. His large nose swelled and began to bleed. His froglike mouth twitched spasmodically as if he were on the verge of tears, but he immediately got control of himself, pulled out a handkerchief and pressed it to his nose, blinked his eyes and laughed. Viktor leaned forward, picked up the glasses and slowly handed them to him.

ALMAN: Right on the beat. It's called syncopation, isn't it? Ha-ha! Isn't it comic? If I had a stop watch, I could have timed the explosion on the nose.

BERIT(screams): Shut up! Shut up! Shut up!

Marianne turned pale. She applied the brakes and slowly stopped the car.

MARIANNE: Maybe this is the terrible truth and maybe it's just what's called letting off steam. But we have three children in the car and for their sake may I ask the lady and the gentleman to get out immediately. There is a house back there; maybe they have a telephone. The walk won't be too strenuous.

All of us were silent after Marianne's speech. Without another word, Sten Alman stepped out of the car. His face was ashen gray and his nose was still bleeding. His wife looked at us and suddenly made a heroic attempt to say something sincere.

BERIT: Forgive us if you can.

Then Berit got out and stood by her husband, who had turned his back on us. He had pulled out a comb and a pocket mirror and was straightening the hair on his white scalp. His wife took his bloody handkerchief and blew her nose. Then she touched his elbow, but he was suddenly very tired and hung his head. They sat down close to each other by the road. They looked like two scolded schoolchildren sitting in a corner.

Marianne started the car, and we quickly drove away from this strange marriage.

The gas station between Gränna and Huskvarna lies on a hill with a wide view over a very beautiful, richly foliaged landscape. We stopped to fill up the tank and decided to have lunch at a hotel some kilometers farther south.

It was with mixed feelings that I saw this region again. First, because I began my medical practice here (incidentally, it lasted for fifteen years; I succeeded the local doctor). Second, because my old mother lives near here in a large house. She is ninety-six now and is generally considered a miracle of health and vitality, although her ability to move around has diminished considerably during the last few years.

The gas-station owner was a big, blond man with a broad face, abnormally large hands and long arms.

AKERMAN: Ah ha! So the doctor is out driving. Shall it be a full tank? Well, well, so it is, and those are children and grandchildren, I know. Have you got the key to the gas tank, Doctor?

ISAK: Hello, Henrik. You recognize me.

AKERMAN: Recognize! Doctor, you were there when I was born. And then you delivered all my brothers. And fixed our cuts and scratches and took care of us, as you did of everybody while you were a doctor around here.

ISAK: And things are going well for you?

AKERMAN: Couldn't be better! I'm married, you know, and I have heirs. (*Shouts*) Eva!

Eva came out of the gas station. She was a young woman, gypsy-like, dark, with long, thick hair and a generous smile. She was in an advanced stage of pregnancy.

AKERMAN: Here you see Dr. Borg himself in person. This is the man that Ma and Pa and the whole district still talk about. The world's best doctor.

I looked at Marianne, who was standing to the side. She applauded somewhat sarcastically and bowed. The three youngsters were in the midst of a lively dispute and pointing in different directions. Eva stepped up and shook my hand.

AKERMAN: I suggest that we name our new baby for the doctor. Isak Akerman is a good name for a prime minister.

EVA: But what if it's a girl?

AKERMAN: Eva and I only make boys. Do you want oil and water too?

ISAK: Yes, thank you. And your father is well, in spite of his bad back?

AKERMAN: Well, it's getting a bit hard for the old man, you know, but the old lady is a little bombshell.

The last was said in greatest confidence as we bent over the measuring rod to see if we needed more oil. We did.

AKERMAN: And now you'll be visiting *your* mother, eh, Doctor?

ISAK: I suppose so.

AKERMAN: She's a remarkable lady, your mother, although she must be at least ninety-five.

ISAK: Ninety-six.

AKERMAN: Well, well, how about that.

ISAK: How much is all this?

AKERMAN: Eva and I want it to be on the house.

ISAK: No, I can't allow that.

AKERMAN: Don't insult us, Doctor! We can do things in the grand manner too, even if we live here in little Granna.

ISAK: There isn't the slightest reason you should pay for my gas. I appreciate your kindness, but . . .

AKERMAN: One remembers things, you know. One doesn't forget one's gratitude, and there are some things that can never be paid back.

Akerman became a little serious and I a little sentimental. We looked at each other quite moved. Eva stepped up and stood beside her husband. She squinted in the sun and beamed like a big strawberry in her red dress.

EVA (*like an echo*): No, we don't forget. We don't forget.

AKERMAN: Just ask anybody in town or in the hills around here, and they remember the doctor and know what the doctor did for them.

I looked around, but Marianne had disappeared. No, she had got into the car. The youngsters were still busy with their discussion.

ISAK: Perhaps I should have remained here.

AKERMAN: I don't understand.

ISAK: What? What did you say, Henrik?

AKERMAN: You said that you should have stayed here, Doctor.

ISAK: Did I say that? Yes, perhaps. Thank you anyway. Send me word and I may come to be godfather for the new Akerman. You know where to reach me.

I shook hands with them and we parted. Marianne called the youngsters and we continued our trip to the inn.

Our lunch was a success. We had a large table on the open terrace and enjoyed a most magnificent view across Lake Vattern. The head-waiter, one of my former patients, did everything to satisfy our slightest wish.

I became very lively, I must admit, and told the youngsters about my years as a country doctor. I told them humorous anecdotes which had a great deal of human interest. These were a great success (I don't think they laughed just out of politeness) and I had wine with the food (which was excellent) and cognac with my coffee.

Anders suddenly rose and began to recite with both feeling and talent.

ANDERS: "Oh, when such beauty shows itself in each facet of creation, then how beautiful must be the eternal source of this emanation!"

None of us thought of laughing at him. He sat down immediately and emptied his coffee cup in embarrassment. Sara was the one who broke the silence.

SARA: Anders will become a minister and Viktor a doctor.

VIKTOR: We swore that we wouldn't discuss God or science on the entire trip. I consider Anders' lyrical outburst as a breach of our agreement.

SARA: Oh, it was beautiful!

VIKTOR: Besides, I can't understand how a modern man can become a minister. Anders isn't a complete idiot.

ANDERS: Let me tell you, your rationalism is incomprehensible nonsense. And you aren't an idiot either.

VIKTOR: In my opinion the modern —

ANDERS: In my opinion—

VIKTOR: In my opinion a modern man looks his insignificance straight in the eye and believes in himself and his biological death. Everything else is nonsense.

ANDERS: And in my opinion modern man exists only in your imagination.

Because man looks at his death with horror and can't bear his own insignificance.

VIKTOR: All right. Religion for the people. Opium for the aching limb. If that's what you want.

SARA: Aren't they fantastically sweet? I always agree with the one who's spoken last. Isn't this all extremely interesting?

VIKTOR (*angry*): When you were a child you believed in Santa Claus. Now you believe in God.

ANDERS: And you have always suffered from an astonishing lack of imagination.

VIKTOR: What do you think about it, Professor?

ISAK: Dear boys, you would receive my opinion with ironic indulgence, whatever I happened to say. That's why I'm keeping still.

SARA: Then think how very unlucky they are.

ISAK: No, Sara. They are very, very lucky.

Marianne laughed and lit my cigar. I leaned back in my chair and squinted at the light filtering down between the table umbrellas. The boys looked surprised as I began to recite.

ISAK: "Where is the friend I seek everywhere? Dawn is the time of loneliness and care. When twilight comes, when twilight comes . . ." What comes after that, Anders?

MARIANNE: "When twilight comes I am still yearning."

ANDERS: "Though my heart is burning, burning. I see His trace of glory . . ."

SARA: You're religious, aren't you, Professor?

ISAK: "I see His trace of glory and power, In an ear of grain and the fragrance of flower . . . ."

MARIANNE: "In every sign and breath of air. His love is there. His voice whispers in the summer breeze . . ."

(*Silence*)

VIKTOR: As a love poem, it isn't too bad.

SARA: Now I've become very solemn. I can become quite solemn for no reason at all.

I rose from the table.

ISAK: I want to pay a visit to my mother, who happens to live nearby. You can remain here and enjoy yourselves for a while. I'll be back soon.

MARIANNE: May I come with you?

ISAK: Of course. Goodbye for now, young friends.

I was in a good mood and felt very happy. Marianne suddenly took my arm and walked beside me. In passing, I patted her hand.

The house was surrounded by an ancient, parklike garden and protected from onlookers by a wall as tall as a man. Inside, everything was quiet and somewhat unreal. The sky had clouded over, and the gray light sharpened the contours of the landscape so that it looked like a skillfully painted set in an old theater.

In a little round drawing room filled with storm-gray light and graced by light, delicate furniture, an old nurse in uniform sat embroidering. On the carpet next to her chair a fat white poodle lay looking at us with sleepy, lidded eyes. When the nurse saw us she immediately arose, smiling politely, to greet us and shake our hands. She introduced herself as Sister Elisabet. I asked her quietly how my mother was and if it was convenient for us to visit her. Sister Elisabet answered that Mrs. Borg was quite well and would be happy with our visit because she was usually rather lonely. I pointed out that it was unfortunate that my visits were rather infrequent, because of the difficult journey, and Sister Elisabet said that she understood. After this hushed introduction, the Sister asked us to wait for a few minutes and disappeared into a nearby room. Marianne became a little nervous with all the solemnity and pulled out a cigarette from a crushed pack and was just about to light it.

ISAK: Please don't smoke. Mother hates the smell of tobacco and her senses are as sharp as those of an animal in the woods.

At the same moment, Sister Elisabet returned and told us that we were welcome.

The room was rather small and oddly irregular, but it had a lofty ceiling. On the walls hung many beautiful and expensive paintings. Heavy draperies covered the doors. In a corner stood a tall porcelain stove with a fire burning. At the room's only window stood an incongruous desk which did not harmonize with the other pieces of furniture. My mother was sitting in a big chair. She was dressed entirely in black and wore a small lace cap on her head. She was busy entering figures in a large blue ledger. When she recognized me, she immediately rose from her seat (although with some difficulty) and walked toward us with many small steps; she seemed to be shoving one foot in front of the other without her soles ever leaving the floor. She smiled cordially and stretched forth both her hands. I grasped them and then kissed her with a son's reverence.

MOTHER: I just sent a telegram to tell you that I was thinking about you today. Today is your big day. And then you come here!

ISAK: Well, I had a moment of inspiration, Mother!

MOTHER: Is that your wife standing back there, Isak? You will ask her to leave the room immediately. I refuse to talk with her. She has hurt us too much.

ISAK: Mother, darling, this is not Karin. This is Evald's wife, my daughter-in-law, Marianne!

MOTHER: Well, then, she can come here and greet me.

MARIANNE: How do you do, Mrs. Borg. (*Curtsies*)

MOTHER: I've seen you in a photograph. Evald showed it to me. He was extremely proud of your beauty. By the way, why are you out traveling this way?

MARIANNE: I've been in Stockholm, visiting.

MOTHER: Why aren't you home with Evald and taking care of your child?

MARIANNE: Evald and I don't have any children.

MOTHER: Isn't it strange with young people nowadays? I bore ten children. Will someone please bring me that large box standing over there.

She pointed at a brown cardboard box on a chair. Marianne picked it up and placed it on the desk in front of the old lady. Both of us helped lift the lid.

MOTHER: My mother lived in this house before me. And you children often visited here. Do you remember, Isak?

ISAK: I remember quite well.

MOTHER: In this box are some of your toys. I've tried to think which of you owned what.

Mother looked bewilderedly into the big box, as if she expected to find all her children there among the toys and things. Then she shook her head and looked up at Marianne.

MOTHER: Ten children, and all of them dead except Isak. Twenty grand-children. None of them visits me except Evald, once a year. It's quite all right — I don't complain — but I have fifteen great-grandchildren whom I've never seen. I send letters and presents for fifty-three birthdays and anniversaries every year. I get kind thank-you notes, but no one visits me except by accident or when someone needs a loan. I am tiresome, of course.

ISAK: Don't look at it that way, Mother dear!

MOTHER: And then I have another fault. I don't die. The inheritance doesn't materialize according to the nice, neat schedules made up by smart young people.

She laughed sarcastically and shook her head. Then she pulled a doll out of the box. It was an old doll, with fine gold hair and a porcelain face (a little scratched) and a beautiful lace gown.

MOTHER: This doll's name is Goldcrown and it belonged to Sigbritt. She got it when she was eight years old. I sewed the dress myself. She never liked it much, so Charlotta took it over and cared for it. I remember it clearly.

She dropped the doll and picked up a little box of bright-colored tin soldiers and poked in it with a small, sharp finger.

MOTHER: Hagbart's tin soldiers. I never liked his war games. He was shot while hunting moose. We never understood each other.

This she said in a matter-of-fact tone, completely without sentimentality. She threw the tin soldiers into the box and fished up a photograph.

MOTHER: Can you see who this is? This is Sigfrid when he was three years old and you when you were two, and here is Father and me. Good Lord, how one looked in those days. It was taken in 1883.

ISAK: May I see that picture?

MOTHER (*uninterested*): Yes, of course, you can have it. It's only trash. Here is a coloring book. Maybe it belonged to the twins, or perhaps to Anna or Angelica. I really don't know because all of them have put their names in the book. And then it says: "I am Anna's best friend." But Anna has written: "I love Angelica." And Kristina has scribbled: "Most of all in the whole world I love Father best." And Birgitta has added: "I am going to marry Father." Isn't that amusing? I laughed when I read it.

Marianne took the book from her and turned the pages. It was partly scribbled on and partly painted with great vitality and strong colors. The light in the small room grew dimmer as the sky darkened outside. In the distance the thunder was already rumbling in the sky. Mother picked up a toy locomotive and looked at it closely.

MOTHER: I think that this is Benjamin's locomotive because he was always so amused by trains and circuses and such things. I suppose that's why he became an actor. We quarreled often about it because I wanted him to have an honest profession. And I was right. He didn't make it. I told him that several times. He didn't believe me, but I was right. It doesn't pay much to talk. Isn't it cold in here? The fire doesn't really warm.

ISAK: No, it isn't particularly cold.

She turned her head toward the darkened skies outside. The trees stood heavy, as if waiting.

MOTHER: I've always felt chilly as long as I can remember. What does that mean? You're a doctor? Mostly in the stomach. Here.

ISAK: You have low blood pressure.

MOTHER: Do you want me to ask Sister Elisabet to make some tea for us so we can sit down and talk for a while? Wouldn't that be . . .

ISAK: No, Mother, thank you. We don't want to trouble you any more. We've just had lunch and we're rather in a hurry.

MOTHER: Look here for a moment. Sigbritt's eldest boy will be fifty. I'm thinking of giving him my father's old gold watch. Can I give it to him, even though the hands have loosened? It is so difficult to find presents for those who have everything. But the watch is beautiful and it can probably be repaired.

She looked anxiously, appealingly, from Marianne to me and back to Marianne. She had opened the lid of the old gold watch and the blank dial stared at me. I suddenly remembered my early-morning dream: the blank clock face and my own watch which lacked hands, the hearse and my dead self.

MOTHER: I remember when Sigbritt's boy had just been born and lay there in his basket in the lilac arbor at the summerhouse. Now he will be fifty years old. And little cousin Sara, who always went around carrying him, cradling him, and who married Sigfrid, that no-good. Now you have to go so that you'll have time for all the things you must do. I'm very grateful for your visit and I hope we'll see each other some time. Give my best regards to Evald. Goodbye.

She offered me her cheek and I bent down and kissed it. It was very cold but unbelievably soft and full of sharp little lines. Marianne curtsied and my mother answered her gesture with an abstract smile. Sister Elisabet opened the door as if she had been listening to us. In a few minutes we were out in the gray daylight, which hurt our eyes with its piercing sharpness.

Once again Marianne took my arm, and when she did so I was filled with gratitude toward this quiet, independent girl with her naked, observant face.

When we reached the inn the youngsters were no longer there. The waitress told us that the young lady was waiting at the car. The headwaiter stood nearby bowing and looking as if he had just had another of his old ulcer attacks.

Sure enough, Sara was leaning against the car looking as though she were ready to cry.

MARIANNE: Where are Anders and Viktor?

Sara pointed without answering. Down on the slope the boys stood glaring at each other with furious expressions on their faces. Every so often one of them would utter some terrible expletive at the other.

SARA: When you left they were talking away about the existence of God. Finally they got so angry that they began shouting at each other. Then Anders grabbed Viktor's arm and tried to twist it off, and Viktor said that was a pretty lousy argument for the existence of God. Then I said that I thought they could skip God and pay some attention to me for a while instead, and then they said that I could stop babbling because I didn't understand that it was a debate of principles, and then I said that whether there was a God or not, they were real wet blankets. Then I left and they ran down the hill to settle things because each of them insisted that the other had hurt his innermost feelings. So now they're going to slug it out.

Marianne put on a very wise countenance and started off to calm down the two debaters. I stepped into the car. Sara looked at the departing Marianne with envy.

SARA: Well, which one of the boys do *you* like the most?

ISAK: Which do you like best?

SARA: I don't know. Anders will become a minister. But he is rather masculine and warm, you know. But a minister's wife! But Viktor's funny in another way. Viktor will go far, you know.

ISAK: What do you mean by that?

SARA (*tired*): A doctor earns more money. And it's old-fashioned to be a minister. But he has nice legs. And a strong neck. But how *can* one believe in God!

Sara sighed and we sank into our own thoughts.

Marianne came up the hill bringing with her the two fighting cocks, barely reconciled. She sat down behind the wheel and we continued our trip.

The sun shone white on the blue-black clouds which towered above the dark, gleaming surface of Lake Vattern. The breeze coming from the open side windows did not cool us any longer, and in the south summer lightning cut across the sky with thin, jagged scratches. Because of the approaching storm, and all the food and wine, I became rather sleepy. I silently blessed my luck in having Marianne beside me as a reliable chauffeur. Anders and Viktor sat in sullen silence. Sara yawned again and again and blinked her eyes.

I fell asleep, but during my nap I was pursued by dreams and images which seemed extremely real and were very humiliating to me.

I record these in the order in which they occurred, without the slightest intention of commenting on their possible meaning. I have never been particularly enthusiastic about the psychoanalytical theory of dreams as the fulfillment of desires in a negative or positive direction. Yet I cannot deny that in these dreams there was something like a warning, which bore into my consciousness and embedded itself there with relentless determination.

I have found that during the last few years I glide rather easily into a twilight world of memories and dreams which are highly personal. I've often wondered if this is a sign of increasing senility. Sometimes I've also asked myself if it is a harbinger of approaching death.

Again I found myself at the wild-strawberry patch of my childhood, but I was not alone. Sara was there, and this time she turned her face toward mine and looked at me for a long time. I knew that I sat there looking old, ugly and ridiculous. A professor emeritus who was going to be made a Jubilee Doctor. The saddest thing about it was that although Sara spoke to me in a grieved and penetrating tone, I couldn't answer her except in stammered, one-syllable words. This, of course, increased the pain of my dream.

Between us stood a little woven basket filled with wild strawberries; around us lay a strange, motionless twilight, heavy with dull expectations. Sara leaned toward me and spoke in such a low voice that I had difficulty grasping her words.

SARA: Have you looked at yourself in the mirror, Isak? You haven't. Then I'll show you how you look.

She picked up a mirror that lay hidden under the small strawberry basket and showed me my face, which looked old and ugly in the sinking twilight. I carefully pushed away the looking glass and I could see that Sara had tears in her eyes.

SARA: You are a worried old man who will die soon, but I have my whole life before me . . . Oh, now you're offended.

ISAK: No, I'm not offended.

SARA: Yes, you are offended because you can't bear to hear the truth. And the truth is that I've been too considerate. One can easily be unintentionally cruel that way.

ISAK: I understand.

SARA: No, you don't understand. We don't speak the same language. Look at yourself in the mirror again. No, don't look away.

ISAK: I see.

SARA: Now listen. I'm about to marry your brother Sigfrid. He and I love each other, and it's all like a game. Look at your face now. Try to smile! All right, now you're smiling.

ISAK: It hurts.

SARA: You, a professor emeritus, ought to know why it hurts. But you don't. Because in spite of all your knowledge you don't really know anything.

She threw away the mirror and it shattered. The wind began to blow through the trees, and from somewhere the crying of a child could be heard. She arose immediately, drying her tears.

SARA: I have to go. I promised to look after Sigbritt's little boy.

ISAK: Don't leave me.

SARA: What did you say?

ISAK: Don't leave me.

SARA: You stammer so much that I can't hear your words. Besides, they don't really matter.

I saw her run up to the arbor. The old house was draped in the gray twilight. She lifted the crying child and cradled it in her arms. The sky turned black above the sea and large birds circled overhead, screeching toward the house, which suddenly seemed ugly and poor. There was something fateful and threatening in this twilight, in the crying of the child, in the shrieking of the black birds. Sara cradled the baby and her voice, half singing, was very distant and sorrowful.

SARA: My poor little one, you shall sleep quietly now. Don't be afraid of the wind. Don't be afraid of the birds, the jackdaws and the sea gulls. Don't be afraid of the waves from the sea. I'm with you. I'm holding you tight. Don't be afraid, little one. Soon it will be another day. No one can hurt you; I am with you; I'm holding you.

But her voice was sorrowful and tears ran down her cheeks without end. The child became silent, as if it were listening, and I wanted to scream until my lungs were bloody.

Now I saw that a door had opened in the house and someone was standing there shouting for Sara. It was my brother Sigfrid.

She ran toward him, gave him the child, and they both disappeared into the house and closed the door.

Suddenly I noticed that the wind had died and the birds had flown away. All the windows in the house shone festively. Over the horizon stood a jagged moon, and music from a piano penetrated the stillness of the strawberry patch.

I went closer and pressed my face against the brightly lit dining-room window. An elegantly laid table stood before me and Sara sat behind the piano, playing. She was wearing an expensive but old-fashioned dress and her hair was piled on top of her head, which made her face look womanly and mature. Then Sigfrid entered the room and they both sat down immediately at the table. They laughed and joked and celebrated some kind of event. The moon rose higher in the heavens and the scene inside became obscure. I rapped on the window so that they would hear me and let me in. But they did not notice me; they were too preoccupied with each other.

On the window sill lay many splinters of glass, and in my eager attempt to get their attention I accidentally cut my hand.

Turning away, I was blinded by the moonlight, which threw itself against me with an almost physical force.

I heard a voice calling my name, and then I saw that the door had been opened. Someone was standing in the doorway and I recognized Mr. Alman. He bowed politely though stiffly and invited me inside.

He led me down a short corridor and unlocked a narrow door. We entered a large windowless room with benches arranged like an amphitheater. There sat about ten youngsters, among whom I immediately recognized Sara, Anders and Viktor. On one of the low walls hung a large blackboard, and on a work table in the center of the room stood a microscope.

I realized that this was the hall where I used to hold my polyclinical lectures and examinations. Alman sat down and asked me to take a seat at the short end of the table. For a few moments he studied some papers in a dossier. The audience remained completely still.

ALMAN: Do you have your examination book with you?

ISAK: Yes, of course. Here it is.

ALMAN: Thank you.

I handed him the examination book and he flipped through it distractedly. Then he leaned forward and looked at me for a long time. After that he gestured toward the microscope.

ALMAN: Will you please identify the bacteriological specimen in the microscope. Take your time.

I arose, stepped up to the instrument and adjusted it. But whatever I did, I couldn't find any specimen. The only thing I saw was my own eye, which stared back at me in an absurd enlargement.

ISAK: There must be something wrong with the microscope.

Alman bent over and peered into it. Then he regarded me seriously and shook his head.

ALMAN: There is nothing wrong with the microscope.

ISAK: I can't see anything.

ALMAN: Sit down.

I sank down on the chair and wet my lips. No one moved or said anything.

ALMAN: Will you please read this text.

He pointed to the blackboard which hung behind him. Something was printed on it in large crooked letters. I made a great effort to interpret what was written: INKE TAN MAGROV STAK FARSIN LOS KRET FAJNE KASERTE MJOT-RON PRESETE.

ALMAN: What does it mean?

ISAK: I don't know.

ALMAN: Oh, really?

ISAK: I'm a doctor, not a linguist.

ALMAN: Then let me tell you, Professor Borg, that on the blackboard is written the first duty of a doctor. Do you happen to know what that is?

ISAK: Yes, if you let me think for a moment.

ALMAN: Take your time.

ISAK: A doctor's first duty . . . a doctor's first duty . . . a doctor's . . . Oh, I've forgotten.

A cold sweat broke out on my forehead, but I still looked Alman straight in the eye. He leaned toward me and spoke in a calm, polite tone.

ALMAN: A doctor's first duty *is to ask forgiveness.*

ISAK: Of course, now I remember!

Relieved, I laughed but immediately became silent. Alman looked wearily at his papers and smothered a yawn.

ALMAN: Moreover, you are guilty of guilt.

ISAK: Guilty of guilt?

ALMAN: I have noted that you don't understand the accusation.

ISAK: Is it serious?

ALMAN: Unfortunately, Professor.

Next to me stood a table with a water decanter. I poured a glass, but spilled a lot of it on the table and the tray.

ISAK: I have a bad heart. I'm an old man, Mr. Alman, and I must be treated with consideration. That's only right.

ALMAN: There is nothing concerning your heart in my papers. Perhaps you wish to end the examination?

ISAK: No, no, for heaven's sake, no!

Alman arose and lit a small lamp which hung from a cord in the ceiling. Under the lamp (very brightly lit) sat a woman wrapped in a hospital robe and wearing wooden sandals on her feet.

ALMAN: Will you please make an anamnesis and diagnosis of this patient.

ISAK: But the patient is dead.

At that moment the woman arose and began laughing as if she had just heard a great joke. Alman leaned across the table and wrote something in my examination book.

ISAK: What are you writing in my book?

ALMAN: My conclusion.

ISAK: And that is . . .

ALMAN: That you're incompetent.

ISAK: Incompetent.

ALMAN: Furthermore, Professor Borg, you are accused of some smaller but nonetheless serious offenses. (*Isak remains silent*) Indifference, selfishness, lack of consideration.

ISAK: No.

ALMAN: These accusations have been made by your wife. Do you want to be confronted by her?

ISAK: But my wife has been dead for many years.

ALMAN: Do you think I'm joking? Will you please come with me voluntarily. You have no choice in any case. Come!

Alman placed the examination book in his pocket, made a sign for me to follow him, opened the door and led me into a forest.

The trunks of the trees stood close together. Twilight had almost passed. Dead trees were strewn on the ground and the earth was covered with decaying leaves. Our feet sank into this soft carpet with every step, and mud oozed up around them. From behind the foliage the moon shone steadily, like an inflamed eye, and it was as warm as inside a hothouse. Alman turned around.

ALMAN: Watch out, Professor Borg. You'll find many snakes here.

Suddenly I saw a small, gleaming body which twisted around and disappeared in one of Alman's wet footsteps. I stepped swiftly aside but nearly trod on a large gray creature which slowly pulled away. Wherever I looked, snakes seemed to well forth from the swampy, porous ground.

Finally we arrived at a clearing in the forest, but we halted at the very edge. The moon shone in our eyes and we hid among the shadows of the trees. The clearing stretched out before us. It was overgrown with twisted roots. At one end a black cliff fell away into a body of water. On the sides, the trees stood lofty and lifeless, as if burdened by each other's enormous shadows. Then a giggling laugh was heard and I discovered a woman standing near the hill. She was dressed in a long black gown and her face was averted from us. She made movements with her hands, as if to ward off someone. She laughed continually and excitedly. A man stood half hidden, leaning against a tree trunk. His face, which I glimpsed, was large and flat, but his eyebrows were quite bushy and his forehead protruded over his eyes. He made gestures with his hand and said some unintelligible words, which made the woman laugh uncontrollably. Suddenly she became serious, and a harassed, discontented expression appeared on her face. She bent over and picked up a small purse. The man stretched out his hand and jokingly began to pull the pins out of her skillfully pompadoured hair. She pretended to be very angry and flailed the air around her furiously. This amused the man, who continued his game. When she finally walked away he followed and took hold of her shoulders. Petrified, she stopped and turned her pale, embittered face toward her pursuer. He muttered something and stretched out his other hand toward her breast. She moved away, but couldn't free herself. When she saw that she was caught, she began to twist and squirm as if the man's grip on her shoulders hurt intensely. The man continued to mutter incoherent words, as if to an animal. Suddenly she freed herself and ran with bent knees and a shuffling step in a semicircle. The man remained standing, waiting and breathless. He perspired heavily and wiped his face over and over again with the back of his hand. The woman stopped as if exhausted and regarded the man, wide-eyed and gaping. She was also out of breath. Then she began running again but pretended to trip and fell on her hands and knees. Her large rump swayed like a black balloon over the ground. She lowered her face between her arms and began crying, rocking and swaying. The man knelt at her side, took a firm grasp of her hair, pulled her face upward, backward and forced her to open her eyes. He panted with effort the whole time. She teetered and nearly fell to the side, but the man straddled her and leaned over her heavily. Suddenly she was completely still, with closed eyes and a swollen, pale face. Then she collapsed, rolled over, and received the man between her open knees.

ALMAN: Many men forget a woman who has been dead for thirty years. Some preserve a sweet, fading picture, but *you* can always recall this scene in your memory. Strange, isn't it? Tuesday, May 1, 1917, you stood here and heard and saw exactly what that woman and that man said and did.

The woman sat up and smoothed her gown over her short, thick thighs. Her face was blank and almost distorted in its puffy slackness. The man had got up and was wandering around aimlessly with his hands hanging at his sides.

WOMAN: Now I will go home and tell this to Isak and I know exactly what he'll say: Poor little girl, how I pity you. As if he were God himself. And then I'll cry and say: Do you really feel pity for me? and he'll say: I feel infinitely sorry for you, and then I'll cry some more and ask him if he can forgive me. And then he'll say: You shouldn't ask forgiveness from me. I have nothing to forgive. But he doesn't mean a word of it, because he's completely cold. And then he'll suddenly be very tender and I'll yell at him that he's not really sane and that such hypocritical nobility is sickening. And then he'll say that he'll bring me a sedative and that he understands everything. And then I'll say that it's his fault that I am the way I am, and then he'll look very sad and will say that he is to blame. But he doesn't care about anything because he's completely cold.

She arose with effort and shook out her hair and began combing it and pinning it up in the same careful way that it was before. The man sat down on a stone a little farther away. He smoked quietly. I couldn't see his gaze below the protruding eyebrows, but his voice was calm and scornful.

MAN: You're insane, the way you're carrying on.

The woman laughed and went into the forest.

I turned around. Alman had a strange, wry smile on his face. We stood quietly for a few moments.

ISAK: Where is she?

ALMAN: You know. She is gone. Everyone is gone. Can't you hear how quiet it is? Everything has been dissected, Professor Borg. A surgical masterpiece. There is no pain, no bleeding, no quivering.

ISAK: It is rather quiet.

ALMAN: A perfect achievement of its kind, Professor.

ISAK: And what is the penalty?

ALMAN: Penalty? I don't know. The usual one, I suppose.

ISAK: The usual one?

ALMAN: Of course. Loneliness.

ISAK: Loneliness?

ALMAN: Exactly. *Loneliness.*

ISAK: Is there no grace?

ALMAN: Don't ask me. I don't know anything about such things.

Before I had time to answer, Alman had disappeared, and I stood alone in the complete stillness of the moonlight and the forest. Then I heard a voice quite close to me.

SARA: Didn't you have to go with them to get your father?

The girl stretched out her hand, but when she saw my face she immediately withdrew it.

ISAK: Sara . . . It wasn't always like this. If only you had stayed with me. If only you could have had a little patience.

The girl did not seem to hear what I was saying but began to look restless.

SARA: Hurry up.

I followed her as well as I could, but she moved so much more easily and faster than I.

ISAK: I can't run, don't you understand?

SARA: But hurry up.

ISAK: I can't see you any more.

SARA: But here I am.

ISAK: Wait for me.

She materialized for a moment and then she was gone. The moon disappeared into darkness and I wanted to cry with wild, childish sorrow, but I could not.

At that moment, I awoke. The car stood still and the storm was over, but it was still drizzling slightly. We were in the neighborhood of the Strömsnäs Foundry, where the road wanders between rich forests on one side and river rapids on the other. Everything was completely silent. The three children had left the car and Marianne sat quietly smoking a cigarette and blowing the smoke through the open window. Gusts of strong and pleasant odors came from the wet forest.

ISAK: What is this?

MARIANNE: The children wanted to get out for a moment and stretch their legs. They are over there.

She made a gesture toward a clearing near the river. All three were busy picking flowers.

ISAK: But it's still raining.

MARIANNE: I told them about the ceremony today, and they insisted on paying homage to you.

ISAK (sighs): Good Lord.

MARIANNE: Did you sleep well?

ISAK: Yes, but I dreamed. Can you imagine — the last few months I've had the most peculiar dreams. It's really odd.

MARIANNE: What's odd?

ISAK: It's as if I'm trying to say something to myself which I don't want to hear when I'm awake.

MARIANNE: And what would that be?

ISAK: That I'm dead, although I live.

Marianne reacted violently. Her gaze blackened and she took a deep breath. Throwing her cigarette out the window, she turned toward me.

MARIANNE: Do you know that you and Evald are very much alike?

ISAK: You told me that.

MARIANNE: Do you know that Evald has said the very same thing?

ISAK: About me? Yes, I can believe that.

MARIANNE: No, about himself.

ISAK: But he's only thirty-eight years old.

MARIANNE: May I tell you everything, or would it bore you?

ISAK: I'd be grateful if you would tell me.

MARIANNE: It was a few months ago. I wanted to talk to Evald and we took the car and went down to the sea. It was raining, just like now. Evald sat where you are sitting, and I drove.

EVALD: Can't you stop the windshield wipers?

MARIANNE: Then we won't be able to see the ocean.

EVALD: They're working so hard it makes me nervous.

MARIANNE (*shuts them off*): Very well.

They sit in silence for a few minutes, looking at the rain, which streams down the windshield quietly. The sea merges with the clouds in an infinite grayness. Evald strokes his long, bony face and looks expectantly at his wife. He talks jokingly, calmly.

EVALD: So now you have me trapped. What did you want to say? Something unpleasant, of course.

MARIANNE: I wish I didn't have to tell you about it.

EVALD: I understand. You've found someone else.

MARIANNE: Now don't be childish.

EVALD (*mimicking her*): Now don't be childish. What do you expect me to think? You come and say in a funereal voice that you want to talk to me. We take the car and go down to the sea. It rains and it's hard for you to begin. Good Lord, Marianne, let's have it. This is an excellent moment for the most intimate confidence. But for heaven's sake, don't keep me dangling.

MARIANNE: Now I feel like laughing. What do you really think I'm going to say? That I've murdered someone, or embezzled the faculty funds? I'm pregnant, Evald.

EVALD: Oh, is that so.

MARIANNE: That's the way it is. And as careless as we've been recently, there isn't much to be surprised about, is there?

EVALD: And you're sure?

MARIANNE: The report on the test came yesterday.

EVALD: Oh. Oh, yes. So that was the secret.

MARIANNE: Another thing I want to tell you. I shall have this child.

EVALD: That seems to be clear.

MARIANNE: Yes, it is!

MARIANNE (*voice over*): We sat quietly for a long time and I felt how the hatred grew big and thick between us. Evald looked out through the wet window, whistled soundlessly and looked as if he were cold. Somewhere in my stomach I was shivering so hard that I could barely sit upright. Then he opened the door and got out of the car and marched through the rain down to the beach. He stopped under a big tree and stood there for a long while. Finally I also stepped out and went to him. His face and hair were wet and the rain fell down his cheeks to the sides of his mouth.

EVALD (*calmly*): You know that I don't want to have any children. You also know that you'll have to choose between me and the child.

MARIANNE (*looks at him*): Poor Evald.

EVALD: Please don't "poor" me. I'm of sound mind and I've made my position absolutely clear. It's absurd to live in this world, but it's even more ridiculous to populate it with new victims and it's most absurd of all to believe that they will have it any better than us.

MARIANNE: That is only an excuse.

EVALD: Call it whatever you want. Personally I was an unwelcome child in a marriage which was a nice imitation of hell. Is the old man really sure that I'm his son? Indifference, fear, infidelity and guilt feelings — those were my nurses.

MARIANNE: All this is very touching, but it doesn't excuse the fact that you're behaving like a child.

EVALD: I have to be at the hospital at three o'clock and have neither the time nor the desire to talk any more.

MARIANNE: You're a coward!

EVALD: Yes, that's right. This life disgusts me and I don't think that I need a responsibility which will force me to exist another day longer than I want to. You know all that, and you know that I'm serious and that this isn't some kind of hysteria, as you once thought.

MARIANNE (*voice over*): We went toward the car, he in front and I following. I had begun to cry. I don't know why. But the tears couldn't be seen in the rain. We sat in the car, thoroughly wet and cold, but the hatred throbbed in us so painfully that we didn't feel cold. I started the car and turned it toward the road. Evald sat fiddling with the radio. His face was completely calm and closed.

MARIANNE: I know that you're wrong.

EVALD: There is nothing which can be called right or wrong. One functions according to one's needs; you can read that in an elementary-school textbook.

MARIANNE: And what do we need?

EVALD: You have a damned need to live, to exist and create life.

MARIANNE: And how about you?

EVALD: My need is to be dead. Absolutely, totally dead.

I've tried to relate Marianne's story as carefully as possible. My reaction to it was very mixed. But my strongest feeling was a certain sympathy toward her for this sudden confidence, and when Marianne fell silent she looked so hesitant that I felt obliged to say something even though I wasn't very sure of my own voice.

ISAK: If you want to smoke a cigarette, you may.

MARIANNE: Thank you.

ISAK: Why have you told me all this?

Marianne didn't answer at once. She took her time lighting a cigarette and puffed a few times. I looked at her, but she turned her head away and pretended to look at the three youngsters, who had picked up some kind of soft drink which they shared in great amity.

MARIANNE: When I saw you together with your mother, I was gripped by a strange fear.

ISAK: I don't understand.

MARIANNE: I thought, here is his mother. A very ancient woman, completely ice-cold, in some ways more frightening than death itself. And here is her son, and there are light-years of distance between them. And he himself says that he is a living death. And Evald is on the verge of becoming just as lonely and cold — and dead. And then

I thought that there is only coldness and death, and death and loneliness, all the way. Somewhere it must end.

ISAK: But you are going back to Evald.

MARIANNE: Yes, to tell him that I can't agree to his condition. I want my child; no one can take it from me. Not even the person I love more than anyone else.

She turned her pale, tearless face toward me, and her gaze was black, accusing, desperate. I suddenly felt shaken in a way which I had never experienced before.

ISAK: Can I help you?

MARIANNE: No one can help me. We are too old, Isak. It has gone too far.

ISAK: What happened after your talk in the car?

MARIANNE: Nothing. I left him the very next day.

ISAK: Haven't you heard from him?

MARIANNE: No. No, Evald is rather like you.

She shook her head and bent forward as if to protect her face. I felt cold; it had become quite chilly after the rain.

MARIANNE: Those two wretched people whom I made leave the car — what was their name again?

ISAK: I was just thinking about Alman and his wife. It reminded me of my own marriage.

MARIANNE: I don't want Evald and I to become like . . ..

ISAK: Poor Evald grew up in all that.

MARIANNE: But we love each other.

Her last words were a low outburst. She stopped herself immediately and moved her hands toward her face, then stopped again. We sat quietly for a few moments.

ISAK: We must get on. Signal to the children.

Marianne nodded, started the motor and blew the horn. Sara came laughing through the wet grass, closely followed by her two cavaliers. She handed me a large bouquet of wild flowers wrapped in wet newspapers. All three of them had friendly, mocking eyes. Sara cleared her throat solemnly.

SARA: We heard that you are celebrating this day. Now we want to pay our respects to you with these simple flowers and to tell you that we are *very* impressed that you are so old and that you've been a doctor for fifty years. And we know, of course, that you are a *wise* and *venerable* old man. One who regards us youngsters with *lenience* and gentle irony. One who knows *all* about life and who has learned all the prescriptions by hearts.

She gave me the flowers with a little mock curtsy and kissed my cheek. The boys bowed and laughed, embarrassed. I couldn't answer. I only thanked them very briefly and rather bluntly. The children probably thought that I had been hurt by their joke.

After a few more hours' travel, we reached Lund. When we finally stopped at Evald's house, a small round woman ran out and approached us quickly. To my surprise and pleasure I discovered that it was Miss Agda.

AGDA: So you did come. Evald and I had just given up hope. It's relaxing and convenient to drive, isn't it? Now, Professor, you'll have to put on your frock coat immediately. Hello, Marianne. I've prepared Evald for your arrival.

ISAK: So, Miss Agda, you came after all.

AGDA: I considered it my duty. But the fun is gone. There's nothing you can say that will make me feel different. Who are these young people? Are they going to the ceremony too?

MARIANNE: These are good friends of ours, and if there is any food in the kitchen, invite them in.

AGDA: And why shouldn't there be? I've had a lot of things to arrange here, believe me.

Evald met us in the foyer. He was already dressed in evening clothes and seemed nervous. Everything was extremely confused, but Miss Agda was a pillar of strength in the maelstrom. Without raising her voice, and dressed in her best dress (especially made for the occasion), she sent the children, the married couple, servants and an old professor in different directions. Within ten minutes, everything was in order.

Just before that, Evald, Marianne and I had a chance to say hello. I wouldn't want to give the impression that our reunion was marked by overwhelming cordiality. This has never been the case in our family.

EVALD: Hello, Father. Welcome.

ISAK: Hello, Evald. Thank you. As you can see, I brought Marianne with me.

EVALD: Hello, Marianne.

MARIANNE: Can I take my things upstairs?

EVALD: Do you want to stay in the guest room as usual, Father?

ISAK: Thank you, that would be just fine.

EVALD: Let me take your suitcase. It's rather heavy.

ISAK: Thank you, I'll take it myself.

EVALD: Did you have a nice trip?

MARIANNE: Yes, thanks, it's been pleasant.

EVALD: Who were those youngsters you had with you?

MARIANNE: Don't know. They're going to Italy.

EVALD: They looked rather nice.

ISAK: They are really very nice.

We had come to the second floor. Evald politely opened the door to the guest room and I entered. Agda came after us as if she were rolling on ball bearings, forced her way in and took the suitcase, putting it on a chair.

AGDA: I bought new shoelaces, and I took the liberty of bringing the white waistcoat to your evening dress if you should want to go to the banquet after the ceremony. And you forgot your razor blades, Professor.

She unpacked, murmuring sounds of worried concern. I didn't listen. Instead I listened to the conversation between Marianne and Evald outside the half-closed door. Their voices were formal and faultlessly polite.

MARIANNE: No, I'll go tomorrow, so don't worry.

EVALD: Do you intend to stay in a hotel?

MARIANNE (*gay*): Why? We can share a bedroom for another night, if you have no objection. Help me to unpack.

EVALD: It was really nice to see you. And unexpected.

MARIANNE: I feel the same way. Are we going to the dinner afterward, or what do you want to do?

EVALD: I'll just call Stenberg and tell him that I'm bringing a lady. He arranges such things.

The door was closed, so I couldn't hear any more of the conversation. I had sat down on the bed to take off my shoes. Miss Agda helped me, but she wasn't very gracious.

Oddly enough, there were three Jubilee Doctors that year. The dean's office had thoughtfully placed us three old men in a special room while the procession was arranged out in the large vestibule of the university hall. I happened to know one of the other two who were going to be honored. He was an old schoolmate, the former Bishop Jakob Hovelius. We greeted each other cordially and embraced. The third old man seemed rather atrophied and declined all conversation. It turned out that he was the former Professor of Roman Law, Carl-Adam Tiger (a great fighter in his time and a man who, according to his students, really lived up to his name).

ISAK: How comforting it is to meet another old corpse. How are you nowadays, dear Jakob?

JAKOB: I enjoy my leisure. But don't ask me if I do it *cum dignitate*.

ISAK: Do you know the third man to be honored?

JAKOB: Of course. It's Carl-Adam Tiger, Professor of Roman Law.

ISAK: The Tiger! Good Lord!

JAKOB: He has three interests left in life. A thirty-year-old injustice, a goldfish, and his bowels.

ISAK: Do you think that we are like that?

JAKOB: What's your opinion? As Schopenhauer says somewhere, "Dreams are a kind of lunacy and lunacy a kind of dream." But life is also supposed to be a kind of dream, isn't it? Draw your own conclusion.

ISAK: Do you remember how in our youth we fought with each other on what we called the metaphysical questions?

JAKOB: How could I forget?

ISAK: And what do you believe now?

JAKOB: I'll tell you, I've ceased thinking about all that. One of these days, knowledge will be achieved.

ISAK: My, how surprised you'll be.

JAKOB: And you. But one has a right to be curious.

TIGER: Gentlemen, do you think I'd have time to make a small secret visit before the great farce begins?

ISAK: I don't know, Professor Tiger.

TIGER (*sighs*): *In dubio non est agendum*. When in doubt, don't, as the old Romans used to say. I'll stay here.

The Festivities

What should I describe? Trumpet fanfares, bells ringing, field-cannon salutes, masses of people, the giant procession from the university to the cathedral, the white-dressed garland girls, royalty, old age, wisdom, beautiful music, stately Latin sentences which echoed off the huge vaults. The students and their girls, women in bright, magnificent dresses, this strange rite with its heavy symbolism but as meaningless as a passing dream.

Then I saw Sara with her two boys among the onlookers outside the cathedral. They waved to me and suddenly looked childishly happy and full of expectations. Among the lecturers was Evald, tall and serious, disinterested and absent. Inside the church, I saw Marianne in her white dress and next to her sat Miss Agda, pale and with her lips pressed tightly together. The ceremonial lecture was dull (as usual). The whole thing went on endlessly (as usual) and the garland girls had to go out and relieve themselves in the little silver pot in the sacristy. But we adults unfortunately had to stay where we were. As you know, culture provides us with these moments of refined torture. Professor Tiger looked as if he were dying, my friend the Bishop fell asleep, and more than one of those present seemed ready to faint. Even our behinds, which have withstood long academic services, lectures, dusty dissertations and dull dinners, started to become numb and ache in silent protest.

I surprised myself by returning to the happenings of the day, and it was then that I decided to recollect and write down everything that had happened. I was beginning to see a remarkable causality in this chain of unexpected, entangled events. At the same time, I couldn't escape recalling the Bishop's words: "Dreams are a kind of lunacy and lunacy a kind of dream, but life is also supposed to be a dream, isn't it . . ."

After the ceremony there was a banquet, but I really felt too tired to go. I took a cab home and found Miss Agda in my room busy making my bed the way I like (very high under my head and folded neatly at my feet). A heating pad was already connected and my sleeping pills stood on the table. Almost at once, Miss Agda began helping me with my shoes and evening dress, and I felt a great warmth toward this extraordinary, faithful, thoughtful old woman. I would really have liked to become friends with her again, and I repented the morning's thoughtless utterances (which, I noticed, she had by no means forgotten).

ISAK: Did you enjoy the ceremony?

AGDA: Yes, thank you.

ISAK: Are you tired, Miss Agda?

AGDA: I won't deny it.

ISAK: Take one of my sleeping pills.

AGDA: No, thanks.

ISAK: Oh, Miss Agda, I'm sorry for this morning.

AGDA: Are you sick, Professor?

ISAK: No. Why?

AGDA: I don't know, but that sounds alarming.

ISAK: Oh really, is it so unusual for me to ask forgiveness?

AGDA: Do you want the water decanter on the table?

ISAK: No, thanks.

We puttered about for a while, silently.

AGDA: Thanks anyway.

ISAK: Oh, Miss Agda.

AGDA: What do you want, Professor?

ISAK: Don't you think that we who have known each other for two generations could drop formality and say "*du*" to each other?

AGDA: No, I don't really think so.

ISAK: Why not, if I may ask?

AGDA: Have you brushed your teeth, Professor?

ISAK: Yes, thanks.

AGDA: Now, I'll tell you. I beg to be excused from all intimacies. It's all right the way it is between us now.

ISAK: But, dear Miss Agda, we are old now.

AGDA: Speak for yourself, Professor. A woman has to think of her reputation, and what would people say if the two of us suddenly started to say "*du*" to each other?

ISAK: Yes, what would people say?

AGDA: They would ridicule us.

ISAK: Do you always act correctly?

AGDA: Nearly always. At our age one ought to know how to behave. Isn't that so, Professor?

ISAK: Good night, Miss Agda.

AGDA: Good night, Professor. I will leave the door ajar. And you know where I am if you should want something. Good night, Professor.

ISAK: Good night, Miss Agda.

I was just going to lie down in bed (I had been sitting on the edge in my old robe) when I heard singing and music from the garden. I thought I recognized the voices and walked over to the window and lifted the blinds. Down there under the trees I recognized my three companions from the trip. They sang to their heart's delight, and Anders accompanied them on his guitar.

SARA: Hey, Father Isak! You were fantastic when you marched in the procession. We were real proud that we knew you. Now we're going on.

ANDERS: We got a lift all the way to Hamburg.

VIKTOR: With a fifty-year-old deaconess. Anders is already sweet on the old girl.

ANDERS: Stop babbling!

VIKTOR: We came to say goodbye.

ISAK: Goodbye, and thank you for your company.

SARA: Goodbye, Father Isak. Do you know that it is really you I love, today, tomorrow and forever?

ISAK: I'll remember that.

VIKTOR: Goodbye, Professor.

ISAK: Goodbye, Viktor.

ANDERS: Goodbye, Professor. Now we have to run.

ISAK: Let me hear from you sometime.

Those last words I said to myself, and rather quietly. The children waved to me and were swallowed up by the summer night. I heard their laughter, and then they were gone.

At the same moment, I heard voices out in the foyer. It was Evald and Marianne. They whispered out of consideration to me and I heard the rustle of Marianne's evening gown. I called to Evald. He entered the room, but stopped at the door.

ISAK: Are you home already?

EVALD: Marianne had to change shoes. Her heel broke.

ISAK: So are you going to the dance?

EVALD: Yes, I suppose so.

ISAK: A-ha.

EVALD: How are you otherwise?

ISAK: Fine, thanks.

EVALD: How's the heart holding up?

ISAK: Excellently.

EVALD: Good night, and sleep well.

He turned and went through the door. I asked him to come back. He looked very surprised. I felt surprised myself, and confused. I didn't really know what to say.

ISAK: Sit down a moment.

EVALD: Is it something special?

He sat obediently on the chair near the bed. His starched shirt rustled and his hands hung a little tiredly across his knees. I realized that my son was becoming middle-aged.

ISAK: May I ask you what's going to happen between you and Marianne? (*Evald shakes his head*) Forgive my asking.

EVALD: I know nothing.

ISAK: It's not my business, but . . .

EVALD: What?

ISAK: But shouldn't . . .

EVALD: I have asked her to remain with me.

ISAK: And how will it . . . I mean . . .

EVALD: I can't be without her.

ISAK: You mean you can't live alone.

EVALD: I can't be without *her*. That's what I mean.

ISAK: I understand.

EVALD: It will be as she wants.

ISAK: And if she wants . . . I mean, does she want?

EVALD: She says that she'll think it over. I don't really know.

ISAK: Regarding that loan you had from me . . .

EVALD: Don't worry, you'll get your money.

ISAK: I didn't mean that.

EVALD: You'll get your money all right.

Evald rose and nodded to me. Just then Marianne appeared in the door. She had a very simple but extraordinarily beautiful white dress.

MARIANNE: How are you, Father Isak?

ISAK: Fine, thanks. Very well.

MARIANNE: I broke a heel, so we had to come home to change. Can I wear these shoes instead?

ISAK: They look fine.

Marianne came up to me. She smelled good and rustled in a sweet, womanly way. She leaned over me.

ISAK: Thanks for your company on the trip.

MARIANNE: Thank *you*.

ISAK: I like you, Marianne.

MARIANNE: I like you too, Father Isak.

She kissed me lightly on the cheek and disappeared. They exchanged a few words outside the door. I heard their steps on the stairs and then the door slamming in the foyer. I heard my heart and my old watch. I heard the tower clock strike eleven, with the light tones designating the four quarter hours and the heavier sounds marking the hour.

Now it began to rain, not very hard, but quietly and evenly. A lulling sound. The street lamp swung on its cord and threw shadows on the light-colored window blinds.

Whenever I am restless or sad, I usually try to recall memories from my childhood, to calm down. This is the way it was that night too, and I wandered back to the summerhouse and the wild-strawberry patch and everything I had dreamed or remembered or experienced during this long day.

I sat under the tree by the wild-strawberry patch and it was a warm, sunny day with soft summer skies and a mild breeze coming through the birches. Down at the dock, my sisters and brothers were romping with Uncle Aron. My aunt went by, together with Sara. They were laden with large baskets. Everyone laughed and shouted to each other and applauded when the red sail went up the mast of the old yacht (an ancient relic from the days of my parents' childhood; a mad impulse of our grandfather, the Admiral). Sara turned around and when she caught sight of me she put down her baskets and ran toward me.

SARA: Isak, darling, there are no wild strawberries left. Aunt wants you to search for your father. We will sail around the peninsula and pick you up on the other side.

ISAK: I have already searched for him, but I can't find either Father or Mother.

SARA: Your mother was supposed to go with him.

ISAK: Yes, but I can't find them.

SARA: I will help you.

She took me by the hand and suddenly we found ourselves at a narrow sound with deep, dark water. The sun shone brightly on the opposite side, which rose softly into a meadow. Down at the beach on the other side of the dark water a gentleman sat, dressed in white, with his hat on the back of his head and an old pipe in his mouth. He had a soft, blond beard and pince-nez. He had taken off his shoes and stockings and between his hands he held a long, slender bamboo pole. A red float lay motionless on the shimmering water.

Farther up the bank sat my mother. She wore a bright summer dress and a big hat which shaded her face. She was reading a book. Sara dropped my hand and pointed to my parents. Then she was gone. I looked for a long time at the pair on the other side of the water. I tried to shout to them but not a word came from my mouth. Then my father raised his head and caught sight of me. He lifted his hand and waved, laughing. My mother looked up from her book. She also laughed and nodded.

Then I saw the old yacht with its red sail. It cruised so smoothly in the mild breeze. In the prow stood Uncle Aron, singing some sentimental song, and I saw my brothers and sisters and aunt and Sara, who lifted up Sigbritt's little boy. I shouted to them, but they didn't hear me.

I dreamed that I stood by the water and shouted toward the bay, but the warm summer breeze carried away my cries and they did not reach their destination. Yet I wasn't sorry about that; I felt, on the contrary, rather lighthearted.

For Consideration

1. Characterize Professor Borg's life as he describes it in the opening lines. He admits to being "withdrawn." Why? What in his life brings him pleasure?

2. The dream is recited to us before we have much understanding of Isak's life and interests. Because of this, it may raise questions more than it resolves uncertainties. What does the dream mean? (Note that the experience is not unique; Isak refers to "all the evil and frightening dreams which have haunted me these last few years.") Particularly since we are in a dream sequence we can be sure that certain objects have symbolic value. What is suggested by the handless timepieces? The faceless figure? The funeral procession and the incident with the coffin? What effect does the presentation of the dream have at this initial point in the screenplay?

3. What is Marianne's estimation of Isak? What distinctions does she make between the man he appears to be and the man he really is?

4. When sitting next to the wild strawberries, Isak has "a strange feeling of solemnity, as if this were a day of decision" and writes that "it was not the only time that day that I was to feel that way." Where else in the play is the day given such importance? What kind of decision is being alluded to? When does that decision become evident?

5. In the dream or reverie which Isak has near the wild strawberries, how is young Isak characterized, especially by Sara? What qualities distinguish Isak from his brother Sigfrid?

6. Sara from the dream merges with Sara of the present, particularly when the latter is first introduced. What is the purpose behind that implied association? How does Isak respond to the present-day Sara?

7. What do Alman and Berit contribute to the play? Why do they appear and disappear so suddenly? What values and characteristics are represented by the three young people? Their age is one obvious contrast to Isak's life. In what other ways do they represent contrasting values?

8. In general, what is Isak's response to the memories from his past? Is he uplifted or depressed by them? In a second dream sequence Sara (his childhood sweetheart) comments to him: "In spite of all your knowledge you don't really know anything." What does she mean? How might this be seen to characterize Isak's life?

9. Of what is Isak accused by Alman in the dream? The examination appears to be one which will test his medical competency. Is that its main concern? What is the connection between the man and woman in the forest and Isak's life? Why must Isak pay a penalty of "loneliness"? A penalty for what?

10. Isak, his son, and his mother are all characterized by Marianne as "lonely and cold," as exemplifying a death-in-life existence. Why? What features of their lives, especially Isak's, are deadly?

11. The ending of the play focuses on ceremony and reconciliation (Evald with Marianne, Isak with Miss Agda) and allows us to see Isak with greater warmth and lightheartedness than before. What has happened to change him? He indicates that he decided to write down his experiences because he "was beginning to see a remarkable causality in this chain of unexpected, entangled events." What links the events together? What is the relationship between the connected events and the "day of decision" Isak referred to earlier? Why do you think the playwright ends his drama with a scene from the past? Is this escapism for Isak? Why or why not?

For Comparison

King Lear and *Wild Strawberries* are both about older men who must relive and in some sense "pay for" mistakes they have made. Both King Lear and Isak Borg are seen as isolated figures, standing apart from family and close friends. What other features of their lives are similar? What is contrasting about their experiences? King Lear dies while Isak Borg does not, a fact which contributes to the tragic effect of Shakespeare's play. What else makes *King Lear* tragic, in contrast to *Wild Strawberries*? Compare Creon and Isak Borg. What is it about their actions, and the final scenes of the two plays, that allows *Antigone* to end on a note of pity and fear, *Wild Strawberries* on a note of reconciliation and "lightheartedness"?

EUGENE IONESCO (1912–   )
The Leader

Translated by Derek Prouse

Characters

THE ANNOUNCER

THE YOUNG LOVER

THE GIRL-FRIEND

THE ADMIRER

THE GIRL ADMIRER

THE LEADER

(*Standing with his back to the public, centre-stage, and with his eyes fixed on the up-stage exit, the* ANNOUNCER *waits for the arrival of the* LEADER. *To right and left, riveted to the walls, two of the* LEADER'S ADMIRERS, *a man and a girl, also wait for his arrival.*)

ANNOUNCER (*after a few tense moments in the same position*): There he is! There he is! At the end of the street! (*Shouts of 'Hurrah!' etc., are heard.*) There's the leader! He's coming, he's coming nearer! (*Cries of acclaim and applause are heard from the wings.*) It's better if he doesn't see us . . . (*The* TWO ADMIRERS *hug the wall even closer.*) Watch out! (*The* ANNOUNCER *gives vent to a brief display of enthusiasm.*) Hurrah! Hurrah! The leader! The leader! Long live the leader! (*The* TWO ADMIRERS, *with their bodies rigid and flattened against the wall, thrust their necks and heads as far forward as they can to get a glimpse of the* LEADER.) The leader! The leader! (*The* TWO ADMIRERS *in unison:*) Hurrah! Hurrah! (*Other 'Hurrahs!' mingled with 'Hurrah! Bravo!' come from the wings and gradually die down.*) Hurrah! Bravo!

(*The* ANNOUNCER *takes a step up-stage, stops, then up-stage, followed by the* TWO ADMIRERS, *saying as he goes: 'Ah! Too bad! He's going away! He's going away! Follow me quickly! After him!'* THE ANNOUNCER *and the* TWO ADMIRERS *leave, crying: 'Leader! Leeeeader! Lee-ee-eader!' (This last 'Lee-ee-eader?' echoes in the wings like a bleating cry. Silence. The stage is empty for a few brief moments. The* YOUNG LOVER *enters right, and his* GIRL-FRIEND *left; they meet centre-stage.*)

YOUNG LOVER: Forgive me, Madame, or should I say Mademoiselle?

GIRL-FRIEND: I beg your pardon, I'm afraid I don't happen to know you!

YOUNG LOVER: And I'm afraid I don't know you either!

GIRL-FRIEND: Then neither of us knows each other.

YOUNG LOVER: Exactly. We have something in common. It means that between us there is a basis of understanding on which we can build the edifice of our future.

GIRL-FRIEND: That leaves me cold, I'm afraid.

(*She makes as if to go.*)

YOUNG LOVER: Oh, my darling, I adore you.

GIRL-FRIEND: Darling, so do I!

(*They embrace.*)

YOUNG LOVER: I'm taking you with me, darling. We'll get married straightaway.

(*They leave left. The stage is empty for a brief moment.*)

ANNOUNCER (*enters up-stage followed by the* TWO ADMIRERS): But the leader swore that he'd be passing here.

ADMIRER: Are you absolutely sure of that?

ANNOUNCER: Yes, yes, of course.

GIRL ADMIRER: Was it really on his way?

ANNOUNCER: Yes, yes. He should have passed by here, it was marked on the Festival programme . . .

ADMIRER: Did you actually see it yourself and hear it with your own eyes and ears?

ANNOUNCER: He told someone. Someone else!

ADMIRER: But who? Who was this someone else?

GIRL ADMIRER: Was it a reliable person? A friend of yours?

ANNOUNCER: A friend of mine who I know very well. (*Suddenly in the background one hears renewed cries of 'Hurrah!' and 'Long live the leader!'*) That's him now! There he is! Hip! Hip! Hurrah! There he is! Hide yourselves! Hide yourselves!

(*The* TWO ADMIRERS *flatten themselves as before against the wall, stretching their necks out towards the wings from where the shouts of acclamation come; the* ANNOUNCER *watches fixedly up-stage, his back to the public.*)

ANNOUNCER: The leader's coming. He approaches. He's bending. He's unbending. (*At each of the* ANNOUNCER'S *words, the* ADMIRERS *give a start and stretch their necks even farther; they shudder.*) He's jumping. He's crossed the river. They're shaking his hand. He sticks out his thumb. Can you hear? They're laughing. (*The* ANNOUNCER *and the* TWO ADMIRERS *also laugh.*) Ah . . . ! they're giving him a box of tools. What's he going to do with them? Ah . . . ! he's signing autographs. The leader is stroking a hedgehog, a superb hedgehog! The crowd applauds. He's dancing, with the hedgehog in his hand. He's embracing his dancer. Hurrah! Hurrah! (*Cries are heard in the wings.*) He's being photographed, with his dancer on one hand and the hedgehog on the other . . . He greets the crowd . . . He spits a tremendous distance.

GIRL ADMIRER: Is he coming past here? Is he coming in our direction?

ADMIRER: Are we really on his route?

ANNOUNCER (*turns his head to the* TWO ADMIRERS): Quiet, and don't move, you're spoiling everything . . .

GIRL ADMIRER: But even so . . .

ANNOUNCER: Keep quiet, I tell you! Didn't I tell you he'd promised, that he had fixed his itinerary himself. . . . (*He turns back up-stage and cries.*) Hurrah! Hurrah! Long live the leader! (*Silence*) Long live, long live, the leader! (*Silence*) Long live, long live, long live the lead-er! (*The* TWO ADMIRERS, *unable to contain themselves, also give a sudden cry of:*) Hurrah! Long live the leader!

ANNOUNCER (*to the* ADMIRERS): Quiet, you two! Calm down! You're spoiling everything! (*Then, once more looking up-stage, with the* ADMIRERS *silenced.*) Long live the leader! (*Wildly enthusiastic.*) Hurrah! Hurrah! He's changing his shirt. He disappears behind a red screen. He reappears! (*The applause intensifies.*) Bravo! Bravo! (*The* ADMIRERS *also long to cry 'Bravo' and applaud; they put their hands to their mouths to stop themselves.*) He's putting his tie on! He's reading his newspaper and drinking his morning coffee! He's still got his hedgehog . . . He's leaning on the edge of the parapet. The parapet breaks. He gets up . . . he gets up unaided! (*Applause, shouts of 'Hurrah!'*) Bravo! Well done! He brushes his soiled clothes.

TWO ADMIRERS (*stamping their feet*): Oh! Ah! Oh! Oh! Ah! Ah!

ANNOUNCER: He's mounting the stool! He's climbing piggy-back, they're offering him a thin-ended wedge, he knows it's meant as a joke, and he doesn't mind, he's laughing.

(*Applause and enormous acclaim.*)

ADMIRER (*to the* GIRL ADMIRER): You hear that? You hear? Oh! If I were king . . .

GIRL ADMIRER: Ah . . . ! the leader!

(*This is said in an exalted tone.*)

ANNOUNCER (*still with his back to the public*): He's mounting the stool. No. He's getting down. A little girl offers him a bouquet of flowers . . . What's he going to do? He takes the flowers . . . He embraces the little girl . . . calls her 'my child' . . .

ADMIRER: He embraces the little girl . . . calls her 'my child' . . .

GIRL ADMIRER: He embraces the little girl . . . calls her 'my child' . . .

ANNOUNCER: He gives her the hedgehog. The little girl's crying . . . Long live the leader! Long live the leead-er!

ADMIRER: Is he coming past here?

GIRL ADMIRER: Is he coming past here?

ANNOUNCER (*with a sudden run, dashes out up-stage*): He's going away! Hurry! Come on!

(*He disappears, followed by the* TWO ADMIRERS, *all crying 'Hurrah! Hurrah!'*)

(*The stage is empty for a few moments. The* TWO LOVERS *enter, entwined in an embrace; they halt centre-stage and separate; she carries a basket on her arm.*)

GIRL-FRIEND: Let's go to the market and get some eggs!

YOUNG LOVER: Oh! I love them as much as you do!

(*She takes his arm. From the right the* ANNOUNCER *arrives running, quickly regaining his place, back to the public, followed closely by the* TWO ADMIRERS, *arriving one from the left and the other from the right; the* TWO ADMIRERS *knock into the* TWO LOVERS *who were about to leave right.*)

ADMIRER: Sorry!

YOUNG LOVER: Oh! Sorry!

GIRL ADMIRER: Sorry! Oh! Sorry!

GIRL-FRIEND: Oh! Sorry, sorry, sorry, so sorry!

ADMIRER: Sorry, sorry, sorry, oh! sorry, sorry, so sorry!

YOUNG LOVER: Oh, oh, oh, oh, oh, oh! So sorry, everyone!

GIRL-FRIEND (*to her* LOVER): Come along, Adolphe! (*to the* TWO ADMIRERS:) No harm done!

(*She leaves, leading her* LOVER *by the hand.*)

ANNOUNCER (*watching up-stage*): The leader is being pressed forward, and pressed back, and now they're pressing his trousers! (*The* TWO ADMIRERS *regain their places.*) The leader is smiling. Whilst they're pressing his trousers, he walks about. He tastes the flowers and the fruits growing in the stream. He's also tasting the roots of the trees.

He suffers the little children to come unto him. He has confidence in everybody. He inaugurates the police force. He pays tribute to justice. He salutes the great victors and the great vanquished. Finally he recites a poem. The people are very moved.

TWO ADMIRERS: Bravo! Bravo! (*Then, sobbing:*) Boo! Boo! Boo!

ANNOUNCER: All the people are weeping. (*Loud cries are heard from the wings; the* ANNOUNCER *and the* ADMIRERS *also start to bellow.*) Silence! (*The* TWO ADMIRERS *fall silent; and there is silence from the wings.*) They've given the leader's trousers back. The leader puts them on. He looks happy! Hurrah! (*'Bravos,' and acclaim from the wings. The* TWO ADMIRERS *also shout their acclaim, jump about, without being able to see anything of what is presumed to be happening in the wings.*) The leader's sucking his thumb! (*To the* TWO ADMIRERS:) Back, back to your places, you two, don't move, behave yourselves and shout: 'Long live the leader!'

TWO ADMIRERS (*flattened against the wall, shouting*): Long live, long live the leader!

ANNOUNCER: Be quiet, I tell you, you'll spoil everything! Look out, the leader's coming!

ADMIRER (*in the same position*): The leader's coming!

GIRL ADMIRER: The leader's coming!

ANNOUNCER: Watch out! And keep quiet! Oh! The leader's going away! Follow him! Follow me!

(*The* ANNOUNCER *goes out up-stage, running; the* TWO ADMIRERS *leave right and left, whilst in the wings the acclaim mounts, then fades. The stage is momentarily empty. The* YOUNG LOVER, *followed by his* GIRL-FRIEND, *appear left running across the stage right.*)

YOUNG LOVER (*running*): You won't catch me! You won't catch me!

(*Goes out.*)

GIRL-FRIEND (*running*): Wait a moment! Wait a moment!

(*She goes out. The stage is empty for a moment; then once more the* TWO LOVERS *cross the stage at a run, and leave.*)

YOUNG LOVER: You won't catch me!

GIRL-FRIEND: Wait a moment!

(*They leave right. The stage is empty. The* ANNOUNCER *reappears up-stage, the* ADMIRER *from the right, the* GIRL ADMIRER *from the left. They meet centre.*)

ADMIRER: We missed him!

GIRL ADMIRER: Rotten luck!

ANNOUNCER: It was your fault!

ADMIRER: That's not true!

GIRL ADMIRER: No, that's not true!

ANNOUNCER: Are you suggesting it was mine?

ADMIRER: No, we didn't mean that!

GIRL ADMIRER: No, we didn't mean that!

(*Noise of acclaim and 'Hurrahs' from the wings.*)

ANNOUNCER: Hurrah!

GIRL ADMIRER: It's from over there! (*She points up-stage.*)

ADMIRER: Yes, it's from over there! (*He points left.*)

ANNOUNCER: Very well. Follow me! Long live the leader!

(*He runs out right, followed by the* TWO ADMIRERS, *also shouting.*)

TWO ADMIRERS: Long live the leader!

(*They leave. The stage is empty for a moment. The* YOUNG LOVER *and his* GIRL-FRIEND *appear left; the* YOUNG LOVER *exits up-stage; the* GIRL-FRIEND, *after saying 'I'll get you!', runs out right. The* ANNOUNCER *and the* TWO ADMIRERS *appear from up-stage. The* ANNOUNCER *says to the* ADMIRERS:) Long live the leader! (*This is repeated by the* ADMIRERS. *Then, still talking to the* ADMIRERS, *he says:*) Follow me! Follow the leader! (*He leaves up-stage, still running and shouting:*) Follow him!
(*The* ADMIRER *exits right, the* GIRL ADMIRER *left into the wings. During the whole of this, the acclaim is heard louder or fainter according to the rhythm of the stage action; the stage is empty for a moment, then the* LOVERS *appear from right and left, crying:*)

YOUNG LOVER: I'll get you!

GIRL-FRIEND: You won't get me!

(*They leave at a run, shouting:*) Long live the leader! (*The* ANNOUNCER *and the* TWO ADMIRERS *emerge from up-stage, also shouting: 'Long live the leader,' followed by the* TWO LOVERS. *They all leave right, in single file, crying as they run: 'The leader! Long live the leader! We'll get him! It's from over here! You won't get me!'*)
(*They enter and leave, employing all the exits; finally, entering from left, from right, and from up-stage they all meet centre, whilst the acclaim and the applause from the wings becomes a fearful din. They embrace each other feverishly, crying at the tops of their voices:*) Long live the leader! Long live the leader! Long live the leader!
(*Then, abruptly, silence falls.*)

ANNOUNCER: The leader is arriving. Here's the leader. To your places! Attention!

(*The* ADMIRER *and the* GIRL-FRIEND *flatten themselves against the wall right; the* GIRL ADMIRER *and the* YOUNG LOVER *against the wall left; the two couples are in each other's arms, embracing.*)

ADMIRER and GIRL-FRIEND: My dear, my darling!

GIRL ADMIRER and YOUNG LOVER: My dear, my darling!

(*Meanwhile the* ANNOUNCER *has taken up his place, back to the audience, looking fixedly up-stage; a lull in the applause.*)

ANNOUNCER: Silence. The leader has eaten his soup. He is coming. He is nigh.

(*The acclaim redoubles its intensity; the* TWO ADMIRERS *and the* TWO LOVERS *shout:*)

ALL: Hurrah! Hurrah! Long live the leader!

(*They throw confetti before he arrives. Then the* ANNOUNCER *hurls himself suddenly to one side to allow the* LEADER *to pass; the other four characters freeze with outstretched arms holding confetti; but still say:*) Hurrah! (*The* LEADER *enters from up-stage, advances down-stage to centre; to the footlights, hesitates, makes a step to left, then takes a decision and leaves with great, energetic strides by right, to the enthusiastic 'Hurrahs!' of the* ANNOUNCER *and the feeble, somewhat astonished 'Hurrahs!' of the other four; these, in fact, have some reason to be surprised, as the* LEADER *is headless, though wearing a hat. This is simple to effect: the actor playing the* LEADER *needing only to wear an overcoat with the collar turned up round his forehead and topped with a hat. The-man-in-an-overcoat-with-a-hat-without-a-head is a somewhat surprising apparition and will doubtless produce a certain sensation. After the* LEADER'S *disappearance, the* GIRL ADMIRER *says:*)

GIRL ADMIRER: But . . . but . . . the leader hasn't got a head!

ANNOUNCER: What's he need a head for when he's got genius!

YOUNG LOVER: That's true! (*To the* GIRL-FRIEND:) What's your name?

(*The* YOUNG LOVER *to the* GIRL ADMIRER, *the* GIRL ADMIRER *to the* ANNOUNCER, *the* ANNOUNCER *to the* GIRL-FRIEND, *the* GIRL-FRIEND *to the* YOUNG LOVER:) What's yours? What's yours? What's yours? (*Then, all together, one to the other:*) What's your name?

CURTAIN

For Consideration

1. This play, like its better known absurdist counterpart, *Waiting for Godot* (Samuel Beckett), depends for its tension and interest on the anticipated arrival of an important figure. In Beckett's play, however, the person never comes; here he does. How does Ionesco suggest that the leader's arrival, even at the beginning of the play, is imminent?
2. What is the Announcer's role in the play? What observed activities of the leader does he describe for us? How extraordinary are those actions?
3. The young lover and the girl-friend provide occasional interludes where love is the subject. What characterizes their relationship in the play? Is it static or progressive? What is implied in the switching of partners between the two admirers and the two lovers?
4. The play utilizes repetition throughout, both in language and in action. What function does the repetition serve here? What does it suggest about the kind of world and people Ionesco is portraying?
5. There are occasional allusions to the leader as a Christ-like individual (e.g., calling the little girl "my child," "He suffers the little children to come unto him.") What is the purpose of the allusions? How serious or complete are the associations between the leader and Christ?
6. What are the responses to the appearance of the headless leader? One critic has suggested that, since the original French term translated here as "leader" is *maitre*, the leader may be a literary figure. What other positions of prominence might the leader represent? Is his exact position of leadership important?

biographical notes

MATTHEW ARNOLD (1822–1888) was a poet, professor, and critic. He was the son of Thomas Arnold, a famous headmaster, and was himself educated at Oxford. He was a teacher and professor of poetry at Oxford for ten years. He wrote numerous critical essays, especially on the arts, society, and education and was a principal leader in the revaluation of the English educational system in the mid-nineteenth century. Best known among his critical works are *Essays in Criticism* (1865, 1888), *Culture and Anarchy* (1869), and *Literature and Dogma* (1873).

W. H. AUDEN (1907–1973) in a pattern the reverse of that of T.S. Eliot, was a native of England but later became a U.S. citizen. He was born in York and was educated at Christ Church, Oxford. In 1939 he emigrated to the U.S.; though he took out U.S. citizenship, he spent much of his later life in Italy and Austria. From 1956–1961 he was professor of poetry at Oxford. His volumes of verse include *The Age of Anxiety* (1948), *The Shield of Achilles* (1959), and *About the House* (1966).

JAMES BALDWIN (1924–   ) was born in Harlem but has been a long-time expatriate in France. Since the publication of *Go Tell It on the Mountain* (1953), he has been regarded as an important American writer and, perhaps, as the leading Black American writer since Richard Wright. His essays and short stories are regarded by some as superior even to his novels; he has also written plays, the best-known of which is *Blues for Mister Charley* (1964). His most recent work is a novel, *If Beale Street Could Talk* (1974).

TONI CADE BAMBARA (1939–   ) has been teaching since 1965 at Livingston College of Rutgers University. She was born in New York City where she presently resides. She has written stories, criticism, and a book for children, and has edited *The Black Woman* (1970) and *Tales and Short Stories for Black Folks* (1971). In her short story volume, *Gorilla, My Love and Other Stories* (1972), she captures the language idioms and the vitality of the lives of contemporary Black Americans in a unique and perceptive manner.

DONALD BARTHELME (1931–   ) is an inspired, witty, outrageous, obtuse, and brilliant writer — with the emphasis falling at different points for different readers. His is largely a surrealistic mode, fragmented and apparently incomplete in its portrayal of characters and incidents. Barthelme was born in Philadelphia, spent some time in Houston as a museum director in the mid-50s, and lives presently in New York, where he has maintained a close association with *The New Yorker* magazine. He has published one novel, *Snow White* (1967), and several short story collections.

INGMAR BERGMAN (1918–   ) was born in Uppsala, Sweden, the son of a Lutheran clergyman. He has written and directed some of the finest films of the last several decades, including *Smiles of a Summer Night* (1955), *The Seventh Seal* (1956), *Wild Strawberries* (1957), *Persona* (1966), and *Cries and Whispers* (1972). Bergman was originally a stage actor and playwright and, as late as 1966, was active in the Royal Dramatic Theater. His reputation has been achieved, however, through his films.

JOHN BERRYMAN (1914–1972) wrote verse that is intensely personal and confessional, often autobiographical. He was himself an intense man, given to many moods and passions, a characteristic which is seen in much of his poetry. Berryman taught principally at Princeton and the University of Minnesota. His best known poems are his Dream Songs, 385 separate selections which reveal the intensity and variety of Berryman's moods. His *77 Dream Songs* won him the 1964 Pulitzer Prize. Berryman committed suicide in 1972 by throwing himself off a bridge in Minneapolis.

ELIZABETH BISHOP (1911–   ) is frequently associated with Marianne Moore, a poet equally concerned with details drawn from the physical world. "The Fish" reveals her interest in presenting and reacting to a particular object or detail and making of it the subject of her poetry. She has written relatively little, and most of her poetry seems intentionally unrevealing about herself. *Selected Poems* appeared in 1967, *The Complete Poems* in 1969.

BYRON BLACK (1940–   ), an American Indian, attended the University of Texas, which provides the locale for "I, the Fake Mad Bomber and Walking It Home Again." The poem was published in *Prairie Schooner* when Black was still a student.

DAVID BLACK (1945–   ) was born in Boston, Massachusetts, and grew up in Springfield, Massachusetts. He attended Amherst College and Columbia University. He has acted five years in Equity summer stock theaters and, in 1965, appeared as Vladimir in a revival of Beckett's *Waiting For Godot* at The Writer's Stage Theater in New York. He has published poems in *Poet Lore, Penache, Grist, Experiment*. Formerly Features Editor of *Zygote*, at present he is a staff writer for *The Metropolitan Review*. He is married and lives in New York City.

PAUL BLACKBURN (1926–1971), like other poets associated with the Black Mountain

School, was attracted to ordinary speech as a vehicle for his poetry rather than remote or stilted language. He was born in Vermont, attended New York University, and graduated from the University of Wisconsin in 1950. He went to France on a Fulbright Fellowship and subsequently taught at the City University of New York. He was also, for a time, poetry editor for *The Nation*. *Collected Poems, 1949–1961* was published in 1972.

WILLIAM BLAKE (1757–1827) was both a poet and engraver; some of his writings are vividly illustrated by his own art work. Discontented with contemporary society and with contemporary views of poetry, he formulated a highly mystical and mythological system which gives meaning to many of his poems, particularly his longer ones. Blake was strongly opposed to the restrictions of society and religion and voiced those objections in his works. *Songs of Innocence* (1789) and *Songs of Experience* (1794), companion volumes, present contrasting views of the prominence of good and evil.

ROBERT BLY (1926–   ) was born in Madison, Minnesota, and presently resides there on a farm. He was educated at Harvard and the University of Iowa. He was influenced in his own writings by Blake and Whitman and by a number of South American and European authors. In addition to writing poetry, he has translated the works of several Eastern and South American figures; he is also the editor of a poetry magazine, *The Seventies*. His work has appeared as *The Light Around the Body* (1967), *The Morning Glory* (1969), *Sleepers Joining Hands* (1972) and other volumes.

ROBERT BRIDGES (1844–1930) was a poet who in many ways was the opposite of his friend and fellow-poet, Gerard Manley Hopkins. Bridges is very traditional, not given to the oddities and experimentation characteristic of Hopkins' verse. Bridges was born in England, attended Oxford University, and spent the last 40 years of his life near the university. He was named Poet Laureate in 1913 and in 1929 received the Order of Merit. Bridges' reputation was secured by the several volumes of his *Shorter Poems* printed between 1873 and 1893; at the other extreme in length, his philosophical poem *The Testament of Beauty* (1929) was equally well received and went through fourteen editions or impressions within one year.

GWENDOLYN BROOKS (1917–   ) is less militant, less strident than other, younger Black poets writing today, but she is no less insistent in her advocacy of human rights and honesty in human relationships. Born in Topeka, Kansas, she has lived most of her life in Chicago, where she presently resides. She won a Pulitzer Prize for her book *Annie Allen* (1949) and was named to succeed Carl Sandburg as Poet Laureate of Illinois. An autobiographical work, *Report from Part One*, appeared in 1972.

ROBERT BROWNING (1812–1889) perfected, as much as any other poet in the language, the difficult form of the dramatic monologue. He wrote other kinds of verse as well, including a book-length narrative titled *The Ring and the Book* (1868-9). In 1846, he married Elizabeth Barret (*Sonnets from the Portuguese*); they spent most of their married life in Italy until her death. During the nineteenth century there sprang up in the United States various clubs and cults made up of Browning devotees; since then, the passionate enthusiasm for his verse has waned but his reputation remains high.

ROBERT BURNS (1759–1796) was a Scotsman noted, in person and in his poetry, for his modest and unassuming manner. His subjects are familiar, even trivial, but he makes them fresh and appealing. In addition to his own volumes of verse, he wrote or adapted numerous songs for two collections of Scottish ballads and songs being edited during his day.

GEORGE GORDON, LORD BYRON (1788–1824) , like his Romantic contemporaries Shelley and Keats, wrote much and died young. Byron especially opposed what he saw as the restrictions and hypocrisy of his native England. Although he wrote a number of short, graceful lyrics, he is best known for his longer works, especially his epic satire, *Don Juan* (1818). The hero of that poem, like Byron himself, was a professed libertine who, by his actions, rebelled against the social and religious limitations of his day. Although Byron's poetry was frequently criticized for moral reasons, it remained popular in England and abroad.

ALBERT CAMUS (1913–1960) was perhaps the most accomplished of the French writers aligned with the "philosophie de l'absurde" which focused on the existential (and often absurd) dilemma facing modern humanity. His works are therefore often grounded on his perception of profound ironies and futilities in human existence. His novels include *The Stranger* (1942) and *The Plague* (1947); an important volume of essays, *The Myth of Sisyphus*, was published in 1942. In 1957 Camus was awarded the Nobel Prize for Literature.

ANTON CHEKHOV (1860–1904) was a Russian author perhaps better known for his plays than for his short stories, but he excelled in both. To further emphasize his achievement, he was, by profession, a doctor and continued to practice medicine while writing and perfecting his stories and plays. His best-known drama, frequently anthologized, is *The Cherry Orchard* (1904).

JOHN CLARE (1793-1864) worked at various jobs and wrote a number of poems, mostly on rural life or natural settings. In 1837 he was declared insane. Poetry published during his lifetime includes *Poems Descriptive of Rural Life* (1820) and *The Rural Muse* (1835).

LUCILLE CLIFTON (1936–   ) has written a number of books for children and adolescents and has published two volumes of poetry, *Good Times* (1970) and *Good News About the Earth* (1972). She attended Howard University and Fredonia State Teacher's College and presently lives in

Baltimore, Maryland. Her poems, like "Good Times," are often short, bittersweet portraits of Black Americans and their experiences in contemporary society.

GREGORY CORSO (1930–   ) is, with Allen Ginsberg and a few others, one of the poets identified with the Beat Generation. His life has been difficult and frenetic since its conception: he was born in Greenwich Village to parents who were seventeen and sixteen and who placed him in foster homes during much of his first ten years. He spent time in prison, underwent a mental examination at Bellevue Hospital, and has seldom settled for long at any one location. Nonetheless, he has, during these years, written some of the best of the "beat" poetry, notably "Marriage." His volumes include *Gasoline* (1958), *The Happy Birthday of Death* (1960), and *Long Live Man* (1963).

STEPHEN CRANE (1871–1900) spent most of his youth in New York, including stints as a reporter for two New York newspapers. He was a war correspondent in Mexico and Cuba and, in 1896, was involved in a shipwreck which furnished the background for "The Open Boat." His novel *The Red Badge of Courage* (1895) has long been known for its realism and its penetration of the psychological trauma of war. During his final years Crane was in poor health, and rumors of alcoholism and drug addiction were prevalent. Crane died in Germany, where he had gone to seek a cure for tuberculosis.

ROBERT CREELEY (1926–   ) has had a varied career as poet and teacher. Born in Massachusetts, he has lived on Cape Cod, on a farm in New Hampshire, at Marjorca, New Mexico, Guatemala, and New York. He joined the faculty of Black Mountain College in 1954 at the request of Charles Olson. Later he taught in New Mexico and Guatemala. Since 1966 he has taught at the State University of New York at Buffalo. Characteristically Creeley's poems are fairly short and unpretentious, for he eschewed remote or pompous language. Among his nearly twenty volumes are *For Love: Poems, 1950–1960* (1962), *Poems 1950–1965* (1966), and *A Day Book* (1972).

E. E. CUMMINGS (1894–1963) was an American poet best known for the unpredictable and idiosyncratic appearance of his verse in printed form. He generally ignored traditional standards of punctuation and capitalization, a quality which frequently frustrates first-time readers. His poetry includes a healthy amount of witty satire, usually directed against the mechanization and dehumanization of modern society. His later volumes of poetry are *95 Poems* (1958), *100 Selected Poems* (1959), *73 Poems* (1963), and *Complete Poems* (1973).

EMILY DICKINSON (1830–1886) was born in Amherst, Massachusetts and was a life-long resident there. She was the grand daughter of one of the founders of Amherst College. She apparently lived a sheltered existence, unmarried and relatively secluded, until her death. Her poetry — in something of a contrast to her life — is characterized by its passionate, unconventional voice. Of her total production of nearly 1800 poems only eight were published during her lifetime.

JOHN DONNE (1572–1631) was the master of the witty and penetrating lyric being written, or attempted, by many poets in the seventeenth century. One of the best practitioners of "metaphysical" poetry, Donne is consistently challenging, cajoling, or questioning another, whether it be a lover, a friend, or God. In 1615 Donne took Anglican orders and proceeded to become one of the outstanding preachers of his day. He was Dean of St. Paul's until his death and frequently preached before the King. Because of his secular and sacred writings a myth has grown about the two John Donnes — "Jack" Donne, young, witty, rakish, and secular, and Dean John Donne, older, more urbane, and intensely religious.

ROBERT DUNCAN (1919–   ) is one of a group of poets (including Robert Creeley and Denise Levertov) who reveal the impact of the earlier modern poet, Charles Olson. Duncan associates poetry with the magical and erudite, and his poetry, particularly that on political subjects such as the Vietnam war, is frequently prophetic and apocalyptic. He has taught at various universities, including a stint with Olson in 1956 at Black Mountain College. Among his published works are *Heavenly City, Earthly City* (1947), *The Opening of the Field* (1960), *Roots and Branches* (1964), *Bending the Bow* (1968) plus some fourteen other volumes of verse.

RICHARD EBERHART (1904–   ) was born in Austin, Minnesota, and was educated at the University of Minnesota, Dartmouth, and St. John's College, Cambridge. He is presently professor of English and poet-in-residence at Dartmouth. His poetic style is occasionally reminiscent of Thomas Hardy's in that some awkwardness of diction or phrasing is combined with the general smoothness of the lyric mode. His *Collected Poems* appeared in 1960 and his *Collected Verse Plays* in 1962. His awards include the Harriet Monroe Poetry Award and the Bollingen Prize.

T. S. ELIOT (1888–1965) wrote a number of works which explore the forces of disillusionment and despair in the early twentieth century, an era which he captured as *The Waste Land* (1922) in one of his important long poems. He was a dominant figure of his age, both in his poetry and his essays. He was born in St. Louis and was educated at Harvard, the University of Paris, and Merton College, Oxford. In 1927 he became a British subject. In his later years he became a convert to the Anglican Church and adopted a more specifically religious tone in his writings. Works from this later period include *The Four Quartets* (1943) and several plays, notably *Murder in the Cathedral* (1935), *The Family Reunion* (1939), and *The Cocktail Party* (1950). In 1948 Eliot was awarded the Nobel Prize for Literature and received the Order of Merit.

RALPH WALDO EMERSON (1803–1882) was a versatile and important writer and speaker — a poet, an essayist, and a public lecturer. His father was a Unitarian minister, a profession young Emerson pursued for a time. In 1832 he resigned the ministry to follow a career as writer and lecturer. His numerous essays and addresses contributed to his prominence and influence even more than his poetry. He was a friend of Henry David Thoreau and was, with Thoreau and others, a leader among American Transcendentalists of the nineteenth century.

WILLIAM FAULKNER (1897–1962) is one of the great writers of modern fiction. His early experiences do not foretell his later success: he did not finish college and spent the first thirty years of his life working at an assortment of jobs. Success and fame came, however, with the writing of such novels as *The Sound and the Fury* (1929), *Light in August* (1932), and *Absalom, Absalom!* (1936). His writing style is complex and highly involved, almost the antithesis of the style of Hemingway, his equally renowned contemporary. A lifelong resident of Oxford, Mississippi, Faulkner created a mythical county (Yoknapatawpha) in which to set his fictional characters. In 1950 he was awarded the Nobel Prize for Literature.

LAWRENCE FERLINGHETTI (1919–) is, with Allen Ginsberg, one of the leaders of the "Beat" movement in modern poetry. He was born in New York and traveled extensively as a young man. In 1951 he opened City Lights Bookstore in San Francisco and later published a number of contemporary poets, including Ginsberg, in his Pocket Poets Series. Like a number of his contemporaries he can be overtly political in his writings, as in his satiric poem on former President Nixon, *Tyrannus Nix?* (1969).

ROBERT FROST (1874–1963) was a poet who, better than most, was able to bridge the gap between the professional, literary poet and the public versifier. His poetry is simple — though deceptively so — and thus has appeal to a broad spectrum of the reading public. He was born in California but spent most of his life on a farm in New England, a region which furnished images and scenes for his poetry. He was frequently honored during his lifetime and won, among numerous awards, three Pulitzer Prizes. Among his popular individual volumes are *A Boy's Will* (1913), *North of Boston* (1914), *West-Running Brook* (1928), *A Masque of Reason* (1945), and *In the Clearing* (1962). *The Poetry of Robert Frost* appeared in 1969.

ALLEN GINSBERG (1926–) is an American poet most readily identified with the Beat Generation. He was born in Newark, New Jersey, and was educated at Columbia University. For a time he worked at a variety of jobs and eventually became identified with the poetry of the counterculture. He achieved great notoriety because of obscenity charges leveled against some early works and because of his advocacy of Zen Buddhism, hallucinatory drugs, and homosexuality. His poetry volumes include *Howl* (1956), *Kaddish and Other Poems 1958–1960* (1961), *Reality Sandwiches* (1963), and *Planet News: 1961–1967* (1968).

NIKKI GIOVANNI (1943–) is an American poet who writes distinctly of her experiences as a black woman. Born in Knoxville, Tennessee, she grew up in a suburb of Cincinnati. She attended Fisk University and, for a time, the University of Pennsylvania. In addition to writing poetry, she has taught literature and poetry in the university. Her poetry volumes include *Black Feeling, Black Talk, Black Judgment* (1970), *Re:Creation* (1971), and *My House* (1972).

URI ZVI GREENBERG (1895–   ) published his first volume of Yiddish verse in 1915. He served in the Austro-Hungarian army during World War I and later was one of the Zionist pioneers in Palestine. He has consistently aligned himself, in his actions and his poetry, with the cause of Israeli independence. He was elected to the Israeli parliament in 1949.

THOM GUNN (1929–   ) is one of a group of English poets emerging in the fifties who sought to make poetry more concrete and its language more familiar. His poems are often about action or movement. One volume is titled *The Sense of Movement* (1957). "On the Move," a further example, is a poem about California motorcyclists. He was born in England, attended Trinity College, Cambridge University, and then moved to California where he entered graduate school at Stanford University. He continues to reside in California where he teaches and writes.

THOMAS HARDY (1840–1928) achieved his reputation for both novels and poetry. His novels include *The Return of the Native* (1878), *The Mayor of Casterbridge* (1886), *Tess of the D'Urbervilles* (1891), and *Jude the Obscure* (1896). He was also an architect, spending time restoring old churches. He was born at Upper Bockhampton in Dorset, England, and spent much of his life there. His writings are characterized by their pessimistic note, resulting fundamentally from Hardy's view that the universe is neither kind nor malevolent but is simply and profoundly indifferent to the affairs of humankind.

NATHANIEL HAWTHORNE (1804–1864) was born in Salem, Massachusetts, and reared in a prominent Puritan family. In his fiction, he frequently depicted the conflict between Puritanical values and individual liberty in New England. He is generally regarded, along with Edgar Allan Poe, as a leader in the development of the short story in American literature. His best known novels are *The Scarlet Letter* (1850) and *The House of the Seven Gables* (1851).

ERNEST HEMINGWAY (1898–1961) exemplified in his life the tough and active virtues which he often wrote about. His life and his writing style are vivid contrasts to those of his contemporary, William Faulkner. His stories and novels are written in a terse, concise style, with little elaboration or extended description. His novels include *The Sun Also Rises* (1926), *A Farewell to Arms* (1929), and *For Whom the Bell Tolls* (1940). In 1954, two years after the publication of *The Old Man and the Sea* (1952), he was awarded the Nobel Prize, more for his total output than for any single work. In 1961, during an extended illness, he committed suicide in a manner characteristic of his life and actions — by shooting himself in the head with a shotgun.

GEORGE HERBERT (1593–1633) wrote poems essentially on one subject: the relationship of man and God. His verse is, in its style, similar to that of his contemporary John Donne. He does not, though, include either the secularism or the degree of incongruity that can be seen in the whole of Donne's works. Herbert's poetry has its quaintness and surprises, but usually within a more moderate, less extravagant tone. Herbert took orders as an Anglican priest and spent the last years of his life as, in a biographer's words, a "country parson."

ROBERT HERRICK (1591–1674) was one of the followers of Ben Jonson in his adherence to a more classical form of poetry. Herrick wrote both sacred and secular verse but is better remembered for the second. His poetry is characterized by a simple, yet appropriately elegant form and by his inclination toward familiar, even trivial subjects. Herrick was born in London, studied at Cambridge, and spent most of his life in Devonshire and Westminster.

RUTH HERSCHBERGER (1917–   ) was born in Philipse Manor, New York, and presently resides in New York City. She attended the University of Chicago, Black Mountain College, and the University of Michigan. In 1953 she received the Harriet Monroe Memorial Prize. In addition to a book of poems (*A Way of Happening*, 1948), she has written several plays: *Adam's Rib*, *Edgar Allan Poe*, *A Ferocious Incident*, and *Andrew Jackson*, the last three written as radio plays.

GERARD MANLEY HOPKINS (1844–1889) was a Jesuit priest whose poetry (with few exceptions) was not published until after his death. In 1918 Robert Bridges, the Poet Laureate and friend of Hopkins, edited Hopkins' poetry and presented it to a generally appreciative audience. Hopkins is thus a nineteenth-century writer who was "discovered" in the twentieth century and who has influenced many poets of the last several decades. His subjects are often religious ones, and his verse is characterized by its close attention to sound effects (notably alliteration) and its relative indifference to traditional expectations about stanzas, meters, and even language.

HENRIK IBSEN (1828–1906) has written some of the best and most influential social dramas of the last hundred years. He was a Norwegian playwright, and, in his finest writings, immersed himself in the problems and attitudes of a restrictive social environment, one which conflicted with and hindered the aims and needs of the individual, notably the individual woman. His plays include *A Doll's House* (1879), *Ghosts* (1881), *An Enemy of the People* (1882), and *The Wild Duck* (1884).

EUGENE IONESCO (1912–   ) was born in Rumania, spent his early childhood in France, and then returned to Rumania at the age of 13. After a university education in Rumania he returned again to France in 1939, where he began working for a publisher. His plays are examples of Absurdist drama and are indicative of his view that fantasy or a surrealistic presentation of character and action may be the most effective, indeed most truthful, representation of the inner realities of human life. His plays, in addition to *The Leader*, include *The Lesson* (1950), *The Chairs* (1951), *Rhinoceros* (1959), and *The Gap* (1962).

SHIRLEY JACKSON (1919–1965) was born in California and was educated at Syracuse University. Her writings tend to be dominated by children in various ways. Her novels include three (*The Road Through the Wall* (1948), *Hangsaman* (1951), and *The Bird's Nest* (1954)) which feature disturbed adolescents; two books (*Life Among the Savages* (1953) and *Raising Demons* (1957)) portray, in a light manner, her own experiences with children. She wrote a book for children, *The Witchcraft of Salem Village* (1956). She also reveals a strong interest in strange, unpredictable or occult experiences. For several years she lived in Vermont with her husband, teacher-critic Stanley Edgar Hyman.

RANDALL JARRELL (1914–1965) was born in Nashville, Tennessee, and studied at Vanderbilt University under John Crowe Ransom. He taught at a number of colleges and universities, including Kenyon College, the University of Texas, and the Women's College of the University of North Carolina at Greensboro. Among his poems, the ones most frequently cited are the several World War II flight poems (though Jarrell himself did not pass flight training) and his poems embodying distinct speaking voices. His volume *Selected Poems* was published in 1955 and 1964; *Complete Poems* appeared in 1969.

BEN JONSON (1572–1637) was a prominent figure of his age and numbered among his literary associates Bacon, Donne, and Shakespeare. His own poetry is, on the whole, classical and unassuming in its style and tone. His best known plays are comedies, including *Volpone* (1606), *Epicoene* (1609), *The Alchemist* (1610), and *The Devil Is an Ass* (1616). Noted for his contentious and sometimes arrogant spirit, Jonson could also be exceedingly kind and generous to others. In 1616 he received a pension from James I, making him, in effect, the first Poet Laureate.

JAMES JOYCE (1882–1941) is largely, though not solely, responsible for the development of the "stream-of-consciousness" technique in modern fiction, an attempt to recount, as exactly as possible, the actual thoughts and images that pass through a character's head. He was born and educated in Dublin but left Ireland for good in his early twenties. In spite of this, Dublin is always the setting for his fiction, though it is specifically a Dublin where political and religious restrictions still exist, restrictions which Joyce vigorously opposed. His fiction, notably *Ulysses* (1922) and *Finnegans Wake* (1939), is difficult and searching, especially in matters of style and technique.

JOHN KEATS (1795–1821) wrote some of the best short lyrics in the English language. In his abbreviated lifetime, he was able to write such lasting works as "The Eve of St. Agnes," "La Belle Dame sans Merci," and the odes — on a Grecian urn, to a nightingale, to autumn, and on melancholy. Keats died of consumption in Rome in 1821, a loss lamented and celebrated by his friend Shelley in the poem "Adonais."

X. J. KENNEDY (JOSEPH CHARLES KENNEDY) (1929–   ) is a poet, teacher, and editor. He was born in Dover, New Jersey, and attended Seton Hall College, Columbia University and the Sorbonne in Paris. He has taught in a number of universities and presently is a professor of English at Tufts University in Medford, Massachusetts. He has been regarded as one of the "academic" poets, knowledgeable, witty and skillful in matters of form. His best known volume of poetry is *Nude Descending a Staircase* (1961). He has also edited a poetry textbook and, recently, an anthology of literature.

THOMAS KINSELLA (1928–   ) was born in Dublin and lived there until 1965. That year he became Writer in Residence at Southern Illinois University, where he presently teaches as Professor of English. His first volume, *Poems*, was published in 1956; a second volume, *Another September* (1958), won the Guinness Poetry Award. He has thus far published eight books of poems, the last being *Nightwalker and Other Poems* (1968).

ETHERIDGE KNIGHT (1933–   ) wrote his *Poems from Prison* (1968) while he was serving a twenty-year term at the Indiana State Prison. Appropriate to the circumstances of the writing, his poems are frequently tense and private reflections. Knight was paroled in late 1968.

STANLEY KUNITZ (1905–   ) won the Pulitzer Prize in 1958 for his volume, *Selected Poems*. Ironically he had some difficulty even getting the book in print. Other volumes include *Intellectual Things* (1930), *Passport to the War* (1944), and *The Testing-Tree* (1970). Kunitz has taught at a number of universities, since 1963 at Columbia. He is also an editor and in 1969 succeeded Dudley Fitts as editor of the Yale Series of Younger Poets.

PHILIP LARKIN (1922–   ) was born in Coventry, Warwickshire, England, and attended Oxford, from which he graduated in 1943. He has been a librarian for much of his life, a profession which is, perhaps, in keeping with the moderate tone and style of much of his verse. He shuns the exaggerated or extreme in his poetry, choosing instead a more familiar, more conversational medium. *Poems* was published in 1954, *The Less Deceived* in 1955, and *The Whitsun Weddings* in 1964.

D(AVID) H(ERBERT) LAWRENCE (1885–1930) is regarded by most critics as one of the two prominent British novelists of the early twentieth century, the second being James Joyce. Lawrence's fiction often depicts lower class working people, reminiscent of the social environment in which he was raised. His writings — both fiction and poetry — are at once vivid and realistic and highly symbolic. His novels include *Sons and Lovers* (1913), *Women in Love* (1920), and *Lady Chatterley's Lover* (1928); the last novel (not, in the view of most, his best) stands as a symbol of his resistance against censorship and restrictions on the arts.

JOHN LENNON (1942–   ) and **PAUL MCCARTNEY** (1940–   ), as members of the British rock group, The Beatles, wrote some of the finest lyrics of the 1960's. The best of their songs, such as "Eleanor Rigby," "A Day in the Life," and "The Fool on the Hill," are particularly skillful in their concise characterizations and their effective images.

DORIS LESSING (1919–   ) was born in Persia and lived for twenty-five years in Southern Rhodesia. She has written a number of novels, including a related series of five volumes, several short story collections, four plays, poetry, and essays. Her books reflect great variety and scope and often focus on male-female relationships. She is probably best known for *The Golden Notebook* (1962), which concerns itself with the problems of writing and with the role of women from what would be judged, in contemporary times, as a feminist perspective.

DENISE LEVERTOV (1923–   ) was born at Ilford, Essex, England, and presently lives in New York. She shares with Robert Duncan and Robert Creeley an interest in less grand, more modest subjects for her poetry. She has an interest in mysticism, in part because of her acquaintance with mystics among past members of her own family. Along with her husband, writer Mitchell Goodman, she actively opposed the Vietnam war, a fact reflected in her poetry of the late Sixties. Her poetry volumes include *The Double Image* (1946), *With Eyes at the Back of Our Heads* (1959), *The Jacob's Ladder* (1961), and *To Stay Alive* (1971) plus some half-dozen others.

ARCHIBALD MACLEISH (1892–   ) is notable for his profound awareness of the conflict between private poetry and public obligation. He is the rare individual who can claim success both as poet and as public servant. He won the Pulitzer Prize in 1932 and later was a professor at Harvard (1949–1962). Between those dates he was Librarian of Congress and held several other government posts, including Assistant Secretary of State. *Collected Poems* was first published in 1952 and revised in 1963, but he has since published additional volumes as well. He has also turned his creative energies toward the writing of verse plays, the best known being *JB* (1958).

BERNARD MALAMUD (1914–   ) was born in Brooklyn and was educated at the City College of New York and Columbia University. His fiction is noted for its wit and satiric humor but also for its compassionate view of human characters. His usual fictional subject is Jewish and, ordinarily, some dilemma or trial must be dealt with. His novels include *The Natural* (1952), *The Assistant* (1958), and *The Fixer* (1966). His short story collection, *The Magic Barrel*, won the National Book Award for 1959.

CHRISTOPHER MARLOWE (1564–1593) was the son of a shoemaker and himself became known as a playwright and poet. His *Tamburlaine* (1590) promoted the development of blank verse in Renaissance drama. Other important plays, in order of their writing, are *Tragedy of Dr. Faustus* (publ. 1604), *The Jew of Malta* (publ. 1633), and *Edward II* (publ. 1594). Marlowe was something of a rebel during his day, holding and espousing atheistic opinions. He was killed in a tavern in 1593 in an action still not fully explained.

ANDREW MARVELL (1621–1678) was born near Hull, England, and was educated at Trinity College, Cambridge. His poems frequently reflect his love of gardens and of rural life, and many are based on his stay as a tutor at Appleton House, beginning in 1650. "The Garden" and "Upon Appleton House" are among the best of these "rural" poems. In 1657 he became an assistant to Milton in the latter's position as Latin secretary. After the Restoration, Marvell entered Parliament and became increasingly involved in political writings and activities.

JAMES ALAN MCPHERSON (1943–   ) was born in Savannah, Georgia, and attended Morgan State College in Baltimore. From there he attended the Harvard Law School and later acted as a recruiter for Harvard. His writing, however, has taken precedent over his training in law. He has worked as a reporter for *The Atlantic* and is presently a contributing editor to that journal. His stories focus on the experiences of blacks in a white society, but his treatment of racial themes are more subtle than overt. His short story volume *Hue and Cry* was published in 1969.

HERMAN MELVILLE (1819–1891) wrote the classic American novel, *Moby Dick* (1851), and other works of fiction and poetry. He was born in New York and spent his youthful years at sea; those experiences provided the seed for several of his fictional efforts, including *Typee* (1846), *Redburn* (1849), and *White Jacket* (1850). During his last years, with the exception of his posthumously published novel *Billy Budd*, he concentrated on writing poetry.

W. S. MERWIN (1927–   ) was awarded the Pulitzer Prize in 1971 for his volume of poems, *A Carrier of Ladders*. A prolific author, Merwin began a distinguished career by being chosen, at age twenty-four, for the Yale Younger Poets series; W. H. Auden selected Merwin's *A Mask for Janus* for publication in the series in 1952. Merwin is a translator and playwright, as well as poet. His poetry frequently deals with the mysterious or mythical, and, as in "Leviathan," a characteristic subject is animals.

JOHN MILTON (1608–1674) contributed to English literature its greatest epic, *Paradise Lost* (1667). He also wrote other poems of various forms, most still highly regarded. Milton's early life was dedicated to his preparation to be a poet. Between 1632, when he left Christ's College, Cambridge with an M.A., and 1637 he had no formal profession; he instead prepared himself to write. Increasingly, though, he was caught up in the political affairs of his day, finally serving as Latin Secretary under Cromwell, whose republican government he supported. After the restoration of the monarchy in 1660, Milton turned back to his poetry. Although by this time he was totally blind, he completed *Paradise Lost, Paradise Regained* (1671), and *Samson Agonistes* (1671), three of his highly regarded works, before his death in 1674.

N. SCOTT MOMADAY (1934–) is an American writer of Indian descent. His best known work is *House Made of Dawn* (1968), a novel about an Indian who, returning to his home from World War II, finds that he can neither fully recover his Indian heritage nor escape from it. Momaday is a professor of English at Stanford University, having earlier received his Ph.D. from that institution. His shorter writings, including poems, stories and essays, have appeared in periodicals such as *The Reporter, Ramparts, New York Times Book Review,* and *New Mexico Quarterly.*

MARIANNE MOORE (1887–1972) was born in St. Louis, ten months before T. S. Eliot was born in the same city. Educated at the Metzger Institute and Bryn Mawr College, she considered becoming a painter but turned, instead, to poetry. Much of her poetry is about animals and she had, by her own admission, "an inordinate interest in animals and athletes." She was, until their move to Los Angeles, one of the leading fans of the Brooklyn Dodgers. Her poetry has an unassuming directness, exemplified by the opening lines of "Poetry": "I, too, dislike it." *Complete Poems* appeared in 1967.

LUIS MUNOZ MARIN (1898–) has combined talents in poetry and politics. Born in Puerto Rico, he spent a number of years in the United States, where he married Muna Lee, a fellow poet, and formed close relationships with several other writers, including Horace Gregory and Vachel Lindsay. His poems have appeared in, among other periodicals, *The Nation* and *Poetry.* His political career was climaxed in 1949 when, having returned to his native land years before, he was elected governor of Puerto Rico.

JOYCE CAROL OATES (1938–) has been a prolific author, having published six novels, four short-story collections, three volumes of verse, and one book of criticism during the ten-year period from 1963 to 1973. The best-known titles are *them* (1969) and *Do With Me What You Will* (1973), novels, and *The Wheel of Love* (1970) and *Marriage and Infidelities* (1972), short-story collections. She was born in Lockport, New York, and attended Syracuse University, the University of Wisconsin, and Rice University. Noted particularly for her fiction, Oates writes of a world characterized by its unconventional and shocking quality; her fictional characters are frequently violent, disturbed, or loveless. She has taught at the University of Detroit and presently teaches at the University of Windsor, Canada.

FLANNERY O'CONNOR (1925–1964) writes of a South peopled by strange, even grotesque characters, a fact rather surprising in view of her traditional, Catholic upbringing and her conventional life on a farm in Georgia. Her works almost always have a religious dimension, particularly in their revelation of mystery or the mystical. That dimension, though, does not mask the harsh reality that O'Connor's fiction always displays. At her death she left a canon fairly small in its volume but impressive in its impact. It includes the novels *Wise Blood* (1952) and *The Violent Bear It Away* (1960), the short story collections *A Good Man is Hard to Find* (1955) and *Everything That Rises Must Converge* (1965), and a miscellaneous volume, *Mystery and Manners* (1969).

MARGE PIERCY (1936–   ) was born in Detroit, Michigan, and was educated at the University of Michigan and Northwestern University, where she obtained an M.A. Her poetry volumes include *Breaking Camp* (1968) and *Hard Loving* (1969). She professes to write poetry which is intended to be read aloud and which blurs the distinction between private and social aims: "I want my poems to be useful to the people I read them to or who read them, and I think they get that way by being as truthful as I can make them."

LUIGI PIRANDELLO (1867–1936), like the Russian Chekhov, may be best remembered as a playwright, but he authored novels and stories as well. As with the hero of "The Captive," Pirandello's characters are frequently caught in an existential dilemma, and their situations are usually marked by important and fundamental ironies. His plays include *Six Characters in Search of an Author* (1921) and *Henry IV* (1922).

ALEXANDER POPE (1688–1744) was a poet of the Neo-Classical era of English literature. Illness as a child affected and impaired his health and led to some physical deformity. Pope was largely self-educated and is best remembered for his achievements in long poems, including *Essay on Criticism* (1711), *Rape of the Lock* (1712), translations of Homer's *Iliad* (1720) and *Odyssey* (1725-26), and the *Dunciad* (1743). He wrote mainly in heroic couplets and was an important contributor to the development of the satiric mode.

SIR WALTER RALEGH (ca. 1552–1618) is perhaps best known as an English explorer and adventurer. He was frequently involved in various kinds of political machinations and spent several years of his life in the infamous Tower of London. He also wrote poetry, though few examples survive to the present day. He was imprisoned a final time after an abortive expedition to Spain, during which a Spanish village was burned. At the request of the Spanish ambassador Ralegh was arrested and, in 1618, executed.

DUDLEY RANDALL (1914–   ) is an accomplished Black American poet but is equally important as editor and owner of the Broadside Press, a publishing outlet for such young Black poets as Don L. Lee, Nikki Giovanni, and Etheridge Knight. Randall had early training as a librarian, and his own poetry reflects both the erudition commensurate with his learning and his skill with language, and his attempt to deal honestly and forcefully with the Black experience. His volumes include *Cities Burning* (1968), *Love You* (1970), and *More to Remember* (1971).

JOHN CROWE RANSOM (1888–1974) was one of the leaders of the Fugitives, a group of Southern writers centered at Vanderbilt University in the 1930's. His students included Allen Tate, Donald Davidson, and Robert Penn Warren. Born in Pulaski, Tennessee, he took a B.A. at Vanderbilt and was a Rhodes scholar at Oxford. He taught at Vanderbilt and Kenyon College, where he founded the influential *Kenyon Review*. In addition to his poetry, he is well known as a critic, particularly because of his volume *The New Criticism* (1941). *Selected Poems* appeared in 1945 and was revised in 1963; *Poems and Essays* appeared in 1955.

THEODORE ROETHKE (1908–1963) was born and educated in Michigan. His father was a florist, one of the factors which contributes to the frequent appearance of vegetative and floral imagery in his verse. He published his first book of poems in 1941 and completed, in all, eight volumes. He was awarded the Pulitzer Prize, the Bollingen Award, and the National Book Award for his poetry. From 1947 until his death he taught at the University of Washington at Seattle. In addition to numerous individual volumes, *Collected Poems* appeared in 1966.

MURIEL RUKEYSER (1913–   ) was born in New York City and has traveled widely as a reporter and correspondent for several publications. Her first volume of poetry, *Theory of Flight*, appeared in 1935. Since then she has published some twelve additional volumes, as well as a novel and several biographies. Two representative poetry volumes are *Selected Poems* (1951) and *Waterlily Fire: Poems 1935–1962* (1962).

ANNE SEXTON (1928–1974) has written poetry which jars and shocks a reader's sensibilities; it is often very physical and usually deals with her life as a woman. She is frequently aligned with the Confessional School of poetry associated particularly with Robert Lowell, for her poetry reveals intimacies and a form of subjective reality in keeping with that mode. Her poetry volumes include *To Bedlam and Part Way Back* (1960), *All My Pretty Ones* (1962), *Selected Poems* (1964), and *The Book of Folly* (1973) plus several others. Sexton committed suicide in 1974.

WILLIAM SHAKESPEARE (1564–1616) was born at Stratford-on-Avon to parents of relative prominence in the village. He spent his first twenty years in Stratford, married Anne Hathaway, and had children. He left for London around 1585, where he soon became famous for his work in the playhouses, as both actor and playwright. He wrote or contributed to some thirty-six dramas, many of them among the most highly regarded in any language. He was also a skillful poet, writing sonnets and longer narrative pieces of lasting significance. He died in Stratford, the birthplace to which he had returned in 1611.

PERCY BYSSHE SHELLEY (1792-1822) was one of the three important Romantic poets (including Byron and Keats) who died at an untimely young age. He was a rebellious figure, particularly in his religious thinking; his espousal of atheism led to his social ostracism and his eventual departure from England in 1814. He wrote a number of important lyrics and odes, several at the time of his friendship with Byron. He also wrote the commemorative poem "Adonais" (1821) which lamented the premature death of Keats. Shelley himself died only a year after Keats; he drowned while sailing off the coast of Italy.

SOPHOCLES (496-406 B.C.) is regarded, along with Aeschylus and Euripides, as one of the three great Greek tragedians. His plays, more than those of his contemporary Aeschylus, emphasize the human rather than heroic dimension of man's experience. Matthew Arnold, in an oft-repeated phrase, described him as a man "who saw life steadily and saw it whole." His best known plays, besides *Antigone*, are *Oedipus the King, Oedipus at Colonus*, and *Electra*.

WALLACE STEVENS (1879-1955) was a lawyer, an insurance company executive and, not least, a poet of the first rank. Since he was not able to devote himself fulltime to his writing, he did not publish his first volume of poems until he was nearly 44. That volume, *Harmonium* (1923), was followed by several others, including *Ideas of Order* (1935), *The Man with the Blue Guitar* (1937), *Notes Toward a Supreme Fiction* (1942), and the *Collected Poems* (1954). His is fundamentally a poetry of ideas, notably, as he expresses it, "ideas of order." In general he wrote slowly but steadily and was, in 1949, awarded the Bollingen Poetry Prize.

JONATHON SWIFT (1667-1745) was born and educated in Dublin and was, throughout much of his life, involved in Irish politics and political affairs. A prolific writer, he authored the well-known satiric work, *Gulliver's Travels* (1726), and a number of other writings which reveal his penetrating, and often bitter, satire against and exposure of human foibles. He also wrote a number of political and religious pamphlets, in each revealing the same perceptive wit and wounding satire that he exhibited in his literary prose and poetry.

JOHN MILLINGTON SYNGE (1871-1909) was an Irish playwright persuaded by W. B. Yeats to devote his creative talents to a revelation of Irish peasant life and folk motifs. He was educated at Trinity College, Dublin, and spent a number of years in Paris. Subsequently, he made several visits to the Aran Islands which were the genesis of his play *Riders to the Sea*. His best known drama is *The Playboy of the Western World* (1907), a play which initially received some criticism on moral grounds.

ALFRED LORD TENNYSON (1809-1892) was educated at Trinity College, Cambridge, and was already writing and publishing poetry as a student. Tennyson was a popular and influential writer of the nineteenth century and, in 1850, was named Poet Laureate to succeed Wordsworth. He wrote many shorter pieces as well as such longer works as *In Memoriam* (1850) (written after the death of his friend, A. H. Hallam) and *Idylls of the King* (1859).

DYLAN THOMAS (1914–1953) is perhaps best remembered for his erratic but brilliant lecture tours in the United States during the final years of his life. He had become an accomplished poet but was also beset by heavy drinking problems; chronic alcoholism contributed to his premature death in New York City. Born in Swansea, Wales, Thomas decided early in his life to be a poet and dedicated himself to that goal. His poetry volumes include *Eighteen Poems* (1934), *Twenty-five Poems* (1936), *Deaths and Entrances* (1946), and *Collected Poems* (1952). He also wrote *Portrait of the Artist as a Young Dog* (1940), semi-autobiographical, and a play, *Under Milk Wood* (1954).

JAMES THURBER (1894–1961) was an American humorist and artist whose reputation was secured in the 1930's and 40's with the publication of a number of volumes of essays, sketches, fables, reminiscences, and satires. Thurber's satire is seldom harsh or riotous; it is, instead, light and disarming, portraying ordinary people moving through any number of ordinary and sometimes extraordinary experiences. His character Walter Mitty ("The Secret Life of Walter Mitty") has come to represent the persistent but incompetent American male trying to escape the dullness and sameness of his life. His volumes number more than 20, including *Is Sex Necessary?* (1929), *My World — and Welcome to It* (1942), *Men, Women, and Dogs* (1943), and *The Thurber Carnival* (1945).

MIGUEL DE UNAMUNO (1864–1936) was a Spanish writer and philosopher. He was a professor of Greek and, later, rector at the University of Salamanca. A frequent critic of Spanish life, Unamuno was dramatically aware of inevitable conflicts between religious ideals and scientific knowledge. His writings present a strikingly modern view of the problematic role of faith in a world not always congenial to it.

JOHN UPDIKE (1932–   ) is the well-known author of *Rabbit, Run* (1960) and its sequel, *Rabbit Redux* (1971); both feature the antics of Harry Angstrom ("Rabbit"), one of the more intriguing characters of contemporary fiction. His stories are equally praised, notably those in *Pigeon Feathers and Other Stories* (1962). Updike was born in Shillington, Pennsylvania, and presently lives in Ipswich, Massachusetts.

JOHN WAIN (1925–   ) is a prolific writer of poetry, fiction, and criticism. It is fair to say, in fact, that he is better known for his fiction and criticism than for his verse. He was born in Stoke-on-Trent, Staffordshire, England, and presently resides, when not travelling, in Oxford. His productivity is indicated by the fact that, during the twenty years from 1950 to 1970 he published five volumes of poetry, ten volumes of fiction, and three volumes of essays. During the same period he was an editor of several other texts and critical studies. He was a university lecturer for a number of years, and his poetry has frequently been compared to that of others (e.g., Kingsley Amis) which reflect an academic bent.

DOUGLAS TURNER WARD (1931–   ) is an actor and a playwright and has received honors for both. He was born in Burnside, Louisiana, and worked for a time in New York City as a journalist. His acting talents have been seen in New York in such productions as *The Iceman Cometh, Lost in the Stars*, and *A Raisin in the Sun*. He also starred in the television production of *Ceremonies in Dark Old Men*. His two plays, *Happy Ending* and *Day of Absence*, gained him the Vernon Rice Drama Award; his acting has won him the Obie Award. He was one of the persons responsible for the creation of the Negro Ensemble Company.

EUDORA WELTY (1909–   ) was born in Mississippi and has lived most of her life there. She faces some of the same problems which confront any writer who focuses on a specific region; unlike the less successful, she both concentrates on her region and transcends it. She is often compared to her fellow Mississippian, William Faulkner, and does share with him a capacity for human compassion and a frequent comic sensibility. Her novels include *The Robber Bridegroom* (1942), *Delta Wedding* (1946), and *Losing Battle* (1970).

WALT WHITMAN (1819–1892) is the American poet most readily identified with American democratic idealism as expressed in nineteenth century United States. His *Leaves of Grass* (1855) remains a classic and influential document in its celebration of the human race and the human individual. In fact, nearly all of existence comes under Whitman's scanning eye in the series of poems collected in *Leaves*; his unbounded enthusiasm and energetic proclamation of individual liberties have continued to influence poets into the twentieth century.

RICHARD WILBUR (1912–   ) was born in New York City and attended Amherst College and Harvard University, receiving an M.A. from the second in 1947. That same year he published his first volume of poems, *The Beautiful Changes*. His poetry has been noted for its difficulty and for its consistent concern with form. Wilbur has also been a university teacher and has, since 1957, taught at Wesleyan University. In 1957 he was also awarded a Pulitzer Prize and the National Book Award. His poetry has been published in *Ceremony* (1950), *Things of This World* (1956), *Poems, 1943–56* (1957), *Walking to Sleep* (1969), and other volumes.

WILLIAM CARLOS WILLIAMS (1883–1963) has been one of the significant influences on post-war American poetry. A medical doctor by profession, Williams was influenced initially by the poets Hilda Doolittle and Ezra Pound, the influence and friendship of the latter being particularly notable. Williams was born in Rutherford, New Jersey, practiced medicine there most of his life, and died in Rutherford in 1963. Among his numerous poetry volumes are *Selected Poems* (1949), *The Collected Later Poems*

(1950, rev. 1963), and *The Collected Earlier Poems* (1951). He was still working on his long epic work, *Paterson*, at the time of his death.

WILLIAM WORDSWORTH (1770–1850) wrote *Lyrical Ballads* (1798) with his friend Samuel Taylor Coleridge, and thereby ushered in the Romantic era of English poetry. His poems reflect his credo that poetry is the "spontaneous overflow of powerful feeling," and that it is written "by a man who . . . had also thought long and deeply." He was a large and influential person of his day and was named Poet Laureate in 1843. Initially a revolutionary in thought and in politics, he later became more conservative, alienating some of his earlier followers.

JAMES WRIGHT (1927–   ) has said that he wants "to make . . . poems say something humanly important instead of just showing off with language." His volume *Collected Poems* won a Pulitzer Prize in 1972. He was educated at Kenyon College and the University of Washington, receiving a Ph.D. from the latter. He has taught at various colleges and universities.

W. B. YEATS (1865–1939) is regarded by most as the finest poet of the twentieth century. Born in Dublin, he continued to feel the effects of his Irish heritage throughout much of his life. He was an Irish nationalist and was involved off and on in politics. That association also furnished the abiding love interest of his life, Maud Gonne, a beautiful and passionate revolutionary who rejected him. Yeats developed a system of symbolism and myth which lies behind, and in some instances is necessary to understand, his poetry. The description of that symbolic system is found in *A Vision* (1925) and is important in such volumes as *Michael Roberts and the Dancer* (1921), *Seven Poems and a Fragment* (1922), and *The Winding Stair* (1929). He was awarded the Nobel Prize in 1923.

index of terms

absurdist drama, 668
accent, 382
allegory, 139, 366–68, 667
alliteration, 393
allusion, 357
anagnorisis, 499
analysis, 399
anapest, 382
antagonist, 29, 495–96
antistrophe, 505n
apostrophe, 349
aside, 497
assonance, 393
auditory imagery, 331–33

ballad, 281
blank verse, 386

caesura, 385
catharsis, 500
character, 9, 28–29, 494–96
climax, 9, 492–93
comedy, 500–1
complication, 9
connotation, 340
consonance, 393
conventional symbol, 366
couplet, 385
crisis, 9

dactyl, 382
denotation, 340
dénouement, 492–93
dimeter, 383
dramatic convention, 496–97
dramatic foil, 495

dramatic irony, 111
dramatic monologue, 313
dramatic poem, 311

elegy, 303
end rhyme, 393
end-stopped line, 385
English sonnet, 306
epic, 281
epistolary novel, 240
exodus, 532n
exposition, 9
expressionistic drama, 668

falling action, 492–93
feminine ending, 385
feminine rhyme, 393
figurative language, 331–57
first-person point of view, 63–64
flat character, 28
foot, 382
foreshadowing, 10
free verse, 386

gustatory imagery, 334

half rhyme, 393
hamartia, 499
heroic couplet, 385
hexameter, 383
hubris, 499
hyperbole, 349

iamb, 382
imagery, 138, 331–34
internal rhyme, 393

interpretation, 6–7
irony, 9, 110–11, 324, 499
Italian sonnet, 306

kinetic imagery, 334

literary ballad, 281
lyric poem, 293

masculine ending, 385
masculine rhyme, 393
metaphor, 340
meter, 377–86
metonymy, 349
monometer, 383
motivation, 495

narrative poem, 281
narrator, 63–64

objective point of view, 63–64
octameter, 383
octave, 306
ode, 299
olfactory imagery, 334
omniscient point of view, 9, 63–64
onomatopoeia, 393
overstatement, 349
oxymoron, 350

paean, 531n
parados, 505n
paradox, 350
pentameter, 383
peripeteia, 499
persona, 318
personal symbol, 366
personification, 349
Petrarchan sonnet, 306
plot, 9–10, 492–93
point of view, 9, 63–65
prosody, 377
protagonist, 29, 495–96
pyrrhic, 384n

quatrain, 386

realistic drama, 668
resolution, 9, 493
rhyme, 393
rhythm, 377
rising action, 492–93
romantic comedy, 500–1
round character, 28
run-on line, 385

satiric comedy, 500–1
scansion, 383-85
selective omniscience, 63–64
sestet, 306
Shakespearean sonnet, 306
simile, 340
situational irony, 111
soliloquy, 497
sonnet, 306
spondee, 382
stanza, 385
stream-of-consciousness novel, 479
stress, 382
strophe, 505n
symbol, 138–39, 363–68
synecdoche, 349
synesthesia, 333
synthesis, 399

tactile imagery, 334
tercet, 385
tetrameter, 383
theme, 7, 493–94
third-person limited point of view, 63–64
third-person point of view, 63–64
tone, 9, 110, 320
tragedy, 498–500
tragic error, 499
tragicomedy, 667
trimeter, 383
triplet, 385
trochee, 382
true rhyme, 393

understatement, 349–50

verbal irony, 110
visual imagery, 331

index of authors and titles